A HISTORY OF GREEK ART

A HISTORY OF GREEK ART

MARK D. STANSBURY-O'DONNELL

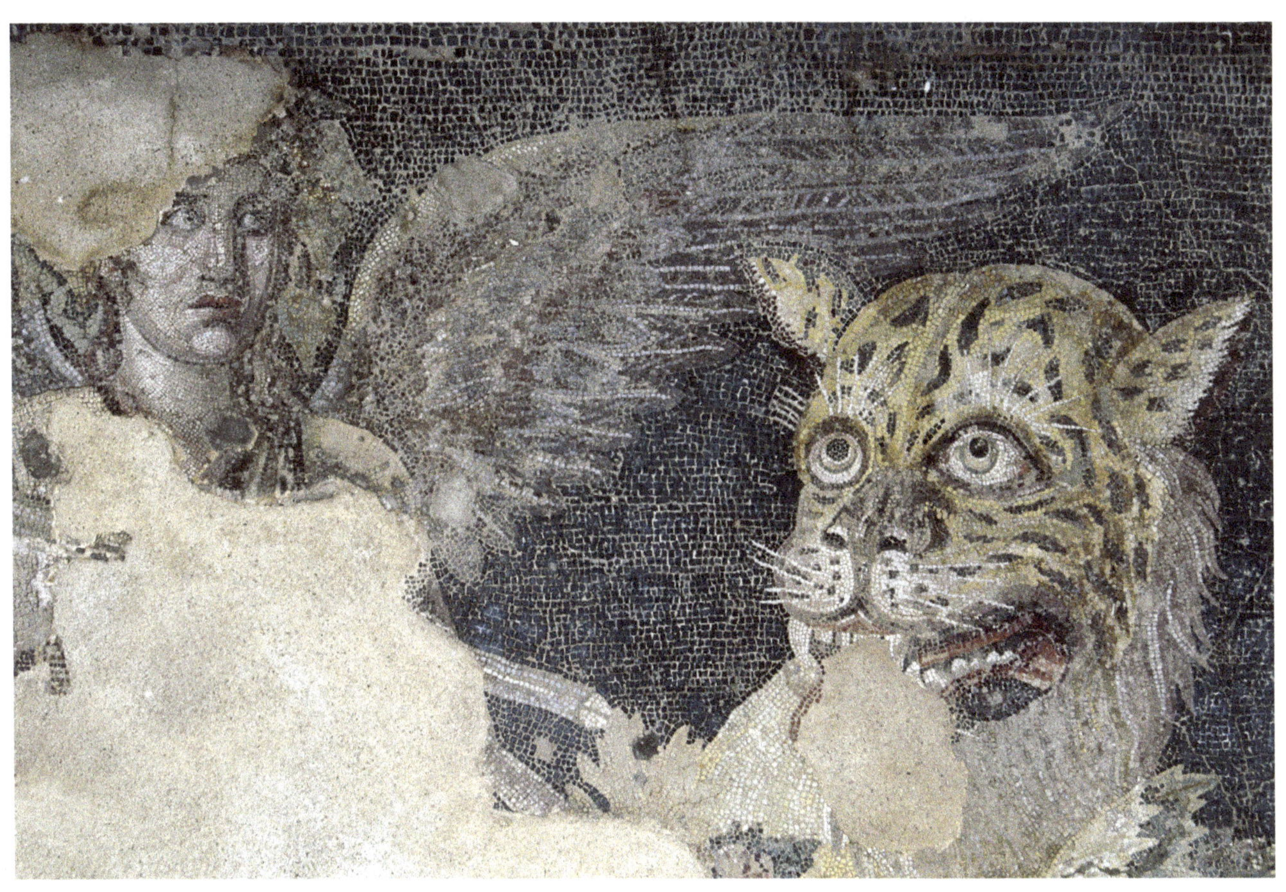

WILEY Blackwell

This edition first published 2015

Registered Office
John Wiley & Sons Ltd, The Atrium, Southern Gate, Chichester, West Sussex, PO19 8SQ, UK

Editorial Offices
350 Main Street, Malden, MA 02148-5020, USA
9600 Garsington Road, Oxford, OX4 2DQ, UK
The Atrium, Southern Gate, Chichester, West Sussex, PO19 8SQ, UK

For details of our global editorial offices, for customer services, and for information about how to apply for permission to reuse the copyright material in this book please see our website at www.wiley.com/wiley-blackwell.

Library of Congress Cataloging-in-Publication Data

Stansbury-O'Donnell, Mark, 1956– author.
A history of Greek art / Mark D. Stansbury-O'Donnell.
pages cm
Includes bibliographical references and index.
ISBN 978-1-4443-5014-2 (cloth) – ISBN 978-1-4443-5015-9 (pbk.) 1. Art, Greek.
2. Art and society – Greece – History – To 1500. I. Title.
N5630.S734 2015
709.38–dc23

2014018396

A catalogue record for this book is available from the British Library.

Cover image: Detail of mosaic from House of Dionysos, Delos, *c.* 166-100 BCE.
Photo © age fotostock / Alamy

Set in 10/13pt Minion by SPi Publisher Services, Pondicherry, India

1 2015

For WENDY

BRIEF CONTENTS

1 INTRODUCTION AND ISSUES IN THE HISTORY OF GREEK ART 1

2 THE EARLY AND MIDDLE BRONZE AGES *C.* 3100–1600 BCE 19

3 THE LATE BRONZE AGE II–III (*C.* 1600–1075 BCE) 48

4 THE SUB-MYCENAEAN, PROTOGEOMETRIC, AND GEOMETRIC PERIODS (*C.* 1075–700 BCE) 68

5 CONTEXTS I: CIVIC, DOMESTIC, AND FUNERARY 97

6 THE SEVENTH CENTURY (*C.* 725/700–625/600 BCE) 130

7 CONTEXTS II: SANCTUARIES AND ARCHITECTURE 152

8 THE SIXTH CENTURY (*C.* 625/600–480 BCE) 179

9 NARRATIVE 209

10 THE FIFTH CENTURY (*C.* 480–400 BCE) 235

11 THE PRODUCTION OF GREEK ART AND ITS MARKETS 265

12 THE FOURTH CENTURY TO *C.* 330 BCE 286

13 IDENTITY 319

14 THE HELLENISTIC PERIOD *C.* 330–30 BCE 341

15 EPILOGUE 380

CONTENTS

Illustrations xiii
Acknowledgments xxi
Timeline xxiii
About the Website xxvii
Maps xxviii

1 INTRODUCTION AND ISSUES IN THE HISTORY OF GREEK ART 1

An Alternative Mini-History of Greek Art 6
Some Questions to Consider for this Book 10
The Plan of this Book 15
A Few Notes About Using this Book 16
Textbox: Stylistic Analysis and Sir John Beazley 17
References 18
Further Reading 18

2 THE EARLY AND MIDDLE BRONZE AGES *C.* 3100–1600 BCE 19

Timeline 20
Chronology, Regions, Periods, and Pottery Analysis 21
Early Cycladic and Minoan Periods, *c.* 3100–2000 BCE 24
Early to Middle Helladic (*c.* 3100–1675 BCE) 27
Protopalatial and Neopalatial Crete 32
The Cyclades 39
Middle Helladic to the Late Helladic I Shaft Graves 43
Textbox: The Eruption of Thera and Debates over Absolute Chronology 46
References 47
Further Reading 47

3 THE LATE BRONZE AGE II–III (*C.* 1600–1075 BCE) 48

Timeline 49
Late Minoan (LM II to LM III) 51

Late Helladic Architecture 52
Late Helladic Pottery and Terracottas 59
Textbox: The Trojan War 66
References 67
Further Reading 67

4 THE SUB-MYCENAEAN, PROTOGEOMETRIC, AND GEOMETRIC PERIODS (*C.* 1075–700 BCE) 68

Timeline 69
Pottery 71
Sculpture 84
Architecture 89
Textbox: What is in a Name? 95
References 96
Further Reading 96

5 CONTEXTS I: CIVIC, DOMESTIC, AND FUNERARY 97

Timeline 98
The City and Its Spaces 99
The Agora 105
Houses and Domestic Spaces 111
Textiles 115
The Symposion 118
Graves 122
Textbox: Agency 127
References 128
Further Reading 129

6 THE SEVENTH CENTURY (*C.* 725/700–625/600 BCE) 130

Timeline 131
Greek Pottery Painting and the Mediterranean 137
Metalwork and Terracotta 143
Architecture and its Decoration 145
Textbox: Network Theory 150
References 151
Further Reading 151

7 CONTEXTS II: SANCTUARIES AND ARCHITECTURE 152

Timeline 153
Sanctuaries 154
Temples and the Architectural Orders 161
A Mini-History of the Greek Temple 167
Other Buildings of the Sanctuary 170
Rituals and Offerings 172
Textbox: Ritual Analysis and *Theoria* 177
References 177
Further Reading 178

8 THE SIXTH CENTURY (*C.* 625/600–480 BCE) 179

Timeline 180
Architecture and Architectural Sculpture 181
Free-Standing Sculpture 190
Other Media 197
Painted Pottery 199
Textbox: Color in Greek Sculpture 207
References 208
Further Reading 208

9 NARRATIVE 209

Timeline 210
Narrative and Artistic Style 212
Narrative Time and Space 214
Viewing Context 220
Art and Literature 222
Choice of Mood and Moment 225
Symbolic and Universal Aspects of Narrative 229
Textbox: Interpretation and Information Theory 233
References 234
Further Reading 234

10 THE FIFTH CENTURY (*C.* 480–400 BCE) 235

Timeline 236
Architecture, Architectural Sculpture, and Relief 244
The Acropolis at Athens 246
Late Fifth-Century Sculpture 253

Painting 255
Textbox: The Parthenon Marbles and Cultural Patrimony 262
References 263
Further Reading 264

11 THE PRODUCTION OF GREEK ART AND ITS MARKETS 265

Timeline 266
Production: Architecture 267
Production: Architectural Sculpture 269
Production: Sculpture 271
Production: Pottery 273
Wares, Markets, and Distribution 276
Artists and Workshops 279
Textbox: The Value of Greek Art 284
References 284
Further Reading 285

12 THE FOURTH CENTURY TO *C.* 330 BCE 286

Timeline 287
Architecture 288
Sculpture 293
Art and Individuals 299
Pottery 305
Mosaic and Fresco 310
Textbox: The Copy Hypothesis 317
References 318
Further Reading 318

13 IDENTITY 319

Timeline 320
Gender 322
Women's Lives 324
Women in Public 329
Men and Youths: Gender and Sexuality 331
Interaction: Class, Civic, and Ethnic Identity 335
Textbox: Money Purses, Sex, and Identity 339
References 340
Further Reading 340

14 THE HELLENISTIC PERIOD *C.* 330–30 BCE 341

Timeline 342
Characteristics of the Hellenistic Period 347
Cities and Architecture 348
Sculptural Styles and Dating 355
Theatricism and Narrative 358
Representations and Portrayal 363
Painting 369
The Private and Personal Realm 374
Textbox: The Riace Warriors as Hellenistic Sculpture 378
References 379
Further Reading 379

15 EPILOGUE 380

Glossary 388
Index 395

ILLUSTRATIONS

1.1 North frieze of the Parthenon, 442–438 BCE
1.2 Attic white-ground calyx krater attributed to the Phiale Painter, *c.* 440 BCE
1.3 Late Geometric I "Hera"-type terracotta figure from Olympia, *c.* 750–725 BCE
1.4 Terracotta woman from a grave at Kamiros cemetery, Rhodes, *c.* 600–540 BCE
1.5 Terracotta figures from girl's tomb in Kerameikos cemetery, Athens, 380–370 BCE
1.6 Terracotta group of women (Demeter and Persephone?), 2nd cent. BCE
1.7 God (Zeus?) from Cape Artemision, *c.* 460 BCE
1.8 God (Zeus?) from Cape Artemision, *c.* 460 BCE, viewed from front
1.9 View of the Acropolis from the Pynx (west)
1.10a Attic pottery from Well J2:4 in the Agora, Athens, *c.* 525–490 BCE
1.10b Attic pottery from Well J2:4 in the Agora, Athens, *c.* 525–490 BCE

2.1 Vasiliki Ware jug with spout, EM IIB
2.2 Folded-Arm Figures (FAF) from Chalandriani cemetery, Syros, EC II/Keros-Syros Group
2.3 "Frying pan" from Chalandriani cemetery, Syros, EC IIB/Keros-Syros Group
2.4 Plan of Myrtos, Crete, EM II
2.5 Sauceboats and bowls from Lerna, EH II
2.6 House of the Tiles, Lerna, EH IIB
2.7 Seals from the House of the Tiles at Lerna, EH IIB
2.8 Minyan ware drinking vessels, MH
2.9 Kamares Ware jug from Phaistos, MM IIB
2.10 Plan of Gournia, Crete, LM I
2.11 Plan of the palace at Knossos, LM I
2.12 View of west side of courtyard at the palace of Minos at Knossos: staircase and throne room (reconstructed)
2.13 "Snake goddess" from Knossos, MM III to LM IA
2.14 Kouros from Palaikastro, LM IB
2.15 Harvester vase, LM IB
2.16 Seal ring from Isopata, LM I
2.17 Marine Style pilgrim's flask from Palaikastro with octopus, LM IB
2.18 Jug from Thera, LC IA
2.19 Landscape and bird fresco from House Delta 2, Thera, LC IA
2.20 Miniature frescoes from Room 5, West House, Akrotiri, LC IA
2.21 Vapheio cup, LM IB
2.22 Dagger from Shaft Grave at Mycenae, LH I
2.23 Wooden box with gold relief from Shaft Grave V, Circle A at Mycenae, LH I

3.1 Palace Style amphora with octopus from Knossos, LM II
3.2 Painted sarcophagus from Hagia Triada, LM IIIA
3.3 Palace of Nestor at Pylos: view of megaron, LH IIIB
3.4 Reconstruction of the megaron interior at Pylos by Piet de Jong, LH IIIB
3.5 Palace of Nestor at Pylos: plan, LH IIIB
3.6 View of walls of Mycenae with Lion Gate, LH IIIB
3.7 "Treasury of Atreus," Mycenae, LH IIIB

3.8 Interior of "Treasury of Atreus," Mycenae, LH IIIB
3.9 Fresco from Cult Center at Mycenae, LH IIIB
3.10 Chamber tomb burial from Agora with three bodies, LH IIIA
3.11 Pottery from chamber tomb burial in the Agora, LH IIIA
3.12 Goblet with floral decoration from Kalymnos, LH IIIB
3.13 Krater with chariot procession from Tomb 70, Enkomi, Cyprus, LH IIIA2
3.14 Terracotta figures (psi, tau, and phi types), LH IIIB
3.15 Stirrup jar with octopus, LH IIIC
3.16 Warrior Vase from Mycenae, LH IIIC

4.1 Sub-Mycenaean Attic amphoriskos from the Kerameikos, *c.* 1100–1050 BCE
4.2 Protogeometric Attic cinerary amphora from the Kerameikos, *c.* 1000–900 BCE
4.3 Early Geometric Attic burial amphora with bent iron sword from Agora (D16:4), *c.* 900 BCE
4.4 Middle Geometric tomb of the Rich Lady in the Agora in Athens (Tomb H16:6), *c.* 850 BCE
4.5 Grave goods from tomb of the Rich Lady, *c.* 850 BCE
4.6 Jewelry from the tomb of the Rich Lady, *c.* 850 BCE
4.7 Late Geometric IA Attic amphora from the Dipylon cemetery (Kerameikos) attributed to the Dipylon Master, *c.* 760–750 BCE
4.8 Detail of prothesis scene in Figure 4.7
4.9 Late Geometric IB Attic krater from Dipylon cemetery (Kerameikos), *c.* 750–735 BCE
4.10 Late Geometric II Attic skyphos from the Kerameikos, *c.* 735–720 BCE
4.11 Late Geometric Euboean lidded krater from Cyprus, *c.* 750–740 BCE
4.12 Late Geometric IB Argive krater fragment from Argos, *c.* 750–740 BCE
4.13 Terracotta centaur from Lefkandi, end 10th cent. BCE
4.14 Ivory figure from Dipylon grave, 750–725 BCE
4.15 Bronze votive horses from Olympia, 8th cent. BCE
4.16 Tripod reconstruction from Olympia
4.17 Bronze warrior from a tripod handle at Olympia, 8th cent. BCE
4.18 Cretan bronze tripod leg from Olympia, end 8th cent. BCE
4.19 Bronze group of man and centaur, mid-8th cent. BCE
4.20 Reconstruction of the House at Lefkandi, 1000–950 BCE
4.21 Plan of the town of Zagora, Andros, 8th cent. BCE
4.22 Plan of houses in Area H of Zagora, Andros
4.23 Late Geometric Attic spouted bowl or louterion, possibly from Thebes, *c.* 730–720 BCE

5.1 Reconstructed view of ancient Athens with view of Agora and Acropolis
5.2 Plan of Athens with ancient structures superimposed on modern city streets
5.3 Plan of Poseidonia/Paestum, founded *c.* 600 BCE
5.4 Plan of Olynthos, *c.* 430–348 BCE
5.5 Reconstructed view of Priene, later 4th–3rd cent. BCE
5.6 View of the Agora in Athens today
5.7 Reconstructed plan of Agora of Athens, *c.* 400 BCE
5.8 Reconstructed plan of Agora of Athens, *c.* 150 CE
5.9 Tyrannicides (Aristogeiton, left; Harmodios, right) of Kritios and Nesiotes, Roman marble copy of Greek bronze original of 477/6 BCE
5.10 Relief commemorating victory of Leontis tribe, early 4th. cent. BCE
5.11 Attic black-figure Panathenaic amphora attributed to Kleophrades Painter, *c.* 490 BCE
5.12 Plan of House A vii 4 at Olynthos, with location of excavated object types
5.13 Reconstruction drawing of House A vii 4 at Olynthos
5.14 Plan of houses, Block 1, Silen's Quarter, Thasos (Phase 4)
5.15 Reconstruction drawing of houses, Block 1, Silen's Quarter, Thasos

5.16 Household pottery found in the Agora at Athens, 6th–4th cent. BCE
5.17 Household finds from Priene, 2nd–1st cent. BCE
5.18 Textile from Tomb II at Vergina, *c.* 336–311 BCE
5.19 Attic red-figure skyphos attributed to the Penelope Painter, *c.* 450–440 BCE
5.20 Reconstruction of dining room with symposiasts in the South Stoa of the Agora at Athens
5.21 Early Corinthian column krater, *c.* 600–590 BCE
5.22 Diagram of vase types
5.23 Middle Corinthian skyphos, *c.* 585–570 BCE
5.24 Kouros from Anavyssos, perhaps from tomb of Kroisos, *c.* 530 BCE
5.25 Late Geometric Tomb XI with part of Tomb XXII, Agora, Athens, end 8th cent. or beginning 7th cent. BCE
5.26 Attic white-ground lekythoi with funerary scenes
5.27 Stelai of Koroibos–Kleidemides family in the Kerameikos, Athens, reconstruction of 4th cent. BCE tomb plot
5.28 Stele of Hegeso, *c.* 400 BCE

6.1 Ivory group of hero with lion, *c.* 700–650 BCE
6.2 Neo-Assyrian relief from the palace at Khorsabad, *c.* 720 BCE
6.3 Kore of Nikandre from Delos, *c.* 650–625 BCE
6.4 Kouros from Sounion, *c.* 590 BCE
6.5 Egyptian male statue, Tjayasetimu, from Giza, *c.* 664–610 BCE
6.6 Egyptian bronze statue of Mut, dedicated at Samos, 7th cent. BCE
6.7 Phoenician ivory plaque from Nimrud, 9th–8th cent. BCE
6.8 Cypro-Phoenician silver gilt bowl with various scenes, *c.* 725–675 BCE
6.9 Protocorinthian aryballos attributed to the Evelyn Painter, *c.* 720–700 BCE; Protocorinthian alabastron from Kamiros, 660–650 BCE
6.10 Protocorinthian aryballos from tomb in Taras/Taranto, *c.* 680–650 BCE
6.11 Protocorinthian olpe attributed to the Chigi Painter, *c.* 650–640 BCE
6.12 Sicilian stamnos from Selinunte, made in Megara Hyblaea, *c.* 660–650 BCE
6.13 Wild Goat-style oinochoe from Rhodes, 625–600 BCE
6.14 Chian "Aphrodite Bowl" from Naukratis, 620–600 BCE
6.15 Protoattic amphora from Eleusis, *c.* 670–650 BCE
6.16 Griffin protome probably from Rhodes, 7th cent. BCE
6.17 Gold plaques with Mistress of Animals from Kamiros, Rhodes, *c.* 660–620 BCE
6.18 Cycladic relief pithos from Mykonos, *c.* 675–650 BCE
6.19 Plan of the sanctuary of Hera at Samos and Temple 1b, *c.* 700 BCE
6.20 Plan of the sanctuary of Hera at Samos and Temple 2, *c.* 650 BCE
6.21 Reconstruction of the stoa and corner of the Hera Temple 2 at Samos, *c.* 650–625 BCE
6.22 Reconstruction of the superstructure of the Temple of Apollo at Thermon, *c.* 630 BCE
6.23 Metope from the Temple of Apollo at Thermon, *c.* 630 BCE
6.24 Lintel from the Temple at Prinias, *c.* 620–600 BCE

7.1 View of the sanctuary at Delphi
7.2 Plan of the sanctuary at Delphi
7.3 Reconstruction drawing of the sanctuary at Olympia
7.4 Plan of the Acropolis and areas to north and east, Athens
7.5 Exterior of the Temple of Concord at Akragas/Agrigento, *c.* 440–430 BCE
7.6 The Doric, Ionic, and Corinthian orders and their components
7.7 Temples of Hera at Poseidonia/Paestum
7.8 Erechtheion, Acropolis, Athens, *c.* 431–405 BCE
7.9 Section of the frieze from the Erechtheion, *c.* 410–405 BCE

7.10 Corinthian capital and entablature from the thymele of the Asklepieion at Epidauros, mid-4th cent. BCE
7.11 General plan of the Greek temple and its components
7.12 Reconstruction of the side and interior of the Temple of Zeus, Olympia
7.13 Interior of the Temple of Concord at Akragas/Agrigento, *c.* 440–430 BCE
7.14 Athenian Treasury at Delphi (reconstructed), *c.* 490 BCE
7.15 Perspective reconstruction of the Siphnian Treasury and Sacred Way at Delphi
7.16 Boeotian black-figure lekane with sacrificial procession to Athena, *c.* 550 BCE
7.17 Attic red-figure volute krater attributed to the Kleophon Painter, *c.* 440–430 BCE
7.18 Kore dedicated by Euthydikos, from Acropolis, Athens, *c.* 490–480 BCE
7.19 Nude male (Apollo?) dedicated by Mantiklos, early 7th cent. BCE
7.20 Objects from votive deposit in the Agora (H 17:4), *c.* 700–625 BCE

8.1 East pediment and frieze from the Siphnian Treasury at Delphi, *c.* 530–525 BCE
8.2 West frieze from the Siphnian Treasury at Delphi, *c.* 530–525 BCE
8.3 Pediment from Temple of Artemis at Korfu, *c.* 580 BCE
8.4 Running Medusa and Pegasos from Temple of Athena, Syracuse/Siracusa, *c.* 575–550 BCE
8.5 Facade of Selinus/Selinunte, Temple C, *c.* 550–530 BCE
8.6 Metopes of Temple C at Selinus/Selinunte, *c.* 550–530 BCE
8.7 Metope from Athenian Treasury at Delphi, *c.* 490–485 BCE
8.8 Ball player base from Themistoklean Wall, *c.* 510–500 BCE
8.9 Kouroi dedicated to Kleobis and Biton at Delphi, *c.* 570 BCE
8.10 Kouros from grave of Sombrotidas, the physician, son of Mandrokles, Megara Hyblaea, Sicily, *c.* 560–550 BCE
8.11 Kouros dedicated by Pytheas and Aeschrion to Ptoan Apollo, Boeotia, *c.* 500 BCE
8.12 Kore dedicated by Cheramyes from Samos, 570–560 BCE
8.13 Kore of Phrasikleia, *c.* 550–540 BCE
8.14 Kore from Acropolis, Athens, *c.* 520–510 BCE
8.15 Color reconstruction of Acropolis Kore 675, “Chiotissa” or Chian kore
8.16 Narrative scenes of bronze shield band from Olympia in Figure 8.17
8.17 Bronze shield band from Olympia, mid-6th cent. BCE
8.18 Chryselephantine statue of Apollo from Delphi, *c.* 550 BCE
8.19 Caryatid mirror from Cape Sounion, *c.* 510 BCE
8.20 Rhodian terracotta scent bottles, *c.* 600–550 BCE
8.21 Painted panel from Pitsa, Corinthia, *c.* 540–530 BCE
8.22 Lakonian kylix attributed to the Hunt Painter, *c.* 555 BCE
8.23 Attic black-figure volute krater signed by Kleitias and Ergotimos (François Vase), *c.* 570 BCE
8.24 Attic black-figure amphora signed by Exekias, *c.* 540 BCE
8.25 Attic bilingual amphora (red-figure side) by the Andokides Painter, *c.* 525–520 BCE
8.26 Attic red-figure calyx krater attributed to Euphronios, *c.* 520–510 BCE

9.1 North frieze from the Siphnian Treasury at Delphi, *c.* 530–525 BCE
9.2 Middle Geometric II Attic skyphos from Eleusis, *c.* 770 BCE
9.3 Attic red-figure pelike near the Pronomos Painter, end 5th cent. BCE
9.4 Frieze from the Great Altar of Zeus at Pergamon, *c.* 180–150 BCE
9.5 Attic black-figure amphora attributed to Exekias, *c.* 540–535 BCE
9.6 Attic black-figure cup, *c.* 550 BCE
9.7 Attic red-figure hydria attributed to the Kleophrades Painter, *c.* 480 BCE
9.8 Attic red-figure kylix attributed to the Kodros Painter, *c.* 440–430 BCE
9.9 Attic red-figure skyphos attributed to the Penelope Painter, *c.* 450–440 BCE

9.10 Attic red-figure kylix attributed to the Briseis Painter, *c.* 480 BCE
9.11 Lucanian red-figure pelike attributed to the Choephoroi Painter, *c.* 350 BCE
9.12 Cabiran black-figure skyphos, late 5th cent. BCE
9.13 Attic red-figure chous attributed to the Group of Berlin 2415, *c.* 460 BCE
9.14 East pediment of the Temple of Zeus at Olympia, *c.* 470–457 BCE
9.15 Attic black-figure amphora from the heroön at Poseidonia/Paestum, attributed to the Chiusi Painter, *c.* 510 BCE
9.16 Attic black-figure column krater, mid-6th cent. BCE
9.17 Metope of Naiskos Tomb from Via Umberto, Taras/Taranto, 300–250 BCE
9.18 Attic red-figure volute krater attributed to the Niobid Painter, *c.* 460 BCE

10.1 "Kritios Boy," after 480 BCE
10.2 West pediment from Temple of Aphaia at Aegina, after 480 BCE
10.3 Color reconstruction by Vinzenz Brinkmann of archer (W11), warrior (W9), and Athena (W1) from west pediment of the Temple of Aphaia at Aigina
10.4 Fallen warrior (E11) from east pediment of the Temple of Aphaia at Aigina, after 480 BCE
10.5 Riace Warriors A and B, *c.* 460–450 BCE
10.6 Argive caryatid mirror, mid-5th cent. BCE
10.7 Doryphoros of Polykleitos, Hellenistic marble copy of Greek bronze original of *c.* 450–440 BCE
10.8 Nike by Paionios, *c.* 420 BCE
10.9 Metope 10 from the Temple of Zeus at Olympia, *c.* 470–457 BCE
10.10 Parthenon, Athens, 447–432 BCE, view from the northwest
10.11 Parthenon, Athens, plan with subjects of sculptural program
10.12 Parthenon, Athens, view of west end
10.13 Parthenon, Athens, drawing of exaggerated architectural refinements
10.14 South metope from Parthenon, 447–442 BCE
10.15 East frieze of the Parthenon, 442–438 BCE
10.16a East pediment of the Parthenon, 437–432 BCE
10.16b East pediment of the Parthenon, 437–432 BCE
10.17 Parthenon, Athens, view of southeast corner with reproduction of Dionysos figure
10.18 Nike figure from the parapet of the Temple of Athena Nike, *c.* 420–410 BCE
10.19 Grave stele of Ampharete from Kerameikos, 430–420 BCE
10.20 Painted wall from the Tomb of the Diver, Poseidonia/Paestum, *c.* 470 BCE
10.21 Attic white-ground kylix attributed to the Sotades Painter, *c.* 460–450 BCE
10.22 Attic red-figure calyx krater attributed to the Niobid Painter, *c.* 460–450 BCE
10.23 Attic white-ground lekythos attributed to the Achilles Painter, *c.* 440 BCE
10.24 Attic red-figure epinetron attributed to the Eretria Painter, *c.* 425–420 BCE
10.25 Attic white-ground lekythos attributed to the Reed Painter, *c.* 420–400 BCE
10.26 Attic red-figure calyx krater signed by Euphronios from Cerveteri, *c.* 520–510 BCE

11.1 West pediment from the Temple of Asklepios at Epidauros, *c.* 370 BCE
11.2 Nike acroterion from west pediment from the Temple of Asklepios at Epidauros, *c.* 370 BCE
11.3 Figures from the frieze of the Erechtheion on the Acropolis at Athens, *c.* 410–405 BCE
11.4 Fragment of a red-figure test piece cut from a krater, attributed to the Methyse Painter, *c.* 460 BCE
11.5 Attic red-figure hydria attributed to Group of Polygnotos, *c.* 450–440 BCE
11.6 Black-glaze ware from the Agora, 5th cent BCE
11.7 Gold phiale dedicated by the Kypselids, 625–600 BCE
11.8 Attic black-figure Nikosthenic amphora signed by Nikosthenes, *c.* 540–510 BCE

11.9 West Slope ware kantharoi, *c.* 275–250 BCE
11.10 Mold-made "Megarian" bowl, *c.* 225–175 BCE
11.11 Unfinished Neoattic marble krater ("Finley Krater"), mid-1st cent. BCE
11.12 Gold pendants from Tekke Tomb 2, Knossos, 9th cent. BCE
11.13 Caeretan hydria attributed to the Eagle Painter, *c.* 530 BCE
11.14 Reconstruction of the sculptural program at Sperlonga, 1st cent. BCE
11.15 Hagesandros, Athenodoros, and Polydoros, Blinding of Polyphemos from Sperlonga, 1st cent. BCE

12.1 Reconstruction of the sanctuary of Asklepios at Epidauros facing to the north, 4th cent. and later BCE
12.2 Reconstruction of the thymele (tholos) at Epidauros, designed by Polykleitos the Younger, *c.* 360–330 BCE
12.3 Theater at Epidauros, designed by Polykleitos the Younger, *c.* 330 BCE
12.4 Reconstruction of the Mausoleion at Halikarnassos, *c.* 350 BCE
12.5 Choreagic Monument of Lysikrates, Athens, *c.* 334 BCE
12.6 Column drum from Temple of Artemis at Ephesos, *c.* 320 BCE
12.7 "Antikythera Youth," *c.* 350–330 BCE
12.8 Agias from the Daochos Monument at Delphi, 337/6–333/2 BCE
12.9 Amazonomachy frieze from the Mausoleion at Halikarnassos, 360–350 BCE
12.10a Head of Telephos from the west pediment of the Temple of Athena at Tegea, *c.* 350–340 BCE
12.10b Head of a warrior from the west pediment of the Temple of Athena at Tegea, *c.* 350–340 BCE
12.11 Aphrodite of Knidos of Praxiteles, Roman copy or adaptation of Greek original of *c.* 350 BCE
12.12 Monument of Dexileos from Kerameikos, Athens, 394/3 BCE
12.13 Reconstruction of Dexileos Monument *in situ*
12.14 Bronze hinged mirror cover, *c.* 330 BCE
12.15 Derveni krater, *c.* 375–350 BCE
12.16 Scepter, ring, and necklace tomb of priestess (?) in Taras/Taranto, *c.* 350–320 BCE
12.17 Attic red-figure Kerch-style pelike attributed to the Wedding Procession Painter, *c.* 360 BCE
12.18 Apulian red-figure calyx krater fragment attributed to the Black Fury Painter, *c.* 400–380 BCE
12.19 Apulian red-figure loutrophoros attributed to the Metope Painter, *c.* 350–325 BCE
12.20 Apulian Gnathian-ware lekythos from Tomb 2, Corso Italia, Taras/Taranto, *c.* 350–325 BCE
12.21 Paestan red-figure krater attributed to Asteas, 350–340 BCE
12.22 Mosaic floor from House A vi 3 at Olynthos, early 4th cent. BCE
12.23 Reconstruction of the facade of Tomb II at Vergina, *c.* 335–315 BCE
12.24 Facade and fresco from Tomb II (of Philip?) at Vergina, *c.* 335–315 BCE
12.25a Fresco from the "Tomb of Persephone" at Vergina, *c.* 336–317 BCE: Abduction of Persephone by Hades
12.25b Fresco from the "Tomb of Persephone" at Vergina, *c.* 336–317 BCE: Demeter
12.26 Praxitelean Hermes and infant Dionysos, Hellenistic copy of 4th-cent. BCE original?

13.1 Attic red-figure kylix attributed to the Gales Painter or the Thorvaldsen Group, *c.* 520 BCE
13.2 Tomb relief of Mnesistrate, mid-4th. cent. BCE
13.3 Attic red-figure chous, *c.* 430–420 BCE
13.4 Attic red-figure pyxis attributed to the Marlay Painter, *c.* 440–430 BCE
13.5 Early Geometric grave goods from a burial (D16:2, "Boots Tomb") in the Agora, Athens, *c.* 900 BCE
13.6 Attic red-figure lekythos attributed to the Brygos Painter, *c.* 480–470 BCE
13.7 Attic red-figure nuptial lebes attributed to the Washing Painter, *c.* 430–420 BCE
13.8 Statue of priestess Aristonoë, from Temple of Themis/Nemesis at Rhamnous (Attica), 3rd cent. BCE

13.9 Grave stele of Phila, daughter of Apollas, from Smyrna/Izmir, 2nd cent. BCE
13.10 Lakonian nude caryatid mirror, 560–540 BCE
13.11 Attic red-figure kylix attributed to the Foundry Painter, *c.* 490–480 BCE
13.12 Attic red-figure kylix attributed to the Euaion Painter, *c.* 450–440 BCE
13.13 Attic red-figure kylix signed by Douris, *c.* 480 BCE
13.14 Campanian red-figure hydria attributed to the Manchester Painter, *c.* 350–330 BCE
13.15 Silver stater from Metapontum/Metaponto, *c.* 540–510 BCE
13.16 Grave goods from Tomb 106, Pantanello Cemetery at Metapontum/Metaponto, *c.* 425–385 BCE
13.17 Reconstruction drawing of "Lucanian" bronze belt from Tomb 106, Pantanello Cemetery at Metapontum/Metaponto, *c.* 425–385 BCE
13.18 Attic red-figure epinetron attributed to the Painter of Berlin 2624, *c.* 450 BCE

14.1 Alexander Sarcophagus from Sidon, *c.* 325–311 BCE
14.2 Alexander Mosaic from the House of the Faun, Pompeii, late 2nd–early 1st cent. BCE
14.3 Plan of early Ptolemaic Alexandria, Egypt, 3rd cent. BCE
14.4 Plan of the acropolis at Pergamon, 3rd cent. BCE and later
14.5 Model of Pergamon: view of western side of acropolis with Great Altar of Zeus to the right
14.6 Great Altar of Zeus at Pergamon, *c.* 180–150 BCE, post-restoration 2004
14.7 Asklepieion at Kos, *c.* 160 BCE
14.8 Temple of Apollo at Didyma, begun *c.* 300 BCE. Exterior with stairs leading to pronaos
14.9 Temple of Apollo at Didyma, begun *c.* 300 BCE. Plan
14.10 Temple of Apollo at Didyma, begun *c.* 300 BCE. Interior
14.11 Odysseus from Antikythera shipwreck, first quarter of 1st cent. BCE
14.12 Eros (once called Agon) from Mahdia shipwreck, late 2nd–early 1st cent. BCE
14.13 "Dancing Dwarf" from Mahdia shipwreck, late 2nd–early 1st cent. BCE
14.14 Nike of Samothrace, later 3rd–early 2nd cent. BCE
14.15 Bronze figure of Tyche of Antioch, 1st–2nd cent. CE Roman copy in bronze after the original by Eutychides, shortly after 300 BCE
14.16 Aphrodite with slipper group from Delos, *c.* 100 BCE
14.17 Aphrodite of Melos, *c.* 150–100 BCE
14.18 Reconstruction of cult statues by Damophon of Messene from the sanctuary of Despoina at Lykosoura, *c.* 200–190 BCE
14.19 Artemis and Demeter from cult statues at Lykosoura, *c.* 200–190 BCE, by Damophon of Messene
14.20 Tripod base fragment from Agora, Athens, *c.* 100 BCE
14.21 Getty athlete (neoclassical), 3rd cent. BCE
14.22 Terme boxer, 2nd–early 1st cent. BCE
14.23 "Hellenistic Ruler," 2nd cent. BCE
14.24 Head of Cleopatra VII, mid-1st cent. BCE
14.25 Statue of Arsinoë II (d. 270) for her posthumous cult, *c.* 150–100 BCE
14.26 Coin of Arsinoë II, *c.* 261–246 BCE, minted by Ptolemy II
14.27 Bronze head of a man, from Delos, early 1st cent. BCE
14.28 Stag Hunt mosaic by Gnosis from Pella, *in situ*, *c.* 330–300 BCE
14.29 Courtyard of the House of Dionysos at Delos with mosaic, *c.* 166–100 BCE
14.30 Detail of Mosaic from House of Dionysos, Delos, *c.* 166–100 BCE
14.31 Painted Stele of Hediste from Necropolis of Demetrias, Greece, *c.* 200 BCE
14.32 Centuripe vase with wedding scene, 3rd–2nd cent. BCE
14.33 Hadra hydria, *c.* 226–225 BCE
14.34 Terracotta woman from Corso Umberto, Taras/Taranto, early 3rd cent. BCE
14.35 Terracotta seated nurse holding child, late 4th cent. BCE

14.36 "Baker Dancer," 3rd–2nd cent. BCE
14.37 Ring with intaglio gem, *c.* 220–100 BCE

15.1 Two Attic mastoi; Attic phiale signed by Sotades, c. 460–450 BCE
15.2 Achaemenid silver griffin rhyton from Erzincan, Turkey, 5th cent. BCE
15.3 East stairway to the Apadana (audience hall) of Darius and Xerxes at the Persian palace at Persepolis, Iran, *c.* 520–460 BCE
15.4 "Mourning Athena" relief, *c.* 470 BCE
15.5 Maya Lin, Vietnam Veterans Memorial, Washington, DC, dedicated 1982

ACKNOWLEDGMENTS

There are many people to thank for conceiving and seeing through this project. From the University of St. Thomas, I would like to acknowledge the support of a three-year University Scholar Grant that provided course releases for time to write and funding for images and permissions for this book. Further funds from Academic Affairs for the John Ireland Professor also helped with travel and permissions. I would particularly like to thank the current and previous Deans of the College of Arts and Sciences for their support of the project, Dr. Terry Langan and Dr. Marisa Kelly. Several graduate students served as readers of draft chapters and helped to focus or clarify the writing: Wendy DePaolis, Chelsea Lynch, and Nicole Sheridan. I would also like to thank Lauren Langan for her careful comments. The Department of Geography provided maps for the book; my thanks especially to Mitchell Schaps, as well as Catherine Hansen and Sarah McNamara for their contribution. Finally, our Visual Resources Curator, Christy Dent, and her gifted student assistants, Magdalena Koebele, MacAulay Steenson, and Samantha Wisneski, provided scanning and image editing that were immensely helpful.

Other institutions also provided fundamental resources or opportunities to develop this project. In particular, a Webster Fellowship at the Institute of Classical Studies, University of London provided the time and resources to outline the project and develop the illustration list at the beginning. The American School of Classical Studies at Athens provided both research resources, especially the Athenian Agora Excavations database, and assistance with images that is invaluable.

There are many thanks for the images and permissions. I list first those by institution and the individuals there: *Aigai (Vergina)*: Dr. Aggeliki Kottaridi, Dr. Dimitrios Papoudas; *AKG-Images*: Stella Calvert-Smith, Stephanie Marsh, Angelika Pirkl; *American School of Classical Studies at Athens*: Ioanna Damanaki, Jan Jordan, Craig Mauzy, Andrew Reinhard, and Natalia Vogeikoff-Brogan; *Archaeological Receipts Fund (Athens)*: Angeliki Voskaki, Pantelis Tsironis; *Art Resource*: Liz Kurtulik Mercuri, Michael Slade; *Bortolami Gallery*: Jillian Clark, Christine Messineo; *Bridgeman Art Library*: Kajette Solomon; *British Museum*: Allyson Carless, Yolande Ferreira, Christopher Sutherns; *British School at Athens*: Amalia Kakissis; *Deutsches Archäologisches Institut, Athens*: Anne Fohgrub; *Deutsches Archäologisches Institut, Berlin*: Prof. Dr. Hans R. Goette; *Deutsches Archäologisches Institut, Rome*: Daria Lanzuolo; *Ecole française d'Athènes*: Calliopi Christophi; *Hirmer Fotoarchiv*: Karen Angne, Irmgard Ernestmeier; *INSTAP Academic Press*: Prof. Philip Betancourt, Dr. Susan Ferrence; *Institute of Classical Archaeology, University of Texas at Austin*: Prof. Joseph Carter; Juan Carlo Fernandez, Lauren Jackson; *Italian Archaeological School of Athens*: Prof. Emanuele Greco; *J. Paul Getty Museum*: Cherie Chen; *Jutland Archaeological Society*: Jesper Laursen; *Musée de Boulogne-sur-Mer*: Fourcroy Florence; *Museo Nazionale Archeologico, Florence*: Dr. Mario Iozzo; *Museo Nazionale Archeologico, Taranto*: Dr. Antonietta Dell'Aglio, Armanda Zingariello; *Museum of Fine Arts, Boston*: Sue Bell; *National Archaeological Museum, Athens*: Dr. George Kakavas, Dr. Alexandra Christopoulou, Dr. Maria Chidiroglou; *Staatliche Antikensammlungen und Glypothek, München*: Irene Boesel, Dr. Astrid Fendt; *Stiftung Archäologie*: Dr. Michael Albert, Dr. Ulrike Koch-Brinkmann; *University of Cincinnati*: Carol Hershenson; *University of Lecce, LAND-LAB*: Prof. Grazia Semeraro, Prof. Francesco D'Andria; *Yale University Art Gallery*: Sarah Cole, Megan Doyon, Susan Matheson.

In addition, I would like to thank the following individuals for sharing their work, drawings, or photos: Bruce Goodman (Agrigento); John Goodinson and Prof. Peter Schultz (Epidauros); Dr. Marina Yeroulanou, Prof. Tyler Jo Smith, and Dan Weiss (Greek architectural orders); Prof. Nicholas Cahill (Olynthos); Prof. Clemente Marconi (Selinus/Selinunte); Prof. Hallie M. Franks and Dan Lamp

(Vergina); Prof. Elena Walter Karydi (Samos); Dr. Michael Squire (Sperlonga); Prof. Alexander Cambitoglou and Dr. Stavros Paspalas (Zagora).

There are several colleagues who wrote on behalf of my university grant that I want to thank for their support: Sheramy Bundrick, Pamela Gordon, Susan Langdon, and Ann Steiner. Elizabeth Langridge-Noti has provided many thoughts and suggestions along the way, and her collegiality and friendship are very much appreciated.

Finally, I would like to thank Haze Humbert for giving me the opportunity to attempt this book, and to the work of Deirdre Ilkson, Allison Kostka, Brigitte Lee Messenger, and Ben Thatcher in sorting out the details and advising on issues. I would also like to express my thanks to the many anonymous peer reviewers of the proposal, sample, and final chapters, and to Deirdre for summarizing and collating them for the editorial process.

As always, this would not have been possible without Wendy.

TIMELINE

3100–2700	***Early Bronze Age I***
2700–2200	***Early Bronze Age II***
2650–2500	Keros-Syros Group (Cycladic Figurines)
2400–2200	House of the Tiles, Lerna (EH II)
2200–2000	***Early Bronze Age III***
2000–1800	***Middle Bronze Age I***
1900–1750	***Protopalatial Crete***
1800–1750	***Middle Bronze Age II***
1750	Destruction of First Minoan Palaces
1750–1500	***Neopalatial Crete***
1750–1700	***Middle Bronze Age III***
1750–1650	"Snake Goddess" from Knossos (MM III–LM IA)
1700/1675–1600	***Late Bronze Age I***
1675–1600	Shaft Graves at Mycenae (LH I)
1700–1625	Frescoes at Akrotiri (LC I)
c. 1625	Eruption of Thera
1600–1430	***Late Bronze Age II***
1430–1300	***Late Bronze Age IIIA***
1450–1340	Painted Sarcophagus from Hagia Triada (LM IIIA)
1300–1190	***Late Bronze Age IIIB***
1300–1190	Lion Gate and Treasury of Atreus at Mycenae (LH IIIB)
1300–1180	Palace of Nestor at Pylos (LH IIIB)
1190–1075	***Late Bronze Age IIIC***
1190–1075	Warrior Vase from Mycenae (EH IIIC)
1075–1025	***Sub-Mycenaean***
1050–900	***Protogeometric***
1000–950	House at Lefkandi
900	Centaur from Lefkandi, Boots and Warrior Grave at Athens

900–850	***Early Geometric***
850	Tomb of the Rich Athenian Lady
850–760	***Middle Geometric***
770	Skyphos from Eleusis (MG II)
760–700	***Late Geometric***
760–750	Dipylon Amphora
750–725	Ivory Figure from Dipylon Cemetery
734	Founding of Syracuse/Siracusa
725–700	Town of Zagora on Andros, phase II
706	Founding of Taras/Taranto
700–600	***Orientalizing Period***
670–650	Eleusis Amphora
651	Founding of Selinus/Selinunte
650–625	Kore of Nikandre
650–640	Chigi Olpe
630	Metopes from Temple of Apollo at Thermon
600	Founding of Poseidonia/Paestum
600–480	***Archaic Period***
590	Kouros from Sounion
580	Temple of Artemis at Korfu
570	François Vase by Kleitias and Ergotimos
550–540	Kore of Phrasikleia
550–530	Temple C at Selinus/Selinunte
540–530	Amphorae by Exekias
530	Kouros from Anavyssos
530–525	Siphnian Treasury at Delphi
520–510	Kraters by Euphronios
490	Battle of Marathon
490–485	Athenian Treasury at Delphi
480/479	Battle of Salamis, Sack of Athens

480–400	***Fifth-Century Classical***
480	Kritios Boy
477/6	Tyrannicides
480–470	Temple of Aphaia on Aigina
470	Tomb of the Diver, Poseidonia/Paestum
470–457	Temple of Zeus at Olympia
460–450	Riace Warriors, Artemision God, Cups by Sotades Painter
450–440	Doryphoros by Polykleitos
447–432	Parthenon
440	Lekythos by Achilles Painter
431–404	Peloponnesian War
431–405	Erechtheion
429	Death of Perikles
420–410	Nike Temple Parapet
400	Stele of Hegeso
400–330	***Fourth-Century Classical***
400–375	Mosaic at Olynthos
394/393	Monument of Dexileos at Athens
375–370	Temple of Asklepios at Epidauros
360–330	Thymele at Epidauros
360–350	Mausoleion at Halikarnassos
350	Aphrodite of Knidos by Praxiteles
350–330	Antikythera Youth
350–340	Temple of Athena at Tegea
359–336	Reign of Philip II of Macedon
348	Destruction of Olynthos
337/6–333/2	Daochos Monument at Delphi
336–323	Reign of Alexander the Great
335–317	Tomb II at Vergina
334	Lysikrates Monument at Athens
331	Founding of Alexandria, Egypt
330	Theater at Epidauros

330–30	***Hellenistic Period***
325–311	Alexander Sarcophagus
300	Founding of Antioch, Statue of Tyche of Antioch
300	Beginning of Temple of Apollo at Didyma
281	Founding of Pergamon
211	Rome sacks Syracuse/Siracusa
200–190	Cult Statues from Sanctuary of Despoina at Lykosoura by Damophon
180–150	Great Altar of Zeus at Pergamon
166–100	House of Dionysos at Delos
160	Asklepieion at Kos
150–100	Aphrodite from Melos
146	Rome sacks Corinth
120–80	Alexander Mosaic from Pompeii
100	Aphrodite with Slipper from Delos
86	Rome sacks Athens
c. 80	Antikythera Shipwreck
70–60	Mahdia Shipwreck
50–25	Sperlonga Sculpture
31	Rome conquers Egypt

ABOUT THE WEBSITE

www.wiley.com/go/greekart

The *Greek Art* companion website features resources created by the author to help you use this book in university courses, whether you're an instructor or a student.

FOR INSTRUCTORS AND STUDENTS

- **Glossary**
- **Timeline**

FOR INSTRUCTORS

- **Slides images included in the book**
- **Sample syllabi**

MAPS

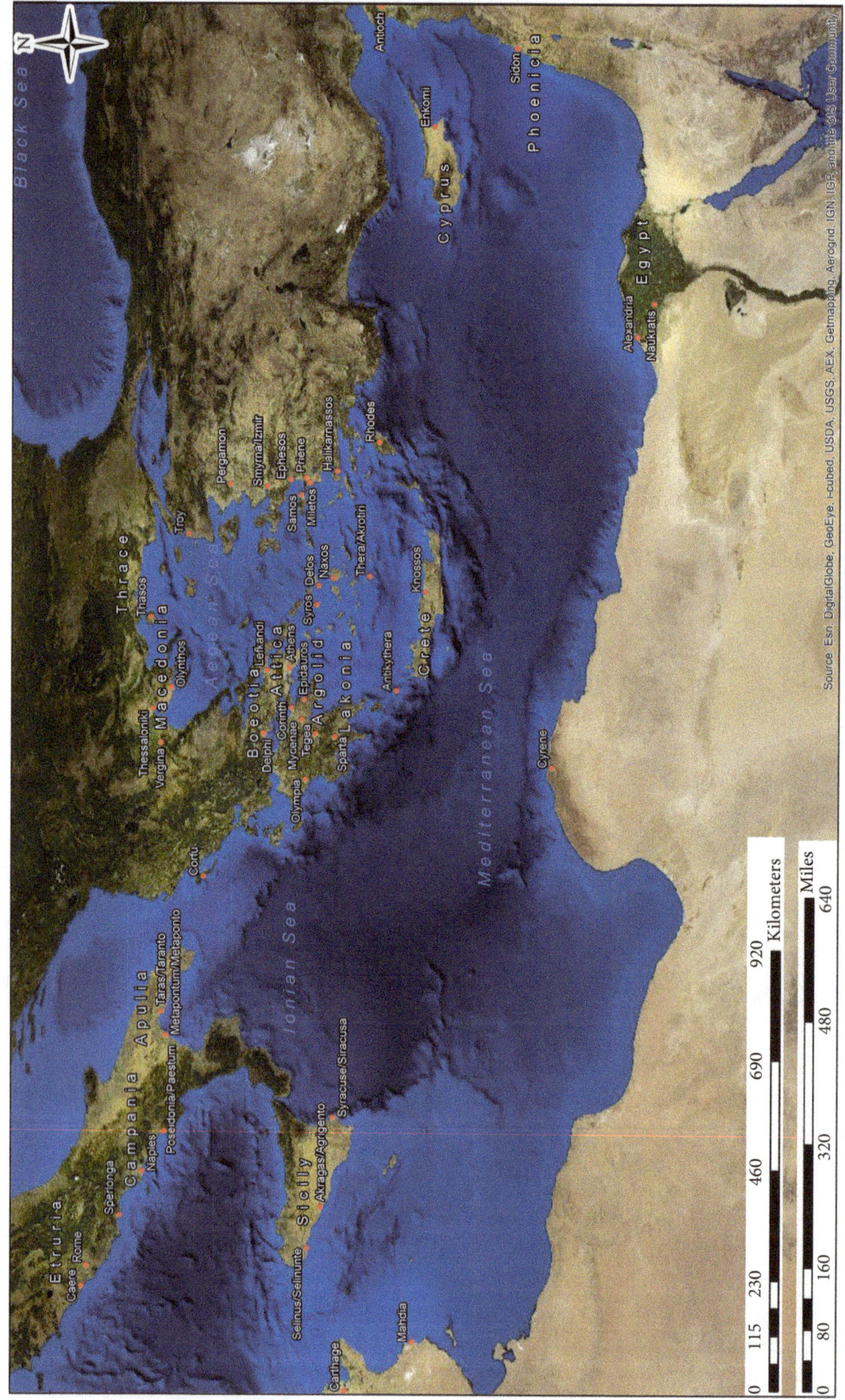

Map 1 Eastern Mediterranean. Source: Environmental Systems Research Institute, Inc. (Esri); map made by Mitchell Schaps, GIS Major, and Sarah McNamara, GIS Minor, Department of Geography, University of St. Thomas.

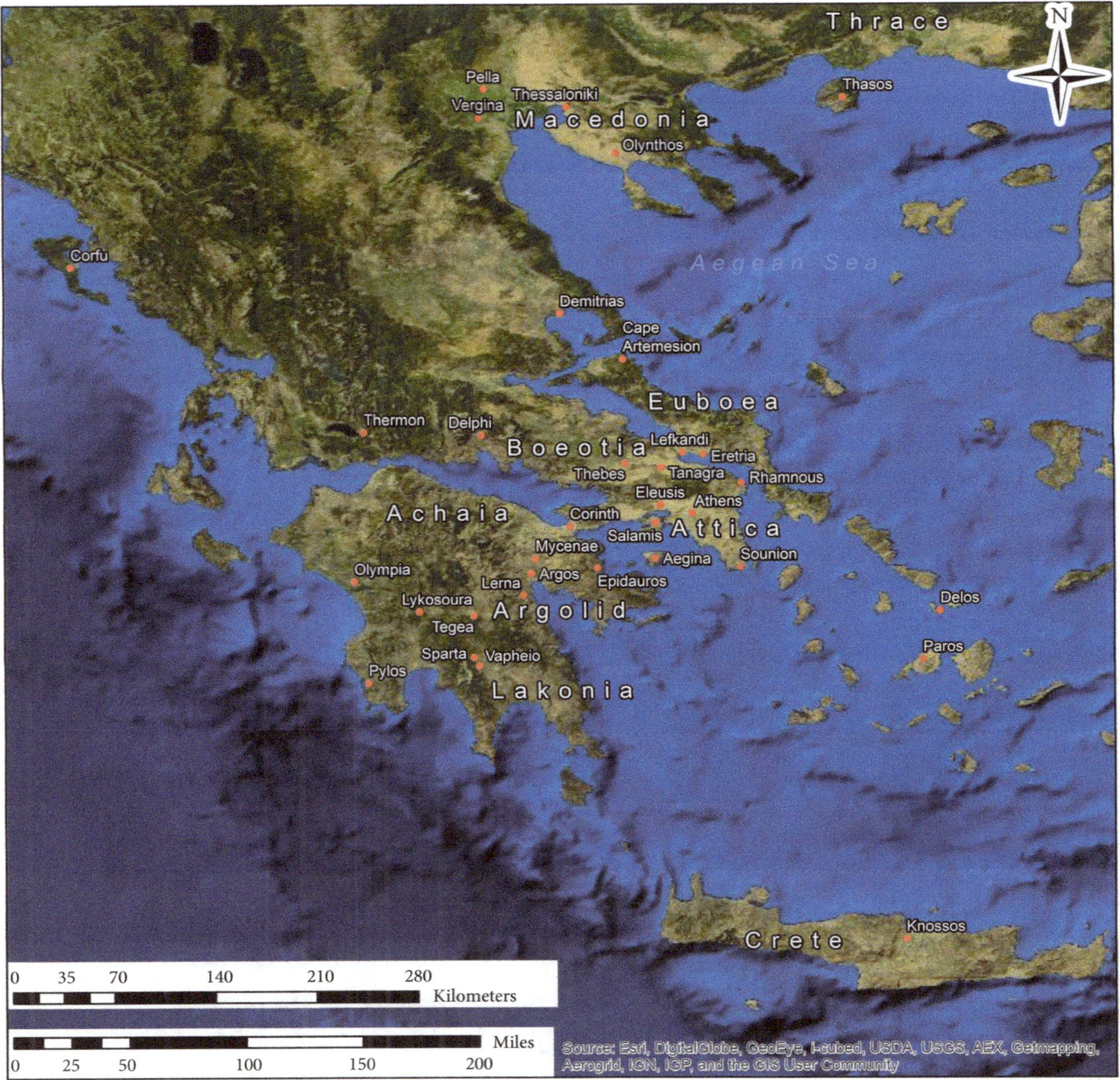

Map 2 Mainland Greece. Source: Environmental Systems Research Institute, Inc. (Esri); map made by Mitchell Schaps, GIS Major, and Sarah McNamara, GIS Minor, Department of Geography, University of St. Thomas.

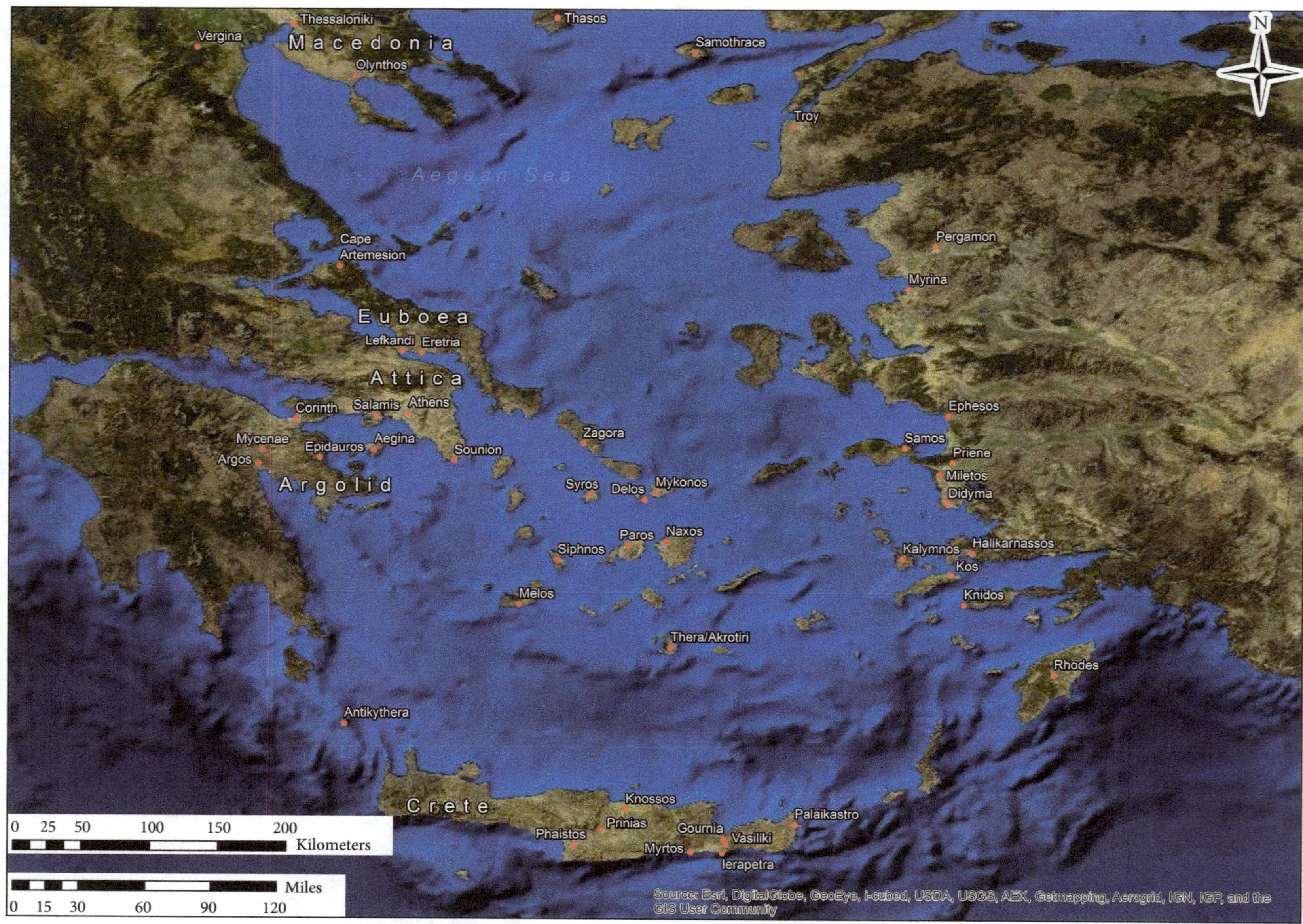

Map 3 Aegean Sea. Source: Environmental Systems Research Institute, Inc. (Esri); map made by Mitchell Schaps, GIS Major, and Sarah McNamara, GIS Minor, Department of Geography, University of St. Thomas.

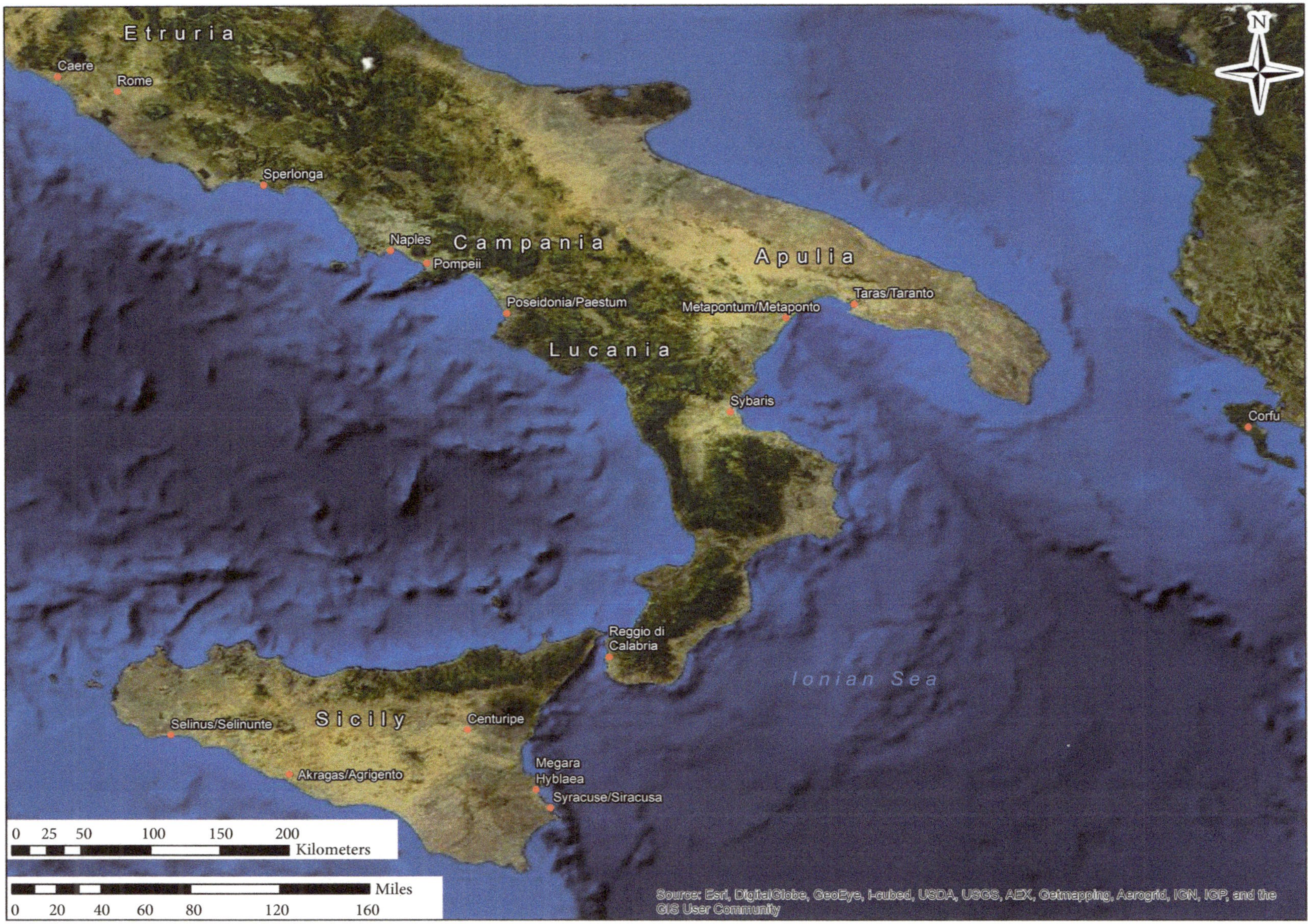

Map 4 Southern Italy and Sicily. Source: Environmental Systems Research Institute, Inc. (Esri); map made by Mitchell Schaps, GIS Major, and Sarah McNamara, GIS Minor, Department of Geography, University of St. Thomas.

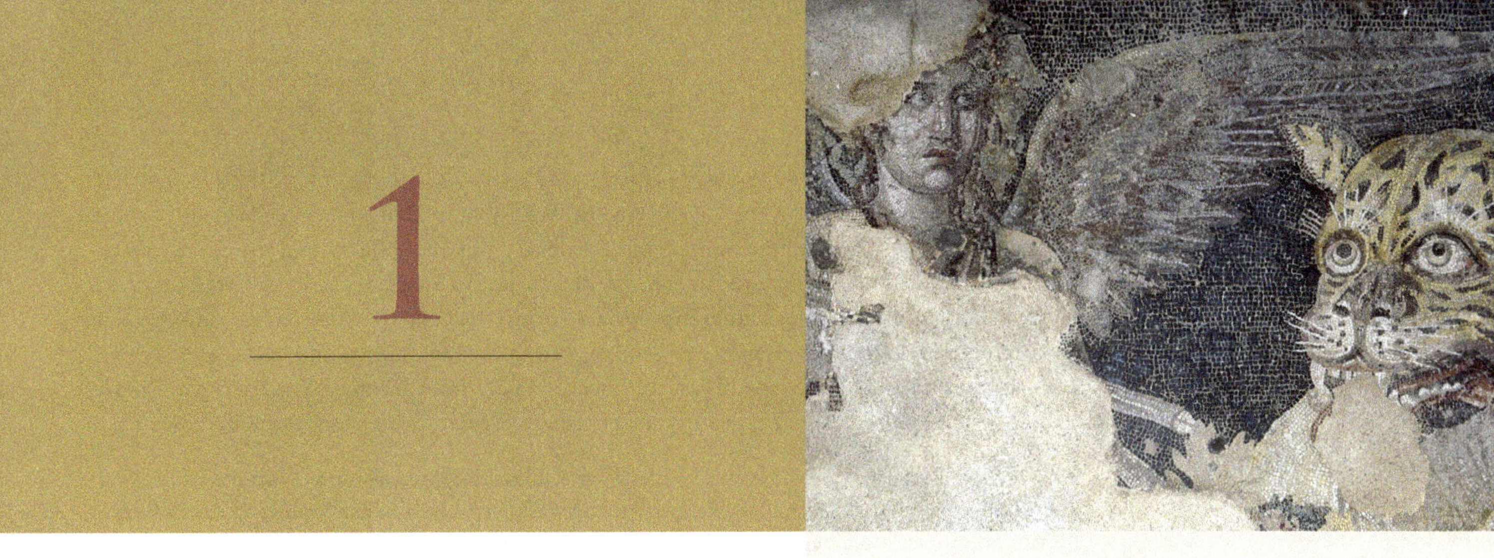

1

INTRODUCTION AND ISSUES IN THE HISTORY OF GREEK ART

An Alternative Mini-History of Greek Art
Some Questions to Consider for this Book
The Plan of this Book
A Few Notes About Using this Book
Textbox: Stylistic Analysis and Sir John Beazley
References
Further Reading

A History of Greek Art, First Edition. Mark D. Stansbury-O'Donnell.

Hellenistic period
Greek art from the time of Alexander the Great (d. 323 BCE) to the reign of the Roman emperor Augustus (r. 31 BCE–14 CE), generally *c.* 330–30 BCE.

The first histories of Greek art were written in the **Hellenistic period** of the third to first centuries BCE, during the last period covered in this book. By that time, Greek art and culture had spread well beyond the borders of the country of Greece today, and the Greeks themselves lived in cities from Russia and Afghanistan in the east to Spain in the west. Greek art was a common sight in Rome, whether statues expropriated from cities that the Romans had conquered or works commissioned from Greek artists by Roman patrons for their homes and villas.

The oldest extant account of the history of Greek art is a "mini-history" written by the Roman orator Cicero around 46 BCE and appearing in his history of rhetoric and orators entitled *Brutus*:

> Who, of those who pay some attention to the lesser arts, does not appreciate the fact that the statues of Kanachos were more rigid than they ought to have been if they were to imitate reality? The statues of Kalamis are also hard, although they are softer than those of Kanachos. Even the statues of Myron had not yet been brought to a satisfactory representation of reality, although at that stage you would not hesitate to say that they were beautiful. Those of Polykleitos are still more beautiful; in fact, just about perfect, as they usually seem to me. A similar systematic development exists in painting. In the art of Zeuxis, Polygnotos, and Timanthes and the others who did not make use of more than four colors, we praise their forms and their draughtsmanship. But in the art of Aëtion, Nikomachos, Protogenes, and Apelles, everything has come to a stage of perfection. (Cicero, *Brutus* 70; tr. Pollitt 1990, 223)

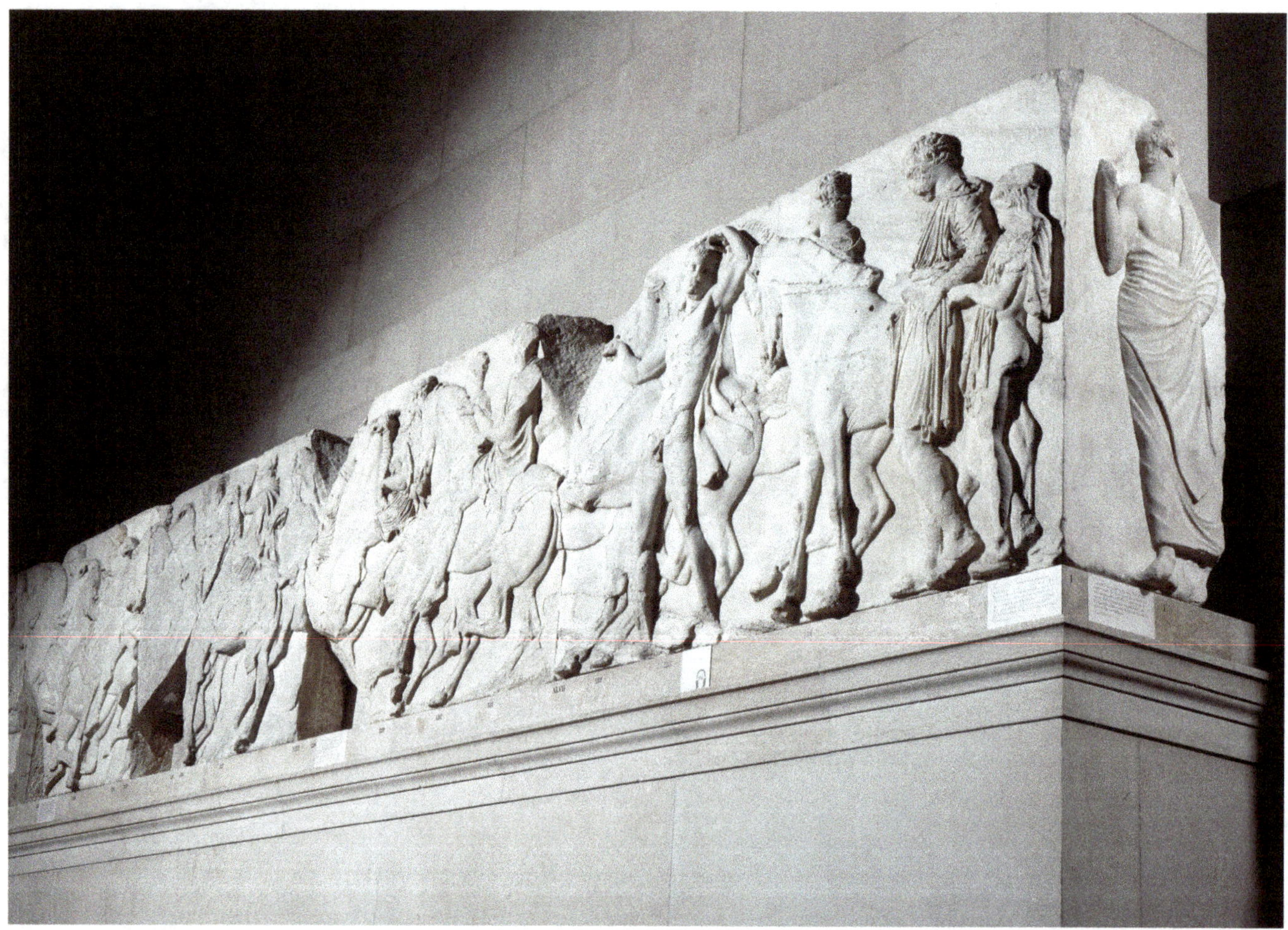

1.1 North frieze of the Parthenon, 442–438 BCE. 3 ft 5¾ in (1.06 m). London, British Museum. Cavalcade. Photo: © The Trustees of the British Museum.

Brief though it is, this passage has the ingredients necessary for a history. Drawing from earlier Greek sources, Cicero names a series of artists in a chronological sequence, presenting us with a **relative chronology** of people and events, rather than an **absolute chronology** based on specific dates. He also tells us about the accomplishments of these artists. The first, Kanachos, created statues of the human figure in rigid postures, whereas his successors developed statues that were increasingly softer and more lifelike in appearance. This happened progressively over several generations, and Cicero singles out **Polykleitos** as nearly perfect in the way he sculpted the human form. We will see later a copy of a bronze statue called the **Doryphoros** or "Spear-Bearer" by Polykleitos **(see Figure 10.7, page 243)**, but for now we can look at a similar figure from the Parthenon frieze that can be given an absolute date between 442 and 438 BCE based on the inscribed accounts of building expenses for the Parthenon **(Figure 1.1)**. The figure standing in front of the horse touching his head with his left arm stands in a very lifelike pose with the weight to one hip and leg. The muscles and anatomy of the body are articulated accurately and precisely, making him lifelike in appearance. Furthermore, he is a graceful, athletic figure whose nudity allows us to admire his beauty. We can see how Cicero might acclaim a Polykleitan statue of the mid-fifth century BCE as both beautiful and "just about perfect."

relative chronology
the dating of a work by its relationship to other works, either before, after, or at the same time

absolute chronology
the dating of a work to a specific calendar year(s) through external evidence, or a range of years on the basis of comparison to works with known dates

Polykleitos
sculptor active in the second half of the fifth century BCE

Doryphoros
"Spear-Bearer," a bronze sculpture of *c.* 450–440 BCE by Polykleitos now found only in copies

In his brief history, Cicero articulates an operating principle for Greek art, and in doing so makes his account more historical and interpretive than simply a chronicle of events and facts. He states, twice, that the purpose of art is to represent reality, and this becomes in turn a standard by which he judges the relative degree of success of the different artists. Not only do statues become more lifelike in their appearance, but they also become more beautiful, making a second criterion by which one can judge art and evaluate the achievements of different artists.

Cicero's two principles, reality and beauty, are not exclusive to Greek sculpture, and are also the standard for his comments on the history of painting. In this even briefer passage, Cicero notes that painters underwent the same type of systematic development, from four-color work that relied on drawing, to presumably a full palette of colors with shading to make two-dimensional figures seem three-dimensional. What Cicero does not tell us directly, however, is that Apelles, the epitome of perfection for painting, was an artist who lived a century after the sculptor Polykleitos, so that the history of painting had a different absolute timetable than the history of sculpture. We have little surviving mural painting from this era, but we might look at a painting done on a ceramic vase about the same time as the Parthenon frieze **(Figure 1.2)**. On the exterior of this vase, a mixing bowl or **krater**, we see Hermes bringing the infant Dionysos to Papasilenos for safekeeping from Hera, who was once again jealous over an illegitimate child fathered by Zeus. The figures are mostly in outline form with just a few added colors, and the effect is somewhat like the four colors of Polygnotos and Zeuxis mentioned by Cicero. There are some of the three-dimensional effects of perspective and shading, but on the whole, this painting would not seem to have met the standard of illusionistic "perfection" achieved by Apelles a hundred years later.

krater
large, open vessel for the mixing of wine and water

Cicero's purpose was not to write a history of Greek art for its own sake, but to use it as an example of parallels to the development of oratory, which was of greater prestige than the "lesser arts" of painting and sculpture. We have to consider that this context filters the principles and protagonists of his history. In writing about oratory, Cicero claims that it reaches its perfection with Roman orators of the first century BCE, surpassing earlier Greek rhetoricians. That Greek painting peaked later than sculpture makes the point that artistic development is not uniform and that oratory in contemporary Rome is just about perfect.

We further have to consider that the Latin terms used by Cicero might have meant something slightly different than the equivalent Greek terms would have meant in his sources. He uses the adjective *verus* and the noun *veritas* to describe the purpose of art, words that mean real and reality, as well as truthful and truth. In colloquial use, the meaning of the term with regard to art is "accurate representation of the natural appearance of a thing," so that a work of art should look like a living

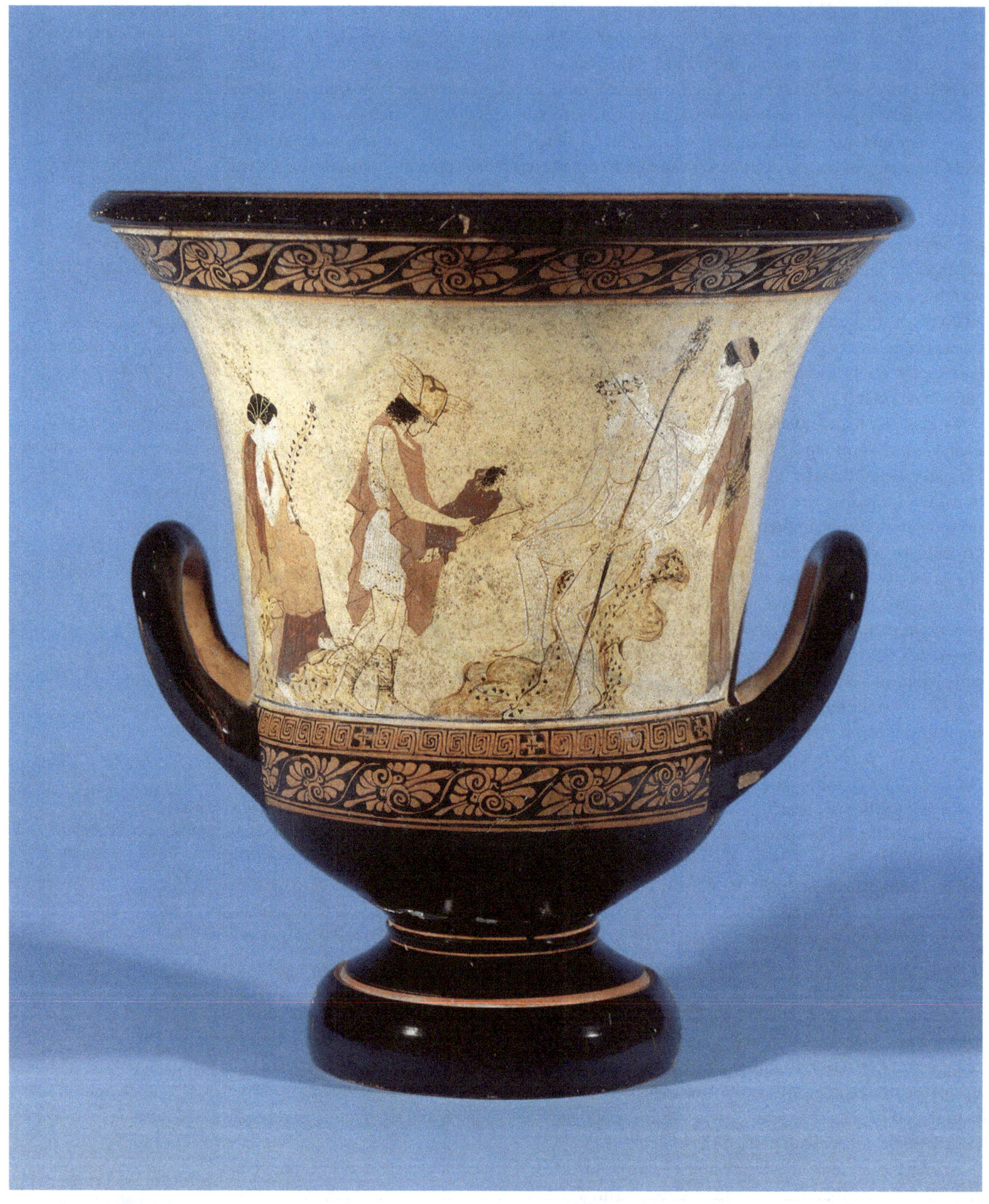

1.2 Attic white-ground calyx krater attributed to the Phiale Painter, *c.* 440 BCE. 12 15/16 in (32.8 cm). Vatican, Museo Gregoriano Etrusco Vaticano 559. Hermes bringing the infant Dionysos to Papasilenos. Photo: Scala/Art Resource, NY.

human being (Pollitt 1974, 138). Comparing the Parthenon frieze to an earlier work like the statues in **Figure 8.9 (page 190)**, we can readily see that the Parthenon figure is more lifelike, more "real" or "true" in appearance. For Cicero as a Roman, however, there was also a tradition of lifelike individual portraits of citizens, frequently elderly men and women with deeply lined faces and receding hairlines. These portraits are also true, but they would hardly be described as beautiful like the Parthenon figure or the Doryphoros of Polykleitos.

Unlike today's histories of Greek art, Cicero did not include any illustrations so that his readers could see what he was saying. Rather, Cicero assumes that his audience is already familiar with a number of these artists and with the general outlines of the history of **style** in Greek art. Indeed, the construct that Cicero presents of Greek art going from less lifelike (stiff) to very lifelike (real) in its representation of the human form, of the human figure being the most important subject of art in both Greece and Rome, and of Greek art of the fifth and fourth centuries BCE achieving a standard of beauty by which Roman or other art was measured, are themes that have dominated the modern histories of Greek art since the eighteenth century, when Johann Winkelmann published what is considered the first modern history of Greek art in 1764.

style
a system of renderings used to form the details of a subject or a set of forms and shapes used to fashion an object

The modern vocabulary of art history, however, has changed. If one were to describe the Parthenon figure as "**realistic**" it would be misleading for a contemporary reader. The youthful male on the frieze is perfectly proportioned and graceful; he does not look like your average, everyday twenty-year-old. We would describe him as **idealized** rather than realistic. The Terme Boxer that we shall see near the end of the book **(see Figure 14.22, page 367)** is realistic in his representation: scarred, cut, and deformed as a result of the boxing contests he has fought. Both figures fit Cicero's stated purpose of art as a representation of reality/truth, but a better modern art historical term for *verus* would be **naturalistic**, lifelike in appearance. Its opposite, the stiff figures of Kanachos, is best described by the term **abstract**, a simplified and schematic rendering of the human figure.

realistic
the representation of a subject as it is, including individual traits or imperfections

idealized, idealistic
the representation of a subject as perfect in its proportions, beauty, or form

naturalistic
the representation of a subject in art as being lifelike in its appearance

abstract
the representation of a subject in art in a simplified, reduced, or schematic form

One might wonder, then, why there should be new histories of Greek art, since it was already an old and well-known story for Cicero. One reason is that Greek art was both familiar and contemporary for Cicero and his audience; it was still being produced when he lived and we have letters from him to Atticus, a friend and agent in Athens, with instructions and comments for purchases of Greek art to be shipped to Cicero's villa in Tusculum, Italy. There the statues would adorn his library and what he called his "**gymnasia**," colonnaded gardens modeled on the sites where Greek youth received physical and philosophical education. Cicero named his two gymnasia the Academy, where Plato had taught in Athens, and the Lyceum, where Aristotle taught. Indeed, Cicero had spent time studying philosophy in Athens as a young man and wanted to replicate the atmosphere of these places at his villa. Greek art was still alive in Cicero's day, even if it had reached its peak much earlier, but for Cicero its purpose was decorative and personal, quite different from the public and purposeful role that Greek art played in its original setting.

gymnasion (pl. gymnasia)
a building associated with physical and philosophical education, usually consisting of an open area flanked by porches or colonnades

Today, Greek art lives mostly in museums and is not part of the visual fabric of daily life, making it even more remote and foreign than it was to Cicero. Our terminology and cultural standards are different from Cicero's and to learn about Greek art today requires much more remedial education about Greek life and culture. Another factor in approaching Greek art history again is that the questions of interest to art historians and archaeologists today have changed. Rather than looking for masterpieces of Greek art mentioned by Cicero and organizing collections by period, place, and subject matter, students of Greek art today are becoming more interested in the context of Greek art: who made something, who paid for it, what purpose did it serve, and what importance did it have in the lives of the ancient Greeks. We need to develop a history that can begin to address some of those questions.

AN ALTERNATIVE MINI-HISTORY OF GREEK ART

Geometric period
Greek art produced between *c.* 900 and 700 BCE

archaic period
Greek art produced between *c.* 720/700 and 480 BCE. From *archaios*, meaning "old"

classical period
Greek art produced between *c.* 480 and 330 BCE

Objects do not come with a certificate of authenticity bearing a date or place of origin. Before we can consider their art historical interest, we have to place each in time by examining and comparing its style to other objects. The shape of a work and its components, the patterns used to ornament or enhance it, and the techniques used in its creation can be distinctive criteria for defining a particular style, as can be its representation of human, animal, and vegetal subjects. As we saw in Cicero's passage, the development of representational style can be a key distinguishing feature of the history of Greek art. Very broadly speaking, Greek art of the tenth to eighth centuries BCE, the **Geometric period**, was very simple compared to contemporary Egyptian art, but by the seventh and sixth centuries BCE, the **archaic period**, Greek artists were producing statues that were comparable in technique and style. By the fifth and fourth centuries BCE, the **classical period**, Greek art developed a consistently lifelike style that was distinctive in the ancient world. In the last three centuries of the millennium, the Hellenistic period, it developed new and even more expressive styles. It is the variation of style from one work to the next that provides a key for identifying its origin and time.

One needs to be cautious, however, about seeing an "evolution" of representational style from abstract to naturalistic as being smoothly progressive or inevitable. Greek art could change dramatically from one region to another, and we can find examples of Greek art in which different artistic styles are combined on the same building or even in the same work. By at least the fifth century BCE Greek artists were producing works that were deliberately older in style, imitating the works of earlier centuries in what would be called today a "retro" style. The lifelike representation of the human figure was not an artistic end in itself and we need to consider the function and context of a work to think about how its appearance might have served a purpose for the artist or the patron.

terracotta
objects made of fired clay, generally small figures, most of which are made with molds and can be painted

votive offering
an offering to a god or shrine to fulfill a vow or recognize a benefit

grave goods
artwork and other objects placed in a grave with the remains of the deceased

techne
the Greek term for art, meaning skill, craft, or cunning of hand

terminus
a fixed calendar date determined by documentary evidence

terminus ad quem
a calendar date at which an object was made

terminus ante quem
a calendar date before which an object was made

terminus post quem
a calendar date after which an object was made

One might construct an alternative to Cicero's grand if short narrative of Greek art by looking at smaller and more modest works, **terracotta** figures that are mostly found in the excavation of sanctuaries where they were **votive offerings**, or in tombs where they served as **grave goods** for the deceased. Such objects fall outside of the traditional "fine arts" of sculpture, painting, and architecture and are more typically labeled "decorative arts." A small bronze figure like that dedicated by Mantiklos that we shall see in Chapter 7 **(see Figure 7.19, page 176)** would generally be placed in the category of decorative art, unlike the large bronze god that we shall see later in this chapter **(see Figure 1.7)**. For its time, however, it is a product that would have been an expensive investment in resources and skill that was worthy of recording the name of the donor/patron on it. Whereas a Greek viewer or patron would recognize the differences in value and visual appeal between a small terracotta and large marble figure, functionally they could serve the same purpose and be invested with similar value in terms of their meaning. Greek art was not made simply for its aesthetic value, but had a social, religious, and cultural purpose that guided its form and content. Accordingly, we need to use a wider definition of what is a work of art. The Greek word for art, ***techne***, is defined as art, skill, craft, or cunning of hand and encompasses the traditional fine arts as well as pottery, metalwork, and shipbuilding. The emphasis is upon the skill required to transform material into something else, whether stone into sculpture, wood into a ship, or words into a speech. For our purposes, we should consider art as an object or work that has been created through the application of skill to materials to create a work that has visual appeal and that serves a cultural or social function. In addition to architecture, painting, and sculpture, this means we shall be looking at jewelry, metalwork, painted and plain pottery, and terracottas throughout this book.

We begin with a terracotta woman that was excavated at the sanctuary at Olympia **(Figure 1.3)**. This figure has been formed from clay that was then fired; the body is flat and schematic, looking as if it were made by a cookie-cutter with blocky arms and legs. The head has been shaped more three-dimensionally with added clay that was worked by hand to make a chin, nose, and hairpiece. Afterward, the details of mouth, nostrils, hair, and genitals were made by incising the clay with a sharp tool, and the eyes, nipples, and navel by pushing a hollow reed or similar device into the clay. The figure is recognizably human but not very lifelike; it has an abstract style that reduces the components and details of the human body to simple forms. Indeed, there are many and more numerous male figures found at Olympia that differ from this "Hera-type" in only a few details like the genitals.

In order to begin to understand this artifact's place in a history of Greek art, we need to observe it closely, analyzing as we did its style – the way in which its details, features, and overall composition and form are made by the artist. The advantage of looking at works like terracotta figures and pottery is that they are mass-produced and artists use familiar techniques and features to make them, somewhat like handwriting. We presume that artifacts that are similar in style are similar in time and origin, and by comparing their archaeological contexts and layers across many sites, archaeologists can establish a relative sequence of their manufacture and designate each grouping as a period in a relative chronology, like Late Geometric I for the Hera-type figure. The relative sequence of chronological periods can sometimes be anchored to more specific calendar dates, or absolute chronology, by comparison with works for which there is external evidence, such as a date of destruction or foundation of a site or building, or the rule of a specific person like a king or tyrant. Such a chronological point is a **terminus**, or fixed point. For example, fragments of inscribed building accounts for the Acropolis allow us to place the Parthenon frieze above into a four-year period of 442–438 BCE, making this a ***terminus ad quem***, a date at which it was made. An object buried in the foundations of the Parthenon as construction fill would date sometime before the beginning of construction of the temple structure; this ***terminus ante quem*** would then be "before 448" when construction began, but how much before that date would not be certain. Finally, a work dedicated inside the Parthenon after it was dedicated in 438 would have a ***terminus post quem***, or date after which: "after 438."

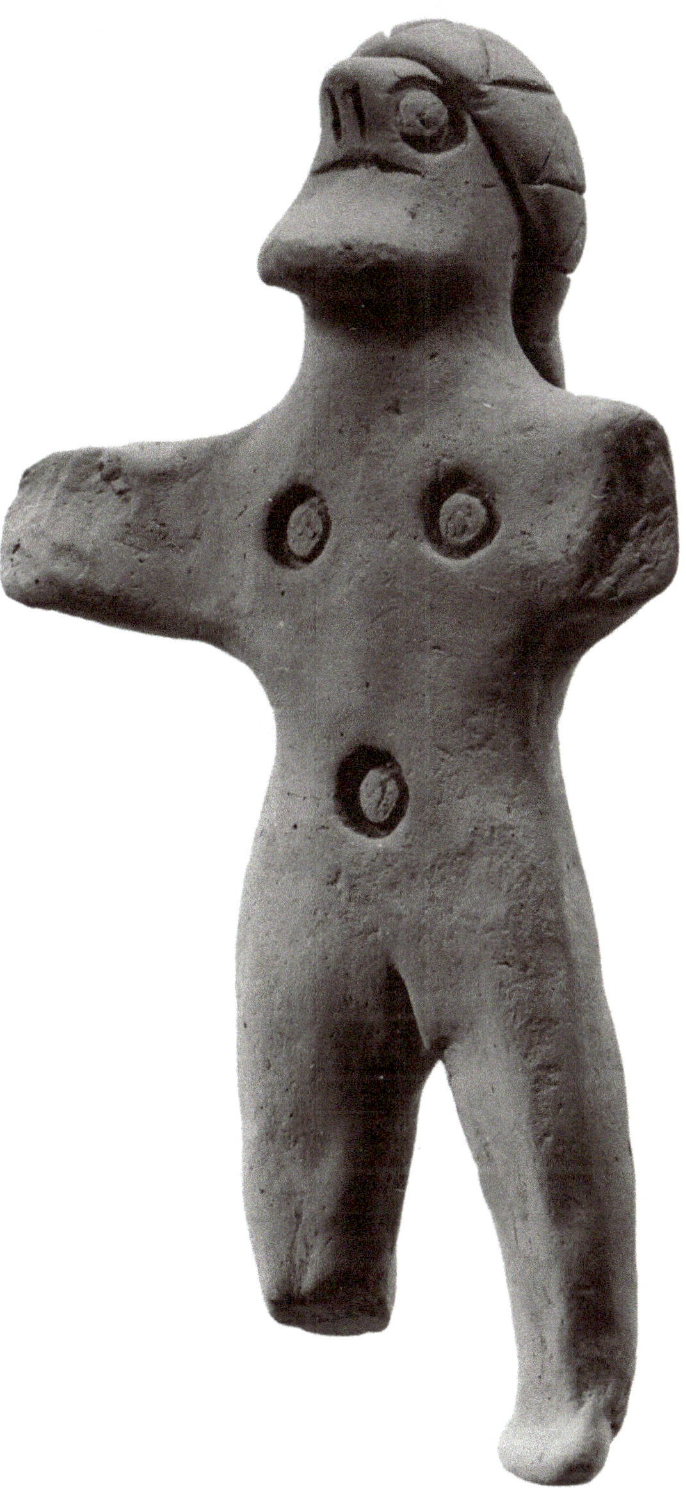

1.3 Late Geometric I "Hera"-type terracotta figure from Olympia, *c.* 750–725 BCE. 6 7/16 in (16.4 cm). Olympia, Archaeological Museum Tc2285 (K151). Photo: Gösta Hellner, DAI-ATH-Neg. 1970/0804.

The number of fixed chronological points for Greek art history, however, is very small and many works, like the Olympia terracotta, can only be dated very generally since there is no external evidence for specific dates at Olympia until much later. These figures, belonging to the Late Geometric I period, are generally dated from the second half of the eighth century by a process of comparison with dates established at other sites and a consideration of the approximate passing of time or generations in the sequence of materials, working backward or forward from whatever termini exist.

The terracotta is roughly contemporary with the ***Iliad*** of Homer, but this modest figure presents a different vantage point about Greek cultural and art history from Cicero's principles of lifelike, perfect beauty in the representation of the human form. What the "Hera-type" figure represents is not certain and it comes from a time when writing was only beginning to be readopted in Greek culture, leaving us with little in the way of contemporary records outside of literature. Since the terracottas and others like it are found at the sanctuary of Zeus, where there was also a cult to his wife Hera, they may represent the goddess as votive offerings. What is unusual about them if they are Hera, however, is that they are nude. Nudity, as we shall see in Chapter 4, becomes standard for representing the male figure in the eighth century, but female nudity develops much later as an artistic subject, and then is associated with Aphrodite, not Hera. Hera, as wife and queen, is shown clothed and regal in later art, where her identification is certain based on inscriptions or attributes. A nude Hera would not seem to be a logical precedent for these later representations based on religious and social continuity, leaving the identification of the figure open to question. If we look outside of Greece in the eighth century, however, we can find examples of female nudity in figures produced in the **Levant**, where fertility figures like **Astarte** were popular. The Olympia figures are far more abstract in style and less three-dimensional in their form, but perhaps there is an influence at work. These are not just idle issues about identifying subject matter, but address questions about gender, religious, social, and cultural identity that are of interest for a history of art.

Iliad
epic poem of Homer recounting the beginning of the tenth year of the Trojan War and the deaths of Sarpedon, Patroklos, and Hektor and the anger of Achilles. Generally dated to the later 8th cent. BCE

Levant
the area of the eastern Mediterranean that includes present-day Israel, Jordan, Lebanon, and Syria

Astarte
Phoenician goddess of fertility and sex often represented as a nude figure

A second terracotta shows a more lifelike representation of the human figure (**Figure 1.4**). This work, found in a tomb in the Kamiros cemetery on the island of Rhodes and acquired by the British Museum in 1861, has much more accurate details of anatomy and its proportions are closer to the human body. The folds and edges of the clothing are shown in a way that suggests the body underneath, and paint helps to distinguish the cloth from the exposed sections of the body. The woman is shown with one foot forward, and she pulls at her skirt to facilitate movement. She holds a small rabbit in her right arm, possibly making an offering or holding it as an attribute. The figure is stiff and closed in silhouette, and this kind of style is generally labeled archaic to distinguish it from the earlier geometric and the later classical periods. Figures like this are generally dated based on the style to the first half of the sixth century BCE, almost two centuries later than the Hera-type figure from Olympia. This style would loosely fit the description that Cicero gives for the statues of Kanachos, "more rigid than they ought to have been if they were to imitate reality." Indeed, the terracotta is probably even more rigid and rudimentary than were the statues of Kanachos.

Again, we can consider some questions about this modest figure. It was found in a tomb, but we have no further information about the context: what type of burial, the identity of the deceased, why it is was placed in the tomb, or whether there were other artifacts in the grave. A slender female figure with braided hair is usually considered to be a young maiden reaching her adolescence, when she takes on important public religious roles and may prepare for marriage. She is an idealized figure, well dressed, modestly posed, and acting piously, but is she meant to signify a goddess or a devotee: is the rabbit an attribute or offering? If the terracotta were from the tomb of a girl, did the deceased die before she was old enough to take on these roles, making the figure a symbol of her and her family's aspirations and feelings at her untimely loss? Is the figure meant to comfort the spirit or ***psyche*** of the deceased in the afterlife? Similar types of figures are also found in sanctuaries; was this artifact made for one purpose, or did it represent a concept that could be appropriate in different situations and could be sold to different purchasers for different purposes? Some of these questions could be answered if we knew more about its **findspot**, and we shall consider this further below, but this would require comparing the work to others to see if there is a consistent pattern in their function or distribution.

psyche
the spirit, soul, or shade of a person

findspot
the location where an object is found, including the site, locale, and the specific deposit or context such as a grave, well, debris pile, or construction fill

assemblage
a group of objects found together in an archaeological context or deposit such as a grave

kithara
a large stringed instrument similar to a lyre, usually with a squared base and curved upright arms

If we look at some figures dating another two centuries later, we can see that the representation of the human figure has shifted again (**Figure 1.5**). This collection of figures was found in the tomb of a girl in the Kerameikos cemetery in Athens and can be dated to about 380–370 BCE based on stylistic comparisons and archaeological context. While smaller and much more simplified compared to the Parthenon frieze, they do show a similar understanding of the body moving and twisting in space and performing more complex actions than the archaic terracotta. The figures were originally painted with white as well as red and blue and show a more naturalistic treatment of the human form. Both these and the archaic terracottas are idealized – poised and composed in their movement and showing a perfect set of proportions and beauty, but their styles and even their ideals are quite different.

This **assemblage** is unusual for grave goods in its number of objects and the variety of deities. While they are not individualized portraits as we think of them, each figure is differentiated from the others in details of action, objects, and attributes, allowing us, for example, to identify Apollo with the ***kithara*** third from right, the goddess Cybele seated in the center, and a priestess or follower of Cybele on the far right, which has been adapted from an Aphrodite-type of figure leaning on a column by the addition of a tympanum. Other figures are more universal in subject: a dancer, a woman carrying a girl, and a woman with a bowl who might be making an offering like a priestess. As grave goods these figures function like the archaic woman from Rhodes, but the assemblage suggests that beliefs in the afterlife might be more prominent in the minds of the family and culture, and that there was some effort to distinguish this burial ritual by the number of grave goods.

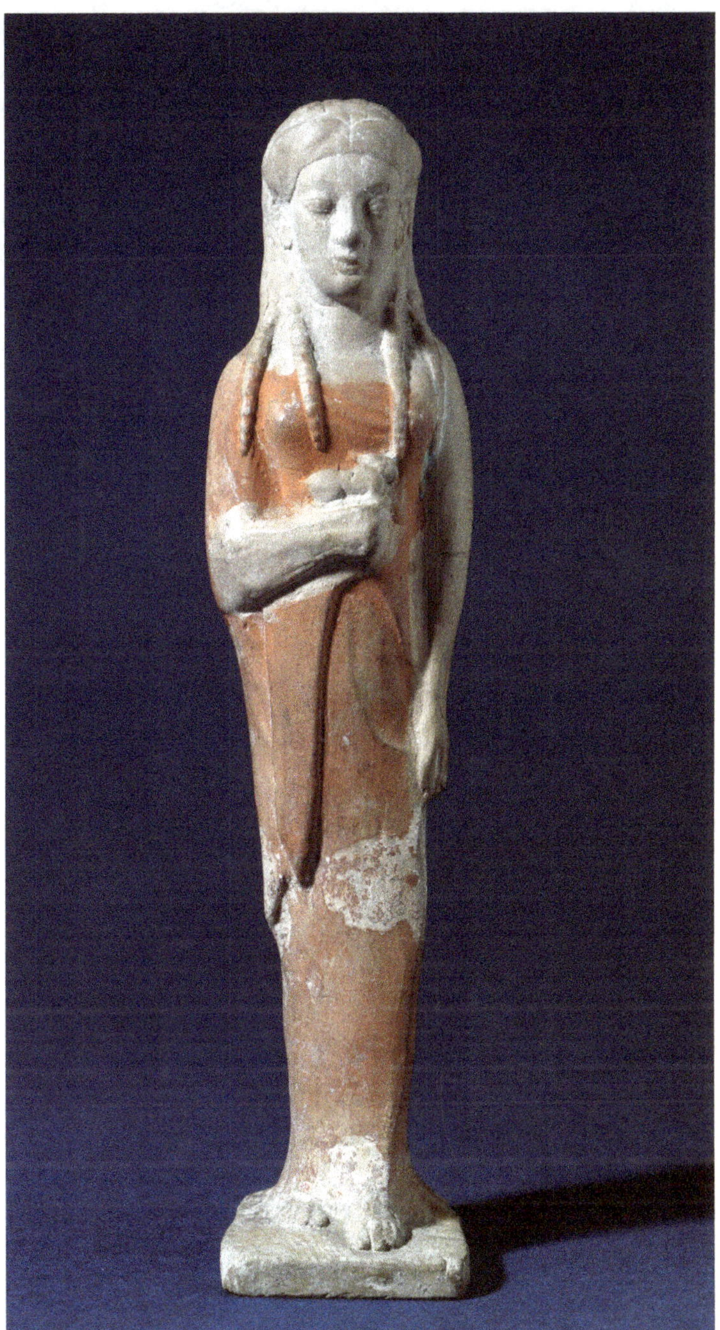

1.4 Terracotta woman from a grave at Kamiros cemetery, Rhodes, *c.* 600–540 BCE. 9³⁄₁₆ in (23.3 cm). London, British Museum 1861,1024.1. Photo: © The Trustees of the British Museum.

One last example of our miniature survey is a terracotta with two seated women that was probably made in Myrina in present-day Turkey (**Figure 1.6**). They are about 3 cm taller than the Apollo in the Kerameikos assemblage, and with their seated posture have a slightly larger scale. These figures are even more detailed in their rendering of the human body and the way that the cloth reacts to the movement of the body. Of particular note is that the figures are wearing double layers of garments and through the manipulation of the depth and direction of folds, the artist has been able to suggest the folds of the lower layer showing through the upper layer, especially on the left knee of the right-hand figure. The women are also shown interacting in an intimate and conversational way that mimics actual human behavior more closely. These are still idealized figures, but they are shown with more realism of behavior. Whether they are Demeter and her daughter Persephone, or a more universalizing pair of women, one might say that they are both real and beautiful, as Cicero praised the art of Polykleitos and Apelles. Curiously, however, these figures are much later than these artists, dating to the second

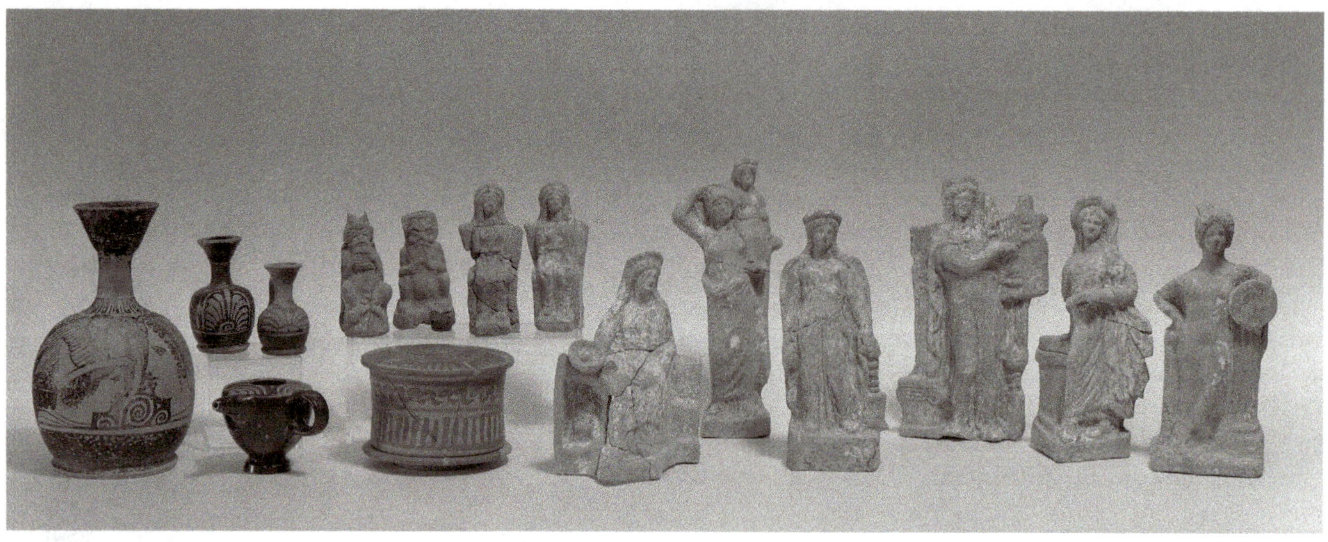

1.5 Terracotta figures from girl's tomb in Kerameikos cemetery, Athens, 380–370 BCE. Height of Apollo with Kithara: 6 15/16 in (17.6 cm). Athens, Kerameikos Museum HS.264. Photo: D-DAI-ATH-Kerameikos-Neg. 07051.

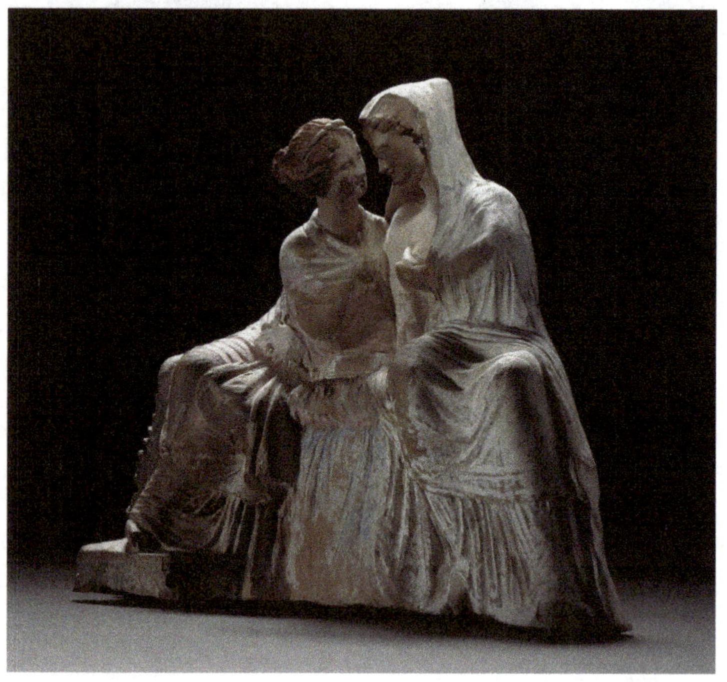

1.6 Terracotta group of women (Demeter and Persephone?), 2nd cent. BCE. 8 1/16 in (20.5 cm). London 1885,0316.1. Photo: © The Trustees of the British Museum.

century BCE. Their type, generally called **Tanagra figures** after a site in Boeotia where many were made and found, represents a high point of terracotta figures in Greek art during the Hellenistic period, a period that Cicero does not include in his list of artists. However, at least in terms of detail, precision, and complexity of figural representation, the seated pair are far more engaging and interesting as a work of art and it could be argued that Hellenistic terracottas surpass those of the classical period. In some ways, these terracottas trace a somewhat different history of Greek art than Cicero and give us an opportunity to consider other issues as well.

SOME QUESTIONS TO CONSIDER FOR THIS BOOK

Beyond style, the terracottas we have discussed have raised questions about the meaning of the figures and how and why they ended up in a tomb or sanctuary. Even when we know that an artifact like the terracotta from Kamiros came from a tomb, we do not know anything about the occupant of the tomb or the other artifacts found in it, as these details were not recorded as they were in the excavation of the Kerameikos tomb. The Tanagra terracotta highlights further the importance of **provenance** for the study of Greek art. This terracotta was purchased in 1885 by the British Museum from a collector, Charles Merlin, who had served as British Consul and later as agent and inspector of the Ionian Bank in Greece and who collected and sold hundreds of works to the museum. Most of these objects appear to have been chance finds, objects found by farmers or land

Tanagra figures
terracotta figures produced from the fourth to first centuries BCE, named after the site in Boeotia where they were first found in large quantities

owners or perhaps amateur archaeologists and then put up for sale, but some were probably dug up by opportunistic excavators simply to make money. The difficulty is that the specific context and purpose for this object, whether grave good, religious offering, or domestic decoration, is lost. Even the origin of the piece can be obscured, as the style is similar to terracottas produced in Myrina in Asia Minor in the second century, but one cannot verify that attribution, made on the basis of stylistic analysis and comparison, through external evidence.

We will consider issues of collecting and cultural patrimony later in the textbox in Chapter 10, but the destruction of archaeological context through grave-robbing and looting from archaeological sites is particularly problematic. In these cases, provenance is either missing or even falsified in order to expedite the transportation and sale of a work; less valuable or more fragmentary objects are discarded and destroyed and restorations to make the prize pieces salable can change the original fabric of the work. As time goes on and contemporary populations grow and spread, there is less chance to find undisturbed ancient sites to provide us with information about the context, and systematic looting accelerates that problem.

provenance the history of findspot and ownership for a work of art

Even when there is an archaeological context for a work of art, one does not always know its origin and purpose. For example, a monumental bronze statue of a god was found in a shipwreck in the sea off Cape Artemision, on the north of the island of Euboea, in 1926–1928 (**Figure 1.7**). The statue, dated by style to the mid-fifth century, about 460 BCE, was found with another, second-century BCE sculpture of a horse and jockey. Both statues were being taken somewhere by ship, perhaps to Rome from Greece. This means that the original context for the statue is lost, even if its archaeological context is better known, and we can only speculate about its original identity and purpose. The statue once held an implement in its right hand, meaning that we have no definitive attribute or other sign to identify the god. Most scholars today favor identifying the figure as Zeus with a thunderbolt, based on the shape and angle of the flange where the implement was once attached to the right hand.

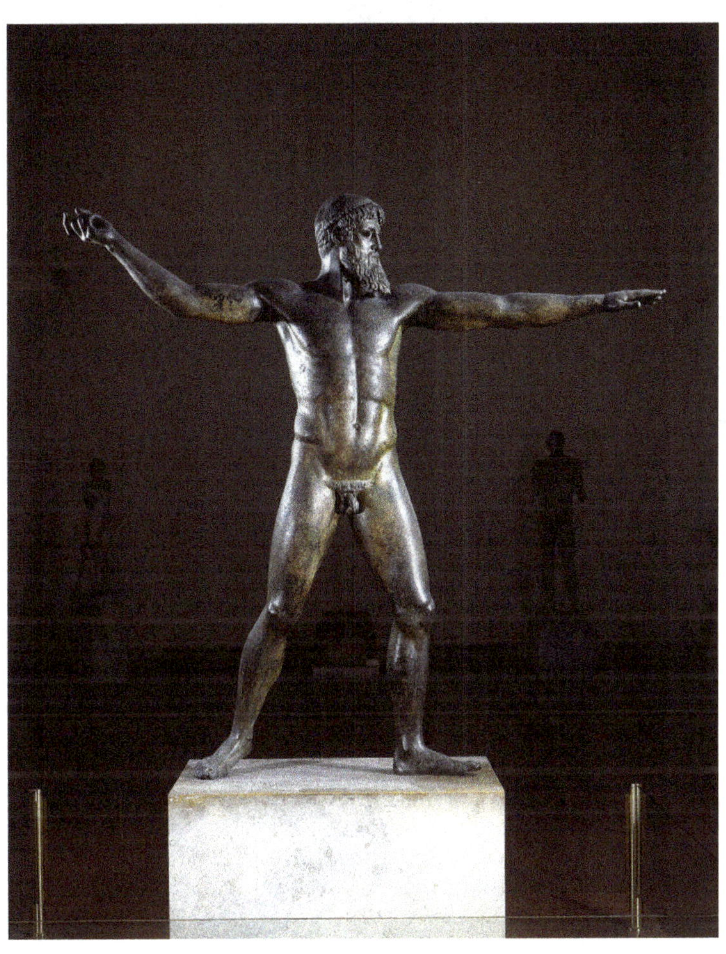

1.7 God (Zeus?) from Cape Artemision, *c.* 460 BCE. Bronze, 6 ft 10¼ in (2.09 m). Athens, National Archaeological Museum Br. 15161. Photo: National Archaeological Museum, Athens (Kostas Xenikakis) © Hellenic Ministry of Education and Religious Affairs, Culture and Sports/ Archaeological Receipts Fund.

Our ignorance of the original context, even when knowing the findspot, is of some importance in that the point of view for this work is critical for understanding how one might approach it. Entering its gallery in the National Archaeological Museum in Athens today, one sees the view in **Figure 1.7**. From this vantage point, the articulation of the anatomy and the strong pose quickly convey the power of a god aiming a weapon. This is the vantage point found in most reproductions, as it provides the clearest possible view of the body and its naturalistic rendering of anatomy and movement, and creates a striking composition for a photograph.

The figure is so lifelike in appearance that it is not immediately apparent to a visitor that his arms are too long; if one were to rotate the left arm down toward the leg, the fingertips would touch the knee rather than the lower thigh as would be normal. The lengthening of the arm enhances the drama of the figure, but it also provides a clue as to how it might have been viewed originally. Such a bronze figure would have been an important dedication in a sanctuary or public area, and so we should think about the viewer approaching the work along a prescribed path. If one were to approach

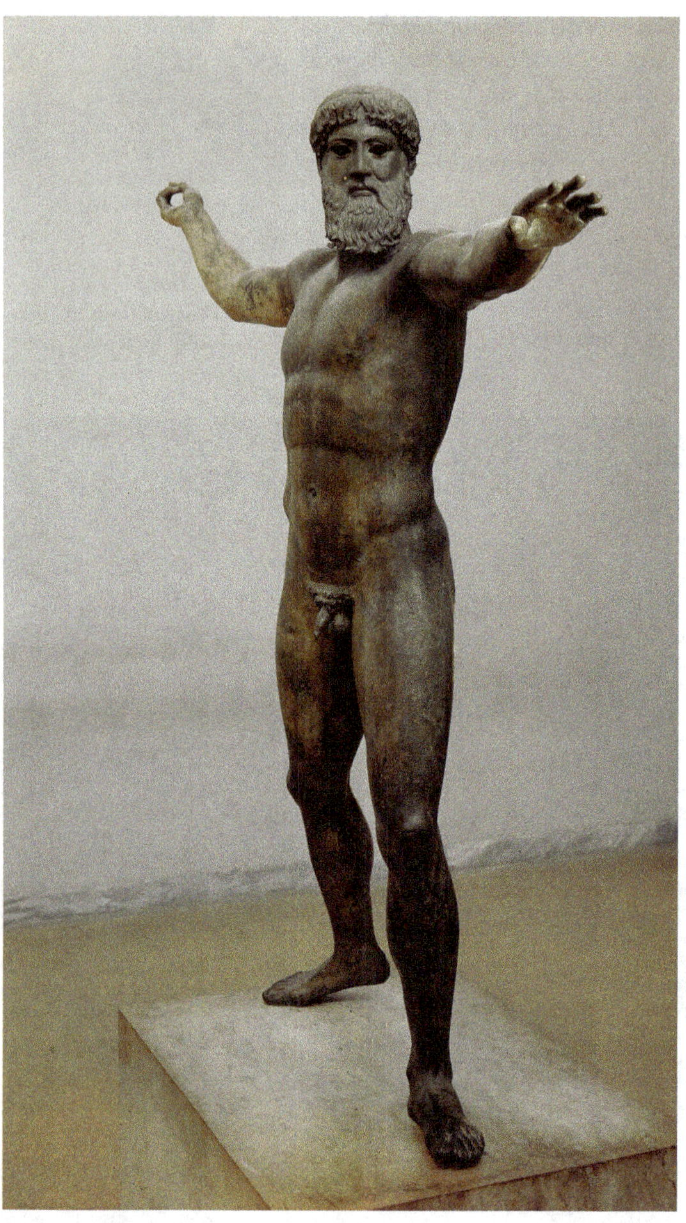

1.8 God (Zeus?) from Cape Artemision, *c.* 460 BCE. Bronze, 6 ft 10¼ in (2.09 m). Athens, National Archaeological Museum Br. 15161. Photo: Erich Lessing/Art Resource, NY.

the god from the front (**Figure 1.8**), one can see the god looking back. The weapon in the right arm would be aimed in the viewer's direction, and the extended left hand would be sighting the target in the viewer's direction too. From this vantage point, the lengthening of the arm adjusts for the foreshortened point of view and appears normally proportioned. This also changes the dynamics of viewing from the previous picture, in that the viewer is now also a target, a participant in the narrative action of the god. This view gives a dramatic vision of the power of a god and of the relationship between the human and divine missing in the other vantage point in **Figure 1.7**.

In other words, we need to consider not only the artist and patron/owner of a work of art, but also the viewer. We shall be discussing the Parthenon extensively in several chapters of this book, in part because of the lavish expenditure in its creation that made it one of the most refined and ornamented buildings in ancient Greece, and further due to its role as a symbol of Athens at its political and cultural height. In selecting a picture of the Acropolis for a book such as this, one usually sees views in which each of the buildings is as completely visible as possible. There is, however, one vantage point that brings them all together in a compact, stage-like view, as can be seen in **Figure 1.9**. In the center is the gateway to the Acropolis, the Propylaia, and just to its side the small Temple of Athena Nike (Victory). To the right and above is the west facade of the Parthenon, while to the left is the Erechtheion. The building to the left of the Propylaia obscures the view of the famous caryatid porch (**see Figure 7.8, page 164**), but contained the first Pinakothek, or painting museum. The buildings blend together, making the picture less suitable as an illustration to discuss their design, but what is significant about this view is that it is taken from the Pynx (**see Figure 5.2, page 101**). This open hillside to the west of the Acropolis is where the ***ekklesia***, the assembly of Athenian voters, would meet to hear speeches and vote on proposals. Standing in the Pynx in the fifth century and later was the height of citizen participation in governance, and from here the claims of Athens to cultural and political leadership became manifest in the marble buildings on the Acropolis to the east. One can imagine the appeals of politicians to the citizens, as we will discuss in Chapter 10, to look upon this and be lovers of the city. The buildings of the Acropolis are spaced so that one can see some of them from almost any part of the ancient city, but it is from the Pynx that they all come together as one ensemble as Athenians carried out some of their most important civic duties.

Nike
the goddess of victory. Also an attribute of another god or goddess who brings victory, such as Athena Nike

caryatid
a statue of a woman that serves as a support in place of a column. It is a feature of the Ionic order of architecture and can also be a support handle for a mirror

The questions that will be of interest in this book, then, will consider meaning, context, viewer, and identity. For example, not only do we want to identify the figures and stories shown in Greek art, but we also want to consider how a story is being told. How does an artist show a narrative in a picture that might be different from the literary versions of tales that we know today? How might the meaning of a picture change when it is found in a sanctuary, a grave, or a house? How were the works of art meant to affect the viewers and frame a point of view or set of beliefs?

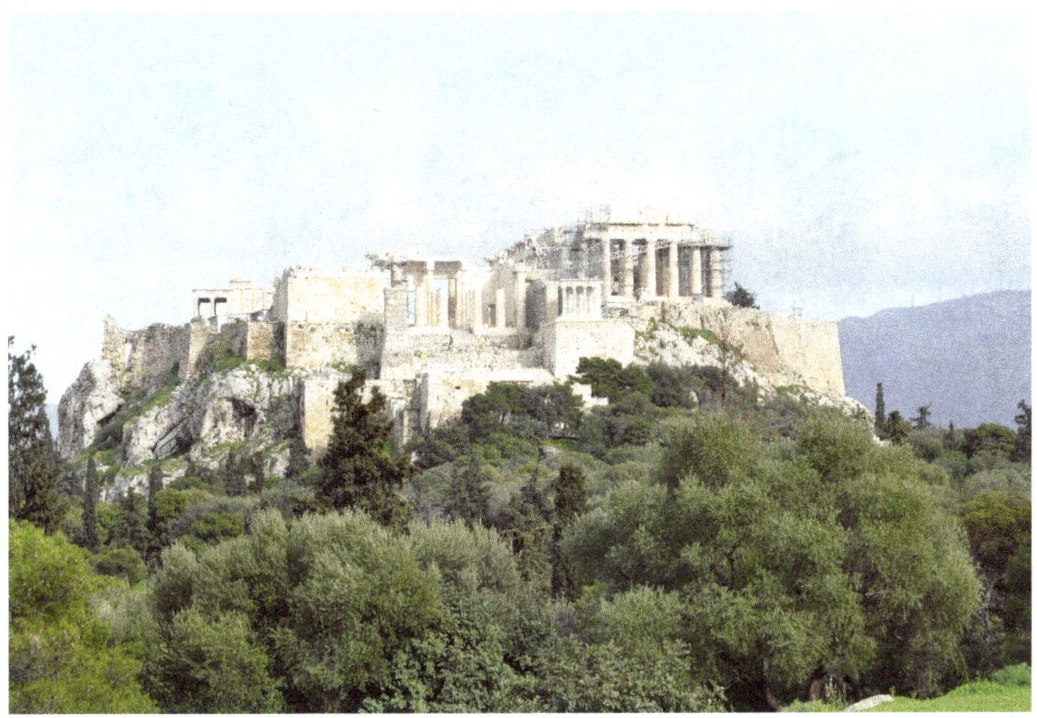

1.9 View of the Acropolis from the Pynx (west). Left: Erechtheion; center: Propylaia and Temple of Athena Nike; right: Parthenon. Photo: author.

Some of these questions have to be answered based on the context, raising further questions that we want to ask. Who made the work of art, where, and how? Was it made for direct sale, export, or by commission? Who purchased it, and if it was transported to a new location from its place of origin, how did that happen and how did trade help to spread ideas, either to other groups of Greeks or to non-Greeks? What was the value of the art and what types of people would have owned it? How did a work of art get used in ritual, whether religious, civic, funerary, or domestic? Why might someone give or dedicate a work of art? How did a viewer interact with art long after the artist and owner had passed into history, and what value might the antiquity of a work have for the society?

In talking about people connected to the art, we also want to consider what it meant to them, recognizing that ancient society was not monolithic, but broken down in smaller, overlapping groups based on gender, age, ethnicity/language, socio-economic-political class, and geographical origin. How might a work of art like the Parthenon frieze or terracotta figures like those above have expressed the identity of the figures who made them, commissioned or owned them, or viewed them? Identity is complex, and made even more so by the long passages of time in Greek history, but the artifacts and images can tell us something about the people by and for whom Greek art was made.

As an example, let us consider a collection of cups that was found in a well that was excavated in the **Agora** in Athens **(Figure 1.10a)**. Stylistically, the cups, a shape called a **kylix (pl. kylikes)**, are designated stylistically as **red-figure** ware since the surface of the clay was painted with a black slip, leaving the silhouette of the figure the red color of the iron-rich clay found in Athens. The one cup without figural decoration is covered with only the black slip, and is called **black-glaze** ware. Looking at the rendering of the figures, a date of 500–480 BCE has been suggested for the cups; the close similarity of the details of the cups and their figural painting suggests that they were obtained from the same or closely related workshops, perhaps in two batches (Lynch 2011).

The pot in the bottom left of **Figure 1.10b** is called a pelike and was used to hold liquid such as wine; stylistically, it is about a decade older than the kylix to the right that also appears in Figure 1.10a. The other three vessels are made in the black-figure technique, in which the silhouette of the figure is painted with black slip and the clay surface is left unpainted. The top right

ekklesia
the assembly of Athenian citizens voting on civic issues requiring a quorum of 6,000

Agora
the central open area of a Greek city where markets and administrative structures were found, as well as dedications and shrines

kylix (pl. kylikes)
a drinking cup with a broad shallow bowl, usually on a stemmed foot, with two handles on the side

red-figure
a style of painted pottery in which the silhouette of the figure is left as the exposed surface of the clay and the background is painted with black slip. Anatomical and other details are drawn or painted on the red figure

black-glaze
a style of painted pottery in which the surface is covered entirely with black slip

(a)

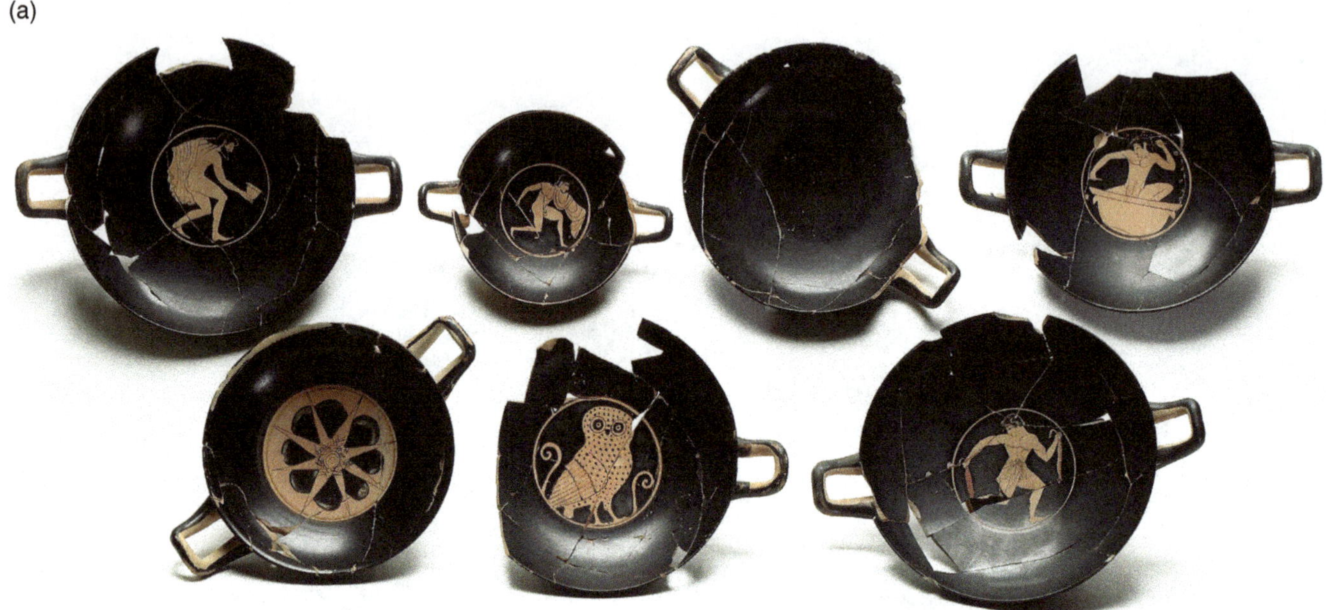

1.10a Attic pottery from Well J2:4 in the Agora, Athens, *c.* 525–490 BCE. Diameter of top left without handles: 7⁹⁄₁₆ in (19.2 cm). Athens, Agora Museum. Top row: red-figure kylikes (P32420, P32411), black-glaze kylix (P32470); red-figure kylix (P32419). Bottom row: red-figure kylikes (P32421, P32422, P32417). Photo: American School of Classical Studies at Athens: Agora Excavations.

(b)

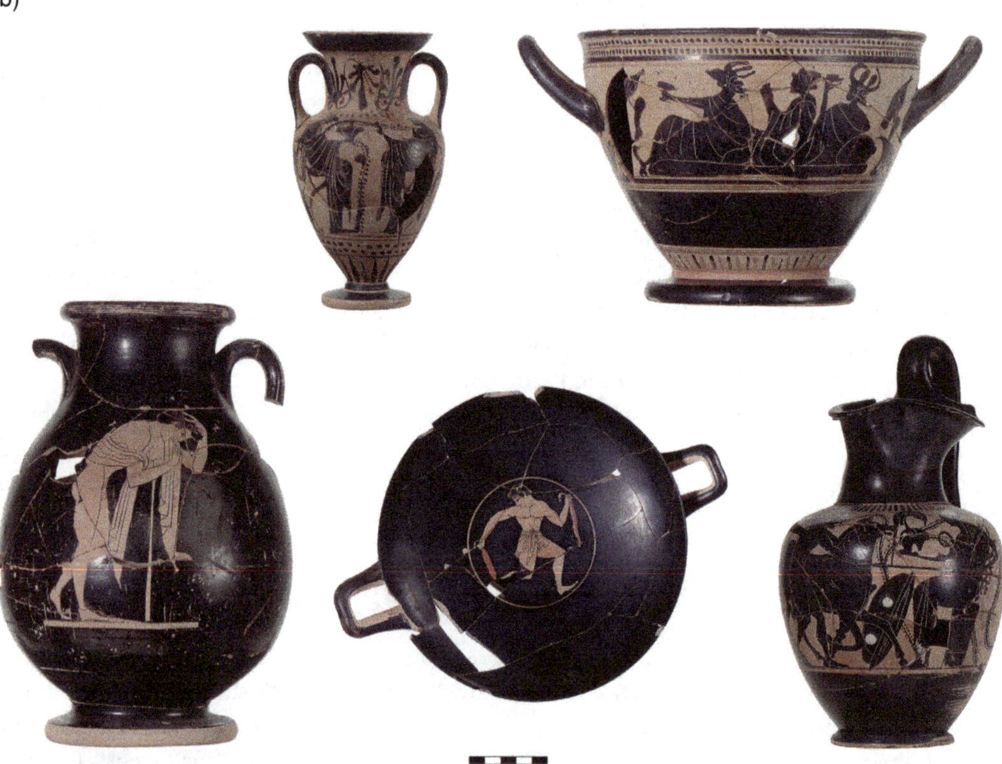

1.10b Attic pottery from Well J2:4 in the Agora, Athens, *c.* 525–490 BCE. Height of top right: 6⅜–6⅝ in (16.2–16.9 cm). Athens, Agora Museum. Top row: black-figure amphoriskos (P32416); black-figure skyphos (P32413). Bottom row: red-figure pelike (P32418); red-figure kylix (P32417); black-figure oinochoe (P32415). Photo: American School of Classical Studies at Athens: Agora Excavations.

vessel is a cup type called a **skyphos**. Holding about 3.5 liters, it is a large version of the skyphos and is a little too big to serve easily as a drinking cup. It might have served as a mixing bowl for wine and water, as the Greeks customarily drank their wine diluted. The small vase on the top left next to the skyphos is a storage container called an **amphoriskos** (a small **amphora**), and might have held liquid such as wine. At the bottom right is a pitcher called an **oinochoe**, which would be used for pouring wine into drinking cups like the kylikes. The black-figure technique is older than red-figure, and the skyphos and oinochoe are dated 525–500 BCE, perhaps two decades earlier than the cups. Here we have all of the pottery that we would need for a **symposion**, or formal drinking party that we will discuss in more detail in Chapter 5, but the small size of the amphoriskos and of the skyphos as a mixing bowl might have made them more suitable for more informal and everyday drinking, perhaps using some of the other smaller and plainer drinking cups found in the same well deposit.

What is of particular interest about this assemblage is that these vessels as well as many other pots were found as fill in a household well and were put there when household debris was cleared for reconstructing the house. The house itself was destroyed as part of the sack of Athens by the Persians in 480–479 BCE, giving us a terminus ante quem for the pottery. This means that some of the pottery, like the black-figure ware, was over a generation old and was still in use at the time the house was destroyed. The kylikes were not very recent purchases, but had likely been bought a decade before the destruction. Stylistically, the cups come from related workshops, so in a sense they make a "matched" household set, even if they are not identical to each other, but the suggestion that they were bought in two or three groups at different times and perhaps from different workshops means that the concept of a matched set, or even a set of drinking ware, did not mean stylistic unity or repetition of subject matter. The kylikes may have been used for household symposia, usually associated with feast days, but there were other sturdier drinking vessels that were used for everyday or private drinking, perhaps along with the black-figure vases in **Figure 1.10B**. Thinking of it in present-day terms, the red-figure cups would be like fine china used on holidays, while the other cups were perhaps less costly and used more frequently and less formally.

The subject matter is mostly universal in nature, with only the oinochoe showing mythological figures (Herakles with the Cretan bull and Athena, one of his twelve labors). The other subject matter is best termed **Dionysiac** since it relates to wine: dancers, drinkers, musicians. The recent excavation of this material and its analysis and publication by Kathleen Lynch offer a rare glimpse at a household assemblage and bring us closer to seeing how art functioned in a Greek household. The existence of different sets of cups for different occasions shows the importance of the symposion as an activity, for which a household would invest its resources in painted pottery, making it something of the mass media of its day.

skyphos
a deep drinking cup with steep sides, a flat bottom or foot, and two handles on the side. Large versions could also be used as mixing bowls

amphoriskos
a small amphora or storage vessel

amphora (pl. amphorae)
a multi-purpose storage vessel with two handles on the side and a narrower neck above a wide shoulder or belly

oinochoe
a pitcher used for pouring wine, with one handle, a defined shoulder, and often a trefoil mouth

symposion (pl. symposia)
a formal drinking party in which men would recline on *klinai* (couches) and drink wine, converse, dance, recite poetry, or otherwise revel. Symposia usually took place after important public festivals or occasions

Dionysiac
subject matter relating to the god Dionysos, his followers of satyrs and maenads, or activities associated with his festivals or the symposion

THE PLAN OF THIS BOOK

If one were to have visited a Greek site like the Acropolis in Athens or the sanctuaries of Delphi and Olympia back in ancient times, one would have had a **synchronic** picture of Greek art, that is, one in which buildings and artwork of vastly different periods and centuries would be set side by side, sharing the same space and possibly even the same function of housing dedications or performing rituals. The contrast between an archaic dedication and one from the Hellenistic period would have been readily apparent, but the **diachronic** narrative of how Greek art changed over time, such as the terracotta figures that we discussed earlier, would not be obvious. For this to happen, we would want to see all of the work from one century or period placed together, and those of other periods set in their own precincts.

A history of Greek art needs both types of narratives, but the pedagogical tradition is to follow primarily a chronological or diachronic scheme, starting at the beginning and going to the end of the first century BCE when Rome and its culture become the dominant civilization of the ancient Mediterranean. Rather than look at contextual issues as digressions from this diachronic history, this book will take a different approach, dividing the chapters into those that are mostly concerned with

synchronic
things and events that exist at the same time, even if they were made at different times

diachronic
looking at things and events in chronological order

specific periods or centuries and those that focus on contextual and other issues. This second group of chapters will be synchronic, mixing works from different periods to see both continuity and change in Greek society and culture. Each set of chapters will refer to issues and illustrations in the other group.

To begin, we will survey briefly the Early and Middle Bronze Age in Chapter 2 and the Later Bronze Age in Chapter 3. This era deserves a text in its own right, but the Bronze Age was the time remembered in the *Iliad* and literally lay under the feet of later Greeks, forming their own ancient history. Chapter 4 will look at the transition from the Bronze to the Iron Age and the first development of the Greek **polis** or city-state (*c.* 1125–700 BCE) and marks the start of the chronological series of chapters on Hellenic or Greek art. The next chapter, Chapter 5, however, will look at the context for Greek art: the city and civic life, the Greek house, and cemeteries, where Greek art and architecture served social and cultural roles from the Geometric period (900–700 BCE) to the Hellenistic period (*c.* 330–30 BCE). Chapter 6 will survey the seventh century BCE, sometimes called the **Orientalizing period**, and Chapter 7 will explore the Greek sanctuary and temple, which first developed its basic configuration during the seventh century. Chapter 8 will look at the sixth and early fifth centuries BCE, when many of the media and orders of Greek art were defined and refined. This is also the period when Greek art began depicting many mythological stories, and Chapter 9 will focus on visual narratives and storytelling in Greek art and how one approaches these pictures.

polis
the Greek city-state

Orientalizing period
Greek art produced from about 720/700 to 625/600 BCE

Chapters 10 and 12 look at classical art and architecture, focusing first on the fifth century BCE and then the fourth century, the periods of the great artists named by Cicero, although virtually none of their works survives today. In Chapter 11 we will look at the economics of Greek art, its production and distribution, drawing upon information that becomes available during the classical period. Chapter 13 looks at issues of identity – gender, sexuality, ethnicity, geography, class – which become particularly important as the Greek world became more multicultural from the fourth century onward. Chapter 14 looks at the Hellenistic period, bringing us to 31 BCE when Augustus defeated Antony and Cleopatra, the Ptolemaic Greek queen of Egypt, and Rome dominated the Greek and entire Mediterranean world for the next four centuries. The epilogue will consider aspects of the relationship between cultures, Greek and non-Greek, and why Greek art might still be of interest to us today.

The book is structured in such a way that one could go through the chronological chapters in order and then turn to the contextual chapters, or the reverse. Both sets of chapters have their own illustrations, but rely heavily on those from other chapters. Indeed, with a limit of just over 300 illustrations, one cannot fully illustrate every chapter independently, but I hope that turning backward or forward in the book to see an illustration (or clicking the link in an ebook edition) will help to emphasize the point that history is complex and both diachronic and synchronic at the same time. Some of the illustrations here will not be well known, and some well-known monuments, like the Delphi Charioteer to name one example, have not been included. This was necessary in keeping the balance and focus of the approach, and most of the well-known works are easily found today in scholarly resources on the web like the Beazley Archive or image databases like Artstor.

My hope is that in going to a museum or visiting a Greek site, the issues and themes raised in this book will help the present-day viewer to look at Greek art and architecture as the fabric of ancient Greek culture. Art can bridge the gaps between people created by time, language, geography, and culture; beginning to understand the complexities, contradictions, and ideals of another people, whether historical or contemporary, helps us to understand our own challenges.

A FEW NOTES ABOUT USING THIS BOOK

There are several ancient sources that are helpful in providing information and context for Greek art and architecture. The citation of ancient sources follows a standardized notation by author and/or work, then book/chapter and section/paragraph/line, such as Herodotos 2.53, which would be Book 2, Chapter 53 of his *History*. This allows consulting different editions or translations whose pagination will vary. The best compilation of these sources in translation is Pollitt 1990, and the most important sources used in this book are:

- Cicero, *Brutus* (cited as Cicero, *Brutus*). Roman orator and politician (106–44 BCE) and author of many letters and works, including *Brutus*, a treatise on rhetoric.
- Herodotos (cited as Herodotos). Greek historian (*c.* 480–420) who wrote a *History*, an account of the wars between the Greeks and Persians.
- Homer, *Iliad* (cited as *Il.*) and *Odyssey* (cited as *Od.*). Late eighth-century poet attributed as author of the *Iliad* and the *Odyssey*, although some hold that these were by different authors.
- Pausanias (cited as Paus.). Greek doctor of the mid-second century CE who wrote *A Description of Greece*, a travel guide in ten books.
- Pliny (the Elder), *Naturalis Historia* (cited as Pliny, *N.H.*). Roman encyclopedist (23–79 CE) whose work, *Natural History*, has three chapters covering materials used in art and includes details on the history of Greek art.
- Plutarch, *Vita Perikles* (cited as Plutarch, *Vita Perikles*). Greek biographer and writer, *c.* 46–120 BCE. Author of the *Lives*, a series of biographies on notable Greek and Roman historical figures, including the life of Perikles (*Vita Perikles*).
- Thucydides (cited as Thuc.). Athenian historian (*c.* 460–400 BCE) who wrote a history of the Peloponnesian War.
- Vitruvius, *de Architectura* (cited as *De Arch.*). Roman architect active in the late first century BCE to early first century CE and author of a treatise on architecture.

The textboxes in this book focus on issues that are currently debated in the field or introduce some recent methodological or theoretical approaches developed in the literature. These are intended to open discussion on the underlying issues about what we think we know, how we might know it, or what we ought to do about something.

There are many terms specific to Greek art or art history generally in this book. These have been defined in the text at their first use, but all have been collected into the glossary at the end. Each chapter has both bibliographic citations for references in the text and suggestions for further reading. The latter are not exhaustive, but are intended as starting points for more detailed exploration or information on the topics in the chapter. The captions also include museum inventory numbers, which allow for finding further information on the work in databases or publications. Finally, all dates are BCE unless otherwise noted.

Attic
art coming from Athens, named for Attica, the name for the city of Athens and its surrounding rural areas

TEXTBOX: STYLISTIC ANALYSIS AND SIR JOHN BEAZLEY

There has been a great deal of attention given to stylistic analysis in this chapter, as it is a necessary methodological approach for suggesting a date and origin for a work of art. When confronted with thousands of examples, as is the case with mass media like terracottas and painted pottery, it is necessary to refine attributions further. If there are sufficient examples for comparison, it is possible to define detailed features to identify individual artists or workshops. Examining how commonly represented features like eyes, ears, and muscles are articulated in the same manner on different objects, like comparing the formation of specific letters on different samples of handwriting, can provide a basis for attributing the works to the same individual or group.

Sir John Beazley (1885–1970), a Professor of Archaeology at Oxford University, began to study Athenian (or **Attic**) pottery in the early twentieth century, making careful and detailed observations of how details of human anatomy were drawn and making lists of vases that he proposed were by the same painter. In the course of his career he studied thousands of vases and published lists organized by painter. For some he could give a name to the artist based on an inscription on one or more vases in the group, such as Exekias or Euphronios. For other groupings, he chose a nickname based on a significant subject, detail, or museum location: the Foundry Painter, the Kleophrades Painter, or the Berlin Painter. He published his complete lists in two books, *Attic Black-Figure Vase-Painters* (1956) and *Attic Red-Figure Vase-Painters* (second edition, 1963), with updates in *Paralipomena* (1971) and additional references compiled by the Beazley Archive in *Addenda* (second edition, 1989). In these lists he included the location and inventory number, subject matter, and publications that illustrated the vase, making these works indispensable references for the study of vase painting. Today, citations of vases typically include the page number and list number of a vase as a universal reference point, such as *ARV²* 1017.54 (page 1017, no. 54 in the list of the Phiale Painter) for **Figure 1.2** above. In cases where there was some uncertainty about the attribution, Beazley would classify a work as "near" or "related to" the list of a named artist.

Attribution requires a degree of judgment, as the variations in details, like those of handwriting, can be considerable. Beazley's lists have held up very well over time and new works have been added to his lists. Today, the lists have been transformed into a searchable database, the Classical Art Research Centre Extensible Database (XDB) maintained by the Beazley Archive and Classical Art Research Centre at Oxford University. With Beazley's lists, it is possible not just to study style and attribution, but also to explore iconography and other approaches to Greek art among thousands of works.

One side effect of attribution is that naming a painter can also increase the appeal of an object for collectors and its value in the market. As we have noted, looting of archaeological sites for antiquities to sell is a critical problem in the study of Greek art. Beazley's work has come under some criticism in connection with the antiquities trade, but it should be noted that his lists do not focus on the best painters alone that would be of the highest interest to dealers and collectors. Beazley made lists of works that would be considered sloppy and second-rate artistically, but including even these groups in his lists gives scholars today an opportunity to consider the roles that Greek art played for many levels of ancient society, and not just the elite.

REFERENCES

Beazley, J. D. 1956. *Attic Black-Figure Vase-Painters*. Oxford: Oxford University Press.

Beazley, J. D. 1963. *Attic Red-Figure Vase-Painters*, 2nd ed. Oxford: Oxford University Press.

Beazley, J. D. 1971. *Paralipomena*. Oxford: Oxford University Press.

Beazley, J. D. 1989. *Beazley Addenda: Additional References to ABV, ARV2 and Paralipomena*, 2nd ed. by T. H. Carpenter with T. Mannack and M. Mendonça. Oxford: Oxford University Press.

Classical Art Research Centre and the Beazley Archive: https://www.beazley.ox.ac.uk/index.htm

Lynch, K. M. 2011. *The Symposium in Context: Pottery from a Late Archaic House near the Athenian Agora. Hesperia* Supplement 46. Princeton: American School of Classical Studies at Athens.

Pollitt, J. J. 1974. *The Ancient View of Greek Art: Criticism, History, and Terminology*. New Haven: Yale University Press.

Pollitt, J. J. 1990. *The Art of Ancient Greece: Sources and Documents*. Cambridge/New York: Cambridge University Press.

FURTHER READING

Beazley, J. D. 1922. "Citharoedus." *Journal of Hellenic Studies* 42, 70–98.

Biers, W. R. 1992. *Art, Artefacts, and Chronology in Classical Archaeology*. London/New York: Routledge.

Marvin, M. 1989. "Copying in Roman Sculpture: The Replica Series." In *Retaining the Original: Multiple Originals, Copies, and Reproductions*. Studies in the History of Art 20. Hanover, NH: National Gallery of Art, Washington, DC, 29–45.

Pollitt, J. J. 1990. *The Art of Ancient Greece: Sources and Documents*. Cambridge/New York: Cambridge University Press.

Stansbury-O'Donnell, M. D. 2011. *Looking at Greek Art*. Cambridge/New York: Cambridge University Press.

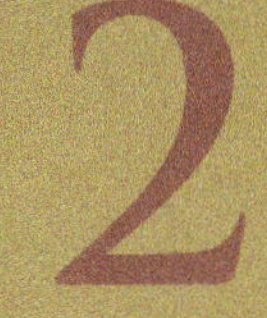

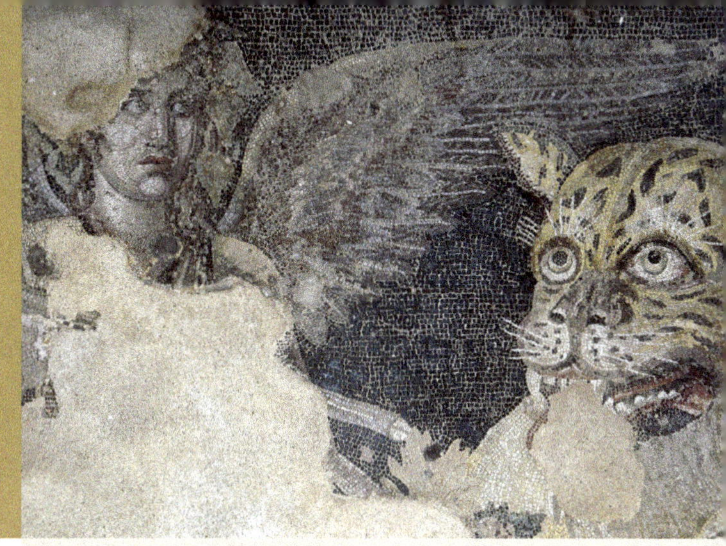

THE EARLY AND MIDDLE BRONZE AGES

C. 3100–1600 BCE

Timeline

Chronology, Regions, Periods, and Pottery Analysis

Early Cycladic and Minoan Periods, *c.* 3100–2000 BCE

Early to Middle Helladic (*c.* 3100–1675 BCE)

Protopalatial and Neopalatial Crete

The Cyclades

Middle Helladic to the Late Helladic I Shaft Graves

Textbox: The Eruption of Thera and Debates over Absolute Chronology

References

Further Reading

A History of Greek Art, First Edition. Mark D. Stansbury-O'Donnell.

TIMELINE

	Cyclades (Cycladic)	Crete (Minoan)	Mainland (Helladic)	Monuments Events
3000	EC I (3100–2700) Gotta-Pelos Group Kampos Group	Prepalatial EM I (3100–2700)	EH I (3100–2700)	
	EC II (2700–2200) Keros-Syros Group	EM IIA (2700–2400)	EH IIA (2700–2400)	Syros figures
	Kastri Group	EM IIB (2400–2200)	EH IIB (2400–2200)	Lerna, Vasiliki Ware
2000	EC III (2200–2000) Phylakopi I Group	EM III (2200–2000)	EH III (2200–2000)	
2000	MC I–II (2000–1700) Phylakopi I Group	Prepalatial MM IA (2000–1900) Protopalatial MM IB (1900–1800) MM II (1800–1750)	MH I–II (2100–1700)	Kamares Ware
1700		Neopalatial MM III (1750–1700)	MH III (1750–1675)	*c.* 1750 Destruction of first palaces on Crete "Snake goddess"
1700 1600	LC I (1700–1600)	Neopalatial LM IA (1700–1600)	LH I (1675–1600)	Frescoes at Akrotiri *c.* 1625 Eruption of Thera, destruction of palaces Shaft Graves at Mycenae
1600 1500	LC II (1600–1400)	Neopalatial LM IB (1600–1500)	LH IIA (1600–1500)	see Chapter 3
1500 1450	LC II (1600–1400)	Final Palatial LM II (1500–1450)	LH IIB (1500–1430)	
1450 1300	LC III (1400–1075)	Final Palatial LM IIIA (1450–1340)	LH IIIA (1430–1300)	
1300 1200	LC III	Postpalatial LM IIIB (1340–1200)	LH IIIB (1300–1190)	
1200 1075	LC III	Postpalatial LM IIIC (1200–1075)	LH IIIC (1190–1075)	
1075 1025		Sub-Minoan (1075–1000)	Sub-Mycenaean (1075–1025)	

The fifth-century BCE historian Herodotos, discussing the origins of the war between the Greeks and the Persians, looked back to the remote past to explain the events leading up to his day. He places Homer four centuries earlier than himself, in the ninth century BCE, about a hundred years earlier than scholars today believe, and dates the Trojan War about four centuries earlier still, in the thirteenth century BCE (Herodotos 2.53, 2.145). Once thought to be mythical, the discovery of Troy and Mycenae in the nineteenth century by Heinrich Schliemann demonstrated that the places were real and that there had been a flourishing civilization in pre-historic Greece, i.e., before the adoption of the alphabet in the eighth century. In order to begin our story about Greek art, we need to go back to this era, now called the **Bronze Age**, and consider what lay under the feet or in ruins above the ground of the Greeks of the first millennium BCE.

Bronze Age
The era of Greek culture characterized by the use of bronze for tools and weapons, *c.* 3100–1075 BCE

This is an era that has been recovered primarily through the work of archaeologists, who have excavated the sites, buildings, and artifacts of two thousand years and reconstructed the era's history without the availability of the literary or documentary sources that we take for granted in later periods. After Schliemann's excavation of Troy and Mycenae, others began looking for sites across Greece. Arthur Evans found a palace at Knossos on Crete, which he named after the legendary King Minos given the scale, complexity, and richness of the building and its arts. Some archaeologists, like Harriet Hawes, focused on smaller towns like Gournia on Crete, which revealed the architecture and art of more ordinary Bronze Age peoples outside of the palaces. New sites continued to be explored throughout the twentieth century, and occasionally open new chapters into our knowledge of Bronze Age civilization. The excavation of Akrotiri on Thera, for example, was begun by Spyridon Marinatos in 1967, revealing a Bronze Age Pompeii with some of the most remarkable wall paintings from the ancient world. In this chapter we will consider the first fifteen hundred years of the Bronze Age, and the five centuries of the later Bronze Age in the next chapter.

CHRONOLOGY, REGIONS, PERIODS, AND POTTERY ANALYSIS

Given the vast range of time covered by the Bronze Age and the lack of documented historical events and signposts, the discussion of Bronze Age art depends heavily on the sequence in which and places where the art has been found. The chronology of Bronze Age art has been constructed through the designation of periods and regions, as can be seen in the timeline for this chapter. As was mentioned briefly in the previous chapter, artifacts do not come with labels telling us when and where they were made and we need to place them in a sequence of periods and sub-periods in a relative chronology. Excavation determines the relative chronology of a site through **stratigraphy**, the layers of deposits and debris at a site, with the older material generally under the more recent material. Material that is sealed underneath a destruction layer of carbonized material could belong to a structure that was destroyed, while material on top would be more recent and belong to a rebuilding or reuse of the site. In order to calibrate the sequence of material across a site, or across an entire region, it is necessary to have **comparanda**. Presumably artifacts that are very similar in form and appearance belong to the same period and/or place, so that two deposits with similar artifacts should be contemporary and linked.

stratigraphy
the analysis of a site by the deposits found in defined layers of remains

comparanda
known works of art that are used as benchmarks to identify or analyze the qualities of a work through comparison

For the Bronze Age (and later), pottery is the key medium for determining the sequence of periods. Pottery was the all-purpose material of the ancient world, used for storage, cooking, drinking, shipping, and, in its finer forms, as gifts, dedications, or grave goods, so it appears in many different contexts. Once fired, it does not deteriorate like organic material. Once broken, it is often useless and so is discarded or used as fill. It may be traded or transported, but rarely is it looted in antiquity since it does not have the material value of metal or ivory. As it is constantly

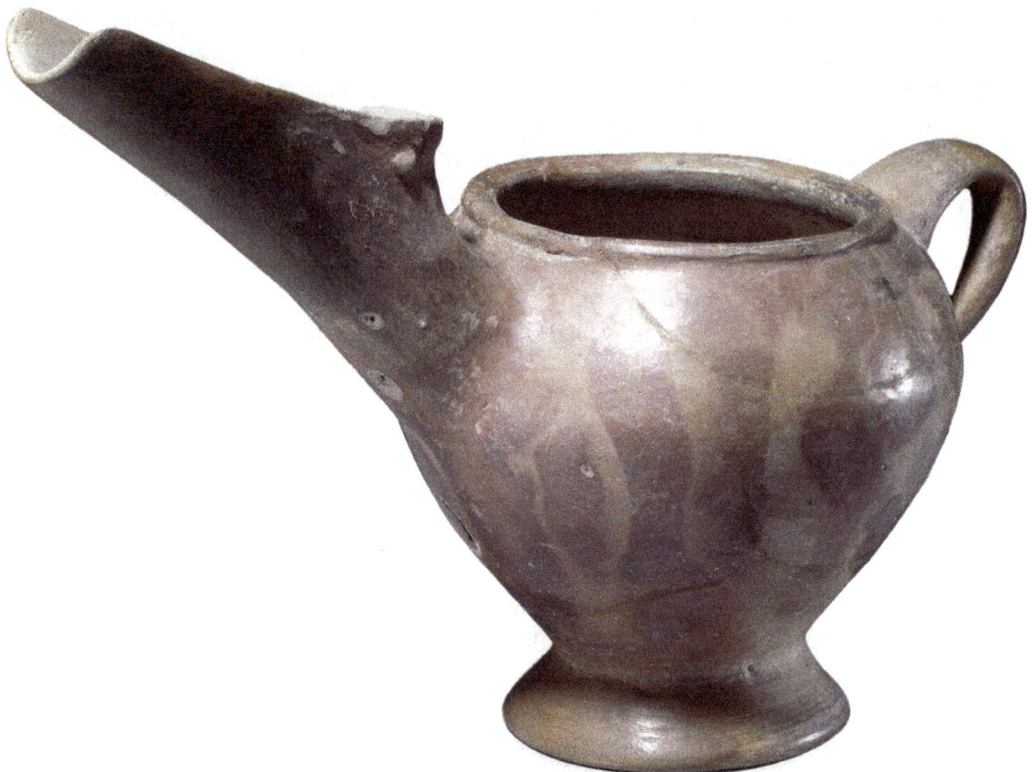

2.1 Vasiliki Ware jug with spout, EM IIB. 6 11/16 in (17 cm). London, British Museum 1921,0515.32 (A425). Photo: © The Trustees of the British Museum.

handmade pottery
pottery made without the use of a wheel, such as through coils

wheel-thrown pottery
pottery made by shaping a vessel as it rotates on a spinning wheel

incision
cutting lines into the surface to create patterns or figural decoration. See also engraving

burnishing
rubbing an unfired, leather-hard vessel with a hard, smooth object to give it a smooth, polished surface

slip
a dilute solution of clay, sometimes with a pigment, that is applied to the surface of a clay vessel to create painted decoration. A slip differs from a glaze, in that the latter is glossy, hard, and relatively impervious. Some slips, like the black of Attic pottery, can vitrify during firing to give a glaze-like appearance

needed, it is produced in batches that follow similar forms, function, and decoration at a particular time and place. Changes in technology, such as firing, glazes and slips, or the use of the wheel, will mean that pottery changes over time, and new shapes will arise in response to new needs or desires, but this type of change is relatively slow. Significant changes in pottery style generally take a generation or more to take hold, so being able to date a pottery sherd, then, will help to date a site or building and their phases of use.

To analyze pottery, one needs to consider several aspects of its physical and stylistic qualities (Rice 1987). The shape and components of a vessel are important features, and key diagnostic elements include the profile and details like the rims, handles, and the transition between the parts. The type of clay and its qualities, such as its refinement and coloring, are also distinctive. One also looks at the way a vessel is fashioned as another set of qualities, whether it is **handmade** or **wheel-thrown**, for example, or the thickness of its walls. The decorative techniques also aid in defining a style, such as **incision**, **burnishing**, or painting the surface with **slips** or glazes. In addition to the techniques of decoration, one can also examine the placement of the decoration and the motifs and compositions used. In the case of figural decoration on pottery, the features of the human anatomy and the representation of action help not only to distinguish the work of one region from another, but even to define the work of different artists.

For example, the small pot in **Figure 2.1** was found in the vicinity of Ierapetra on Crete. The main body of this vessel, usually called a "teapot," has a globular shape, with a loop handle on one side and an elongated spout opposite. The foot is conical in shape and the rim has a slightly raised lip. The handle tapers from flat and wide at the top to narrower and more cylindrical at its bottom, while the spout is nearly the same length as the body and projects upward at about a 40° angle. The parts blend together at their joints. The clay is generally smooth and refined, but shows some working by hand and the marks of tools. The vessel is handmade, rather than wheel-thrown, and the thickness of the clay is notable. In terms of its decoration, this teapot has slips of red and black applied to its surface in irregular shapes that have fired unevenly in the kiln, giving it a mottled effect. One finds similar patterns in stone that is used to make vessels, and perhaps the patterning and color were meant to mimic stone. The surface has also been burnished to give it a smooth and polished look. Also distinctive of this ware are the the small knobs that appear near handles or on the spouts that look like rivets, and this similarity has led to suggestions that the pottery is imitating shapes in metalwork.

Works like this teapot are found at a number of sites in southern and eastern Crete, and the type is called **Vasiliki Ware**, after one of the first sites where it was excavated. A quick comparison to the nearly contemporary "sauceboats" found on the mainland at Lerna show some similarities **(see Figure 2.5, page 28)**, but many more differences from Vasiliki Ware in Crete. The presence of the pottery in different sites in Crete allows one to place the levels where they are found, and the other objects with them, into the same time period and to construct a relative chronology across the region.

For the Bronze Age in Greece, archaeologists have constructed a relative chronology based on changes in pottery style, dividing Greece into three regions. As can be seen in the timeline, the area of the mainland is designated as Helladic, the Aegean islands as Cycladic, and Crete as Minoan, after the legendary King Minos. The chronology of each area is divided into sequential phases based on chronological sequence, starting with a tripartite division into Early–Middle–Late, followed by further subdivisions as necessary based on the archaeological record: I–II–III, A–B–C, 1–2–3, etc. Thus, the Early Bronze Age on Crete is labeled EM (Early Minoan) and divided into three periods (I, II, III) and two sub-periods (IIA and IIB). Thus, we have a sequence of EM I, EM IIA, EM IIB, and EM III, with Vasiliki Ware falling into EM IIB. The Early Cycladic chronology is similar, but without sub-periods: EC I, EC II, EC III. For the mainland, the Early Helladic (EH) is similar to Crete in the sequence of periods: EH I, EH IIA, EH IIB, EH III. The movement of artifacts across the regions, such as discovering a Cycladic object like a frying pan at a mainland site, helps to correlate the different phases across the three regions.

The three-phase model was established early in the history of archaeology, but more recent work has developed alternative period schemes that correspond better to the archaeological material. For the Early Cycladic period, an alternative sequence of five "groups" has come into use, named after important sites. As can be seen in the timeline, these groups span EC into MC I but do not always fit well into the traditional EC I–II–III divisions. Of these five groups, the **Keros-Syros Group** is particularly noteworthy for the production of marble figures, while the **Kastri Group** in the same EC II period represents a different population that succeeded the Keros-Syros Group.

For Crete, an alternative to the tripartite division of EM, MM, and LM is a five-part sequence based on the establishment of large palaces as central administrative and artistic centers. Hence, archaeologists speak of the **Prepalatial period** (roughly EM I to MM IA), the **Protopalatial** (first palaces, MM IB–MM II), the **Neopalatial** (the new palaces, rebuilt following the widespread and nearly simultaneous destruction of the first palaces, MM III–LM IB), and the **Final Palatial**, when only one site, Knossos, continued to function after a second wave of destructions and then invasion from the mainland (LM II–LM IIIA). The **Postpalatial** follows until the end of the Bronze Age (LM IIIB–LM IIIC). The need to have smaller chronological groupings, however, means that both systems will sometimes be used in the same discussion.

Finding a terminus to establish an absolute chronology is difficult for the first millennium BCE, but even more so in the Bronze Age. As we will see throughout this book, finding an absolute date is rare and when one does, it becomes the anchor for the relative chronology established by excavation, analysis, and comparison of artifacts. For the Bronze Age, the external evidence was originally derived from other Mediterranean cultures, particularly Egypt. However, more recent evidence based on the eruption of Thera near the beginning of the Late Bronze Age has created an alternate terminus that does not correspond with the traditional chronology, leading to controversy over dates as we shall see.

The early phases of each region – EM, EC, EH – are generally dated between *c.* 3100 and 2000 BCE. These dates and those of the subdivisions are approximations working back from dates established for the Middle and Late Bronze periods, but have general confirmation from radiocarbon

Vasiliki Ware
a pottery ware found in eastern and southern Crete in the period EM IIB, *c.* 2400–2200 BCE, and characterized by mottled slip surfaces and so-called teapots with long angular spouts

Keros-Syros Group
a phase of Early Cycladic culture named after the cemetery on Syros, *c.* 2700–2200 BCE

Kastri Group
a phase of Early Cycladic culture named after the site at Kastri on Syros and representing a new group of people in the area, *c.* 2200–2000 BCE

Prepalatial
the period of Bronze Age Minoan culture before the establishment of the palaces, *c.* 3100–1900 BCE

Protopalatial
the period of Bronze Age Minoan culture that saw the establishment of the first palaces, *c.* 1900–1750 BCE. The period ended in a cataclysmic destruction of the palaces, which were rebuilt

Neopalatial
the period of Bronze Age Minoan culture that saw the rebuilding of the palaces following their destruction at the end of the Protopalatial period, *c.* 1750–1490 BCE

Final Palatial
the period of Bronze Age Minoan culture following the second destruction of the palaces, during which only the palace at Knossos continued to be active, LM II–LM IIIA, *c.* 1490–1300 BCE

Postpalatial
the period of Bronze Age Minoan following the Mycenaean control of Crete and their center at Knossos, *c.* 1300–1075 BCE

testing. For the Middle Minoan period, dates were originally established by the discovery of pottery from Crete in Egypt. This pottery had been brought to Egypt most likely through trade, and was found in excavations of contexts belonging to the Middle Kingdom of Egypt. Since there were extensive king lists for Egypt going back from Roman times, the calendrical dates of the Egyptian dynasties provided potential termini for the Minoan pottery. Using this material, the period MM II was dated between 1900 and 1700 BCE. Such correlation with Egypt also resulted in a dating of the two waves of palace destruction, and the end of the Protopalatial and Neopalatial periods, to about 1750 and 1500 BCE respectively. This last destruction, the division between LM IA and LM IB, is also linked to the massive eruption of the volcanic island of Thera, which destroyed much of that island and sent tsunamis, ash, and destruction across the eastern Mediterranean. Recent scientific dating of the Thera eruption, however, places it between 1650 and 1600 BCE, not 1500 BCE, creating a discrepancy and controversy for dating the Middle and Late Bronze Ages **(see Textbox, page 46)**. For our purposes, we will use the so-called "high" dating based on Thera, placing the beginning of the Late Minoan period at 1700 BCE rather than 1600 BCE in the traditional chronology.

This discussion of chronology, and especially of the difficulties in finding absolute dates for periods or monuments, highlights how much we have yet to learn about Greek art and archaeology. While the sequence of periods remains intact despite the controversy over the absolute dating of Thera, the development of alternative phases and nomenclature, such as Keros-Syros Group or Neopalatial, points out that history, society, and material culture are complex and resist fitting into neat schemes and boxes. Digging deeper will reveal both inconsistency and complexity, not just about chronology but about the cultures and artifacts that we study.

EARLY CYCLADIC AND MINOAN PERIODS, *C.* 3100–2000 BCE

Humans have been living in Greece for millennia, and the archaeological remains of their early habitation in the **Neolithic** period, or new stone age, have been found in all of the three main regions. There was, at least in the late Neolithic, some knowledge of metals such as copper, pottery, and textiles, but the development of bronze marks a change in culture. Bronze, a combination of about 90 percent copper and 10 percent tin, requires greater technological expertise than working with copper and also requires a more complex social and economic organization since the source materials, especially tin, are not widely available and would need to be acquired through trade and communication. In the Near East and Egypt, where the Bronze Age began in the fourth millennium, this period corresponds to the rise of the great cities, monuments, and writing. The Early Bronze Age in Greece starts later and is more modest in scale.

The most well-known artworks from the early Bronze Age are the marble figures from the Cyclades **(Figure 2.2)**. The earliest versions of these are simple, fiddle-shaped works with a flaring neck for the head, similar to the top rows of the figures found at the Chalandriani cemetery on the island of Syros. These are similar to figures found in Anatolia, suggesting a connection to that mainland culture. In the Keros-Syros Group of the EM II period, the figures develop into a more defined form of a nude, frontal woman with articulated arms, legs, breasts, genitals, and head. The bent arms are crossed over the abdomen in a form labeled the **Folded-Arm Figure (FAF)**. The abdomen is generally rounded and only the nose is defined sculpturally; additional facial details were originally painted on the marble. The figures range in height from 10 cm to life-size, but most are under 40 cm. There is some variety in proportions and detailing by period and location, but some of the figures are similar enough to suggest that a workshop or artist was responsible

Neolithic period
literally the new stone age, characterized by the use of stone tools, farming, and domesticated animals. It is the last period before the Bronze Age, *c.* 7000–3100 BCE in Greece

Folded-Arm Figure (FAF)
marble female figure produced in the Early Cycladic period, characterized by arms folded across the torso, a pubic triangle, a flat curved face with nose ridge, and slightly bent legs

cist grave
a form of burial in which the grave is lined with stone slabs, leaving an open cavity for the body or ossuary and associated grave goods

stamp and stamped designs
making a decorative motif or design by pressing an incised, hard stamp into the surface of clay, metal, or other malleable material

for producing a number of the works and some have been attributed to "masters" with titles like the Goulandris Master.

The Cycladic islands are rich in marble deposits, as well as obsidian and other stones used for cutting, which may help to explain the appearance of marble sculpture as a medium at this early time; marble statues will be rare after the Early Cycladic period until they begin to be produced in the seventh century (see Chapter 6). Most of the Early Cycladic settlements were very small; their cemeteries were located outside the habitation area and most of the burials were in individual, shallow **cist graves**. Most of the excavated FAF have been found in tombs, and it is possible that they were a means of showing the deceased's prestige through the grave goods, which also included marble vases. Some FAF have also been found in the villages nearby, so it is not clear what their function was or what they represent. The abstract form and pristine lines and surfaces of the figures were much admired by artists and collectors in the early twentieth century, leading to many being dug up and put on the market without provenance. Additional forgeries further complicate the FAF record. In the absence of historical records and with limited examples from controlled excavations, the meaning and purpose of the works will remain speculative even as their aesthetic appeal continues to be strong.

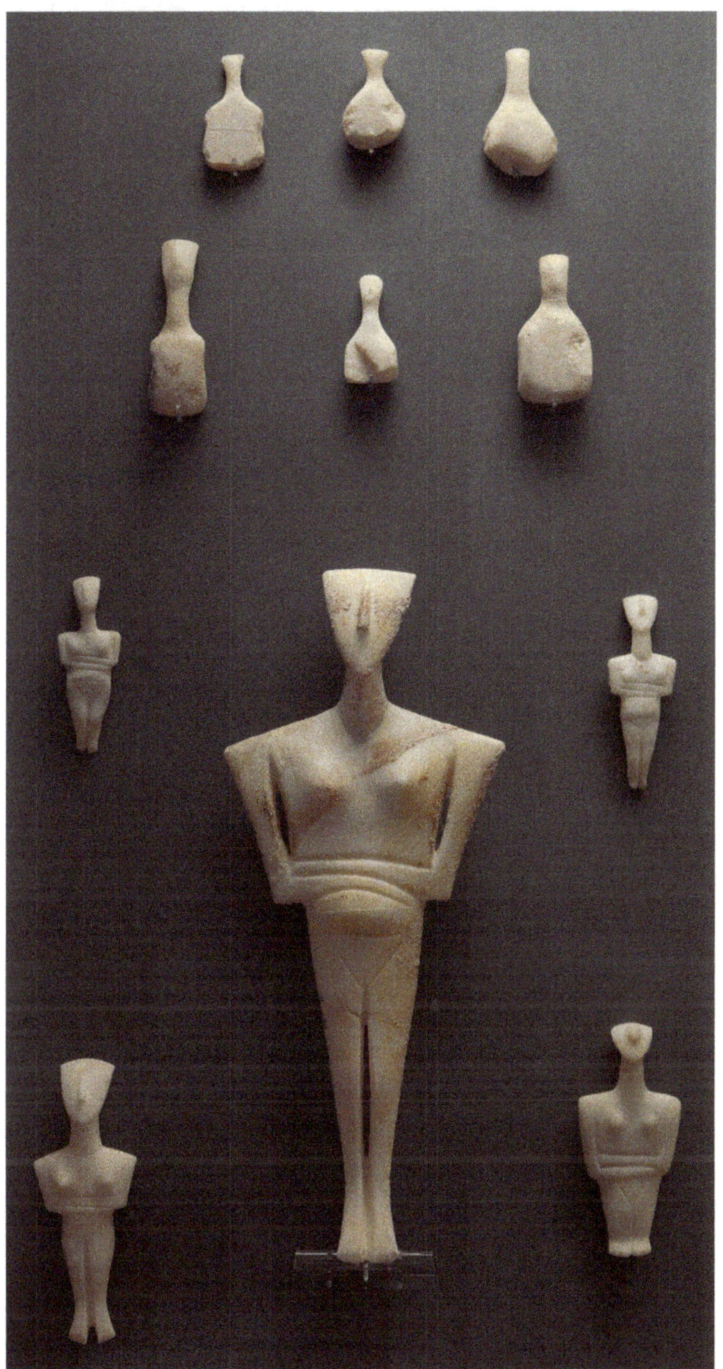

2.2 Folded-Arm Figures (FAF) from Chalandriani cemetery, Syros, EC II/ Keros-Syros Group. Athens, National Archaeological Museum. Largest figure: 18⅛ in (46 cm). Photo: © Vanni Archive/Art Resource, NY.

Also enigmatic are a class of terracotta objects called "frying pans" based on their shape, flat disks with flanges like short handles (**Figure 2.3**). The objects, however, show no signs of having been used for cooking. They have been found primarily in graves in the Cyclades, where presumably they had some funerary function or symbolism that remains unclear. Interestingly, examples of the frying pans have also been found on the Greek mainland, where they appear in domestic rather than funerary contexts. Their appearance outside of the Cyclades is an example of inter-regional contact and trade during the Early Bronze Age, and also of the repurposing of an object when it enters a new context. The frying pan would have had no practical purpose in an Early Helladic household, but its status as an imported good may have been appealing to its owner, as well as the different quality of its shape and decorative designs. EC pottery is found also on Crete, and its broader distribution in Greece suggests that the Cyclades may have been an influential culture during this period.

The decoration of the disks is made with incised lines or **stamped** designs pressed into the clay before firing. Some of the disks, such as this example from the Chalandriani cemetery on Syros, show simplified boats with lines for oars incised on both sides. The ships are not symmetrical

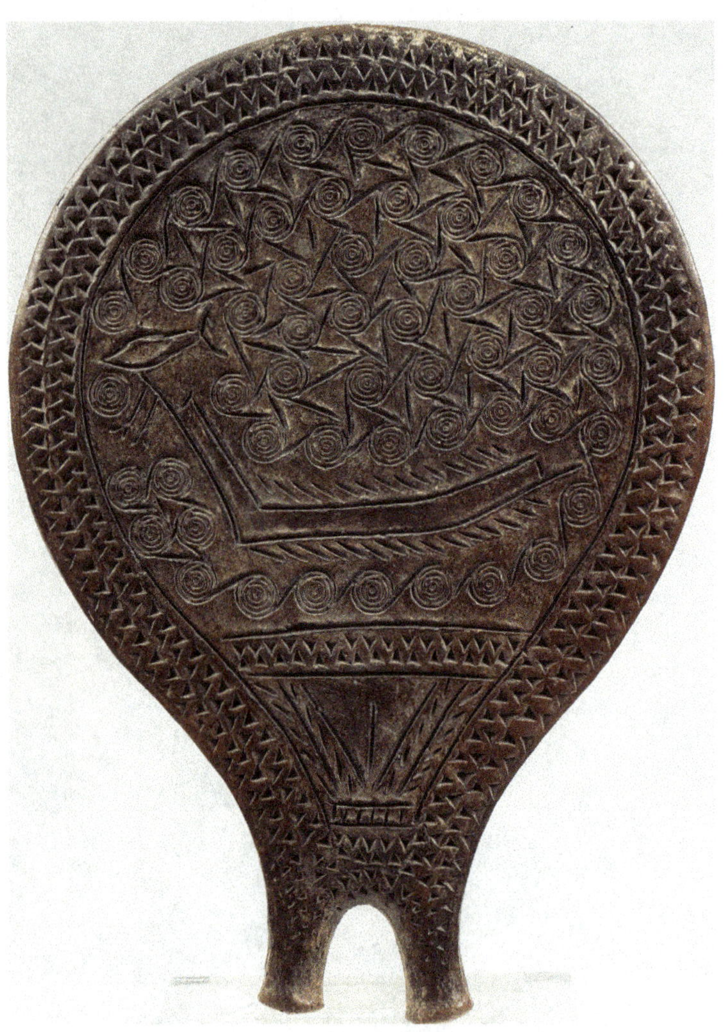

2.3 "Frying pan" from Chalandriani cemetery, Syros, EC IIB/Keros-Syros Group. 11 in (28 cm). Athens, National Archaeological Museum 4974. Photo: National Archaeological Museum, Athens (George Fafalis) © Hellenic Ministry of Education and Religious Affairs, Culture and Sports/Archaeological Receipts Fund.

and have one much higher end, perhaps with steering oars. Surrounding the ship are concentric circles made by a stamp and then linked by lines to make the design look like running spirals. Perhaps, in conjunction with the ship and the small fish in the upper left, the pattern is meant to represent the sea, but the pattern also appears as a simple decorative scheme that fills up the entire surface on other pans without any reference to the sea or ships.

Early Cycladic villages consisted of houses made of **mud brick** and stone built on rough stone foundations and lower courses. A similar type of architecture appears on Crete, and the village of Myrtos is the best excavated example of an Early Minoan (EM) site **(Figure 2.4)**. The site was first occupied in EM IIA (2700–2400 BCE) and was then expanded in EM IIB (2400–2200 BCE); it was destroyed at the end of EM II and the site was abandoned, probably by 2170–2150 BCE. The settlement was placed on the top of a hill, above the arable land, and consisted of a half-dozen houses set irregularly together, with lower stone courses surmounted by mud brick for walls and timbers and reeds for roofing. The oldest structure is in the center (in hatched lines), and the other houses were built incrementally during the second phase. Each of the houses had kitchen, storage, and living areas, with some rooms having benches that might have been used for storage or work surfaces. Clustering the houses together like this made them more secure and limited the number of entry points both to the village and to each dwelling. The spaces marked 13/14, 64/65, and 67 are passages and made navigating through the village like a maze. At some other sites, fortification walls surround the houses. As in the Cyclades, the cemetery was outside of the habitation. Unlike the Cyclades, Minoan tombs are communal rather than individual, with circular chambers being used for multiple burials.

The village of Myrtos may have had only about fifty residents who were closely related to each other. Loom weights were found in several areas, showing weaving as one of the important activities of the settlement. Some of the spaces were specialized in their function. For example, 49 was a pottery production area, with vats of clay to be used for making pottery. Room 92 had a semicircular platform and eighteen vessels, as well as a terracotta female figure holding a jug in her arms. These features suggest that the room and its building were some type of shrine that served the community.

The pottery at Myrtos shows a change in style from dark lines on a light surface in EM IIA to a more burnished and mottled surface in EM IIB. As we saw earlier in this chapter, the new style is labeled Vasiliki Ware, after another site where it was found in large quantities. The teapot in **Figure 2.1** **(see page 22)** is like examples found at Myrtos, with similarly elongated, asymmetric, or imbalanced elements and mottled surface patterns. The appearance of Vasiliki Ware at sites across Crete shows that even though the settlements were small, trade and communication spread new artistic ideas and practices across the region.

mud brick
building bricks made of mud, clay, and/or sand mixed with straw and dried hard in the sun. Walls of mud brick would be covered with plaster to make them more durable

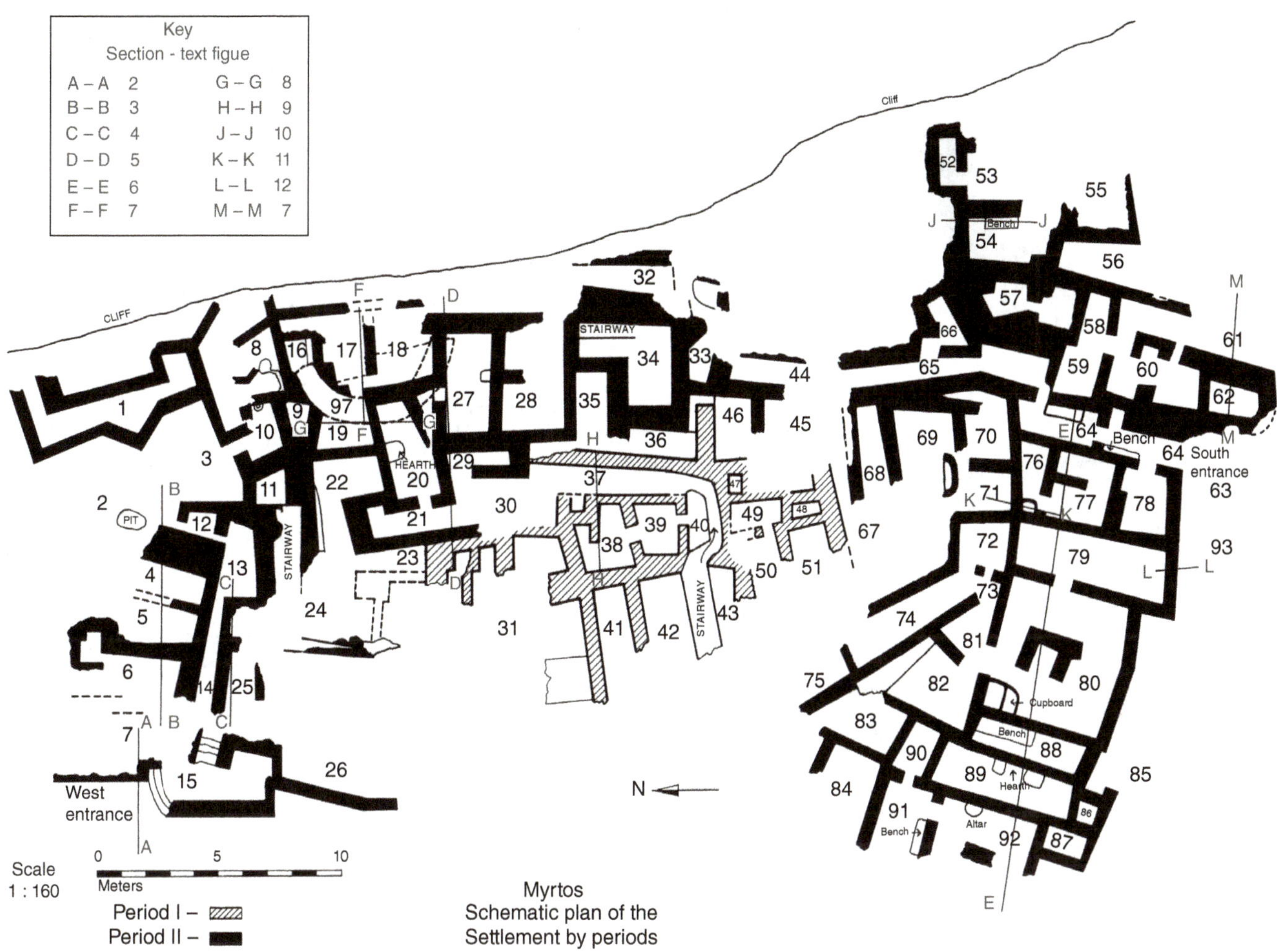

2.4 Plan of Myrtos, Crete, EM II. After P. Warren, *Myrtos: An Early Bronze Age Settlement in Crete* (London, 1972), insert. Reproduced with permission of the British School at Athens.

EARLY TO MIDDLE HELLADIC (C. 3100–1675 BCE)

Turning to the Early Helladic Greek mainland, we also see important developments in the middle of the third millennium in the period EH II. The archaeological evidence suggests that there were new peoples moving into the area at the end of EH I, and there is additional evidence of trade with the Cyclades in EC II/EH II, as mentioned earlier with the Cycladic frying pans. Among the most distinctive EH pottery products of this period are terracotta "sauceboats," like the examples found at the Peloponnesian site of Lerna **(Figure 2.5)**. The earliest version of the shape (I in the drawing) is very similar to examples of Cycladic sauceboats in EC II. Later Lerna versions of the sauceboat are more vertical in their proportions (II–IV in the drawing), with the spouts stretched and angled out and upward, a stylization that is found elsewhere in EH II. Most of the ware is undecorated and plain, which focuses attention even more on the form itself. Like the EC frying pans, we remain unsure about the function of the sauceboats, which virtually disappear as a product at the end of EH II. Figure 2.5 also shows some characteristic bowls and saucers from EH II, some used for drinking

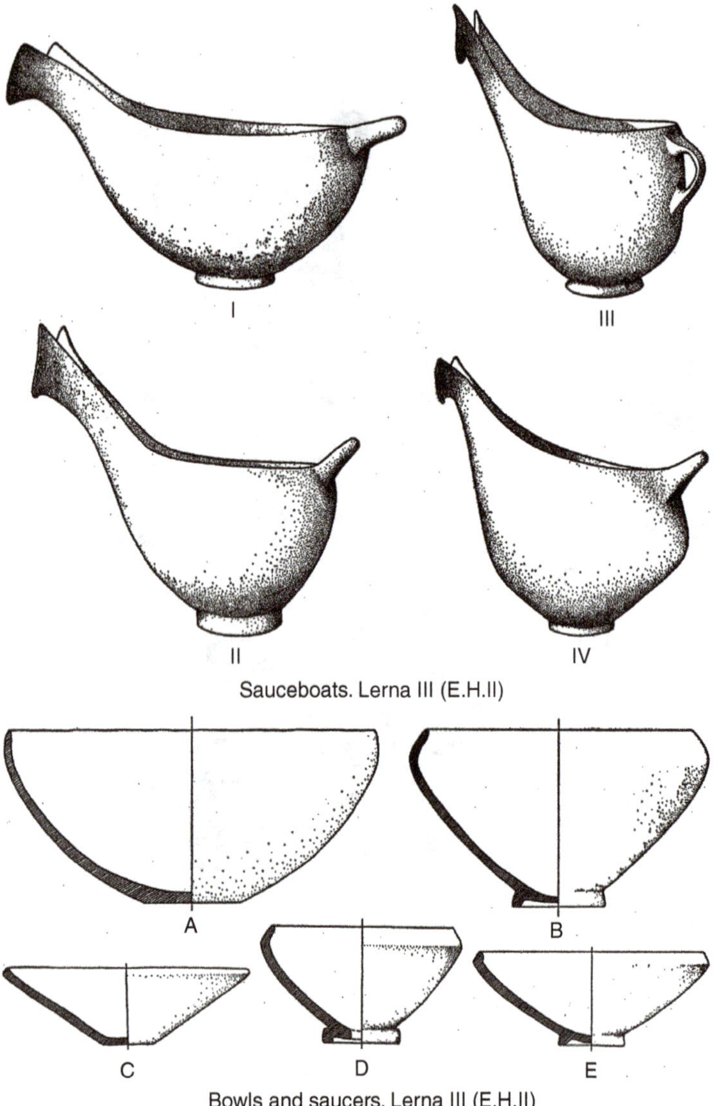

2.5 Sauceboats and bowls from Lerna, EH II. After J. L. Caskey, "The Early Helladic Period in the Argolid," *Hesperia* 29 (1960), 291, Fig. 1, used with permission.

(A–E in the drawing). While these shapes are more practical in form and function, one can see a stylistic consistency, with turned-in rim and proportions that distinguish EH II pottery from other later periods (for example, compare these to the later MH **Minyan ware** in **Figure 2.8, page 31**).

Lerna is an important Early Helladic site for its well-documented excavation and because the site was destroyed and not rebuilt in later periods, preserving much of the EH occupation. The first two phases of the town, Lerna I and II, belong to the period EH I, and there appears to have been a smooth transition to Lerna III, the high point of the site in period EH II. There is evidence for the use of the plow at this time, and so likely greater agricultural production. The houses grew larger, being typically rectangular in shape, with a door on one short wall and either a squared end or rounded apse at the other end. A large town wall offering defense for Lerna was constructed, consisting of a double wall with space between.

The most distinctive structure in the later stages of Lerna III is the large House of the Tiles, named after the fired terracotta tiles that made up the roof of the structure (**Figure 2.6**). Tiles provided a more waterproof and durable roof than reed and thatch, but also increased considerably the weight on the walls of the structure, requiring more careful construction techniques. The house is much larger, 25 meters long and 12 meters wide, than the typical house and had a second story. The main entrance, marked by its framing and larger width, remained on the short end, and led past a short portico into a large square room. Smaller doors in the back of the large room and on the other end of the house led to additional rooms and access to the corridors at the side of the house, which provided stairs to the upper stories and give the name **Corridor House** to this type of building. Some of the walls were plastered, and the presence of a large collection of seal impressions in a self-contained small room on the south long side of the house suggests that the structure served as both residence and administrative center. The House of the Tiles and the settlement were destroyed at the end of EH II, *c.* 2200. The succeeding buildings were much smaller, rectangular buildings with apsidal ends, and a large circular **tumulus** was set up over the remains of the house, indicated by the circular line in the plan.

The Corridor House would have dominated the town visually, being both larger and taller than the other houses in the town. The large rooms on the first floor would have provided spaces in which groups could have assembled, while the rooms on the second floor would have provided restricted but elevated living quarters for the occupants. Its large scale and more costly structure and materials suggest that there had been changes in the social structure of the town from earlier phases. The presence of the storeroom with numerous seals, as we shall see next, suggests an administrative role for the building, and probably the emergence of an elite ruling family or group in the town. Whereas the plans of houses and towns in the first phases of the Bronze Age in Greece, like Myrtos, suggest a more horizontal type of social structure, the Corridor House at Lerna may indicate the emergence of social and political hierarchies in the middle of the third millennium.

Minyan ware
a smooth, burnished, gray or yellow, wheel-thrown pottery produced on the Greek mainland in the Middle Helladic period

Corridor House
a type of Early Helladic structure with main rooms on the first floor that were flanked by corridors on either side that led to the upper story of the structure

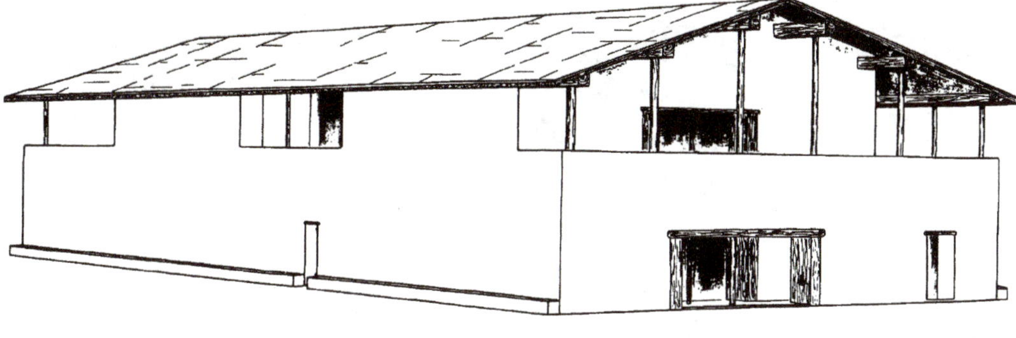

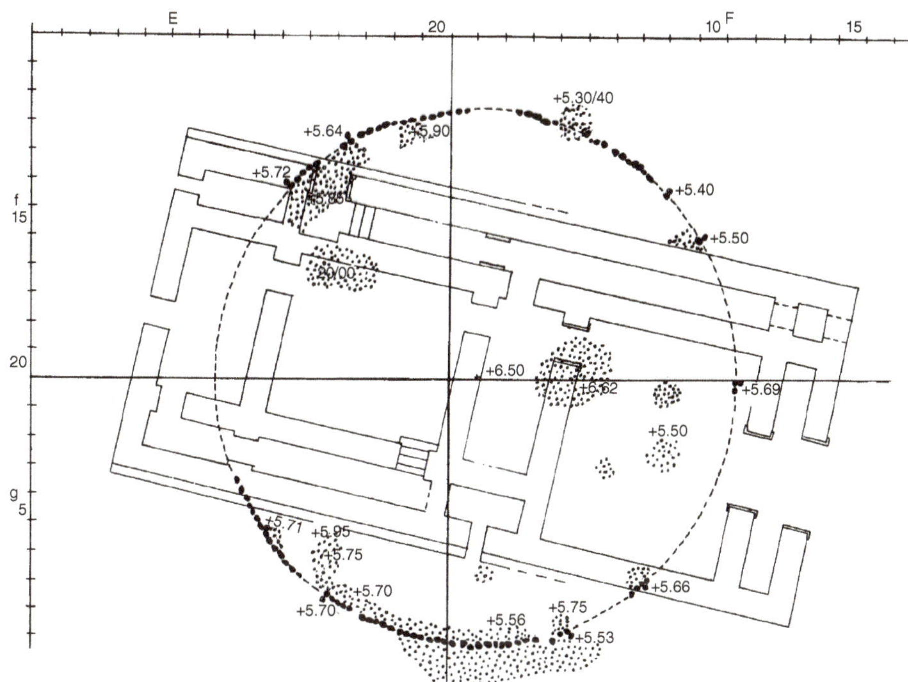

2.6 House of the Tiles, Lerna, EH IIB. Plan and reconstruction. After M. H. Weincke, *Lerna IV: The Architecture, Stratification, and Pottery of Lerna III* (Princeton, 2000), Fig. I.107, used with permission.

As mentioned above, the small room on the south side of the Corridor House is only accessible from the exterior; inside were found 143 fragments of sealings on clay, with 120 different seal designs, some of them seen in **Figure 2.7**. Seals, made of stone or other materials, served an important role in the Bronze Age by serving to secure the tops of jars with clay to prevent tampering with their contents, and additionally signaled individual ownership of the contents. In the absence of writing, the unique design of a seal served throughout the ancient world to signal ownership and identity. Circular seals and seal impressions like those at Lerna are found throughout Bronze Age Greece, although not in these numbers in one location. These seals may have served an administrative purpose as a means for tracking payments of goods or crops of members of the community. The concentration of seals in a room of the Corridor House suggests that the building and its occupants served an administrative role. Whether the seals and house supported a ruling elite, who drew from the production of the residents, or served a communal function as a repository is debated, but in either case there was a centralized point of record-keeping and meeting space for the town.

As can be seen in the illustration of the seal impressions, most of the designs radiate from a central point to fill up the circular surface of the seal. Carved *intaglio* lines of a seal created raised lines in the impressions that they made when pressed in the clay, as can be seen in the drawings. Some of the designs use a swastika or bent pattern to create a more whirligig composition (S25, S26, S27), while

tumulus
a large mound built over a grave or structure

seal
a small object made of stone or metal used to make impressions on clay or wax used to seal containers, marking ownership and security of the contents. Seals were decorated with designs to distinguish individual owners

intaglio
the creation of a design by incision or engraving on a surface, producing raised lines when pressed into a soft surface like clay

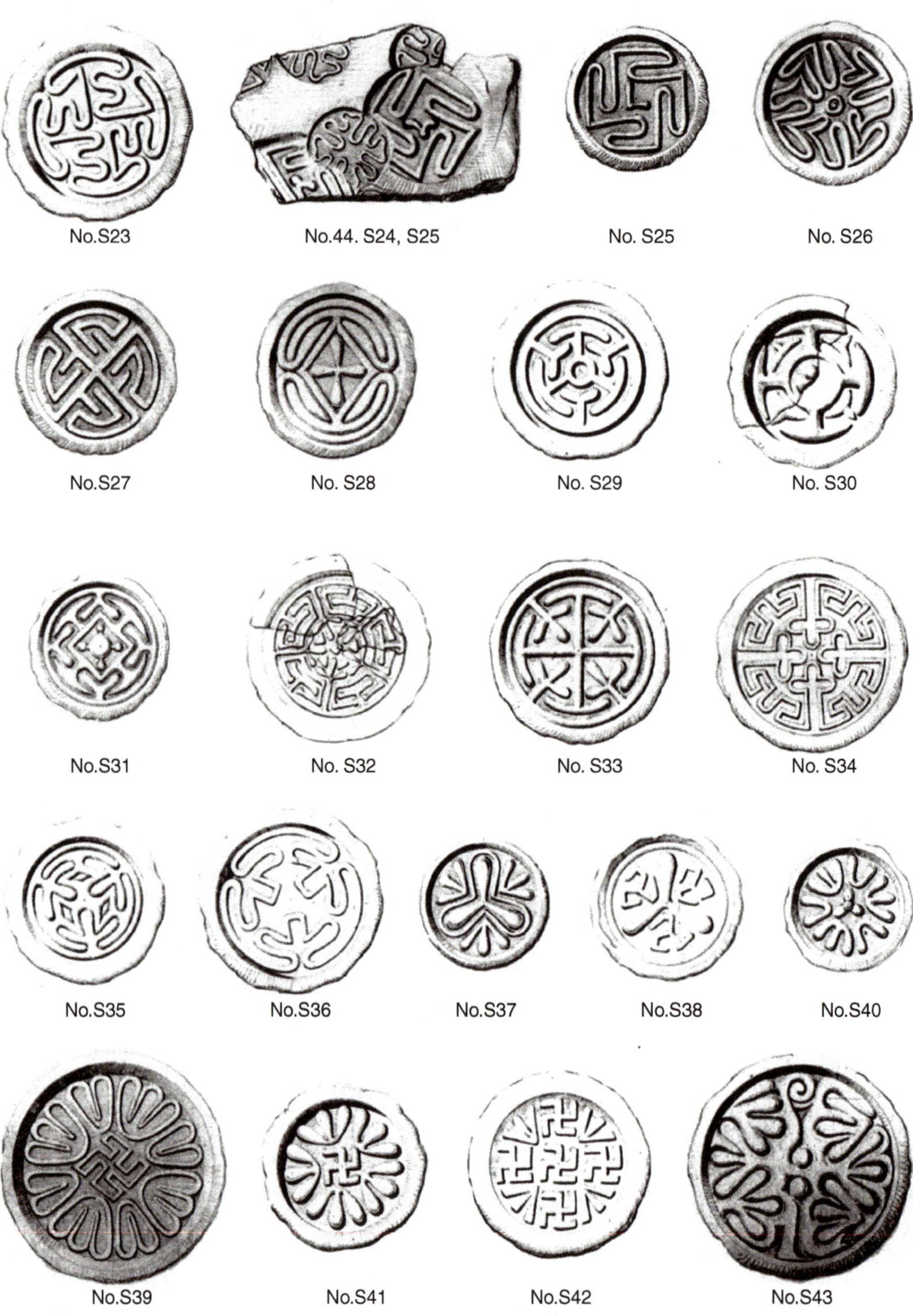

2.7 Seals from the House of the Tiles at Lerna, EH IIB. After M. C. Heath, "Early Helladic Clay Sealings from the House of the Tiles at Lerna," *Hesperia* 27 (1958), pl. 21, used with permission.

meander
a rectilinear design also known as a key pattern that creates a motif that winds or doubles back on itself before going forward

the symmetry of the other patterns might be better described as radial or centrifugal (S33, S40). Some of the seals, such as S34 and S32, show a bent-key motif that looks forward to the **meander** pattern found frequently in later Greek art, starting in the Early Geometric period as we shall see in Chapter 4. Some of the designs are tripartite and others quadripartite. Even within the limitations of the small field and the use only of engraved lines, one can still see that there was a wide range of designs and variations possible that would make each design unique and recognizable to both owner

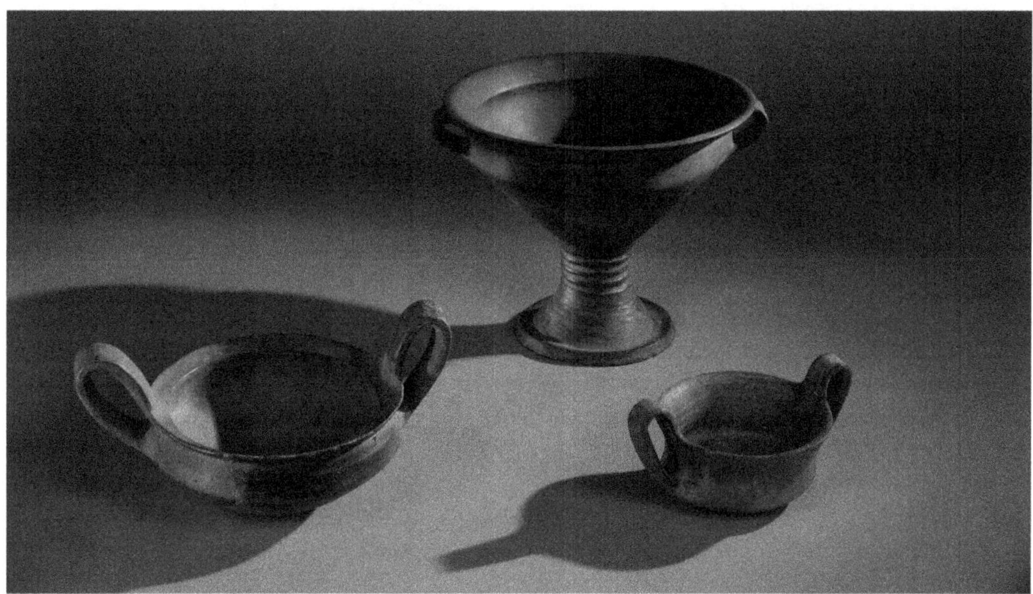

2.8 Minyan ware drinking vessels, MH. $4\frac{7}{16}$ in (11.2 cm), $7\frac{5}{16}$ in (18.6 cm), $3\frac{1}{8}$ in (8 cm). London, British Museum. Left: 1912,0626.307; middle: 1912,0626.35; right: 1912,0626.55. Photo: © The Trustees of the British Museum.

and recipient of goods marked by the seal. Seals continued to be used into the first millennium and we will see that in the Middle Bronze Age intricate figural compositions would be used on elite seal rings and gems **(see Figure 2.16, page 39)**.

Just how and why Lerna III was destroyed or by whom is uncertain. The succeeding periods, EH III, MH I, and MH II, appear to have been more modest in the number and size of settlements, not only at Lerna, but throughout mainland Greece. Shapes like the sauceboats disappear from pottery production, and there is a change in pottery technology that may indicate larger-scale social changes. Pottery from Lerna III had been handmade with coils, but in the EH III period the pottery wheel was adopted to finish the vessel and the surface is more burnished and glossy, techniques that had been developed in the Levant and Anatolia and made their way to the Aegean at this time.

One theory is that new people arrived in EH III who displaced the earlier population, resulting in the destruction of Lerna and other sites and a general decrease in the population. The discovery that the writing on tablets from the Late Helladic period was a very old form of Greek led to the hypothesis that it was a Greek-speaking people who settled on the mainland in EH III, but there is no evidence from this period to confirm what language the people of Early Helladic Greece spoke. It is possible that Greek-speaking peoples arrived even earlier, or that there were several waves of migration rather than a single invasion that resulted in the destruction of Lerna. Recent study has also indicated that there were significant environmental changes that took place during EH III, and this might explain the depopulation and abandonment of sites as agricultural production declined.

On the Greek mainland, the Middle Helladic period is certainly more modest generally, with many of the EH sites abandoned, especially in the interior of the region. There is an increase in settlements, population, and wealth beginning in MH III, and especially in LH I, that we will discuss later. One of the most distinctive products of the MH period is gray Minyan ware, like the three heavily restored drinking cups in **Figure 2.8**. These vessels are made using a potter's wheel and have sharply defined edges and components like rims and feet; the surface is burnished, giving the cups a polished appearance. The two-handled design for a drinking cup is significant, in that their presence indicates a practice of shared or communal drinking. With two handles a host or pourer can use one handle to give the cup to a drinker, unlike a one-handled mug or goblet without handles. Two-handled cups first appear in the the later phases of the Early Bronze Age, and continue to be common and even predominant in later Greek art, as we saw in the kylikes in Chapter 1, reminding us of the social context in which drink was consumed.

PROTOPALATIAL AND NEOPALATIAL CRETE

Kamares Ware
a Minoan pottery style produced in the Protopalatial period and featuring a dark slip background with painted motifs in white, yellow, and red

During the first phase of the Middle Minoan period we see the development of large palaces throughout Crete, giving rise to the term Protopalatial for the time corresponding to MM IB through MM II in the traditional chronology (*c.* 1900–1750 BCE). These palaces featured a large central courtyard surrounded by buildings, dwarfing in scale earlier houses and signaling the development of more centralized administration and a much greater degree of wealth. There is also evidence of more extensive trade contacts, both through the presence of materials like gold and ivory imported into Crete and through the export of Cretan works, like **Kamares Ware** pottery, to places like Egypt. These palaces were all destroyed around 1750 BCE, possibly due to earthquakes, but then rebuilt at a larger scale than before. The Neopalatial structures likely followed the general plan of their predecessors, but the vigorous rebuilding obliterated much of the remains of the Protopalatial structures. The Neopalatial period encompasses both the end of the Middle Minoan period (MM III) and the beginning of Late Minoan (LM I). Most of the palaces are destroyed at the end of LM IA, probably due to damage associated with the eruption of Thera around 1625 BCE, and only the palace at Knossos is rebuilt and continues to function until the end of LM IB around 1490 BCE, when the Neopalatial period concludes. The palatial period on Crete not only marks a high point of art and architecture, but also signals a change from the less complex settlements of the Early Minoan period. Specialization of production at the palaces suggests an elite culture that reflects more centralized organization of agriculture, economic production, and trade, providing the resources and patronage necessary for the skills and materials used in the production of art and architecture.

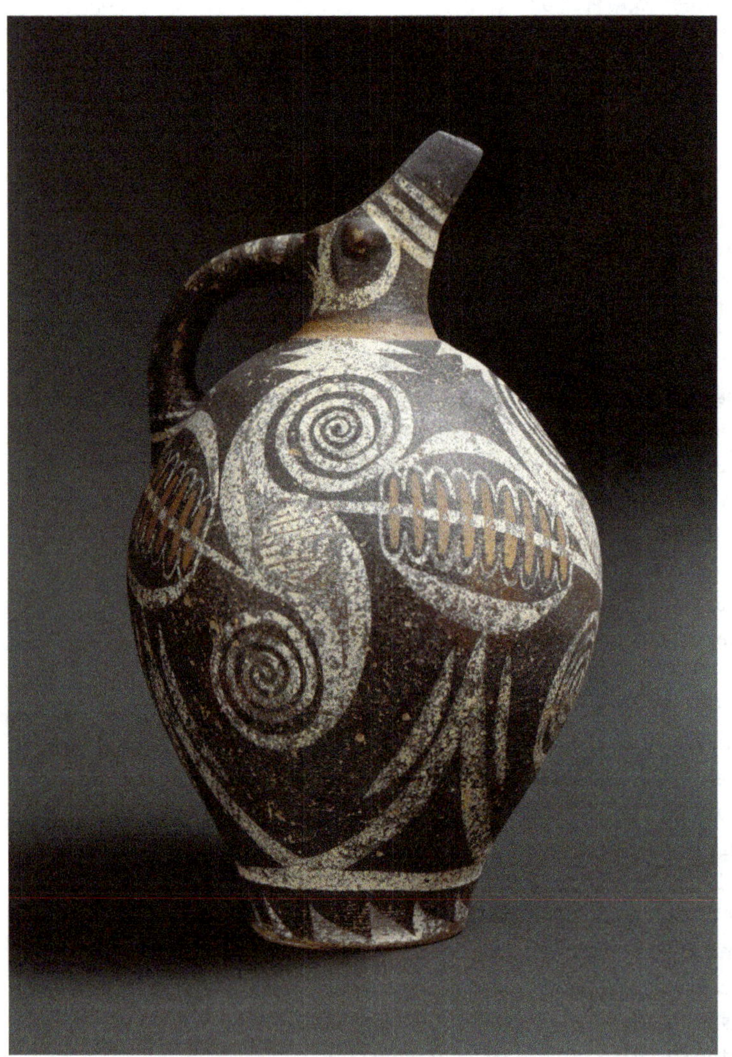

2.9 Kamares Ware jug from Phaistos, MM IIB. 10$^{5}/_{8}$ in (27 cm). Herakleion, Archaeological Museum. Photo: Nimatallah/Art Resource, NY.

We can readily see the change in artistic culture by examining a different approach to form and decoration in Middle Minoan pottery. Beginning in EM III, Minoan potters painted a coat of dark slip over the vase, and then added decoration in white on top of it. This fashion continued into the Protopalatial period (MM IB and MM II), by which time these wheel-thrown vases were both sharply defined in terms of their shape and architectural form and decorated with vibrant swirling designs by use of white and red paint on the dark surface **(Figure 2.9)**. These Kamares Ware vessels, like this pitcher from the town of Phaistos, feature abstract motifs that derive from plant forms, but the emphasis is upon an energetic and visually dynamic design that leads the eye around and over the vase following the repeated linear patterns. The shape retains some of the stylized features that we saw in Vasiliki Ware, like a projecting and angular spout, but the shape is more vertical, adding to the sense of potential movement of the vase. Kamares Ware appears during the Protopalatial period and continues to be produced in a more restrained fashion into MM III and the Neopalatial period, suggesting that the destruction of the palaces did not destroy the system that built them.

To survey Minoan architecture and towns, we have to look at buildings from the Neopalatial period, but these probably follow the forms and functions of the earlier Protopalatial phase. The town of Gournia shows an increase in both the area and population of Minoan towns during the Palatial period compared to Early Minoan sites like Myrtos **(Figure 2.10)**. The town is organized around a large square (3 in the plan), above which was a modest "palace" (5–6) that was probably more like a governor's residence than the large palaces found at sites like Knossos and Phaistos. While more modest in scale than the large palaces like Knossos that we shall discuss next, the palace at Gournia dominates visually the town around it by its central and higher position and the use of

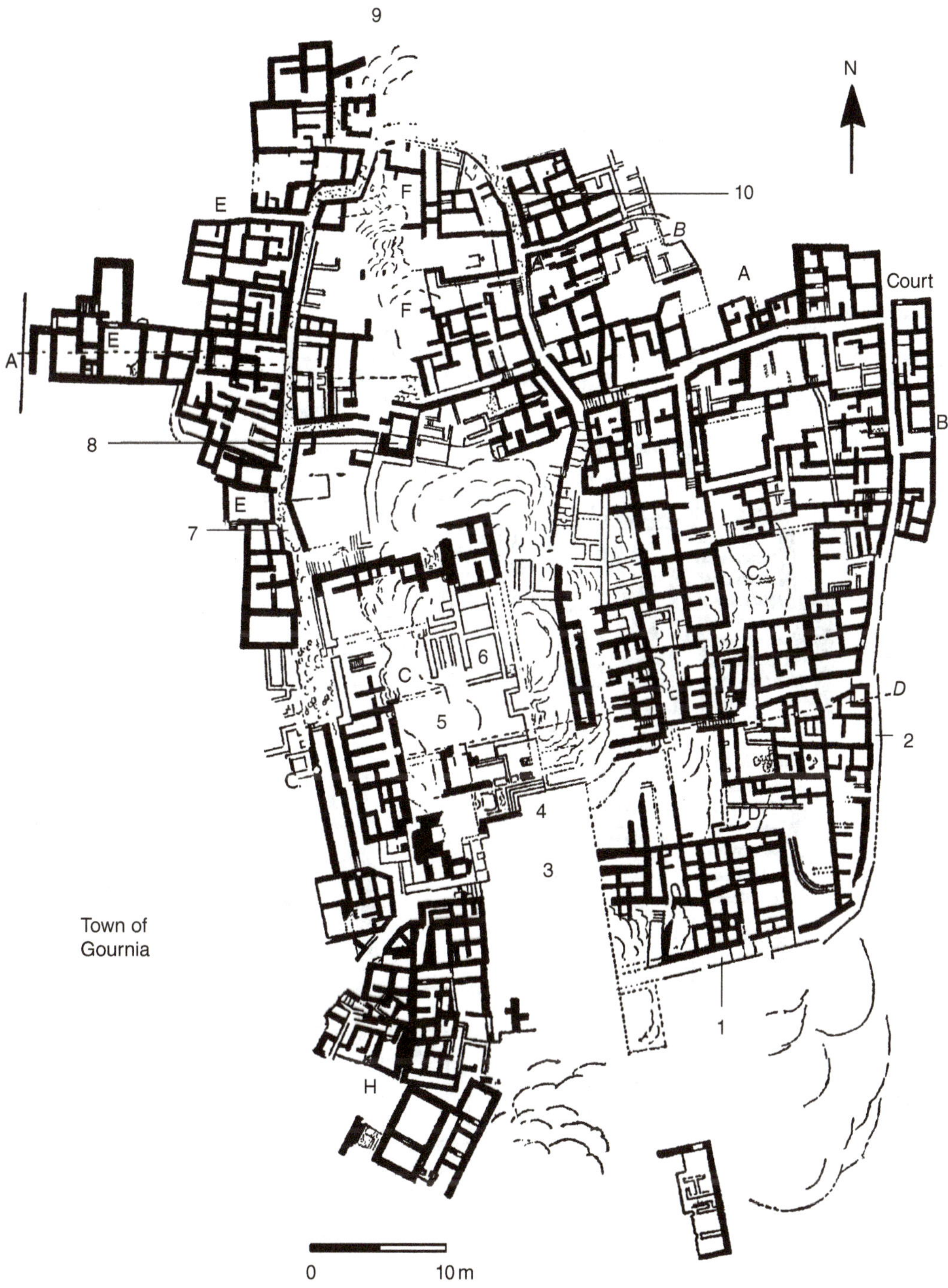

2.10 Plan of Gournia, Crete, LM I. Drawing from P. P. Betancourt, *Introduction to Aegean Art* (Philadelphia: INSTAP Academic Press, 2007), Fig. 5.7. Image provided by INSTAP Academic Press.

ashlar masonry
square-cut stone, usually in the form of long rectangular blocks

ashlar masonry. The open square could have been used for public functions like markets, as well as for rituals, but sitting above it, the palace would have dominated the activities of the square.

Gournia is built on a slope above a harbor, and three main roads run along the ridges, looping from the main square and back again (7, 10, and 2). Stairs and sharp inclines run east–west between the main traffic arteries. As in Myrtos, the houses are quite varied in their plans and configuration, but most were two stories with six to eight rooms, with storage on the lower floor and living quarters above. The houses continue to use many of the same materials as earlier, rough stone, mud brick, timber, and reeds. Many of the houses share exterior walls, unlike the isolated exterior walls of the palace, giving further visual distinction to the palace and showing the importance of a centralized administration in Minoan Crete.

It is in the palaces of the Neopalatial period that we see the use of more finely worked stone and larger-scale rooms. The palace at Knossos, often called the Palace of Minos after the legendary king of Crete who built the labyrinth to imprison the Minotaur, is the largest of the palaces. As can been seen in the plan (**Figure 2.11**), the palace was built around a large rectangular courtyard (25 m x 50 m) set along a north–south axis. The surrounding structures were built two, three, or four stories high, with a shrine, throne room, and staircase on the west side of the court (13/14, 12, 11) and residential

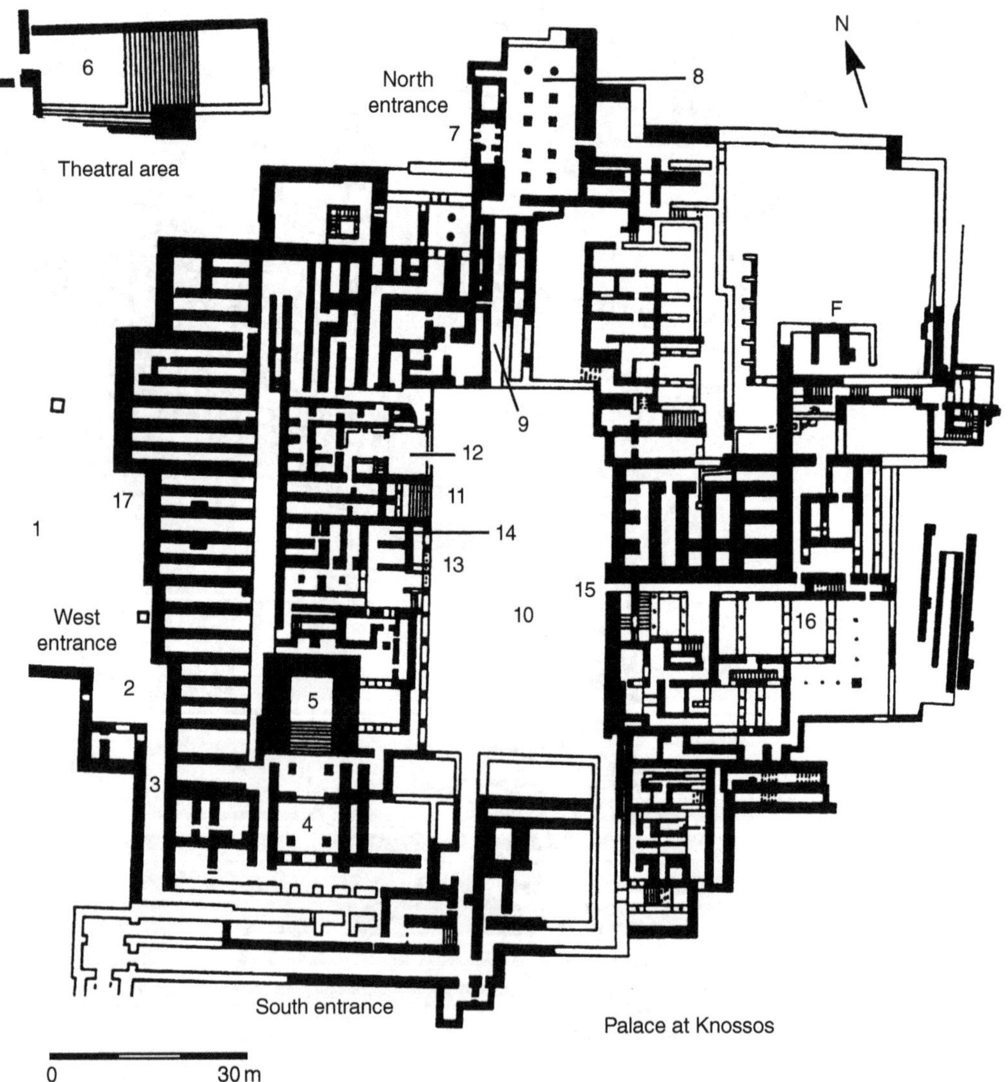

2.11 Plan of the palace at Knossos, LM I. Drawing from P. P. Betancourt, *Introduction to Aegean Art* (Philadelphia: INSTAP Academic Press, 2007), Fig. 5.2. Image provided by INSTAP Academic Press.

area to the east (15). The walls were made of ashlar blocks of stone, as well as rougher stone, timber, rubble, mud brick, and plaster **(Figure 2.12)**. Large wooden columns had a particular form that is distinctly Minoan: a smooth shaft that tapers downward from a large bulbous capital that is painted red and black. The plaster was made from burned limestone, making a durable coating to the walls. The plastered walls in Minoan palaces were covered with frescoes to make truly impressive rooms and passageways. The processed materials and their combination in construction to create staircases, corridors, windows, and openings required a skilled team of architects and builders and are by themselves a sign of the increased prosperity of Crete during this period. Indeed, at an area of roughly 20,000 square meters, the palace at Knossos is larger than the town of Gournia.

It is during the Protopalatial period that a writing system was developed, labeled **Linear A**, that remains mostly undeciphered today. Linear A inscriptions are found on sealings, tablets, storage vessels as well as other objects, which suggests that it served an administrative role in signaling ownership and inventory of goods and agricultural produce. As the palaces contained large storage areas (no. 17 at Knossos, no. 6 in the small palace at Gournia), it is thought that the palaces served a redistributive function: gathering commodities from the surrounding territory and distributing them to members of the palace and town, including those producing specialized products like potters, builders, and metalworkers. Production centers were concentrated around the palaces, and in the Protopalatial and Neopalatial period these workshops produced luxury items of gold, ivory, and other materials for the elite.

Linear A
a writing script developed by the Minoans in Protopalatial Crete

Entrance to the palace at Knossos must have resembled something like a journey through a labyrinth. The west entrance (1, 2, 3) led to a monumental doorway (4) and stairs to the upper floors, but also to the storage rooms of the palace (17). The north entrance (7) led into a long ramped corridor (9) that brought the visitor into the central court and was probably used for ceremonial processions and entries, while a kitchen and dining room above at 8 could entertain a large assembly. The throne room and palace shrine (12 and 13/14) could be accessed from the courtyard but looked out over it

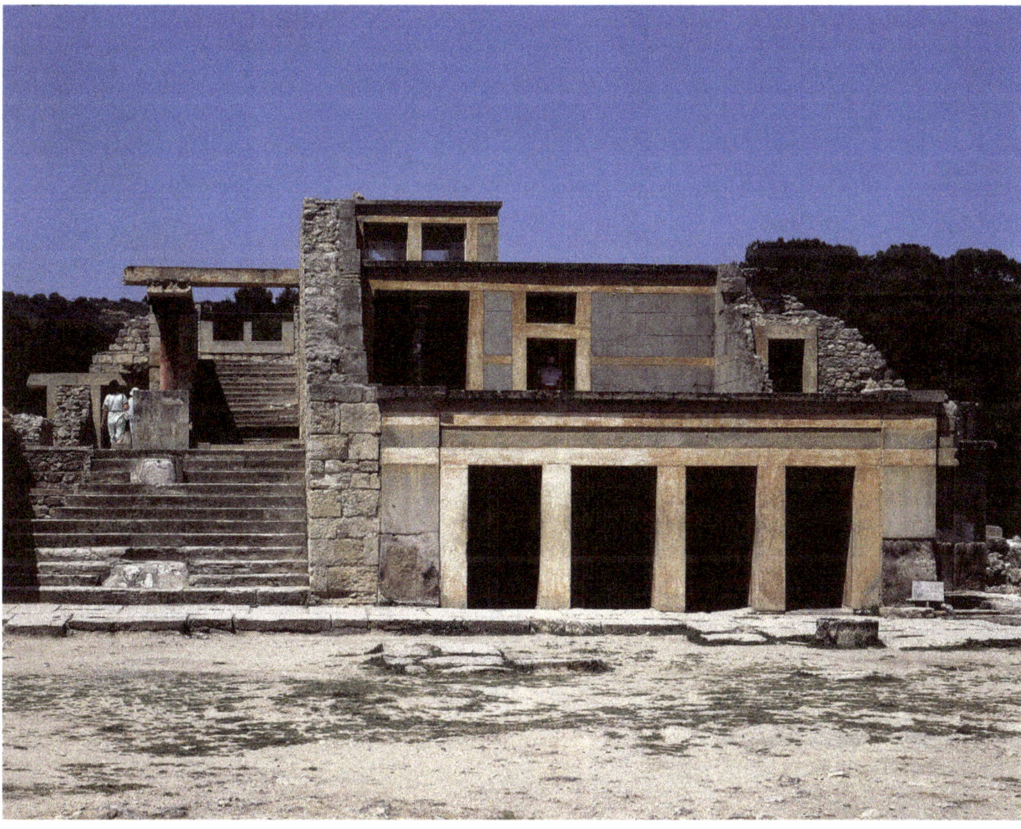

2.12 View of west side of courtyard at the palace of Minos at Knossos: staircase and throne room (reconstructed). Photo: Gianni Dagli Orti/The Art Archive at Art Resource, NY.

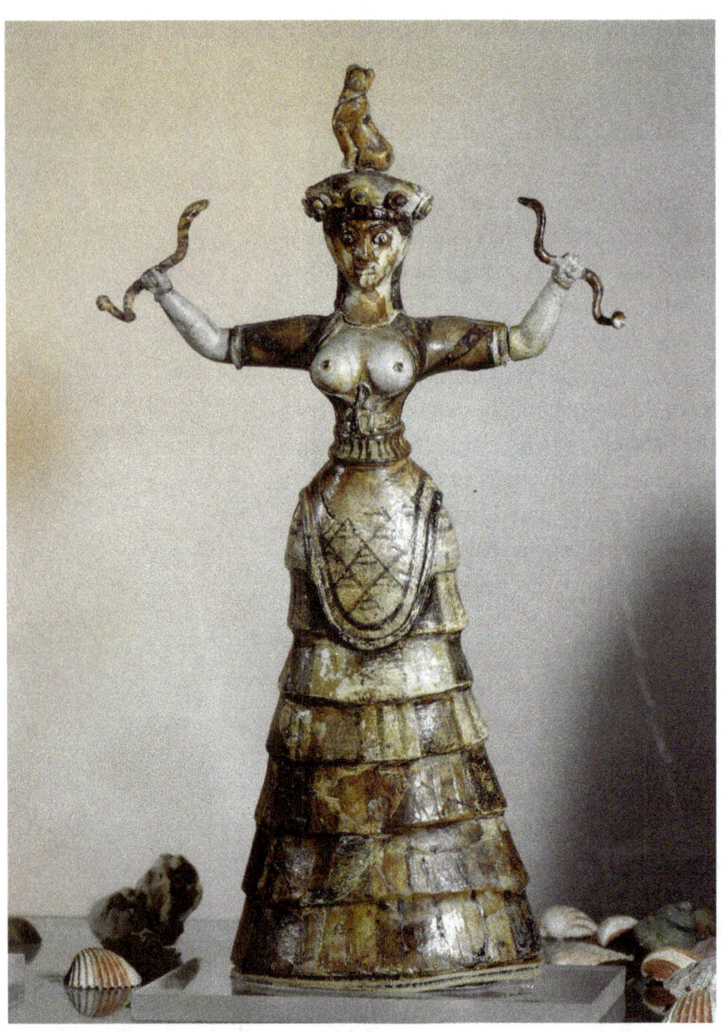

2.13 "Snake goddess" from Knossos, MM III to LM IA. Faience, 11⅝ in (29.5 cm). Herakleion, Archaeological Museum. Photo: Erich Lessing/Art Resource, NY.

from a second story. The central courtyard was probably the center of activity and would have been big enough to accommodate a large number of people and activities, with the ability of observers to watch from the upper floors.

The arts of the Neopalatial period include a broad range of materials and a distinct interest in the human figure. We can see this in one of the iconic works of Minoan sculpture, a female figure found buried in a repository (14) in the palace shrine at Knossos **(Figure 2.13)**. The work is made of **faience**, a material imported from Egypt that vitrifies into a colorful glass-like surface. Like much of Minoan art, the color and sheen must have been quite appealing, especially in combination with an animated style for representing the human figure. This figure, like others of men and women that we will see, combines a very narrow waist with shoulders that are broadened by the projecting arms that hold two snakes. The neck and face are animated and she balances a headdress with an animal on top of her head. For female figures the heavy, flounced skirt is cone-shaped, and the bodice is open to reveal the breasts. The painted lines remind us that the fabric of her garments would have been richly patterned or embroidered, and it would appear from surviving paintings that Minoan textiles were elaborate and rich materials that were exported. The figure is called a "snake goddess," but is one of several such statues found together that could be goddesses or might be priestesses performing a ritual. Certainly the small scale of the figure would seem to argue against its serving as a cult statue, and the costume is, as we shall see in other media, typical of women performing ritual.

Another cult figure is the so-called **kouros** found at Palaikastro in eastern Crete **(Figure 2.14)**. The figure is a half-meter high and is one of the largest surviving Minoan sculptures. The body and face are made of hippopotamus ivory, another Egyptian import, along with gray serpentine stone for the hair and skull, rock crystal for the eyes, and gold leaf for bracelets, kilt, and sandals. **Chryselephantine** statues are found in later periods of Greek art as cult statues, including the statue of Zeus in the temple at Olympia and of Apollo excavated at Delphi **(see Figure 7.12, page 168 and Figure 8.18, page 200)**. The Palaikastro kouros, too, may have served as a cult statue in a town shrine, elevated on a base. Although the figure is not nearly as large as later cult statues, within its small room and with its precious materials it would have been visually distinctive. One hypothesis is that the figure is Diktaian Zeus, or Zeus born on Mount Dikte, where the god was born and raised according to later mythological accounts. The rituals of the shrine would then be focused on rites of transition from adolescence to adulthood. The statue was broken and burned sometime at the end of LM IB along with the rest of the town itself, perhaps at the hands of invading Mycenaeans. The town of Palaikastro was mostly abandoned afterward.

The kouros shares the narrow waist and vigorous pose of the snake goddess, here with the elbows out and clenched hands bent back before the body. The hips flare out from the waist and taper through the thigh to the foot, and the left foot is positioned slightly forward. Attention to the tendons

faience
glazed ceramic ware produced by a mixture of sand, fluxes, water, and calcium carbonate compounds

kouros (pl. kouroi)
a male youth, used to denote statues of standing nude young men

chryselephantine
a work made of gold and ivory, often used for cult statues

and veins in the arms and legs conveys a feeling of tension and animation in the figure that is distinctive of the Minoan style.

Mortal humans are depicted in other media and works, including reliefs such as the stone Harvester vase (**Figure 2.15**). This vessel, called a **rhyton,** had a narrow, pointed foot (missing and restored) and was carved with a scene of men carrying harvesting tools and singing on its shoulder. Even at this small scale, we see the distinctive Minoan physique of small waists, broad shoulders, and tensed, extended arms. The men wear belts and kilts, as did the Palaikastro kouros originally, the male equivalent to the flounced skirt of Minoan women. Unlike the statues, these men are shown in vigorous action, marching briskly in procession. The figure at the center opens his mouth in song and shakes a bow-shaped metal device with crossbars and beads that is an Egyptian rattle called a **sistrum**.

Even at the smallest scale we can find these animated features of Minoan representations of the human figure. A gold intaglio seal ring from a tomb in Isopata by Knossos is just over 1 cm in height, but shows a full landscape with lilies and plants and four female figures wearing flounced skirts and open bodices (**Figure 2.16**). The two on the left are dressed like the snake goddess, but both hold their arms forward and up rather than out. At the top center is a partly frontal women dressed the same as the first two, but she has one arm bent and the other down. Between these three women is a tiny figure in a skirt hovering in the air. Finally at the right is another three-quarter female figure facing back toward the others and on the same groundline as the first two. She has both arms bent and held up in a pose similar to the snake goddess. Even at this miniature scale, with each figure less than 1 cm high and formed by tiny incisions into the gold surface, the figures are recognizably Minoan and made by a highly skilled workshop or artist. The ring functions like other seals, but the object itself conveys the wealth and status of its elite owner and perhaps reflects the rituals in which its owner participated.

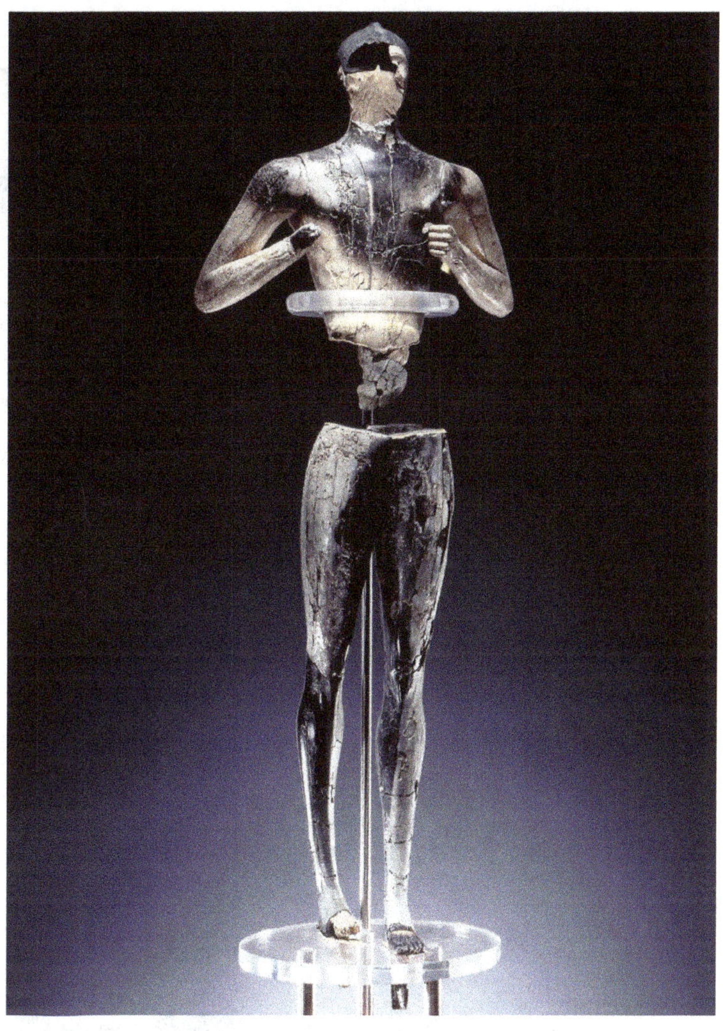

2.14 Kouros from Palaikastro, LM IB. Ivory, gold, serpentine, rock crystal, 20¼ in (51.5 cm). Siteia Museum. Photo: British School at Athens.

rhyton
a conical shape drinking cup, sometimes with a base in the shape of an animal, head, or figure

sistrum
a rattle made in Egypt with beads set on wires stretched between U-shaped or squared arms

Special Palace Tradition
Minoan pottery produced in the LM IB period at Knossos. It has several different stylistic divisions: Marine, Floral, Abstract or Geometric, and Alternating

More difficult to decipher is whether the scene is meant to be entirely symbolic or whether there is a narrative taking place. The pair of women to the left are surely mortal and performing some type of ritual, and the small figure who hovers above them must be divine, but are the other two women mortal or divine? Is the figure on the far right shown twice, once appearing in the skies on the left side and then appearing on the ground as an epiphany for the three worshipping mortal women? Or is the figure to the right a choral leader and the one in the center a lead performer, dancing while the other women sing? Undoubtedly the meaning of the gestures and the relationship of the figures to each other was clear to the owner of the ring, but without a guide to Minoan religion, its ritual actions and beliefs, we are left with a puzzle of large proportions in spite of the intricate detail.

We have concentrated on Neopalatial art that would have been for the elite, but pottery also developed new styles of decoration, particularly in LM IB after the eruption of Thera. Rather than the light on dark scheme of Kamares Ware, late Minoan pottery of the **Special Palace Tradition** used

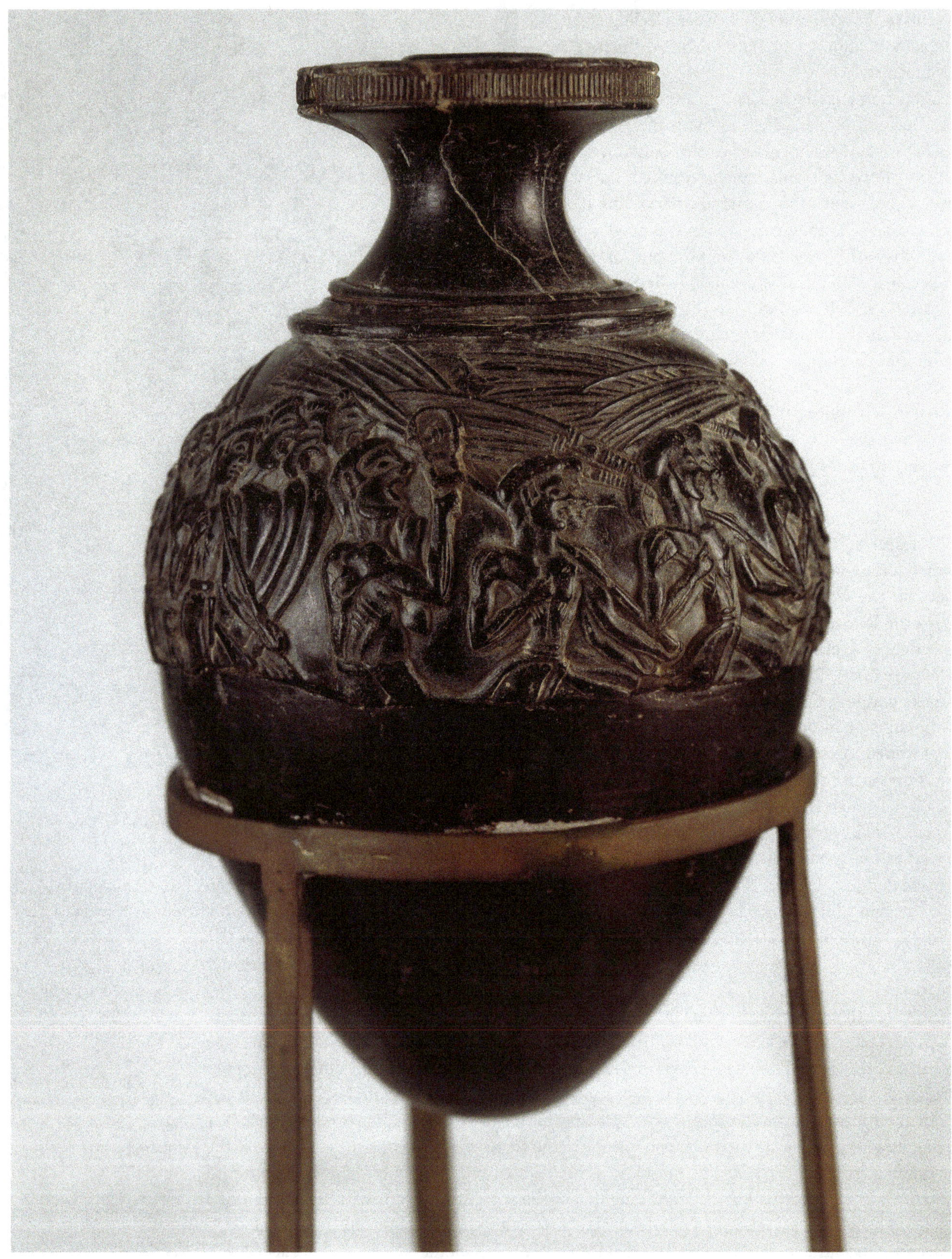

2.15 Harvester vase, LM IB. Height of preserved section, 3¾ in (9.6 cm). Herakleion, Archaeological Museum. Photo: Marie Mauzy/Art Resource, NY.

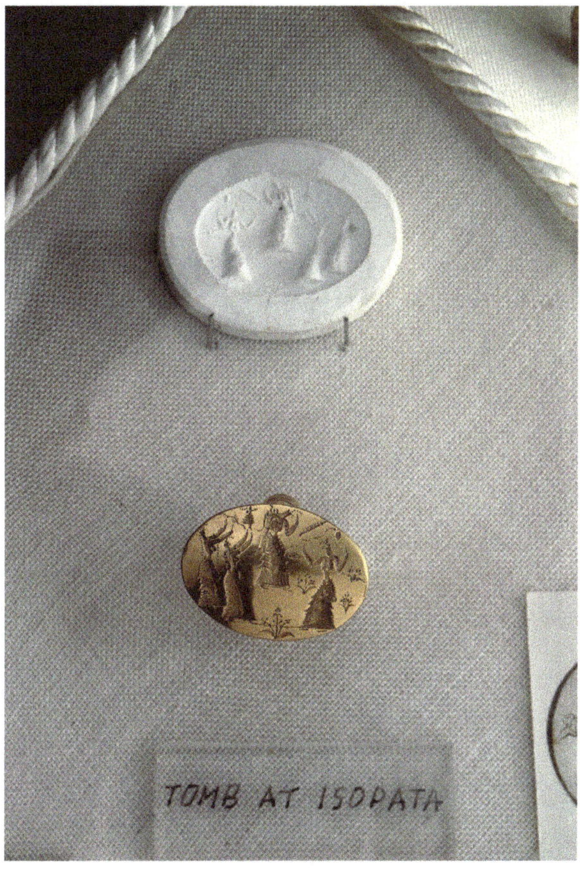

2.16 Seal ring from Isopata, LM I. Gold, ⅞ in × $^{7}/_{16}$ in (2.25 cm x 1.16 cm). Herakleion, Archaeological Museum. Photo: Scala/Art Resource, NY.

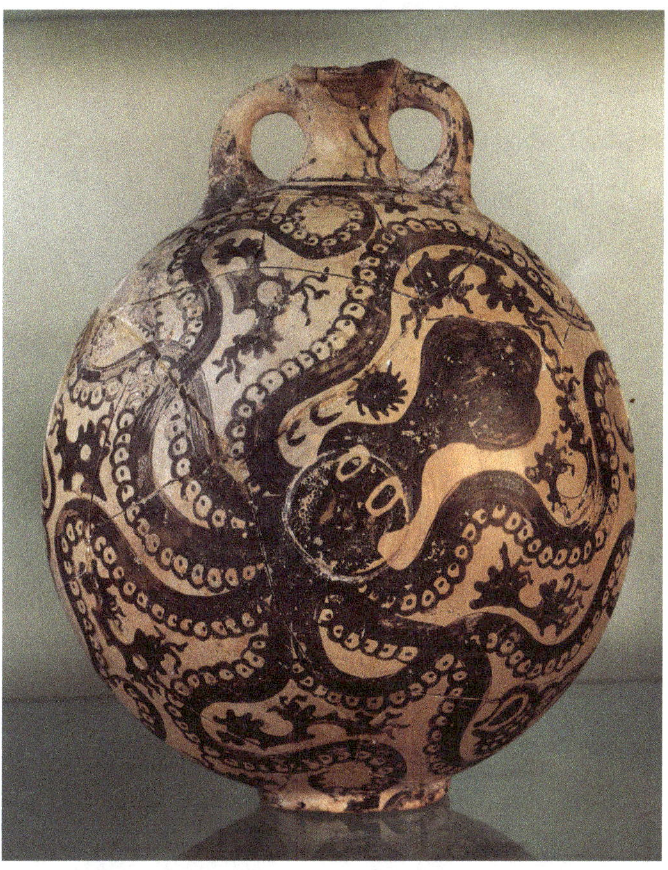

2.17 Marine style pilgrim's flask from Palaikastro with octopus, LM IB. 11 in (28 cm). Herakleion, Archaeological Museum. Photo: Marie Mauzy/Art Resource, NY.

dark forms on a light surface. The pottery was fired at a higher temperature and was more refined in its fabric, and the iron oxide slips used for the dark painting gave a more lustrous surface quality to the vase, which was also burnished. New decorative fashions were developed, with stylistic categories labeled Marine, Floral, Abstract or Geometric, and Alternating. An example of the Marine style is a flask having two loop handles flanking an opening at the top of a spherical body, a shape called a **pilgrim's flask** **(Figure 2.17)**. Filling up the hemispherical body is an octopus painted in dark slip on the pale surface. Its head is set at the center and the arms and body radiate and undulate outward to fill the vessel's surface. In the gaps between the arms are craggy forms that are abstracted rocks or coral. The asymmetry and serpentine lines give a strong sense of movement and animation to the octopus, which is painted in a simplified but still naturalistic form.

pilgrim's flask
a small vessel with a round body and narrow neck and two loop or stirrup handles at the neck

THE CYCLADES

The Cycladic islands are more modest in their artistic production during the Middle Cycladic period compared with contemporary Crete, and there is evidence of the greater influence of Minoan art and culture. The most significant archaeological site is Akrotiri on the island of Thera. The eruption of the volcano destroyed the island and sealed the town in volcanic debris, making it a Bronze Age Pompeii. The remains of the town belong mostly to the first phase of period LC I (i.e., LC IA), contemporary with the last phase of the Neopalatial period on Crete. Minoan and Mycenaean

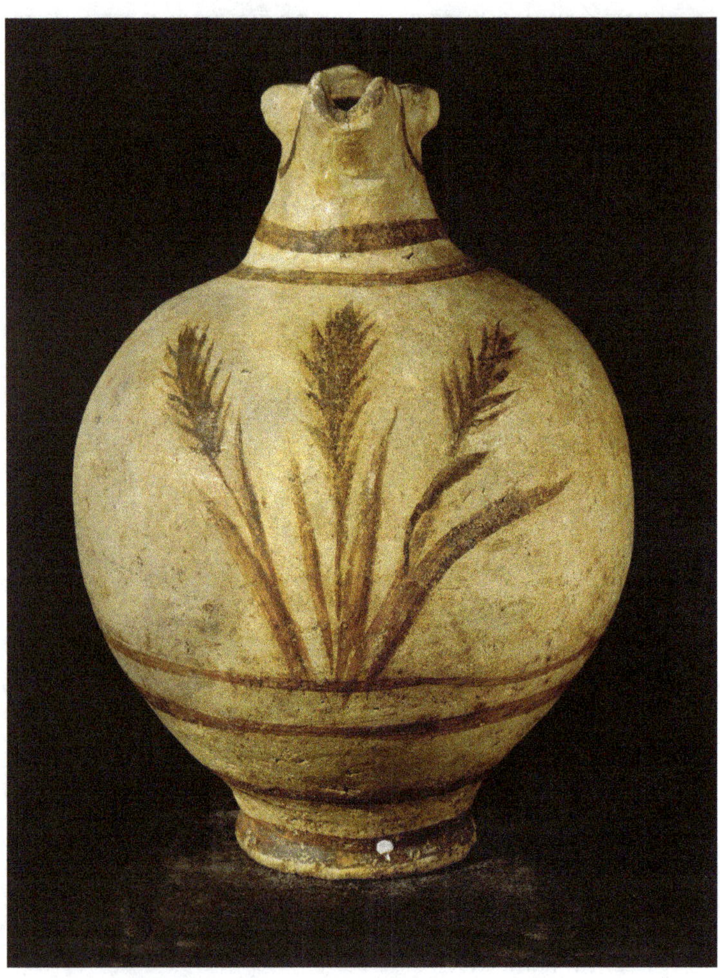

2.18 Jug from Thera, LC IA. 8⅛ in (20.7 cm). Athens, National Archaeological Museum. Sheaves of grain. Photo: Erich Lessing/Art Resource, NY.

pottery was found on the island, as well as locally produced Cycladic pottery. The local Theran ware shows Minoan influence in several ways (**Figure 2.18**). The pottery's painting style features dark painted slip on a light surface, like the octopus flask, and also uses Minoan production techniques of higher temperature firing and iron oxide slips. The range of decorative themes includes marine motifs, flying birds, geometric patterns, and floral motifs, such as the jug with sheaves of grain. As can be seen in this example, Theran painting has a sketchy quality to it, with quick, uneven, and overlapping strokes that give a sense of movement and depth to the plants.

The most remarkable find at Akrotiri, however, was the frescoes in its houses. At least every house had one fresco, painted in true **fresco** technique, in which the dissolved pigments are applied to the surface of the wet plaster, bonding them chemically into the wall. The excavated palaces in Crete also preserved fragments of frescoes, but at Akrotiri the state of preservation in some cases is striking, giving us a sense of the vibrancy of Aegean architecture and its decoration. The landscape fresco from Delta House has three well-preserved walls of a first-story room entered from the house's courtyard (**Figure 2.19**). The bottom section is a rocky landscape with an irregular series of outcroppings. Dark lines suggest striations in the rock, but the color is more artificially applied, with irregular bands of blue, red, and yellow painted vertically on the rocks. Clinging to the rocks are lilies that sway and bend in different directions. In the air are several flying swallows, painted with strokes of dark paint on the light wall and a dab of red for the head. The curving lines have a calligraphic quality, making the looping tails and uneven wings convincing naturalistic representations of birds turning and twisting in three dimensions as they fly. Called the Spring Fresco, it has been pointed out that the birds' behavior belongs to a later season in the year as the adult birds feed their offspring in mid-flight.

fresco
wall painting in which the pigments are applied to the wet plaster (true or buon fresco) or applied with a binder on the surface of dry plaster (dry fresco)

An upstairs room in West House preserves sections of miniature-scale frescoes that ran along the upper part of the four walls above the exterior windows (**Figure 2.20**). The friezes, now preserved like panel paintings, show a scene of ships arriving at an island (top), a battle scene before a city (bottom), and a winding river landscape with trees and animals, called a Nilotic landscape after similar motifs in Egypt (bottom right). The landscapes are continuous – the action changes from departure from an island on the right side of the ship fresco to the arrival on the left side. In the battle scene we see women fetching water and a herder near the top, a structure from which warriors march in the middle, and at the bottom and down below a battle at a harbor with the dead floating in the water. The ships in the better preserved fresco show two towns with small inhabitants watching the ships depart on one side and greeting their arrival on another. The ships have some oarsmen and many oars, with awnings stretched above them and small cabins near the stern. Following Egyptian conventions, men are shown with dark, red-brown skin and women with white. The landscape shows mountains and animals running and has the same colorful irregularity as the landscape fresco in Delta House. As we shall see, landscape is not of special interest for most Greek art after the Bronze Age, but in Thera we see it both with and without humans, and at large and small scales.

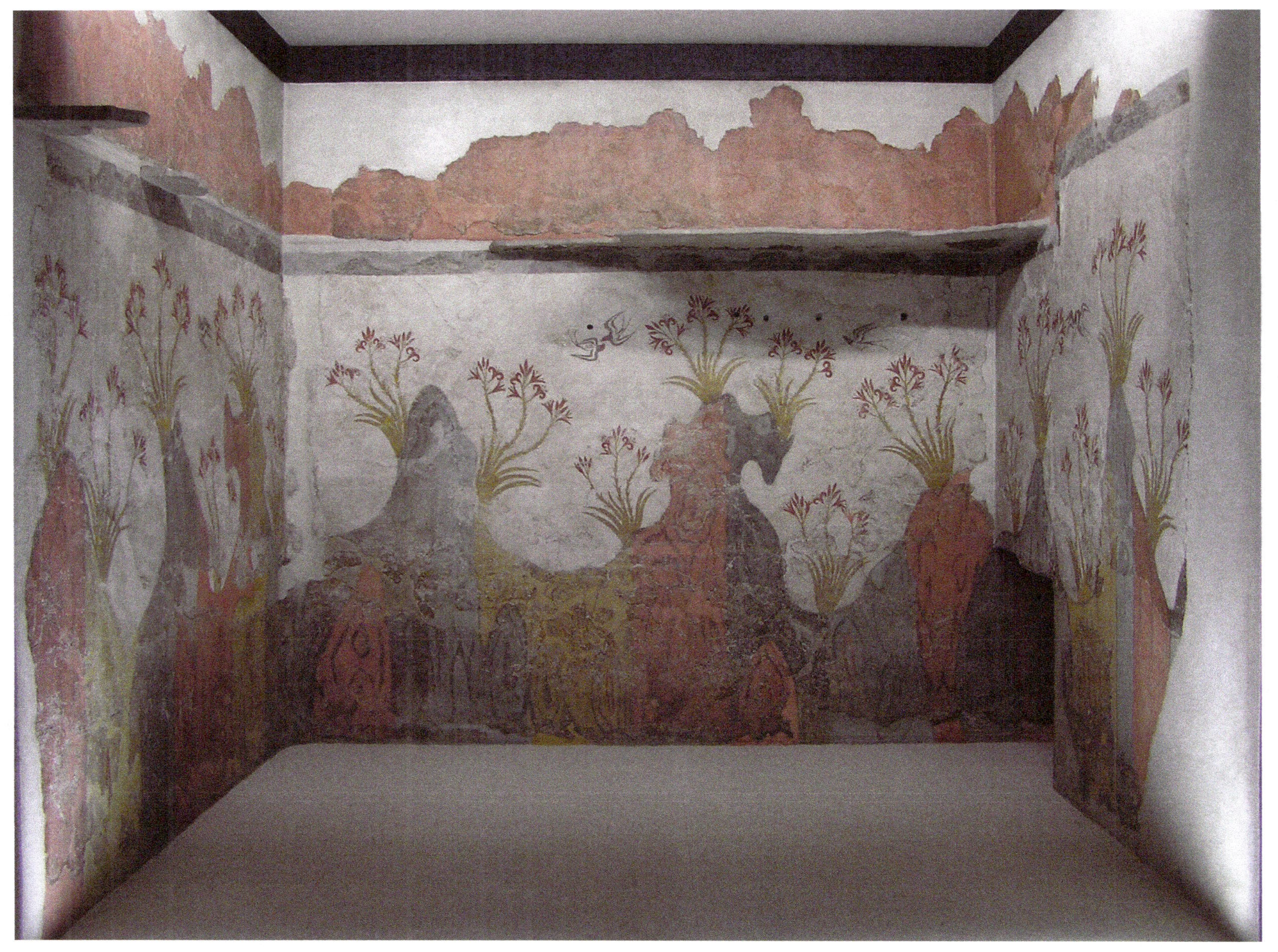

2.19 Landscape and bird fresco from House Delta 2, Akrotiri, LC IA. Athens, National Archaeological Museum. Photo: National Archaeological Museum, Athens (George Fafalis) © Hellenic Ministry of Education and Religious Affairs, Culture and Sports/Archaeological Receipts Fund.

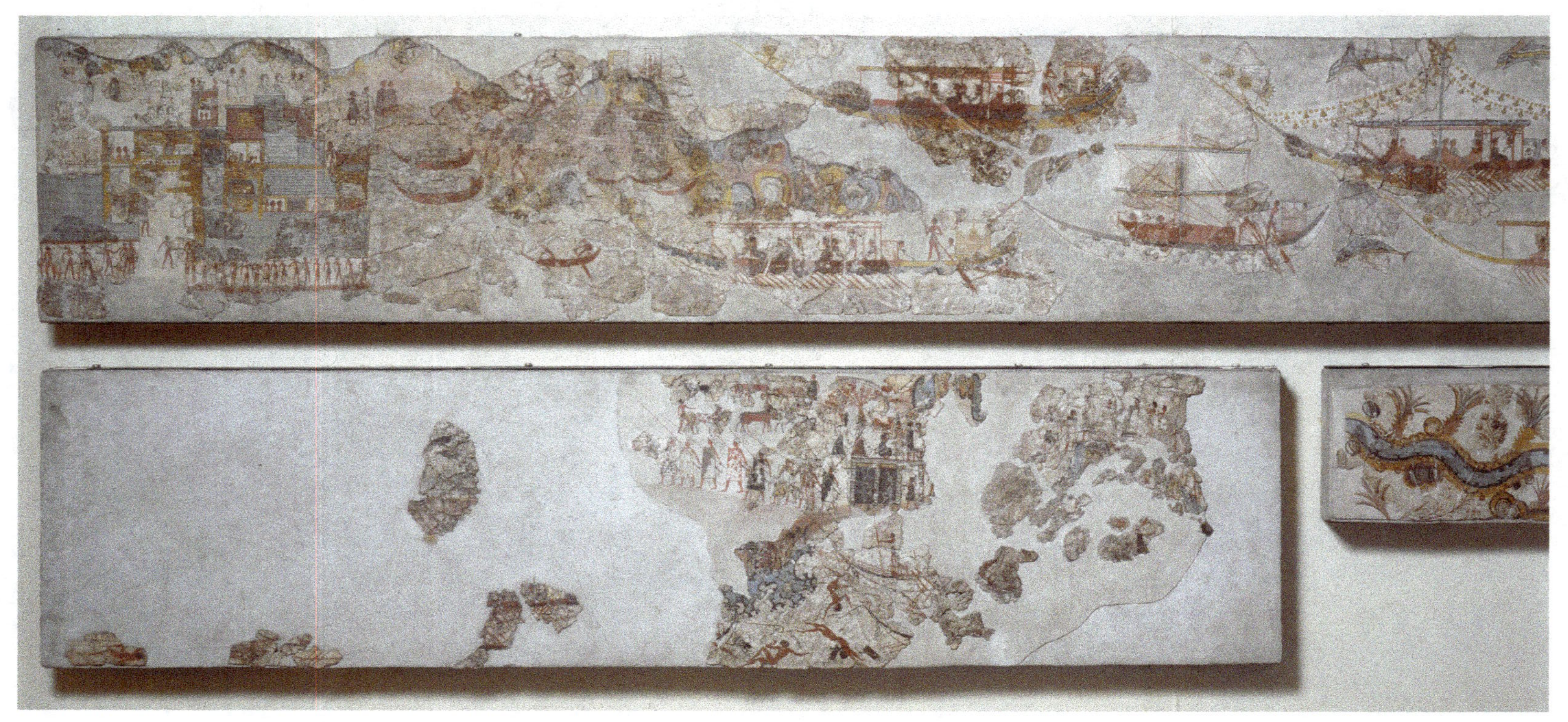

2.20 Miniature frescoes from Room 5, West House, Akrotiri, LC IA. 15¾ in (40 cm) (ship fresco). Athens, National Archaeological Museum. Ship scene; battle scene; Nilotic scene.

The ship and battle frescoes are unique in their subject matter, raising a question as to whether these represent specific scenes that relate to the owner of the house or are more general in their meaning. The frescoes of Thera are found in regular domestic buildings rather than palaces, and we should consider the idea that fresco painting might have been well established in the Cyclades and did not have to be associated in all cases with elite, large palaces.

MIDDLE HELLADIC TO THE LATE HELLADIC I SHAFT GRAVES

We will look at one final work of Minoan art, a gold cup found at Vapheio showing a kilted youth holding a rope tethered around one back leg of a bull **(Figure 2.21)**. The youth is similar in physique and dress to the Palaikastro kouros, although he has long tresses of hair down his back. The scene is set in a rocky landscape whose stylized rocks are similar to the fresco from Delta House **(see Figure 2.20)** or the octopus flask **(see Figure 2.17, page 39)**. This is one of two cups that show young men capturing or working with bulls; scenes of bull jumping are found in various media of Minoan art and reflect some type of ritual activity. The Vapheio cup is made through a combination of ***repoussé*** work, hammering the forms from behind using a mold so that the figures project in relief, and **engraving** or **punching** to create some of the surface detail.

It is not difficult recognizing the style of the cup as Minoan, but the find context was a Late Helladic (LH I) tomb in Vapheio, in Lakonia on the Greek mainland. This cup and its companion were among the grave goods placed into a **tholos** tomb of a Mycenaean elite. On the one hand this circumstance shows that Minoan art was considered valuable and worthy of elite ownership outside of Crete. It also signals a change in the social and economic conditions on the mainland, which had been very modest at the beginning of the MH period. Elite burials by the period LH I became far more lavish, with individual chambers set below ground and accessed through a shaft (**shaft grave**) or in a vaulted stone chamber tomb (tholos). The Vapheio ruler's grave, set in a chamber under the floor of a tholos, also contained weapons and other jewelry, amber from the Baltic region, vases of Egyptian or Syrian alabaster, and an Egyptian axe derived from a Syrian design. Along with the Minoan goods, the assemblage reveals a taste for luxury international goods that demonstrated the prestige and connections of their owner.

By LH I, the Mycenaeans, named after the site that was the citadel of Agamemnon, leader of the Greeks against Troy, had begun building palaces on prominent hills and developing a centralized administrative system in their palaces. The core structure of the palace was the **megaron**, a rectangular structure with an entry porch on one end that led to a central room with hearth and columns supporting a roof. The megaron's form and decoration became more elaborate in the LH II and III palaces, as will be seen in the next chapter, and the palace complex would grow larger too. The development of these palaces and the rich graves of their elite occupants point to the eventual dominance of Mycenaean culture in the late Bronze Age.

There were two sets of graves set within circles at Mycenae that show the development of an elite, wealthy culture. The graves in Circle B belong to the Middle Helladic period and consist of small cist graves with the bodies placed in a crouched position along with some grave goods. Later graves become larger in size, and in the Late Helladic period develop into shaft graves set in a new Circle A. In these tombs the deceased was fully laid out with lavish grave goods that included gold, amber, and ostrich eggs, all of which had to be imported great distances from the north and south. The tombs were marked by stone **stelai** carved with reliefs. Like the tomb at Vapheio, the Shaft Graves at Mycenae reveal the new wealth, power, and aspirations of its rulers.

repoussé
a metalwork technique in which the decoration is hammered from behind to create a raised relief

engraving
a metalwork technique in which lines are incised into the metal to create details or patterns

punch or punching
a metalwork technique in which a tool is pressed into the surface to create a design. The end of the tool can be carved with a design that is transferred to the surface

tholos
a circular-shaped building, including vaulted tombs or free-standing structures, sometimes with exterior colonnades as at Epidauros

shaft grave
a tomb with a chamber below ground that is accessed through a vertical shaft filled in after burial

megaron
a rectangular structure featuring a square room with four columns, a small vestibule, and a porch with two columns set on a longitudinal axis

stele (pl. stelai)
a vertical stone slab used as a tomb stone or commemorative marker; it could be covered by relief, inscription, or painting

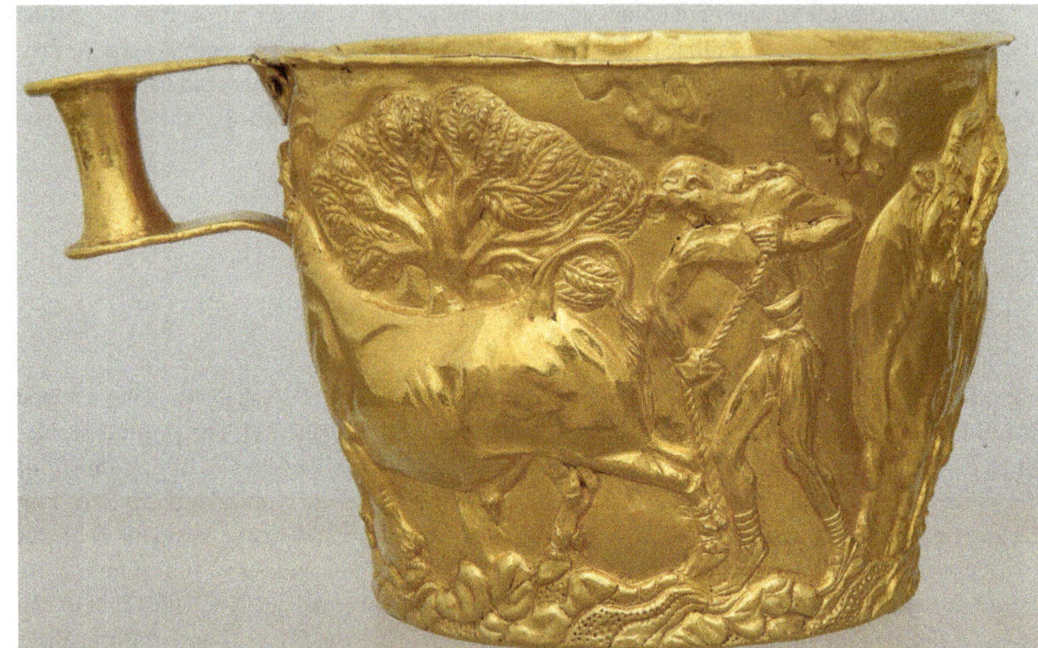

2.21 Vapheio cup, LM IB. Athens, National Archaeological Museum 1759. 3⅛ in (7.9 cm). Youth and bull. Photo: National Archaeological Museum, Athens (George Fafalis) © Hellenic Ministry of Education and Religious Affairs, Culture and Sports/ Archaeological Receipts Fund.

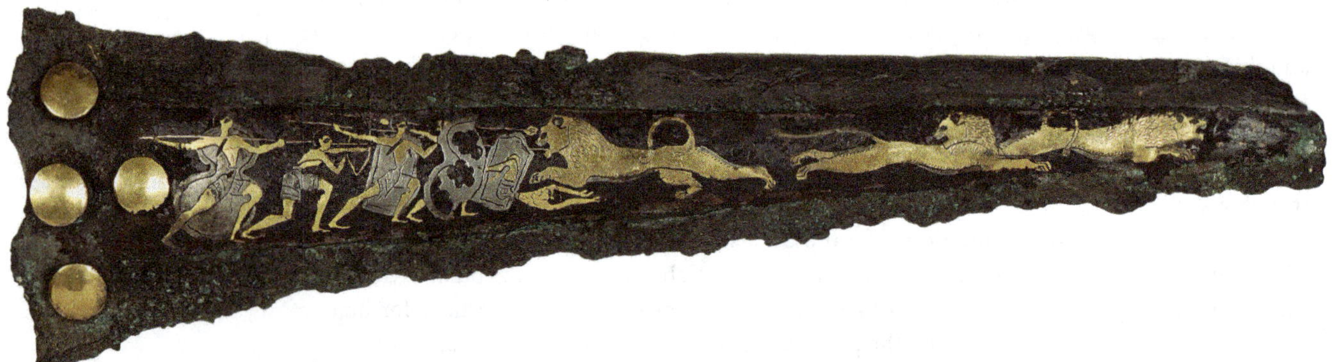

2.22 Dagger from Shaft Grave at Mycenae, LH I. Length 8 7/16 in (21.4 cm). Athens, National Archaeological Museum 394. Lion hunt. Photo: National Archaeological Museum, Athens (Giannis Patrikianos) © Hellenic Ministry of Education and Religious Affairs, Culture and Sports/Archaeological Receipts Fund.

Among the grave goods are some unusual works whose origin is hard to identify. Several bronze dagger blades have scenes inlaid with gold, silver, and a sulfurous compound called niello, which takes on a lustrous black appearance (**Figure 2.22**). On the lion hunt blade, found in Grave IV of Circle A, we see four hunters facing a charging lion. Three of the hunters bear large shields and aim spears at the lion, while one figure crouches to shoot an arrow. A fifth hunter already is dead, his body slumped before his shield. Two other lions run away toward the tip of the blade, one looking back at the scene. The hunters have the same stylistic features as the bull handler on the Vapheio cup or the figures in the West House frescoes, but the lion hunt is not a scene found in the Minoan repertory. Furthermore, the figure 8-shaped shield of the hunters is found only in Mycenaean art. The emphasis on war-like actions is more common in Late Helladic art than in Late Minoan,

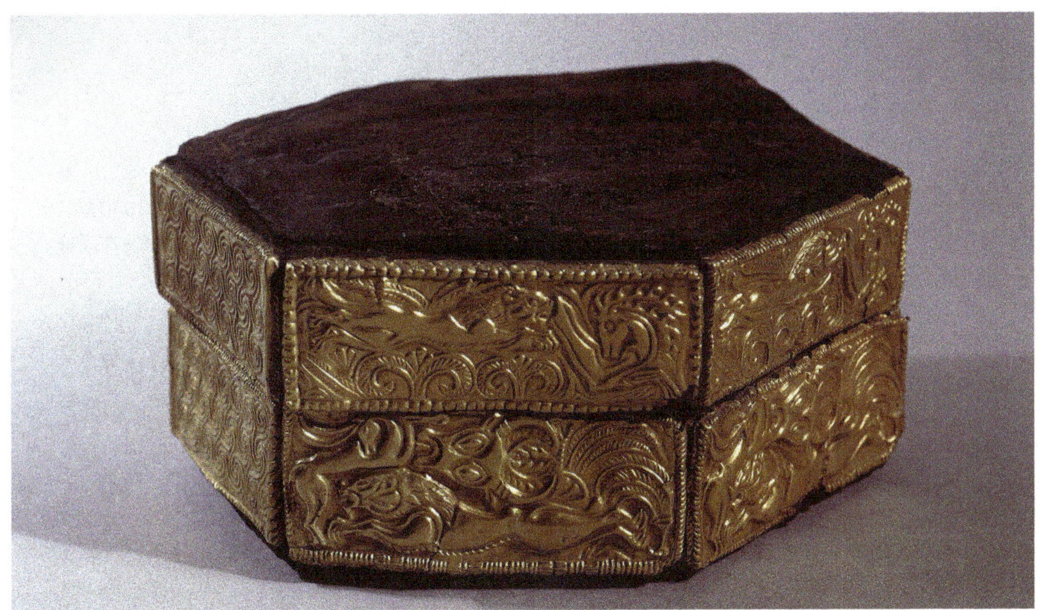

2.23 Wooden box with gold relief from Shaft Grave V, Circle A at Mycenae, LH I. Length of box: 3 11/16 in (9.4 cm). Athens, National Archaeological Museum. Lions hunting deer. Photo: Gianni Dagli Orti/ The Art Archive at Art Resource, NY.

although it is found in the nearly contemporary frescoes at Thera. Niello and the inlay technique have their origins in Syria and the Levant, rather than Crete. Ultimately, the dagger is a hybrid, a combination of Helladic, Minoan, and Near Eastern elements. Whether the artist was Minoan or a Mycenaean who might have been trained by a Minoan, clearly the patron was using this dagger and the other grave goods to create an identity as an elite Mycenaean, a ruler of an area that had been, during the Middle Helladic period, fairly insignificant. Whether they had acquired their wealth through trade, piracy, or warfare, or a combination of those activities, the grave goods of the Mycenaean elite demonstrated their extensive network of contacts in the Mediterranean and beyond.

Other objects from the Shaft Graves show the eclectic tastes and agenda of the Mycenaean elite. A hexagonal wooden box from Grave V is covered with gold relief panels (**Figure 2.23**). The panels with running spirals are at home with other gold objects decorated with spirals in the graves, but the scenes of lions chasing deer are unusual. The chase is set in a lush landscape, with palm fronds, palmette shapes, and a lily–lotus hybrid flower below the lion in the top panel. The lions recall those on the hunt dagger in action, but are more schematic in style. The deer look very schematic and stylized in their contorted pose and sharply turned head. Although similar in technique to the Vapheio cup, the origin of this style is harder to place, and seems more at home in the Near East than in Crete or Greece. Perhaps this work too is a hybrid, and it certainly foretells in hindsight the greater involvement of mainland Greece in the Mediterranean world in the later Bronze Age that we will discuss in the next chapter.

As we have seen in this chapter, the Middle Bronze Age sees the development of elite, palatial cultures from the smaller-scale culture of the Early Bronze Age. These elites controlled sufficient resources to develop the architecture of the palaces, which, beyond providing a visual expression of their power, also served as their industrial, administrative, and religious centers. There was an emphasis in art on valuable and imported materials, and in some cases interesting or unusual subject matter or styles that would also serve to distinguish the palatial cultures visually. The Minoans could be said to be the dominant culture of the Middle Bronze Age, but the Mycenaean tombs show the emergence of a potential rival that will, in the Late Bronze period, dominate the Aegean, including the political control of Crete, as we shall see in the next chapter.

TEXTBOX: THE ERUPTION OF THERA AND DEBATES OVER ABSOLUTE CHRONOLOGY

When Bronze Age sites like Troy, Knossos, and Mycenae were excavated, there were initially no means for the phases of these cultures to be dated. Once the relative chronology based on pottery styles was established, examples of Minoan ceramics could be identified in Egyptian contexts. Presuming that the pottery was placed into tombs near the time of its production, this provided a correlation between two periods of Minoan and Egyptian chronology. MM II pottery was found in contexts associated with the Egyptian Dynasty XII, dated by king lists to the years *c.* 1963–1786 BCE. LH IIIA2 pottery was found in the New Kingdom city of Tell el-Amarna, which was built as the new capital under the Pharaoh Akhenaten, who reigned *c.* 1353–1337 BCE. Unfortunately, the period between *c.* 1750 and 1550 was the Second Intermediate Period in Egypt, when it was under the rule of the Hyksos and there was little import of pottery or other Aegean artifacts. Still, this allowed a chronology to be worked out by correlating Egyptian and Aegean contexts and estimating the intervening periods.

Scientific methods of dating have advanced considerably and archaeologists have collected more organic samples in their excavations, including seeds, wood, and carbon from burnt material. Analysis of the material excavated on Akrotiri, which was destroyed in the eruption of Thera at the end of LC IA, and elsewhere in the Aegean would seem to provide an opportunity for confirming the dating of the gap between MM II and LM IIIA. Since LH I and IIA as well as LM IA pottery was found at Akrotiri, this would allow calibration of all three chronologies during this period. The analysis showed, however, that the eruption of Thera took place between 1660 and 1613 BCE, with a 95.4 percent probability, and most likely between 1639 and 1613. This has ignited a controversy over chronology, since the traditional chronology placed the end of LM IA around 1500 BCE, about 100 years later. If LM IA lasted from *c.* 1700–1600, then MM III must have been very short and LM IB must have been much longer; if LM IA were from 1600–1500, then MM III was longer and LM IB shorter, affecting roughly a 300-year period overall.

This debate continues, but it may be some time before a resolution is possible between the two bodies of evidence and assumptions. The ice cores of Greenland do record a major volcanic eruption around 1642 BCE +/– 5 years, but there is no certainty that this is the eruption of Thera or another volcano from a different part of the globe. Scientists have also studied dendrochronology, which is based on measuring the growth rings in trees. Since annual growth rates will vary according to environmental conditions, it is possible to create a sequence of growth rings based upon the pattern of wide and narrow rings. In the aftermath of an event like Thera, there would have been very slow growth for several years and there are several periods of such growth anomalies – 1652–1648, 1628–1626, and 1619–1617 BCE – that might correspond to Thera if the radiocarbon dating is correct. There are also anomalies in the next century, so by itself the dendrochronology does not identify a specific set of dates for Thera, only possible overlap.

The difficulty is that both chronologies were developed following a systematic process and data-based evidence, either from analysis of organic materials or from the classification of thousands of pottery sherds from across the Mediterranean. In this chapter we have used the so-called "high" chronology based on the radiocarbon dates, but this still depends on estimates about how long a period lasted based on the rate of change in pottery styles. Whichever chronology is used, all assume that LM IA lasted about 100 years, but until we can get an external date, that will remain conjecture. Considering how quickly scientific methods of testing have changed, we should be cautious about being too certain about absolute dates.

See *Aegean Prehistoric Archaeology*; Manning 2010a and 2010b; Shelmerdine 2008, 1–18.

REFERENCES

Aegean Prehistoric Archaeology, Chronology and Terminology Resources: http://www.dartmouth.edu/~prehistory/aegean/?page_id=185

Manning, S. W. 2010a. "*Chronology and Terminology*." In Cline 2010, 11–28.

Manning, S. W. 2010b. "*Eruption of Thera/Santorini*." In Cline 2010, 457–474.

Rice, P. M. 1987. *Pottery Analysis: A Sourcebook*. Chicago: University of Chicago Press.

Shelmerdine, C. W., ed. 2008. *The Cambridge Companion to the Aegean Bronze Age*. Cambridge: Cambridge University Press.

FURTHER READING

Aegean Prehistoric Archaeology. Website. http://www.dartmouth.edu/~prehistory/aegean/

Betancourt, P. P. 2007. *Introduction to Aegean Art*. Philadelphia: INSTAP Press.

Cline, E. H., ed. 2010. *The Oxford Handbook of the Bronze Age Aegean*. Oxford: Oxford University Press.

Doumas, C. 1992. *The Wall-Paintings of Thera*. Athens: Thera Foundation-Petros M. Nomikos.

Immerwahr, S. A. 1990. *Aegean Painting in the Bronze Age*. University Park, PA: Pennsylvania State University Press.

Krzyskowska, O. 2005. *Aegean Seals: An Introduction*. London: Institute of Classical Studies.

MacGillivray, J. A., J. M. Driessen, and L. H. Sackett. 2000. *The Palaikastro Kouros: A Minoan Chryselephantine Statuette and its Aegean Bronze Age Context*. British School at Athens Studies, 6. London: British School at Athens.

Renfrew, C. 1972. *The Emergence of Civilisation: The Cyclades and the Aegean in the Third Millennium B.C.* London: Methuen.

Shelmerdine, C. W., ed. 2008. *The Cambridge Companion to the Aegean Bronze Age*. Cambridge: Cambridge University Press.

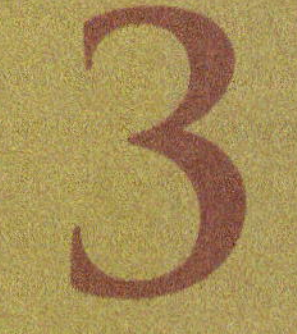

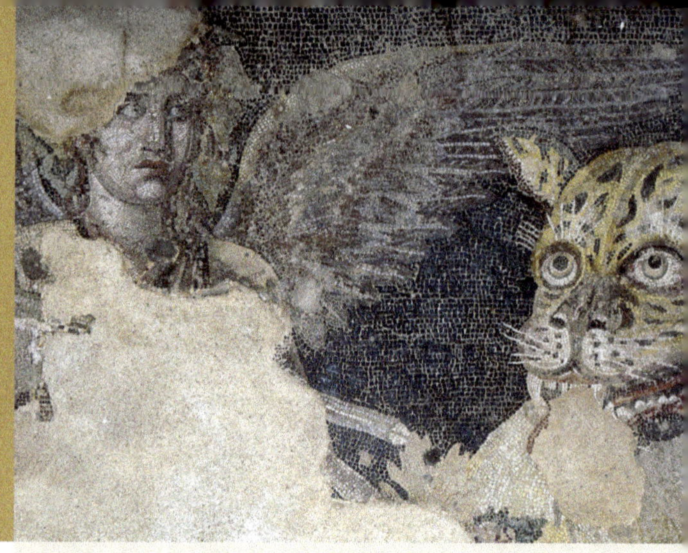

THE LATE BRONZE AGE II–III

(*c.* 1600–1075 BCE)

Timeline
Late Minoan (LM II to LM III)
Late Helladic Architecture
Late Helladic Pottery and Terracottas
Textbox: The Trojan War
References
Further Reading

TIMELINE

	Cyclades (Cycladic)	Crete (Minoan)	Mainland (Helladic)	Monuments Events
1600 1500	LC II (1600–1400)	Neopalatial LM IB (1600–1500)	LH IIA (1600–1500)	*c.* 1625 Eruption of Thera
1500 1450	LC II (1600–1400)	Final Palatial LM II (1500–1450)	LH IIB (1500–1430)	Palace Style pottery
1450 1300	LC III (1400–1075)	Final Palatial LM IIIA (1450–1340)	LH IIIA1 (1430–1390) LH IIIA2 (1390–1300)	Hagia Triada sarcophagus; Agora Tomb III
1300 1200	LC III (1400–1075)	Postpalatial LM IIIB (1340–1200)	LH IIIB (1300–1190)	Lion Gate and Treasury of Atreus at Mycenae
1200 1075	LC III (1400–1075)	Postpalatial LM IIIC (1200–1075)	LH IIIC (1190–1075)	*c.* 1180 Destruction of Pylos Warrior Vase
1075 1025		Sub-Minoan (1075–1000)	Sub-Mycenaean (1075–1025)	

As mentioned in the last chapter, the eruption of Thera had a devastating impact on the Minoan sites in Crete, with widespread destruction near the end of Late Minoan (LM) IA. Most of the palaces on the island, such as Phaistos and Malia, were not rebuilt, but there is evidence of rebuilding in towns like Palaikastro during LM IB, when the Palaikastro kouros was made. Knossos was the only major palace to be reconstructed, although the quality of construction, such as the use of ashlar masonry, declined. At the end of LM IB there is evidence that the Mycenaeans were becoming more heavily involved in Crete. Whether they took control at this time or somewhat later is debated, but there is evidence for destructions at the transition between LM IB and LM II, including at Knossos and Palaikastro. Knossos continued to serve as an administrative center in LM II with some rebuilding and new frescoes being painted, and this phase of Minoan archaeology is sometimes called the Final Palatial period. It lasted until the end of LM IIIA, when the palace at Knossos was destroyed again and the Postpalatial period began.

Linear B
writing script developed by the Mycenaeans in the Late Bronze Age that proved to be an old form of Greek

The final destruction of the palace at Knossos preserved a large number of clay tablets written in a script called **Linear B**, a writing system unlike the earlier and as yet undeciphered Minoan script Linear A. Arthur Evans had attempted to decipher the script after the tablets' discovery in the early twentieth century but was unsuccessful. Efforts to decode Linear B were later undertaken by Alice Kober and John Chadwick, but in the early 1950s Michael Ventris, a young British architect, was able to decipher the Linear B inscriptions and define their sounds and vocabulary. In collaboration with Chadwick, Ventris demonstrated that Linear B was an old form of Greek (see Ventris and Chadwick 1973; Chadwick 1990). Previous theories, based on ancient stories, that the Greeks had arrived in the late second millennium as part of the so-called Dorian invasion, therefore had to be revised. The Linear B tablets were basically bureaucratic accounts of inventory and administration, but the relationship of some of the vocabulary to words in the Homeric poems suggested that the stories of Bronze Age palaces and kings might have some kernel of historical reality to them. The presence of Linear B tablets at Knossos indicates that the Mycenaeans were in charge of administration at Knossos when it was destroyed and had taken control of Crete after LM IB, either in LM II or LM IIIA. Linear B did not exist in the LH I Shaft Graves at Mycenae or other elite tombs; the script may have been developed by the Mycenaeans from Linear A to serve their extensive administrative needs on Crete and elsewhere as they expanded their network of kingdoms and palaces.

Other evidence for expanded Mycenaean presence in the Mediterranean during the Late Bronze Age is found in the late fourteenth-century shipwreck at Ulu Burun on the southwest coast of Turkey. The finds include Mycenaean pottery and weapons among the large cargo of copper, pottery, and other material originating from Egypt, the Levant, and Cyprus. The finds at Ulu Burun may be more indicative of Mycenaeans being among the crew of the ship, which was diverse in its nationalities, than of the ship's itinerary including the Greek mainland. Nevertheless, the wide distribution of Mycenaean pottery from Italy to the Near East and Black Sea is substantial evidence of their activity as traders and perhaps settlers/invaders/raiders during the Late Bronze Age.

In looking at the Late Helladic period, we need to consider its art and architecture not only as products of that period, but also as what was literally under the feet of the Greeks of the first millennium. The poems recounting the Trojan War and its aftermath were long regarded as myths, and therefore fictional. Schliemann's discovery of Troy and Mycenae showed not only that these places were real, but also that they were the sites of a Bronze Age palace culture that had some features resonating with the poems. The discovery that Linear B was a form of Greek further linked Bronze Age Helladic with later Greek culture. Some Greeks of the later archaic and classical periods looked back at the poetic heroes and claimed them as ancestors, viewing the monumental remains of the walls and tombs as the places where they had lived and died.

In this chapter, we can consider the following questions about Late Helladic art and architecture:

- What transformations take place in Late Minoan art and how might these reflect the influence of Mycenaean art?
- How do Mycenaean palaces carry out similar or different functions from Minoan palaces? What differences or similarities can be found in specific spaces and their organization and decoration?
- How does monumental Mycenaean art and architecture reflect power and the ruling elite?
- Finally, how does more everyday art like pottery and terracottas reflect the interaction of the Mycenaeans in the Mediterranean and respond to historical changes during the period?

LATE MINOAN (LM II TO LM III)

Palace Style
term for the LM II style of pottery produced at Knossos

We will begin by looking at Minoan pottery of the LM II period that is labeled the **Palace Style**, recognizing Knossos as the dominant center of production. The LM II amphora from Knossos with an octopus **(Figure 3.1)** continues a decorative theme found in the Marine Style of the preceding period, LM IB **(see Figure 2.17, page 39)**, but there are some significant changes that show a new sensibility in design. In profile, the vase can be considered top-heavy, with the widest section at the shoulder of the vessel, about three-quarters of the vessel's height. Combined with the narrow foot and wide mouth, this is a different approach to proportions when compared with earlier Minoan pottery, even in those vessels that had highly stylized spouts or handles and tall proportions **(see Figure 2.9, page 32)**. The painted octopus fills up the central decorative panel, but in a different way from the Palaikastro octopus. The Knossos octopus is bilaterally symmetrical along a vertical axis in the arrangement and configuration of its body and tentacles. When compared to the Palaikastro octopus, the design is more formal, abstract, and rigid in concept; the idea of a rocky and undulating seascape as habitat is missing. The variation in the size and undulating curves of the arms and the thin coils at the end still give the design some sense of movement, but it has lost the naturalism of the Palaikastro octopus (and sprouted an extra pair of arms) and the asymmetrical composition. As we shall see, this increased abstraction and compartmentalization of the design elements are a feature of late Mycenaean pottery, and we can see the Knossos octopus as being influenced by Mycenaean art and perhaps patronage at the palace.

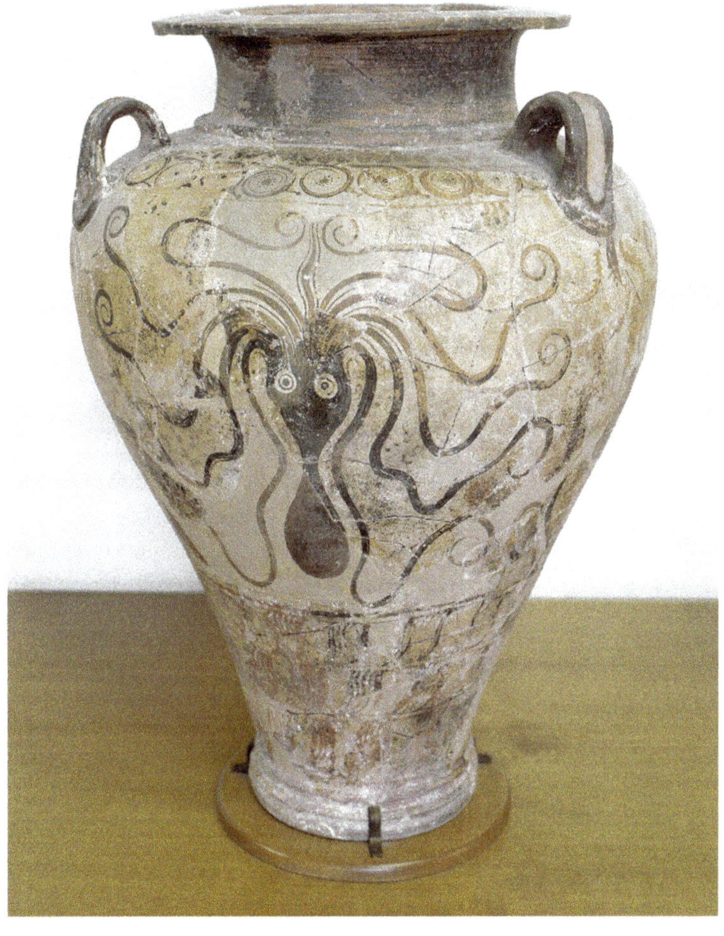

3.1 Palace Style amphora with octopus from Knossos, LM II. 28½ in (72.5 cm). Herakleion, Archaeological Museum. Photo: Album/Art Resource, NY.

Indeed, in looking at pottery during this period we can see that Mycenaean pottery had a stylistic influence on Minoan pottery, reversing the cultural relationship found at the time of the Shaft Graves in Mycenae. In this chapter we will begin by looking at a few examples of Late Minoan art before turning our attention to the architecture and art of the Late Helladic period.

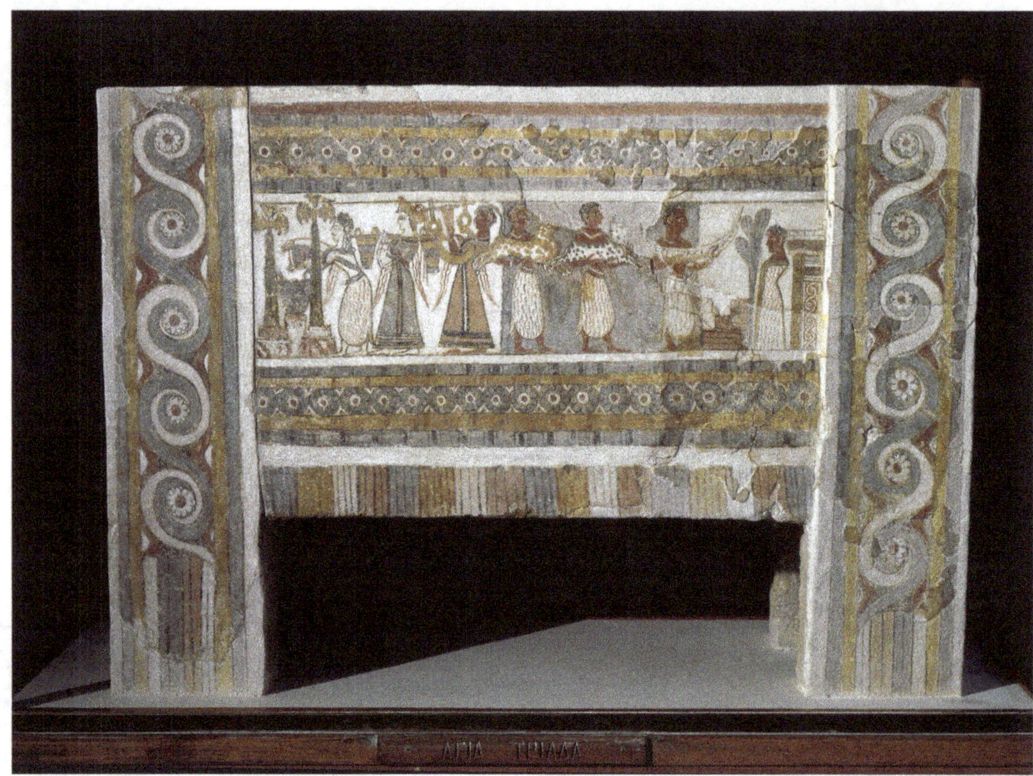

3.2 Painted sarcophagus from Hagia Triada, LM IIIA. Length 4 ft 5 15/16 in (1.37 m). Herakleion, Archaeological Museum. Photo: Nimatallah/Art Resource, NY.

sarcophagus
a stone coffin for inhumation burial sometimes set into a chamber tomb and having relief decoration on the exterior

Frescoes continued to be painted at Knossos until LM IIIA, including the famous bull leaper's fresco. Elite burials also continued, and a tholos tomb at Hagia Triada included a well-preserved stone **sarcophagus** that was covered in plaster and then painted like a fresco **(Figure 3.2)**. The subject matter is ritualistic, but enigmatic. On the right we can see a tomb with ornate painted door and a wrapped male figure in front of it, presumably the deceased. Three men in kilts bring offerings of animals and an unidentifiable long object. To the left are two women and a male musician who are processing in the other direction toward an altar. There is a krater on top of it and it is flanked by a pair of standing double axes, a common ritual motif for Minoan art. The lead woman pours an offering into the krater and appears to be dressed like a Minoan priestess; the woman behind her carries two more vessels on a pole over her shoulder. We are not sure if the ritual is connected with the deceased in the other part of the picture, or perhaps shows other members of the deceased's family carrying out an elite public ritual.

The figures are recognizably Minoan in some ways, including details of the hairstyle, poses, narrow waists, and costumes. The figures are drawn with heavy outlines and are more schematic in their anatomy and stiff in their postures than earlier paintings. The awkwardness of the priestess's arms shows the difficulty or disinterest in rendering animated, three-dimensional figures compared to earlier Neopalatial representations like the Harvester vase or even the miniature Isopata seal ring **(see Figures 2.15 and 2.16, pages 38, 39)**. Certainly the style shares features with Mycenaean fresco and pottery painting during this period, as we shall see later in this chapter, and it is possible that Mycenaean patronage and rule in Crete played a role in the development of LM III style.

LATE HELLADIC ARCHITECTURE

As the Linear B tablets recount, the Mycenaean palaces were administrative centers that collected and distributed commodities and goods produced in their territory. The palaces included storage areas, as well as workshops for the production of pottery and more luxurious goods for the elite, and areas for ritual and feasting. Minoan palaces served most of these same functions, but Mycenaean palatial architecture is different in the most important architectural features and their organization. As we shall see, the palaces were impressive both in creating effective housing for the political and economic administration of the kingdom and for projecting an image of kingly power.

Whereas the open courtyard was the main organizational feature of the Minoan palace, the Mycenaean palace centered around the megaron, a rectangular structure in the center of the palace. One of the best preserved of these is the megaron at Pylos, the so-called Palace of Nestor, one of the elder kings of Homer's *Iliad* (**Figure 3.3**). The main room of the megaron was slightly rectangular and had a single doorway on the long axis. In the middle of the room was a circular hearth. To one side (left in the picture) was a throne for the king or ***wanax***, as he was called in the Linear B tablets. Four columns, originally made of wood, flanked the hearth and supported a second floor and **clerestory**, as can be seen in the reconstruction drawing by Piet de Jong (**Figure 3.4**). The lower section of the walls was made of ashlar blocks of stone and the upper stories a mixture of materials, including rubble, timber, and plaster, which was painted with **tempera** or dry frescoes. The columns tapered upward and had bulbous capitals, like Minoan columns (**see Figure 2.12, page 35**). The fresco on the throne wall features lions and griffins, who symmetrically flank and guard the throne in a **heraldic composition**. Such compositions can be seen as an **apotropaic** device, protecting the room or doorway that they guard, but they are also an expression of kingly power, particularly in a large-scale and colorful composition. They draw the viewer's eye to the *wanax* and his throne. We have already seen the association of lions and griffins with the elite burials of the Shaft Graves (**see Figures 2.22 and 2.23, pages 44, 45**), and this is a theme that continues in the later Mycenaean palaces and their art. Both motifs and the heraldic composition have origins in Near Eastern art, and their use at a monumental scale in the palaces provided a stage for the king that set him apart from the ordinary.

As can be seen in the plan of the palace (**Figure 3.5**), the main chamber of the megaron (4) was preceded by a small vestibule (3) and then a porch (2) that opened into a small courtyard (1).

wanax
Linear B/Mycenaean word for king

clerestory
an upper story of a wall with openings or windows into the main space

tempera
painting technique in which the pigments are dissolved in egg white and applied to the surface. When applied to plastered walls it is called dry fresco, to distinguish it from true fresco (see **fresco**)

heraldic composition
symmetrical composition that shows figures like lions or sphinxes facing toward a central axis, which might include an object such as a column or sacred tree. Often used as an apotropaic device

apotropaic
a visual composition or motif that serves to protect a person or place from harm

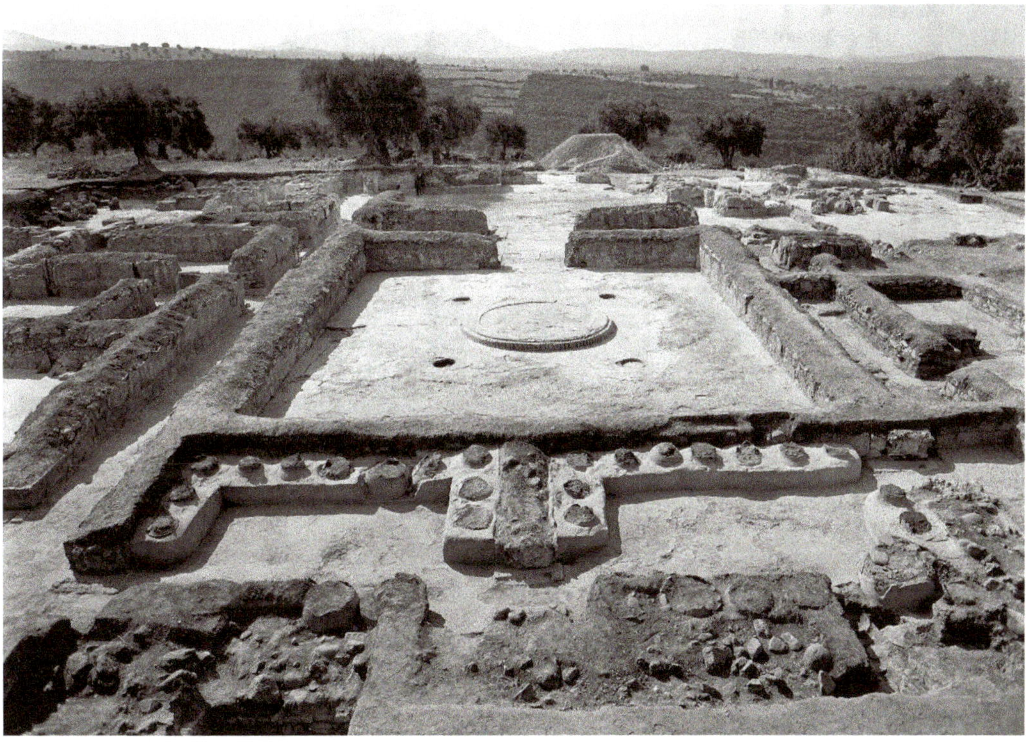

3.3 Palace of Nestor at Pylos: view of megaron, LH IIIB. After C. W. Blegen and M. Rawson, *The Palace of Nestor at Pylos in Western Messenia I: The Buildings and their Contents* (University of Cincinnati and Princeton, 1966), Vol. 1, Pl. 22. Image courtesy of the Department of Classics, University of Cincinnati.

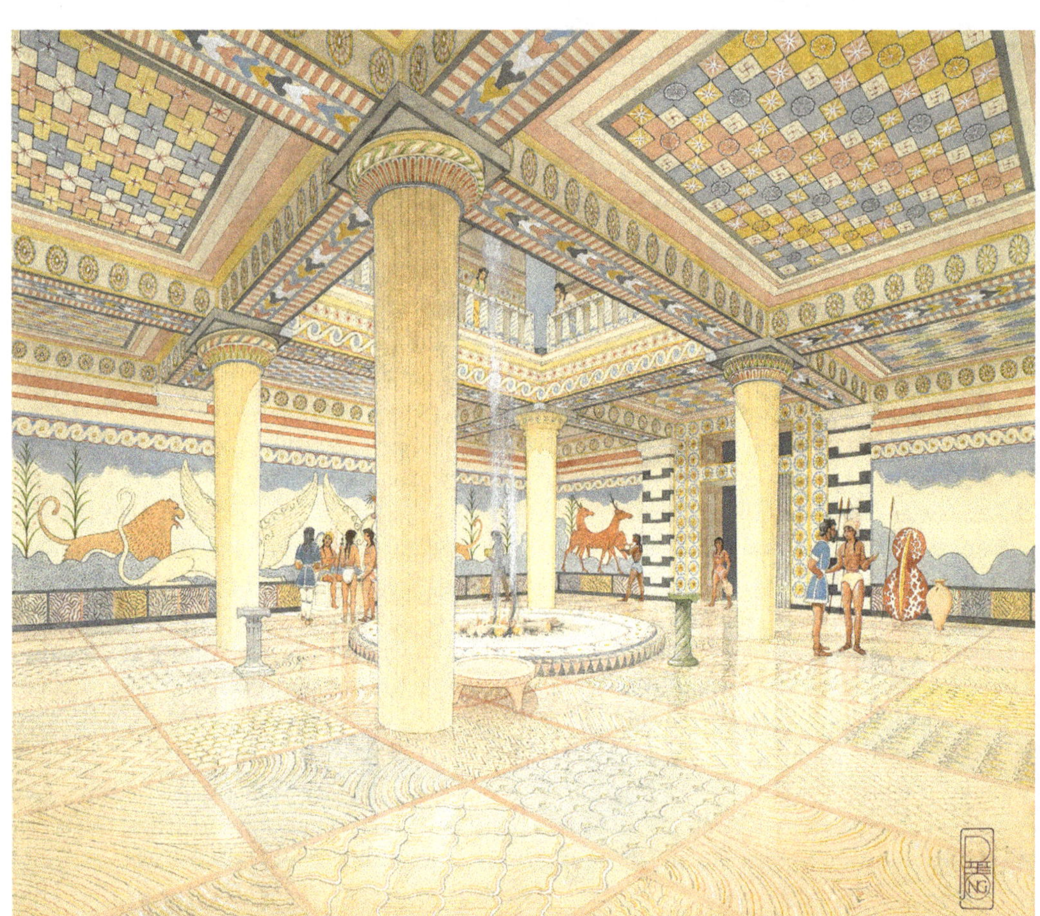

3.4 Reconstruction of the megaron interior at Pylos by Piet de Jong, LH IIIB. Photo: American School of Classical Studies at Athens: Agora Excavations.

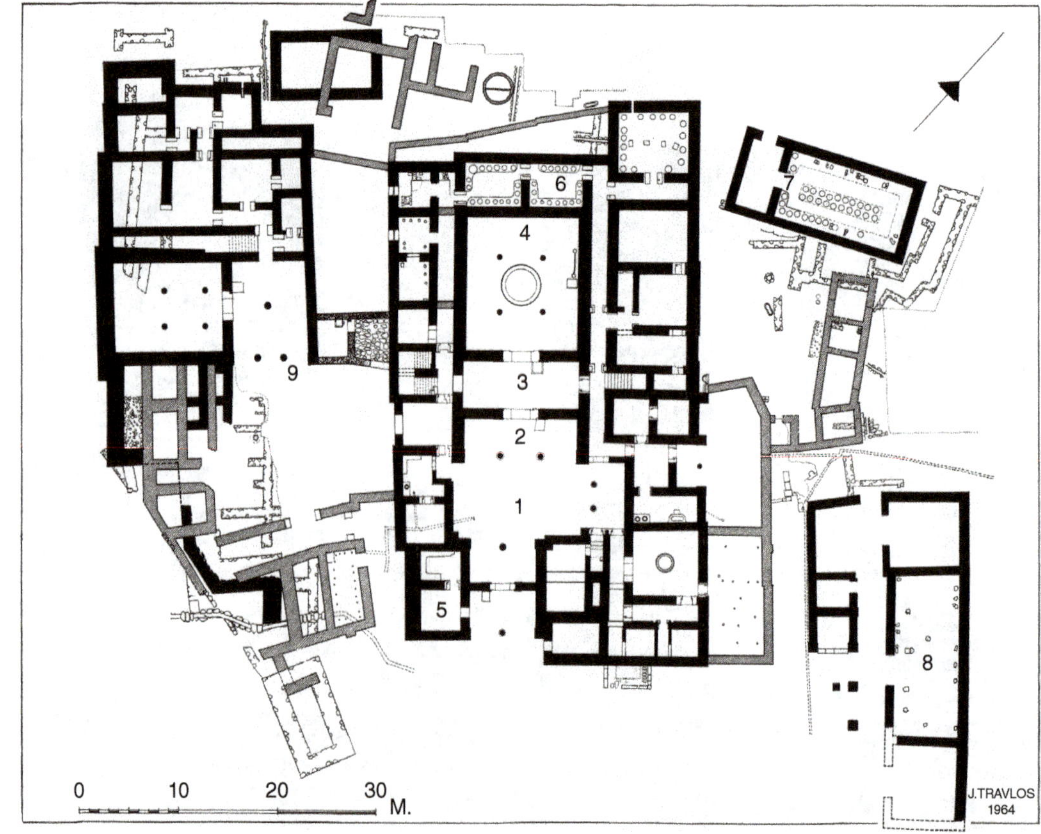

3.5 Palace of Nestor at Pylos: plan, LH IIIB. After C. W. Blegen and M. Rawson, *The Palace of Nestor at Pylos in Western Messenia I: The Buildings and their Contents* (University of Cincinnati and Princeton, 1966), Vol. 1, Pl. 416. Image courtesy of the Department of Classics, University of Cincinnati.

Surrounding the megaron was a series of halls and smaller rooms that included storage areas. The bases for the large terracotta jars of olive oil in the room directly behind the megaron (6) can still be seen today; a wine magazine lay in a separate building just to the north (7). The archive, containing a deposit of clay Linear B tablets, lay next to the gate entering the palace court (5). The tablets, which were burnt and fired hard in the destruction of the palace, survived in great numbers at Pylos, adding to the larger cache of surviving tablets at Knossos. The tablets track the flow of commodities and storage at the palace, the circulation of materials, and the manufacture of products in the workshops of the palace. In this sense, the Mycenaean palace, like the Minoan palaces, functioned both for storage and for artisan workshops, and these would be located in the peripheral sections of the palace surrounding the megaron core. The tablets also document that the king and elite were important participants in ritual practices and provided wine and food, including meat, for feasts that took place in the palace.

The outer buildings are less clear in their function and probably had multiple roles. The northeast building (8) contained a shrine and perhaps workshops, while the southwest building (9) also had a smaller megaron set at a 90° angle to the axis of the main megaron. Other palaces also had smaller megarons, which have sometimes been called the queen's megaron. It has been proposed that a second high official mentioned in the Linear B tablets, the *lawagetas* or "leader of the people," perhaps a war leader, might have held office here.

lawagetas
Linear B/Mycenaean term meaning "leader of the people," perhaps a war leader

The palace at Pylos was placed on a ridge overlooking a bay. The site had been used since at least the MH period but had been built up extensively by LH II, with several buildings using ashlar masonry facades under the influence of contemporary Minoan palaces. These buildings burned near the beginning of LH III, around 1400 BCE, and were then rebuilt in the plans seen above. The entire site was violently burned around 1180 at the end of LH IIIB and never built up again, marking the start of the collapse of Mycenaean culture during the LH IIIC period and leading eventually to the so-called Dark Ages that we will discuss more fully in Chapter 4.

The Linear B tablets provide some insight into the organization of artistic production in the palaces and outside of them. Four different potters are mentioned in the tablets, with one of them named as *pi-ri-ta-wo* and described as royal (*wa-na-ka-te-ro*, compare to *wa-nax*), meaning that he produced for the palace and received a landholding as part of his office (Hruby 2013). Of the pottery excavated at Pylos, about half was undecorated fine ware that belongs to the same hand or workshop, and is likely to be associated with the court potter. Another potter also seems to have worked as a smith for the palace. Finally, there are two other potters from a place named *re-ka-ta-ne* who appear on a list of craftsmen. These potters may have been independent artists who produced pottery on occasion for the palace, perhaps for special needs or as tribute or taxes to the palace from their production. Curiously, as Hruby points out, the quality of the pottery produced by the palace potter, including a large number of cups, is not very high. Late Helladic pottery can be of high quality, as we shall see later, and more work needs to be done to understand the mechanisms of production and markets in the Late Bronze Age. Recent research and analysis suggest that there were forms of markets outside of the palaces where pottery and other goods could be traded or acquired for use outside of the palaces.

Estimates of the population at Pylos put it around 3,000 inhabitants, while the larger and more fortified citadel and palace of Mycenae had about 6,000. Like the other palaces, the core of Mycenae was its megaron, set on the top of a prominent hill. The terrain is more difficult than at Pylos, and the shaft grave circles mentioned in Chapter 2 were lower down near the entrance to the citadel. Mycenae expanded during LH IIB and at the beginning of LH IIIB construction began on huge fortification walls to protect the palace. The walls were expanded outward to the south and west toward the end of LH IIIB when the famous Lion Gate was built (**Figure 3.6**). This expansion brought Grave Circle A with the shaft graves within the citadel, as well as some houses and a cult center. The fortification walls, about 5 meters thick, were made of massive, roughly shaped blocks

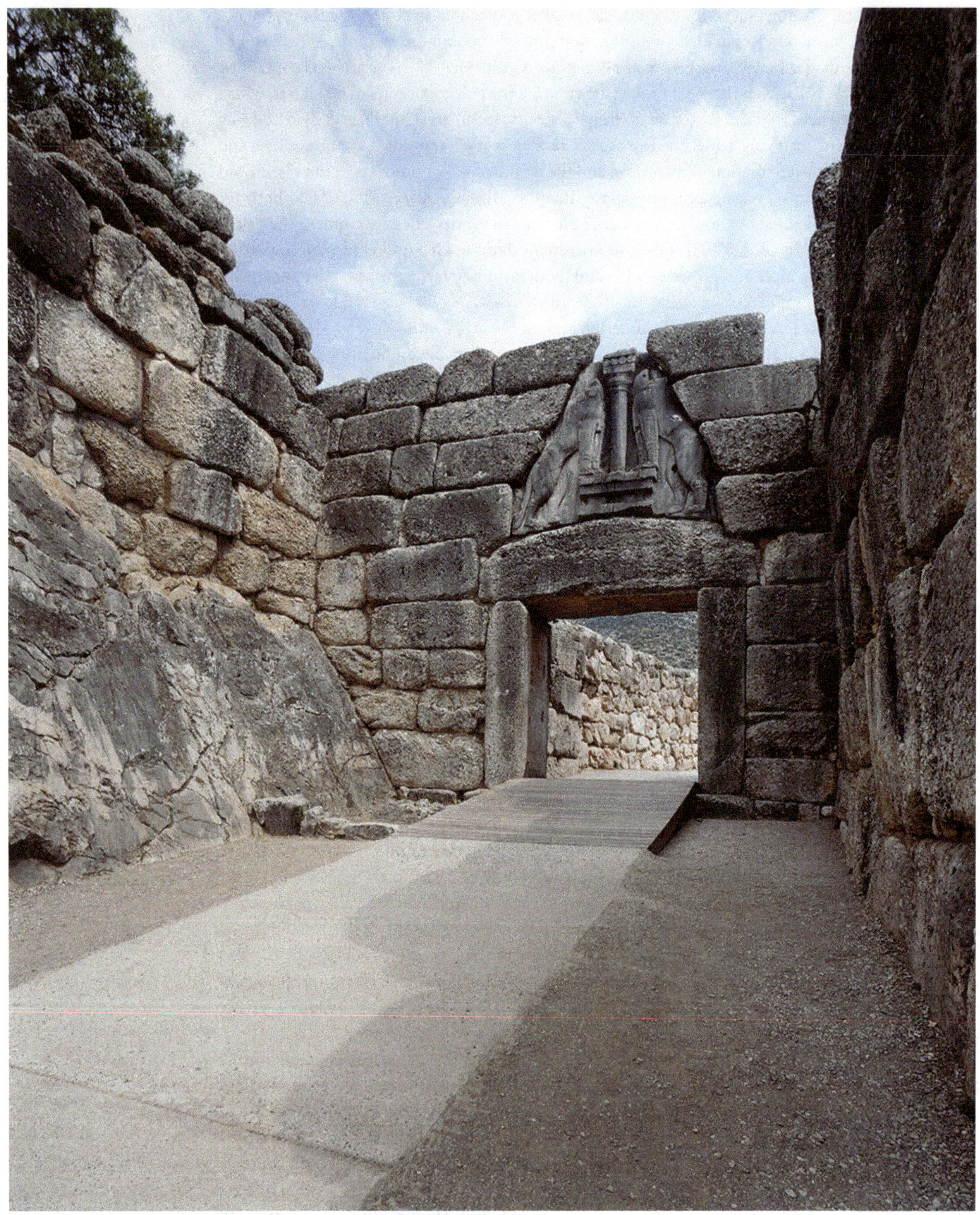

3.6 View of walls of Mycenae with Lion Gate, LH IIIB. Photo: © Vanni Archive/Art Resource, NY.

on the inside and outside and then filled with rubble between the faces of stone. Seeing these walls about 1,500 years later, Pausanias tells us that:

> Parts of the fortification wall [of Mycenae], however, still remain, and also the gate, on which lions stand. They say that these are the works of the Cyclopes, who made the wall for Proitos in Tiryns ... There is a tomb of Atreus, and also the graves of those whom Aigisthos entertained and slew upon their return from Troy with Agamemnon ... Another tomb is that of Agamemnon, another that of Eurymedon the charioteer ... (Paus. 2.16.5–7; in Pollitt 1990, 11)

The stones of the walls, indeed, are huge in size, and are called **Cyclopean** after the legend of their building.

Cyclopean
walls made of massive, roughly worked stones, often with uneven courses

corbel
a form of vaulting in which each course of the vault projects progressively further inward until it meets the sloping ceiling from the other side

The Lion Gate is formed by a massive stone lintel set on two huge pillars, and the courses of stones above the lintel are **corbeled** to create a triangular space that relieves the weight on the opening. In this case, the builders used this as an opportunity to create an usual monumental stone relief to fill the triangle. In the center is a Minoan-style column set on two Minoan-style altars like that on the Hagia Triada sarcophagus. Two lion bodies in high relief face the column with their forelegs set on the altars. The heads of the lions were made separately and set by dowels on the bodies; these do not survive, but may have faced away from the column (see Blackwell 2014). The figures undoubtedly served as an apotropaic device, guarding the citadel; the symmetrical and inward-facing heraldic composition is common in Near Eastern art and architecture serving similar purposes, including the contemporary Hittite empire. The column would symbolize the megaron of the palace, and together with the altars would proclaim the political and religious authority of the *wanax*. It should be noted that the scale of the stone relief at Mycenae is unprecedented in Late Helladic art, and its size and sculptural quality would have been striking to a visitor approaching the gate, as it was to Pausanias even as a ruin centuries later. This unusual monumental display would create an impression of power and authority, and the soldiers watching traffic from the top of the walls on both sides of the passage would have confirmed that projection of power.

Equally impressive as architecture are the tholos tombs at Mycenae built in LH II and III. These replaced the shaft graves for elite burial and consisted of large circular chambers (the tholos) with a

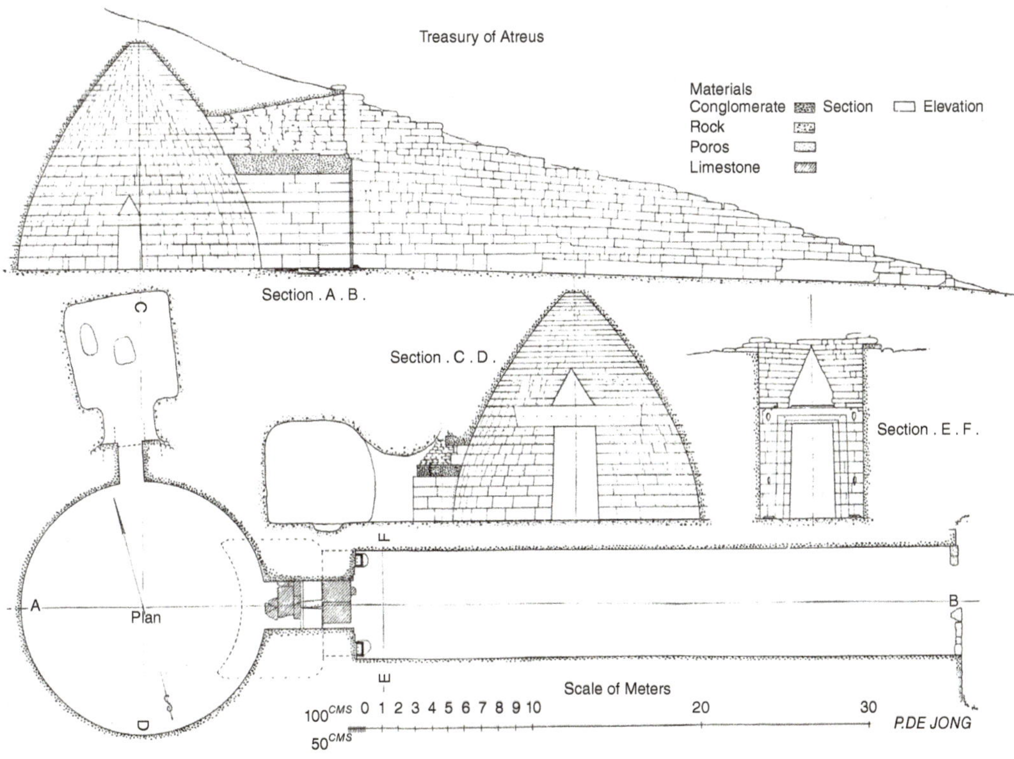

3.7 "Treasury of Atreus," Mycenae, LH IIIB. Plan and section. After A. J. B. Wace, "Excavations at Mycenae IX: The Tholos Tombs," *Annual of the British School at Athens* 25 (1921), pl. LVI. Reproduced with permission of the British School at Athens.

dromos
a long and narrow passage leading to the vaulted chamber of a tholos

stomion
entrance to a tholos tomb at the end of the dromos

long causeway (**dromos**) leading to their entrance (**stomion**). These were built into hillsides and then covered, creating an impression of beehives, as the tomb type is sometimes called. The masonry of the later tholoi is Cyclopean like the walls of the Lion Gate, and the best known example is the so-called Treasury of Atreus at Mycenae, built in LH IIIB (**Figure 3.7**). As the plan and section of the tomb show, the long dromos funnels the visitor to the massive doorway, which uses a lintel even larger than that of the Lion Gate and is estimated to weigh 100 tons or more. The dromos is over 30 meters in length and seems to lead into the earth as the walls rise higher on either side, although the ramp is actually sloped upward as the section drawing shows. The facade of the stomion originally had half columns and ornament set against the stones, and the emphasis on monumental entranceways and long, narrow processional avenues is a recurring feature of Mycenaean architecture.

The space inside the tholos is unexpected for its height and volume (**Figure 3.8**). The interior vault is built through corbeling, so that the walls create a pointed arch profile that produces a stronger verticality. The top of the vault is 13.4 meters (almost 44 ft) in height, a truly remarkable achievement for a vaulted interior space. A side chamber with a small door and relieving triangle opens on the right side as one enters the tomb, and it is here, probably under the floor, that the deceased was buried. As the most impressive of the tholos tombs at Mycenae, it was named the Treasury of Atreus, the father of Agamemnon, but we have no evidence for who was actually buried in the structure since its contents were looted thousands of years ago. If multiple burials were made within the tomb, as was common in Mycenaean practice, the large central chamber would have been a clearly impressive stage for the secondary interment of Mycenae's kings and members of the royal family at the height of its power and grandeur as a citadel.

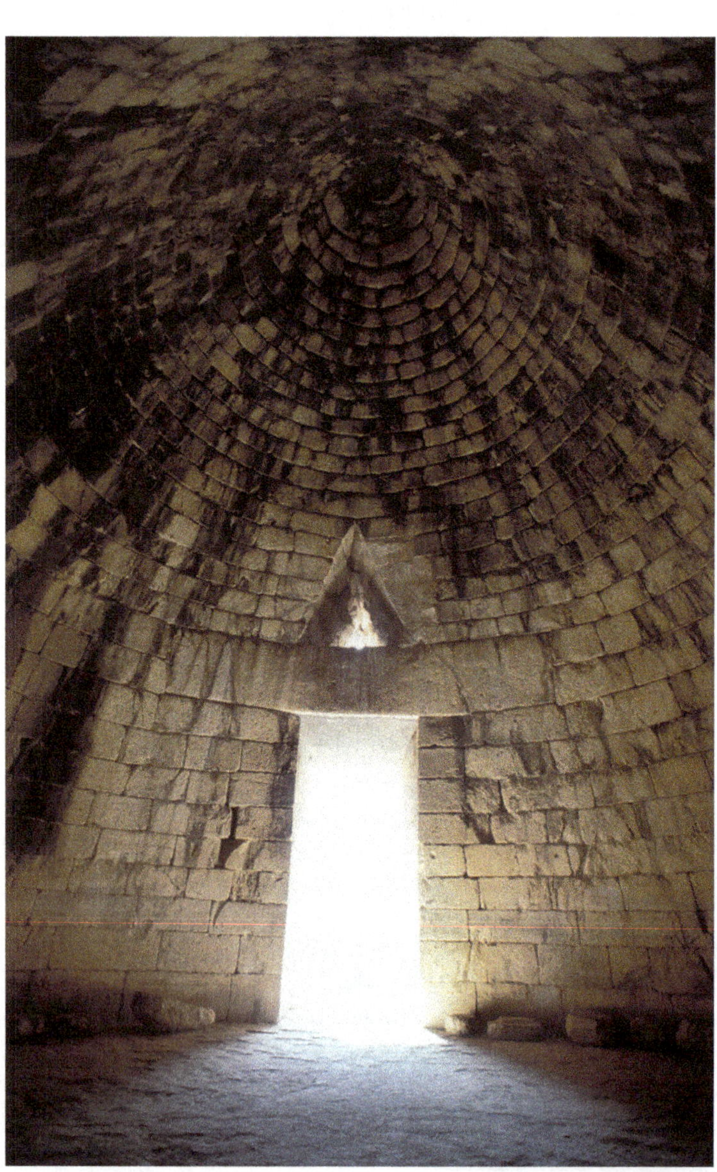

3.8 Interior of "Treasury of Atreus," Mycenae, LH IIIB. Photo: © Vanni Archive/Art Resource, NY.

Like Pylos, the walls of the palace were painted with frescoes but survive only in small fragments. There were additionally frescoes found in one room of the cult center south of the Lion Gate and Grave Circle A. The complex housed four main shrines along with passages, storerooms, and workshops. The Room with the Fresco complex was built in LH IIIB and repaired after an earthquake before being destroyed by fire at the end of LH IIIB. In the room with frescoes was a bench, a hearth, and an altar in the corner. Above the altar on the wall were the remains of the bottom half of two dressed female figures facing each other, holding a sword and spear. They could be goddesses, being above the altar, but their identities are uncertain. In front of the altar and lower than the pair was a third figure, a woman holding sheaves of grain facing the altar (**Figure 3.9**). The frescoes were covered after the earthquake and the room apparently went out of use, but this helped to preserve some of the frescoes when fire finally destroyed the cult center.

The woman holding grain wears a headdress similar to one of the women on the Hagia Triada sarcophagus (**see Figure 3.2, page 52**), but her dress hangs from one shoulder, leaving her arms bare. There are traces of a griffin below her, and the pose with both arms held outward recalls images of

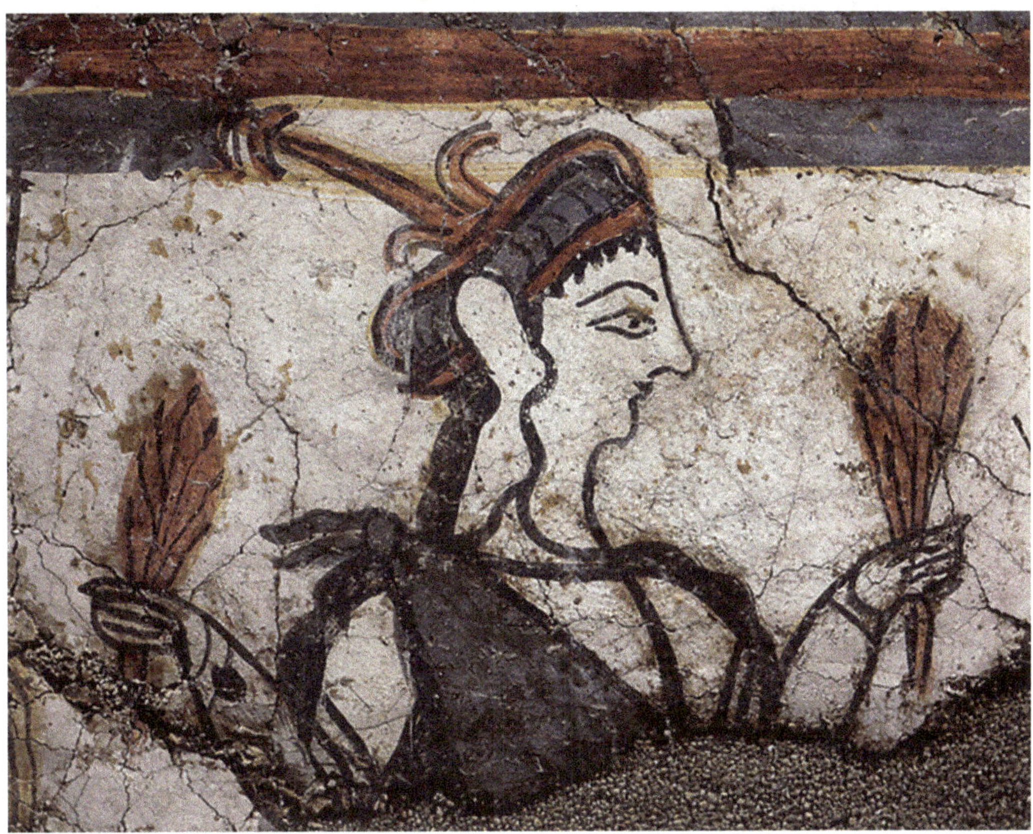

3.9 Fresco from Cult Center at Mycenae, LH IIIB. Nauplia, Archaeological Museum. Photo: Gianni Dagli Orti/The Art Archive at Art Resource, NY.

the Mistress of Animals motif that is common in Near Eastern art. A Linear B tablet found at the center mentions a Mistress of the Grains, and perhaps that is who this figure is. Whether the woman is a goddess or priestess is uncertain, but the location of the figure in front of the altar would place her in a position of offering or acting at the altar, making a priestess seem more appropriate. Even in its fragmentary condition, the fresco shows the prevalence of colorful wall painting in elite Mycenaean buildings. The painting is rather sketchy and quick in its quality, with the flowing black lines that define the figure overlapping with the blue, red, and yellow used for the clothing, sheaves, and borders. While in some ways the drawing and coloring are less precise than the Hagia Triada sarcophagus, the rendering of the arms and torso is more convincing.

The monumental scale, expensive materials, colorful frescoes, and subject matter of palatial art and architecture set themselves apart from the ordinary and express the power and privilege of elite Mycenaeans. Curiously, there are no images or portraits of kings in the surviving art. The megaron and its throne create a platform for the kings and the Linear B tablets document their wealth and activities as hosts and leaders, but images of rulers that are a common feature of some Near Eastern and Egyptian royal art do not seem to occur in Greece.

LATE HELLADIC POTTERY AND TERRACOTTAS

Mycenaean decorated pottery has been systematically studied and categorized, and its abundant production during the Late Helladic period provides a good picture of the stages of its development in terms of both the favored shapes and their decoration. The relative chronology of the pottery has been worked out through excavations and comparisons across sites, but the broad artistic phases do not always line up neatly with the traditional period nomenclature. Four major phases have been identified (Rutter 2010):

- *Phase 1: LH I–LH IIA.* This corresponds to the period of the Shaft Graves and shows the influence of Late Minoan techniques and decoration on Mycenaean pottery.
- *Phase 2: LH IIB–LH IIIA1.* This is the period when the Mycenaeans expand their control to Crete (Final Palatial Knossos) and we see the development of the palace complexes on mainland Greece. The pottery in this period becomes more independent of Minoan style and shapes, with increasing abstraction in the natural motifs. This period corresponds to the Palace Style on Crete (**see Figure 3.1, page 51**).
- *Phase 3: LH IIIA2–LH IIIB.* This is the high point of Mycenaean pottery production and distribution, with greater abstraction in the decorative motifs.
- *Phase 4: LH IIIC.* This follows the destruction of the palaces and the decline of Mycenaean power and influence. Curiously, it sees some rise in the quality of painted decoration on pottery, even while major art media such as fresco and stone sculpture virtually disappear.

To explore these last three phases in this chapter and to broaden our scope beyond the palaces, we will begin with a chamber tomb from the Agora in Athens. There was a Mycenaean citadel on top of the Acropolis in the Late Helladic period, but few traces of Mycenaean building remain due to the later building programs there. A number of Mycenaean graves have been found below the Acropolis in the Agora and provide a glimpse of the use of tombs and the disposition of grave goods. Tomb III was one of the richer burials in terms of its grave goods, but the **chamber tomb** is small in size compared to the tholos tombs of Mycenae. While it did contain some metal, its grave goods are very modest when compared to those of the Shaft Graves and other LH I tombs. There appears to be a scaling back in the luxury of grave goods in elite tombs during LH II and III, even while their architecture is becoming more monumental in form.

chamber tomb
a burial in which the remains are placed inside an open chamber, either vaulted or cut into rock or soil

Tomb III contained three bodies set on the floor of the tomb (**Figure 3.10**). As can be seen in the excavation plan, there was a dromos leading to the stomion, which had been blocked with a stone wall after the last burial in the chamber. The bodies (A, B, C) were placed at the sides and back of the chamber and grave goods were placed before them. The bones of A were interred first and were later disturbed; the next burial was of a woman (B), and the last was of a man (C). The heads of B and C were turned toward the center of the tomb when placed in the chamber and their arms positioned across their abdomens. The burials probably took place in a relatively short period of time, and the stone wall was then built in the stomion to seal the tomb.

The grave goods included a bronze sword, dagger, razor, and bowl for the man (C), set on a wooden table, possibly with ivory inlays (Immerwahr 1971, 170–177). Gold rosettes and steatite buttons were also found in the tomb and associated with bodies A and B. There were sixteen pottery vessels in the tomb, most of them undecorated (**Figure 3.11**). Some of the undecorated cups were unusual in being covered with tin foil, probably as a cheaper alternative to metal vessels. There were three painted vessels in the tomb, a small **pithoid** jar in fragments, a large pithoid jar in the middle of the tholos (seen in the drawing), and a pilgrim's flask (a variation on the shape of the Minoan octopus pilgrim's flask seen in **Figure 2.17, page 39**). The decorated jar contained the ashes and remains of a sacrificial offering to one of the deceased, probably C, that was enclosed in the tomb before it was sealed.

pithos (pl. pithoi), pithoid
a storage vessel with high shoulders and a pointed bottom, usually set into a circular opening in a bench or floor

Both of the larger jars feature a high profile and narrow foot and have three handles on the shoulders, showing the standardization of vessel types and shapes of Mycenaean pottery. The dark-on-light painted floral motifs on the large jar, an ivy leaf and papyrus blossom set on tripled curvilinear stems in each panel, can be placed stylistically into period LH IIIA1, during the second phase of Late Helladic pottery. In comparison, the decoration of the pilgrim's flask in **Figure 3.11** is more abstract and its concentric circles emphasize quite strikingly the shape of the body. These features place it in

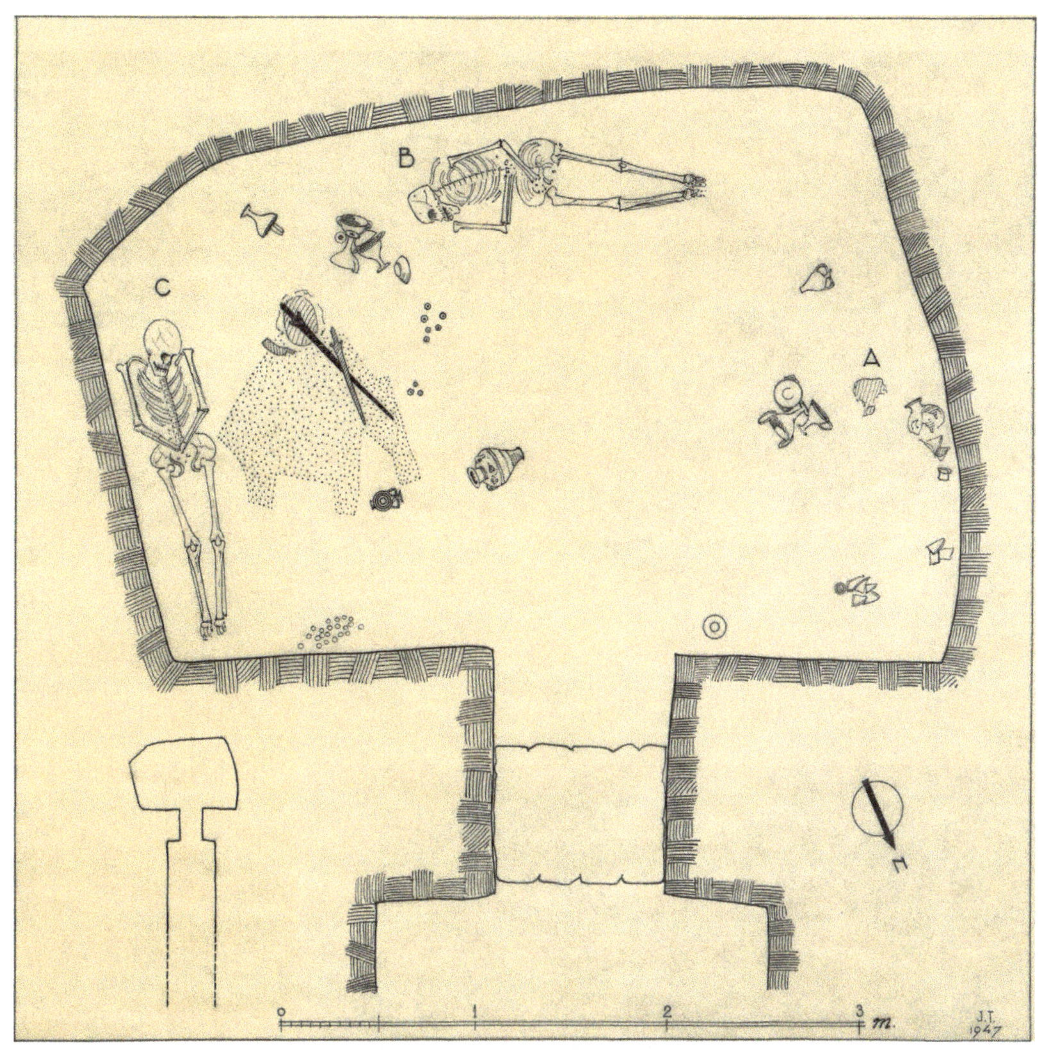

3.10 Chamber tomb burial from Agora with three bodies, LH IIIA. Photo: American School of Classical Studies at Athens: Agora Excavations.

period LH IIIA2, during Phase 3 of Late Helladic pottery. Very similar sherds from a pilgrim's flask were found in the excavations of Amarna in Egypt, providing a date of about 1375–1350 BCE based on Egyptian chronology. Since both vases were found near the entrance but belong to different periods, there is a question of how they came to be part of the same assemblage, a question that we considered for a much later set of pottery in Chapter 1 (**see Figure 1.10, page 14**). In this case, the smaller pilgrim's flask seems to be associated with the last burial, C. The Agora excavation report suggests that the larger jar had been placed in the tomb with an early burial, perhaps A, and was then reused for the last burial (C) when the ashes from the sacrifice were placed inside it. It was then placed in the center of the tomb near the entrance, which was then closed. By correlating vessel styles and multiple burials over time, it becomes possible to work out a relative chronology and to consider potential anomalies in that sequence.

As the Mycenaean sherds from Amarna indicate, Mycenaean pottery was widely distributed from Italy to the Near East and Black Sea areas during Phase 3 (LH IIIA2–LH IIIB) and is strong evidence of the trading and cultural connections of the Mycenaeans. A cup found on the island of Kalymnos near Rhodes, for example, is representative of a popular shape of the goblet (**Figure 3.12**). The cup type was used in domestic contexts for drinking and included in burials as grave goods, as we saw in the Agora tomb above. This example shows the more elongated and curvilinear shape of Late Helladic cups when compared to their Middle Helladic, Minyan-ware predecessors (**see Figure 2.8, page 31**). The very high stem and sharp flaring of the bowl in a double curve create a sinuous and energetic

(a)

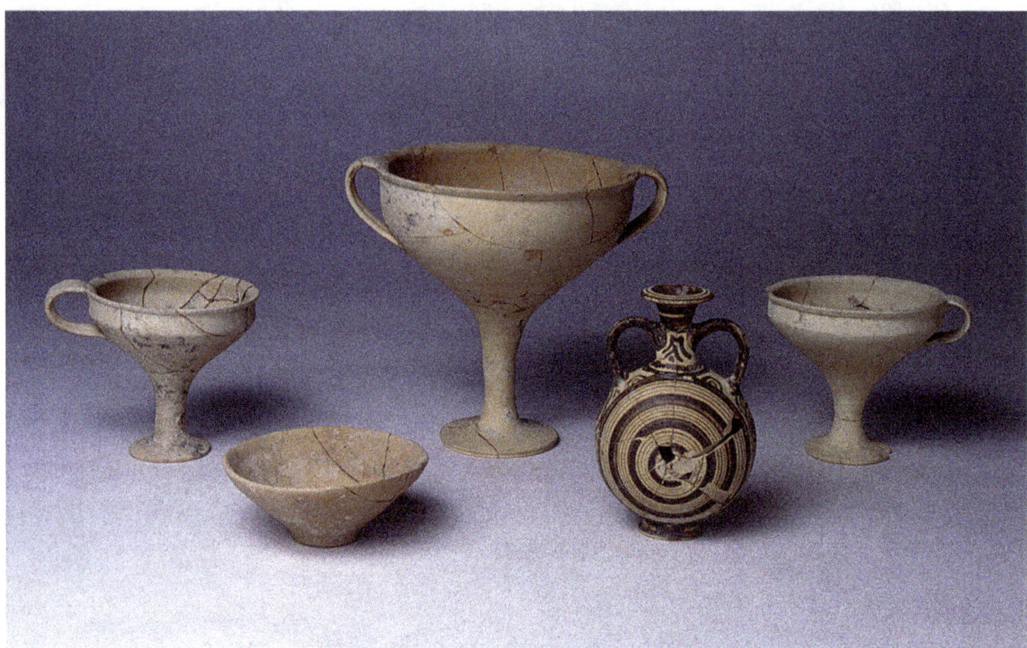

(b)

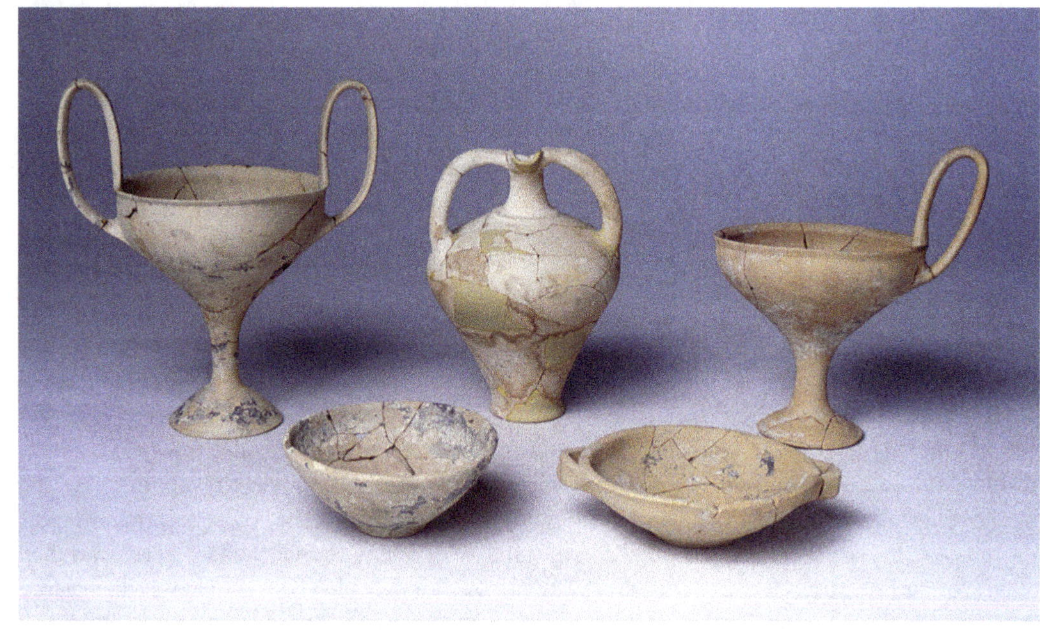

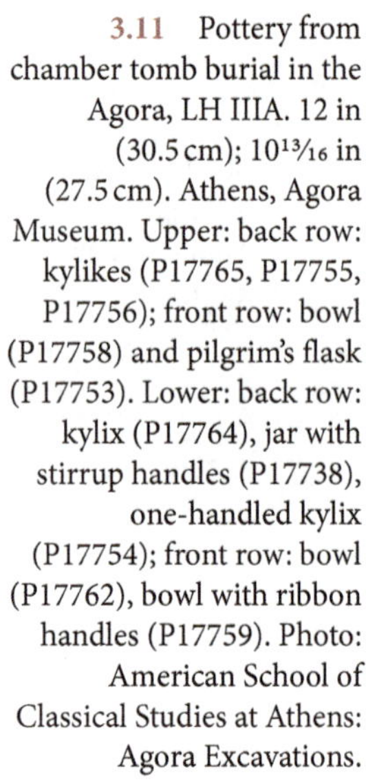

3.11 Pottery from chamber tomb burial in the Agora, LH IIIA. 12 in (30.5 cm); $10\frac{13}{16}$ in (27.5 cm). Athens, Agora Museum. Upper: back row: kylikes (P17765, P17755, P17756); front row: bowl (P17758) and pilgrim's flask (P17753). Lower: back row: kylix (P17764), jar with stirrup handles (P17738), one-handled kylix (P17754); front row: bowl (P17762), bowl with ribbon handles (P17759). Photo: American School of Classical Studies at Athens: Agora Excavations.

profile for the cup, giving it the same top-heavy and seemingly precarious balance found in the Mycenaean-influenced Palace Style pottery on Knossos **(see Figure 3.1, page 51)**. It also has more stylized and sharper drawing than the previous phase of Mycenaean pottery. The floral decoration is very abstracted, almost like a cut-away diagram of a flower stem, which conforms to the profile of the vessel. The petals stretch out to either side, curving sharply upward before bending slightly downward and then ending in upturned curls. The sepals (the small leaves that enclose the flower before it blossoms) bend out and down. The entire design is simple but fits the shape of the vessel well. The slight differences in symmetry between the two sides and the variation in the thickness or tapering of the drawn lines hold visual interest even in such a simple decorative scheme. When compared with earlier LH pottery, it seems to have higher production values and a visual appeal that would correspond to its wide distribution.

Most decorated Mycenaean pottery from Phase 3 (LH IIIA2–LH IIIB) has abstracted motifs like this, but there is also a pictorial style of pottery that developed and seems to have been very popular in Cyprus, where a number of Mycenaean Greeks settled, especially at Enkomi (**Figure 3.13**). This krater has two handles and a wide shoulder zone, providing a particularly suitable surface for a figural scene. Like abstractly decorated pottery, horizontal bands divide the vase into distinct sections of neck, shoulder, belly, and foot. The figural decoration, consisting of a chariot carrying three men and followed by a fourth walking man, is applied over and above the triple band in the center of the vase, leaving the feet of the horses suspended below and the chariot wheel resting well above on the lowest band. The chariot riders are wrapped in their cloaks, creating lozenge-shaped silhouettes that recall the deceased figure in the Hagia Triada sarcophagus (**see Figure 3.2, page 52**). These figures, like the flower on the goblet, are strongly abstracted and show little trace of body structure. The chariot is pulled by two horses, as can be seen from the doubled muzzles, tails, and legs, though at first glance they seem to share a single body. Various linear patterns fill up the surfaces between the figures, and a large blossom sprouts from the top band at the right of the picture to close the scene. The kraters appear to have been popular for tombs, whether as grave goods or perhaps as burial urns, but the chariot procession would be an appropriate theme for a funerary offering in either case.

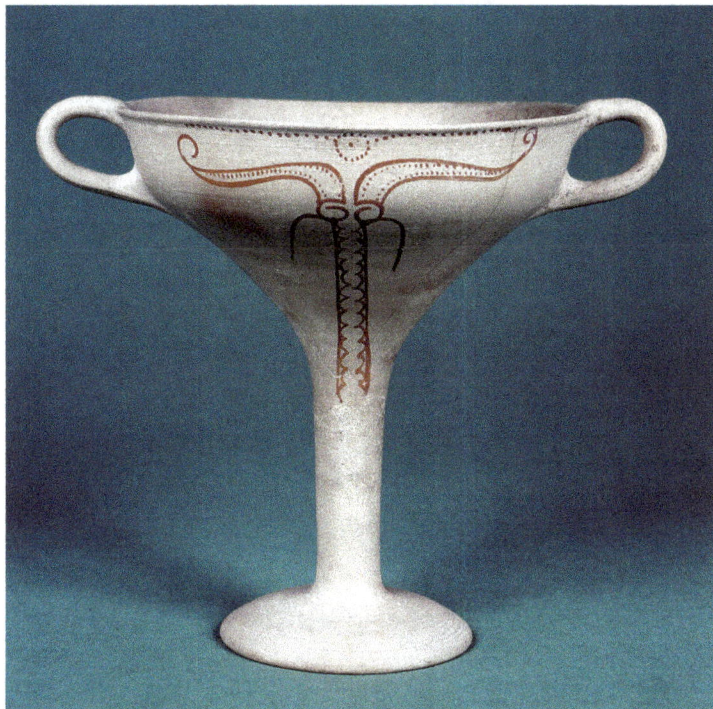

3.12 Goblet with floral decoration from Kalymnos, LH IIIB. 7³⁄₁₆ in (18.2 cm). London, British Museum 1886,0415.15. Photo: © The Trustees of the British Museum.

It is during the LH IIIB period that we also see the emergence of a new class of small terracotta female figures (**Figure 3.14**). Like the chariot figures, these are highly abstracted in form, with a sharp ridge for the nose, dots or holes for eyes, rudimentary arms, and paint applied to indicate clothing and details of hair and headdress. Based on the arm configuration, these have been named by types based on Greek letters: psi (ψ) with upward-lifted arms, phi (φ) for arms held over the abdomen, and tau (τ) for arms akimbo. The figures have a rounded base for feet and a long cylinder for legs, giving them a verticality and top-heaviness similar to the pottery vessels. What the figures represent is less certain. They are frequently found in shrines and might be a goddess, but the figures are also found in domestic contexts and graves as well. The psi-type with the upward-lifted arms would more likely suggest a praying figure like a priestess, rather than a divinity receiving prayer, and some of the phi-figures hold infants, suggesting a mother or nurse. They were sufficiently generalized in their form that they could be adapted for use in different contexts. The figures are widely found throughout the Mycenaean world, so we have to assume that their meaning was understood by their makers and users, if not by us. While the figurines conform to a few limited types, they, like the goblet, have enough hand-applied elements in each case to make each work slightly different from another.

As we noted in the discussion of the palace at Pylos, many of the Mycenaean palaces show evidence of destruction at the end of LH IIIB, roughly the first quarter of the twelfth century BCE. Some of the sites have small-scale towns rebuilt on or near the ruins, but the palaces are essentially abandoned, and with them, monumental architecture and art. There is a scaling back and simplification in the quality of metalwork, whose production had been concentrated in the palaces.

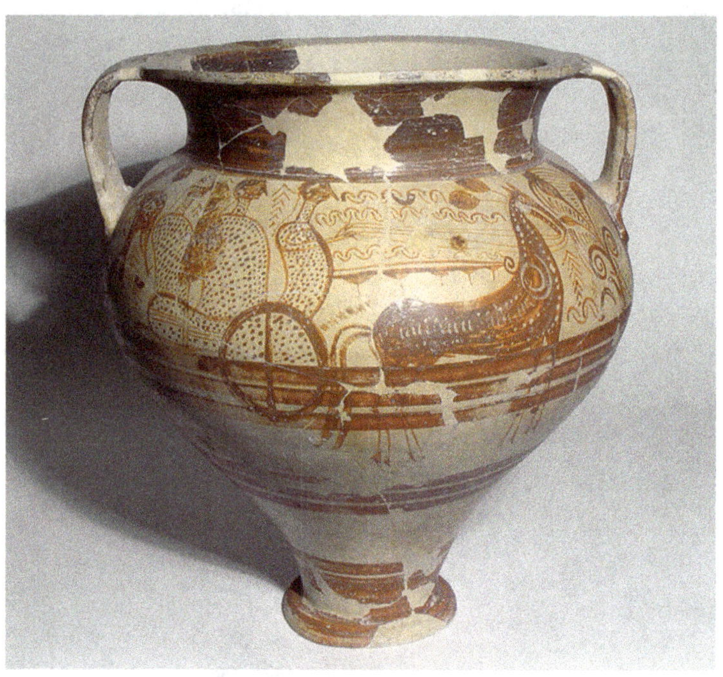

3.13 Krater with chariot procession from Tomb 70, Enkomi, Cyprus, LH IIIA2. 11¹¹⁄₁₆ in (29.7 cm). London, British Museum 1897,0401.1113. Photo: © The Trustees of the British Museum.

Curiously, pottery during Phase 4 (LH IIIC) shows signs of more careful production than in Phase 3. A **stirrup jar** in the Metropolitan Museum of Art, for example, belongs to this last period of Mycenaean art **(Figure 3.15)**. Looking at it, one could readily argue that it shows greater skill and precision than the earlier chariot krater. Once more we have an octopus for the design, a motif that allows the painter to fill the surface of the vase very fluidly. The octopus is more symmetrical than the flower on the goblet from Kalymnos, but it is painted with greater detail and pattern and so more costly in terms of the labor. The colored areas of black paint are even and consistent in tone, also evidence for the care in its making. The profile is squatter than earlier vessels, but the parts of the vase are still precisely articulated. When comparing this to other octopus vases, one can see that it is far more abstract than the Marine style Minoan flask **(see Figure 2.17, page 39)**, but that it has a more lively and carefully articulated design than the Palace Style amphora **(see Figure 3.1, page 51)**. One might not guess that the palatial infrastructure behind the production of art in earlier periods had deteriorated.

There are still pictorial vases made during this period, including the well-known Warrior Vase found at Mycenae and today in the National Archaeological Museum in Athens **(Figure 3.16)**. Here we see six warriors marching out to war, while behind them a woman raises a hand to the top of her hair. This is a gesture that we will associate in later Greek art with the tearing of hair while mourning the deceased **(see Figure 4.8, page 79 and Figure 5.26, page 125)**, and certainly it would appear to be a gesture of distress as she watches the warriors marching away. While at first glance the representational style seems simplified and cartoon-like, it is done with greater attention to figural anatomy and

stirrup jar
a small liquid container with a narrow opening and stirrup-shaped handles between the neck and body, sometimes with a third handle at right angles

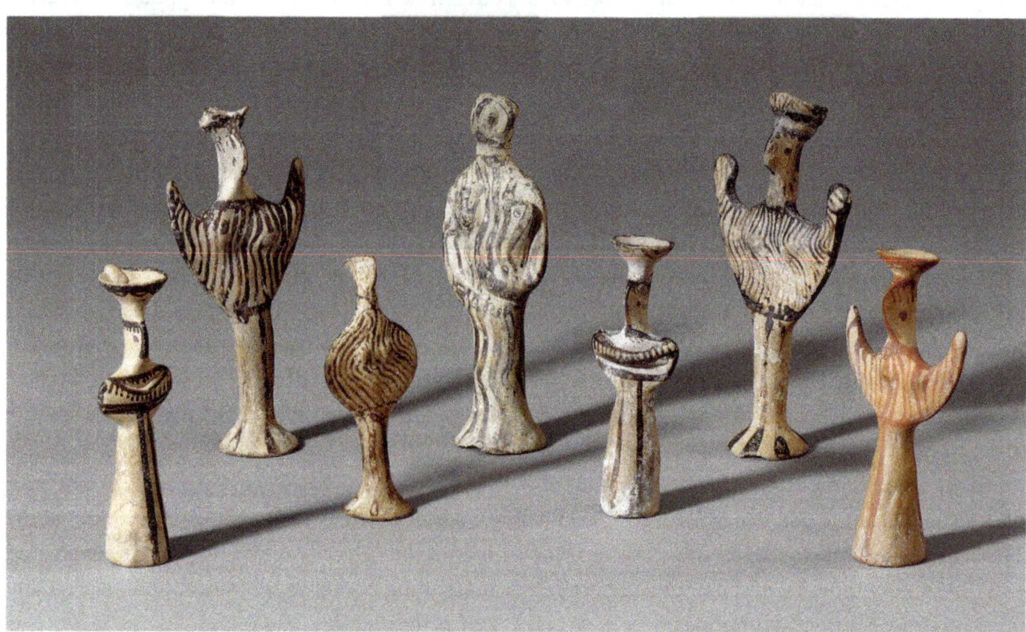

3.14 Terracotta figures (psi, tau, and phi types), LH IIIB. Height of second from left: 5 in (12.7 cm). London, British Museum 1875,0512.3–5 and 1864,0220.32–33. Photo: © The Trustees of the British Museum.

details of armor and weapons than the earlier chariot kraters and the fresco from the cult center at Mycenae. The figures use the top of the triple band of lines marking the base of the handle and defining the picture zone as a ground line for walking, and they march evenly spaced as a troop of soldiers should. The figures show some similarity to some earlier fresco fragments from the palaces, and it has been suggested that fresco painters turned their skill to pottery in the absence of frescoes to paint in the post-palace world. Given the circumstances of the palace destructions, this would have been a much less secure age, which is also demonstrated in the fact that Mycenaean pottery no longer shows up in quantity outside of Greece as it had previously.

There was another wave of destructions at the end of LH IIIC, at which point many of the Late Helladic sites are abandoned or are reduced to agricultural villages. This period of the so-called Dark Ages is one that we will consider in the next chapter. Who destroyed the palaces and caused the collapse of Mycenaean culture is not clear. The period coincides with a larger series of devastations and invasions in the eastern Mediterranean, bringing an end to the Bronze Age generally. Greek legends spoke of the invasion of Dorian Greeks at about this time, but the Linear B tablets show that Greeks had already arrived by the Late Bronze Age. Many of the palaces were burned within a small span of time, and the construction of huge and expensive fortification

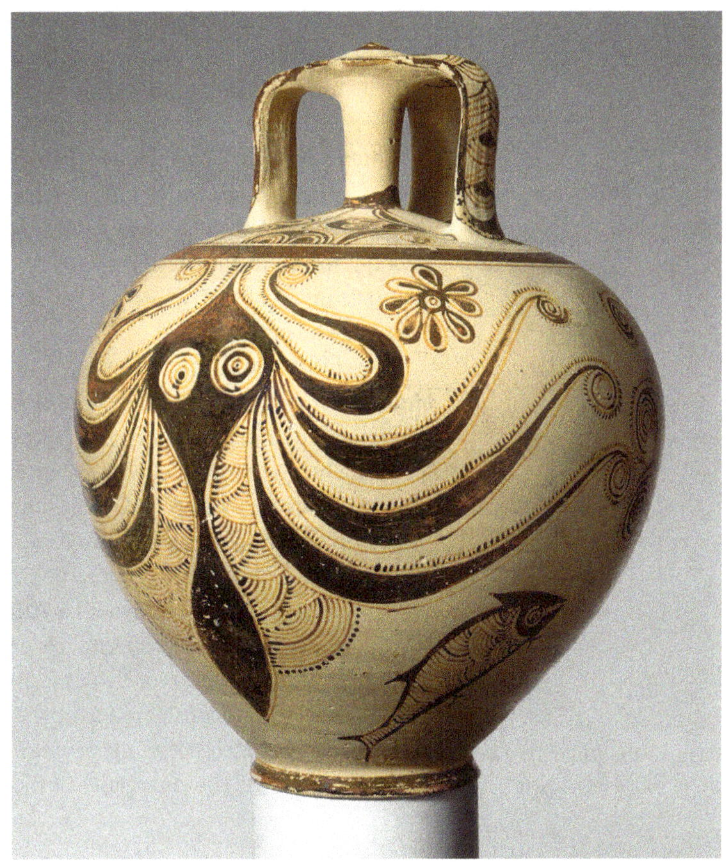

3.15 Stirrup jar with octopus, LH IIIC. 10¼ in (26 cm). New York, Metropolitan Museum of Art 53.11.6. Photo: Image copyright © The Metropolitan Museum of Art. Image source: Art Resource, NY.

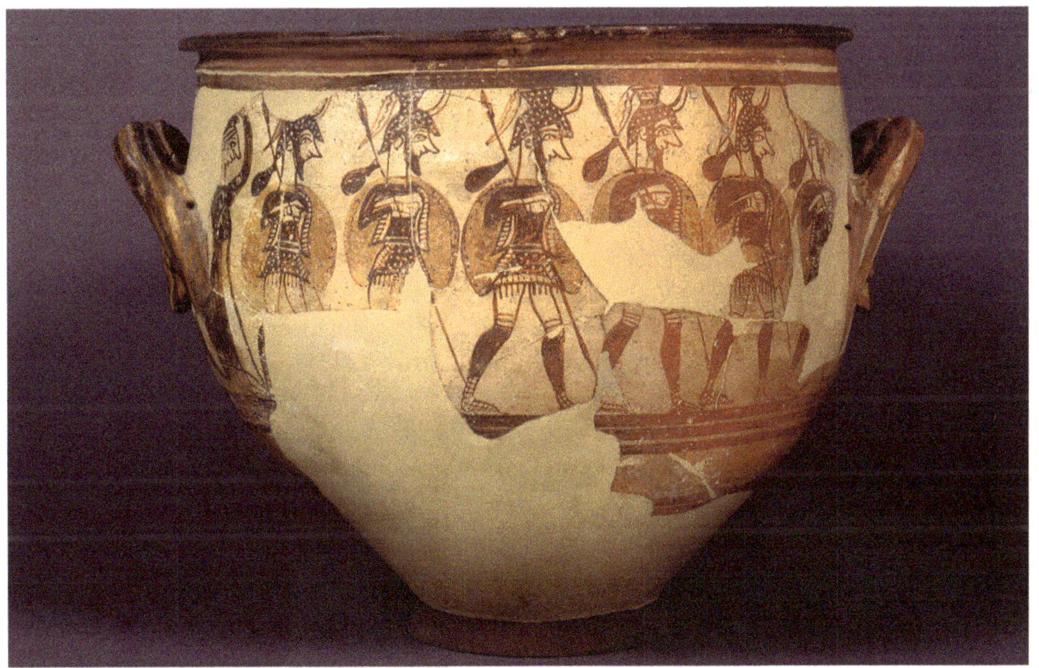

3.16 Warrior Vase from Mycenae, LH IIIC. 16⅛ in (41 cm). Athens, National Archaeological Museum 1426. Photo: National Archaeological Museum, Athens (Athanassios Miliarakis) © Hellenic Ministry of Education and Religious Affairs, Culture and Sports/Archaeological Receipts Fund.

walls in LH IIIB shows that security was both uncertain and a concern of the rulers. Still, some palaces were not fortified and some were not burned, so the idea of a climactic invasion does not offer a full explanation (Dickinson 2010). It is possible that some of the destruction was the result of local warfare, but why then did the victors not rebuild their newly conquered citadel?

Other theories have been proposed, including widespread earthquakes, drought, or environmental degradation. There is evidence in the Levant of problems with drought, which might well explain why sites would be abandoned if there were no crops, but this would not account for their destruction by fire. The bureaucracy described in the Linear B tablets may also have become oppressive, ineffective, or rigid, resulting in a systems collapse when triggered by an event like one of these.

It would seem most likely that the reason for the collapse of Bronze Age Greek culture is multidimensional and complex. Prolonged drought and environmental stress may have forced migrations or raids on more prosperous neighbors; the palace administrative system may have been unable to respond effectively or creatively to new challenges. Cascading problems over the course of a decade or two might have reached a tipping point where the palace culture collapsed. Access to distant materials would have been limited and the skills needed for manufacturing may have vanished. In the end, Greece was a less populous and more decentralized place at the end of the Bronze Age (see generally Cline 2014).

Still, the ruins of the great citadels were visible in the landscape and memories of a heroic and expansive age were preserved through epic poetry such as the *Iliad*. The world that the eighth-century poem describes was considered to be the long distant past. The memories and artifacts of the Bronze Age became the ancestry and genealogy of Greek art in the succeeding millennium. In place of the palaces, we will see the emergence of the polis in the next periods of Greek art.

Iliupersis
term for the fall of Troy or Ilium as it was known

TEXTBOX: THE TROJAN WAR

Troy looms large in Greek poetry and art. The *Iliad* recounts about two weeks at the beginning of the tenth year of the siege of Ilium, as Troy was called, but it was just one of an entire cycle of epic poems composed between the later eighth and sixth centuries that told the tale of the entire war. The tragedians of the fifth century retold the stories for the stage, and there are numerous references to the characters and incidents of the war in lyric and other poetry. Other than representations of Herakles, it may well be the most common subject in Greek art and was shown in a range of media, from small items such as gems to monumental painting and sculpture like the Parthenon. Certainly the ***Iliupersis***, the fall of Troy, with its many subplots such as the death of Priam and the rape of Kassandra, was an important subject in Greek art, as were other episodes involving Achilles, such as his fights against the Amazon queen Penthesileia, the Ethiopian king Memnon, and his killing of the Trojan prince Troilos at the beginning of the siege. Curiously, in spite of the status of the *Iliad*, its events are much more rarely represented than other episodes from the war.

For the Greeks, the Trojan War was part of their remote history and some families claimed descent from its participants. As noted in Chapter 2, Herodotos dated the Trojan War 800 years before his time, but he also doubted whether the king of Troy would risk the destruction of his city for Paris's abduction of Helen. Indeed, he was told by his Egyptian sources that Paris and Helen had spent the war in Egypt, a fact the Greeks only discovered after they had sacked the city. The historicity of the city was doubted for many centuries, but Schliemann's excavation at the Turkish site of Hisarlik found a walled city whose inhabitation went back well into the third millennium BCE. Later and more systematic excavations led by Carl Blegen and now Ernst Pernicka and Brian Rose found Late Helladic pottery at the site, showing that there was contact between the Mycenaeans and Troy.

Whether there was a decade-long Trojan War is another issue. The walls of Troy VI certainly would appear to resemble the legendary poetic walls that distinguished Troy from many contemporary cities, but this phase of Troy was destroyed, apparently by an earthquake, during the first half of the thirteenth century. This is also a time when the

Mycenaean palaces were being fortified, seemingly concerned for their own defense rather than overseas expansion. Letters preserved in the archives of the contemporary Hittite Empire in Anatolia speak of the Ahhiyawa. This people are troubling Hittite vassals along the Anatolian coast and could be the Mycenaeans (Achilles led the Achaians). The difficulties caused by the Ahhiyawa do not seem to rise to the level of epic, at least from the Hittite perspective, but they do show that the Mycenaeans were a force in international relations.

It is conceivable that there was conflict in the Bronze Age between Troy and the Mycenaeans, and perhaps as far back as the fifteenth century, as Emily Vermeule once suggested. Certainly Troy's position on the Bosporus is strategic for trade, and there may well have been a rivalry as Mycenaean ships came to the area. Perhaps some early successes were magnified in song and remembered long after both Troy and Mycenae had fallen. What is remarkable about the Greek viewpoint on Troy in literature and art is that many of the Greeks and Trojans are honorable characters and not cartoons. Indeed, as the stories about Agamemnon and both Ajax the Greater and Lesser attest, the Greeks themselves did behave badly at Troy, whereas Hektor is noble and receives a heroic burial with the help of the gods.

See Güterbock 1983; Mellink 1983; Project Troia; Rose 2013, 8–43; Vermeule 1986.

REFERENCES

Blackwell, N. G. 2014. "Making the Lion Gate Relief at Mycenae: Tool Marks and Foreign Influence." *American Journal of Archaeology* 118, 451–488.

Chadwick, J. 1990. *The Decipherment of Linear B*, 2nd edition. Cambridge: Cambridge University Press.

Cline, E. 2014. *1177 B.C.: The Year Civilization Collapsed*. Princeton: Princeton University Press.

Dickinson, O. 2010. "The Collapse at the End of the Bronze Age." In Cline 2010, 483–490.

Güterbock, H. G. 1983. "The Hittites and the Aegean World: Part 1. The Ahhiyawa Problem Reconsidered." *American Journal of Archaeology* 87, 133–138.

Hruby, J. 2013. "The Palace of Nestor, Craft Production, and Mechanisms for the Transfer of Goods." *American Journal of Archaeology* 117, 423–427.

Immerwahr, S. A. 1971. *The Neolithic and Bronze Ages*. The Athenian Agora, 13. Princeton: American School of Classical Studies at Athens.

Mellink, M. J. 1983. "The Hittites and the Aegean World: 2. Archaeological Comments on Ahhiyawa-Achaians in Western Anatolia." *American Journal of Archaeology* 87, 138–141.

Pollitt, J. J. 1990. *The Art of Ancient Greece: Sources and Documents*. Cambridge/New York: Cambridge University Press.

Project Troia. Website: http://www.uni-tuebingen.de/troia/eng/

Rose, C. Brian. 2013. *The Archaeology of Greek and Roman Troy*. Cambridge: Cambridge University Press.

Rutter, J. B. 2010. "Mycenaean Pottery." In Cline 2010, 415–429.

Ventris, M. and J. Chadwick. 1973. *Documents in Mycenaean Greek*, 2nd edition. Cambridge: Cambridge University Press.

Vermeule, E. D. T. 1986. "'Priam's Castle Blazing': A Thousand Years of Trojan Memories." In M. J. Mellink, ed., *Troy and the Trojan War: A Symposium held at Bryn Mawr College, October 1984*, 77–92. Bryn Mawr: Bryn Mawr College.

FURTHER READING

Aegean Prehistoric Archaeology. Website: http://www.dartmouth.edu/~prehistory/aegean/

Betancourt, P. P. 2007. *Introduction to Aegean Art*. Philadelphia: INSTAP Press.

Cline, E. H., ed. 2010. *The Oxford Handbook of the Bronze Age Aegean*. Oxford: Oxford University Press.

Immerwahr, S. A. 1990. *Aegean Painting in the Bronze Age*. University Park, PA: Pennsylvania State University Press.

Shelmerdine, C. W., ed. 2008. *The Cambridge Companion to the Aegean Bronze Age*. Cambridge: Cambridge University Press.

Vermeule, E. D. T. 1972. *Greece in the Bronze Age*. Chicago: University of Chicago Press.

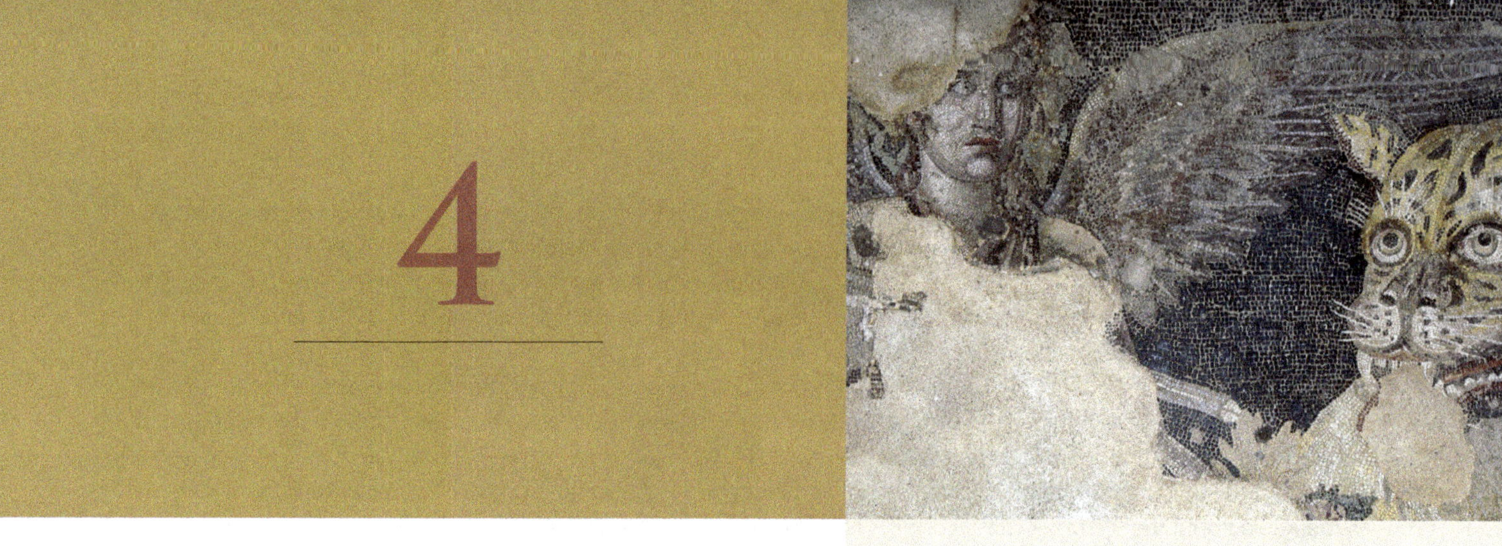

4

THE SUB-MYCENAEAN, PROTOGEOMETRIC, AND GEOMETRIC PERIODS

(*C.* 1075–700 BCE)

Timeline
Pottery
Sculpture
Architecture
Textbox: What is in a Name?
References
Further Reading

TIMELINE

	Period	Pottery	Architecture and Sculpture
1085/80–1050/25	Sub-Mycenaean	Amphoriskos fr Kerameikos	
1050–900	Protogeometric	Amphora fr Kerameikos	House at Lefkandi Lefkandi Centaur, *c.* 900
900–850	Early Geometric	Amphora with Spear Boots Grave [13.5]	
850–800	Middle Geometric I	Tomb of the Rich Lady in Athens, *c.* 850	
800–760	Middle Geometric II	Skyphos from Eleusis [9.2]	
760–735 760–750 750–735	Late Geometric I LG IA LG IB	Dipylon Amphora Dipylon Krater Euboean Krater Argive Krater	Olympia bronzes Dipylon Ivory Zagora I
735–700 735–720 720–700	Late Geometric II LG IIA LG IIB	Louterion from Thebes LG II Skyphos	Zagora II
700–675	Sub-Geometric		Mantiklos Apollo [7.19]

To speak about Greek art around the year 1050 BCE, one has to be broad about defining what art is. The works that we saw in the Bronze Age Mycenaean palaces included monumental forms of architecture, sculpture, and painting that we typically associate with "art," but the landscape of Greece around 1050 was quite different than it had been two centuries earlier. Many of the palaces such as Mycenae, Tiryns, and Pylos had been destroyed by 1175 and lay in ruins, although the large citadel walls, such as the Lion Gate at Mycenae, were still visible **(see Figure 3.6, page 56)**. Mycenaean culture continued for a time after 1175, but writing disappeared and the production of mural paintings or luxury items like gold and ivory in the palace workshops ceased. By 1075, the population had declined dramatically, with people living in small clusters; travel and trade were severely limited. This period, broadly lasting from the eleventh until the eighth century BCE, is sometimes labeled the Dark Ages, signifying the reduction in the scale of material culture and the relative lack of archaeological and historical evidence. An alternative term for the period is the Early Iron Age, signifying the use of a more durable and versatile metal for tools and weapons that was technologically more difficult to make than bronze. As we shall see in the textbox for this chapter, the name of a period can affect our perception of it, whether in this era or another.

Whereas the material remains of this period do not rival in scale or luxury those of the periods before and after it, this is a period that is transformative and inventive. During the eighth century, Homer composes the *Iliad* and we see the rise of Panhellenic sites such as Olympia and Delphi that will play an important role in Greek culture for many centuries. The adoption and adaptation of the alphabet from the Phoenicians created a form of writing that had much wider use than tracking palace inventories. Perhaps the most significant cultural development was the initial establishment of the polis, rather than the restoration of the palace, as the model for civic life. Rather than a rigid hierarchical organization of political rule by a small elite class and their control of agricultural and production, the polis came to emphasize political rule through laws, constitutions, and collective decision-making. For individuals and households, there was a sense of citizenship and community; even with large differences in wealth and connections, there was an expectation of household autonomy and social leveling.

In the *Iliad*, Homer describes the Shield of Achilles, which was made by Hephaistos to replace the hero's original shield after it had been borrowed by his companion Patroklos and then taken by Hektor after the Trojan killed him. The new shield had many figural scenes on it, and in one there is a description of a scene in a peaceful city:

> But the people were crowded together in the agora. And there a quarrel had arisen, for two men were arguing on account of the penalty of slaying a man. The first had been swearing to have made full atonement [by] making declaration to the people; the other had declined to accept. But both then had sent forth the issue to an arbitrator to decide. (*Il.* 18.497–501; tr. Stansbury-O'Donnell 1995, 322)

It is clear that someone has been killed, and that the restitution by or punishment of the killer was rejected as insufficient by the victim's family or associates. Both make their arguments before the elders of the town seated in a circle in the agora, while the population of the town watches and voices its opinions. The remarkable aspect of the story is that the scene describes a system of justice that has its authority based on the prerogative of the community, the polis, to assert its judgment and rights in arguments between members of the community. Further, the scene does not take place inside a megaron or palace, but in the public space of the city before all of the citizens. The polis, its households and population, are the foundation of the social structure. Further, one could argue that this is the foundation for the monumental architecture and art of succeeding centuries, in which the temple and agora rather than the palace are the monumental forms of cultural expression.

The art from the Protogeometric and Geometric periods is modest in scope when compared to earlier and later art. The work that continued to be produced after the Bronze Age served a practical purpose, such as houses, textiles, and pottery, but in the archaeological record, it is only the latter that survives in any quantity and degree of preservation. Looking at the style and quality of pottery, though, can reveal developments in the contemporary social fabric. Indeed, the utilitarian aspect of pottery means that whatever the material circumstances, pottery is needed for activities like cooking, storage, drinking, eating, and so on. The quality of a vessel's fabric – the refinement of the clay, the way that it is formed into a shape, its decoration, the firing temperature, etc. – does not need to be high in order for a terracotta product to function. If a potter invests additional time and resources in the visual qualities and refinement of an object, and if a patron is willing to spend additional resources to acquire a decorated and higher-quality pot than one that is purely utilitarian, this can indicate something about the well-being of a society and the identity of its members. We can also see in pottery the emergence of distinct regional variations in style within Geometric Greece. Indeed, as we shall also see in later centuries, there are strong regional styles within each period of Greek art even when producing the same type of object or using the same materials and techniques. Given its consistent production during this period, then, we will look at the pottery of these four centuries before turning to sculpture and architecture.

POTTERY

Excavations at the Kerameikos and Agora areas of contemporary Athens have provided the most complete survey of developments in pottery from about 1085/80 BCE, when the sub-Mycenaean period begins, down through the Protogeometric and Geometric periods (see timeline for period subdivisions and dates). The area called the Kerameikos today was a prominent burial area on the northwest side of Athens, as well as the place where Athenian pottery was later made. Before the classical period, however, the area known today as the Agora was not yet the marketplace, but a mixture of residential, funerary, and workshop activity.

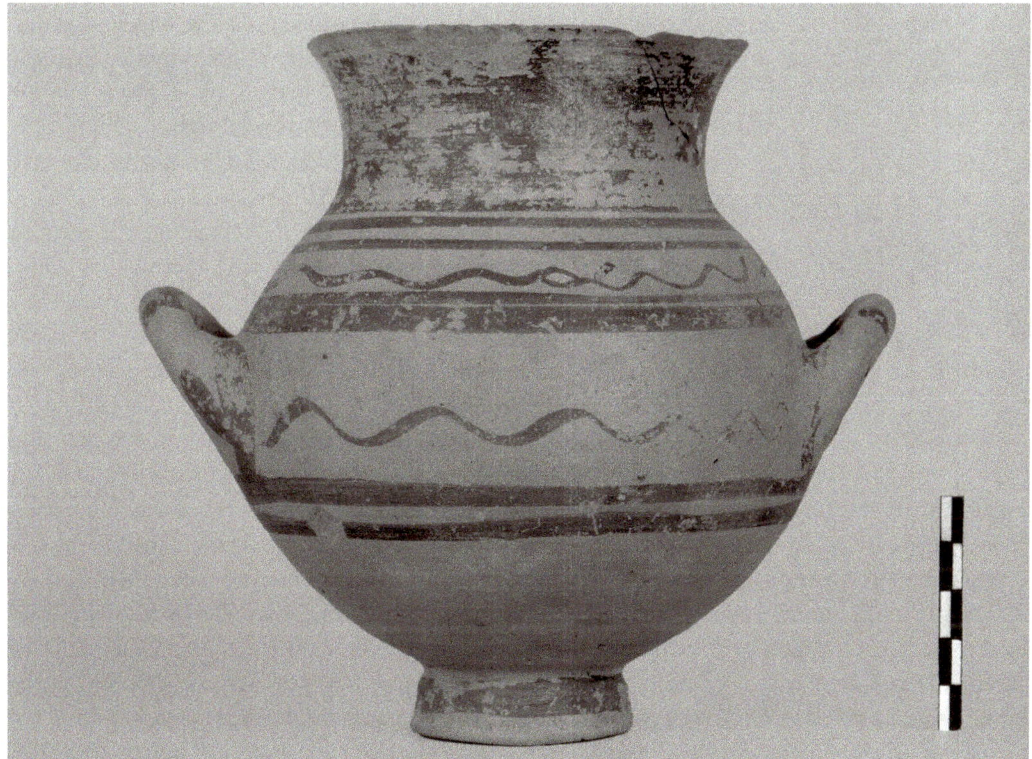

4.1 Sub-Mycenaean Attic amphoriskos from the Kerameikos, *c.* 1100–1050 BCE. Athens, Kerameikos Museum T108 (inv. 466). 5¹³⁄₁₆ in (14.8 cm). Photo: Hermann Wagner, D-DAI-ATH-Kerameikos-Neg. 03218.

During the sub-Mycenaean period, we no longer see chamber tombs as in the Mycenaean era **(see Figures 3.10 and 3.11, pages 61, 62)**, but instead find bodies placed in a trench or pit (known as a ***fossa* tomb**), sometimes with slabs surrounding it to make a cist grave. Frequently vases such as amphorae, drinking cups, and oil containers (either a stirrup jar or a new shape called the **lekythos**) were left in the grave for the dead. Taking a look at one of these vessels, an amphoriskos (**Figure 4.1**), offers a strong contrast with the vases of even the latest Mycenaean era, such as the Late Helladic (LH) IIIC octopus stirrup jar seen in the last chapter **(see Figure 3.15, page 65)**. The clay surface of this sub-Mycenaean amphoriskos is not as smooth and even in texture as the octopus stirrup jar; the shape is thicker and the edges less sharp, as can be seen at the transitions between the parts of the vessel like the join of the neck to the shoulders. The painted decoration is not only far simpler, but the lines are more uneven and inconsistent in their application. The even, thick quality of the paint on the octopus stirrup jar, its more symmetrical composition, and its detailed drawing took considerably longer to do, and required a greater application of skill than is apparent in the sub-Mycenaean vessel. This pot is functional, but not much more than that, and bears witness to a decline in the resources that society was willing to invest in pottery at that time.

***fossa* tomb**
Italian term designating a tomb made by digging a hole or trench into the ground for the body or ashes, and then covered over, sometimes with a stone slab on the surface. Also called trench or pit burial

lekythos
an oil container, usually with a cylindrical body, with a foot and single handle attached to a narrow neck and flanged opening. A more spherical body is called a squat lekythos

The sub-Mycenaean period lasted to the middle of the eleventh century, at which time we can begin to see some changes in both the style of the pottery and its context. The placement of graves in the Kerameikos was moved further away to the northwest in an area that was used continuously as a cemetery into the eighth century and later. Rather than inhumation, there was a change to cremation burial, with the ashes placed in a large amphora (**Figure 4.2**). This was set into a pit along with other vessels for the dead, and the tombs were then covered, as before, by a small mound of dirt and sometimes stone. Changes in burial custom, from inhumation to cremation and from group burials to individual tombs, are significant as they must reflect changes in social or religious attitudes. Cremation burials occur elsewhere in Greece at this time in places like Lefkandi and Argos, but are used alongside inhumation burials. The coincidence of these changes with an increase in the quality of pottery and grave goods may reflect new attitudes about social status or structure. In the *Iliad*, cremation is the only form of burial and the ritual and offerings associated with the burials of Patroklos and Hektor make it a heroic form of burial. Perhaps the changes in burial customs reflect a desire to emphasize the status of the deceased and family within the civic burial ground.

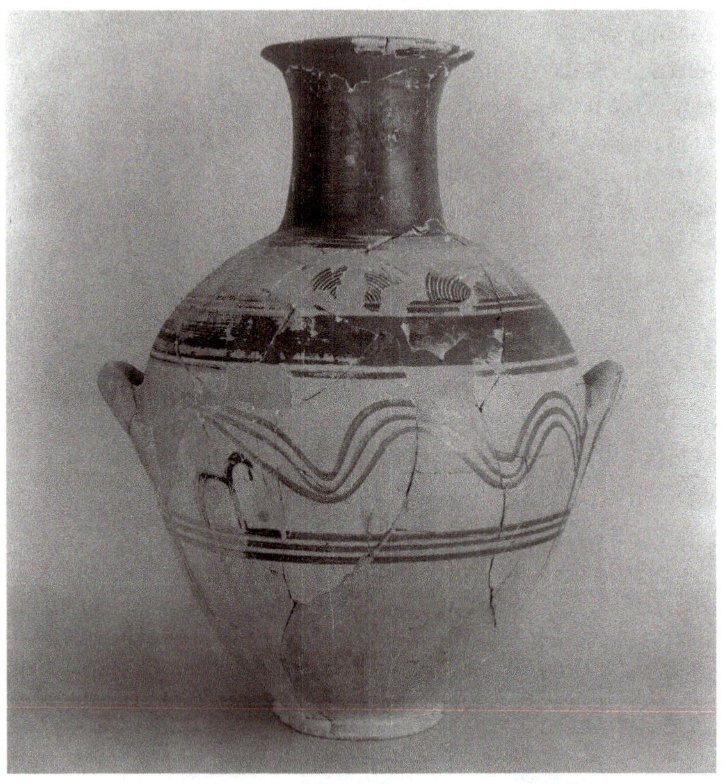

4.2 Protogeometric Attic cinerary amphora from the Kerameikos, *c.* 1000–900 BCE. 18⁹⁄₁₆ in (47.2 cm). Athens, Kerameikos Museum T 18/I (inv. 560). Photo: Karl Kübler, D-DAI-ATH-Kerameikos-Neg. 03394. All rights reserved.

A distinct change of style in the pottery coincides with the change of burial practice. The fabric of the clay is now more refined and the paint is more evenly and thickly applied to the surface. The neck is more sharply articulated from the shoulders and the proportions are more vertical than the earlier amphoriskos. The handles are placed at the widest part of the body of the vessel and their ends are flattened to make a more gradual transition into the body. The shoulder is set off as a decorative field by the thick bands of dark paint below and above on the neck. While the wavy lines are a motif that continues from sub-Mycenaean times, two new decorative motifs appear. On the shoulder, facing upward toward the viewer, is a series of concentric half-circles. These were not made free-hand but with a multiple-point compass that gives them a precise and even appearance. This use of regular geometric forms for decoration has given to the entire period the name "Geometric" and to the earliest pottery the label "Protogeometric," first or beginning geometric.

This geometric approach to decoration can also be seen in the small horse that appears near the left handle. Indeed, this is among the first animal forms found in Greek art since the end of the Mycenaean period more than a century earlier. The neck and body of the horse have been formed like the arcs of a circle, very abstract but very recognizable and precise in their drawing. This horse is not a casual sketch, and the size, quality, and decorative motifs of the amphora show a greater willingness to invest in the visual appeal of a pot by both potter and patron, particularly considering that once seen during the funerary ritual and then buried, it would no longer be visible.

The number and value of grave goods in Athens increase over time, as a glance at the contents of a tomb from the north side of Areopagos Hill just to the west of the Acropolis demonstrates. This tomb, part of the Agora excavations, dates to about 900, at the beginning of the Early Geometric period (*c.* 900–850). Like the Protogeometric amphora, this is also a cinerary urn, which contained the remains of a male in his mid-thirties **(Figure 4.3)**. An iron sword has been bent around the neck of the amphora. In addition, the grave goods included two pitchers, three cups, a pyxis (lidded container), carbonized figs and grapes, and various iron implements, including bits for a horse, an axe, a chisel, two knives, and two spearheads (Blegen 1952). The placement of weapons in the tomb signifies the importance of individual arms to a warrior, as the struggles over the armor of a dead hero such as Patroklos or Hektor in the *Iliad* attest. Bending the sword renders it useless except to the deceased, making it his permanently. There were also two iron bits for a horse among the grave goods, perhaps identifying the deceased as a member of the elite who could afford to own a horse and possibly serve in a cavalry unit. In this light, we can consider that the earlier Protogeometric horse, in view of its rarity and newness as a motif, could also have signaled elite status for the deceased whose ashes were inside the amphora.

pyxis (pl. pyxides)
a small cylindrical container with a lid used to store small items such as jewelry

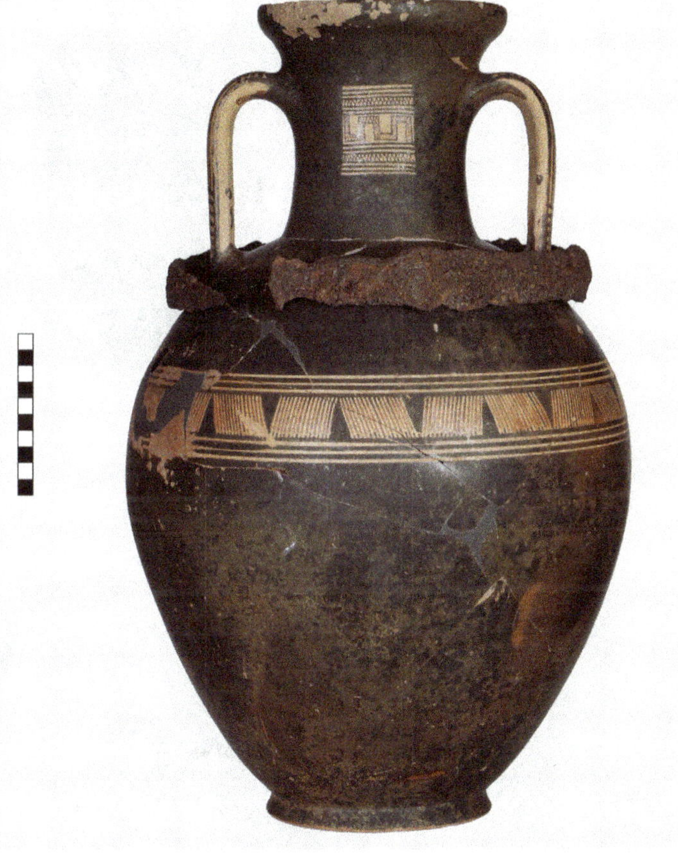

4.3 Early Geometric Attic burial amphora with bent iron sword from Agora (D16:4), *c.* 900 BCE. 20½ in (52 cm). Athens, Agora Museum P20177 and IL1058. Photo: American School of Classical Studies at Athens: Agora Excavations.

The handles of the Early Geometric amphora are located at the neck and project outward, in contrast to the handles on the belly of the Protogeometric amphora. This is not just a stylistic distinction, but also a signifier of the gender of the deceased. Handles on the belly or shoulders of a vase are found with female graves, whereas a neck-handled amphora like this example is found with male tombs. Stylistically, the amphora is proportionally taller than Protogeometric amphorae, a trend that would continue throughout the Geometric period. Finally, the decorative scheme of the amphora also changes in the Early Geometric period. Most of the vessel is now painted dark, setting off the reserved decorative bands on the neck and belly. The latter features a tooth pattern with hatching framed by three lines. The neck has a meander or key pattern made up of a hatched-pattern line that moves at 90° turns from upper left to lower right; a smaller frieze of zig-zags above and below creates a complex frame for the major pattern.

Another nearby grave in the Agora excavations was for a woman, as can be seen in the different shape and handle placement for the cinerary amphora **(see Figure 13.5, page 326)**. We will consider this distinction of gender more fully in Chapter 13, but for now one can note that whereas the goods of the first grave are associated with warfare, the goods in the so-called "Boots Grave" include more pyxides, some earrings, and two sets of terracotta shoes. Shoes are sometimes included in grave goods as part of a "maiden's kit," representing objects given up with the transition from childhood to adulthood; here they may symbolize the marriage that death cut short (Langdon 2008, 136–137). Susan Langdon further suggests that the inclusion of two pairs of boots may relate to the cult of Demeter and Persephone, who are also important deities for marriage. While the shoulder-handled amphora marks the grave as belonging to a woman rather than a man, its decorative style is similar to the amphora in **Figure 4.3**, dating them to about the same time, around 900 BCE. Both amphorae share the emphasis

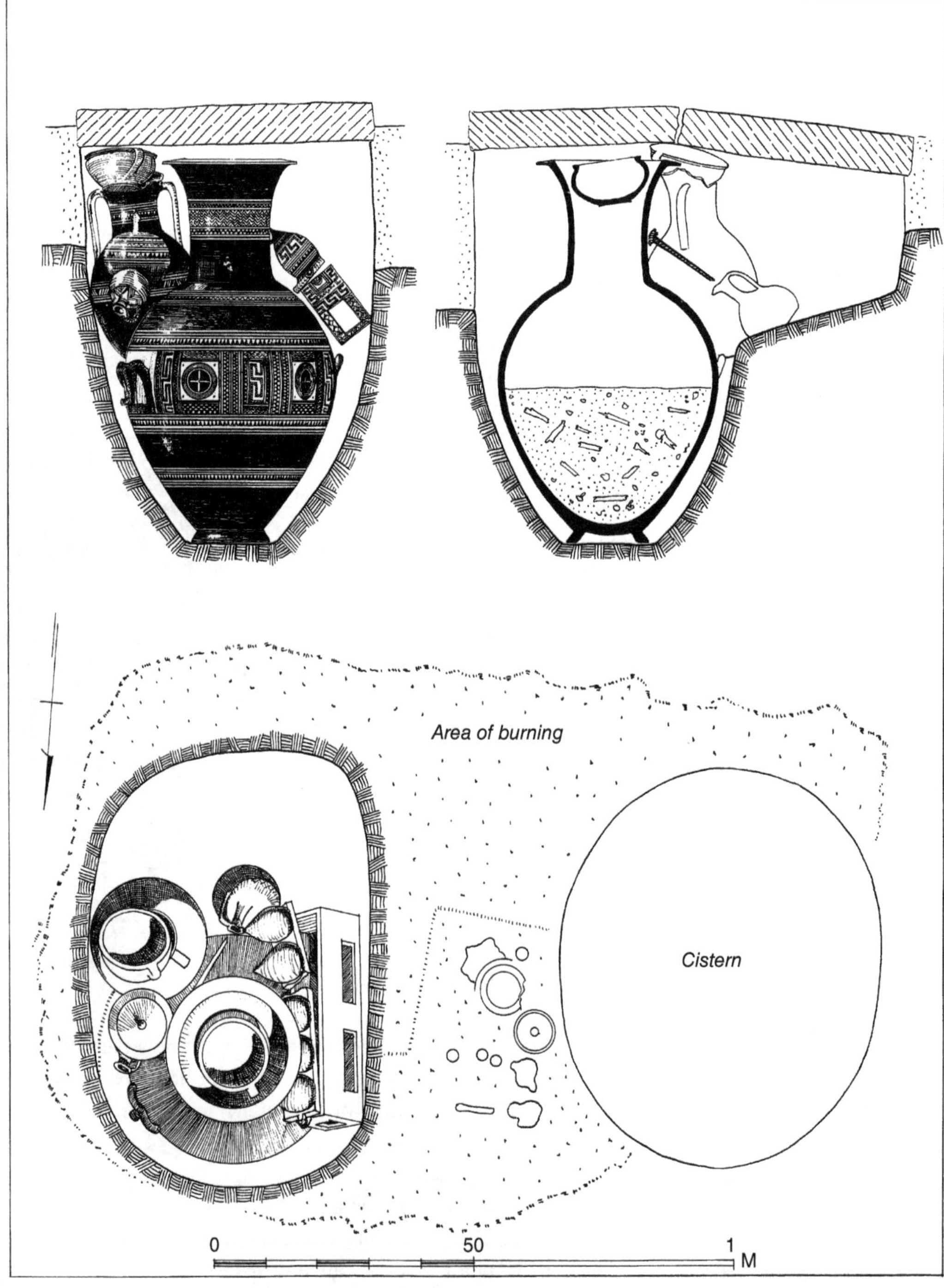

4.4 Middle Geometric tomb of the Rich Lady in the Agora in Athens (Tomb H16:6), *c.* 850 BCE. Drawing of grave and grave goods in situ. Photo: American School of Classical Studies at Athens: Agora Excavations.

on the dark surfaces framing similarly placed decorative motifs; the meander pattern goes continuously around the neck since the handles do not interrupt the decorative zone.

In the succeeding Middle Geometric period (*c.* 850–760), there is an increase in the decorative complexity and vertical proportions of pottery. The tomb of the "Rich Lady" from the Agora dates to the beginning of the Middle Geometric period (MG I, *c.* 850–800), but surpasses many contemporary tombs for the wealth and unusual qualities of its grave goods. The cinerary amphora is large (72 cm) and was placed in a pit dug through one side of the trench used to cremate the body **(Figure 4.4)**. The tomb was then filled and covered by a slab. Recent analysis of the bones found in the amphora not only confirmed that the deceased was a woman, but also found the bones of a fetus of seven or eight months in age, suggesting that the Rich Lady was pregnant when she died (Liston and Papadopoulos 2004).

The cinerary amphora is decorated with a complex ensemble of patterns and shapes. The primary decorative zone is now the belly rather than the neck, and two smaller decorative friezes break up the shoulder and foot of the amphora **(Figure 4.5)**. Circles drawn with a multiple-point compass appear

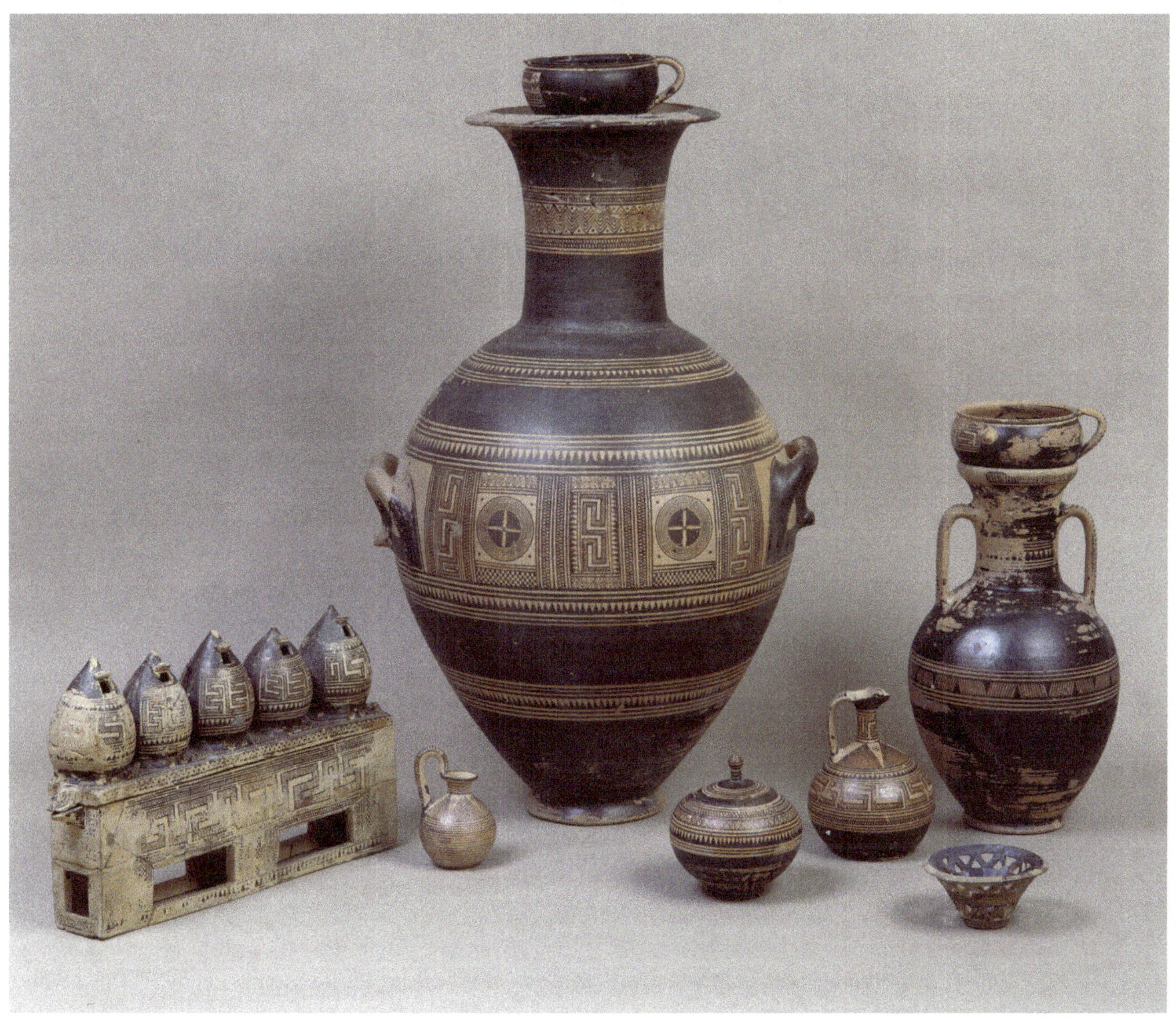

4.5 Grave goods from tomb of the Rich Lady, *c.* 850 BCE. Athens, Agora Museum. Height of amphora: 28⅜ in (72 cm). Photo: American School of Classical Studies at Athens: Agora Excavations.

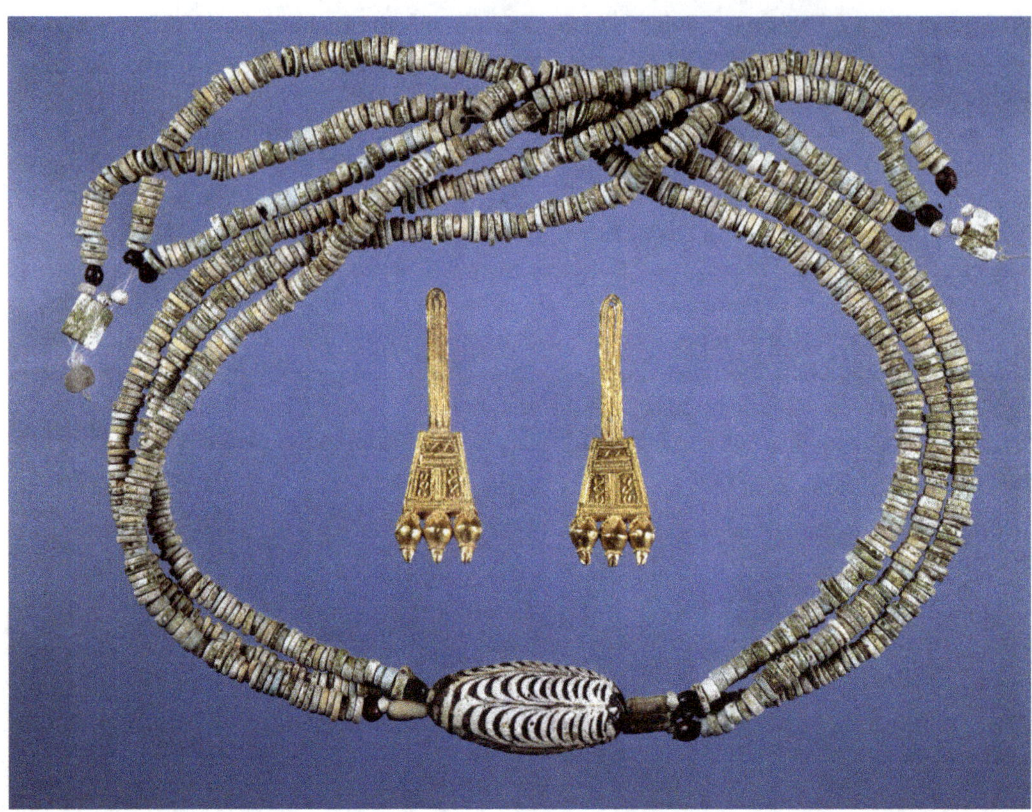

4.6 Jewelry from the tomb of the Rich Lady, *c.* 850 BCE. Necklace of glass and faience beads; earrings. Photo: American School of Classical Studies at Athens: Agora Excavations.

twice on each side, framed by meanders and other patterns. The effect is like that of a complex carpet, and some scholars have wondered if the patterns of Geometric textiles, none of which have survived, might have been similar to those in pottery.

Stacked on top of the amphora in the grave pit was a terracotta chest with five pointed-bulb shapes that has been identified as a model granary and a small openwork terracotta basket that is a ***kalathos*** or wool basket, indicating the elite status of the deceased through agricultural landholdings. This high status is also suggested by the jewelry in the tomb, such as the faience-bead necklace with a glass pendant that probably came from Syria (**Figure 4.6**). The gold for the rings and earrings was also imported, but the simple engraving technique and angled or zig-zag patterns of the rings point to local manufacture. The earrings use two techniques that originate in the Near East at this time: **filigree** work, in which wires are twisted into shapes and soldered to the surface, and **granulation**, in which small beads of gold are soldered to the surface. The rectilinear style and patterns of the earrings, though, suggest either that they were made in Syria or Phoenicia for a Greek market by adapting the Geometric style, or that a Greek goldsmith had learned these foreign techniques to produce them locally with imported gold. In either case, the materials and craft are distinctive and must have demonstrated the wealth and connections of the deceased for the mourners gathered at the funeral. The inclusion of a partial stamp seal among the grave goods also suggests that the woman buried here may have overseen property and goods.

kalathos
a basket to hold wool during its preparation for weaving. Small terracotta versions with openwork sides could serve as grave goods

filigree
metalworking technique in which wires are twisted into shapes and soldered to a surface

granulation
metalworking technique in which small beads of gold are soldered to a surface as decoration

The second part of the Middle Geometric period (MG II, *c.* 800–760) saw a diminishment in metal grave goods, but there was a new development in the use of human figures for decoration on pottery, including scenes that can be described as having narrative action. On a small skyphos (cup) from Eleusis near Athens there are two scenes, one of a ship with helmsman and archer on it, and the other of a battle between two pairs of warriors fighting over a third pair of fallen warriors (**see Figure 9.2, page 213**). This scene, which we shall consider further in Chapter 9 on narrative in art, treats the human figure in a more rubbery fashion than the Protogeometric horse in **Figure 4.2**. The technique can be described as both linear and **silhouette**, meaning that there is emphasis on the shape of the limbs, head, and torso but little anatomical detail, leaving only the action to be emphasized. These first figural scenes appear in association with graves, and we have to consider that their innovative subject matter, simple as it is, could distinguish the tomb of the deceased. The number of tombs with these visual markers is not representative of the entire community but of the land-owning elite who could afford, quite literally, to throw away their wealth on or in a grave to demonstrate their standing. Indeed, the association between elite tombs and stylistic developments of the period leads to the hypothesis that elite patrons worked with the potters/painters in Athens to develop increasingly distinctive forms of visual display that signified their status within the community (Whitley 1991, 181–183).

silhouette
painting technique in which the figure is shown as a silhouette with no or minimal anatomical detail other than limbs and head

In the first decades of the Late Geometric period (LG I, *c.* 760–735) the use of painted pottery to distinguish the elite transforms the large burial amphora into a truly monumental grave marker. The so-called Dipylon amphora, attributed to an anonymous artist called the Dipylon Master and dated in the decade 760–750 (LG IA), takes its name from the cemetery found by the later Dipylon gate in the Kerameikos (**Figure 4.7**). At 1.55 meters (61 in) in height, it is a truly monumental work, one of two such amphorae that along with a couple dozen kraters come from the same area of the cemetery. These monumental vases created external visual markers of elite status that continued to be seen long after the funeral. The Dipylon amphora was made in three sections and joined, and its proportions are carefully controlled. The neck is half the height of the body, creating a 1:2 proportion, and the vase's widest diameter is in this same proportion to its height, 1:2. The ornamental bands have now taken over the entire surface of the vase, with single, double, and triple meanders arranged in a varied and rhythmic pattern that frames the central figural scene placed between the handles.

This picture shows a **prothesis**, or laying out of the body on a bier with mourners surrounding it (**Figure 4.8**). The figures, like the vase itself, follow a regular ratio of proportions. Taking the head as a single unit, the triangular torso is about two units in height, the upper legs and hips from the narrowest part of the waist a bit more than that, and the lower legs a bit less, with a head:body ratio of 1:7. The width of the shoulders is about the same as the height of the neck and head, and we can say of these figures that they live up to the label geometric. The checked area above the body is the burial shroud, but it is placed like a panel so that we can see the body that it covered. The mourners are spread out below and to the sides to be clearly visible, but were surrounding the bier in reality. This schematic approach very legibly presents all the elements that one might expect at an elite funeral. The hands of most of the mourners are placed on top of the head in a mourning gesture we know from later art as tearing at the hair in grief. Several figures raise up a hand, as if directing the funeral song or **threnody**, or making a prayer. There is no indication of the gender of these figures, neither breasts nor genitals, but the mourners are likely women and the deceased must be the woman whose grave was marked by the vase. The other side of the vase has a much simpler picture of eight mourners, so that we can call the prothesis the "front" of the vase that must have been directed toward the main point of access to the grave.

prothesis
funerary rite in which the body of the deceased is laid on a bier and prepared for burial. The body is usually flanked by mourners

threnody
a song sung at the burial lamenting the deceased

The workshop of the Dipylon Master continued to produce monumental grave markers into Late Geometric IB (*c.* 750–735), including a krater currently in New York that stood over the tomb of a man (**Figure 4.9**). The figural scenes here are more complex and tailored to expressing the gender and elite status of the deceased. A prothesis scene is placed again between the handles, and the posts of the bier serve to focus the viewer's attention on the deceased. The mourners to either side of the bier now have two small projecting lines on their torsos to indicate breasts; the hair of these women is also pulled up and out as if they were tearing it. The head of the figure is now a circle with a dot in the middle; together with the projection that resembles a nose, these figures give a little more sense of being able to see as well as to act. Under the deceased are funerary offerings, and an elaborate, woven burial cloth is draped above the figure as it is prepared for burial. There are two half-size versions of the figures that can be seen with the adults, perhaps the children of the deceased? The changes in representing the figure here are relatively slight, but they create an opportunity to represent a more complex scene and a greater range of the participants' identities.

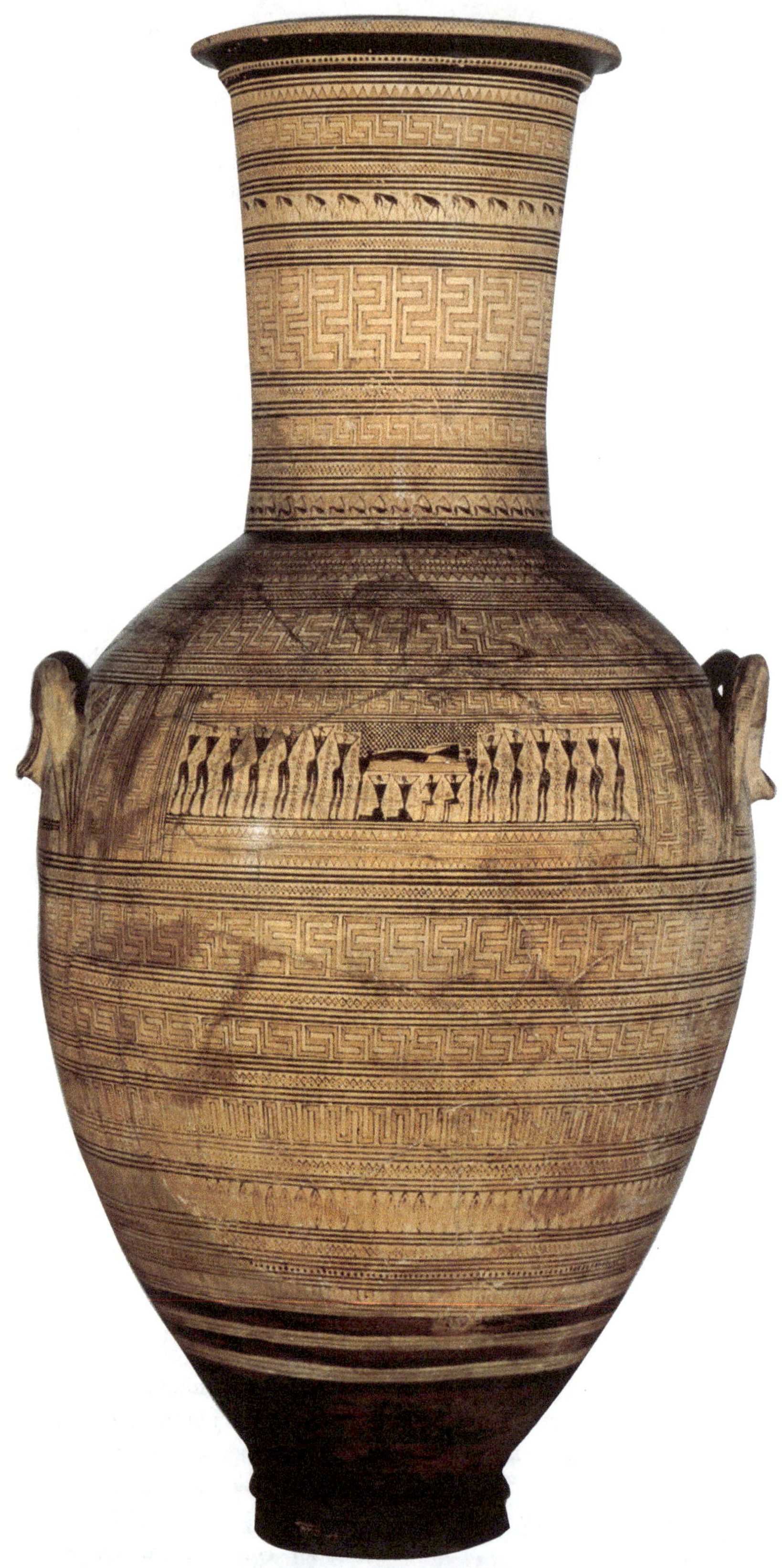

4.7 Late Geometric IA Attic amphora from the Dipylon cemetery (Kerameikos) attributed to the Dipylon Master, *c.* 760–750 BCE. 5 ft 1 in (1.55 m). Prothesis. Athens, National Archaeological Museum 804. Photo: National Archaeological Museum, Athens (Giannis Patrikianos) © Hellenic Ministry of Education and Religious Affairs, Culture and Sports/Archaeological Receipts Fund.

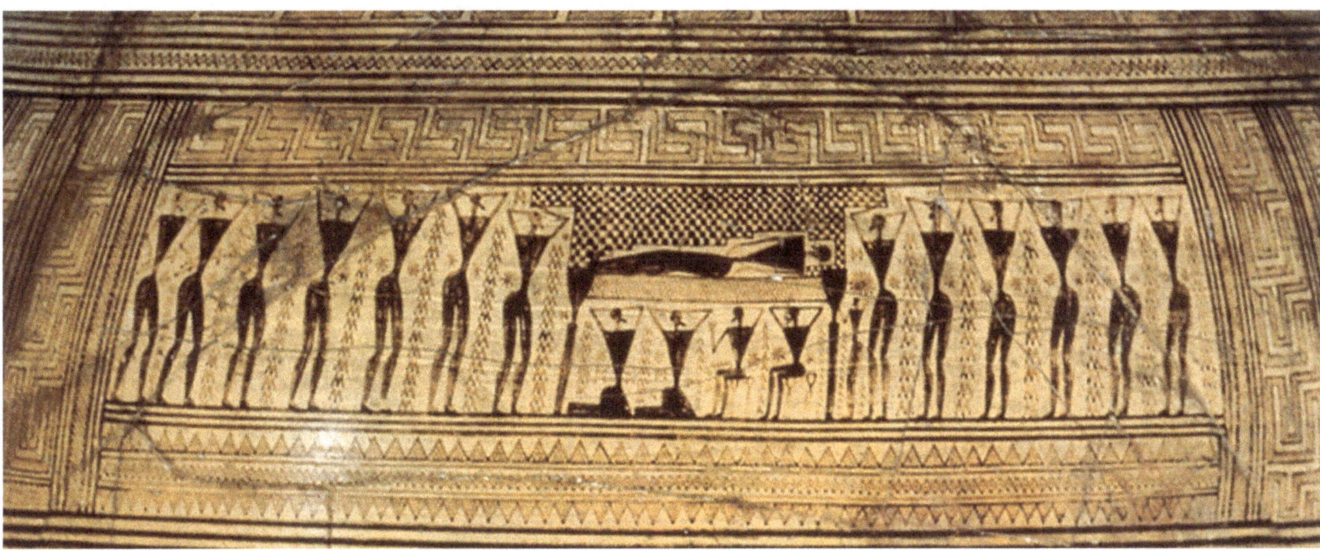

4.8 Detail of prothesis scene in Figure 4.7.

Below the prothesis is a second figural frieze with chariots carrying male charioteers, indicated by their plumed helmet crests. In between the chariots are walking warriors whose body is formed of a circular shield cut with notches in the side that has been called a "Dipylon" shield, after the cemetery where so many of these painted figures were found. Each warrior has two spears and a sword, recalling the grave goods from the Early Geometric warrior's tomb above **(Figure 4.3, page 73)**. The marching warriors and chariots are probably an honorific procession, perhaps circling the prothesis above as part of the funerary ritual. Funeral games were also part of the elaborate funerary rites for the elite, as can be read in the description of the funeral of Achilles's companion Patroklos recounted in *Iliad* 23, and the chariots may also refer to that later celebratory event of the funeral.

The fashion for monumental vases as elite grave markers does not continue beyond the middle third of the eighth century. During the Late Geometric II period we see other changes, including the return of inhumation burial in Athens and the use of vases as grave goods in a larger number of graves **(see Figure 5.25, page 124)**. Figural scenes become more numerous in the later eighth century and appear on smaller objects, such as drinking cups, pitchers, and small amphorae. The skyphos in **Figure 4.10** shows a row of **tripods** separated by groups of vertical lines on the exterior, looking like the later arrangements of **triglyphs** and **metopes** of the **Doric order** of architecture (see Chapter 7). On the inside of this cup we see processional lines of men wearing swords at their waists and women wearing long checked skirts. The addition of skirts helps to distinguish the gender of the figures more readily, but also creates a disparity between the nude and clothed figures. Some of the figures hold hands as they dance together, separated by figures bearing half-discs thought to be lyres. There are three groupings of men and women on the frieze, and it has been suggested that these are choruses competing against each other as part of a festival, with the tripods on the exterior to be awarded to the victors. The development of non-funerary subject matter on vases that are not exclusively grave goods, but could also have been used in a domestic or other context, reflects the development of a new civic identity during the late Geometric period, with the roles of men and women in the polis defined through ritual performance such as dances (see Langdon 2008).

Up to now we have been looking solely at Attic vases, but Geometric pottery was produced in many regions. Euboea, a large island off the eastern mainland to the north of Athens, was an important area in the Protogeometric period and maintained contact with the Mediterranean world through the Early Iron Age. We shall discuss later some architecture and sculpture from the Euboean

tripod
a bronze or ceramic vessel with a cauldron supported by three legs and having handles on the shoulder. Originally used as cooking vessels, monumental bronze tripods became prizes in competitions and dedications in sanctuaries

triglyph
vertical panel with three vertical bands that stands between metopes in the Doric frieze

metope
a square panel between triglyphs in a Doric frieze that is frequently used for painted or sculpted decoration

Doric order
one of the orders of Greek architecture developed particularly for temples. It features columns with cushion capitals and no bases and a frieze made up of alternating triglyphs and metopes

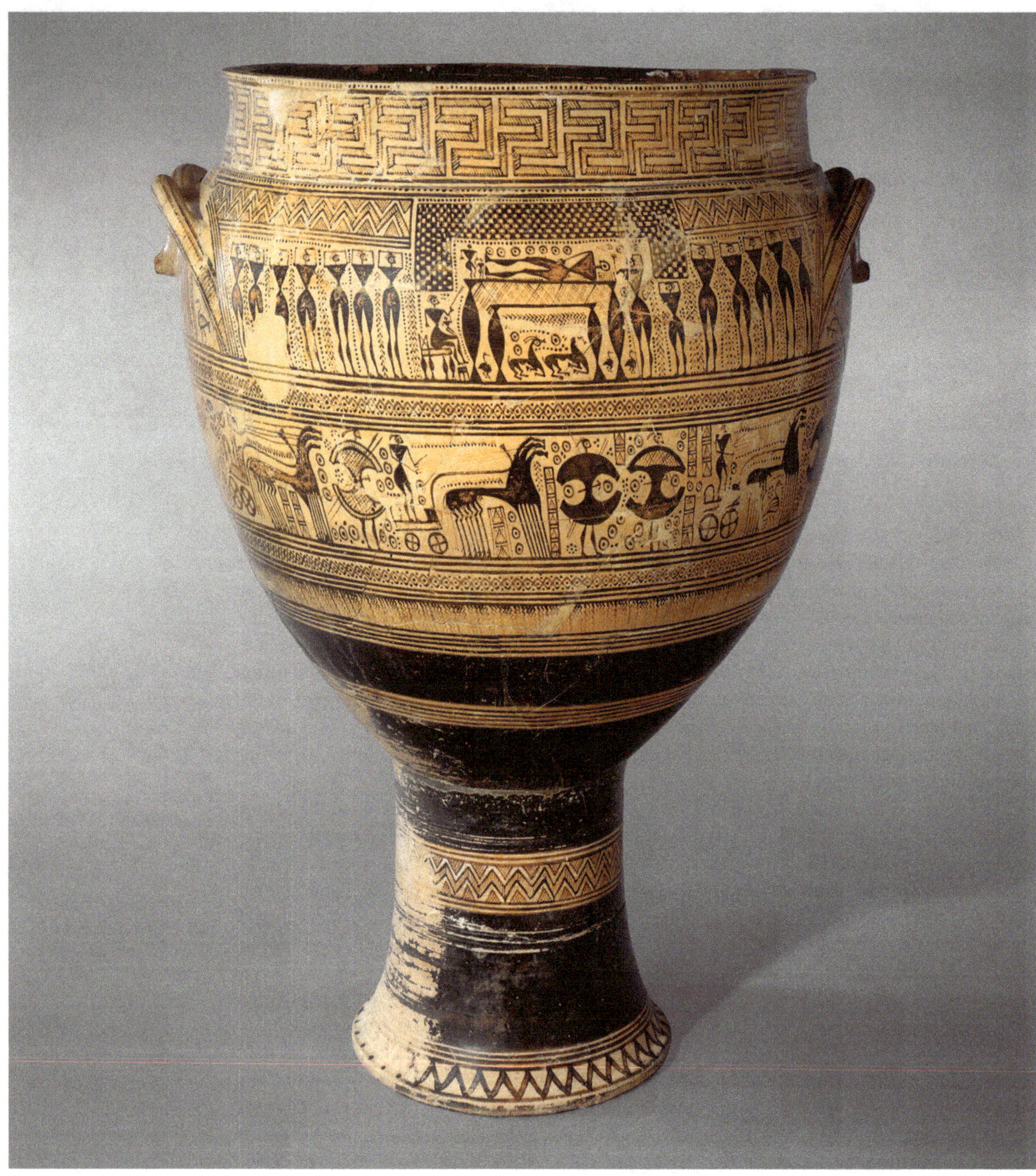

4.9 Late Geometric IB Attic krater from Dipylon cemetery (Kerameikos), *c.* 750–735 BCE. 3 ft 6⅝ in (108.3 cm). Attributed to the Hirschfeld Workshop. New York, Metropolitan Museum of Art, Rogers Fund, 1914, 14.130.14. Prothesis and chariot procession. Image © The Metropolitan Museum of Art. Image source: Art Resource, NY.

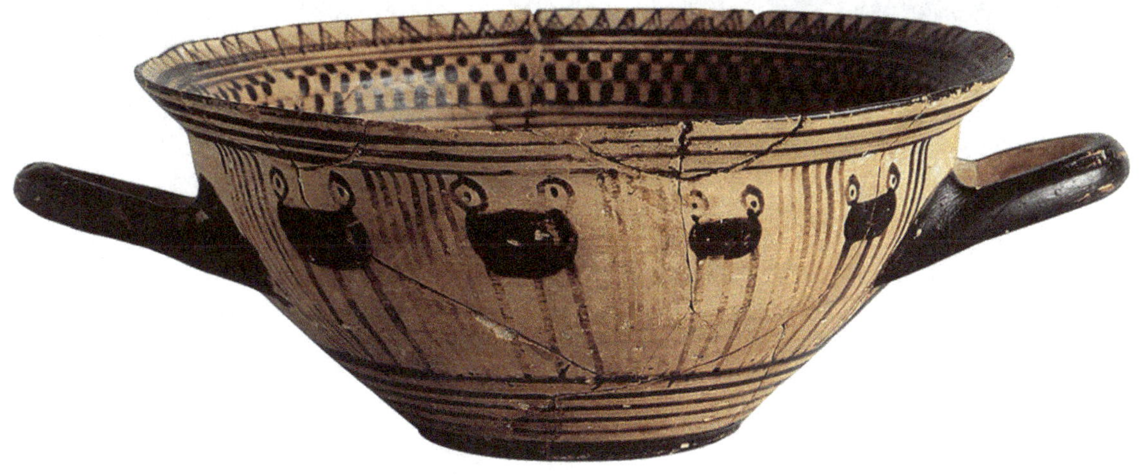

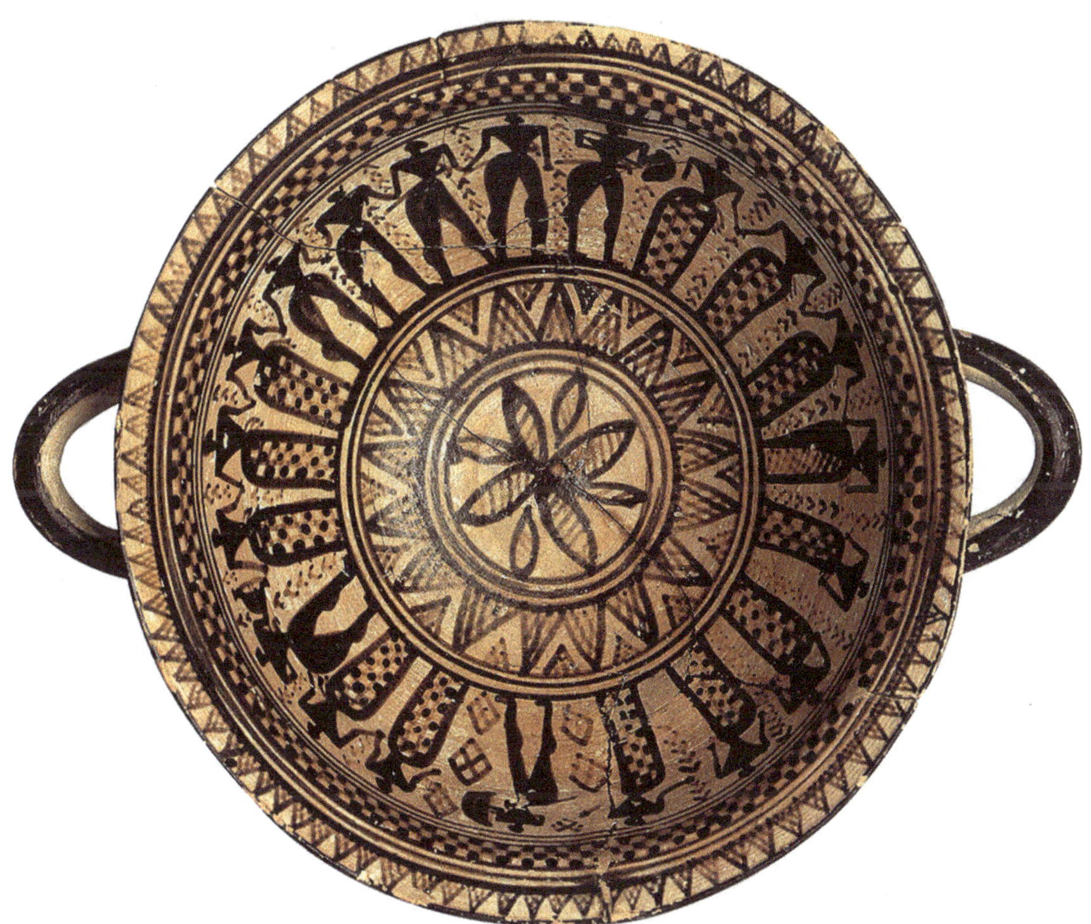

4.10 Late Geometric II Attic skyphos from the Kerameikos, *c.* 735–720 BCE. Diameter 6¹⁹⁄₆₄ in (16 cm). Interior: musician with male and female chorus; exterior: tripods. Athens, National Archaeological Museum 874. Photo: National Archaeological Museum, Athens (Giannis Patrikianos) © Hellenic Ministry of Education and Religious Affairs, Culture and Sports/Archaeological Receipts Fund.

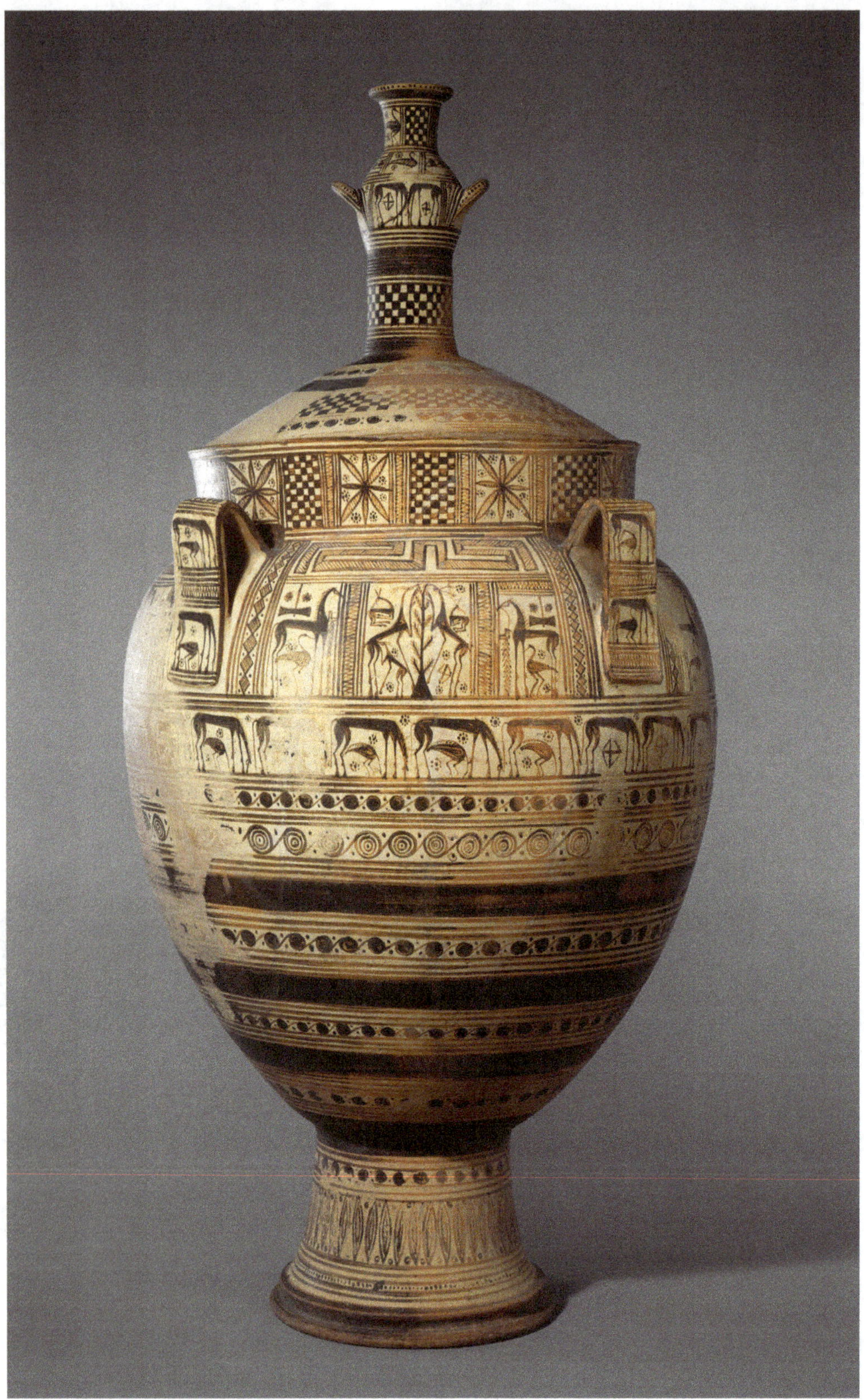

4.11 Late Geometric Euboean lidded krater from Cyprus, *c.* 750–740 BCE. 3 ft 9¼ in (114.9 cm). New York, Metropolitan Museum of Art, Cesnola Collection, purchased by subscription, 74.51.965. Stags flanking sacred tree. Image © The Metropolitan Museum of Art. Image source: Art Resource, NY.

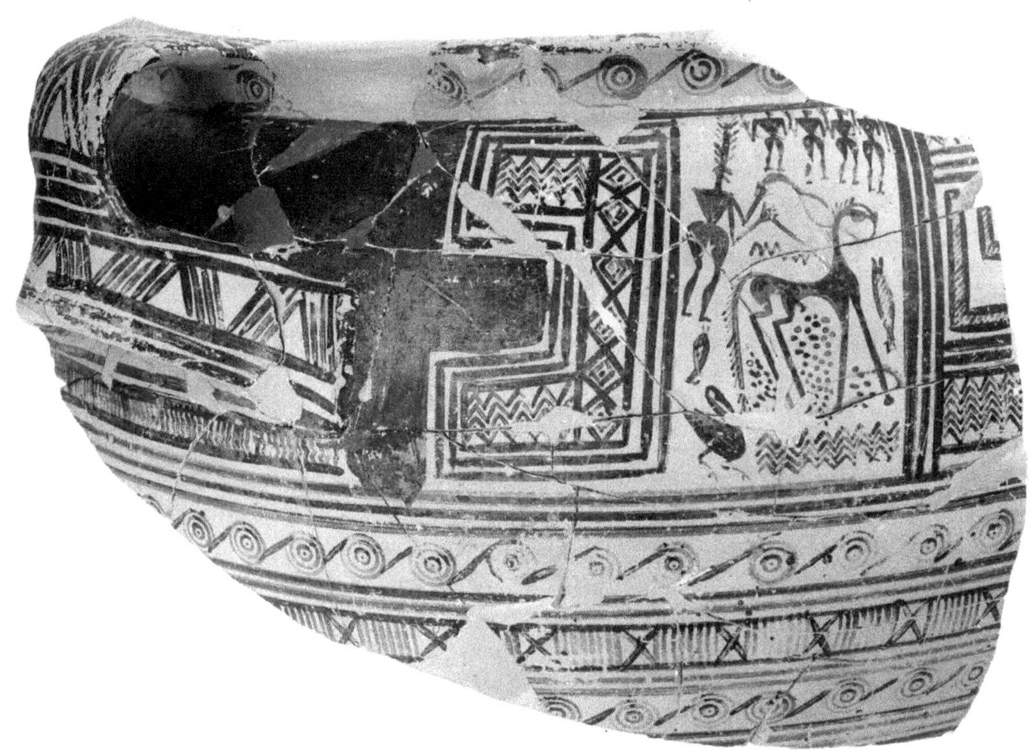

4.12 Late Geometric IB Argive krater fragment from Argos, *c.* 750–740 BCE. 10⅛ in (25.7 cm). Argos, Archaeological Museum C.240. Photo: EfA/E. Sérafis.

site of Lefkandi, but for now will turn to the production of Geometric vases during the middle of the eighth century. Contemporary with the monumental krater from the Dipylon cemetery is a large, lidded krater in the Metropolitan Museum (**Figure 4.11**). Both vases feature the spread of the decorative bands across the whole vase and share several motifs such as meanders, deer, and checked patterns, but the Euboean work is distinctive in its use of running spirals, more complex animal scenes, and a subdivision of friezes into metope panels. The central panel here shows two deer reaching up symmetrically around a thin tree while a young deer suckles. This type of symmetrical, inward-facing heraldic composition was very popular in Near Eastern art in Syria, Phoenicia, Cyprus, and Mesopotamia, where a variety of animals and deities flank a sacred tree (**see Figure 6.8, page 138**). The Euboean picture reflects an awareness of eastern motifs and a willingness to translate them into a Geometric style using familiar animals such as deer. On either side of the central metope are panels with a tethered horse and bird and above them a double axe, a motif that had been common in Minoan art, as on the Hagia Triada sarcophagus (**see Figure 3.2, page 52**) and could possibly reflect that tradition.

The evidence for eastern contact lies not only in the motifs and compositions of the decoration, but also in the fact that this vase was itself found in Kourion, Cyprus, and so is a Euboean export, a repackaging of eastern formulae for an eastern market. Mycenaean potters had exported large vases to Cyprus, as we saw in Chapter 3 (**see Figure 3.13, page 64**), and the resumption of exports to Cyprus reminds us that trade is an exchange of both goods and ideas. Phoenician material and Cypriote pottery have been found at the Euboean site of Eretria, and Euboean pottery has also been found at al-Mina in Syria. We have to consider that Greek artists borrowed, adapted, and exchanged visual ideas within the Mediterranean during the Geometric period.

Turning to the southern section of mainland Greece, the Peloponnesus, we also find the use of human figures on pottery coming from the Argive region, such as the fragment of a krater from Argos from the middle of the eighth century (**Figure 4.12**). While many of the Argive kraters with figural decoration are from graves, like those from Athens, their subject matter is based on religious ritual and horse-taming scenes rather than the funeral rites. In the main panel we see a figure holding reins and a prod over a horse. The multiple zig-zag lines below, the small dots, fish, and water bird combine to signify that the horse is on a beach and being driven into the water to tame it. The elaborate headdress marks the horse tamer as elite, as do his action, scale, and connection to the horse as a status symbol. The importance of the action is further signified by the four figures holding branches in the "background" at the top of the picture. These are thought to be a female chorus performing a ritual dance as part of the taming ceremony. The emphasis upon horse-taming ritual and choral performance, earlier than the subject appeared in Attic pottery, seems to reflect a particularly Argive agenda in the decoration of Geometric pottery.

In looking at these three large vases painted between about 750 and 740 (**Figures 4.9, 4.11, and 4.12**), we can see there is a common style that links the three regions where they were produced, but also differences in motifs, subjects, and purpose of the vases. All are Late Geometric and emphasize decorative bands covering the entire surface of the vase. The Attic vase emphasizes continuous figural friezes wrapped around the vase, the Argive krater makes more use of the metope panel for figural compositions, and the Euboean vase has elements of both. Running spirals are found in the later two, but the drawing of the horses differs. Here, the Euboean and Attic horses are closer to each other in style of drawing, more static, vertical, and streamlined, while the Argive horse is looser, more curvilinear, and given texture with the hairy mane and tail. Sorting out the potential relationships and influences between regional styles is not easy. Certainly there are common stylistic elements that show a shared approach across regions, but the regional differences suggest exchange rather than centrifugal influence, going outward from a single center. For example, the use of figural imagery on Argive funerary vases comes later than its appearance in Attic art, but the appearance of dance scenes on vases is earlier in Argos than in Athens. Each region's vases can be said to serve their own purposes, and when we add to this the connections with Cyprus and the Levant demonstrated in Euboean and other wares, we should see the Late Geometric period as one of ferment, change, and potentially cross-influences among the various centers of production.

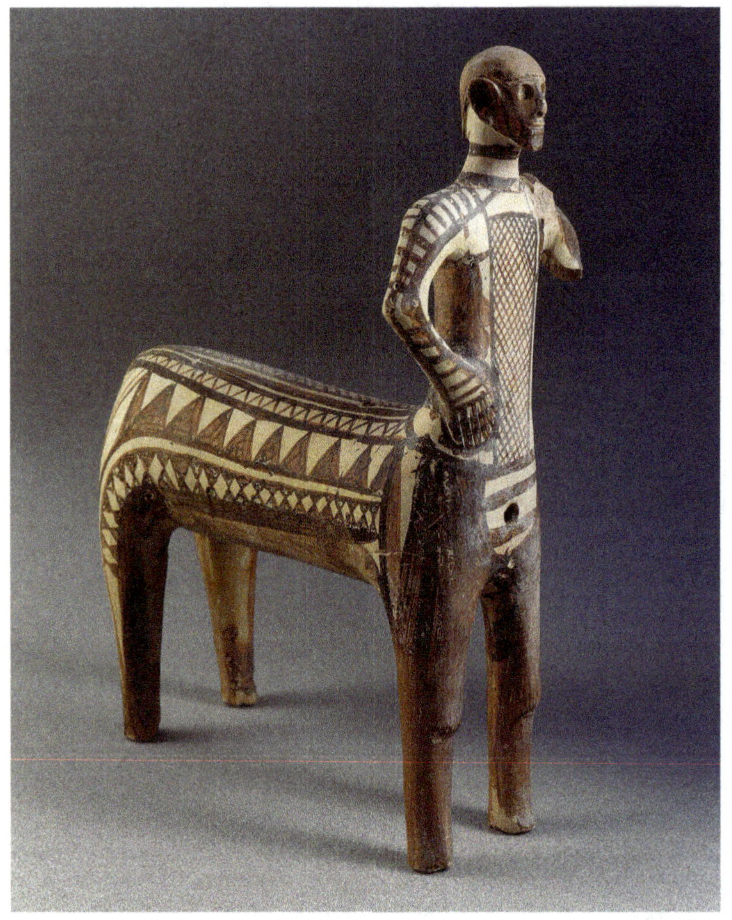

4.13 Terracotta centaur from Lefkandi, end 10th cent. BCE. 14 3/16 in (36 cm). Eretria, Archaeological Museum 8620. Photo: Gianni Dagli Orti/The Art Archive at Art Resource, NY.

SCULPTURE

Small votive statues of animals or humans/gods, made out of terracotta or bronze, are the most common type of sculpture for the Geometric period, but there are a few remarkable figures found in graves to consider first. The Euboean terracotta statue of a centaur from the cemetery at Lefkandi dates to about the year 900 (**Figure 4.13**). The horse body was thrown like a pot and its decoration recalls that of late Protogeometric and Early Geometric pottery, but the centaur is remarkable both for its context and as a figural representation. First, there are individualized features, such as six fingers on the right hand, perhaps a sign of wisdom, and an intentional vertical gash on his left knee that appears to represent a scar. The left arm is broken, but was likely holding something that rested on the shoulder, such as a branch. The hand-modeled torso and head are fully three-dimensional and articulated. The face, in particular, has an appearance of attentiveness, quite unlike the typically unruly character of centaurs in Greek mythology. It has been suggested that this centaur may be Cheiron, the wise centaur who was the tutor of Achilles and Asklepios and was wounded by Herakles, but this is conjectured on the basis of much later, identifiable representations of Cheiron.

The work was found in two pieces, the head in one grave and the body in a nearby grave in the Toumba cemetery at Lefkandi, just west of the remains of the large building discussed below. The head had been deliberately broken off before the burial, and the excavators have suggested that this represents some type of **chthonic** (i.e., concerning the underworld) ritual, and that a centaur at this time represents a guardian or protector for the deceased. Both the centaur and the context are unique, however, and without comparanda from other tombs or representations of centaurs, we cannot be sure of what it meant, only that it was a special type of creation that had particular meaning for the deceased and their family. Why the work was broken into two pieces, what was the relationship of the two deceased in the tombs, and whether the two burials were nearly simultaneous or separated by some time are questions that remain unanswered.

chthonic
related to or belonging to the underworld

polos
a small cylindrical hat worn by women

Whereas the Lefkandi centaur uses a common medium of the Geometric period to create sculpture, a group of five female figures from a Late Geometric tomb in Athens uses an imported material, ivory (**Figure 4.14**). The largest of the five figures is the most detailed and shows a standing woman with both arms at her sides. The body is shaped like a three-dimensional version of the mourners on Late Geometric vases, but the higher waist and longer legs are closer to the mourners on the krater in **Figure 4.9** than the earlier amphora in **Figure 4.8**. Like those women, this one is nude. This representation of female nudity becomes atypical in later Greek art, but in the case of the ivory statue it would not be unusual in sculptures of the Near Eastern goddess Astarte made in Syria or Phoenicia, the likely source of the ivory. The small cylindrical cap, usually called a **polos**, is also a feature of the goddess. Given that the proportions are similar to painted Geometric figures and that there is a meander carved into the polos, it is more likely that the artist was in Athens; whether Greek, Near Eastern, or Greek trained by a Near Eastern sculptor is less clear. The tomb also contained two faience lions that are Egyptian imports, more testimony to some of the cross-cultural currents at this time.

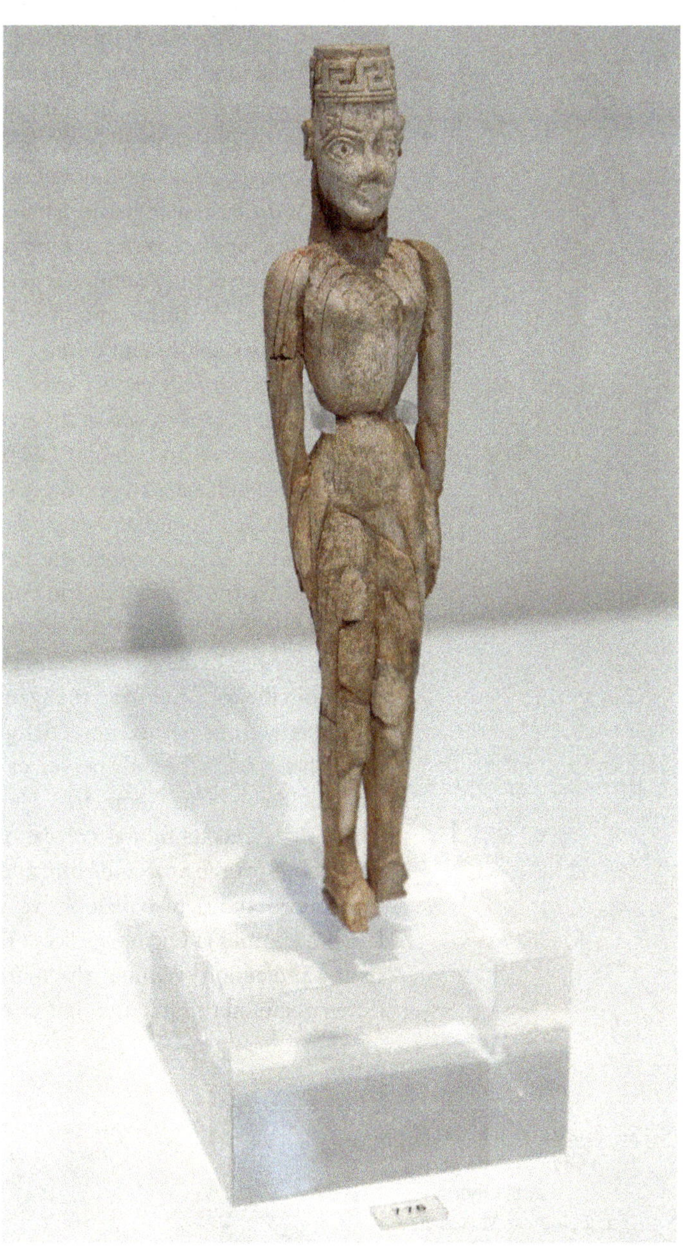

4.14 Ivory figure from Dipylon grave, 750–725 BCE. 9½ in (24 cm). Athens, National Archaeological Museum 776. Photo: © Vanni Archive/Art Resource, NY.

Other works show not only that was there trade in materials and finished work with the eastern Mediterranean, but also that there were foreign artists living and working in Greece during this period. A gold pendant found in a tholos tomb at Tekke, near Knossos in Crete, was part of a deposit of gold buried there when the chamber was appropriated by a Near Eastern family or group of goldsmiths as a storage vault and workshop (**see Figure 11.12, page 281**). We will discuss this work again when considering the relationship of Greek art and culture to the Mediterranean more broadly, but the pendant's techniques, such as the use of filigree and granulation, and the subject matter, including the polos hats on the two heads and the heraldic type of composition, suggest that the goldworkers were from north Syria and came to Crete sometime in the last half of the ninth century, perhaps as a result of the Assyrians subjugating that area, as John Boardman has suggested (Boardman 1967, 66–67).

Most Geometric sculpture is found outside of tombs in sanctuaries. The appearance of dancers and rituals on Late Geometric pottery reminds us that, whereas religion and ritual continued through the Early Iron Age, our evidence for its beliefs and practices is meager. Before 700, there is little evidence of temples as buildings and, before 800, there are relatively small traces of artifacts. Indeed, the ritual of Greek religion, which we shall discuss more in Chapter 7, involved animal sacrifices and offerings to the gods or heroes. One needed a place for burning the sacrificial victim, pouring the libations, and depositing the gifts, but a permanent structure for these rituals was not necessary. Mostly ritual took place out of doors where an altar and fire could be made and people could gather, hence an open space was more important than a structure. Unless a stone altar were built, there is little imperishable material from these acts unless the same spot is used repeatedly and the deposits develop into a tumulus or mound, or buildings are created to support the ritual or store the gifts.

This is the case at Olympia, where the second-century CE writer Pausanias (Paus. 5.13.8–11) tells us that the altar of Zeus at that sanctuary was 22 feet (6.7 m) high and made up of the ashes from the burning of the sacrificial animals. There are differing foundation accounts by Pausanias (Paus. 5.7.10 and 5.8.2) and the fifth-century BCE poet Pindar (*Ol.* 1.67–88, 6.67–69, 10.24–25 and 57–59) that attribute the establishment of the cult at Olympia to Herakles honoring Zeus and Pelops, to Pelops honoring Zeus for his victory over king Oinomaos, or to Zeus honoring his victory over his father Kronos. Recent excavations in the area of the Pelopeion at Olympia have found terracotta and bronze figures of humans and animals, as well as pottery that can be dated back into the tenth century, showing that cult activity here dates from at least the Protogeometric period. The games at Olympia, too, have various foundation legends, but the custom of using the numbering of the Olympiads as a means for marking a chronological event or period in Greek history allows us to work backward to arrive at a traditional foundation date for the first Olympiad in 776 BCE. Whether or not there was such a specific or single founding, the excavations at Olympia have revealed an increase in the number of offerings in the eighth century that corroborates the early importance of the site to Greeks not only from the area, but from many other regions of Greece as well.

The terracotta figures from Olympia are fairly simple and consist primarily of animals, including bulls, sheep, and especially horses, as well as human figures of charioteers, warriors, men, and some women, like the Late Geometric "Hera"-type discussed in the first chapter **(see Figure 1.3, page 7)**. The early terracotta figures consist of very simplified and flattened shapes for the torso and limbs, projections for the nose and chin, and circular indentations to mark the eyes, nipples, and belly button. Indeed, the Hera-type looks very similar in form and detail to the "Zeus"-type figure found in larger quantities at Olympia, except that the genitals on the Hera-type are marked with a line rather than a projection. Without the marking of the genitals on these figures, they would be hard to differentiate, not unlike the figures on contemporary LG IA Attic funerary vases, where we often

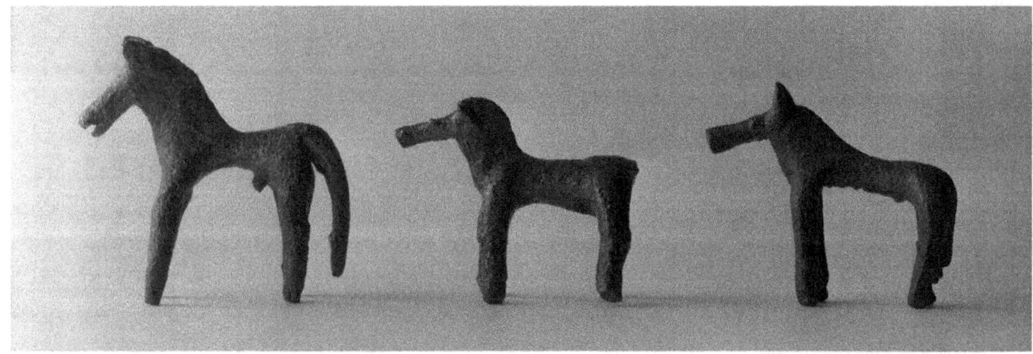

4.15 Bronze votive horses from Olympia, 8th cent. BCE. Olympia, Archaeological Museum. B5353/B6167/B1314. Height of left horse: 2⁷⁄₁₆ in (6.2 cm). Photo: Gösta Hellner. D-DAI-ATH-Olympia-Neg. 7295.

distinguish gender on the basis of action rather than anatomy. Both Hera- and Zeus-types also look quite different from the terracotta figures of the late Mycenaean period **(see Figure 3.14, page 64)**.

Many of the eighth-century votive figures are made out of bronze rather than terracotta, and include bulls and horses as common subjects **(Figure 4.15)**. These figures are very clay-like in their form: tubes with swellings, pinches, and bends to define the body parts and small appendages for ears, horns, and tails. These figures are solid-cast bronze pieces, and this early work in bronze shows the influence of working with clay and wax in making the models and molds for casting. In spite of the differences in media, we can readily see a similarity between the votive terracotta and bronze sculptures and the animals and humans in contemporary vase painting.

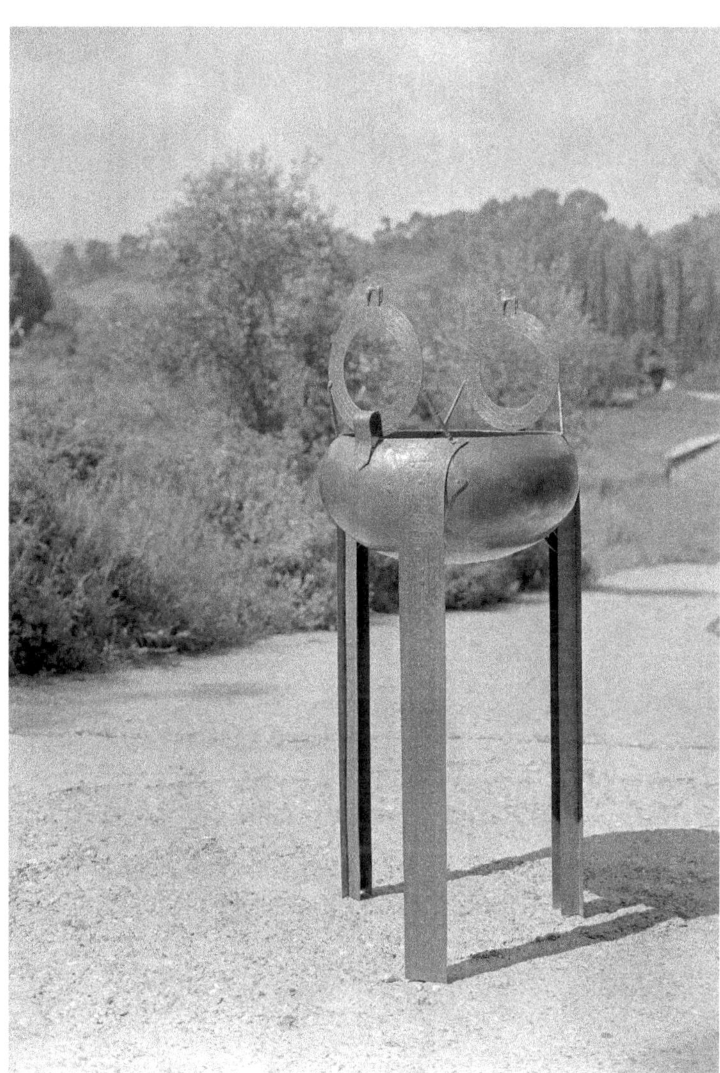

4.16 Tripod reconstruction from Olympia. After M. Maass, *Die geometrischen Dreifüsse von Olympia*, Olympische Forchungen 10 (Berlin: Walter de Gruyter, 1978), no. zu201. Photo: Gösta Hellner, D-DAI-ATH-Neg. 1973/1458.

The rapid increase in the use of bronze figures as votive offerings in the eighth century is interesting in reflecting some of the changing social purposes of art during the Late Geometric period. We have already noted that the amount of metal as grave goods declines in the eighth century, and even the creation of monumental vases as grave markers does not continue beyond the Late Geometric I period. If these earlier uses of art in burials were to distinguish their elite patrons, then the growth in offerings, especially in the second half of the eighth century, suggests a new avenue for their patronage in sanctuaries rather than cemeteries. These small votives were relatively expensive items to acquire and then give away, but the ever accumulating deposits showed the social and religious importance of the gifts. Many were made by metalworkers at the site and sold to visitors to the sanctuary, but some may also have been brought to the site by visitors. Since the patrons were from all over Greece, this shared act of acquiring and giving these small bronzes helped to create a visual culture that was Panhellenic, forming bridges across regions and a shared social structure, particularly one that emphasized the elite as a class.

The second major type of bronze artifact found at Olympia is the tripod. Originally a three-legged cooking pot that could be set over a fire, the bronze tripod became an elite and monumental prize in contests and a gift to sanctuaries. The reconstruction of a late eighth-century tripod **(Figure 4.16)** shows the legs made out of sheets of metal that join to a bowl made of a hammered sheet of bronze. Ring handles are a practical legacy of its cooking function, but now these have been made into thin disks with cast and engraved patterns on them. Solid-cast figures further decorate the handles, including horses and human figures, usually in pairs holding the sides of the ring. One such handle support is a nude warrior wearing a crested helmet **(Figure 4.17)**. The warrior is quite similar in its proportions and abstraction to figures in contemporary vase painting or the ivory woman from Athens **(Figure 4.14, page 85)**.

In the *Iliad*, a tripod is the top prize for the chariot race at the funeral games of Patroklos (23.698–702), and we should consider that the combination of form, size, and material made this an important and expensive work of art, one that was likely commissioned and brought to Olympia rather than

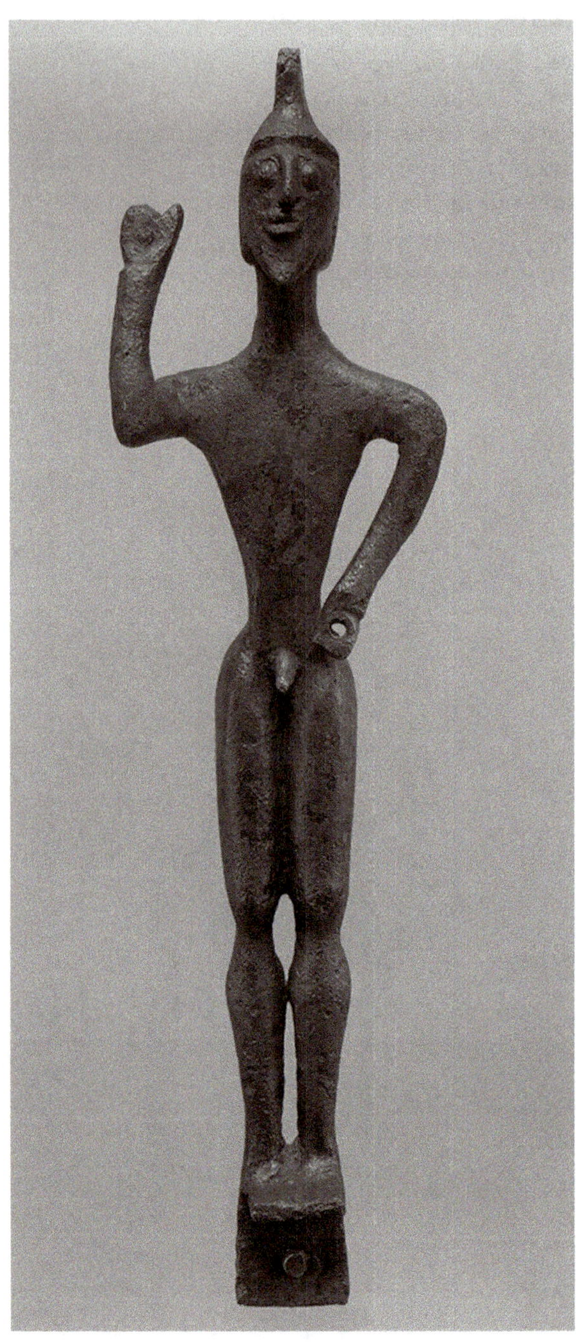

4.17 Bronze warrior from a tripod handle at Olympia, 8th cent. BCE. 9³⁄₁₆ in (23.3 cm). Olympia, Archaeological Museum B5600. Photo: Gösta Hellner. D-DAI-ATH-Olympia-Neg. 5816. All rights reserved.

ethos
Greek word meaning character

purchased there. On a leg from a tripod made in Crete and dedicated at Olympia near the end of the eighth century, we see action scenes like those in Late Geometric II vase painting (**Figure 4.18**). The surface of the leg is divided vertically into metope panels, with two helmeted warriors fighting over a tripod in the upper panel and two "lions" fighting each other below. The warriors are identical in form, leaving the viewer to wonder if this is meant to be a prototypical scene of competition and struggle, perhaps symbolizing the competitions that the tripod celebrated, or is this an early effort to represent a mythological story, such as the struggle of Apollo and Herakles over the Delphic tripod? Since the warriors are nearly identical, a mythological interpretation is probably less likely since we cannot determine who is the god and who is the hero. We should certainly see the predators fighting below like a Homeric simile, in which the poet compares a warrior's prowess and actions to an animal like a lion. Perhaps we should think of the warriors, too, as a simile for the donor of the tripod, perhaps given in honor of a victory at Olympia.

We should note that these bronze warriors are nude, and briefly consider nudity more broadly as a recurring feature of Greek art. Clearly, real warriors did not fight nude, but the nude warriors of Geometric art begin a long tradition of heroic nudity in art in which gods and heroes are shown fighting and otherwise interacting in the nude. The question of nudity is more complex than simply a reference to heroes and myths, however, in that the Greeks did actually compete athletically in the nude. According to one tradition, a runner lost his loincloth in an early footrace at Olympia but won, starting a new custom. The nudity in art, however, is earlier than this, and is further complicated by considerations of gender. While early terracotta figures distinguished male and female by indicating the genitals, the earliest painted human figures did not have any signals of gender: no genitals, no breasts, and no clothing. The mourners on the Dipylon amphora must include women, but there is no sign of their sex, and only the gender association of their action. The proportions of the figures in the earliest figural representations are the same for men and women, whether terracotta or painted figures.

It is not until the last half-century of the Geometric period when we begin to see a more systematic distinction of nude versus clothed figures, as on the LG II Attic skyphos we saw earlier (**see Figure 4.10, page 81**). We should, then, consider the question of nudity and clothing as reflecting a differentiation of gender roles in the emerging polis. Men fight and compete in athletics; nudity emphasizes their physical action even in the silhouette style of the Geometric period. That many of the men wear helmets while nude emphasizes their role as warriors, and the popularity of nude warriors at Olympia emphasizes the importance of athletics as part of a warrior *ethos*. Women's roles, at least in Geometric art, are more limited to ritual, either dancing or singing in public performances, or as mourners. We will consider gender in Greek art further in Chapter 13, but we should note its early, if still inconsistent, differentiation here in the Late Geometric period.

The developing interest in action and the recurring debate as to whether some Geometric scenes are mythological or not can be found in a bronze group showing a nude warrior confronting a centaur (**Figure 4.19**). The arms of the two figures interlock with one another, but the right forearm of the man is broken off and the point of a spear protrudes from the left side of the centaur's torso, surely showing the man has struck the centaur with his weapon. The man wears a conical hat but is otherwise nude, like the warrior from the tripod handle. The front part of the centaur is virtually a replica of the hero, including the hat, but at a smaller scale; the hind quarters of a Geometric horse stick out from his back to make him a centaur. Furthermore, the centaur has human rather than horse genitalia and can be seen not so much as a truly hybrid creature as a pastiche. Of course, the artist is free to imagine a centaur in any number of ways, and this is not the only centaur to be so configured with a human front half in Greek art, so its identity, like the Lefkandi centaur, remains a mystery.

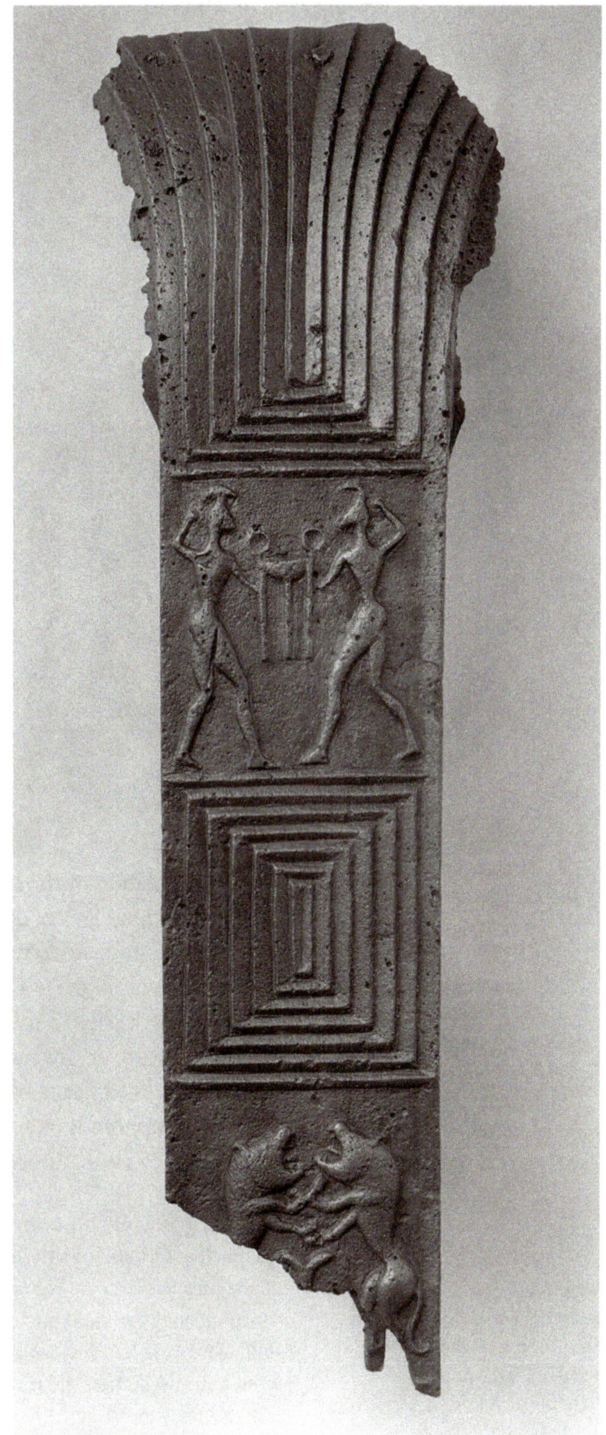

4.18 Cretan bronze tripod leg from Olympia, end 8th cent. BCE. 18⁵⁄₁₆ in (46.5 cm). Olympia, Archaeological Museum B1730. Photo: Hermann Wagner. D-DAI-ATH-Olympia-Neg. 2032.

ARCHITECTURE

Our knowledge of Geometric architecture is very limited. Most of the building material was perishable: wood, mud brick, and thatch. Furthermore, places with long histories of settlement such as Athens have seen most of the earliest levels obliterated in the rebuilding and developments over many centuries. Later buildings constructed out of stone, for example, needed large foundations for support, and the builders dug through the layers beneath the ground, destroying much of what was there. Given the general impoverishment and lack of monumental work in the Protogeometric period, the discovery of a large, tenth-century building in the Toumba cemetery at Lefkandi came as a surprise. The building, shown in reconstruction **(Figure 4.20)**, was more than 50 meters long and had a porch on the east end and a rounded apse on the opposite western end, much of it missing. The walls were made of mud brick with timber that rested on a large socle of roughly worked stones about 1 meter high. Wooden columns ran down the center of the building, and columns lined the exterior wall supporting the eaves of the roof. A timber roof frame supported a steep thatch roof. The floors and walls were at least partially finished with plaster, but there was not much sign of wear from long habitation.

The building was divided into three main sections. A porch led into a square room at the east end. Beyond that was a large rectangular room about 22 meters long in the center of the structure. Beyond that was a passageway with two small rooms that led into the apse, that likely served for storage. In almost the center of the building were two shafts cut into the floor of the central room, one holding the remains of four horses along with bronze and iron objects. The second shaft contained two burials. One was a cremation burial of a man, with the ashes placed in a bronze amphora from Cyprus dating to the late thirteenth or twelfth century BCE and a sword and spear placed next to it. The other was a female inhumation burial, with elaborate jewelry and disks placed over the breasts of the woman and other offerings such as an iron knife with ivory handle placed around her. Both tombs date to about the middle of the tenth century. This means that the bronze cinerary amphora was about 200 years old at the time it was used for the burial, and so rare both by

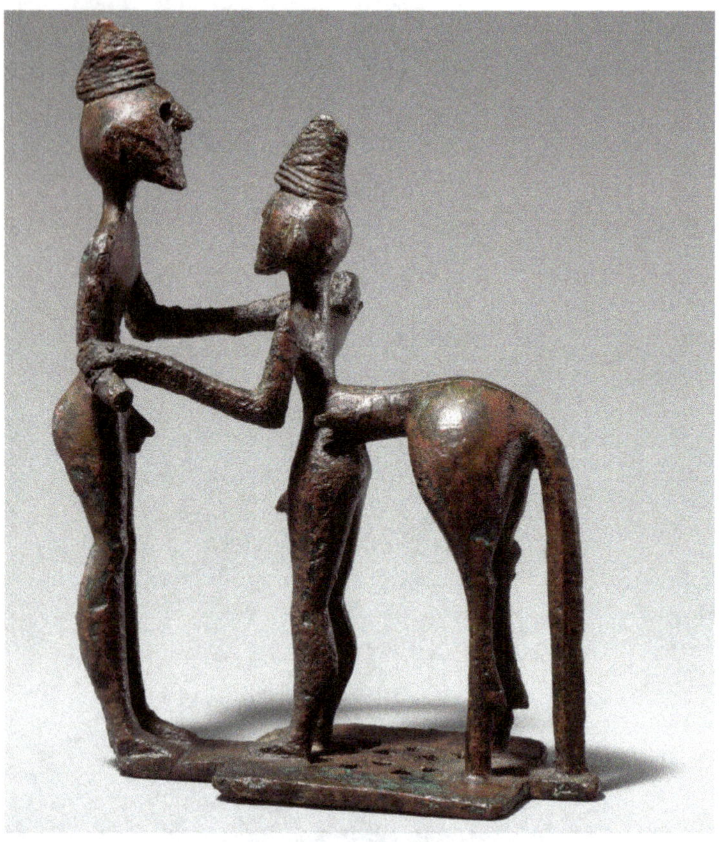

4.19 Bronze group of man and centaur, mid-8th cent. BCE. 4⅜ in (11.1 cm). New York, Metropolitan Museum of Art, Gift of J. Pierpoint Morgan, 17.190.2072. Image copyright © The Metropolitan Museum of Art. Image source: Art Resource, NY.

age, material, and origin. Above the graves was set a contemporary ceramic krater made by a Euboean potter.

The relationship of the pair of tombs to the building is uncertain from the excavation. The building is unusual in that it was deliberately demolished not long after the burials to create a mound over the tombs. One theory is that the building was built over the tombs, perhaps as a **heroön** or hero shrine, although there is no evidence of later cult activity associated with the building. The second theory is that the structure was a residence that had been built for the deceased, who were buried under its floor, and the building was then demolished and made into a tumulus. If so, the building had not been used for long and might have been unfinished at the time of the burials. Whichever theory is correct, the building is certainly monumental in scale, easily seven times the size of a typical house such as those at Zagora that we will discuss below. The grave goods are extraordinary, and whether a house or tomb, the grand scale and large central room recall the megaron of the Mycenaean palaces. Whether the man buried beneath the floor fashioned himself as a king or "big man," the monumentality of the buildings sets up a contrast to the scale of later Geometric architecture.

After the creation of the tumulus, the site then became the focal point of a large cemetery to the east of the building. Two of the earliest graves there, dating around 900, contained the head and body of the centaur discussed earlier **(see Figure 4.13, page 84)**. Many other elaborate grave goods, including contemporary imported work from the Near East, were found in the cemetery.

Was the man buried in the building/tumulus regarded as a hero of the community and the subject of a cult afterward, or was he perhaps the ruler and founder of a ruling family whose members were later buried in the adjacent cemetery? The cremation of the man's body and placement of his ashes in a bronze amphora look forward to the cremation of Patroklos described over a century later in *Iliad* 23.250–257 (tr. Lattimore 1951, 457):

heroön
a shrine dedicated to a hero, frequently a Bronze Age tomb in later periods

> First with gleaming wine they put out the pyre that was burning,
> as much as was still aflame, and the ashes dropped deep from it.
> Then they gathered up the white bones of their gentle companion,
> weeping, and put them into a golden jar with a double
> fold of fat, and laid it away in his shelter, and covered it
> with a thin veil; then laid out the tomb and cast down the holding walls
> around the funeral pyre, then heaped the loose earth over them
> and piled the tomb, and turned to go away.

For now, we have to recognize that the circumstances at Lefkandi are highly unusual and difficult to interpret with certainty, except to say that the scale and extravagance of the building and its contents, as well as its demolition, signify the importance of the deceased to the community, both at the time of death and afterward.

While the Lefkandi building was atypical, we have a few surviving examples of town architecture during the Geometric period that tell us about more ordinary villages and houses. Excavations at Zagora on the island of Andros have revealed a town that was built in two phases on the top of a hill

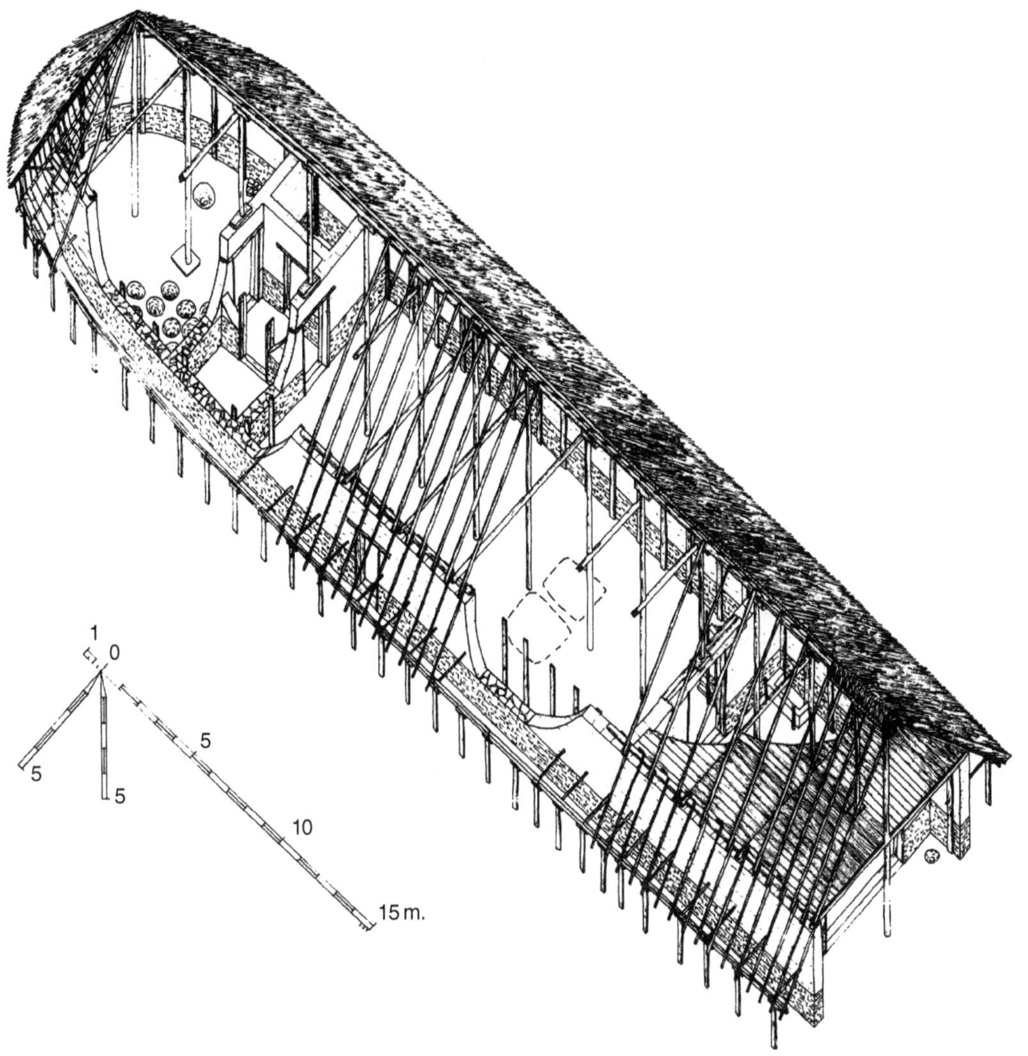

4.20 Reconstruction of the House at Lefkandi, 1000–950 BCE. After M. R. Popham, P. G. Calligas, L. H. Sackett, J. Coulton, and H. W. Catling, *Lefkandi II: The Protogeometric Building at Toumba. Part 2: The Excavation, Architecture and Finds*, British School at Athens. Supplementary Volumes, 23 (Athens, 1993), pl. 28. Reproduced with permission of the British School at Athens.

overlooking the sea, well suited for defense but without a water supply within the perimeter walls **(Figure 4.21)**. The first phase of the town was built in the middle of the eighth century (*c.* 775–725) and consisted of one-room houses with a porch or pronaos in front of them, clustered in rows facing outward in the same direction **(Figure 4.22, top)**. The rooms are modest in size, about 6–7 meters wide and 7–8 meters deep. Many of the rooms served as both living and storage areas, the latter consisting of stone benches with circular openings that could hold large terracotta storage pithoi or jars. The houses underwent extensive remodeling between 725 and 700, after which the town was abandoned. In this second phase, additional rooms were built and interior courtyards were formed for each house, separating living from storage areas **(Figure 4.22, bottom)**. This created a series of houses, each of which had a central focus on the courtyard. While it created more functional space for the inhabitants and their activity and storage needs, the new plan also served to isolate each house from activities in the others.

pronaos
an open porch on the end or side of a building leading to the naos, the interior room

This scheme of rooms arranged around a central court would become the predominant house type in Greek architecture, as we will see in several examples in the next chapter. The development of this dense clustering of independent but similar houses has been linked to the development of the social structure of the polis. Rather than a town dominated by elite individuals who ruled on the basis of their personal and family connections and lived in palatial structures, power in the polis was invested in institutions and laws emphasizing corporate oversight and communal participation, with the citizens

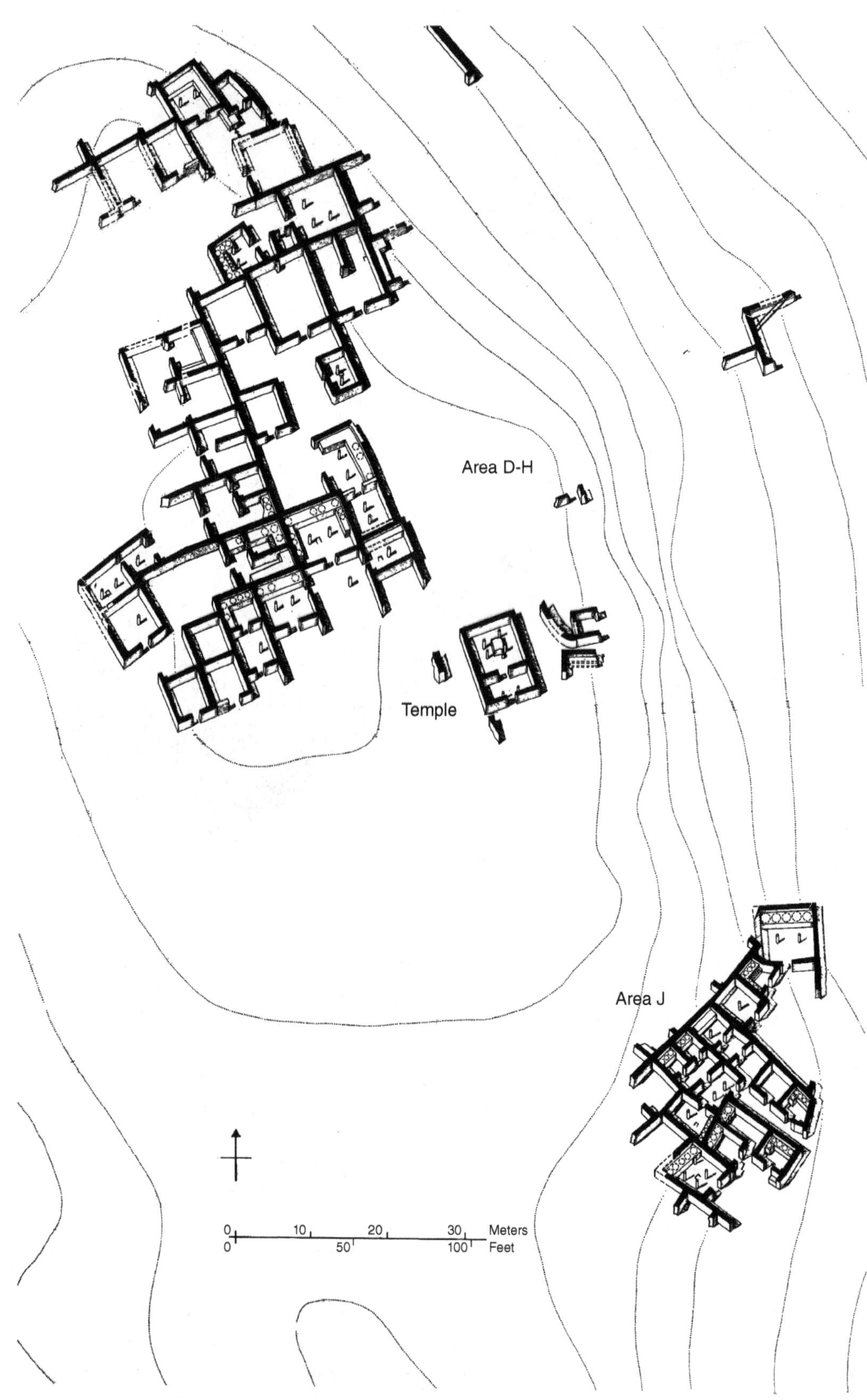

4.21 Plan of the town of Zagora, Andros, 8th cent. BCE. Drawing by J. J. Coulton, reproduced by permission from A. Cambitoglou, *Archaeological Museum of Andros* (Athens, 1981), fig. 4.

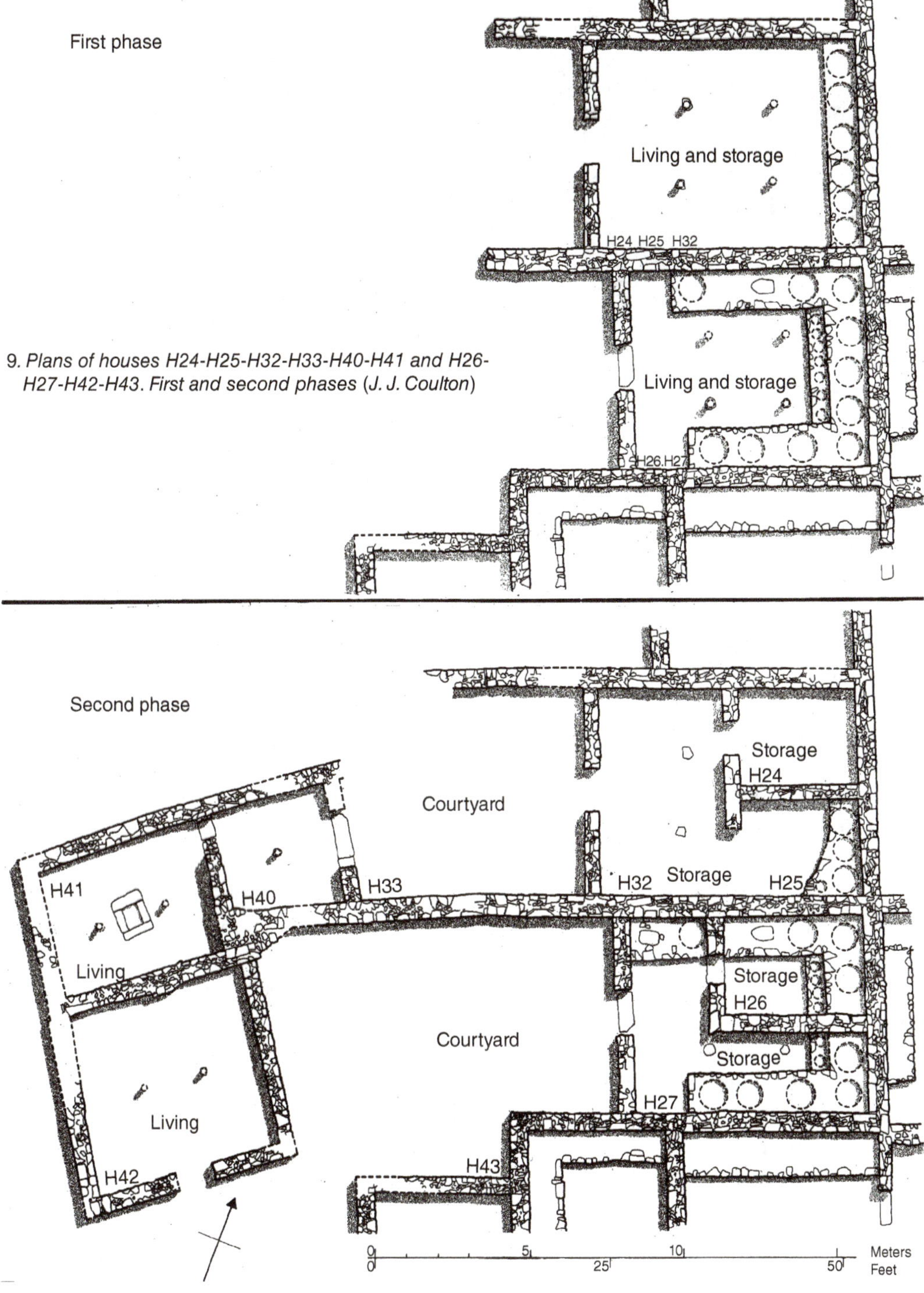

4.22 Plan of houses in Area H of Zagora, Andros. Top: Phase 1, before 725 BCE; bottom: Phase 2: 725–700 BCE. Drawing by J. J. Coulton, reproduced by permission from A. Cambitoglou, *Archaeological Museum of Andros* (Athens, 1981), fig. 9.

being roughly equivalent before the law (***isonomia***). Citizenship was limited to freeborn men, excluding women, immigrants, and slaves, although each of these groups had some legal status and protections. The houses of citizens in classical Greece were inwardly focused, autonomous units without great distinction in terms of size or exterior decoration. The housing at Zagora has some of these same features, built at the same time that we see emerging signs of the polis in the *Iliad* and other sources.

As the remains of vase painting, sculpture, and architecture suggest, the long centuries of the Protogeometric and Geometric periods witness the beginnings of the development of the polis in place of the Bronze Age palace as the basic structure of society. While the elite continuously find

isonomia
Greek term designating the equality before the law of citizens

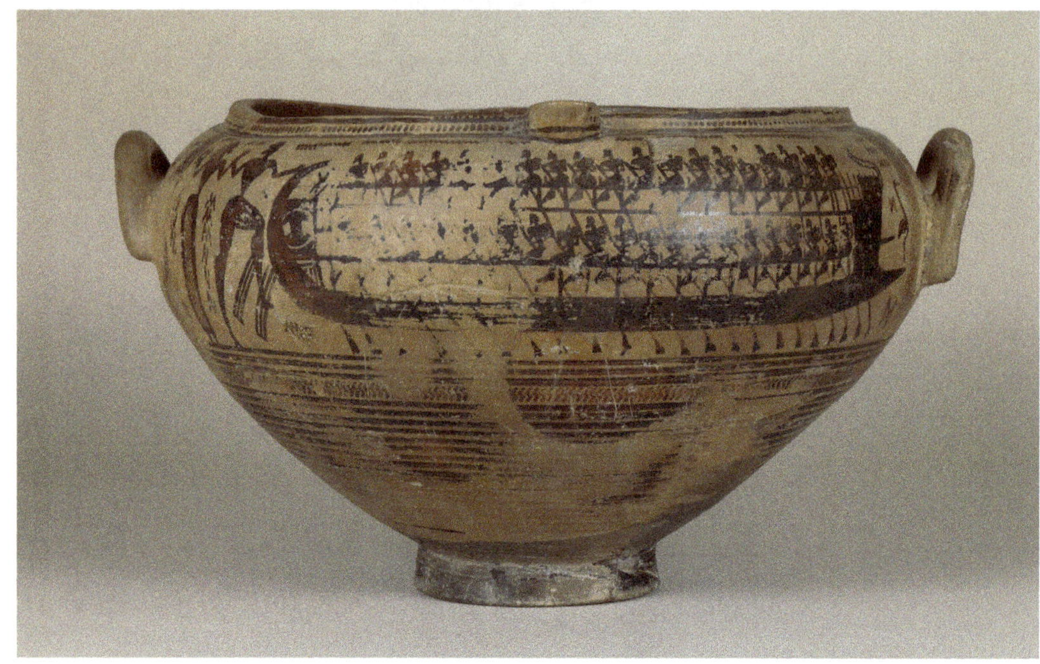

4.23 Late Geometric Attic spouted bowl or louterion, possibly from Thebes, c. 730–720 BCE. 12 in (30.5 cm). London, British Museum 1899,0219.1. Man and woman boarding a ship. Photo: © The Trustees of the British Museum.

ways of distinguishing themselves, at first through elaborate grave goods, followed by grave markers and then their dedications in sanctuaries, the artistic developments that they patronized gradually became more diffuse and common. In the latter half of the eighth century new scenes emerge that reflect the emerging collective identity of the polis and the important activities of the lives of its members. One final example shows both how Geometric art could express the events and identity of its users and how the abstract and silhouette forms and their formulaic composition were limited in their ability to develop new meanings.

louterion
a basin made of metal or clay used to heat water for a bath or ritual purification

A large bowl in the British Museum that is thought to have been found in Thebes is a product of an Attic workshop around the year 730 (**Figure 4.23**). The bowl is a special shape, a **louterion**, associated with heating water for washing, and so would be appropriate for a ritual like the washing of a bride, corpse, or guest. The decoration on the shoulders of the vase includes some of the largest figures painted in the Geometric period. A large ship with two lines of rowers in a combination of profile and bird's-eye type of view takes up most of the panel between the handles, while two very large figures, a man and woman, stand before a ramp at the ship's stern, preparing to board it. He is nude and grabs hold of her by the wrist, leading her to the ship. She holds up a wreath in her hand and wears a dress.

The question that has puzzled scholars is whether this is one of the abductions found in Greek myth, such as when Theseus abducts Helen before her marriage to Menelaos, or Paris takes Helen to Troy after her marriage? Is it Theseus taking Ariadne, whose "crown of light" helped him to slay the Minotaur? No story quite fits the image and it has been viewed consequently as a generic abduction/marriage scene, equivalent to later marriage scenes in which the bridegroom leads the bride by the wrist from her home to his (**see Figure 13.4, page 326** for the procession part).

More recently, Susan Langdon has proposed that this bowl might have been commissioned for an Athenian bride who was marrying a man from outside Athens, perhaps Thebes, and so the pot, which would be appropriate for use in the ceremonial washing of the bride, would be an idealized representation and marker of the actual wedding (Langdon 2008, 19–32). The atypical subject matter would suggest that the work was a special commission, and would proclaim the status of both bride and groom on the occasion. The artistic difficulty is that the specific meaning, whether mythological or social, created by its commissioning and use is lost once there is no one left to remember and explain the story and circumstances to a viewer.

Indeed, while the style of Geometric art allows artist, patron, and viewer to express some ideas, the lack of detail severely limits the ability of the images to be very specific and connected to individuals, stories, and events. A tripod certainly represents a substantial gift and shows one's status, but it does not preserve one's name and deeds very well for later generations. Writing, also a late Geometric development in Greece, helped to record possession and donation, and there are a few examples of inscriptions on Geometric objects that record their ownership and purpose. Indeed, an early seventh-century bronze figure of a man (**see Figure 7.19, page 176**), who still shows many of the features of the Late Geometric style, has an inscription on his legs that reads "Mantiklos dedicated me as a tithe to Apollo of the silver bow; do you, Phoibos, give some pleasing favor in return." We do not know who Mantiklos was, or even whether the figure is meant to be Apollo or an idealized man, but we at least know and remember Mantiklos's existence and offering. Such inscriptions were made on the objects after they were produced, and in effect demonstrate that patrons were aware of the limitation of Geometric art to communicate effectively and permanently simply through image or subject matter. New techniques, materials, and style in the next century would expand the range and accessibility of Greek art considerably, as we shall see in Chapter 6.

archaios
Greek word for old, used to denote something old in style, such as art of the seventh and sixth centuries, hence the archaic period

TEXTBOX: WHAT IS IN A NAME?

We have seen two different terms used to designate the centuries covered in this chapter, the Dark Ages and the Early Iron Age, and the differences in connotation give us a chance to consider the usefulness and limitations of names for such broad stretches of time throughout this book. "Dark Ages" captures the scaling back that follows the destruction of the palaces and the loss of Linear B and monumental art. The same term is used for the period after the fall of the Roman empire and for other similar episodes in history. But as we have seen, it was not a cultural wasteland and we could argue that any era that developed the idea of the polis and saw the composition of the *Iliad* was not dark. The "Early Iron Age" has the advantage of recognizing a new technology, but is this the most important feature of the period? Geometric might also be a descriptive label, but none of these terms is as evocative or useful as Palatial to signify the period.

The problem is not just limited to the periods discussed so far. The next 700 years of Greek art are divided into three phases: archaic, classical, and Hellenistic, and there have been efforts to divide each of these into three phases of early, middle, and late as in the Bronze Age. Archaic derives from the Greek word **archaios**, meaning old, and is a term that Greek writers used generally to describe things that dated before the fifth century BCE. Classical, however, derives from the Latin adjective *classicus*, which signified a division of the Roman people into groups according to wealth and family in order to prepare for military action, hence to classify the population. By extension, *classicus* came to signify a group that was authoritative and excellent, set apart from the common. As an historical term, then, our adjective "classical" has served to distinguish the cultures of ancient Greece and Rome from others, such as early medieval Europe, which was once considered a "dark" age by comparison with the "classical" age. In this sense, it is also a qualitative term, making a judgment about the value of something classical. It has a narrower but similarly double meaning when used for Greek art, distinguishing "classical" Greek art from the earlier, more "primitive" archaic and the later, more "excessive" Hellenistic periods, establishing the classical as a high point of artistic achievement. For the Greeks of the fifth and fourth centuries, however, classical art was contemporary art and its lack of a uniform and constant style suggests that it did not articulate a standard that was meant to be followed to the exclusion of newer and more expressive styles.

Even within a period, there can be nomenclature problems. "Late archaic" has been typically applied to art of *c.* 530–480 BCE. By itself, the label does not have an evaluative significance, but when it follows "high archaic" or "ripe archaic," two names frequently found in the literature rather than "middle archaic," then "late" cannot but mean an abandonment of the principles or achievements of the preceding period. The same applies in the classical period, when the period of the Parthenon is termed the "high classical" and all that follows is "late classical." Indeed, that short period is a "classic moment" or, in the words of one witness before the Select Committee of the British Parliament that was considering the purchase of the Parthenon marbles, "so high a point of perfection." The use of high archaic or high classical also means that the "early" period is still developmental and not fully formed, which might have surprised its practitioners.

Some terms, such as Daedalic in Chapter 6, have continued in use in spite of their difficulties. Indeed, one problem with changing terminology or labels that have been used for decades is that it disrupts continuity in communication. In some ways, terms can be artifacts that reflect an older way of thinking while simultaneously referring to newer understandings. Any label will have the baggage of the framework that coined it, and that is something to consider whenever using terms for any period.

REFERENCES

Blegen, C. W. 1952. "Two Athenian Grave Groups of about 900 B.C." *Hesperia* 21, 279–294.

Boardman, J. 1967. "The Khaniale Tekke Tombs, II." *Annual of the British School at Athens* 62, 57–75.

Homer, *Iliad*. 1951. *The Iliad of Homer*, tr. R. Lattimore. Chicago: University of Chicago Press.

Langdon, S. 2008. *Art and Identity in Dark Age Greece, 1100–700 B.C.E.* Cambridge/New York: Cambridge University Press.

Liston, M. A. and J. K. Papadopoulos. 2004. "The 'Rich Athenian Lady' Was Pregnant: The Anthropology of a Geometric Tomb Reconsidered." *Hesperia* 73, 7–38.

Stansbury-O'Donnell, M. D. 1995. "Reading Pictorial Narrative: The Law Court Scene of the Shield of Achilles." In J. B. Carter and S. P. Morris, eds. *The Ages of Homer: A Tribute to Emily Vermeule*. Austin: University of Texas Press, 315–334.

Whitley, J. 1991. *Style and Society in Dark Age Greece: The Changing Face of a Pre-Literate Society 1100–700 BC.* Cambridge: Cambridge University Press.

FURTHER READING

Hurwit, J. M. 1985. *The Art and Culture of Early Greece, 100–480 B.C.* Ithaca: Cornell University Press.

Langdon, S., ed. 1993. *From Pasture to Polis: Art in the Age of Homer*. Columbia, MO: University of Missouri Press.

Langdon, S. 2008. *Art and Identity in Dark Age Greece, 1100–700 B.C.E.* Cambridge/New York: Cambridge University Press.

Snodgrass, A. M. 2000. *The Dark Age of Greece: An Archaeological Survey of the Eleventh to the Eighth Centuries BC*, new edition. New York: Routledge.

Whitley, J. 1991. *Style and Society in Dark Age Greece: The Changing Face of a Pre-Literate Society 1100–700 BC.* Cambridge: Cambridge University Press.

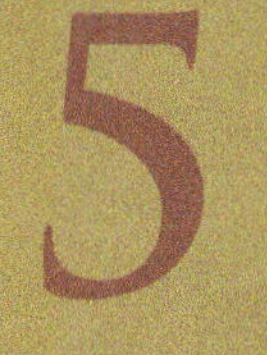

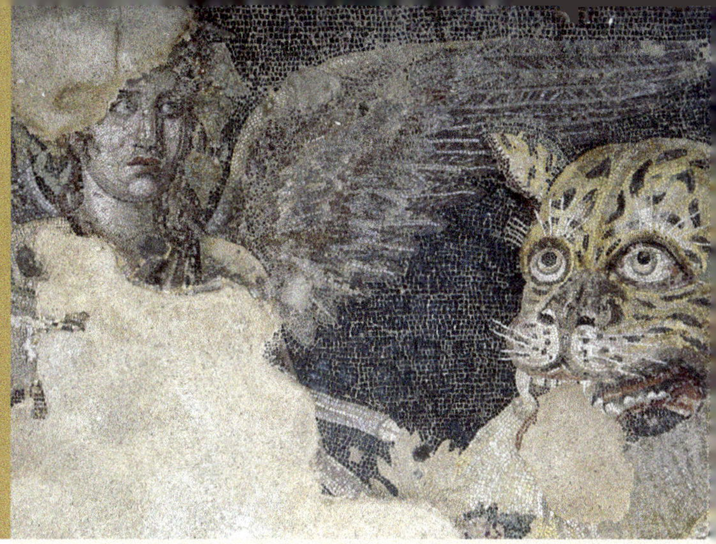

5

CONTEXTS I: CIVIC, DOMESTIC, AND FUNERARY

Timeline
The City and its Spaces
The Agora
Houses and Domestic Spaces
Textiles
The Symposion
Graves
Textbox: Agency
References
Further Reading

TIMELINE

	Sculpture/Tombs	Pottery/Tombs	Buildings/Cities
800–700		760–750 Dipylon amphora [4.7] end 8th cent. Tomb XI in Agora at Athens	775–725 Zagora, phase I [4.22] 725–700 Zagora, phase II [4.22]
700–600			
600–500	*c.* 550 Kore of Phrasikleia [8.13] *c.* 530 Kouros from Anavyssos	600–590 Early Corinthian krater with symposion 525–490 Pottery from Well 2:4 in the Agora, Athens [1.10]	600 Founding of Poseidonia/ Paestum
500–400	477/476 Tyrannicides	450–420 Attic white-ground lekythoi	480–400 Development of the classical Agora in Athens *c.* 430 Founding of Olynthos
400–300	*c.* 400 Stele of Hegeso	*c.* 336–311 Tomb II at Vergina	348 Destruction of Olynthos mid-4th cent. Founding of Priene
300–200			
200–100			*c.* 150 Stoa of Attalos in Athenian Agora

As we saw in Chapter 4, Greek works of art served a purpose, whether as grave goods, grave markers, votive offerings, or potential wedding gifts. In some cases they were made specifically for the function and occasion, such as the monumental Dipylon amphora that served as a funerary marker (**see Figure 4.7, page 78**), or they might have been taken from one context and then repurposed, such as the jewelry of the rich lady buried in the Agora becoming her grave goods (**see Figure 4.6, page 76**). Context and function not only shape the form and subject matter of artworks, but also help to frame meaning for their makers, owners, and viewers. The setting and purpose of a work, then, are essential to understanding its role as both art and artifact. Broadly speaking, there are four major contexts in which Greek art is found: sanctuaries, civic spaces such as the agora, domestic spaces, and finally graves and cemeteries. Already we have seen that in the Geometric period these contexts were not static, but changed to meet the needs of Greek society and culture. We will begin by looking at the overall plan of the city and its main public space, the agora, and then turn to housing and cemeteries. We will return in Chapter 7 to the developments to be found in sanctuaries, including the temple and the development of the architectural orders.

In exploring the civic, domestic, and funerary realms, we will review some of the works in the Geometric period, but mostly we will be looking ahead to some of the developments that take place in later periods. In taking a more diachronic view, we can see how the contexts either changed or remained the same over time. Accordingly, some important examples of context are found in other chapters focused upon chronology, so we will be making reference throughout this and the other contextual chapters in this book to works in other chapters. Admittedly, looking ahead or behind at images in other chapters can be time-consuming, but one may also regard it as a reflection of the multiple layers of monuments and artifacts that accumulated in the Greek city and that a stroll through the ancient agora or sanctuary was a historical as well as immediate experience. In this chapter, then, we will pick up with the emerging polis that we see in Zagora and observe the archaic, classical, and Hellenistic developments that followed in the key areas of civic life and spaces.

THE CITY AND ITS SPACES

The growth in population and economic activity during the Geometric period led not only to the expansion of towns like Athens, which had been continuously settled since the Bronze Age, but also to the foundation of new towns like Zagora, and, beginning in the eighth century, to new settlements throughout the Mediterranean as Greek cities founded colonies in southern Italy, Sicily, Asia Minor, and elsewhere. As we saw at Zagora (**see Figures 4.21 and 4.22, pages 92, 93**), houses were laid out in clusters with some common walls, but the overall plan is asymmetrical and uneven. A defensive wall helped to define the boundary of the city as well as to protect it. Besides housing, a town also had to have spaces for markets and civic gatherings, an area usually labeled the *agora*, but at least at Zagora this did not require specific buildings. There was also an area for an altar and religious rituals, but there was not an actual temple until later, after the settlement itself had been abandoned. Towns also needed places for burials, and these were located outside the inhabited area, usually along or near roads leading to the city.

Zagora is important because it gives us a picture of the earliest development of the city, particularly in terms of its housing. The earliest phases of Athens are much harder to recover because of the vast expansion of the city in later periods and the rebuilding/destruction of its earliest civic and domestic buildings. Looking ahead to the fourth century, we can see that the basic division of the city's interior into sanctuaries, the agora and civic spaces, and housing still holds. In the reconstruction drawing by John Travlos, looking from the northwest, the city is dominated by the Acropolis in the upper center of the picture, with the Parthenon in the middle of the view and the Propylaia or entrance on the right (west) side (**Figure 5.1**). We will discuss the sanctuary in more detail in Chapter 7, but this view shows that the temple was the largest and tallest standing structure of the city and was distinguished

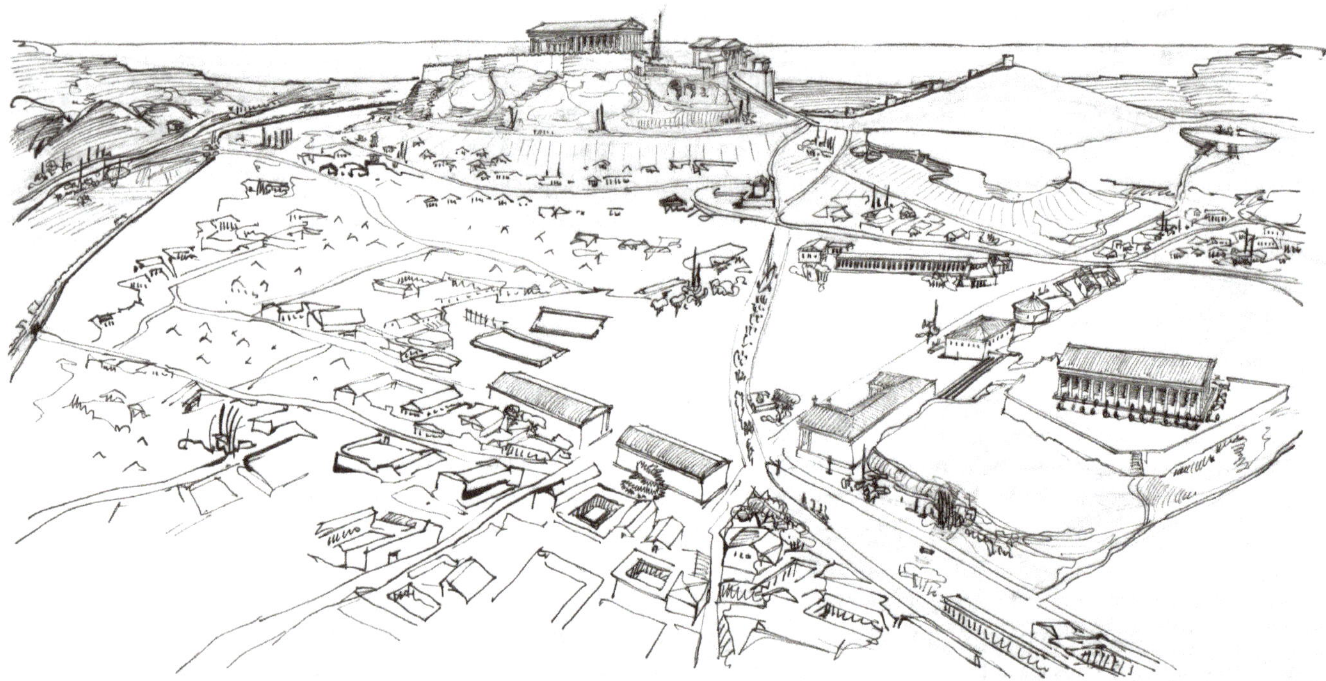

5.1 Reconstructed view of ancient Athens with view of Agora and Acropolis. Drawing by John Travlos. Photo: American School of Classical Studies at Athens: Agora Excavations. Top: Acropolis with (left to right) Parthenon (Erechtheion in front); statue of Athena Promachos, Propylaia with Temple of Athena Nike. Lower right: Agora with Panathenaic Way; Stoa Poikile and Stoa Basileos; Temple of Hephaistos. Upper right: Pynx.

Panathenaic Way the processional route of the Panathenaia in Athens, going from the Dipylon Gate to the Acropolis and going through the agora

stoas a rectangular colonnaded porch, sometimes with a second story, that served a variety of civic or religious needs in the agora or sanctuary

visually by the colonnade that surrounded it. The road leading to the Acropolis was the **Panathenaic Way**, the route followed by the procession of Athenians from the Dipylon Gate in the city walls to the Acropolis.

The Panathenaic Way cuts diagonally in the picture and goes through the large open space of the Agora. The most noteworthy feature about an agora is that it is an open space within the densely packed streets and houses inside the city walls. This provided an area where markets, processions, and contests could be held. By the fifth century, the area today known as the classical Agora in Athens was taking shape and included a variety of buildings. Most characteristic were the series of long rectangular buildings with open colonnades called **stoas** that were built along the boundaries of the Agora. In the drawing, these line the north and south sides of the Athenian Agora and the northwest corner. Along the west boundary of the Agora were buildings dedicated to the city government, as we shall see later in this chapter. Beginning in the middle of the fifth century the Athenians also built the Hephaisteion above the Agora on its west side, a temple dedicated jointly to Hephaistos and Athena. Like the Acropolis to the southeast, this sanctuary is on a high place with the temple as the central focal point with limited access points to the sanctuary. There were also altars, memorials, and other monuments in the Agora, some of which we shall see later in this chapter.

The upper right section of the drawing shows the line of hills that bounded Athens on the southwest. At the far upper right is an area that was originally the bowl-shaped slope of the Pynx Hill. This is where the *ekklesia* of Athenian citizens met to make decisions as part of the democratic constitution of the city in the fifth century. At the beginning of the fourth century, the area was transformed by a large retaining wall to create theater-like seating for the citizens to hear speeches and proposals. From here, as we saw in **Figure 1.9 (page 13)**, Athenians were in a position to see the full splendor of the Periklean building program while considering the polis's affairs. A road leads from the Pynx to the southwest corner of the Agora, linking markets and governance.

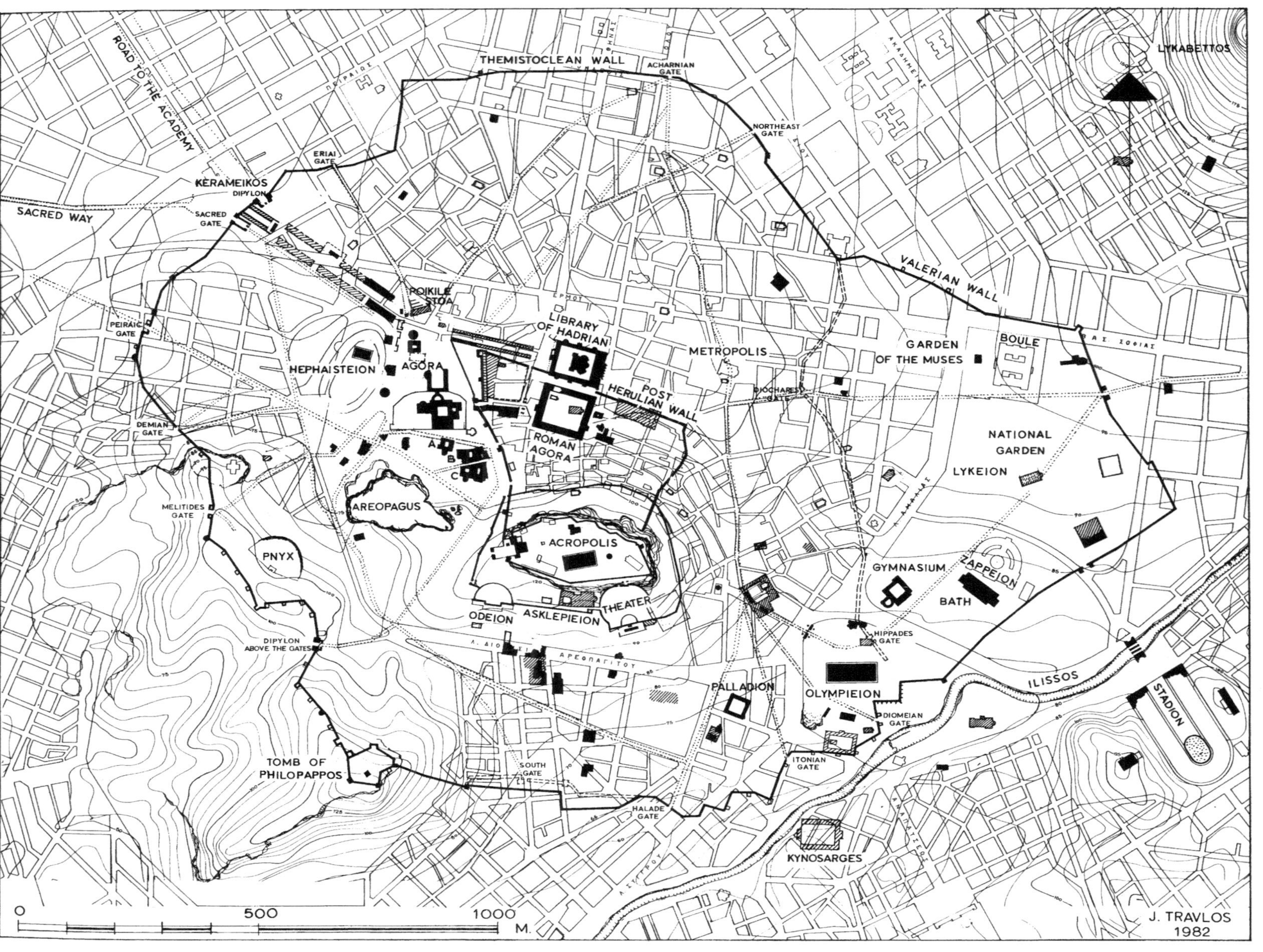

5.2 Plan of Athens with ancient structures superimposed on modern city streets. Ancient streets in dotted lines. Drawing by John Travlos; Photo: American School of Classical Studies at Athens: Agora Excavations.

The remaining areas of the city were filled with smaller houses and much less open space, densely clustered together along irregular roads that navigated around the terrain, particularly the hills of the Acropolis, the Areopagos, and the Pynx, seen on the top right of the drawing.

The irregularity of Athens is a reflection of its long history and dramatic expansion. John Papadopoulos has recently suggested that most of the Dark Age population of Athens lived on the Acropolis, with the semi-industrial pottery production area and cemeteries located below in the area of what became the classical Agora (Papadopoulos and Schilling 2003). There may have been additional small settlements or neighborhoods below the Acropolis with their own cemeteries, such as those found in the area of the Dipylon Gate (**Figure 5.2**). As the city expanded in population, it would have had to build up areas below the Acropolis, and the archaic Agora was probably located to the east of the Acropolis, along with housing. The Acropolis during the sixth century became more exclusively a sanctuary with a temple dedicated to Athena and other buildings.

The destruction of the city by the Persians in 480/479 BCE required not only rebuilding, but also apparently a reorganization of the city. The classical Agora, the one dominated today by the rebuilt second-century Stoa of Attalos housing the site's museum (**see Figure 5.6, page 105**), was founded and became a new focal point of commercial and civic activity. The pottery industry moved further out to the area of the Dipylon Gate and gave the name to this quarter of the city, the Kerameikos. The Agora housed the meeting buildings of the civic government, with the larger area for the *ekklesia* located on the plateau of the Pynx.

The terrain and episodic development of a city like Athens makes its overall plan and organization irregular. In founding new colonies, however, cities were planned in a more regular and precise fashion. Usually these colonies were established in areas with flatter, arable land, as agriculture was initially the primary economic activity of the new sites. The land, called the *chora*, was divided by a grid into parcels for farms. Rural sanctuaries were often used to mark the boundaries of the territory. Some land was set aside for a city and laid out using a grid system, as can be seen in the plan of Poseidonia (modern Paestum) in southern Italy (**Figure 5.3**). This city was founded around 600 BCE by colonists from Sybaris, itself an Achaian colony founded in the late eighth century on the south coast of Italy. The boundaries of the city, marked by walls, were mostly straight, but meandered on the western boundary due to the coastline and marsh. Within the walls, a regular grid established long rectangular blocks running north–south. The central north–south section of the city was defined by three large areas about 5.5 blocks deep. Two of these, at the north and south end, were made into sanctuaries. The oldest temple, dedicated to Hera, was built around 550 BCE on the south section (1 on the plan) (**see Figure 7.7, page 163**). The sanctuaries had enough space for subsequent temples to be built as the city developed, including a second temple to Hera in the south (2) and one to Athena in the north (4). At the center were the civic spaces of the agora (around 3), now built over by the remains of the Roman forum and its structures. The main roads of the city intersected at the southwest corner of the agora and led out to the four main gates. The rest of the city was dedicated to housing and workshops and much more densely packed buildings, but it is probable that only some of this land was used initially. In planning their cities, the colonists allowed room for future growth of the population that would conform to the original design. Cemeteries, the last major requirement for civic planning, were located outside the city walls, primarily along the roads leading to the north and south.

chora
the area of the Greek countryside and farmland outside of the polis

The city of Olynthos shows a combination of planned and unplanned development (**Figure 5.4**). A small town had developed on the south hill of the modern site by the Geometric period and remained irregular in plan. Just before the start of the Peloponnesian War, several cities on the Chalkidian peninsula rebelled against the rule of Athens and fought against it in the ensuing conflict. At that time there was an *anoikismos*, or "moving inland" of some of the population of these cities to a larger and more defensible place with good agricultural land. Like the colonies in Italy, Sicily, and elsewhere, this new foundation was laid out on a grid, in this case along the north hill below the older settlement. The population was a mixture of the natives as well as Bottiaians, Chalkidians, and other immigrants. An agora was marked out along the west side of the city near the city wall, and cemeteries

anoikismos
the founding or relocation of a city or cities by the movement inland of previously settled populations

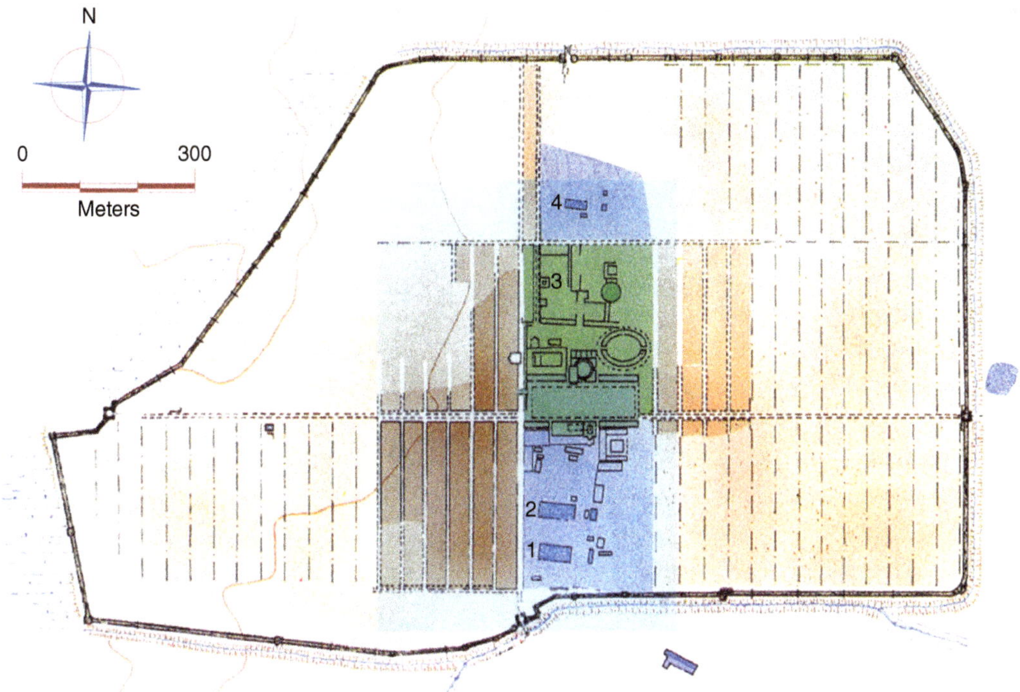

5.3 Plan of Poseidonia/Paestum, founded *c.* 600 BCE. After E. Greco and F. Longo, *Poseidonia Paestum: La Visita della Città* (Paestum, 2002), fold-out plan. Reproduction permission granted by the Scuola Archeologica Italiana di Atene. Selected points: (1) Temple of Hera I; (2) Temple of Hera II; (3) Heroön; (4) Temple of Athena.

were placed beyond the wall to the west. The excavations found no sanctuaries within the city, and these may have been all extramural. The rectangular grid blocks ran east–west and were filled with rows of houses set back to back. As the city expanded, a new area, the "Villa Section," was built outside the walls but mostly aligned with the original grid. The houses of Olynthos are among the best preserved in mainland Greece due to the fact that Philip of Macedon besieged and destroyed the city in 348 BCE, leaving the houses in ruins that were not rebuilt, as they were in Athens and other sites. We will look at the design of these houses and some of their contents later in this chapter, but for now it is important to note that the houses are equal in the size of their lots and are oriented toward the south to take advantage of the sun for light and warmth in the winter. One advantage of the grid plan is that it provides an opportunity to make equal provision to the residents of the city. This did not prevent strife from developing in some cities, but it did accord with the principles of government and rule that were later articulated by Plato and Aristotle.

The grid plan is often associated with Hippodamos of Miletos, who was active in the second half of the fifth century and, according to Aristotle (*Pol.* 1267b22–1268a14), laid out the harbor town of Piraeus near the city of Athens. As we have seen, grid planning is found in new foundations much earlier than that, and it continued to be used when possible into the Hellenistic period, as can be seen in the city of Priene in Asia Minor **(Figure 5.5)**. The city was initially planned as a deep-water port by the ruler of Halikarnassos, Mausolos, in the mid-fourth century, but most of its construction took place after the conquest of the area by Alexander the Great in 334 BCE. Despite the uneven terrain of the site, the city was laid out on a grid within the city walls. An agora was placed at the center of the city on flatter land, with stoas on the north side facing south. There are two major sanctuaries inside the city. A small sanctuary of the healing god Asklepios is to the east of the agora, but is entered from the residential area on the east side. A large temple dedicated to Athena is to the northwest of the agora on a terrace. North of the agora is a theater, built against the rising slope toward the high acropolis. A gymnasion is between the theater and the Asklepion, while just inside the city walls on the south side is a race course. As the reconstruction drawing shows, the houses were densely packed within the blocks, but the slope provided additional exposure to sunlight for each of the houses. We will look at some of the finds from the houses later in this chapter.

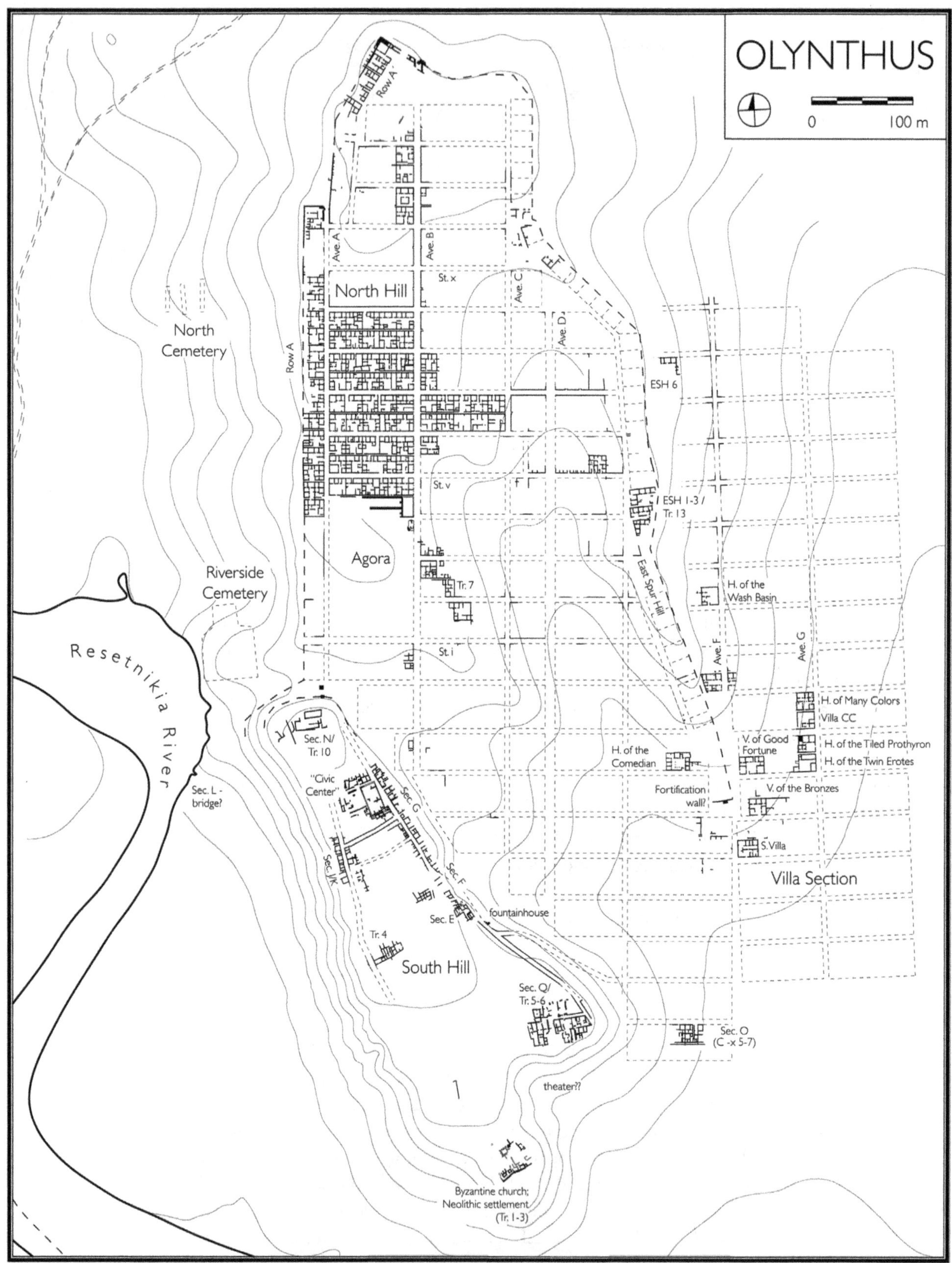

5.4 Plan of Olynthos, *c.* 430–348 BCE. After Cahill 2002, fig. 6. Reprinted with permission of author.

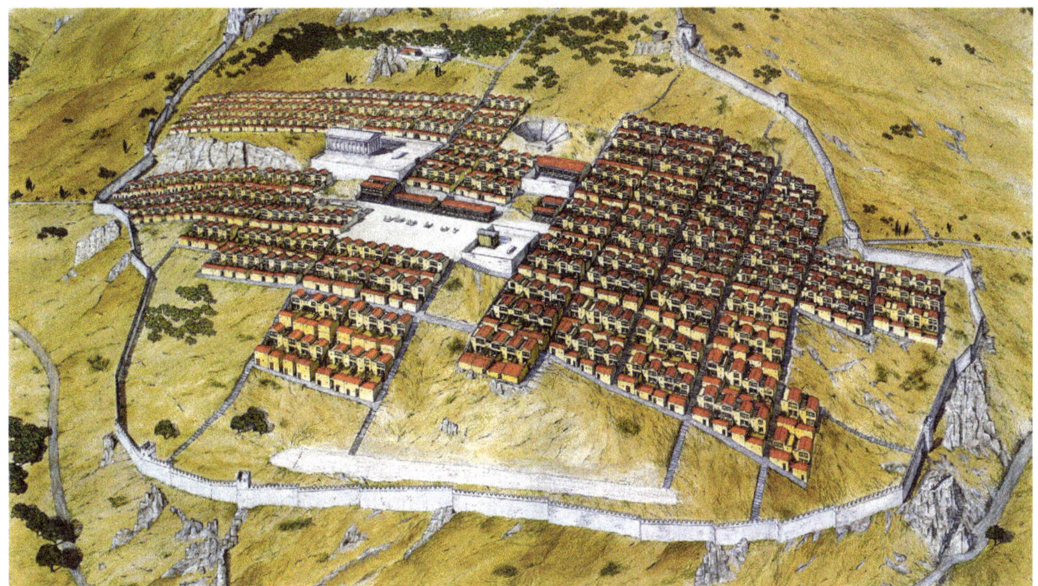

5.5 Reconstructed view of Priene, later 4th–3rd cent. BCE. Drawing by Z. Wendel, from W. Hoepfner and E.-L. Schwandner, *Haus und Stadt im klassischen Griechenland* (Berlin/Munich: Deutscher Kunstverlag, 1994), Fig. 183. Used with permission of Hans Goette and the Deutsches Archäologisches Institut, Berlin.

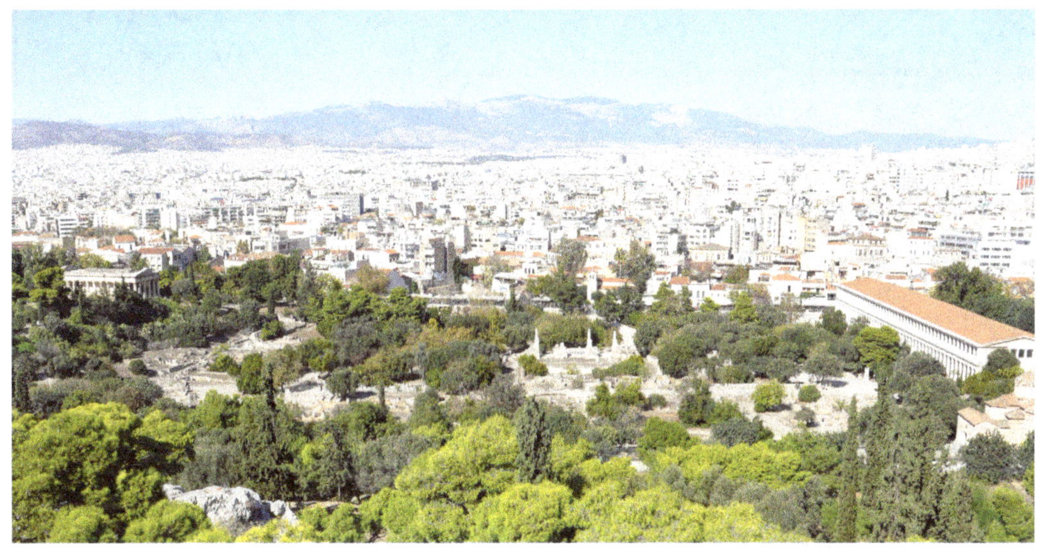

5.6 View of the Agora in Athens today. Left: Temple of Hephaistos; right: reconstructed Stoa of Attalos. Photo: author.

THE AGORA

The agora was the open area in the heart of the Greek city hosting markets, governmental offices, and meeting chambers, as well as some sanctuaries, shrines, and altars. In looking at a view of the Agora in Athens today from the Areopagos Hill **(Figure 5.6)**, one can see to the left/west the Temple of Hephaistos, which was begun in the 450 s BCE on a hill bordering the west side of the Agora. The Panathenaic Way, the path of the Panathenaic festival procession from the city gate to the Acropolis, cut diagonally through the center of the Agora; early on there was also a race course for the Panathenaic Games in the central area. Other buildings included fountain houses, offices, mints, jails, and assembly halls. Stones marked the boundaries of the area, and shafts with male genitals and a head of Hermes, called herms, marked entrances. While the modern buildings that bound the Agora today are taller than the houses of ancient times, the contrast between the dense concentration of residential areas and the open space of the Agora is still apparent.

On the right/east is the reconstructed Stoa of Attalos, originally built in the mid-second century and reconstructed 1952–1956 CE. The stoa is the major building type of an agora, and is essentially a colonnaded portico open on one long side. Like the Stoa of Attalos, it can have a second story and/or a series of rooms along the back for dining, offices, and other functions **(see Figure 5.20, page 119)**. The stoas are rather simple structures, but many had paintings, sculpture, or other objects on display inside them. For example, the Stoa Poikile at the Agora, built in the 460 s, had four monumental paintings showing fallen Troy and battles with Amazons, Persians, and Spartans, along with shields dedicated from the Athenian victory over the Spartans at Sphacteria in 425. It was here in the fourth century that philosophers that we now call Stoics lectured, deriving their name from the building where they gathered.

The plan of the Agora as it stood around 400 BCE shows a concentration of structures on the south and west sides **(Figure 5.7)**. Small stoas and the Altar of the Twelve Gods flank the northwest entrance on both sides of the Panathenaic Way that cuts diagonally through the area on the way to the Acropolis. The Stoa Basileos, or Royal Stoa, is the oldest structure, but suggestions for its dating range from 500 BCE to after 480. The Stoa Poikile was built in the 460 s and the Stoa of Zeus in the 420 s. On the hill to the west of the Agora was built the Temple of Hephaistos and below it a small

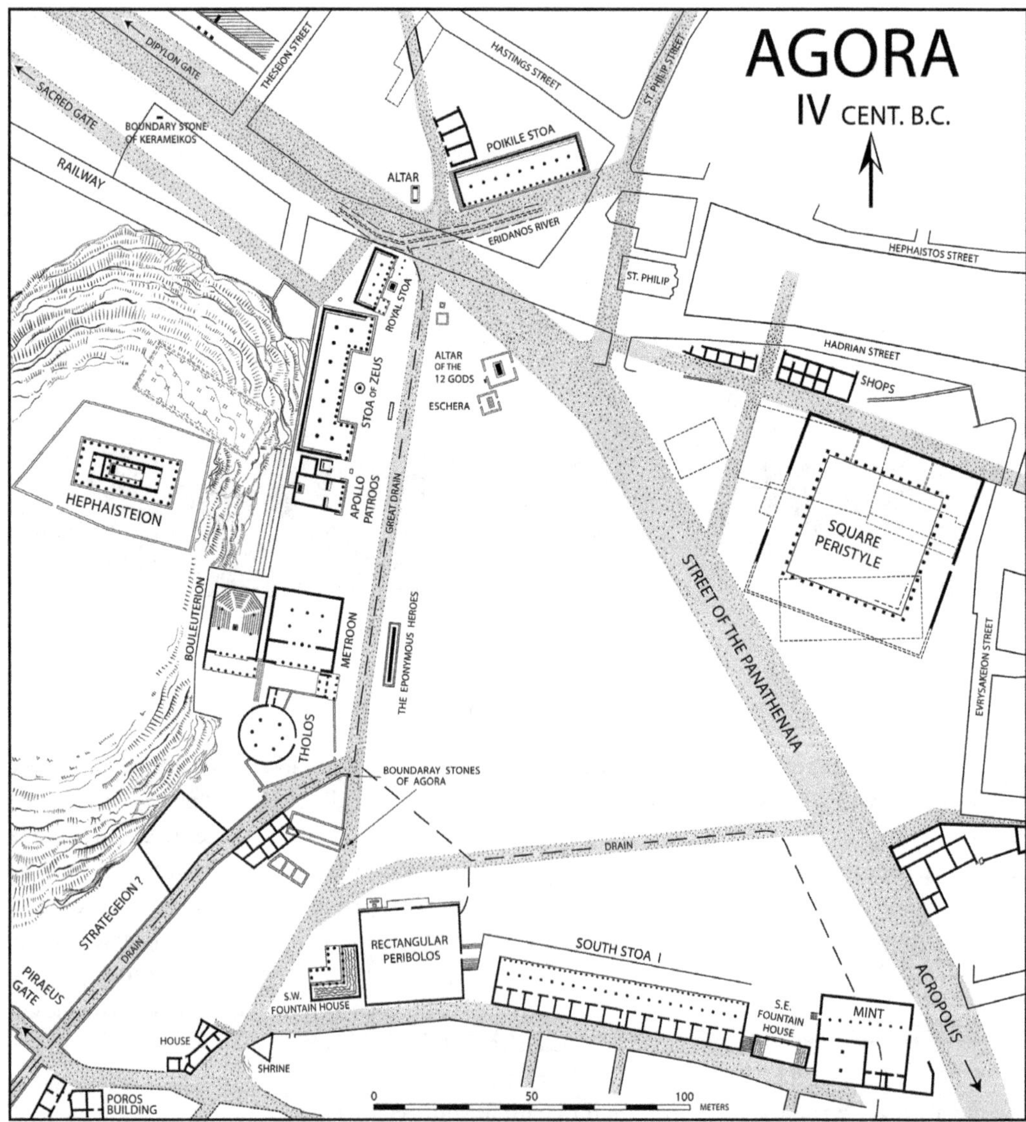

5.7 Reconstructed plan of Agora of Athens, *c.* 400 BCE. Photo: American School of Classical Studies at Athens: Agora Excavations.

temple to Apollo. Further south of these were three buildings that served the city council. The round structure, called a tholos, was a dining hall and administrative center for the ***boule***, the council of 500 Athenian citizens chosen to make decisions for a year. The round shape is unusual and how the building was arranged on the interior is not certain. The square structure directly north was built as a ***bouleuterion***, or meeting place of the *boule*, but was converted into the archive or **metroon** after a new bouleuterion was built in the 410 s. The new structure was more rectangular in plan and enclosed banked semi-circles of seats for the members of the *boule*. This small complex was entered by a porch facing the Agora across from the monument of the Eponymous Heroes who represented the twelve tribes of Athens. Once inside the porch, the entrances of the metroon and bouleuterion faced toward each other within the enclosure. On the south side of the Agora were fountain houses, the South Stoa with dining rooms along the back side, and the city mint. The South Stoa was built at the same time as the new bouleuterion and housed the officials in charge of weights and measures, reflecting the commercial importance of the Agora for the city. On the other side of the Panathenaic Way was a square building open in the center with colonnades; this Square **Peristyle** was a law court built in the fourth century.

boule
a council of citizens chosen to make decisions for the polis. This was a smaller group than the *ekklesia*

bouleuterion
the meeting place of the *boule*

metroon
building housing the civic archive

peristyle
a structure with columns that enclose it, such as a peristyle temple with columns on all four sides of the exterior or a peristyle courtyard with colonnaded porches on all four sides

The Agora continued to be developed into the Hellenistic and Roman periods (**Figure 5.8**). A plan of the site around 150 CE shows several new stoas on the south and east. The new South Stoa lies at an angle over its predecessor and has additional wings to make an enclosure. Immediately in front of it was another stoa, the "Middle Stoa," that now was the boundary of the central open space. On

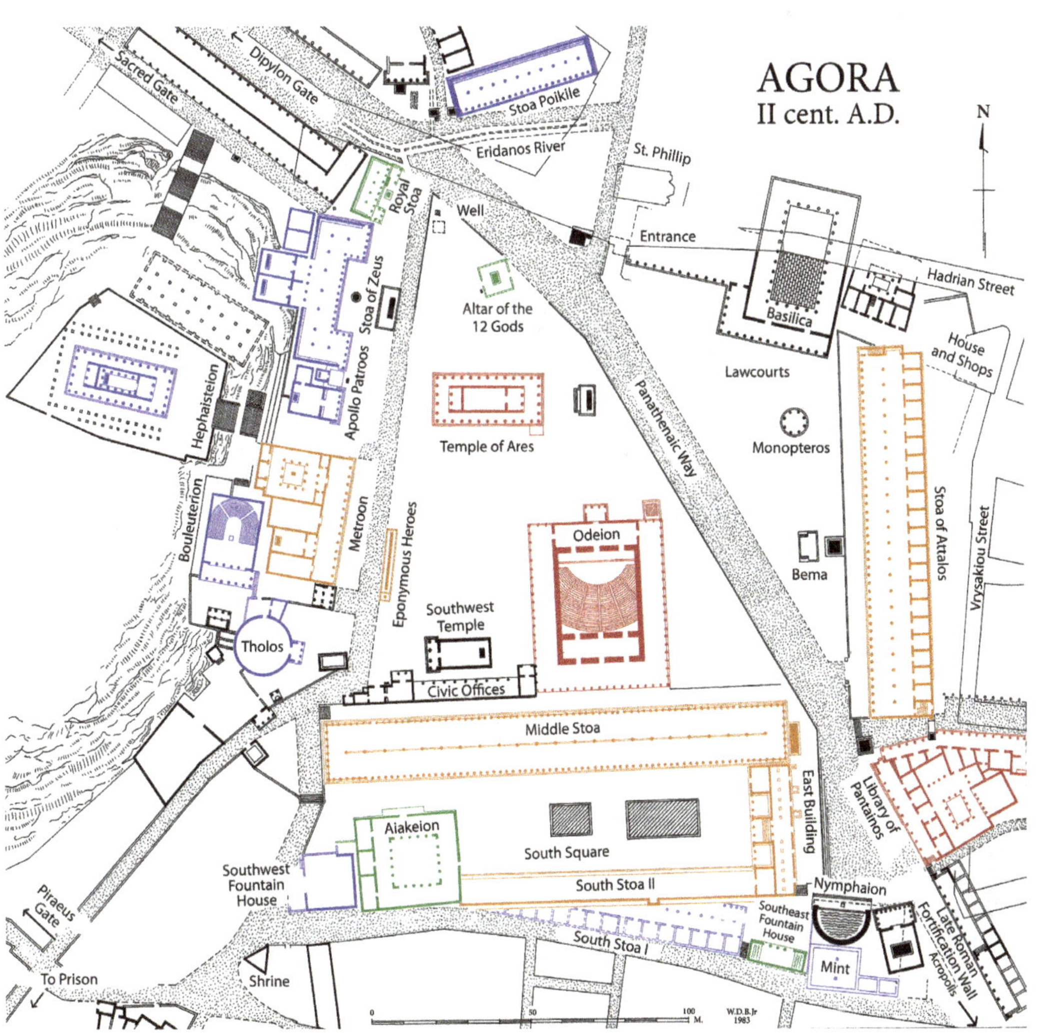

5.8 Reconstructed plan of Agora of Athens, *c.* 150 CE. Photo: American School of Classical Studies at Athens: Agora Excavations.

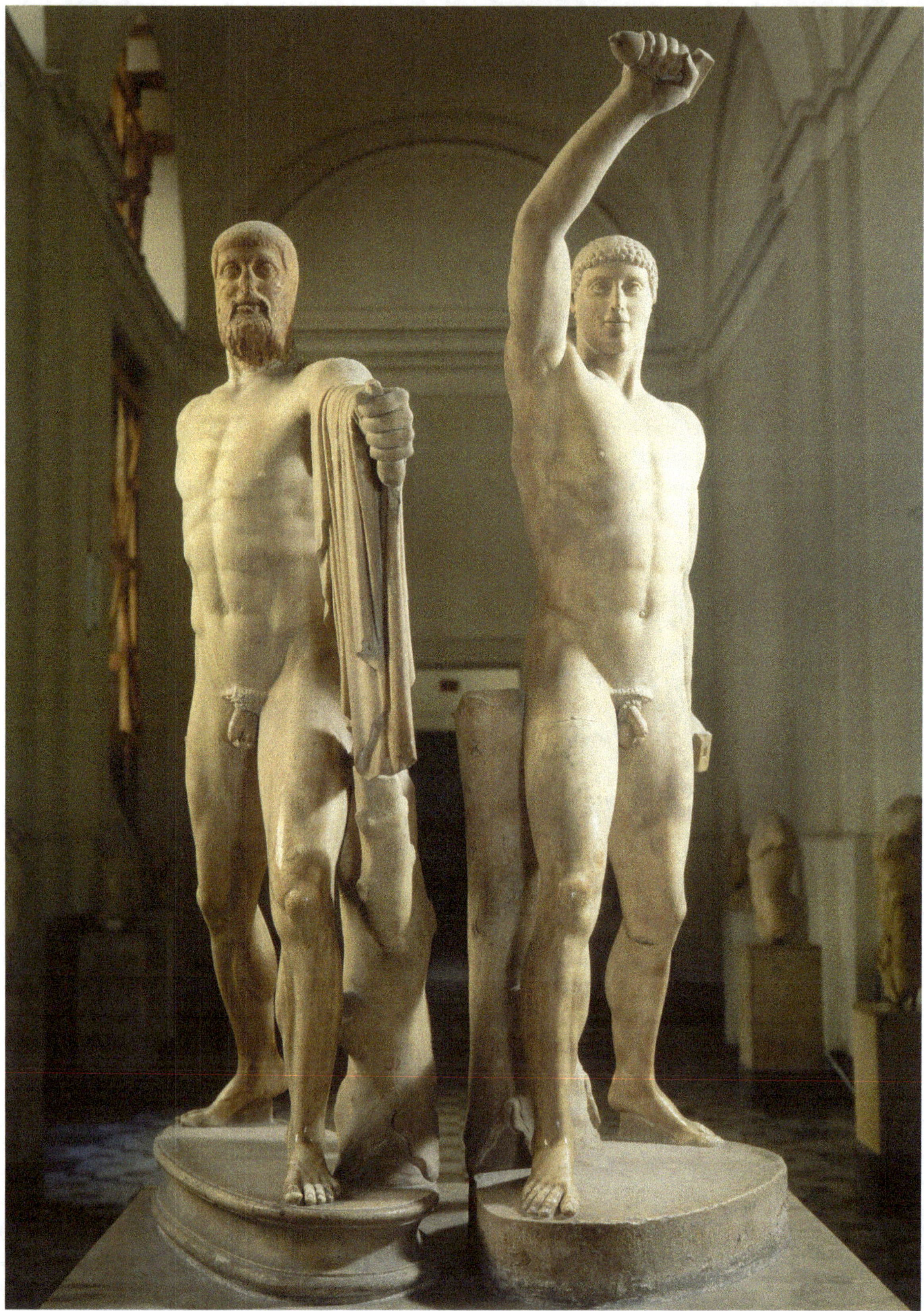

5.9 Tyrannicides (Aristogeiton, left; Harmodios, right) of Kritios and Nesiotes, Roman marble copy of Greek bronze original of 477/6 BCE. 6 ft 4¾ in (1.95 m). Naples, Museo Archeologico Nazionale. Photo: Alinari/Art Resource, NY.

the east is the Stoa of Attalos, built by the ruler of Pergamon over the Square Peristyle with the law courts. On the east the tholos remains, but the bouleuterion and metroon were rebuilt, with the metroon now facing toward the Agora. The space became more congested under the Romans. Marcus Agrippa (d. 12 BCE), son-in-law of the first emperor Augustus (reigned 31 BCE–14 CE), built an Odeion or concert hall in the open space in front of the Middle Stoa. The Romans also dismantled a fifth-century BCE temple dedicated to Ares and reassembled it in the central open space during the late first century BCE.

In addition to buildings, an agora was an important public place for the display of sculpture and painting. Monumental paintings, sculpted reliefs, and statues were found in the stoas and shrines, as well as free-standing works in the open areas. One of the most famous in the Athenian Agora was the statue group commemorating the **Tyrannicides**, or Tyrant-Killers, by Kritios and Nesiotes. Fragments of the base for the sculpture have been found in the excavations, but the original bronze statues are gone and the original location for the base is uncertain. We do have marble copies of the original bronze statues that give us a very good idea of their appearance (**Figure 5.9**). In the composition we see the young man Harmodios (right) stepping forward with a sword over his head and the bearded adult Aristogeiton (left) holding a mantle and sword straight out, as they step out of the crowd along the Panathenaic Way to strike the tyrant Hipparchos in 514 BCE.

Tyrannicides
"Tyrant-Killers," a term used for Harmodios and Aristogeiton who killed the tyrant Hipparchos in Athens in 514 BCE

To understand the importance of the dedication and its subject, we need to remember the story and its context. Peisistratos had taken control of Athens in 546 BCE and established himself as a tyrant, that is, someone who illegally usurped the power of the polis and ruled individually. After his death in 527, his sons Hippias and Hipparchos succeeded him as tyrants. According to historical sources, Hipparchos had sought the affection of the young Harmodios in a pederastic relationship, an aspect of Greek culture and identity that we will discuss in Chapter 13. Upon being rejected in favor of Aristogeiton, Hipparchos alleged that Harmodios's sister was not a virgin, forcing her to be dropped from her role as the ***kanephoros*** in the **Panathenaia**. To avenge the insult to the family, Harmodios and Aristogeiton plotted to attack the tyrants and managed to step out of the crowd and stab Hipparchos during the Panathenaia. When Hippias was later expelled from Athens in 510 and a new democratic constitution was established under Kleisthenes in 507, the city commissioned a statue group to honor Harmodios and Aristogeiton, now labeled as the Tyrannicides or Tyrant-Killers. These statues, made by Antenor in bronze, were taken by the Persians when they sacked Athens in 480/479. On its return, the city government commissioned a replacement sculpture from Kritios and Nesiotes that was dedicated in 477–476. It is this second statue group that was copied in the marble statues we see today.

kanephoros
basket-bearer, an important role in a ritual in which a woman bears a basket of sacrificial instruments in the ritual procession

Panathenaia
the annual ritual in Athens honoring Athena as patron goddess of the city. It featured an elaborate procession from the Dipylon Gate to the Acropolis on the Panathenaic Way

The work commemorated individuals who were model citizens, but were not true-to-life portraits as we think of them. Their importance to the city can be seen in the quick replacement of the original statues, and in the frequent literary references to their actions and the mimicking of their poses in art, such as the figure of Theseus attacking the Kremmyon Sow in the Kodros Painter kylix modeled on Aristogeiton (**see Figure 9.8, page 220**). The inscription was apparently placed on the front side of the base with the figures, and in reading it, the viewer would be in the position of the tyrant Hipparchos, about to be murdered. The statues not only honor heroes of the polis, but also serve as warnings when the viewer reads the inscriptions about the potential fate of tyrants.

Other statues, such as the Doryphoros or Spear-Bearer made by Polykleitos and originally in the agora in the city of Argos (**see Figure 10.7, page 243**), were more universalizing but idealistic models. We will discuss this work more extensively in the chapter on fifth-century art, but for now can note that it is a representation of the heroic-athletic ideal of the Greek man set in a place where citizens would see it as they conducted their business in the city. Statues of women or goddesses are rarer, but the Aphrodite of Melos from the second century came from a gymnasium in the agora at Melos (**see Figure 14.17, page 362**).

Smaller reliefs were dedicated in the agora to commemorate events and victories by groups or individuals. A fragmentary fourth-century relief from the Athenian Agora, for example, shows five

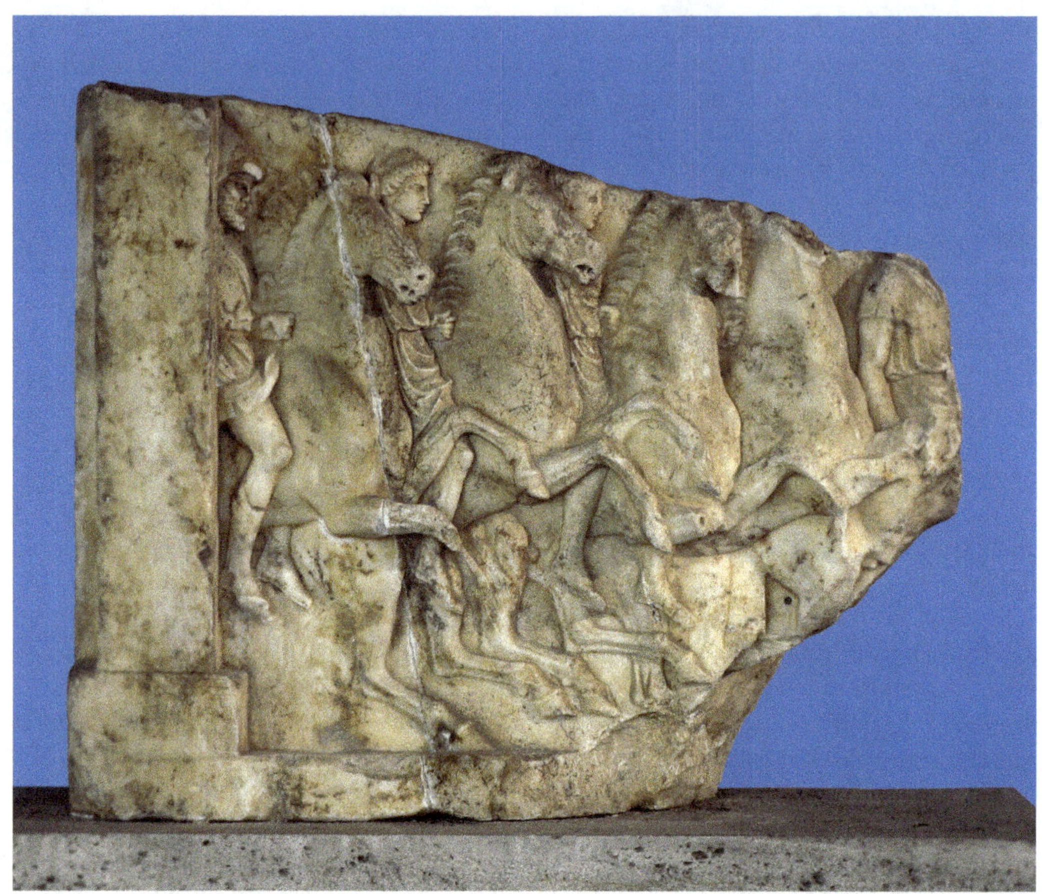

5.10 Relief commemorating victory of Leontis tribe, early 4th. cent. BCE. 18⅞ in (48 cm). Athens, Agora Museum S 7167. Photo: American School of Classical Studies at Athens: Agora Excavations.

riders in a cavalcade, their horses rearing synchronously **(Figure 5.10)**. The back side of the relief shows a crouching lion and the inscription *Leontis enika*, "the Leontis (tribe) was victorious." The relief probably commemorates the group's victory in the *anthippasia*, the cavalry contest of the Panathenaia. It was found at the west end of the Agora and may have originally been placed near the entrance where the contest was held. The figures are about 42 cm high and probably included a dozen riders originally. The work is more modest in scale than the Tyrannicides, but proclaimed both the victory and the civic involvement of the tribe for those who passed by in their business in the Agora. The Panathenaic Games, like those at Olympia and Delphi, were part of religious festivals, but the civic importance of victories in these contests is proclaimed by monuments such as this. We know from literary accounts and statue bases that these commemorative dedications were means for acknowledging both individual and polis and their interrelationship.

Panathenaic amphora
special Attic black-figure amphora with a pointed end that contained oil as prize for victory in the Panathenaic Games. The amphora had Athena and an owl on one side and a representation of the event on the back

Athena Promachos
Athena "foremost fighter," featuring an armored Athena striding forward with a spear

This is also the place to mention a particular type of storage jar, the **Panathenaic amphora**, that was commissioned by Athens to award victors in the games **(Figure 5.11)**. The value of the prize was not the vase, but the oil that it contained. The decoration of the vase, large and with a pointed end so that it could be placed securely in a circular opening in the floor or bench for storage, served to identify the special source of the contents. On one side is a picture of Athena striding forward with a spear, the **Athena Promachos** (foremost fighter). On either side are columns with cocks on them, and to the left is the inscription *Ton Athenethen athlon*, "from the games at Athens." On the reverse side we see a charioteer driving his team of four horses at full gallop. The style is deliberately more archaic than other work by the same artist, the Kleophrades Painter (to compare it to another work of the artist, **see Figure 9.7, page 219**), but this is typical of these amphora, whatever workshop was commissioned to make them. Greek viewers used the term *archaios* to describe statues and paintings such as this. For them, it had associations with old cult statues and heirlooms, and so had a status

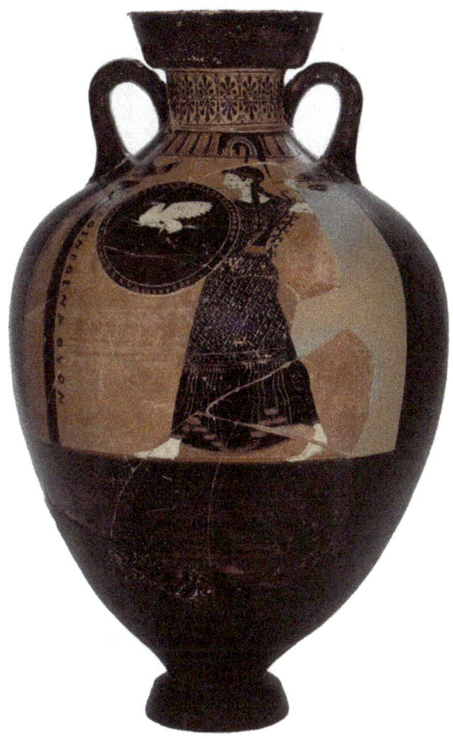

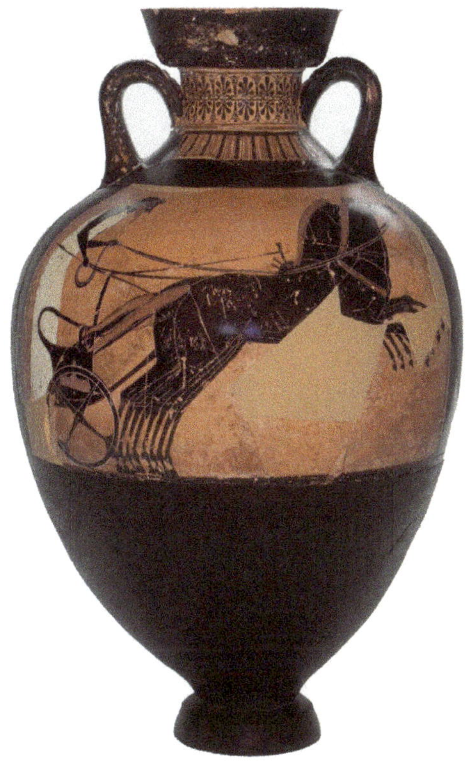

5.11 Attic black-figure Panathenaic amphora attributed to Kleophrades Painter, *c.* 490 BCE. 25¹¹⁄₁₆ in (65.2 cm). Side A: Athena; side B: racing chariot. New Haven, Yale University Art Gallery, Gift of Frederic W. Stevens, B.A. 1858, 1909.13.

connected with religion and ritual. The continuation of an archaic style on Panathenaic amphorae, which continued to be done in the black-figure technique long after it had fallen out of favor, remind us that there is a religious element to contests and competitions.

HOUSES AND DOMESTIC SPACES

The Greek household is less well known than its public spaces and architecture, as there is no site like Pompeii where both the houses and their contents have been well preserved. Since much of the material used to build houses – timber, mud brick, and roughly worked stone – does not endure or remain in place, most houses are known only by their foundations and floors. Houses at some sites like Priene, gradually abandoned after its harbor silted up, and Olynthos in northern Greece, destroyed in a military campaign of Philip II of Macedon in 348 BCE, have been excavated with some household remains, but luxury items such as jewelry and metalwork would have been salvaged or looted, the furniture broken and decayed except for metal fittings. Much of the pottery used in the household was utilitarian and discarded when broken, and sometimes valuable items were placed in the graves of household members, making it difficult to gauge the full extent of art in a domestic context. Most houses would seem to have been plainly decorated on the exterior, but there was not much in the way of large-scale work to be found inside given the modest scale of the houses and their rooms. It is only in the fourth century and later that larger houses, including villas and palaces, began to be built that could feature mosaics and statues.

Most Greek houses were organized around a courtyard, usually facing to the south so that the sun could provide light and warmth. As can be seen in the plan of a house from Olynthos, labeled A vii 4, access to the house was restricted to one main door that led from the street to the courtyard **(Figure 5.12, i)**. Many Greek houses had a porch or colonnade on one side that made a transition from the open courtyard to the enclosed rooms of the house. In this Olynthos house, this took the form of a long porch (f on the plan) with two columns flanking the courtyard; the porch continued

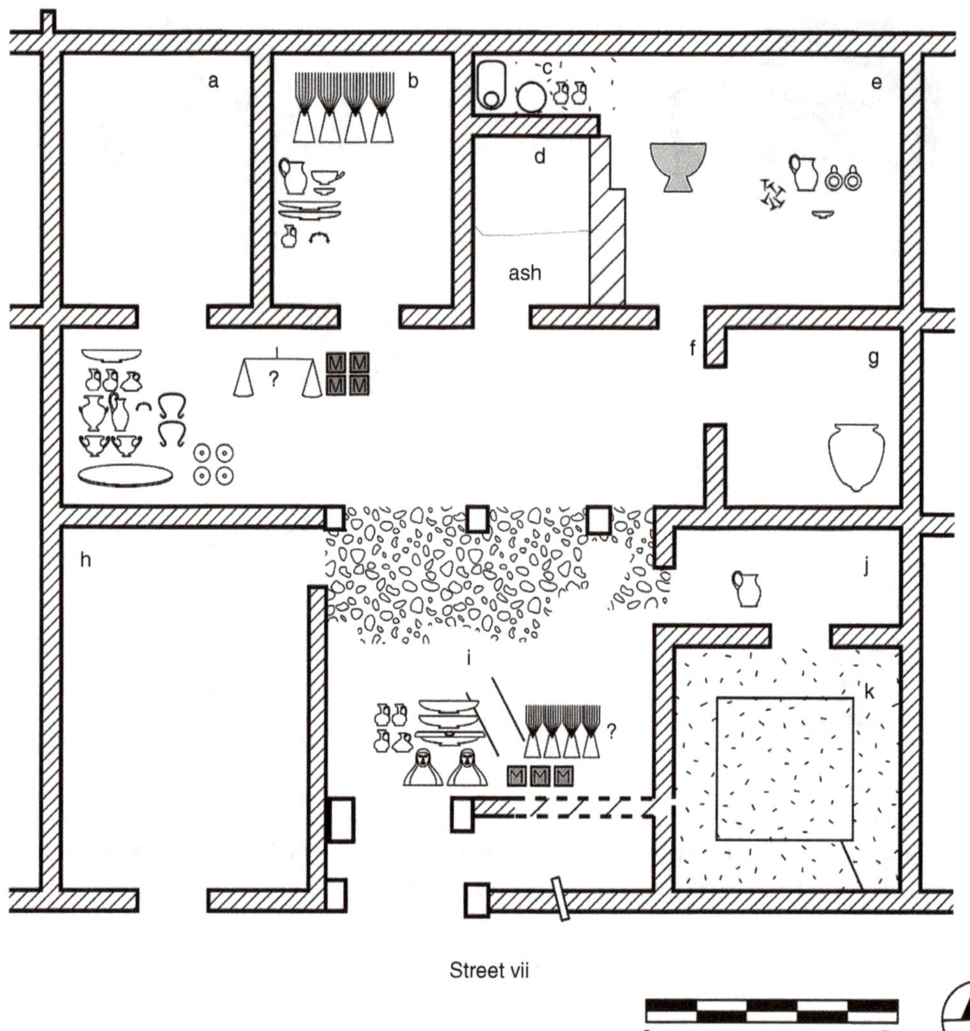

5.12 Plan of House A vii 4 at Olynthos, with location of excavated object types. After Cahill 2002, fig. 22. Reprinted with permission of author.

***pastas* house**
house with a colonnaded porch across one side of the courtyard that continued as a hall across the house

***prostas* house**
house with a small porch on the courtyard and usually no columns

***peristyle* house**
house whose courtyard is flanked by colonnaded porches on three or four sides

andron
word meaning men's room, used to designate the dining room in the house where the symposion was held

on into a hallway, creating a corridor and transition space that ran across the middle of the house **(Figure 5.13)**. This feature is called a ***pastas***, and houses like this are usually called *pastas*-type. Most of the houses at Olynthos, and elsewhere in Greece, are *pastas*-type, but two other types are also found. The ***prostas***-type features a smaller porch, often without a column, and is found at sites like Priene. The ***peristyle***-type was usually larger and had colonnaded porches on three or four sides of the courtyard. Some of the later villas in the southeast section of Olynthos, such as the House of the Comedian and the House of the Tiled Prothyron, are *peristyle*-type **(see Figure 5.4, southeast section)**.

The courtyard of the Olynthos house A vii 4 was paved with cobblestone and had stairs to an upper floor. The rooms to the east and west of the courtyard were single-story and the most publicly oriented rooms of the house. Room h has a separate door to the street. Small weights found in several nearby rooms suggest that it was used as a shop/workshop by the household, thus making the street door convenient for dealing with the public without disturbing the rest of the household. On the southeast side were a square, paved room (k) and forechamber (j) that was the dining room or **andron** (men's room), where the symposion would be held, which we will consider in more detail below. Couches would have lined the walls of the andron, leaving the center open. The north end of the house was two-story, with the columns of the *pastas* supporting a balcony above, as can be seen in the reconstruction. This arrangement meant that sunlight would reach the courtyard and the

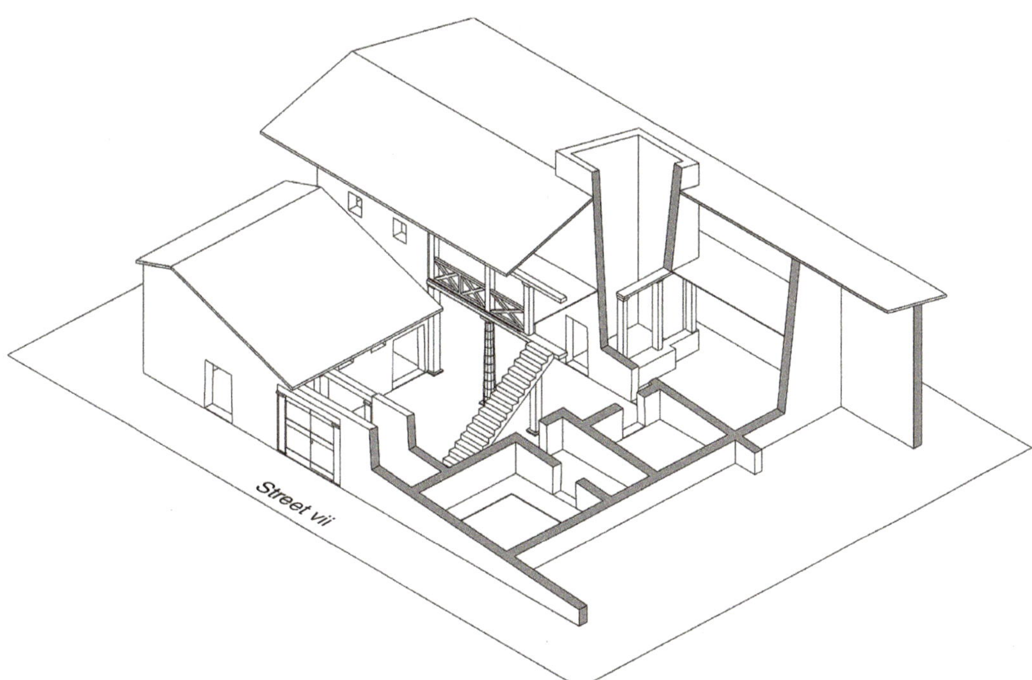

5.13 Reconstruction drawing of House A vii 4 at Olynthos. After Cahill 2002, fig. 23. Reprinted with permission of author.

upper story throughout the year. The upper floors are not preserved but probably had bedrooms that could serve other purposes. The first floor had two rooms on the northwest side (a, b) and a kitchen/flue/bathroom complex at the northeast (c, d, e). A small storeroom (g) at the end of the *pastas* had a single large pithos set into a hole in the floor.

Many excavated houses in Greece are not as regular as the houses of Olynthos and underwent many alterations in the course of their existence. For example, some houses near the Silen Gate at Thasos in northern Greece were built in the mid-fourth century BCE on the remains of some shops and were later remodeled in the Hellenistic period. These houses were much narrower and rectangular in plan than those at Olynthos **(Figure 5.14)**. House A on the left had a courtyard (3) set back from the street with a narrow hall (2) leading to it. Room 5 resembles a *pastas* opening into the back rooms (6–7), but had walls facing the courtyard rather than columns. Room 1 may have served as an andron. The remains of a staircase in the courtyard suggest that a second floor was added to this house by the third century, as shown in the reconstruction **(Figure 5.15)**.

House B had a similar hall (2) from the street leading to its courtyard (5); room 1 had a doorway to the street as well and may have served as a shop. The north side of this house (7–9) is similar in plan to House A, but the area around the courtyard has been subdivided into three rooms (3, 4, 6) rather than one. Both houses, then, have a more private and enclosed section to the north and their public spaces to the south next to the street. A second floor was not put onto this corner house, but during a remodeling the doorway was moved from the south and was closed off and a new doorway was opened on the east side (5), giving direct access from the street into the courtyard.

House C across the road was much simpler than these, and consisted of an enclosed courtyard with an entrance on the south side, and a house with two rooms on the north side, each opening to the south and the courtyard, which constitutes the largest area of the house. Indeed, the plan of this house recalls the remodeled houses at Zagora from the late eighth century **(see Figure 4.22, lower, page 93)**, with small rooms for storage and living set off an irregular courtyard. It would appear that the owners of this house had more modest means than those of the other two, but have the essential features of a courtyard with limited access, storage, and living/work space.

We can get a sense of the objects to be found in a domestic context by looking again at the plan of the house in Olynthos **(see Figure 5.12)**. The icons on the plan show the type of artifacts found in

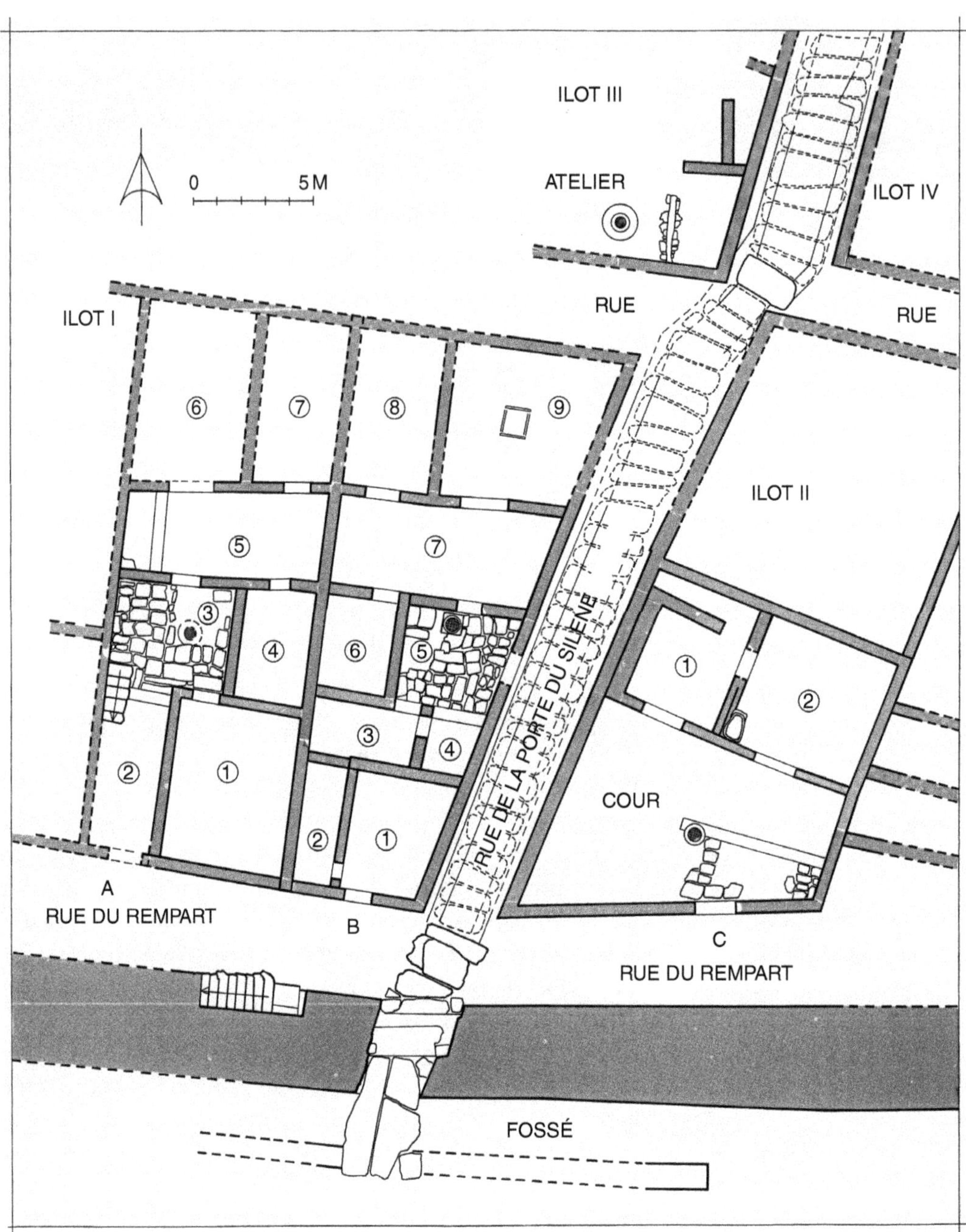

5.14 Plan of houses, Block 1, Silen's Quarter, Thasos (Phase 4). Source: plan no 25.368, EfA/M. Wurch-Kozelj.

each location. The west end of the *pastas* (f) had a variety of eating and drinking vessels, fragments of bronze vessels and traces of furniture, and small oil containers. The courtyard (i) was probably used for a variety of purposes. Loom weights, small weights tied to the end of vertical threads on a loom that maintain the tension needed for weaving, suggest weaving took place there. A simplified rendering of such a loom with a series of loom weights can be seen in a skyphos showing the meeting of Odysseus and Kirke **(see Figure 9.12, page 226)**. Kirke's loom was set up in the courtyard of her house, where light and ventilation were suitable, especially in the warmer months. Small bronze weights found in the courtyard may have been connected with the shop (h) adjacent to the courtyard. Indeed, the openness and light of the courtyard would have made it a flexible workspace for the entire household, as these finds suggest. Other dishes and loom weights were found in room b, which seems to have been a multipurpose space. Unlike other rooms, the walls of the andron (k) were

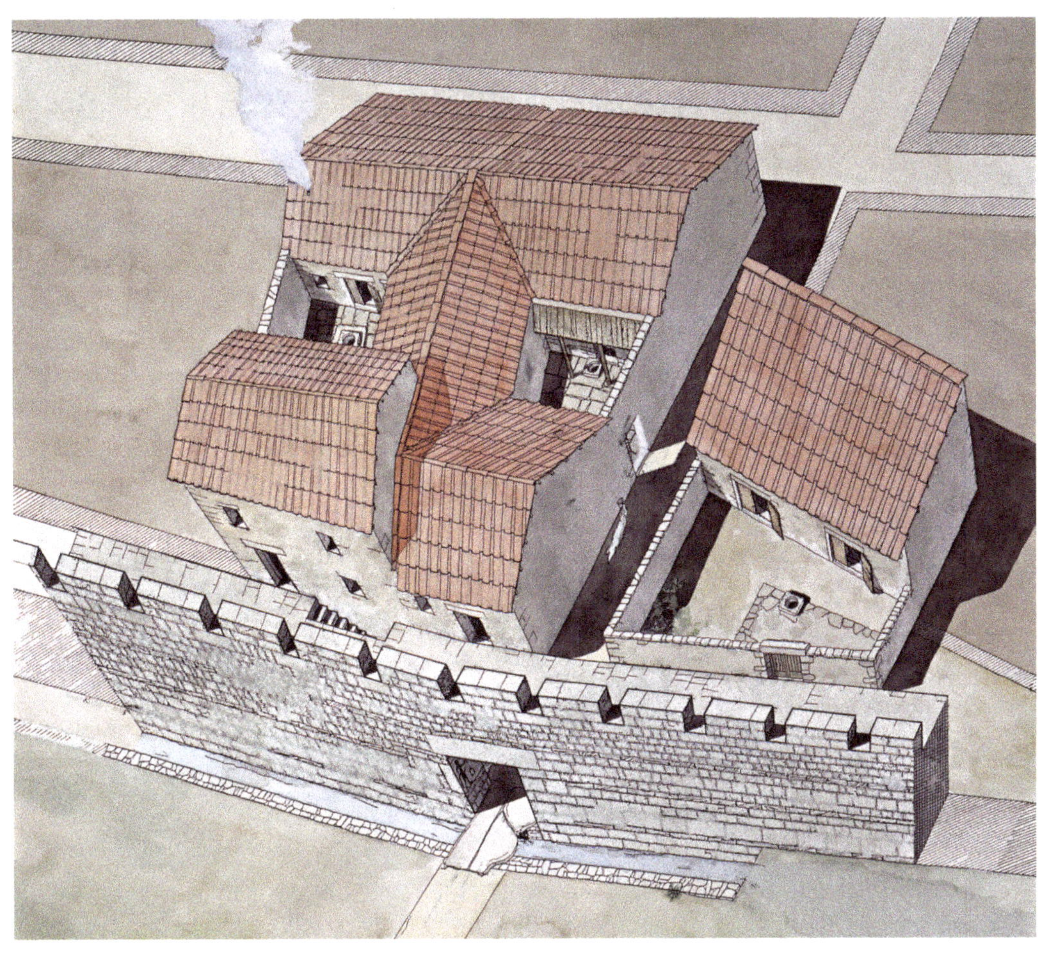

5.15 Reconstruction drawing of houses, Block 1, Silen's Quarter, Thasos. Source: slide no. X.822, EfA/P. Collet.

plastered and painted with black, yellow, and red, but only one piece of broken pottery, a pitcher, was found in its anteroom (j); pottery for the symposion held in the andron was likely stored in the other rooms of the house.

Examples of these types of objects are found at other sites. Drinking, eating, and cooking vessels have been found in the Agora excavations (**Figure 5.16**). Cooking and household vessels in the bottom row were plain and utilitarian. Vessels used in the symposion, such as pitchers and drinking cups, could be more finely made with a black glaze, thinner walls, more elaborate handles, and some painted and incised decoration. There are examples of pottery in the black-figure and red-figure techniques with figural decoration from households, but usually in a very fragmentary state and much less common than the plain and black-glaze ware seen here. The ensemble found in the debris from the destruction of a house in the Agora that we saw in Chapter 1 provides a glimpse of these wares and how they were accumulated over the course of years (**see Figure 1.10, page 14**). The household finds from Priene mostly date to the Hellenistic period (**Figure 5.17**). These include both plain pottery and a small fragment of red-figure work, mold-made bowls, lamps, and small metal objects such as spoons, lamps, tools, bells, and weapons.

TEXTILES

The presence of loom weights in houses shows the importance of weaving and textile production in the house, a task performed by its women. Most textiles would have been utilitarian and plain, but we know from literary sources that some were very elaborate and could feature intricate patterns and

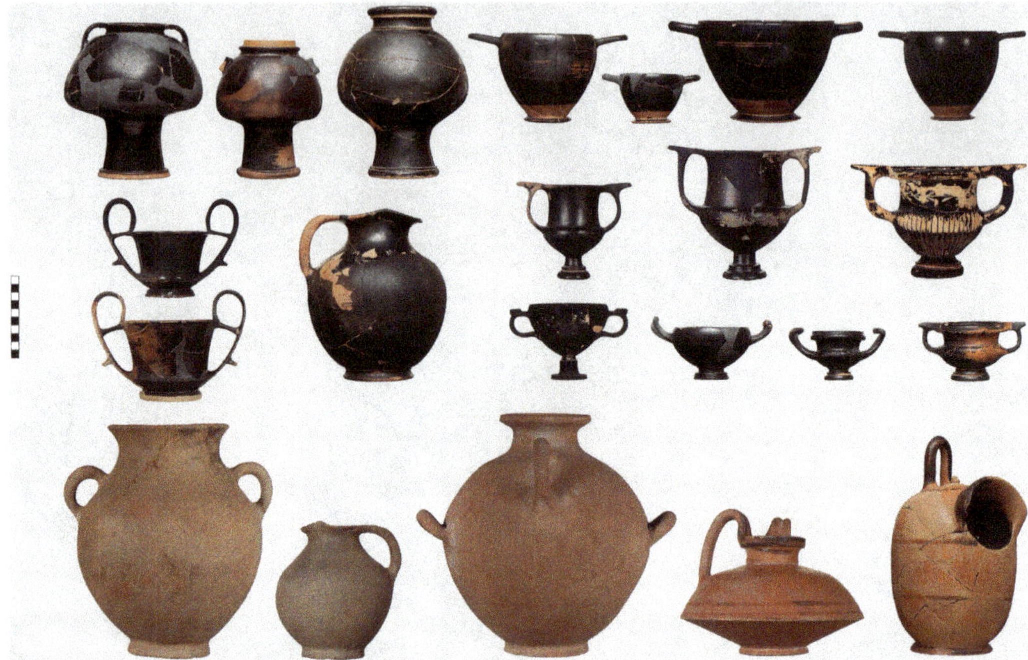

5.16 Household pottery found in the Agora at Athens, 6th–4th cent. BCE. Athens, Agora Museum. Photo: American School of Classical Studies at Athens: Agora Excavations.

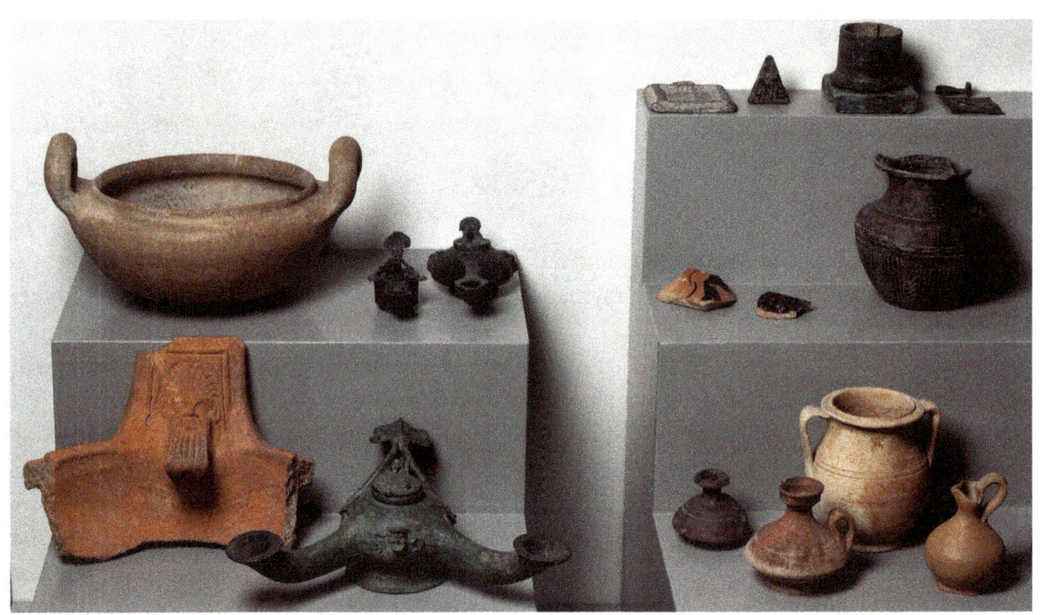

5.17 Household finds from Priene, 2nd–1st cent. BCE. Berlin, Antikensammlung AV1167. Photo: bpk, Berlin/ Antikensammlung, Staatliche Museen, Berlin, Germany/Ingrid Geske/Art Resource, NY.

colors and even narrative scenes. Fine and skillfully woven textiles could be very costly and an important resource of the household that had the advantage of being lightweight, easy to transport and store, and not prone to spoilage like most agricultural products. Unfortunately, textiles are perhaps the rarest of archaeological artifacts because they deteriorate so quickly, even in tombs.

The excavations of the royal tombs at Vergina have provided a rare example of the most costly type of weaving (**Figure 5.18**). The trapezoidal cloth has a wave-motif border around its edge, framing lush vegetal forms of leaves, flowers, tendrils, and birds that fill out the interior compartment. The use of threads made of gold and purple, a rare and expensive pigment, would have made this a costly work and a truly royal grave good. Color and shine would have been important visual qualities

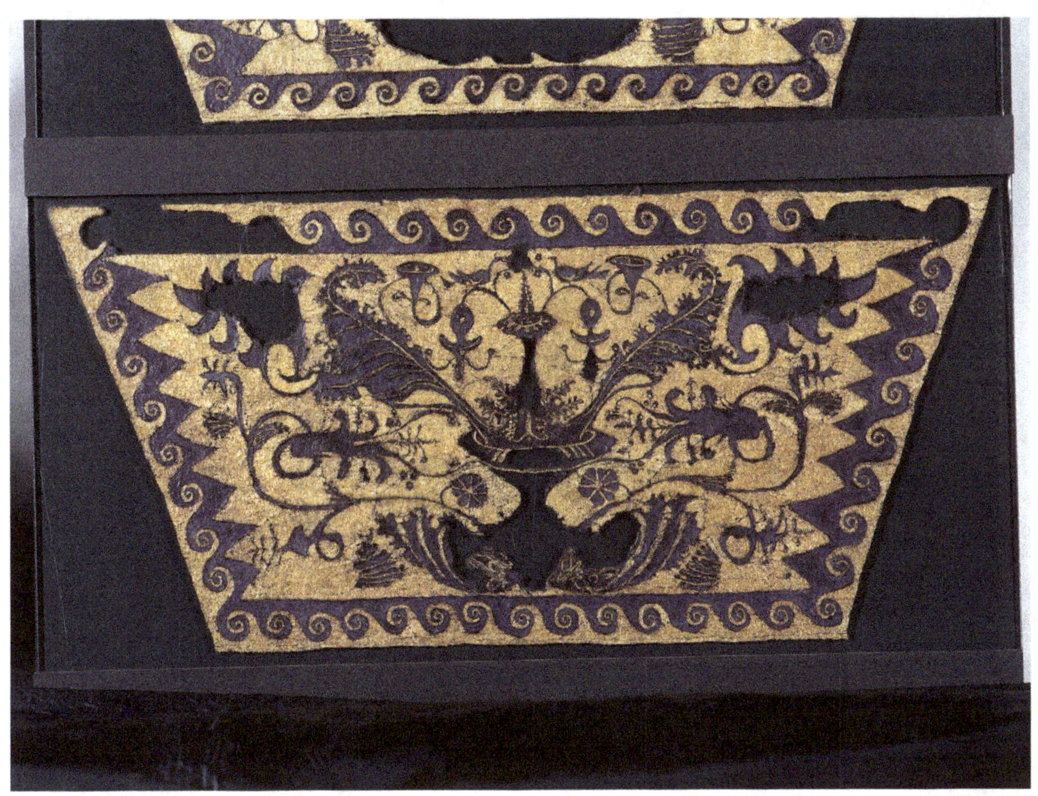

5.18 Textile from Tomb II at Vergina, *c.* 336–311 BCE. Aigai, Museum of the Royal Tombs. Photo: 17th Ephorate for Prehistoric and Classical Antiquities.

of the textile, and the use of gold thread would have created an interesting visual effect if worn or used in the sunlight. The importance of such cloth for grave goods and votive offerings means that their disappearance is a lost chapter of the history of Greek art.

The regard for elaborate textiles can be glimpsed through literary sources. The garment woven for the statue of Athena on the Acropolis that was presented during the Panathenaia was made by specially selected women and girls in a designated building and featured the battle of the gods and giants on it. The incident surrounding the Tyrannicides, when the sister of Harmodios was removed from the procession, shows how much prestige and care would have been worked into the gift to the goddess. Euripides, in his play *Ion*, has a servant recount how Ion, the son of Apollo and Creusa, set up a tent for a feast at Delphi:

> He took from store some sacred tapestries, a wonder to behold. And first he cast above the roof [of the tent] a wing of cloth, spoil from the Amazons, which Heracles, the son of Zeus, had dedicated to the god. And there were figures woven in design: For Uranus was mustering the stars in heaven's circle; and Helios drove his horses toward his dying flame and trailed the star which shines bright in the West. While black-robed Night, drawn by a pair, urged on her chariot, beside the stars kept pace with her. The Pleiades and Orion, his sword in hand, moved through the Sky's mid-path; and then, above, the Bear who turned his golden tail within the vault. The round full moon threw up her rays, dividing the month; the Hyades, the guide most sure for sailors; then light's herald, Dawn, routing the stars. (Euripides, *Ion* 1141–1158; tr. Willetts)

We can get an indirect picture of these high-end works in their domestic context by turning to a skyphos showing Penelope, the wife of Odysseus, with their son Telemachos (**Figure 5.19**). Penelope sits in a chair in her quarters of the house and contemplates the pressure on her to marry one of the suitors who are staying there, eating and drinking the provisions of the house. Odysseus has been gone ten years since the end of the Trojan War, and he has been given up for dead by all but his family. A loom is set up behind her and we see the end border hanging from the rolled fabric. On it

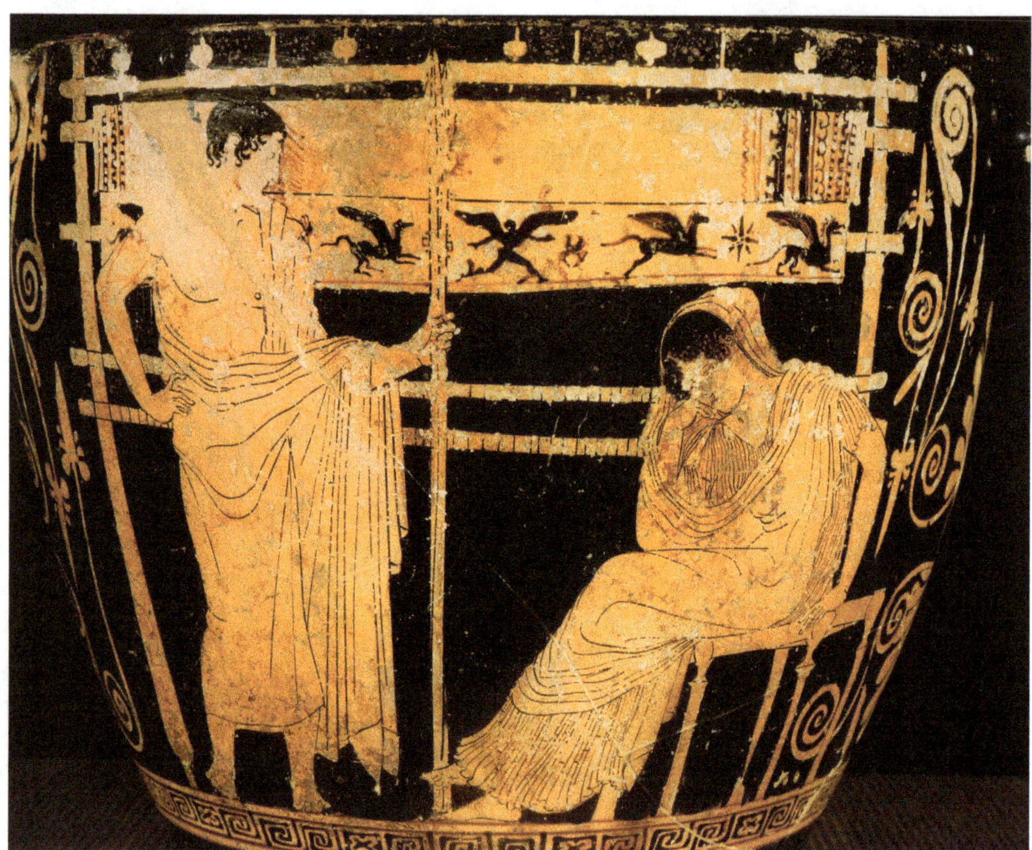

5.19 Attic red-figure skyphos attributed to the Penelope Painter, *c.* 450–440 BCE. 8 1/16 in (20.5 cm). Penelope and Telemachos at the loom. Chiusi, Museo Archeologico 1831. Photo: Erich Lessing/Art Resource, NY.

are depicted winged horses, griffins, and a winged deity running to the right. While the miniature picture of the cup can only sketch the elaborate detail possible with a finely woven garment, the quality of its work is a symbol of the work of Penelope in maintaining her household in Odysseus's absence and of the wealth and prestige of the household generally.

The tunic on the *kanephoros* at Delphi on a fifth-century Attic krater **(see Figure 7.17, page 174)** is another example of prestige textiles, and its intricate motifs and fringe distinguish this woman from those around her in the procession, and from the more plainly dressed maenads below. Some idea of the rich coloristic effects of textiles can be seen in the clothing of the seated king Priam on a large Apulian krater fragment from the fourth century **(see Figure 12.18, page 307)**. Yellow, red, brown, and white set on the red surface of the clay reveal an interest in both pattern and color, and a similarly ornate cloth is worn by Hermes who reaches to touch the king. The display of richly ornamented cloth would signify the status and wealth of its owner as he or she moved through the city. That most of them were undoubtedly designed and made by women also means that we have lost a significant group of Greek artists and their art as well.

THE SYMPOSION

It is within the context of the house that we should also consider the symposion of the Greeks. This was a gathering of men who would be invited to the house of the host in the evening. The symposion was held in a modest-sized room, such as the rooms at the back of stoas in the Agora or in a specially designated room in the house called the andron or men's room. The reconstruction in **Figure 5.20** shows a dining room in the South Stoa of the Agora at Athens, but its configuration and size are nearly the same as the andron at Olynthos that we saw earlier **(see Figure 5.12, k)**. The

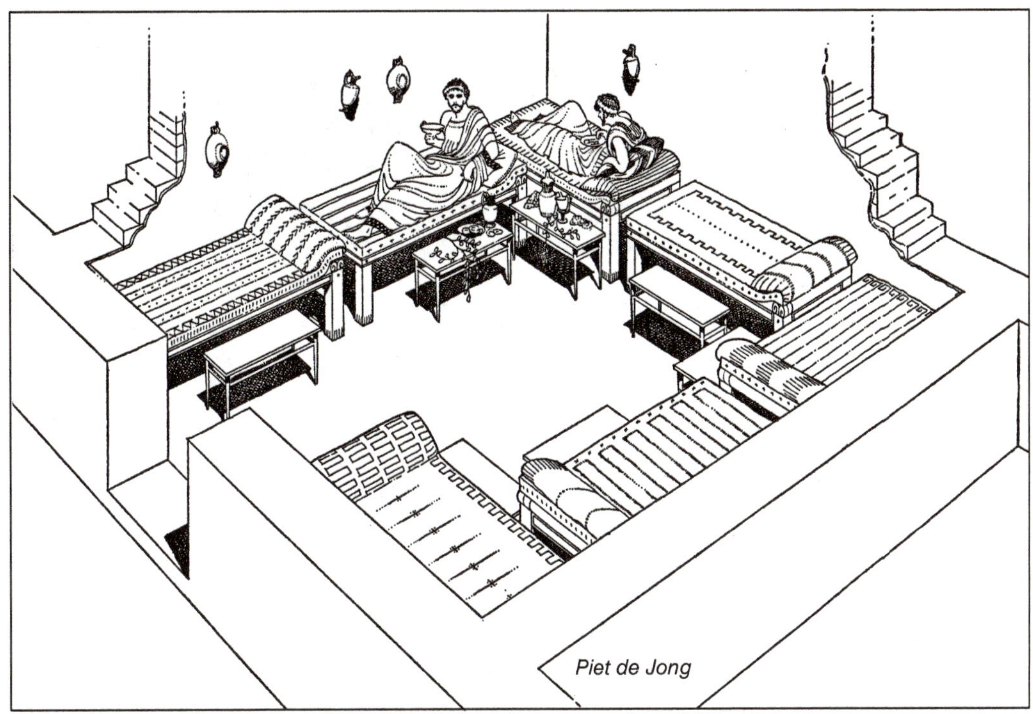

5.20 Reconstruction of dining room with symposiasts in the South Stoa of the Agora at Athens. Drawing by Piet de Jong. Photo: American School of Classical Studies at Athens: Agora Excavations.

symposiasts would recline on one-armed *klinai* or couches, drinking wine and interacting with each other. One or two men would recline on each *kline*, resting his weight on the left arm and using the right hand to hold the cup. Before each *kline* is a small table on which food and cups could be placed. The *klinai* were set against the wall of the room, leaving the center open and the symposiasts facing one another.

***kline* (pl. *klinai*)**
wooden couches with one arm and covered with cushions that were used for dining and drinking in the symposion. They might also serve as a bier for the prothesis

Based on descriptions in literary accounts, the symposion began with the welcoming of guests and washing in the courtyard, after which the guests would go to the andron to eat lightly. Following the meal, the symposiasts would have a drinking party that would start with a poured libation and a hymn. Slaves or servants would mix the wine with water and then serve the symposiasts. There might also be entertainers hired for the occasion, who might include women. Activities could include conversation, debate, singing, recitals of poetry, dancing, and/or sex **(see Figure 13.1, page 321)**. Literary sources suggest that the women of an elite family would typically be sequestered from the proceedings in other areas of the house. We will discuss the household relations of men and women further in Chapter 13.

Many of the vases used in the symposion are themselves decorated with sympotic pictures. One of the earliest examples is a Corinthian krater from the beginning of the sixth century **(Figure 5.21)**. Six men sit on four *klinai*, with a woman standing in front of them. The inscriptions identify this as a mythological scene, with king Eurytios seated in the left-center *kline* talking to his son Didalon. His other sons, Toxos and Klytios to the left and Iphitos to the right, are helping to entertain Herakles, who sits alone on the couch at the far right end. The woman is not a slave but Eurytios's daughter, Iole. While the symposion seems orderly here, in the end Herakles kills Eurytios and his sons and sacks the city of Oichalia, perhaps because of drunkenness or because Iole had been promised to him as the prize in an archery contest. This and other pictures are reminders that events at the symposion can get out of hand and require balance and moderation by the symposiasts.

Wine was the center of the symposion and its service required a number of different vases, whose variety can be seen in the diagram **(Figure 5.22)**. Wine would be stored in a necked jar called an amphora; the pelike, distinguished by its wider belly, is also used for storing and pouring liquids, as is the wider-mouthed stamnos. Wine was always mixed with water in proportions of 1:2 or 1:3; the

stamnos
a large storage vessel with two side handles and a wide mouth that could be used for storing or serving wine

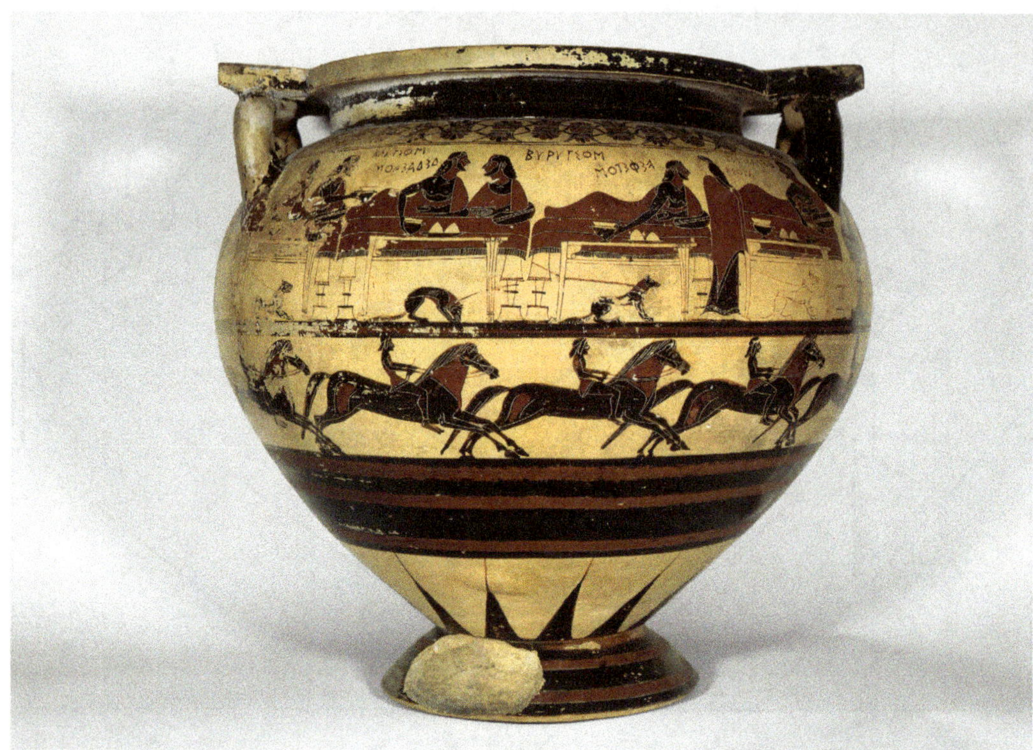

5.21 Early Corinthian column krater, *c.* 600–590 BCE. Banquet of Eurytios. 18⅛ in (46 cm). Paris, Musée du Louvre E635. Photo: © RMN-Grand Palais/Art Resource, NY.

water came in a three-handled jar called the **hydria**. The mixing of wine and water took place in a large krater that sat on the floor or on a table; the Eurytios krater is a version called the column krater for the configuration of the handles. Another mixing vessel called a **dinos** consisted of a spherical bowl without handles that sat on a stand; one of these can be seen on the far right of the Eurytios krater and on a Corinthian skyphos of about the same time period as the krater (**Figure 5.23**). The krater had several varieties, the *column krater*, *volute krater*, and *bell krater*, based on their features or shape, and the *calyx krater*, based on its resemblance to the kylix.

A pitcher, either an oinochoe or **olpe**, was dipped into the krater and then used to pour wine into cups. There is a wide range of cup shapes, some deep and large and others shallow and more delicate. The kylix was a shallow, broad bowl on a stemmed foot with handles projecting from the bowl; there was also a stemless kylix. This type of cup had to be handled carefully by the drinker if the wine were not to be spilled. Pictures of symposiasts holding a kylix up at an angle, as in the painting from the Tomb of the Diver (**see Figure 10.20, page 255**), show them either signaling the need to be refreshed with wine or playing a game called ***kottabos***, in which the sediment from the wine is flung at a target. The skyphos was a steep bowl with two handles that was sturdier and less likely to spill. The **kantharos** had high vertical handles and was a more elaborate shape related to metal vases (**see Figure 5.16**). We will be seeing examples of these types of vessels throughout this book.

While drinking, the symposiasts could sing or converse or be entertained by musicians, singers, or acrobats. The symposiasts could also rouse themselves from their couches to move around the andron, the house, or into the streets. The Corinthian skyphos (**Figure 5.23**) shows the ***komos***, a boisterous dance of symposiasts around a dinos. Some painted cups show symposiasts throwing up from too much drinking, reminding viewers of the sympotic pictures that the gifts of the gods needed to be consumed with balance and thought. This prompts us to remember, when looking at images on all vases, that these were objects that were used in specific ways, setting up a visual relationship with the viewer. With a cup, some pictures, such as inside the bowl, could only be seen by the drinker, while some on the outside could only be seen by other symposiasts. Motion and sharp angles of viewing would frame or limit what a viewer could see, so considering the sympotic context is

hydria
a three-handled vessel used for carrying and pouring water

dinos
a spherical mixing bowl without handles that sat on a stand

olpe
a pitcher used for pouring wine, usually with a round opening and continuously curved body

kottabos
a symposion game in which the sediment or dregs from the wine are tossed at targets in the andron

kantharos
a steep-sided, footed drinking cup with high projecting handles

komos
the movement of revelers at a symposion, which might take the form of a procession, boisterous dancing, and carousing

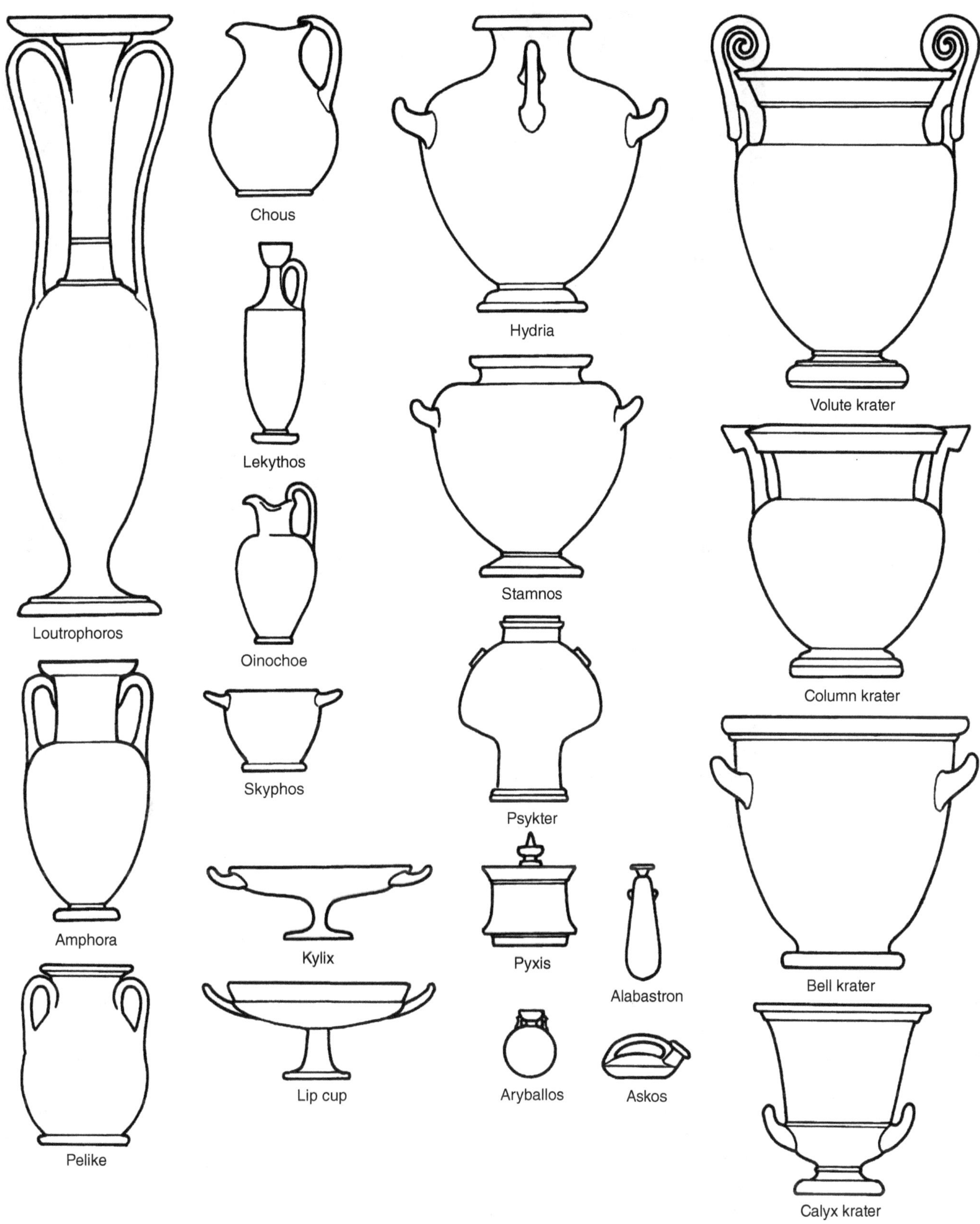

5.22 Diagram of vase types. After S. Bird and S. Woodford, *Greek Designs* (London: British Museum, 2003), p. 90.

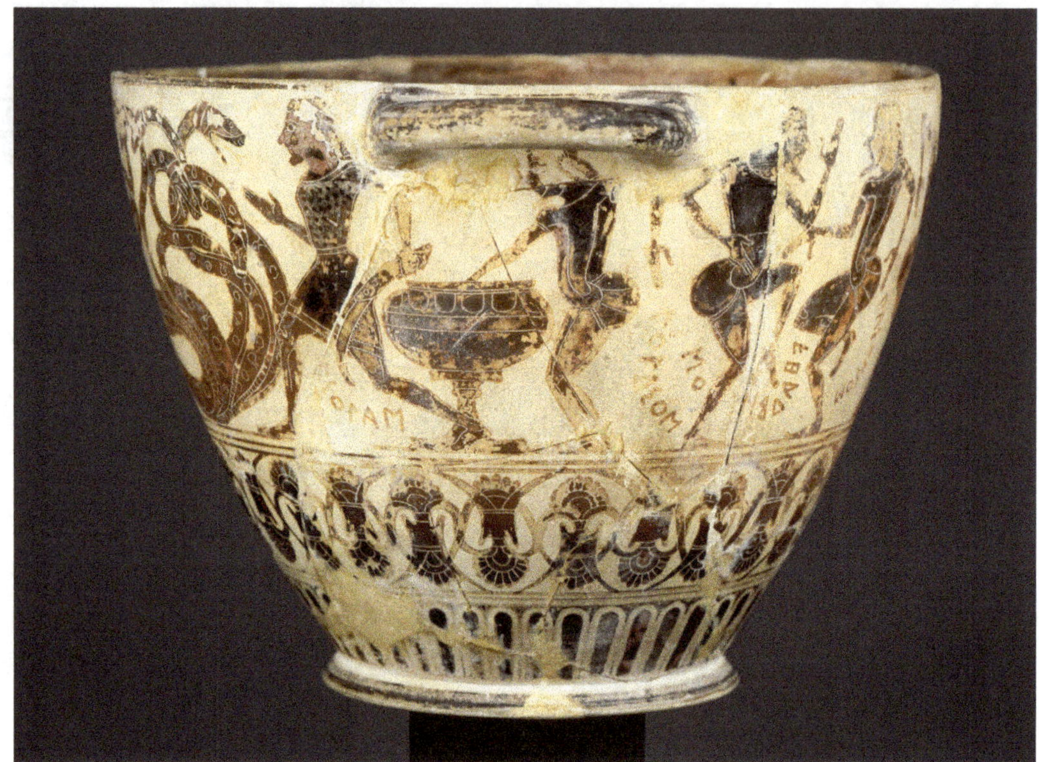

5.23 Middle Corinthian skyphos, *c.* 585–570 BCE. Paris, Musée du Louvre CA3004. 4½ in (11.5 cm). Left: Herakles and Hydra: center/right: komasts. Photo: © RMN-Grand Palais/Art Resource, NY.

important in considering the experience of the many images to be found on vases generally, including the narratives that we will explore in Chapter 9.

Before leaving the context of the symposion, one must remember that it was a formal and ritualistic activity, one in which the guests would bond with each other as members of the polis. Events could be boisterous and get out of hand, but the symposion could also be a venue in which serious thought or the performance of poetry and music helped to articulate the ideas of the participants. Many of the literary works of Plato and Xenophon are set in a symposion, with the participants engaging in a conversation with each other. That aspect of the proceedings continues on today in the use of the word symposium for a gathering of individuals to hear papers and discuss important topics.

GRAVES

grave offerings
objects left by mourners at a tomb, either on it or in an offering trench, as part of a ritual sacrifice or visit to the tomb

It was important to the Greeks for the dead and their names to be remembered and honored. Grave goods placed inside a tomb and **grave offerings** at or around the tomb are one way to do so, and a grave marker would be a still more visible sign to those who passed the cemeteries that were typically located just outside the walls of a town along the main roads. The Late Geometric I vases from the Dipylon cemetery in Athens were an early effort to distinguish the tombs of the elite, but this did not preserve their individual identity for someone who did not know or remember the deceased (**see Figures 4.7 and 4.9, pages 78, 80**). By the sixth century, large stone statues like those found in sanctuaries could be used as markers for elite tombs, such as the kouros statue found at a cemetery near Anavyssos, close to the tip of the Attic peninsula southeast of Athens (**Figure 5.24**). The nude youth is typical of works produced in this period, presenting an idealized, athletic male figure. The middle stone of a three-step base associated with the statue, but not certainly belonging to it, is inscribed: "Stay and mourn at the monument for dead Kroisos whom violent Ares destroyed, fighting in the front rank" (tr. Boardman 1991, 104). To die in battle, like Achilles, was to be heroic and ideal. The inscription, which by early custom would have been read aloud by the viewer rather than silently, evokes the name and deed of the deceased, perpetuating his memory. This statue is not a portrait but a representation of the ideal Greek male, and this is how Kroisos is to be remembered. The expense of a life-size marble statue testifies to the importance placed on his remembrance by the family and, if the inscription belongs to the statue, helps anyone visiting the tomb to know Kroisos.

Upon death, the body of the deceased would be washed and prepared and then laid out in the home on a couch or bier, a process called the prothesis that we saw on Geometric vases and continues to be seen in all periods of Greek art **(see Figures 4.7 and 4.9, pages 78, 80)**. Family and others would grieve and mourn over the dead, and then would accompany the body to the cemetery in a procession called the ***ekphora***.

What happened next depended on the type of burial, cremation or inhumation. If cremation, the body would be burned at the cemetery, and the ashes collected and placed in a container like an amphora or krater, usually ceramic but sometimes bronze or precious metal like gold. The tomb of the Rich Lady in the Athenian Agora is an excellent example of a cremation burial, as we saw in the last chapter **(see Figures 4.4–4.6, pages 74, 75, 76)**. Other vases or offerings for the dead sometimes show signs of being burned in the fire, but in many cases not. The ashes and other grave goods would be placed in the tomb, which could consist of a simple pit or trench in the ground (*fossa* tomb), or a trench or pit lined with terracotta panels (***a cappucina* tomb**) or stone slabs (cist tomb).

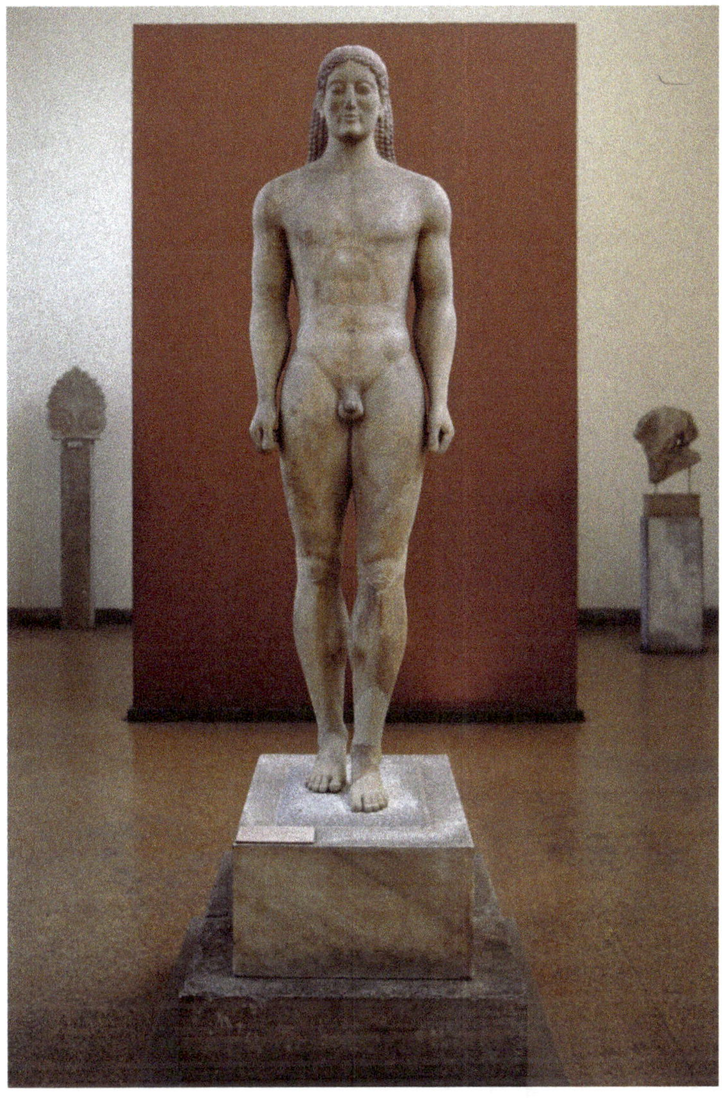

5.24 Kouros from Anavyssos, perhaps from tomb of Kroisos, *c.* 530 BCE. 6 ft 4⅜ in (1.94 m). Athens, National Archaeological Museum 3851. Photo: © Vanni Archive/Art Resource, NY.

With inhumation burial, the body was placed into the tomb, which was usually rectangular in shape so that the body was stretched out. As with cremation burials, the tomb could be a simple trench in the ground (*fossa*) or lined with terracotta (*a cappucina*) or stone slabs (cist). In addition, the body could be placed into a stone coffin called a sarcophagus **(see Figure 14.1, page 344)**, either set into the ground or placed in a chamber or vault. Even large vases like a pointed amphora and a pithos **(see Figures 6.15 and 6.18, pages 144, 146)** could be used as a coffin, although each was likely intended for another purpose, such as a grave marker and storage container respectively.

Grave goods could be placed next to or on the body, and also on top of a slab covering the tomb. A drawing made during the excavation of the Late Geometric IIB Tomb XI in the Athenian Agora shows a *fossa* inhumation burial of a man with a large number of vases as grave goods placed at his feet **(Figure 5.25)**. In making the trench, the diggers cut through an earlier tomb and the lower legs of its occupant (the later well in the drawing cut through the upper part of the same grave). The grave goods in Tomb XI included two amphorae, some bowls and drinking cups, a terracotta mourning figure, an iron knife, and a number of other vase fragments. Some of these show signs of burning, and must be offerings in a sacrificial pyre at the tomb site that were gathered and buried with the

ekphora
the procession bearing the body of the deceased from the home to the tomb

***a cappucina* tomb**
Italian term designating a tomb made by lining a pit or trench with terracotta panels

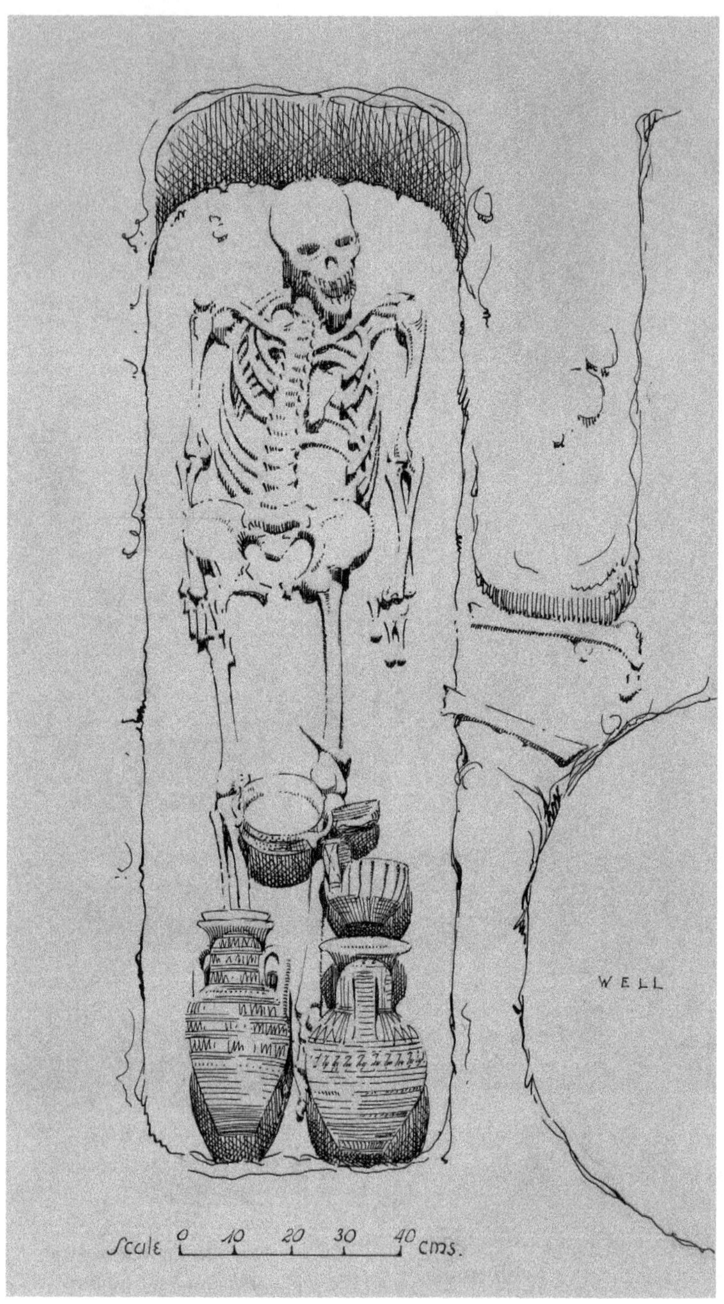

5.25 Late Geometric Tomb XI with part of Tomb XXII, Agora, Athens, end 8th cent. or beginning 7th cent. BCE. Drawing by Piet de Jong. Photo: American School of Classical Studies at Athens: Agora Excavations.

deceased. Other assemblages of grave goods can be seen in other chapters **(see Figures 12.16, page 305; 13.5, page 326; 13.16, page 337)**. Indeed, many of the sympotic vessels found in museums today come from tombs, either in Greek sites or in those of other cultures like the Etruscans, who purchased these objects in large quantities. Being sealed in a tomb can help to preserve an object, unlike a domestic context in which breakage and discarding in the trash is a more likely fate for pottery.

A wide variety of objects and materials could be placed in the grave with the deceased. Vessels for drinking were common, as were kraters, which could also be used as ossuaries for cremation burials. Some vases found in tombs have been mended with drill holes and lead clamps, showing that vases in the household could find their way into graves, whereas other vases could be bought for the occasion. The jewelry and metal objects found in tombs likely came from domestic contexts before they were used in the tomb, so we find some overlap between objects found in tombs and those originally used in houses. Small terracotta figures like those in sanctuaries could also be placed into graves, showing further overlap among contexts **(see Figures 1.4–1.5, pages 9–10)**. Whatever their source, grave goods and grave offerings are reminders of the rituals associated with funerals and the importance of tombs and their dead for the living.

After the burial, there were return visits to the grave on days 3, 9, and 30 after death, and then monthly or annually after that. A special category of vases made in Athens, white-ground lekythoi, contained oil and were left at the tomb on these visits, and the paintings that cover their white surface give us a synopsis of funerary practices and beliefs **(Figure 5.26)**. The lekythos on the left shows the prothesis in the house, with a young man lying on a *kline* or bier. At his head is a standing youth who claps his hand to his hair in grief; as a youth, he has not yet developed the restraint expected of adult men at the funeral. Leaning over the deceased is a woman who holds the chin of the deceased and gestures toward the youth. Unseen at the foot of the couch is a second woman in a pose like the standing youth. The action is similar to what is represented more schematically on the Geometric prothesis scenes, but is essentially the same on a reduced scale at a time when there were restrictions of lavish public displays of grief at funerals.

The lekythos on the right shows a stone funeral stele, on which garlands brought by the visitors have been tied. The woman to the left carries a basket, from which garlands or ribbons can be seen hanging; she will leave these offerings at the tomb. Wreaths, lekythoi, and a kylix stand on the steps as offerings left at the tomb, as can be seen on another lekythos from the same time **(see Figure 10.25, page 261)**. The youth on the right leans on a stick, as is common in conversational types of scenes, but we do not know whether this youth is the deceased or another family member. So, too, the woman

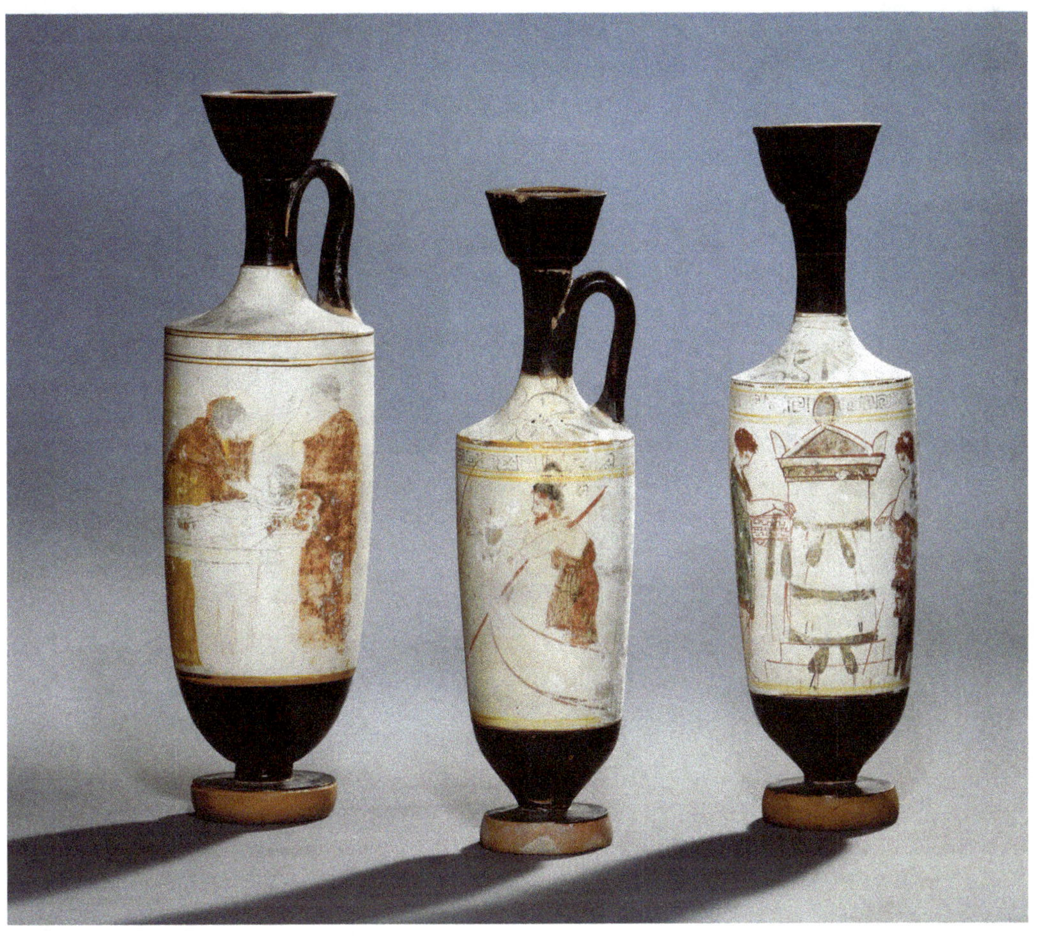

5.26 Attic white-ground lekythoi with funerary scenes. London, British Museum. Left: attributed to the Sabouroff Painter, c. 450–440 BCE. 13 in (33.02 cm). Prothesis and mourning. D62. Center: attributed to the Reed Painter, c. 420–410 BCE. 11½ in (29.2 cm). Charon. D61. Right: attributed to the Reed Painter, c. 420 BCE. 12½ in (31.7 cm). Woman and youth at tomb. D73. Photo: © The Trustees of the British Museum.

seated before the stele in **Figure 10.25** is likely to be the deceased, but mourners such as Elektra have also been known to sit in a similar pose. These pictures convey the importance of continued visits to the tomb, and the identity of the figures remains flexible to allow "reading" the picture according to the specific circumstances in which the lekythos is purchased and used.

The middle lekythos shows Charon in his boat, reaching out to take the shade of the deceased to the underworld. These are melancholy scenes, and the picture painted of the underworld in literature is generally somber. What gladdened the spirits of the dead were the rites and offerings made at their tombs and that they were remembered by their families. These vases would both honor the dead by their use and recognize the continuing attention to the dead by tomb visits. An indication that the act and appearance of the ritual are more important than the actual gift is seen in the fact that many of these lekythoi have plugs just below their neck, so that a small amount of oil would make the container look full, while in fact it was mostly empty.

The **kore** statue could also be used as a grave marker, although less frequently. Rather than recognizing heroic deeds, these inscriptions tend to emphasize the domestic context. The statue of Phrasikleia (**see Figure 8.13, page 195**), for example, tells us that she "will always be called kore," or maiden, since she died before she was married. She is dressed with fine garments whose woven decoration is shown by paint and incision, and wears a crown like a bride.

kore (pl. korai) a young woman or maiden, used to denote statues of clothed standing female figures in the seventh, sixth, and fifth centuries

The excavations at the Kerameikos cemetery in Athens give us a good idea of the arrangement of grave markers and how they were situated for viewing by people entering and leaving the city. Today, reproductions of original grave markers from the classical period line the embankment along the road from the Dipylon Gate leading to the sanctuary of Demeter at Eleusis. Three of these stelai belonged to the plot of a family from the neighborhood of Melite in western Athens (**Figure 5.27**).

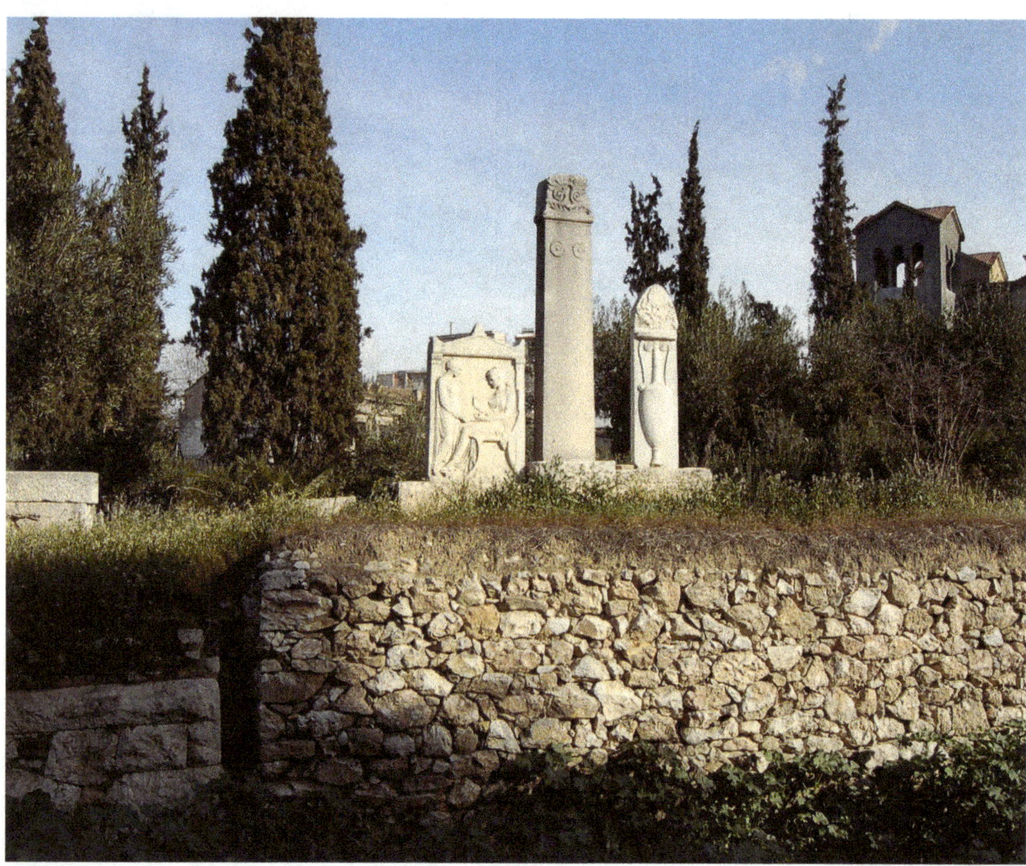

5.27 Stelai of Koroibos–Kleidemides family in the Kerameikos, Athens, reconstruction of 4th cent. BCE tomb plot. Photo: author.

The central stele has five inscriptions in different hands, added over the course of several generations, that record the names of the deceased:

> Koroibos son of Kleidemides, of Melite
> Kleidemides son of Koroibos, of Melite
> Koroibos son of Kleidemides, of Melite

Two more names follow these:

> Euthydemos, son of Sosikles of Eitea
> Sosikles, son of Euthydemos

The first three names are three generations of the male head of the family, with given names alternating by generations. The fourth individual, Euthydemos, may have married a sister or daughter of Koroibos II, and assumed the role of head of the family, which then passed to his son Sosikles. The stele to the right features a relief of a special long-necked vase called a **loutrophoros**. This vessel, used for ritual washing, was particularly appropriate for commemorating the dead and its inscription tells us that it is for Kleidemos, son of Kleidemides, probably the brother of the first Koroibos (the alternation of names by generation makes this uncertain). He appears to have died unmarried and was good in battle, and perhaps died fighting like Kroisos. The nearby monument of Dexileos **(see Figures 12.12 and 12.13, pages 301, 302)** tells us that he died in a battle in 394–393 and shows him triumphant riding a horse, even though he was killed in battle (**see also Figure 9.17, page 231** for another battle funerary monument).

loutrophoros
a tall closed container with a long and narrow neck. The *loutrophoros-hydria* with three handles was generally used for water in ritual washing of the bride; the *loutrophoros-amphora* with two handles served funerary purposes

The left stele shows a woman seated on a chair with a female attendant, probably a slave **(Figure 5.28)**. She holds something like a necklace in her hand; the inscription tells us that she is

"Hegeso, [daughter of] Proxenos." Given its date, about 400 BCE, it is thought that she could be the wife of the first Koroibos mentioned on the adjacent stele. While more naturalistic in appearance than Phrasikleia or Kroisos in the mid-sixth century, this is still an idealized and universal representation, now of a woman who, as wife, manages the household. She is beautiful, poised, and modest. As the only woman represented by image or name in the family plot, one can see the relative importance of male lineage, but the interruption in the male line on the middle stele also reminds us that women had a role to play in the continuity of the family and household, as we shall discuss further in Chapter 13. Indeed, the fortune of Koroibos, like that of Euthydemos, might have been made by his marriage to the daughter of Proxenos, if she were Proxenos's only descendant, prompting a special monument for the female line of the family (Stewart 1997, 124–129).

These three monuments were set up near each other in time, in the late fifth and early fourth centuries, but the four added inscriptions on the central stele are testimony to the continuing involvement of the family in honoring their ancestors. In their original condition, we have to imagine the stelai festooned with ribbons and offerings of vases by attendants, like the scene on the earlier lekythoi. Set up high along the road to Eleusis, these and other monuments would testify to the position and devotion of the family, and the role that both its men and women played in the city. Sculpted stelai would be an expensive commemoration, but one that would endure and be worth the investment for the family.

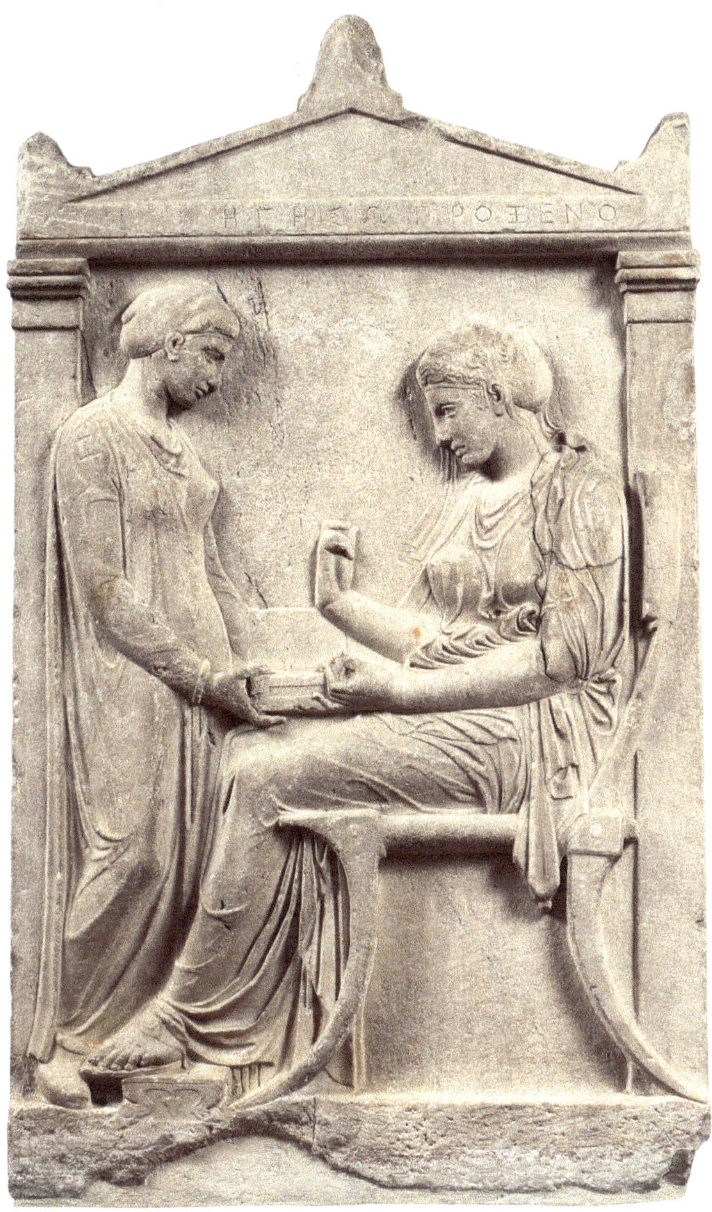

5.28 Stele of Hegeso, *c.* 400 BCE. 5 ft 2$\frac{3}{16}$ in (1.58 m). Athens, National Archaeological Museum 3624. Photo: National Archaeological Museum, Athens (Giannis Patrikianos) © Hellenic Ministry of Education and Religious Affairs, Culture and Sports/Archaeological Receipts Fund.

TEXTBOX: AGENCY

Art history as a discipline has been built around two primary methodologies: stylistic or formal analysis and iconography. Emphasizing context as we have in this chapter means that we need other approaches that focus our attention on the social or religious role that a work of art plays. Alfred Gell developed one contextual methodology that is called agency. He maintained that

> art is a system of action, intended to change the world rather than encode symbolic propositions about it. The "action"-centred approach to art is inherently more anthropological than the alternative semiotic approach because it is preoccupied with the practical mediatory role of art objects in the social process, rather than with the interpretation of objects "as if" they were texts. (Gell 1998, 6)

To maintain focus upon action, he defined four components of the art "nexus," the chain of actions that center on the work of art. These are:

- Index (the object or work of art)
- Artist (maker of the work of art)
- Prototype (the idea, concept, or thing represented)
- Recipient (the viewers and/or purchasers of the work of art)

Every stage of action involves two of these components, with one serving as the Agent (who causes the action to happen) and the other as the Patient (who receives the action).

For example, in making a work of art, the Artist is Agent while the Index (work of art) is the Patient. However, if a patron commissions a work, then the Recipient is the Agent, and the Artist is the Patient. Who acts upon whom can be designated by arrows. So, we might say that for the grave stele of Hegeso, presuming that it was commissioned by her family, we would have the following chain of actions:

Hegeso (Prototype) → → → → → Family (Recipient) → → → → → Sculptor (Artist) → → → → → Relief (Index) → → → → → Viewer (Second Recipient)

The death of Hegeso and the need to commemorate her are the initial action that causes the family to act, commissioning the artist who produces the relief. Once set up, it is then on display to viewers, who through this chain of action understand the virtue and importance of Hegeso.

By focusing on the actions in its creation and use, one can begin to understand the intention and purpose of a work outside of its aesthetic quality. Working through such a defined system allows us to consider how actions create meaning and importance for a work of art, whether it is a small terracotta purchased as a modest votive offering or a monumental bronze sculpture group like the Tyrannicides commissioned by a city.

See Tanner 2007; Stansbury-O'Donnell 2011, 149–154; Whitley 2012.

REFERENCES

Boardman, J. 1991. *Greek Sculpture: The Archaic Period: A Handbook*. London: Thames and Hudson.

Cahill, N. 2002. *Household and City Organization at Olynthus*. New Haven: Yale University Press.

Euripides, *Ion* in D. Grene and R. Lattimore, eds. 1958. *Euripides III*, tr. R. F. Willetts. Chicago: University of Chicago Press.

Gell, A. 1998. *Art and Agency: An Anthropological Theory*. Oxford: Oxford University Press.

Papadopoulos, J. K. and M. R. Schilling. 2003. *Ceramicus Redivius: The Early Iron Age Potters' Field in the Area of the Classical Athenian Agora. Hesperia Supplements* 31. Princeton: American School of Classical Studies in Athens.

Stansbury-O'Donnell, M. D. 2011. *Looking at Greek Art*. Cambridge/New York: Cambridge University Press.

Stewart, A. 1997. *Art, Desire, and the Body in Ancient Greece*. Cambridge/New York: Cambridge University Press.

Tanner, J. 2007. "Portraits and Agency: A Comparative View." In R. Osborne and J. Tanner, eds. *Art's Agency and Art History*, 70–74. Oxford: Blackwell.

Whitley, J. 2012. "Agency in Greek Art." In T. J. Smith and D. Planzos, eds. *A Companion to Greek Art*, Chapter 30. Oxford: Blackwell.

FURTHER READING

Boardman, J. 1991. *Greek Sculpture: The Archaic Period: A Handbook.* London: Thames and Hudson.

Cahill, N. 2002. *Household and City Organization at Olynthus.* New Haven: Yale University Press.

Camp, J. M. 1986. *The Athenian Agora: Excavations in the Heart of Classical Athens.* London: Thames and Hudson.

Camp, J. M. 2001. *The Archaeology of Athens.* New Haven: Yale University Press.

Kurtz, D. C. and J. Boardman. 1971. *Greek Burial Customs.* Ithaca: Cornell University Press.

Lissarrague, F. 1987. *The Aesthetics of the Greek Banquet: Images of Wine and Ritual (Un Flot d'Images),* tr. A. Szegedy-Maszak. Princeton: Princeton University Press.

Mee, C. 2011. *Greek Archaeology: A Thematic Approach.* Chichester: Wiley Blackwell.

Nevett, L. C. 1999. *House and Society in the Ancient Greek World.* Cambridge: Cambridge University Press.

Nevett, L. C. 2010. *Domestic Space in Classical Antiquity.* Cambridge: Cambridge University Press.

Stansbury-O'Donnell, M. D. 2011. *Looking at Greek Art.* Cambridge/New York: Cambridge University Press.

Topper, K. 2012. *The Imagery of the Athenian Symposium.* Cambridge/New York: Cambridge University Press.

Young, R. S. and J. L. Angel. 1939. *Late Geometric Graves and a Seventh Century Well in the Agora. Hesperia Supplements* 2, 44–55. Princeton: American School of Classical Studies at Athens.

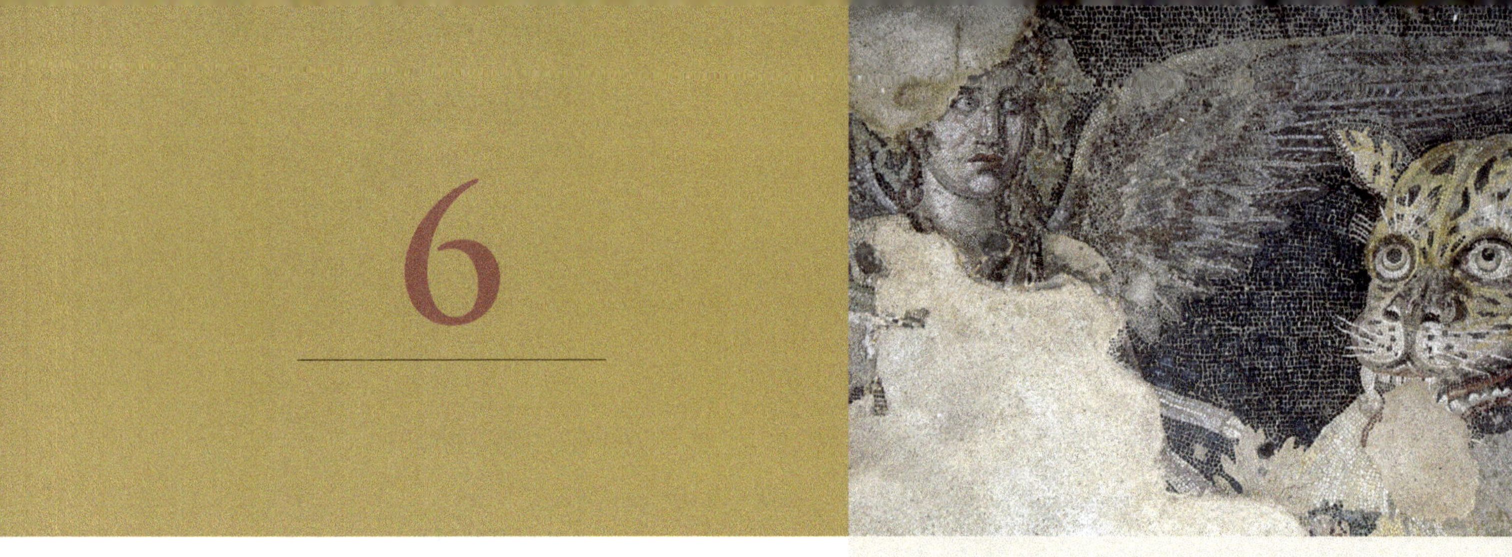

6

THE SEVENTH CENTURY

(*c.* 725/700–625/600 BCE)

Timeline

Greek Pottery Painting and the Mediterranean

Metalwork and Terracotta

Architecture and its Decoration

Textbox: Network Theory

References

Further Reading

A History of Greek Art, First Edition. Mark D. Stansbury-O'Donnell.

TIMELINE

	Sculpture	Pottery	Architecture	Events
725–700		Protocorinthian Evelyn Painter aryballos		734 Founding of Syracuse/Siracusa 706 Founding of Taras/Taranto
700–675	Mantiklos Apollo [7.19]		Temple of Hera 1b at Samos	
675–650	Mykonos relief pithos	Protocorinthian aryballoi Sicilian stamnos Protoattic amphora at Eleusis		664–610 Reign of Psammetichos, founding of Naukratis 651 Founding of Selinus/Selinunte
650–625	Nikandre's kore	Protocorinthian Chigi olpe	Temple of Hera 2 at Samos Temple at Thermon	
625–600		Wild Goat-style oinochoe	Temple at Prinias	*c.* 600 Founding of Poseidonia/Paestum
600–575	Sounion kouros			

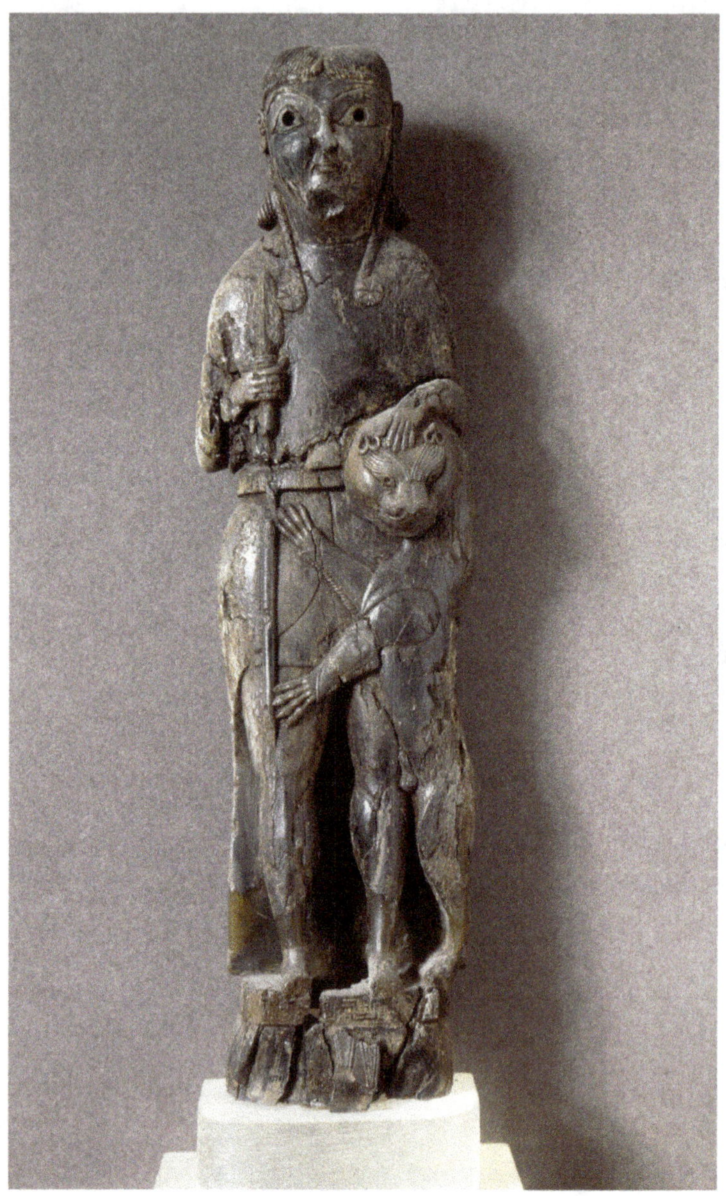

6.1 Ivory group of hero with lion, *c.* 700–650 BCE. 9½ in (24 cm). Delphi, Archaeological Museum 9912. Photo: Nimatallah/ Art Resource, NY.

rosette
a circular ornamental motif made of petals, with lines converging to the center

The seventh century is generally called the Orientalizing period due to the much closer interactions between Greece and the eastern Mediterranean, particularly with the peoples of Asia Minor, the Levant, and Egypt. During this time, one can see new developments in the style of Greek art, especially in the more precise detailing that makes human and animal figures more naturalistic in their appearance than their Geometric predecessors. New subjects appear, and there is a more widespread effort to represent pictorial narratives. The objects made by Greek artists include new shapes, new materials, and new techniques, and their works find new markets in both the eastern and central Mediterranean. We have already seen that Geometric art from Greece did find its way to Cyprus **(see Figure 4.11, page 82)**, while works, material, and even artists from the Levant ended up in Athenian graves and Crete **(see Figures 4.6, 4.14, 11.12, pages 76, 85, 281)**. The scale of interaction with other regions and cultures increases significantly beginning in the late eighth century, and many of the new subjects, techniques, and materials of the seventh century suggest that Greek artists were influenced by these other cultures. The question of cultural interaction is complex, and we will consider the forms that it takes – imitation, copying, originality, influence, adaptation – more generally in this chapter.

These issues present themselves in an ivory statue of a man and lion that was found with other ivory and gold artifacts buried in Delphi under the Sacred Way, the path that led through the sanctuary to the Temple of Apollo **(Figure 6.1)**. The figure has more lifelike proportions than earlier Geometric bronzes **(compare Figures 4.17 and 4.19, pages 88 and 90)** and his costume and anatomy are more detailed, including jointed fingers, knees, and plaits of the hair. The figure is still frontal and the arms are compressed to hold a spear and head of a lion while keeping close to the body and minimizing the carving of the ivory surface. The small mouth and cheeks are more rounded, the overlarge eyes have tear ducts and pupils, and the ears are formed by spirals, details lacking in the Geometric bronzes. Two circles are formed at the end of the front braid and are divided into eight segments, a motif called a rosette that becomes popular in Orientalizing art. The lion's head is also frontal and its snout, eyes, eyebrows, and ears create a dynamic X-shaped composition that gives some real energy to its face. The claws and tendons are given detailed attention, although the tops of both feet are shown, as if it had two left feet. The top ledge of the base has a meander/battlement pattern like those we saw in the Geometric period, but the curved section below has a more curvilinear, leaflike pattern.

The object was likely a votive offering to the sanctuary at Delphi, which had become an important Panhellenic site by the eighth century BCE. Like the sanctuary of Olympia that we discussed in Chapter 4, Panhellenic sanctuaries were important cultural exchanges for Greek art and Delphi's prominence grew through the seventh century and afterward. As we shall see more fully in the next chapter, visitors came to Delphi from all over the Greek world and some from the non-Greek

Mediterranean, bringing offerings to Apollo in the hopes of an oracle and guidance. Visual motifs, subjects, and styles could be observed and dispersed by exchange of goods and ideas.

The ivory statue was likely brought to Delphi from somewhere else, but trying to determine its origin is difficult since it has a pastiche of traits from different artistic traditions. In terms of its subject and composition, the closest parallel for the ivory is found in monumental Assyrian sculpture, such as the guardian figure holding a small lion from a courtyard in the palace at Khorsabad in modern Iraq (**Figure 6.2**). This figure wears a short tunic and its beard, face, and hairstyle differ from the Delphi ivory. The lions are similar, but the legs of the Assyrian lion move more convincingly in three dimensions to wrap around the body of the guardian. There is no parallel for the composition in small sculpture, and it is not likely that the ivory carver had seen the Assyrian palaces for it to be a direct influence. The style and some of the details, such as the ornament on the bottom level of the base, can be found in the art of Lydia in Asia Minor, but the battlement pattern appears to be more Greek in origin. The ivory itself likely originated in western Asia, but it could have been carved elsewhere. The face, especially its triangular chin, has some affinity with the "Daedalic" face found in Greek sculpture of the seventh century, such as the votive figure of the "Mantiklos Apollo" that we will see in the next chapter (**see Figure 7.19, page 176**), but is otherwise more rounded. While it has a belt like the Mantiklos Apollo, this is not a Greek device; and the Mantiklos Apollo's nudity is more typical of Greek male figures, unlike the Delphi man. The subject of man controlling or fighting a lion is also unusual for Apollo, but not necessarily for his sister Artemis, who is often shown as a mistress of the animals, holding a beast in each hand (**see Figure 6.16, page 145**).

We might call this ivory figure syncretic or a hybrid, blending motifs and styles of different contemporary artistic traditions. Certainly this work looks very different than the ivory woman from the Dipylon cemetery (**see Figure 4.14, page 85**), which itself was already "Orientalizing" in its depiction of a nude female figure like the representations of the goddess Astarte in art of the Levant. Here there is more borrowing and blending, perhaps done by an eastern Greek artist who was familiar with small works of art from various Mediterranean cultures.

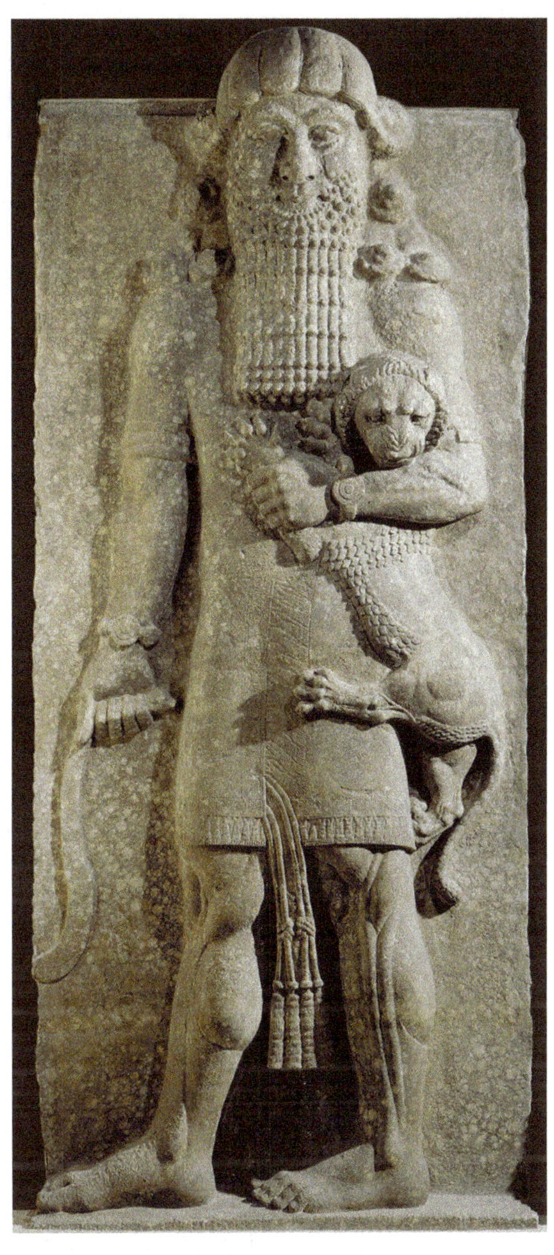

6.2 Neo-Assyrian relief from the palace at Khorsabad, *c.* 720 BCE. 14 ft 7³⁄₁₆ in (4.45 m). Paris, Musée du Louvre. Photo: Erich Lessing/Art Resource, NY.

A more certainly identifiable Greek sculpture of the period is still surprising in the new features it presents. Done around 650–625 BCE, it is a monumental marble statue, dedicated by a woman named Nikandre on the island of Delos as a votive offering to Artemis, for whom Nikandre may have served as a priestess (**Figure 6.3**). The work is one of the earliest in a series of female stone statues, called kore or "maiden." The scale of the figure is striking compared to earlier sculpture; at 1.75 meters, it is life-size or a bit larger (5 ft 6 in = 1.68 m). This larger size is made possible by using marble from the island of Naxos as the medium. While the statue now appears very worn, the use of marble allowed the work to endure years of exposure to the elements and to preserve the inscription that we can still read today: "Nikandre dedicated me to the far-shooter of arrows [Artemis], the excellent daughter of Deinodikes of Naxos, sister of Deinomenes, n[ow?] wife of Phraxos."

The figure is very shallow, almost slab-like, and much of the surface is flat. The kore is wearing a simple, long garment that is belted at the waist. The arms are straight at the side, with drill holes in the rolled fingers that held some type of attachment, perhaps an offering (if she is a mortal figure like

Daedalic
a term derived from the mythological figure of Daidalos, used to signify early sculpture and relief of the seventh century, particularly the flat heads and triangle-shaped hair and faces

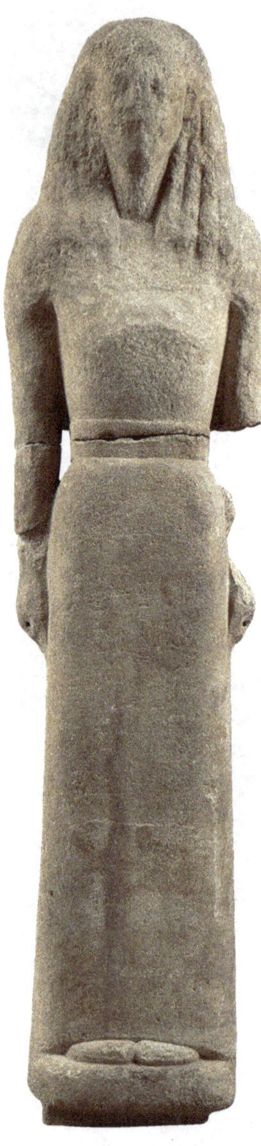

6.3 Kore of Nikandre from Delos, *c.* 650–625 BCE. 5 ft 8¹¹⁄₁₆ in (1.75 m). Athens, National Archaeological Museum 1. Photo: National Archaeological Museum, Athens (Giannis Patrikianos) © Hellenic Ministry of Education and Religious Affairs, Culture and Sports/Archaeological Receipts Fund.

Nikandre) or an attribute such as a bow (if the goddess Artemis). The head is representative of what is called the Daedalic type, with a flattened cranium, a triangle pointing downward for the face inside a larger triangle, formed by the braids of hair, pointing upward. The figure was once painted, which would have emphasized these features and additionally given some pattern to the flat surfaces of the dress.

A striking point about Nikandre's kore is that the production of a large marble sculpture and its transportation to Delos would have been a significant expenditure and undertaking, since there was no established infrastructure for the production of large sculpture at this time. Although it had been commonly used for Cycladic figures two millennia earlier in the Bronze Age, its use as a material is new in the third quarter of the seventh century. To cut and polish the stone required the development of techniques that were not found in previous stonework, such as the rough stones used in the walls of Zagora. To make this sculpture, a block of marble had to be cut out of a quarry bed using wedges, splints, and hammers, and then shaped with a variety of points and chisels. At 160 pounds per cubic foot, transportation of the marble from the quarry to the harbor in Naxos, and then by ship to Delos, would require planning and care. In other words, creating a well-made marble statue requires an infrastructure of source material, skilled labor, and transportation that did not exist in the earlier Geometric period.

There are a number of fragmentary marble and limestone statues of female and male figures dated between 650 and 600 BCE, but the earliest surviving complete statues of the standing nude male counterpart to Nikandre's kore, the kouros statue, date to just after 600, like the kouros found in the sanctuary at Cape Sounion (**Figure 6.4**). This statue is nearly twice life-size in scale, standing 3.05 meters high, and like Nikandre's kore it is made of Naxian marble. There is more detail preserved of the anatomy of this figure, including deeper ridges for the knees and groin line and shallower incisions for the muscles on the abdomen, legs, and arm. The figure still has the Daedalic shape of head, and the facial features share some similarities to the Delphi ivory. The figure is not deeply carved, but the projection of the left leg forward and deeper chin give it more three-dimensionality than Nikandre's kore. The appearance of these statues in the sanctuaries would have created a lasting impression on visitors, considering the far more modest scale of Geometric votive offerings. By using marble, the votives could be placed more readily in the open areas and, with inscriptions like Nikandre's, would have conveyed the piety and lineage of elite donors.

The similarity of the marble kouros and kore statues to Egyptian statues has led to debate about the influence of Egyptian art in Greece. For example, a slightly earlier limestone Egyptian statue from Giza has the same striding pose with the left leg forward and hands held at the sides (**Figure 6.5**). This statue of Tjayasetimu, however, has less modeling of the knees and less detailing of the abdominal muscles than the Sounion kouros, but otherwise is similarly naturalistic in the treatment of the body, with an idealized emphasis on broad shoulders and narrow waist. The head of Tjayasetimu is more lifelike and less stylized than the Sounion kouros, and overall has less abstract patterning. There are some other noteworthy differences: the stone of the Sounion kouros between the legs and the arms and torso has been removed and its back is fully carved, rather than left as a slab. As a sanctuary dedication, the kouros would be in the open and seen from multiple angles, unlike the Egyptian statue that was made to stand against a wall in a tomb. Finally, the Egyptian figure wears a kilt, while the Sounion kouros follows the Greek convention of male nudity.

The rectangular forms of Egyptian and Greek statues at this time are partly the result of their production techniques. Both were made from blocks of stone. Egyptian sculptors marked the block into gridlines and placed major features like the shoulders, waist, hands, and knees at specific points on that grid, whether the statue was 1 meter or 3 meters high. This was one factor giving Egyptian art its much-noted consistency. The use of a grid system for laying out the figure was almost certainly used by the Greeks, although gridlines on unfinished sculpture do not survive as they have in Egypt.

There have been studies comparing the proportions of Greek and Egyptian statues that suggest some Greek sculptors used the Egyptian system itself, but recent reevaluation of the data does not suggest a widespread direct copying of the Egyptian canon (Carter and Steinberg 2010). Greek figures tend to be proportionally taller and narrower and their heads more elongated than their Egyptian counterparts.

Much later Greek literary sources refer to the sculpture of Daidalos, who created the mythical labyrinth hiding the minotaur, among many other works. The first-century Greek historian Diodoros, for example, states "the *rhythmos* of the ancient statues of Egypt is the same as that of the statues made by Daidalos among the Greeks" (1.97.5; tr. Pollitt 1990, 15). By ***rhythmos***, Diodoros refers to the compositional pattern of the work, and certainly comparing the two works here one can see the similarity in proportions and forms. While Daidalos is legendary, there were early works attributed to him by the Greeks, and their comparison of his reputed work to Egyptian statues suggests the Greeks saw some noteworthy similarities between an early kouros and Egyptian statues. Daedalic persists as a term to describe seventh-century sculpture, but it implies a greater unity of style and concept than exists. Rather, we should consider it in light of the relationship of Greek art to the eastern Mediterranean, as one aspect of the Orientalizing and innovative character of seventh-century art (Morris 1992, 255–256).

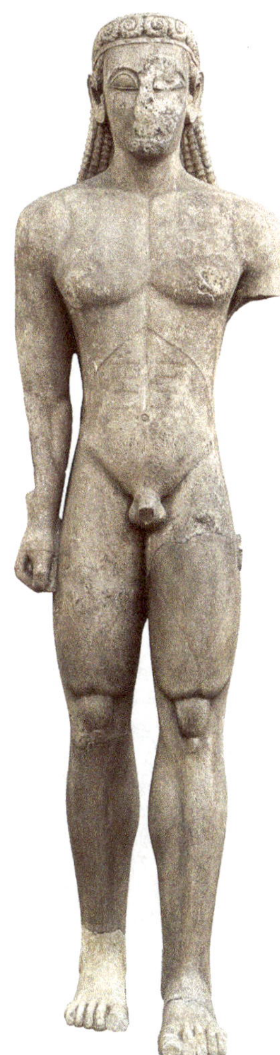

6.4 Kouros from Sounion, c. 590 BCE. 10 ft 1/16 in (3.05 m). Athens, National Archaeological Museum 2720. Photo: National Archaeological Museum, Athens (Giannis Patrikianos) © Hellenic Ministry of Education and Religious Affairs, Culture and Sports/Archaeological Receipts Fund.

Diodoros (1.98.5–9) also tells us of two Greek sculptors, the brothers Theodoros and Telekles, who spent time in Egypt. Together they made a statue of Apollo, Telekles making half of the statue on Samos and Theodoros making the other half at Ephesos, so that "when the parts were fitted together with one another, they corresponded so well that they appeared to have been made by one person. This type of workmanship is not practiced at all among the Greeks, but among the Egyptians it is especially common" (Pollitt 1990, 28). While these artists are said to have worked in the sixth century, the passage describes the use of a grid and proportional system to ensure conformity of the parts, and the association of this technique with Egypt. Further, it links the striding pose with hands at the side to Egypt.

There is historical evidence of emerging connections developing between Egypt and Greece in the seventh century. The Egyptian pharaoh Psammetichos inherited the throne in 664 BCE, hiring Ionian Greek mercenaries, among others, to consolidate his power by 656. The pharaoh established the trading settlement of Naukratis in the Nile delta by the year 620, and excavations at the site have found imports of Greek pottery and other goods **(see Figure 6.14, page 143)**, showing there was two-way trade and Greek settlers in Egypt by the late seventh century.

One can see that there would have been an opportunity for Greeks to become familiar with Egyptian art, and it is plausible that Greek sculptors could have learned the skills needed for marble and limestone sculpture by training in Egypt. Evidence from quarrying techniques, however, suggests that Greek quarrying methods were more similar to those found in southern Anatolia and northern Syria. The similarity in the process of making something can lead to similarity in the finished product, but is this a case of mimicry and copying, in which a Greek sculptor sought to replicate Egyptian work, or is it a case of adaptation, in which some elements are changed to conform with existing artistic practice in Greece? Related to this question is one of motivation. Is this a case of two cultures interacting freely, or is it a case of one culture dominating the other? In recognizing an influence of one culture on another, is its purpose to elevate the status of the source or of the borrower? The question of the relationship and dependence of Greek stone sculpture on Egyptian is complex, but the purposes of Greek stone sculpture appear to have been different from its inception. Egyptian statues serve primarily as furnishings inside an offering chamber of a tomb and are meant to be placed against a wall. Greek sculpture appears first in sanctuaries and stands out in the open; its purpose, based on the inscription for Nikandre, is to enhance the prestige of the donor and/or donor's family. As its inscription notes, the kore of Nikandre praises her as the "excellent" daughter, sister, and wife of her father, brother, and husband, someone who likely served a prominent role in the worship

rhythmos
a Greek term that signifies the compositional pattern of a work or figure, and, in connection with movement, an expression of how the parts of the body move to carry out an action

of Artemis at Delos. The votive statue, by its material, scale, style, and inscription, distinguishes it among the other dedications at Delos.

Undoubtedly stories of monumental Egyptian statues circulated through travelers to Egypt, but there were also expensive works of Egyptian art dedicated in sanctuaries in Greece, such as the seventh-century bronze statue of the goddess Mut found at the Heraion on the island of Samos (**Figure 6.6**). This work shares similarities to Nikandre's kore in the frontal, plank-like composition and in details like the arm at the side, with a hole in the hand for an attachment. Mut's dress clings more to the body, the breasts are articulated, unlike Nikandre's kore, and the hairstyle, crown, and face are different. Unlike Egyptian stone sculpture, the bronze is made as a fully three-dimensional object with a fully worked back like Nikandre's kore. In comparing these two works, one can see that Greek artists were adapting Egyptian techniques and subject matter in a way that made Greek statues consistent with earlier Greek representations. In the effort to distinguish Nikandre's dedication as "excellent," Egyptian art might provide both a model for the form of the statue and an association of prestige for the Greek patron and artist.

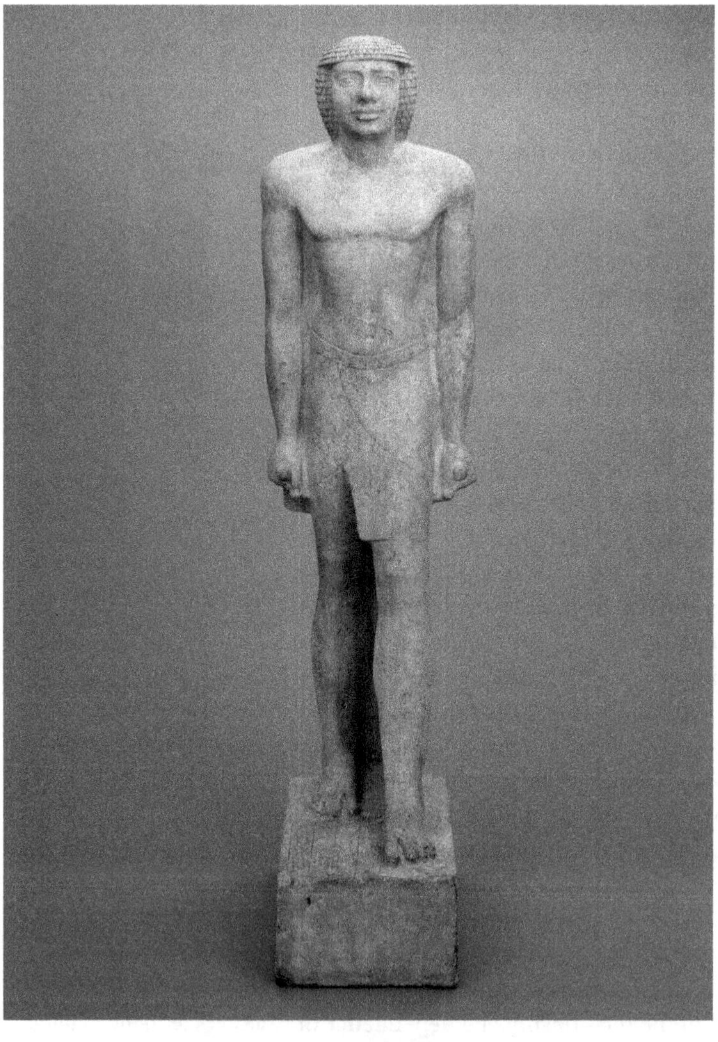

Egypt was not the only source of art, techniques, and motifs for Greek art. As we noted with the Delphi lion and man, there are also strong connections to Asia Minor, the Levant, and Syria. The Phoenicians specialized in producing metal and ivory work that included motifs derived from both Egypt and Mesopotamia, as can be seen in an ivory panel that was part of the decoration for a piece of furniture (**Figure 6.7**). The ivory is from Syria or further east, but the sphinx and the pharaoh's double crown with cobra uraeus come originally from Egypt. There are intertwining plants with blossoms that are a combination of the lotus and palmette, which are common decorative motifs in Egyptian art. One modification to the Egyptian sphinx, however, is the addition of wings, which is more common in hybrid creatures in Mesopotamian art. The ivory itself was found in the Assyrian capital at Nimrud, along with many other Phoenician works. The muscular rendering of the lion's body is similar to that found in Assyrian reliefs (**see Figure 6.2**), and Assyrian sculpture and seals feature a range of hybrid creatures. The Phoenician sphinx could be said to be a syncretic creation, one that would have been appealing for its formidable rendition of a mythical creature and for the value of its material and craft in an international market. Phoenician art would also have been appealing to Greek artists and patrons and another source of ideas for Greek art.

6.5 Egyptian male statue, Tjayasetimu, from Giza, *c.* 664–610 BCE. 4 ft 1³⁄₁₆ in (1.25 m). Limestone. London, British Museum EA1682 (1921,0507.1). Photo: © The Trustees of the British Museum.

Other luxury objects from Phoenicia are metal bowls or plates that feature a wealth of figural decoration and ornamental motifs. A large number of these come from Cyprus but have many similarities to Phoenician work, so they are usually labeled Cypro-Phoenician ware since their origin is uncertain (**Figure 6.8**). This bowl, now in the Metropolitan Museum of Art, has raised or *repoussé* figures hammered out in the silver from behind and then gilded; details of the contour, anatomy, and costume were incised on the surface. The outer rim of the dish shows heraldic units of animals flanking a sacred tree, including griffins and sphinxes. A number of Egyptianizing warriors are shown, and in the upper right is a pharaoh about to club some captives while Horus, the falcon-headed figure, watches. The middle frieze has mythical and real animals, including lions killing men. In the center medallion is a winged **genius** fighting a lion. His wings, costume, and headdress are more Assyrian in form, but an Egyptian Horus falcon flies overhead in a truly syncretic combination. The luxury status, intrinsic value, and portability of objects like these meant that they would circulate, carrying visual ideas from the eastern Mediterranean and making them models worth emulating.

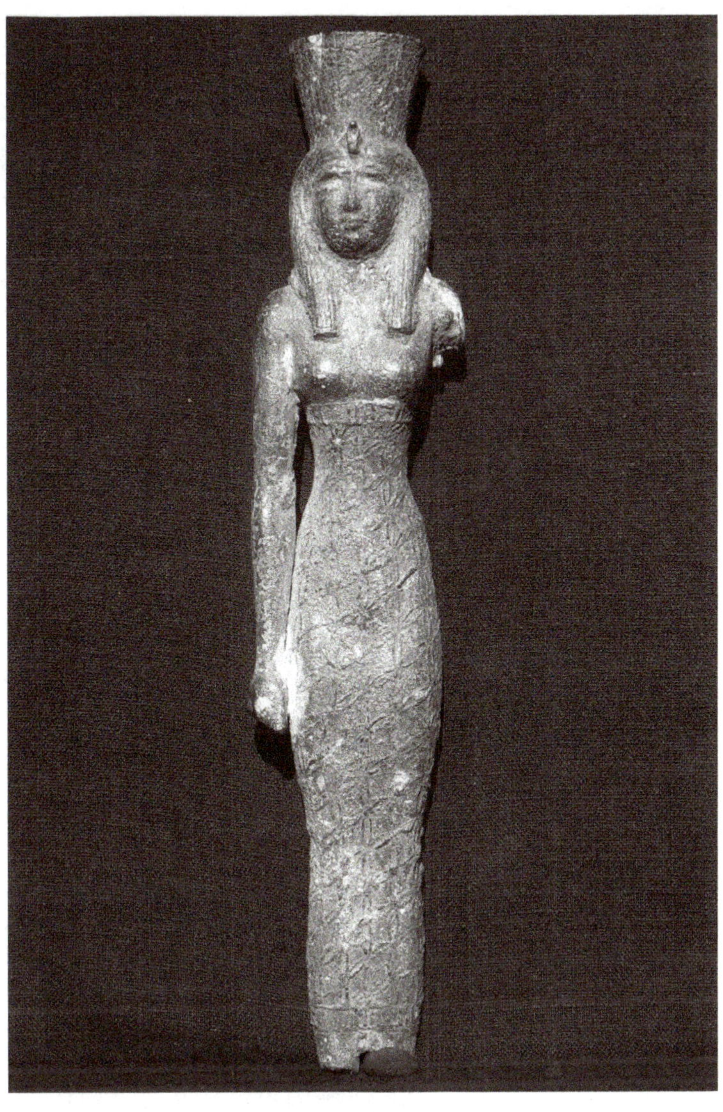

6.6 Egyptian bronze statue of Mut, dedicated at Samos, 7th cent. BCE. 6⅞ in (17.4 cm). Samos, Vathy Museum B148. Photo: Hermann Wagner. D-DAI-ATH-Samos-Neg. 0721. All rights reserved.

GREEK POTTERY PAINTING AND THE MEDITERRANEAN

How the statue of Mut ended up at Samos is uncertain, but there are several possibilities that speak to the movement of art and its motivations during this period. Samos had close connections to Egypt during the seventh century and there was an unusually large number of Egyptian works dedicated there. It is possible that some of these were donated by Egyptians at Samos, who were taking advantage of the trade between the two regions, just as the Greeks were doing at Naukratis. It is also possible that the work was obtained by a Greek traveling in Egypt and then dedicated on returning to Samos, perhaps to acknowledge the protection of the gods. It is also possible that the work belonged to a family for a time and was then rededicated in the sanctuary. In all three cases, not only would the material, subject, and work quality of the object reflect upon the prestige of the donor, but as a public gift it would be viewable to other visitors to the sanctuary. In other words, Egyptian art could be seen by Greeks locally, and its status as a distinctive artwork could have stimulated adaptations of subject, style, and materials.

Indeed, we should consider that the developments of Greek art in this period reflect the wider movement of art and peoples. Whereas Phoenician and Greek merchants sailed around the Mediterranean, particularly in search of metal, during the last third of the eighth century BCE, Greek cities began establishing colonies that eventually spread from the Black Sea to Spain and south to Egypt and Libya. Euboean trading outposts could be found at al-Mina in Syria during the Geometric period, and at Pithekoussai on Ischia, an island near Naples. Around 735–734 BCE, Euboeans founded a city at Naxos near the Messina Strait between Italy and Sicily, and Corinthians founded Syracuse/Siracusa in Sicily, and a bit later Korfu on modern Korkyra. Taras (modern Taranto) in southern Italy was founded by the Spartans in 706, and many other colonies followed in the seventh century. Sometimes the story of the colony's founding includes a crime by a leading member of the mother city, expulsion, and consultation with the oracle at Delphi on the act of founding a new city. In practice, these colonies were mostly independent of the mother city and their artwork is frequently a combination of imports from Greece and local products.

genius (pl. genii)
a winged human figure, often a guardian, having its origins in Near Eastern art

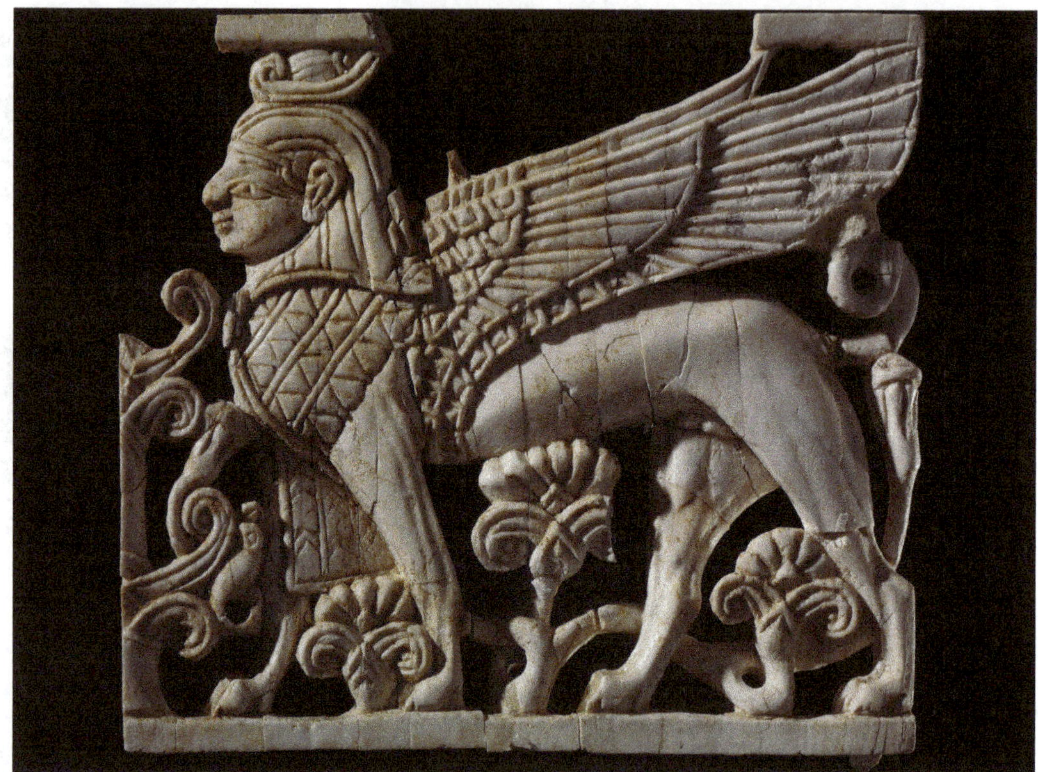

6.7 Phoenician ivory plaque from Nimrud, 9th–8th cent. BCE. 2¾ in (6.9 cm). London, British Museum WA134322 (1963,1214.8). Photo: © The Trustees of the British Museum.

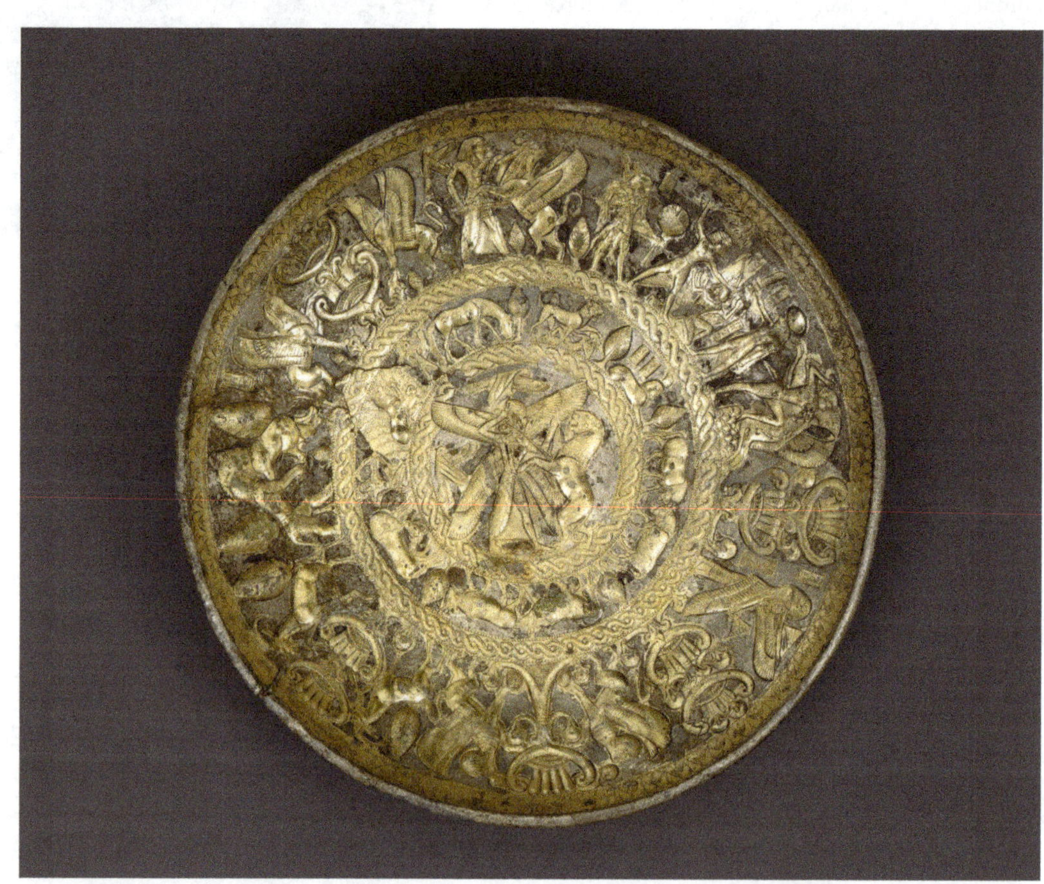

6.8 Cypro-Phoenician silver gilt bowl with various scenes, *c.* 725–675 BCE. 6⅝ in (16.8 cm) diameter. New York, Metropolitan Museum of Art, The Cesnola Collection 74.51.4554. Image copyright © The Metropolitan Museum of Art. Image source: Art Resource, NY.

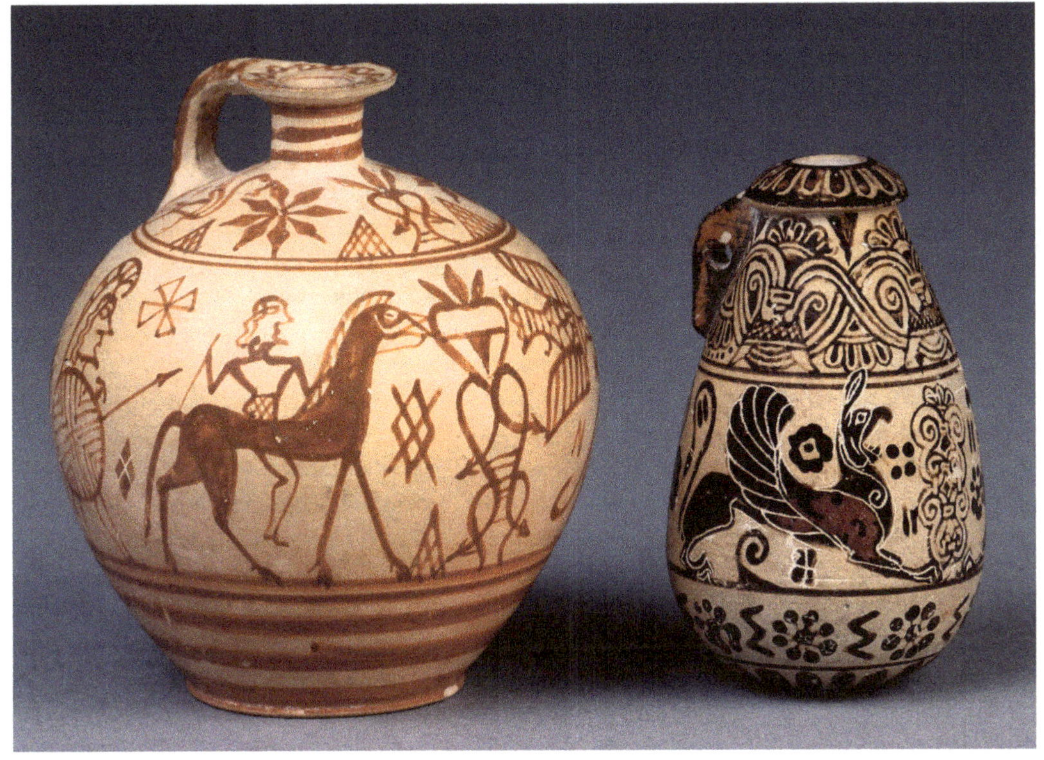

6.9 Left: Protocorinthian aryballos attributed to the Evelyn Painter, *c.* 720–700 BCE. 2¹¹⁄₁₆ in (6.8 cm). London, British Museum 1969,1215.1. Rider and warrior. Right: Protocorinthian alabastron from Kamiros, 660–650 BCE. Griffins. 2¼ in (5.8 cm). London, British Museum 1860,0201.30. Photo: © The Trustees of the British Museum.

We can see the currents of trade between these old and new sites by looking at Corinthian pottery during this period. Corinth became a major center of pottery manufacture in the late eighth century, producing a large number of small perfume vessels. These would be filled with scented oil and were then shipped throughout the Mediterranean world. The round **aryballos** on the left in **Figure 6.9** dates to about 720–700 BCE, the beginning of what is called the **Protocorinthian** pottery, or "first-Corinthian," another term for Orientalizing art from that city. While the horse is painted in a silhouette technique like Geometric figures, the rest is done in an outline technique drawn in lines of slip. This allows more anatomical details, such as nose, mouth, beard, and eyes. To the right is a stacked series of heart shapes that is an abstraction of the eastern sacred tree such as we saw in the Cypro-Phoenician bowl in **Figure 6.8**. Some of the decoration recalls Geometric work, but the eight-pointed form in the upper register looks to the rosette motif that becomes popular in seventh-century painting.

aryballos
a small perfume container with a single handle and narrow spout and with a pointed or globular body

Protocorinthian
the period of Corinthian art following the Geometric period, *c.* 725–625 BCE

alabastron
a small perfume container, with a tall profile and rounded bottom

The small vessel to the right is a more vertical shape called an **alabastron**, a bottom-heavy shape derived from alabaster stone vases. This vase is dated about fifty years later, *c.* 660–650 BCE, and was found at the Kamiros cemetery on the island of Rhodes. This vase uses a new technique called black-figure painting, in which the silhouette of the form, like the griffin, is painted and then internal details of anatomy, such as the wing feathers, ears, eyes, mouth, and muscles, are incised by a sharp point. This vase also uses a second color of red slip, giving it a richer and more dynamic effect. To the right of the griffin are intertwining vines with a crowning palmette, like those on the Phoenician ivory (**see Figure 6.7**), to make a sacred tree. On the other side of the tree is a second griffin facing in to create a symmetrical, heraldic composition. The typically buff-colored surface of the Corinthian vase is filled with ornamental patterns, including rosettes and a complicated outline chain of alternating spiked lotus blossoms and rounded palmettes.

A contemporary Protocorinthian pointed aryballos comes from a tomb in Taras/Taranto in south Italy. It features a sculpted spout made of three women's heads in the Daedalic style (**Figure 6.10**). The center frieze, less than 2 cm high, shows a horse race on the front, with the last-place rider seen on the right side of the picture. Below the handle on the left one can see a judge, who stands behind the prize tripods at the finish line. A sphinx fills in the space between the race and the judges. Below

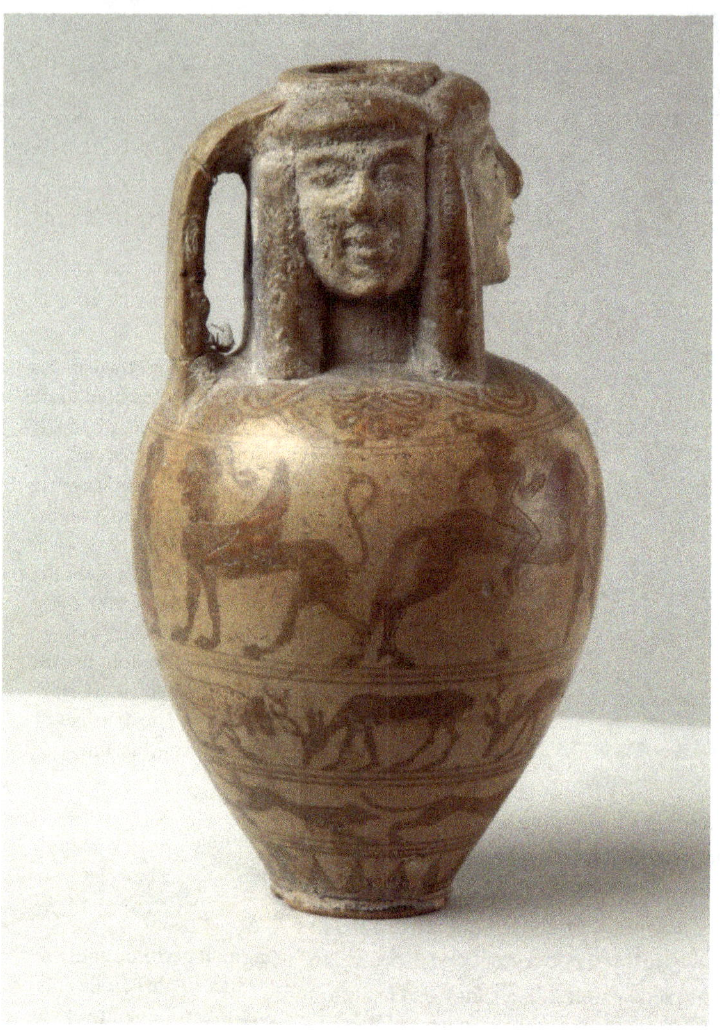

6.10 Protocorinthian aryballos from tomb in Taras/Taranto, *c.* 680–650 BCE. Riders, animal frieze, dogs chasing hare. 2⅜ in (6.1 cm). Taranto, National Archaeological Museum 4173. Photo: Museum.

the race is an animal frieze made up of deer, a leopard, and a winged lion (not visible in the picture). The bottom frieze has four dogs running after a hare. Details of the sphinx's wings and horse's manes are in red over the brown slip, and another lotus/palmette chain is on the shoulder. Both the animal frieze and the running dogs are typical of Protocorinthian decoration and last into the next century.

Hundreds of Protocorinthian aryballoi have been found throughout the Mediterranean, primarily in graves or as sanctuary offerings. They were made in batches in Corinth and then exported to sites both east and west, such as Rhodes and Taras/Taranto. Like Nikandre's kore, they show a combination of new techniques (outline and black-figure drawing), new subjects derived ultimately from Near Eastern or Egyptian art, and imitate shapes that are found in metalwork. The black-figure technique, especially with secondary coloring, makes a more complicated and subtle drawing system than the silhouette or outline techniques, and in appearance it is similar to engraving on metal objects like gilded-silver vessels, such as the Cypro-Phoenician bowl that we saw earlier **(see Figure 6.8, page 138)**. Metalware such as this might have served as an inspiration for Corinthian painters, but the technique and decoration had to be adapted and transformed for a different shape and medium such as painted pottery. In the process, Protocorinthian pottery becomes quite distinctive in its appearance and it has been suggested that this was in some sense a "brand," a distinctive category of work that was recognized and consumed throughout the Mediterranean (Rasmussen 1991, 65–66).

One of the most richly decorated Protocorinthian vases is a wine pitcher or olpe dating to about 650–640 BCE. It was found in a very large tomb in Etruscan Italy and is now in the Villa Giulia in Rome **(Figure 6.11)**. The painter, called the Chigi Painter after a previous owner of this vase, or the MacMillan Painter after another work in the British Museum, used a combination of black-figure incision and three colors – black, red-purple, and yellow-brown – not only to create a rich coloristic effect, but also to show multiple layers of figures. Nine warriors overlap one another as they advance as one of three waves of warriors, called **hoplites**, fighting in closed ranks. This is a more lifelike type of warfare than the heroic single combats that we have seen and will see as typical artistic representations of battles. The middle frieze shows riders and a chariot going toward a lion hunt on the other side of the vase, while under the handle is a lone mythological scene, the judgment of Paris. Finally, a hare hunt is shown in the bottom frieze, with the already successful hunter crouching with his dogs behind a bush. An incised lotus and palmette chain on the spout is typical of seventh-century work, and the flared disks at the handle are probably imitations of metal shape in clay. The hare hunt and battle are scenes drawn from the experiences of Greek men, while the lion hunt recalls elements of mythic as well as Egyptian and Assyrian hunting scenes. As a wine pitcher for the symposion, the subject matter would reflect an idealized male life. Like most Protocorinthian pottery, this vessel was exported and its discovery in an Etruscan tomb, along with other Greek as well as Etruscan pottery, is an example of the cross-currents of visual culture during this period.

hoplite
term for Greek infantry soldier whose equipment included a helmet, breastplate or cuirass, and metal greaves on the shins. Hoplites carried one or two spears and wore a sword on a belt

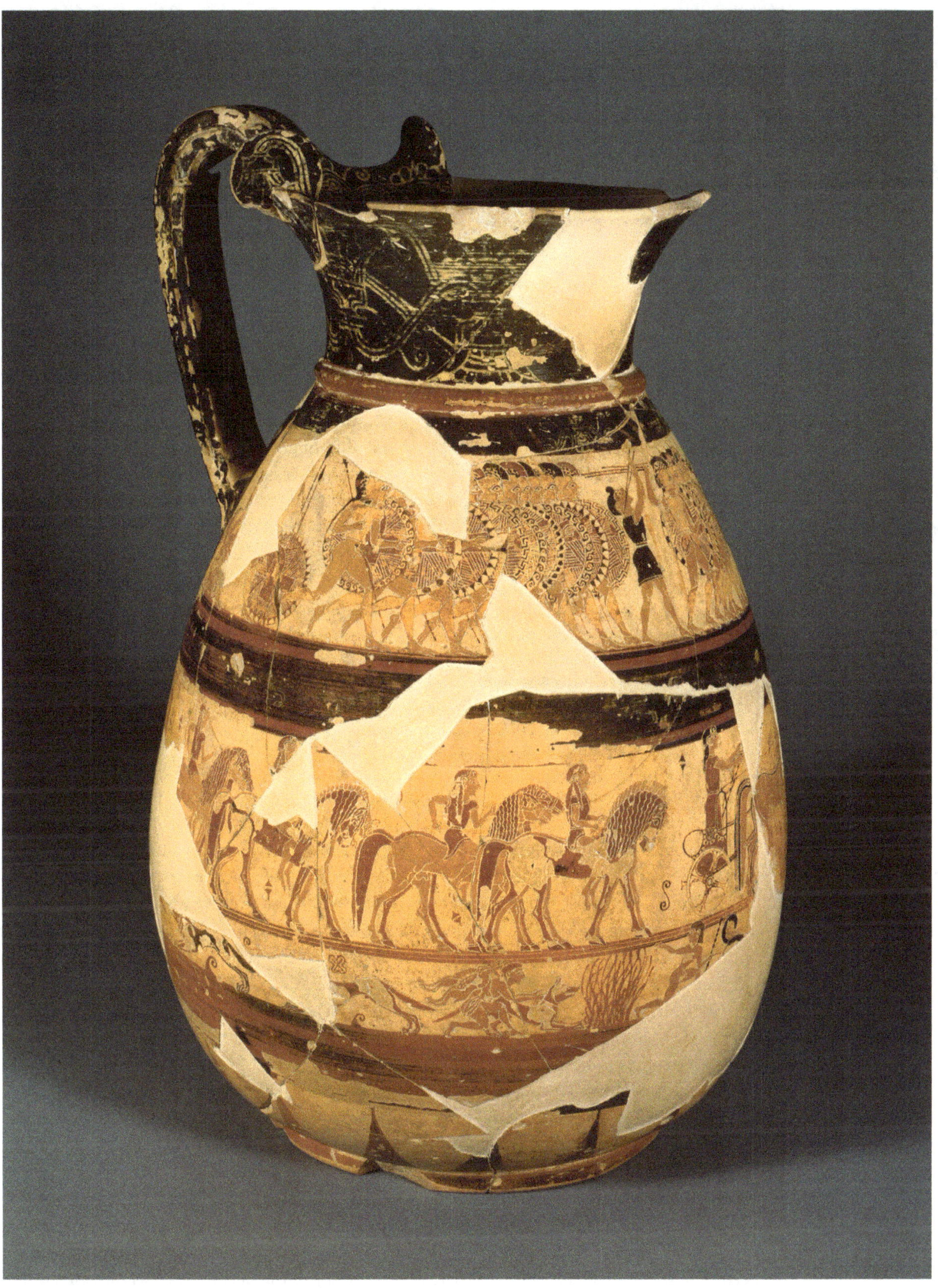

6.11 Protocorinthian olpe attributed to the Chigi Painter, *c.* 650–640 BCE. Battle; lion hunt; hare hunt. 10⁵⁄₁₆ in (26.2 cm). Rome, Villa Giulia 22679. Photo: Scala/Art Resource, NY.

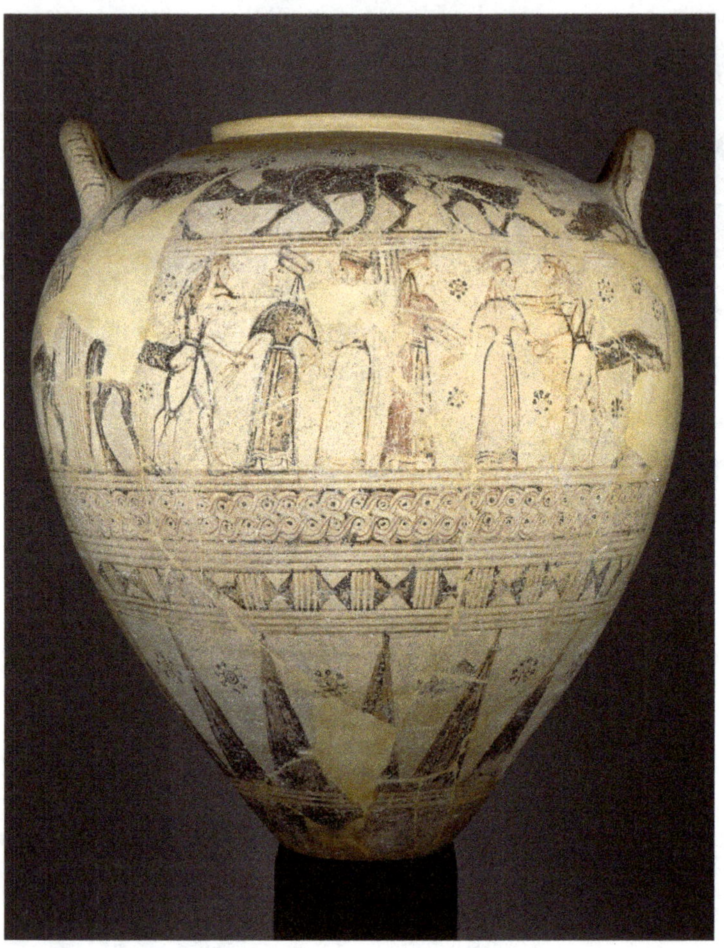

6.12 Sicilian stamnos from Selinunte, made in Megara Hyblaea, *c.* 660–650 BCE. Centaurs and women. 20½ in (52 cm). Paris, Musée du Louvre CA3837. Photo: © RMN-Grand Palais/Art Resource, NY.

Other areas of Greece and Magna Graecia, the Greek settlements of the central and western Mediterranean, developed their own distinctive styles of pottery during this period. For example, a stamnos or storage container found in Selinus (modern Selinunte) in Sicily **(Figure 6.12)** uses an outline polychrome technique with larger-scale figures. The vase was made in the Greek colony of Megara Hyblaea in Sicily, just north of Syracuse/Siracusa and also founded in the later eighth century, and then exported to its daughter colony of Selinus/Selinunte. An animal frieze appears at the top and several mythological scenes below it; on the one side we see pairs of centaurs grabbing hold of elaborately dressed women. Early mythological scenes like this are sometimes hard to identify because of their experimental formulation, but this might be the wedding of the Lapith prince Peirithoös, friend of Theseus. Peirithoös invited the local centaurs to the wedding feast, at which they got drunk and tried to abduct the women present, a scene called the centauromachy that became very popular in later Greek art. The figures are more stilted in appearance than contemporary work by the Chigi Painter, but are more monumental in form and represent a local alternative technique for painting. While rosettes fill in the space of the figural friezes, one of the lower ornamental bands uses a double-axe and three-line pattern that recalls Geometric decoration.

centauromachy literally, a centaur-battle, a term used to describe battles between centaurs and humans, and particularly the battle of the centaurs with the Lapiths at the wedding of their king, Peirithoös

At the eastern end of the Mediterranean we find the Wild Goat style, produced on Chios and other eastern Aegean islands during the last half of the seventh century **(Figure 6.13)**. This work is another type of wine jug, an oinochoe, that also features disks on its handles like metalwork. The decoration is mostly in outline and polychrome painting and features animal friezes with goats, deer, birds, sphinxes, and a profusion of filler ornament. An open-and-closed lotus chain at the bottom derives ultimately from Egyptian art. Wild Goat pottery was widely distributed, with findspots in Bulgaria, Aigina, al-Mina in Syria, Cyprus, and in Naukratis in Egypt. Some of the pottery found in Naukratis, such as the special-handled bowl found in the sanctuary of Aphrodite at Naukratis **(Figure 6.14)**, was produced specifically for export there. This particular bowl was dedicated by a Greek named Sostratos, who inscribed his dedication on the inner rim. Interestingly, this ware features Geometric decoration like the meander that had gone out of style in other seventh-century pottery.

Given its prominence as a center for Geometric pottery, it is surprising that pottery produced in Athens during the seventh century, Protoattic pottery, is less common and was mostly consumed in the home region of Attica and on the neighboring island of Aigina. One of the best examples is a pointed amphora from Eleusis near Athens **(Figure 6.15)**. It is a very large vase and may have been intended as a grave marker like the Geometric kraters and amphora from the Dipylon cemetery **(see Figures 4.7 and 4.9, pages 78, 80)**. Ultimately, however, it ended up as a coffin for a young boy. The openwork handles are likely an imitation of metalwork, and the repertory of decorative motifs is similar to other pottery in the period, such as the lion confronting a boar on the shoulder. The figures in the main frieze are about a half meter in height and show two Gorgons chasing Perseus, with Athena standing between them. The painting is a combination of black/brown outline and silhouette, but the heads of the Gorgons are imagined like cauldrons with snake handles, similar to the griffin protome we shall see below **(see Figure 6.16, page 145)**.

On the neck is Odysseus and two of his sailors blinding Polyphemos, one of the Cyclops. The scene is described in *Odyssey* 9 and is found on several seventh-century vases from different regions, but each imagines the story in its own way. Here the giant Cyclops sits to fit into the panel; he holds a drinking cup, alluding to his drunkenness. His inebriation allows Odysseus to run a stake into his eye to blind him, later enabling Odysseus's eventual escape from the cave where he and his sailors were trapped. We presume that Odysseus is the lead figure, distinguished by added white and sketches of black line that give him a more three-dimensional appearance to our eye, but if so, this differs from his position and action in the *Odyssey*, reminding us that artists were not illustrating poems but telling stories in their own right.

METALWORK AND TERRACOTTA

Greek metalwork became more accomplished during the seventh century. A new form of the tripod, with a large ovoid bowl placed on a separate openwork stand, replaced

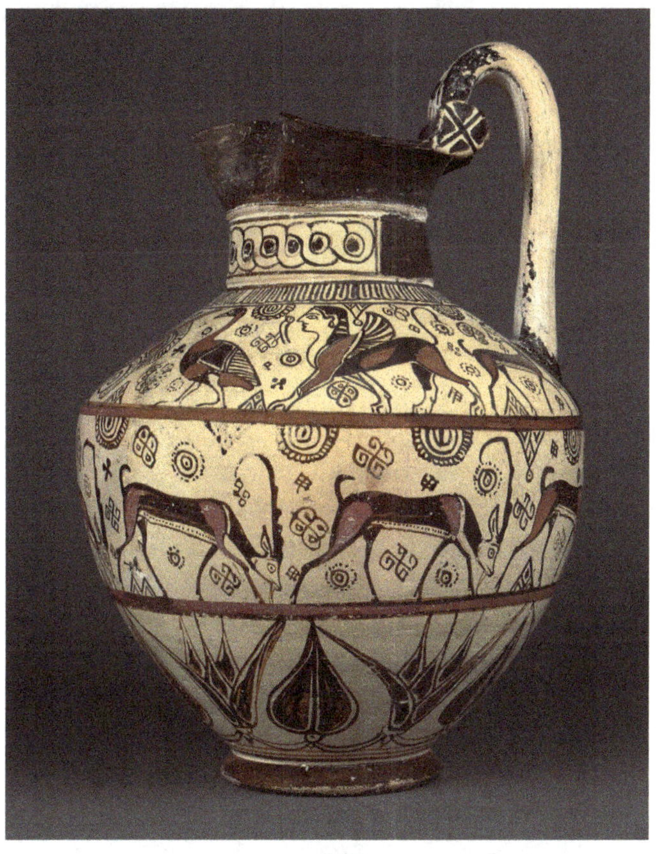

6.13 Wild Goat-style oinochoe from Rhodes, 625–600 BCE. 12 in (30.5 cm). Paris, Musée du Louvre A312. Photo: © RMN-Grand Palais/Art Resource, NY.

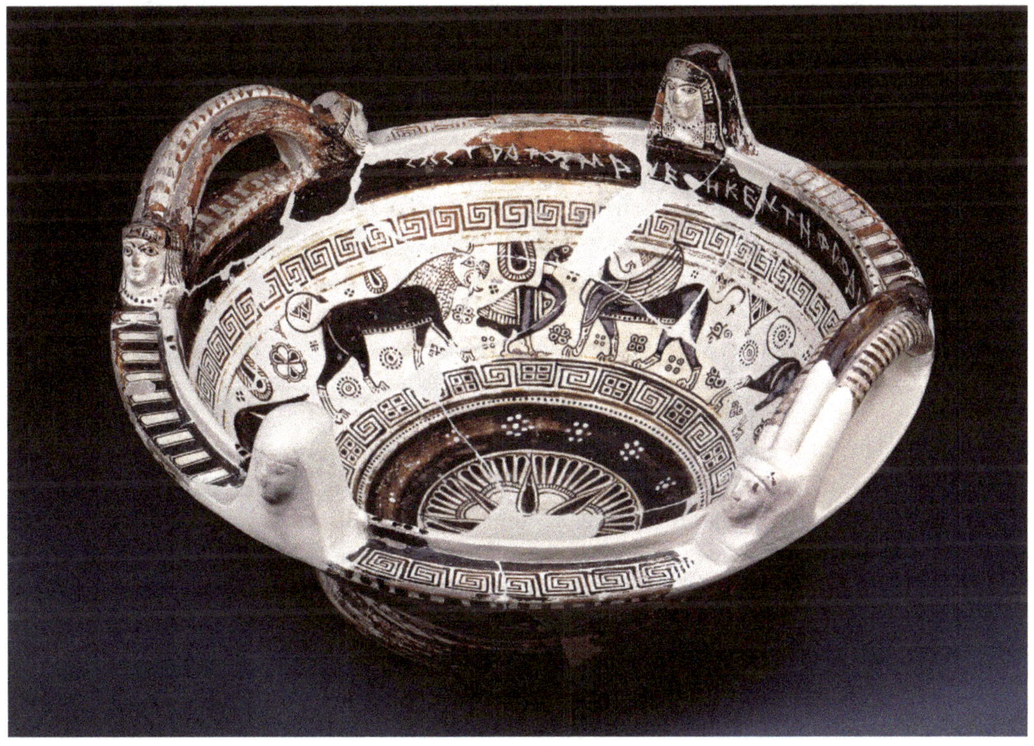

6.14 Chian "Aphrodite Bowl" from Naukratis, 620–600 BCE. Diameter 15¼ in (38.8 cm). London, British Museum 1888,0601.456. Photo: © The Trustees of the British Museum.

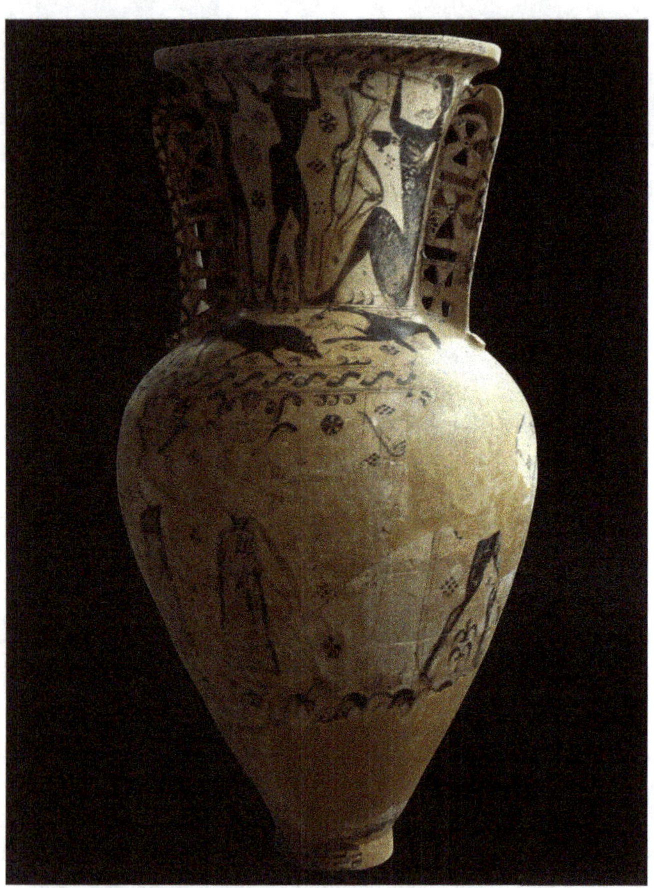

6.15 Protoattic amphora from Eleusis, *c.* 670–650 BCE. Blinding of Polyphemos; Gorgons chasing Perseus. 4 ft 7 15/16 in (1.42 m). Eleusis, Archaeological Museum. Photo: Gianni Dagli Orti/ The Art Archive at Art Resource, NY.

the Geometric type. There was a new type of figural-shaped handle called a protome, consisting of creatures like griffins, sirens, and lions that were attached to the bowl with rivets. One example is a griffin's head and neck from Samos (**Figure 6.16**). A raptor's head is perched on a snake-like neck, with two ears and a knob on the head that reflect its hybrid nature (bird, lion) as a mythical beast. The S-curve of the figure, the sharp beak, and bulging eye give it a vigorous attack posture like a rearing snake. The surface is incised with overlapping U-shaped lines that recreate scale-like tips of feathers. Riveted onto the bowl of the tripod, we have a new subject and more refined style used on an important ceremonial object of Greek culture, giving it a new vitality.

We can also see the appearance of the Daedalic style and form in sculpture in a miniature version with goldwork produced in eastern Greece during this period. The plaques, found on Rhodes, formed part of a necklace and were made by stamping the gold sheet from behind with a raised relief form (**Figure 6.17**). Surface details were made by granulation to create patterns on the clothing and spots on the animals. In terms of style, the heads are typically Daedalic, but the subject matter is derived from images of the Mistress of Animals, or ***Potnia Theron***, that have a long history in Levantine and Mesopotamian art. The image can serve as an apotropaic device, like a Gorgon's head, and the figure is later associated with the goddess Artemis. Small pomegranates hang as pendants from the plaques, and rosettes also feature among the motifs.

Potnia Theron
term meaning "Mistress of the Animals," usually a frontal female figure holding two animals in either hand

hekatompedon
a term designating a large, or 100-foot, temple

The Orientalizing style is found in terracotta figures and relief plaques as well as large terracotta storage vessels that were found in many storage areas and were usually undecorated and functional. During the seventh century there were experiments with putting figural reliefs rather than paint on the surface of these large pithoi, some of which feature the earliest representations of specific mythological stories in Greek art. Usually called the Tenian-Boeotian group, these were produced in the northern Cycladic islands. Of particular interest is a pithos found on the island of Mykonos. This vessel has a large panel on the neck and three registers on the body, subdivided into twenty individual panels; the other side of the vessel is blank and would have faced the wall (**Figure 6.18**). When it was found, it had been used as a coffin, but it is thought that it had earlier been used as a storage vessel and repurposed, perhaps like the Eleusis amphora discussed earlier (**see Figure 6.15**).

The scene on the neck is instantly recognizable as the Trojan horse, as the horse is on wheels and small windows reveal the heads of warriors inside. One warrior reaches out of the window to hand a helmet to one of the standing warriors outside the horse. These must be Greeks who have already disembarked, ready to attack the citizens of Troy. Scenes of the subsequent attacks on the men, women, and children of Troy follow in the panels below, with Greek warriors stabbing or violently flinging their victims to the ground. One panel shows a warrior confronting a woman who opens her mantle toward him, and is probably Menelaos confronting Helen, whose anger at his wife will subside when he glimpses her beauty once again. The meaning of the scenes has been much debated, ranging from Greek triumph to a recent theory that the scenes show the devastation that results from the death of a city's protectors (Ebbinghaus 2005). Whatever the intention, the simple and rubbery figures convey the action very graphically and constitute a strong narrative experiment with the grand theme of the fall of Troy.

ARCHITECTURE AND ITS DECORATION

Experimentation with materials, design, and subject matter is also found in architecture of the seventh century BCE. We will examine the planning and architecture of sanctuaries in more detail in the next chapter, but for now will look at the developments in the sanctuary of Hera on the island of Samos, where the bronze figure of Mut discussed earlier was dedicated **(see Figure 6.6, page 137)**. According to foundation accounts for the site, Hera was born under a lygos tree on Samos. Cult activity there goes back at least to the tenth century. There is no evidence of a temple at that time, but evidence for an altar and votive offerings dating to the ninth century have been found.

The first temple was built during the eighth century. This structure was a long rectangular building, consisting of the solid walls shown in the plan **(Figure 6.19)**. This temple, designated 1a in the sequence of temples built on the site, was 32.86 meters long and 6.50 meters wide with thirteen columns down the middle to support the roof. It was open at one end and the cult statue of Hera, described in literary sources as plank-like in form, was placed at the other, closed end. The building is a **hekatompedon**, a "100-foot" temple. Like the Protogeometric building at Lefkandi **(see Figure 4.20, page 91)**, it is monumental in scale and would have been the largest building at the site. The surviving lower courses of stone for the building were roughly worked and the columns were wooden; their placement down the center axis of the building meant that the cult statue had to be positioned off axis if it were to be visible. The altar, the fourth in its sequence, was to the east and a little north, but its entrance faced to the northwest, meaning that the temple served more as a backdrop for the sacrifices and that public ritual was focused on the open area before the temple. The lygos tree was next to the altar, and these two features were the principal focal points for ritual activity in the sanctuary. At the end of the eighth century an exterior peristyle of wooden posts was added around the exterior of the hekatompedon, making this phase 1b. While we do not know why this was done (perhaps because the original roof had to be replaced), it was an important innovation in that it made the temple building not only larger than any other structure, but also more visually distinctive compared with the plain-wall structures that then were typical of Greek buildings.

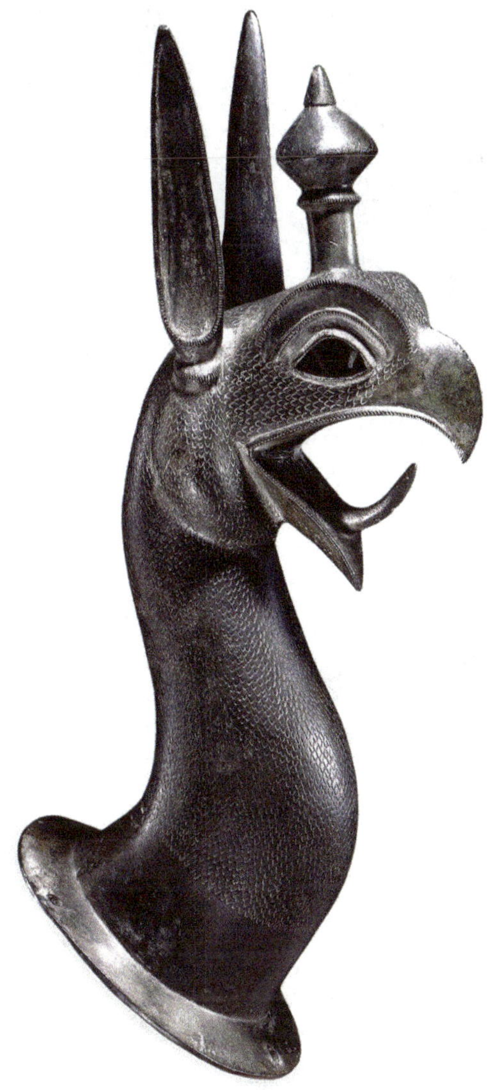

6.16 Griffin protome probably from Rhodes, 7th cent. BCE. 9 3/16 in (23.4 cm). London, British Museum 1870,0315.16. Photo: © The Trustees of the British Museum.

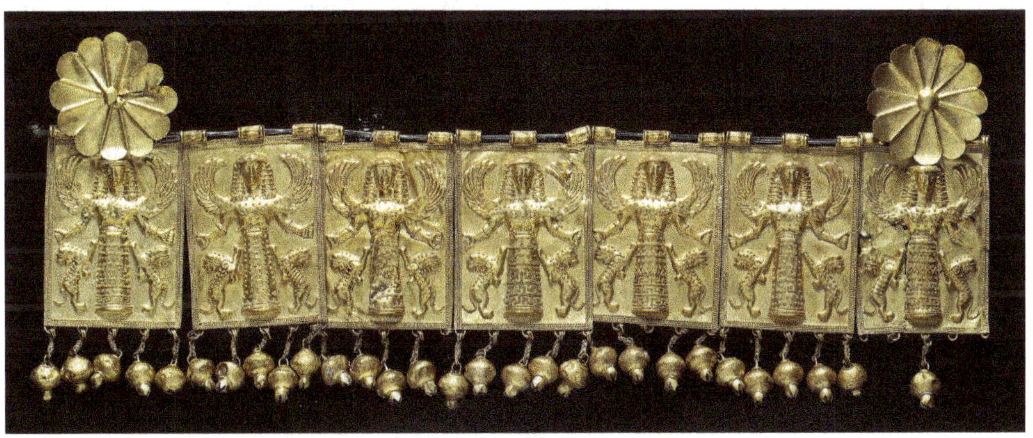

6.17 Gold plaques with Mistress of Animals from Kamiros, Rhodes, *c.* 660–620 BCE. 1 5/8 in (4.2 cm). London, British Museum 1861,1111.4. Photo: © The Trustees of the British Museum.

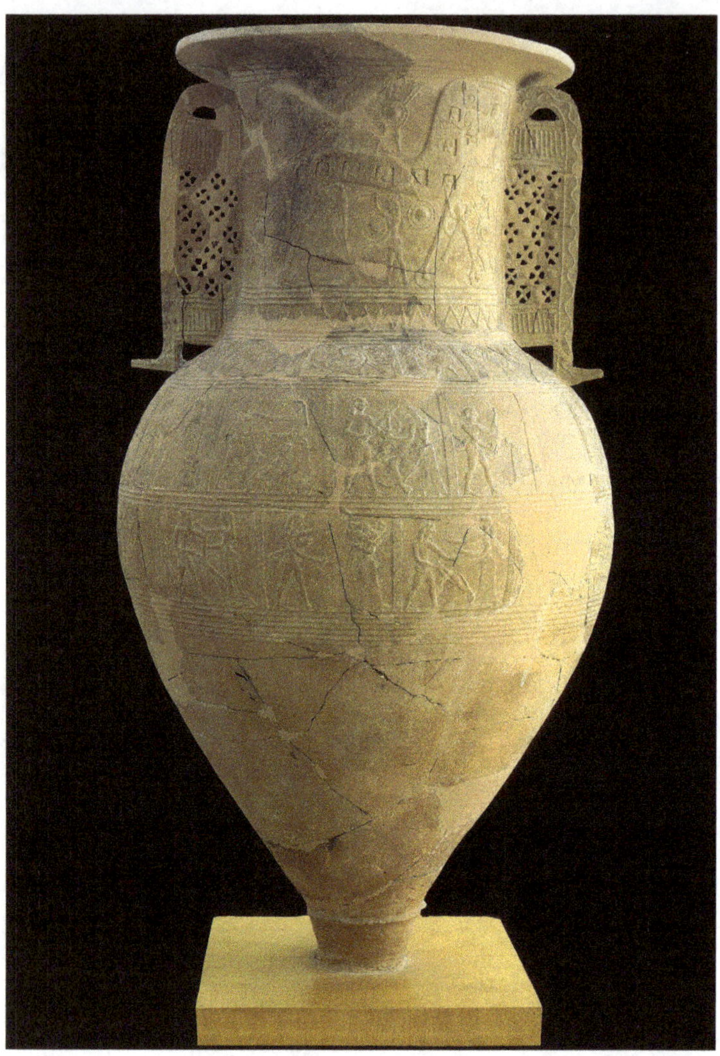

6.18 Cycladic relief pithos from Mykonos, *c.* 675–650 BCE. 4 ft 5 in (135 cm). Trojan horse and *Iliupersis*. Mykonos, Museum 2240. Photo: Gianni Dagli Orti/ The Art Archive at Art Resource, NY.

In the middle of the seventh century the first temple was reconstructed as a new building, Temple 2 **(Figure 6.20)**. The core of the building remained a long rectangular hall, called the **cella** or **naos**, but the surviving portions of the wall now used ashlar masonry, that is, rectangular blocks carved with flat surfaces. This development in masonry coincides with the development of stone sculpture and created a more durable building material. Posts along the side of the interior walls allowed for the elimination of the interior columns on the central axis of the first temple, creating an open view to the cult statue at the west end of the naos. The wooden columns of the peristyle on the exterior were placed on circular stone bases and located further from the naos wall, making a more usable area for circulation. The west corner of the new, enlarged altar was placed on line with the central axis of the temple, and a new processional avenue led from the south to the space between the temple and altar. Besides the processional avenue, the boundary or **temenos** of the sanctuary was defined by a wall and a stoa was built to the south **(Figure 6.21)**. This building, a rectangular structure open on the long end with rows of supports in the middle and along the open end, was almost 70 meters long and divided into three sections. The stoa provided a sheltered area that could house dedications and provide space for the activities of the large number of visitors to the sanctuary, away from the area for sacrifices at the altar.

It is thought that the roof of the structures at Samos were still using perishable materials such as thatch. A more durable roofing material, fired terracotta tiles, was developed during the seventh century, but the added weight that resulted from their use meant that the structure of the roof had to change, from the high pitch necessary for thatch **(see Figure 4.20, page 91)** to a lower profile with much thicker supporting walls, columns, and rafters. The effects of this can be seen in the reconstruction drawing of the Temple of Apollo at Thermon in mainland Greece **(Figure 6.22)**. The naos of this temple is about the same hekatompedon size as the Heraion at Samos, but it has a porch at the back end. Whereas Temple 2 at Samos eliminated the central columns, these are retained at Thermon in order to support the heavier terracotta tile roof. The exterior colonnade was made of wooden columns like Samos, but their diameter was almost double (0.65 m to 0.35 m).

cella
the central room of a temple where the cult statue would be placed. Also called a naos

naos
the central room of a temple where the cult statue would be placed. Also called a cella

temenos
the boundary of a sanctuary

The wooden superstructure consisted of beams running across the columns and a frieze zone above it that had beams running perpendicular. This second zone was covered by painted terracotta metopes, which become standard in the Doric order of architecture that we will discuss in the next chapter **(Figure 6.23)**. Several of these have been recovered and their style and fabric show similarities to Corinthian vase painting of the period, including the use of multiple colors and outline drawing as on the Chigi olpe **(see Figure 6.11, page 141)**. One of the metopes shows Perseus fleeing from the Gorgons, who were likely shown on one or two adjacent metopes. Perseus wears the cap of invisibility and winged boots provided to him by Hermes, and the head of the decapitated Medusa peeks out of the purse slung over his right shoulder. His arms and legs are drawn at sharp

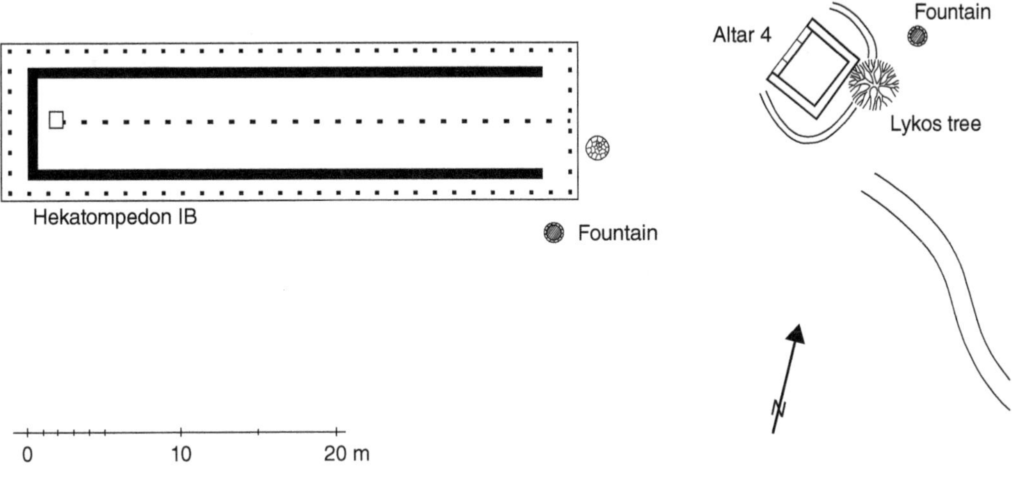

6.19 Plan of the sanctuary of Hera at Samos and Temple 1b, *c.* 700 BCE. After H. Walter, *Das Heraion von Samos* (Munich, 1976), fig. 39, used with permission.

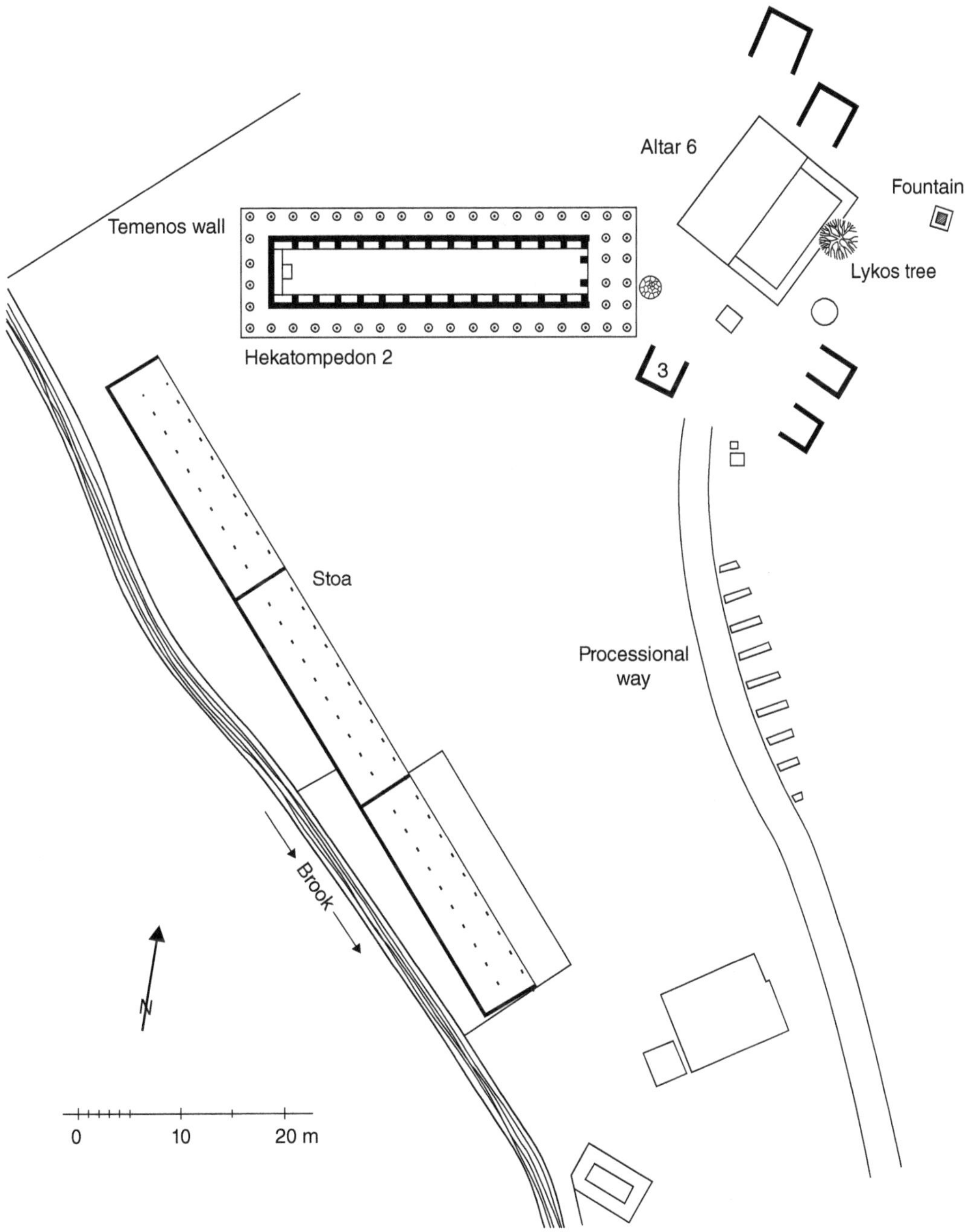

Altar 6
Fountain
Temenos wall
Lykos tree
Hekatompedon 2
3
Stoa
Processional way
Brook
0
10
20 m

6.20 Plan of the sanctuary of Hera at Samos and Temple 2, *c.* 650 BCE. After H. Walter, *Das Heraion von Samos* (Munich, 1976), fig. 45, used with permission.

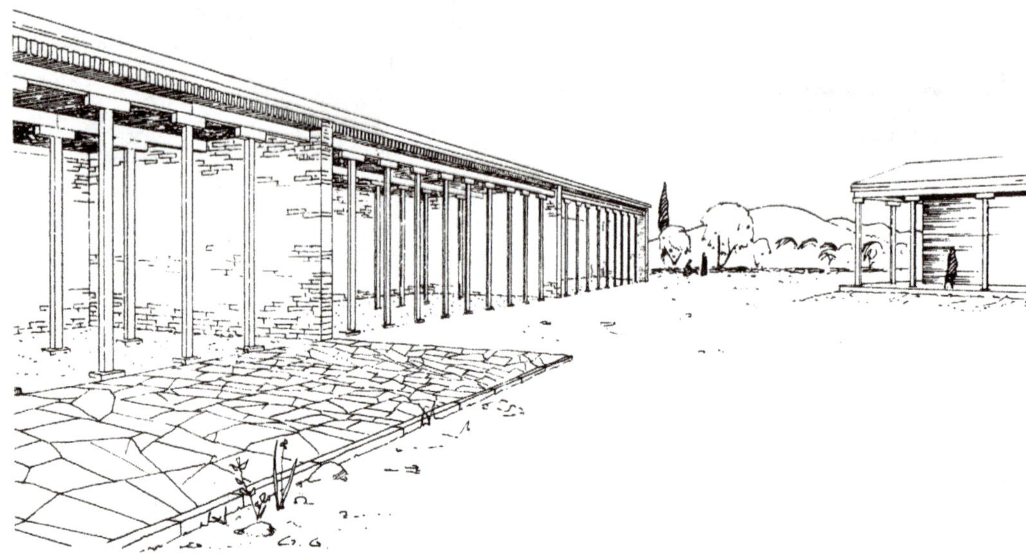

6.21 Reconstruction of the stoa and corner of the Hera Temple 2 at Samos, *c.* 650–625 BCE. After H. Walter, *Das Heraion von Samos* (Munich, 1976), fig. 47, used with permission.

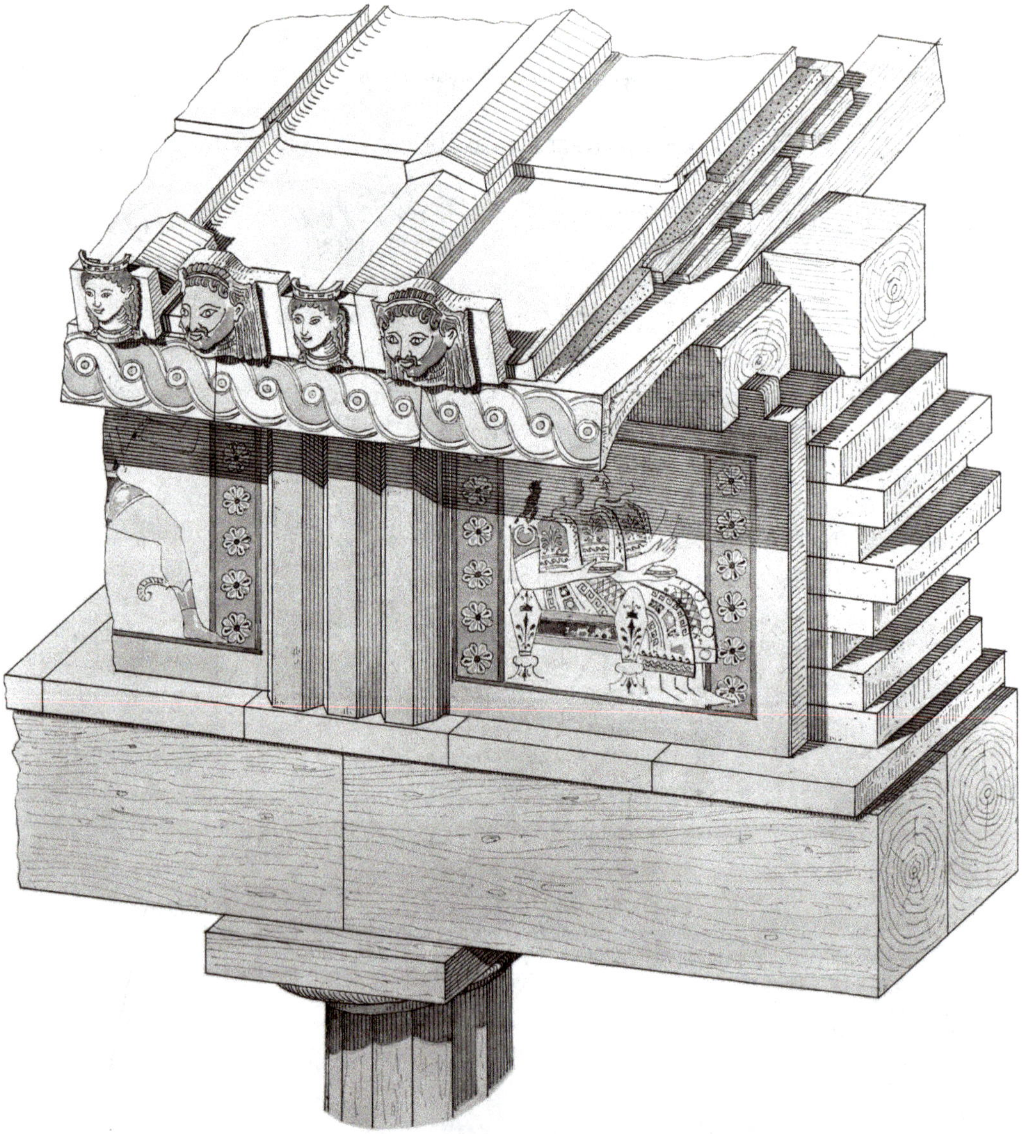

6.22 Reconstruction of the superstructure of the Temple of Apollo at Thermon, *c.* 630 BCE. After G. Kawerau, *AntDenk* 2 (1908), pl. 49. Photo: D-DAI-ATH-Aetoloakarnanien-Neg. 0155. All rights reserved.

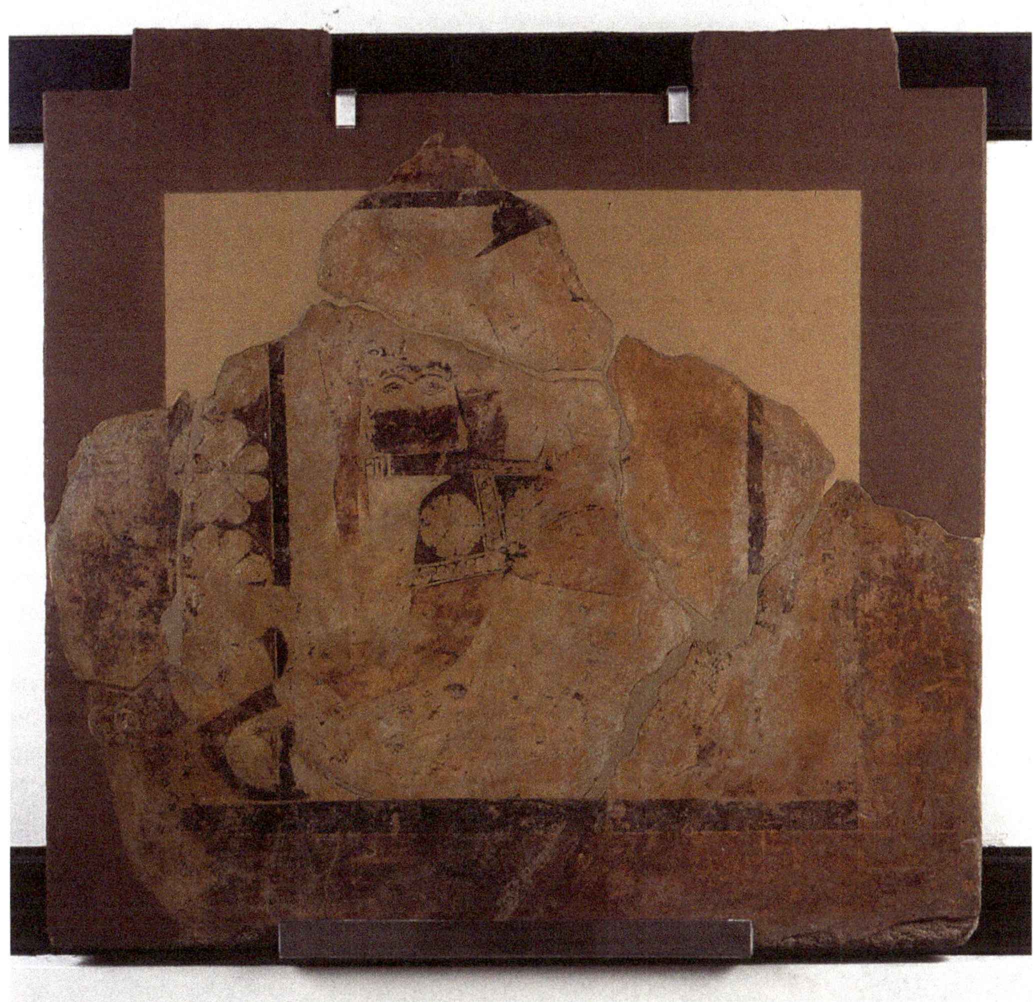

6.23 Metope from the Temple of Apollo at Thermon, *c.* 630 BCE. 34⁹⁄₁₆ in (87.8 cm). Perseus fleeing. Athens, National Archaeological Museum 13401. Photo: National Archaeological Museum, Athens (Klaus-Valtin von Eickstedt) © Hellenic Ministry of Education and Religious Affairs, Culture and Sports/Archaeological Receipts Fund.

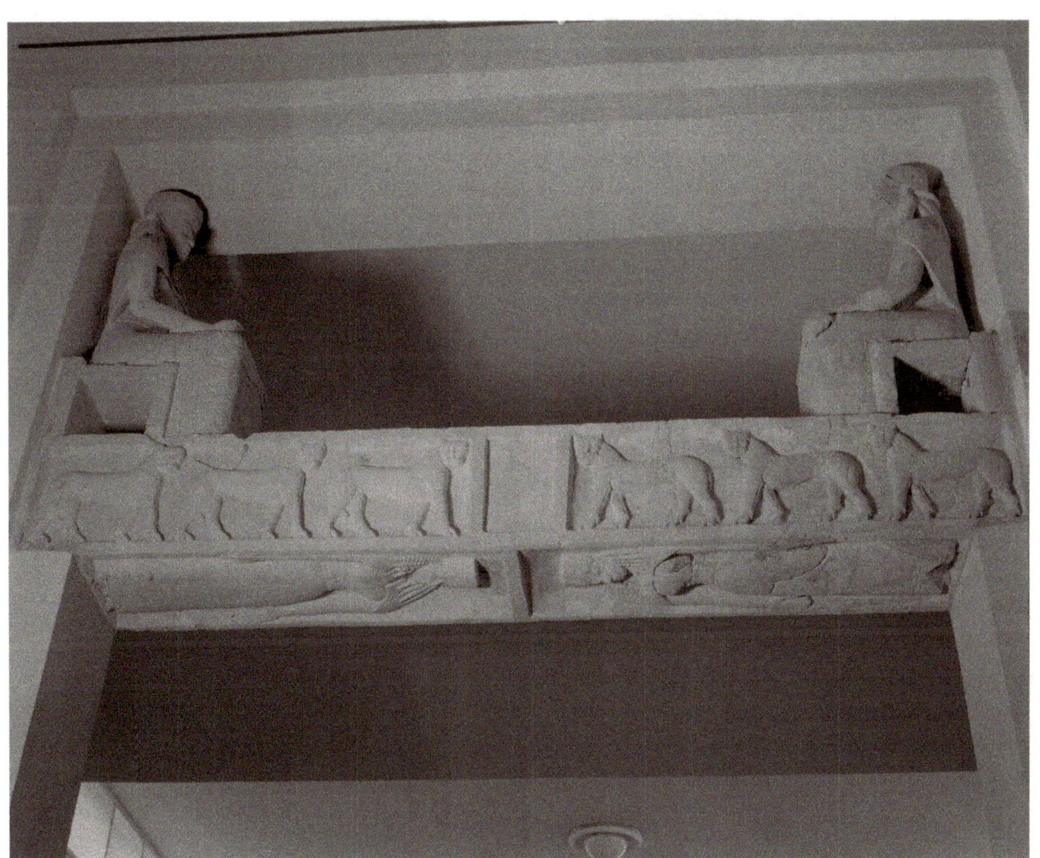

6.24 Lintel from the Temple at Prinias, *c.* 620–600 BCE. Heraklion, Archaeological Museum 231–232. Height of seated woman: 32¼ in (82 cm). Photo: Alison Frantz, courtesy of the American School of Classical Studies in Athens.

angles in a "whirligig" posture to indicate strong motion. Rosettes create a frame around the panel. The color palette is limited to the same range of reds, browns, and yellows found in pottery, but the figure is monumental in scale, about one-half meter in height and visible from a distance. The rich color, scale, and variety of subjects decorating the frieze would have further distinguished the temple as a visual focal point and something quite different from ordinary Greek architecture.

Smaller temples with a naos and porch that are closer to their Geometric predecessors continued to be built, but the availability of stone transformed their appearance. The Temple A at Prinias on Crete dates to the end of the seventh century and was built with ashlar masonry even in the upper courses. The door and lintel that separated the porch from the naos were decorated with relief sculpture featuring female figures and a frieze of panthers that is more symmetrical and repetitive than the animal friezes in contemporary vase painting, but is otherwise very similar **(Figure 6.24)**. The figural style is Daedalic, and its frequent use in stone architectural sculpture from Crete, where Daidalos is said to have created many innovative works, makes it an appropriate name for the style of this period. The figures are in low relief and share similarities with the kore figures of the period such as that of Nikandre **(see Figure 6.3, page 134)**. Framing the entrance into the naos, these figures create a monumental gateway marking the boundary of the god's enclosure and demonstrate the new possibilities for art that arose through developments in materials, techniques, and subject matter.

In conclusion, the seventh century is a period of great change and experimentation in Greek art, one in which Greek art is both influenced heavily by the art of other cultures, particularly the Levant and Egypt, and finds a much wider range of manufacture and distribution throughout the Mediterranean.

TEXTBOX: NETWORK THEORY

As we have seen in this chapter, the Greeks established colonies throughout the Mediterranean and Black Sea, in some cases during the Geometric period. The term colony, however, conjures up the idea of a satellite that orbits around and is controlled by a center in a hierarchical system. In fact, Greek colonies were more independent than the term implies and could be important centers in their own right. The center–periphery model that goes with the idea of colonization is predicated on the assumption that significant developments and ideas take place at the center and trickle down to the dependent colonies.

The Greek world was much more decentralized than the center–periphery model implies. Cities like Syracuse/Siracusa became leading centers of Greek culture, rivaling cities like Athens in terms of their wealth, power, and culture, and they acted in their own interests, not as dependents. Syracuse/Siracusa had connections to Corinth, its mother city, but it would trade extensively with Athens and send its own citizens to represent it at Panhellenic sites like Delphi and Olympia. It would interact with other Greek and non-Greek cities in Sicily and southern Italy, and its citizens, being diverse, would have contacts throughout the Mediterranean.

Rather than a center–periphery model, it is more fruitful to think of the Greek world and its connections as a decentralized network in a system that Ian Malkin compares to the structure of the world wide web today (Malkin 2011, 9). Communication and exchange can take place directly with other sites or through hubs that could connect with more distant places. Furthermore, it is important to remember that networks communicate in both directions. In terms of the history of art, some centers like Corinth or Athens may produce much more for export than others and seem influential in a center–periphery model. However, much art and architecture were locally made and both individuals and commodities could move along the network, leading to new centers of production in the case of Caeretan pottery or goldwork on Crete, as we shall see in Chapter 11.

Network theory also illuminates how the Greeks developed multiple identities, as we shall see further in Chapter 13. As Malkin notes (2011, 18–19), a Syracusan would consider himself/herself as a citizen of Syracuse/Siracusa, a colonist of Corinth, a Dorian (one of several dialects of Greek), a Greek (Panhellenic), and also a Sikeliote (a Greek living in Sicily). While Athens always looms large in a history of Greek art due to the scale of production and export of art, one must remember that Greek art is not Athenian art and that networks go in multiple directions, meaning that Athenian art would need to be responsive to the interests of its network clients if it were to continue to be in demand.

REFERENCES

Carter, J. B. and L. J. Steinberg. 2010. "Kouroi and Statistics." *American Journal of Archaeology* 114, 103–128.

Ebbinghaus, S. 2005. "Protector of the City, or the Art of Storage in Early Greece." *Journal of Hellenic Studies* 125, 51–72.

Malkin, I. 2011. *A Small Greek World: Networks in the Ancient Mediterranean*. Oxford: Oxford University Press.

Morris, S. B. 1992. *Daidalos and the Origins of Greek Art*. Princeton: Princeton University Press.

Pollitt, J. J. 1990. *The Art of Ancient Greece: Sources and Documents*. Cambridge/New York: Cambridge University Press.

Rasmussen, T. 1991. "Corinth and the Orientalising Phenomenon." In T. Rasmussen and N. Spivey, eds. *Looking at Greek Vases*, 57–78. Cambridge: Cambridge University Press.

FURTHER READING

Boardman, J. 1998. *Early Greek Vase Painting: 11th–6th Centuries. A Handbook*. London: Thames and Hudson.

Boardman, J. 1999. *The Greeks Overseas: Their Early Colonies and Trade*, 4th ed. London: Thames and Hudson.

Burkert, W. 1992. *The Orientalizing Revolution: Near Eastern Influence on Greek Culture in the Early Archaic Period*. M. E. Pinder and W. Burkert, tr. Cambridge, MA: Harvard University Press.

Gunter, A. C. 2009. *Greek Art and the Orient*. Cambridge/New York: Cambridge University Press.

Hurwit, J. M. 1985. *The Art and Culture of Early Greece, 1100–480 B.C.* Ithaca: Cornell University Press, 125–202.

Malkin, I. 2011. *A Small Greek World: Networks in the Ancient Mediterranean*. Oxford: Oxford University Press.

Morris, S. B. 1992. *Daidalos and the Origins of Greek Art*. Princeton: Princeton University Press.

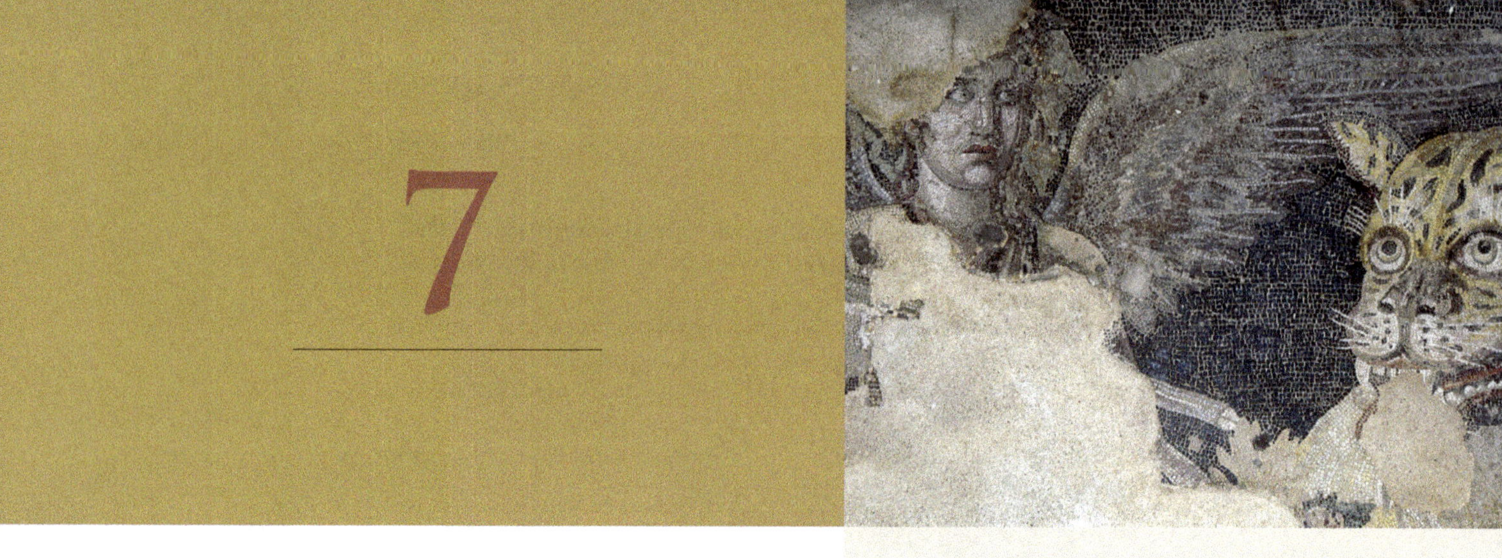

CONTEXTS II: SANCTUARIES AND ARCHITECTURE

Timeline
Sanctuaries
Temples and the Architectural Orders
A Mini-History of the Greek Temple
Other Buildings of the Sanctuary
Rituals and Offerings
Textbox: Ritual Analysis and *Theoria*
References
Further Reading

A History of Greek Art, First Edition. Mark D. Stansbury-O'Donnell.

TIMELINE

	Sculpture	Buildings
800–700	Geometric Tripods at Olympia, 750–700	
700–600	Mantiklos Apollo, 700–675 Kore of Nikandre, 650–625 [6.3]	Temple of Hera 1b at Samos, 700 [6.19] Temple of Hera 2 at Samos, 650–625 [6.20, 6.21] Temple of Apollo at Thermon, 630 [6.22]
600–500	Kouros from Sounion, 590 [6.4]	Temple of Hera I at Poseidonia/Paestum, 550 Temple of Apollo (archaic) at Delphi, 548–510 Temple C at Selinus/Selinunte, 550–530 [8.5] Siphnian Treasury at Delphi, 530–525
500–400	Kore of Euthykides, *c.* 490 Olympia sculpture, 470–457 [9.14; 10.9] Parthenon sculpture, 447–432 [10.14–10.16]	Athenian Treasury at Delphi, 490–485 Temple of Zeus at Olympia, 470–457 Temple of Hera II at Poseidonia/Paestum, 460 Parthenon at Athens, 447–432 Temple of Concord at Akragas/Agrigento, 440–430 Erechtheion at Athens, 431–405
400–300	Aphrodite of Knidos, mid-4th cent. [12.11]	Temple of Asklepios at Epidauros, 375–370 [12.1] Thymele at Epidauros, 360–330 [12.2] Temple of Apollo (classical) at Delphi, 373/2–327/6
300–200	Nike of Samothrace, later 3rd–early 2nd cent. [14.14]	Temple of Apollo at Didyma, begun 300 (unfinished)
200–100	Cult statues at Lykosoura, 200–190 [14.18–19]	Great Altar of Zeus at Pergamon, 180–150 [14.6] Asklepieion at Kos, 160 [14.7]

The sanctuary was a gathering point for Greeks, in both urban and rural areas. At least since the Geometric period, some sanctuaries served even larger groups from across Greece and its colonies, as attested by the offerings at Olympia that we have discussed in earlier chapters (**see Figure 1.3, page 7; Figures 4.15–4.18, pages 86–89**). Sacrifices at altars, contests, and other rituals made these areas the most public spaces in the Greek environment, places where individuals, by participating or witnessing the activities and by giving gifts to the gods, defined themselves as members of the community. Besides the altar and temple, additional structures like the stoa served to meet the needs of visitors to a sanctuary. Sanctuaries outside of a city helped connect the citizens of the polis to the *chora*, while Panhellenic sites like Olympia and Delphi connected them to the broader world.

In this chapter we will look at the components and organization of the sanctuary. In the previous chapter we saw that during the seventh century the temple became a much more prominent structure in the city, much larger than other buildings and further distinguished by its use of dressed stone as a building material, its large-scale decoration, and the use of an exterior colonnade to support the edge of the roof. We will, here, explore further the design of the temple, and in particular the architectural orders or systems used in their construction that created one of the most distinctive visual forms of Greek architecture. Finally, we will look at some of the other buildings found in the sanctuary and examine some of the ritual activity and offerings performed at these sites that made them virtual museums.

SANCTUARIES

Sanctuaries exist in a variety of locations and sizes, but all can be said to be places that are set apart from ordinary life in which humans can connect with the divine. In Greece, this interaction took place at both a group and individual level. In festivals, the community collectively celebrated its relationship with a god through ritual actions and offerings. Communal acts could include, especially at the most prominent sites and cults, processions, performances of choral songs or plays, dancing, sacrifices of animals or harvest followed by communal feasting, dedications of gifts, and competitions in both athletics and the arts, including music, poetry, drama, and dance. At a more personal level, an individual asked or thanked a god for well-being, healing, protection, or intervention, either at a local sanctuary or via a pilgrimage to a distant but potent place like Delphi or Epidauros. Individuals, too, left gifts and made sacrifices, but at a smaller scale. In addition, individuals could make demands on the resources and organization of a sanctuary if they had to wait there for a prophecy or a course of healing.

A sanctuary, therefore, had to be able to handle both small and large groups of people in activities that took both short and long periods of time to complete. It had to accommodate the performance of these activities, as well as provide space for spectators to watch. If someone were staying for a period, a sanctuary needed to provide shelter in addition to worship space. Finally, a sanctuary had to store and keep safe the gifts dedicated to the gods. Most communal activities took place in the open air, so that sanctuaries were generally defined precincts with paths for circulation and open areas for gathering, as well as a collection of support structures that additionally served as a stage setting for the activities.

Over the course of time, sanctuaries become more complex spaces, as the success or wealth of a city or site led to an accumulation of gifts and structures that could crowd the limited space. Occasional events such as earthquakes or fires could reshape a site by reorganization and rebuilding, but this also created a vertical layering as destroyed material had to be buried or reused on the site since it belonged to the deity. In looking at a sanctuary, then, one has to consider it both diachronically, as it developed from one point in time to the next, and synchronically, as a pastiche of works and buildings from different periods that existed concurrently with each other.

The sanctuary or temenos is usually defined by walls or boundary markers to distinguish the sacred space clearly. Entrances are limited and regulate the flow of traffic, which will be set on pathways that provide an order to the visit or ritual. The most essential ritual feature of the sanctuary is its altar, where sacrifices take place outside before the assembled participants. The space around the altar is open to provide room for the congregation, while the altar itself is often elevated to provide a view of the sacrifice. The most prominent building of the temenos is the temple, which is typically located across an open space from the altar. Larger and taller than anything else, it housed the cult statue of the deity and served as a storehouse for many of the most valuable offerings. Together, the altar and temple are the primary focal points for a sanctuary and the stage for the most important activities.

As we shall see, sanctuaries contained many other buildings. Temples and altars for other gods can be found at some sanctuaries, but usually at a smaller scale and not as visually prominent as the main altar and temple. Gifts were also found in smaller buildings with porches called **treasuries**; most of these were built by poleis and served as markers of civic status and ambitions. Other buildings can be found either inside the temenos or, more commonly, just outside of it. Stoas, dining halls, gymnasia, and hostels shelter the feasts and provide places for individual devotions and activities. The performance of drama, including both tragedy and comedy, in festivals dedicated to the deity took place at the theater, usually on the slope of a hill to provide the bank for seating. Athletic competitions were held at the **stadion**, usually just outside of the temenos boundary and featuring a long course for racing with sloped earthen sides to seat the spectators.

treasury
a small building housing dedications at a sanctuary, usually rectangular in plan with a naos and pronaos with columns in antis

stadion
a race course in a sanctuary, with banked sides for spectators

We can see most of these features at Delphi (**Figure 7.1**), one of the most important religious sites in ancient Greece. According to mythology, Delphi was the center of the earth, the *omphalos*, which was guarded by a serpent, Python, son of Gaia. He was killed by Apollo, who took over the sanctuary and, most important, its prophetic function. The priestess, called the **Pythia**, pronounced the oracles, which frequently had an obtuse and hard-to-decipher quality about them. These oracles were

Pythia
the priestess of Apollo at Delphi

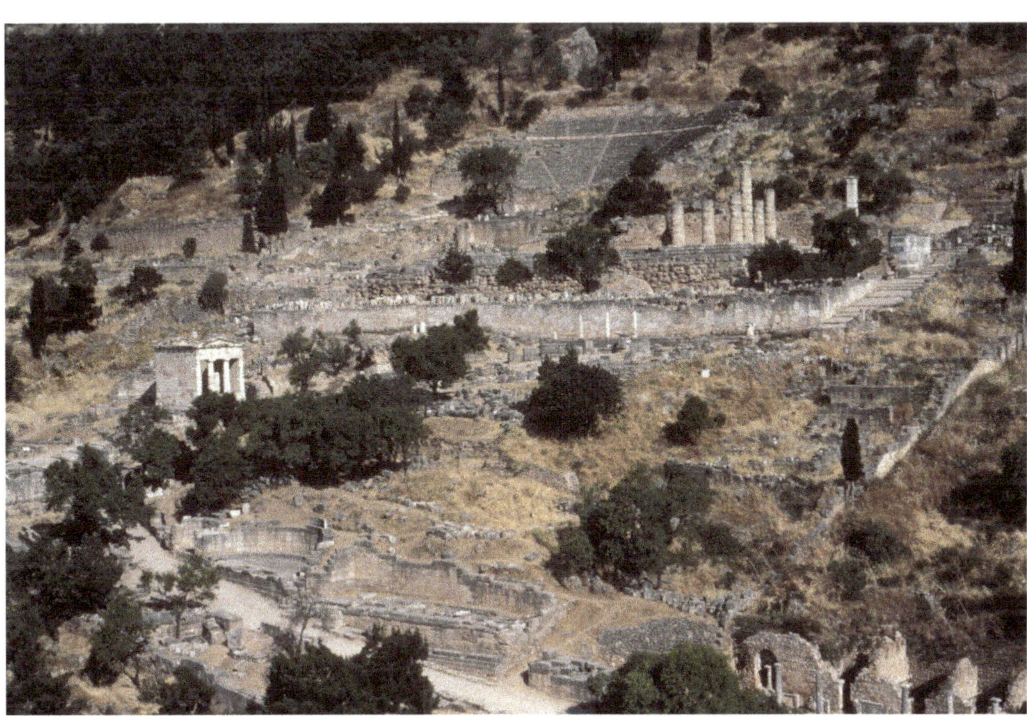

7.1 View of the sanctuary at Delphi. Photo: EfA/P. Amandry.

held as sacred by cities throughout Greece, who often sent for a pronouncement from the Pythia before a major undertaking such as war or colonization. As a rural site that was not associated with a specific major city, the sanctuary became Panhellenic. The sanctuary at Delphi also hosted the Pythian festival, initially a contest of hymns called **dithyrambs**, performed by a singer with a chorus. After a reorganization around 582 BCE, quadrennial athletic games took place midway between the Olympic Games. Additional athletic contests were organized in the sixth century at Isthmia and Nemea during the odd years between the Olympic and Pythian games, and the sites together constituted the four crown games of ancient Greece, referencing the crowns of olive, laurel, or celery awarded at each site.

dithyramb
a hymn that was sung and danced by a chorus

Looking at the site today, one can see six re-erected columns of the fourth-century temple (**upper right in Figure 7.1, 422 in Figure 7.2**). This fourth-century temple was set on a terrace bounded by a wall with **polygonal masonry** (329), irregularly shaped stones that fit together closely and have some resistance to earthquakes. This temple was built after an earthquake in 373 BCE destroyed the earlier sixth-century temple; the fourth-century building followed the siting and general plan of its predecessor but was not finished until about 320. The archaic temple itself had been built following the destruction by fire of a still earlier temple in 548 BCE. The archaic temple, too, took a long time to construct and was not finished until sometime after 513, when the Alkmaionid clan of Athens undertook completion of the project and provided marble rather than limestone sculptures for its pediments. The temple before 548 was likely smaller and not made completely out of stone since it was severely damaged by the fire. Pausanias, our source for the date of the fire, also mentions three still earlier temples, including the first of laurel and the third of bronze, made by the god Hephaistos (Paus. 10.5.9–13). Like the founding of the Olympics, the earliest origin stories of sanctuaries are often mythological, but nevertheless the claims convey both the antiquity and importance of the site. Indeed, excavations at Delphi have found Geometric bronze figures and tripods like those at Olympia being left as offerings, so that by the eighth century the site had begun to function as a Panhellenic sanctuary. Although no traces of the oldest structures survive, it appears the physical spot where the oracle was induced had had some type of structure over it from very early on in the history of the site, and was rebuilt as events made it necessary.

polygonal masonry
walls made of irregularly shaped stones that are finished with a smooth surface, giving the appearance of polygonal shapes

To return to the plan of the Delphi sanctuary (**Figure 7.2**), the temenos is defined by a boundary wall marking off the space. Before 548 BCE, the temenos was smaller and not defined by a wall, but following the fire it was expanded and a new main entry point established at 103. The Sacred Way climbs steeply along the southeast border, between the old and new boundaries and lined on both sides by monuments (104–118) and small treasuries (121, 122, 124, 223, 219). The path switches back and winds up the hill to the corner and northeast side of the temple platform, passing more buildings and monuments, before turning into an open area between the temple (422) and its altar (417). Above the temple is a fourth-century theater (538) with half-circle stone banks of seating built into the rising hillside. The theater testifies to the importance of music and poetic performances in ritual life, as well as the worship of Dionysos at the sanctuary. Earlier, these performances would have taken place in more irregular, open areas with sloped banks for spectators. Above the theater is a winding path that leads further up and away to the west where the stadion for the athletic races is found. As we shall see at Olympia, the stadion was usually adjacent to the temenos, but the topography made this impossible at Delphi. The plan shows in black the buildings that still existed in the second century CE when the traveler Pausanias visited the site and recorded what he saw. By this time it was a very congested site with monuments and small buildings crowding the Sacred Way, such as the Athenian Treasury (**see Figure 7.14, page 170**) and the Siphnian Treasury (**see Figure 7.15, page 171**) that were constructed more than six centuries previously.

The monuments and buildings at a sanctuary like Delphi competed for visual prominence along the Sacred Way. The placement of the Athenian Treasury (225) at the switchback of the

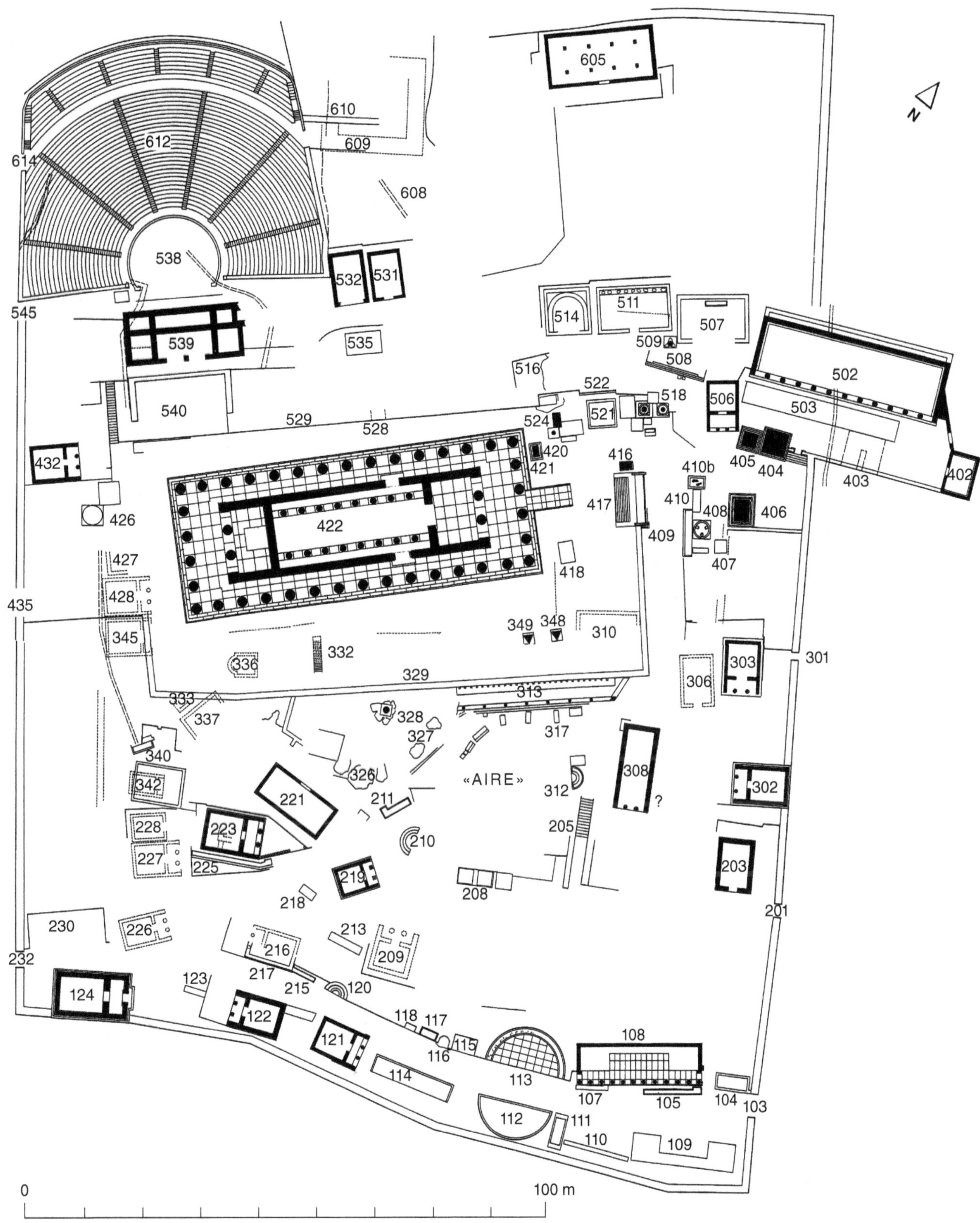

7.2 Plan of the sanctuary at Delphi. Structures with black lines are those that still existed in the 2nd cent. CE. Source: plan no. 19.639, EfA/D. Laroche. Selected points: 122: Siphnian Treasury; 223, 225: Athenian Treasury and Marathon trophy base; 313: Stoa of the Athenians; 329: polygonal wall of temple platform; 417: altar; 422: Temple of Apollo; 511: Daochos Monument; 538: theater.

path exposes the entire south side of the building and its adjacent dedication of spoils from Marathon directly to the viewer's eyes. So too the stoa (313) stands open in front of the temple platform; it would have appeared to support the temple rising above it, and promoted the importance of Athens. The Lesche, or dining room, of the Knidians (605) was built on the north side of the temenos in the 460 s after another victory over the Persians, this time at Eurymedon. It is isolated, but would have provided a good spot for smaller gatherings and was decorated with monumental mural paintings of the fall of Troy and Odysseus's visit to the underworld by Polygnotos.

The competition for the visual and physical prominence of monuments was perhaps at its highest in the crowded area to the north side of the temple platform (507–524). This defined the boundary of the space in front of the altar and temple facade; here visitors approached the priests serving the Pythia and sacrifices were made at the altar. During the fourth century, cities and states vied for the placement of new monuments in this space at the time the temple was being rebuilt, making rival claims for dominance in Greece. A similar set of competing claims is found in the sculptural monuments dedicated by Sparta and other poleis in the fifth century along the first leg of the Sacred Way (105–118).

This pattern is found in other sanctuaries. At Olympia, the altar of Zeus was on the level plain between the Kladeos and Alphaios rivers, called the Altis, and was the focal point of the site even before the Olympic Games were founded **(Figure 7.3, 3)**. Sometime in the seventh century, the ashes from the altar and debris consisting of the terracotta and bronze votives were collected and buried in the sanctuary and new monumental structures were built, including the first temple. Starting in the early sixth century, the first temple was rebuilt and its foundations were reused for the sixth-century Temple of Hera, whose lower interior wall and partial colonnade stand on the site today (5). Afterward on the north side were built treasuries (6) with prime vantage

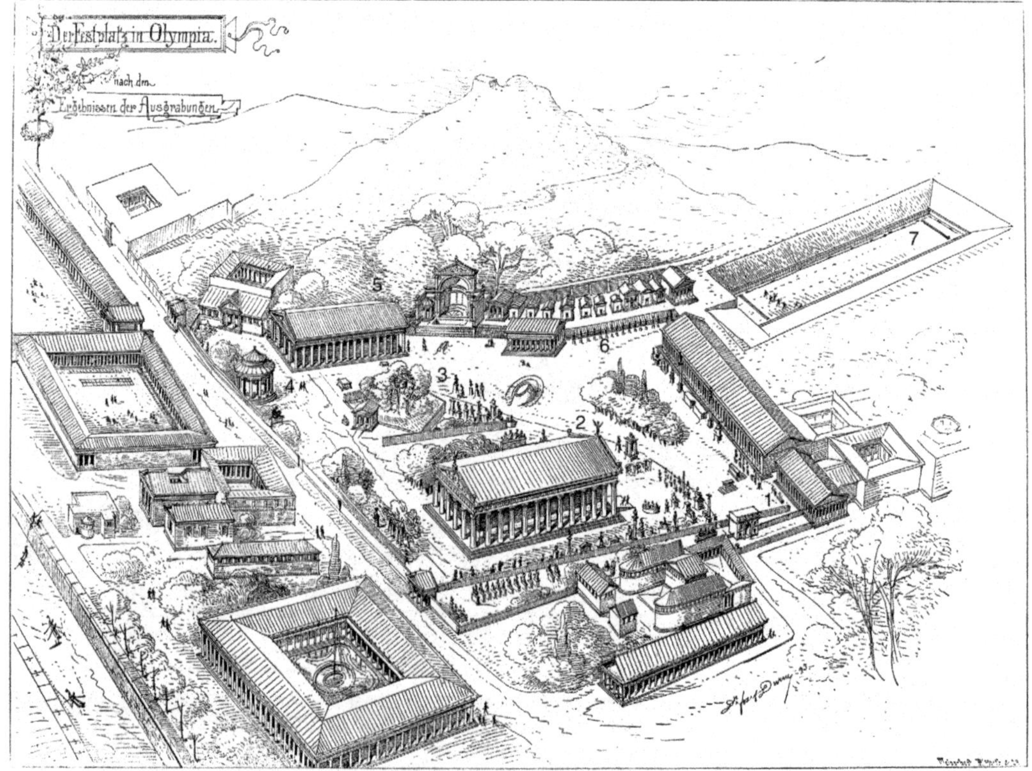

7.3 Reconstruction drawing of the sanctuary at Olympia. Date of photo: 1900. Photo: D-DAI-ATH-Olympia-Neg. 194. All rights reserved. 1: Entrance to temenos; 2: Temple of Zeus; 3: Altar of Zeus; 4: Philippeion; 5: Temple of Hera; 6: Treasuries; 7: Stadion.

points of the stadion to the east of the altar of Zeus. Around 470 BCE a Temple to Zeus (2) was started, built by Libon of Elis and completed around 457 after the city of Elis gained control of the sanctuary. The stadion was moved further to the east amid earthen banks for the spectators (7). Some additional treasuries were built, and these now lined a formal processional path from the temenos to the stadion. While much of the construction at Delphi was motivated by competition among poleis, the new phases of construction at Olympia were linked to struggles among neighboring cities for control of the sanctuary, with a new victory prompting deconstruction of existing structures and the construction of new ones. For example, the Philippeion, or shrine of Philip (4), was set just to the south of the temple and west of the Zeus altar in the fourth century, after the conquest of Greece by Philip of Macedon and his son Alexander the Great.

Additional support structures were built outside of the temenos to house athletes and visitors, and their numbers multiplied in the late classical and Hellenistic periods. The paths along the temenos wall and in front of the temple with Zeus were populated with numerous dedications of statues, as was the path below the treasuries leading to the stadion. One can see that the area outside of the temenos became crowded with buildings, but the boundary wall kept open the space inside the sanctuary where sacrifices and the oath of the athletes would take place.

Both Olympia and Delphi were not constrained by surrounding cities in their expansion, although the boundaries of the temenos, the topography, and previous structures meant that these important sites experienced somewhat uneven and irregular growth. This was also true of sanctuaries like the Acropolis in Athens, which had housed the Mycenaean palace and probably most of the city's population into the Geometric period. Literary sources suggest that the Acropolis began to be transformed into a sanctuary in the seventh century, and by the middle of the sixth century a temple dedicated to Athena had been constructed, along with numerous smaller buildings whose sculpture survives. After the Battle of Marathon in 490 BCE, the city began to build a new temple to Athena, the Parthenon, to the south and east of the archaic temple. This building was still under construction when the entire site was destroyed by the Persians in 480–479. The site was not rebuilt for thirty years, reportedly as a monument to the sacrilege of the Persians, but in 451 plans were made to build a new and larger Parthenon on the remains of the uncompleted building **(Figure 7.4)**. Inscribed building accounts tell us that construction began in 447 and that the building was completed by 438, with the pedimental sculpture taking until 432 to complete. At the same time as the pediments a new gateway, the Propylaia, was constructed at the west end. From here, both visitors and the Panathenaic procession would walk along the north side of the Parthenon with walls defining the path. The altar of Athena was to the north, and a large gathering area was defined by a wall to the west alongside the present-day Erechtheion **(see Figure 7.8, page 164)**. Additional buildings were placed mostly along the walls of the Acropolis, and a temple to Athena Nike was built above the processional entrance at the west end. On the south slope of the Acropolis was a temple of Dionysos and a theater area that was replaced by a stone theater in the fourth century.

We will discuss the Parthenon and Erechtheion in more detail below and in Chapter 10, but for now we should note that one of the buildings is generally visible from most spots in the city below and one can see their symbolic importance as signs for the city. Indeed, perhaps the best view of the Periklean building program is from the Pynx to the west, where the citizens of Athens would gather in assembly to hear speeches and vote on important actions **(see Figure 1.9, page 13)**. From there one can see all the major buildings and recall the words of Perikles in his funeral oration of 431 BCE, at the end of the first year of the Peloponnesian War, urging his fellow citizens to look around and become lovers of the city. The idea that even in ruins, the buildings of Athens would still impress later peoples, unlike their rival Sparta, indicates the significance of these places for the Greeks and explains their heavy investment in the cost of building the sanctuaries and their temples.

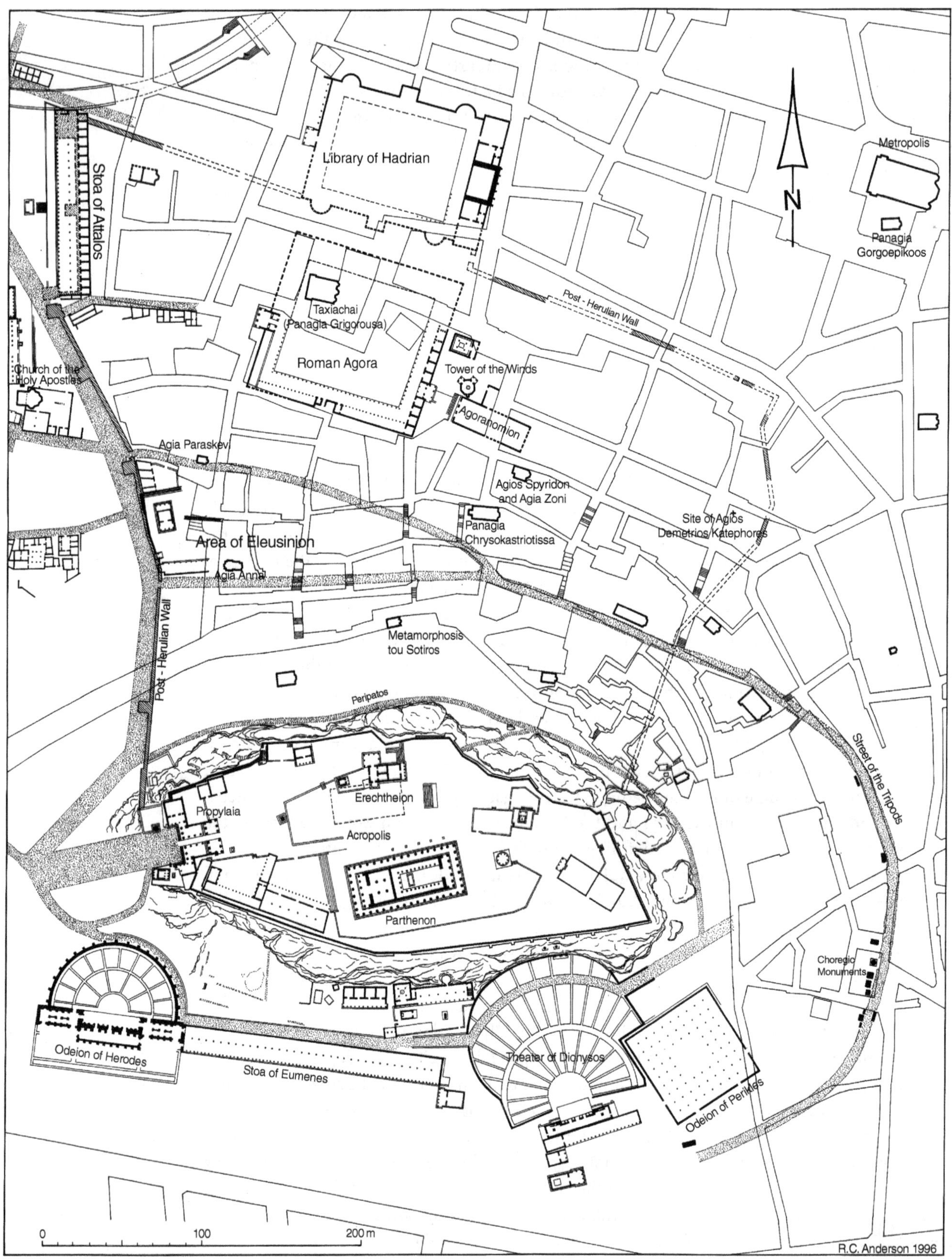

7.4 Plan of the Acropolis and areas to north and east, Athens. Photo: American School of Classical Studies at Athens: Agora Excavations.

TEMPLES AND THE ARCHITECTURAL ORDERS

Even in its ruined state, the visual dominance of a sanctuary by the temple through its height and size is apparent. In this section we will focus on the design of the Greek temple itself, its component parts, and the system of its forms and decoration that constitute the Greek "orders." These systems of design provided some standardization to the temple throughout the Greek world that made it the most recognizable and influential of Greek buildings, but still allowed many variations of style, proportions, and materials. We can begin by looking at a temple that is one of the best preserved, the Temple of Concord in the ancient city of Akragas (modern Agrigento) in Sicily (**Figure 7.5**). This building was constructed around 440–430 BCE, but in the late sixth century CE it was converted into a church. Although the interior walls were cut to provide arch windows, this conversion still preserved more of the original fabric, especially of the interior, than is the case today at Delphi, Olympia, and most other sites.

The most distinctive feature of its exterior is the **peripteral** colonnade, or columns that run around the exterior of the building, supporting the edge of the roof and enclosing a central rectangular chamber called the naos or cella. The colonnade rests on a stepped base called the **stereobate** that elevates the temple above the surrounding terrain; this and the other components of the elevation of the temple are shown in the diagram (**Figure 7.6**), with the Doric order found at Akragas/Agrigento on the left and the Ionic order to its right. The columns are set on the **stylobate** platform formed by the stereobate. The columns are built in sections or drums and are joined by dowels set in the center; after completion, the columns are then fluted, accentuating the vertical lines. The columns are not cylindrical but taper inward from the base to the top, a feature called **entasis** that gives the column more of a visual "lift." The top block is the capital and makes the transition between the circular column and the rectangular roof. Horizontal grooves mark the boundary of column shaft and the round section of the capital called the **echinus**. The cushion shape of the capitals here is distinctive of the Doric order, in contrast to the volute scrolls of the Ionic order that we will discuss later. Above the round echinus is a rectangular block, the **abacus**, that completes the transition to the rectangular blocks of the superstructure.

The horizontal upper section of the temple is called the **entablature** and consists of the **architrave**, the blocks or lintels that connect the columns, the frieze above it, and finally the sloping roof making

peripteral
a colonnade that goes all the way around a building, especially in the case of temples

stereobate
steps defining the platform of the temple

stylobate
platform of the temple on which the colonnade sits

entasis
the vertical tapering and swelling of columns

echinus
the round cushion-shaped section of the Doric capital

abacus
the square block that sits on top of the capital and supports the architrave

entablature
the superstructure of a building above the colonnade, which includes the architrave, frieze, cornice, and pediment

architrave
the lower section of the entablature that rests on column capitals

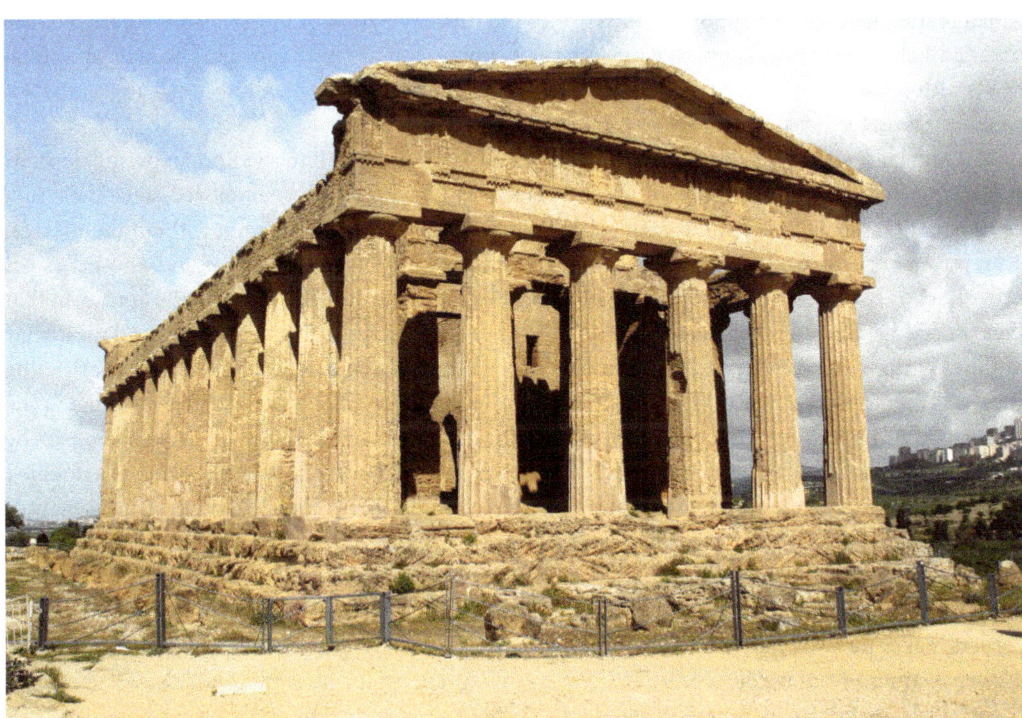

7.5 Exterior of the Temple of Concord at Akragas/Agrigento, *c.* 440–430 BCE. Photo: Bruce Goodman.

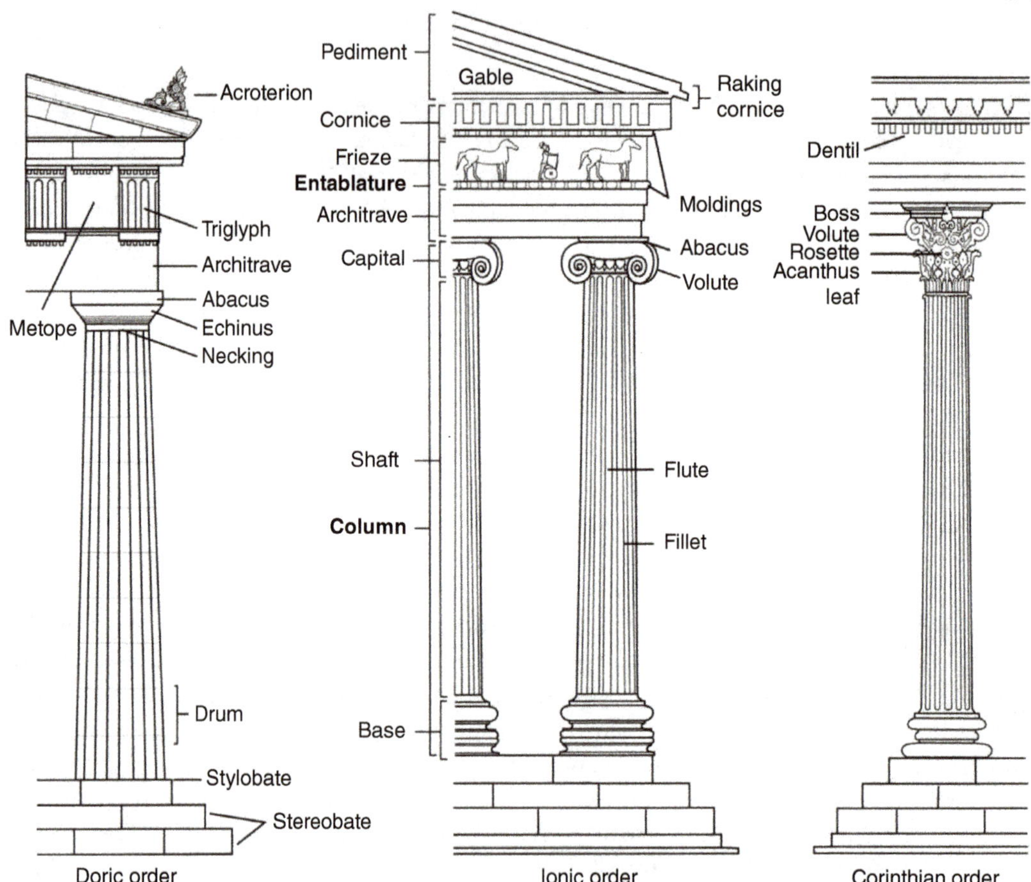

7.6 The Doric, Ionic, and Corinthian orders and their components. Drawing by D. Weiss, after Tyler Jo Smith and Dimitris Plantzos (eds.), *A Companion to Greek Art* (Oxford: Blackwell Publishing, 2012), fig. 6.3.

pediment
the triangular gable at the ends of a building, part of the entablature

frieze
the second course of the entablature, between the architrave and cornice

regula
peg-shaped elements below the triglyph

mutule
decorative element above the triglyph and below the cornice

cornice
the edge of the roof or pediment, called a raking cornice when sloped

sima
gutter inside the edge of the roof

antefix
vertical tile of terracotta or stone that covers the ends of the roof tiles. Antefixes can also serve as rain spouts

the triangular gable at the ends called the **pediment**. The Doric **frieze** is divided into alternating forms called triglyphs, the three-part projecting rectangles, and the square panels of the metopes. The triglyphs are framed by the peg-shaped element called **regula** underneath and the **mutule** above, which marks the **cornice** supporting the edge of the roof. The **sima** or gutter forms the edge of the roof and helps to channel the water to a series of spouts, usually in the form of human or animal heads with open mouths called **antefixes** for the water to exit. Finally, a sculpture call an **acroterion** could be set on the peak of the roof or on pedestals at the corners.

The regularity of these features in temples from the sixth century into the Roman period demonstrates that these forms constitute an order or rule that Greek architects employed since their first development in the late seventh to early sixth centuries BCE. The rules were not without their issues, however. For example, the triglyph is placed over the center of each column, and another is set between two columns, with metopes filling in between them. A problem occurs at the corner, in that the corner edge of the entablature, while set back from the abacus, still extended beyond the center of the column, so that the triglyph at the corner could not be centered over the column, as can be seen in the temple at Akragas/Agrigento. Designers had to compensate for this either by fudging the placement of the first few triglyphs and widening the metopes to fill in the uneven spacing, or by adjusting the spacing of the columns. While the alternating triglyphs and metopes provide a doubled rhythm from the colonnade below that balances the horizontal and vertical elements, the anomaly of the rule would seem to be unsatisfactory. Recalling the organization of the sanctuaries, however, reminds us that temples were meant to be seen from multiple angles, especially from the corners. From this vantage point, the uneven spacing is less apparent and the meeting of two triglyphs at the corners makes for a stronger corner, continuing the rhythm from one side of the building to another.

One distinct advantage of an order is that it is not limited to a specific size of building. The Temple of Concord is moderate in size, 16.91 meters across the end and 39.44 meters down the side. The end side has six columns, while the long side has thirteen. This proportion follows a colonnade ratio of x:2x + 1 [6:2(6) + 1, or 6:13]. The same formula is found in the larger Parthenon, which has an 8:17 ([8:2(8) + 1] colonnade. This rule is not universal, but the articulation of the Doric order is flexible in being applied to small treasuries or gigantic temples of varying proportions. It is perhaps this combination of consistency and variability with the Doric order and its Ionic counterpart that led to the long history of their use in Greek architecture.

acroterion (or akroterion) (pl. acroteria) ornament or sculpture placed at the corners or peak of a roof

The development of the Doric order has been the subject of much debate. It was called Doric because it developed on the mainland where Dorian Greek was spoken, particularly at Corinth and the northeast Peloponnesos. According to the Roman architect Vitruvius, the Doric order evolved from wooden architecture in a process of petrification (*De Arch.* 4.2.2–3). Triglyphs are the ends of beams set perpendicular to the architrave and the metope was a panel covering the gap between the beams, as can be seen in the reconstruction of the entablature for the seventh-century Temple of Apollo at Thermon (**see Figure 6.22, page 148**). The mutules are the remnants of the rafters rising up from the cornice to form the roof. While we have seen that in the Geometric period buildings were made primarily of wood, mud brick, and thatch, and that early exterior columns at Lefkandi and Samos were made out of wood, the theory of petrification has difficulties. Recent analysis of the archaeological evidence suggests that the Doric order evolved within a couple of generations between 625 and 575 BCE at a number of sites throughout Greece, and that its components have varied sources (Barletta 2001). The cushion capital has similarities to Mycenaean capitals, an example of which was visible in the pediment over the Lion Gate at Mycenae (**see Figure 3.6, page 56**). Technological developments such as ashlar masonry and the production of terracotta tiles also played a role. Similarly, Near Eastern and Egyptian sources may have played a role in developments of some forms or motifs. As Barbara Barletta has suggested, the development of the orders was a process of experimentation and adaptations as Greek builders at many different sites sought to create a system over a short period of time.

Even once a system was developed, there was change in its deployment. We can see this readily by comparing the two temples dedicated to Hera at Poseidonia/Paestum (**Figure 7.7**). The temple on the left, Hera I, was built around 550 BCE, within a couple of generations of the founding of the city (**see Figure 5.3, page 103**). Its colonnade has nine columns across the front and eighteen down the side, for a ratio of 1:2. The odd number of columns on the end is unusual, but was also found at Thermon and might have accommodated a two-chamber cella on the interior. The second temple,

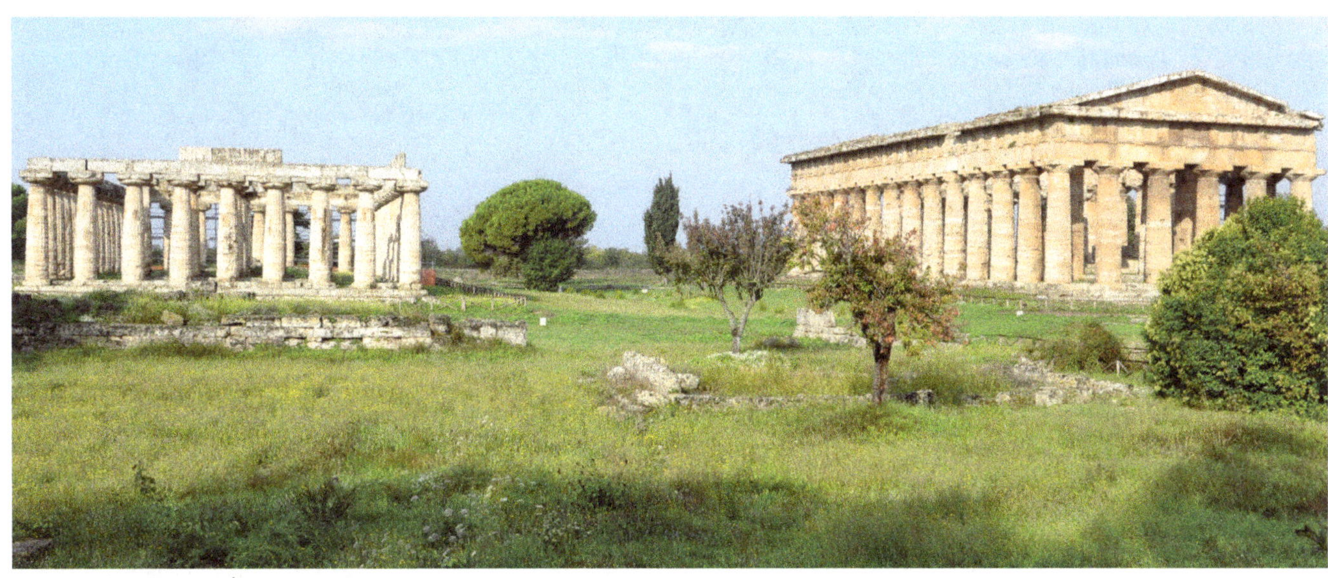

7.7 Temples of Hera at Poseidonia/Paestum. Left: Temple of Hera I, *c.* 550 BCE (width 80 ft 5 in/24.51 m). Right: Temple of Hera II, *c.* 460 BCE (width 79 ft 7 in/24.26 m). Photo: author.

Hera II, dates to *c.* 460, but its colonnade is 6:14 rather than the "canonical" 6:13. Comparing the columns, one can see that there is a more pronounced bulge or entasis in the Hera I columns, its capitals are wider and proportionally flatter, and the proportions of the columns somewhat squatter. Hera II has a more subtle entasis and pronounced verticality in its columns, capitals, and the overall proportions of the building. One can readily see that there is a system at work that gives the Greek temple a distinctive visual identity, but also a range of variation and flexibility that makes each building individual and local.

Turning to the Ionic order (**Figure 7.6**), we can see that it has the same three-part elevation of base, colonnade, and entablature. The stylobate is the same, but the columns are more complex and ornate. The columns have a square plinth block and above it a three-part circular base, with a projecting, rounded molding called the **torus** sandwiching a receding molding called the **scotia**. The fluting consists of channels carved between ridges. The capital consists of a circular echinus with projecting volute scrolls facing to the inside and outside, with a square and ornamented abacus block to make the transition from the circular column to the rectilinear entablature. This section has the same layers as the Doric order: architrave, frieze, cornice, and sima, but the decoration differs. The architrave has three staggered horizontal bands called **fascia**, while the frieze is left undivided. Like the Doric order, the frieze could be filled with relief or painted decoration **(see Figure 7.15, page 171)** that runs along the length of the building. The cornice and sima project outward as in the Doric order to enclose the roof, but rather than mutules as a decoration the Ionic order has small block-like teeth called dentils. The Ionic order, too, is not without its inconsistencies. Especially in a peripteral temple, one has a problem in that the Ionic capital has two faces with the volute scrolls. The scroll ends face each other in a colonnade until one reaches the corner. Here, one has two volute faces meeting each other, forcing the corner scroll to project more diagonally and making the corner columns inconsistent with the rest.

torus
a convex or rounded molding, especially on the base of an Ionic or Corinthian column

scotia
a concave molding, especially on the base of an Ionic or Corinthian column and sandwiched by a torus molding above and below

fascia
a series of long, flat moldings, especially on the architrave of the Ionic and Corinthian orders

There are no peripteral Ionic temples that are as well preserved as the temple at Akragas/Agrigento to give us a good view of the overall effect of the exterior. The Erechtheion on the Acropolis in Athens does give us a feeling for the ornateness of an Ionic building **(Figure 7.8)**. Possibly designed by Mnesikles, it was started in 431 BCE and after several delays completed about 405. The building is actually several temples with a facade facing east, a south porch supported by statues of women called caryatids, and a porch on the lower north side. The facade

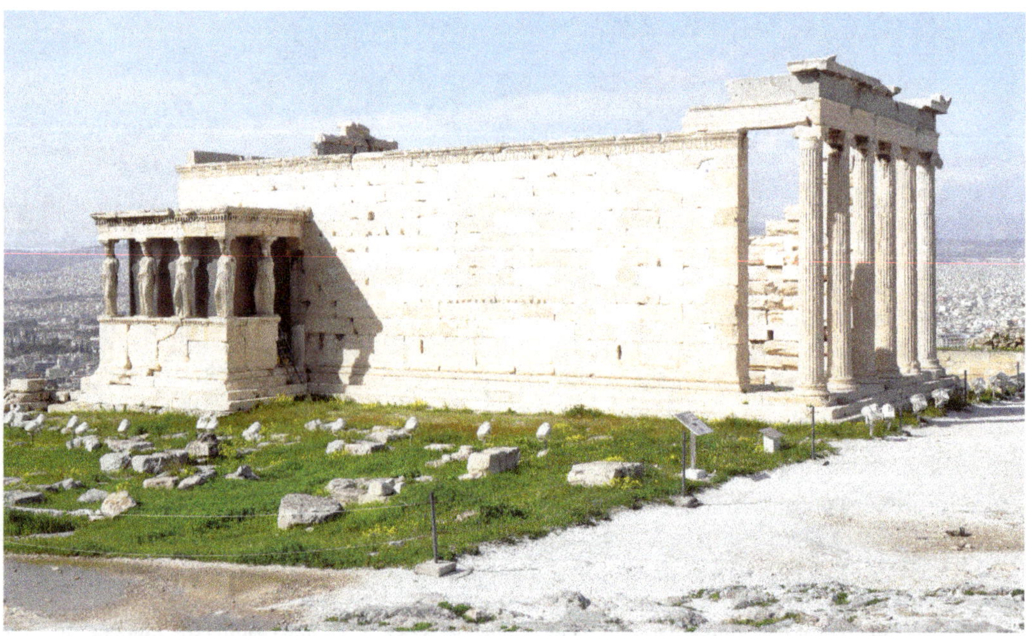

7.8 Erechtheion, Acropolis, Athens, *c.* 431–405 BCE. Possibly by Mnesikles, architect. Photo: author.

has six columns sitting in front of the main chamber, making this a **prostyle** (columns before) rather than a peripteral temple. The three-step platform supports the columns, which have the three-part torus and scotia base but lack a plinth block. The columns are proportionally taller than those of the Doric order, and overall the building has more verticality. The columns have a decorative band at their top that marks the transition to the capitals. The architrave and its fascia are intact on the east end, but the frieze was once decorated with white marble figures set against the blue stone.

On the walls of the cella an additional and lavish ornamental frieze was added below the architrave, as can be seen in one of its blocks now in London **(Figure 7.9)**. The frieze is divided into horizontal sections with a **lotus and palmette** chain in the lower half, an **egg-and-dart** molding above it, and a variant **leaf-and-tongue** pattern at the top. The three larger bands are separated by a thin **bead-and-reel** runner. The basic units of the top moldings align with each other in a 1:1 ratio and in a 1:2 ratio with the bead-and-reel molding. The lotus-and-palmette chain, however, has a different rhythm. It takes four of the lotus-palmette units to align with fifteen of the egg-and-dart units, creating a regular but syncopated pattern of 4:15:30 overall.

Vitruvius (*De Arch.* 4.1.6–8) tells us that the proportions of the Doric order were based on the ideal male figure, while those of the Ionic order were based on the female figure. The famous caryatid porch of the Erechtheion suggests a visual, symbolic linkage of Ionic proportions and female figures, but it is not likely that there was such a precise correspondence in proportional systems as Vitruvius suggests. The Ionic order, like the Doric, developed over a few decades, about 600–550 BCE, in several places; its early proportions were varied, like those of both the Doric order and korai from the same period.

prostyle
temple or structure with columns projecting on the end or ends of the building

lotus and palmette
ornamental pattern consisting of alternating lotus blossoms with spiked petals and palmettes with a fan of rounded fronds

egg-and-dart
decorative molding made of alternating ovoid eggs framed by fanning spikes (darts)

leaf-and-tongue
decorative molding made of alternating leaf shapes framed by a running tongue

bead-and-reel
decorative pattern made of alternating round or ovular beads and narrow vertical disks (reel)

One other major order evolved at the end of the fifth century, the Corinthian, which is distinguished by its much taller proportions and the carving of acanthus leaves covering an underlying bell shape **(Figure 7.10)**. According to Vitruvius (*De Arch.* 4.1.9–10), this was developed by the sculptor Kallimachos, who had observed a basket that had been set on an acanthus plant in a cemetery. The basket contained drinking vessels used by a young woman who had died and were left as a tomb offering, with a tile placed over the top of the basket to protect them. The plant's leaves and tendrils grew around and over the surface of the basket, and it is said that Kallimachos rendered this into a stone capital and created the Corinthian order from it. This story may have some element of truth in it, although basically the Corinthian order is adapted from the Ionic, with the biggest change being in the tall, bell-shaped capital, giving it a more vertical proportion than the Ionic. Since the Corinthian capital does not have volutes at the corners, it did not have the problems of consistency that the Ionic order faced, and it became very common in Roman architecture. Its use in Greece was more limited to interiors at the beginning. At Epidauros it was used on the interior colonnade of the tholos or thymele, but not on the exterior **(see Figure 12.2, page 290)**. An early example of it on the exterior is seen in the Lysikrates monument, where it forms essentially a false colonnade for the cylindrical shape of the monument **(see Figure 12.5, page 293)**.

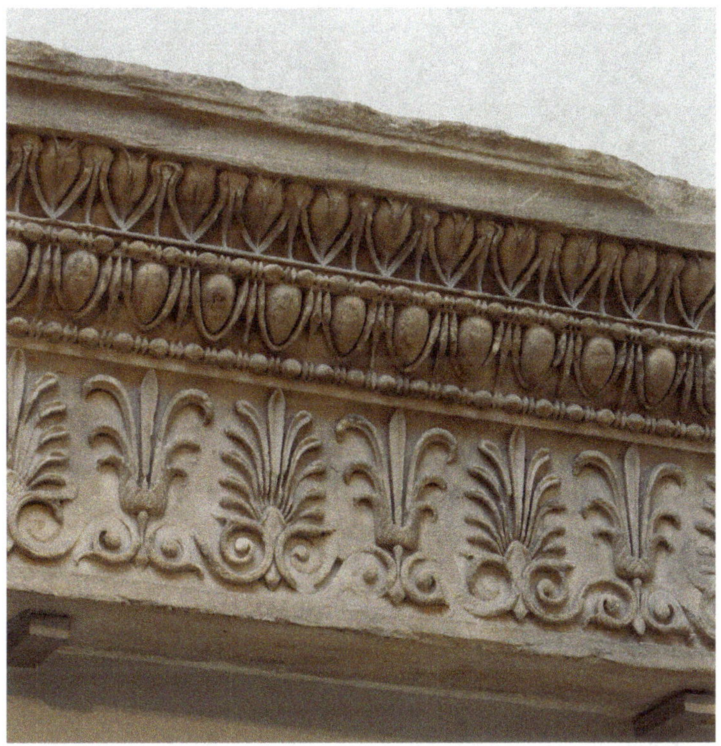

7.9 Section of the frieze from the Erechtheion, *c.* 410–405 BCE. 20½ in (52 cm). London, British Museum. Photo: © The Trustees of the British Museum.

The exterior of the Greek temple masks a simpler interior, as we can see by looking at a generic plan of the temple (**Figure 7.11**). The top of the stylobate (6) is a rectangular platform with the columns along its edge in a peristyle or colonnade (5). In the case of very large temples, such as the Temple of Apollo at Didyma (**see Figures 14.8–14.10, pages 353–354**), it is necessary to double or even triple the rows of columns to support the superstructure, but this just adds another unit or layer to the plan without changing the basic concept. Once past the peristyle, the naos consists of a long, rectangular space with solid walls on the long sides and columns replacing the walls on the ends. This arrangement of columns in antis (anta is the term for the ending of the wall) creates a porch opening at both ends (7, 8). At the back side this is an enclosed chamber called the opisthodomos (3) that is often used as a storage or display space for offerings. The other porch, or pronaos (1, before-the-naos), has a door in its back wall leading to the naos proper (2).

anta (pl. antis)
term for the projecting end of a wall

opisthodomos
the back room of a Greek temple. It abuts the naos but does not usually open to it

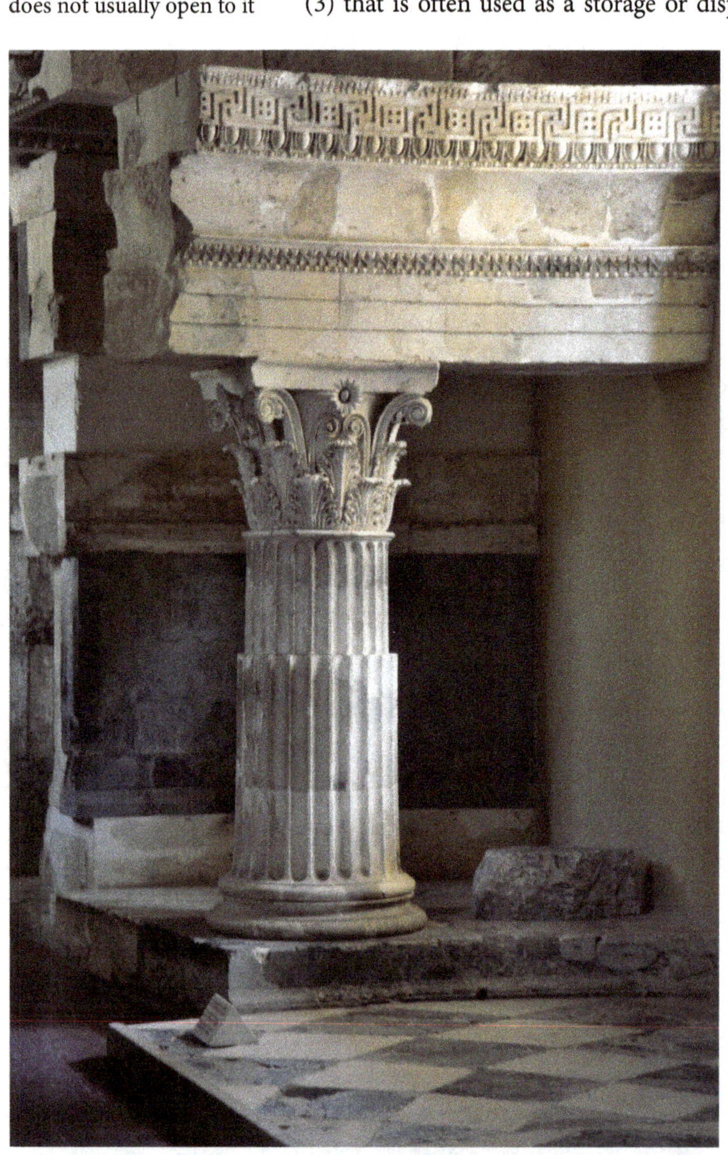

7.10 Corinthian capital and entablature from the thymele of the Asklepieion at Epidauros, mid-4th cent. BCE. Epidauros, Archaeological Museum. Photo: Vanni/Art Resource, NY.

In the naos would be found the statue of the deity and other important cult objects or treasures, as can be seen in the reconstruction of the Temple of Zeus at Olympia (**Figure 7.12**). The statue here, made of gold and ivory by Pheidias in the 430 s, completely filled the interior to create a glittering and overwhelming sight of the god. Long lost, reconstructions based on literary accounts, excavations (including the workshop of Pheidias), and representations on coins only hint at the wonder-inspiring nature of the experience. To support the roof in large temples like this, tiers of small, superimposed columns would line the sides of the naos, since a standard column would be too wide and reduce the interior space. The interior was not well illuminated since natural light could only indirectly reach the interior. Reflecting stone floors or pools and lamps would supplement the lighting, but the interior of the temple was not a place intended for large-scale ritual and was meant to invoke a sense of awe or reverence. Most cult statues were more modest in size than the Olympian Zeus, such as the group from Lykosoura (**see Figures 14.18 and 14.19, page 364**) or copies of the Aphrodite of Knidos (**see Figure 12.11, page 300**), and some of the oldest cult statues were small wooden statues that resembled planks.

Whatever the scale, the temple interior was not designed for large group rituals but was meant to convey a sense of awe in the visitor as he or she entered the dwelling of the deity, leaving the bright open area in front of the temple and entering the darker, enclosed interior. At Delphi, the cella was the place of the oracle itself, and so was modified. An underground chamber below the level of the naos enclosed the *omphalos*, the stone that was the "navel" of the earth, a tripod set over the fissure, and a statue of Apollo. The Pythia would sit in the tripod to await the trance in which the oracle would be received from Apollo. The oracle would then be pronounced to the petitioner.

The interior of the Temple of Concord at Akragas/Agrigento does give a sense of the enclosed and removed space of the naos (**Figure 7.13**). Many temples today have only the exterior colonnade left

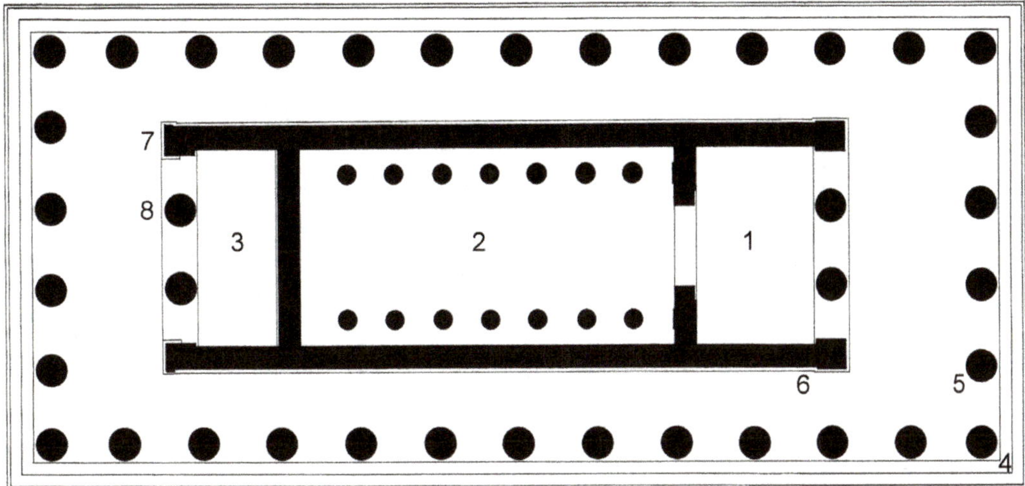

7.11 General plan of the Greek temple and its components. Adapted by Christine Dent from J. Travlos, *Pictorial Dictionary of Ancient Athens* (New York, 1971), fig. 263. 1: Pronaos; 2: Naos or Cella; 3: Opisthodomos; 4: Stereobate; 5: Colonnade or Peristyle; 6: Stylobate; 7: Anta; 8: Columns in Antis.

since the regular ashlar blocks of the interior were taken as building material in later centuries. This temple's conversion into a church, with rounded arch openings cut on the sides to allow light into the interior, preserved much of the interior walls. Today, with the roof gone, it is more well lit than it would have been originally, but even with these losses and modifications, one can still see that the interior is more vertical than the exterior and set off from the outside. With only the doorway or lamps providing any significant light in the original building, the naos would feel like a space removed from the exterior world. The placement of an exhibition of contemporary sculpture as part of a UNESCO-sponsored festival in 2011 gives a sense of the visibility of the cult statue and the dedication of many other works in the temple's interior, making them repositories for the actions of individuals over the centuries.

A MINI-HISTORY OF THE GREEK TEMPLE

Given its visual prominence in a sanctuary and its importance as a civic undertaking, as we shall see further in Chapter 11, we might take a diachronic view of the temple's development. The earliest temples of the polis appear to have been similar in conception to houses, as the small temple built at Zagora in the seventh century shows **(see Figure 4.21, page 92)**. Consisting of a pronaos and a rectangular naos with four columns and a hearth, it recalls the Mycenaean megaron that was the core of the Late Bronze Age palaces **(see Figures 3.5 and 3.6, pages 54, 56)**. The earlier house at Lefkandi is much larger and more complex, and whether intended as a house or a heroön, it represents the idea of the temple as a house distinguished by its size. We see the further development of this symbolism in the hekatompedon, or hundred-footer, in the first Temple of Hera built at Samos **(see Figure 6.19, page 147)**. The addition of an exterior colonnade in the seventh century further served to mark the building visually **(see Figure 6.20, page 147)**.

The greater use of stone as a more prominent building material created the need for more systematic construction techniques and stimulated the development of the orders during the late seventh and early sixth centuries **(see Figure 6.22, page 148)**. In the first half of the sixth century we see the construction of temples built completely of stone and the use of the Doric and Ionic orders throughout the Greek world. The early buildings, like the Temple of Hera I at Poseidonia/Paestum **(see Figure 7.7)**, were squatter in proportion and profiles, but later temples followed more vertical proportions, as can be seen in the adjacent Temple of Hera II. As we shall discuss further, a number of optical refinements were introduced during the fifth century, including the

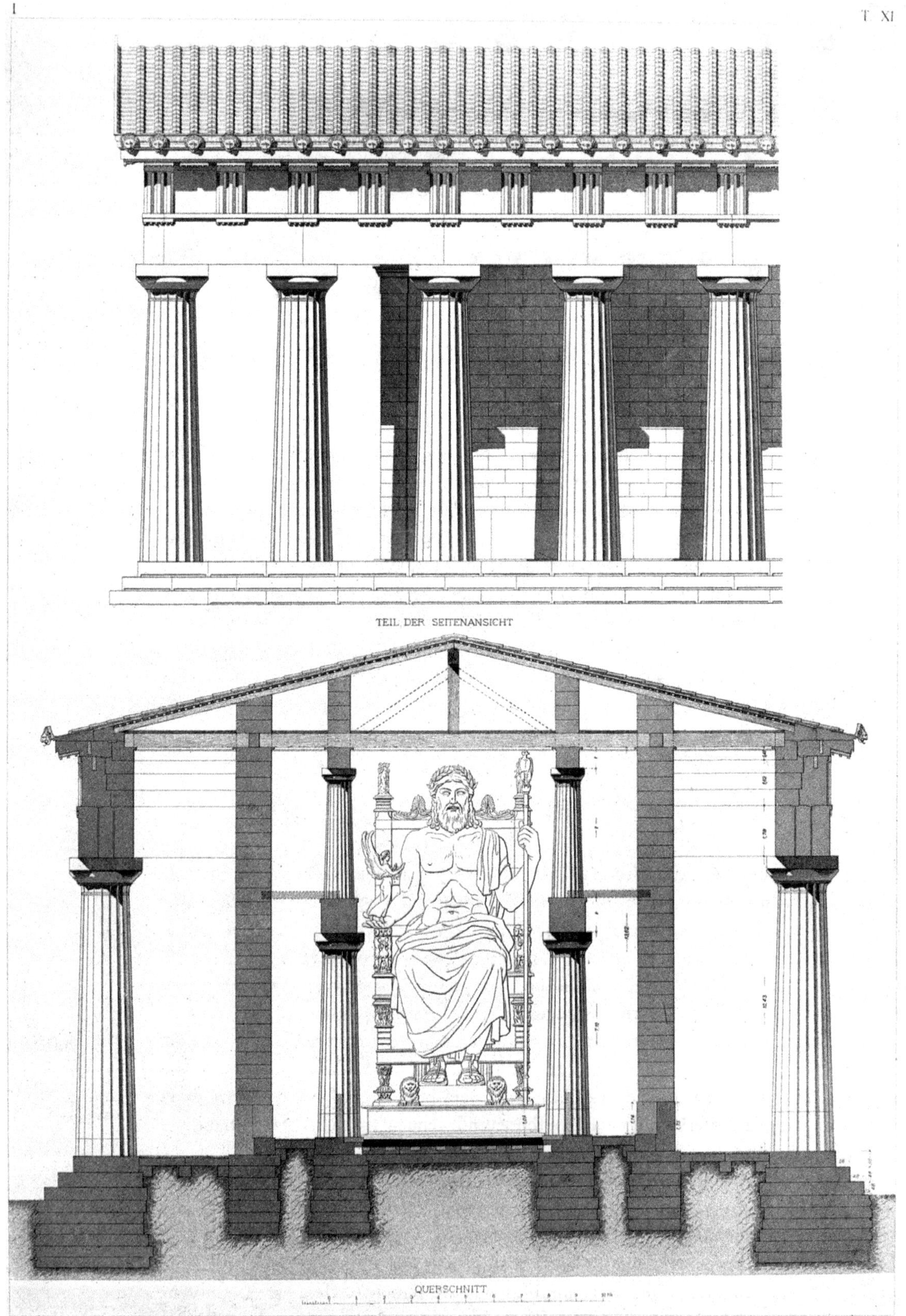

7.12 Reconstruction of the side and interior of the Temple of Zeus, Olympia. Height of naos about 46 ft 11 in (14.3 m). Photo: DAI-Athen-Olympia-0175.

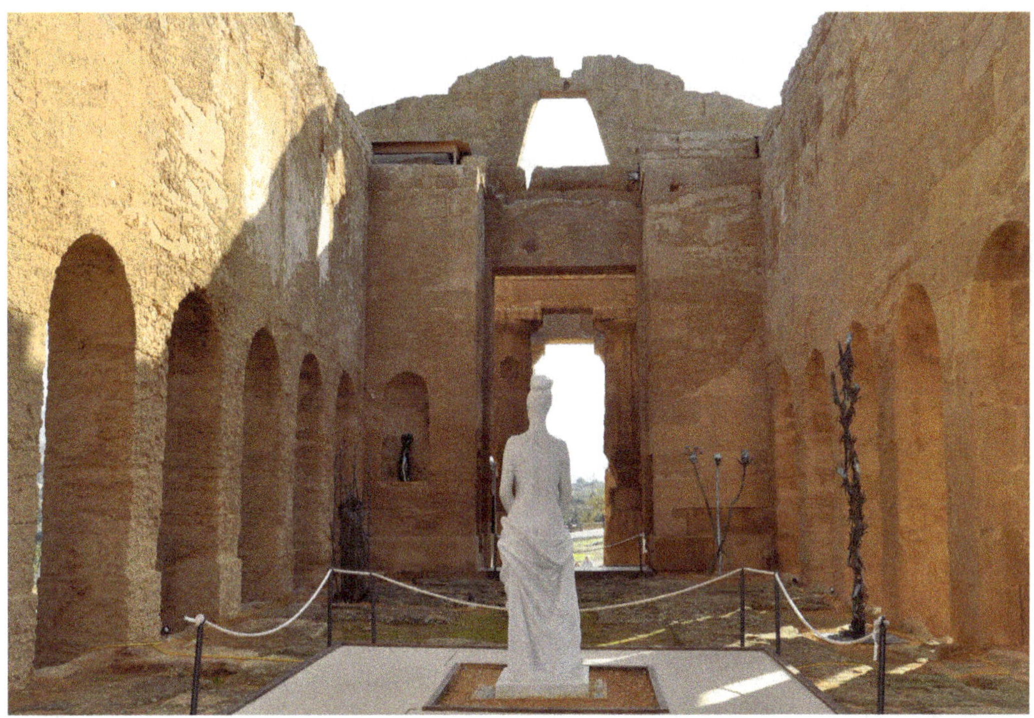

7.13 Interior of the Temple of Concord at Akragas/Agrigento, *c.* 440–430 BCE. Sculpture: Piergorgio Colombara, *In Prison*, 2009; Aaron Young, *Purple Rain*, 2009; Francesco Messina, *Bianca*, 1938–1990; Daniel Spoerri, *The Skull Tree*, 1993; Paolo delle Monache, *Eulogy of the Hands*, 2009. Photo: author. Reproduction courtesy of the artists and Bortolami Gallery, New York.

curvature of the stylobate, the adjustments of intercolumnation dimensions, and having columns lean in slightly. These are particularly evident in the Parthenon **(see Figure 10.13, page 249)**, but appear earlier in Sicily and Magna Graecia.

Later temples show some changes from the fifth-century standards of proportions. Both the Temple of Asklepios at Epidauros **(see Figure 12.1, page 289)** and the Temple of Athena Polias at Priene **(see city view in Figure 5.5, page 105)**, for example, have six columns on the end but eleven rather than thirteen down the side, making them appear more vertical in proportion than temples like the Hephaisteion in Athens **(see Figure 5.6, page 105)**. The Temple of Apollo at Bassae in the Peloponnesos was the earliest building to use the Corinthian order on the interior, and that new order is a prominent feature of the fourth-century tholoi that were built in sanctuaries at Epidauros **(see Figure 12.2, page 290)**, Delphi, and Olympia.

Siting continues to be a major consideration and can be seen in Hellenistic examples of temple architecture. The Temple of Asklepios at Kos was modest in scale, but gained visual prominence through the construction of terraces lined with stoas and the creation of a more longitudinal avenue leading to it from the nearby city **(see Figure 14.7, page 352)**. Some Hellenistic temples, such as the unfinished Temple of Apollo at Didyma, were huge in both size and scale, with columns over 20 meters high and bases made up of seven large steps rather than the more traditional three **(see Figure 14.8, page 353)**. The interior of Didyma was also exposed to the open air and enclosed a small shrine and grove, but could only be accessed indirectly through a dark stairway and ramp **(see Figure 14.10, page 354)**. While conforming to the rules of the orders, these buildings focused on dramatic presentations. During the second century the Corinthian order was used for the exterior of a temple for the first time at the Temple of Olympian Zeus in Athens.

To summarize, the temple is the most distinctive building type developed by the Greeks and becomes a visual mark of their identity. Temples are among the earliest structures built in a city, and even though they serve mainly a supporting role in communal ritual, they help to distinguish the Greek sanctuary and city. The orders provided a system for their design and construction, but one that could be adapted or varied to make each temple potentially distinctive. Certainly a city would

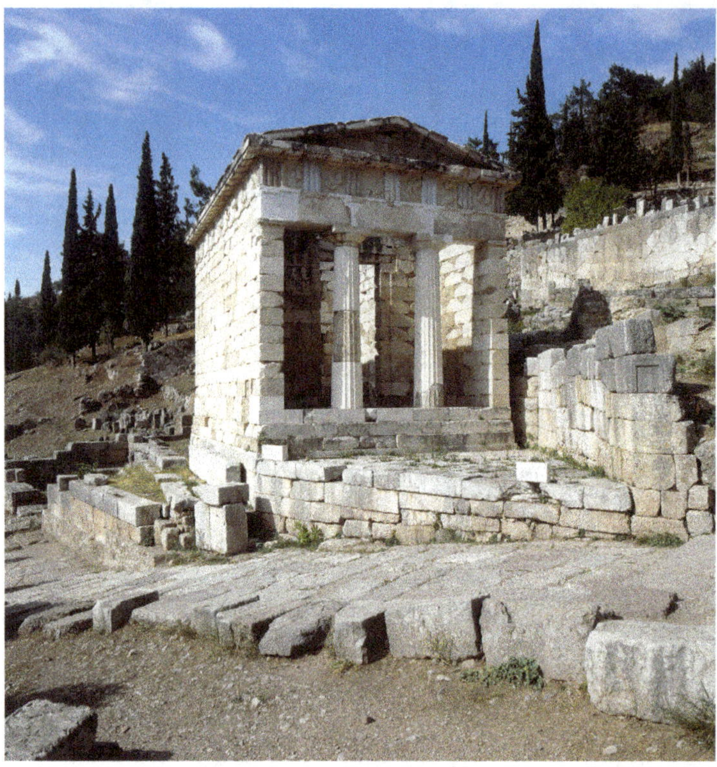

7.14 Athenian Treasury at Delphi (reconstructed), *c.* 490 BCE. Photo: Marie Mauzy/Art Resource, NY.

strive to build temples that rivaled those of other cities, as we shall see in other chapters, but this would be through the manipulation of materials, proportions, furnishings, and siting within the framework of the orders.

OTHER BUILDINGS OF THE SANCTUARY

As the views and plans of Olympia, Delphi, and the Acropolis show, sanctuaries were filled with a number of other structures besides temples and altars. At Panhellenic sites like Delphi and Olympia, treasuries were quite prominent and were placed in highly visible locations. A treasury was a relatively small structure made of marble or limestone, and typically consisted of a rectangular naos with a pronaos and columns in antis, virtually a replica of the temple interior, as can be seen in the reconstructed Athenian Treasury at Delphi **(Figure 7.14; see 223 in Figure** 7.2, **page 157)**. Indeed, their plan recalls the earliest temple structures before the development of exterior colonnades.

The function of the treasuries was limited but important for the polis. At Panhellenic sanctuaries like Delphi and Olympia, treasuries were built by poleis and housed their civic dedications, as well as those made by their citizens. Indeed, just as the polis claimed the prerogative for law in early Greece, it also claimed authority over the dedications of its citizens at sites like Delphi. The treasury and its contents were meant to proclaim the status and preeminence of the city among the Greeks. For example, Pausanias (10.11.5–6) tells us that the Athenians built their treasury with spoils from their victory at the Battle of Marathon in 490 BCE, and a platform on the south side of the building displayed trophies of that battle. The Siphnian Treasury, seen in the reconstruction in **Figure 7.15**, was built with revenues from the silver mines on the island of Siphnos, whose citizens erected the treasury as an offering to the gods for their fortune (Paus. 10.11.2). Unfortunately, the mines were flooded around 525 when, according to Herodotos (3.57), pirates attacked the island. Both of these buildings would have been conspicuous along the Sacred Way, impressing the visitor with the importance and piety of the cities dedicating them.

The placement of a treasury, or of a major sculptural monument, would have been a key factor in its motivation and construction. As the plan at Delphi shows, some monuments have greater visibility than others and the construction of buildings like these would have required negotiation with the **amphictyony**, the group that oversaw that sanctuary. The Siphnian Treasury was one of the earliest buildings following the destruction of 548 BCE, and originally would have been visible for some distance along the first leg of the Sacred Way when it was built around 525 **(see Figure 7.2, 122, page 157)**. The construction of a new building, like the Sikyonian Treasury **(121, at the left side of Figure 7.15)**, would have obscured much of the visitor's view of its slightly earlier neighbor when it was built about a quarter-century later. In placing the Athenian Treasury, that city was able to secure a spot at the switchback, so that its southern side was completely exposed to the viewer when turning to ascend toward the Temple of Apollo. The trophies from the victory at Marathon would have been prominently displayed, reminding the visitor of the triumph and importance of Athens. Its visibility and prominence at the site, reflected in its currently

amphictyony
a group made up of members of neighboring states that oversaw a sanctuary such as Delphi

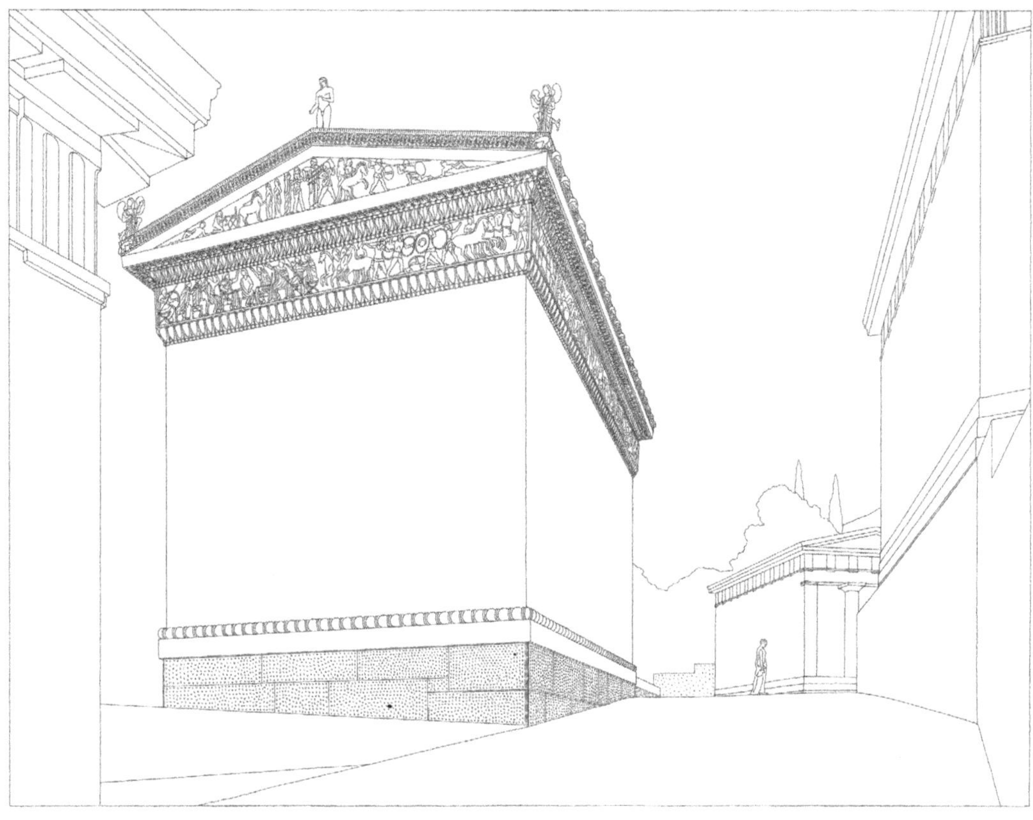

7.15 Perspective reconstruction of the Siphnian Treasury and Sacred Way at Delphi. Source: plan no. 18082, EfA/E. Hansen.

reconstructed state (**see Figure 7.1, page 155**), was surely not accidental and must have been the result of negotiation between Athens and the sanctuary.

There were other special building types in sanctuaries. A glance at the reconstruction of Olympia shows a round building inside the western temenos wall (**see Figure 7.3, page 158**). This type of small structure, generally featuring a cylindrical cella surrounded by a circular colonnade, is called a tholos after earlier Bronze Age tombs (**see Figure 3.7, page 57**). At Olympia it was begun by and dedicated to Philip of Macedon after the Battle of Chaironeia in 338 BCE and called the Philippeion in his honor. It had an Ionic colonnade on the exterior; inside were statues of Philip and the Macedonian royal house framed by a decorative colonnade made up of Corinthian half-columns projecting from the wall. Earlier round structures from the fourth century are found at Delphi and Epidauros (**see Figure 12.2, page 290**); the exterior of these had a Doric colonnade, with a Corinthian colonnade on the interior. The dedication and purpose of the Delphic tholos are uncertain, but the tholos at Epidauros served the cult of Asklepios and the labyrinth underneath its center may have contained the cultic snakes. An even earlier round structure was built in the Agora at Athens (**see Figure 5.7, page 106**). This non-sanctuary structure served as an administrative and dining area for the Athenian *boule*. The remains of the entablature of an archaic sixth-century round structure were also found beneath the Sikyonian Treasury at Delphi, so that the history of the circular building is long and varied. These tholoi would have stood out visually from the other buildings in the sanctuary, but they seemed to have served no consistent purpose.

We can also see at many sanctuaries a theater (**see Figure 7.2, page 157; Figure 7.4, page 160; Figure 12.3, page 291**). While today we think of theater as a secular art form, tragedy and comedy both originated in the performance of choral songs in the festivals of Dionysos. The early theaters were generally a rectangular open space flanked by slopes for the spectators, but by the fourth century a specific design was developed. We will discuss the design of the theater at Epidauros in more detail in Chapter 12, but the distinctive architectural elements are a circular performance area, the

orchestra
the circular area at the center of the theater where dramas were performed

orchestra, a structure on one side that housed the scenery, and banks of circular seating rising above. The theater at Athens, which may have been the model for Epidauros and may have been designed by the same architect, Polykleitos the Younger, was next to a small Temple of Dionysos on the slope of the Acropolis. Other open structures in sanctuaries, such as the stadion, were for races and athletic competitions and can be seen in the reconstructions of Olympia and Epidauros (**see Figure 7.3, page 158; Figure 12.1, page 289**).

RITUALS AND OFFERINGS

lekanis
a broad shallow bowl used for food. It can have a lid or cover

kanous
basket for ritual instruments carried in a procession by a kanephoros

aulos
a double flute played through a mouthpiece set on the ends and strapped around the neck, with each flute held in a different hand

Before looking at the offerings of individuals at sanctuaries, we need to emphasize that the physical setting has to be considered along with the rituals that were performed there and framed the experience of both participants and visitors. Sports and comedies provided thrills and entertainment, but these were parts of larger ritual performances and served to negotiate the relationships of individuals within the community and to the gods. The gods could provide many blessings, but also many difficulties, and one's behavior needed to be mindful of one's place in the *kosmos*, a word that originally meant order.

We can get a sense of the qualities of these rituals by looking at representations in vase painting. A sixth-century Boeotian **lekanis** (**Figure 7.16**), for example, shows a sacrificial procession. Starting at the handle on the right side, we see a woman with shield and spear that must be Athena. Behind Athena is a snake and column; before her is an altar that has a bird perched on it and flames rising up. The figure of Athena must be intended as a statue, rather than the goddess herself, and some later representations make that clear by adding a base (**see Figure 9.7, page 219**). In front of the altar is a woman who carries a **kanous** or basket on her head. She is the *kanephoros*, and the *kanous* contains the equipment needed for the ritual, including the knife for the sacrifice. Behind her a man walks with a bull, the sacrificial victim. Six men make a line behind them, led by an **aulos** (double-flute) player.

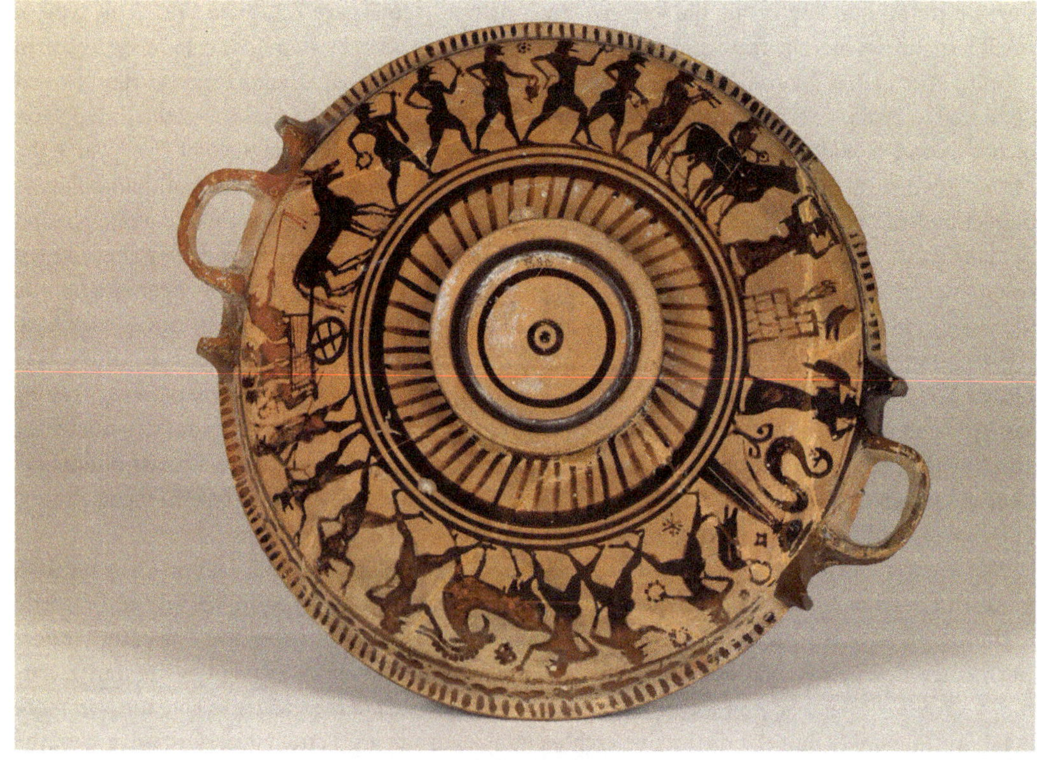

7.16 Boeotian black-figure lekane with sacrificial procession to Athena, *c.* 550 BCE. 12 in (30.5 cm) diameter. London, British Museum B80 (1897,1004.1). Photo: © The Trustees of the British Museum.

The men carry wreaths, knives, a pitcher, and tethers to assist with the sacrifice. Under the left handle, the end of the procession is marked by a cart drawn by donkeys with three figures and a driver, followed by a man with a staff.

The column behind Athena might be a symbolic reference to a temple building that would house a cult statue, but freestanding columns could also be found in sanctuaries. If it signifies an entire building, it shows the greater significance of the altar for ritual and worship and the temple's role as a stage. The statue and column signify the goddess's awareness and acceptance of the sacrifice. The differing roles of the ritual's participants on the dish remind us that these were organized and defined proceedings that involved offerings (the bull), invocations, libations, music, and solemn behavior, particularly when compared to the more boisterous figures on the other side of the dish. These figures may represent another aspect of the ritual, perhaps at a later and more celebratory moment, or a different occasion altogether. In either case, it is a reminder that rituals included festivities and celebration as well as solemnity. The feasting, athletic games, plays, and other performances were both engaging and formal and served as shared experiences to define religious, civic, and social identity.

Another procession from a red-figure krater a century later is more true-to-life in its representational style, but equally symbolic (**Figure 7.17**). From the left side, we see three men wearing robes and laurel crowns, paused with a bull in front of an incense burner. One of them holds a **phiale**, a shallow bowl used to pour libations of wine. A youth turns back to look at them while a *kanephoros* advances to the right, carrying a very elaborate *kanous* of implements on her head. She is wearing several layers of clothing, including an ornately decorated tunic on top. On the right side we can see two Doric columns supporting a lintel, a clearer sign of a temple structure. Before it stands a bearded priest who receives the procession, looking upward toward the top of the basket. Between the columns sits Apollo on a throne holding a laurel branch. Two tripods flank him, one of which stands on a round stone, the *omphalos* of Delphi. The picture, then, signifies the tripod that stood on the *omphalos* inside the Temple of Apollo at Delphi, in which the priestess would sit waiting to receive the god's prophecy. Apollo sits on a platform, and it is ambiguous whether we are to understand his figure as a statue, like the seated figure of Zeus at Olympia, or the god himself, or both simultaneously. The more naturalistic style makes the ambiguity of statue or deity even stronger than in archaic art, and given the context of the importance of the oracle at Delphi, serves to remind the viewer of Apollo's role as source of the oracles.

phiale
a wide shallow bowl, usually with a knob in the center, used for pouring libations

The scene on the other side of the vase shows the return of Hephaistos to Mount Olympos, in which Dionysos used wine to help persuade the god to come back and free Hera from the chair he had made as a trap for her. Dionysos also had a festival at Delphi, and the performances in the theater there would be part of his cult. As a mixing bowl for wine and water, a scene with Dionysos would be quite suitable for the krater, and the lower frieze shows satyrs chasing maenads all the way around the vase. The maenads, female followers of Dionysos, carry either a torch or a large podded branch called a *thyrsos*. The central satyr has dropped his drinking horn to chase the maenads, making this a ritual that has now deteriorated into chaos. The scene is festive and amusing, but also a reminder for celebrators drinking wine from the krater of the line between revelry and disorder.

Sacrifices were not the only offerings that could be made to the gods. As we have seen, the treasuries were built by poleis as gifts, and we saw in Chapter 4 that sanctuaries like Olympia were filled with small bronzes, terracottas, and tripods even in the Geometric period. These offerings are usually called votives or votive offerings, a term that in a limited sense means something done in fulfillment of a vow, but more broadly represents an offering dedicated to the gods. These could be civic, group, or individual gifts, and consisted of statues in a wide range of materials and sizes according to the means of the giver, of vessels made from precious metals and large in size, and of textiles and other works of art. For example, a statue of a young woman was made about 490–480 and dedicated on the Acropolis in Athens (**Figure 7.18**). The statue was one of dozens of kore statues that had been damaged when Athens was sacked by the Persians in 480–479 and is now missing its center section. As gifts to Athena, the statues

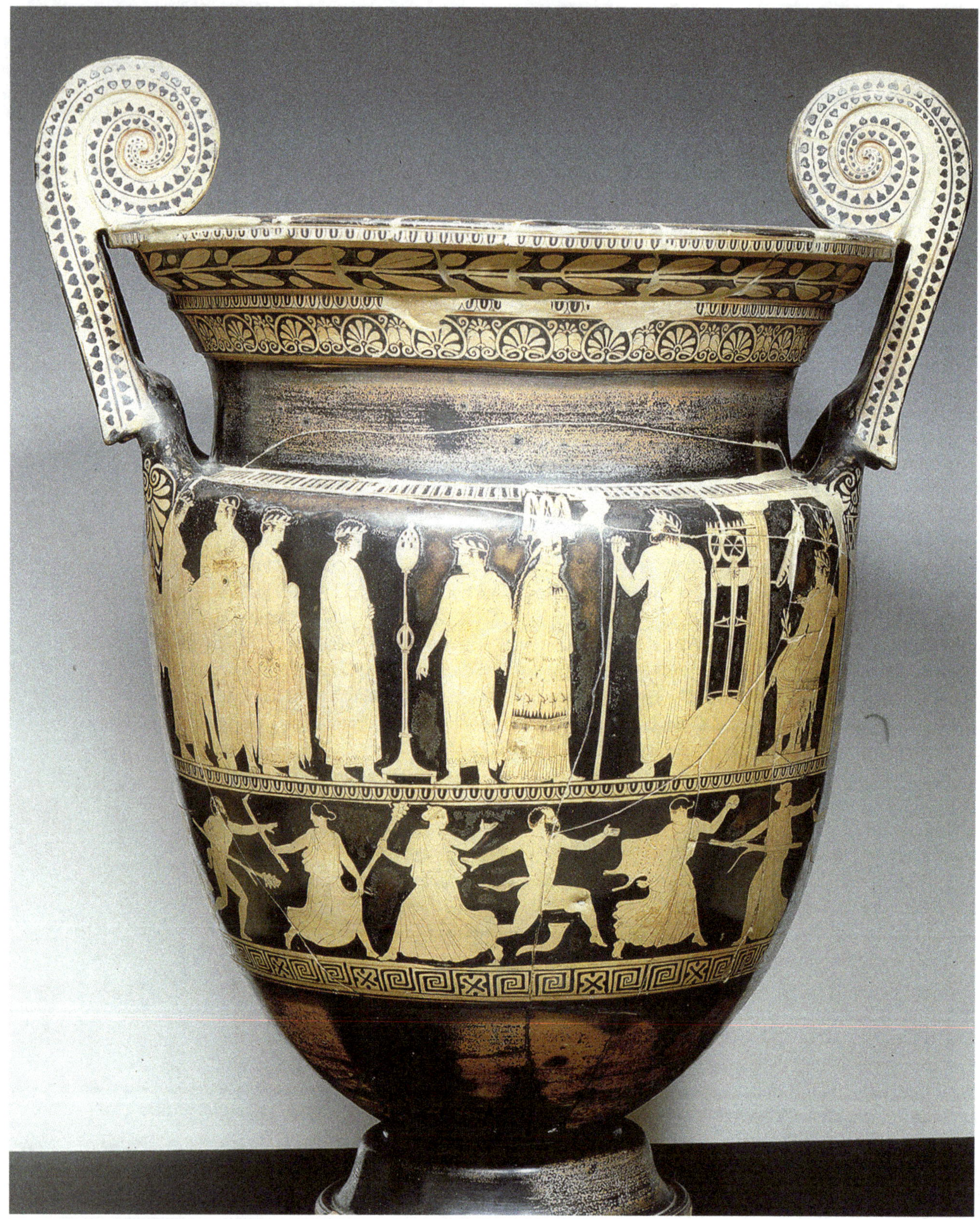

7.17 Attic red-figure volute krater attributed to the Kleophon Painter, *c.* 440–430 BCE. 30⁵⁄₁₆ in (77 cm). Procession to Apollo; satyrs pursuing maenads. Ferrara, Museo Nazionale di Spina 44894, T57CVP. Photo: Alfredo Dagli Orti/The Art Archive at Art Resource, NY.

belonged to the goddess and were buried in trenches on the Acropolis, some serving as fill in the eventual reconstruction of the sanctuary that included the building of the Parthenon. The inscription on the base states: *Euthydikos o Thaliarchou anetheken*, "Euthydikos, son of Thaliarchos, dedicated [me]." The verb recognizes not only that the statue is given, but also that it was formally set in place, a ritualistic action that gives significance to the work. A later viewer visiting the Acropolis would see this offering, or **anathema**, and learn of the action of Euthydikos from the inscription by reading it aloud, as was the custom at the time, see the expense of the work, and recognize by all of this the piety of Euthydikos.

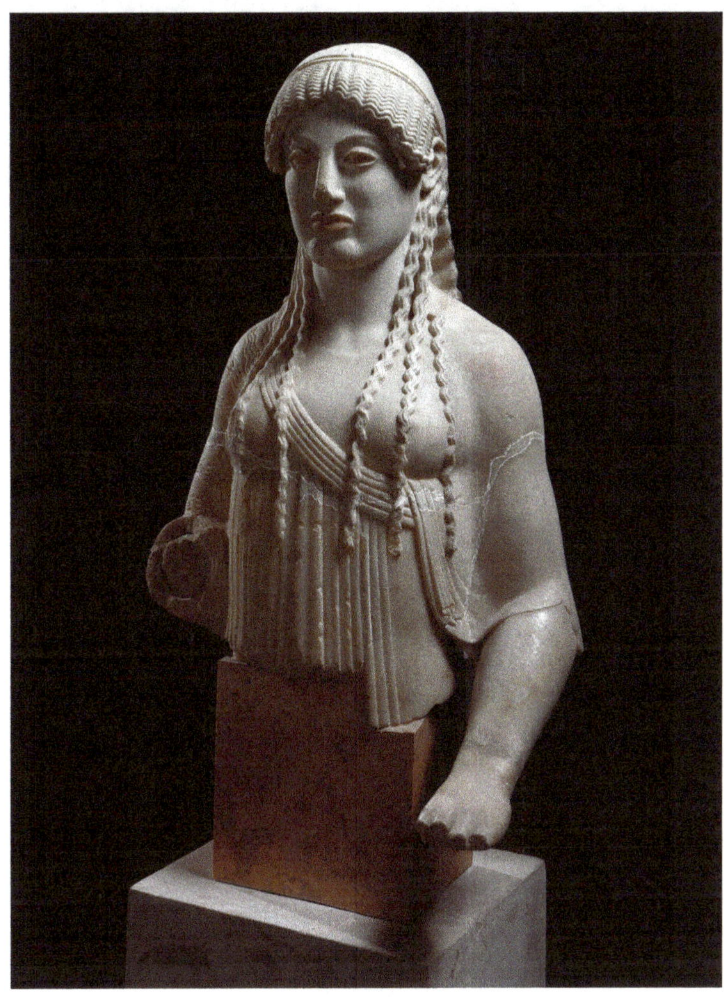

7.18 Kore dedicated by Euthydikos, from Acropolis, Athens, *c.* 490–480 BCE. 22 13/16 in (58 cm). Athens, Acropolis Museum 686 and 609. Photo: Universal Images Group/Art Resource, NY.

Most statues from sanctuaries cannot be connected with a specific inscription naming an individual, but some can. The kore of Nikandre **(see Figure 6.3, page 134)** tells us "Nikandre dedicated (*anetheken*) me to the far-shooter of arrows [Artemis], the excellent daughter of Deinodikes of Naxos, sister of Deinomenes, n[ow?] wife of Phraxos." A kore from Samos **(see Figure 8.12, page 193)** records: "Cheramyes dedicated (*anetheke*) me to Hera as an offering (*agalma*)." The word **agalma** in this inscription means not only an offering, but one that is pleasing to the gods. These inscriptions remind us that the statues are not portraits, since both Euthydikos and Cheramyes were men, but that these korai would be appropriate gifts for the goddess. Nikandre was a woman, and her work was dedicated to Artemis at her sanctuary on the island of Delos. Nikandre was likely a priestess or administrator at the sanctuary, and the statue commemorates her service to the goddess, whether or not the female figure is meant to be the goddess, a priestess, or an individual. This statue, too, has much to ponder in terms of both its style and gender identity, and we will consider it further in later chapters.

Other reasons for offerings were to recognize that wealth and success came from the gods. These could be either a "first-fruit" offering, or **aparche**, or a tithe, **dekate**, as surviving inscriptions inform us. For example, the small bronze statue from Thebes of a nude man is generally called the Mantiklos Apollo **(Figure 7.19)**, based on the inscription that runs up and down across its thighs: "Mantiklos dedicated (*anetheke*) me as a tithe (*dekatos*) to Apollo of the silver bow; do you, Phoibos, give some pleasing favor in return." The inscription sounds more demanding of the god than it is, but it reminds us that votives offered not only thanks for benefits received but also hopes for future benevolence. The figure, appropriately male for both the god and donor, continues the use of the ideal nude male seen in the Geometric period. As at Olympia, though small, the bronze figure would have been a significantly expensive dedication at the time. Even more expensive dedications like the tripods at Olympia can be found with dedications of armor, including helmets and shields, or objects made of gold and silver **(see Figure 11.7, page 275)**.

Terracotta figures and plaques fulfill the same function as their metallic counterparts, but were for those of more modest means and rarely have inscriptions. These are found in all periods

anathema
Greek word indicating the setting up or dedication of something for the gods

agalma
term meaning an object of delight such as a statue dedication

aparche
an offering of "first fruits," that is, from the initial success or harvest

dekate
a tithe offering

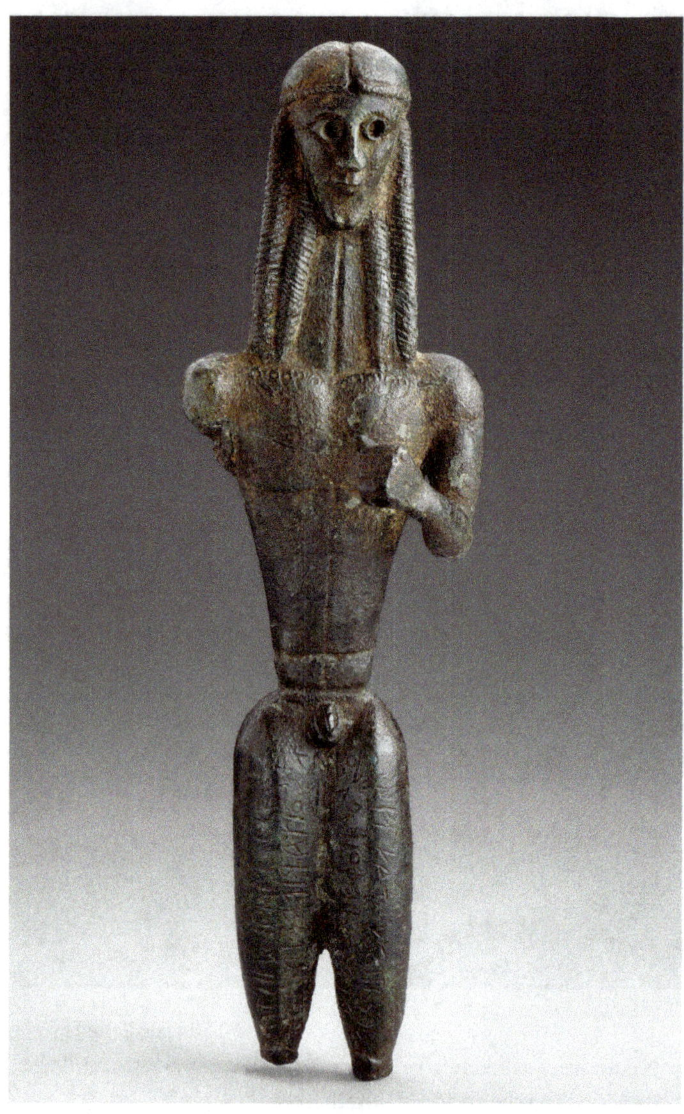

7.19 Nude male (Apollo?) dedicated by Mantiklos, early 7th cent. BCE. 8 in (20.3 cm). Boston, Museum of Fine Arts 03.997. Photograph © 2014 Museum of Fine Arts, Boston.

of Greek art, using simpler versions of the current styles. Those that do have inscriptions, such as the bowl from Naukratis in Egypt that we saw in the last chapter (**see Figure 6.14, page 143**), show that they serve a similar purpose. Scratched on the surface of the interior is the phrase *Sostratos me anetheken taphroditei*, or "Sostratos dedicated me to Aphrodite." The verb, *anetheken*, is the same used by Euthydikos, Nikandre, and Cheramyes for their statues and signifies that the actions are equivalent in terms of ritual, even if they differ dramatically in terms of cost and visibility.

A collection of votives from a shrine in the Agora in Athens shows the range of subjects, styles, and forms of objects, but gives us a sense too of the accumulative nature of votive offerings in sanctuaries (**Figure 7.20**). The objects belonged to a deposit on top of an abandoned Geometric house in the Agora, and range in date from 700 to 625 BCE. It has been suggested that they belong to a small sanctuary dedicated to cults of the dead or to deities like the Furies associated with the earth. The offerings included terracotta figures of horses and men, cups, oil containers, and miniature shields. Some of these, such as the small Protocorinthian aryballos on the bottom row, are imported, but most were made locally in Athens. The most remarkable work is the painted terracotta plaque that shows a frontal woman with raised arms and snakes to either side. Holes in the upper corners show it was meant to be hung, and the raised, modeled head is similar in style to Mantiklos's Apollo. This might be a representation of one of the chthonic or underworld deities, since snakes are associated with deities who go between this

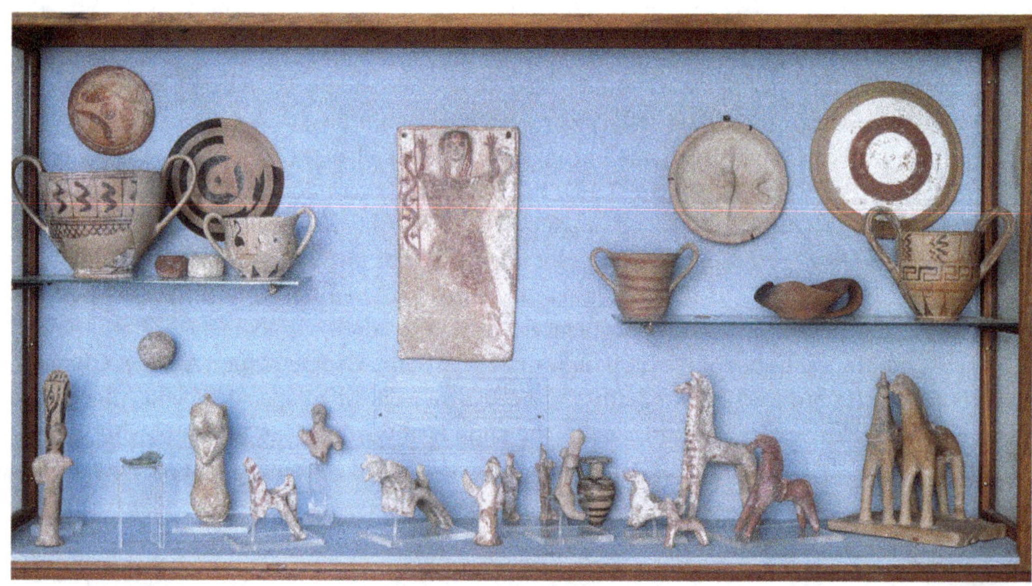

7.20 Objects from votive deposit in the Agora (H 17:4), *c.* 700–625 BCE. Height of central plaque: 9¾ in (24.8 cm). Athens, Agora Museum. Photo: American School of Classical Studies at Athens: Agora Excavations.

world and the underworld, but there is not enough specific information to be sure. While from a local and modest shrine, unlike the grander sanctuaries and works of the Acropolis, Delphi, and Olympia, these offerings were individually important and functioned ritualistically in the same manner.

Indeed, while many of the offerings at sanctuaries are modest, it is the setting and the action that give them a special meaning, as we saw in the discussion of agency theory in Chapter 5 (pp. 127–128). The accumulation of offerings over time only enhanced the authority of and reverence for a site, and the building of temples, smaller structures, and other monuments reflects both the status of the site and the donor, and stimulated competition among cities and individuals for the impressiveness of their offering and commemoration of their piety.

theoria
viewing or being a spectator at a ritual performance

TEXTBOX: RITUAL ANALYSIS AND *THEORIA*

When one thinks of ritual, one tends to consider a lengthy and solemn gathering, elaborate script directions, and very old and/or very long texts and songs. One might think of ritual as something that is controlling, but the history of ritual shows rather that it can be creative and adaptive, a way for members of a community to forge a pact or relationship with one another. By performing a ritual, it creates a contract or bond among its participants, whether that ritual is a religious sacrifice, a wedding, an inauguration, or an athletic contest. Some rituals are clearly more important or awe-inspiring than others, but it is the actions of the participants that lend significance to the places where they are performed, to the objects used and given, and to the attire that the participants wear.

In considering ritual, one has to consider it as a performance. One needs to identify the setting or stage for the event, the cast of participants and individual or group roles, the actions and words of each participant or group, how they move in order to carry out these actions, their dress and demeanor, and finally the equipment or type of objects needed to carry out the ritual. Much of ritual is ephemeral physically, leaving few traces in the archaeological record. Architecture clearly plays an important role in creating the setting for the event, but it also needs to facilitate the movement through space and the actions that are performed, such as sacrifices, the dedication of gifts, or the performance of plays and contests. Ritual equipment also leaves a physical record of the ritual, whether dedications such as votives or implements used in the ritual, such as a cult statue, a phiale used for a libation, or a cup placed in the grave for the deceased. For the Greeks, watching a ritual was not a passive action, but one that signaled participation and belonging. The term ***theoria***, from which we derive the word theory, meant being not just a witness, but also a member of the community able to make judgments on its action. As Athena Kavoulaki has summarized *theoria* for democratic Athens, "the term and practice of *theoria* aligns most closely the aspect of viewing with participation: watching the *heorte* (festival), seeing what was taking place, meant actually participating in the *heorte*" (1999, 311). Indeed, vision was considered as a species of touch, so that witnessing a ritual was akin to being physically involved in the ritual, even as a spectator.

The importance of rituals helps to explain the investment of resources made by a community in its civic planning, buildings, and memorials. The Tyrannicides are an effective symbol of democratic Athens, but they had added importance by being placed on the Panathenaic Way going through the Agora. When processing along with other Athenians, one participated in the same ritual as Harmodios and Aristogeiton, affirming a shared identity as a member of the polis.

See Stansbury-O'Donnell, 2006, 89–127; 2011, 154–163.

REFERENCES

Barletta, B. A. 2001. *The Origins of the Greek Architectural Orders*. Cambridge/New York: Cambridge University Press.

Kavoulaki, A. 1999. "Processional Performance and the Democratic Polis." In S. Goldhill and R. Osborne, eds. *Performance and Culture and Athenian Democracy*, 293–320. Cambridge: Cambridge University Press.

Stansbury-O'Donnell, M. D. 2006. *Vase Painting, Gender, and Social Identity in Archaic Athens*. Cambridge/New York: Cambridge University Press.

Stansbury-O'Donnell, M. D. 2011. *Looking at Greek Art*. Cambridge/New York: Cambridge University Press.

FURTHER READING

Barletta, B. A. 2001. *The Origins of the Greek Architectural Orders.* Cambridge/New York: Cambridge University Press.

Barringer, J. M. 2008. *Art, Myth, and Ritual in Classical Greece.* Cambridge/New York: Cambridge University Press.

Jensen, J. T., G. Hinge, P. Schultz, and B. Wickkiser, eds. 2009. *Aspects of Ancient Greek Cult: Context–Ritual–Iconography.* Aarhus: Aarhus University Press.

Keesling, C. M. 2003. *The Votive Statues of the Athenian Acropolis.* Cambridge/New York: Cambridge University Press.

Lawrence, A. W., with revisions by R. A. Tomlinson. 1996. *Greek Architecture,* 5th ed. New Haven: Yale University Press.

Pedley, J. 2005. *Sanctuaries and the Sacred in the Ancient Greek World.* Cambridge/New York: Cambridge University Press.

Scott, M. 2010. *Delphi and Olympia: The Spatial Politics of Panhellenism in the Archaic and Classical Periods.* Cambridge/New York: Cambridge University Press.

Simon, E. 1983. *Festivals of Attica: An Archaeological Commentary.* Madison: University of Wisconsin Press.

Stansbury-O'Donnell, M. D. 2006. *Vase Painting, Gender, and Social Identity in Archaic Athens.* Cambridge/New York: Cambridge University Press.

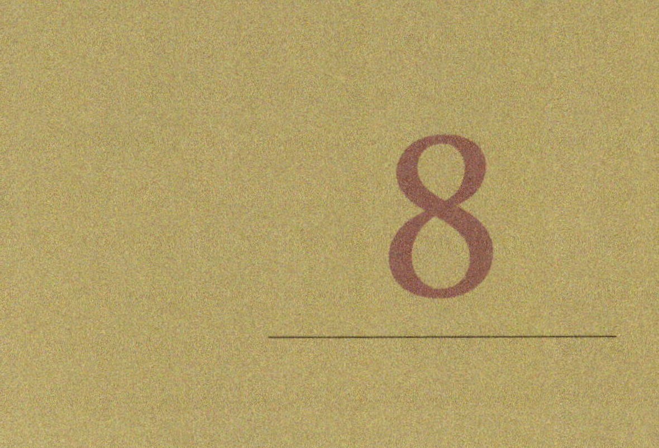

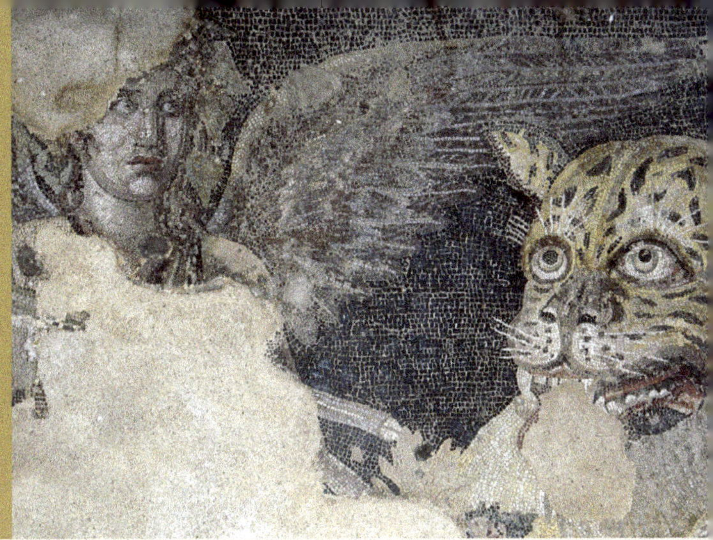

8

THE SIXTH CENTURY

(C. 625/600–480 BCE)

Timeline
Architecture and Architectural Sculpture
Free-Standing Sculpture
Other Media
Painted Pottery
Textbox: Color in Greek Sculpture
References
Further Reading

A History of Greek Art, First Edition. Mark D. Stansbury-O'Donnell.

TIMELINE

	Architecture and Relief	Statues	Pottery
600–570	Temple of Artemis at Korfu, *c.* 580	Kouros from Sounion, 590 [6.4]	Early Corinthian krater, 600–590 [5.21] Middle Corinthian skyphos, 585–570 [5.23]
570–550	Temple of Athena at Syracuse/Siracusa, 575–550	Kore of Cheramyes, 570–560 Kouros of Sombrotidas, 560–550	François Vase, 570 Lakonian BF kylix, 555 Attic BF kylix with Kirke, 550
550–530	Temple C at Selinus/Selinunte, 550–530	Kore of Phrasikleia, 550–540	Attic BF amphora by Exekias, 540
530–520	Siphnian Treasury at Delphi, 530–525 [7.15]	Kouros from Anavyssos, *c.* 530	Attic bilingual amphora, 525 Attic BF Nikosthenic amphora, 540–510 [11.8] Caeretan BF hydria, *c.* 530 [11.13]
520–500	Ball player base, 510–500	Kore from Akropolis, 520–510	Attic RF krater by Euphronios, 520–510 Attic BF amphora, 510 [9.15]
500–480	Athenian Treasury at Delphi, *c.* 490–485	Kore of Euthydikos, *c.* 490 [7.18]	Berlin Painter amphora Attic RF kylix by Foundry Painter, 490–480 [13.11]

The word archaic derives from the Greek *archaios*, meaning "ancient" or "old," as well as "beginning." The second-century CE traveler Pausanias used the term to refer to art produced before the early fifth century BCE, but as an art historical term it has since come to designate more narrowly the period between the late seventh century, 625–600 BCE, and 480, the year that the Persians invaded Greece and after which we see the advent of the classical style. Very broadly, one could look at the archaic period as one of standardization, refinement, and elaboration, following the expansion of the Greek world in the late eighth and seventh centuries and the concurrent experimentation in the forms of art, its media and subject matter. The architectural orders, discussed in the last two chapters, continue to be refined in their appearance and proportions, while the kouros and kore constitute the main form of monumental statues.

It is not, however, a static period, and we can see in the art of this time a development of more lifelike figures in all media. In pottery, the black-figure technique dominates, but we see the development of the reverse red-figure technique, which will flourish in the fifth century. Athens, a less important artistic center in the seventh century, becomes a major producer of sculpture and painted pottery in the sixth century, exporting pottery throughout the Mediterranean to both Greek and non-Greek sites, especially to Etruria. Architectural sculpture and painted pottery become major platforms for visual narratives, creating, in a sense, the mass visual media for the time. One might liken the art of the period to the idea of a theme and variations in music. There is a modest range of types of art forms and techniques, but a quite wide range of expression through the appearance and movement of the human form and the choice of narrative action.

One difficulty in discussing the history of this period, particularly in terms of its stylistic changes, is that its chronology has very few fixed points. Most works are dated through relative chronology and stylistic comparison, but without a number of works with fixed dates, it is difficult to know how much a difference in style between two objects is due to a difference in date, or region, or perhaps the age of the artist. While art historians agree that the representation of the human figure at the end of the period is far more lifelike than at the beginning, this development was unlikely to have followed a linear and progressive evolution. Given the problem of dating, we shall begin by looking at one major chronological terminus for the period, the Siphnian Treasury at Delphi. From this point we can then examine other architectural sculpture, both earlier and later. Afterward, we will survey other media and forms: stone figural statues, three-dimensional work in other media, and finally painted pottery.

ARCHITECTURE AND ARCHITECTURAL SCULPTURE

The development of the monumental Doric and Ionic orders and the adoption of stone as the primary building material for religious structures such as temples and treasuries, as discussed in the previous chapter, created specific areas for sculpted decoration, whether ornamental or figural. The triangular pedimented gables offered a prominent space for placing large reliefs or free-standing figures that could be set in front of the back wall of the pediment. Below it, the frieze presented panels for relief sculpture, whether square metopes in the Doric order or the continuous band found in the Ionic order. The ridge and corners of the roof also supported free-standing figures, called acroteria. Few buildings used all of the available areas for figural decoration, but the full potential for sculptural ornament can be seen in the small Siphnian Treasury at Delphi **(see Figure 7.15, page 171)**. As the reconstruction drawing of this Ionic building shows, it featured two pedimental ensembles, friezes on all four sides of the building, six acroteria, as well as two caryatids in the place of columns on the pronaos, the earliest surviving examples of this statue type. The building was constructed of marble imported from the islands of Siphnos and Paros, making this building a very lavish and expensive undertaking.

Both Pausanias, the second-century CE traveler, and Herodotos, the fifth-century BCE historian, mention the Siphnian Treasury. According to Herodotos (3.57–58), the building was a tithe offering of the Siphnians from their gold and silver mines. These were flooded around 525 BCE, when the island was attacked by Samians who had unsuccessfully sought a loan from the wealthy Siphnians. Siphnos was not able to recover from this loss for decades. This suggests that the attack on the island is a *terminus ante quem* for the building's start, since the funds for construction had to have been at Delphi by 525. Therefore a date of 530–525 is usually assigned to the building and its sculpture, and this becomes the anchor for sixth-century chronology through stylistic comparison.

The east pediment, on the back side of the building but seen first in approaching on the Sacred Way, **(Figure 8.1)** shows the struggle between Apollo and Herakles over the Delphic tripod, the seat of the god's prophecy, as we saw in the previous chapter. Herakles had gone to Delphi, seeking purification or healing over his murder of Iphitos. According to some accounts, he seized the tripod when his request was refused. The scene of Apollo wrestling with Herakles over the tripod becomes popular in archaic art, often with Artemis and Athena supporting the two and Zeus in the center intervening. The figures are in high relief and fully in the round in their upper sections. The corners of the pediment have unidentified combat scenes, with the figures set in smaller scale to fit in the narrower corners.

The east frieze below shows a council of the gods on the left and a battle from the Trojan War between Memnon (left) and Achilles (right) over the corpse of Antilochos. These figures are strongly muscular and project from the background as if they were on a stage, an effect that would have been even stronger when they were originally painted, with dark blue for the background and reds on the insides of the shields and the groundline (for a restoration of color in sculpture **see Figure 8.15, page 197 and Figure 10.3, page 239**). The gods lean forward and gesture as they vigorously debate which warrior will win. Zeus, enthroned in the center, once held a bronze scale in which the souls of both warriors would have been set to determine who would live (Achilles) and who would die (Memnon). Each warrior has an ally fighting with him, and chariot teams flank both sides. The sculptor has arranged the horses' heads in a combination of profile and three-quarter views that conveys an agitated, twisted movement in space. When compared with seventh-century sculpture, one can see more detailed rendering of anatomy and drapery and more varied movement **(see Figure 6.24, page 149)**.

Looking at a section of the west frieze, from the front of the building, one can see some differences in both horses and human figures **(Figure 8.2)**. The subject is uncertain; a scene like the abduction of the daughters of Leukippos by the Dioskouroi has been suggested. The composition is not as dense, with less overlapping than in the east frieze. The horses are completely in profile and, rather than rounded contours where the figure projects from the background, these figures have sharper edges that look more like cut-outs. The riders are slenderer than the warriors on the east side, and one might describe the detail of muscles, hair, and reins as linear across the top surface. Overall, there is less suggestion of a three-dimensional compositional space.

Gigantomachy the battle between the giants, sons of Gaia and Uranus, and the Olympian Gods

These stylistic differences are explained by an inscription on the shield of a giant on the north frieze, which states that "[missing name] made these subjects and those at the back [east]." Indeed, the style of the Gigantomachy on the north frieze is very similar to the combat on the east frieze, except that there is even more overlapping, stronger movement and further experiments with three-quarter views **(see Figure 9.1, page 212)**. Of particular note is the lion wrapping his limbs around a giant dressed as a hoplite warrior, who looks backward and down toward the viewer standing below on the Sacred Way. Since all four friezes were carved at the same time, both sculptors were contemporaries, but elements of the south and west friezes appear to be older in approach, while the east and north friezes look ahead to later developments in the representation of movement and space in both sculpture and vase painting. By comparing the style of the Siphnian reliefs to sculpture and painting in the sixth century, the degree of difference in either direction becomes the basis for assigning dates throughout the archaic period. However, the differences between these two sculptors working at the same time on the same monument caution us against seeing developments in naturalistic representation, i.e., showing a lifelike human figure, as a smooth, progressive evolution.

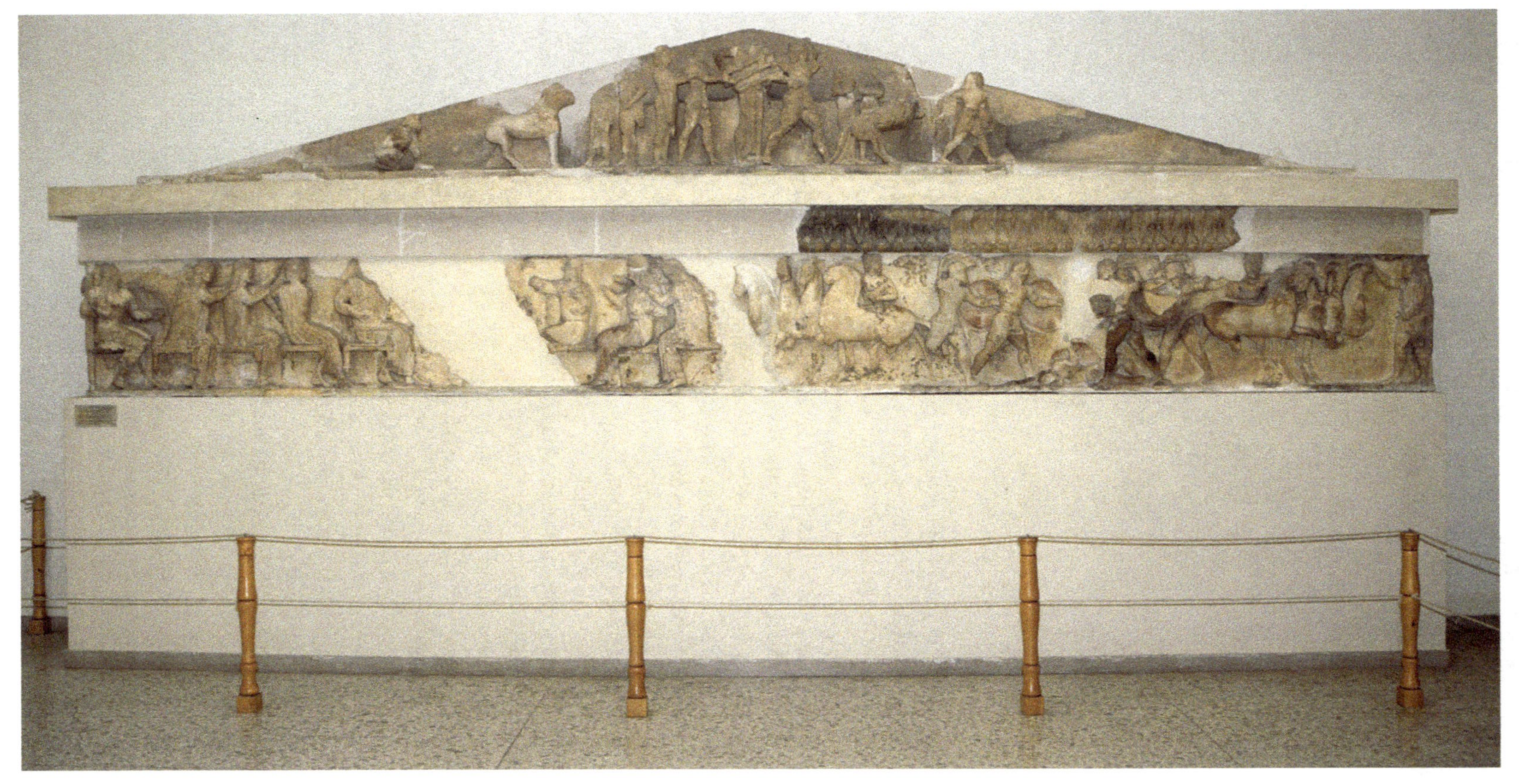

8.1 East pediment and frieze from the Siphnian Treasury at Delphi, *c.* 530–525 BCE. Delphi Museum. Height of frieze: 25 3/16 in (64 cm). Herakles and Apollo struggling over the tripod; council of the gods and battle of Memnon and Achilles. Photo: © Vanni Archive/Art Resource, NY.

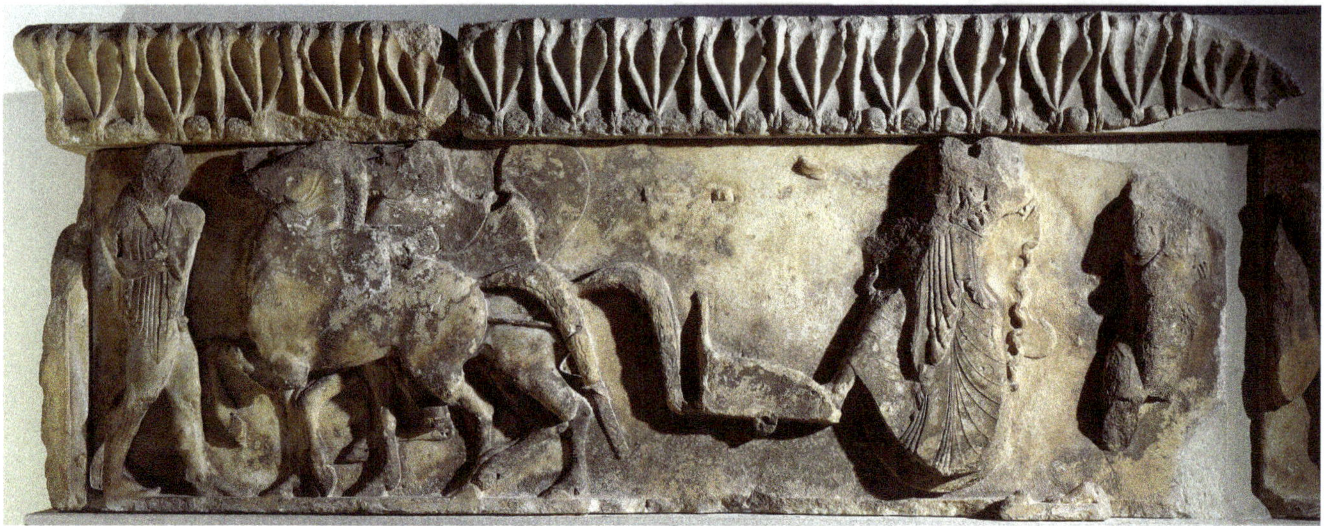

8.2 West frieze from the Siphnian Treasury at Delphi, *c.* 530–525 BCE. 25³⁄₁₆ in (64 cm). Delphi Museum. Abduction scene? Photo: Gianni Dagli Orti/The Art Archive at Art Resource, NY.

In considering architectural sculpture, we also have to give some thought to the relationship of the viewer to the work. The sculptor of the east and north frieze has composed the figures to address the viewer walking up the Sacred Way at Delphi **(see Figure 7.15, page 171)**. On the east frieze, Achilles is the foremost warrior on the right side. Usually a victorious warrior is shown on the left, moving rightward **(see Figure 6.15, page 144; Figure 6.18, page 146; Figure 9.17, page 231)**. By placing Achilles on the right, however, the sculptor puts the viewer down below on the side of the victor, standing behind him figuratively as his ally. Continuing along the north frieze, the visitor moves in the same direction as the victorious gods, who are shown in the more typical left-to-right direction. Thus the giants flee away from the viewer, and the giant being mauled by the lion looks down, back, and outward toward the viewer. The narrative unfolds as the viewer walks alongside the building, with wave after wave of giants fighting and being defeated by the gods. Reverence toward the gods, implicit in a pilgrimage to Delphi, puts the viewer on the compositional side of both heroes and the gods, from whom the visitor is seeking divine counsel through the oracle. In developing visual narrative in the sixth century, we will see in this chapter and the next that artists often took account of the viewer in structuring their compositions.

Turning now to earlier architectural sculpture, the Temple of Artemis at Korfu, an important early colony of Corinth, is considered to be the earliest temple made entirely with stone **(Figure 8.3)**. It has two identical pediments carved in high relief. In the center is a running Medusa flanked by two lions; under her arms is her son Chrysaor on the right and the remains of Pegasos on the left. At the corners are large fallen figures, and toward the center are fighting scenes, carved at a smaller scale, showing the Olympian gods battling the Titans (Titanomachy), the older generation of gods whom the Olympians overthrew. Medusa runs in the conventional whirligig or running/kneeling pose that we saw in the painted metope of Perseus at Thermon **(see Figure 6.23, page 149)**. While done in deep relief, the edges of the figures recede sharply into the pedimental wall, giving them a strong and projecting silhouette whose effect is heightened by Medusa's monumental scale at over 3 meters high. The faces and bodies are flat planes with a variety of incised patterns on the surface for the details of the hair and garment borders. The figure of Chrysaor, who is roughly life-size, is similar in the detailing of his anatomy to the Sounion kouros **(see Figure 6.4, page 135)**, with some indication of the chest and hips but little articulation of muscles on the surface of the stone. The Korfu pediment and Sounion kouros are both considered to be a couple of generations earlier than the Siphnian Treasury, with the kouros about 590 BCE and the Korfu pediment about 580 BCE.

Titanomachy
the battle of the gods and the Titans, the generation of gods before the Olympians. They included Kronos, Oceanus, Rhea, Themis, and Mnemosyne

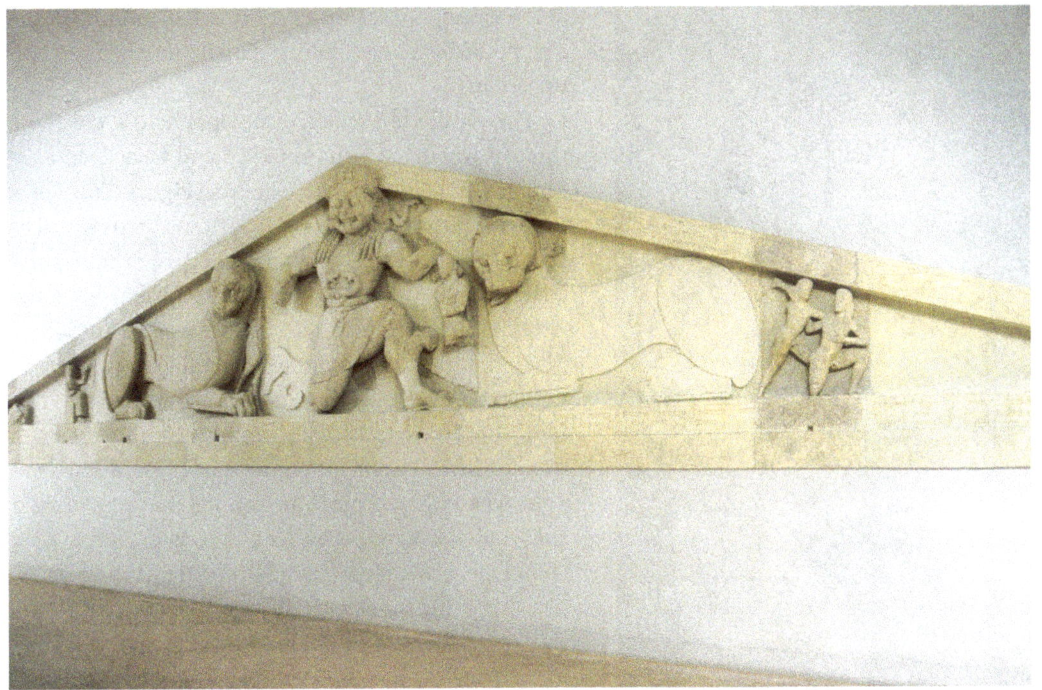

8.3 Pediment from Temple of Artemis at Korfu, c. 580 BCE. Height in center: 10 ft 4 in (3.15 m). Korfu Museum. Medusa with Pegasos and Chrysaor; Titanomachy. Photo: © Vanni Archive/Art Resource, NY.

The bodies of Medusa, Chrysaor, and the lions are in profile, but their heads are turned frontally to look out toward the viewer. While this looks awkward, the function of the sculpture on the temple overrides its narrative purpose. The representation of deities is meant to be an epiphany, a visualization of the divine that engages the viewer. Like a cult statue, this means that the figure should look toward the viewer. A second function of the decoration is also to serve as an apotropaic device, that is, a sign that protects and guards a place or person from harm. The heraldic mistress of animals composition can serve this function **(see Figure 6.17, page 145)**, as can the lions flanking a column on the Lion Gate at Mycenae **(see Figure 3.6, page 56)**. We can look at the combination of lions and Gorgon here as similarly guarding the temple's entrance. The decapitated head of Medusa, called a **gorgoneion**, becomes a highly favored apotropaic device, since it turned those who looked at it to stone. The placement of Medusa's frontal head, still attached to her body, at the central peak of the pediment, even breaking beyond its upper frame, points to the apotropaic function of the gorgoneion, even though it creates a narrative problem. Chrysaor and Pegasos are both offspring of Medusa, born from her spilled blood after her head was severed by Perseus, who is nowhere present on the pediment. Nevertheless, Medusa's heroic offspring bring order to the world by defeating fearsome beasts and malevolent deities, as do the Olympian gods. These symbolic roles of the sculpture are more important than narrative consistency.

gorgoneion the decapitated head of the Gorgon Medusa, shown frontally and used as a shield device or apotropaic figure

Medusa and the gorgoneion are also favored subjects for Greek temples in Sicily. A terracotta plaque with a running Medusa and Pegasos was found at an archaic temple of Athena in Syracuse (modern Siracusa) **(Figure 8.4)**. The black, red, and cream colors create a rich display of details, patterns, and movement that reminds us of the effect of color in sculpture. The plaque is 56 cm high and has four holes where it was attached to the building. Whether it was mounted on the pediment or attached to a beam projecting above the gable of the temple like an acroterion is uncertain. The work is also an example of the importance of terracotta as a large-scale sculptural medium, especially at the Greek sites in southern Italy and Sicily.

A larger gorgoneion was placed on a temple at Selinus (modern Selinunte), a colony in western Sicily founded by settlers from the older, eastern Sicilian colony at Megara Hyblaea. The Doric building, as seen in the reconstruction by Marconi and the University of Lecce, is designated as Temple C, one of several temples found at Selinus/Selinunte **(Figure 8.5)**. Based on Corinthian pottery found

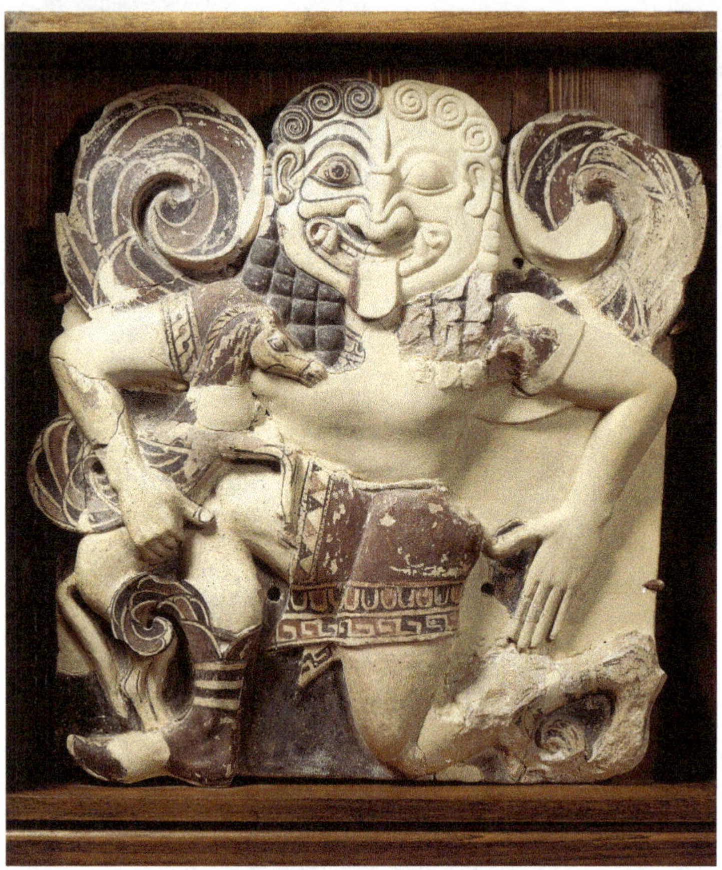

8.4 Running Medusa and Pegasos from Temple of Athena, Syracuse/Siracusa, *c.* 575–550 BCE. Terracotta, 22 in (56 cm). Syracuse, Paolo Orsi Museum. Photo: Scala/Art Resource, NY.

at the foundations, construction of the building began around 560–550 BCE, but its completion date remains uncertain.

There were ten sculpted metopes across the front, three of which are well preserved and have been reassembled at the museum in Palermo (**Figure 8.6**). These occupied positions 6–8, counting from left to right. The left metope shows Apollo in a **quadriga**, or four-horse chariot, with two female figures, probably his sister Artemis and mother Leto. Next is Perseus killing Medusa, with Athena standing behind him and Pegasos in Medusa's arms. The last metope shows Herakles carrying the Kerkopes, trickster brothers who attempted to steal the hero's armor. He bound them upside down to a pole, where they commented on his tanned or blackened buttocks; according to a very late source, their comments made Herakles laugh and he let them go.

Comparing the style of the figures to those at Korfu, we can see that the poses are somewhat more convincing, the anatomical details more numerous and lifelike, and the edges more rounded against the stone background. The compositions also adapt to their position on the temple facade, with the quadriga metope at the center being fully frontal, and the narrative metopes moving more strongly rightward as the viewer glances toward the corner of the temple. The dating of the metopes has also been debated, since some of the fragmentary metopes at the corners appear later in style, which might have been a result of a slow building campaign. Many have dated the metopes to the middle of the sixth century, but Clemente Marconi has more recently suggested a date of 540–530 BCE, just before the Siphnian Treasury (Marconi 2007, 175–176). While none of the Siphnian Treasury figures uses a frontal head, this may be due to both a greater importance for narrative in later archaic architectural sculpture and the different function of a treasury compared to a temple. A temple like Selinus/Selinunte houses a cult statue and is a focal point for ritual and votive offerings that communicate with the gods. Like the Korfu pediment, all of these figures at Selinus/Selinunte are turned frontally, serving both epiphanic and apotropaic functions. A treasury, on the other hand, does not have a cult statue and is only a repository, so the cultic significance as well as the need to present a divine epiphany for its sculpture is less prominent.

quadriga
term for a chariot drawn by four horses

The choice of subject matter for Temple C appears very eclectic, particularly the Kerkopes metope. It has been suggested that the metopes as an ensemble represented all of the gods and heroes worshipped in the city, but this still leaves unresolved the choice of individual scenes, such as Kerkopes, which is not one of the most heroic stories. Most interpretations treat it as a comic episode, but Marconi has suggested that we should regard it more seriously, with the brothers being viewed as liars and thieves rather than tricksters, hence as menaces like others that Herakles subdued in many of his labors (Marconi 2007, 150–159). The story took place at Thermopylai in northern Greece; like the other episodes in the metopes, it occurred in the "Old World" of the Greek colony, reasserting its connection to the motherland (Marconi 2007, 204). Whereas the story may seem secondary to us today, it was widely known in sixth-century art and used for a metope on the Temple of Hera at Foce del Sele near Poseidonia/Paestum. Certainly the unusual subject and composition would have had its own appeal and perhaps have reflected some of the concerns of the colonists in their new land.

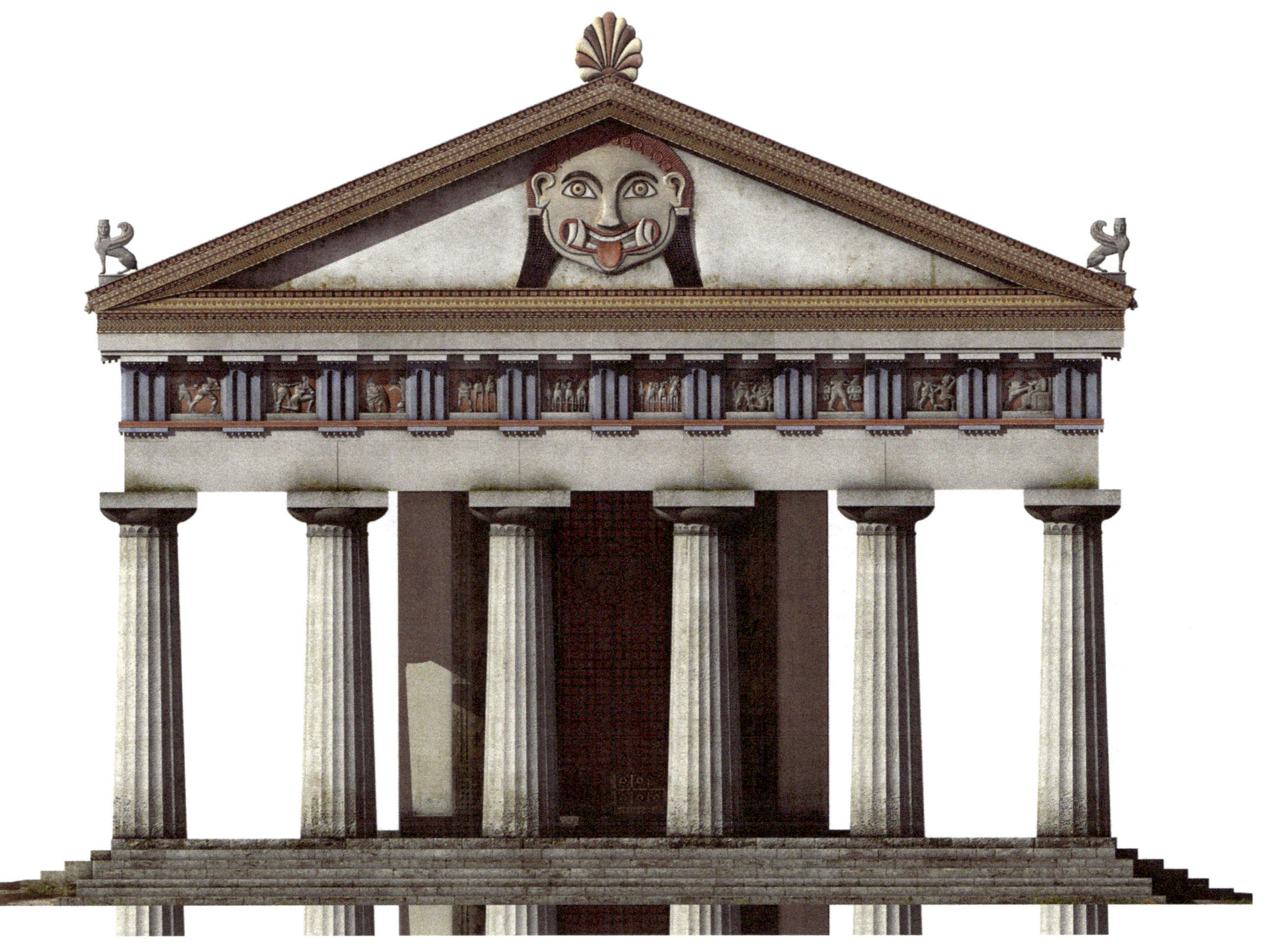

8.5 Facade of Selinus/Selinunte, Temple C, *c.* 550–530 BCE. New restoration by University of Lecce (Progetto LAND-LAB, http://landlab.unisalento.it) and Clemente Marconi. Image courtesy of Grazia Semeraro, Francesco D'Andria, and Clemente Marconi.

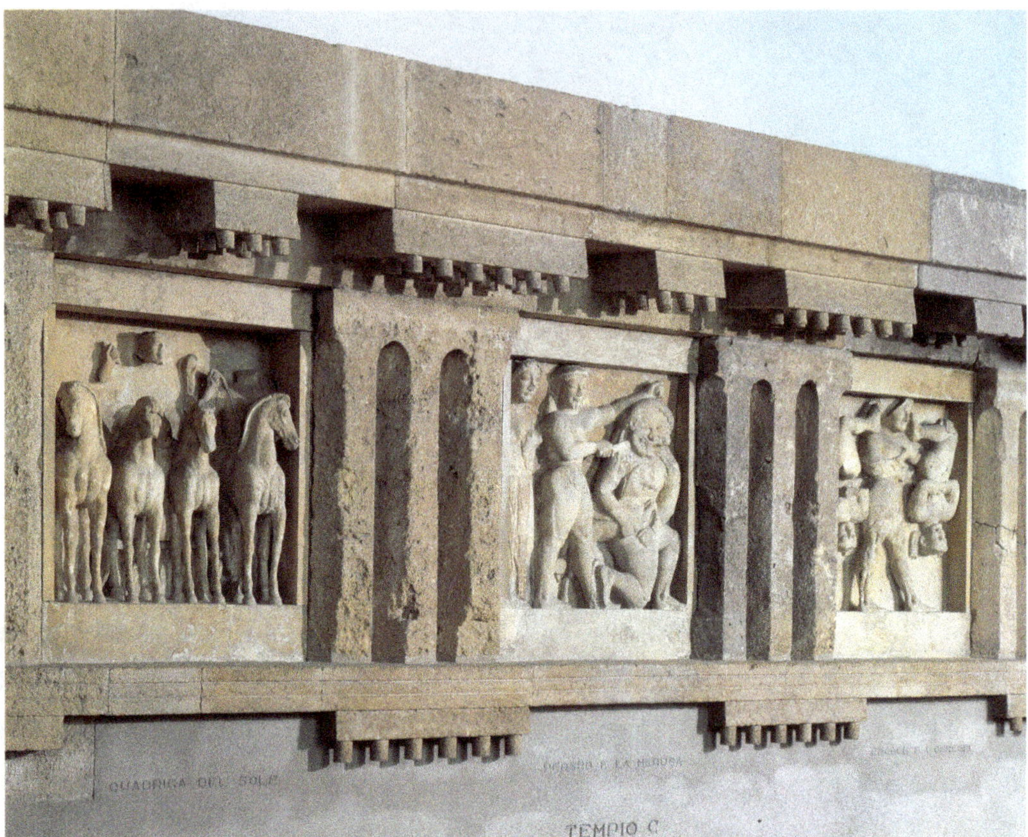

8.6 Metopes of Temple C at Selinus/Selinunte, *c.* 550–530 BCE. Metope height: 4 ft 9⅞ in (1.47 m). Palermo. Quadriga with Apollo and two goddesses; Perseus slaying Medusa; Herakles and the Kerkopes. Photo: Nimatallah/Art Resource, NY.

The narrative potential of architectural sculpture becomes more developed with the increasing ability and effort of sculptors to show complex poses and movement in the later sixth and early fifth centuries, as we can see in the metopes of the Athenian Treasury at Delphi. Pausanias (10.11.5–6) states that the treasury was built with the spoils of the victory over the Persians in the Battle of Marathon in 490 BCE **(see Figure 7.14, page 170)**, giving us a *terminus post quem* for the beginning of the construction. There is indeed a base on the south side of the treasury for the display of battle trophies, but there has been debate over the years as to whether the base was added to a preexisting treasury or not. Recent archaeological analysis of the foundations favors the idea that base and treasury were built at the same time, and so the sculpture would date shortly after 490.

The sculptural program was dedicated to Herakles, the paramount Panhellenic hero, and Theseus, the hero of Athens. The deeds of Herakles were placed on the west and north sides, away from the main lines of sight on the Sacred Way, while the deeds of Theseus were placed in the nine south metopes facing the switchback of the Sacred Way, and his fight against the Amazons filled the six eastern metopes over the building's entrance. The deeds of Theseus are in two groups: the first four show him fighting with brigands who plagued the road from Troizen, his home town, to Athens, where he came to claim his inheritance as the son of king Aigeus. The middle metope shows him being greeted by Athena on his arrival in Athens. The last four show later scenes, including the fight with the Minotaur and with an Amazon on the last metope **(Figure 8.7)**. Thus, as the viewer walks along the Sacred Way, the metopes show an unfolding heroic biography.

Although fragmentary, one can readily see that the figures are in far more complicated poses than on the nearby, earlier Siphnian Treasury. As can be seen in the metope with Theseus and the Amazon, both figures twist and move in space, and rather than a combination of profile and frontal views, there is use of a three-quarter view. This is more of an artistic challenge, in that a body at an oblique angle is not symmetrical like the frontal Athena at Selinus/Selinunte. It diminishes in scale as it recedes from the viewer, making a more lifelike pose. The more active figures show the asymmetry and bulging of muscles that vigorous poses create. The term *rhythmos*, which means pattern of movement or the combination and sequence of small actions required to carry out an action, describes this interest in how bodies move and work. The wrestling figures of the first metope are a good example, as Theseus wraps his arm around the waist of Kerkyon, who is in an unstable pose and will be thrown down by Theseus. Rather than the impassive faces of many archaic figures, the face of Skiron in the second metope is distorted by the pain caused by Theseus, who jerks his head in the opposite direction in which his body is twisting.

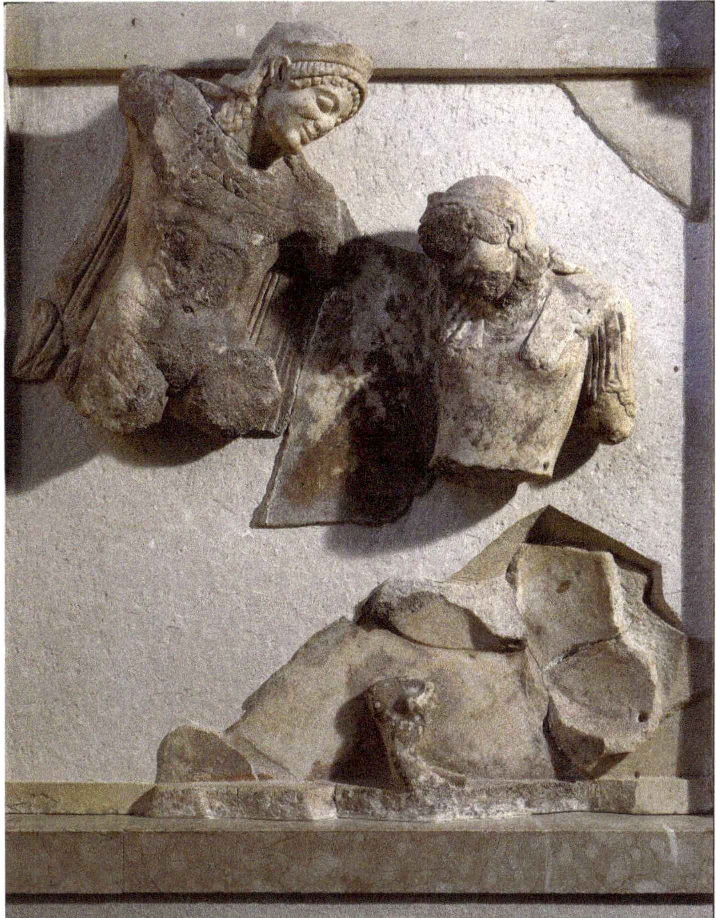

8.7 Metope from Athenian Treasury at Delphi, *c.* 490–485 BCE. 26³⁄₈ in (67 cm). Delphi Museum. Theseus fighting an Amazon. Photo: Marie Mauzy/Art Resource, NY.

This interest in *rhythmos* can also be seen in other late archaic reliefs, such as the so-called ball player base **(Figure 8.8)**. This work, found in a defensive wall built by Themistokles in 478 after the Persian destruction of Athens, was originally a base for a statue in the Kerameikos cemetery (this reuse gives us a *terminus ante quem* for the work, which is usually dated to 510–500 BCE). The range of poses and movements shows strong interest in how the body works in various actions, even though the ability to show three-quarter views and foreshortening is less convincing than on the treasury. As we will see later in this chapter, this interest in *rhythmos* is also found in contemporary Athenian painted pottery, especially in the new red-figure technique. Indeed, the similarities of the ball player base to the Euphronios krater **(see Figure 8.26, page 206)** and to the metopes provide one reason that a date around 510–500 BCE was initially proposed for the metopes of the Athenian Treasury, in spite of the testimony about the Marathon dedication. Perhaps the Theseus metopes appear stiff when compared with some other works after 490, but the Athenian Treasury metopes are good examples of the developments in rendering the human figure at the end of the archaic period.

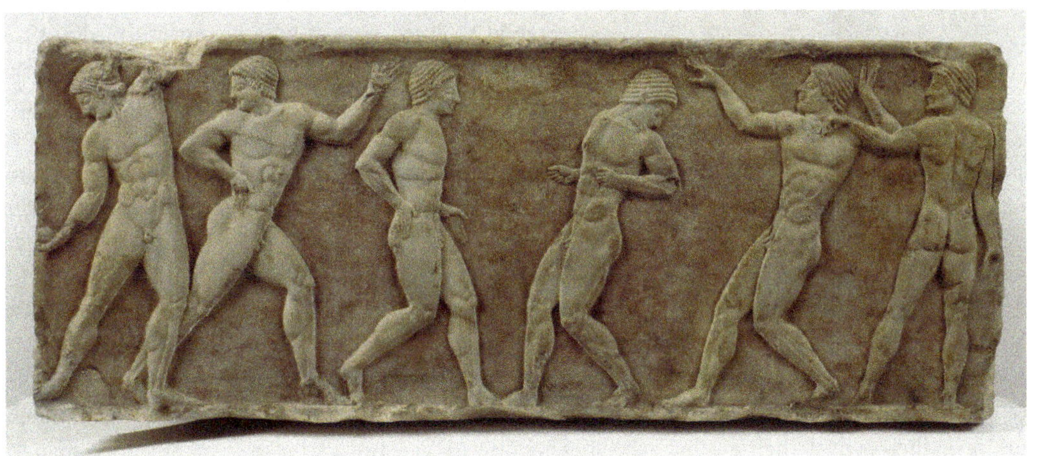

8.8 Ball player base from Themistoklean Wall, *c.* 510–500 BCE. 12⁵⁄₈ in (32 cm). Athens, National Archaeological Museum 3476. Photo: National Archaeological Museum, Athens (Giannis Patrikianos) © Hellenic Ministry of Education and Religious Affairs, Culture and Sports/Archaeological Receipts Fund.

FREE-STANDING SCULPTURE

There are two dominant types of free-standing sculpture in the sixth century, which have been given the general terms of kouros and kore, both of which have their origins in the seventh century. The kouros follows a formula of a standing, nude, beardless male, generally youthful in age, with long braided hair. Like one of the earliest surviving versions in marble, the monumental kouros from Cape Sounion **(see Figure 6.4, page 135)**, the pose has the left leg forward and the arms held at the sides, with the stone between the middle of the arm and body removed. The major divisions of the body, such as the pelvis, knees, pectoral region, and collar bone, are articulated by strong ridges, while other details such as the abdominal muscles are shallow surface grooves. The hair, ears, and even the eyes are abstracted, geometric designs. The figure is conceived more as an assemblage of parts and combination of front, back, and side views, rather than as an organic body.

The earliest kouroi, as well as korai, are associated with sanctuaries, and early interpretations of the kouroi were that they represented Apollo. There are, however, no attributes identifying them as Apollo and they are found in sanctuaries of other gods and goddesses. By the early sixth century they also serve as grave markers. There are also examples that are clothed or carry an animal like a ram or calf over the shoulders as an offering, but that otherwise share many of the stylistic features and formulas of nude statue. The use of the term kouros may imply a stronger precision and identity of subject matter than is actually the case. As we have seen, the standing male nude has a long tradition in Greek art going back to the Geometric period, and perhaps we should think of the appeal and success of the formula of the standing male nude as the result of its universality, idealism, and variability. The type could represent a god, a hero, or a mortal who had achieved fame or virtue; it could be used as a commemorative funerary monument or a votive offering. Its context and/or inscription would provide the cues for its specific purpose and identity.

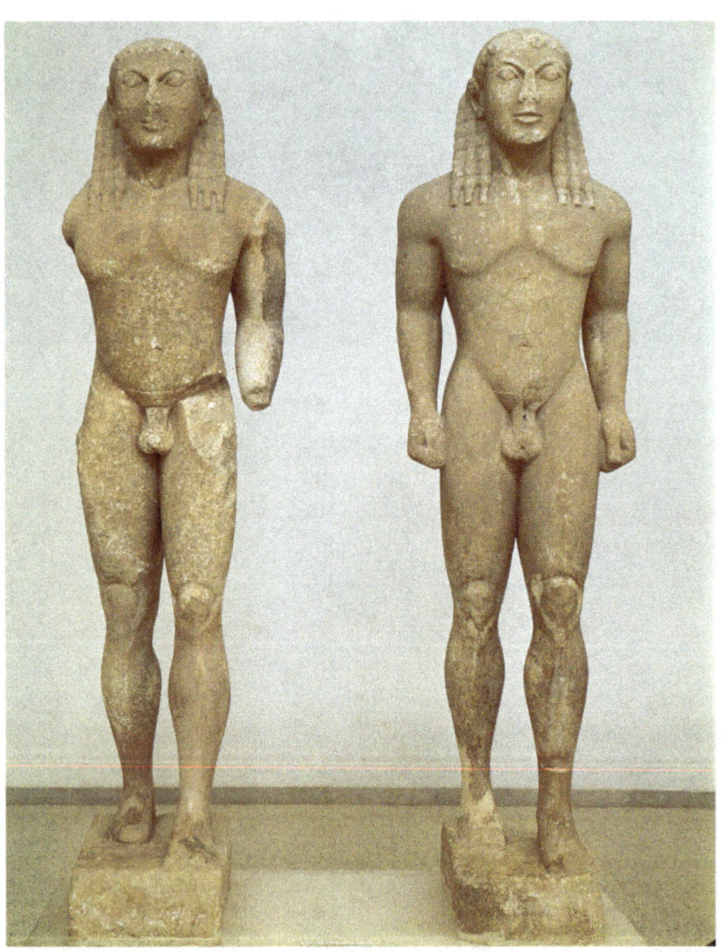

8.9 Kouroi dedicated to Kleobis and Biton at Delphi, *c.* 570 BCE. 6 ft 5⁹⁄₁₆ in (1.97 m). Delphi Museum. Photo: Scala/Art Resource, NY.

While following a formula, kouroi do vary widely in their appearance, both by time and by region. Two kouroi found at Delphi are dated around 570 BCE, not long after the Sounion kouros **(Figure 8.9)**. They are made of marble from Naxos, but are products of an Argolid sculptor, part of whose name, [-]medes, survives on the plinth (Palagia and Herz 2002, 243). These figures are more muscular in their proportions and their heads are less elongated than the Sounion kouros. While not completely "Daedalic," they look back to that earlier style of the seventh century. They also offer a variation on the typical kouros, in that they wear boots rather than being barefoot and there is a suggestion of an armor breastplate on their chests. What is interesting about these statues is that Herodotos mentions two statues at Delphi in a story told by Solon about blessings for men. The mother of Kleobis and Biton had to go to the feast at the Heraion in Argos; with the farm animals unavailable to pull her wagon, her sons pulled it themselves for 45 *stade* (about 8.3 km). After receiving much praise on their arrival, their mother asked the goddess to "give them whatsoever is best for a man to win." Accordingly, they died in their sleep while resting at the sanctuary, renowned as forever youthful and pious. According to Herodotos, "The Argives made statues of them and dedicated them at Delphi, as of two men who were the best of all" (1.31, tr. Grene, 46). By dedicating them at Delphi, the Argives promoted their own excellence in a Panhellenic context, much as victor statues did at Olympia. While not true portraits, they commemorate the two brothers as ideal men.

There has been some debate as to whether the kouroi are indeed Kleobis and Biton, and an alternative identification based on a new reading of the inscription suggests that they might instead be the mythological Dioskouroi, the twin brothers of Helen (Faure 1985). Whether or not this theory is eventually accepted, it points out that the formula of the nude male could serve a variety of purposes; without more evidence, either reading is plausible and the key to the specific meaning depends upon inscription and context.

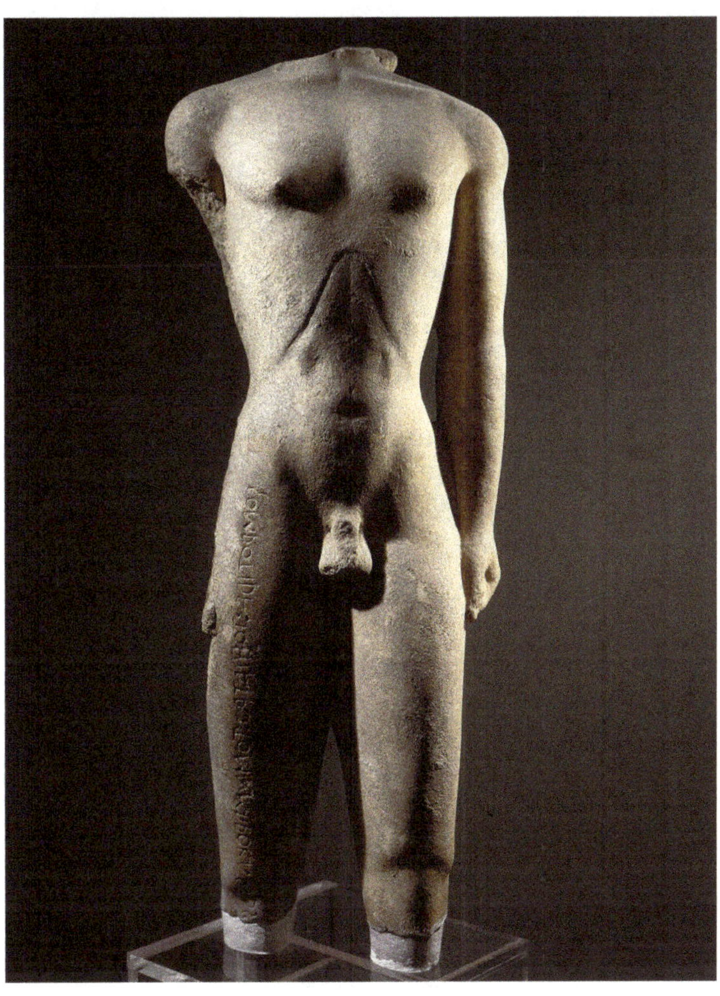

8.10 Kouros from grave of Sombrotidas, the physician, son of Mandrokles, Megara Hyblaea, Sicily, *c.* 560–550 BCE. 3 ft 10⅞ in (1.19 m). Syracuse, Paolo Orsi Museum 49401. Photo: Gianni Dagli Orti/The Art Archive at Art Resource, NY.

A slightly later kouros has much more slender proportions and demonstrates less interest in the articulation of the body parts and musculature **(Figure 8.10)**. This is more typical of Ionian kouroi, made in the eastern Greek islands. This particular statue was found in the cemetery at Megara Hyblaea, north of Syracuse/Siracusa, Sicily. Marble was rare in Sicily and limestone was the predominant material for architectural sculpture, so this is likely an import. When set up as a grave marker, an inscription was carved on its leg: "[tomb] of Sombrotidas, the physician, [son of] Mandrokles." Sombrotidas may have been an Ionian immigrant, as inscriptions on a statue leg are an Ionian tradition. As a practicing physician, however, Sombrotidas would not have been young when he died. His prominence derives from his profession, but the kouros gives him the appropriate visual symbol of male excellence. It is likely that the expense of the statue was covered by the family of Sombrotidas, and as we shall see in Chapter 11, a nearly life-size and imported statue would have been a significant financial undertaking for the family. The personal importance and social value of commemoration and offerings are clearly signaled by works like this.

This was also the case for the statue associated with the grave of Kroisos discussed in Chapter 5 **(see Figure 5.24, page 123)**. As the inscription found near that statue indicates, Kroisos was killed in battle: "Stay and mourn at the monument for dead Kroisos whom violent Ares destroyed, fighting in the front rank" (tr. Boardman 1991, 104). Although he might have been relatively young when he died, he is not remembered visually as a warrior, but as an ideal youth. Whether or not this statue belongs to the base, we see the same formula as in other kouroi. The surface of the figure has become more complex and subtle in the articulation of the muscles, bones, and body divisions, while the figure is becoming more rounded and three-dimensional in concept. The structure of the face is more complex, and the eyes bulge outward from the eye socket less than earlier kouroi.

There were many kouroi dedicated to Apollo in his sanctuary of Ptoön in Boeotia. One of the latest was dedicated by Pytheas and Aeschrion, around 500 BCE **(Figure 8.11)**. The figure still has the so-called archaic smile that we have seen on the other statues and the hair is highly stylized, but now is tied up above the neck. The eyes are set further back into the head and the articulation of the

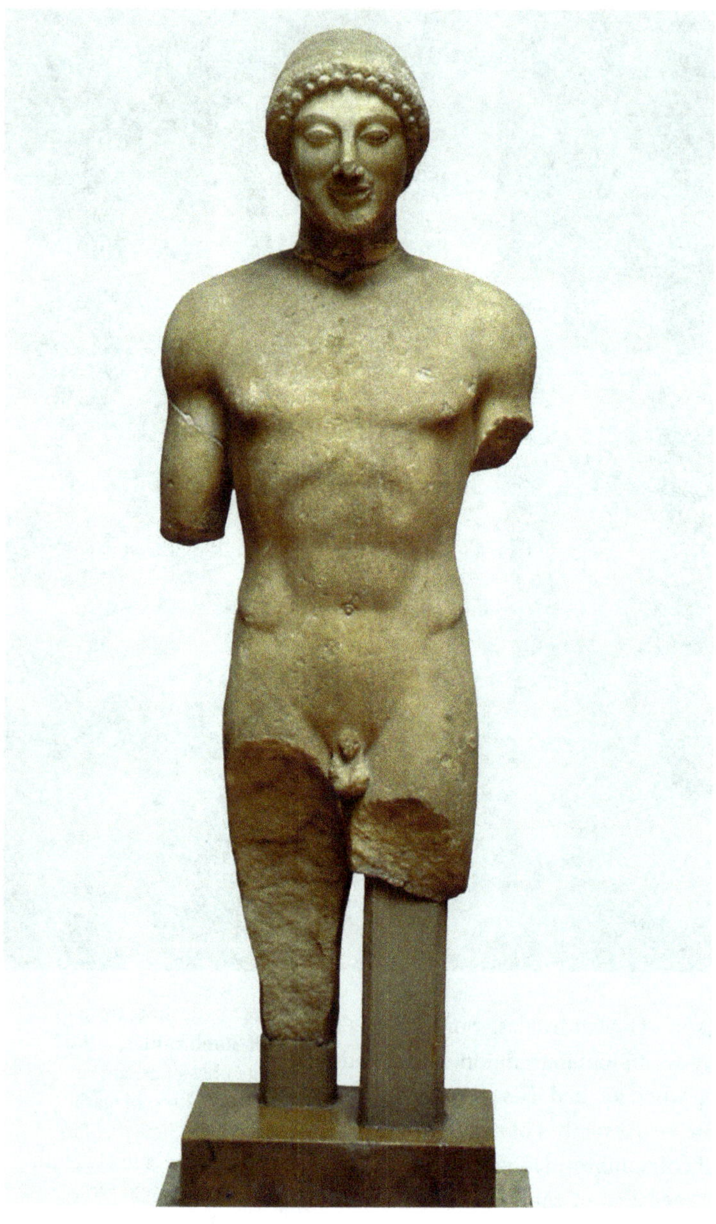

8.11 Kouros dedicated by Pytheas and Aeschrion to Ptoan Apollo, Boeotia, c. 500 BCE. 3 ft 4⁹⁄₁₆ in (1.03 m). Athens, National Archaeological Museum 20. Photo: National Archaeological Museum, Athens (Athanassios Miliarakis) © Hellenic Ministry of Education and Religious Affairs, Culture and Sports/Archaeological Receipts Fund.

muscles and bones is achieved through more subtle undulations in the surface of the stone. This figure is more rounded and unified as a body.

Late archaic sculptors did create a more naturalistic figure while retaining the kouros formula, that is, the anatomical structure and proportions become more lifelike and there are more details of skeleton and musculature on the surface that mimic human figures more closely. Why this development of naturalism took place, however, is less certain. Given that we will see further innovations toward lifelike representation of the human figure in the fifth century, it has been a theorem of classical art history that Greek art strived steadily toward increasing naturalism and that this eventually led to the abandonment of the kouros formula after 480 BCE in favor of more lifelike figures. This may have less to do with an inherent desire for naturalism over abstraction in art, as the traditional theory implies. Rather, we should consider that statues like these were uncommon and expensive products, usually associated with elite social classes. The statues were meant to impress the viewer and to interact with him or her, whether by the viewer gazing at the figure, reading an inscription aloud, or performing a ritual offering. While they follow a formula, we should note that there is very little in the way of duplication from one statue to the next, except when they are made as a set like Kleobis and Biton. Differences in size, proportions, and details would have made a distinct impression on the viewer, who could see each statue as a unique work among many in a cemetery or sanctuary. Each was meant to evoke wonder and contemplation on the part of the viewer, thus the creation of a new work in a new style would be one way to maintain a balance between formula and individuality.

There is a similar pattern of type and variation in the sixth-century kore statues, and a similar difficulty with the terminology. Like the early statue dedicated by Nikandre on Delos **(see Figure 6.3, page 134)**, the kore is a clothed, standing female figure who is young and wears an elaborately woven garment. Early korai used paint and incised lines to articulate the clothing, but in the sixth century the drapery and its folds become more sculptural in their articulation. The kore dedicated by Cheramyes at Samos is an Ionian work, like the kouros of Sambrotidas, with the inscription carved on the statue **(Figure 8.12)**. The sculptor uses precisely carved grooves to show the folds of the clothing, with fine lines along the skirt to indicate the thinner under-layer of the **chiton**, smooth surfaces with flat and more thickly carved borders for the **himation** (mantle) worn over the chiton, and finally, widely spaced, deep grooves for the **epiblema** (shawl) over her top. The lines create a dynamic pattern of movement around the figure while also drawing attention to the curves of the body underneath the drapery. Typical of the regional Ionian style of the kore, the figure is cylindrical in conception, rather than the more rectilinear forms of contemporary statues like Kleobis and Biton.

A second, nearly duplicate kore was later found on Samos along with a common base. A pair of korai would be appropriate dedications for the sanctuary of Hera. Since Cheramyes was a man

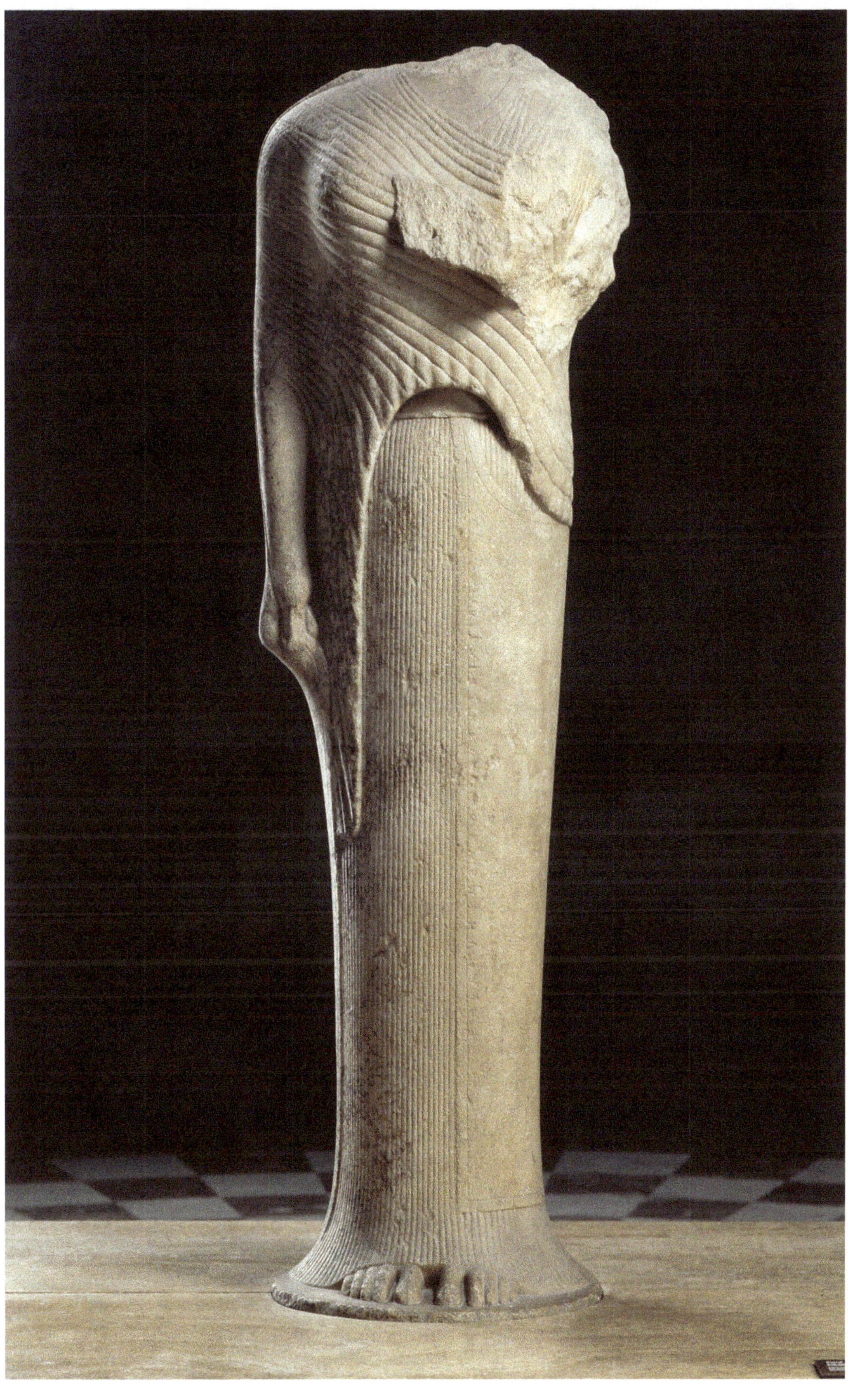

8.12 Kore dedicated by Cheramyes from Samos, 570–560 BCE. 6 ft 3⁹⁄₁₆ in (1.92 m). Paris, Musée du Louvre MNB3226. Photo: © RMN-Grand Palais/Art Resource, NY.

chiton
a thin rectangular garment that is buttoned at the shoulders and hangs down, sometimes belted at the waist. Warriors can wear a short chiton under armor. Long chitons are worn by both women and men, although more rarely by the latter

himation
term used to designate a heavy cloth mantle worn over another garment, usually over one shoulder and hanging at an angle

epiblema
a large and heavy mantle

nymphe
term designating a wife or bride

(he also dedicated an inscribed kouros at Samos), the figure does not represent him, but it is possible it could symbolize the women of his family. The pose of the figure, with the left arm drawn up and across the chest, suggests that it might be making an offering or performing a ritual. The inscription states that the statue is an agalma, a work that is a pleasing gift to the deity as we saw in Chapter 7. With its over-life-size scale and precisely carved details, it would have served that purpose well and would have commemorated the piety and prominence of Cheramyes and his family.

The kore could also be used as a grave marker, like the kore of Phrasikleia (**Figure 8.13**). The statue was discovered in 1972 in the cemetery of Merenda in Attica, along with a kouros, where it had been set in a trench in antiquity, presumably due to the destruction of the tomb. The base, found built into a nearby church and known since the eighteenth century, tells us:

> *Sema* [memorial] of Phrasikleia, *kore* I shall always be called,
> having received this name from the gods instead of marriage.

Using the first person, we understand the statue is speaking directly to us as viewers. The word *sema* means tomb or memorial, but it also means more broadly a "sign," a visual equivalent to Phrasikleia. The inscribed name, read aloud, and the sculpted figure together evoke Phrasikleia in the ears and eyes of the viewer. On the side of the base is inscribed the name of the artist: "Aristion of Paros made me." It is during the sixth century that we begin to see the names of artists written on sculpture and painted pottery, but phrased as if the work itself is telling us who made it.

The statue still preserves some of the red paint of the fabric. Decorative motifs of meanders and rosettes are marked by incised lines and were painted yellow and blue. Phrasikleia's dress is simpler than Cheramyes's kore, a chiton belted at the waist. The overfold above the belt has slight undulations that capture the fall of fabric hanging on a body. She pulls her skirt at the thigh, a gesture that would have allowed her to walk in procession, but would have also pulled the hem up and revealed her ankle. Phrasikleia's hem is not disturbed, but it is an effect found in other korai and would have signified their desirability. She holds a closed lotus bloom in her left hand and wears elaborate jewelry, including a crown made up of lotus blossoms and pearls. Phrasikleia is dressed as a bride, a maiden (kore) who would be presented on her marriage day to become a wife (**nymphe**). As the inscription tells us, she did not marry, but she is shown in what we can regard as an ideal female form, youthful, poised, and elegant, able to be a bride or serve a goddess. Indeed, Kore is also a name for Persephone, wife of Hades, so the use of the term in the inscription might have additional meaning for Phrasikleia in the underworld.

Late archaic korai become more complicated and intricately carved, such as the kore from the Athenian Acropolis dated around 520–510 BCE (**Figure 8.14**). It is one of a large assembly of votive dedications on the Acropolis between 520 and 480, and while most share similar features of costume and style, each is quite different and individual in proportions and details. This kore is wearing a thin chiton that hugs the body in crisp, raised, undulating lines. A heavier mantle hangs from one shoulder and creates a series of large, smooth folds. The edges create another, deeper undulating pattern reinforced by painted decoration. She holds out an apple or pomegranate in one hand, which is carved separately and inserted into a socket at the elbow; she also pulls her garments with her left hand, creating a pinwheel pattern of folds.

With its original paint, the figure was lavishly decorated. Recent study of the pigments still embedded in the marble has led to new reconstructions of the original coloring of Greek sculpture, and we can see the result in another contemporary kore from the Acropolis that is sometimes called the "Chian Kore" (**Figure 8.15**). Analysis of the original work has shown the use of pale yellow ochre and lead yellow as pigments for the yellow garment, cinnabar for red, and azurite for blue. These pigments have been applied to a replica of the original. The impression is startling at first glimpse, conditioned as we are to think of Greek sculpture as purely marble. Even when the traces of the pigment and even the details of the ornamented patterns of the cloth are visible on the marble statue, the fading and changing color mutes what must have been a rich coloristic effect in Greek sculpture

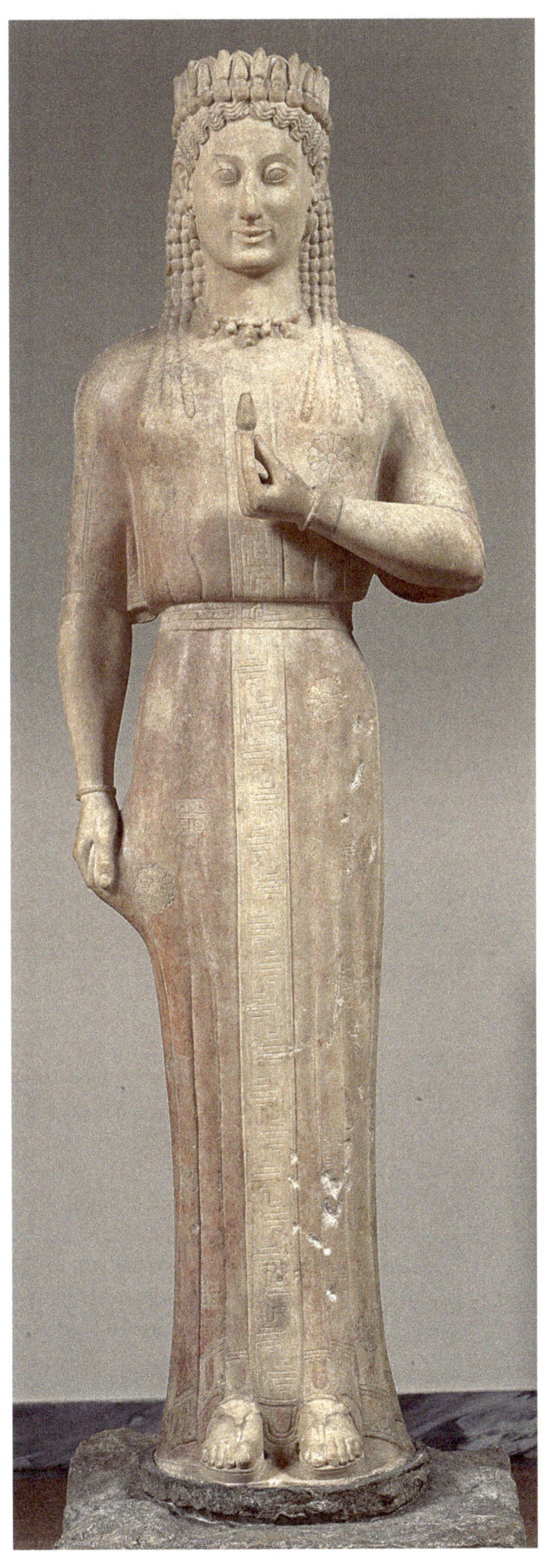

8.13 Kore of Phrasikleia, *c.* 550–540 BCE. Signed by Aristion of Paros. 5 ft 9⁵⁄₁₆ in (1.76 m). Athens, National Archaeological Museum 4889. Photo: National Archaeological Museum, Athens (Giannis Patrikianos) © Hellenic Ministry of Education and Religious Affairs, Culture and Sports/Archaeological Receipts Fund.

originally. This has generated some debate and reassessment, as is considered in the textbox for this chapter, but undoubtedly the paint provided not only rich color, but also an impression of the intricate patterns in textiles, particularly those that would have been worn by women in important public rituals.

Indeed, the kore would have been a *kalon agalma*, or beautiful object of delight, as many of the votive dedications for such statues testify. Some works, such as a kouros dedicated by Cheramyes in addition to his kore **(see Figure 8.12)**, go further in calling themselves *perikalles agalma*, a very beautiful object of delight. In addition to coloring and pattern, the polish and reflection of the marble surface of the sculpture, its **aglaos** or brilliance and radiance, would have been appealing. Youthful figures and the limbs of warriors are often described in poetry as *aglaos*, and the kouroi and korai that stand in for these humans are meant to be equally brilliant. The shine of marble, **mamoros** in Greek, must have been one of its attractive qualities that justified its expensiveness as a material, and indeed the related word *marmairein* means generally to shine and sparkle. Bronze, gold, and ivory held similar visual appeal.

aglaos
term signifying brilliance or radiance, especially of sculpture

mamoros
term designating the shine of marble

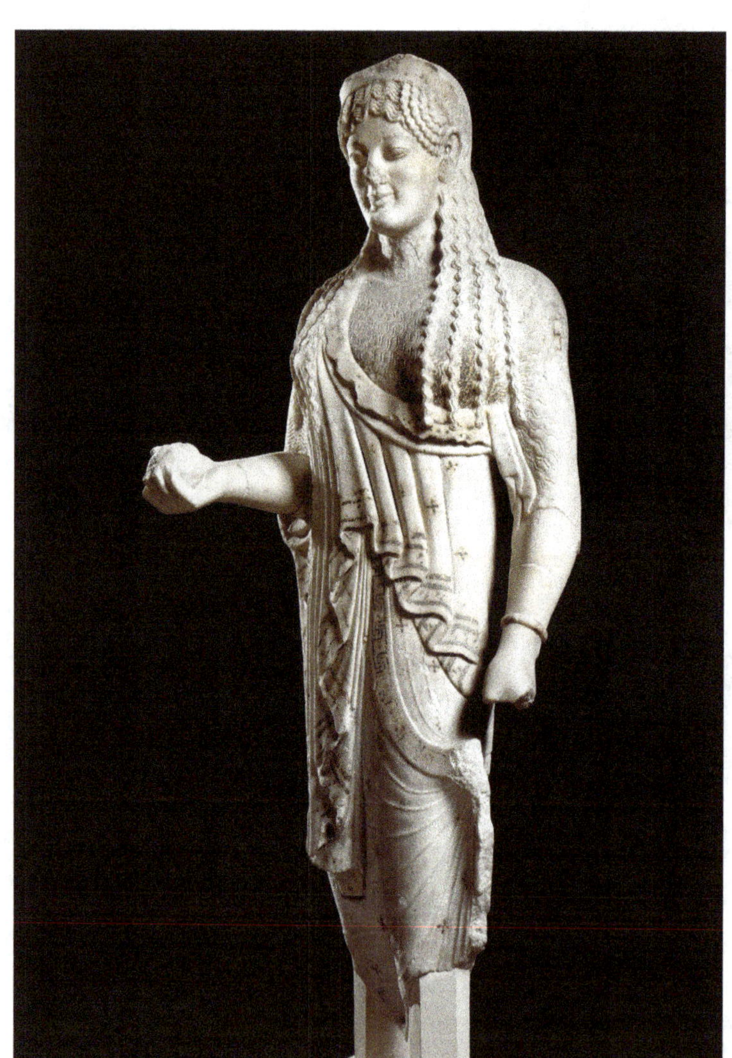

8.14 Kore from Acropolis, Athens, *c.* 520–510 BCE. 3 ft $10^{1}/_{16}$ in (1.17 m). Athens, Acropolis Museum 680. Photo: University Images Group/ Art Resource, NY.

Like the kouroi, there has been debate about who or what the korai represent. In some cases votive statues commemorate family members even if dedicated by a male, and certainly a funerary kore like Phrasikleia's is a sign for the deceased woman. Many, if not most dedicators of korai are men without reference to their family, so with these votives, the kore might be a goddess, such as Hera or Athena, or an idealized representation of the women who made offerings and performed rituals on behalf of the community. Many of the late korai on the Athenian Acropolis modify the formula by extending one arm out and holding something in the hand, but whether the object is an attribute signifying a goddess or an offering identifying a worshipper is debated. This ambiguity might be part of the reason for the success of the kore, in that it could be both typical and individualized simultaneously, whether through details or an accompanying inscription.

The kore of Euthydikos, which we saw in Chapter 7, is one of the last of the series dedicated on the Athenian Acropolis **(see Figure 7.18, page 175)**. While it follows the formula found in **Figure 8.14**, the figure no longer has the archaic smile, and the drapery patterns are more subdued, with graduated folds that mimic the behavior of cloth more closely. The eyes are set further back into the head, and the doughy quality of the body looks ahead to the Severe Style of the early classical period **(see Figure 10.1, page 237)**. This kore, along with the others on the Athenian Acropolis, was destroyed in 480 BCE in the sacking of Athens; the statues were buried, used as fill in the reconstruction of the sanctuary. When new dedications were made on the Acropolis after that time, the kore was no longer used.

Indeed, after 480 we see that both the kore and kouros figures give way to new types that feature greater animation and reveal more character. As can be seen in the Kritios Boy from just after 480 **(see Figure 10.1, page 237)**, the archaic smile is gone, and the pose of the body is more like that of an actual person poised at rest but attentive to his surroundings. The nude male continues to be a dominant subject, but there is more variation in poses and actions. We shall explore these aspects of fifth-century sculpture in Chapter 10.

OTHER MEDIA

Three-dimensional works in other media, including bronze, were produced during the archaic period but survive more rarely. From literary testimony we know of the visual appeal of statues made of gold and ivory, called chryselephantine, in antiquity, including the Palaikastro kouros from the Late Minoan period **(see Figure 2.14, page 37)**. Indeed, the fifth-century colossal chryselephantine statue of Zeus at his temple in Olympia was one of the seven wonders of the ancient world **(see reconstruction in Figure 7.12, page 168)**. Such statues were highly valued not only for the preciousness of their materials, but also for the radiance and shine that they produced. An important set of such archaic statues, about life-size in scale and dated to the middle of the sixth century, was found at Delphi, buried along with other objects in two pits under the Sacred Way **(Figure 8.18, page 200)**. The ivory is blackened from being burned, so the statues were likely damaged in some unknown incident and then, belonging to the god, buried within the temenos of the sanctuary. The surviving fragments, which would have been attached originally to a wooden core, have been placed in position in the museum at Delphi. The figure here is Apollo, with his head, part of an arm, the arm of a throne, and two feet made of ivory. Gold sheets with relief-work make up his hair and costume, as well as parts of the throne, and he held a gold phiale in his right hand.

One has to imagine such a figure set inside a building. As such, it would have faced the door looking out toward the viewer. The light from the doorway would have reflected off the gold and polished ivory, so that the figure would have stood out, glistening, from its surroundings. Lamps, if present, would have added sources of illumination, and the flickering quality of the flame would have given animation to the light reflecting on the gold and ivory. Given the enclosed environment, the expensive materials, and their visual qualities, we can consider the sense of wonder or awe provoked in the viewer as even greater than that produced by the sculpture decorating the exterior of the buildings or the statues populating the open areas of the sanctuary.

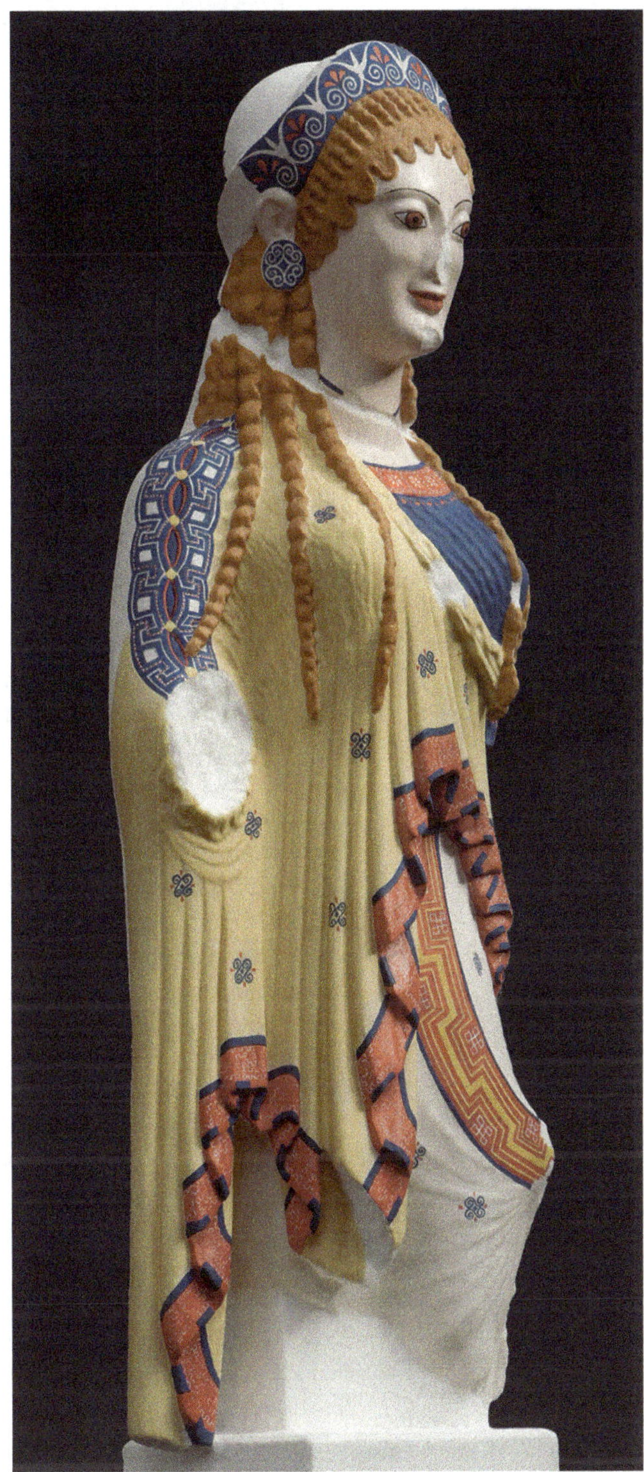

8.15 Color reconstruction of Acropolis Kore 675, "Chiotissa" or Chian kore, from Acropolis, Athens, by Stiftung Archäologie, 2012 (Brinkmann and Brinkmann). Photo: Vinzenz Brinkmann.

Other precious objects were placed in sanctuary buildings. Bronze shields and helmets were common dedications, and some of the arm bands from the interior of shields have *repoussé* and engraved figural scenes on them, such as a shield band from Olympia contemporary with the chryselephantine statues at Delphi **(Figures 8.16 and 8.17)**. The band is divided into squares like metopes, with narrative scenes. Observing from top to bottom, the viewer notices a number of

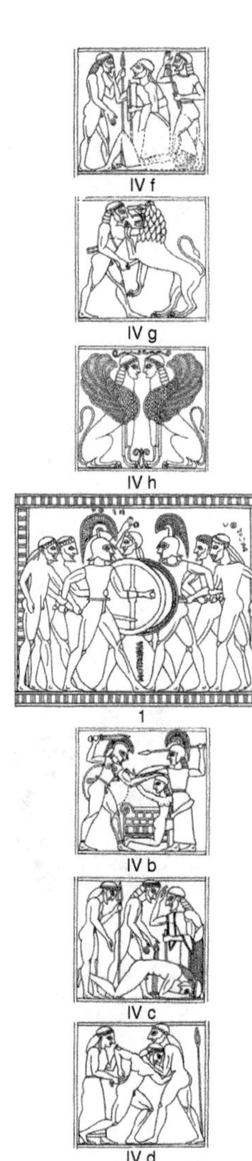

8.16 Narrative scenes of bronze shield band from Olympia in Figure 8.17. From top: ransom of Hektor; Herakles and a lion; sphinxes; strife of Amphiaraos and Lykourgos (plate); Ajax and Kassandra; suicide of Ajax; murder of Agamemnon; Theseus and the Minotaur. Drawings after E. Kunze, *Archaische Schildbänder (Olympische Forschungen* 2) (Berlin, 1950), pl. 19 IV f–g; insert 13 IV 1; pl. 18 IV a–e. Used by permission of DAI and Prof. Hans Goette.

mythological scenes: Priam pleading with Achilles for the body of his son Hektor; Herakles and a lion; a heraldic pair of sphinxes; the strife between Amphiaraos and Lykourgos from the Seven against Thebes; Ajax the Lesser attacking Kassandra at the statue of Athena; the suicide of Ajax the Greater; the murder of Agamemnon; and Theseus attacking the Minotaur. Like the metopes at Selinus/Selinunte, the choice of subject matter is eclectic but focuses upon protective figures like the sphinxes as well as heroes and warriors, examples of excellence and virtue that would be appropriate for a shield and its dedication at a sanctuary.

Unlike the Selinus/Selinunte metopes, a shield band does not have the same epiphanic function as temple sculpture and the compositions do not use frontally facing figures. Somewhat curious is the choice of the suicide of Ajax the Greater, son of Telemon, the second greatest warrior at Troy after Achilles. Ajax had tried to kill the leaders of the Greeks in a fit of anger and madness, after which he killed himself, making this scene less triumphant than the others. The composition, with a horizontal warrior lying on an upright sword, is unusual, and so easily identifiable, but this more common narrative version stands in sharp contrast to the same subject on a slightly later pot painter Exekias, as we will see in the next chapter **(see Figure 9.5, page 216)**. Other oddities include the murder of Agamemnon by his wife Klytaimnestra and his cousin Aigisthos; this subject is not very common in archaic art, but is included on a metope in the Temple of Hera at Foce del Sele near Poseidonia/Paestum and shows the wide range of interest in mythological stories in art. The scene with Herakles and the lion might be the Nemean lion, but since that predator could not be killed by a weapon, the use of a sword is untypical of the narrative formulas that show the hero wrestling the lion. A shield is an expensive and personal type of object to leave as an offering at a sanctuary, and perhaps the mix of typical and unusual narrative scenes reflects not only the growing interest in narrative art in the sixth century, but an individual interest in specific stories.

Bronze mirrors become more common during the archaic period, particularly in the form of the caryatid mirror like that found at Cape Sounion **(Figure 8.19, page 201)**. The female figure serves as a handle and supports the reflective disk above, like the maidens serving as columns on the Erechtheion or the Siphnian Treasury. Today, the mirrors seem dull with their darkened and rough surface, but originally these were polished and gleaming. To support the flat disk of the mirror, the caryatids often wear elaborate, architectural headdresses, and small figures to the sides serve to brace the disk further. The drapery and pose of the female figure recall the Acropolis kore **(see Figure 8.14)** and she holds a flower like Phrasikleia **(see Figure 8.13)**. We can readily understand the appeal of the figure as an exemplar for its owner as she looked at herself, and the erotes serve to acclaim her beauty. The tugging of the garment pulls the hem of the chiton up to the ankle, a hint of movement, grace, and erotic appeal implied in some lines by the poet Sappho (fr. 57): "And what country girl melts your sense … wearing rustic clothes … not knowing how to draw up her long robe to her ankles?" (Stieber 2004, 121). As objects used by women, the mirrors could also serve as votive offerings or grave goods. While most caryatids are clothed, there are examples of nude female figures, such as an earlier sixth-century mirror from Hermione **(see Figure 13.10, page 331)**. We will discuss issues of nudity and gender identity in Chapter 13, but it should be noted here that a female nude could be an ideal form, although not as a monumental sculpture before the fourth century.

Terracotta figures and vessels were more affordable objects than bronzes or stone statues. The terracotta figure of a woman holding a hare that we saw in Chapter 1 was a grave offering found on Rhodes **(see Figure 1.4, page 9)**; she resembles the columnar form and smooth surface of the korai from Samos **(see Figure 8.12, page 193)**, but with much less detail. Some of the more delightful objects from this period include scent bottles from Ionian Greece in the shape of animals, heads, and figural busts **(Figure 8.20, page 201)**. As grave goods, votive offerings, or household items, these objects show how far archaic style and subject matter were used, from the small and mass-produced terracottas to the individual and large monumental marble statues. They also preserve the richness of color in Greek art, even if they do not have the luster of metalwork or marble.

The first major painters whose names and works are recorded in literary sources worked in the sixth century. According to these accounts, painting started out as outline drawing, to which interior lines were added to define parts of the body, and then finally color, applied as flat monochrome. As in all periods, panel and wall painting only rarely survive, but several fragments of archaic painted wooden panels were found in a cave above the town of Pitsa near Corinth. The most well known shows a family in a sacrificial procession to an altar **(Figure 8.21, page 202)**. Without comparanda, dating the panel is difficult, but a date of 540–530 BCE seems reasonable. The blues and reds of the garments are still vivid, and the yellow of the sheaves of grain and garlands on the head creates light accents across the panel. The faces are in profile, but the eyes are frontal. The painter here distinguishes the skin of men and women by using a light brown and white respectively, a distinction found in Egyptian and other ancient art as well as contemporary black-figure vase painting, as we shall see next. The names of the figures are written above; the varied size of the figures gives us a sense of a real family, even if these are not true-to-life portraits. Itself a votive offering, the scene eternalizes the piety of the family. Painted on a small panel of wood, the offering would have been vivid but much more modest than something like a kore statue.

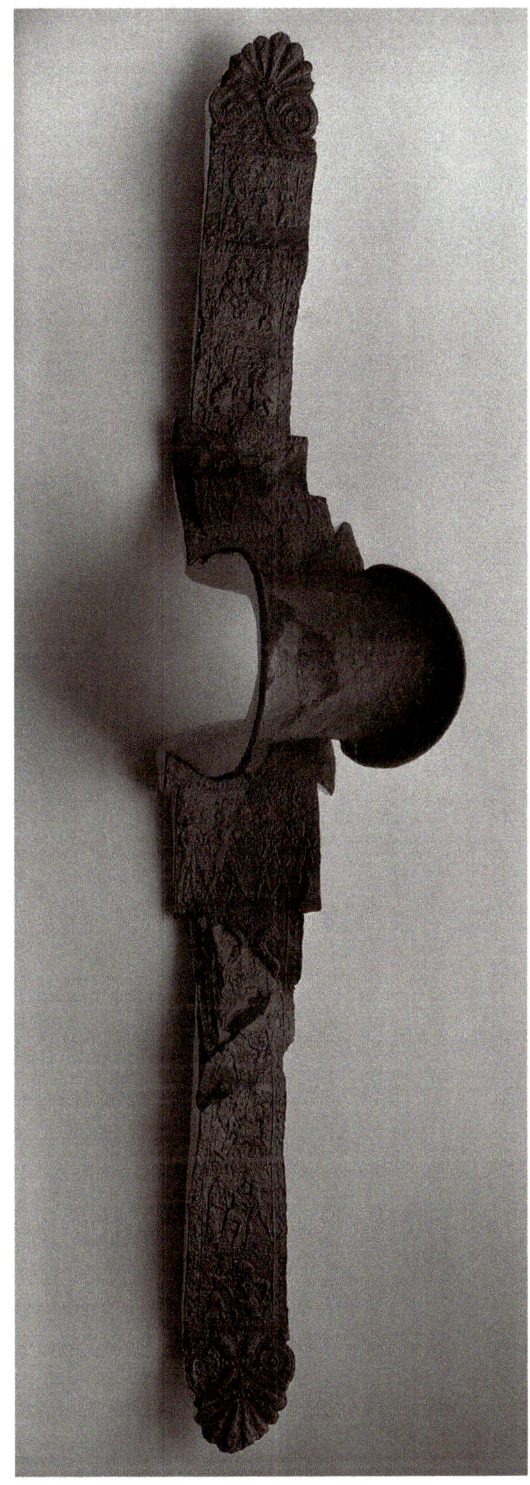

8.17 Bronze shield band from Olympia, mid-6th cent. BCE. Length: 33¹¹/₁₆ in (85.5 cm). Olympia, Archaeological Museum B1654. Photo: Eva-Maria Czakó.D-DAI-ATH-Olympia-4336A. All rights reserved.

PAINTED POTTERY

As we saw in Chapter 6, painted pottery from Corinth was made and distributed in large quantities in the seventh century, and Corinth continued to be a major producer and exporter into the sixth century. The range of shapes expanded, but the emphasis upon friezes of animals painted in the black-figure technique, with added red on the buff background, continued. A new subject related to the symposion, *komasts*, became popular. These were scenes of drinkers, musicians, and padded dancers cavorting, usually with a krater or dinos and other sympotic material in the picture. On the skyphos that we saw in Chapter 5, we can see two men on the right dancing, with padding on their bodies and buttocks **(see Figure 5.23, page 122)**. Behind, another man dips a pitcher into the mixing bowl of wine. Other komasts dance boisterously around the right side of the cup. To the left we see Herakles attacking the hydra; the scene is apparently unrelated, but the left foot of Herakles crosses in front of the dinos, almost as if he is charging out of the sympotic space to deal with the monster. **(See also Figure 5.21, page 120.)**

Other areas of Greece produced figured pottery for brief periods or in modest quantities during the sixth century. Lakonian pottery, produced in Sparta, developed some black-figure workshops during the sixth century, mostly cups and kraters that were exported both to Italy and to Greek colonies such as Cyrenaica (Libya) and Naukratis (Egypt) **(Figure 8.22, page 202)**. The scenes and ornament are precisely drawn and the black and red slips stand out against the pale fabric of the clay. The subject matter or composition of Lakonian painted pottery is frequently unusual. For example, the cup attributed to the Hunt Painter shows a boar hunt, probably the mythical Calydonian boar that required a group of heroes to kill it. The same scene appears on the top frieze of the François Vase discussed below, where we see pairs of heroes four

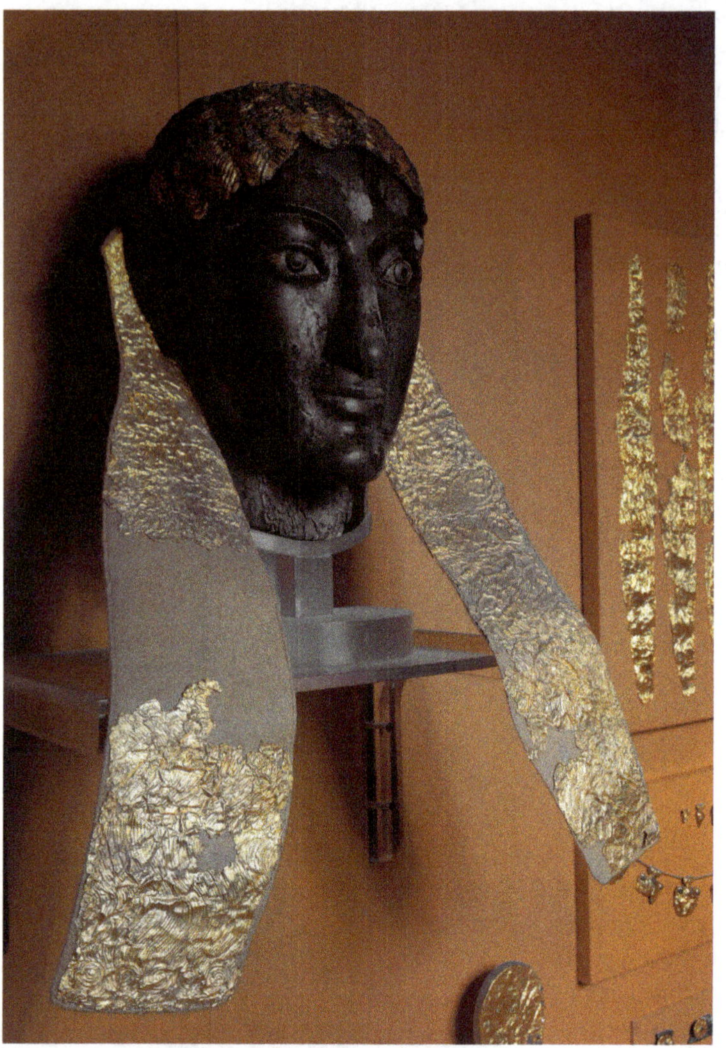

8.18 Chryselephantine statue of Apollo from Delphi, *c.* 550 BCE. Height of face: 7⁷/₈ in (20 cm). Delphi, Archaeological Museum 10413. Photo: University Images Group/ Art Resource, NY.

ranks deep attacking the boar from front and behind. On the Lakonian cup only a detail of the scene appears, with a pair of hunters attacking the rear with spears. The interesting aspect of the picture is that its border serves as a frame, and the way that it cuts off the view of the boar implies that the picture space continues beyond what we can see, as if the frame were a window into this other world. This is an assumption that a Renaissance perspective picture would make, but it is highly unusual for an archaic vase picture to do this, especially before the development of perspectival systems in the later fifth century. Cropping the composition like this does put the hero rather than the boar into focus as the central element, and this device is used on some other Lakonian vases as well.

In Etruria, there were a few workshops of immigrant Greek artists who produced distinctive pottery, called Caeretan ware, for the local market in the last half of the sixth century. The hydria by the Eagle Painter features animated figures, rich coloring, and very rounded forms with boisterous action **(see Figure 11.13, page 282)**. The figures seem more comical than serious, as we see king Eurystheus hiding in a pithos from the hound of hell, Kerberos, brought to the palace by Herakles in one of his labors. The production of these workshops, primarily hydria, lasted a couple of generations.

None of these areas produced as much figural pottery as Athens in the sixth century. Whereas in the seventh century Athens had been a minor pottery center, in the sixth century it became a major producer and exporter, dominating the market by the middle of the century. Early Attic production abandoned the black-and-white style of the Orientalizing period **(see Figure 6.15, page 144)** for the black-figure technique developed in Corinth, and much of its early archaic works favored long figural friezes at a small scale like Corinthian pottery. Because Athenian clay was richer in iron than that of Corinth, the background color of Attic vases is a distinctive red-orange. In the early sixth century Athenian potters and painters also began signing their wares, such as the so-called François Vase **(Figure 8.23, page 203)**. It has two inscriptions: *Kleitias m'egraphsen*, or "Kleitias painted me," and *Ergotimos m'epoiesen*, or "Ergotimos made me," which is taken to mean that Ergotimos was the potter. There are dozens of other inscriptions on the vase, naming virtually every figure and many of the objects.

The figures are precise and detailed, with much incised patterning of clothing, wings, and equipment. The skin of women is painted in added white slip. The figures are thinly proportioned and use very angular gestures. The scenes are virtually an encyclopedia of mythological stories, including on one side narratives related to the family history of Achilles. The reception for the marriage of Peleus and Thetis, Achilles's parents, runs around the entire vase at the shoulder, with Peleus receiving the wedding guests at the far right near the handle. Because of its prominence, it is thought that the vessel may have been made for a wedding, but it was at some point exported to Etruria and ended up in a tomb near Chiusi.

The François Vase was produced at a time in the 570 s when Attic pottery began to represent narrative scenes in large numbers. Most of the pottery was exported to other Greek cities in the Aegean, Black Sea, and southern Italy, and especially to the Etruscans in northern Italy, where the

François Vase itself was found. We will examine narrative in Greek art more fully in the next chapter, but we can consider here just how unusual it is for painted pottery to feature narrative images rather than straightforward ornament. Indeed, the focus on the human figure and narrative in Attic pottery made it distinctive from contemporary Corinthian pottery and would appear to have made it a popular commodity for purchase across the Mediterranean in the sixth century and afterward. As we shall see in Chapter 11, figural pottery would have been an affordable commodity for many, and narrative would have been an appealing decoration (see Osborne 2001 and 2007). In some cases, Attic producers also imitated shapes from their markets, such as the neck amphora signed by Nikosthenes and dated to the third quarter of the sixth century **(see Figure 11.8, page 277)**. This work, with its flared mouth and strap handles, copies earlier Etruscan bucchero-ware vases like that next to it in the picture. Whereas bucchero ware had a highly polished black glaze with incised or stamped relief decoration rather than painted figures, the Attic potters copied the shape but applied a lively black-figure decoration, in this case dancing satyrs and maenads in a miniature style.

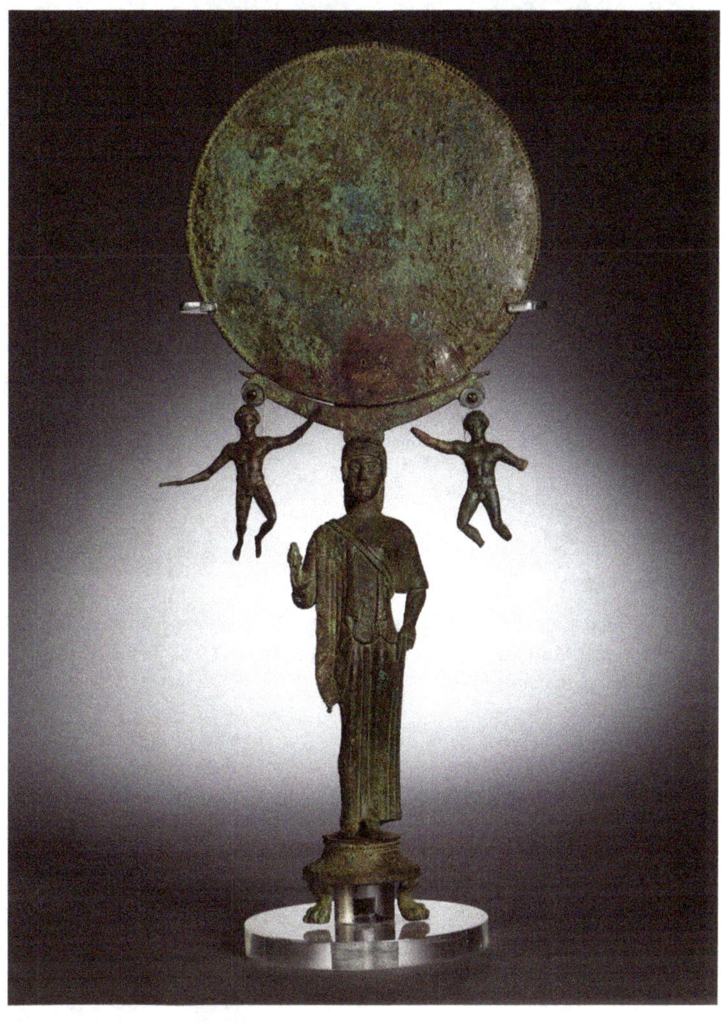

8.19 Caryatid mirror from Cape Sounion, *c.* 510 BCE. 16 in (40.64 cm). London, British Museum 1851,0507.13. Photo: © The Trustees of the British Museum.

Looking at the François Vase, some of the scenes follow formulas that become conventional in the sixth century and must have been widely recognized across the markets. The Calydonian boar hunt on the top frieze, for example, shows a large number of hunters attacking a huge boar from both sides, with a dog and hunter already dead. An excerpt from this formula might be seen in the Lakonian kylix, which is about fifteen years later in date **(see Figure 8.22)**. Given the longer frieze to fill, Kleitias could add a full complement of hunters that would have been impossible on the kylix. The scene second from the bottom shows Achilles chasing the Trojan prince Troilos, who is riding a horse. This, too, becomes very popular in the sixth century and would be instantly recognizable for having a warrior running

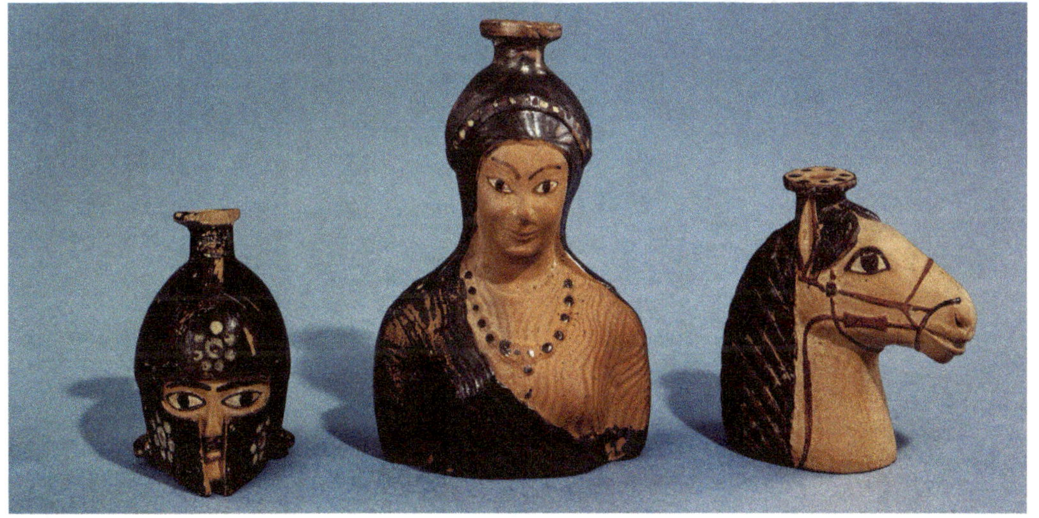

8.20 Rhodian terracotta scent bottles, *c.* 600–550 BCE. Warrior, 2 9/16 in (6.5 cm); woman, 4 3/4 in (12 cm); horse, 3 in (7.6 cm). London, British Museum 1860,0201.41; 1836,0224.365; 1860,0404.27. Photo: © The Trustees of the British Museum.

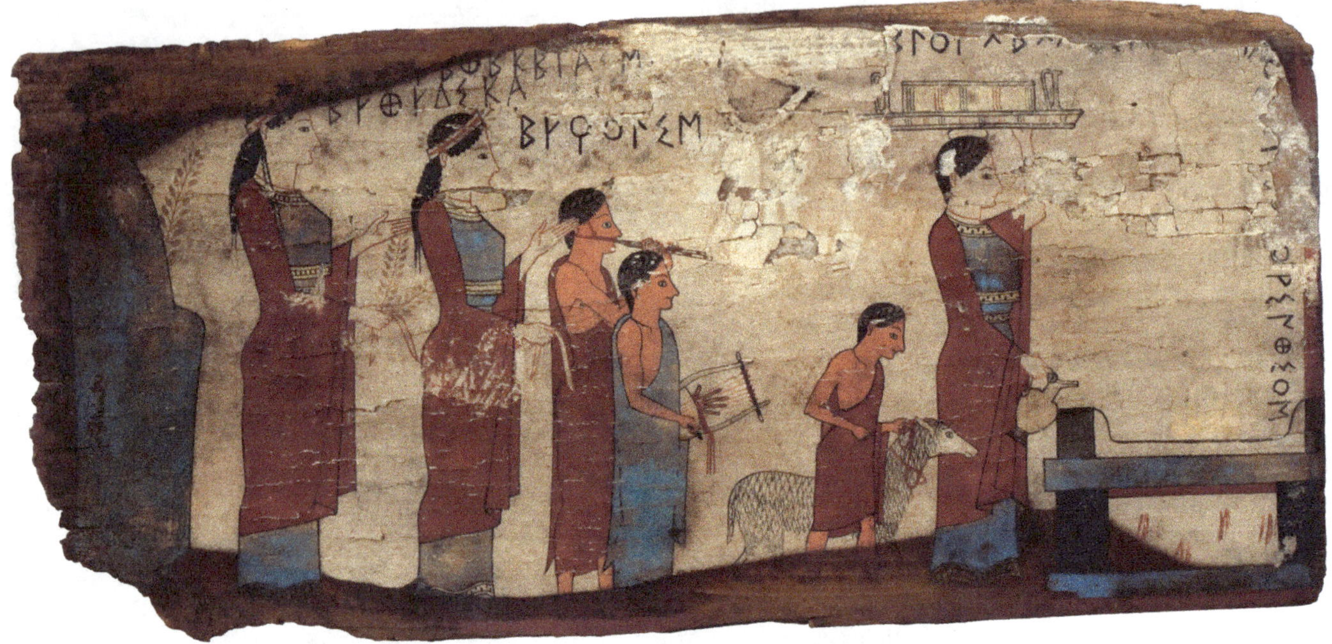

8.21 Painted panel from Pitsa, Corinthia, *c.* 540–530 BCE. $5\frac{15}{16}$ in (15 cm). Athens, National Archaeological Museum 16464. Photo: National Archaeological Museum, Athens (Giannis Patrikianos) © Hellenic Ministry of Education and Religious Affairs, Culture and Sports/ Archaeological Receipts Fund.

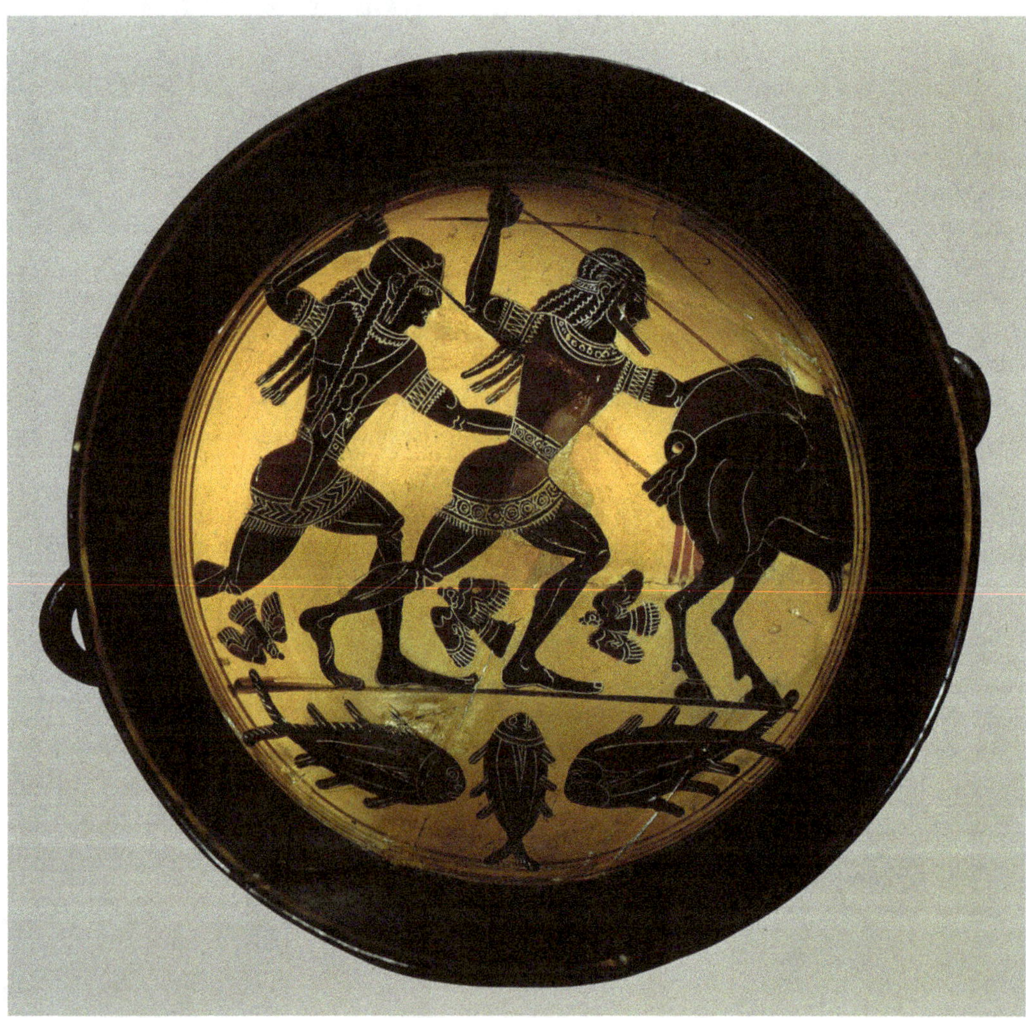

8.22 Lakonian kylix attributed to the Hunt Painter, *c.* 555 BCE. $7\frac{11}{16}$ in (19.5 cm) diameter. From Cerveteri. Paris, Louvre E670. Calydonian boar hunt. Photo: Gianni Dagli Orti/The Art Archive at Art Resource, NY.

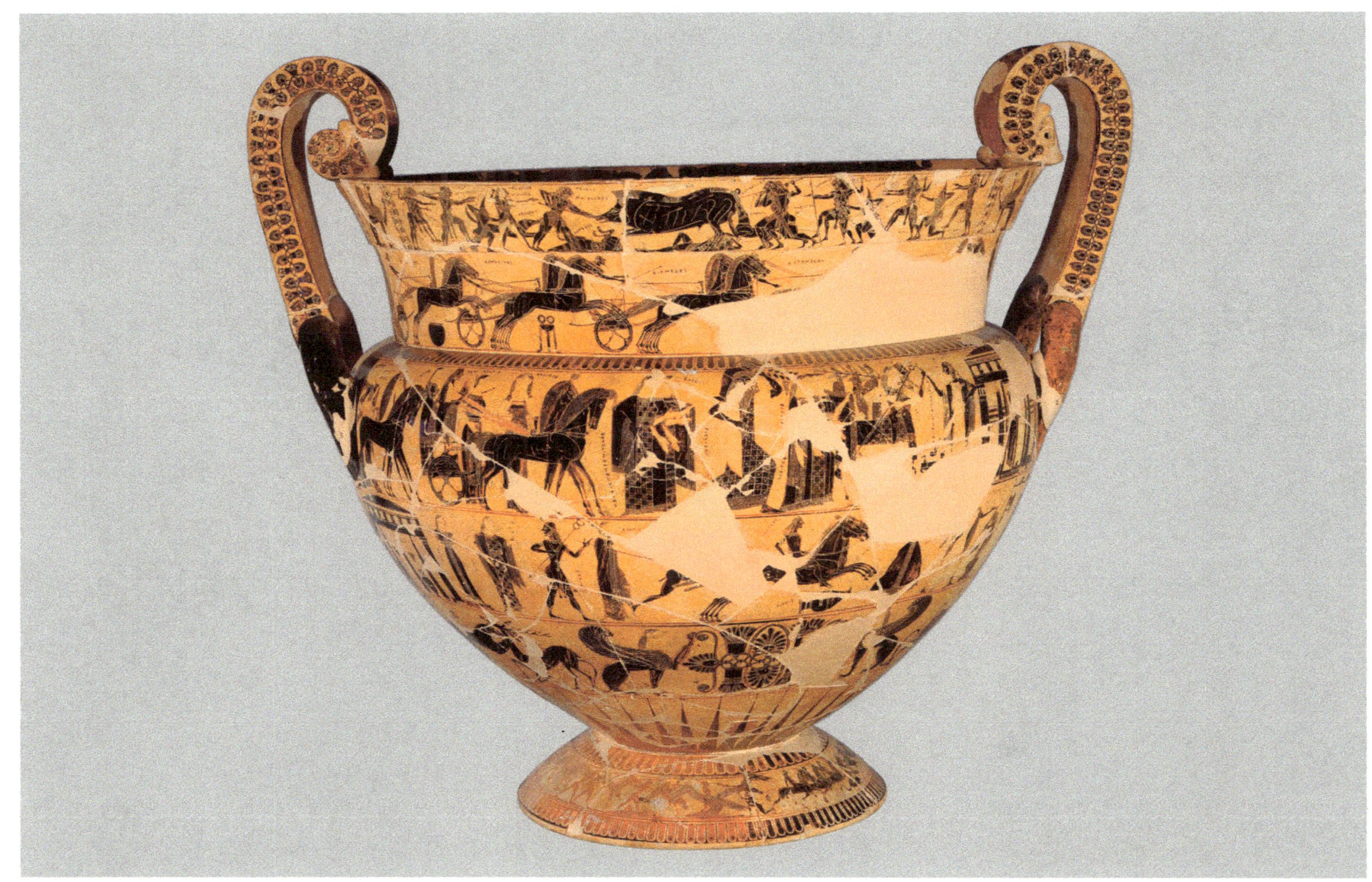

8.23 Attic black-figure volute krater signed by Kleitias and Ergotimos (François Vase), *c.* 570 BCE. 26 in (66 cm). Florence, Museo Archeologico Nazionale 4209. Top to bottom: Calydonian Boar Hunt; Funeral Games of Patroklos; Wedding of Peleus and Thetis; Achilles pursuing Troilos; animal frieze; Battle of Pygmies and Cranes. Photo courtesy Museo Archeologico Nazionale, Florence.

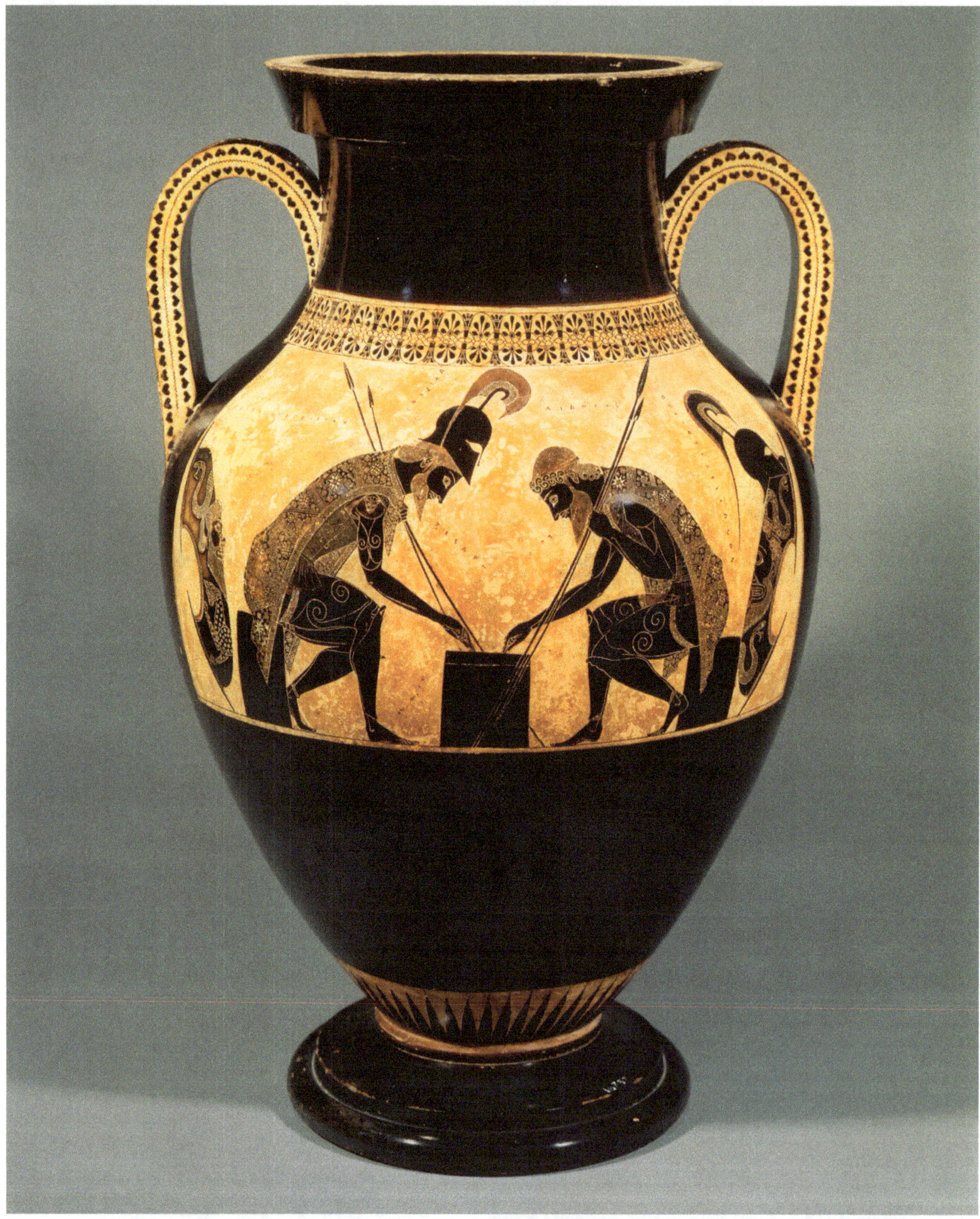

8.24 Attic black-figure amphora signed by Exekias, *c.* 540 BCE. Vatican 344. Achilles and Ajax gaming. 17⁵⁄₁₆ in (44 cm). Photo: Scala/Art Resource, NY.

down a rider, an apt image for "swift-footed Achilles" as Homer calls him. Other scenes, like the chariot race in the funeral games of Patroklos, are much rarer, but whether or not a viewer knew the *Iliad*, the chariot race would have a universal appeal as a theme. The wedding reception of Peleus and Thetis is likewise uncommon after 570, but as an encyclopedia of the gods, it would have been an interesting frieze to contemplate. Full literacy would have been limited among both Greeks and Etruscans, but the ability to sound out the names would have been more common and allowed some-one to identify the figures. The François Vase is highly unusual for the vast quantity of narrative and figures, but it is a suitable exemplar for the widespread interest of narrative in sixth-century art and for its adoption as a distinctive feature of Attic pottery.

Around the middle of the sixth century, Attic artists increased the scale of their figures, so that each vase often had only one or two scenes that dominated the vase. For example, a black-figure cup in Boston shows the sorceress Kirke mixing a potion for the sailors of Odysseus, who runs in from the left to confront her **(see Figure 9.6, page 217)**. The larger scenes are more visible from across a room than the earlier miniature-scale scenes and the details of the action among the figures more legible. The most well-known painter of the third quarter of the sixth century is Exekias, who signed the amphora in the Vatican Museum as both potter and painter **(Figure 8.24)**. The larger figures could bear more detail, and the drawing of the anatomy becomes more subtle: the details of the hands as they move their pieces are precisely engraved through the black silhouette. There is still an interest in pattern and texture, but even with their frontal eye, there is a sense of focus and concentration. The orange-red color of the clay surface, a result of the high iron content of Athenian clay, is no longer cluttered with filling ornament, and the figures stand out as if they were on a stage.

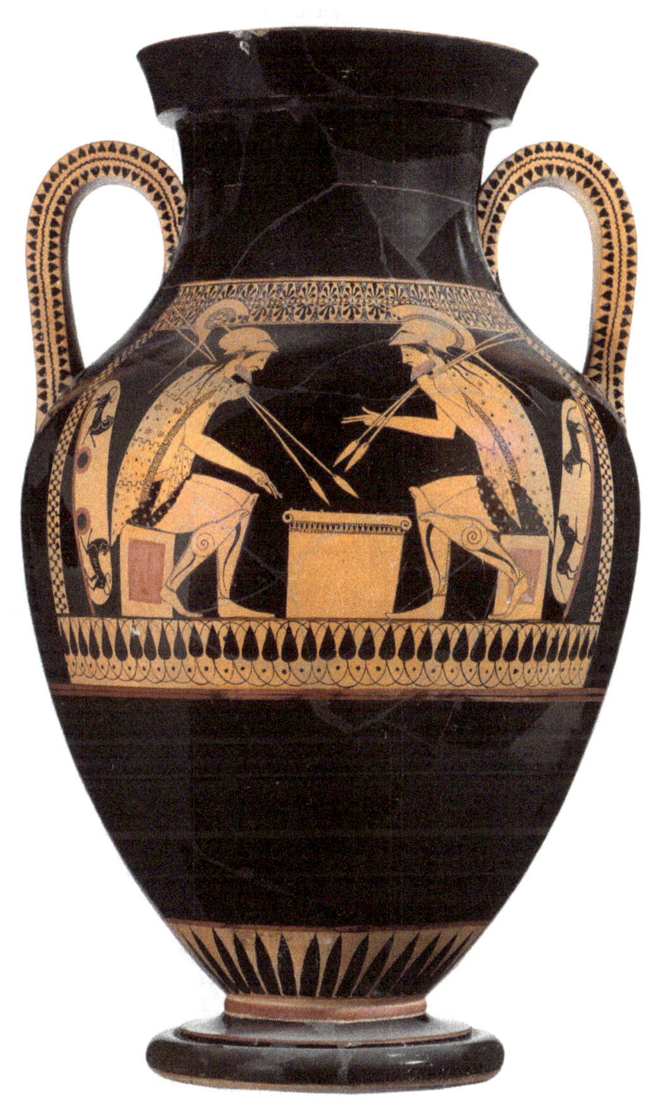

8.25 Attic bilingual amphora (red-figure side) by the Andokides Painter, *c.* 525–520 BCE. 21⅞ in (55.5 cm). Boston, Museum of Fine Arts 01.8037. Ajax and Achilles gaming. Photograph © 2014 Museum of Fine Arts, Boston.

On this pot we see Achilles and Ajax playing a board game while resting from their duties. They call out their rolls in inscriptions, like a modern comic strip, with Achilles on the left having a four (*tesara*) and Ajax a three (*tris*). This subject is unusual and new in Attic art, and it is thought that this story of heroes gaming, for which we have no surviving literary source, might be an invention of Exekias. Susan Woodford has proposed that Exekias has created a scene that reflects the life of the warriors at Troy, including the tedium and the diversion through board games, which Palamedes was renowned for inventing (Woodford 1982, 178–179). In this light, we have to see artists as narrators in their own right, free to imagine a story that could have its own appeal and might catch the interest of viewers. In this case, his composition was the first of more than 150 surviving examples of the scene in Attic art, showing that it was not only popular with viewers, but was also copied by other painters in the Athenian potters' quarter.

Among the earliest copies are in workshops associated with Exekias, where we also see the development of a new technique, red-figure painting. As can be seen on an amphora in Boston by the Andokides Painter, it is essentially a reversal of the black-figure composition **(Figure 8.25)**.

The figure's outline is now defined by a thick brushstroke of paint and the background is then painted with black slip. Inside the outline, the silhouette of the figure is then the bare, red surface of the clay. Lines are drawn in the silhouette, thick black lines for major parts of the figures and lighter, dilute red-brown lines for finer details, as can be seen in the pot sherd of a test piece from the fifth century (see **Figure 11.4, page 273**). Additional applications of red and white slip can also appear. Some of the earliest vases in this technique, like the Boston amphora, feature black-figure on one side and red-figure on the other, and are called **bilingual**. Their style is very similar to the figures on the Siphnian Treasury, as can be seen by comparing the poses and details of anatomy to the scene of Achilles fighting Memnon from the east frieze (**see Figure 8.1, page 183**) or the Gigantomachy from the north frieze (**Figure 9.1, page 212**). This similarity to the earliest red-figure painting suggests a date of 530–520 BCE for the invention of the red-figure technique. Since the painter is no longer engraving through the black silhouette, but is applying slip directly to the surface, it is more like free painting, like the painted panel with sacrificial procession from Pitsa (**see Figure 8.21**).

bilingual vase painting vases in which one side is painted in black-figure technique and the other in red-figure technique, often with the same subject matter

The change to red-figure technique might at first have been a novelty for the market, since the style remained similar to black-figure work, but in the last two decades of the sixth century a group of artists labeled the Pioneers began to use the new technique to develop more complicated, three-dimensional poses and actions. For example, a calyx krater by Euphronios shows Herakles wrestling the giant Antaios (**Figure 8.26**). Whereas Herakles's pose is all in profile (and even the pupil of his eye has moved forward slightly, changing the frontal eye of Exekias), Antaios's body is in a frontal view at the hips, somewhat three-quarter at the shoulders, and profile at the head. His left leg is crossed over in front of his right, with the effect that Herakles is twisting him like a corkscrew. Herakles's mouth is closed with his gaze forward, but Antaios's mouth is open and his teeth show. Antaios's eyes look upward, as if the life were being squeezed out of him; indeed, his right hand lays

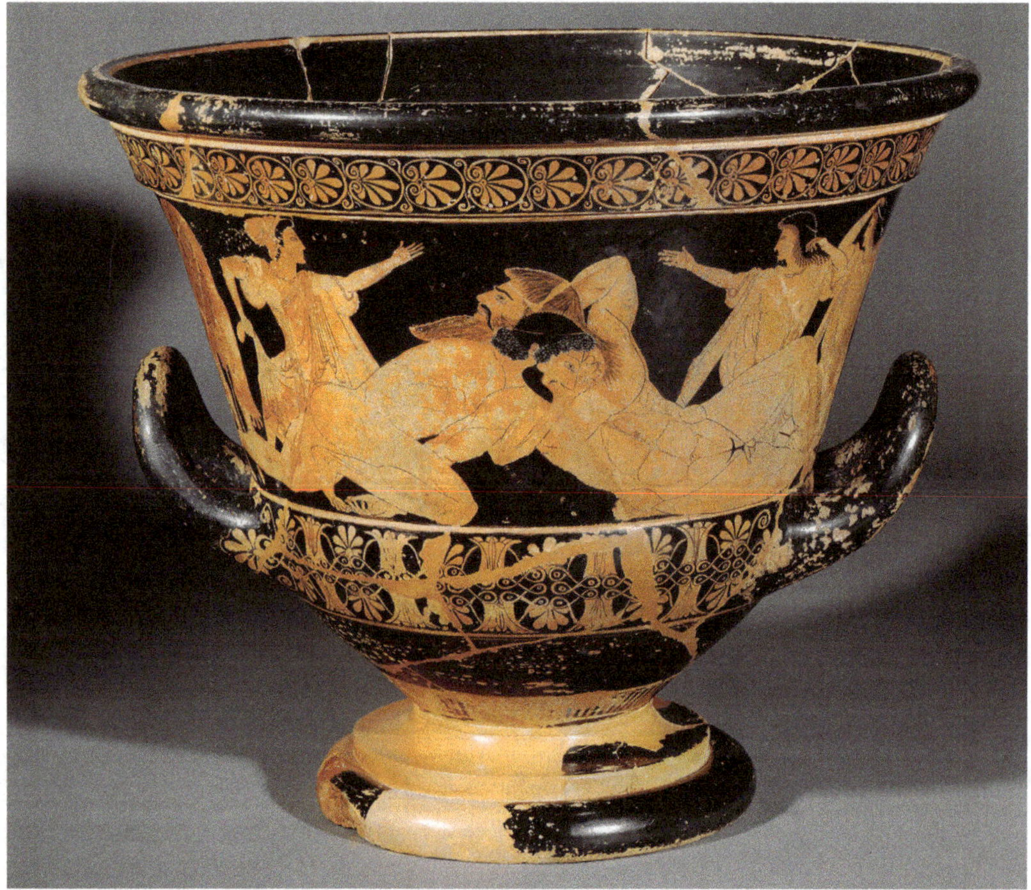

8.26 Attic red-figure calyx krater attributed to Euphronios, *c.* 520–510 BCE. $17^{5}/_{8}$ in (44.7 cm). Paris, Musée du Louvre G103. Herakles and Antaios. Photo: Erich Lessing/Art Resource, NY.

on the ground lifeless. Many of the muscles of the figures are shown with dilute line and heighten the sense of exertion. There is still some awkwardness in how the parts of Antaios's body connect where the view is blocked by Herakles, but Euphronios here is attempting to show the body's movement and exertion, the concept of *rhythmos* that we have already discussed with the Athenian Treasury **(see Figure 8.7)** and the ball player base **(see Figure 8.8)**.

The experimentation with poses, gestures, and expressions can be seen in a contemporary cup with a symposion scene **(see Figure 13.1, page 321)**. Rather than wrestling, the painter here is attempting to show a more erotic scene, but one that requires twisting figures and extended limbs as the figures interact. Again, there is a bit of awkwardness in the drawing of the anatomy, but later red-figure painters of the end of the sixth century and beginning of the fifth master the representation of more complex movement and poses and how to foreshorten a figure to adjust for the viewing angle. The cup by the Foundry Painter showing two young and inexperienced boxers has a very poised youth observing the main action, turning back to view the comic slapping of the young trainees in the center **(see Figure 13.11, page 332)**. The muscles of his abdomen are drawn in dilute red and are shown in a three-quarter view to make the transition from frontal right foot to profile left foot below. The contrast between his demeanor and that of the boxers also suggests a difference in the emotional state of the figures, as the standing youth appears and behaves in a more mature, calm, and perhaps superior attitude. The *Iliupersis* scene by the Kleophrades Painter uses this juxtaposition to offer a sharp contrast between the grieving king Priam, who has lost his grandson and his city, and Neoptolemos, the son of Achilles, who is about to kill him **(see Figure 9.7, page 219)**.

This second generation of red-figure painters brings us into the developments of the fifth century, which we shall explore in Chapter 10. It also highlights the continuing interest in and development of narrative art in Attic vase painting, since with red-figure painting there is an expansion in the production and export of narrative images. The technique opened new possibilities for showing the human figure in action, and we shall explore narrative art more specifically in the next chapter.

TEXTBOX: COLOR IN GREEK SCULPTURE

When the korai on the Acropolis in Athens were excavated, the preservation of the original coloring was striking to the excavators **(see Figure 8.14)**. Whereas literary sources and earlier discoveries had indicated that the Greeks painted their sculpture, the coloring was rarely visible in any detail in the works. Since then, discoveries of new statues like the kore of Phrasikleia added to the list of works that preserved some of their coloration **(see Figure 8.13)**. There were attempts at reconstructing the original appearance of some of these statues, but without detailed analysis of the actual pigments these efforts could only be an approximation.

Our knowledge about ancient color and painting has advanced considerably in the past two decades with the use of non-invasive analytical techniques, such as concentrated raking light, ultraviolet fluorescence, infrared spectrography, and X-ray diffractometry (for a summary see Brinkmann 2008). Vinzenz Brinkmann has used these techniques to study the traces of polychromy that are nearly invisible to the naked eye and to identify the actual pigments used in the original paint, as well as the painting techniques. Based on this analysis, he and his colleagues at Stiftung Archäologie in Munich have made replicas of the original works and applied the colors and details found to recreate the appearance of the originals, as can be seen in the Chian kore reconstruction **(see Figure 8.15)** and the Aigina pediment figures **(see Figure 10.3, page 239)**. Their work has been featured in a number of museum exhibitions in the past decade, such as *The Gods in Color*, and has a powerful impact on visitors, especially when an original and its replica are displayed together for study (see Brinkmann and Wünsche 2007). Their work also includes analysis of Roman sculpture as well as bronze statues, whose metals have changed color through chemical reaction with the environment but were once more colorful and shining in appearance. Other scholars have looked intensively at the range of color in vase painting, a medium in which color was important, rich, and subtle (see Cohen 2006).

In comparing the two korai from the Acropolis in **Figures 8.14 and 8.15**, the contemporary viewer, conditioned to thinking of Greek sculpture as unpainted marble, is struck by the vivid colors. The reconstruction is helpful in reminding us that Greek art was much more colorful than the remains indicate, but there are still some issues to ponder. For example, applying paint to a marble surface creates a different effect than applying it to another material, particularly given the luminescence of marble. Another issue concerns how well the colors would have worn over time, exposed to the sun and weather. Painted architectural surfaces could be more protected than a kore in the open, but how would the ancient viewer have reacted to a statue whose color was fading or flaking? Would this be considered as a sign of neglect, or would it enhance the antiquity and value of the work, as some ancient cult statues were regarded?

REFERENCES

Boardman, J. 1991. *Greek Sculpture: The Archaic Period: A Handbook.* London: Thames and Hudson.

Brinkmann, V. 2008. "The Polychromy of Ancient Greek Sculpture." In R. Panzanelli, ed. *The Color of Life: Polychromy in Sculpture from Antiquity to the Present*, 18–39. Los Angeles: J. Paul Getty Museum.

Brinkmann, V. and R. Wünsche, eds. 2007. *The Gods in Color: Painted Sculpture of Classical Antiquity. Exhibition at the Arthur M. Sackler Museum, Harvard University Museums in Cooperation with Staatliche Antikensammlungen and Glyptothek Munich, Stiftung Archäologie Munich. September 22, 2007–January 20, 2008.* Munich: Stiftung Archäologie.

Cohen, B., ed. 2006. *The Colors of Clay: Special Techniques in Athenian Vases.* Los Angeles: J. Paul Getty Museum.

Faure, P. 1985. "Les Dioscures à Delphes." *L'Antiquité Classique* 5, 56–65.

Herodotos. 1987. *The Histories*, tr. D. Grene. Chicago: University of Chicago Press.

Marconi, C. 2007. *Temple Decoration and Cultural Identity in the Archaic Greek World: The Metopes of Selinus.* Cambridge/New York: Cambridge University Press.

Osborne, R. 2001. "Why Did Athenian Pots Appeal to the Etruscans?" *World Archaeology* 33, 277–295.

Osborne, R. 2007. "What Travelled with Greek Pottery?" *Mediterranean Historical Review* 22, 85–95.

Palagia, O. and N. Herz. 2002. "Investigation of Marbles at Delphi." In J. J. Herrmann, Jr., N. Herz, and R. Newman, eds. *Asmosia 5: Interdisciplinary Studies on Ancient Stone*, 240–248. London: Archetype Publications.

Stieber, M. 2004. *The Poetics of Appearance in the Attic Korai.* Austin: University of Texas Press.

Woodford, S. 1982. "Ajax and Achilles Playing a Game on an Olpe in Oxford." *Journal of Hellenic Studies* 102, 173–185.

FURTHER READING

Beazley, J. D. 1986. *The Development of Attic Black-Figure.* Berkeley: University of California Press.

Boardman, J. 1974. *Athenian Black Figure Vases: A Handbook.* London: Thames and Hudson.

Boardman, J. 1975. *Athenian Red Figure Vases: The Archaic Period. A Handbook.* London: Thames and Hudson.

Boardman, J. 1991. *Greek Sculpture: The Archaic Period: A Handbook.* London: Thames and Hudson.

Hurwit, J. M. 1985. *The Art and Culture of Early Greece, 1100–480 B.C.* Ithaca: Cornell University Press.

Marconi, C. 2007. *Temple Decoration and Cultural Identity in the Archaic Greek World: The Metopes of Selinus.* Cambridge/New York: Cambridge University Press.

Rasmussen, T. and N. Spivey, eds. 1991. *Looking at Greek Vases.* Cambridge: Cambridge University Press.

Shapiro, H. A., ed. 2007. *The Cambridge Companion to Archaic Greece.* Cambridge/New York: Cambridge University Press.

Snodgrass, A. 1980. *Archaic Greece: The Age of Experiment.* London: J. M. Dent.

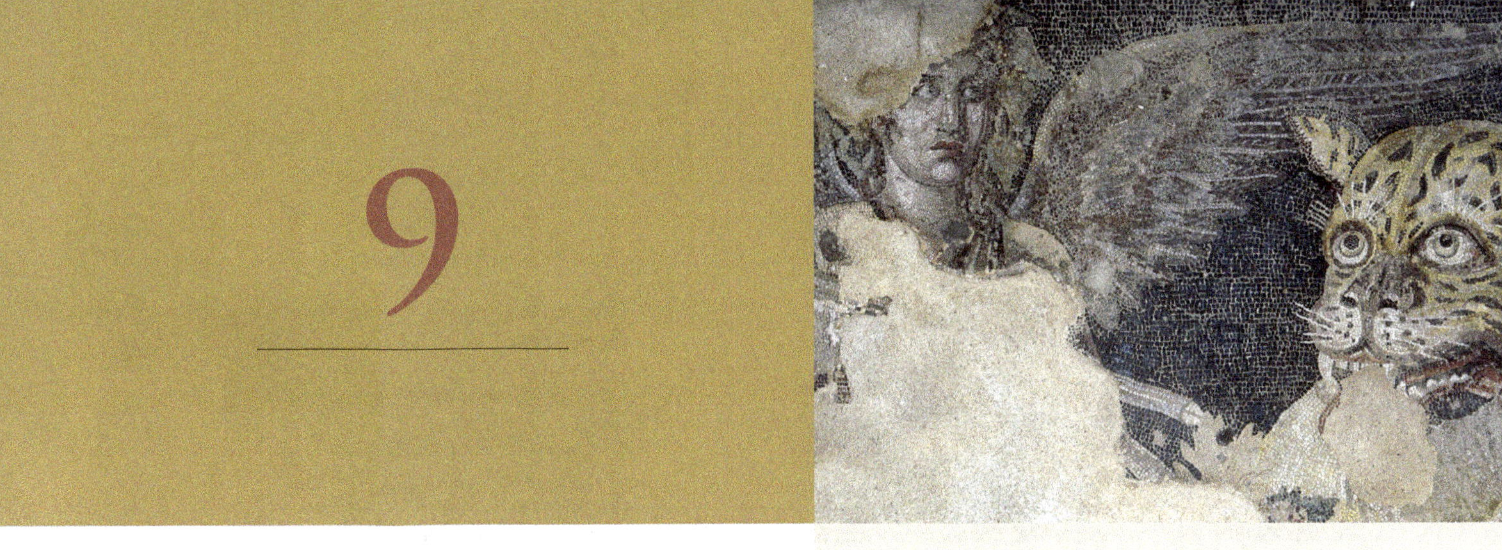

9 NARRATIVE

Timeline
Narrative and Artistic Style
Narrative Time and Space
Viewing Context
Art and Literature
Choice of Mood and Moment
Symbolic and Universal Aspects of Narrative
Textbox: Interpretation and Information Theory
References
Further Reading

A History of Greek Art, First Edition. Mark D. Stansbury-O'Donnell.

TIMELINE

	Sculpture	Pottery
800–700		MG II skyphos from Eleusis, 770
700–625/600		Eleusis amphora, 670–650 [6.15] Chigi olpe, 650–640 [6.11]
625/600–480	Temple C at Selinus/Selinunte, 550–530 [8.6] Siphnian Treasury, 530–525 [8.1–8.2]	François Vase, 570 [8.23] Attic BF kylix with Kirke, 550 Attic BF amphora by Exekias, 540–535
480–400	Temple of Zeus at Olympia, 470–457 Parthenon frieze, 442–438 [1.1, 10.15]	Attic RF hydria by Kleophrades Painter, 480 Attic RF krater by Niobid Painter, 460 Attic RF skyphos by Penelope Painter, 450–440 Attic RF pelike by Pronomos Painter, 410–400 Cabiran skyphos, 410–400
400–330	Monument of Dexileos, 394/393 [12.12]	Lucanian RF pelike by Choephoroi Painter, 350 Paestan RF krater by Asteas, 350–340 [12.21]
330–30	Tomb relief from Taras/Taranto, 300–250 Great Altar of Zeus at Pergamon, 180–150	

As we noted in the last chapter, Greek narrative pictures became more common during the sixth century and were widely distributed throughout the Mediterranean and Black Sea areas. "Reading" these stories, however, is different from reading a text. Poets and writers can explain a sequence of actions in minute detail; the *Iliad* covers just over two weeks of the decade-long Trojan War, although it recounts many other earlier events through speeches and descriptions. Most pictorial narratives are a single image that captures only some of the story's action and calls upon the viewer to fill in the missing parts. The descriptive capacity of images, however, has its own narrative power that can appeal across barriers of language and culture. It is one thing to describe a battle, but to see the agony of the defeated or the perfect body of the hero creates an engagement with the viewer that is different from a text and partly explains the power of film as a narrative medium today.

There are several critical challenges for the modern viewer in deciphering an ancient Greek narrative. First, many ancient Greek stories and their variations do not survive in literary accounts. Some narratives were composed and preserved, like the *Iliad*, but many more poems and written accounts are known only from fragments or are lost entirely. Whereas we depend upon these surviving texts as a source for our knowledge of Greek narrative, the Greeks did not. Most people experienced epic poems like the *Iliad* and *Odyssey* or dramas like the plays of Aeschylus, Sophocles, and Euripides as performances and did not consult texts. Oral traditions, tales told by parents and grandparents or stories told by guides at sanctuaries, were a fundamental part of both individual and collective knowledge. Furthermore, Greek literature did not focus on the creation of new stories and characters, but reworked or elaborated upon the stories that the culture had shared for centuries or adapted narratives from other cultures. Like the poets, artists rarely invented completely new narrative images, but drew upon the same sources as the poets. They could repeat or adapt a common visual formula, introduce a new variable or twist that might capture a viewer's attention, or develop a new scene and their own version of a story.

The second challenge when looking at narrative pictures is that the ancient Greeks shared a visual language that we can only partially recover. While today many people can recognize and decode a sign like the Apple computer logo without effort, contemporary students of Greek art do not have that shared cultural experience of ancient art to identify figures and stories without effort. By examining and comparing numerous examples of a scene, however, we can decode some of the visual language with a degree of certainty. For example, we have seen several representations of the Gorgon Medusa in the past few chapters and of Perseus attacking her **(see Figure 6.15, page 144; Figure 6.23, page 149; Figure 8.3, page 185; Figure 8.4, page 186; Figure 8.5, page 187; Figure 8.6, page 188)**. Even with variations in detail, some features, such as Medusa's face, the use of a sword to behead someone while turning away, and the flight with the head as a trophy, permit quick recognition of the story. As we see in these examples, both protagonists do not even need to be present for recognition of the scene, nor is the presence of some other characters such as Athena, Hermes, Chrysaor, or Pegasos necessary. Greek artists and viewers shared this visual language, which allowed a single image to evoke recollection of an entire story.

In this chapter we will consider not only the story being represented in an image, but also the different ways in which narrative pictures can interact with the viewer. Having seen the development of a more naturalistic style of representation during the archaic period, we will first consider the impact that style has upon a narrative image. We will then observe the various strategies that artists used to deal with action in time and place, fundamental elements of any story. Finally, we will explore the role of the viewer in a pictorial narrative, consider the viewing context, the choice of narrative moment, and narratives that are more universalizing in theme and call upon the viewer to contribute specificity.

NARRATIVE AND ARTISTIC STYLE

We can broadly define a pictorial narrative as a picture of an action that leads to a change in the situation of the participants. A mythological battle scene, such as the gods and the giants fighting on the Siphnian Treasury (**Figure 9.1**), the Gigantomachy, fulfills that definition. The Giants, children of Gaia (Earth) and Uranus described in literature sometimes as monsters and sometimes as warriors, challenged the Olympian gods for supremacy. With the aid of a mortal, Herakles, the gods were able to defeat the giants. In art, the story is usually shown as a duel between one or two gods and opposing giants, but on a long frieze like the Siphnian Treasury we see a series of interlocking fights. In this section, we see Dionysos with his leopard skin behind a chariot driven by Themis; Dionysos and a giant are aiming spears at each other, while the lion pulling the chariot mauls a second giant. Ahead of the chariot Apollo and Artemis draw arrows at a triad of giants; in the background a fourth giant runs away while looking backward, perhaps at Dionysos and Themis. Another giant lays dead on the ground. The dead body shows that the battle has been going on for a while, but by showing one giant dead and another fleeing, the artist indicates that while the battle is still raging at the moment, the gods have the advantage and will be victorious.

The ability of an archaic artist to depict a complex composition, show space through the overlapping of the figures into receding planes, and vary the details of the actions makes visual narratives of the seventh and sixth centuries far more effective than scenes from the Geometric period. If we look at another combat scene on a skyphos found in a grave at Eleusis and dating to *c.* 770 BCE, we can see two pairs of warriors fighting (**Figure 9.2**). The pair on the right has an archer in front and a spearman behind taking aim at their opponents. On the left side there is a second archer in front, but the warrior behind him holds some type of large pole, perhaps an epic weapon like the spear of Achilles that was made from a tree trunk and could only be thrown by Achilles himself. In the middle of the picture lie two figures set at an angle who are likely corpses that the fighting warriors are trying either to rescue or to strip of their armor. There is no indication that this is a mythological picture, lacking clear signs such as the inscriptions and attributes on the Siphnian Treasury, but like the Gigantomachy scene, it does show forceful actions that have had and will have consequences.

As we saw in the discussion of Chapters 4 and 6, the Geometric style, unlike the archaic, does not allow for detail or specificity of action, and this problem has led to debates about the

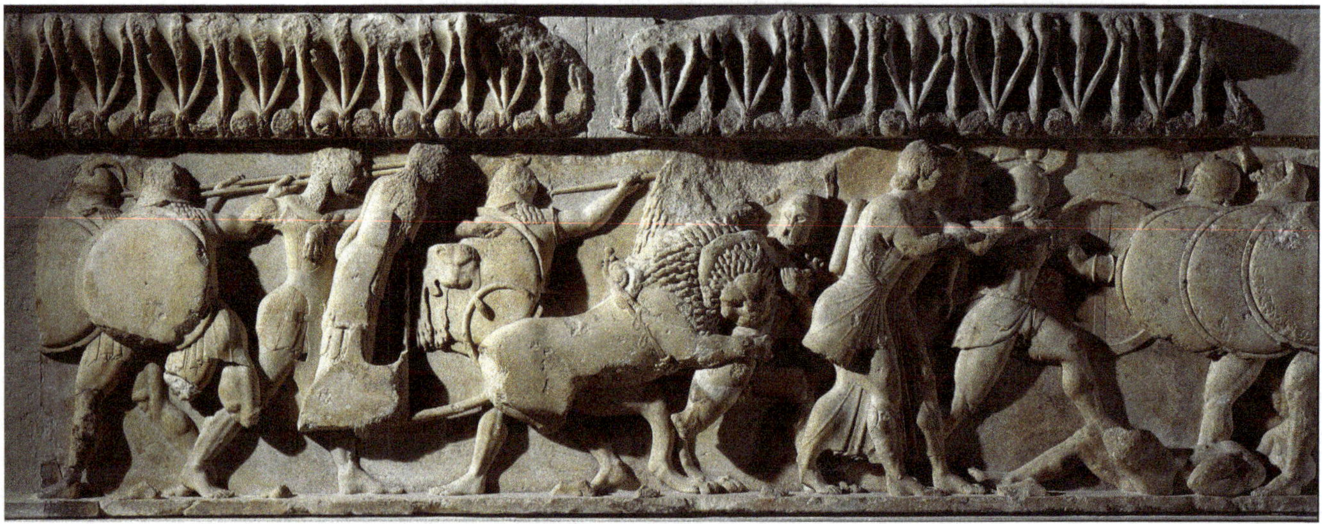

9.1 North frieze from the Siphnian Treasury at Delphi, *c.* 530–525 BCE. 25¼ in (64 cm). Delphi Museum. Gigantomachy. Photo: Gianni Dagli Orti/The Art Archive at Art Resource, NY.

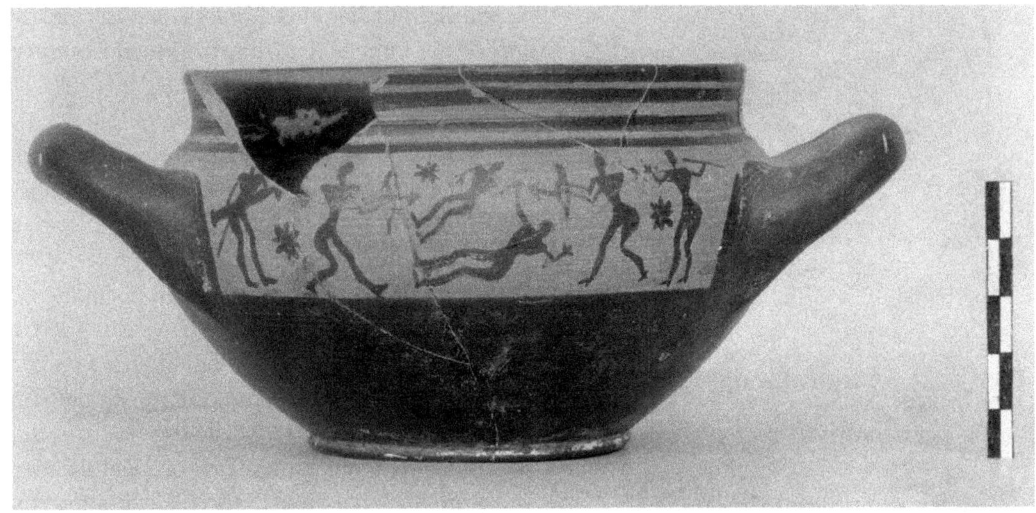

9.2 Middle Geometric II Attic skyphos from Eleusis, *c.* 770 BCE. Battle over fallen warriors. 2½ in (6.4 cm). Eleusis, Archaeological Museum 990. Photo: Hermann Wagner. D-DAI-ATH-Eleusis-512A.

existence of mythological narrative during this period. It is possible to "read" some Geometric pictures as mythological narratives, but there remains uncertainty as to whether a specific story rather than a universal situation is represented. It took the development of a more intricate style in both sculpture and painting for artists to show narratives that were unambiguously specific. Whether or not an image is mythological is not the same, however, as whether it is a narrative. For example, the battle scene on the Chigi olpe **(see Figure 6.11, page 141)** is more complex and detailed in its action than the Eleusis skyphos, and has a variety of actions spanning a range of moments in time similar to the later Siphnian Treasury. For example, at the far left of the frieze a warrior is still putting on his armor. The last three warriors in the phalanx have longer strides than those ahead of them, showing that they are rushing up to join in the rank. At the head of the group, the warriors march in tight, rhythmic formation, ready to meet their opponents. Viewing the frieze from left to right, one can see unfold the initial response to the call to battle and then the subsequent joining and locking in formation. It is an effective representation of a battle and easily as complex as the Gigantomachy on the Siphnian Treasury, but there is no sign that it is a mythological or specific scene. Nevertheless, as a story of battle, it is quite an effective narrative.

We will discuss these more universalizing narratives like the Chigi olpe further at the end of this chapter, but for now we can turn to a late fifth-century representation of the Gigantomachy to see how changes in style over the century showing movement and space affect a narrative. On a late fifth-century pelike linked to the Pronomos Painter, we see three duels **(Figure 9.3)**. In the center top is Ares, who has struck his spear through the shield of a giant, who grasps its point. To either side are the Dioskouroi (the Gemini twins), one on horseback and one on foot, fighting other giants. The scene is set in a rocky, three-dimensional landscape, with the god and heroes on the high ground attacking downward. The giant on the left has collapsed under the weight of the assault, while the one in the middle is being driven back and the two on the right are attempting a counterattack. The body posture of the nude youth and his action suggest that he is changing his position tactically, giving ground slightly in order to counter the attack of two giants. The picture, then, allows one to see the narrative as figures moving through space in three dimensions, rather than simply moving two-dimensionally across a shallow stage like the Siphnian Treasury. We also see convincing back and three-quarter views of the figures that reinforce this sense of the picture as a three-dimensional world. The greater naturalism in the rendering of muscles and anatomy conveys the fighters' physical effort, and the perspectival consistency of the face and eye provides a sense of their gaze and focus. The greater range and subtlety of actions make each duel different and the overall action more life-like and varied than archaic narrative.

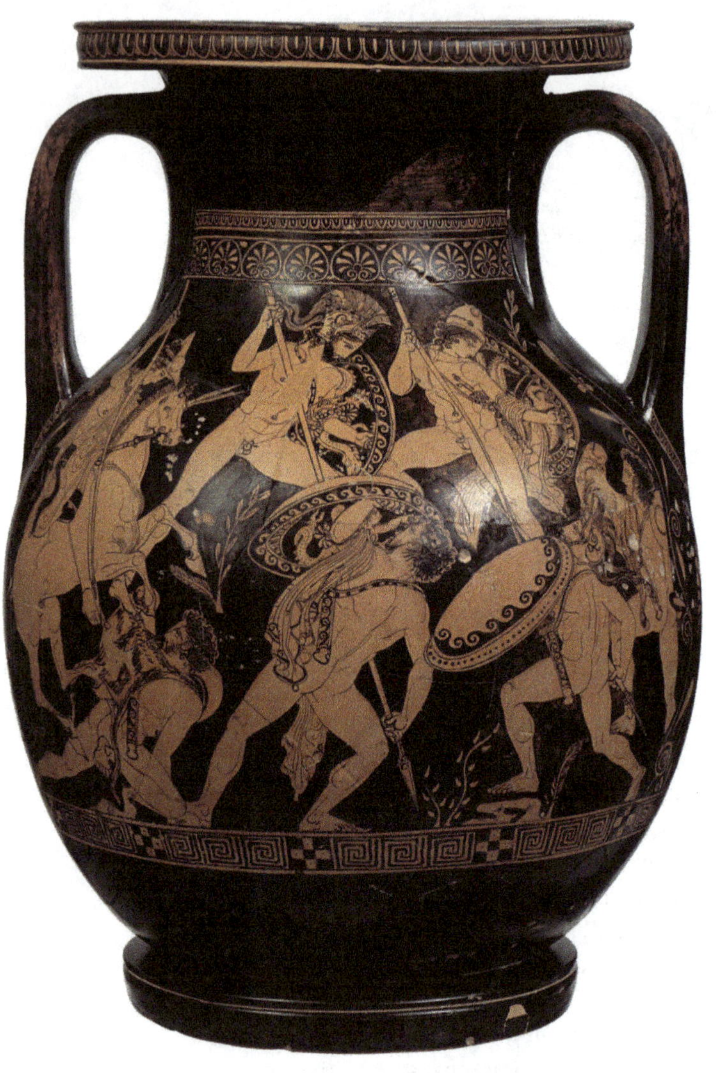

9.3 Attic red-figure pelike near the Pronomos Painter, end 5th cent. BCE. 16½ in (42 cm). Athens, National Archaeological Museum 1333. Gigantomachy. Photo: National Archaeological Museum, Athens (Giannis Patrikianos) © Hellenic Ministry of Education and Religious Affairs, Culture and Sports/Archaeological Receipts Fund.

We can skip further ahead to look at a Hellenistic version of the same story from the second century BCE. A monumental Gigantomachy filled the frieze of the Great Altar of Zeus at Pergamon **(Figure 9.4)**. Here the figures are over life-size and cover the three sides and the wings flanking the front stairs, almost 120 total meters of frieze with close to 100 figures (see the view of the altar in **Figure 14.6, page 352)**. On the front side, we see at the right end Amphitrite moving leftward away from the stairs, subduing a giant falling away from her; on the other side is the god Triton, who moves rightward toward Amphitrite and strikes down a second giant between them. In the section of the frieze along the stairs we see at the corner the bearded Nereus, god of the sea, who supports a goddess in front of him, probably his wife Doris, although the inscription is missing, moving toward the right (upstairs). Doris moves rightward (upstairs) and has grabbed the hair of a giant who has fallen to his knees; she pulls on the head so that the giant's body arches back violently. His eyes are deeply set in his skull and convincingly roll upward; with his open mouth and slack hand trying to pull her wrist away, we see a figure that is expressing an emotional anguish and pain to match the physical trauma his body is experiencing. The figures are carved in very deep relief, and many of the anatomical features, especially the bulging muscles, are exaggerated to increase the sense of exertion and movement. We will discuss the Hellenistic "baroque" style in more detail in Chapter 14, but one can readily see that this style makes the Gigantomachy more dramatic, violent, and imposing than the other two gigantomachies, even though the basic storyline is similar.

NARRATIVE TIME AND SPACE

As we have seen, a narrative needs to suggest a sequence of actions in time and space. The place does not have to be geographically specific, but the viewer needs to understand how the figures move through space to interact with each other. This can be simple, as with two warriors on a simple groundline, but it can also be more complex, as we saw in the classical Gigantomachy **(Figure 9.3)**. A time sequence is more challenging. In movies or videos, time is built into the experience of the medium, so that story time and viewer time run together, although not always synchronously. For Greek artists, multiple pictures or complex compositions could provide an element of storytelling time like movies or cartoons. However, most narrative pictures are single panels, leaving an artist the choice between showing a snapshot of time and action or cheating time and space to show multiple actions or moments.

monoscenic narrative narrative picture in which the action occurs at a single time and place

An amphora by Exekias depicting the story of the suicide of Ajax is an example of the snapshot approach, called a **monoscenic narrative**: action taking place at a single time and place **(Figure 9.5)**. We have already seen on the shield band from Olympia **(see Figure 8.16, page 198)** a very late moment in the story, when the Greeks discover the body of Ajax impaled on his sword. In that panel, the

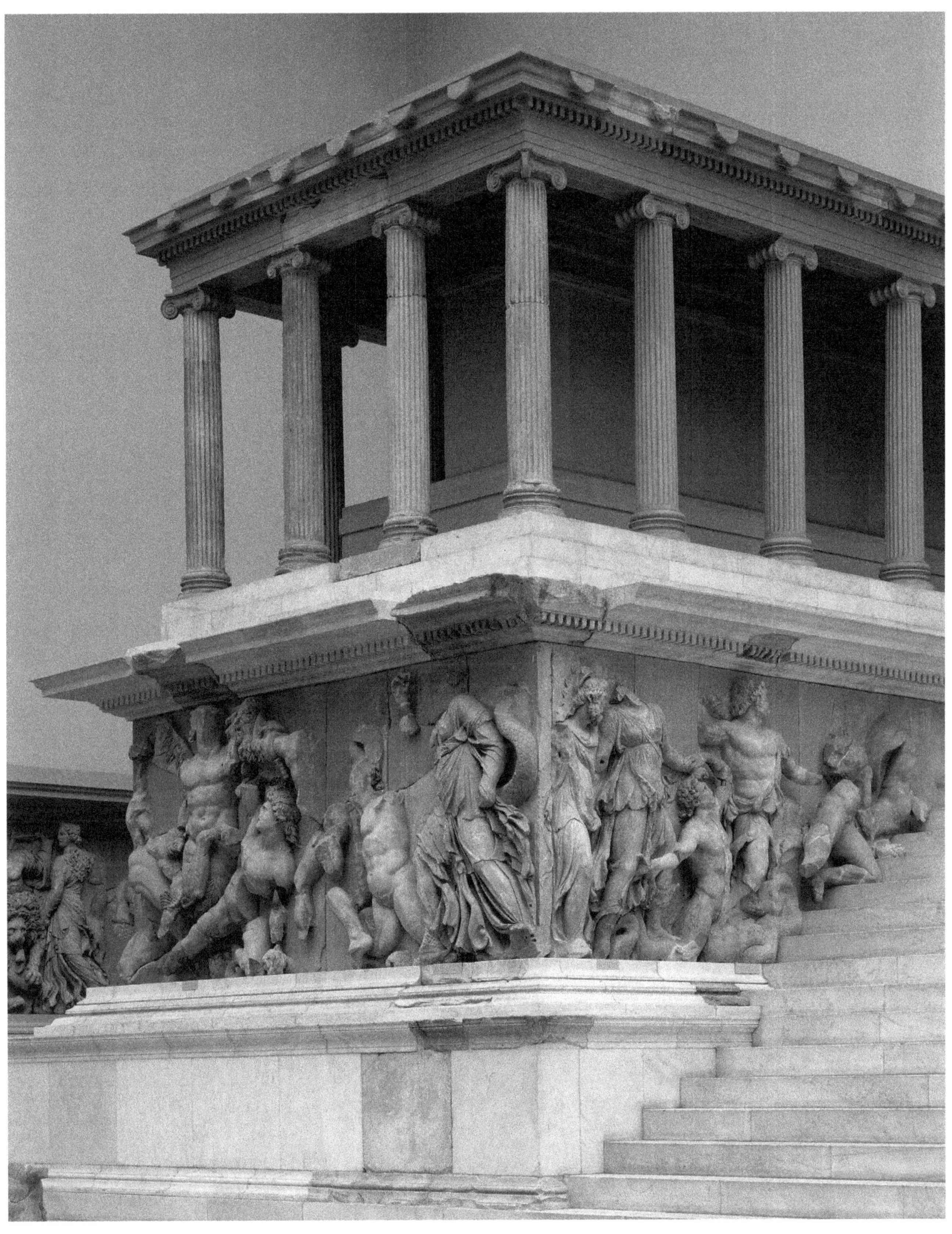

9.4 Frieze from the Great Altar of Zeus at Pergamon, *c.* 180–150 BCE. Height of frieze: 7 ft 6½ in (2.3 m). Berlin, Pergamonmuseum. Gigantomachy. Photo: Erich Lessing/Art Resource, NY.

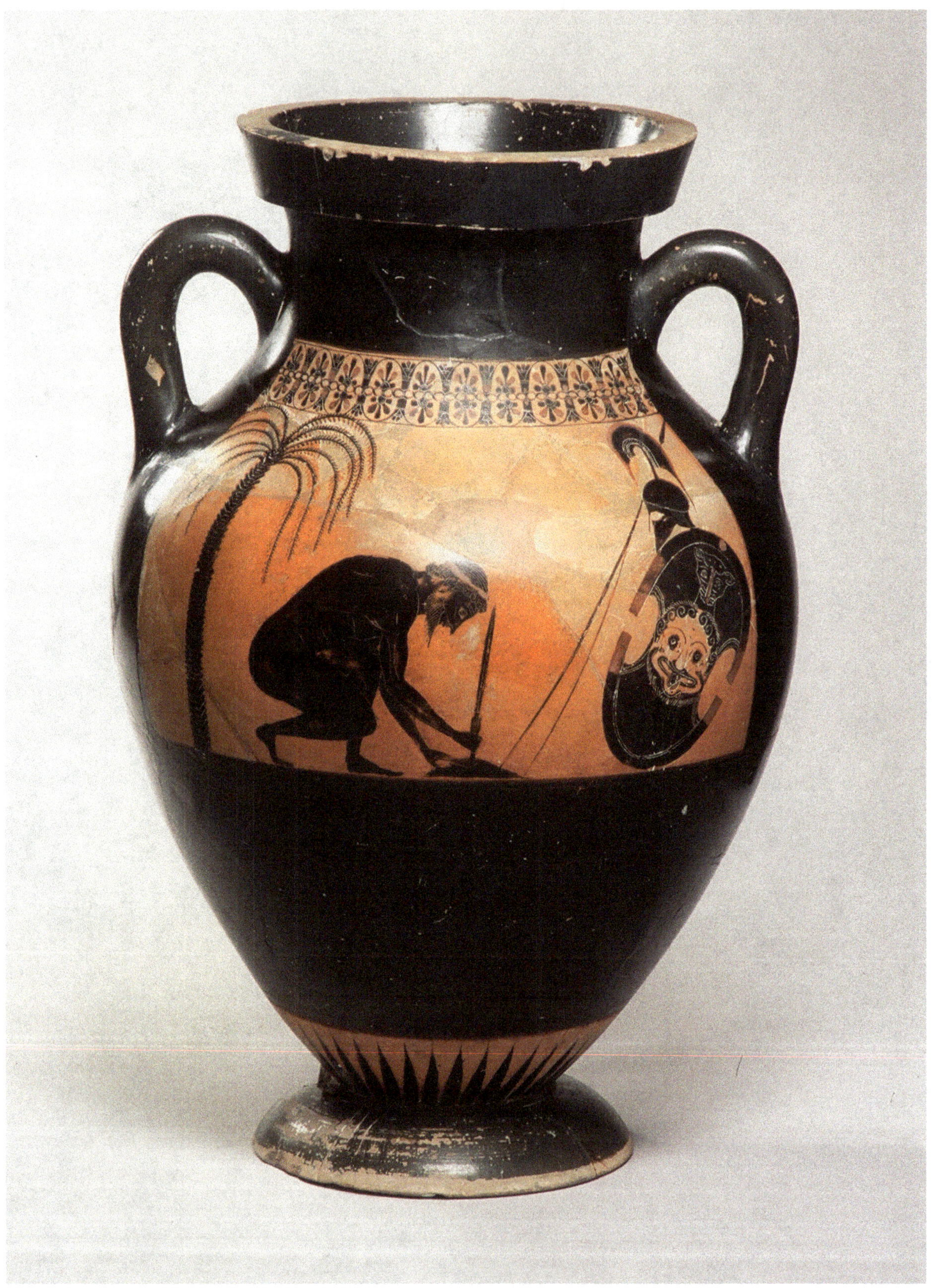

9.5 Attic black-figure amphora attributed to Exekias, *c.* 540–535 BCE. Height of picture: 6¼ in (15.8 cm). Collection of the Museum of Boulogne-sur-Mer 558. Suicide of Ajax. Photo © Museum Service Boulogne-sur-Mer.

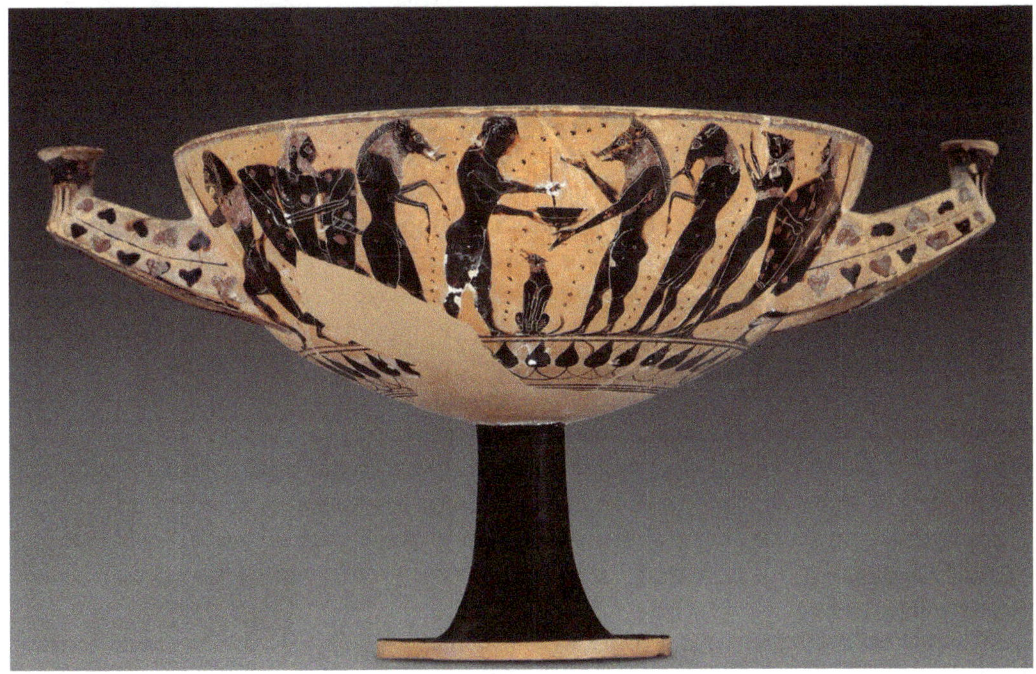

9.6 Attic black-figure cup, *c.* 550 BCE. 5¼ in (13.2 cm). Boston, Museum of Fine Arts 99.518. Kirke, Odysseus, and his sailors. Photograph © 2014 Museum of Fine Arts, Boston.

action is nearly finished except for the decision about what type of funeral to give Ajax. In his picture, Exekias has chosen an earlier moment when Ajax is planting his sword and patting the sand to hold it in place. The palm tree signifies a beach location, and it has been suggested that its bent form perhaps symbolizes the hero's sorrow (Hurwit 1982, 198 and 1983; contra Madden 1983). Certainly his distinctive and unusual action leads one to recall from our knowledge of the story and other pictures that he will throw himself on the sword and die at a moment in the future.

By showing this moment, Exekias makes us think even more about events leading up to this scene. Since Ajax has already removed his armor, we know that he is not going to battle. We can then ponder the reasons for this: a dispute over who was to get the armor of the dead Achilles, Ajax's proud anger at the award going to the eloquent Odysseus in a vote of the army, his attempt to kill the leaders of the Greeks in retaliation, and the madness brought on Ajax by Athena that caused him to kill a flock of sheep instead. We now see the moment when he has regained his senses and takes what he feels is the only honorable course of action left to him. None of these events is in the picture, but the armor cues us that he is no longer the warrior who led the Greeks in battle against the Trojans and rescued the body of Achilles, and reminds us of the prize of Achilles's armor that he lost. Exekias's style is not sufficiently naturalistic to suggest emotion and thought through Ajax's facial expression, but the choice of action, gesture, pose, and objects in the picture presents a narrative that truly deserves the label tragic, even if the dramatic medium of tragedy itself had not yet been developed.

Artists can also include in a composition objects or actions that belong to different places or times to make more direct reference to the passage of narrative time. In a well-known example in the scholarly literature, a black-figure kylix in Boston shows the story of Odysseus and Kirke (**Figure 9.6**). As we know the story from *Odyssey* 10.222–385, Odysseus arrived at an island and some of his men, led by Eurylochos, went to seek hospitality at the home of Kirke. She welcomed them with a drugged drink, and then turned them into pigs with a touch of her wand. Eurylochos escaped and ran back to tell Odysseus. The hero, after eating an herb that Hermes gave him, went to the house and drank the potion, but did not turn into an animal. After threatening Kirke, he went to bed with her. Eventually, Kirke turned the sailors back into their human form and they, along with Odysseus, stayed on the island for a while before continuing the journey home.

Looking at the picture, we see in the center a nude Kirke mixing her potion in a wine cup in her left hand. In front of her is a figure with a human body and a boar's head, a sailor who has already drunk the mixture and is transforming into an animal. Behind him are two other sailors who also have animal legs in place of arms, having drunk the potion earlier. These hybrid sailor-animals differ from the pigs in the *Odyssey* account, but are an effective visual cue, reminding the viewer of their metamorphosis (Davies 1986). At the far right, a completely human figure runs away, the sailor Eurylochos. On the left side of the cup we see two more hybrids, one with a lion's head and human arms running away, and another boar-sailor behind Kirke. In between is a figure charging with drawn sword, who could only be Odysseus. This, however, introduces a narrative anomaly, in that Eurylochos has not yet got away to tell Odysseus what has happened. Thus, actions from two different times of the story are shown in the picture, a pastiche called **synoptic** narration. This inconsistency of time and place is not unusual, and is a way for artists to compensate for the limitations of the medium and object in showing time and action. We have already seen examples of it in the Temple of Artemis at Korfu, where Medusa holds her posthumous children (**see Figure 8.3, page 185**), and the amphora from Eleusis in which the supposedly unconscious Polyphemos is seated with a cup still in his hand while Odysseus drives a stake into his eye (**see Figure 6.15, page 144**). It is much less common after the archaic period, but examples can be found in all periods.

synoptic narrative
narrative picture that includes figures, actions, or objects that belong to different moments of a narrative

More complex or larger-scale pictures can introduce multiple moments or places to show more of a story. In a long frieze, for example, the early stage of an action can be shown at one end and a later moment at another without having to repeat any figures. This **progressive narrative** type we have already discussed in the battle scene on the Chigi olpe (**see Figure 6.11, page 141**). Viewing the scene from left to right, we can see a call to arms, the formation of the rank, the march forward, and then finally the engagement in battle. The Parthenon frieze uses the same type of approach, with youths assembling their horses to prepare for a procession on the west side of the frieze, the cavalry riding forward in procession on the north and south sides (**see Figure 1.1, page 2**), and the ending presentation of the peplos to Athena on the east side (**see Figure 10.15, page 250**). Whether or not this is a unified subject or several, as we shall discuss in the next chapter, as one walked along the Parthenon the actions of the narrative would unfold in time with the viewer's progress.

progressive narrative
narrative image in which time progresses as one moves from one part of the image to another, but without repetition of any characters

One could also arrange a frieze that showed multiple actions taking place simultaneously but in different places, a **panoramic narrative**. A red-figure hydria by the Kleophrades painter, for example, shows five scenes of the *Iliupersis* on a frieze stretching all the way around the shoulder, making it impossible to see the entire composition at once (**Figure 9.7**). The center scene shows Neoptolemos, the son of Achilles, about to strike Priam, the king of Troy, with his sword. The king's grandson, Astyanax, lies dead in his lap and blood flows from wounds on both. Priam sits on an altar, which would be the household altar in the palace, grasping his head in a gesture of mourning. To the left, the warrior Ajax, son of Oileus (or the lesser Ajax to distinguish him from the other, greater Ajax who committed suicide), strides to our right and grabs a nude woman clutching a statue. This is the rape of Kassandra, the daughter of Priam, who had sought refuge in the Temple of Athena. Out of sight on the left one would see Aeneas fleeing Troy with his father and son. To the right of Priam, we see a woman armed only with a pestle attacking a fully armed Greek warrior, who cowers before her attack. She is usually identified as Andromache, the wife of Hektor and mother of Astyanax, whose name literally means "man-fighter." To the far right one would see two warriors helping up a seated old woman. They are the sons of Theseus, Akamas and Damophon, rescuing their grandmother Aithra, who had been forced to serve as Helen's slave.

panoramic narrative
narrative image in which different actions take place at the same time but in different places

All of these scenes of Troy's fall could have occurred at the same time narratively, but they clearly took place in different locations. Turning the vase to view one scene after another, one gets a more vivid impression than in a lengthy poem of the scale and scope of the carnage in the destruction of a

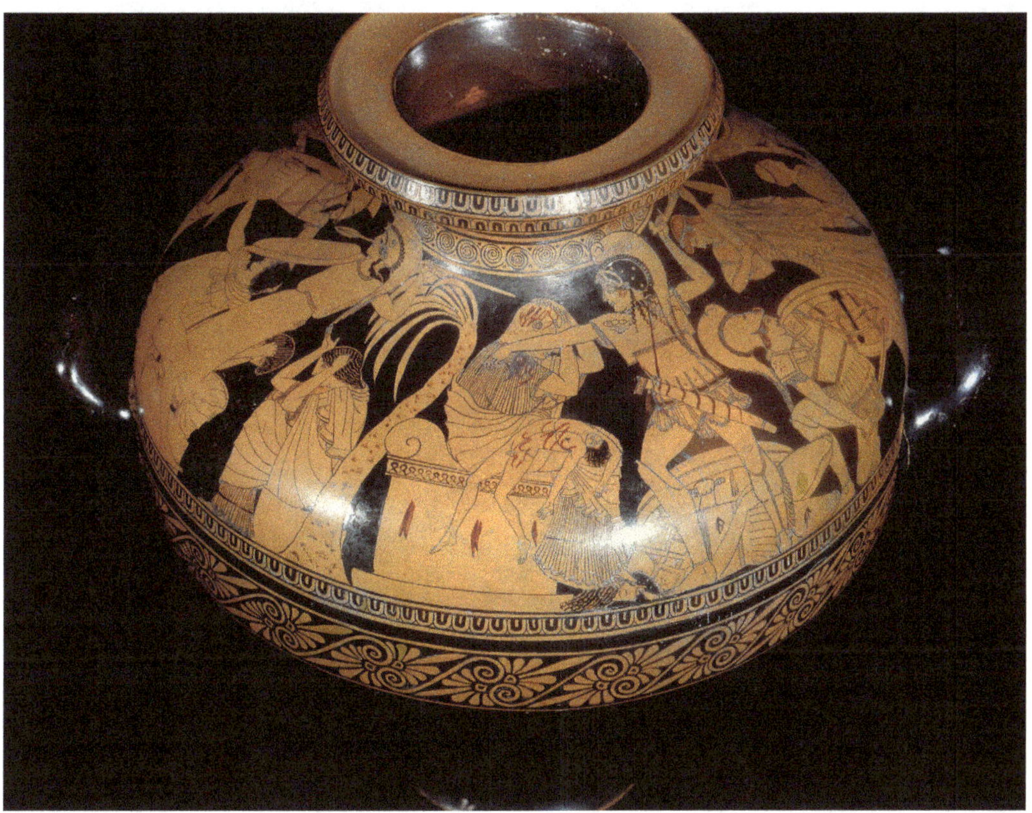

9.7 Attic red-figure hydria attributed to the Kleophrades Painter, *c.* 480 BCE. 16½ in (42 cm). Naples, Museo Nazionale Archeologico 2422. *Iliupersis* scenes. Photo: Fotografica Foglia; Credit: Scala/Art Resource, NY.

city and its people. Other versions of this panoramic strategy can also be seen in the east frieze of the Siphnian Treasury, where Achilles and Memnon fight at Troy while the gods debate their fate on Mount Olympos **(see Figure 8.1, page 183)**.

If there is sufficient room on a monument or object, one could also show multiple scenes that repeat one or more characters, with each action set at a different time (and possibly location). The interior of a mid-fifth-century cup shows six deeds of Theseus in the circular frieze, and a seventh in the central tondo **(Figure 9.8)**. In each case Theseus is repeated, signaling that we have a new major action at a different time than the scenes on either side. Five of the scenes take place on his way to Athens, while the scene with the bull of Marathon in the bottom of the cup takes place after his arrival, as does the Minotaur episode in the tondo. Since each of his opponents is different, there is a sequence of both time and place on this cup. The figures in the scenes overlap, and this lack of visual division gives the name **continuous** narration to this composition. Turning to the metopes of the Athenian Treasury from the last chapter **(see Figure 8.7, page 189)**, we find some of the same scenes, but now each composition is framed in its own panel. This approach with separate framed scenes is called **cyclical** narration, but features the same approach to character, time, and space as continuous narrative.

continuous narrative
narrative image in which multiple scenes are set in a continuous frieze or picture, repeating some of the participants from one scene to the next

cyclical narrative
narrative image in which multiple scenes are set in separate panels or pictures, repeating some of the participants from one scene to the next

As we have seen, there are objects and buildings featuring multiple scenes that do not belong to a single story but are from different narratives. The metopes of Temple C in Selinus/Selinunte depicted a variety of gods and heroes, some in narrative scenes and others not **(see Figure 8.6, page 188)**, but the thematic connection between them is debated, as we saw in the last chapter. The narratives on one side of the François Vase depict stories connected with members of Achilles's family **(see Figure 8.23, page 203)**. From top to bottom these are the Calydonian boar hunt, featuring his father Peleus next to Meleager going head to head with the boar; the funeral games hosted by Achilles for his dead friend/lover Patroklos; the wedding of Achilles's parents, Peleus and the goddess Thetis; and finally Achilles attacking the Trojan prince Troilos at the beginning of the Trojan War.

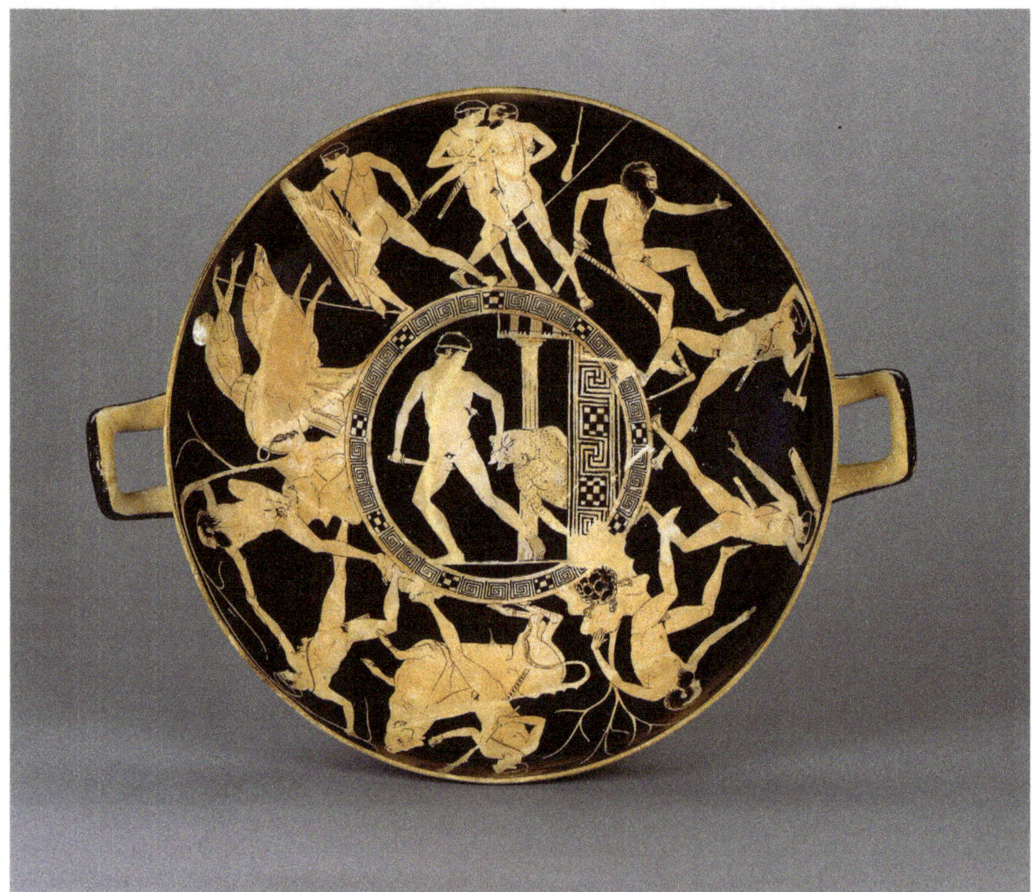

9.8 Attic red-figure kylix attributed to the Kodros Painter, *c.* 440–430 BCE. 13 in (33 cm) diameter. London, British Museum E84. Deeds of Theseus: clockwise from top: Kerkyon, Prokrustes, Skiron, Marathonian Bull, Sinis, and Kremmyon Sow; tondo: Minotaur. Photo: © The Trustees of the British Museum.

The theme here could be the heroic pedigree and accomplishments of Achilles, which would be suitable for a wedding reception, as has been suggested for this krater (Stewart 1983). There are many pictures on objects, however, that have no apparent connection, or only the vaguest link, such as "gods" or "heroes." The scene on the other side of Exekias's amphora showing the suicide of Ajax, for example, has two youths departing on a chariot with onlookers, which has no discernible direct connection to the other side of the pot.

When looking at pictorial narratives, we have to think about the single picture and how it structures action, time, and place. We can then consider additional pictures or scenes on the object or building and how they connect to each other narratively, thematically, or not at all.

VIEWING CONTEXT

Narrative pictures do not exist in isolation but as part of an artwork that exists within a context. The physical properties of an artwork impose conditions on what a viewer can see at one time and the order in which one sees other parts. What someone is doing, and where, while looking at one or more pictures also affects the viewer. In this section we will consider the potential effect of context on a viewer's experience of a narrative.

First, we shall consider the function of an object and its physical interaction with the viewer. For example, the kylix with the scene of Kirke and Odysseus **(see Figure 9.6)** is for drinking wine. The drinker would hold the cup by the foot or handle, probably below eye level like the symposiasts in

Figure 5.20 (page 119) or **Figure 5.21 (page 120)**. In this position, one could not see the entire picture, only its upper section. Only when the cup is empty could one readily hold it up to view the picture more clearly, either before the wine is poured, while getting a refill, or after drinking. The cup held by Kirke is located at the center, where one would put one's lips to drink from the real kylix. It is a playful irony, then, that the sailors have already turned into animals after drinking from Kirke's cup, and we could consider the placement of Kirke's cup to be a reminder to the drinker of the power of Dionysos's gift, to bring euphoria but also chaos. The scene on the kylix's other side holds a similar caution, showing Polyphemos in the center getting drunk on wine provided by Odysseus, which will lead to the hero blinding the Cyclops after he passes out.

Other guests in the room would be able to see the picture on the other side of a cup since it would be tilted when drinking, whereas only the drinker could see an interior picture, such as the Theseus scenes in **Figure 9.8**. Viewing them, however, would not be for long since the cup would have to be quickly leveled after sipping or risk spilling. The pictures, then, are only seen in glimpses and in motion over the course of a social occasion like the symposion. This actually makes the placement of the Minotaur scene a clever artistic choice, in that the picture would be covered with wine until drinking, when it would emerge before the viewer as Theseus emerges from the door of the dark labyrinth.

An artist can also use the three-dimensional quality of an object to emphasize a point about the narrative. In Chapter 5 we saw a skyphos that showed Penelope, the wife of Odysseus, seated in front of a loom with their son Telemachos (**see Figure 5.19, page 118**). Penelope's head rests on her hand in a pose that has been interpreted as brooding or pensive. Certainly she is in a difficult situation because of the demands of dozens of suitors for her to declare Odysseus dead and to pick one of them as her new husband. The other side of the cup shows Odysseus disguised as a beggar at the door to the house, having his feet washed by an old woman who was once his nurse (**Figure 9.9**). She realizes that the beggar is Odysseus by a scar on his leg from a childhood boar hunt, and she looks up at him in recognition. She is ordered to keep his identity a secret, as it is part of Odysseus's scheme to kill the suitors, who are armed and outnumber him and his son. The placement of the scenes on the skyphos means that the two scenes cannot be seen at the same time. While the viewer becomes aware that Penelope is to be reunited with Odysseus by turning the skyphos, she cannot see what is going to happen or realize that Odysseus has arrived.

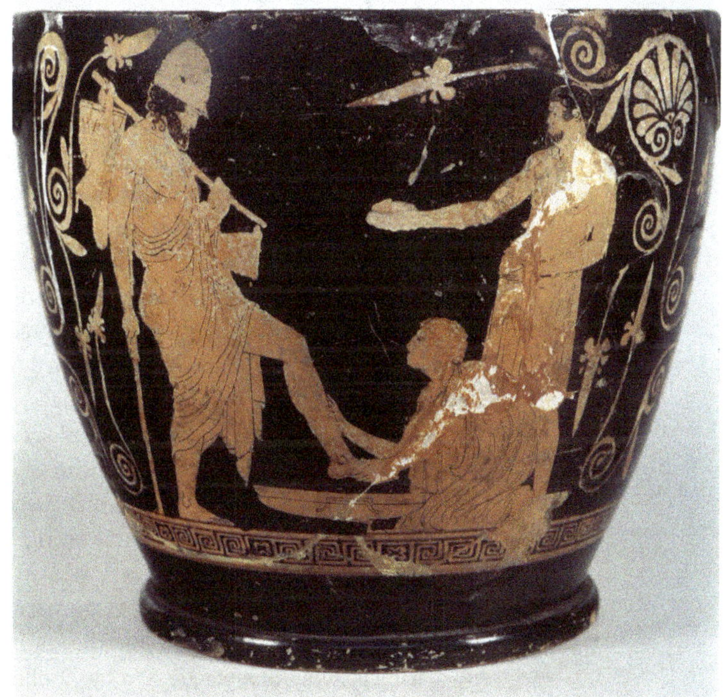

9.9 Attic red-figure skyphos attributed to the Penelope Painter, *c.* 450–440 BCE. 8 1/16 in (20.5 cm). Chiusi, Museo Archeologico 1831. Nurse recognizing Odysseus disguised as a beggar. Photo: Scala/Art Resource, NY.

These examples show that a viewer may only be able to see part of a narrative, and that its composition may be arranged to take advantage of that circumstance. We have already seen in architectural sculpture how the viewer can be engaged with the narrative by the position of the figures. On the Siphnian Treasury, the viewer is on the side of Achilles and the gods in the friezes above walking up the Sacred Way (**see Figure 7.15, page 171; Figure 8.1, page 183; Figure 9.1, page 212**). On the Parthenon frieze, the stages of the procession and ritual unfold as the viewer walks along the building, with both art and viewer heading toward the entrance to the naos on the east side of the building (**see Figure 1.1, page 2; Figure 10.15, page 250**). A viewer could also be put into the narrative itself, as is the case with the Tyrannicides set up in the Agora in 477/6 BCE (**see Figure 5.9, page 108**). This group shows a man (Aristogeiton) and youth (Harmodios) charging out of the crowd during the Panathenaia to slay the tyrant Hipparchos in the Agora. Standing in front of the statue, which is a primary viewing point and where the inscription would be read, the viewer is put into the position of the tyrant or crowd of the Panathenaic procession, and so becomes part of a reenactment of the original event and an actor in the drama.

These examples demonstrate that the kinds of activities in which viewers engage while looking at a visual narrative vary, from drinking at a symposion to a religious procession to conducting business in the agora. To these we can add a funerary context, which would include objects buried as grave goods, the commemoration of the dead by a tomb marker, and objects left as offerings at the tomb. A specific narrative scene, such as the blinding of Polyphemos, would not necessarily have the same meaning in a funerary context as it would in a symposion. Whereas the kylix with scenes of Kirke and Polyphemos reflects upon the symposion and drinking (**see Figure 9.6**), the same story on the Eleusis amphora (**see Figure 6.15, page 144**) would have to be interpreted in light of its use either as a grave marker, likely its original purpose, or as a burial container. We then have to consider attitudes toward death and the triumph of heroes, whose memory is perpetuated by the narratives of their deeds, as factors for interpreting a scene (Osborne 1988). Context, then, makes each narration, that is the telling and reception of the story, potentially unique.

ART AND LITERATURE

In this chapter and earlier we have had to summarize stories based on literary sources like the *Iliad* or *Odyssey* in order to analyze how the artist has chosen to construct the visual narrative. This is unavoidable for us, but it does create an interpretive problem. When comparing pictures and texts, there is a tendency today to look at images as illustrations of a text, rather than as narrative works in their own right. However, it is unlikely that any artist read a complete *Iliad* or other poem or play, or would have consulted texts when designing a picture, at least before the fourth century. The poems and plays that we have were performed publicly and so could have been known to both artist and viewer. However, in many cases the earliest narrative picture of a story predates the earliest literary version that survives, making problematic our use of later literary sources to explain early images. Indeed, both poet and artist developed their narratives from the vast repertory of stories belonging to Greek culture from the earliest days, and then altered these to create narratives that suited their purpose, sometimes with new details or actions. This means that the "facts" of some surviving literary accounts are not consistent with one another, or with the surviving pictorial narratives either. Unfortunately, the oral culture that sustained this rich narrative repertory is lost to us, so we must cautiously rely on literary sources while looking at the pictures but keep in mind that the artist did not rely on these same sources.

We can look at an example of the narrative differences between texts and images by turning to the beginning of the *Iliad* and the story of Briseis being taken from Achilles. To paraphrase, the Greek army is dying of a plague sent by Apollo, who is angry that the leader of the Greeks, Agamemnon, has taken as a war prize and concubine Chryseis, the daughter of the priest of Apollo. In order to save the army, he must give her back, an action that Achilles urges. Agamemnon, however, is angry at being without a war prize and so threatens to take the war prize of Achilles, Briseis. Achilles's anger leads him first to threaten Agamemnon and then to withdraw to his encampment, vowing not to fight anymore. Later, Agamemnon sends two heralds to take Briseis away:

> They [the heralds] went against their will beside the beach of the barren
> salt sea, and came to the shelters and the ships of the Myrmidons.
> The man himself they found beside his shelter and his black ship
> sitting. And Achilleus took no joy at all when he saw them.... (1.327–330)

[Achilles speaks to the heralds and orders Patroklos to fetch Briseis]
He [Patroklos] led forth from the hut Briseis of the fair cheeks and gave her
to be taken away; and they walked back beside the ships of the Achaians,
and the woman all unwilling went with them still. But Achilleus
weeping went and sat in sorrow apart from his companions
beside the beach of the grey sea looking out on the infinite water. (1.346–350)

(Homer, *Iliad*, tr. Lattimore)

The poet creates a vivid scene that emphasizes the anger and grief of Achilles together with the reluctant participation of the heralds and Briseis.

The scene is rarely shown in Greek art, but appears on a red-figure kylix in the British Museum **(Figure 9.10)**. On the left side of the picture we see the two heralds flanking Briseis and leading her away. On the other side of the cup, the trio is repeated, now reaching the tent of Agamemnon, an example of cyclical narrative with the handles dividing the scenes. This arrival scene, though, is not mentioned in the *Iliad*. As Briseis and the heralds exit to our left, the right half of the picture shows the tent of Achilles, with two wooden posts supporting a woven covering. Two adult men stand to either side, while inside is a beardless figure wrapped almost completely in a himation. The right hand grasps the front of the head in a gesture that is like the female mourners at a funeral pulling their hair **(see Figure 4.8, page 79 and Figure 5.26, page 125)**.

At first glance, considering this figure's heavy clothing, gesture, and placement inside the tent, one might think that this is a woman, thus Briseis, but it is rather Achilles. While Achilles sits outside the tent in the *Iliad*, placing him inside is an effective visual way for the artist to suggest the grief and tears of Achilles mentioned in the poem. There are no common visual precedents for a weeping man in art, so when trying to capture such a "non-masculine" and emotional mood in the character, the artist uses a visual vocabulary that suggests women grieving at a funeral to describe the hero's anger and loss. The artist has also borrowed from wedding imagery to show one of the heralds leading Briseis by the arm, another action not described in the poem. Since Briseis is to become Agamemnon's war trophy, the leading gesture signifies to the viewer that the woman is being led to a new situation that has aspects of marriage or concubinage about it. The destination tent on the

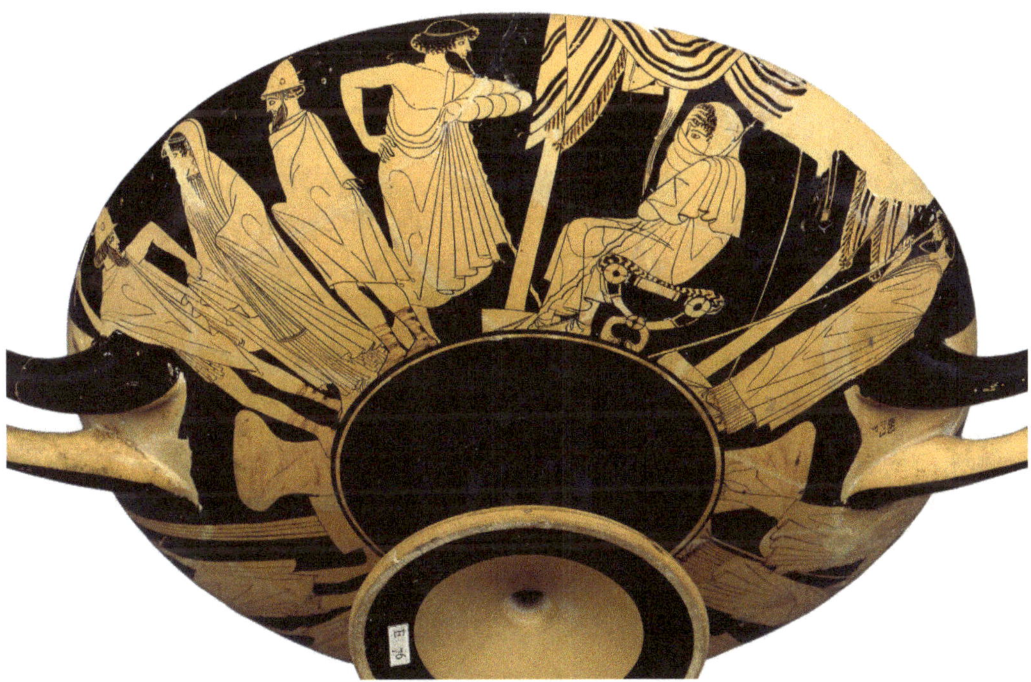

9.10 Attic red-figure kylix attributed to the Briseis Painter, *c.* 480 BCE. 11¾ in (30 cm) diameter. London, British Museum E76. Briseis led away from Achilles. Photo: © The Trustees of the British Museum.

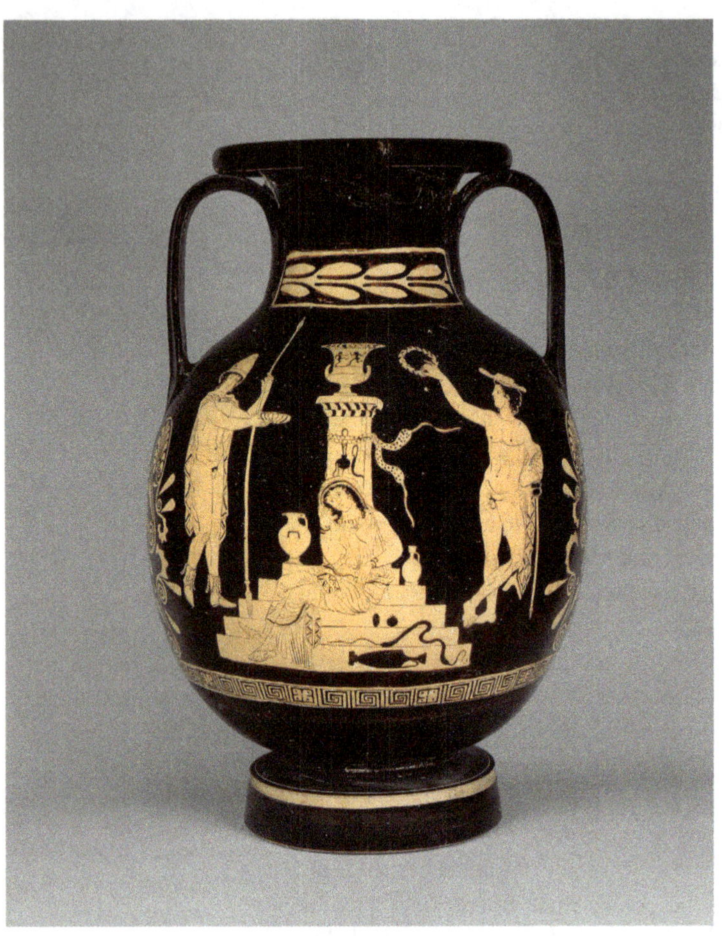

9.11 Lucanian red-figure pelike attributed to the Choephoroi Painter, *c.* 350 BCE. 16¹⁵/16 in (43 cm). Paris, Musée du Louvre K544. Elektra and Orestes at tomb of Agamemnon. Photo: © RMN-Grand Palais/Art Resource, NY.

other side is a further reference from wedding processions, in which the house of the groom is the destination. It is possible, given the rarity of the scene, that the artist may have been inspired by a performance of the *Iliad* in representing this story, but there might be other sources or reasons, whether literary or having to do with contemporary culture or circumstances. Regardless of the source of inspiration, the painter uses a visual language, in particular funerary and wedding imagery, that is independent of whatever textual sources were known either to the artist or to the viewer and creates an autonomous pictorial narrative. The wrath of Achilles is strong, and the atypical composition of the narrative captures that point.

Although dramatic performances in Athens were a key element of fifth-century Athenian culture, they are very limited instances of the direct influence of a play on the representation of a narrative in vase painting. There are, however, some vase paintings that appear to be inspired by dramas in fourth-century southern Italy. Interestingly, this was also a period and place where dramas first produced in fifth-century Athens by poets such as Aeschylus, Sophocles, and Euripides were revived on local stages. Some of these south Italian vases, which we will discuss more broadly in Chapter 12, seem to be related to surviving plays, although we have to consider that it is the performance of the play rather than the text which might be the source. For example, a Lucanian pelike attributed to the Choephoroi Painter and dated to about 350 BCE recalls the opening scene of Aeschylus's play *Libation Bearers* (*Choephoroi*) **(Figure 9.11)**. In the opening scene of the play, set at the tomb of Agamemnon, we see his son Orestes visiting the tomb with his friend Pylades. They hide when Orestes's sister Elektra comes to bring her own offerings to the tomb. She notices that someone else has been there and discovers a lock of hair that is like hers. After this Orestes steps out and reveals himself to her, as well as his plot to avenge their father's death.

The pelike shows a three-step tomb with a pillar on top. On the pillar is a krater and on the steps are a hydria and lekythos, for washing the tomb and leaving an offering of oil. Ribbons and an athlete's strigil and aryballos are tied to the pillar. Earlier offerings appear to be scattered on the ground and lower steps. Elektra is in front of the tomb, but rather than standing to make an offering, she is seated on the steps with her head in her hand like Penelope **(see Figure 5.19, page 118)**. This pose, which is found in representations of Penelope in fifth- and fourth-century art, would be well known to viewers and would evoke Elektra's isolation and forlorn hope. This is a good visual choice for Elektra, who has to live in the household of her adulterous mother and uncle Aigisthos, lovers who murdered her father. The appearance of Orestes, as yet unknown to her, will be her deliverance. The painter has made use of three-dimensional representation of the picture space to show Orestes with a phiale, unseen behind and to the side of the tomb in the landscape background. While all of this can be related to the play, Pylades and an attendant for Elektra are missing. The male figure on the right is not Pylades but Hermes, as identified by his **kerykeion** and hat. Hermes does not appear in the play, although he is invoked in the opening speech of Orestes: "Hermes, lord of the dead, who watch over the powers of my fathers, be my savior and stand by my claim" (Aesch., *Cho.* 1–2, tr. Lattimore). Visually, the painter effectively represents the

kerykeion
the wand held by Hermes or a herald, topped by a closed circle and open circle at its top. Also called the *caduceus* in Latin

act of making an offering while invoking a god's help by showing Orestes holding the phiale, while Hermes, unseen by either Orestes or Elektra, offers a wreath toward the tomb of Agamemnon as if to fulfill the plea.

All of the pictures that can be associated with this scene in south Italian pottery show some degree of variation from the play and each other (Taplin 2007, 49–57). Perhaps the revival of older plays stimulated an interest in paintings showing selected scenes, making a closer connection between art and literature than is typical. But even here in the late classical period, paintings are still adaptations that draw upon motifs known to viewers through other visual narratives, like the pose of Penelope, to convey a specific sense of the narrative.

There are some pots that more self-consciously show a play as it is being performed, but these are usually comedies. For example, the krater painted by Asteas in Poseidonia/Paestum shows two actors in padded costumes, fake phalluses, and masks pulling at the legs of an old miser who clings to a chest containing his hoard (**see Figure 12.21, page 310**). The figures stand on an elevated platform with columns in front, like the front of a stage, and a door to the side leads off stage. This is unlike the circular orchestra of the Greek theater, like that at Epidauros (**see Figure 12.3, page 291**), and perhaps represents a different type of local performance setting.

CHOICE OF MOOD AND MOMENT

With this last example, we can also consider the genre or mood of a visual narrative. Comic narrative is clearly intended to amuse, and can take various forms such as satire and parody, visual puns, exaggeration, and slapstick. Most of the narratives we have seen are more serious and straightforward. Pictorial narrative can also emulate some of the features of dramatic tragedies, involving sudden changes of situation and a focus on the choices of the characters rather than strenuous action, such as the scene at the tomb of Agamemnon in **Figure 9.11**. We might also include more universalizing scenes such as the departure of a warrior, warriors fighting, or a marriage scene as a genre of narrative as well.

Judging from the plays and other testimony, comedy was very popular both as a theatrical medium and in poetry. Identifying humor in art is difficult, in that comic devices such as puns are harder for us to recognize or understand today. The dress of comic actors (**see Figure 12.21, page 310**) provides a cue to us that there is a comic rather than serious narrative intent, but we should consider that comedy could be created by pictures through the demeanor of the figures and the choice of moment shown.

One way to identify a comic narrative would be through its contrast to more standard representations of a scene. For example, we saw earlier Kirke transforming the sailors of Odysseus as the hero charges toward her in a straightforward synoptic narrative (**see Figure 9.6**). There is a trace of irony, given the context of the symposion, since Kirke's cup doubles for the actual cup in the hands of the drinker/viewer, but the scene itself is not particularly comic in its action. Another representation of the scene, on a late fifth-century, black-figure skyphos from Boeotia, is quite different (**Figure 9.12**). The deep cup is one of many examples that are connected to the sanctuary at Cabiros, called Cabiran Ware, that feature a much more caricature-like style than contemporary red-figure pottery from Athens. On the right is a loom, a symbol of domesticity that we saw in the Penelope skyphos (**see Figure 5.19, page 118**), but in the case of Kirke it is somewhat deceptive given her powers. She holds out a skyphos and wand toward Odysseus on the left. Both faces have exaggerated eyes, noses, and mouths like the masks of the actors on the Paestan krater, and Odysseus has a fake enlarged phallus as well. As in other representations of the story, Odysseus has charged in with a drawn sword, but now he is stopped in his tracks and stumbles backwards, defying the expectations of the viewer. Rather than being in control of the

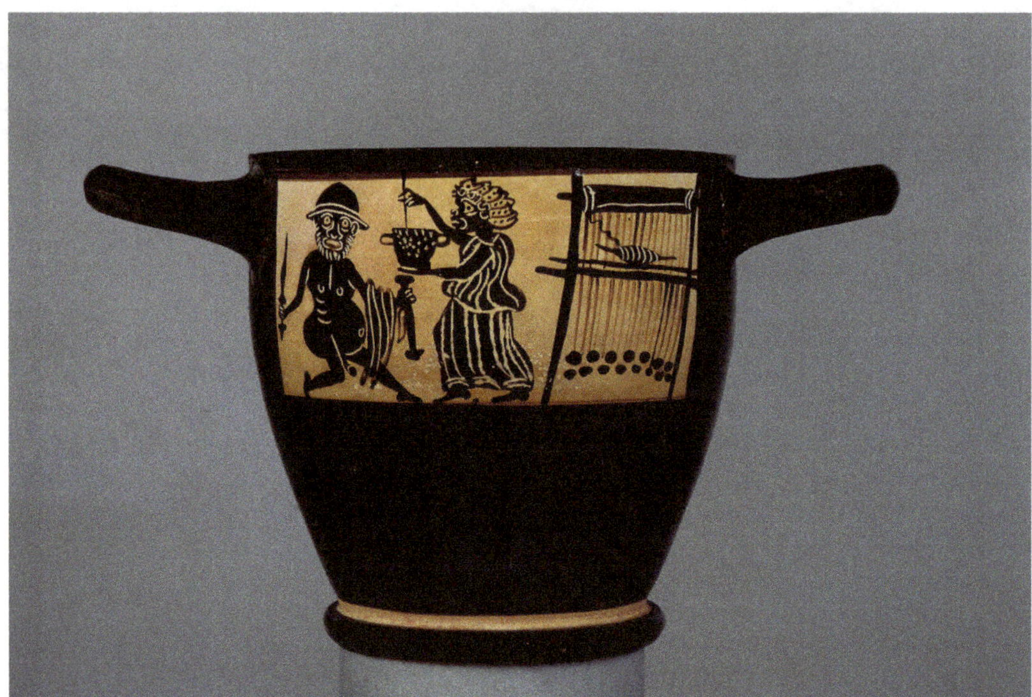

9.12 Cabiran black-figure skyphos, late 5th cent. BCE. 6¹⁄₁₆ in (15.4 cm). Oxford, Ashmolean Museum G.249. Kirke and Odysseus. Photo: Ashmolean Museum/The Art Archive at Art Resource, NY.

situation, Odysseus is rebuffed by an unarmed woman. We are not entirely sure about the nature of the Cabiran mysteries, but it is possible that they involved humor and satire that ridiculed heroes or gods.

Satyrs are good for humorous antics as well **(see Figure 11.8, page 277)**, and can be effective for satire by mocking the behavior of heroes and gods. A red-figure chous, a special pitcher used in the Anthesteria festival of Dionysos that celebrated the new year's new wine, shows a satyr with a club and cloak attacking a snake in a tree **(Figure 9.13)**. Rather than fruit, the tree bears pitchers like the chous itself. The scene is a parody of Herakles getting the apples of the Hesperides from a tree guarded by a dragon, one of his twelve canonical labors (Walsh 2009, 238). The satyr's club is an attribute of Herakles, so the satyr is substituting for the hero, but attacking a curious snake rather than a hostile monster. Instead of apples, the satyr desires the wine of the chous pitchers in the tree and is willing to endure this "heroic" trial for his prize. His pose is heroic and muscular, but his satyr head hardly fits with the heroic body, and the prize is not the means to immortality that are the apples.

For a tragic narrative mood, we might look for pictures that concentrate on a moment of decision. For example, we saw that Exekias's version of the suicide of Ajax **(see Figure 9.5)** was quite different from much archaic narrative, in that Exekias represented the moment of decision to take action by planting the sword, rather than the more climactic result of lying on the sword that is more typical of representations of the story. Although Exekias worked before the time when drama first developed, attributed to Thespis in the later sixth century, Exekias's composition could be called tragic in mood by focusing on choice and character rather than climactic action.

We see a similar approach to the story of Pelops and Oinomaos on the east pediment of the Temple of Zeus at Olympia, dated to 470–457 BCE **(Figure 9.14)**. This is not a common subject for Greek narrative art, but it is appropriate for the Temple of Zeus at Olympia. The basic story is that there was a prophecy that Oinomaos, king of nearby Pisa, would be killed by his son-in-law. He tried to prevent this by challenging all suitors to a chariot race in which he would give a head start to the suitor, but would kill him if he caught up. Since he had horses provided by Ares, this gave him an advantage and so far a number of suitors had died. Pelops was successful, and in the race Oinomaos lost his life, leaving the kingdom to Pelops (who also gave his name to the southern peninsula of Greece, the Peloponnesos). Since the city of Elis had defeated Pisa for control of the sanctuary in 470 and began the temple immediately afterward, featuring the race that the king of Pisa had lost would be an appropriate subject symbolizing the victory of Elis.

Our literary sources have different reasons as to why Pelops won. In Pindar's account (*Olympian* 1), our earliest version dating to 476 BCE and hence before the temple was started, Pelops was given horses by Poseidon, a former lover; with these he was successful in neutralizing the unfair advantage of Oinomaos. A slightly later version, *c.* 440, by the Athenian mythographer Pherekydes, states that Pelops bribed Myrtilos, charioteer of Oinomaos, to sabotage the wheel of Oinomaos's chariot, causing it to fall off during the race and precipitate the king's death. Pelops later killed Myrtilos when he tried to collect the bribe, and the charioteer called a curse down on the family. Certainly the family of Pelops was cursed. Atreus, the oldest son and Pelops's successor, killed the children of his brother Thyestes, serving them to their father in a stew, apparently because Thyestes plotted to overthrow Atreus by sleeping with his wife. Thyestes was exiled along with his remaining son, Aigisthos. The curse continued into the next generation when Agamemnon, the son of Atreus, sacrificed his daughter Iphigeneia to sail to Troy. While he was away, his wife Klytaimnestra slept with Aigisthos and together they plotted to murder Agamemnon on his return. Finally, the son of Agamemnon, Orestes, acting on the word of Apollo, killed his uncle and mother but was set upon by the Furies, who were finally appeased by the intervention of Athena. The story of the house of Agamemnon is the subject of a trilogy composed by Aeschylus in 458 BCE that serves as a foundational story for trial by jury in the polis. With such a legacy, the oath of Pelops and Oinomaos at Olympia and its interpretation become entangled in the competing versions of the oath and its aftermath.

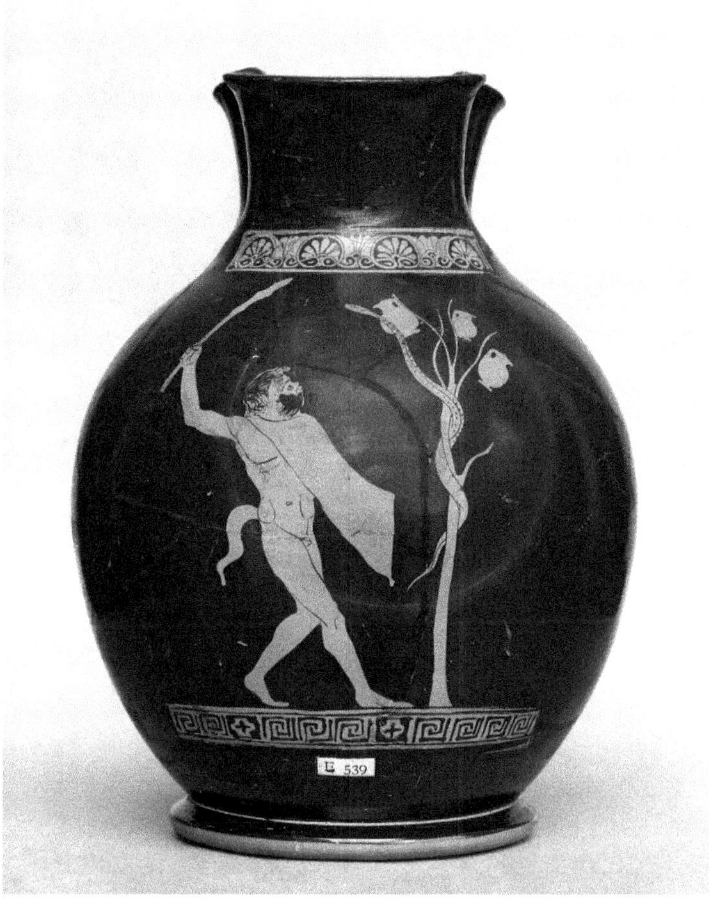

9.13 Attic red-figure chous attributed to the Group of Berlin 2415, *c.* 460 BCE. 9½ in (24.1 cm). From Capua. London, British Museum E539. Satyr attacking tree with jugs (mocking Herakles and apples of Hesperides). Photo: © The Trustees of the British Museum.

The sculpture at Olympia was found dispersed across the site during the excavations there, and controversies persist to this day regarding the placement of the figures and determining the narrative direction. The identity of the five main figures seems well established, and we will discuss the composition as it appears in the current installation in the museum at Olympia. In the center stands Zeus, at a larger scale than the mortals around him. Before him, on our left, king Oinomaos of Pisa sets out the terms of a race, while Pelops listens to our right. Oinomaos is bearded whereas Pelops is not, and so is designated the senior figure. Flanking Oinomaos is his wife Sterope, mother of Hippodamia, who stands next to Pelops and pulls at her mantle in a gesture associated with the *anakalypsis*, the revealing of the bride in marriage. On either side of the central group are the chariot teams being readied by the attendants for the race. Beyond them are two seated figures who are seers; the one on the right, called the Old Seer, holds his hand to his face and has opened his mouth in what is seen as a gesture of concern. Personifications of the river gods lie at the corners of the pediment.

anakalypsis
the gesture in the wedding in which the bride unveils herself to the groom. In art this is typically seen as a reference when a woman pulls her mantle away from her face or shoulder

Looking at the pediment, the emphasis is not upon the race but upon the oath taken by the participants beforehand setting out the terms. Oinomaos's pose is strident and has been seen as

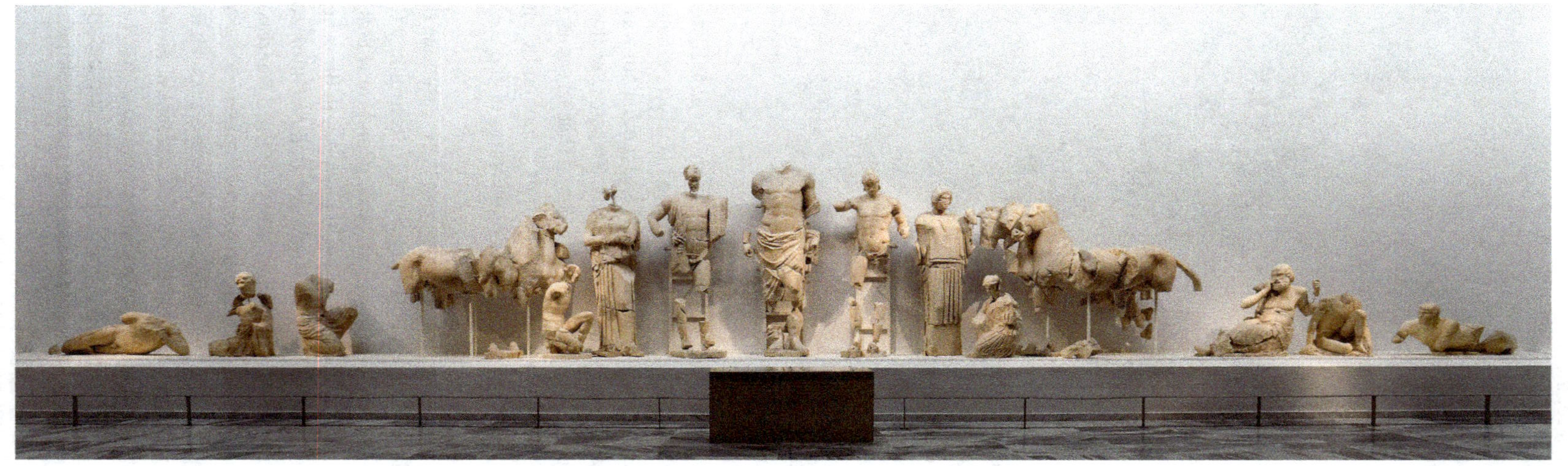

9.14 East pediment of the Temple of Zeus at Olympia, *c.* 470–457 BCE. Height of central figure: 10 ft 2 in (3.1 m). Olympia Museum. Oath of Pelops and Oinomaos. Photo: © Vanni Archive/Art Resource, NY.

arrogant, particularly as he is attempting to defy a divine prophecy and is also denying the opportunity for an heir to the kingdom by preventing the marriage of his daughter. Whether Pelops is competing fairly or not is hard to say based on what we see. The Old Seer is certainly expressing concern at what he sees. A viewer could read this as shock at Oinomaos, who will die, Pelops, who may be cheating, or at both for violating or intending to violate their oath. Whatever the case, it is the oath that is the important action of the narrative. Zeus, as arbiter of oaths, becomes central in overseeing the consequences of the action.

The ritualistic context of the temple also helps to explain why the oath would be an appropriate narrative, in that the open area in front of the temple is where the Olympic athletes swore their competition oaths (**see Figure 7.3, page 158**). In either version of the story, Oinomaos has been cheating by having divine horses, and his eventual demise is the consequence of his false oath. Given that the Temple of Zeus was built by the Eleans, who had defeated the nearby Pisans for control of the sanctuary, this makes Pelops's triumph over Oinomaos a metaphor for the Eleans' victory over the Pisans. As Judith Barringer has pointed out, it is not likely that the Eleans would suggest that Pelops, too, cheated, as he was worshipped at the site (Barringer 2008, 51–52). However, by focusing on the moment of decision rather than the consequent action, it is possible for a viewer to regard Pelops in the same light as Oinomaos and give a very different direction to the story, one that encompasses the many murders that plague the house of Pelops. Ultimately, the viewer has to fill in the gaps of the narrative to develop a reading of the story, whatever the original intentions of the designers may have been.

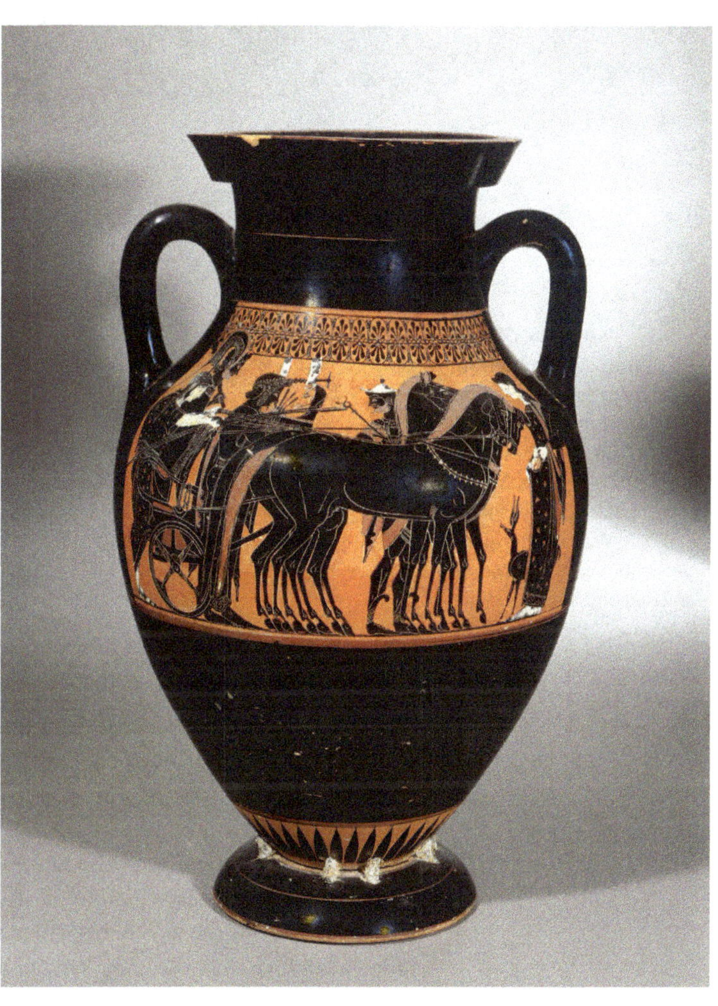

9.15 Attic black-figure amphora from the heroön at Poseidonia/Paestum, attributed to the Chiusi Painter, *c.* 510 BCE. 22⅞ in (58 cm). Paestum, Museo Archeologico Nazionale 133153. Apotheosis of Herakles. Photo: Scala/ Ministero per i Beni e le Attività culturali/Art Resource, NY.

SYMBOLIC AND UNIVERSAL ASPECTS OF NARRATIVE

In looking at Greek narrative, we have to think not only about the immediate story and viewing circumstances, but also about the symbolic value of narrative for contemporary culture and events. Whereas there were many decisive events in Greek history, such as the battles of the Persians and Greeks, Athenians and Spartans, the sack of Athens in 480 BCE, and others, rarely did Greek artists show these events as narrative pictures. Rather, battles such as those of the Lapiths and Centaurs, the Greeks and Amazons, the Trojan War, and the Gigantomachy served sometimes as metaphors for historical events. To end this chapter, we will explore some of the symbolic value of Greek narrative art and consider its appeal to a non-Greek audience like the Etruscans.

An Attic black-figure amphora with a scene of the apotheosis of Herakles was discovered in Poseidonia/Paestum just north of the agora (**Figure 9.15**). It and eight bronze vases were excavated in a roofed, rectangular chamber that was dug into the ground within a temenos (**see Figure 5.3, page 103**). Inside the vases had been placed around a stone platform with remains of

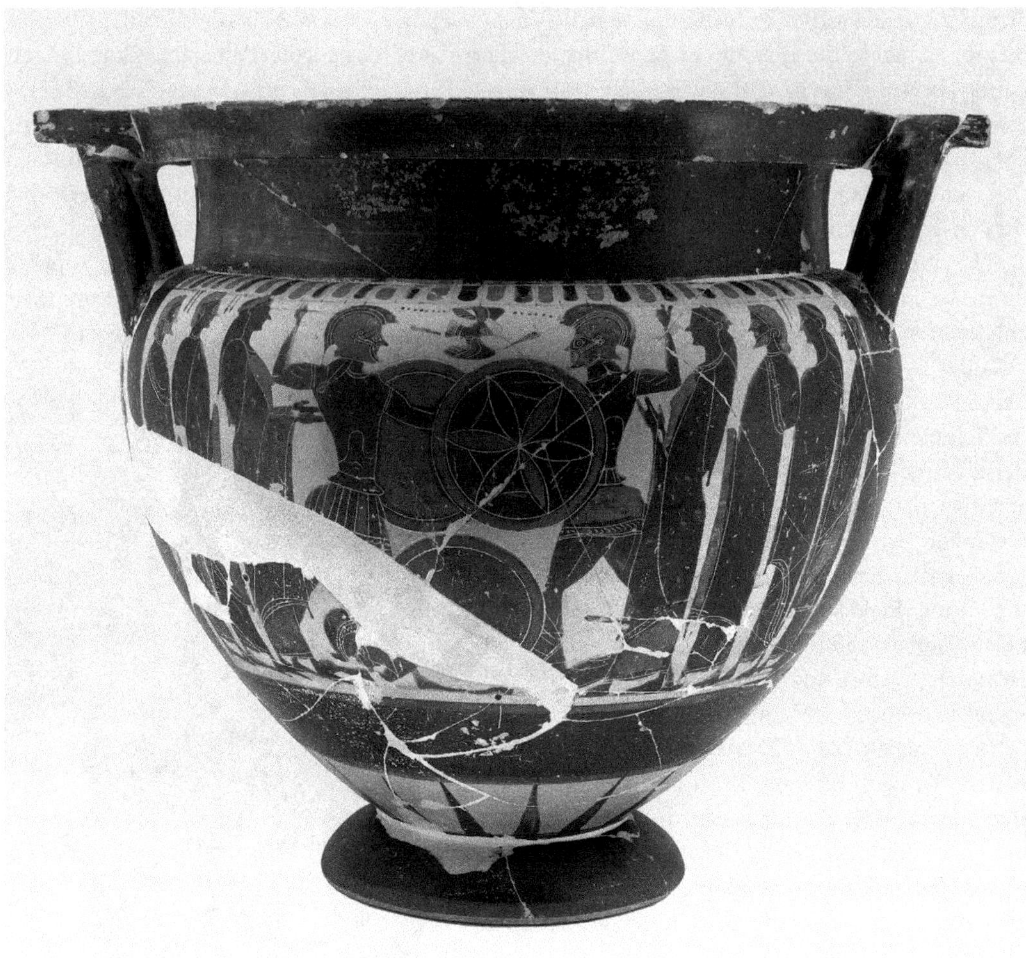

9.16 Attic black-figure column krater, mid-6th cent. BCE. From the Tomb of the Panathenaic Amphorae, Orvieto. Florence, Museo Archeologico Nazionale 22203. Warriors fighting. Photo courtesy Museo Archeologico Nazionale, Florence.

iron, cloth, and lead, possibly the remains of a bed or couch. There is no inscription to identify the chamber or its dedication, but it is thought to be a heroön, built as a tomb but without a body, perhaps in honor of a founder of Poseidonia/Paestum or its mother city, Sybaris. Some of the bronze vessels contained offerings of honey sealed with wax, but the subject of the single figured amphora is symbolically interesting. As a reward for his assistance to the gods and for his heroic deeds, Herakles was granted immortality and married to the goddess Hebe. In the sixth century scenes of the apotheosis, or deification, of Herakles became common in Athenian art, following a formula of Athena driving him in a chariot. This subject becomes particularly meaningful within the context of the Poseidonia/Paestum heroön, since its dedicatee was honored by the citizens of the town as a deified hero, who lives on through their veneration and memory, as does Herakles. It is not always possible to hypothesize a symbolic connection between a narrative and context, but it is important to remember that narrative could function as a metaphor, relying upon its symbolic value to link the present with the past.

Another vase, an Attic black-figure column krater, was found in an Etruscan tomb in Orvieto, the Tomb of the Panathenaic Amphorae (**Figure 9.16**). On one side of the vase is a scene of a warrior departing, a theme we will examine below. The other is a universal scene of two warriors fighting over a fallen warrior who lies at their feet. There are a few dots in front of the warriors' helmets that look a bit like inscriptions, but these are anonymous warriors like those on the Middle Geometric skyphos from Eleusis (**see Figure 9.2, page 213**). Clearly the artist could have provided an attribute or inscription if necessary, but we can consider what value it might have to leave the subject ambiguous. The vase was exported from Athens around the middle of the sixth century, about two decades after the François Vase **(see Figure 8.23, page 203)** when foreign markets, especially in Etruria, had become an important outlet for Attic painted pottery. Orvieto was a common destination for such pottery, but it is well inland from the coast, making transportation of such a large vessel to its destination an added effort and expense.

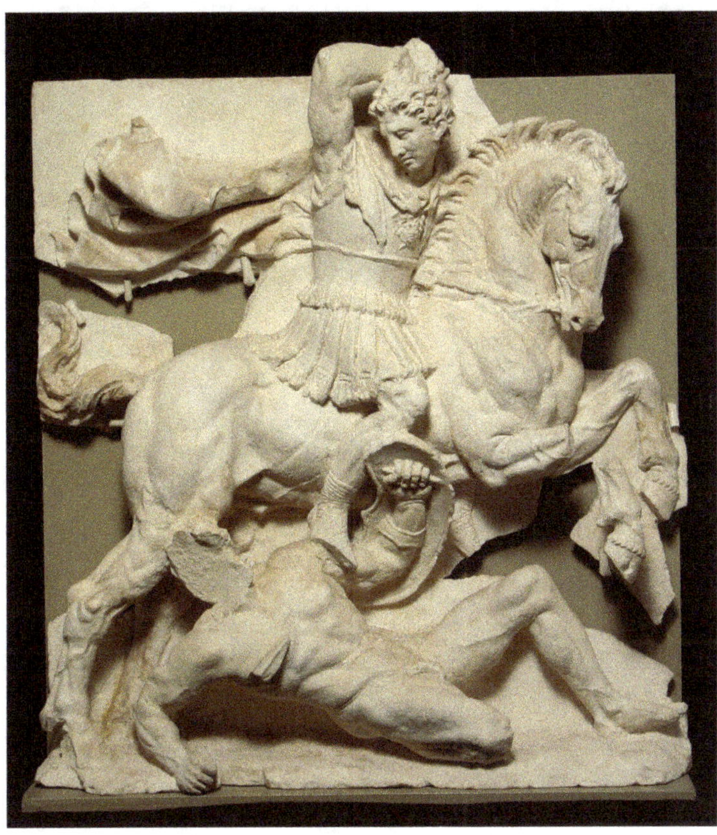

9.17 Metope of Naiskos Tomb from Via Umberto, Taras/Taranto, 300–250 BCE. Taranto, Museo Archeologico Nazionale 113768. 20¼ in (51.5 cm). Battle scene with rider. Photo: Museum.

As we have noted in Chapter 8, Attic pottery did distinguish itself by representing a very large number of narrative scenes that were otherwise unavailable in competing wares. Mythological pictures would have had an appeal, particularly for Etruscans who had some familiarity with Greek mythology, but the images could have had a broader attraction. Even if a scene like the warriors fighting on this krater was not transformed into a mythological scene like Achilles and Memnon by the addition of inscriptions, as on the Siphnian Treasury, the action itself would have had value for the deceased and the family. Just as in Greek cities, members of a household would leave for war and fight in battle. Actual battles did not feature the duels represented in most battle scenes like this. The focus on elite warriors fighting conferred a heroic scale on the anonymous figures for the viewer. As if to reinforce this, the warriors are watched by a variety of spectators: adult men, youths, and women, the members of the city who would witness and remember the deeds of a city's soldiers. Vases such as this might have been used in a household as part of the Etruscan equivalent of the symposion and then placed into the tomb in honor of the deceased. In either case, the narrative picture mirrors on a heroic scale the actions of its users and culture, a symbolic value that would appeal to both Greek and non-Greek viewers according to their situation.

Many of the action scenes in Greek pottery are not specific subjects, like the deeds of Herakles, but are formulaic and can represent the action of an individual within a more universal setting. For example, the third-century metope from a tomb in Taras/Taranto shows a warrior on horseback attacking a fallen soldier **(Figure 9.17)**. The rider is shown in armor and gear like a real cavalryman, but the opponent is nude except for his shield. This is a formulaic battle composition that was common in art from the sixth century onward and can also be seen in another work, the cenotaph of Dexileos from 394/3 BCE **(see Figures 12.12 and 12.13, pages 301, 302)**. The metope in Taras/Taranto is one of six combats on the tomb, but none shows details that would link them to a specific individual or battle. Indeed, the inscription for Dexileos's monument tells us that he died fighting, so the triumphant rider in battle is not a true-to-life representation of Dexileos in battle either. Rather, the triumphant rider composition creates a heroic narrative for the deceased that becomes, like a kouros or kore figure, an idealization of the individual. We might call narrative representations such as this universalizing, in that rather than showing specific contemporary events, a heroic formula symbolizes the achievements of the deceased.

Indeed, many if not most of Greek narrative pictures are similarly universal. The body of a red-figure krater of the middle of the fifth century shows a young man in armor and cloak and holding a spear, reaching out to touch the hand of a woman who holds a second spear and helmet **(Figure 9.18)**.

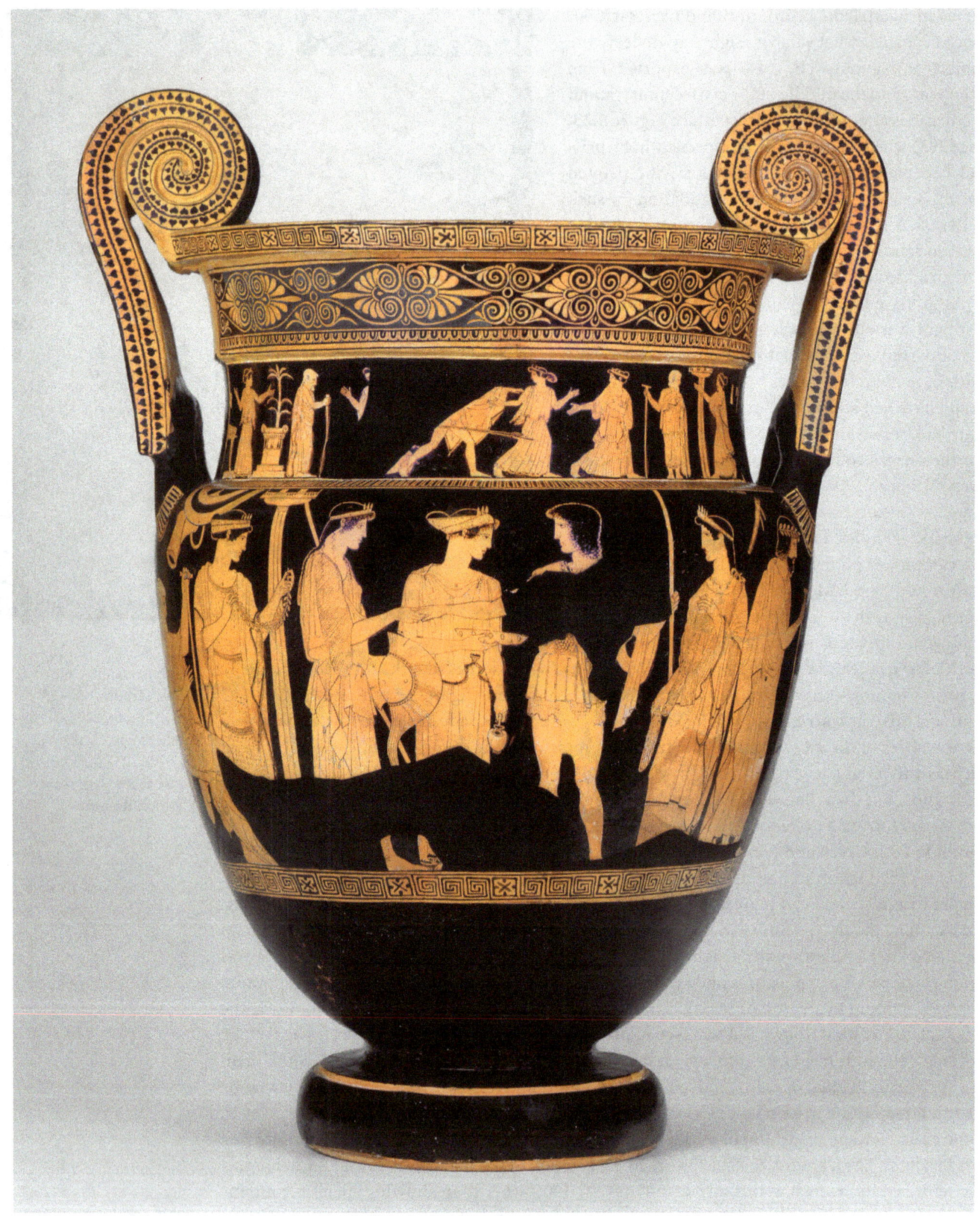

9.18 Attic red-figure volute krater attributed to the Niobid Painter, *c.* 460 BCE. 26¾ in (68 cm). Boston, Museum of Fine Arts 33.56. Body: departure of warrior; neck: Peleus pursuing Thetis. Photograph © 2014 Museum of Fine Arts, Boston.

Between them is another woman holding a phiale and oinochoe to pour a libation. Other women and an old man seated at the far left look on, while an adult man wearing a wreath walks away. The scene shows the warrior's departure from his home to fight in the army. The women might include a wife, mother, sister or other relations, while the old man could be his father, or grandfather if the departing man is the head of the household. The ages and relationships of the figures are ambiguous, but this is part of the appeal of the narrative composition for the viewer. In purchasing such a vase, whether to use in a symposion or to put into a tomb as a grave good, the owner can identify these idealized figures according to his or her particular circumstances. Most men who owned such a vase as this would have fought in the army and participated in a departure ceremony, although not as rich or elaborate as this one, as would most of the women in a family. Making a pot like this for export, the painter uses narrative scenes that can become specific through the actions of the viewer/owner of the vase.

Turning back to the battle scene on the Middle Geometric skyphos from Eleusis **(see Figure 9.2, page 213)**, itself a grave good, we can understand even these simple action pictures of the Geometric period in the same way, as idealized and universal narratives that show the story of actual lives in a heroic, timeless way. In looking at hunting scenes **(see Figure 6.11, page 141)** or wedding scenes **(see Figure 13.4, page 326)**, we should consider how the narrative represents the *ethos* or character of its participants, and, by extension, the *ethos* of the viewers or recipients of the work. Context, then, shapes the results or "readings" of the narrative, even to the present day.

TEXTBOX: INTERPRETATION AND INFORMATION THEORY

The traditional approach to analyzing the meaning of a work of art, called iconography, involves analysis of the actions, attributes, and characters in an image and, consulting literary sources for the story, the development of an interpretation of a scene. In cases where our literary sources are vague or nonexistent, as with the scene of Achilles and Ajax playing a game **(see Figure 8.24, page 204)**, we are left to consider the story or its meaning based mostly on the image itself. In some cases, iconography can yield competing theories, particularly when the literary sources are fragmentary or contradict the image. For example, the Parthenon frieze has long been associated with the Panathenaic procession, but there are discrepancies between participants in the image and what we learn from literary sources, all of which are much older. An alternative theory was proposed by Joan Breton Connelly based on fragments of a play by Euripides, arguing that the central scene **(see Figure 10.15, page 250)** shows the daughters of Erechtheus preparing to sacrifice themselves to save the city from an invasion (see Connelly 1996, 2014). This theory has generated considerable controversy in the scholarship, particularly as it involves human sacrifice.

Given the limitations in our sources and considering artists as independent storytellers, alternative approaches to meaning have been developed that can supplement iconography (see Stansbury-O'Donnell 2011, 57–109). One example is Ann Steiner's use of information theory for "reading" Greek vases (Steiner 2007). This is based on understanding how, in language or communication, humans can filter out the noise of a signal to identify a message or intention. In particular, information theory focuses upon various forms of repetition in a message to create a structured and meaningful communication. Repetition signals an intentionality or pattern for decoding a message, and can also be used to emphasize specific parts of the message as important.

This is a useful framework for looking at narrative images, especially when considering that an Athenian vase painter was usually making an image on a vase for export, whether to a Greek colony or to a non-Greek people like the Etruscans. An effective narrative depends not only upon the creation of the narrative image, but also upon its successful recognition and reception. Since storyteller and viewer may not share a common language or set of stories, a successful narrative would depend upon the inclusion of enough signals for some type of story to be conveyed, even if the artist's intention and the viewer's understanding diverged. Repetition in an image can help the viewer, as can repeated exposure to the story on multiple objects. In the case of Ajax and Achilles playing a game, many images of which were exported to Etruria, the continued production of such scenes shows us that it was a successful story that continued to be of interest in the market. Thus it can provide a key for understanding the reception of the narrative image by the ancient viewer.

REFERENCES

Aeschylus, *Choephoroi*. 1953. In *Oresteia: Agamemnon, The Libation Bearers, The Eumenides*, tr. R. Lattimore. Chicago: University of Chicago Press.

Barringer, J. M. 2008. *Art, Myth, and Ritual in Classical Greece*. Cambridge/New York: Cambridge University Press.

Connelly, J. B. 1996. "Parthenon and Parthenoi: A Mythological Interpretation of the Parthenon Frieze." *American Journal of Archaeology* 100, 58–80.

Connelly, J. B. 2014. *The Parthenon Enigma*. New York: Alfred A. Knopf.

Davies, M. 1986. "A Convention of Metamorphosis in Greek Art." *Journal of Hellenic Studies* 106, 182–183.

Homer, Iliad. 1951. *The Iliad of Homer*, tr. R. Lattimore. Chicago: University of Chicago Press.

Hurwit, J. M. 1982. "Palm Trees and the Pathetic Fallacy in Archaic Greek Poetry and Art." *Classical Journal* 77, 193–199.

Hurwit, J. M. 1983. "Professor Hurwit Replies." *Classical Journal* 78, 200–201.

Madden, J. D. 1983. "The Palms Do Not Weep: A Reply to Professor Hurwit and a Note on the Death of Priam in Greek Art." *Classical Journal* 78, 193–199.

Osborne, R. 1988. "Death Revisited, Death Revised: The Death of the Artist in Archaic and Classical Greece." *Art History* 11, 1–16.

Stansbury-O'Donnell, M. D. 2011. *Looking at Greek Art*. Cambridge/New York: Cambridge University Press.

Steiner, A. 2007. *Reading Greek Vases*. Cambridge/New York: Cambridge University Press.

Stewart, A. 1983. "Stesichoros and the François Vase." In W. Moon, ed. *Ancient Greek Art and Iconography*, 53–74. Madison: University of Wisconsin Press.

Taplin, O. 2007. *Pots and Plays: Interactions between Tragedy and Greek Vase-Painting of the Fourth Century* B.C. Los Angeles: The J. Paul Getty Museum.

Walsh, D. 2009. *Distorted Ideals in Greek Vase-Painting: The World of Mythological Burlesque*. Cambridge: Cambridge University Press.

FURTHER READING

Carpenter, T. H. 1991. *Art and Myth in Ancient Greece*. London: Thames and Hudson.

Giuliani, L. 2013. *Image and Myth: A History of Pictorial Narration in Greek Art*, tr. J. O'Donnell. Chicago/London: University of Chicago Press.

Junker, K. 2012. *Interpreting the Images of Greek Myths*, tr. A. Künzl-Snodgrass and A. Snodgrass. Cambridge: Cambridge University Press.

Mitchell, A. G. 2009. *Greek Vase-Painting and the Origins of Visual Humour*. Cambridge: Cambridge University Press.

Shapiro, H. A. 1994. *Myth into Art: Poet and Painter in Classical Greece*. London: Routledge.

Small, J. P. 2003. *The Parallel Worlds of Classical Art and Text*. Cambridge/New York: Cambridge University Press.

Snodgrass, A. 1982. *Narration and Allusion in Archaic Greek Art*. Eleventh J. L. Myres Memorial Lecture. Oxford: Leopard's Head Press.

Squire, M. 2009. *Image and Text in Graeco-Roman Antiquity*. Cambridge: Cambridge University Press.

Stansbury-O'Donnell, M. D. 1999. *Pictorial Narrative in Ancient Greek Art*. Cambridge/New York: Cambridge University Press.

Steiner, A. 2007. *Reading Greek Vases*. Cambridge/New York: Cambridge University Press.

Taplin, O. 2007. *Pots and Plays: Interactions between Tragedy and Greek Vase-Painting of the Fourth Century* B.C. Los Angeles: The J. Paul Getty Museum.

10

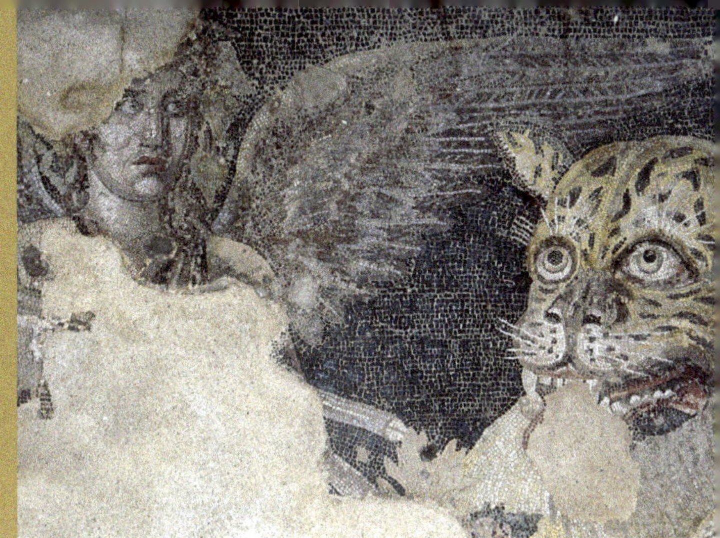

THE FIFTH CENTURY

(*C.* 480–400 BCE)

Timeline

Architecture, Architectural Sculpture, and Relief

The Acropolis at Athens

Late Fifth-Century Sculpture

Painting

Textbox: The Parthenon Marbles and Cultural Patrimony

References

Further Reading

A History of Greek Art, First Edition. Mark D. Stansbury-O'Donnell.

TIMELINE

	Architecture	Sculpture	Painting	Events
480–450	Temple of Aphaia at Aigina, after 480 Temple of Zeus at Olympia, 470–457	Kritios Boy, *c.* 480 Tyrannicides, 477/6 [5.9]* Artemision God, 460 [1.7]	Attic RF hydria by Kleophrades Painter, 480 Tomb of the Diver, 470 Attic RF krater by the Niobid Painter, 460 Sotades Painter Cup, 460–450	480 Sack of Athens, Battle of Salamis 479 Battle of Plataia 462–451 Athens fighting Sparta 454 Removal of Delian Treasury to Athens 450 Peace treaty with Persia
450–430	Parthenon, 447–432* Propylaia, 437–432	Doryphoros, 450–440 Parthenon metopes, 447–442* Parthenon frieze, 442–438* Parthenon pediments, 437–432*	Attic WG lekythos by Achilles Painter, 440	Perikles as leader of Athens; peace with Persia and Sparta
430–400	Erechtheion, 431–404 Nike Temple, 430–420	Nike of Paionios, 420 Nike Temple parapet, 420–410	Attic RF epinetron by Eretria Painter,425–420 Attic WG lekythos by Reed Painter, 420–400	431–404 Peloponnesian War 429 Death of Perikles

*Works for which an absolute chronological date can be suggested.

As we saw in Chapter 8, the archaic kouros and kore statues became considerably more naturalistic in their appearance by the early fifth century. Whereas the torso of the kouros of Pytheas and Aeschrion is modeled to make it look more lifelike **(see Figure 8.11, page 192)**, the pose is still symmetrical (with the exception of the slightly advanced left leg), the structure of the face is still spherical, the eyes protrude from the skull, and he still bears the archaic smile. While not truly a smile in the sense of being an expression of joy or pleasure, it makes the face mask-like and prevents the viewer from reading the facial expression for signs of the figure's emotions or thoughts. Around 480 BCE, we can see a changing conception of the human figure in art, one that mimics in stone, bronze, or painting both the physical movement and the emotional expression of the human body. Aeschylus uses the term ***mimesis*** in one of his satyr plays to describe the image of a satyr that is being presented as a votive offering by a "real" satyr: "This imitation [*mimema*] of Daidalos lacks only a voice … It would challenge my own mother! For seeing it she would clearly turn and [wail] thinking it to be me, whom she raised. So similar is it [to me]" (tr. Morris 1992, 218). The idea behind mimesis is that the image both resembles the object it is imitating and can evoke a response in the viewer akin to seeing the real thing (Stansbury-O'Donnell 1999, 111–114). Thus the experience and engagement of the viewer are transformed in fifth-century art, along with the appearance of the human figure.

mimesis
the imitation or representation of an object in a work of art so that it resembles the original model

Severe Style
a style of the early classical period that, while more lifelike than archaic art, was characterized by simplified body features and less ornamental surfaces

contrapposto
representation of the human figure showing the shifting and balancing of weight, usually with the weight borne on one leg and the other leg bent

We can see an early example of the more naturalistic treatment of the movements of the human figure in a half life-size statue from the Acropolis called the "Kritios Boy" **(Figure 10.1)**. The statue is named after the sculptor Kritios, who along with Nesiotes made the bronze originals of the Tyrannicides in 477/6 BCE that has some stylistic similarities to the youth, even in the Roman copies preserved today **(see Figure 5.9, page 108)**. The doughy quality of the cheeks and flesh, in particular, has led to the term **Severe Style** being applied to the works of the early classical period, *c.* 480–450.

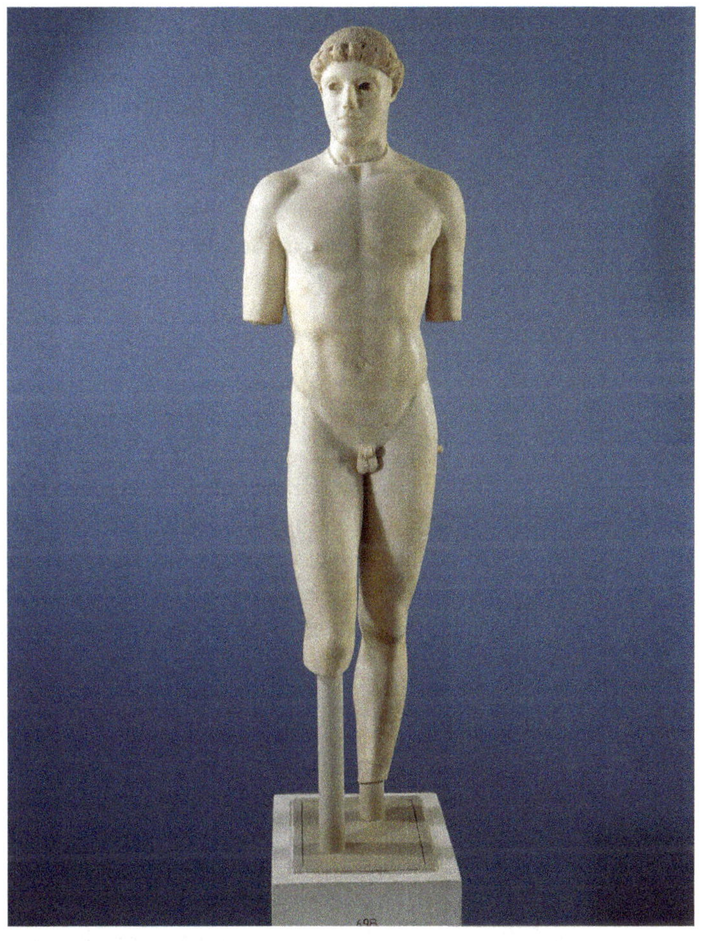

10.1 "Kritios Boy," after 480 BCE. Marble, 33⅞ in (0.86 m). Athens, Acropolis Museum 698.
Photo: Marie Mauzy/Art Resource, NY.

The most striking difference in the Kritios Boy from the kouros is the pose. Instead of the left leg being advanced, the left leg here is positioned directly under the torso while the right leg is forward and is bent at the knee rather than straight like a kouros. In a human body this would mean that most of the weight of the body would be on the straight left leg, rather than evenly distributed on two feet. The pose is typical of the way that humans stand and move around, unlike the stiffer posture of the kouros. While this shifting of the weight to one limb seems straightforward, anyone who has watched an infant learn to stand and then to walk realizes how complex are the adjustments in the human body to maintain balance. To represent the dynamic balance of a standing figure, the sculptor has had to make many small adjustments in the composition of the body. The hips are not level, with the figure's right hip lower compared to the left. The plane defined by the shoulders is not parallel to that defined by the buttocks, and the figure's right shoulder is slightly lower and brought forward, resulting in a slight torsion or twisting of the boy's torso to his left while his head turns slightly to the right. The result is a figure represented as actively standing, perhaps ready to take a step. This effect of balanced movement and counter-movement is usually labeled with the Italian term ***contrapposto***.

There are also differences between the Kritios Boy and the kouros in the rendering of the head. The mouth is now set in a more neutral position and the lips seem firmly closed as if the boy is consciously not speaking or reacting to what he sees. The cheeks are smoothed out, and the eye sockets (once filled with inset eyes) are truly recessed into the skull as they are in life. Along with the slight turn of the head, the eyes seem to be looking out into his surroundings and have the potential to react to what he sees.

The precise date of the Kritios Boy is uncertain. The statue was damaged not long after it was set up on the Acropolis in Athens; wear along the break between neck and torso suggests it lay exposed for a while. It was later buried in the construction trenches made during the Periklean rebuilding of the Acropolis starting around 451 BCE, as were many other statues like the kore of Euthydikos discussed in Chapters 7 and 8 **(see Figure 7.18, page 175)**. Whether the Kritios Boy was destroyed when the Persians sacked Athens and the Acropolis in 480 or was set up after the return of the Athenians in 479 and damaged not long afterward is undeterminable, but the later scenario seems more likely (Hurwit 1989). The issue may seem relatively unimportant, but the destruction of Athens caused a break in its artistic production followed by a surge in rebuilding and new artistic projects. Was the classical style associated with the Kritios Boy already being developed before 480, or was it an innovation that belongs to the rebuilding of the city? To push the question further, was the classical style developed gradually out of the archaic, or was its development sudden? The kore of Euthydikos already shows elements of simplification that belong to the new style, but its pose does not have the complexity of the Kritios Boy. If it and the Kritios Boy belong after 480, as Andrew Stewart has argued, then the Kritios Boy may indeed reflect an innovative change (Stewart 2008a, 2008b).

The issue is more than simply a question of periods and boundaries. In labeling the naturalistic and idealized style of the Kritios Boy "classical," we use a term that designates more than a time period and has several simultaneous layers of meaning – historical, stylistic, and qualitative – as we discussed in the textbox to Chapter 4 (see page 95). As Cicero's mini-history of Greek art mentioned in Chapter 1 suggests (see pp. 1–4), viewers recognized that these new statues were losing their "hardness." But whereas the Greeks used *archaios* or archaic to describe material from the seventh and sixth centuries, they themselves did not designate succeeding works as "classical" and we should be careful to recognize that there was no uniform standard that ruled art in this period. For the artists making and the viewers looking at "classical" art, it was contemporary art that was full of variations and new features, not unlike preceding periods.

The Tyrannicides **(see Figure 5.9, page 108)** reveal another important aspect of mimesis and the relationship between the work of art and the viewer in fifth-century art. The Tyrannicides are shown in action, stepping forward to attack and kill the tyrant Hipparchos. As we saw in the last chapter, this statue group creates a narrative tableau that engages the viewer in the story, either as a spectator or, from a certain position, as a stand-in for their target. This engagement of the viewer in the action is different from archaic sculpture, and we can consider that the *contrapposto* pose of the Kritios Boy also creates a potential for action and involvement different from the kouros. Indeed, as Richard Neer has argued, this narrative quality of classical sculpture is one of its key distinguishing features (Neer 2010).

We should not conclude that the archaic style stopped overnight. The sculptures from the Temple of Aphaia on Aigina, an island just south of Athens, have long been regarded as late archaic works that dated before 480 BCE. The temple had two pediments, the east showing the first sack of Troy under Herakles and the west showing the sack of Troy under Agamemnon. Based on stylistic analysis, the archaic features of the west pediment figures, like the smile and twisted pose of the fallen warrior in the right corner, have caused that pediment to be dated between 500 and 480 **(Figure 10.2)**. The figures were brightly painted, as seen in the reconstruction by Vinzenz Brinkmann, which gives a vivid sense of the richly colored korai and relief sculpture of the sixth century **(Figure 10.3)**. By comparison, the fallen warrior from the east pediment is a more convincing representation of a mortally wounded soldier who struggles to move and live **(Figure 10.4)**. This led to the hypothesis that the east pediment group is about a decade later than the west, but still probably before 480.

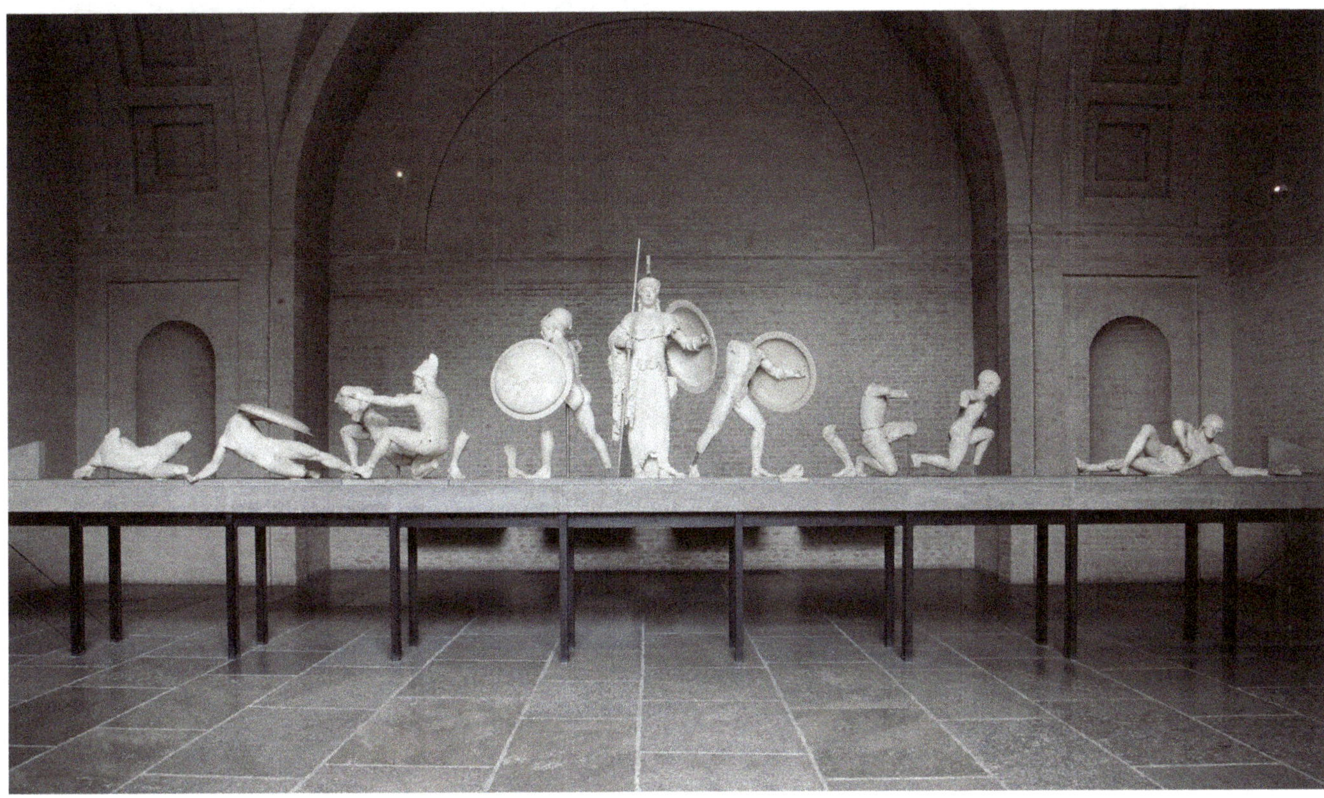

10.2 West pediment from Temple of Aphaia at Aegina, after 480 BCE. Height of pediment 5 ft 7¾ in (1.72 m). Munich, Glyptothek. Photo: © Vanni Archive/Art Resource, NY.

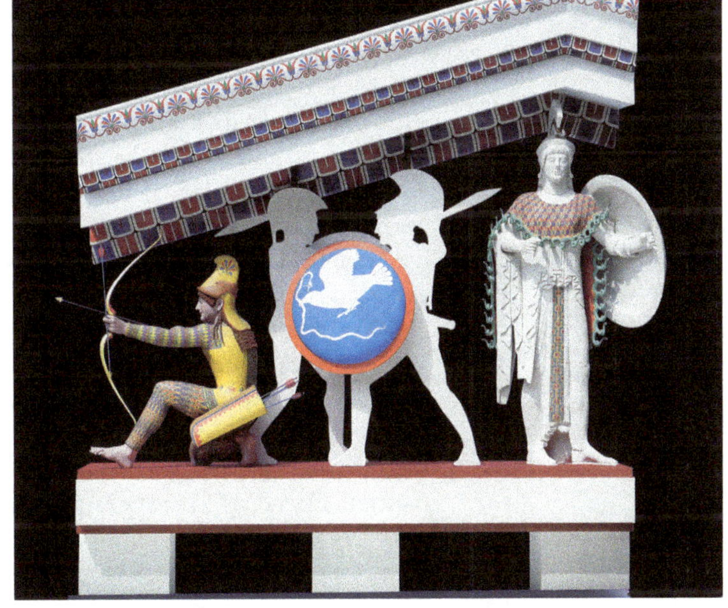

10.3 Color reconstruction by Vinzenz Brinkmann of archer (W11), warrior (W9), and Athena (W1) from west pediment of the Temple of Aphaia at Aegina. Munich, Glyptothek.

Recent review of the excavation of the temple's foundations, however, has led Andrew Stewart to argue that the building was constructed after 480 BCE and that both pediments must be nearly contemporary with or slightly later than the Tyrannicides and Kritios Boy (Stewart 2008b, 2008c). Indeed, Stewart has suggested that the stylistic differences between the east pediment and the west are divergent reactions to the work of Kritios and Nesiotes in nearby Athens, and do not indicate a difference in time. Comparing the fallen warriors in the two pediments does reflect a change in the viewer's engagement between the two groups. The west fallen warrior, on the far right of the pediment in **Figure 10.3**, looks straight out into space, like archaic architectural sculpture **(see Figure 8.6, page 188)**. The east warrior (**Figure 10.5**), however, looks down and turns his head outward, so that a viewer standing below in front of the temple entrance would look up and make eye contact with the figure. While the pose and anatomy of the east warrior are more life-like, they still have some archaic elements; it is the engagement with the viewer that most clearly signals a different relationship between image and viewer. Of course, such viewer engagement was not an invention of the classical period, as we saw heads turned toward the viewer in the Siphnian Treasury a half-century earlier **(see Figure 9.1, page 212)**, but in the classical period it becomes a dominant mode of presentation.

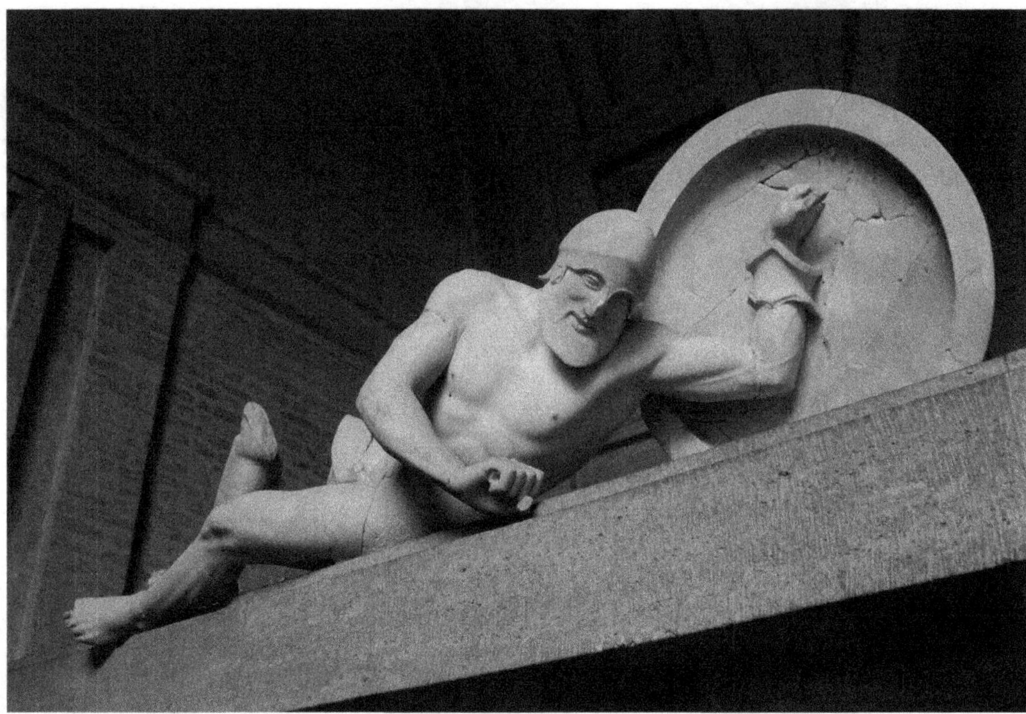

10.4 Fallen warrior (E11) from east pediment of the Temple of Aphaia at Aegina, after 480 BCE. Munich, Glyptothek. Photo: author, used by permission.

This engagement with the viewer can also be seen in one of the rare monumental bronze statues that survive from this period, a god found in the sea at Cape Artemision **(see Figure 1.7 and Figure 1.8, pages 11, 12)**. The figure, standing 2.09 meters high (about 6 ft 10 in), is more than a head taller than a normal person and its scale can be described as heroic, or larger-than-life, typical of monumental works found in sanctuaries or public spaces like an agora. This work is representative of the early classical style; there is still a stiffness in the figure when compared to later fifth-century works, as we shall see. Compared to the Kritios Boy and Tyrannicides, however, there is more subtlety in the representation of movement or *rhythmos*, and a greater awareness of optical effects. The left arm of the figure is actually about a hand-length too long, but when seen from the front, the foreshortened angle makes the arm appear more normal in proportion but highly dramatic in the vector that it creates. Indeed, this statue was probably meant to be viewed from the front, so that the weapon/attribute that was once held in the throwing hand would be pointed toward the viewer. Like the Tyrannicides, this statue confronts the viewer with an action, and can even implicate the viewer as the target that the god, likely Zeus, is measuring with his gaze and outstretched left arm.

Two other bronzes were found in the sea off the coast of southern Italy and are now called the Riace Warriors **(Figure 10.5)**. The size, pose, and anatomical structure of the figures are virtually duplicates and were probably made with master molds formed from the same original model (Mattusch 1996, 64). In making these bronzes, the interior of the master mold, made of fired terracotta, would be lined with wax and then liquid clay to create a new working model. Surface details, such as the bulges of muscles and tendons, would be carved in the wax. This wax/clay working model would then have pins and wax channels set for pouring and venting and be placed inside a new clay container called the investment. When the molten bronze is poured, it dissolves the wax and fills the space where the wax used to be. With statues like these, the figure was cast in several pieces and then soldered together. In the case of the Riace Warriors, the wax surface of the working model was more articulated and defined on warrior A than on B, but it is the differences in the heads that really distinguish the figures for the viewer. Warrior B has a smooth domed skull where a helmet rested; his mouth is closed and neutral and his head tilted slightly to his right, as if he were listening. Warrior A's head is turned more sharply to his right; his mouth is open and teeth are showing as if he were speaking to a group.

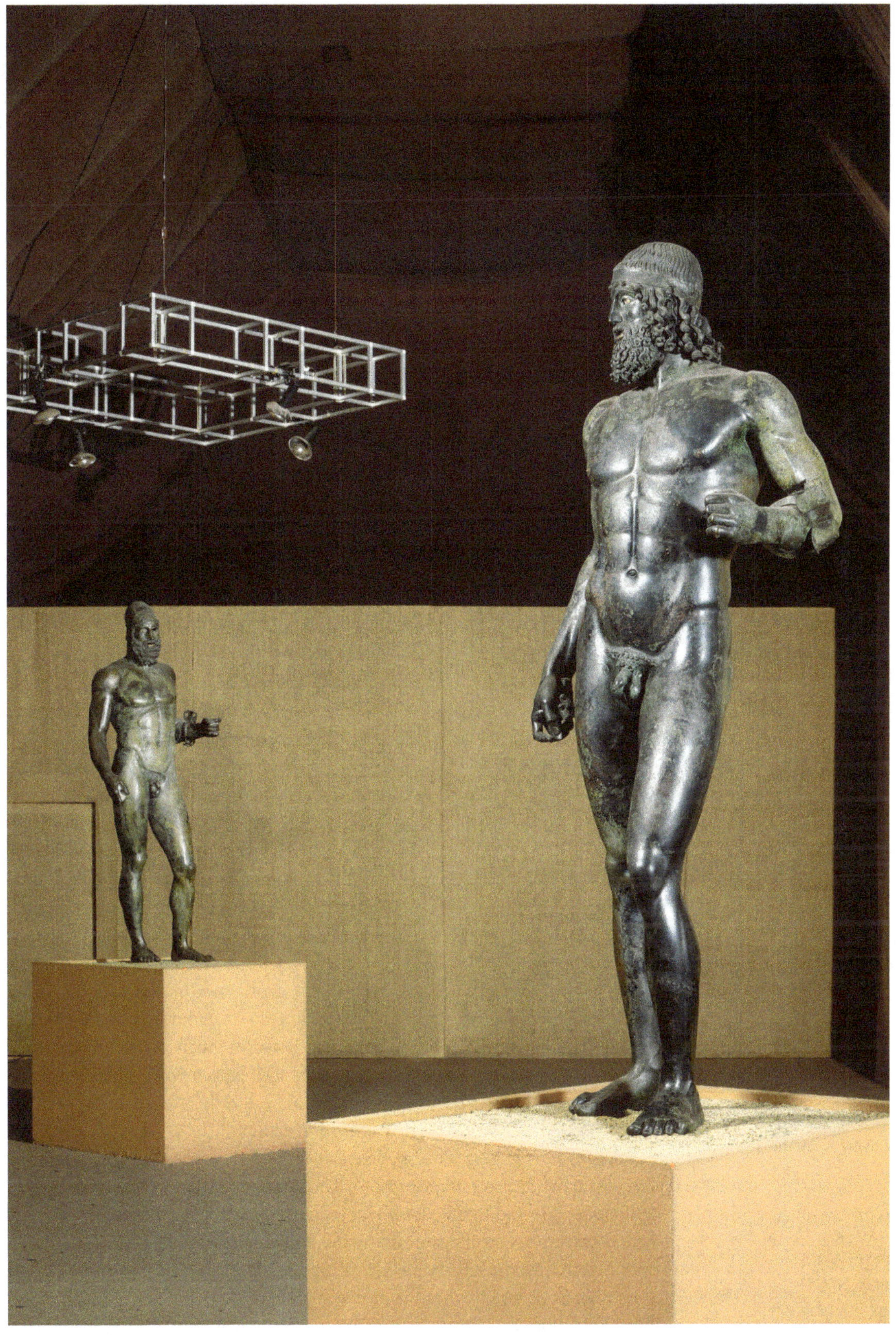

10.5 Riace Warriors A (right) and B (left), *c.* 460–450 BCE. Bronze, 6 ft 5½ in and 6 ft 6 in (1.97 m and 1.98 m). Reggio di Calabria, Museo Archeologico Nazionale. Photo: Scala/Art Resource, NY.

neoclassical or neoclassicizing
a style that imitates the qualities of fifth- and fourth-century classical sculpture but is produced in later periods like the Hellenistic

With few comparanda in bronze and without an original context, the identity and dating of the works are hypothetical. Most scholars date the works to just before 450 BCE, but there is a proposal that these statues are **neoclassical** works made in the first century BCE, and not fifth-century originals, an issue we will address in the textbox in Chapter 14 (see pp. 378–379). Regardless of date, the two statues were most likely part of an ensemble showing a scene such as a debate among heroic warriors. Several such fifth-century groups are described by Pausanias at both Olympia and Delphi, and presumably the statues were being taken from somewhere in Greece to Rome, possibly as loot, when they were lost at sea. For a spectator standing and observing this group in its original setting, it is as if one were a member of the Greek army, listening to a debate among the leaders, who tower over everyone because of their heroic scale (and being set on a base). The figures are like the actors on a stage performing a drama, and it is indeed during this period that tragedy, performed by two and then three actors with a chorus, became an important new literary medium.

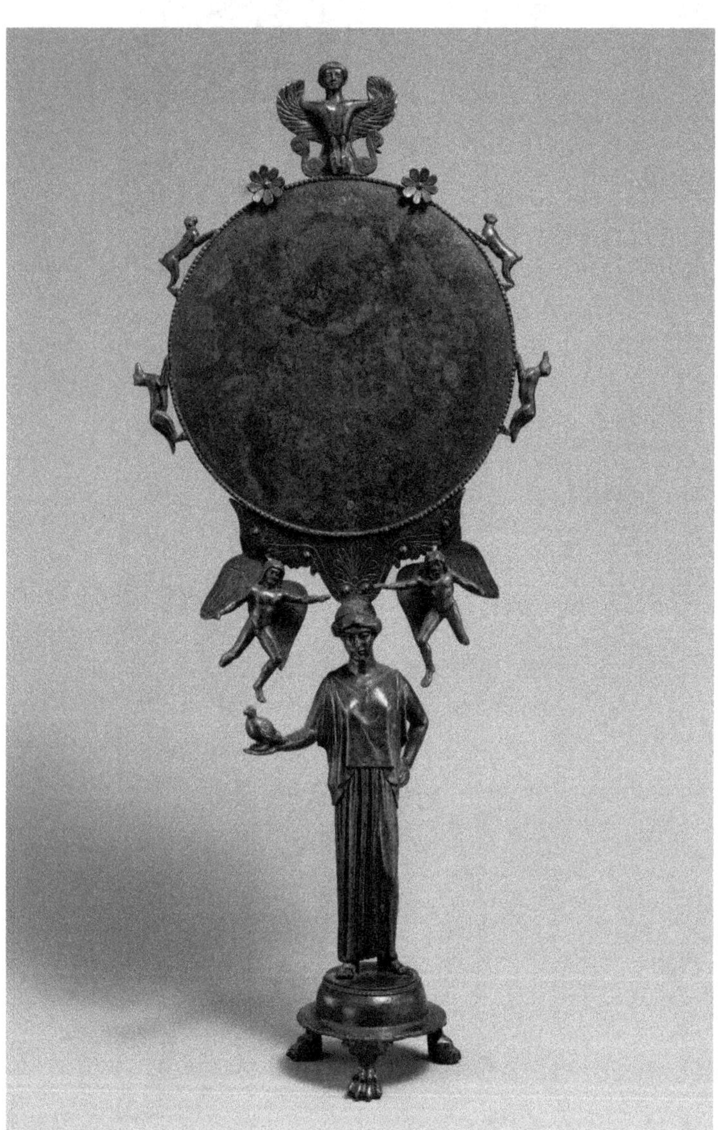

10.6 Argive caryatid mirror, mid-5th cent. BCE. Bronze, 15 15/16 in (40.4 cm). New York, Metropolitan Museum of Art, bequest of Walter C. Baker, 1971, 1972.118.78. Photo: Image copyright © The Metropolitan Museum of Art. Image source: Art Resource, NY.

Looking at the Artemision god and Riace bronzes, we can see that Greek sculptors had by 450 BCE mastered the ability to show *rhythmos*. They were also more adept at showing through gesture and facial expression the emotional state of the figure, its ***pathos***, and differentiating their attitudes. This ability to represent both physical and psychological movement gave artists the opportunity to express the character of a figure, its *ethos*. This was of particular importance for narrative art, as we saw in the last chapter with the *Iliupersis* scene by the Kleophrades Painter **(see Figure 9.7, page 219)** and the contrast between the heroic Theseus and his less noble opponents on the Kodros Painter cup **(see Figure 9.8, page 220)**. Contemporary playwrights such as Aeschylus and Sophocles were also interested in showing the *ethos* of their characters, as revealed by their words, choices, and actions. Looking at the Riace Warriors, one wonders if the speaking figure does not also display some sense of anger or arrogance, like the figure of Agamemnon in contemporary drama. Without a specific context or knowledge of the identity of the figures, however, such readings remain speculative, although the expectation would have been for the viewer to discern the character of the subject through pose and action.

The stylistic changes in large-scale sculpture also appear in smaller bronze and terracotta works, such as an Argive caryatid mirror **(Figure 10.6)**. The woman here wears a heavy **peplos**, rather than the combination of chiton and mantle found on many archaic korai. The drapery falls in fewer folds but they are more asymmetric and responsive to the body underneath the clothing. The woman is set in a *contrapposto* pose with the left knee bent, causing the fabric to pull and smooth against her leg. The feet are set at an angle and the head is turned slightly to her right, in the direction of the bird in her hand. The *erotes* move as vigorously as those on the archaic mirror in **Figure 8.19 (page 201)**, about a half-century earlier, but their bodies and heads are turned more toward her. The face has lost its stiffness and smile and appears more contemplative and engaged while making her offering.

The Doryphoros, or Spear-Bearer, of Polykleitos was a bronze statue created in Argos around 450–440 BCE and is likely the same as the statue called the Canon, which was a demonstration of the principles of design written down by Polykleitos in a lost treatise of the same name (**Figure 10.7**). The treatise is known only indirectly from remarks and quotations by other writers, but what we know of it tells us that it articulated a system of proportions in which one unit, such as the fingertip, became the module that determined the length of the digits and hand using a series of mathematical ratios. This system embodies the concept of *symmetria*, translated as commensurability or the appropriate relationship and proportions among parts, as described by the Roman-era doctor Galen:

> Beauty [*kallos*], he [Chrysippos] believes, arises not in the commensurability [*symmetria*] of the constituent elements [of the body], but in the commensurability of the parts, such as that of finger to finger, and of all the fingers to the palm and the wrist, and of these to the forearm, and of the forearm to the upper arm, and, in fact, of everything to everything else, just as it is written in the Canon of Polykleitos. For having taught us in that work all the proportions of the body, Polykleitos supported his treatise with a work of art; that is, he made a statue according to the tenets of his treatise, and called the statue, like the work, the "Canon." (*De placitis Hippocratis et Platonis* 5; tr. Pollitt 1990, 76)

pathos
Greek term indicating the emotions of a figure, which can be read through facial expression and body movement

peplos
a heavier woman's garment made of wool, consisting of a single piece of cloth folded over to create a double layer over the chest and pinned together

symmetria
regarding proportions in art, commensurability or the appropriate relationship among the parts

The ratios, now lost, were probably based on harmonic intervals in music, such as 1:2 (so that dividing a string in half creates a tone one octave higher), 2:3, and so on. Since the statue is known only through later copies, we cannot be sure how precisely the ratios are used in the surviving examples. Of course, the use of numbers and ratios is not new in Greek art and was also featured in the grid system used by the Egyptians, but what is new is the link between visual proportions and philosophical, mathematical, and musical principles to express a more universal order, what Polykleitos labeled *eu* (perfection or goodness).

Polykleitos is also said to have been a follower of the philosopher Pythagoras. The Pythagorean theorem ($a^2 + b^2 = c^2$) can be seen as another example of the proportional order underlying nature and the world, but the philosopher also articulated a concept of the world as being balanced between pairs of opposite values, such as light/dark, motion/rest, straight/curved, male/female, and so on. The mean (*to meson*) was the point between these opposites, and we can readily see this balancing principle even in the copies of the Doryphoros. Notice that the *contrapposto* pose makes the right leg straight while the left is bent or curved. The right arm is also straight, while the left arm was originally bent and carrying a spear, so that there is a balance between straight and curved lines. The weight-bearing limbs (left arm, right leg) are set diagonally opposite, creating a dynamically balanced chiastic (X-shaped) composition. The left heel is raised rather high, and in describing the figure's movement, it seems balanced between motion and rest; he is either stopping from movement, or resting and beginning to move. The figure is neither young like the Kritios Boy nor old like the Riace Warrior, but at the perfect balance of youth and experience. He is neither too thin nor thickly muscled, and he could be the ideal warrior or athlete. One can see how such an idealized figure, representing both the mean and *symmetria*, became canonical as a standard for later artists.

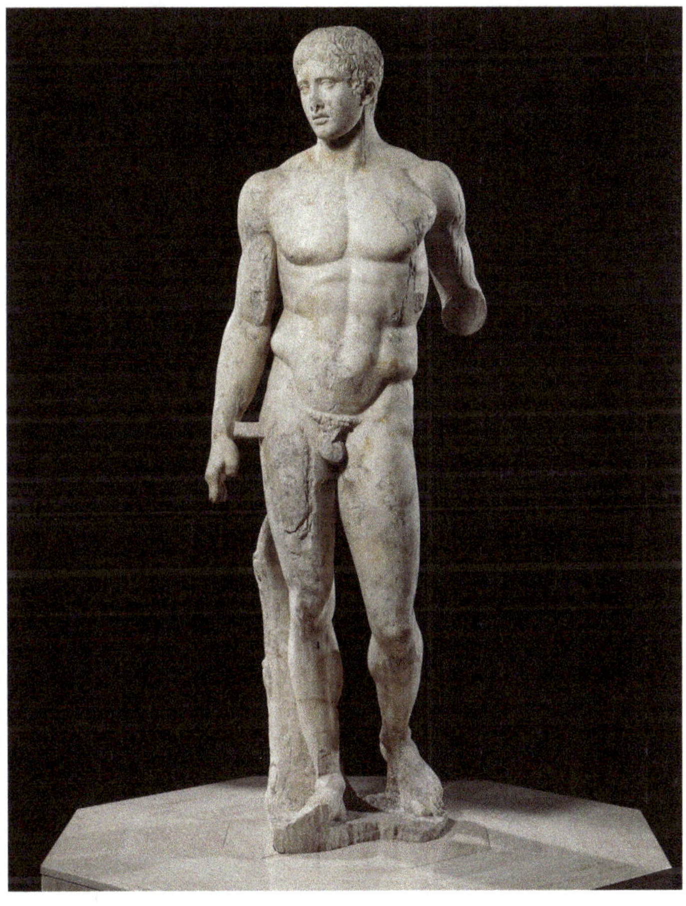

10.7 Doryphoros of Polykleitos, Hellenistic marble copy of Greek bronze original of *c.* 450–440 BCE. 6 ft 6 in (1.98 m). Minneapolis Institute of Arts, Minnesota 86.1. Photo: Bridgeman Art Library.

Sculpture in the last part of the fifth century becomes more sensual and decorative. It is a time when artistic production is disrupted by the struggles of the Peloponnesian War (431–404 BCE), when the reality of destruction and death often stood in sharp contrast to the idealistic figures of contemporary art. A good example of the stylistic change is seen in a statue of Nike that was the top of a victory monument dedicated in Olympia (**Figure 10.8**). As the inscription tells us, "The Messenians and Naupactians dedicated this to Olympian Zeus, a tithe from the spoils of war. Paionios of Mende made this, and was victor to make the acroteria for the Temple." This victory was likely in a battle against the Spartans, and both cities fought with Athens in the Battle of Sphacteria in 425 BCE, making the statue a bit later in date. Rather than a calm and poised figure like the caryatid in **Figure 10.6** or the women in the Parthenon frieze (**see Figure 10.15**), we see a winged figure rushing to earth to bring victory to one side. The fabric is pushed back by Nike's speed and clings to the body like wet drapery, revealing much of the anatomical structure underneath. The light ridges and smooth surfaces of the front contrast with the deeply drilled ridges and shadows of the billowing drapery behind the figure, creating a complicated and calligraphic pattern of drapery that is labeled the **florid style**. While the figure is quite effective at representing the thrill of a triumphant moment, it no longer has the balance and moderation of works like the Doryphoros. Emotion and sensuality aptly describe much of the work found in painting and relief sculpture of this time, as we shall see later in this chapter.

florid style
term used for late classical art in which drapery is shown thin and tightly clinging to the body, often with many small folds that reveal the anatomy

ARCHITECTURE, ARCHITECTURAL SCULPTURE, AND RELIEF

We have already seen a number of the best examples of fifth-century architecture in Chapter 7. The Temple of Hera II at Poseidonia/Paestum, a Greek colony in southern Italy, dates to around 460 BCE; construction on a temple of this size would probably have taken about ten years (**see Figure 7.7, page 163**). The colonnade is six columns wide and fourteen long, with overall dimensions of 24.26 meters × 59.98 meters. The columns are both higher and proportionally taller than those of the archaic Temple of Hera I, which is virtually the same width (24.51 m). The intercolumnation, or distance between the columns, is less at the corners than in the rest of the colonnade, making the visual transition around the corner more rhythmic and adjusting for the problem of metope placement. This practice of **contraction** in Doric design appeared first at the Temple of Hera at Olympia in the early sixth century, and then spread throughout Greece and westward to Italy. Inside, the ceiling of the naos was supported by two rows of columns set vertically, an arrangement that is also found on the contemporary Temple of Zeus at Olympia (**see Figure 7.12, page 168**).

contraction
the practice in Doric architecture of adjusting the distance between columns at the corners to compensate for the placement of the triglyphs and metopes

Pausanias (5.10.2–3) tells us that the Temple of Zeus at Olympia was built by the Eleans as an offering to Zeus for their victory over the Pisans to control the sanctuary, implying that construction started after 470 BCE. Pausanias also records an inscription on the Nike acroteria over the pediment that it was a votive offering from the Spartans for their victory over the Athenians at Tanagra in 457, providing a *terminus ante quem* for the building. The architect was Libon of Elis, who designed a 6 × 13 colonnade made from local limestone that was covered with stucco. The temple was about 15 percent wider (27.7 m) than the Temple of Hera II at Poseidonia/Paestum and proportionally just a little taller. The architectural sculpture consisted of two pedimental groups: on the west a Centauromachy and on the east, looking over the open area where the athletes took their oaths, the oath of Pelops and Oinomaos before their chariot race that we saw in Chapter 9 (**see Figure 9.14, page 228**). In addition there were twelve metopes, six each above the pronaos and opisthodomos showing the twelve deeds of Herakles, the first time there had been a canonical set. Rather than using the poor local stone for the sculpture, these works were made on the island of Paros and shipped to Olympia at very great cost, as we shall see in the next chapter (see p. 269).

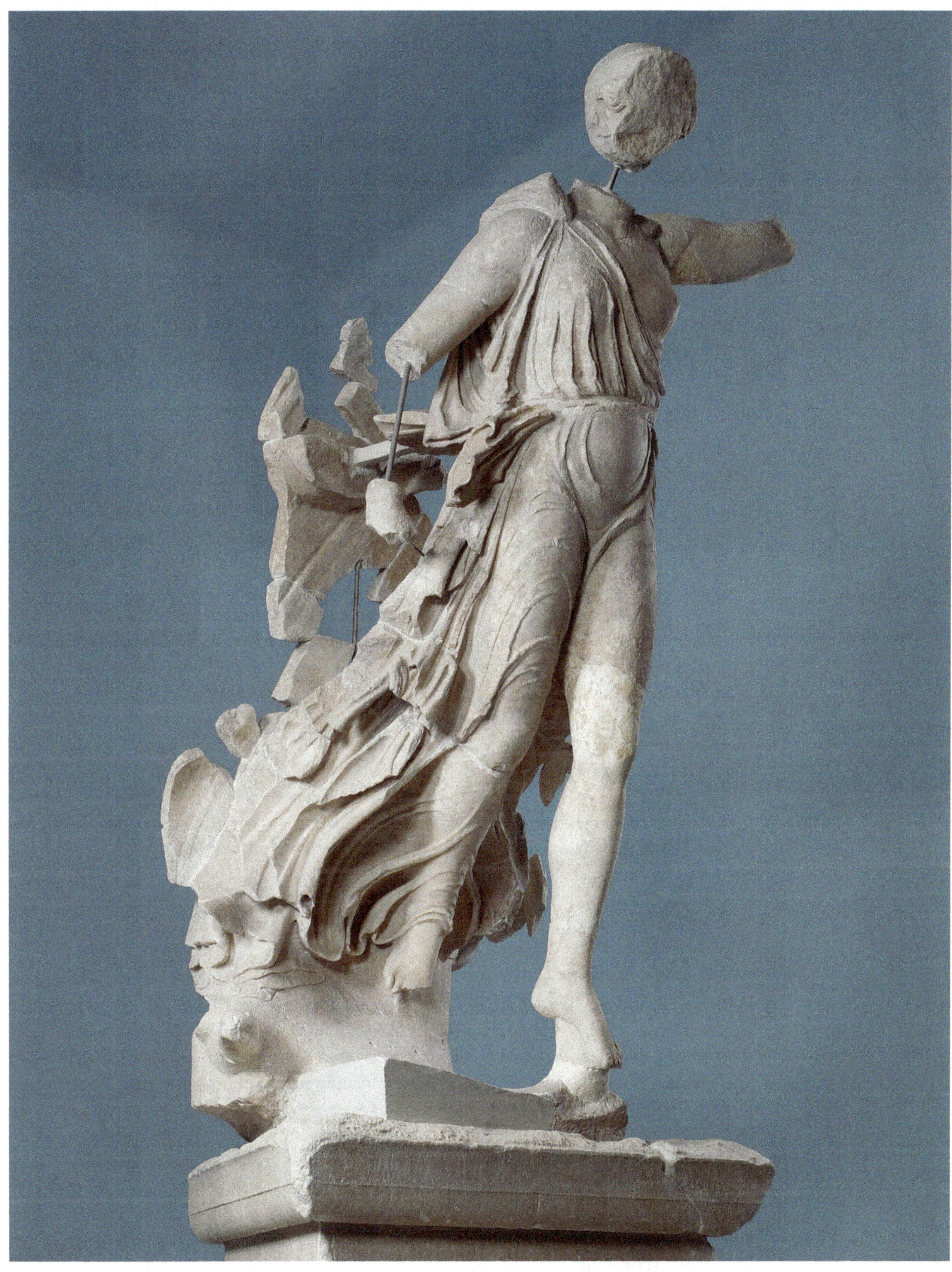

10.8 Nike by Paionios, *c.* 420 BCE. Marble, 6 ft 4¾ in (1.95 m). Olympia Museum. Photo: Marie Mauzy/Art Resource, NY.

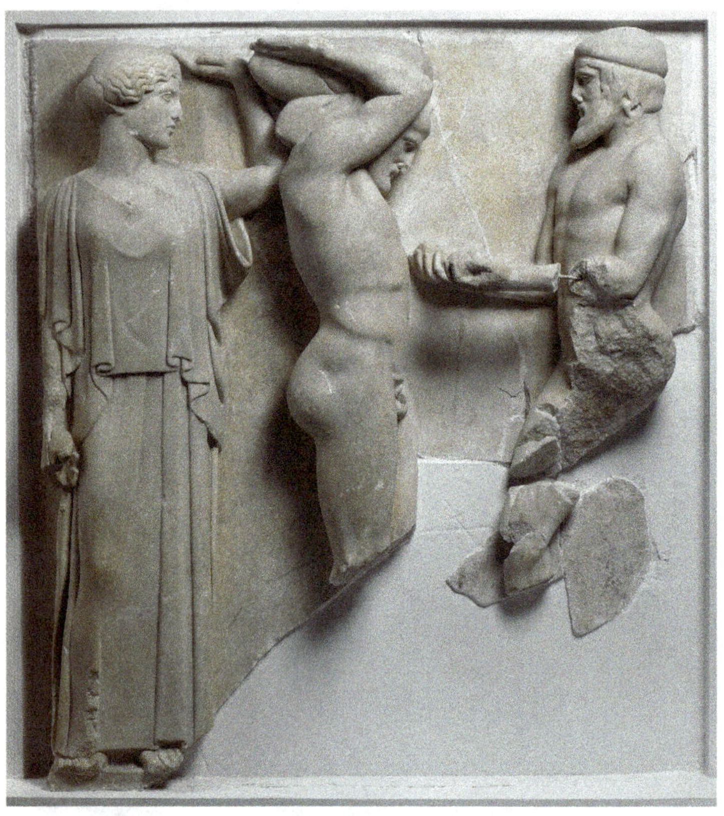

10.9 Metope 10 from the Temple of Zeus at Olympia, *c.* 470–457 BCE. 5 ft 3 in (1.60 m). Athena, Herakles, and Atlas with apples of the Hesperides. Olympia, Archaeological Museum. Photo: Marie Mauzy/Art Resource, NY.

We can study stylistic change in architectural sculpture by turning our attention to one of the metopes from the cyclic narrative of the labors of Herakles. Metope 10, which stood just to the right side of the opening of the opisthodomos, shows the retrieval of the apples of the Hesperides **(Figure 10.9)**. The style of the figures has often been called doughy, as is characteristic of the Severe Style, but it has been recently argued that in fact the figures are mostly unfinished (Younger and Rehak 2009). To lessen the weight for transportation, much of the carving was done in the quarry and workshop on Paros. Apparently the sculptures were set into place without being finished completely on site, hence the hair, faces, and clothing lack some of the detailing seen in free-standing sculpture of the period.

On the right side of the metope we see Atlas, who has fetched the apples that provide immortality and holds them before Herakles. The hero is holding up the weight of the sky with both arms; although he has a cushion, his neck and back are bent and pressed down by the weight. Behind him Athena gives support, but clearly her lack of exertion demonstrates the different power of a god compared to a mortal. What is interesting about the narrative is that Herakles faces a problem: he cannot reach for the apples without being crushed, and so cannot rely on his physical strength as he does in most of his labors. He must think of a way out of the situation, since Atlas is in no hurry to resume his labors. The viewer might recall the story that Herakles tricked Atlas, asking him to hold up the sky so that Herakles could adjust his cushion, but then Herakles escaped with the apples. This wiliness is more typical of Odysseus than Herakles, but Athena is here to help Herakles think through the problem, which was not his greatest strength. Given his very human and mortal difficulty, it is noteworthy that Herakles not only looks down toward the apples, but also down and slightly outward toward the viewer below, who would also be seeking the wisdom and assistance of the gods in a visit to the sanctuary.

THE ACROPOLIS AT ATHENS

The first half of the fifth century was basically one of constant conflict in Greece. Athens and other cities were fighting the Persians most of the time, and between 462 and 451 BCE Sparta and Athens were fighting each other as well. Following a truce with Sparta, Athens and Persia concluded a peace treaty in 450, so that for the first time in many years there was peace in Greece. Much of this was the result of the work of Perikles, who became prominent in Athenian politics when he was one of the prosecutors of Kimon in 463/2 that led to Kimon's ostracism and exile. In the next year he was allied with Ephialtes in reforming the Athenian democratic constitution and, after the murder of Ephialtes, dominated Athenian politics until his death in 429. Under his leadership, jury pay of a half drachma was instituted for trials and Athenian citizenship was limited to those who had both an Athenian father and mother. He also oversaw the transformation of the Delian League from a defensive alliance of poleis against the Persians into an empire. Although he was challenged and at times charged with crimes like embezzlement, he was acquitted and continued to have the support of most of the citizens of Athens.

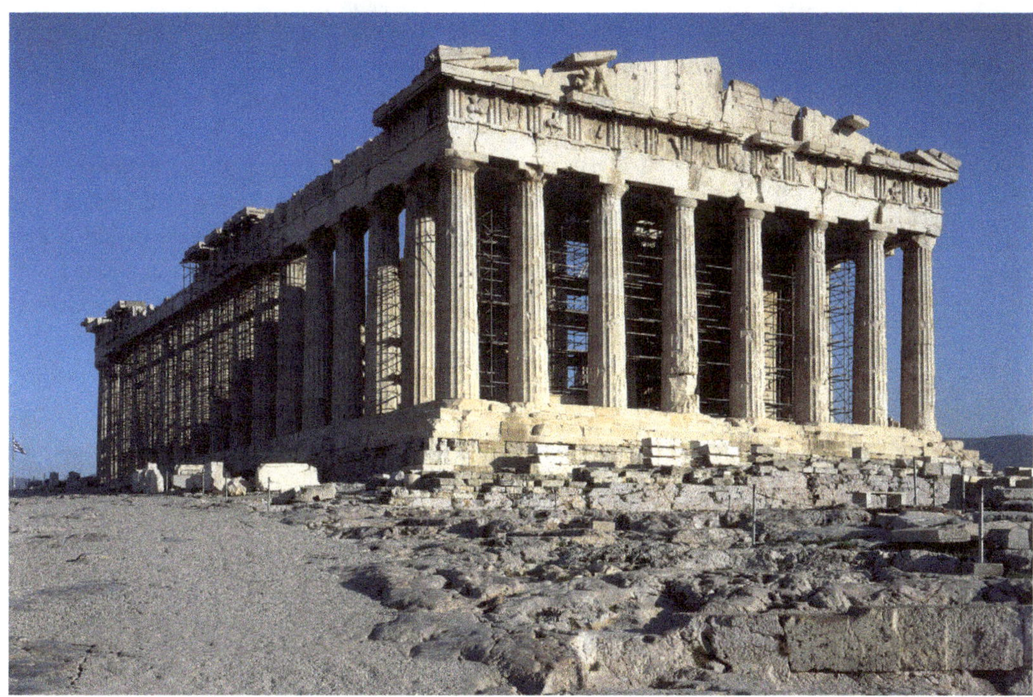

10.10 Parthenon, Athens, 447–432 BCE, view from the northwest. Architects Iktinos and Kallikrates. Width 101 ft 3¾ in (30.88 m). Photo: Marie Mauzy/Art Resource, NY.

In 449 BCE, Perikles proposed a massive building program on the Acropolis and elsewhere in Athens, creating some of the key monuments in the history of Greek art. To help pay for this work, Perikles used revenue from the silver mines and also appropriated funds from the treasury of the Delian League, the confederacy led by Athens to fight the Persians, which had been moved from Delos to Athens for safekeeping in 454. This appropriation was opposed without success by the allies of Athens, who had, in reality, become tribute states of an Athenian empire. The public nature of the expenditure led to the building accounts being inscribed on marble tablets on the Acropolis, some of which still survive and give us more precise information about the Acropolis buildings and sculpture than almost any other monument of Greek art. From these, we can determine that work began clearing and preparing the site and extending the bastion on the south side by 448. The Parthenon was designed by the architects Iktinos and Kallikrates between 447 and 438, with the metopes and colonnade built first, 447–442, and then the cella and frieze made in 442–438. Finishing work and the pedimental sculptures were completed 437–432.

The Parthenon is larger than the Temple of Zeus at Olympia and has eight columns across the front and seventeen down the side **(Figures 10.10, 10.11)**. This larger size allowed the naos of the building to be just over 100 Attic feet in length, a hekatompedon, which would hold a massive gold and ivory statue made by Pheidias. The 8:17 colonnade ratio, like 6:13, follows a formula of x:2(x) + 1. Using 4 as "x" in the formula, one gets a proportion of 4:9, the squares of 2:3, and the basic ratio for the entire Parthenon. For example, this 4:9 proportion determines the width and length of the building (30.88:69.51 m). It also determines the height of the colonnade and entablature to the width (13.73:30.88 m). The diameter of the columns and the distance between the centers of the columns (1.91:4.29 m at the center) also is a ratio of 4:9. This use of ratio created *symmetria* in the building, as it had in the contemporary sculpture of the Doryphoros.

One particularly striking aspect of the Parthenon is the range of subtle adjustments made to account for viewer perception. Like earlier fifth-century temples, it uses contraction to make the intercolumnation at the corner (3.68 m) less than at the center (4.29 m), but this adjustment is carried out gradually across the first three columns, as can be seen in a view of the facade, creating an A:B:C:C:C:B:A spacing **(Figure 10.12)**. To the eye, this makes the spacing appear regular when one first views the Parthenon upon entering the Acropolis and seeing its northwest corner **(see Figure 10.10)**.

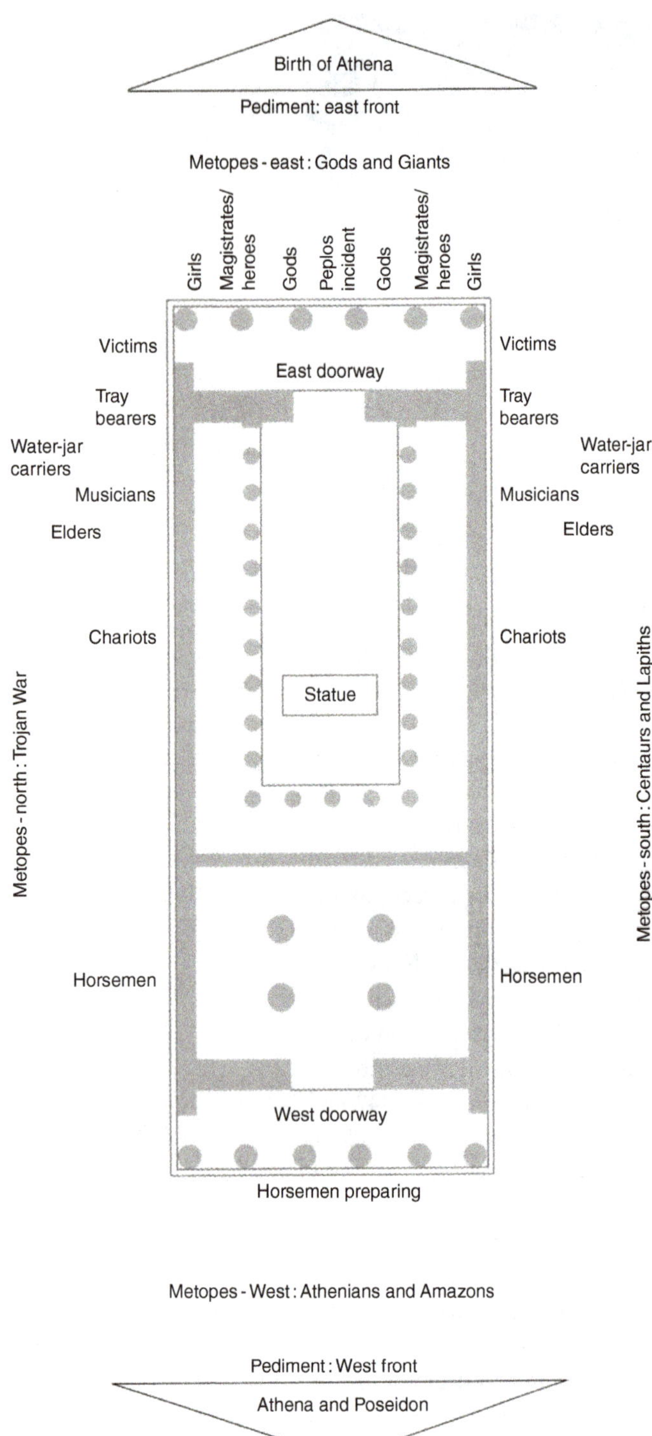

10.11 Parthenon, Athens, plan with subjects of sculptural program. After I. Jenkins, *Greek Architecture and its Sculpture* (London: British Museum Press, 2006), Fig. 67, drawing by K. Morton. © The Trustees of the British Museum.

The columns are also not perfectly vertical but lean inward about 2 inches (5 cm) from plumb. The effect is to make them appear vertical, since tall walls and objects can often appear to be leaning outward when seen up close from below. The corner columns are thicker than the others to make them appear to be the same diameter. Finally, it is when standing at the corner looking down the length of the steps on either side that one realizes the stylobate is actually curved and is about 4 inches (10 cm) higher in the center of the long side than at the corners. The effect is subtle but visible to the knowledgable eye at the site; the drawing in **Figure 10.13** exaggerates these effects to make them more visible at a small scale.

The later Roman architect Vitruvius (*De Arch.* 3.4.5) tells us in his treatise on architecture that this optical refinement is necessary to make the line of the stylobate appear straight and not bent, and in the Parthenon this extends up into the entablature. Additional explanations for these adjustments were to make the building appear larger than it is, or that the inconsistencies create a tension in the mind of the viewer between rule and perception, forcing attention on the building and making it a more dynamic sight (Pollitt 1972, 75–78). Undoubtedly, the importance of the viewing experience would seem to be a foremost concern for the design and the enormous expense these adjustments entailed.

The Parthenon was the first large temple to be built entirely out of marble, which came from the quarries on the slopes of Mount Pentelikon, about 17 kilometers from the Acropolis. The marble was used in creating one of the largest ensembles of architectural sculpture for a temple: ninety-two metopes on all four sides of the building, a frieze wrapping around all 159.7 meters of the naos, two pedimental groups, and acroteria. On the west, back side of the Parthenon, the first side that a visitor would see, the pediment showed the contest between Poseidon and Athena for naming Athens **(see subjects in Figure 10.11)**. The metopes below had an **Amazonomachy**. The metopes on the north side showed the *Iliupersis*, while those on the south had a Centauromachy. Finally on the east side, where one entered the naos, the metopes featured the Gigantomachy and the pediment showed the birth of Athena. The pediments thus represent the relationship of Athens to its patron goddess, while the metopes show various Greek groups fighting their enemies (Amazons, Centaurs, and Trojans) and the Olympian gods imposing their order over the giants. The frieze on the exterior of the naos shows a procession of Athenians, beginning with the assembly of riders on the west end, followed by parallel cavalcades on the first half of the north and south sides **(see Figure 1.1, page 2)**. Next are contests with hoplites jumping into chariots (called the ***apobates***), and then a sacrificial procession with animals and attendees. These figures round the corner to the east side of the building, where a peplos is being handled by a priest, priestess, and three younger figures while the Olympian gods watch from the wings **(see Figure 10.15)**.

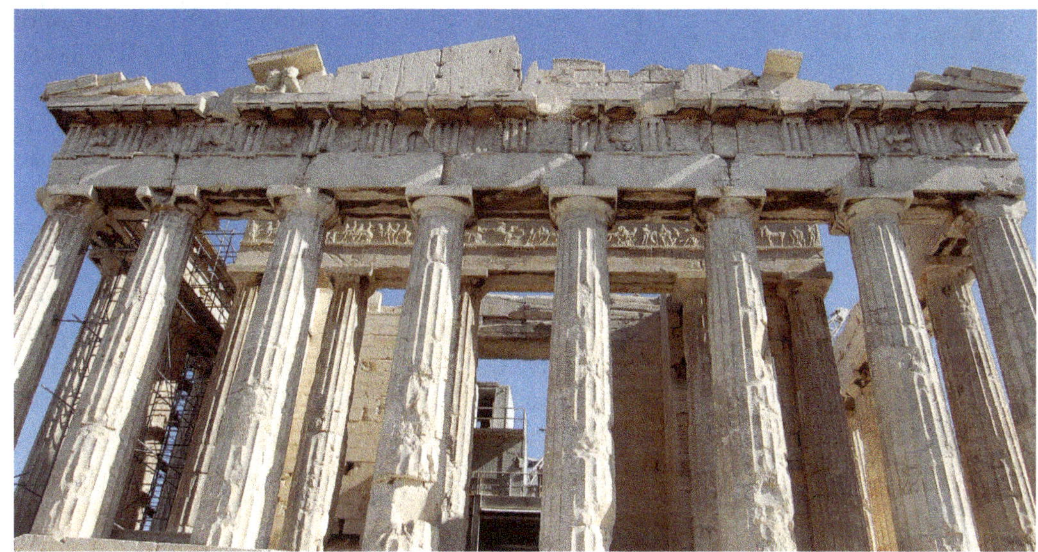

10.12 Parthenon, Athens, view of west end. Photo: author.

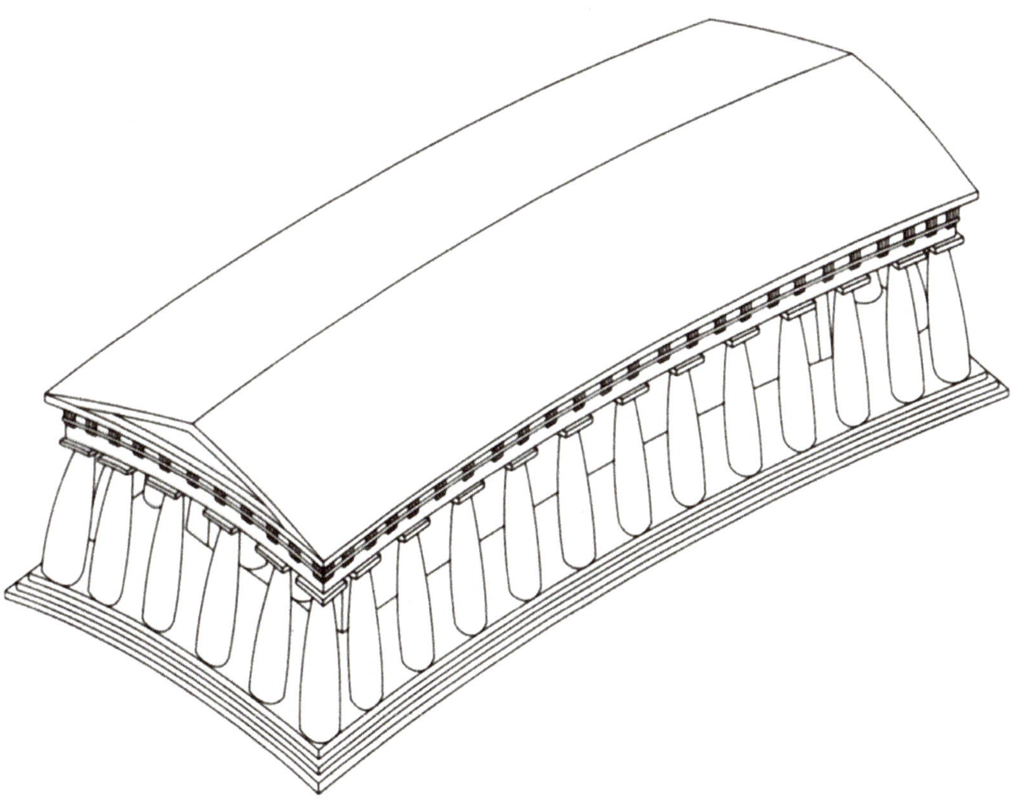

10.13 Parthenon, Athens, drawing of exaggerated architectural refinements. After I. Jenkins, *Greek Architecture and its Sculpture* (London: British Museum Press, 2006), Fig. 65, drawing by K. Morton. © The Trustees of the British Museum.

Stylistically the figures of the metopes, dated to 447–442 BCE, have some similarities to bronze and marble sculpture like the Riace Warriors and the Olympia metopes, but some of them reveal a greater emphasis on more graceful and fluid movement in the figure and slightly thinner body proportions **(Figure 10.14)**. This is even clearer in the frieze, where the figures exhibit a poise and gravity like the Doryphoros **(Figure 10.15; see Figure 1.1, page 2)**. The men and women of the frieze are idealized Athenians, showing their piety toward the gods. As mentioned in the last chapter, there has been much debate about whether the frieze represents an actual Panathenaic procession, in which the citizens of Athens bought a new peplos for the cult statue of Athena on the Acropolis, or

Amazonomachy
term for a battle between Amazons and Greeks

***apobates* (pl. *apobatai*)**
a competition that involved a fully dressed warrior jumping out of and into a moving chariot

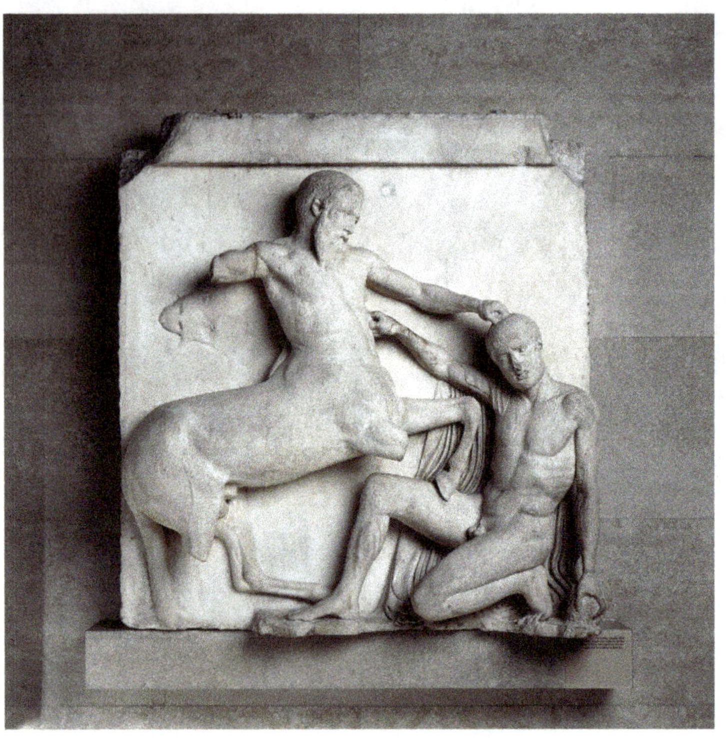

10.14 South metope from Parthenon, 447–442 BCE. 4 ft 5½ in (1.36 m). London, British Museum 1816,0610.14. Lapith and Centaur fighting. Photo: © The Trustees of the British Museum.

perhaps a mythological narrative showing the sacrifice of the daughters of Erechtheus (see p. 233). One can also consider the frieze as composed of universalizing scenes, models of what makes Athens special. As J. J. Pollitt has proposed, Perikles himself made such an argument in his funeral oration of 431, when eulogizing those who had died fighting Sparta in the first year of the Peloponnesian War (Thuc. 2.38–39; Pollitt 1997). According to Perikles, what distinguished the Athenians from others was the quality of their institutions and way of life, their contests (seen in the *apobatai*), their sacrificial offerings and piety (the procession and peplos scene), and their military training (the cavalcade).

In looking at the frieze, one can see that the sculptors were aware of the procession of viewers below and alongside the building, walking from west to east. The youth who stands at the northwest corner next to his horse turns his head back and down and looks at the viewer below (**see Figure 1.1, page 2**). The depth of the relief is higher at the top of the frieze than at the bottom, allowing the figure to project visually and be seen more clearly at the sharp upward angle. Not only does this figure engage the viewer, but other riders turn their heads in the same direction in a periodic rhythm as one walks along the frieze, as do attendants with the chariots and sacrificial animals as one approaches the east end of the building. Since the viewers' actions below mimic those of the relief, a visual bond is established between the idealized and real Athenians. The frieze itself is composed as a progressive narrative, moving from the early stages of assembly and organization to the end presentation and keeping pace with the viewer walking along the building.

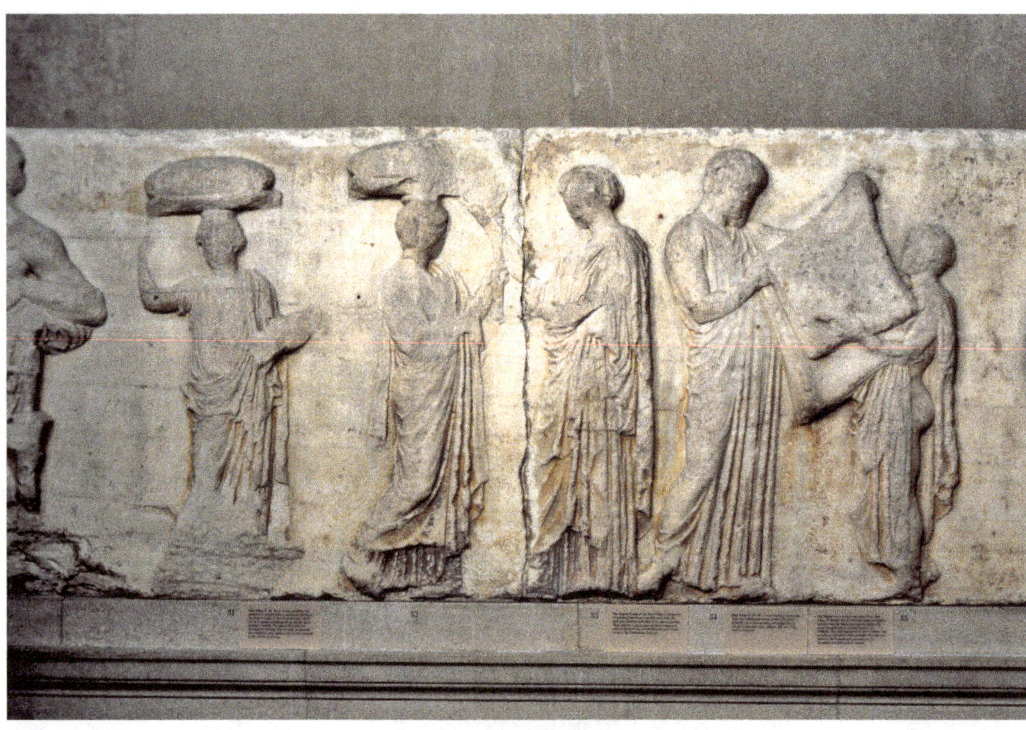

10.15 East frieze of the Parthenon, 442–438 BCE. 3 ft 5¾ in (1.06 m). London, British Museum. Presentation of peplos. Photo: © The Trustees of the British Museum.

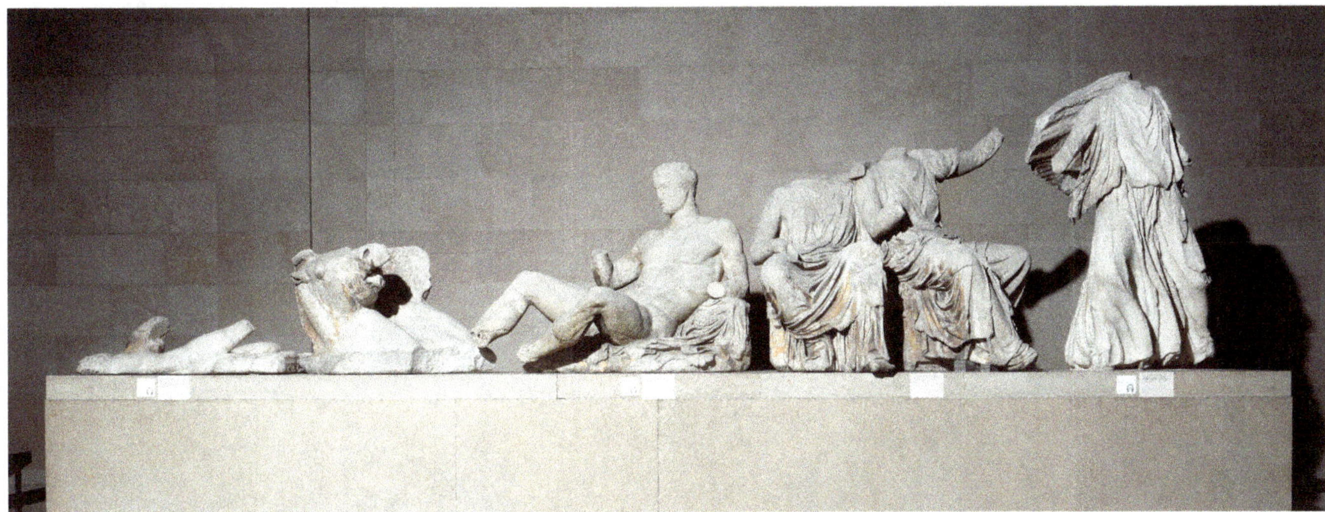

10.16A East pediment of the Parthenon, 437–432 BCE. Height of tallest figure (G): 5 ft 8⅛ in (1.73 m). London, British Museum. Birth of Athena, left side. From left: Helios with chariot team (labeled in the literature as figures A–C), Dionysos (?) (D), Kore/Persephone (E), Demeter (F), Artemis (G). Photo: © The Trustees of the British Museum.

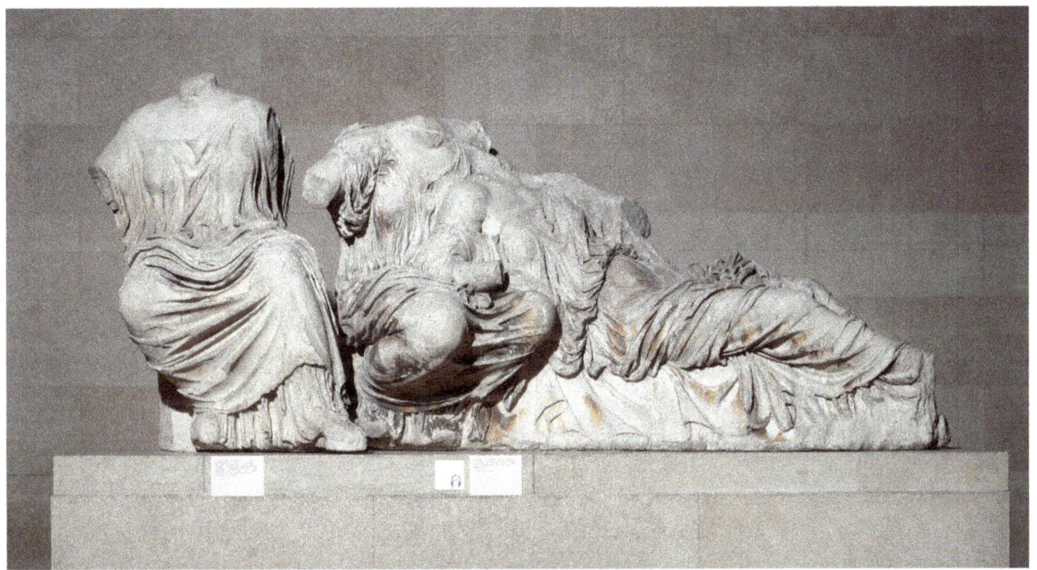

10.16B East pediment of the Parthenon, 437–432 BCE. Height of tallest figure (K): 4 ft 3⅛ in (1.30 m). London, British Museum. Birth of Athena, right side. From left: Hestia (K), Dione or Themis (L), Aphrodite (M). Photo: © The Trustees of the British Museum.

Turning the corner to the east pediment, its center once showed the birth of Athena, but only the two wings are left **(Figures 10.16A and 10.16B)**. On the right are three reclining goddesses, labeled K, L, and M, probably Hestia, Dione, and Aphrodite respectively. On the left side is Artemis (G) moving away from the center, Demeter (F) and Kore (E) seated, and finally a reclining man labeled D. The seated figures toward the center are turned in that direction, as if they have just become aware of the birth of Athena, goddess of wisdom and craft. The reclining figures, D and M, show no awareness of this event and have their backs turned against it. The composition is a dramatically staged metaphor, with the reclining figures set in opposition to the center of the composition. If these reclining figures are Dionysos, as many scholars have seen as probable, and Aphrodite, one would have the gods of wine and love at the wings of the tableau, and wisdom and industry in the center. The divine gifts of wine and love are necessary for humans, but they can also bring chaos if used unwisely. Athena brings order and balance, the Pythagorean mean, to the citizens of her city below. Of course, this specific interpretation depends on the identification of the figures, especially

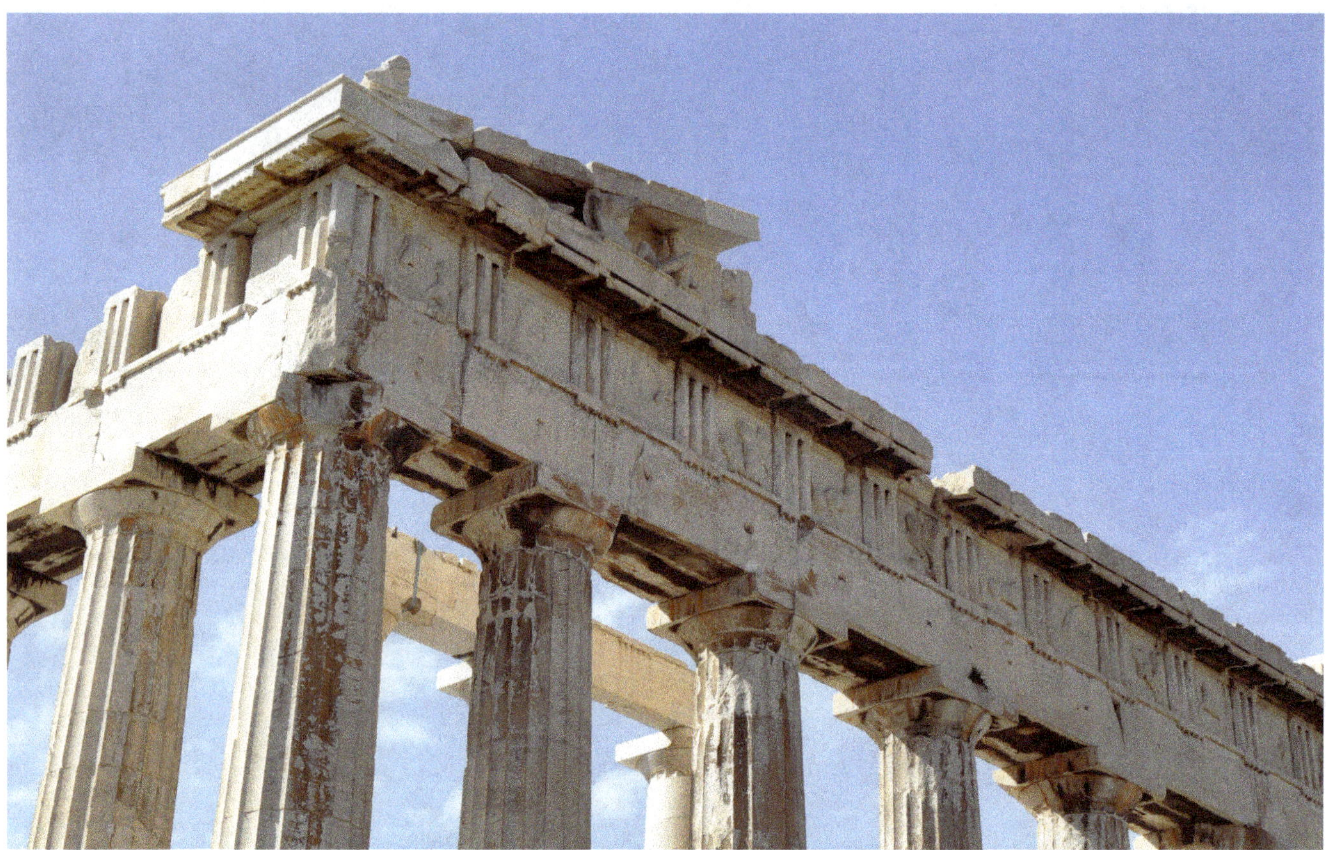

10.17 Parthenon, Athens, view of southeast corner with reproduction of Dionysos (D) figure. Photo: author.

Dionysos, who has also been identified by some scholars as Theseus, Herakles, and most recently by Dyfri Williams as Ares (Williams 2013). The pairing of Ares and Aphrodite could also be oppositional and disruptive like that of Dionysos and Aphrodite, with Athena providing the resolution, but the continued debate over the identity of figure D reminds one of the element of uncertainty in interpreting ancient art.

That the pedimental composition is like a play that engages the audience can be seen by looking at the replicated figure of Dionysos (or D) in the corner of the pediment today **(Figure 10.17)**. Not only is he turned away from the central action, he is also looking down toward the viewer and is the first to greet the viewer as he or she rounds the southeast corner. Although Aphrodite has no head today, her position is similar to Dionysos and she would have faced the main processional traffic turning the northeast corner to enter the naos. In a way, they tempt the viewers with their gifts, but the piety and civic life of the viewer create balance as he or she moves along and sees Athena in the pediment above and the presentation of her peplos over the door to the naos **(see Figure 10.15)**.

The presentation of the peplos reminds us that the Parthenon is a religious building and that some of the most important Athenian rituals, including the Panathenaia, took place on the Acropolis. In the aftermath of the Persian destruction the site was not rebuilt immediately, allegedly as part of the Oath of Plataia by the victorious Greeks as a testimony to the sacrilege of the Persians. A small sanctuary had been refashioned at the sixth-century Temple of Athena on the Acropolis, but as we saw in Chapter 7, most public ritual required open space, so that the Acropolis continued to serve its religious functions. In undertaking its reconstruction, Perikles was also making an ideological statement about the pious character and power of Athens. In looking at the Parthenon, both up close and from various sites in the city, one can see that the agenda of Perikles was not just to beautify the city, but to project an image of its power and prestige. This is particularly visible from the Pynx, where Athenian male citizens gathered to vote and make decisions such as the construction of the Acropolis, whose major buildings can all be seen from there when looking eastward (**see Figure 1.9, page 13**).

In his history of the Peloponnesian War, Thucydides provides the text of Perikles's funeral oration of 431 BCE, which eulogized the Athenians who had died in the first year of the war. While presented as a quotation, it more likely represents an approximation of some of what Perikles said. According to Thucydides, Perikles asked the citizens of Athens to look upon their city, recently transformed with new buildings, and by looking at it become lovers of the city, willing to sacrifice their lives on its behalf:

> you must yourselves realize the power of Athens, and feed your eyes upon her from day to day, till love of her fills your hearts; and then, when all her greatness shall break upon you, you must reflect that it was by courage, sense of duty, and a keen feeling of honour in action that men were enabled to win all this. (Thuc. 2.43.1; tr. Crawley)

Earlier in his history, Thucydides tells us of Sparta and Athens:

> For I suppose if Lacedaemon [Sparta] were to become desolate, and the temples and the foundations of the public buildings were left, that as time went on there would be a strong disposition with posterity to refuse to accept her fame as a true exponent of her power.... Whereas, if Athens were to suffer the same misfortune, I suppose that any inference from the appearance presented to the eye would make her power to have been twice as great as it is. (Thuc. 1.10.2; tr. Crawley)

With the fifth-century building program, Athens created both a stage for its rituals and piety and an expression of Athenians' perceived preeminence among the Greek poleis.

LATE FIFTH-CENTURY SCULPTURE

The drapery style of the pedimental figures, especially Aphrodite, has the combination of thick folds and smooth surfaces clinging to the body that we saw on the slightly later Nike of Paionios, and this style is prevalent in architectural sculpture and relief for the remainder of the century. One well-known example is from the small Temple of Athena Nike that was set on a bastion next to the Propylaia and built after it in the 420s (**see Figure 1.9, page 13**). Between 420 and 410 BCE, a parapet wall was added around the bastion that featured reliefs on each side of multiple Nikes bringing a sacrifice to a seated Athena (**Figure 10.18**). In the example, we see a Nike adjusting the straps of her sandal, a familiar type of pose that recalls the recumbent Aphrodite from the Parthenon pediment. The unsteady and twisting pose makes the fabric stretch and clump over her body, and the effect around the breasts and abdomen leaves little to the imagination. The long hanging curves of the garment folds create a very decorative ripple effect, giving a very different and more sensual impression than the Parthenon frieze figures.

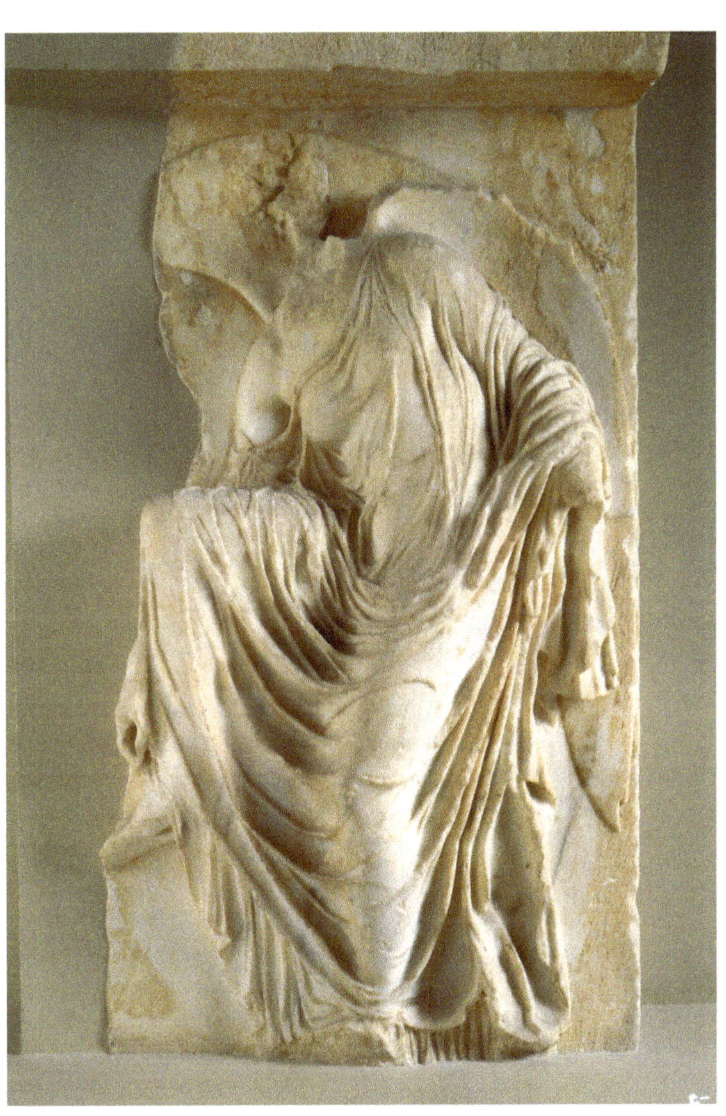

10.18 Nike figure from the parapet of the Temple of Athena Nike, *c.* 420–410 BCE. 3 ft 3¾ in (1.01 m). Athens, Acropolis Museum. Photo: Nimatallah/Art Resource, NY.

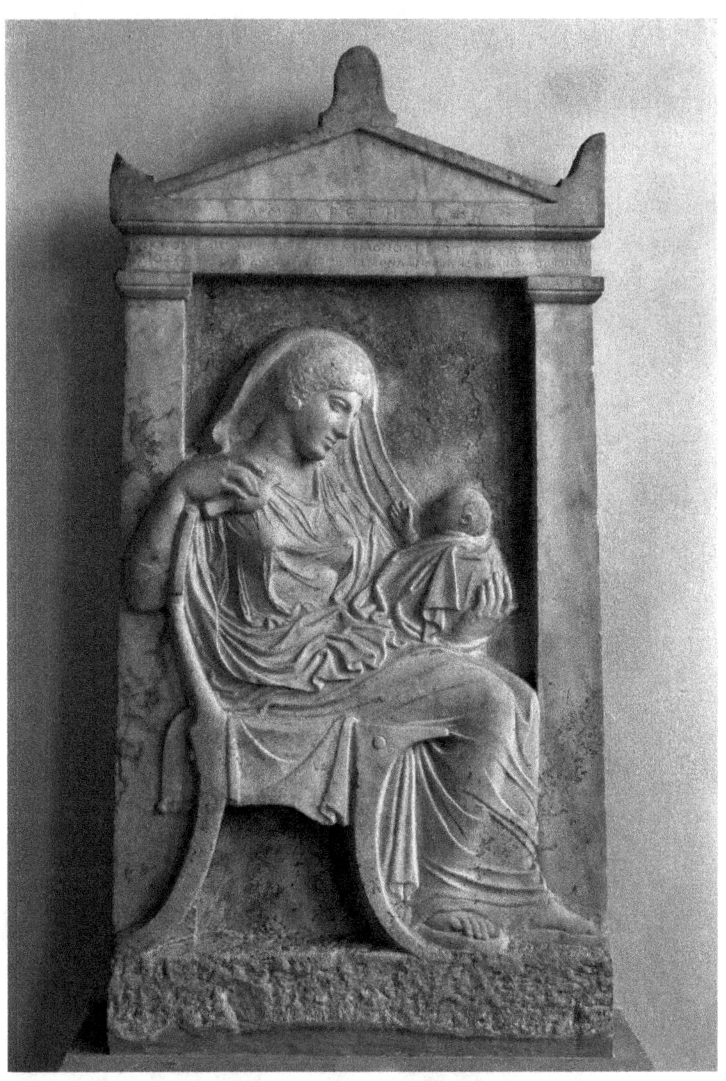

10.19 Grave stele of Ampharete from Kerameikos, 430–420 BCE. 3 ft 11¼ in (1.20 m). Athens, Kerameikos Museum P999. Photo: Foto Marburg/Art Resource, NY.

The last building to be completed on the Acropolis was the Erechtheion **(see Figure 7.8, page 164)**. Whereas the Parthenon and Propylaia had Doric exteriors and Ionic interior columns, this building was completely in the Ionic order and included the famous Caryatid porch. As we saw in Chapter 7, the building itself is very irregular as a temple, but its decorative relief does convey the richness of Ionic architecture **(see Figure 7.9, page 165)**. The building was not completed until about 405 BCE, and its frieze showed a series of white marble figures that were set into a blue marble background **(see Figure 11.3, page 272)**. While smaller and not quite as detailed as the Nike parapet, they continue the florid style on the Acropolis. Since some of the payments for these figures survive on the Acropolis building tablets, we will discuss these reliefs further in the next chapter since they are important for understanding the economics of sculpture production (see pp. 270–271).

During the last three decades of the fifth century there is a change in burial customs that revives an important category of relief sculpture in Athens, funerary monuments. While these were found in archaic Attica, as we have seen, they had apparently been banned by the city during the fifth century as too extravagant for private expenditure. Such legislation, typically called sumptuary laws, is often intended to prevent a small group of wealthy or privileged citizens from distinguishing their elite status; for the new democratic constitution of Athens in the late sixth century and following, a ban on elite funerary monuments emphasized the prerogative of the polis. For whatever reason, these prohibitions relaxed around 430 BCE and later, and there is a growing use of reliefs for commemoration of the deceased by families, such as the grave stele of Ampharete (**Figure 10.19**). Ampharete sits on a chair as if in an interior setting, holding an infant in her hand. The drapery does clump and pull tightly, but is not quite as revealing as the Nike Temple figure and the pose is quieter and more contemplative, as would be appropriate for commemorating the deceased. Ampharete's veil makes her seem like a bride, making her an idealized Athenian woman. The inscription on the architrave, however, tells us that Ampharete is a grandmother holding her dead grandchild: "I hold here the beloved child of my daughter, which I held on my knees when we were alive and saw the light of the sun, and now dead, I hold it dead." It is possible that this monument was made for a mother and child in a workshop and then adapted by inscription to its final use for a grandmother, but the ideal of bride and mother that Ampharete had attained still makes this youthful idealization appropriate for her grave monument.

Indeed, grave reliefs, while being individual purchases, use a small range of figural types that were adapted through details or inscriptions to serve their individualized purpose. We have already seen the stele of Hegeso from the end of the century, seated as a matron like Ampharete but engaged with pulling jewelry from a box **(see Figure 5.28, page 127)**. While far more naturalistic than their archaic predecessors like Phrasikleia **(see Figure 8.13, page 195)**, the message remains similar and conforms to an idealized type. The detachment of the figures continues the idea of grandeur seen in the Parthenon frieze, but there is a more intimate appeal of quiet emotion and domesticity in these grave reliefs.

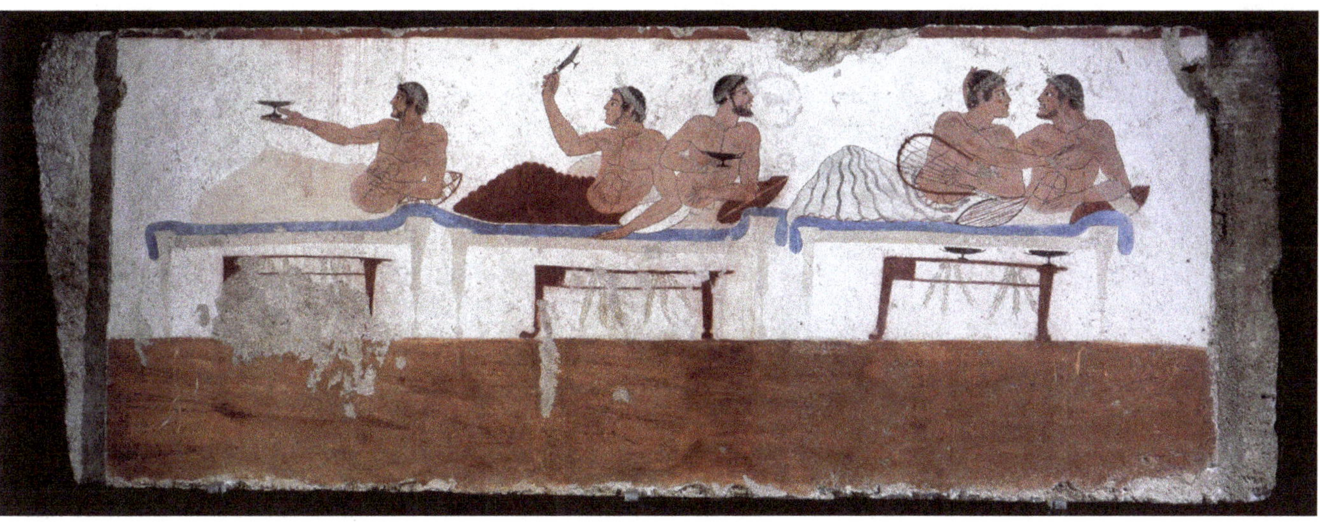

10.20 Painted wall from the Tomb of the Diver, Poseidonia/Paestum, *c.* 470 BCE. 30 11/16 in (78 cm). Symposion scene. Paestum, Museo Archeologico Nazionale. Photo: Gianni Dagli Orti/The Art Archive at Art Resource, NY.

PAINTING

The elements of human representation that we found in fifth-century sculpture, such as *contrapposto*, *rhythmos*, *pathos*, and *ethos*, are also found in painting of the fifth century. Additionally painters have two other challenges to naturalistic representation: how to show a body with mass and volume on a two-dimensional surface, and how to represent a three-dimensional space in which the figures move not just from side to side, but forward and backward relative to the two-dimensional picture plane. These challenges become even more complicated for vase painters, who work on a curving rather than flat surface. By the end of the fifth century, we will see that some of the features of illusionistic pictures that we take for granted, such as foreshortening, ***skiagraphia*** (shading to create volume), and ***skenographia*** (perspective), become common in painting.

skiagraphia
Greek term meaning "shadow painting or drawing," it refers to the use of highlights and shading (chiaroscuro) to suggest the three-dimensionality of an object in a painting

skenographia
Greek term meaning "scene painting," it refers to the use of a perspectival system to represent a three-dimensional space in a picture

In the last chapter we looked at a hydria by the Kleophrades Painter with scenes from the *Iliupersis* that is nearly contemporary with the Kritios Boy and Aigina pediments **(see Figure 9.7, page 219)**. The warrior Neoptolemos is poised to bring his sword down upon king Priam, who grasps his head with his hands. He is not shielding himself but is tearing at his scalp in mourning for his dead grandson, Astyanax, who lays on his lap. While Neoptolemos still has traces of the archaic smile, his emotional state contrasts sharply with the grieving, doomed residents of Troy. The Greek warrior behind him, however, cowers before a woman holding only a large pestle, who attacks him with her makeshift weapon. The parts of the body in these figures are more coordinated with each other than in the early experiments with *rhythmos* and foreshortening that we saw in the earlier work of Euphronios **(see Figure 8.26, page 206)**.

It is during the fifth century that large-scale painting became a prominent medium. Some of the new buildings constructed in Athens between 475 and 450, such as the Theseion and the Stoa Poikile (painted stoa), had monumental paintings on their walls, either large wooden panels or frescoes. Literary sources record some details of the paintings of Polygnotos and Mikon in these and other buildings that became famous in the following centuries. Even 400 years later, these artists are still mentioned by writers such as Cicero as the first great painters in the history of Greek art, whose figures were less "hard" than those of the archaic period, and more closely represented reality (see Chapter 1).

None of these paintings survive, but there is a rare example of wall painting from the Tomb of the Diver in Poseidonia/Paestum showing a youth diving into a pool on the tomb's ceiling, and below a symposion scene on the four walls of the cist tomb **(Figure 10.20)**. The treatment of anatomy and pose is similar to that of the Kleophrades Painter, with a greater sense of three-dimensionality and movement compared to the panel from Pitsa about a half-century earlier (**see Figure 8.21, page 202**). The contour of the figures is defined by a thick dark line, helping the flesh color to stand out from the white background, and the major anatomical features are also defined by lines as they are in vase painting. The medium does make it easier for the painter to suggest the wispy fringes of hair and beard than in red-figure painting, but it is the use of color that stands out from red-figure painting. Being able to use red for lips against the tan color of the skin, for example, gives more expressiveness to the mouth, and the distribution of colors creates more visual variety in the composition. We get a more vivid sense of the adult man on the far right professing his feelings to his younger companion, with the clearly open mouth and the light fingers moving through the black hair.

The Tomb of the Diver is unique and likely shows a pastiche of influences or sources. The tomb itself was from a small cemetery outside of Poseidonia/Paestum and near a settlement of Etruscans. In Etruria wall paintings in chamber tombs had become a major art form in the sixth century, and the painting technique in the Tomb of the Diver is consistent with Etruscan practices. However, the cist form of the tomb is more local or Greek in form. Whether the tomb's occupant was Etruscan, Greek, or Lucanian, the native Italic residents of the area, is uncertain. The krater depicted on one of the short walls is more Lucanian in form, but the symposion scene would appear to be derived from Greek practices and perhaps from vase paintings of the symposion that could have been available for the painters, who were likely local (Holloway 2006). Perhaps the best way to view the tomb paintings is as a nexus, one that combines multiple artistic influences and reflects multiple aspects of identity, a theme that we will explore further in Chapter 13.

There is not much sense of volume in the figures in the Tomb of the Diver since the paint is generally applied in a flat monotone. It is by setting darker and lighter tones next to each other to mimic the play of light on a three-dimensional form, modeling or *skiagraphia* in Greek, that a painter can create a sense of volume and mass. In the absence of fifth-century mural paintings, we can find some examples of this on **white-ground vase painting**, in which a white calcareous layer like plaster coats the surface of the vase, as can be seen on the interior of a cup attributed to the Sotades Painter (**Figure 10.21**). This painting technique developed in the sixth century when some black-figure painters applied the coating over the red surface of the vase, but in the fifth century painters began to paint directly on the white surface with colored pigments. While it looks like a wall painting, this cup is only 13.3 cm in diameter, a truly miniature painting. In the picture, a young boy labeled Glaukos, crouching on the right, wears a brown-purple himation pulled over his head. Darker lines create the impression of deep folds in the fabric, while white lines on the garment's edges and creases simulate light catching the ridges of fabric. So too the hair is lighter brown around the temple and darker where it is thicker on top of the head. The effect is to give a sense of mass and volume to the figure. This use of tone to suggest three-dimensionality would become more refined into the fourth century as *skiagraphia*.

white-ground vase painting
form of vase painting, especially in Athens, in which a slip of white calcareous clay was placed on a vase. Figures were then drawn with outlines and washes of color

The same effect can be seen in the arched line that represents the tumulus enclosing the figures. Multiple, thicker lines of yellow at the edge and thinner lines inside create the effect of a curved wall so that we get the sense of looking inside something like a tholos tomb. The figures are not set on a single groundline but on a ground plane with added bits of clay to give it a pebbly texture. This is like the texture of the beach described in the contemporary mural paintings at Delphi by Polygnotos. The arch and ground features give the picture a rudimentary three-dimensional space, both receding and projecting forward.

The mural painter Polygnotos had a reputation in literary sources as a painter of *ethos*, but this is a quality that we can also see even in this miniature painting by the Sotades Painter. In particular, it is the choice of the moment of action that captures the thought and decision-making that define character. Glaukos was the son of king Midas and had disappeared, but was found drowned in a vat of honey by the seer Polyeidos. The distraught king buried his son and the seer in the tomb, and the only hope of escape for Polyeidos was to bring Glaukos back to life. A snake appeared in the tomb and was killed by Polyeidos; it lays coiled at the lip of the cup. When a second snake appeared with an herb in its mouth, Polyeidos hesitated before killing it reflexively and observed its action. The snake placed the herb in the mouth of the dead snake and revived it, thus providing Polyeidos with his means of escape by reviving Glaukos. In the picture Polyeidos is poised with his staff in hand,

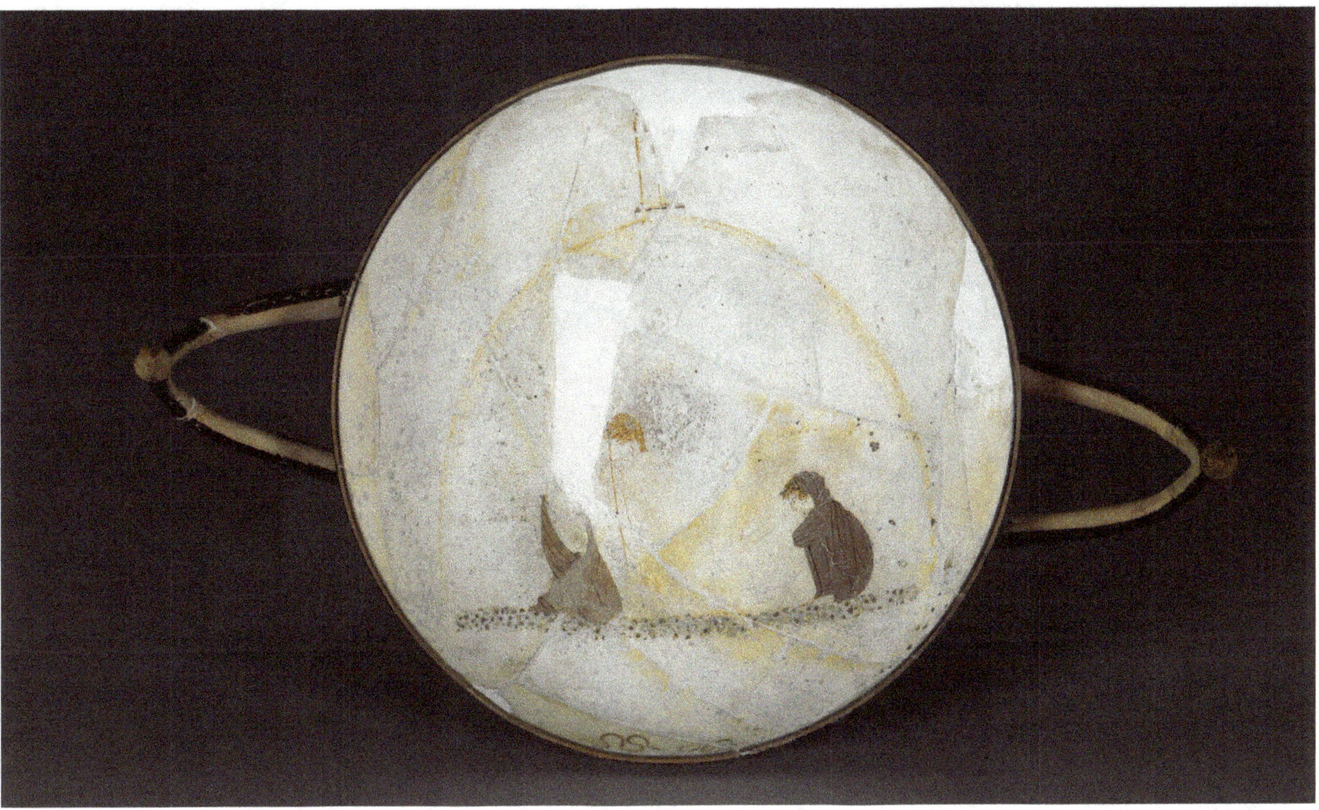

10.21 Attic white-ground kylix attributed to the Sotades Painter, *c.* 460–450 BCE. 5¼ in (13.3 cm) diameter. Polyeidos and Glaukos in the tomb. London, British Museum D5. Photo: © The Trustees of the British Museum.

ready to crush the second snake, drawn at the very rim of the cup, but pauses to observe. This is a moment of decision that will determine his life or death, and he acts with thought rather than fear, revealing his *ethos* as a seer. This focus upon the choice of action as the key to revealing character was apparently present in the painting of Polygnotos, and is a component of the plots in the contemporary tragedies of Aeschylus and Sophocles. It is, indeed, a broad concern of the fifth century, but we should also remember that the focus on a pivotal moment of choice to reveal character is something that could appear earlier, as in Exekias's painting of the suicide of Ajax (**see Figure 9.5, page 216**).

Another innovation attributed to Polygnotos regarding picture space was the placement of figures on multiple groundlines, with figures in the background or distance being higher up in the picture than figures in the foreground. This effect is seen on a pot in the Louvre known as the Niobid krater for its representation of the killing of the children of Niobe on one side. It is better known for its scene of heroes on the other side (**Figure 10.22**). The specific story is uncertain, although Herakles and Athena are easily identified in the center and left, and the seated figures in the foreground are probably Theseus and Peirithoös. The figures are set on undulating lines that represent an uneven terrain. Herakles is higher than the two seated figures below and in front of him, as can be seen by their overlapping limbs, making him further back in space. Athena is lower than Herakles and closer to the picture plane, but still behind Theseus and Peirithoös. Behind Athena is the top half of a warrior; his lower half is hidden by the hillock that is behind Athena, so he is even deeper in the picture and moving toward the front and center. This use of levels to represent depth of space is not a true perspectival system, which would be more precisely measurable and also involve the reduction in size of figures in the background compared to the foreground. That development would take place later in the fifth century, as we shall discuss below.

A white-ground lekythos attributed to the Achilles Painter brings us to the third-quarter of the fifth century, contemporary with the Doryphoros and Parthenon frieze (**Figure 10.23**). In this

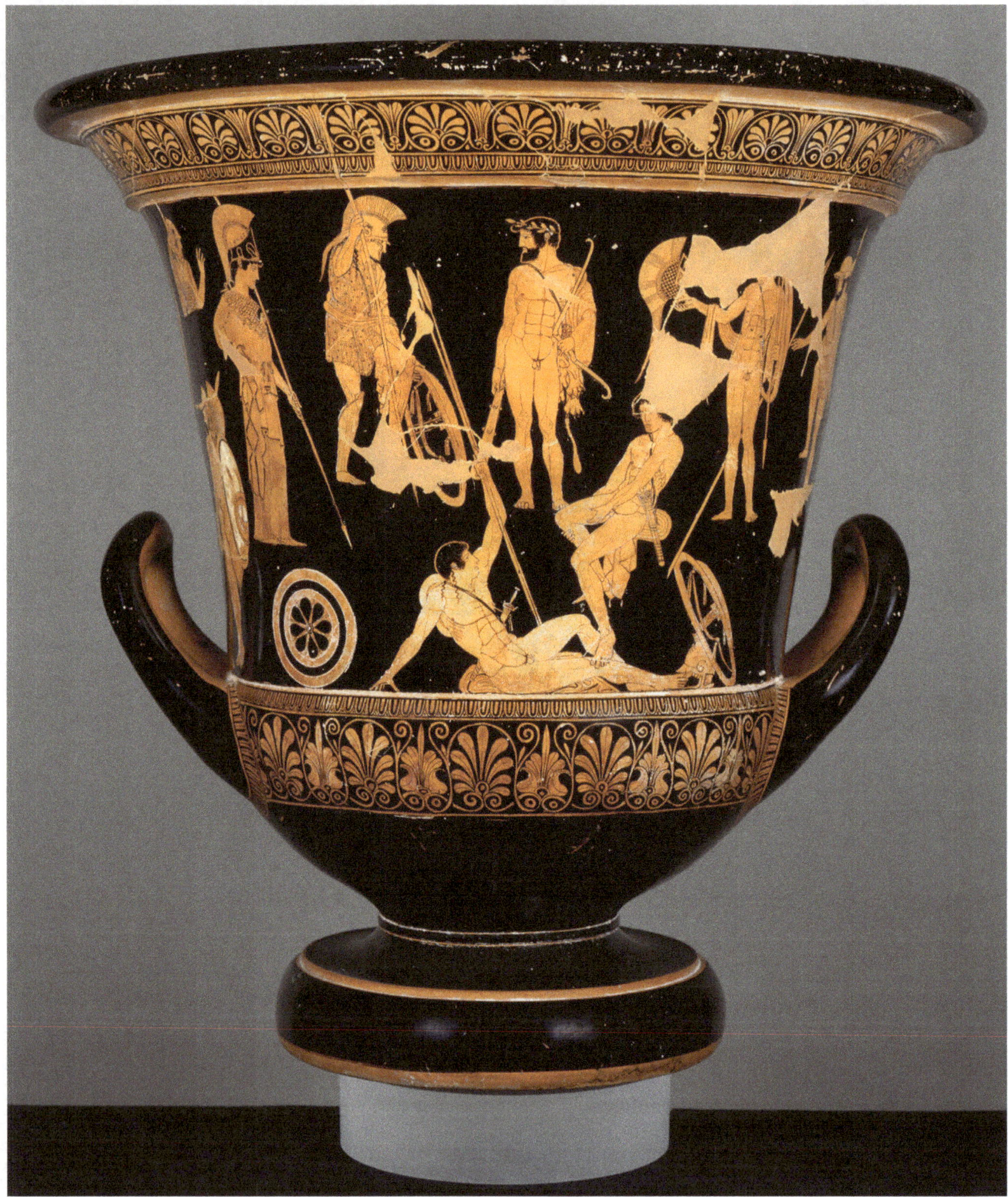

10.22 Attic red-figure calyx krater attributed to the Niobid Painter, *c.* 460–450 BCE. 21¼ in (54 cm). Paris, Musée du Louvre, G341. Scene with heroes. Photo: © RMN-Grand Palais/Art Resource, NY.

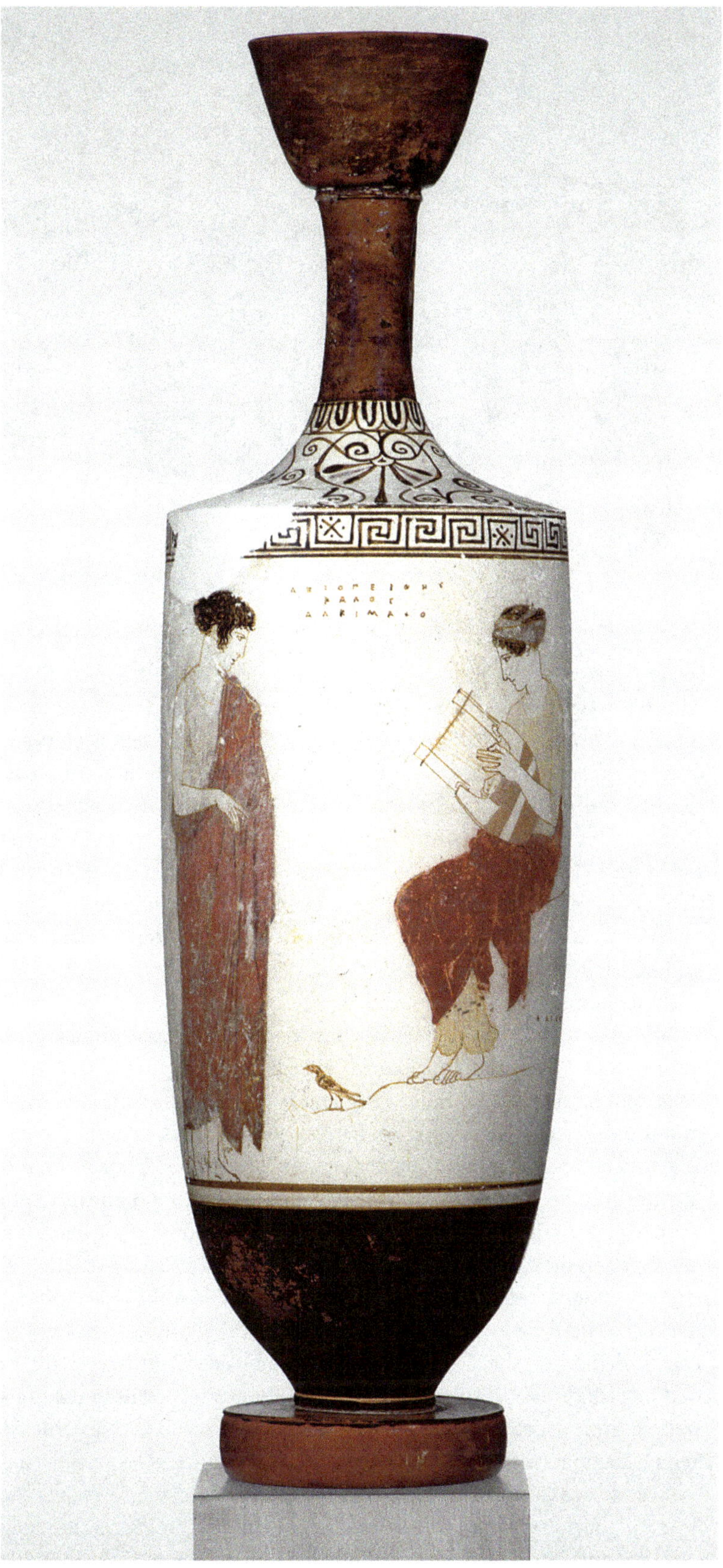

10.23 Attic white-ground lekythos attributed to the Achilles Painter, *c.* 440 BCE. Height of picture 6⅛ in (15.5 cm). Muses on Mount Helikon. Munich, Staatliche Antikensammlung und Glyptothek, Schoen 80. Photo: Renate Kühling.

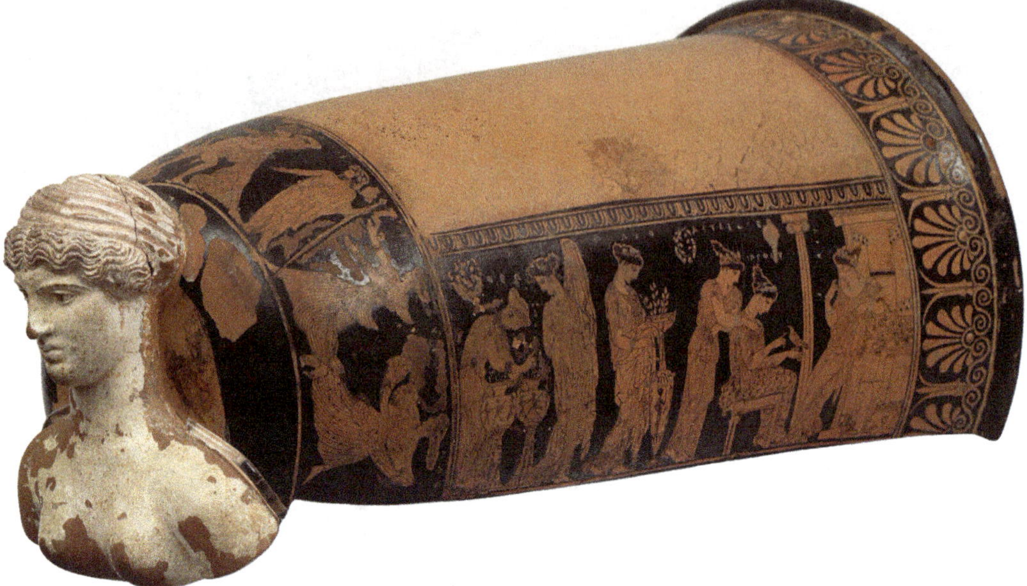

10.24 Attic red-figure epinetron attributed to the Eretria Painter, *c.* 425–420 BCE. 6⁵⁄₁₆ in (16 cm). Athens, National Archaeological Museum 1629. Bridal reception of Alkestis (*epaulia*). Photo: National Archaeological Museum, Athens (Giannis Patrikianos) © Hellenic Ministry of Education and Religious Affairs, Culture and Sports/Archaeological Receipts Fund.

scene of two muses on Mount Helikon, we see that the standing figure is in a *contrapposto* pose, with her weight on her left leg and the right leg turned outward toward the viewer. The second muse is seated on a ledge and plucks a lyre. She wears a yellow chiton under a red mantle, and the drapery of both figures has a sense of movement as well as the mass under it, created in part through the traces of the brown contour lines under the paint that define the body's features. Details of the toes, fingers, and face show a mastery of different viewing angles, including a frontal foot with heavy foreshortening, and the eye is now drawn in a completely profile view. These figures have the same poise and grandeur as the participants in the Parthenon procession and figures found in the later grave stelai, as would be appropriate for a funerary object like a white-ground lekythos.

A contemporary red-figure work is the skyphos by the Penelope Painter that we have seen before, with Penelope and her son Telemachos on one side **(see Figure 5.19, page 118)** and Odysseus returning to Ithaca and being recognized by his nurse on the other **(see Figure 9.9, page 221)**. Penelope crosses her legs while seated and rests her head against her hand; her face and shoulders are in a three-quarter view that suggests real volume and certainly pathos as she waits for Odysseus. Telemachos's pose is assured and convincing like the Doryphoros. An interesting touch is the red slip that has been hatched on the surface of the textile in front of the line defining his profile. This would seem to be a shadow cast from a light source in front and to the left. This is rare, but helps to suggest the recession into space.

epinetron
a device worn over the knee to protect against abrasion and cuts from working with wool

epaulia
term designating the reception held by a bride in her new home on the day after the wedding procession

As in sculpture, the last quarter of the century sees the development of a wet drapery style, the florid style, and a more delicate sensibility in the figures. The **epinetron** attributed to the Eretria Painter depicts on the side the mythological bride Alkestis receiving her friends the day after her wedding (the ***epaulia***) **(Figure 10.24)**. The figures relax within the household in languorous poses, isolated from the cares of the world outside. The work is a little earlier than the Nike from the Nike Temple parapet **(see Figure 10.18)**, but is similar in its effort to show a thin garment that clings to a body and reveals the anatomy underneath. Since red-figure details have to be drawn by contour lines, the florid style in vase painting results in a web of lines that makes the shape of the breasts awkward and can obscure the contours of the limbs more than in sculpture. The style is sometimes more effective with partly clad figures like the Gigantomachy in the late fifth-century pelike in Chapter 9 **(Figure 9.3, page 214)**.

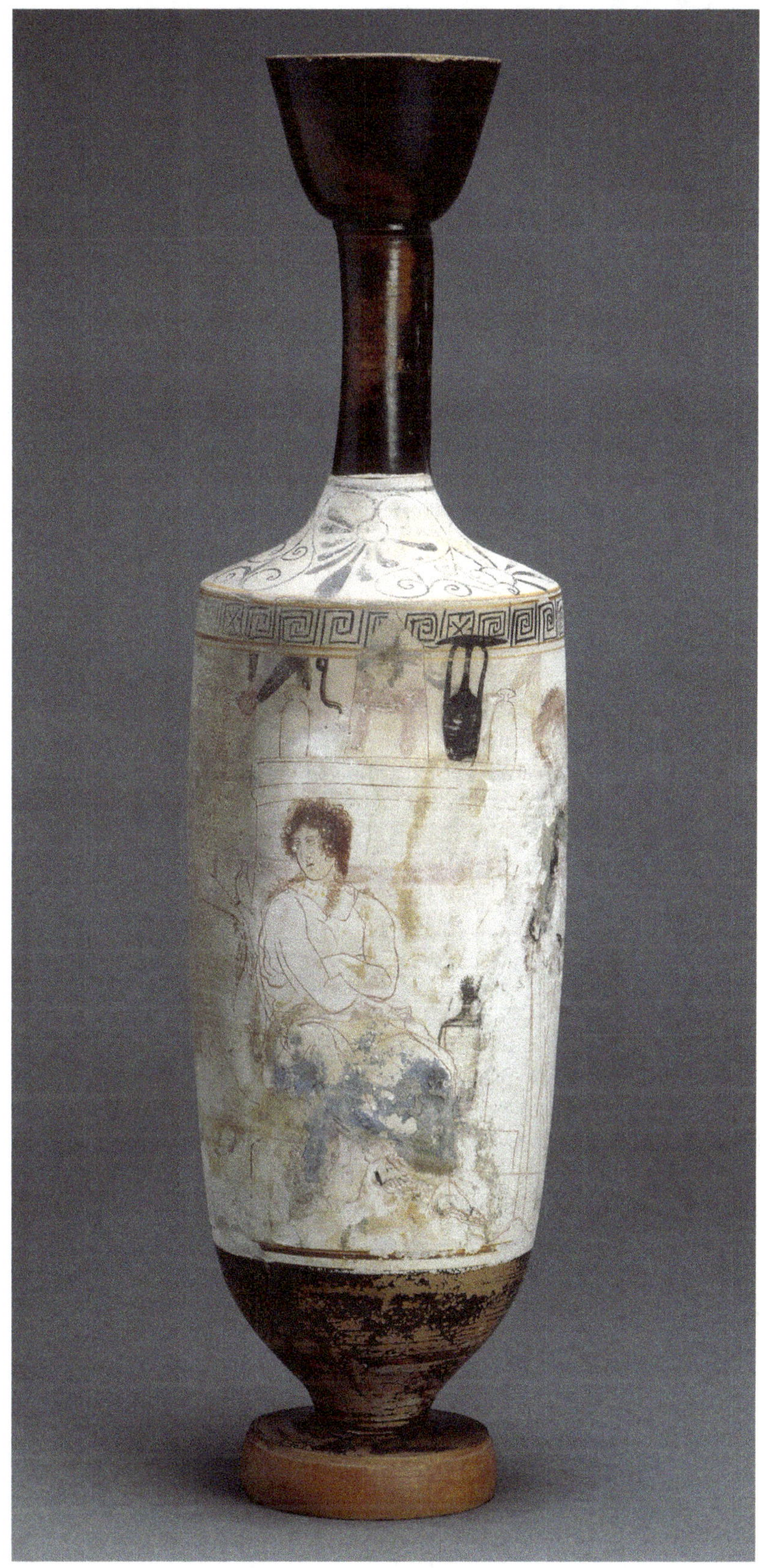

10.25 Attic white-ground lekythos attributed to the Reed Painter, *c.* 420–400 BCE. 20 in (50.8 cm). London, British Museum D71. Woman at tomb. Photo: © The Trustees of the British Museum.

Vitruvius (*De Arch.* 7.11) credits the invention of *skenographia*, or spatial perspective, to the painter Agatharchos, who was active in the second half of the fifth century. He developed a system for painting stage scenery that was similar to one-point linear perspective and included the diminishment of scale with distance. As with the painting of Polygnotos, none of his work survives, nor does the treatise that he wrote on the subject. As a system being used in large public spectacles like theatrical dramas, however, it would become part of the visual vocabulary of the classical period and was refined by other painters. It is difficult to find detailed traces of such a system in vase painting, but a late fifth-century lekythos shows the habit of a perspective view in its drawing of a tomb and its offerings **(Figure 10.25)**. A woman, probably the deceased, sits in front of the tomb on its plinth. Behind her rises the front of a stone stele with a cornice molding on top. On the top ledge is set an obelisk-shaped slab and three vases, including two stone alabastra on the ends. The bottoms of the vessels are cut off by the cornice, since from a vantage point from below, it would cut off that view. The mouths of the alabastra are foreshortened as ovals and are seen from below, but tilted so that they remain parallel to the ground plane. The drawing is only an approximation of a perspective system that was sketched rather than plotted on the picture surface, but it gives a hint of how *skenographia* could define a picture space in late fifth-century painting that worked with foreshortening and *skiagraphia* to create a three-dimensional picture.

To conclude, we might consider that Greek art has changed from its emphasis upon schemata and formulas in the sixth century to the exploration of mimesis in fifth-century art. Pictures develop means for representing a three-dimensional world on a flat surface, while buildings and sculpture adjust their proportions to create a visual effect upon the viewer. Artists articulate the human body as one in dynamic motion and balance even when at rest, and represent nuances of facial expression, gaze, and gesture to reveal the *pathos* of the person being represented. Together, these express the *ethos* of a figure, particularly when the narrative moment focuses on an instant of choice and decision. In these ways, fifth-century visual art shared similar concerns and themes with Greek drama and the other mimetic arts.

TEXTBOX: THE PARTHENON MARBLES AND CULTURAL PATRIMONY

As we have seen, the provenance of an object is important for all aspects of its study; the collecting or looting of antiquities over the centuries has erased much of our knowledge of contexts. In the case of the Parthenon marbles, their context is well known but the circumstances of their acquisition have generated controversy since Lord Elgin offered them to the British Museum (see Fitz Gibbon 2005 for review). By the standards of the early nineteenth century, their removal from the Parthenon, shipment back to England, and their sale and installation in a museum were not remarkable, but by modern standards they present a particularly difficult ethical problem regarding cultural patrimony.

As defined by UNESCO in 1970, "the term 'cultural property' means property which, on religious or secular grounds, is specifically designated by each State as being of importance for archaeology, prehistory, history, literature, art or science" (UNESCO 1970, Article 1). In Article 2, it proclaims that those adopting the convention "recognize that the illicit import, export and transfer of ownership of cultural property is one of the main causes of the impoverishment of the cultural heritage of the countries of origin of such property and that international co-operation constitutes one of the most efficient means of protecting each country's cultural property against all the dangers resulting there from." The Convention was not intended to cover the restitution of cultural property legally owned at the time it came into effect, but to provide a means for halting the trade in antiquities that was leading to a huge loss of cultural patrimony, as has been amply documented in journalistic investigations in recent years (see Felch and Frammolino 2011; Watson and Todeschini 2007).

One of the most famous recent examples of the problem is a krater signed by Euphronios that was bought by the Metropolitan Museum of Art in 1972 for about $1,000,000 **(Figure 10.26)**. Claims quickly emerged that the work had been illegally procured from an Etruscan tomb north of Rome, but counterclaims of another provenance were offered by the dealer. With the discovery of documentation for the krater in the warehouse of a middleman who acquired objects from *tombaroli* or tomb raiders and provided them to dealers, it was clear that the work was acquired contrary to the guidelines of the UNESCO Convention. Finally, in 2008, the museum sent the krater and other works back to Italy. A constructive development, however, was the offer by the Italian government to lend significant works to the museum as part of a long-term agreement.

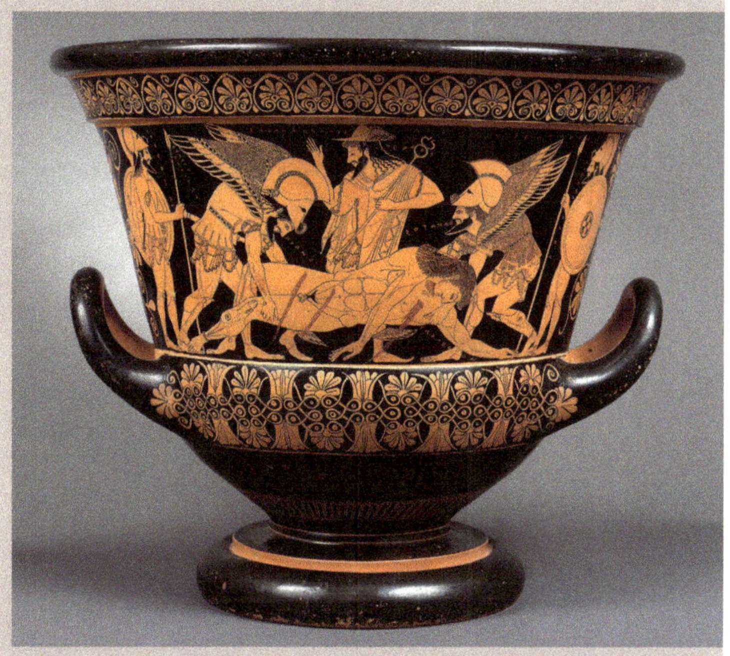

10.26 Attic red-figure calyx krater signed by Euphronios from Cerveteri, *c.* 520–510 BCE. Death of Sarpedon. Rome, Museo Nazionale di Villa Giulia. Photo: Scala/Ministero per i Beni e le Attività culturali/Art Resource, NY.

This act of diplomacy, in light of the decades of difficulties, claims, and counterclaims, is encouraging for a long-term solution. It is perhaps worthwhile, then, to recall the law court scene on the Shield of Achilles (*Il.* 18.497–501) mentioned in Chapter 4 (see p. 70). As Homer describes the debate over a murder and its consequences, it is the polis that is to decide the outcome. In other words, one might say that the solution to problems concerning key monuments of cultural patrimony needs to be decided politically. Although politics has become a dirty word today in many countries, in the context of the polis, debate and compromise are vital for developing a global solution to the issue of cultural property and patrimony. The UNESCO Convention of 1970 is one example of a positive step toward protecting and preserving cultural property, and national laws and museum practices are gradually catching up to fulfill its principles. Dealing with what happened before 1970 will require even greater efforts by the next generation.

REFERENCES

Felch, J. and R. Frammolino. 2011. *Chasing Aphrodite: The Hunt for Looted Antiquities at the World's Richest Museum*. Boston/New York: Houghton Mifflin Harcourt.

Fitz Gibbon, K. 2005. "The Elgin Marbles: A Summary." In K. Fitz Gibbon, ed. *Who Owns the Past? Cultural Policy, Cultural Property, and the Law*, 109–121. New Brunswick, NJ: Rutgers University Press.

Holloway, R. R. 2006. "The Tomb of the Diver." *American Journal of Archaeology* 110, 365–388.

Hurwit, J. M. 1989. "The Kritios Boy: Discovery, Reconstruction, and Date." *American Journal of Archaeology* 93, 41–80.

Mattusch, C. C. 1996. *Classical Bronzes: The Art and Craft of Greek and Roman Statuary*. Ithaca: Cornell University Press.

Morris, S. B. 1992. *Daidalos and the Origins of Greek Art*. Princeton: Princeton University Press.

Neer, R. 2010. *The Emergence of the Classical Style in Greek Sculpture*. Chicago: University of Chicago Press.

Pollitt, J. J. 1972. *Art and Experience in Classical Greece*. Cambridge: Cambridge University Press.

Pollitt, J. J. 1990. *The Art of Ancient Greece: Sources and Documents*. Cambridge/New York: Cambridge University Press.

Pollitt, J. J. 1997. "The Meaning of the Parthenon Frieze." In D. Buitron-Oliver, ed. *The Interpretation of Architectural Sculpture in Greece and Rome*. Studies in the History of Art, 49, 51–65. Hanover/London: National Gallery of Art, Washington.

Stansbury-O'Donnell, M. D. 1999. *Pictorial Narrative in Ancient Greek Art*. Cambridge/New York: Cambridge University Press.

Stewart, A. F. 2008a. "The Persian and Carthaginian Invasions of 480 B.C.E. and the Beginning of the Classical Style: Part 1, The Stratigraphy, Chronology, and Significance of the Acropolis Debris." *American Journal of Archaeology* 112, 377–412.

Stewart, A. F. 2008b. "The Persian and Carthaginian Invasions of 480 B.C.E. and the Beginning of the Classical Style: Part 2, The Finds from Other Sites in Athens, Attica, Elsewhere in Greece, and on Sicily; Part 3, The Severe Style: Motivations and Meaning." *American Journal of Archaeology* 112, 581–616.

Stewart, A. F. 2008c. *Classical Greece and the Birth of Western Art*. Cambridge/New York: Cambridge University Press.

Thucydides. *The History of the Peloponnesian War*, tr. Richard Crawley. 2009. Project Gutenberg eBook 7142: http://www.gutenberg.org/files/7142/7142-h/7142-h.htm (last accessed May 11, 2014).

UNESCO. 1970. *Convention on the Means of Prohibiting and Preventing the Illicit Import, Export and Transfer of Ownership of Cultural Property 1970*. Paris: UNESCO, November 14, 1970: http://portal.unesco.org/en/ev.php-URL_ID=13039&URL_DO=DO_TOPIC&URL_SECTION=201.html (last accessed May 11, 2014).

Watson, P. and C. Todeschini. 2007. *The Medici Conspiracy: The Illicit Journey of Looted Antiquities, from Italy's Tomb Raiders to the World's Greatest Museums*. New York: Public Affairs.

Williams, D. 2013. *The East Pediment of the Parthenon: From Perikles to Nero*. Bulletin of the Institute of Classical Studies Supplement 118. London: Institute of Classical Studies.

Younger, J. G. and P. Rehak. 2009. "Technical Observations on the Sculptures from the Temple of Zeus at Olympia." *Hesperia* 78, 41–105.

FURTHER READING

Hurwit, J. 2004. *The Acropolis in the Age of Pericles*. Cambridge/New York: Cambridge University Press.

Mattusch, C. C. 1996. *Classical Bronzes: The Art and Craft of Greek and Roman Statuary*. Ithaca: Cornell University Press.

Oakley, J. H. 2004. *Picturing Death: The Evidence of the White Lekythoi*. Cambridge/New York: Cambridge University Press.

Pollitt, J. J. 1972. *Art and Experience in Classical Greece*. Cambridge: Cambridge University Press.

Robertson, M. 1992. *The Art of Vase-Painting in Classical Athens*. Cambridge: Cambridge University Press.

Stansbury-O'Donnell, M. D. 2014. "Reflections of Monumental Painting in Greek Vase Painting of the 5th and 4th Centuries BC." In J. J. Pollitt, ed. *The Cambridge History of Painting in the Classical World*, 1143–1169. Cambridge: Cambridge University Press.

Stewart, A. F. 2008. *Classical Greece and the Birth of Western Art*. Cambridge/New York: Cambridge University Press.

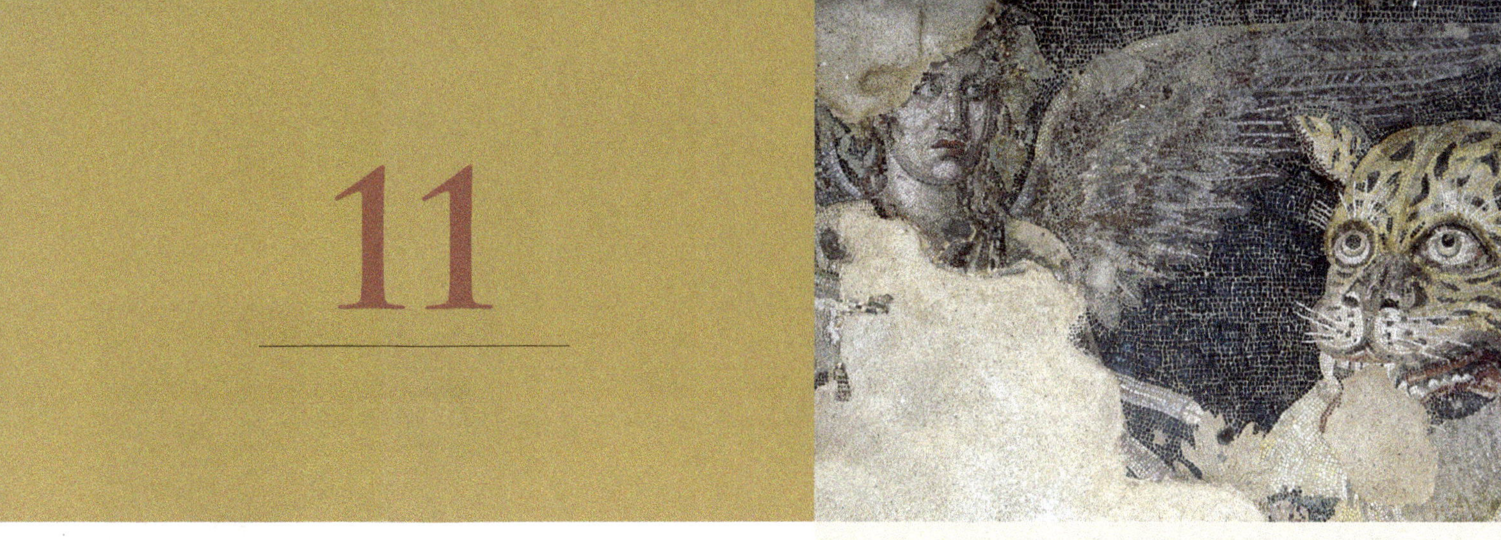

11

THE PRODUCTION OF GREEK ART AND ITS MARKETS

Timeline
Production: Architecture
Production: Architectural Sculpture
Production: Sculpture
Production: Pottery
Wares, Markets, and Distribution
Artists and Workshops
Textbox: The Value of Greek Art
References
Further Reading

A History of Greek Art, First Edition. Mark D. Stansbury-O'Donnell.

TIMELINE

	Architecture and Relief	Pottery Production
800–700		Dipylon Master
700–600		Protocorinthian black-figure Protoattic Eastern Greek pottery
600–500		Corinthian black-figure Attic black-figure Attic red-figure (from 530)
500–400	Parthenon, 447–432 Polykleitos, active 450–430 Grave stele of Ampharete, 430 Erechtheion reliefs, 410–406	Attic black-figure (early) Attic red-figure Attic white-ground Attic black-glaze ware Lucanian red-figure (late)
400–300	Temple of Asklepios at Epidauros, 370 Praxiteles, active mid-4th cent.	Attic red-figure and Kerch style Black-glaze ware Gnathian ware Apulian red-figure Lucanian red-figure
300–200		Apulian red-figure Gnathian ware West Slope ware Paestan red-figure
200–1	Damophon of Messene, early 2nd cent. Hagesandros, Polydoros, Athenodoros, later 1st cent.	Mold-made wares

As we saw in the last chapter, the Parthenon was part of an ambitious rebuilding program undertaken by the leader of Athens, Perikles, and supervised by Pheidias (see Figure 10.10, page 247). In addition to the buildings on and around the Acropolis, the Athenian building program between 455 and 430 BCE included other temples, such as the Hephaisteion in the Agora (see Figure 5.6, page 105), the Telesterion in Eleusis, the Temple of Poseidon on Cape Sounion, the Temple of Athena at Pallene, and the Temple of Nemesis at Rhamnous. This was a highly unusual amount of construction for a single polis in a period of just a few decades. Financing the program was made possible by the revenue from the silver mines at Laurion, which had in wartime paid for the large naval fleet that was the foundation of Athenian military power. According to his Roman-era biographer Plutarch, Perikles also appropriated funds from the Delian Treasury, which was the common defense fund for the alliance of states against the Persians, to the consternation of and in the face of futile protests from the tributary states (Plutarch, *Vita Perikles* 12).

Large building projects, ancient as well as modern, generate costs, benefits, and debates, and it is important to consider the economics of art and architecture in addition to their design, function, and meaning. A larger than average temple made out of marble like the Parthenon would cost much more than the nearly contemporary and smaller Temple of Concord at Akragas/Agrigento (see Figure 7.5, page 161), which was more typical in size and used softer sandstone, making it a much less expensive public undertaking. Considering the cost and organization of production can help us appreciate the investment made in a building and its decoration, and understand the source of pride or meaning that it could represent for the ancient citizen. Indeed, according to Thucydides, this is what Perikles had prompted the citizens of Athens to do, to look upon their city as its lovers, as we saw in the last chapter. We can extend this examination from civic projects to the production and distribution of objects bought and used by individuals, such as pots, to gauge their value within Greek culture. Whereas an attributed pot today could sell for $1,000,000 and more, its original value was quite different, as we shall see. Attempting to calculate past values helps us put these works into context.

In this chapter we will consider aspects of production first, focusing on buildings and then sculpture and pottery. Greek art, as we have seen, circulated widely, so that its users were often far from its producers. We will look at the distribution of both sculpture and pottery, not just as a way of spreading a style or narrative, but also as part of the commercial network that tied artist and viewer together. Finally, artists themselves were mobile, and we will explore some examples of artists who moved into and away from Greece, as well as the status of the artist in antiquity.

PRODUCTION: ARCHITECTURE

The documentation of building costs during the first millennium BCE is meager, but there are two important sets of inscriptions that provide information on the organization and cost of construction. We have already noted the fragmentary records for the Acropolis that provide us with precise dating for the Parthenon, but the tablets also record some of the costs of specific items. A more complete set of inscriptions was found at Epidauros, which recorded contracts and expenditures for the fourth-century building program there, including the Temple of Asklepios, which was built in a five-year period about 370 BCE. As can be seen in the reconstruction of the site in the next chapter (see Figure 12.1, page 289), the temple was of a modest size, 11.76 meters wide and 23.06 meters long with a 6 × 11 peristyle, and was built of limestone. Based on the inscriptions, the temple was constructed in a sequence of phases over this five-year period (Younger and Rehak 2009):

Phase/Year 1: quarrying, colonnade foundations

Phase/Year 2: construction of colonnade, foundations of cella

Phase/Year 3: construction of cella

Phase/Year 4: construction of ceiling and roof, installation of doors and floors

Phase/Year 5: fluting of columns, roof tiles, finishing work

This sequence would be typical of other temples, but the length of time would vary by size, materials, and financing. By comparison, the Epidauros temple is smaller than the Temple of Concord at Akragas/Agrigento (16.93 m × 39.42 m) **(see Figure 7.5, page 161)**, but that structure was made with softer sandstone that was available almost within sight of the temple, whereas the limestone for Epidauros had to be carted from nearby Corinth. The Hephaisteion in the Athenian Agora **(see Figure 5.6, page 105)** was also larger (13.71 m × 31.77 m), but its use of marble, a harder stone to quarry and finish than limestone, would have required more labor and expense.

For a much larger building like the Parthenon (30.88 m × 69.51 m) that was also made of marble, a longer construction period was necessary, even with lavish resources. The building accounts for the Acropolis tell us that the work was mostly completed, except for the pedimental sculptures, in ten years, between 447 and 438 BCE. This ten-year period for construction was probably typical for other large projects like the Temple of Zeus at Olympia (27.68 m × 64.12 m) or the Temple of Hera II at Poseidonia/Paestum (24.26 m × 59.97 m), even though these buildings used limestone rather than marble for the structure. Based on written accounts, the Temple of Zeus was begun after 470 BCE and the acroteria dedicated about 457, so a ten-year period seems quite reasonable for the construction.

The Epidauros accounts are valuable not only for understanding the phases and timing of construction, but also for the costs associated with the different activities. Most of the costs are associated with labor rather than ready-made materials: quarrying and shaping the stone, transportation from the quarry to the building site, construction of the building, and finishing work. It is estimated that, typically, about half of the labor costs for a temple are consumed by quarrying and one-fourth by transportation. The refinements that we see in the architectural details and sculptural programs of a temple, as well as its painting, thus consume a small part of the overall building costs, despite receiving the bulk of art historians' attention.

According to the accounts at Epidauros, the Temple of Asklepios cost a total of 23–24 talents. Translating ancient monetary units into modern equivalents is very difficult. A talent was a specific weight; this varied by polis, but in Athens it was about 26 kilograms, and as a monetary unit it would be equivalent to that weight of silver. One talent would equal 6,000 drachmas, each drachma weighing about 4.3 grams of silver, and a drachma could be subdivided into 6 obols. The price and, more important, the purchasing power of silver in antiquity are not the same as now, making direct comparison by the value of silver misleading. An alternative approach would be to look at the drachma as a measure of household income since workers and contractors, like those at Epidauros, were paid in drachmas. According to sources, a drachma was about the wage paid for a single day of labor; one-half drachma was the amount set for jury pay in Athens under Perikles, which allowed its citizens to participate in the judicial process without undue financial sacrifice in lost wages. Allowing about sixty days for festivals and rest, a household income would be around 300 drachmas per year. If we consider that 300 drachmas represented the median income of an ancient Greek household, we could compare it to the median household income today. In the United States this is currently about $50,000/year, so that 300 dr = $50,000, making one drachma equal to about $167, or somewhere between $150 and $180. A talent, 6,000 drachmas, would be about the same as $1,000,000 ($167 × 6,000 dr).

The temple at Epidauros cost 23–24 Aiginetan talents, so for comparison to the Attic monetary standards used in the Parthenon, this would be about 34 Attic talents. The total cost of the Temple of Asklepios, then, would be about $34,000,000. While this comparison is only a rough approximation, it does give us an idea of the relative cost of a building like the temple at Epidauros, and a guide for other temples without building accounts. While the Temple of Concord at Akragas/Agrigento was larger than Epidauros, it was also made of a softer material (sandstone) and the quarry was much closer to the site, so the total costs may have been on a similar scale to the temple at Epidauros.

Temples like these were certainly significant civic undertakings, but in scale they are not too different from a large campus or civic building today. Their construction would require planning and some additional resources, but not necessarily a heavy tax or special levy.

By comparison with the work at Epidauros and based on the more incomplete Acropolis inscriptions, estimates of the cost of the Parthenon are about 470 talents, although this might be a little low and does not include the cost of the monumental chryselephantine sculpture of Athena on the interior, which may have been 800 talents more. The Parthenon, then, cost fourteen times more than the temple in Epidauros, and was just one of several major building projects being funded by Athens at that time. Using the figure of $1 million = 1 talent, the cost of the Parthenon's construction would be roughly $470 million, about the same as a new sports stadium without a roof. The total annual revenue for Athens around this time is estimated to have been 400 talents, which was far more than was available to other cities. The Parthenon, then, would have consumed at least 10 percent of the total annual city budget over the ten years of its basic construction, and was one of only several simultaneous building projects underway. Given the controversies over funding such large projects today, one can see the advantage for Perikles of using revenue from both the silver mines and the Delian League Treasury to help fund the Parthenon and all of the rest of his building program, rather than relying on the city budget or imposing additional taxes on the citizens of Athens. While this was not popular with the members of the Delian League, who had essentially become tributary states in an Athenian empire, it meant that the building program would provide substantial income for the city's workers and residents and could be politically advantageous for Perikles, enabling him to remain in power.

PRODUCTION: ARCHITECTURAL SCULPTURE

The accounts at Epidauros provide finer details about parts of the building costs. For example, the contract to a man named Marsyas for the fluting of the interior and exterior columns in the last year of construction showed a payment of 1,336 Aiginetan drachmas, or 1,908 Attic drachmas. Thus, an expenditure of 1,900 drachmas would equal approximately 1,900 worker-days. At 300 worker-days per year, this would suggest that Marsyas had a team of six workers for the year, probably including himself.

For the pediments at Epidauros, sculpture workshops were set up in Phase/Year 3 and work on the sculpture occurred mostly in Phase/Year 4. Payment was made for the west pediment, half of the east pediment and acroteria that year, and for the rest of the east pediment in Phase/Year 5. The subject of the west pediment is an Amazonomachy (**Figure 11.1**) and that of the east pediment an *Iliupersis*. Both pediments originally had about twenty figures, each carved in the round and using Pentelic marble from Athens, rather than the limestone from Corinth that was used for the temple's structure. Marble was harder both to quarry and then to carve, but would give greater durability, detail, and luster to the sculpture. For the architectural sculpture at Epidauros, then, the materials would have created additional costs for quarrying and transportation. There are other cases, such as the archaic temple at Delphi and the Temple of Zeus at Olympia, where marble was imported from afar and used for the architectural sculpture rather than limestone. For example, John Younger and Paul Rehak calculate that the marble sculpture at Olympia (**see Figure 9.14, page 228; Figure 10.9, page 246**), which was made with marble from the island of Paros, would have cost 2.40 talents for the carving, between 7 and 10.67 talents for the quarrying, and 40–80 talents for the transportation, much more than the cost of the entire temple at Epidauros (Younger and Rehak 2009).

For the carving of the pedimental figures at Epidauros, the building accounts tell us that each pedimental group cost 4,300 Attic drachmas (3,010 Aiginetan drachmas) and the acroteria for each end were 3,200 Attic drachmas (2,240 Aiginetan drachmas), with the total cost of the sculptural program coming to 15,000 Attic drachmas, or 2.5 talents, about 7.3 percent of the total building cost.

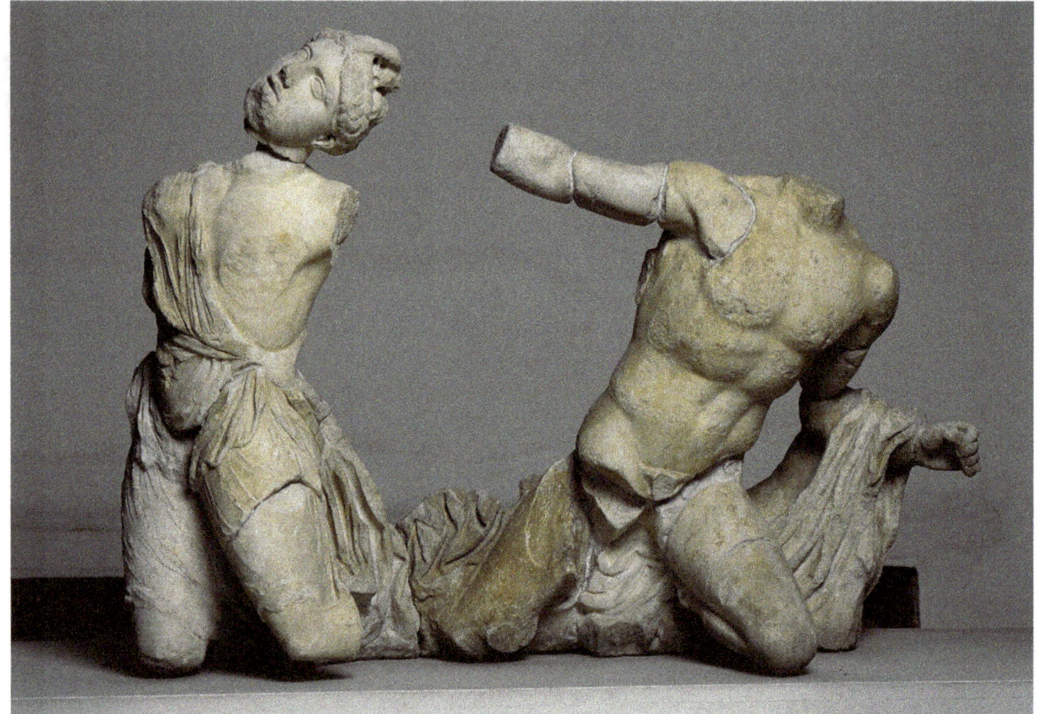

11.1 West pediment from the Temple of Asklepios at Epidauros, *c.* 370 BCE. Detail of warrior and Amazon. 21⅝ in (0.55 m). Athens, National Archaeological Museum 139, 140, 149, 4752. Photo: National Archaeological Museum, Athens (Kostas Xenikakis) © Hellenic Ministry of Education and Religious Affairs, Culture and Sports/Archaeological Receipts Fund.

The contract for the west pediment was given to Hektoridas in two parts, and seems to have taken two years to complete, while the contract for the east pediment was given for one year to someone whose name is missing from the tablets. Each of the pedimental figures at Epidauros would, then, have cost about 215 drachmas for the carving (Schultz 2009; Younger and Rehak 2009). Such an amount is about three-fourths of the median annual wage; since the figures are three-quarters life-size, this would generally agree with estimates that it would take about a working year for one sculptor to carve a life-size marble statue. Since the ensemble was finished within a year, this indicates that the contractors had teams of sculptors working for them; Hektoridas's workshop may have been smaller, which is perhaps why that work was divided over two years.

As we shall see with the Erechtheion frieze, the wages for the pedimental sculptors at Epidauros would generally be about the same as for other skilled labor. For the acroteria sculpture, however, there was a higher wage rate. The two sculptors for these, Timotheos and someone whose name began Theo--, were paid 3,200 Attic drachmas each, about 800 drachmas per figure **(Figure 11.2)**. While the acroteria figures are a bit larger than the pedimental figures, they are made of the same material, so that the time to carve them was not four times greater. This means that Timotheos and his colleague were paid at a higher wage rate than the pedimental sculptors. As Peter Schultz has argued, the style of the acroteria figures is more complex, intricate, and finished than that of the pedimental figures (Schultz 2009). Some of the additional cost of the figures, then, must be attributable to the greater labor involved, but some of that labor includes the effort demanded of a more accomplished technique and style. This may be a case where a premium is paid for a higher level of skill and artistry. Even so, given the longer time needed for fabrication, it still amounts to no more than a doubling of the wages. Whereas Hektoridas and his crew seem to have been paid the same wage as those who did the quarrying and transportation, Timotheos was paid more.

The costs for the sculpture at Epidauros generally match those in the Acropolis accounts, which include payments made for the relief sculpture on the frieze of the Erechtheion during the last decade of the fifth century (**Figure 11.3**). The inscriptions record payments to specific individuals by the finished piece, such as "[payment to] Phyromachos of Kephisia for the young man with the breastplate: 60 drachmas" (Pollitt 1990, 192). Other sculptors received different amounts for other subjects, but all working out to a standard rate of 60 drachmas per figure. The reliefs were originally about 65 cm in height and made to be set into a blue marble block; consequently they were not part of the building fabric and were more readily transported. The price and size would suggest that it took about two months to make each figure, which would have cost about $10,000 by our earlier estimates of the modern comparative value of the drachma ($167 × 60).

In conclusion, we can see that from the patron's point of view, architectural sculpture could be more expensive proportionally than other construction costs and was a notable if relatively small part of the total cost of a project. Most of the time, however, the wages paid to the sculptors were the same as those paid to other skilled workers, including those who carved the architectural ornament and painted the building. There were probably cases, such as cult statues or highly prominent pieces such as acroteria, where some premium was paid for more accomplished work, but even this was probably eclipsed by the cost of the quarrying and transportation in the final expenditure on the project.

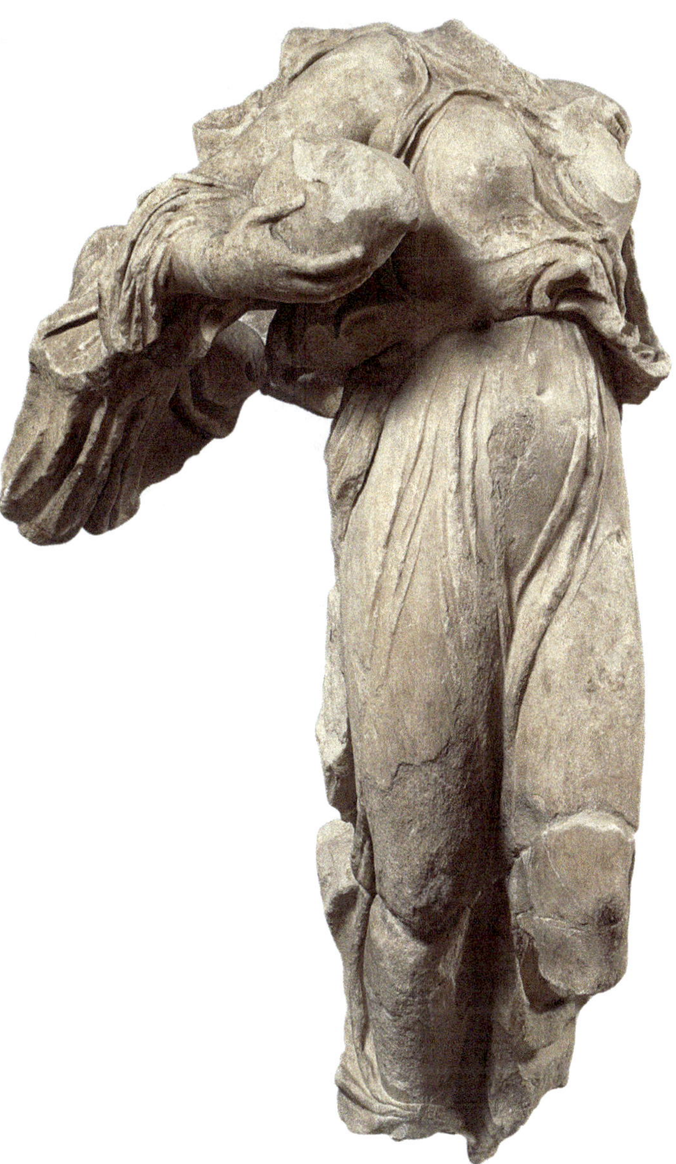

11.2 Nike acroterion from west pediment from the Temple of Asklepios at Epidauros, *c.* 370 BCE. 33½ in (0.85 m). Athens, National Archaeological Museum 155. Photo: National Archaeological Museum, Athens (Giannis Patrikianos) © Hellenic Ministry of Education and Religious Affairs, Culture and Sports/ Archaeological Receipts Fund.

PRODUCTION: SCULPTURE

The accounts for the Erechtheion and Epidauros are also of interest for what they tell us about the status of artists, and more particularly sculptors. Looking at the Erechtheion accounts, the names of the sculptors fall into two forms. One gives the name followed by the *deme* or tribe to which they belonged, such as Phyromachos of Kephisia or Hiasos of Kollytos. The other states their residence, such as Praxias living in Melite and Mynnion living in Argyle. The distinction is between Athenian citizens and **metics**, or foreign (non-Athenian) residents living and working in Athens. Overall, about three-fifths of the names in the Erechtheion accounts are metics. In some cases a name is followed by that of a master, indicating a slave, or the name is common for a slave; most of these were employed as masons or carpenters rather than sculptors or painters (Randall 1953).

metic
term for a foreign resident in a city. These were free individuals, but with limited legal rights

The Epidauros accounts also include Athenian sculptors such as Timotheos who worked on site. Sculptors had to be mobile if they were interested in working on large projects, but how they were selected is less clear. The public nature of the contracts would mean that the project would have to be announced and a proposal or offer made before an award could be granted. It is possible that sculptors and their workshops might have competed against one another. A story in Pliny's *Natural History* (34.53) records that Polykleitos, Pheidias, Kresilas, Kydon, and Phradmon all made statues of a

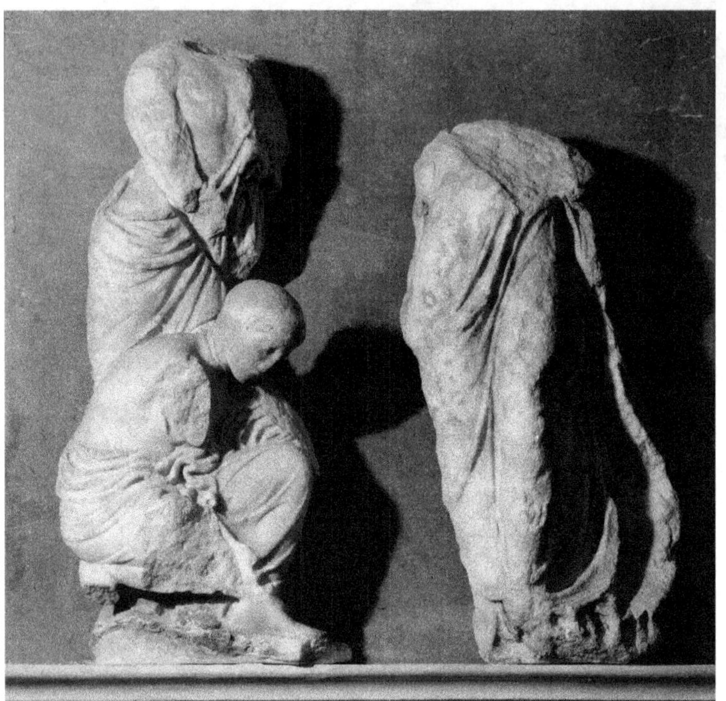

11.3 Figures from the frieze of the Erechtheion on the Acropolis at Athens, *c.* 410–405 BCE. 19 5/16 in (0.49 m). Athens, Acropolis Museum. Photo: Werner Forman/Art Resource, NY.

wounded Amazon for the Temple of Artemis at Ephesos, and that the winner of the competition, Polykleitos, was chosen by a tally of the votes of the sculptors for second-best entry (after they had each selected their own work first). Whatever the historicity of the story, it does suggest a certain amount of collegial competitiveness among artists.

The payments connected to architectural sculpture help us to consider the cost of free-standing statues and funerary reliefs produced in the late fifth and fourth centuries. A life-size statue (about 165–175 cm high) would be three times as high as the Erechtheion figures and would have both front and back sides, representing about six times the amount of labor. This would suggest that a life-size statue in marble might cost about 360 drachmas and take about a year to make. A heroically scaled figure in marble (about 200 cm in height), like the figure of Agias from Delphi **(see Figure 12.8, page 296)**, might have cost eight times the amount of the Erechtheion figure, or 480 drachmas. A funerary relief, such as that of Ampharete in the last chapter **(see Figure 10.19, page 254)**, is about twice as high as the Erechtheion figures (120 cm vs. 65 cm) and includes an additional figure, so that it might have cost 150 drachmas based on the Erechtheion payments. A much larger funeral monument like that of Dexileos **(see Figure 12.12, page 301)**, at 175 cm high and with two figures in very deep relief, might well have cost the same or a bit more than a life-size statue. Ampharete's grave stele would represent about half of the annual income of a worker at the time, so it is likely that such funerary monuments were made by sculptors for wealthier and more elite clients.

We have less information, direct or indirect, on the costs for statues made out of bronze. The labor process would be more complicated and involve more equipment and energy for melting the bronze to pour into the mold. The two metals that constitute bronze, tin and copper, would have to be mined and the ore smelted to produce the raw material. Since the sources of copper and especially tin were far off in places like Cyprus, this would mean both had to be transported long distances to reach the foundry, although sufficient ingots of metal to make a bronze statue would be lighter, easier, and cheaper to transport than the marble needed for a stone sculpture. Undoubtedly there would have been a premium to pay for a bronze statue as compared to a marble one due to the cost and reusability of the material.

Based on Hellenistic sources, Andrew Stewart estimates a monumental-scale bronze portrait statue about 2 meters high would have cost 3,000 drachmas, with about 550 drachmas for the bronze alone and probably more than 2,000 drachmas for the labor of the sculptor and his workshop (Stewart 1990, 67). This figure might also serve as an estimate for classical bronze statues like the Riace Warriors **(see Figure 10.5, page 241)** or the youth from the Antikythera shipwreck **(see Figure 12.7, page 295)**. This is the most technically challenging type of bronze work, and it is possible that the price would represent a more significant profit and premium for skill for the elite bronze-maker than for the marble sculptor. Such statues would have to be commissioned by a city, as Athens had done with the original bronze Tyrannicides, or by a very wealthy individual. It is less likely, however, that smaller-scale and simpler bronze work, like figures **(see Figure 7.19, page 176)** and mirrors **(see Figure 10.6, page 242)**, would have had as much of a premium on labor given the simpler manufacturing process. The makers of small bronzes might have earned more of a standard wage like marble sculptors.

PRODUCTION: POTTERY

Pottery was a much more modest commodity in ancient Greece than surviving Greek pottery is in the art market today. Clay is much less difficult to dig and refine and transportation from the source of the material to the place of production, the pottery workshop, is usually shorter than is the case with marble and limestone. Firing the pot required fuel and a kiln, but pottery is fired in batches to make production more efficient. It is likely that workshops were generally small and may well have been family enterprises, with extra workers like painters hired as needed to finish large batches.

Potters had to produce a wide range of products to meet daily needs, much of it utilitarian and undecorated as we saw in Chapter 5 (**see Figures 5.16 and 5.17, page 116**). Many of the products were either haphazardly or sketchily decorated, but they still had value as wares since a vessel was functional even if it were not beautiful. Like most artistic professions, learning to become a potter was a process of apprenticeship, with the less skilled individuals performing less intricate work as they learned. Recently, Susan Langdon has argued that some small vessels with unskilled decoration might be the work of children learning to make and decorate a pot, training within the family enterprise. Typically, such works were small in scale to be suitable for small hands (Langdon 2013).

Some pottery pieces, such as the krater fragment in **Figure 11.4**, that appear unfinished were probably test pieces, placed into the kiln during firing to gauge if the temperature and conditions were sufficient for producing the color effects of the slips. These are still useful for understanding the process of red-figure painting today, as we discussed in Chapter 8.

For estimating the value of fine finished pottery, we can look to graffiti on pots. These are scratches and marks made in the surface of the clay, often on the underside, and consist of letters, numbers, and other signs that record trademarks, ownership, and occasionally prices. For example, a mid-fifth-century hydria attributed to the Group of Polygnotos (not the same person as the mural painter) has a graffito that reads "hy[dria] 2 drach[mos] poi[kile]," or, painted hydria, 2 drachmas

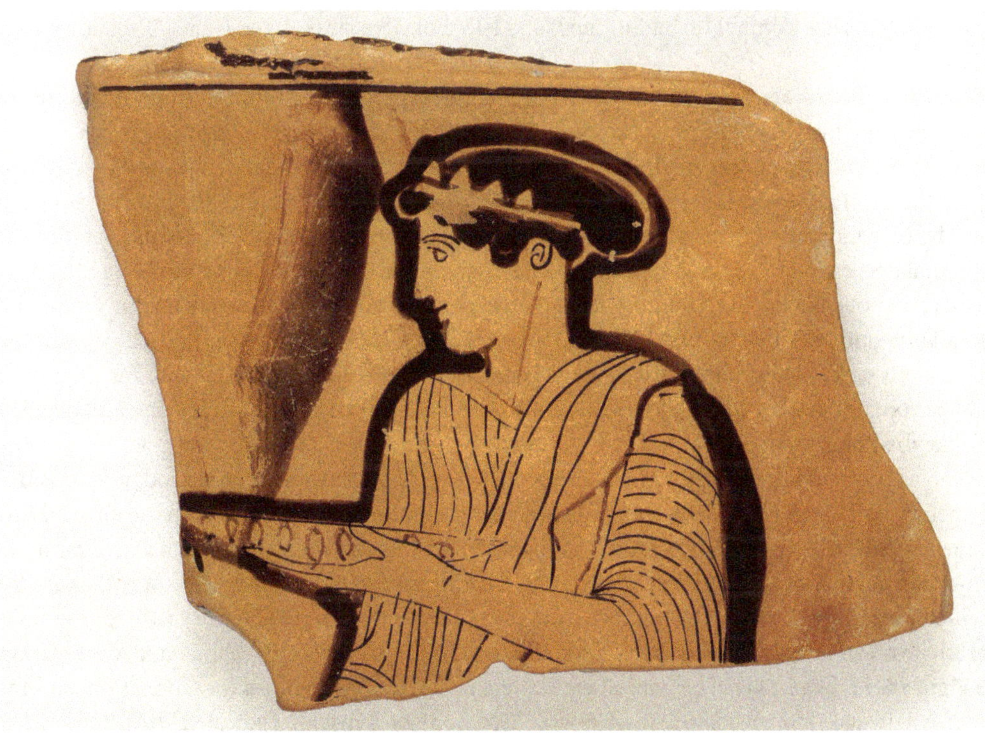

11.4 Fragment of a red-figure test piece cut from a krater, attributed to the Methyse Painter, *c.* 460 BCE. 2½ in (6.5 cm). Berlin, Antikensammlung V.I.3362. Photo: bpk, Berlin/ Staatliche Museen, Antikensammlung/Art Resource, NY.

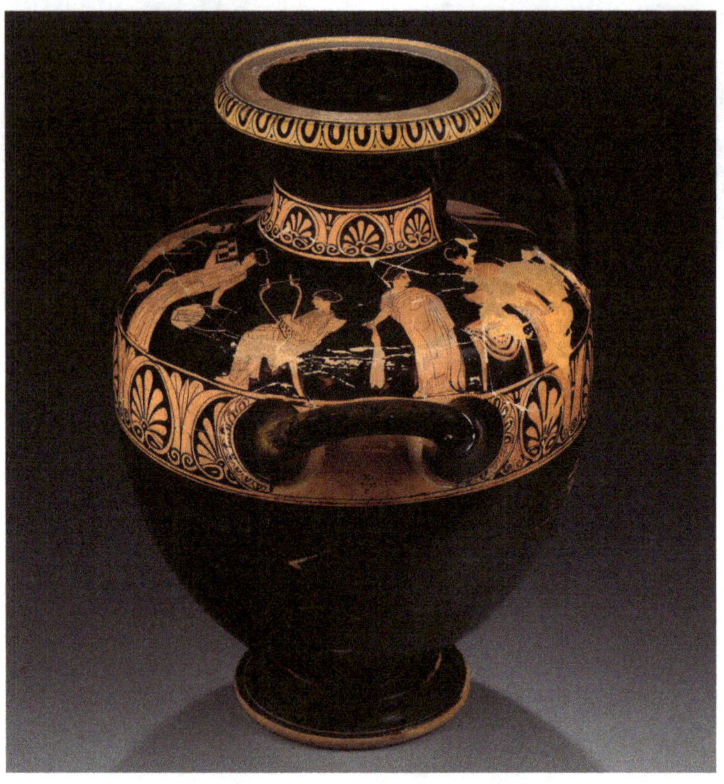

11.5 Attic red-figure hydria attributed to Group of Polygnotos, *c.* 450–440 BCE. 16⅛ in (41 cm). London, British Museum 1921,0710.2. Musical scene with women. Photo: © The Trustees of the British Museum.

emporion
Greek term for a large market or trading center

(Figure 11.5). Marks like this are made after firing and show up on pottery sold in both Greek colonies and Etruria, so it is probable that the mark represents the price in Athens. A trader coming to Athens and its harbor, Piraeus, would have bought a number of works and then taken them by ship to markets elsewhere, perhaps selling them along the way or bringing an entire batch to a single destination or **emporion** for sale. How much of a mark-up there would be at the retail end is unknown, but allowing for loss in breakage during transportation, the final price should not be more than two or three times as much as the cost in Athens.

The price of 2 drachmas would likely be close to the retail price in Athens if the pot had been sold locally, and if we consider the drachma as being worth about $150–180 based on a median household income of $50,000 in the United States, the hydria would have cost about $300–360. This would be a significant purchase for an Athenian consumer, but not unreasonable, equivalent perhaps to an iPod or a couple of place settings of very fine china such as Wedgwood or Noritake today. If we consider that a pot like this could be used to serve water at a symposion, it would be equivalent in both price and formal use to the fine china used today on special holiday gatherings like Thanksgiving.

The price of the Polygnotan hydria is at the high end of the recorded prices. Some stelai in Athens record prices of 2.4–3.7 obols for Panathenaic amphorae that presumably were empty **(see Figure 5.11, page 111)**. Since a drachma is equivalent to 6 obols, a 3-obol pot (½ drachma) would be about $75–90 based on our $50,000 median household income. Stamnoi are about the same price, but smaller items like skyphoi (drinking cups) and lekythoi were far cheaper, from 1 obol down to ⅙ obol ($4–5).

The lowest prices are probably for non-figured pottery. Athens produced large quantities of black-glaze ware that was consumed both locally and exported at the same time as red-figure ware **(Figure 11.6)**. The cost of making the basic shape in clay and firing it would be the same as a figured pot, but the painted decoration would be simpler. Small vessels like the salt cellar and dishes would indeed be very modestly priced. Comparing figured and non-figured pots, Alan Johnston estimates that figural decoration would add about one-third to the value of the pot (Johnston 1991, 228). This suggests that pot painters, like sculptors, were paid at a rate of a drachma for a day's work. One could make a large number of simple and small pots, or take more time for a larger, figured pot, but the price in both cases would reflect the labor needed to do the work and the income for the potter would be roughly similar, although there might have been a modest premium for fine and detailed work like the Polygnotan hydria.

Whereas painted pottery with figural scenes fetches high prices in the market today, vessels like Panathenaic amphorae would have been most valuable in antiquity when filled with the olive oil that was the prize for winning a competition. Vessels made from metal would have been worth far more intrinsically because of the cost of their material, whether bronze, silver, or gold, as was the case for metal sculpture over marble. A gold phiale from the late seventh century (**Figure 11.7**), for example, is much less complicated in its decoration than the Chigi olpe made about a decade earlier **(see Figure 6.11, page 141)**. The lobe shape is unusual but straightforward for fabrication, and the surface is left plain except for the inscription: "The sons of Kypselos dedicated [this bowl] from

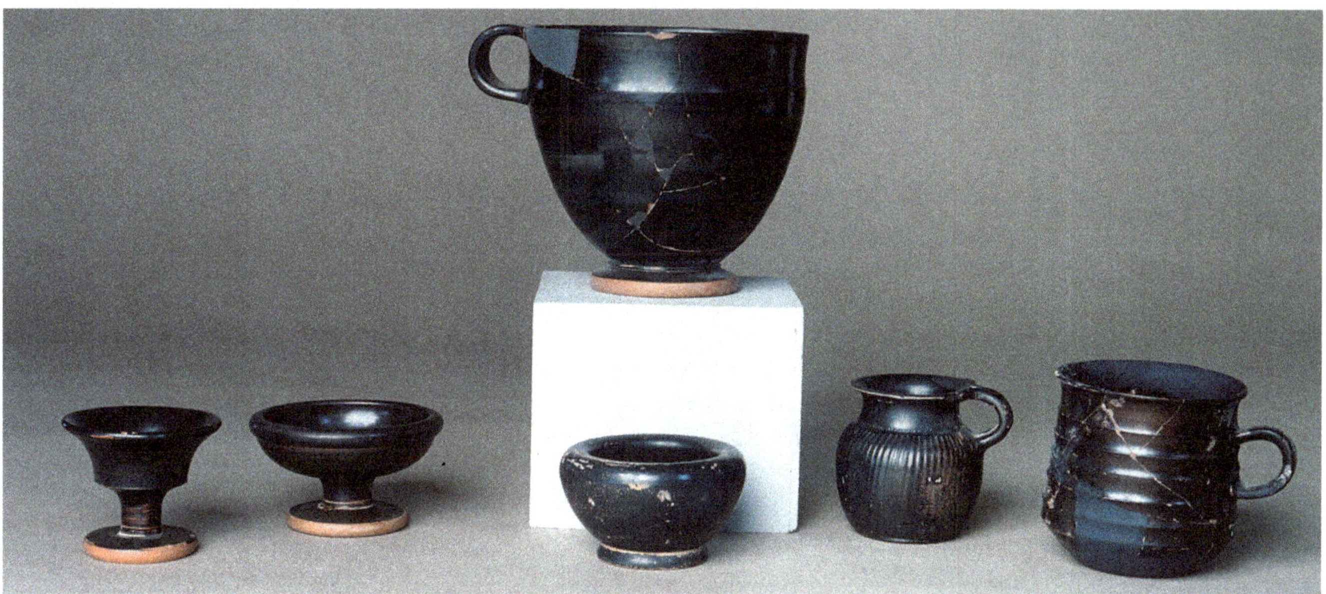

11.6 Black-glaze ware from the Agora, 5th cent. BCE. Athens, Agora Museum. Stand: mug, 500–480 BCE. 4½ in (11.5 cm). P14972. Bottom, left to right: stemmed dish, *c.* 500 BCE. 2⅛ in (5.5 cm). P1195; stemmed dish, 500–480 BCE. P24612; salt cellar, 425–400 BCE. 1¾ in (4.6 cm). P14822; ribbed mug, 450–425 BCE. 2⅝ in (6.7 cm). P2340; mug, 450–425 BCE. 3⅛ in (8 cm). P4876. Photo: American School of Classical Studies at Athens: Agora Excavations.

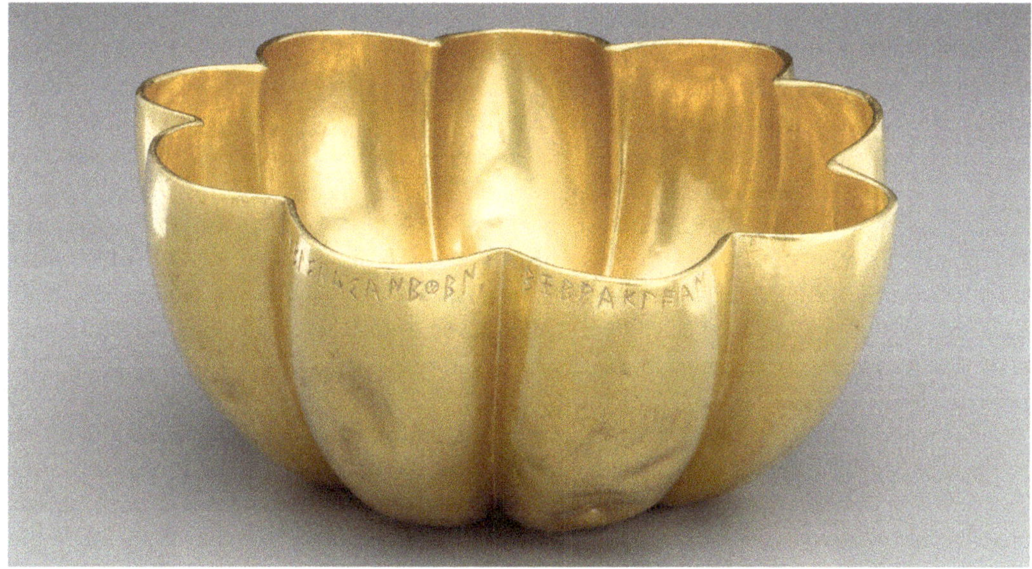

11.7 Gold phiale dedicated by the Kypselids, 625–600 BCE. 5$\frac{15}{16}$ in (15 cm). Boston, Museum of Fine Arts 21.1843. Photograph © 2014 Museum of Fine Arts, Boston.

Heraclea." The decoration of the interior of the bowl has a simple row of beads between lines at the base of the lobes and around the circular omphalos in the center, so overall the detailing of the object is rather minimal. The bowl, however, weighs 835 grams (29.5 oz), and would have been a noteworthy object to own or to dedicate in a sanctuary because of its size and material.

The bowl is without specific provenance but was said to come from Olympia, where Pausanias (5.17.5–5.19.10) records a cedar, ivory, and gold chest of Kypselos, a tyrant of Corinth *c.* 655–625, that was dedicated in the Temple of Hera. Temple and sanctuary inventories frequently mention metal vases, including large kraters, and typically signify their value in terms of their weight and material rather than their artistry. That is not to say that a more modest work like the Chigi olpe was not admired by its owner or that producing painted pottery did not provide a livable income. It is only to remind us that what we value today from antiquity is not necessarily the same as what the original makers and owners would have prized most.

WARES, MARKETS, AND DISTRIBUTION

Once a work like a pot is produced, it must be distributed and sold in a market. If the market is local, pot producers are immediately aware of what sells and what does not and can make adjustments in their wares to meet the needs or interests of consumers. When pottery is exported, there is a middle person, a merchant with access to transportation like a ship or cart, who buys wholesale and sells retail. Merchants on returning to Corinth or Athens would have provided feedback to producers about what was successful abroad and what was not. We have little direct evidence of this process, but by looking at changes in production and wares we can get an idea of the relationship that existed between artists and consumers and consider the links between artistic style and market.

Looking first at Corinthian pottery, we saw in Chapter 6 that its painters developed a black-figure technique with added color that appeared on small perfume vessels such as aryballoi and alabastra (**see Figure 6.9, page 139; Figure 6.10, page 140**). The painting technique, the division of the vase into multiple friezes with miniature-scale figures, and a limited range of subjects like animals, hunts, races, and fighting (**see Figure 6.11, page 141**) mean today that one can readily recognize Corinthian vessels from the seventh century. The vessels were valuable because they contained perfume and scented oil that had been imported to Corinth and then produced, packaged, and shipped around the Mediterranean. Corinth was not the only producer of these luxury goods, but its pottery gave its products a distinct identity in the market. Tom Rasmussen (1991) likens the style and deployment of Corinthian pottery to a trademark or brand identification, allowing a consumer to identify Corinthian perfume in the marketplace.

As time went on, Corinthian potters and painters produced other wares, including drinking cups and vessels associated with wine and the symposion, like the Chigi olpe, creating another source of revenue for their workshops independent of the perfume trade (**see Figure 5.23, page 122; Figure 6.11, page 141**). These new shapes of figured pottery continued with the same black-figure technique and many of the same compositions and subjects as the perfume containers, and would have been markedly different from local wares available in the markets of Italy. The less precise style and execution of late Corinthian pottery in the sixth century may indicate that they were being mass produced for a lower-end market.

After adopting the black-figure technique in the late seventh century, mostly on wares sold within the region, Athenian potters and painters began to make works that were exported, such as the François Vase (**see Figure 8.23, page 203**), while continuing to produce for their local market. The introduction of new shapes and subjects, as well as larger figural compositions, kept their wares distinctive in the marketplace from other Greek pottery, such as Corinthian black-figure. In some cases, Attic pots were produced solely for export, based on the distribution of findspots, and we even see Athenian potters imitating foreign shapes and then exporting their wares back to that market. For example, the black amphora in **Figure 11.8** is Etruscan bucchero ware. The wide strap handles, embossed relief, and profile are different from Athenian amphorae and reflect metalware forms, while the glossy black finish gives a luster to the vessel. Bucchero ware is a distinctive Etruscan product, and in the last half of the sixth century we see a workshop associated with the Athenian potter Nikosthenes producing imitations of Etruscan shapes, like the black-figure amphora on the left, signed by Nikosthenes as potter. Rather than black glaze, its decoration uses the current Athenian black-figure style to show satyrs and maenads dancing, a universally popular theme for both domestic and export markets. Whereas Nikosthenic amphorae are unusual for their explicit demonstration of Athenian

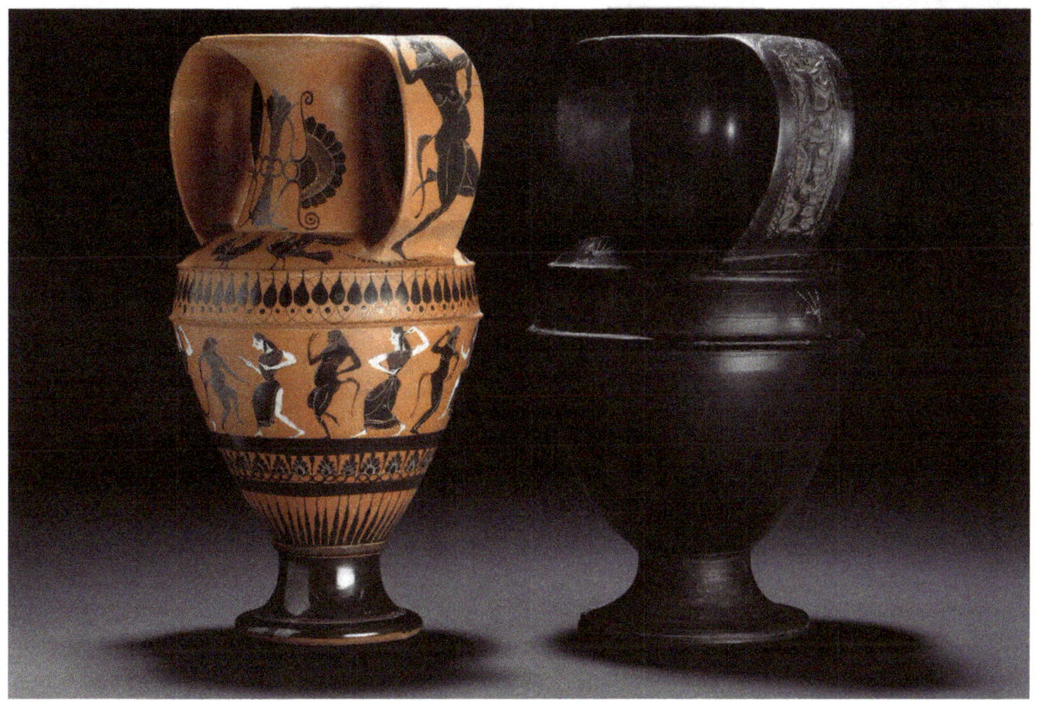

11.8 Attic black-figure Nikosthenic amphora signed by Nikosthenes, *c.* 540–510 BCE. 13 in (33 cm). London, British Museum B296. Etruscan bucchero-ware amphora, 560–530. 13⅛ in (33.4 cm). London, British Museum 1984,1023.1. Photo: © The Trustees of the British Museum.

responsiveness to foreign markets, we should consider that ancient trade networks were paths of communication, with both works of art and visual ideas being exchanged in reciprocal directions.

The history of Athenian pottery production consists of a series of wares that appeared, flourished, and then were replaced by new wares, keeping the pottery industry active in the city and in export markets for centuries. Much of Attic black-figure ware was exported to Etruria in the sixth century. It continued to be produced for about seventy-five years after the invention of red-figure painting around 525, but after 500 was relegated mostly to small and hurriedly painted objects like cups and lekythoi produced in large quantities. The fifth century saw the domination of red-figure ware. In terms of its distribution, red-figure pottery is found in greater proportions than black-figure ware outside of Etruria, as Athenian potters expanded their markets in the fifth-century to include more of southern Italy and Sicily. Locally in Attica, they developed the multicolor white-ground technique, primarily on larger lekythoi used in funerary contexts **(see Figure 5.26, page 125)**. Some of these lekythoi were exported, but not in nearly the same quantities as red-figure wares.

By the end of the fifth century there is a sharp decline in the number of red-figure vessels being produced in Athens, and it is reasonable to suppose that the Peloponnesian War may have disrupted trade routes and therefore production. Indeed, as we shall see in the next chapter, at the end of the fifth century red-figure pottery in Lucania and Apulia in southern Italy becomes locally made, production probably being stimulated initially by the migration of Attic artists and the disruption of trade, and subsequently takes hold as new wares in their own right. Red-figure pottery continued to be produced in Athens during the fourth century, but in more modest quantities and typically less carefully painted. Attic workshops at this time developed a new red-figure ware called the **Kerch style**, named after a site in the Crimea. The Black Sea had long been a market for pottery, but its importance as an export destination grew in the fourth century. Kerch pottery is very fine work with a rich use of color and complex figural poses, as we shall see in Chapter 12 **(see Figure 12.17, page 306)**.

Kerch style
Attic pottery produced in the fourth century featuring a rich use of color and exported in large numbers to the Black Sea

Apart from Panathenaic amphorae produced for the games, figural pottery is replaced by new products at the end of the fourth century. A more simply decorated type of ware called **West Slope** becomes a new line in the third century BCE **(Figure 11.9)**. Some of its shapes, like kantharoi, follow forms found in metal, including some specific features like ribs, flanges, and high-looping handles.

West Slope ware
overpainted pottery ware produced in Athens during the third century

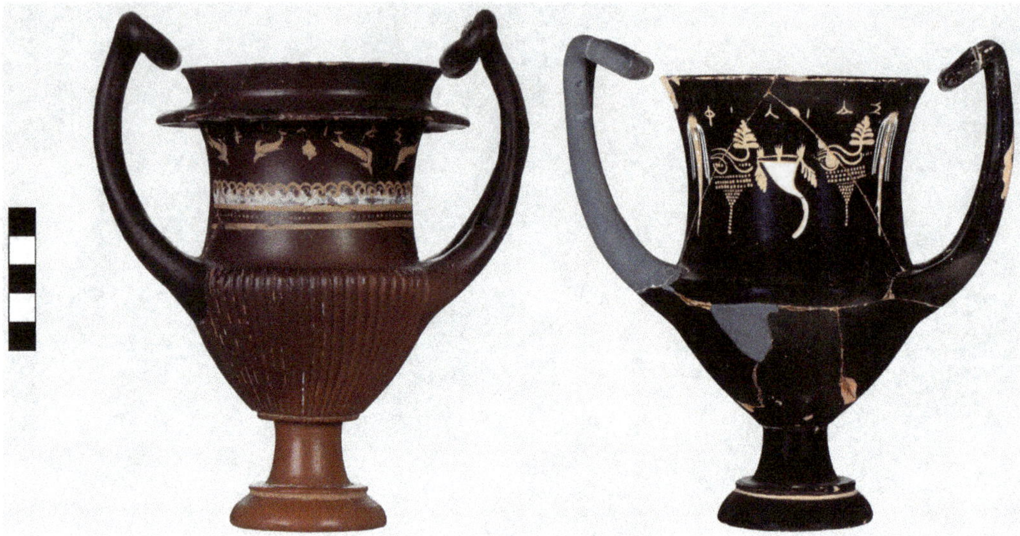

11.9 West Slope ware kantharoi, *c.* 275–250 BCE. 6⅝ in and 6⅜ in (16.9 cm and 16.3 cm). Athens, Agora Museum P5719 and P5811. Photo: American School of Classical Studies at Athens: Agora Excavations.

overpainting
pottery painting technique in which the colored pigments are painted on the glazed or slip surface, rather than put on the bare surface of the clay

Gnathian ware
overpainted pottery ware produced in Apulia in the fourth and third centuries

Megarian bowl
term for a mold-made bowl with relief decoration on the exterior and produced during the Hellenistic period in Athens and other centers

The pot is covered with a black slip and then **overpainted**, mostly with ornamental motifs in whites and light reds. This type of pottery was widely distributed to the north and east, but not as much to Italy where a competing product, called **Gnathian ware**, featured a larger range of themes and colors, as can be seen in a small lekythos found in Taras/Taranto **(see Figure 12.20, page 309)**. The overpainting technique of West Slope ware was once thought to have originated in Athens, but whether Athenian potters were imitating Gnathian ware needs further study. Curiously, the human figure remains a subject in Gnathian ware, while it all but disappears from the Athenian workshops.

Beginning in the last quarter of the third century Athenian potters also began producing mold-made bowls, sometimes called **Megarian bowls**. These are mass-produced works made with fired terracotta molds, and then covered with black slip to give them a lustrous gloss like black-glaze ware. The bowls feature a range of ornamental friezes, including some Egyptianizing motifs, which led to their original association with Alexandria as a place of origin. Since few of the bowls have been found there, it is more likely that they were developed in Athens using Alexandrian metal wares as sources (Rotroff 1982, 6–13). Some bowls also include figural scenes, such as one example found in Thebes **(Figure 11.10)**. In the center we see a striding male figure before a chariot. This is Hermes leading Hades, who is driving a chariot and holding the abducted Persephone in his arms. Further around the cup we find Demeter, Athena, and other figures reacting to the action. The bottom of the cup has vegetation, while the upper rim features rosettes, palmettes, spirals, and egg-and-dart ornamental motifs.

Not only pottery was exported far from its place of production. Small terracottas that were light and readily transported, either by individuals or by merchants, were also widely distributed, but even large and heavy works like statues and reliefs ended up a great distance from their point of origin. The archaic kouros of Sombrotidas, for example, was found at Megara Hyblaea in Sicily, but its marble comes from the Greek islands and it is probable that it was exported as a finished or nearly finished work, since this would cut down on the weight and shipping cost **(see Figure 8.10, page 191)**. As mentioned earlier, the metopes and pedimental sculpture at Olympia were quarried and carved nearly to completion on the island of Paros in the Aegean Sea, sent by ship to Corinth, and, after transfer to the other side of the isthmus, shipped further to Olympia on the west side of Greece **(see Figure 9.14, page 228)**. These were works that were certainly made to order on commission, but we are less certain about works like the kouros of Sombrotidas, since a formulaic work such as this did not require special treatment or subject matter and the inscription could have been carved at the destination.

Athens in the fourth century and later was a large-scale exporter of sculpture as well as pottery. During the last two centuries of the Hellenistic period Athenian sculptors produced many classical-style works for export to Roman clients. By this time, Rome had conquered the Greek cities of Italy

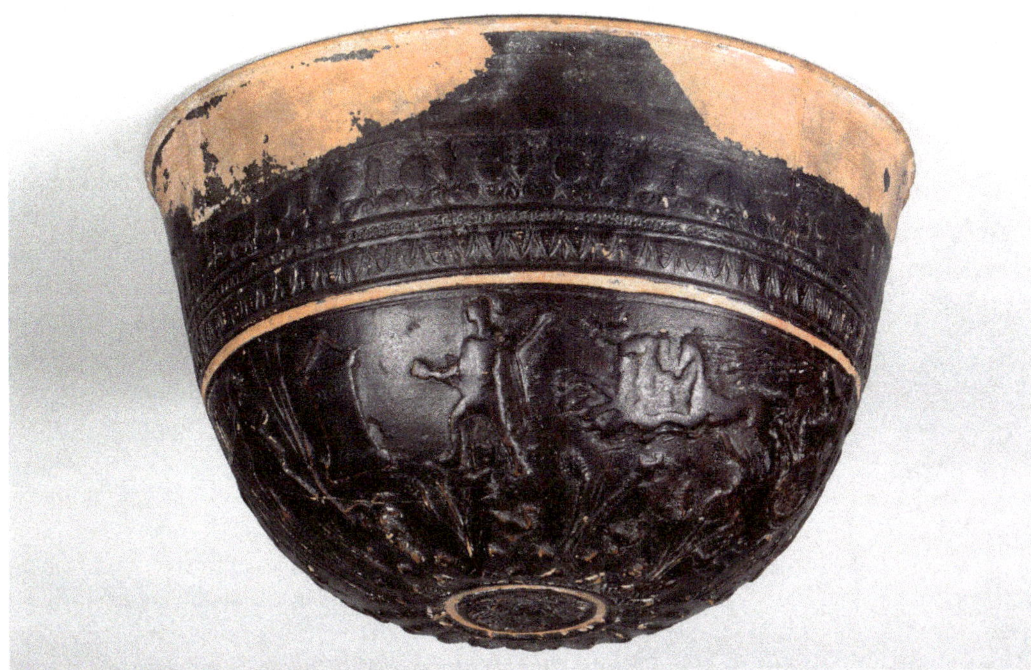

11.10 Mold-made "Megarian" bowl, *c.* 225–175 BCE. 4¼ in (10.8 cm). London, British Museum 1897,0317.3. Hades abducting Persephone. Image rotated 180°. Photo: © The Trustees of the British Museum.

and Sicily and all of mainland Greece, which had sent a steady supply of important artwork to Rome as loot; this is possibly the case with the Riace Warriors if they are fifth-century originals **(see Figure 10.5, page 241)**. Roman sources speak of public interest in Greek sculpture among the elite as well as the population that frequented the forum and public buildings like baths, and this created new markets for Greek sculpture. An unfinished, monumental marble krater found in Athens, for example, was the type of work popular with Roman patrons for the gardens of their houses and villas **(Figure 11.11)**. The relief decoration is a copy of the early classical sculpture of Athena and the satyr Marsyas made by Myron, which is mentioned in some literary sources but survives only in copies like this. These works are labeled **Neoattic** and belong to the classicizing style of the Hellenistic period that produced works purchased by prominent Romans such as Cicero, whose letters to his agent discuss the types of statues that he wanted purchased in Athens and shipped to him in Rome. Neoattic sculpture supplied new work imitating the themes and styles of classical Athens, once looting as a cheap and ready source of works had dried up.

Neoattic term for classicizing sculpture produced in Athens for export, especially in the first century BCE

ARTISTS AND WORKSHOPS

It was not only art like pottery, terracottas, and sculpture that could be made in one place and exported. Artists and their workshops were also mobile. For example, the workers at Epidauros were mostly Corinthians, so both stone for the building and the masons came from a relatively nearby city in the region (about 70 km). Since an architectural project requires work on site, this means that the workers would have had to relocate, at least temporarily, to the construction site. The Pentelic marble for the pediments and acroteria came from Attica (about 200 km away), as did the three sculptors who carved the figures on site. The names of the sculptors for the reliefs on the Erechtheion on the Acropolis include Athenians and non-Athenians, and the vast scale of the Pheidian program of the fifth century must have brought a number of workers to Athens from elsewhere to find work on the projects there.

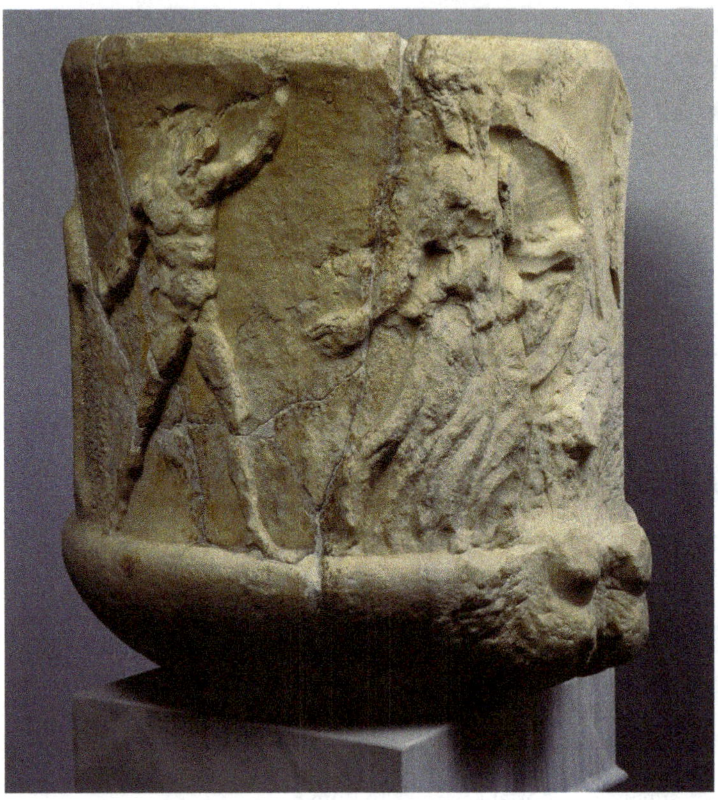

11.11 Unfinished Neoattic marble krater ("Finley Krater"), mid-1st cent. BCE. Copy of Myron's sculpture group Marsyas and Athena of *c.* 460–450 BCE. 18⅛ in (46 cm). Athens, National Archaeological Museum 127. Photo: National Archaeological Museum, Athens (Kostas Xenikakis) © Hellenic Ministry of Education and Religious Affairs, Culture and Sports/ Archaeological Receipts Fund.

These were temporary relocations, but there are other examples of more permanent movements of artists who settled in a new city to provide work for the local market. A very early example discussed in Chapter 4 (see pages 85–86) comes from a tholos tomb in Crete that was used as a workshop in the ninth century by goldsmiths, probably from northern Syria **(Figure 11.12)**. These metalworkers brought with them new techniques and subjects that they began producing for a local market. Eventually these innovations were adopted by other metalworkers in Greece, whether through training or imitation. This example shows the portability of skills and designs from one part of the Mediterranean to another and indicates another means for the transmission of ideas and motifs.

We can see other examples of foreign artists taking up residence in Athens in the sixth century through the names of potters such as Lydos, "the Lydian," or Amasis, who shares the name of an Egyptian pharaoh of the sixth century. Their contemporary Exekias may have been himself from the island of Salamis. It is thought that Exekias, who signed some pots as both maker (**Εχσεκιας εποιεσε** *Exekias epoiese* or Exekias made [this]) and painter (**Εχσεκιας εγραφσε** *Exekias egrapse* or Exekias painted me), directed a workshop in Athens and employed others as potters and painters. While we consider that Attic black-figure is a distinctive product of Athens, it is interesting to note that many of its artists were not Athenian and were active in developing markets in Etruria and elsewhere.

Not only did Greek potters and painters make wares for export to foreign markets, but some also migrated to non-Greek areas like Etruria. One example is the workshop that began producing finely made hydria in the Etruscan city of Caere (modern Cerveteri), giving the name of Caeretan ware to this product **(Figure 11.13)**. This ware had at least two recognizable artists, but its origin is uncertain. The black-figure technique is supplemented with a rich use of added reds and white, as we can see in the hydria attributed to the Eagle Painter. The picture shows Herakles bringing Kerberos, the three-headed hound of hell, to king Eurystheus, who gave the tasks to Herakles that make up his cycle of twelve heroic deeds. In this scene, Eurystheus has jumped into a large storage pithos and throws up his arms in fear, having assumed that Herakles would be killed by the beast rather than successfully capturing it. The humor of a scared king acting in an undignified way gives a comic gloss to the scene that is somewhat different from Attic versions of this story, although it is similar to Attic versions of Herakles bringing the Erymanthian boar back to Eurystheus, who hides in a pithos. The rounded bodies and extended limbs of the figures are distinctive of the Caeretan style, which has similarities to Etruscan pottery painting and appears to have appealed to local clientele.

As mentioned earlier, in the last part of the fifth century red-figure workshops were set up in southern Italy. The earliest workshops of Lucanian red-figure ware, made in Metapontum/Metaponto, show strong connections in terms of style and subject matter to contemporary Attic red-figure painting, and the uncertainty over classifying some of these artists, like the Amykos Painter, as either Attic or Lucanian suggests that Athenian potters/painters may have migrated to set up workshops in western Greek markets, thereby satisfying pottery demand locally. By the beginning of the fourth century, the style of Lucanian red-figure had developed more distinctly, adopting a few new shapes and compositions for the narrative pictures that it produced. By this time, local workshops had seized control of their markets from Athenian potters and painters, no doubt aided by the disruptions of the Peloponnesian War. The pelike showing Elektra and Orestes at the tomb of Agamemnon **(see Figure 9.11, page 224)** reveals the particular interest in stories featured in tragic plays that were very popular in southern Italy, including the revival of fifth-century tragedies by Aeschylus, Sophocles, and Euripides. At its best, the figural pottery of Apulia, Lucania, Poseidonia/Paestum, and Sicily rivaled or bettered that of contemporary Athens.

Sculptors, too, could relocate on a more permanent basis. During the Hellenistic period, when the workshops of Athens were producing sculpture for export to Rome, other artists migrated to Rome to work for Roman clients. One such case may be three artists named Hagesandros, Athenodoros, and Polydoros. The first-century CE writer Pliny (*N.H.* 36.37), whose work *Natural History* includes many details on the history of Greek sculpture and painting, mentions these sculptors as the creators of the Laocoön Group in the palace of Nero, which was found *in situ* during the Renaissance. Pliny tells us that the sculptors were from Rhodes, but we otherwise have no literary record of them. There has been much scholarly debate as to whether these figures were second-century BCE artists in Rhodes whose work was taken to Rome, or whether the statue in Rome was copied from a Greek original by the sculptors in Rhodes.

11.12 Gold pendants from Tekke Tomb 2, Knossos, 9th cent. BCE. Width of pendants: 2⅝ and 2⅛ in (6.7 and 5.5 cm). Herakleion, Archaeological Museum. Photo: Gianni Dagli Orti/The Art Archive at Art Resource, NY.

Excavations at the grotto in Sperlonga south of Rome in the 1950s, however, brought to light five more ensembles in the same style, including one with an inscription bearing the names of the same three sculptors **(Figure 11.14)**. As can be seen in the reconstruction, the floor of the grotto cave was crossed by a series of walkways between pools drawing water from the sea. The sculptural groups seem to have been designed for the space, making it less likely that the artists were copying older originals but were, rather, creating these works in a particular stylistic tradition. The monumental group with Polyphemos shows the Cyclops lying unconscious from drinking, while Odysseus and his sailors prepare to drive a stake into his eye to blind him and aid their escape from the cave in which they were imprisoned **(Figure 11.15)**. The works are in a full Hellenistic baroque style that we will discuss in Chapter 14. Recent scholarly opinion suggests that they were created in the first century BCE by the workshop that also did the Laocoön Group and perhaps worked for other Roman clients at the time.

Most of the artists that we have been considering were likely to have been skilled workers who earned the type of normal wages we discussed earlier in the chapter. While they were accomplished, we know little about the lives or achievements of Exekias or Hagesandros outside of their extant works. The status of artists, both social and economic, throughout most of the history of Greek art was relatively modest. For some artists during the classical period, however, there were greater financial and social rewards that for a time made the most successful among them members of the elite class. Kephisodotos, the son of the fourth-century sculptor Praxiteles, is said to have outfitted three Athenian warships from his own resources, a civic act limited to the wealthiest elite families of Athens. His father Praxiteles, whose Aphrodite of Knidos might well be the most famous statue of antiquity and which we will discuss in the next chapter **(see Figure 12.11, page 300)**, had apparently achieved great financial success as an

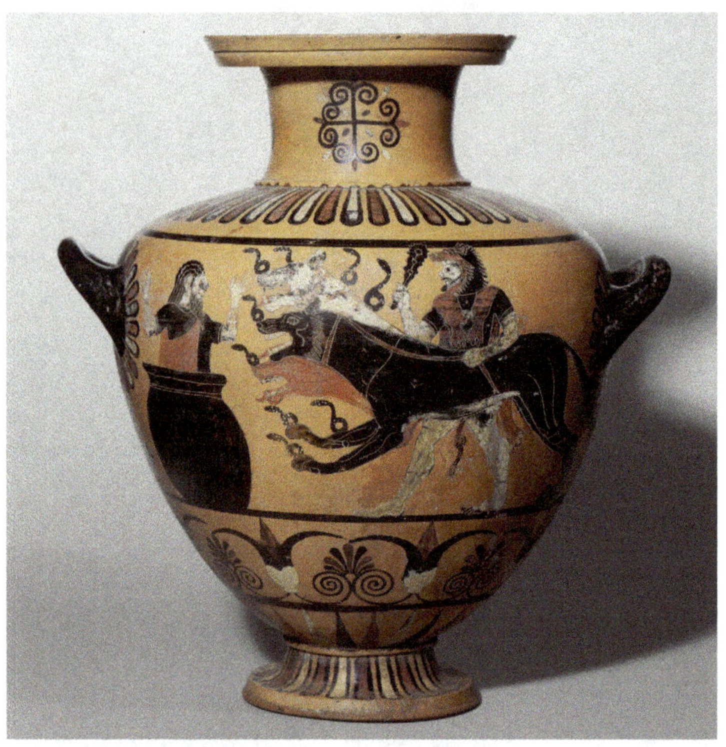

11.13 Caeretan hydria attributed to the Eagle Painter, *c.* 530 BCE. $16^{15}/_{16}$ in (43 cm). Paris, Musée du Louvre E701. Herakles bringing Kerberos to Eurystheus. Photo: © RMN-Grand Palais/Art Resource, NY.

artist and was able to charge a premium for the quality and reputation of his work. Pliny (*N.H.* 35.62) tells us that a fourth-century painter, Zeuxis, "acquired such great wealth that he showed it off at Olympia by exhibiting his name woven into the checks of his cloaks in gold letters. Afterwards he decided to give away his works as gifts, because he maintained that no price could be considered equal to their value" (tr. Pollitt 1990, 149). Cloth with threads of gold was a luxurious item, associated with royal burials such as the cloth found at the tomb in Vergina **(see Figure 5.18, page 117)**, so we have to conclude that Zeuxis was extremely wealthy.

As Jeremy Tanner (2006) has discussed, this change of social status is tied to a change in the intellectual status of artists. As we saw in the previous chapter (p. 243), Polykleitos wrote a treatise, the *Canon*, that explained the principles of his work, which were rooted in both mathematics and philosophy **(see Figure 10.7, page 243)**. Whereas there is testimony that architects had written treatises on architecture since the sixth century, the small workshops of sculptors did not require written manuals or references, making the *Canon* of Polykleitos unusual and possibly groundbreaking. A statue was not simply a mimesis of the human form, but had a deeper and more intellectually expressive meaning at its core that could only be explained through the written word. That some artists were writing treatises and not just recording their names, in an era when genuine literacy belonged to a minority, supports the claim to higher status for those who were able to study and use contemporary theories in their work. Some artists also became teachers whose students, like those of Plato and Aristotle, came from elite and wealthy families. Once again, Pliny tells us that one fourth-century painter, Pamphilos of Sikyon, could charge 500 drachmas a year for tuition for one student, more than the annual income of the sculptors of the Parthenon and Epidauros (*N.H.* 35.76). Pliny continues that "as a result of his prestige, it came about that, first in Sikyon and then in all Greece, free-born boys were given lessons in drawing on wooden tablets, although the subject had been previously omitted, and thus painting was received into the front rank of the liberal arts" (tr. Pollitt 1990, 158).

Pliny's account regards the period after the fourth century to have been a time when the merit of artists was well below that of the classical period, and certainly our literary sources have fewer names and details of artists of the Hellenistic period than of the fifth and fourth centuries. The social and intellectual claims of artists appear to have retreated, but some artists continued to prosper, and the patronage of Hellenistic rulers provided new sources of opportunity that were absent before the fifth century. Some artists did achieve recognition, such as the second-century sculptor Damophon of Messene, who produced a number of works in southern Greece that are mentioned by Pausanias. The civic value of his work was recorded not in literary sources like Pliny, but in an inscription found on a Doric column in Messene. It records the honors given to Damophon by seven cities, including Lykosoura, for whom he made its cult statues **(see Figures 14.18 and 14.19, page 364)**. Lykosoura even erected a bronze statue to honor Damophon, in recognition of his making their cult statues and postponing or forgiving payment of 3,546 silver tetradrachms (4-drachma pieces) due to him (Themelis 1994). The enormous debt forgiven by Damophon was a mark of civic largess, like that of Kephisodotos outfitting warships, and is a sign of his wealth and prestige. Nevertheless, the status of artists during the Hellenistic period never rivaled that of Polykleitos, Praxiteles, and others during the fifth and fourth centuries, and we must think of that phenomenon as atypical of the experience of most artists during the first millennium BCE.

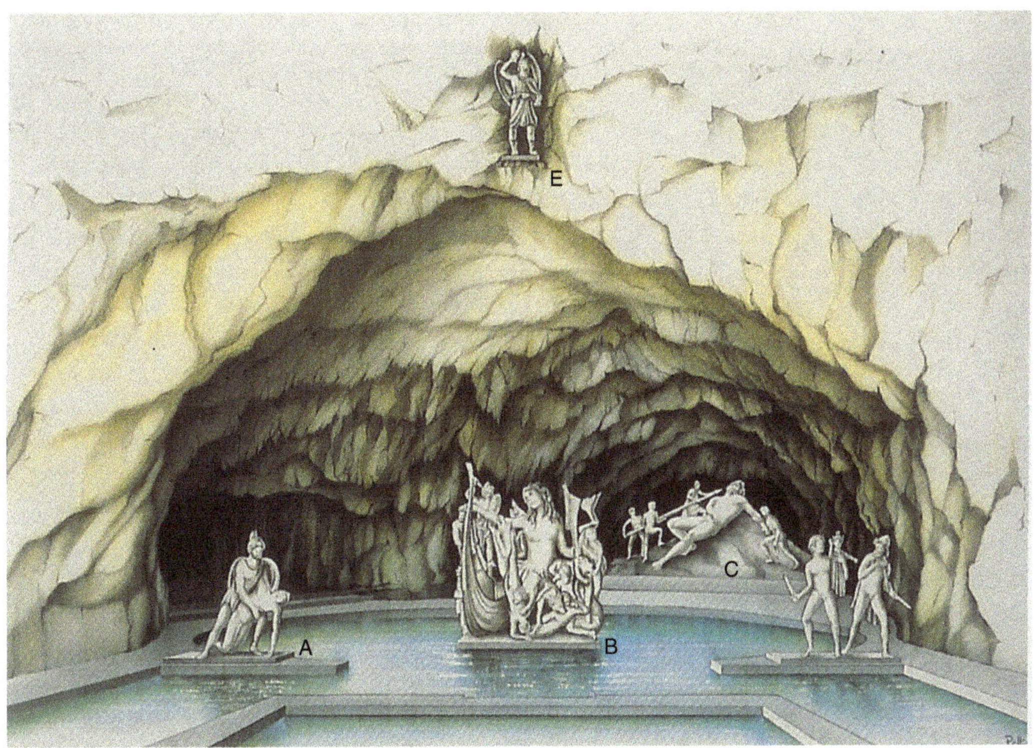

11.14 Reconstruction of the sculptural program at Sperlonga, 1st cent. BCE. Reconstruction by G. Lattanzi, after B. Conticello and B. Andreae, *Die Skulpturen von Sperlonga* (Berlin: Mann, 1974), fig. 11, modified, photo by Michael Squire.

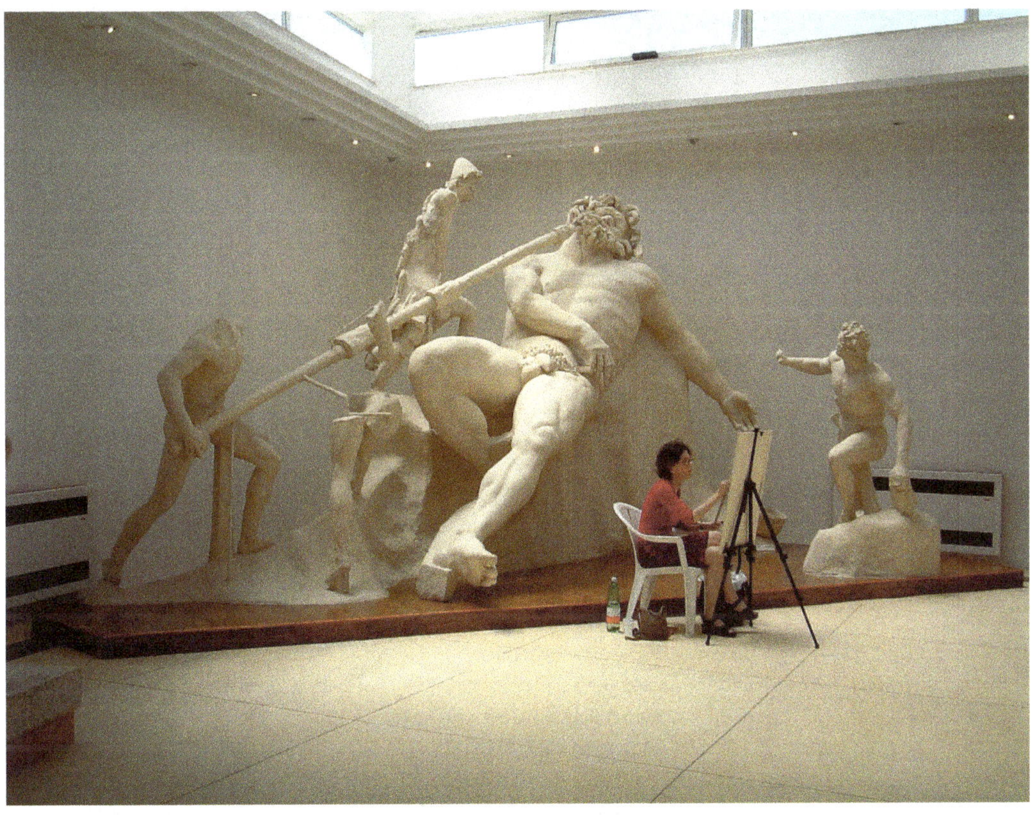

11.15 Hagesandros, Athenodoros, and Polydoros, Blinding of Polyphemos from Sperlonga, 1st cent. BCE. 11 ft 5¾ in (3.5 m) (Polyphemos). Sperlonga, Museo Archeologico. Photo: Michael Squire.

TEXTBOX: THE VALUE OF GREEK ART

Much of our discussion in this chapter has considered the value or cost of Greek art for its original owners. There has been some scholarly debate about this, generated in part by the value of Greek art for current owners. By assigning works ranging from Cycladic sculpture to Attic pottery to specific artists, with actual or invented names, the value of noteworthy artists with limited production, like Exekias and Euphronios, can be as high as painters or sculptors of more recent periods of art.

According to the published accounts of the parliamentary hearing to determine whether the British Museum would buy the Parthenon marbles, Lord Elgin submitted that he had spent at least £33,200 to acquire the works and bring them to England (House of Commons 1816). According to the National Archives Currency Converter, based on spending value, this amount would be equivalent to £1,127,000 in 2005, a very substantial sum. Prices paid today for pottery, however, can reach that level for a single pot. When the Metropolitan Museum of Art bought the krater by Euphronios in 1972 (see **Figure 10.26, page 263**), it spent $1,000,000, which was several times the high price previously paid for a painted pot. In June 2000 a kylix painted by Douris (see an example of his work in **Figure 13.13, page 334**) sold at Christie's for $1,766,000. The record price for a vase was set in December 1993 at Sotheby's in London, which auctioned a Caeretan hydria attributed to the Eagle Painter for over £2,000,000 (see an example of his work in **Figure 11.13, page 282**).

It is safe to say that modern consumers of art place greater value on these works than their original makers and purchasers, and it is the temptation of prices such as these that helps to drive the looting of antiquities that occurs throughout the world today, whether through illegal excavations of archaeological sites or through the ransacking of museums such as the Iraq Museum in Baghdad in 2003 or thefts from the Corinth Archaeological Museum in 1990 and the Museum of the History of the Olympic Games in Olympia in 2012 (see Felch and Frammolino 2011; Watson and Todeschini 2007). This is not simply a problem for Greek art but concerns our world heritage. Developing a global solution to the continuing problem of art theft is as urgent as dealing with the issues of past collecting if more cultural property is not to be lost.

REFERENCES

Felch, J. and R. Frammolino. 2011. *Chasing Aphrodite: The Hunt for Looted Antiquities at the World's Richest Museum*. Boston/New York: Houghton Mifflin Harcourt.

House of Commons. 1816. *Report from the Select Committee of the House of Commons on the Earl of Elgin's Collection of Sculptured Marbles, &c.* London: John Murray.

Johnston, A. W. 1991. "Greek Vases in the Marketplace." In T. Rasmussen and N. Spivey, eds. *Looking at Greek Vases*, 203–232. Cambridge: Cambridge University Press.

Langdon, S. 2013. "Children as Learners and Producers in Early Greece." In J. E. Grubbs and T. Parkin, eds. *The Oxford Handbook of Childhood and Education in the Classical World*, 172–194. Oxford: Oxford University Press.

National Archives Currency Converter. http://www.nationalarchives.gov.uk/currency/default0.asp#mid (last accessed May 13, 2014).

Pollitt, J. J. 1990. *The Art of Ancient Greece: Sources and Documents*. Cambridge/New York: Cambridge University Press.

Randall, R. H., Jr. 1953. "The Erechtheum Workmen." *American Journal of Archaeology* 57, 199–210.

Rasmussen, T. 1991. "Corinth and the Orientalizing Phenomenon." In T. Rasmussen and N. Spivey, eds. *Looking at Greek Vases*, 57–78. Cambridge: Cambridge University Press.

Rotroff, S. I. 1982. *Hellenistic Pottery: Athenian and Imported Moldmade Bowls*. The Athenian Agora, 22. Princeton: American School of Classical Studies in Athens.

Schultz, P. 2009. "Accounting for Agency at Epidauros: A Note on *IG* IV^2 102 AI-BI and the Economies of Style." In P. Schultz and R. von den Hoff, eds. *Structure, Image, Ornament: Architectural Sculpture in the Greek World. Proceedings of an International Conference Held at the American School of Classical Studies 27–28 November 2004*, 70–78. Oxford: Oxbow Books.

Stewart, A. F. 1990. *Greek Sculpture: An Exploration*. New Haven: Yale University Press.

Tanner, J. 2006. *The Invention of Art History in Ancient Greece: Religion, Society and Artistic Rationalisation*. Cambridge: Cambridge University Press.

Themelis, P. 1994. "Damophon of Messene: New Evidence." In K. A. Sheedy, ed. *Archaeology in the Peloponnese: New Excavations and Research*, 1–37. Oxford: Oxbow Books.

Watson, P. and C. Todeschini. 2007. *The Medici Conspiracy: The Illicit Journey of Looted Antiquities, from Italy's Tomb Raiders to the World's Greatest Museums*. New York: Public Affairs.

Younger, J. G. and P. Rehak. 2009. "Technical Observations on the Sculptures from the Temple of Zeus at Olympia." *Hesperia* 78, 41–105.

FURTHER READING

Burford, A. 1969. *The Greek Temple Builders at Epidauros: A Social and Economic Study of Building in the Asklepian Sanctuary, during the Fourth and Early Third Centuries B.C.* Toronto: University of Toronto Press.

Hasaki, E. 2012. "Workshops and Technology." In T. J. Smith and D. Planzos, eds. *A Companion to Greek Art*, Chapter 14. Malden, MA/Oxford: Blackwell Publishing.

Langridge-Noti, E. 2013. "Consuming Iconographies." In A. Tsingarida and D. Viviers, eds. *Pottery Markets in the Ancient Greek World (8th–1st Centuries B.C.). Proceedings of the International Symposium held at the Université libre de Bruxelles, 19–21 June 2008*. Études d'archéologie 5, 61–72. Brussels: CReA-Patrimoine.

Papadopoulos, J. 2003. *Ceramicus Redivivus: The Early Iron Age Potters' Field in the Area of the Classical Athenian Agora. Hesperia Supplement 31*. Princeton: American School of Classical Studies at Athens.

Stansbury-O'Donnell, M. D. 2011. *Looking at Greek Art*, 110–133. Cambridge/New York: Cambridge University Press.

Tanner, J. 2006. *The Invention of Art History in Ancient Greece: Religion, Society and Artistic Rationalisation*. Cambridge: Cambridge University Press.

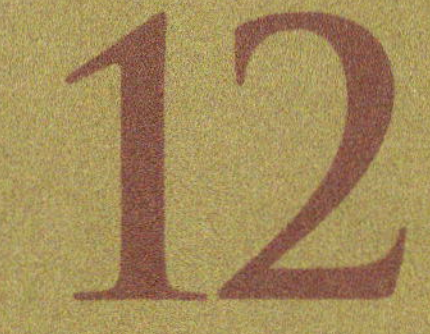

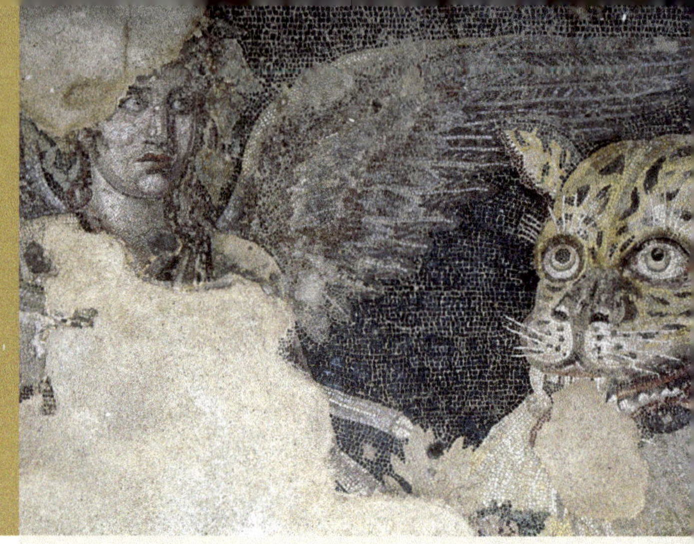

12

THE FOURTH CENTURY TO *C.* 330 BCE

Timeline
Architecture
Sculpture
Art and Individuals
Pottery
Mosaic and Fresco
Textbox: The Copy Hypothesis
References
Further Reading

A History of Greek Art, First Edition. Mark D. Stansbury-O'Donnell.

TIMELINE

	Architecture	Sculpture	Painting	Events
400–375		Dexileos Monument, Athens, 394/393*	Early Apulian painting	395–386 Corinthian War (Athens, Thebes, Corinth vs. Sparta) 394 Battle of Corinth and rebuilding of Long Walls to Piraeus 386 Plato founds Academy
375–350	Temple of Asklepios, Epidauros, 375–370* Thymele (tholos) at Epidauros, 360–330 Beginning of reconstruction of Temple of Apollo at Delphi	Pediments and acroteria from Temple of Asklepios at Epidauros, 370* Mausoleion at Halikarnassos, 360–350*	Kerch-style pelike, 360	373 Earthquake at Delphi, destroying Temple of Apollo 371–366 Thebes defeats Sparta at Battle of Leuktra and invades Lakonia 362 Battle of Mantinea 359–336 Reign of Philip II of Macedon 353 Death of Mausolos of Caria
350–325	Temple of Athena Alea at Tegea, 350–340 Lysikrates Monument, Athens, 334* Theater at Epidauros, 330	Aphrodite of Knidos, 350? Antikythera Youth, 350–325 Daochos Monument (Agias) at Delphi, 337–332*	Late Apulian painting Tomb II at Vergina, 335–315 Tomb of Persephone at Vergina, 350–325	348 Philip II destroys Olynthos 346–336 Macedon takes control of Greece 338 Macedon defeats Athens and Thebes at Battle of Chaironeia 336 Assassination of Philip II 336–323 Reign of Alexander the Great 332 Founding of Alexandria, Egypt
325–300		Drum from Temple of Artemis at Ephesos, 320*		Establishment of Hellenistic kingdoms in Greece, Egypt, and Near East

*Works for which an absolute chronological date can be suggested.

The Peloponnesian War ended in 404 BCE with the victory of Sparta and a dictatorship of aristocrats called the "Thirty Tyrants" taking control of Athens. The city was forced to dismantle its so-called Long Walls that had lined the road to its harbor at Piraeus; these and the city's circuit walls had protected Athens since its sack by Persia in 480 and all through the years of war with Sparta. While Sparta's victory seemed nearly total, within a year the Athenians overthrew the imposed government and reinstated a democracy; by 391 Athens had rearmed and rebuilt its walls. The city of Thebes in Boeotia rose to greater political and military prominence at this time, and during the fourth century there was a complex and shifting pattern of alliances and wars that was only brought to a temporary end by the rise of Macedonia in northern Greece. That kingdom had grown under Philip II (r. 359–336), who formed a powerful army that defeated the various alliances of Greek cities and imposed unified control over Greece. Following Philip's assassination in 336, his son Alexander the Great (r. 336–323) reasserted control of Greece and then expanded outward, creating one of the largest empires of the ancient world, stretching from the Balkans in the north to Egypt in the south and the Indus Valley in the east. With the establishment of many new cities by Alexander and his successors, the Greek world became significantly broader. Alexander's reign is typically regarded as a marker for the transition from the classical period of the fifth and fourth centuries to the Hellenistic period.

The changes in fourth-century culture from the fifth century are perhaps less dramatic, but are distinctive nevertheless. Fourth-century art is less Athenocentric than fifth-century art, surpassing it in some ways, departing from several of its principles, and inaugurating qualities that will dominate the Hellenistic period. Athens continued to be a primary artistic center, but the changes in the political and social landscape parallel important developments in patronage and artistic activity in new places like Epidauros and Macedonia. Culturally, new schools of philosophy such as the Cynics and the Stoics articulated a different type of relationship between the individual and the world. The Cynics taught that happiness resulted from living as close to a natural state as possible, rejecting the demands of social institutions and norms; the Stoics held that happiness resulted from virtue based on human reason and understanding the nature of the world. As J. J. Pollitt has described, the fourth century is a period in which there is less emphasis on what it means to be a member of a community (polis) than on what it is to be an individual and a human being (Pollitt 1972, 137–143). As we will see, for art and architecture this meant a greater emphasis on monuments for individuals rather than cities. Art became more diverse in both its style and mood, with a new concentration on expression, emotion, realism, and sensuality. Fourth-century art remains classical in terms of its mimetic and idealistic qualities, but relaxes some of the canon inherited from artists like Polykleitos and stresses visual effects and illusionism to a greater extent.

ARCHITECTURE

There is less construction of monumental buildings such as temples in the fourth century BCE than in the fifth, and almost nowhere are fourth-century buildings as well preserved as their predecessors in Athens, Poseidonia/Paestum, or Sicily. The most significant sanctuary building program is found at the sanctuary of Asklepios at Epidauros, which included a new temple, a theater, and a circular tholos. As we saw in the last chapter, the building expenditures at Epidauros were modest in scale compared to the massive building program in fifth-century Athens (see pages 267–270). Nevertheless, there are several important innovations in fourth-century architecture at Epidauros and elsewhere that are of particular interest.

The site is an extra-urban or rural sanctuary 13 kilometers inland from the actual town of Epidauros, which was located on the Saronic Gulf and had a relatively small population. Archaeological evidence shows there was religious activity at the site in the Geometric period, but it was not until the fifth century BCE that we have the first clear evidence for the cult of Asklepios at Epidauros and a

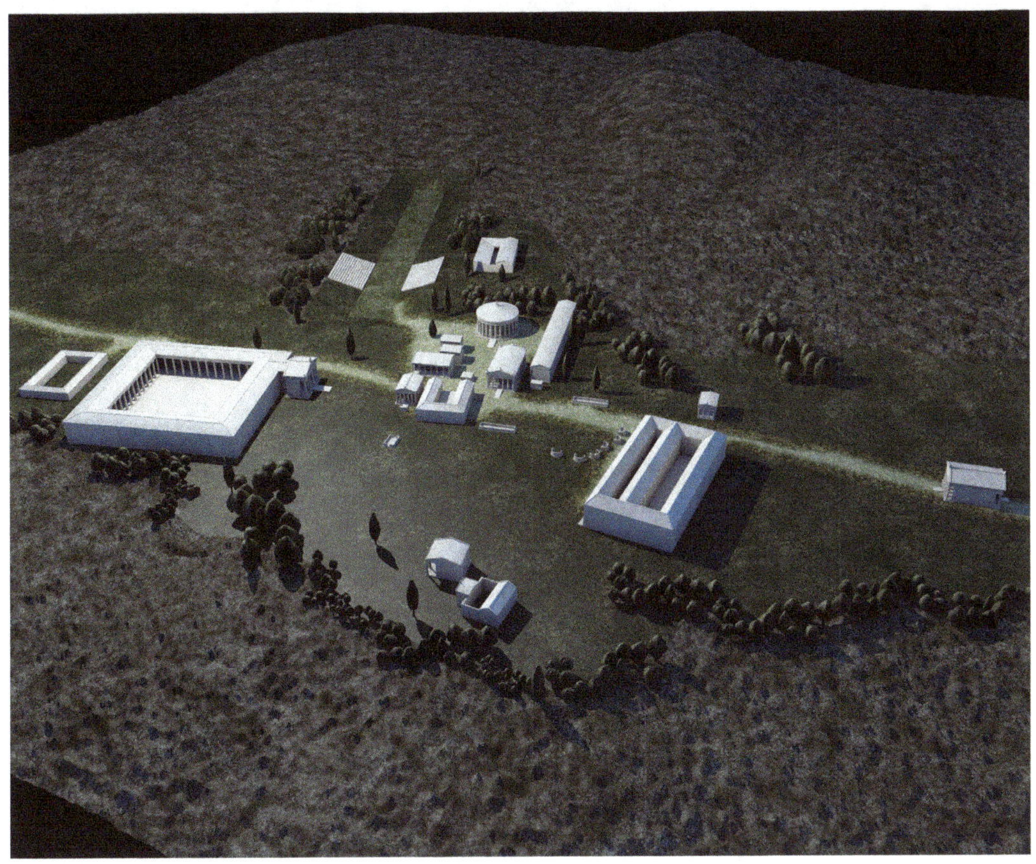

12.1 Reconstruction of the sanctuary of Asklepios at Epidauros facing to the north, 4th cent. and later BCE. 3D model: John Goodinson. Scientific advisor: John Svolos. Image courtesy of John Goodinson. Center: Thymele (tholos); Temple of Asklepios, Abaton (stoa). Center–left: Stadion. Far right: Propylaion.

significant growth in religious activity. Asklepios, a mortal son of Apollo and Coronis, was a physician and healer who was deified after his death. His cult began to receive wide attention in Greece in the fifth century as a source of healing for diseases and afflictions, including an **Asklepieion** that was established in Athens around 420 in the aftermath of the plague that had hit the city at the beginning of the Peloponnesian War. Sometime in the early fourth century, the city of Epidauros began to raise funds to rebuild its sanctuary, resulting first in the construction of the Temple of Asklepios and the carving of its sculpture. The building of the temple was begun in the 370s and construction continued on many other buildings through most of the fourth century.

Asklepieion
a temple dedicated to Asklepios

As can be seen in the reconstruction of the site (**Figure 12.1**), the sanctuary has the typical features discussed in Chapter 7, including an entry or propylaion on the east side (far right in the picture), a temple at the corner of the central cluster of buildings, a stoa on the northeast (upper-right) side of the temple and an altar to the west (left), and a stadion to the northwest. A theater, which we will discuss later, is 500 meters southwest of the main sanctuary area. Public worship at the festival honoring Asklepios was similar to festivals elsewhere, with processions, sacrifices, and performances. Private worship, however, played a very important role throughout the year, particularly for those who were sick and came to be healed. Suppliants began with a three-day period of purification and abstinence. After this, there were offerings: the sacrifice to Apollo of an animal and cakes for the other gods. Next, there was the sacrifice of a piglet at the main altar of Asklepios and a monetary offering. Finally, there was a period of incubation for the suppliant, in which he or she would stay in the sanctuary while waiting for the response of the god. The suppliant would wear a laurel wreath, offer more cakes in the evening, and sleep in the **abaton**, a stoa-type structure in the central area. Here suppliants were to receive a vision of the god, either through sleep or by being approached by a sacred snake. If there were a cure, the god would be thanked and more offerings made; numerous surviving slabs record some of these cures, which confirmed the effectiveness of the cult for

abaton
the building in a sanctuary of Asklepios where the sick would be "incubated" as part of the healing ritual

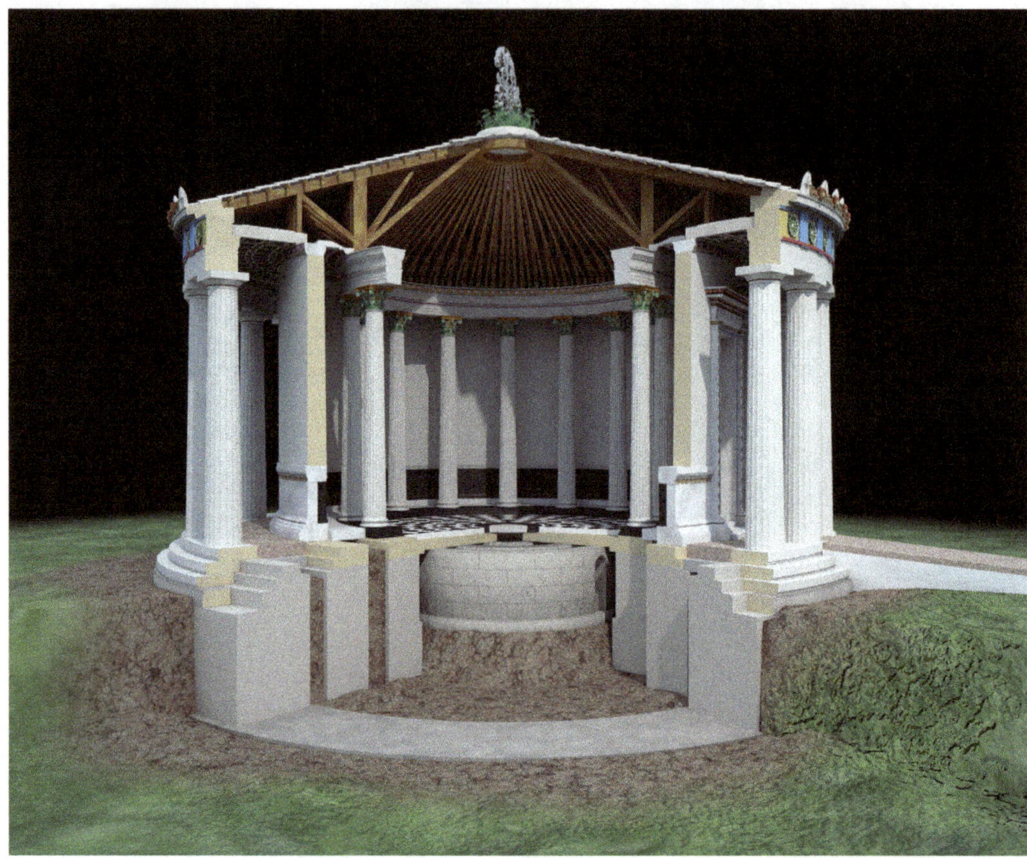

12.2 Reconstruction of the thymele (tholos) at Epidauros, designed by Polykleitos the Younger, *c*. 360–330 BCE. 3D model: John Goodinson. Scientific advisor: John Svolos. Image courtesy of John Goodinson.

subsequent visitors. This steady stream of worshippers in search of healing made Epidauros one of the most prominent religious centers in fourth-century Greece and afterwards.

The Doric temple is modest in size and was one of the first parts of the new building program; its accounts and contracts are preserved, as we saw in the last chapter. The temple was constructed in the 370 s with limestone from Corinth, but its pediments **(see Figure 11.1, page 270)** and acroteria **(see Figure 11.2, page 271)** were made of Pentelic marble from Athens. There was a chryselephantine statue of Asklepios in the interior, but it was less than half the height of similar statues in the Parthenon or the Temple of Zeus at Olympia **(see Figure 7.12, page 168)**. The building accounts tell us that the temple cost 23–24 talents to construct, with another 50 talents being estimated for the cost of the cult statue. This is only a fraction of the 470 talents spent on the Parthenon's building, not including its chryselephantine statue, an indication of the more restrained scope of building projects in the fourth century.

It is in some of the other buildings at Epidauros that we see significant innovations in fourth-century architecture. The first is the round building called the *thymele*, or hearth, in the ancient accounts. In form, the building is a tholos, a type that begins to appear in sanctuaries in the fourth century, first at Delphi around 375 BCE, and later at Olympia where it was a Philippeion, dedicated to Philip II of Macedonia **(see Figure 7.3, page 158)**. In form, the tholos consisted of a cylinder defined by a solid wall with one doorway; at Epidauros there were both interior and exterior colonnades and a conical-shaped roof **(Figure 12.2)**. The thymele at Epidauros was probably started around 360 according to the building accounts, but its construction was more intermittent and it was probably not completed until 330. Pausanias (2.27.5) tells us that the architect was Polykleitos, who is usually called Polykleitos the Younger to distinguish him from the earlier fifth-century sculptor of the same name. Since names are often repeated in families, it is possible that he was a descendant of the sculptor.

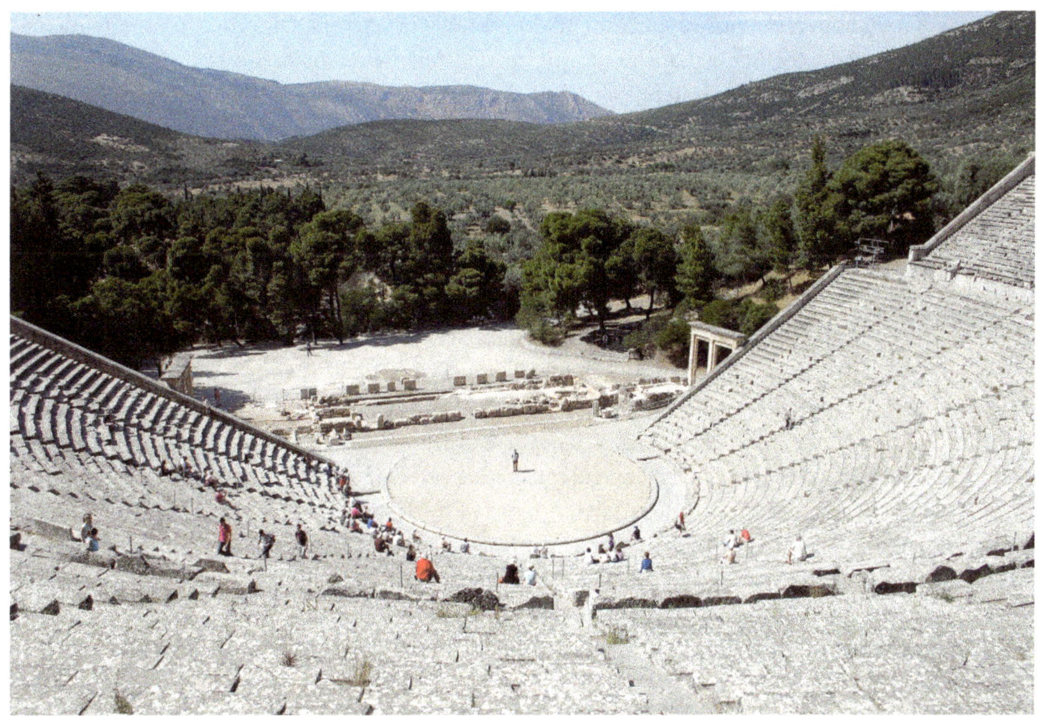

12.3 Theater at Epidauros, designed by Polykleitos the Younger, *c.* 330 BCE. Photo: author.

Only the foundations of the building are well preserved, along with some elements of the superstructure, but the computer-generated reconstruction gives a good idea of its original appearance. On the exterior was a ring of twenty-six Doric columns that created a porch around the solid wall defining the interior. The single doorway was on the east side, leading from the open space framed by the abaton and the back of the temple into the interior chamber. Here there was a second circular colonnade of fourteen Corinthian columns **(see Figure 7.10, page 166)**. The foundations preserve three rings of walls in the center of the building under the main floor that created a basement area. The doors in these walls are set at different points of orientation and the space was probably used for some type of ritual, but its character or purpose is not well known.

The thymele was both wider and taller than the Temple of Asklepios, and its unusual form would have been quite distinctive to a visitor. Furthermore, it also dominated the functioning of the site by its placement. The entry to the temple was off the road leading into the central area, making the entrance to the tholos the main point of transit off the open area flanked by the altar, the abaton, and the rear of the temple. The circular space and the central opening in the floor would have been unusual visual points to consider once inside the building. Richard Tomlinson (1983) suggests that the thymele symbolized the tomb of the mortal Asklepios; the round shape would be analogous to Bronze Age tholoi or tombs that had become hero shrines in later times. The nearby temple, then, would recognize the deified Asklepios. Both buildings were visible from the abaton as signs of Asklepios's powers.

Polykleitos the Younger is also credited with the design of the theater in Epidauros, which is the best preserved of all Greek theaters and dates to the later fourth century, about 330 BCE **(Figure 12.3)**. Early theaters were built into hillsides with the slopes providing seating; the stage or orchestra where the actors and chorus performed was usually oblong. During the fourth century, perhaps initially in the rebuilding of the theater at Athens **(see Figure 7.4, page 160)**, the design became more geometric, with the orchestra becoming circular. The seats were laid out in segments of concentric circles at a steady upward angle, about 26° at Epidauros, and were divided by aisles radiating like spokes from the center of the orchestra. Across the open end of the theater was the stage set or skene, which made a tangent to the orchestra. At Epidauros the seats were arranged in two sections divided by an ambulatory, with thirty-four rows in the lower auditorium and

skene
stage housing behind the orchestra in the Greek theater

twenty-one rows above, providing space for 12,000–14,000 spectators. One effect of this geometric transformation of the theater is that sound projects naturally from the orchestra to all of the seats. Not only were the acoustics excellent, but all of the seats were angled toward the stage and each seat in a row had an equal view of the theatrical action. This design became standard for theaters in the Greek world.

Another major development in fourth-century architecture is the large personal monument. Perhaps the most famous is the tomb of Mausolos, the king of Caria. Mausolos had become king of Caria in 377 BCE and ten years later moved his capital to Halikarnassos. He likely started the tomb at that time as part of the orthogonal grid design of the town; the tomb was finished after his death in 353 by his wife and sister Artemisia, who was later buried in the structure as well. The plan of the Mausoleion, the root of our word mausoleum, easily overshadowed in scale most temples like Epidauros and rivaled buildings like the Parthenon in its lavish sculptural program.

propylon
term signifying a gate marking the entry into the temenos of a sanctuary

The Mausoleion was set within a rectangular temenos entered by a **propylon**, sequestering it from the rest of the city (**Figure 12.4**). Ancient descriptions of the structure are inconsistent in details, but the Mausoleion consisted of a high podium with relief sculpture, a colonnaded story, and then a pyramidal roof that supported a colossal quadriga (see summary in Jenkins 2006, 203–235). In all, the structure must have been over 40 meters tall, and would have dominated the cityscape and the view for ships entering the harbor. The king's sarcophagus occupied a relatively small space on the inside, and most attention was focused on the exterior, where there were four sets of sculpture decorating all four sides of the building. The smallest, a half-life-size frieze with an Amazonomachy that we shall discuss later, was at the top of the podium just below the colonnade (**see Figure 12.9, page 297**). There were also small friezes of the Gigantomachy and chariots whose positioning is uncertain. In addition, there were life-size figures of Greeks battling Persians, heroic-scale (about 2.3 m high) standing figures, and colossal-scale (about 3 m high) figures that included dynastic portraits and scenes of hunting and sacrifice.

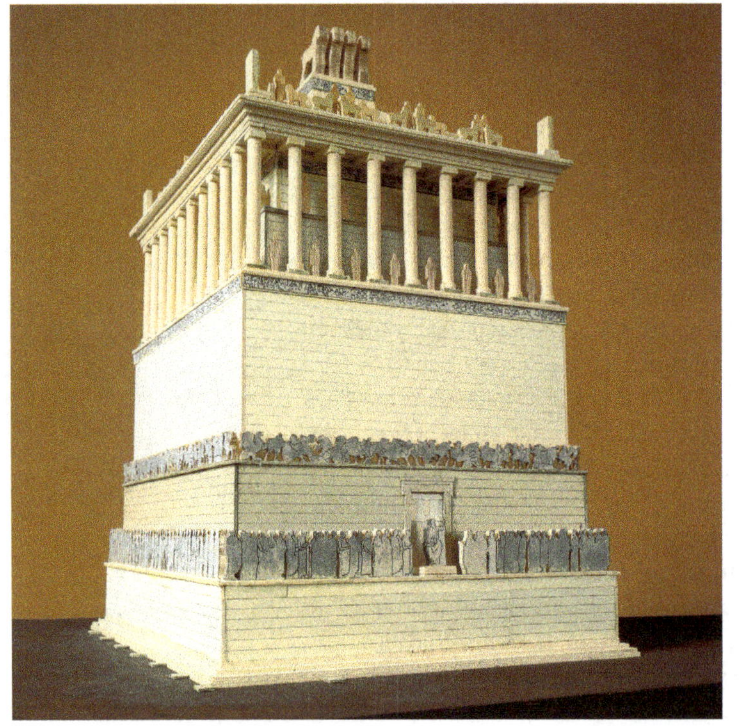

12.4 Reconstruction of the Mausoleion at Halikarnassos, *c.* 350 BCE. After K. Jeppesen, *The Maussolleion at Halikarnassos*, vol. 5, Jutland Archaeological Society Publications XV:5 (Højbjerg, 2002). Used by permission.

The Mausoleion was essentially a shrine to the king and his dynasty and became one of the seven wonders of the ancient world. As Jeremy Tanner (2013) has pointed out, the monument is a *mnema*, a memorial, and so like the funerary monument of Kroisos (**see Figure 5.24, page 123**), and of Dexileos that we shall see later (**see Figure 12.12, page 301**). The inclusion of the mythical battles of the Amazonomachy and Centauromachy on the tomb forms a legendary framework for the achievements of Mausolos, in a similar way to the Centauromachy and Amazonomachy on the Parthenon serving as frameworks for the Greeks fighting the Persians. Unlike the Parthenon, this is a personal and not a civic monument. It reflects Mausolos's agency, and the inclusion of multiple images of himself seeks to establish a future dynastic legitimacy for his successors.

In a similar way, the tholos at Olympia also served the agency of the Macedonian dynasty (**see Figure 7.3, page 158**). Begun by Philip II after his victory at Chaironeia in 338 BCE, it was finished by his son Alexander and contained five chryselephantine statues of Alexander, his parents Philip and Olympias, and his paternal grandparents Amyntas III and Eurydike. Considering that gold and ivory statues had been reserved for deities in the sixth and fifth centuries, and that the tholoi at

Delphi and Epidauros were cult buildings, the Philippeion did in effect deify the Macedonian dynasty individually in a way that was quite different from previous customs.

Smaller individual monuments were also constructed in the fourth century that show this shift in decorum, such as the Choreagic Monument of Lysikrates in Athens (**Figure 12.5**). This monument, which originally had a bronze tripod on its roof, commemorated a victory in 334 BCE at the festival of the Greater Dionysia in Athens by a chorus of boys financed by a man named Lysikrates. On top of a block-like pedestal is a miniature, slender variation of a tholos. Rather than a Doric exterior colonnade, there are half-columns of the Corinthian order set against the drum, making this the oldest surviving exterior use of the Corinthian order. The entablature includes a miniature relief frieze of satyrs with Dionysos. The acanthus foliage on the roof supported the bronze tripod. At about 10.6 meters high (and higher still with its original bronze tripod), the lushly ornate monument has an unusual verticality that would have drawn the attention of passers-by. Choral and theatrical competitions were important civic events, but even as the inscription on the architrave commemorates an individual's patronage and triumph, it is the lavish form and scale of the Lysikrates monument that first attract the attention of the viewer, before one is able to read the inscription with his name. Indeed, its prominence prompts a viewer to seek its owner, and it is possible that as a distinctive landmark the monument was known by word of mouth as the Lysikrates monument, even as we refer to it today.

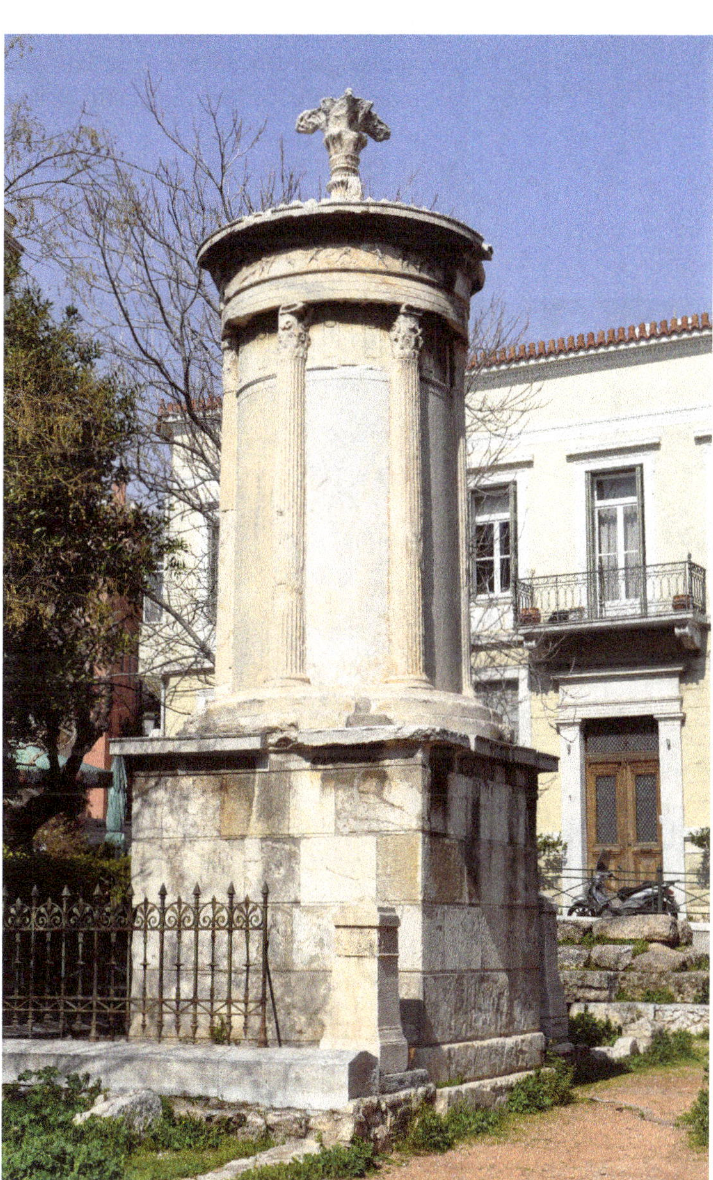

12.5 Choreagic Monument of Lysikrates, Athens, *c.* 334 BCE. Photo: author.

SCULPTURE

While fifth-century artists such as Polykleitos and Pheidias became renowned for their individual accomplishments in later ancient histories of art, the fame and personalities of fourth-century sculptors such as Skopas, Praxiteles, and Lysippos were even greater. Even while continuing the classical style of their predecessors, each was noted for perfecting some aspect of artistic style that made their work both celebrated and admired long afterward in the Roman empire. While none of their original work survives, we can see in extant fourth-century sculpture as well as some later copies elements of the refinements that they introduced. Overall, fourth-century art continued with the highly naturalistic human figure as its primary focus, but introduced elements of expression, emotion, and sensuality that made the figures less idealized than they had been in the fifth century. Sculptural style also became more diverse, so that one has to speak of sculptural "styles" that exist concurrently (see Ridgway 1997). The consequence of this, however, is that without stylistic uniformity, the ability to date sculpture on the basis of style is more difficult, and one sees in the scholarly literature strong disagreements over dating for works of the fourth century and later. Rather than look at fourth-century sculpture in chronological order, we shall instead look at it in groups of similar style or type.

We will begin at the end of the period with a column drum from the Temple of Artemis at Ephesos, now in the British Museum **(Figure 12.6)**. The monumental sixth-century Temple of Artemis at Ephesos had been destroyed by fire in 356 BCE, and the new temple was still under construction when Alexander the Great conquered the area in 334. His offer of financial assistance for the reconstruction was turned down. This incident is helpful in terms of dating the relief drums from the bases of the columns; the reliefs, like the fluted drums of the columns above them, would have been carved near the end of construction to prevent damage from the construction of the interior. On this basis, the single surviving drum is dated around 320, after Alexander had moved on (and died in 323). The subject matter is uncertain, but we can identify Hermes by his kerykeion, standing in a Doryphoros-type pose and looking upward. Indeed, the proportions of the body and the articulation of the musculature and anatomy are very similar in style to the Doryphoros **(see Figure 10.7, page 243)** and show that the Polykleitan classical style continued to be used more than a century after the original. There are some differences that show it belongs to the fourth century, particularly the greater torsion of the figure around its central axis, the placement of the left arm to the small of the back, and the more expressive open mouth, but this figure possesses more similarities than differences in relation to the Doryphoros.

The Antikythera Youth, named after its recovery from a shipwreck near the island of Antikythera between the mainland and Crete, is a rare example of an original bronze statue from the fourth century BCE **(Figure 12.7)**. Dating the statue by its archaeological context, however, is difficult since the ship was carrying a cargo of both bronze and marble sculpture when it sank, some dating from the fourth century but others from the first century **(see Figure 14.11, page 355)**. Coins found at the underwater site suggest that the ship may have been coming from Asia Minor and heading toward Rome in the first century BCE, bringing both new work and older statues appropriated, whether looted or purchased, from other contexts.

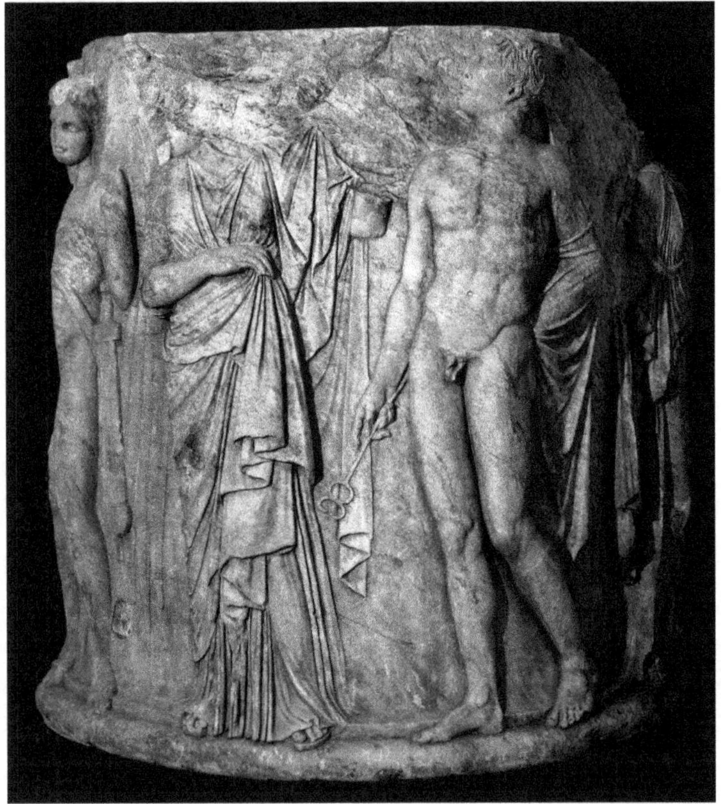

12.6 Column drum from Temple of Artemis at Ephesos, *c.* 320 BCE. 5 ft 4⅝ in (1.64 m). London, British Museum 1206. Photo: © The Trustees of the British Museum.

The youth has been identified by some scholars as Perseus, once holding the head of the Gorgon Medusa, but there is no agreement on this and no trace of the winged sandals that Perseus would have worn. The youth has a stance similar to the Doryphoros, but his right arm is extended and once held an object, as did the curled left hand to his side. Comparing the figure's proportions to the Doryphoros, we can see that the youth's head is smaller in relation to the body, making the figure appear more elongated. This is a refinement of the canon of proportions associated with the sculptor Lysippos (Pliny, *N.H.* 34.65), who is reported to have made more than 1,500 stone and bronze sculptures (Pliny, *N.H.* 34.37). His straight left arm and leg are shorter than their counterparts on his right, drawing attention to the youth's right side, both in terms of size and the use of a projecting diagonal angle. This distortion is along the vector of the figure's gaze, and if we consider this to be the primary vantage point, the elongated arm would be an optical correction for the foreshortened angle to make it look correct; such use of perspective adjustments is also associated with Lysippos in literary sources. While no original work can be attributed to the sculptor, the Antikythera Youth evokes the Lysippan canon of the late classical period. Dating by stylistic comparison is difficult in an era of widespread variation

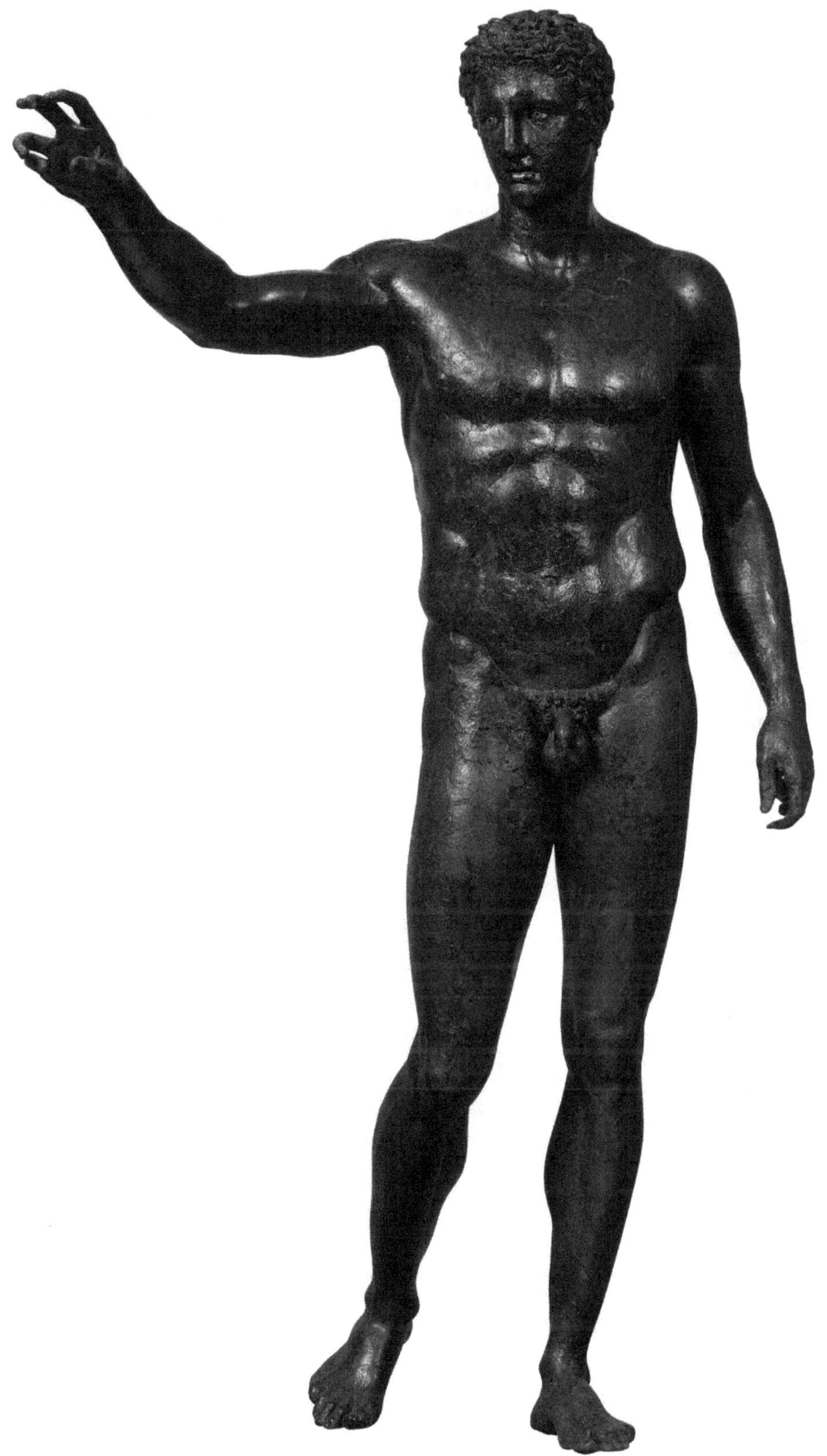

12.7 "Antikythera Youth," *c.* 350–330 BCE. 6 ft 4⅜ in (1.94 m). Athens, National Archaeological Museum Br 13396. Photo: National Archaeological Museum, Athens (Giannis Patrikianos) © Hellenic Ministry of Education and Religious Affairs, Culture and Sports/ Archaeological Receipts Fund.

and few bronze comparanda. A date of 350–325 BCE is usually cited, placing it slightly earlier than the more Polykleitan drum from Ephesos.

An original marble sculpture associated with the Lysippan canon is the statue of Agias from the Daochos Monument at Delphi (**Figure 12.8**). This ensemble included nine statues set on a long base within an enclosure, prominently located to the northeast of the Temple of Apollo (**see Figure 7.2, 511, page 157**). Based on the inscription, Daochos dedicated the monument between 337/6 and 333/2 BCE, and its nine statues included a portrait of himself and his grandson, as well as Apollo and six of Daochos's royal ancestors. Agias had been a victor in the Olympics in the 480 s and his ears are deformed from his activity as a boxer ("cauliflower ears"), but this cannot be a true portrait since Agias had died at least a century beforehand. The head is small compared with the height of the body, but additionally there are some features that suggest qualities of realism associated in literary sources with the art of Lysippos. Although the figure has a *contrapposto* pose, both feet are set flat to the ground, making the figure firmly at rest. Looking at the shoulders, they sag more acutely from the neck than either the Ephesos or Antikythera figures. Finally, the mouth is turned down slightly and the eye socket is more deeply arched and inset. Altogether, these details suggest a strong figure who is affected by his exertions, like an athlete who is triumphant but tired after the contest. This is an element of realism not found in the Doryphoros or Parthenon frieze, whose figures never seem to tire; this is probably the sense behind Pliny's account that Lysippos had said "men were made by those earlier sculptors as they were, but by him [Lysippos] as they appeared" (*N.H.* 34.65; tr. Pollitt 1990, 99).

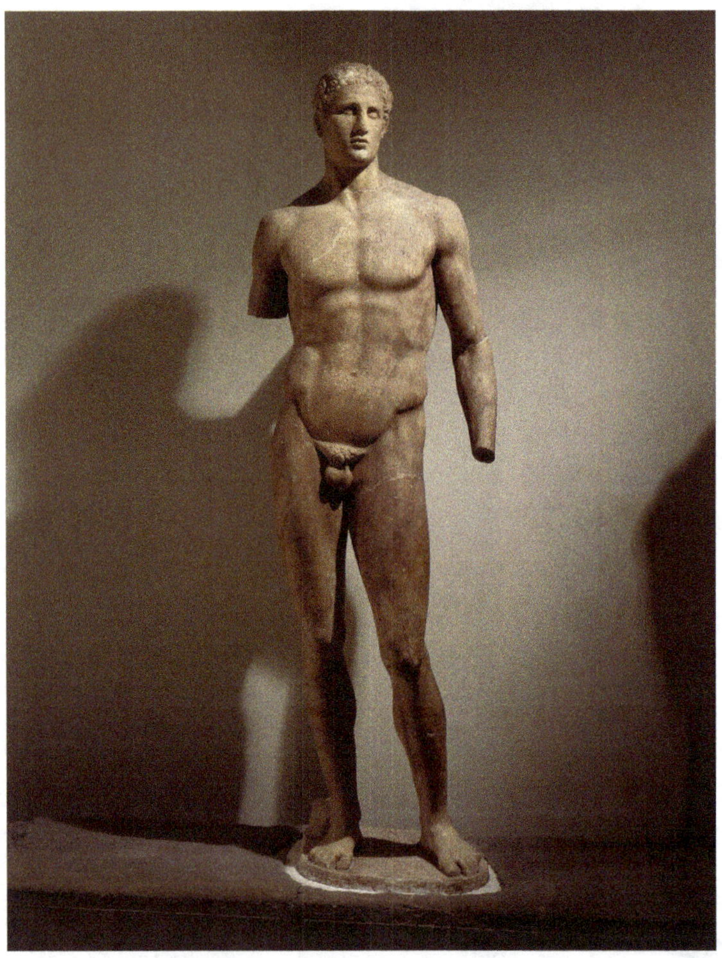

12.8 Agias from the Daochos Monument at Delphi, 337/6–333/2 BCE. 6 ft 6¾ in (2 m). Delphi, Archaeological Museum. Photo: Gianni Dagli Orti/ The Art Archive at Art Resource, NY.

These three statues date to the last half of the fourth century and show both the continuation and refinement of the Polykleitan style of the fifth century, but there are additional styles that coexisted with or predated these. Dating to the 370 s BCE, the sculpture of the Temple of Asklepios at Epidauros has examples of two other stylistic trends. The Nike acroterion (**see Figure 11.2, page 271**), probably carved by Timotheos of Athens according to the contracts, is a successor to the florid style of drapery found on the late fifth-century Nike by Paionios at Olympia and the Aphrodite of the Parthenon east pediment even earlier (**see Figure 10.8, page 245; Figure 10.16B, page 251**). The drapery pulls across the breasts, abdomen, and thighs to be almost transparent at the same time as it piles and swirls elsewhere to create strong visual effects. The style in the pediment is different in spirit as well as execution (**see Figure 11.1, page 270**). The cloth on the Amazon does pull and bunch, but with less precision and detail. There is more interest in the twisting and pulling of the figures and the drama created in their fight. The Greek warrior grabs the head and hair of the Amazon and pulls it back; the forward momentum of the rest of her body results in a sharp backwards bend in the neck. Her eyes bulge outward, and one can see in her face an interest in the *pathos* of a struggling warrior.

One can contrast the Epidauros Amazonomachy with the more ballet-like treatment of the same theme on the friezes of the Mausoleion at Halikarnassos (**Figure 12.9**). These reliefs, carved in the 350 s BCE, show well-muscled bodies and vigorous poses, but without marring their idealized beauty

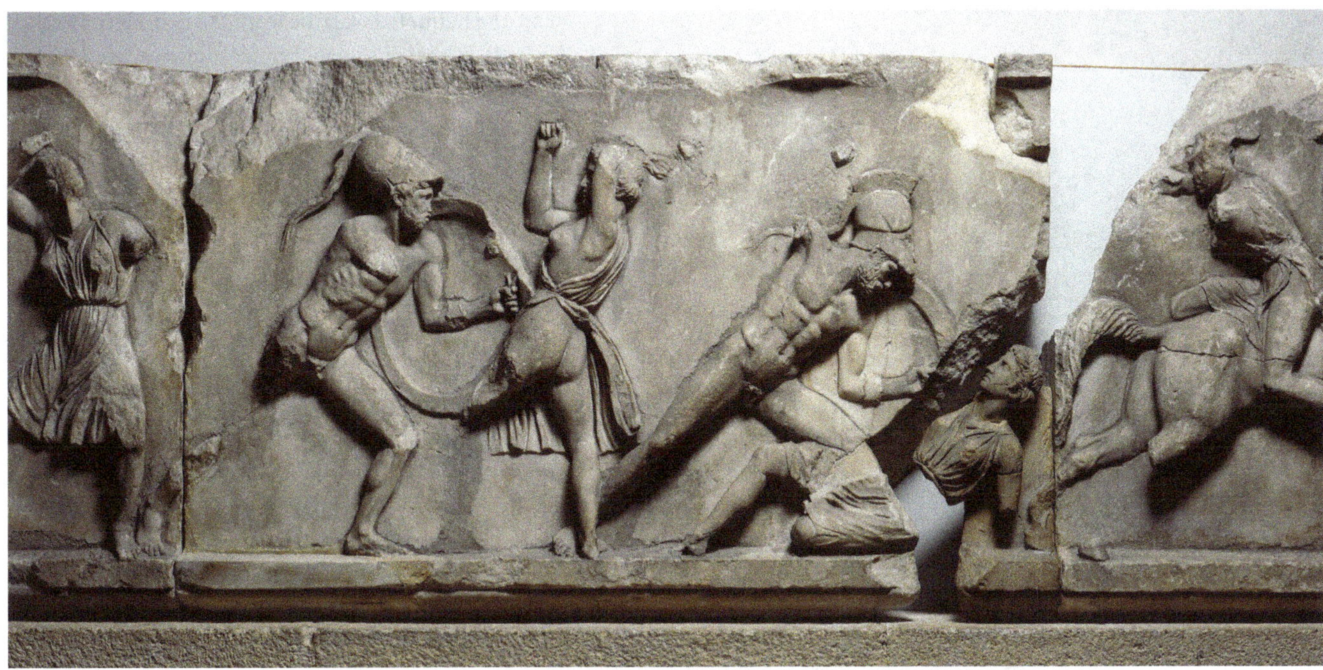

12.9 Amazonomachy frieze from the Mausoleion at Halikarnassos, 360–350 BCE. 35 in (89 cm). London, British Museum. Photo: © The Trustees of the British Museum.

through emotional expression or tortuous positioning of the body. These figures are relatively impassive and remain undisturbed in their idealism. Indeed, one has to wonder at the expected response of a viewer looking at the short chiton of the Halikarnassos Amazon, which has blown back to reveal her buttocks and thighs, a vision antithetical to the pain and death of the Epidauros Amazon. Even though the figures were very high at the top of the Mausoleion's base, the contrast between the painted cloth and the flesh-colored body would have enhanced the visibility of the figures.

The interest in *pathos* is very strong in the sculpture of the west pediment from the Temple of Athena Alea at Tegea. Pausanias (8.45.5; 8.47.1) writes that the temple and its cult statue were designed by Skopas after a fire had destroyed the previous building in 395 BCE; the attribution and dating of the architectural sculpture, almost certainly done by a workshop, is less clear. If Skopas were involved in the Tegean pedimental sculpture, it would likely be later than Halikarnassos, where he and Timotheos are said to be among its four sculptors (Pliny, *N.H.* 36.30), making a date in the 340 s possible. The subject of the west pediment was the combat between Achilles and Telephos, the son of Herakles and Auge and ruler of Mysia, a city in northwest Asia Minor. The Greeks in sailing to Troy had landed at Mysia and, mistakenly thinking it to be Troy, attacked the city but were forced to withdraw. During the fight, Telephos was wounded by Achilles. Telephos's wound would not heal, however, and he had to force Agamemnon, the leader of the Greek forces, to make Achilles heal him, after which Telephos led the Greeks to Troy.

The head from the pediment with the lion skin headdress has been identified as both Herakles and Telephos, but it is more likely that Telephos wears it to show his heroic lineage **(Figure 12.10A)**. If so, we have to place him in the center of the pediment, being attacked by Achilles, who would be to his left and our right. Telephos was moving away from Achilles but turns his head back sharply to his left to look back at his opponent, as the bulging neck tendons indicate. The face has furrows around the cheeks and across the forehead and the lips are pulled down and back, but it is in the eyes that one can sense the pain of Achilles's spear striking the king. The eyebrow forms a ridge over the eyeball, and the undercut fold of skin above the upper eyelid droops to obscure the eyelid, almost a visual parallel to Homer's phrasing of "night descending on a warrior's eyes" as he dies. A second

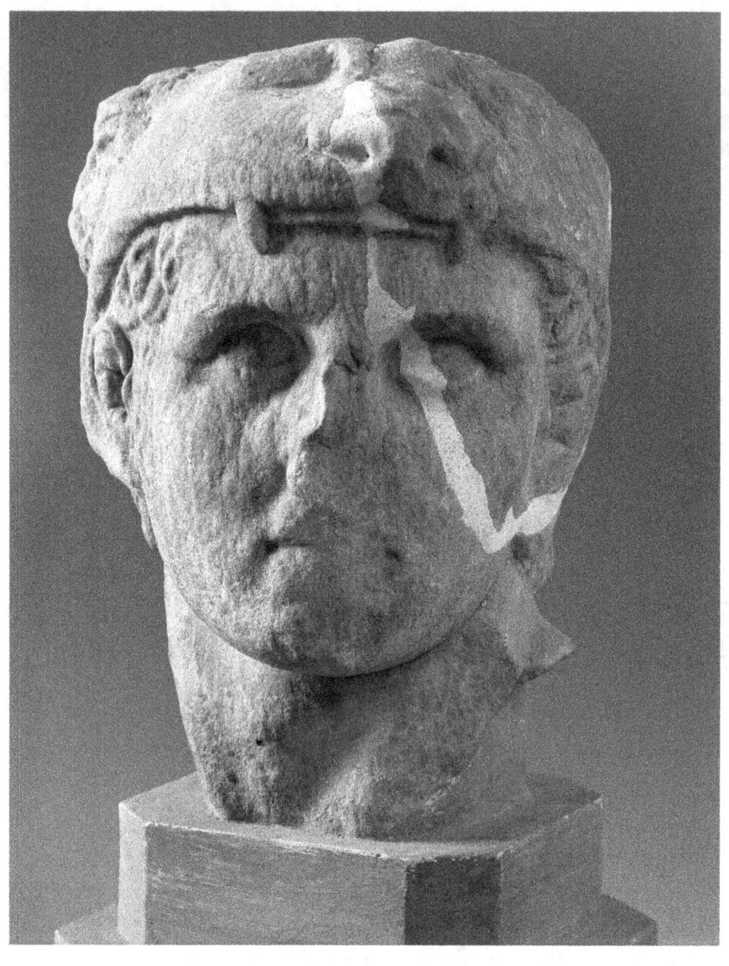

12.10A Head of Telephos from the west pediment of the Temple of Athena at Tegea, *c.* 350–340 BCE. 12⅜ in (31.4 cm). Tegea Museum. Photo: Eva-Maria Czakó. D-DAI-ATH-Arkadien-0493.

head of a helmeted warrior from the pediment (**Figure 12.10B**) is sharply turned upward as well as twisted, and his eyes would seem to be rolling up into their sockets in the throes of death in a stronger display of *pathos*.

Based on the sculpture from Tegea, Skopas is characterized as particularly interested in emotion, but literary sources also record that he did a number of cult statues that were likely more idealized in their style. Such disparity in style, along with a lack of detailed literary sources, has raised difficulties in assessing Skopas's work.

We will end our survey of sculpture by considering the work of Praxiteles of Athens, who was best known for his statue of Aphrodite at Knidos (**Figure 12.11**). He is also linked with the sculpture of Hermes and Dionysos that we will consider in the textbox for this chapter. For the Aphrodite, Praxiteles had been commissioned by the community on the island of Kos to make a cult statue of the goddess of love; our sources tell us that he made two works, one clothed and one nude (Pliny, *N.H.* 36.20). We have seen that male nudity was commonplace in Greek art, but female nudity outside of narrative or symposion scenes was rare. The people of Kos took the clothed version, while the island of Knidos bought the nude version, which subsequently became one of the most famous works of art in antiquity and afterward.

The original statue was set at the center of an open circular colonnade in her sanctuary, making it open to view from all directions. The original is lost, but there are dozens of literary references and literally hundreds of copies and adaptations that give us some idea of the work's reputation and appearance. The goddess is shown in a *contrapposto* pose with a strong S-curve contour; her head turns to her left and there is a slight torsion in the figure. She is picking up a cloth that has been resting on a hydria, a reference to her act of bathing. The features of her face are very softly modeled and tranquil, and her hair is drawn back on both sides to create a triangle framing her face; the rich texture of the hair further sets off her smooth skin. Here Praxiteles essentially defined an ideal of female beauty that lasted throughout the Hellenistic period and into the Roman era, as reflected in later works such as the Aphrodite of Melos (**see Figure 14.17, page 362**) and the portrait of Cleopatra (**see Figure 14.24, page 369**).

We shall explore issues of gender and sexuality in more detail in the next chapter, but the differing artistic treatment of the male and female body in the preceding centuries of Greek art certainly points to different social attitudes about modesty and virtue in men and women. Praxiteles's creation of a canonical female nude was certainly revolutionary in artistic terms, but whether social conventions adapted to this new idea is harder to evaluate. Certainly there has been a tendency in scholarship to see in the Aphrodite a hint of modesty as she pulls her garment up to clothe herself, but is she doing this in response to being disturbed at her bath in a feeling of shame? This would typically be expressed through lowering your eyes while someone is looking at you. Without the original statue, it is difficult to know if Aphrodite is looking straight out at something or someone to her left and the viewer's right, or if she is looking downward and turning her head away from a viewer who stands in front of her body, which would suggest shame and modesty. Given that this was a cult statue and likely elevated slightly on a base, her gaze appears level and even to look over the head of the viewer toward an unseen, perhaps divine presence. Within a religious sanctuary, a leering attitude would be inappropriate, and Greek myth has many tales of the dangers of inappropriate attitudes of human intruders toward goddesses, and of the potential dangers of this statue in particular to its viewers.

The beauty and fertility that Aphrodite epitomizes were essential for society, as we saw in the Parthenon pediment (**see Figure 10.16B, page 251**), but here they are revealed in their own right. In this sense, what we see is another dimension of the fourth-century transformation of the classical style by an interest in sensuality and sensual experience. The cult of Aphrodite, like that of Asklepios, had both public and personal dimensions. Whereas the suppliant at Epidauros sought physical healing, one might say that the visitor to Knidos sought beauty and love and was meant to be emotionally moved by the sight of the goddess. A Roman-era writer, Lucian, wrote a long account of two friends who visited the sanctuary and admired the goddess from both the front and the back. Their rapture over the statue, both physical and verbal, conveys to us that in their eyes the goddess embodied both female beauty in her graceful limbs and parted lips and, from the rear view, male beauty in the flowing line of her thighs, buttocks, and back (Stansbury-O'Donnell 2014). To see beauty was to experience *pathos*, and perhaps a temporary release or euphoria from harsher images of reality.

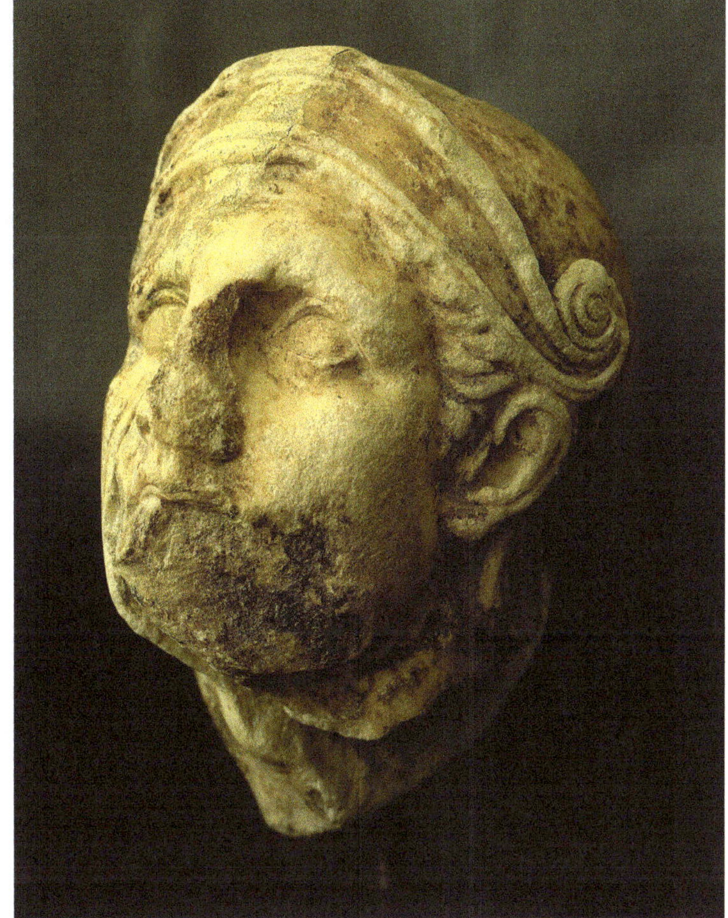

12.10B Head of a warrior from the west pediment of the Temple of Athena at Tegea, *c.* 350–340 BCE. 12⅜ in (31.4 cm). Athens, National Archaeological Museum 180. Photo: Gianni Dagli Orti/The Art Archive at Art Resource, NY.

ART AND INDIVIDUALS

The contexts of the works that we have considered up to now have been highly visible and public. Looking at art that has a more personal or private context, such as a tomb or individual possessions, we can see a similar range of styles and interests, from idealistic naturalism to more realistic, emotional, or sensual expression. We can begin by looking at the stele of Dexileos from the Kerameikos in Athens (**Figure 12.12**). The inscription on the base informs us that Dexileos died fighting the Spartans at the Battle of the Nemea River in 394/3, just a decade after Athens' defeat in the Peloponnesian War. The inscription is unusual in also giving us a birth year, making Dexileos twenty when he died. The relief is larger than fifth-century stelai like those of Ampharete (**see Figure 10.19, page 254**) and Hegeso (**see Figure 5.28, page 127**). Indeed, it is about the size of the Parthenon metopes and, like them, carved in high relief. Stylistically, the figure has an idealized naturalism similar to the Parthenon riders (**see Figure 1.1, page 2**). The stele was placed upon a stepped, curved wall that stood on a square stone platform at a fork on the street of tombs just outside the Dipylon Gate (**Figure 12.13**). In this location, standing at least 4 meters above the ground and angled toward those approaching from the city's Dipylon Gate, the monument was visually prominent, more so than others along the same road such as the Koroibos–Kleidemides family (**see Figure 5.27, page 126**).

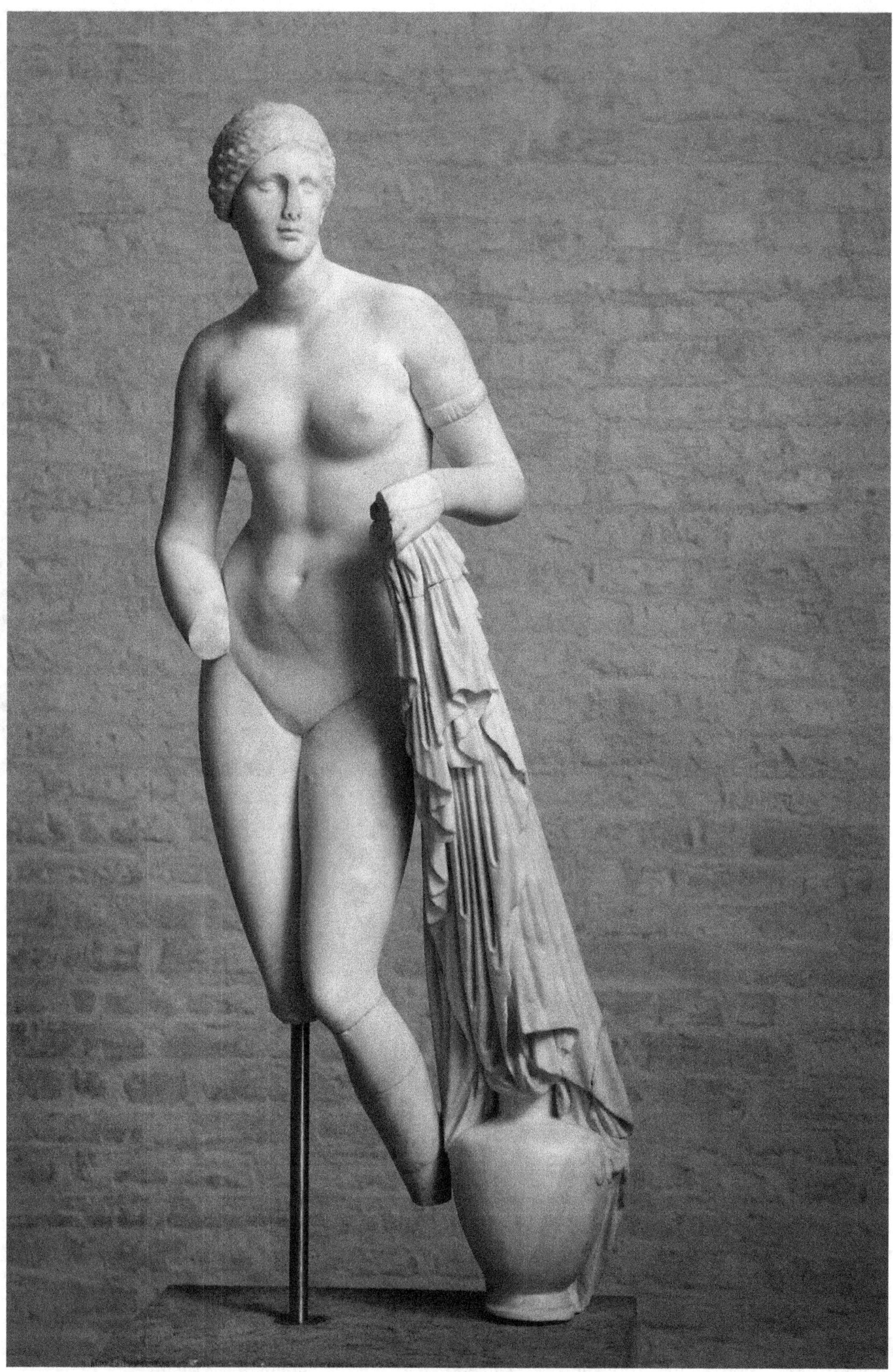

12.11 Aphrodite of Knidos of Praxiteles, Roman copy or adaptation of Greek original of *c.* 350 BCE. 5 ft 8½ in (1.74 m). Munich, Staatliche Antikensammlungen und Glyptothek. Photo: © Vanni Archive/Art Resource, NY.

While it looks and functions like a grave monument, Dexileos was not actually buried here. As was customary, his ashes and bones were placed with the other fallen warriors in the state burial ground of the Demosion Sema, further west outside the Dipylon Gate toward the Academy. It was here that those who died in battle for Athens were buried and their names, the casualty list, were inscribed annually on a stele. This practice of a civic tomb began sometime in the second quarter of the fifth century BCE and became an important ritual of the polis, taking precedence over entombment in a family burial plot. There were also sculptural monuments at the Demosion Sema, and Dexileos was included on a second public monument near the tomb dedicated to the eleven cavalrymen who had died in the Battle of the Nemea River.

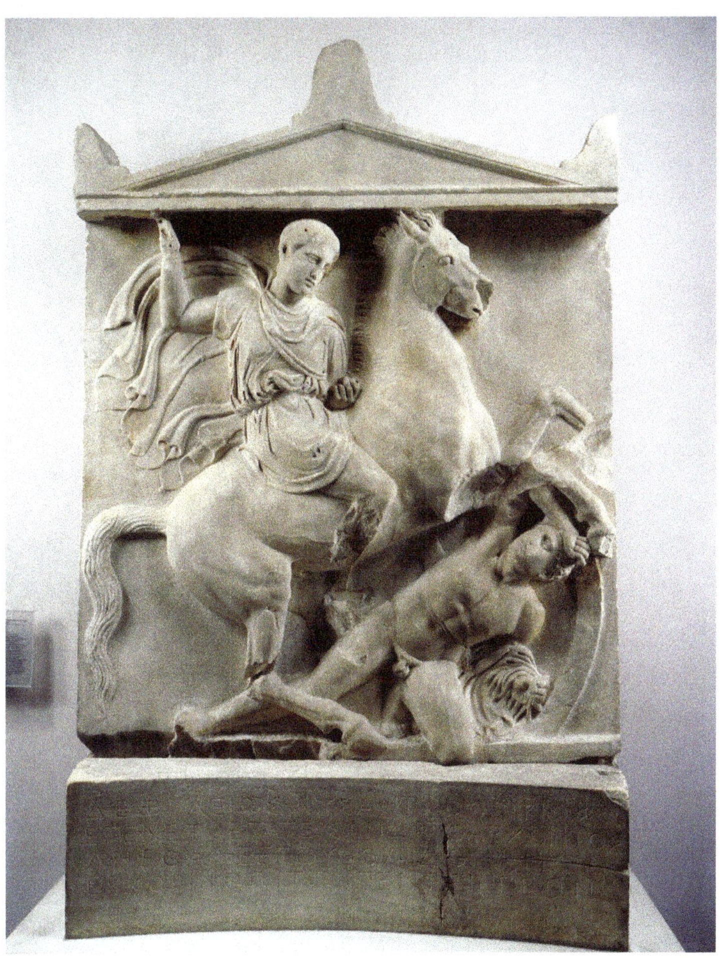

12.12 Monument of Dexileos from Kerameikos, Athens, 394/3 BCE. 5 ft 8⅞ in (1.75 m). Athens, Kerameikos Museum P1130. Photo: Marie Mauzy/Art Resource, NY.

Dexileos's personal monument is, strictly speaking, a cenotaph set up by the family in addition to his state-funded tomb and cavalrymen monument and explicitly commemorates an individual rather than a group. As can be seen in the reconstructed tomb, it is part of a family plot and would serve as both a personal and family commemoration, like the nearby tombs of the Koroibos-Kleidemides family. Dexileos is shown as a *hippeus* or knight raising his arm to deliver the final blow to an opponent collapsing under his horse. Curiously, Dexileos is clothed, as he would have been in battle, while his opponent is unrealistically nude, reversing the heroic nudity of works like the Amazonomachies seen above. That his enemy is given heroic nudity amplifies Dexileos's triumph. Sitting high and angled to face the street, the monument elevates the individual and family to a heroic status.

The monument does, however, create an ambiguity around Dexileos himself (see Hurwit 2007). Like his victim, Dexileos was a casualty of war and ultimately did not triumph in battle as the image suggests, although he might have been a successful fighter before being killed. An image that showed him attacking an opponent on equal terms could have been read as either triumphant or not, but this image shows a victorious climax over a heroic foe that contrasts with the facts recounted in the inscription below: he is shown triumphant, but actually died in battle. There are other ambiguities. Dexileos died fighting for the democratic regime of Athens against Sparta, but his status as a *hippeus* places him among the aristocratic elite who had supported the Thirty Tyrants that controlled Athens briefly after its defeat by Sparta in 404 BCE. Perhaps his cenotaph helped to confirm the place of his family in the fourth-century polis.

Later tombs from Athens and elsewhere show this oversized representation of the individual. From the middle of the fourth century in Salamis comes the grave stele of Mnesistrate, whose name appears in the cornice above her on the left **(see Figure 13.2, page 322)**. A bearded man, presumably her husband, is shown as speaking with her. She is modestly clothed, but her S-shaped pose and her gaze are not unlike the Aphrodite of Knidos. The cloth of her chiton and himation pull more tightly across her thigh and buttock and her head is turned slightly outward from the background plane and looks directly at her husband, unlike the more modest pose, clothing, and gaze of Ampharete and

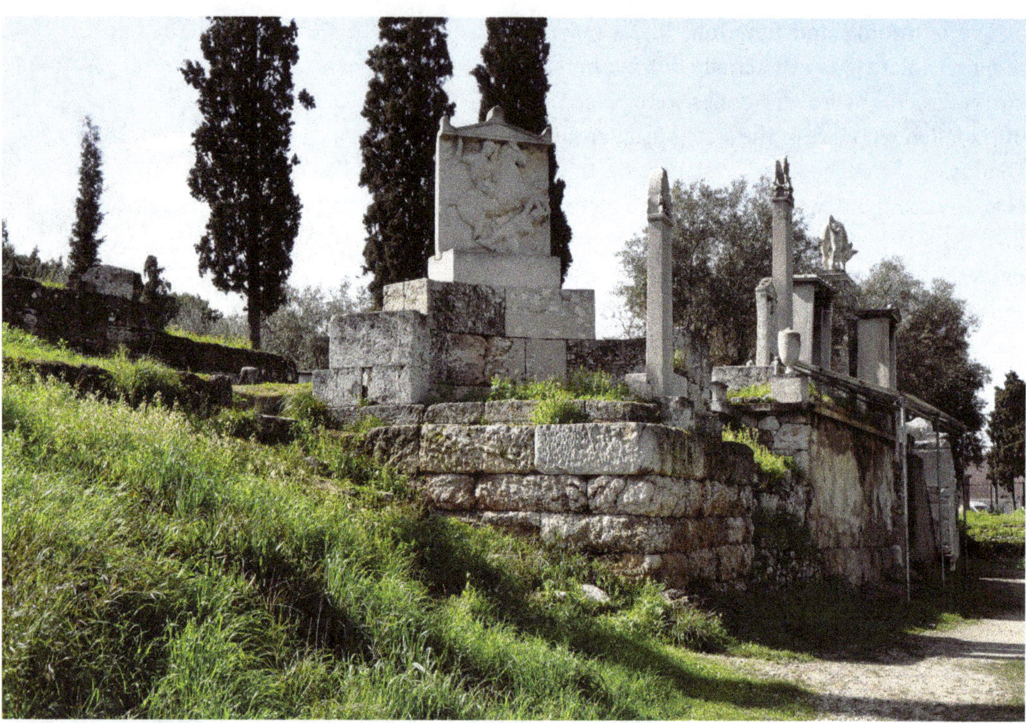

12.13 Reconstruction of Dexileos Monument *in situ*. Photo: author.

Hegeso. It should also be noted that the scale of the figures is life-size; they are about 1.75 meters high (5 ft 9 in), which would be bordering on heroic scale. The scene and figures are rather conventional, but their scale makes them monumental.

Terracottas also show the animation and decorative quality of fourth-century styles. The collection of figures from a girl's tomb in the Kerameikos cemetery includes Apollo playing the kithara, a seated figure with a phiale, a woman carrying a child on her shoulders, a priestess of Kybele with a tambourine, and a dancer next to an altar **(see Figure 1.5, page 10)**. This is an unusual assortment of tomb figures for this time, but it becomes much more common in the Hellenistic period and the emergence of what are called Tanagra figures. The pose of the priestess of Kybele is of particular interest in that she is nude and leaning against a column like a figure of Aphrodite. She has the same strong S-contour that we see in Praxiteles's Aphrodite, although this figure is a couple of decades earlier than Praxiteles. The flowing drapery of the dancer recalls the Nike figures that we have seen, and the terracottas in general show the willingness to adapt features associated with specific deities to new contexts.

We also see changes in the figural imagery associated with mirrors. The caryatid mirror of the sixth and fifth centuries is replaced by hinged mirrors with relief covers as the prevailing type **(Figure 12.14)**. This example, from a tomb in Elis, shows the drunken Herakles grabbing the maiden Auge, whom he will rape and by whom he will father Telephos, whom we saw as an adult in the pediment at Tegea **(see Figure 12.10A)**. Auge is usually shown in art as resisting, backing or pulling away from Herakles, but her action here is more ambiguous. While Herakles's right hand grabs her garment, he is falling back and is not really able to bear his own weight, nor are his eyes focused on her. Her hands actually cup under his arm, as if she were trying to support him rather than resist. Like the Amazon at Halikarnassos, her drapery falls away behind her body, revealing her in near total nudity. The scene is very sensually composed, but raises a question, as with the Aphrodite of Knidos, as to whether the situation is shameful (in the story, her father king Aigeus will set her and the child adrift in a box to perish at sea) or is an epiphany of beauty and desire that suggests her power over Herakles. The mirror was found in a tomb and a mirror's viewer would almost certainly be a woman. As an example of an ideal figure, however, Auge sends a quite different message than the caryatid of fifth-century mirrors, nearly nude and directly interacting with men **(see Figure 10.6, page 242)**.

A similar sensuality is featured on the main scene of a large volute krater found in Tomb B at Derveni, about 10 kilometers northeast of Thessaloniki (**Figure 12.15**). The krater had been set on a pedestal in a stone-lined cist tomb, one of several that probably belonged to an elite family, along with a variety of bronze and ceramic washing and sympotic vessels. The krater contained the ashes and bones of a man aged thirty-five to fifty years and a younger woman, presumably his wife. Based on the military and horse gear in the tomb, he was probably a soldier and possibly a cavalryman. An inscription in the Thessalian dialect, placed on the vessel's rim sometime after its manufacture, states that it is the "krater of Astioun, son of Anaxagoras from Larissa," a town in Thessaly. Based on the grave goods, the tomb dates to 325–300 BCE, but the vessel is dated earlier to 375–350 based on style and motifs. Beryl Barr-Sharrar suggests that the vessel was commissioned by Anaxagoras and later used by his son, or possibly grandson, as a funerary urn (Barr-Sharrar 2008, 182).

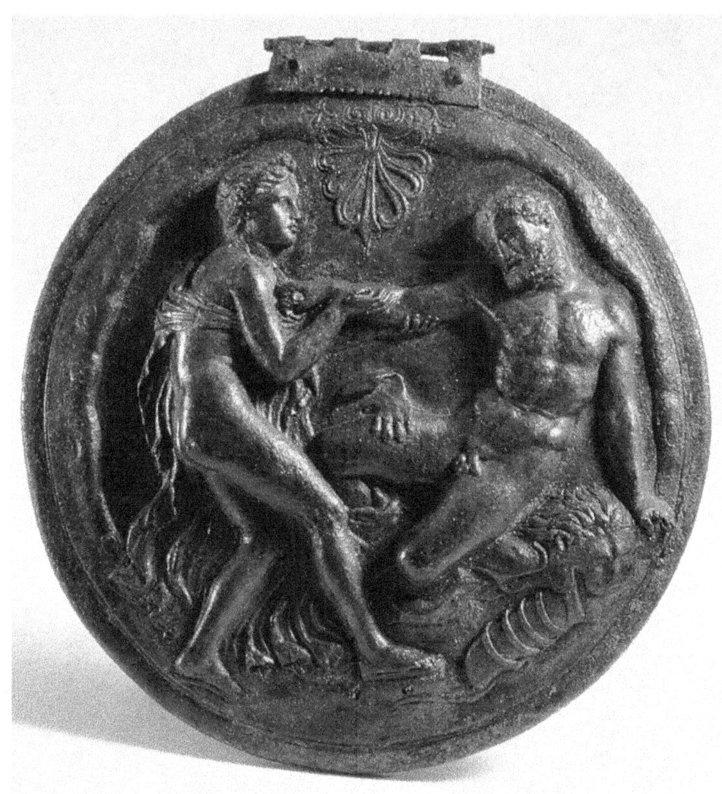

12.14 Bronze hinged mirror cover, *c.* 330 BCE. Diameter: 6⅛ in (15.5 cm). Athens, National Archaeological Museum, Stathatos Collection 312. Herakles and Auge. Photo: National Archaeological Museum, Athens (Kostas Xenikakis) © Hellenic Ministry of Education and Religious Affairs, Culture and Sports/Archaeological Receipts Fund.

The main frieze shows Dionysos and Ariadne seated, while to either side around the vessel are energetically dancing maenads, a satyr, and a hunter. This Dionysiac scene is a common and appropriate choice for a mixing bowl for wine, but the composition is unusual in representing Dionysos at a larger scale than Ariadne, about the difference between a heroic-scale figure and one who is life-size. Her clinging drapery reveals her voluptuous figure, and she pulls her veil forward to signify her status as bride and wife. More provocative is the way in which Dionysos's right leg is draped over her left thigh, giving a decided sexual tone that is not typical of this scene. Around them the cloaks of the maenads billow out while their chitons cling to their bodies or fall away. Certainly one could compare the style to the Nike acroterion from Epidauros (**see Figure 11.2, page 271**) and suggest that the vessel originated in Athens, but with such an expensive work, we have to consider the importance of the patrons in northern Greece, the Thessalian and Macedonian elite, in supplying commissions for such a work.

The krater's subject matter and use in a cremation burial, and the presence of ritual and sympotic vessels in the tomb, are thought to be the result of the owners' belief in the afterlife and the possibility of a luxurious, heroic feast. An Orphic papyrus text found in Tomb A is also associated with mystery cults that looked to the afterlife and heroizing the dead. Certainly the lavish cost of the grave goods is in sharp contrast to the more modest tomb furnishings of fifth-century Athens, emphasizing the significance of the afterlife for the deceased and family and creating a heroic setting for the funerary rituals.

Another example of costly tomb furnishings is the regalia said to have come from a tomb in Taras/Taranto (**Figure 12.16**). The restored necklace features female heads and seeds as pendants. The ring shows in low relief a seated female figure holding a scepter, who could be a priestess or a goddess. The very rare scepter is a significant indicator of status and authority. It has an intricate gold net sleeve that covered its original wooden core, now replaced by a resin rod. The top finial is a Corinthian capital that supports acanthus leaves enclosing a glass fruit, a lavish topping decoration like the acanthus on the Lysikrates Monument (**see Figure 12.5**). Based on the ring's image, it is thought that the ensemble might have belonged to a priestess in Taras/Taranto, and surely to a member of the aristocratic elite.

This disposition of luxurious grave goods in the fourth century, from southern Italy to the Black Sea region, provides us with rare examples of metalwork from the classical period. It also shows that

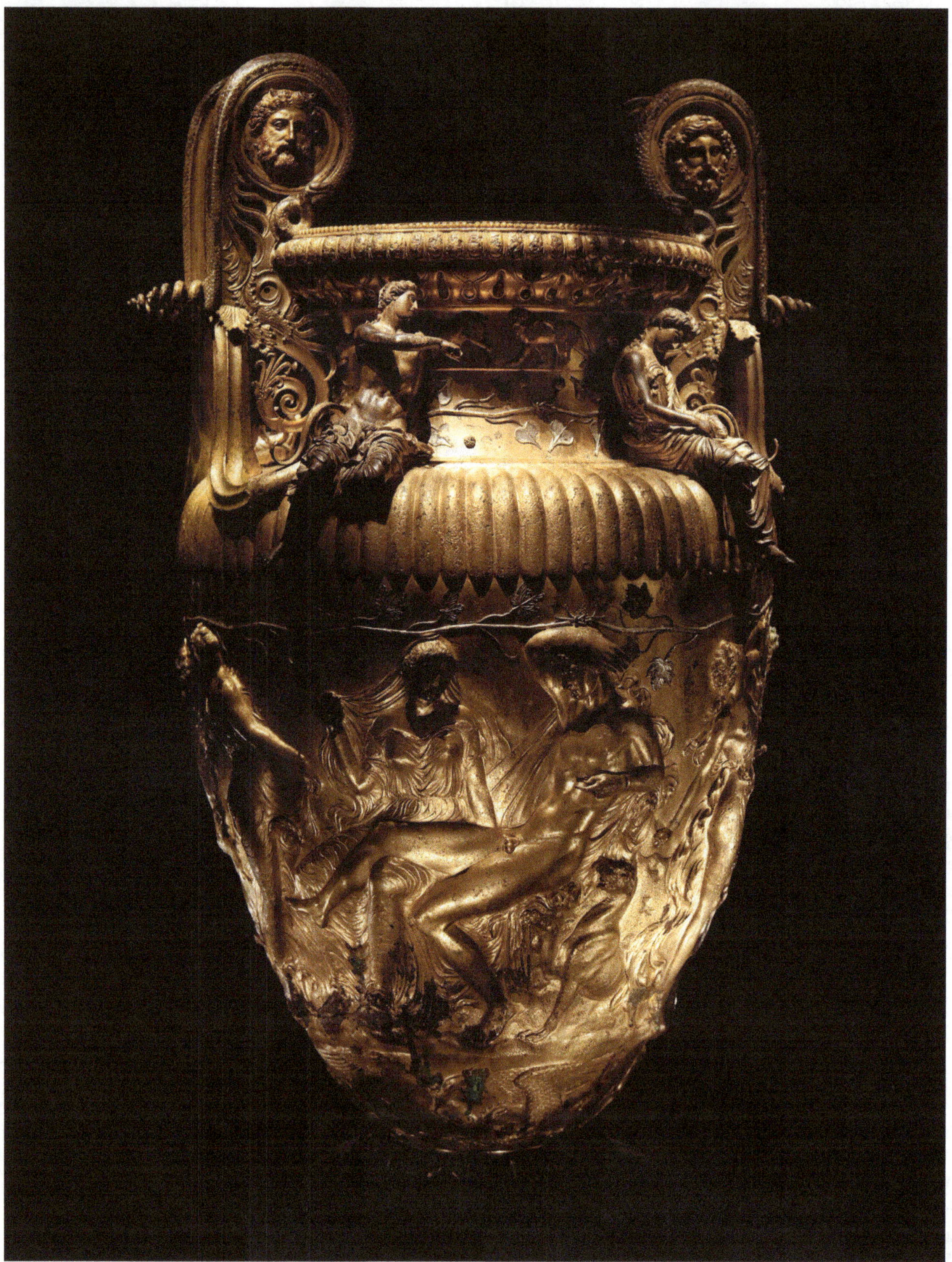

12.15 Derveni krater, *c.* 375–350 BCE. 35⅝ in (90.5 cm). Thessaloniki, Archaeological Museum. Dionysos and Ariadne with maenads. Image: © Vanni Archive/Art Resource, NY.

the restraint practiced in burial customs in fifth-century Athens was no longer as pronounced and elite families would provide elaborate furnishings and tomb markers for the dead, for their care in the afterlife, for their commemoration in contemporary times, and for the enhancement of the family's prestige.

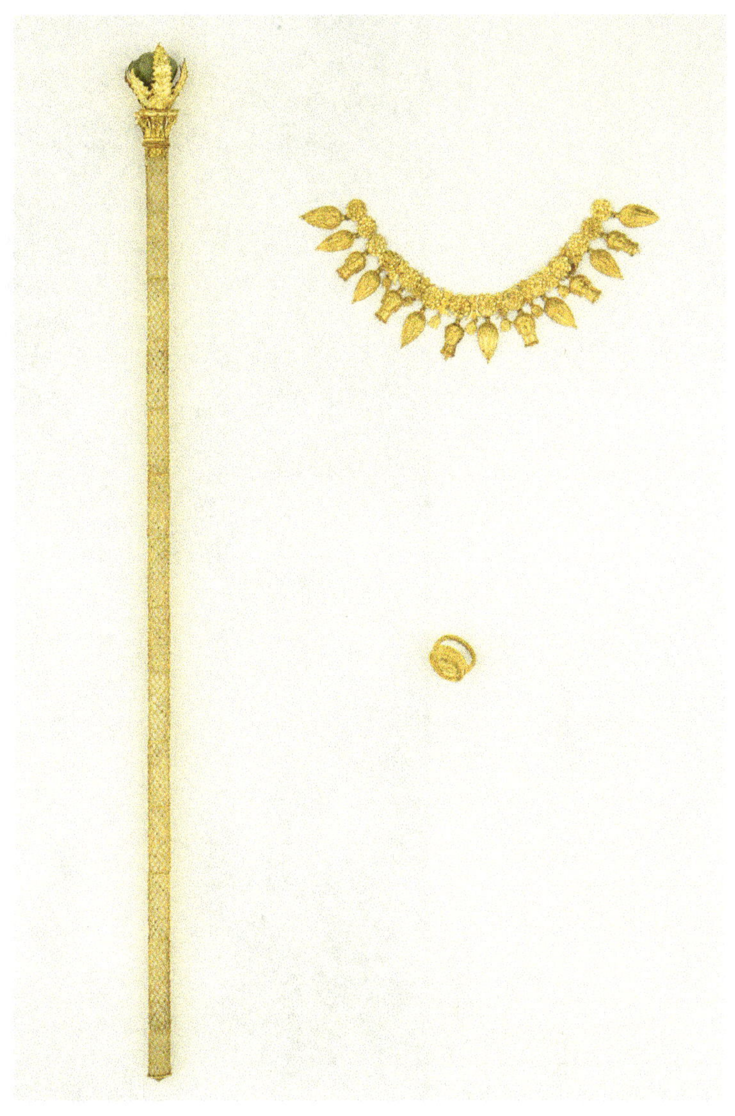

12.16 Scepter, ring, and necklace tomb of priestess (?) in Taras/Taranto, *c.* 350–320 BCE. 20¼ in (51.4 cm) (scepter); ⅞ in (2.1 cm) (height of ring bezel); 7$\frac{1}{16}$ in (18.0 cm) (length of necklace). London 1872,0604.842, 146, 667. Photo: © The Trustees of the British Museum.

POTTERY

Literary accounts suggest that the fourth century was a high point of achievement in wall and panel painting. The simulation of three-dimensional objects in a perspectival space made some pictures appear to act as windows into the world. Feats of illusionistic painting mentioned in literary sources include a purported encounter through painting between Zeuxis and his rival Parrhasios:

> [Parrhasios] is reputed to have entered into a contest with Zeuxis, and when the latter depicted some grapes with such success that birds flew up to the scene, he [Parrhasios] then depicted a linen curtain with such verisimilitude that Zeuxis, puffed up with pride by the verdict of the birds, eventually requested that the curtain be removed and his picture shown; and, when he understood his error, he conceded defeat with sincere modesty, because he himself had only deceived birds, but Parrhasios had deceived him, an artist. (Pliny, *N.H.* 35.65; tr. Pollitt 1990, 150)

However exaggerated the account may be, it demonstrates that there was an expectation that a two-dimensional painting could create the illusion of three-dimensional mass and space and might even fool a viewer with its veracity at just a quick glance. In other sources we can read about the expressiveness and emotions of individual figures in paintings, and we can catch glimpses of such work in some surviving tomb paintings that we will discuss at the end of the chapter.

Painted pottery continues as a medium in the fourth century, but its production in both quality and quantity begins to decline significantly in Athens during this century. There are several important regional schools of vase painting that develop in southern Italy and Sicily, including Apulian, Lucanian, Campanian, and Paestan, but by the end of the fourth century, figural painting essentially disappears as decoration for pottery.

Ceramics remained an important industry in fourth-century Athens, but there was less red-figure work and no white-ground painting during the fourth century. Some potters began to shift production to terracotta figures, such as those from the girl's tomb in the Kerameikos discussed above **(see Figure 1.5, page 10)**. Black-glaze ware was produced in large quantities, as well as gold-decorated variations, and in the third century glazed pottery with overpainted ornament called West Slope ware began to be produced **(see pages 277–278 and Figure 11.9, page 278)**. The demand for red-figure Attic pottery in Italy was far less than it had been in the fifth century, and much of the figural painting exported there became more schematic and hurried in its quality. Attic painters did produce more carefully painted vases for the market in the north Black Sea area, and the fourth-century Kerch style is named for one of the sites in that region.

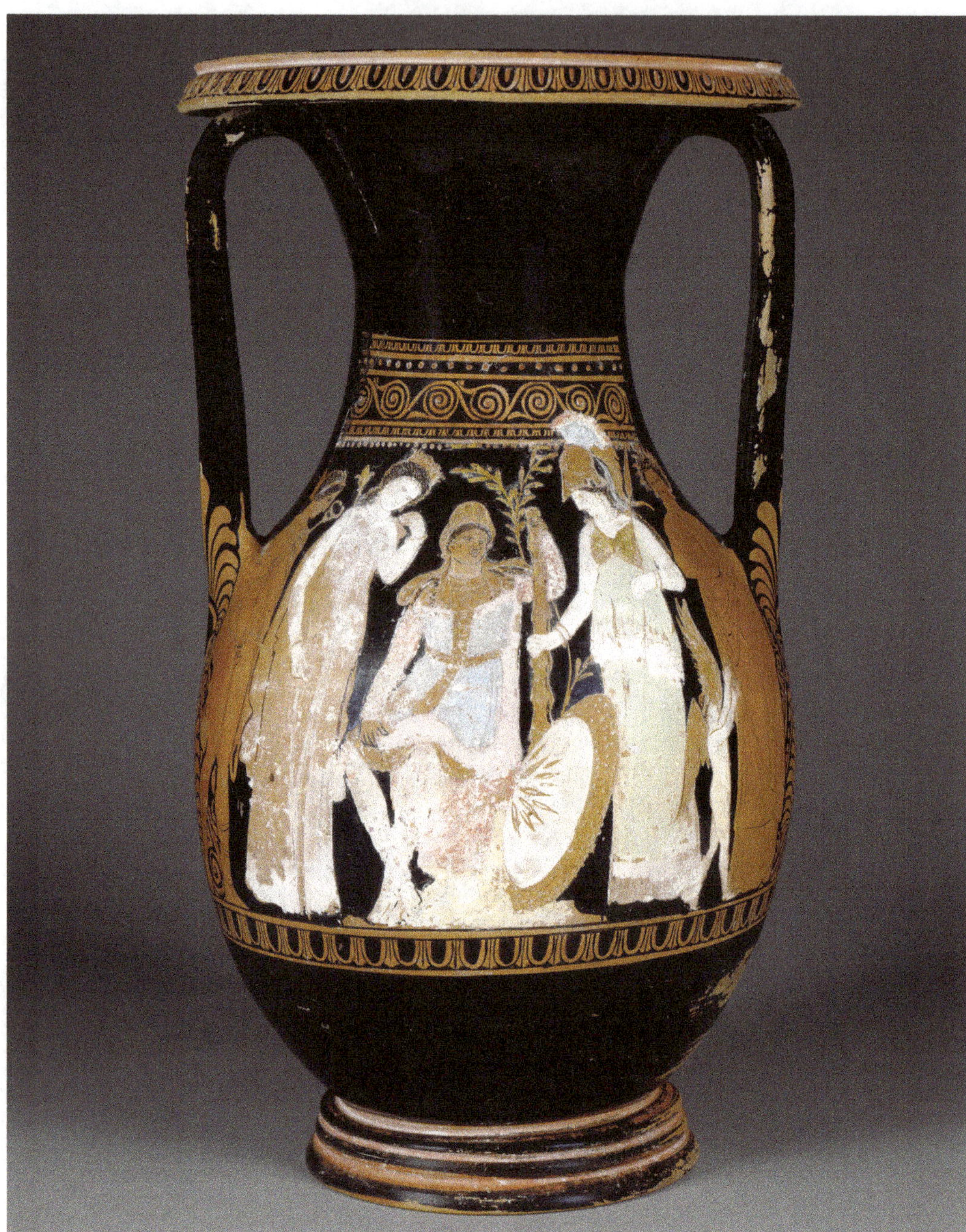

12.17 Attic red-figure Kerch-style pelike attributed to the Wedding Procession Painter, *c.* 360 BCE. 19 in (48.3 cm). Malibu, Getty Villa 83.AE.10. Judgment of Paris. Photo: The J. Paul Getty Museum, Villa Collection, Malibu, California.

Some of the best of these Kerch-style vases are large pelikai that are richly colored and include gold leaf applied to the surface (**Figure 12.17**). The use of a wider range of colors on vase painting is characteristic of the Kerch style, and of particular note in this example is the range of pastel colors in pink, green, and blue. These are perhaps related to the so-called "florid" colors that Pliny says mural painters developed during this period. The scene on the obverse of this pelike is the judgment of Paris, with Paris seated between Hermes, Hera, Athena, and Aphrodite, from left to right. The figures are serene in their poses, as the goddesses set out their offers to Paris as he judges which of the three is the most beautiful. Three of the figures have faces in three-quarter view, rather than the profile view that was preferred in the fifth century. This aspect is harder to draw convincingly because of the asymmetry and foreshortening of the facial features, but it is more effective in showing facial expression and interaction among the figures. Paris, for example,

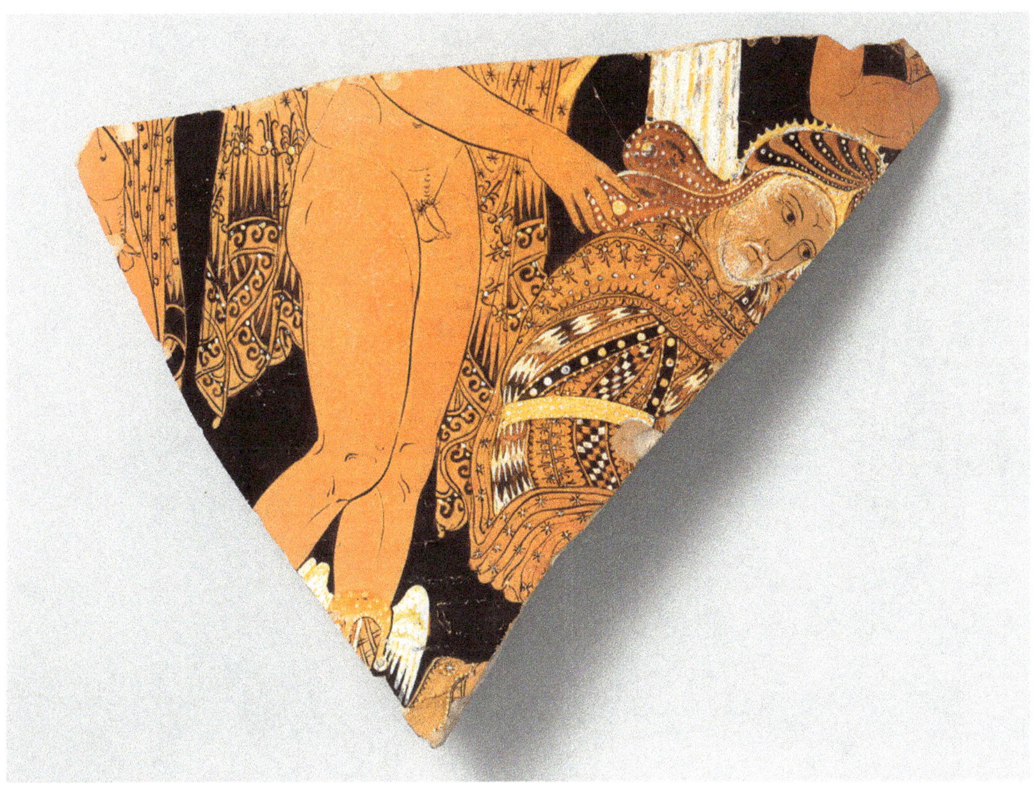

12.18 Apulian red-figure calyx krater fragment attributed to the Black Fury Painter, *c*. 400–380 BCE. 7¾ in (19.7 cm). New York, Metropolitan Museum of Art 20.195. Priam at ransom of Hektor. Image copyright © The Metropolitan Museum of Art. Image source: Art Resource, NY.

is looking behind and past Athena toward Aphrodite, who covers her mouth and looks as if she were conspiring with Paris, as indeed she was as she offered him the most beautiful woman in the world, Helen, and consequently started the Trojan War. Interestingly, Aphrodite is painted in simple red-figure technique with just a bit of gold leaf for her wreath, unlike the other figures who have even more gilding and added colors on the red clay. She almost blends into the background while being the key protagonist in the story.

The demand for painted pottery in southern Italy and Sicily was now met primarily by regional workshops that had begun to appear in the late fifth century. At first these workshops produced pottery that was closely related in style and subject matter to contemporary Attic vase painting, but by the fourth century more distinctive regional styles and interests had developed to meet local needs and tastes. Apulian pottery, produced for the southeast region of the "heel" of Italy, was the most prolific of the regional schools. An early example of Apulian red-figure work is the fragment of a krater by the Black Fury Painter showing Priam in the tent of Achilles, attempting to ransom the body of his dead son Hektor **(Figure 12.18)**. Priam wears a Phrygian cap and highly embroidered clothing befitting an eastern monarch in the Greek imagination, but he kneels looking downward, presumably before Achilles, while Hermes stands protectively behind him. The painter uses more added white, yellow, and red than was typical in Attic red-figure work in the early fourth century, and this is characteristic of Apulian work, as is the depiction of architectural features such as the column just behind Priam. The detail and precision of the work easily match anything produced in Athens, and the rendering of the three-quarter face is effective both as a three-dimensional drawing and in conveying the mood of Priam. Indeed, his pose resembles that of Penelope waiting for Odysseus **(see Figure 5.19, page 118)** and captures the feelings of the king and father who has lost the greatest defender of Troy.

Much Apulian pottery has been found in tombs throughout the region, and many of the largest and most elaborate shapes, like the loutrophoros in **Figure 12.19**, were made as grave goods. There has been debate about where in Apulia such pottery was produced, with some favoring the single large Greek colony of the region, Taranto (ancient Taras) since it had connections with Athens during

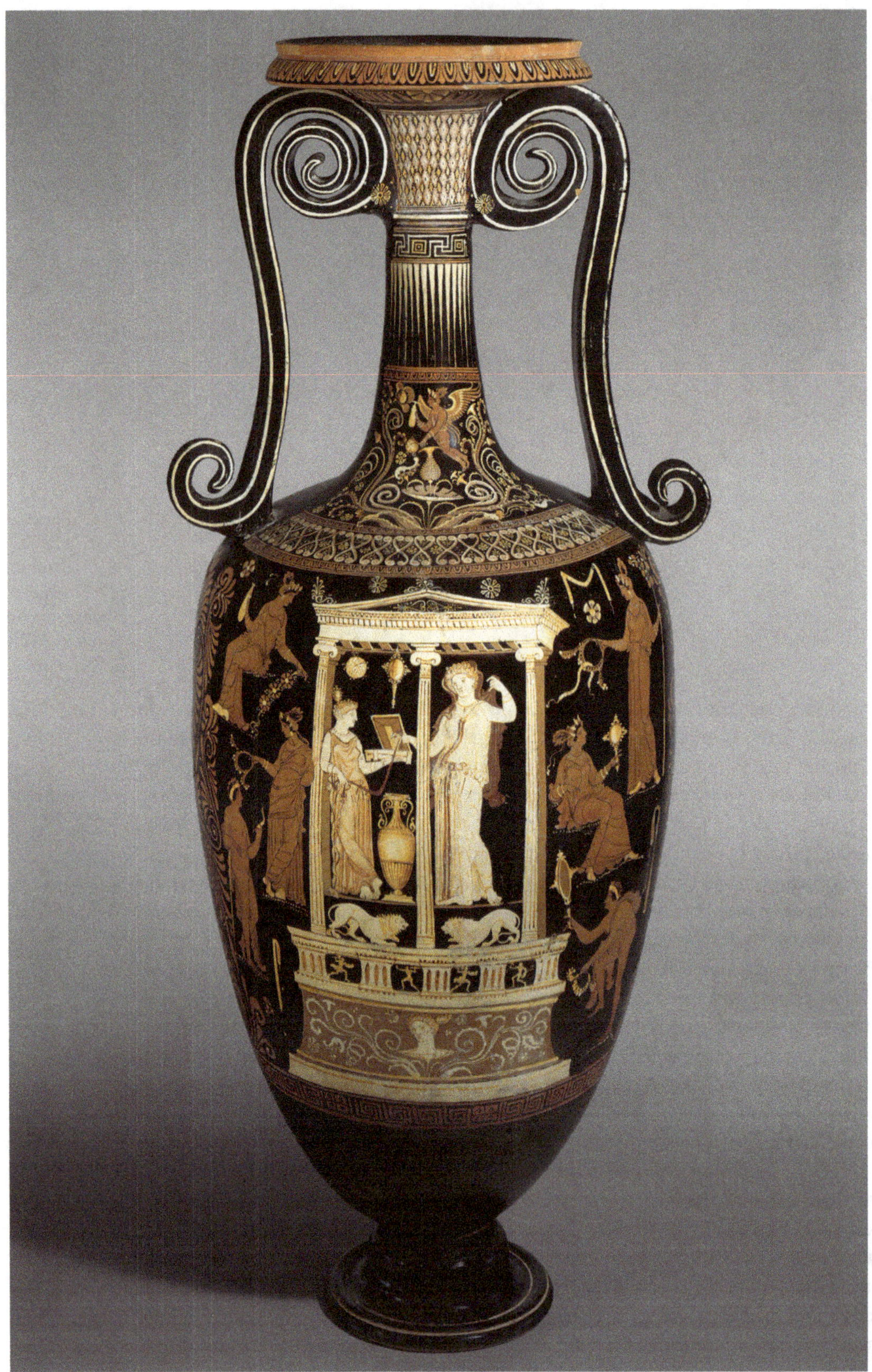

12.19 Apulian red-figure loutrophoros attributed to the Metope Painter, *c.* 350–325 BCE. 34¾ in (88.3 cm). New York, Metropolitan Museum of Art 1995.45.1. Grave naiskos scene. Image copyright © The Metropolitan Museum of Art. Image source: Art Resource, NY.

the fifth century. Since many of the vases are found further north and in tombs of indigenous, non-Greek people, there is a question now as to whether the pottery might not have been produced in the central or northern areas of Apulia, closer to where many of the largest and most fragile vases were used. Given that these tombs are primarily for non-Greek Apulians, it is possible that the potters and painters might have been non-Greeks as well but had learned the techniques and repertory from earlier Greek artists. In any case, there is strong interest in Hellenic culture in Apulian pottery, but its forms, styles, and subject matter are adapted to local interests (see Carpenter 2009).

The loutrophoros by the Metope Painter shows a typical scene of late Apulian pottery, with a funerary shrine called a **naiskos** in the center and women in the landscape around it. The naiskos encloses two figures, a mistress and her slave/servant, who assists her in dressing. A lavish metal loutrophoros, a duplicate of the actual vase, is rendered with yellow and white paint to give it a three-dimensional appearance with reflected light. The use of several shades of white, yellow, and brown on the drapery gives it a tangible, naturalistic quality. The painter has also used a simplified version of linear perspective to show the recession of the ceiling to create depth in the naiskos. Around the naiskos are women and a couple of men in a rocky landscape, with white dots rather than lines to indicate the ground; the man at the lower right brings an offering of a mirror and wreath to the tomb. These figures are mostly in red-figure, contrasting with the color and brightness of the central naiskos figures; they are also smaller in size than the woman in the naiskos, making her monumental in scale like a statue, similar to the funerary stele of Mnesistrate mentioned earlier (**see Figure 13.2, page 322**). The depiction of a large landscape has the consequence of diminishing the scale of the human figure, which is a striking departure from the dominance of the human figure in Attic pottery painting.

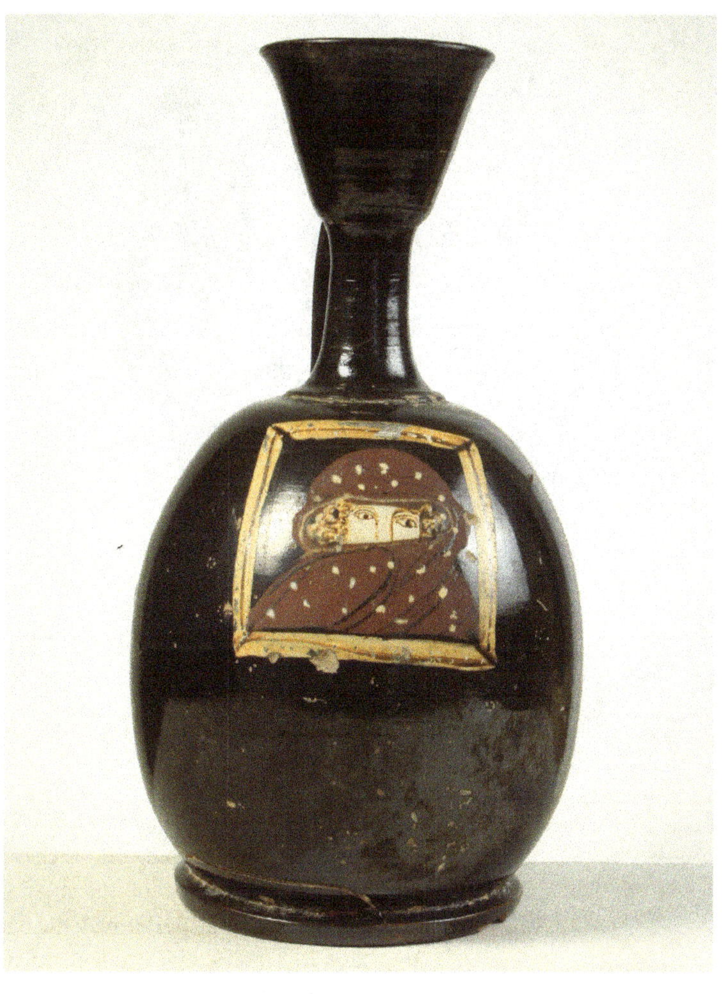

12.20 Apulian Gnathian-ware lekythos from Tomb 2, Corso Italia, Taras/Taranto, *c.* 350–325 BCE. Taranto, National Archaeological Museum 99195. Woman in window. Photo: Museum.

naiskos
a small, temple-like enclosure with a shallow space, frequently used for shrines or grave monuments and enclosing sculpted figures

Apulian potters also developed a black-glaze ware that was overpainted, with the colored pigments placed on the glazed surface and leaving no bare clay. Called Gnathian ware after a site in southern Apulia, the best examples are more like free painting than red-figure and are lustrous in their appearance (**Figure 12.20**). The squat lekythos from a tomb in Taras/Taranto shows the motif of a woman's face looking out of a window. The painting has a sketchy quality to it that could be described as more painterly than linear red-figure painting. From the literary accounts there was a debate over the better of these two main approaches to painting: whether one should draw figures precisely with line and then fill with color, or whether one should rely on brush strokes of paint set against each other to create a more impressionistic rendering of an object or figure. The wood of the window frame uses variation in line and tone that is less precise as an architectural rendering, but approximates the appearance of wood better than linear drawing. This technique of overpainting may have influenced the development of later Athenian West Slope ware in the third century.

Other centers of painted pottery include Sicily, Lucania (on the instep of the Italian peninsula), Campania (the area around modern Paestum), and Poseidonia/Paestum itself. Lucanian pottery began to be produced in the late fifth century. Like Apulian painting, it showed a great interest in scenes related to tragic and comic performances (**see Figure 9.11, page 224**). Many fifth-century plays were revived in

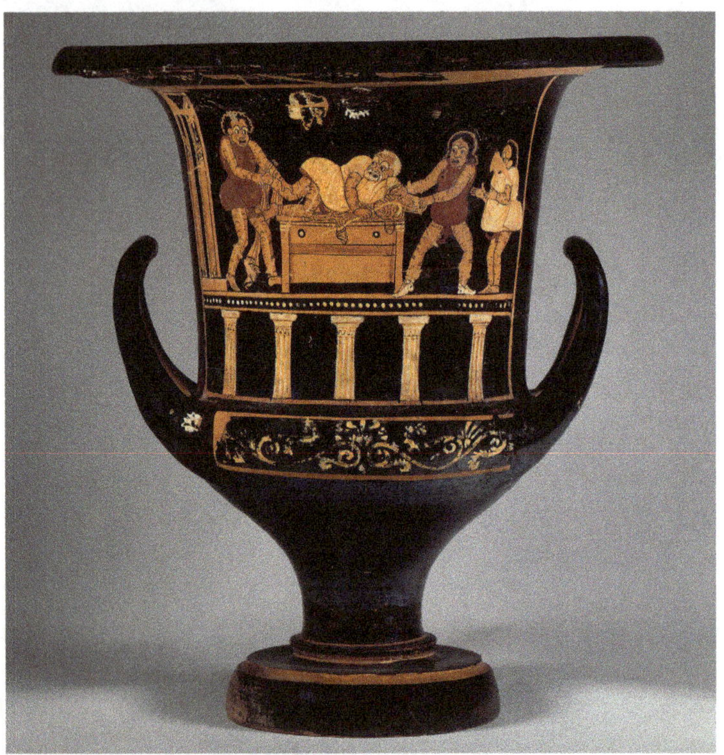

12.21 Paestan red-figure krater attributed to Asteas, 350–340 BCE. 14½ in (37 cm). Berlin, Staatliche Museen, Antikensammlung F3044. Phlyax play with scene of miser being robbed. Photo: bpk, Berlin/ Staatliche Museen, Antikensammlung/ Johannes Laurentius/Art Resource, NY.

performances throughout Italy, and some actors became famous for their work in this repertory. Much of Lucanian painting, like the pelike with Elektra and Orestes at the tomb of their father Agamemnon, is predominantly red-figure in technique. The figures are shown at different levels to indicate a landscape setting, and the three-quarter views of the faces provide a sense of emotion and gaze among the characters, as if they were acting on a stage. The Choephoroi Painter did five versions of this scene, which is the opening of the tragedy *Libation Bearers* by Aeschylus. It is not an illustration of the play or necessarily of its performance, but it does capture the essence of the scene in showing Elektra despondent when attending the tomb of her father, unaware that her brother has returned secretly to avenge their father's murder.

Campanian pottery is primarily red-figure with much added white and yellow, and shows a number of idyllic or Dionysiac scenes (**see Figure 13.14, page 335**). This school of painting was developed by painters emigrating from Sicily, making the connection to Attic red-figure painting indirect. The town of Poseidonia/Paestum became an important center for painted pottery in the later fourth century, and the work of one painter, Asteas, is especially noteworthy (**Figure 12.21**). The small Paestan-ware krater shows a **phlyax** play, with an old miser who has been sleeping on his chest of valuables in the center. Two robbers have broken into the house and are pulling him off the chest, while a slave looks on helplessly to the right. Here Asteas has shown a comedy being performed; the figures all wear the masks and padded costumes of comedy and the actors are set on a stage that is elevated and supported by a row of columns below. While they appear distorted, the figures are well drawn and capture the stilted but animated quality of comic acting.

phlyax
a type of comic or burlesque play popular in fourth- and third-century southern Italy

The phlyax scenes and actors should be seen as reflecting the interests of Greek culture in southern Italy and an example of the responsiveness of artists to the interests of their local communities. By the fourth century, Poseidonia/Paestum was under the control of Lucanians and the city had a significant Italic as well as Greek population. The elaborate Apulian kraters and amphorae have been found primarily in tombs and were made as grave goods, but interestingly, most of these tombs are in the areas of Apulia outside of Taras/Taranto where there were no Greek colonies and their owners were not Greek. These factors point to the increasingly complex relationship between Greeks and non-Greeks throughout the Mediterranean and the growing importance of new patronage outside of the traditional centers for Greek art.

MOSAIC AND FRESCO

We have paid little attention to the floors of Greek buildings up to now, but with the development of a new medium, **mosaic**, as a floor in the fourth century, we need to look at what images were literally under foot. The earliest mosaic appears at the end of the fifth century in Corinth and consisted of small pebbles set into mortar to create a durable and permanent flooring. The use of the medium spread in the fourth century and can be found at Sikyon, Eretria, and Olynthos. With the use of small pebbles rather than paving stones, mosaicists could divide a floor into panels and create a wide range of decorative borders and panels, as can be seen in the mosaic from the andron in House A vi 3 in Olynthos (**Figure 12.22**). The central part of the floor is a medallion framed by a vine band and corners; these are framed by panels of meanders and waves. The klinai along the walls of the andron

mosaic
a medium used for decorating floors in which small pebbles or tesserae are set in mortar to create decorative and figurative compositions

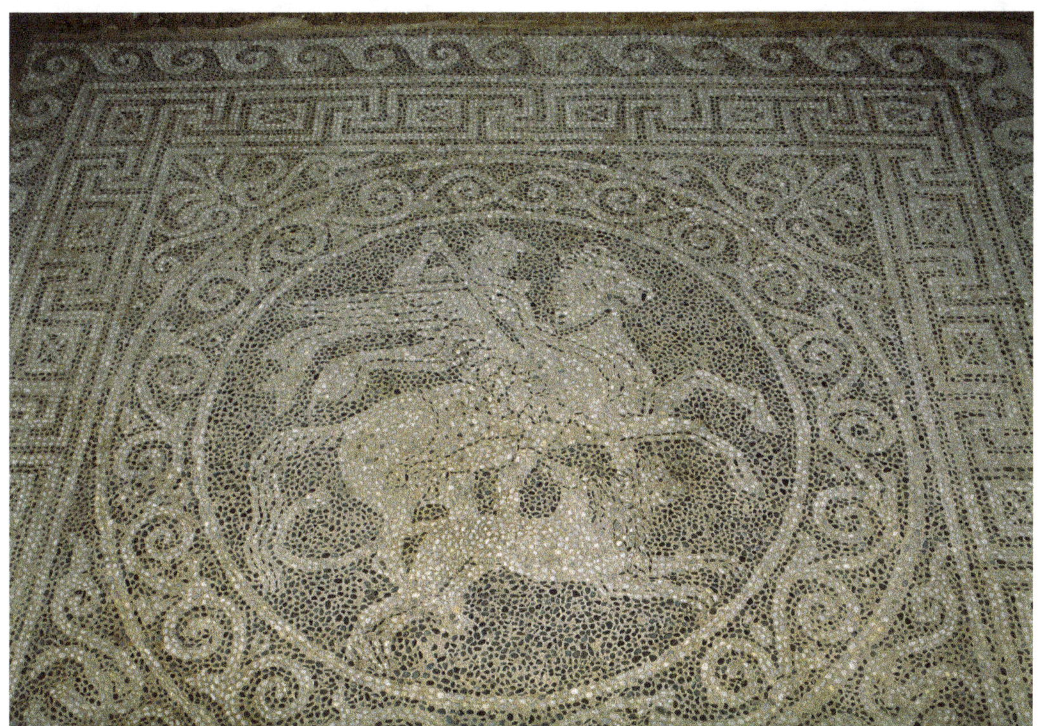

12.22 Mosaic floor from House A vi 3 at Olynthos, early 4th cent. BCE. Diameter of medallion about 4 ft 5⅛ in (1.35 m). Bellerophon and Pegasos attack the Chimaera. Photo: akg-images/Rainer Hackenberg.

would have covered the edge of the mosaic, leaving the central scene of Bellerophon on Pegasos attacking the Chimaera visible to all of the symposiasts.

The mosaicists had a limited palette of dark and light pebbles, supplemented with reddish stone in some examples. The medium was essentially two-tone, so that there is not as much sense of three-dimensionality as we see in contemporary vase painting. The medium works well for the decorative borders and geometric patterns, but is initially less successful with figural compositions. In order to draw lines to define the human form, the mosaicist had to use a line of dark pebbles, which did not allow for much subtlety or detail when working in the relatively small surface area available in the andron. We need to consider, however, that the mosaic floor would have been a very significant and expensive undertaking for the owner of the house. Few houses had mosaic floors, and their polished and durable appearance would have been impressive. It is also worth remembering that being placed in the andron, they would be on display to guests for extended periods of time, creating a distinctive experience for the symposiasts. Since the exterior of houses was relatively unadorned, walking into and on a decorated mosaic floor would signal the status or aspirations of the house's owner. In time, as we shall see in the Alexander Mosaic from Pompeii, the pictorial quality of the medium could rival fresco painting **(see Figure 14.2, page 346)**.

As mentioned earlier, the fourth century was regarded in antiquity as the great age of wall and panel painting, with Zeuxis, Parrhasios, and Apelles among the most illustrious names in the literary record. None of the works mentioned in the sources survived, but in 1977 several tombs buried under a great tumulus at Vergina in Macedonia were excavated by Manolis Andronikos, providing a glimpse of what we have lost in this medium. The largest tomb, Tomb II, is a barrel-vaulted structure with two chambers and a Doric facade **(Figure 12.23)**. The tomb contained the cremated remains of a man and woman, each set in a gold box inside a stone sarcophagus, along with other offerings of ivory, wood, gold, and rare luxury textiles **(see Figure 5.18, page 117)**. There has been much dispute about the identity of the deceased, with Andronikos proposing that it is the tomb of king Philip II (assassinated in 336) and his second wife Cleopatra, but alternatives have been proposed, such as Philip III Arrhidaios (murdered in 317) and his wife Eurydike. The evidence is not conclusive, although alternative theories to Philip II have been recently rejected on the basis of forensic examination of the skeletal remains. Certainly these are royal Macedonian burials and a date for the tomb in the last third of the fourth century is likely.

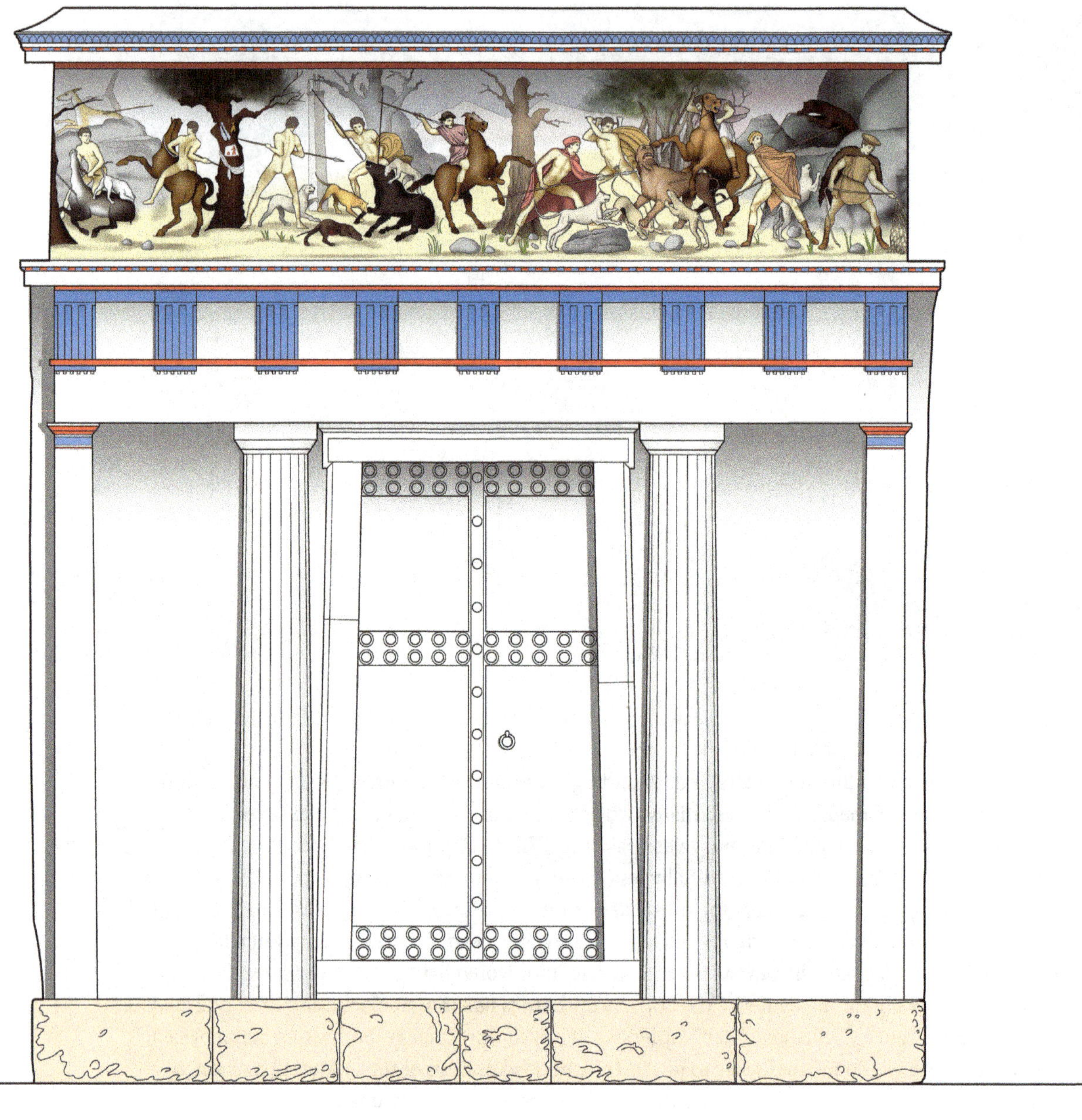

12.23 Reconstruction of the facade of Tomb II (of Philip II?) at Vergina, *c.* 335–315 BCE. Drawing by Daniel R. Lamp, from Hallie M. Franks, *Hunters, Heroes, Kings: The Frieze of Tomb II at Vergina* (Princeton, 2012), Fig. 3. Used by permission.

The attic story above the entablature was painted in fresco (**Figure 12.24**). Although much of the surface has been lost, the fact that the facade was buried in the tumulus has preserved enough to study the composition and style of the painting. The scene is an animal hunt, with hunters on horseback and foot killing deer, a boar, and a lion from left to right. In the center is a youth wearing a rose costume on a rearing horse; he aims a spear and moves toward our right. On the right, two youths on foot and a bearded rider attack a lion. The figures are about half of the height of the frieze and move through a detailed wooded landscape with rocks, puddles, trees, and mountains in the background. The use of light and dark creates the illusion of three-dimensional bodies moving through the landscape. Unlike vase painting, most of these figures move diagonally within the picture space, and the youthful rider to the left is shown in three-quarter view from behind, moving into the picture depth. We have here a fully realized world in which three-dimensional figures move in all directions through a space that extends into our own, in other words, a window onto another world. While this is how we look at images, conditioned by Renaissance perspective and our experience of photography and film, it is not the convention by which earlier ancient viewers looked at images. Before this, the figures and their action dominated the picture; they acted on a shallow stage that did not appear as an extension of the viewer's world. The developments in perspective and modeling from the mid-fifth century onward gradually transformed this convention and we can see its result in the hunt fresco.

The figure on the central rearing horse resembles in pose Alexander from the second-century mosaic in Pompeii and on the Alexander Sarcophagus that we will discuss in Chapter 14 (**see Figure 14.1, page 344; Figure 14.2, page 346**). Were this the tomb of Philip II, as seems possible, it would make sense, particularly if Alexander were overseeing the creation of the tomb after his father's assassination, to show the son and heir in the center, perhaps making the bearded rider attacking the lion to the right Philip himself. While illusionistic in style, a hunt with so many victims in such close proximity can only be a staged type of event or constructed image, essentially a panoramic type of narrative where different hunts have been set into the same landscape, which here takes a far more prominent pictorial role than in earlier narratives. The fresco was intended to show Macedonian royalty engaged in a regal activity, making them the equals of the great kings of Persia and elsewhere, and legitimizing the passing of the crown. Whereas images of the hunt were collective activities of members of the polis in earlier imagery, such as the Chigi olpe, hunting imagery is now a royal prerogative and symptomatic of the changes taking place in the fourth-century culture.

The smaller Tomb of Persephone (Tomb I) at Vergina is named for the painting on its interior showing Persephone's abduction by Hades (**Figure 12.25A**). The tomb had been robbed, with only bones and some fragments of pottery and marble left behind. The bones included those of a woman, a man, and an infant, making it a family burial like Tomb II and Derveni Tomb B. One short end wall shows Demeter seated (**Figure 12.25B**); to her left is a badly preserved scene that recent study suggests is Persephone and Aphrodite with Adonis (D'Angelo 2012), while to her right is her daughter Persephone being abducted by Hades in a chariot.

The abduction of Persephone shows a companion crouched on the right, holding up her hand against the terrifying sight of Hades in his chariot. He holds the reins of the horses with one hand while holding Persephone in the other. Persephone reaches out both arms; with the foreshortened angle they appear to be reaching out toward her mother on the adjacent wall. This painting is surely an example of the painterly style of the fourth century, with large brushstrokes that sketch the strong movement of bodies and drapery. The contrast between dark and light tones gives the bodies solidity, but there is a very strong emphasis upon facial expression and gesture that captures the distress of the women and the aggression of Hades. The chariot is set at a three-quarter angle to the picture plane, and it appears as if it is headed out of the picture into the space of the tomb and down to the underworld. This and the three-quarter views of faces and bodies give a full three-dimensionality to the picture.

We do not know the names of the painters at Vergina, but given that they were working for powerful royal patrons, it is probable that they were highly skilled and conversant with the current trends in painting mentioned in the literary sources. Indeed, Apelles, who is sometimes named as the greatest of all painters, worked for Alexander the Great and had a monopoly on his painted portraits according

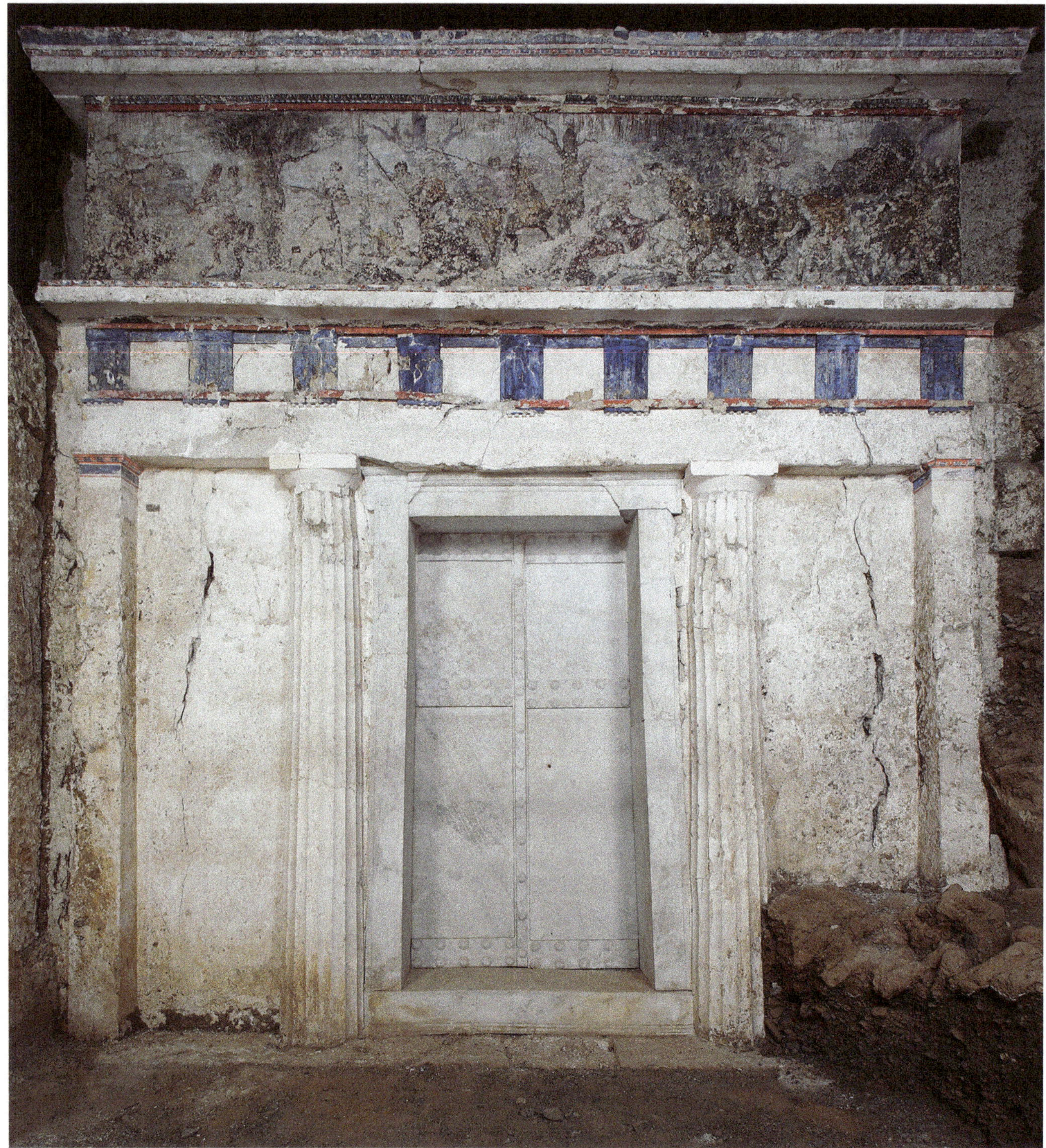

12.24 Facade and fresco from Tomb II (of Philip II?) at Vergina, *c.* 335–315 BCE. Height of painted frieze: 3 ft 9 11/16 in (1.16 m). *In situ*. Hunt. Photo: 17th Ephorate for Prehistoric and Classical Antiquities.

(a)

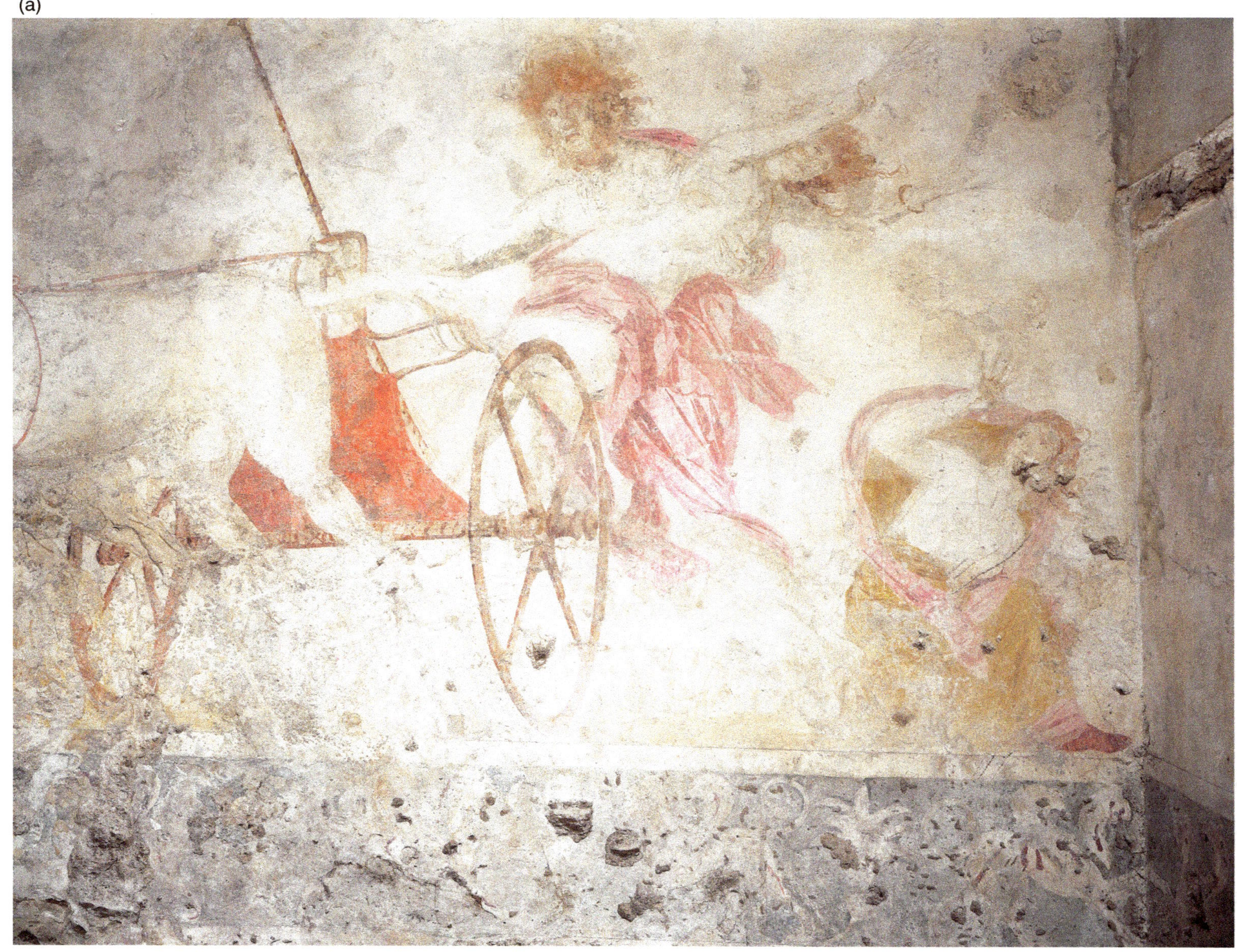

12.25a Fresco from the "Tomb of Persephone" at Vergina, *c.* 336–317 BCE. Height of frieze, 3 ft 9 11/16 in (1.16 m). *In situ*. A: Abduction of Persephone by Hades. Photo: 17th Ephorate for Prehistoric and Classical Antiquities.

(b)

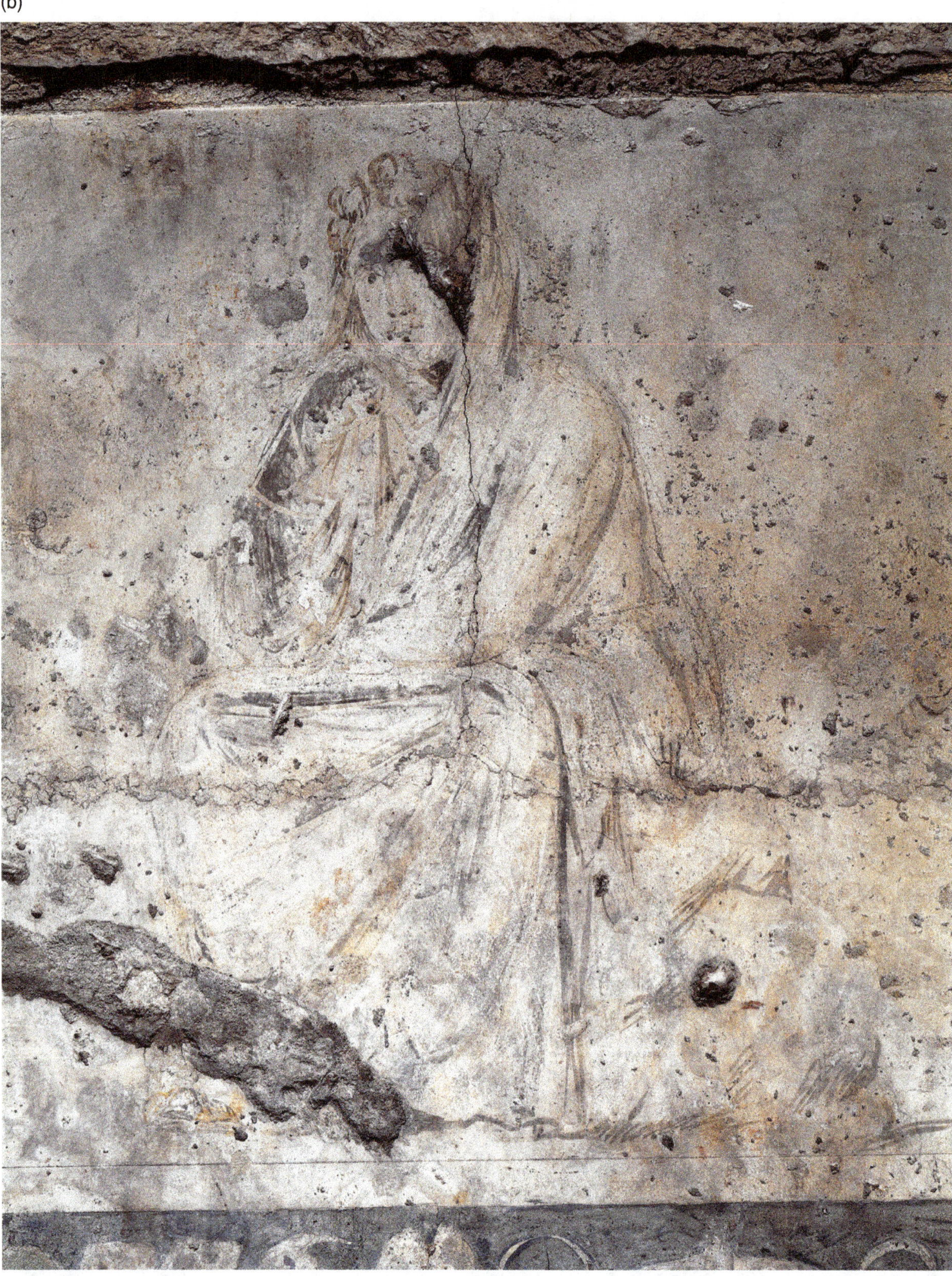

12.25b Fresco from the "Tomb of Persephone" at Vergina, c. 336–317 BCE. Height of frieze, 3 ft 9 11⁄16 in (1.16 m). *In situ*. B: Demeter. Photo: 17th Ephorate for Prehistoric and Classical Antiquities.

to literary sources. As we have seen in this chapter, Athens continued to be a very important center of art production in the fourth century, but the examples of metalwork and fresco from northern Greece show that the impetus of patronage had shifted, bringing some of the best artists to the Macedonian royal court. With Alexander's conquests, new centers in Antioch, Alexandria, and elsewhere would develop, and the Greek art world of the Hellenistic period is one that would be more cosmopolitan.

TEXTBOX: THE COPY HYPOTHESIS

Several works discussed in this and earlier chapters have been identified as Roman copies of Greek originals, including the Tyrannicides **(see Figure 5.9, page 108)**, the Doryphoros **(see Figure 10.7, page 243)**, and the Aphrodite of Knidos **(see Figure 12.10)**. The idea that statues excavated in Roman contexts were copies of Greek statues rather than Roman originals was realized early in the study of Greek history, including by Winckelmann. Art historians noted that many statues were identical to one another and the hypothesis was that these were all made after the same original. In a methodology that followed the process of *Kopienkritik* in the study of Biblical texts, it was thought that study of the variations among the statues could identify what the common elements were and thus "restore" the original. In the process, the study of Roman sculpture often resembled a hunt for lost Greek works.

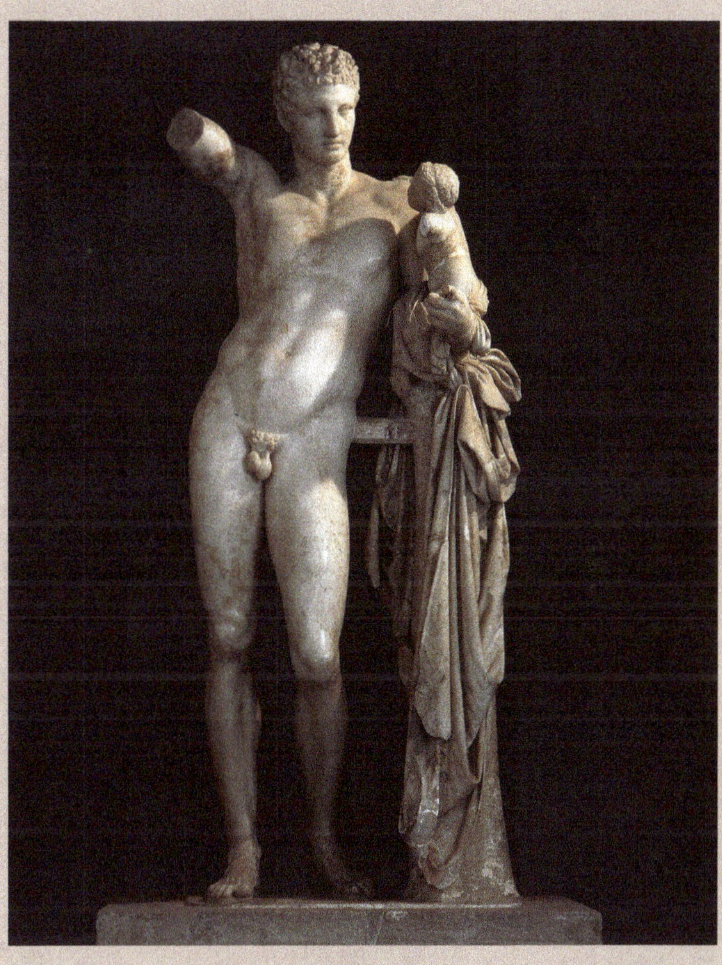

12.26 Praxitelean Hermes and infant Dionysos, Hellenistic copy of 4th-cent. BCE original? 7 ft ⅝ in (2.15 m). Olympia, Archaeological Museum. Photo: Gianni Dagli Orti/ The Art Archive at Art Resource, NY.

There are several difficulties with this approach. The first is that the classical style never went out of production after the classical period and was passed down to Hellenistic and Roman sculptors. The second is that Greek art always relied very heavily on types that could be repeated with slighter or greater variations, so that in one sense, looking for a Greek "original" in our sense of the word is a misguided search. Idealizing sculpture of later periods continued to refine, adapt, and develop types. In some cases there is external evidence to conclude that a work like the Doryphoros is a copy: literary testimony, fragments of plaster casts used for making copies in a sculptor's studio in Baie on the Bay of Naples, and a bronze bust of the Doryphoros from the Villa of the Papyri in Herculaneum that has the title inscribed on it. That the name of the artist, Polykleitos, was not as important as we think it should be, is shown by the fact that the Herculaneum bust was inscribed "Apollonios son of Archias of Athens made it." This was undoubtedly the maker of the bronze and an advertisement for his skill in making a Doryphoros, but there is no reference to the original artist, suggesting that the subject was at least as important as the artist.

One marble statue has been thought to be an original by Praxiteles, the Hermes with the infant Dionysos found at Olympia **(Figure 12.26)**. Pausanias (5.17.3) describes this statue and the attribution when he sees it in the Temple of Hera at Olympia: "at a later time still other works were set up in the temple of Hera, among them a Hermes of stone, who carries the infant Dionysos, the work of Praxiteles" (tr. Pollitt 1990, 89). When the statue was found in that area during excavations in 1877, it was seen as corroboration for a Greek original. This opinion was not universal, but became more tenuous when K. D. Morrow, in a study of Greek footwear and its history, noted that the sandals of Hermes had some odd features: notches between the big and second toe, square-end straps, and decorated tongue (Morrow 1985). These features only became used in sandals in the second century BCE, meaning that the statue could not date earlier to the fourth century. The statue could be a copy of a work by Praxiteles, perhaps replacing one damaged for some reason. If ordered from a workshop in Athens that did not know the original well, it might explain stylistic discrepancies noted by some scholars. The statue might also be a later work by a different sculptor named Praxiteles. Finally, it might be a misattribution by the guide at Olympia, who would have been Pausanias's source. Needless to say, the probable loss of a Greek original has generated controversy in the scholarly literature since so many of our claims about Praxitelean style were based on the Hermes.

REFERENCES

Barr-Sharrar, B. 2008. *The Derveni Krater: Masterpiece of Classical Greek Metalwork.* Princeton: American School of Classical Studies at Athens.

Carpenter, T. 2009. "Prolegomenon to the Study of Apulian Red-Figure Pottery." *American Journal of Archaeology* 113, 27–38.

D'Angelo, T. 2012. "Adonis in Vergina: The Frescoes of Tomb I Reconsidered." *113th AIA and APA Annual Joint Meeting, January 5–8 2012*, Philadelphia, PA.

Hurwit, J. M. 2007. "The Problem with Dexileos." *American Journal of Archaeology* 111, 35–60.

Jenkins, I. 2006. *Greek Architecture and Its Sculpture in the British Museum.* London: British Museum Press.

Morrow, K. D. 1985. *Greek Footwear and the Dating of Sculpture.* Madison: University of Wisconsin Press.

Pollitt, J. J. 1972. *Art and Experience in Classical Greece.* Cambridge: Cambridge University Press.

Pollitt, J. J. 1990. *The Art of Ancient Greece: Sources and Documents.* Cambridge: Cambridge University Press.

Ridgway, B. S. 1997. *Fourth-Century Styles in Greek Sculpture.* Madison: University of Wisconsin Press.

Stansbury-O'Donnell, M. D. 2014. "Desirability and the Body." In T. K. Hubbard, ed. *A Companion to Greek and Roman Sexualities*, 31–53. Malden, MA/Oxford: Wiley Blackwell.

Tanner, J. 2013. "Figuring Out Death: Sculpture and Agency at the Mausoleum of Halicarnassus and the Tomb of the First Emperor of China." In L. Chua and M. Elliot eds. *Distributed Objects: Meaning and Mattering after Alfred Gell*, 58–87. New York/Oxford: Berghahn Books.

Tomlinson, R. A. 1983. *Epidauros.* Austin: University of Texas Press.

FURTHER READING

Ajootian, A. 1996. "Praxiteles." In O. Palagia and J. J. Pollitt, eds. *Personal Styles in Greek Sculpture.* Yale Classical Studies 3, 91–129. Cambridge: Cambridge University Press.

Boardman, J. 1995. *Greek Sculpture: The Late Classical Period and Sculpture in Colonies and Overseas.* London: Thames and Hudson.

Franks, H. M. 2012. *Hunters, Heroes, Kings: The Frieze of Tomb II at Vergina.* Princeton: American School of Classical Studies in Athens.

Marvin, M. 2008. *The Language of the Muses: The Dialogue between Roman and Greek Sculpture.* Los Angeles: The J. Paul Getty Museum.

Mattusch, C. C. 2004. "Naming the 'Classical' Style." In A. P. Chapin, ed. *Charis: Essays in Honor of Sara A. Immerwahr. Hesperia Supplement* 33, 277–291. Princeton: American School of Classical Studies at Athens.

Ridgway, B. S. 1997. *Fourth-Century Styles in Greek Sculpture.* Madison: University of Wisconsin Press.

Ridgway, B. S. 2001. *Hellenistic Sculpture I: The Styles of ca. 331–200 B.C.* Madison: University of Wisconsin Press.

Trendall, A. D. 1989. *Red Figure Vases of South Italy and Sicily.* London: Thames and Hudson.

13

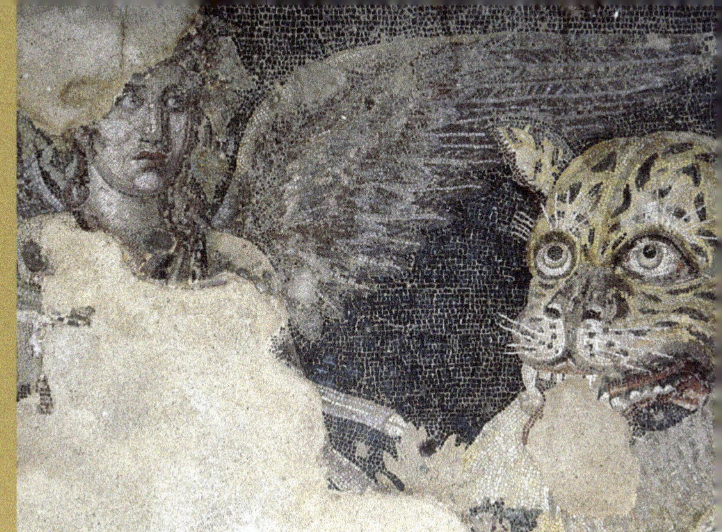

IDENTITY

Timeline
Gender
Women's Lives
Women in Public
Men and Youths: Gender and Sexuality
Interaction: Class, Civic, and Ethnic Identity
Textbox: Money Purses, Sex, and Identity
References
Further Reading

A History of Greek Art, First Edition. Mark D. Stansbury-O'Donnell.

TIMELINE

	Sculpture	Pottery and Painting
900–700		"Boots Grave" in Athens, 900 Dipylon amphora and krater, 760–735 [4.7, 4.9] Thebes bowl, 730–720 [4.23]
700–600	Kore of Nikandre, 650–625 [6.3]	Chigi olpe, 650–640 [6.11]
600–480	Lakonian mirror, 560–540 Kore of Phrasikleia, 550–540 [8.13]	Panel from Pitsa, 540–530 [8.21] Kylix with symposion scene, 520
480–400	Grave stele of Ampharete, 430 [10.19] Grave stele of Hegeso, Koroibos-Kleidemides family, 400 [5.28]	Kylix with male courtship, 480 Krater by Niobid Painter with departure, 460–450 [9.18] Pyxis with wedding procession, 440–430 Lebes with domestic scene, 430–420 Chous with girl, 430–420 Grave goods from Metaponto, 425–385
400–330	Dexileos Monument, 394/3 [12.12] Grave stele of Mnesitrate, 350	Campanian hydria with ritual procession, 350–330
330–30	Statue of Aristinoë, 3rd cent. Grave stele of Phila, 2nd cent.	

Looking at the kylix in **Figure 13.1**, we can compare its red-figure technique to the calyx krater by Euphronios **(see Figure 8.26, page 206)**. The rendering of anatomical features such as the eyes and the attempt to show two bodies in a complicated and intertwined action are characteristic of the style of the Pioneers at the end of the sixth century BCE. Turning to the subject, we can see that is a symposion (see Chapter 5), with a youth reclining on a couch with cushion and a young woman reclining against him, holding an *aulos* with which she had been providing musical entertainment. The picture is an excerpt from a group activity like the symposion scenes we have already discussed **(see Figure 5.21, page 120; Figure 10.20, page 255)**, and may have taken place in the andron of a house (see the reconstruction of a public andron in **Figure 5.20, page 119**). As a drinking cup, the representation of a sympotic scene on its interior would provide the drinker with a picture of a symposion while he drank from it. The picture, then, nicely aligns the function of the vase with its decoration and setting.

We can consider the scene beyond its style and sympotic subject, since it also represents two people whose individual and social identities differ. The young woman, for example, is either a slave or a hired entertainer for the event, placing her in a different social class than the young man, who is a guest at the symposion. There is also a difference in gender between the two figures, not just in terms of their biological sex, but also in the relationship between men and women. His nudity is not unusual, as we have seen throughout the history of Greek art, but her nudity, a century and a half before the Aphrodite of Knidos, is strikingly different. He wraps his right leg around her hips and his right arm around her head, essentially controlling her like a wrestler, but fondling her breast and bringing her face close; he clearly has a sexual intent. Her reaction to the situation is more ambiguous. The right arm holding up the *aulos* suggests surprise, but she also reaches behind his head as if to pull him closer while her body and head twist around. Whether she was hired for both musical and sexual entertainment at a symposion, or was a slave who essentially had to submit to her owner's whims is not certain, but it is not likely that he would behave this way if she were his social equal. The necklace or collar that she wears is unusual and has been identified as the Egyptian Broad Collar, which consisted of rows of beads and tubes in a semi-circular shape (Cole 2013). With her shorn hair, these markers suggest that she is a foreigner and likely an Egyptian or perhaps an Egyptianizing Ionian Greek, introducing a level of ethnic identity to the mixture of social class, sexual, and gender issues in the scene.

On one level images such as this might appear as everyday genre scenes. They are, in fact, staged pictures that express the complex web of identities of the artists and viewers who used, owned, and

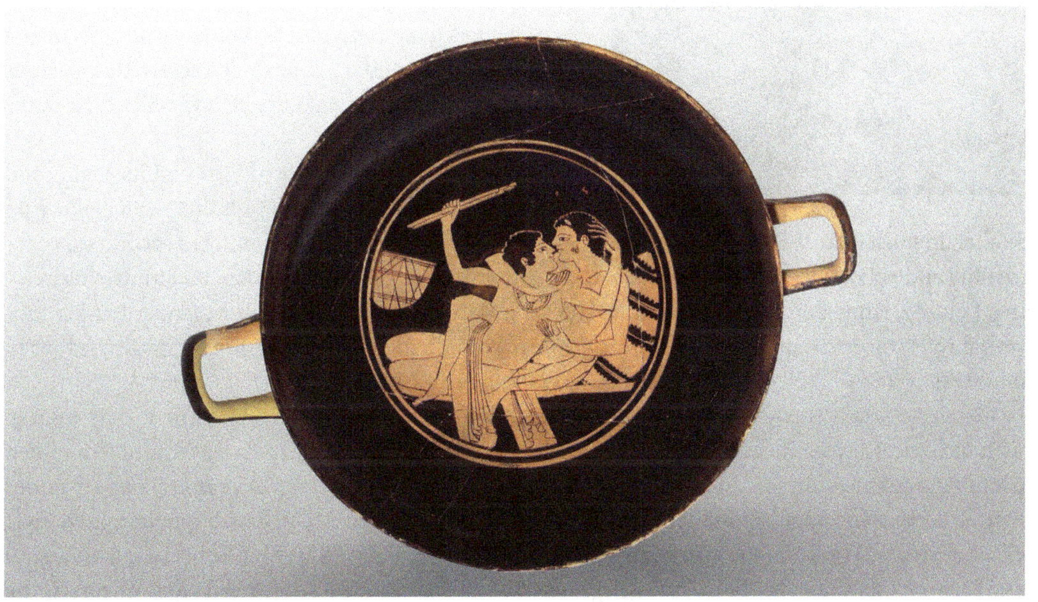

13.1 Attic red-figure kylix attributed to the Gales Painter or the Thorvaldsen Group, 520 BCE. Diameter 8¾ in (22.3 cm). Symposion scene. New Haven, Yale University Art Gallery, Gift of Rebecca Darlington Stoddard, 1913, 1913.163. Photo: Yale University Art Gallery.

looked at the objects and their images. We will explore these different aspects of identity in this chapter, beginning with gender. In doing so, we should consider how visual elements mark identity. In pictures, we can look at signs such as hair, clothing, and attributes that mark the identity of the figure for the viewer; such an image presents a construction of identity through this combination of signs. At another level, though, we can consider that the works themselves are chosen by individuals and so can express identity by their selection, whether through the image on an object like a kylix or grave stele or through its function. If a cup like the Yale kylix, for example, were purchased for a symposion in Athens, it would be used by a man. By selecting it, the user would act as an agent and be expressing his identity through the use of the cup. If the cup were bought and used by an Etruscan, however, its use and meaning for identity might be different. The identity signified by the image and by the actions of the viewer may vary, then, as the context and agent changes.

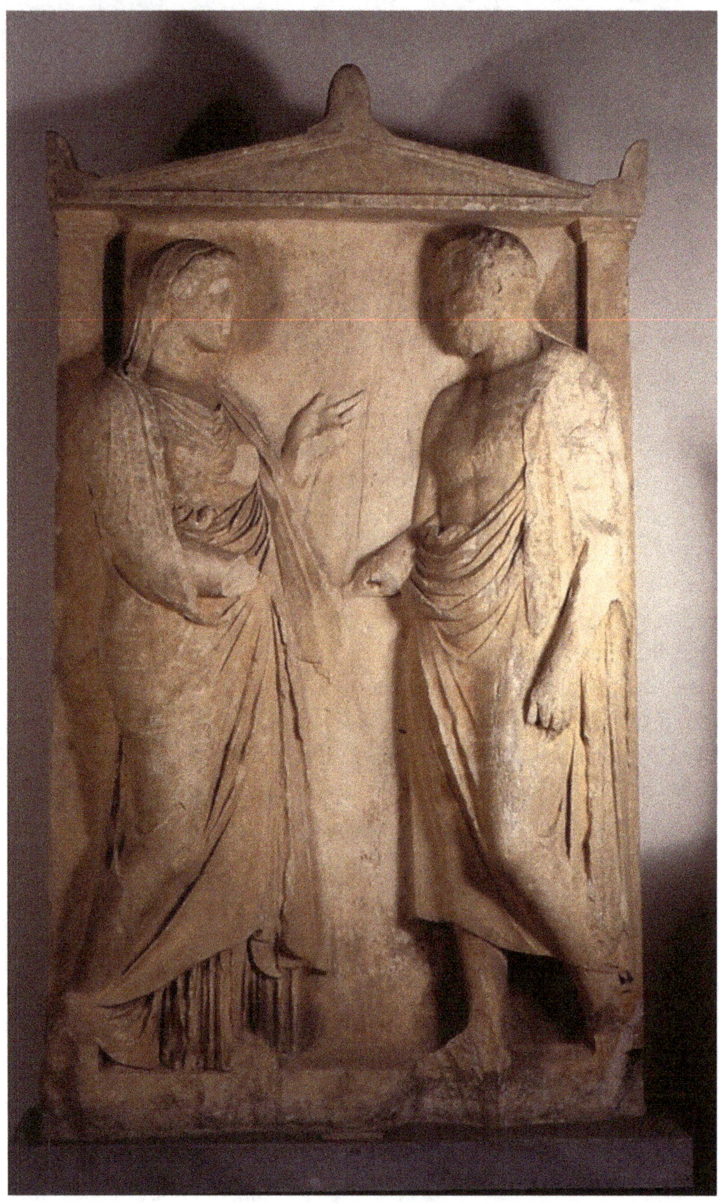

13.2 Tomb relief of Mnesistrate, mid-4th. cent. BCE. 6 ft 8¹¹⁄₁₆ in (2.05 m). From Salamis. Athens, National Archaeological Museum 826. Photo: National Archaeological Museum, Athens (Demetrios Gialouris) © Hellenic Ministry of Education and Religious Affairs, Culture and Sports/Archaeological Receipts Fund.

GENDER

In discussing gender in art, we first have to distinguish between biological sex, gender, and sexuality. Biologically one is typically born either male or female, although there are some individuals with more ambiguous sex type. Most of these differences relate specifically to reproduction, so that childbearing and nursing are biological functions that women carry out based on their biological sex. The vast majority of human anatomy is similar in both women and men, but some external anatomical differences, such as genitals and breasts, provide immediate visual cues to an individual's biological sex. There are in addition secondary sexual characteristics, such as beards and baldness, that are also visually distinctive by sex.

Childrearing, as opposed to childbearing and nursing, is a socially defined task that, while falling on women in most cultures, is not biologically determined. The term gender signifies a second aspect of identity and encompasses the social roles and relationships of men and women, including childrearing, fighting, labor, and production, as we shall see in this section. The third component of identity, sexuality, is the orientation of sexual behavior toward individuals of the same or opposite sex, or to both sexes. We will look at representations of sexuality in a later section of the chapter.

Gender, then, is the social definition or translation of sexual differences. While it may overlap with biological sex, gender definitions and roles will vary considerably from one culture to another. Clothing, activities, physical location, legal and political rights, education, and cultural opportunities may all serve to distinguish one gender from another. We can turn to the fourth-century grave stele of Mnesistrate to consider the visual manifestations of gender (**Figure 13.2**). The beard is a biological marker that identifies the figure on the right as a man. As we have seen in previous chapters, the beard is also a social indicator of maturity, of full legal rights and citizenship, so it is not simply a biological marker. Men can start growing a beard in their late teens, but the presence of a beard here signifies that the man is the head of a household, either the husband or father of the other figure, and is a mature citizen, thirty or more years old.

Since men can be clean shaven, either in reality or in art, there are other ways of visually distinguishing gender through hairstyle and clothing. Adult Greek men generally have shorter hair than adult women, although women's hair is frequently tied up or covered like that of the woman Mnesistrate on the left. Younger men and women often have longer, hanging hair, so Mnesistrate's hairstyle suggests she is an adult like the man, although there may be a wide difference in terms of their actual age. The clothing of the figures also differs. The man, who is not named, wears a long himation draped over one shoulder and falling at the calves, while Mnesistrate wears two garments, a thin, full-length chiton and a himation draped over both shoulders and the back of her head. Women are typically more heavily covered than men, and this reflects differing social conventions regarding the display of the body and modesty, or ***aidos***, a term that can also suggest shame. Even when wearing a single garment like the peplos, as in the classical caryatid mirror (**see Figure 10.6, page 242**), its heavier fabric provides a similar or greater degree of covering than the chiton and himation.

aidos
term meaning modesty or sense of shame, usually signified by a downward gaze

Hair and clothing are culturally specific and need to be interpreted by ancient Greek standards. For example, men can also wear full-length chitons like Mnesistrate. The adult figure folding the peplos from the east Parthenon frieze is a male priest, wearing a long chiton as a religious marker (**see Figure 10.15, page 250**), as does the figure of Zeus standing between Apollo and Herakles in the Siphnian Treasury (**see Figure 8.1, page 183**). The fourth-century Amazons at Epidauros (**see Figure 11.1, page 270**) and Halikarnassos (**see Figure 12.9, page 297**) wear a short chiton that to a modern eye looks like a woman's dress, but was actually a garment worn by Greek men, especially warriors, as can be seen in the Niobid krater (**see Figure 10.22, page 258**) and the Parthenon frieze (**see Figure 1.1, page 2**). For a contemporary Greek viewer, the Amazons were clearly cross-dressing even without armor, transgressing the visual boundaries marking male and female appearance and gendered behavior. Men, too, could also adopt female clothing, as male actors did playing female roles and as Spartan husbands did when furtively leaving the army barracks to visit their wives at home.

Beyond clothing, there are visual signs that women are in a secondary position to men socially. The virtual nudity of the sympotic couple in **Figure 13.1** may be equivalent, but their actions, with the youth controlling and limiting her movement, place the woman in an inferior physical position. She does not act in the modest and restrained manner of Mnesistrate. There are a number of such scenes in Greek art, especially in sympotic pottery painting, and there has been debate about whether a woman in such a scene is a ***porne***, or prostitute, or a ***hetaira***, a woman hired to provide entertainment and possibly sex as well. Literary sources suggest that respectable women avoided contact with men who were not their close relatives, leading to the use of the term *hetairai* in scholarship to label women in scenes like the Yale kylix. This label is frequently applied to women in scenes where they simply converse with men, who may offer them small gifts or hold small pouches that probably contained coins. If they are *hetairai*, the discussions in these circumstances would be about the services they will provide at an event, but we will see in the textbox for this chapter that the meaning of money purses is not certain.

porne
Greek term for a prostitute

hetaira
Greek term for a woman who was hired to provide entertainment for the symposion, which could include sex as well

Aidos was expressed not only through clothing, but also by the way that individuals looked at their surroundings and other people. Women were expected to lower their gaze when in public or mixed company, since their glance could be sensually exciting and provocative to a man. This lowering of the gaze, seen even in the slightly downturned heads and eyes of some of the idealized mirror caryatids, is said to signify a sense of shame as well as modesty in women. Young men, too, who might be displayed before the public eye when being crowned as athletic victors, were also expected to lower their gaze with modesty and not look directly at the crowd, even while the spectators were looking at them with admiration and even desire.

It is interesting, then, that on her grave stele Mnesistrate looks directly at the man before her. Their missing right arms might have been joined in a handshake associated with departure and farewell, a gesture frequently found in funerary monuments. Of greater interest is that she also raises her left arm as if she were speaking to the man, giving her the more active role in the scene. While Mnesistrate is clothed appropriately for a respectable, elite woman, her behavior suggests an equivalence with the man and is a reminder that gender relationships have more variation in practice than the limited range of literary sources, mostly written by elite men for each other, would suggest. That only her name is written on the stele indicates that this is her grave monument; her actions and the monumental scale give Mnesistrate a striking social prominence.

WOMEN'S LIVES

pais (pl. *paides*)
Greek term for child

chous (pl. choes)
small wine pitcher used in the Anthesteria

Anthesteria
Dionysiac festival celebrating the new wine from the fall harvest

In order to place artistic representations of women into context, we need to consider the stages in a woman's life. The Greeks used the word ***pais* (pl. *paides*)** to refer to both boys and girls. Both were essentially viewed as immature adults who had to develop physically and intellectually to take on their adult roles. Gender distinction began at birth, with an olive wreath hung at houses for a newborn boy and wool for a girl, if she were accepted into the family and not left exposed after birth to die, a not uncommon fate. While the number of representations of young boys, under age five, is greater in Greek art than that of girls, the activities of boys and girls are similar, including scenes of play and pretending to do adult activities. One large source of such images is on the small wine pitcher called a **chous (pl. choes)**, which was used in the Dionysiac festival of the **Anthesteria** that celebrated the opening of the new wine from the fall harvest. The pitchers were actually used as drinking vessels, and small versions were made for children to carry and use. In the chous from a grave in the Kerameikos cemetery **(Figure 13.3)**, we see a girl in a long chiton (the standard costume of a charioteer) driving a small cart pulled by two deer. Deer are sacred to Artemis, who was a patron of unmarried girls, and goddesses

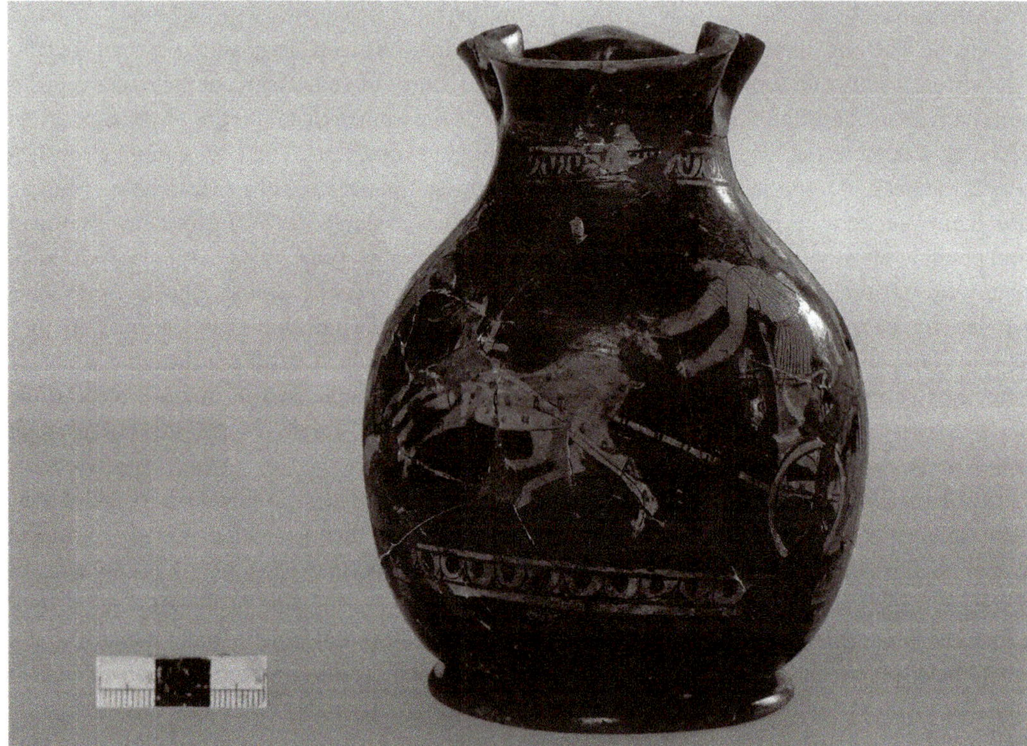

13.3 Attic red-figure chous, 430–420 BCE. Athens, Kerameikos 1067; Tomb 593/VII. Girl driving chariot pulled by deer. Photograph: D-DAI-ATH-Kerameikos-Neg. 06640.

such as Artemis and Athena are shown driving chariots in mythological pictures. Amazons, too, could drive chariots, but modeling the behavior of a goddess in this image suggests a more appropriate form of childhood play and mimicry.

Between five and seven years, children began to learn the tasks and roles that they would need at maturity. For girls, this included the many preparatory tasks associated with weaving. As we saw in Chapter 5, wool-working and weaving were a primary task of Greek women and this role is acknowledged early, with objects like the spindle becoming symbols of that domestic gender role. There were also important roles in religious ritual that would introduce girls to the community as they approached puberty. The comic poet Aristophanes mentions some of these pertinent to Athens in his play *Lysistrata*, when the chorus of women states:

> Once I was seven I became an arrephoros [bearer of sacred vessels].
> Then at ten I became a grain grinder for the goddess [*archegetis*].
> After that, wearing a saffron robe, I was a bear [*arktos*] at Brauron.
> And as a lovely girl [*pais kale*] I once served as a basket-bearer [*kanephoros*], wearing a string of figs.
> (*Lysistrata* 641–647; tr. Fantham et al. 1994, 84)

Each role assumed more responsibility in the performance of ritual, and the last is one of the most prominent duties, bearing the basket of implements used in the ritual sacrifice. The Attic krater showing a Delphic procession in Chapter 7 shows an elaborately dressed *kanephoros* at the head of the procession, standing before the sacred tripod and omphalos of Delphi **(see Figure 7.17, page 174)**, and the two girls behind the priestess in the Parthenon frieze may be *arrephoroi* **(see Figure 10.15, page 250)**. The rituals and roles would vary by region, but in each case the succession of rituals would ultimately present the young women of a town carrying out some of its most important rituals just as they reached the age of puberty. Aristophanes uses the word *pais* to describe the *kanephoros*, but we can also use the word *kore* or maiden for this figure, the term that has been applied generically to the statues of young women.

After puberty, around age fifteen in Athens but several years later in Sparta, a young woman would be married, becoming a *nymphe* or wife. Her husband was usually much older, about thirty, after he had achieved full legal rights and become head of an ***oikos***. The marriage ritual served to mark publicly this change in status for both bride and groom. Typically the groom would go to the house of the bride, lead her from it to his cart or chariot, and then, accompanied by a retinue, bring the bride to his house with her belongings. A number of wedding scenes are shown on black-figure and red-figure pottery, such as a red-figure pyxis in the British Museum **(Figure 13.4)**. On the rolled-out picture that wraps around the cylinder, we see on the left a procession bearing the bride's goods and a torch-bearer following the chariot. The bride, with her mantle over her head but her face exposed, stands in the cab while the groom mounts to drive her to his home. A man leads the way to a set of double doors with one panel open; this serves doubly as the destination and the departure, and the woman inside could be the mother of either bride or groom, but since she looks to the right, she is more likely the bride's mother watching her daughter leave. One unusual feature of this scene is that the groom is beardless, and so by normal visual convention a man who is not a full adult over thirty years of age. Most grooms in wedding scenes are bearded, but in the late fifth century BCE and afterward beardless grooms begin to appear more frequently in painting, often on ritual vases or objects used by women such as this pyxis. Since marriage was closely tied to property ownership, the change in appearance of the groom in the picture does not suggest a dramatic change in the reality of marriage.

oikos
Greek term designating the household and its activities

Looking at the wedding scene, one can compare it to scenes of maidens being abducted by gods and heroes, such as the abduction of Persephone at Vergina **(see Figure 12.25a, page 315)**. In a slightly different form, it also resembles the man leading a woman onto a ship on the Geometric bowl from Thebes **(see Figure 4.23, page 94)**. In one sense, the wedding procession is a ritualized abduction that reminds the viewer that the bride has lost her home and family. In another sense, chariots are also markers of status that elevate the wedded pair as they process through the town.

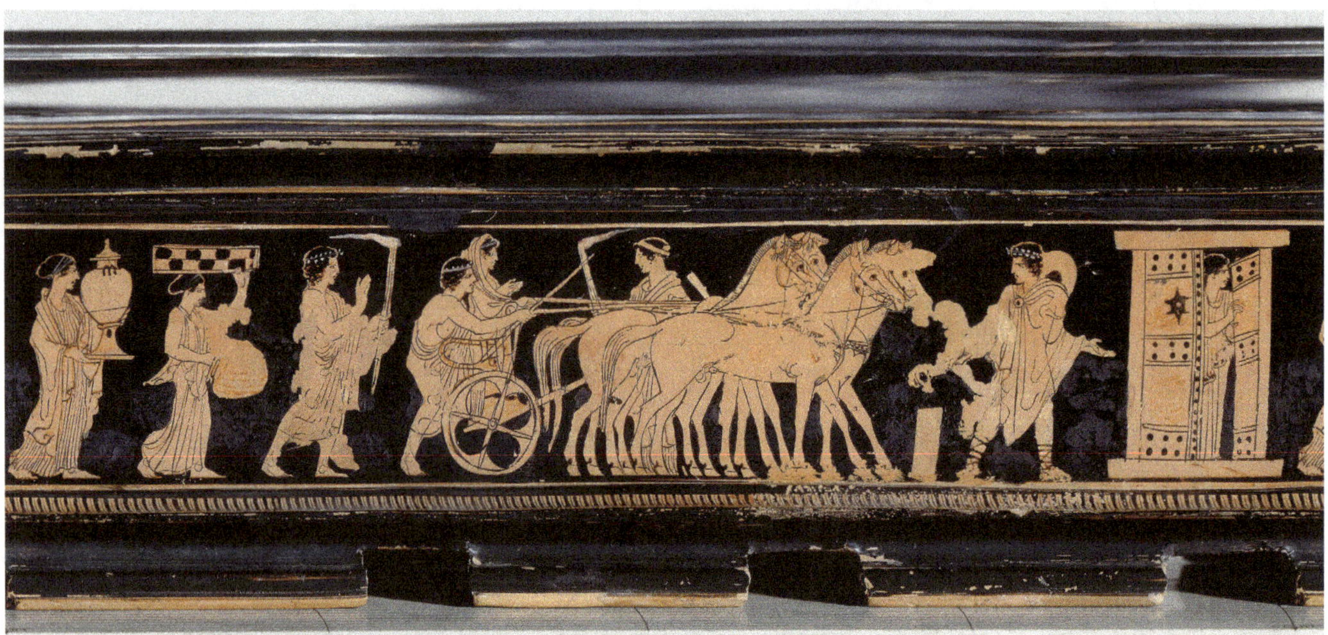

13.4 Attic red-figure pyxis attributed to the Marlay Painter, 440–430 BCE. 6¹¹⁄₁₆ in (17 cm) high (with lid). London, British Museum 1920,1221.1. Wedding procession. Photo: © The Trustees of the British Museum.

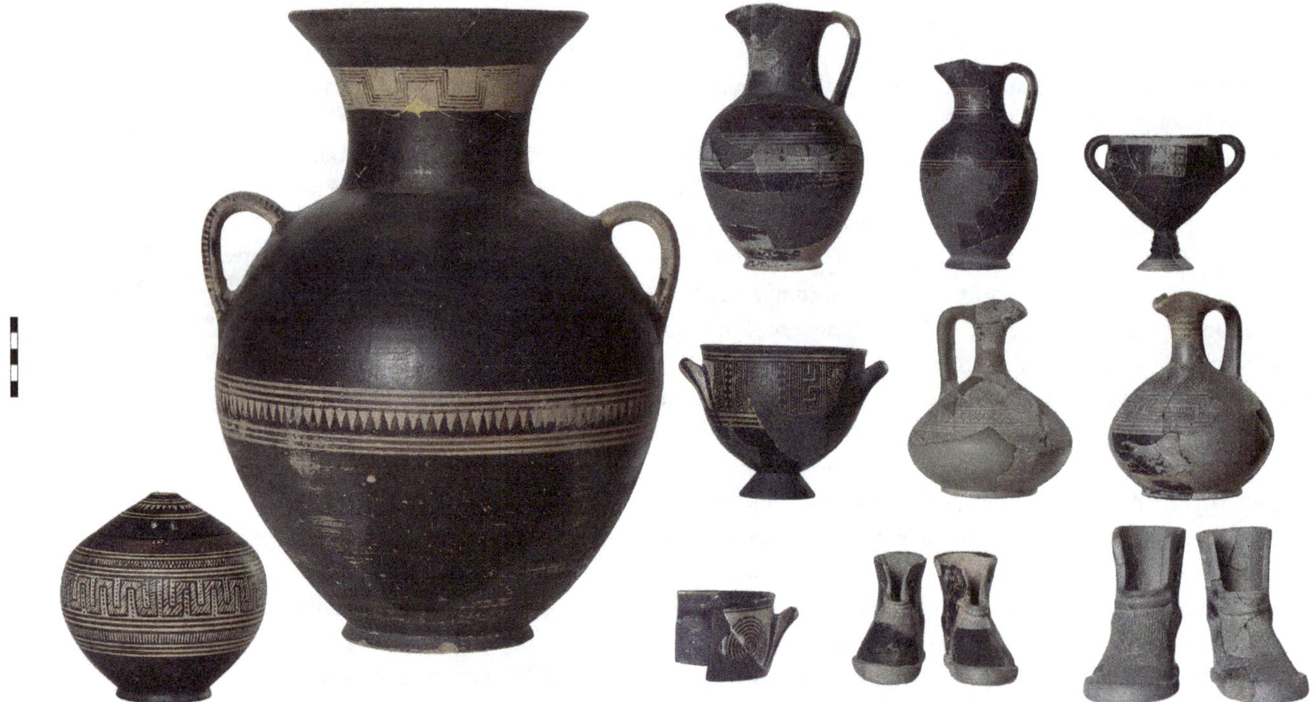

13.5 Early Geometric grave goods from a burial (D16:2, "Boots Tomb") in the Agora, Athens, 900 BCE. Athens, Agora Museum. Photo: American School of Classical Studies at Athens: Agora Excavations.

The wedding, therefore, marked a visible but complex transition in identity and status. The inscription on the base of the kore of Phrasikleia (**see Figure 8.13, page 195**) makes it clear that she died before she could marry, but her statue gives her the perpetual identity of the bride for the visitor to her tomb. In addition to taking on a new identity by the drive to her husband's house, there were also personal items, such as mirrors and shoes, that were surrendered and offered at sanctuaries to mark the transition from childhood to maturity. Susan Langdon, for example, has suggested that the two pairs of terracotta boots found in the Early Geometric "Boots Grave" in the Athenian Agora (**Figure 13.5**) were not intended to speed the journey of the dead to the afterlife, but marked the childhood boots given up by a woman on her marriage (Langdon 2008, 134–137). Shoes and clothing like these were dedicated by brides at shrines to Artemis. Perhaps the deceased in this tomb died before marriage, but the model boots were given as grave goods as signs of a mature identity.

sakkos
hair net or bag worn by mature women to cover their hair when worn up

Following the procession to the husband's house, the bride would receive guests in her new quarters. Mythological versions of the scene are found on the François Vase, where Peleus and Thetis receive the gods at their home, with Peleus outside and Thetis inside, partly hidden by the door (**see Figure 8.23, page 203**). The epinetron by the Eretria Painter (**see Figure 10.24, page 260**), a device worn over the knee to protect against abrasion and cuts from working with wool, shows the mythological *epaulia* of Alkestis, where she received her friends and family in her new home. Once established, the new wife was responsible for taking on the management of the house and its provisions, supervising slaves and work such as the production of textiles, and ultimately bearing a child, preferably male, to continue the line of the *oikos*. There are many domestic scenes on painted pottery that symbolize this activity, such as a red-figure lekythos in Boston (**Figure 13.6**). Here a fully dressed woman sits on a chair with a *kalathos* in front of her, from which she pulls the heavy strand of wool through her hands. On such a narrow shape, the full representation of all weaving activities would be difficult, and there would be little room for a loom such as we saw in other pictures (**see Figure 5.19, page 118; Figure 9.12, page 226**). The *kalathos*, the spindle, and the strand of wool become metonyms for the entire process of textile production in the Greek household.

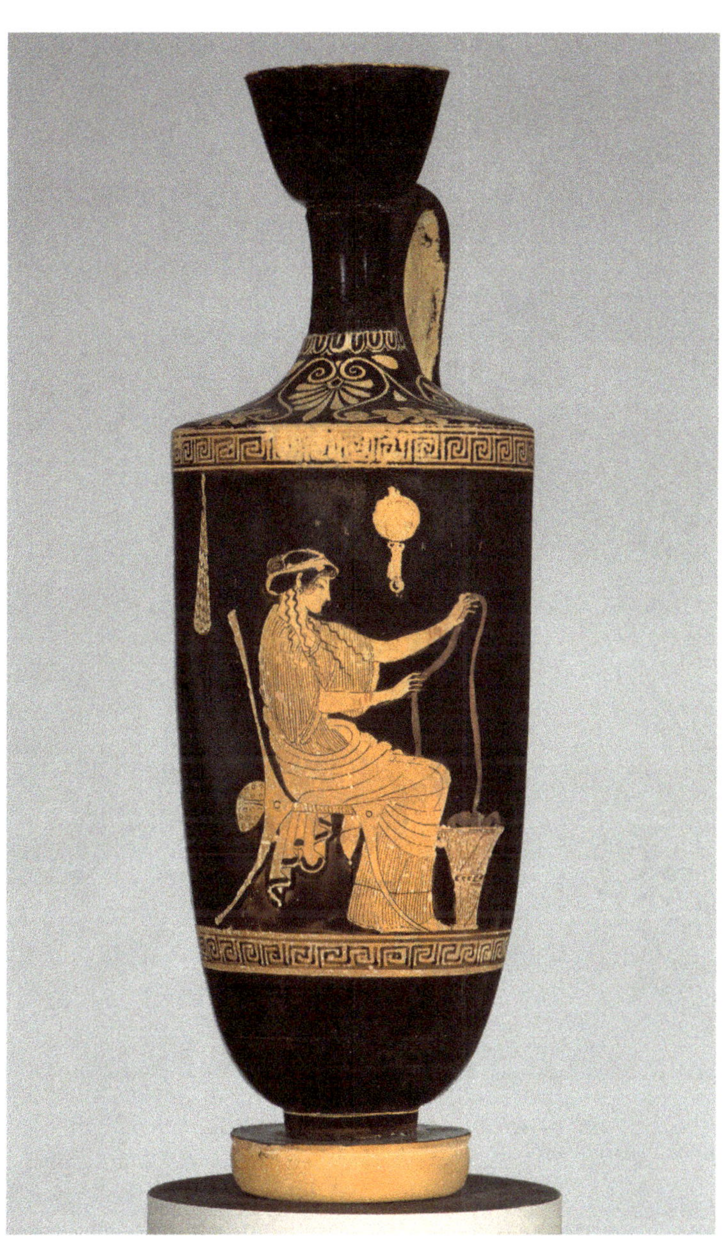

13.6 Attic red-figure lekythos attributed to the Brygos Painter, 480–470 BCE. 13$\frac{1}{16}$ in (33.2 cm). Boston, Museum of Fine Arts 13.189. Woman working wool. Photograph © 2014 Museum of Fine Arts, Boston.

A *sakkos*, or net bag that mature women often use to tie up their hair, hangs behind her from a background wall, as does a mirror, similar to caryatid mirrors, with a profile engraved on its back side. The diadem and earrings suggest that this is a mature or married woman, but the inscription reads "*he pais*," or "the [girl] child." Greek artists did not frequently distinguish fully grown women by age, so that a young maiden of fourteen, a wife of twenty, and a mother of thirty or forty years usually look alike; the picture represents an idealized picture of all women. This lekythos was used for grave offerings and ritual, which may explain the inscription. Like Phrasikleia, artists represented individuals not as they were, but as they strived to be. A lekythos like this could be an offering for a girl who died before marriage or for a woman who had been a wife, but the image serves to idealize either. The vase is said to have been found in Gela, Sicily, and it was undoubtedly a good strategy of the Athenian painter to be somewhat ambiguous in decorating a lekythos for export and an unknown purchaser.

lebes gamikos
a vase consisting of a deep bowl with handles on a stand, used for a wedding

A more complete domestic picture is found on a nuptial lebes, or *lebes gamikos*, in the Metropolitan Museum of Art (**Figure 13.7**). The shape is a variation of the lebes or dinos used as a mixing bowl for wine and water since the sixth century; the more elaborate version seen here is associated with weddings, but its specific function in the ceremony is not certain. The vase is also used as a grave offering, but whether it belonged to the deceased or is offered as a substitute for an unmarried woman is not certain. On the lebes, we see a well-dressed seated woman wearing a fillet (head band) and playing a harp. Behind her is a woman carrying a loutrophoros, which was used for ritual washing, either of the bride before the wedding or of a corpse before the burial. In front of her are other women carrying an array of chests; some are dressed like the seated woman and others wear just a chiton. Under each handle is a winged woman flying in toward the center picture and holding tendrils, a sash, and a box. Down below on the stand are two standing women, one holding a *kalathos* in her hand and the other a piece of cloth.

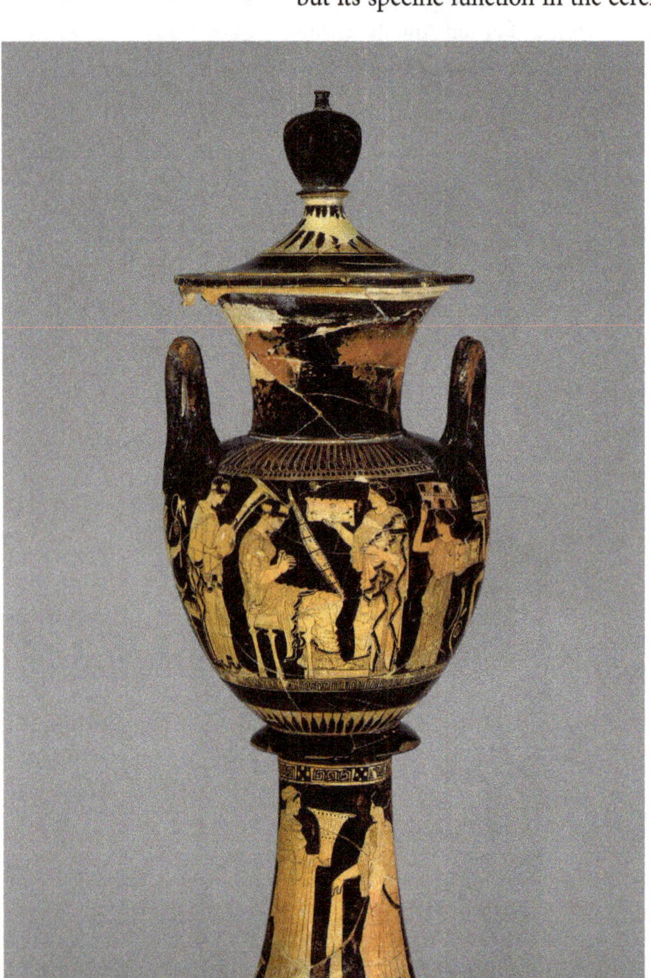

13.7 Attic red-figure nuptial lebes attributed to the Washing Painter, 430–420 BCE. 20⅛ in (51.1 cm). New York, Metropolitan Museum of Art 07.286.35a, b. Wedding preparations; seated bride playing harp. Image copyright © The Metropolitan Museum of Art. Image source: Art Resource, NY.

The scene on the bowl may represent the *epaulia*, as the bride sits in her new home. Given the chair and footrest, the scene is set in an interior space. The chests would be filled with her possessions and the winged figures serve to acclaim her new status. The scene on the stand below looks ahead to the work of the matron in running the household, especially supervising the production of textiles. Whether the standing women in the main scene are family members or slaves is less clear. The shorter figure on the right is of inferior status, but the other two standing women are virtually identical except for the fillet.

According to the literary sources, these women would be in the women's quarters of the house, the *gynaikonitis*. These sources suggest that there was a strict segregation of men and women in the Greek house, with women essentially being sequestered and kept respectable by avoiding going out in public or having contact with men who were not close relatives. Some of the sources also suggest that the interaction of wife and husband was limited, with men spending time in the andron and in public with other men. More recent analysis of houses and their use, however, suggests that such segregation was not rigorously enforced in the ancient Greek house and that there was fluidity and flexibility in the organization of the work of the *oikos* and the interaction of family members (Nevett 1999).

Finally, we should note the function of the bride and wife is to become a mother, for which we can use the term *gyne*. On a number of wedding vases we see a woman holding a small child, which would look ahead to the ideal result of marriage. The ambiguity of images and the difficulty of interpreting them individually, however, is highlighted by the grave stele of Ampharete that we saw in Chapter 10 (**see Figure 10.19, page 254**). That image of a seated woman holding a toy bird before a small child seems the perfect picture of motherhood, but we know from the inscription that the image signifies Ampharete and her granddaughter, both of whom apparently died about the same time. Since age was not commonly distinguished in representations of women, this might have been a gravestone made for any of several situations, including mother and child. Whatever the actual circumstances, images of women and children would epitomize the Greek social ideal for women.

WOMEN IN PUBLIC

gynaikonitis
the women's quarters of the household

gyne
term designating an adult married woman and mother

Contrary to the picture of women's seclusion in the literary sources, women did have important public roles to perform, in civic and religious processions, cult rituals, and funerary rites. In funerals, women were responsible for cleansing and preparing the body of the deceased. At the same time, this is a sign of their inferior status since the risk of pollution from tending to the dead was deemed lower for women than men because of their differing biological natures. The prothesis constitutes one of the first common scenes in Greek art beginning in the Geometric period, and women are the primary participants in this activity of laying out and mourning the dead **(see Figure 4.7, page 78; Figure 4.9, page 80)**. Women were also the primary mourners of the deceased, wailing the threnody and pulling and tearing their hair in grief, whether genuine or dramatic **(see Figure 5.26, page 125)**. Indeed, women could be hired as mourners to make a funeral more elaborate and sensational, a practice that was sometimes proscribed by law. Men typically are more restrained in funerary scenes and acknowledge the deceased through salutes or chariot processions. The still immature nature of non-adult males can be seen in some of these scenes, such as in the gesture of the youth in the fifth-century prothesis scene that we saw in Chapter 5 **(see Figure 5.26, left)**, where he grasps at the hair on his forehead in a powerful expression of grief. After burial, women were responsible for bringing offerings to the tomb regularly and decorating it with ribbons **(see Figure 5.26, right)**.

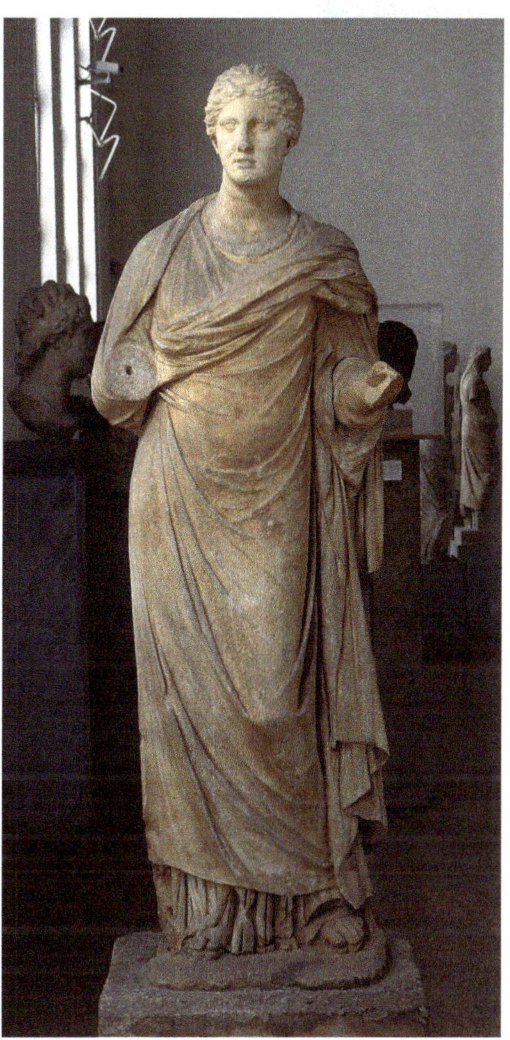

13.8 Statue of priestess Aristonoë, from Temple of Themis/Nemesis at Rhamnous (Attica), 3rd cent. BCE. 5 ft 3¾ in (1.62 m). Athens, National Archaeological Museum 232. Photo: National Archaeological Museum, Athens (Kostas Xenikakis) © Hellenic Ministry of Education and Religious Affairs, Culture and Sports/ Archaeological Receipts Fund.

We have already seen many examples of women participating in religious processions, whether at important Panhellenic sites such as Delphi **(see Figure 7.17, page 174)** or at smaller sacred sites with just family members, as shown on the painted panel from Pitsa **(see Figure 8.21, page 202)**. In the latter, a woman serves as *kanephoros* and pours a libation from a pitcher over an altar. The taller women behind her wear diadems and carry sheaves of grain, perhaps signaling their status as adults. A more important religious role for a woman was as priestess, which would involve greater responsibility for the supervision of ritual, the preparation of participants, and care for the shrine or precinct. While only a few, usually elite, women could become priestesses, the role brought a level of public visibility. The significance of this function is reflected in the statues that were erected in public spaces to honor priestesses. The kore of Nikandre, for example, is thought to have been set up at Delos in the mid-seventh century, where she likely served a prominent role, perhaps as priestess, in the cult of Artemis **(see Figure 6.3, page 134)**.

Nikandre's inscription does not mention any title and defined her status through her relationship to her father, brother, and husband: "Nikandre dedicated me to the far-shooter of arrows [Artemis], the excellent daughter of Deinodikes of Naxos, sister of Deinomenes, n[ow?] wife of Phraxos." Public statues of priestesses become more common in the fourth century BCE and later; these more clearly recognize the status or office of the individual. The statue of Aristonoë from the third century **(Figure 13.8)**, for example, was placed inside the cella of the small Temple of Themis/Nemesis at Rhamnous in Attica. The inscription states that it was dedicated by her son Hierokles (son of Hieropoios) and that she was the daughter of Nikokrates of Rhamnous, so there is still some definition of her identity through her male relatives. An important difference from the inscription for Nikandre, however, is that she is identified as the priestess (*hiereia*) of Nemesis, and so carries a title in her own right. She once held a phiale in her missing right arm, and therefore is shown in the act of making a

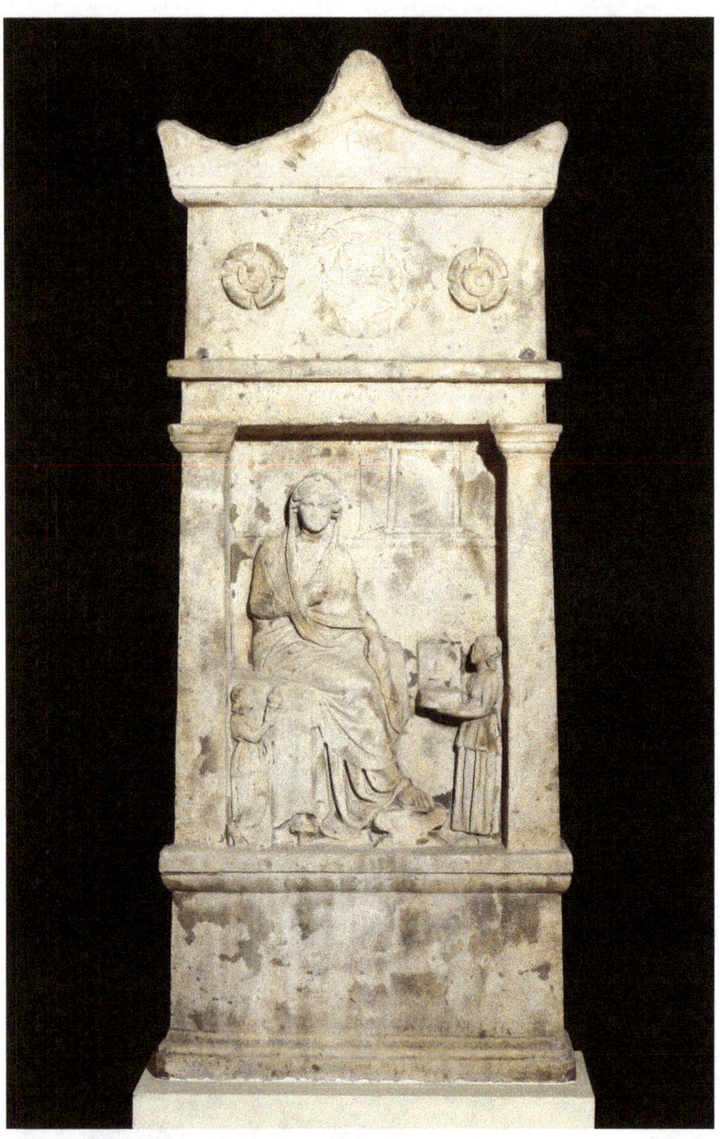

13.9 Grave stele of Phila, daughter of Apollas, from Smyrna/Izmir, 2nd cent. BCE. 4 ft 8¹¹⁄₁₆ in (1.44 m). London, British Museum 1947,0714.2. Photo: © The Trustees of the British Museum.

libation to the goddess whom she served. The marble statue is life-size and standing on its base would have looked over all visitors to the temple.

We can see further recognition of the public roles of women in funerary monuments of the Hellenistic period. The stele of Phila, daughter of Apollas (**Figure 13.9**), dates to the second century and comes from Smyrna (present-day Izmir in Turkey). Phila is shown seated in a room with an open cabinet in the background. The two small figures in the corners are not children, but slaves shown in a hierarchical scale. One holds an open chest like that in the fifth-century stele of Hegeso (**see Figure 5.28, page 127**), while the other holds a spindle, a symbol of wool-working like the *kalathos*. Unlike Hegeso, Phila does not look at either object, implying that she may supervise the slaves but does not participate in their work. More evocative, however, is the frontal positioning of the head that looks directly at the viewer. Rather than a tableau within the funerary relief that keeps the space distant from the viewer, like the stele of Mnesistrate (**see Figure 13.2**), Phila engages directly with the viewer and does not lower her gaze. There is no mention of husband or children in the short inscription, but the wreath in the attic section of the stele bears the inscription *o demos* or "the people." This signifies that Phila has received some type of civic honor for her service to the city. Contemporary records indicate that wealthy and elite women could serve as substantial patrons of public projects in Hellenistic cities, and there are records of a few women holding public office or receiving honors for their literary achievements. While these examples are very modest in number compared to those of men, they do indicate that gender limitations and expectations were complex and variable by period and region.

One notable example of regional differences in gender is the case of Sparta. Here the number of citizens in the polis was small, while a much larger population, called helots, labored on the estates and workshops of the Spartans, essentially as serfs. Control over the territory and the helots depended upon a highly trained, essentially professional army whose fitness and discipline could defeat much larger forces. While Sparta's regime was more authoritarian than the democratic government of Athens, Spartan women were better off than their Athenian counterparts judging by modern standards. There was public education for women, which included exercise. Spartan women married later, closer to twenty years old rather than fifteen, making them more mature and physically fit for bearing children. There were athletic contests for Spartan women, and some of the religious rituals appear to have been performed in the nude or nearly so, as they could be for men.

We have already seen some examples of caryatid mirrors which would have been idealized presentations of female identity, but there is a group of mirrors associated with Sparta that show a nude rather than clothed female figure for the handle (**Figure 13.10**). The figure on this example is young like the other caryatids, around the age of puberty, and wears elaborate jewelry and a headdress like that seen on other caryatid mirrors whose figures are clothed (**see Figure 8.19, page 201;**

Figure 10.6, page 242). This nude caryatid holds a bud in her hand and would appear to be making an offering or performing a ritual, and should be seen within a ritualistic context in either case. The sirens next to her are metaphors for her allure, and their singing reminds us that the young women would also be singing and dancing in front of the city. This is a quite different attitude toward nudity and gender identity than in Athens during the sixth and fifth centuries.

Female nudity, however, presents challenges different from male nudity, both for the ancient viewer and today. The Aphrodite of Knidos (**see Figure 12.11, page 300**) established a canon of the female nude that was even more popular than the Doryphoros (**see Figure 10.7, page 243**) based on the number of copies and imitations, but questions linger about the direction of her gaze and whether she is looking downward in both modesty and shame. In the majority of cases, female nudity occurs in scenes of sexual violence, like the rape of Kassandra (**see Figure 9.7, page 219, left side**), or in more ambiguous sexual situations in which women were not equals with men, like the symposion scene in **Figure 13.1**. The double layers of clothing on elite women in tomb reliefs and statues show that the display of their body and sexuality was more restrained than that of men.

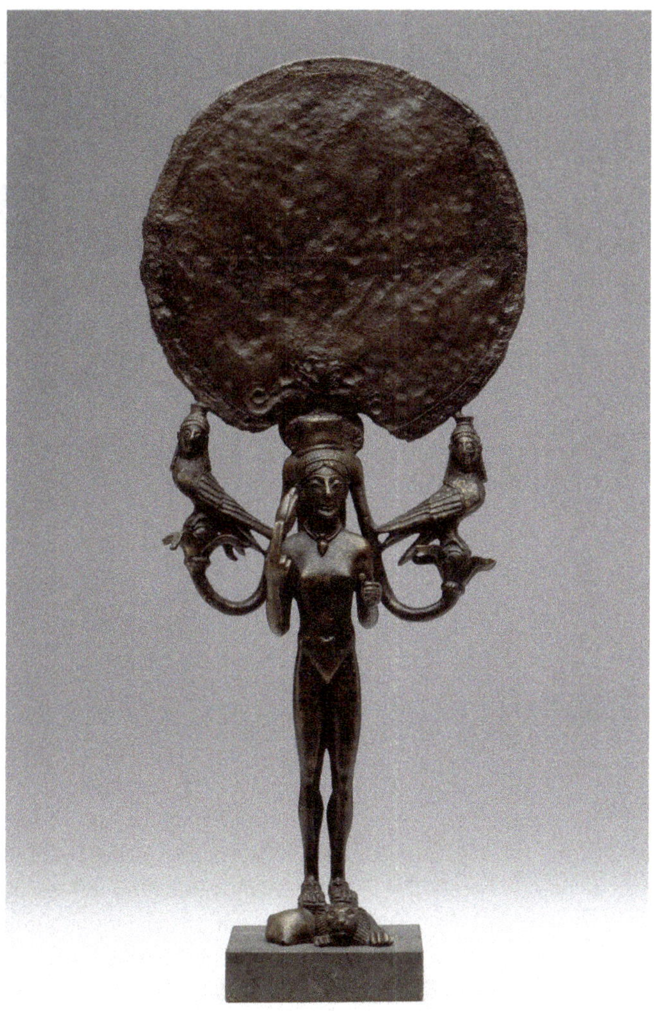

13.10 Lakonian nude caryatid mirror, 560–540 BCE. About 13⅝ in (34.5 cm). From Hermione, Greece. Munich, Staatliche Antikensammlung und Glyptothek 3482. Photo: Renate Kühling.

MEN AND YOUTHS: GENDER AND SEXUALITY

Boys went through a similar sequence of stages as children, although rather than being taught the work of the household, such as weaving and cooking, they began to learn a craft or, in more elite families, were sent to schools. Pictures of school scenes were popular in Attic vase painting in the first half of the fifth century and show a teacher (***paidagogos***) instructing both young boys and teenagers in reading, writing, music, and athletics. On the cup by the Foundry Painter (**Figure 13.11**) one can see two youths being taught to box, their awkward gestures suggesting that they are unpracticed and new to this sport. The bearded adult man holds a forked stick that is the typical implement of trainers. The youth to the right is winding his hand and wrist in the leather straps of boxers, while a fourth youth appears on the left carrying a helmet and shield. The armor reminds the viewer of the close association between athletics and military service; training prepares the boys for the roles that they will assume in the city. Similar athletic scenes can also be seen on the ball player relief from a base that supported a kouros statue, probably for a tomb (**see Figure 8.8, page 189**). Other vases show scenes of youthful activity, including the hunting scenes on the Chigi olpe (**see Figure 6.11, page 141**). In the lowest frieze, youths and dogs work together to chase and trap hares; in the middle frieze youths ride to a lion hunt, and around the other side of the vase they attack the lion from all sides. As the choice of subjects for the Chigi olpe's three friezes shows, group hunting and warfare are closely linked, with the scene of the hoplites marching and fighting in the top frieze being the result of the lessons learned from athletics and hunting.

Turning back to the youth with armor on the Foundry Painter's cup, he seems better developed and more poised than the other youths, and may have moved on to the next stage of becoming an adult. At sixteen, a son was introduced by his father to the **phratry** or other group or tribe to which

paidagogos
term for teacher of boys and youth

phratry
term designating a social or tribal group within the Greek polis

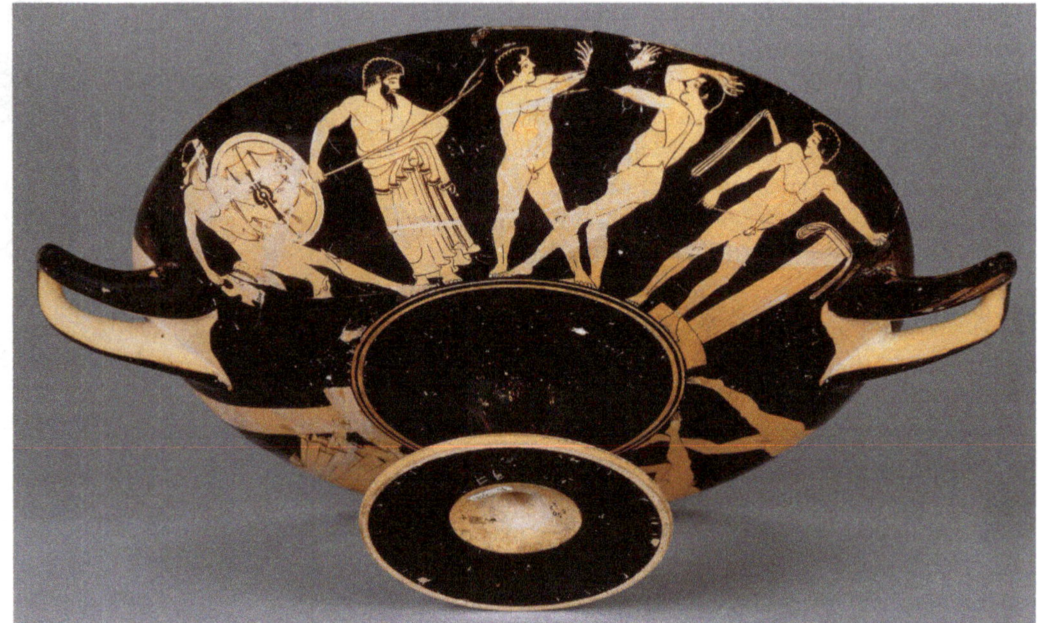

13.11 Attic red-figure kylix attributed to the Foundry Painter, 490–480 BCE. Diameter 12 in (30.4 cm). London, British Museum E78. Boxers with trainers. Photo: © The Trustees of the British Museum.

ephebos
term for a young man of eighteen to twenty years in age

his family belonged. At eighteen, he would formally become an ***ephebos*** and would begin military training. By age twenty or so, the young man would be ready for service in the army, whether as a hoplite or as a cavalry rider like the youths in the Parthenon frieze or Dexileos, who was twenty when he died in battle **(see Figure 12.12, page 301)**. Attic vase painting has many scenes showing warriors departing, either bearded adults or beardless men who could be in their twenties (although in reality most men in their twenties would have been bearded, especially when wearing a helmet). On the volute krater by the Niobid Painter **(see Figure 9.18, page 232)**, a youth in armor holds a spear while touching the hand of a woman holding his helmet and second spear. A second woman holds a phiale and oinochoe for a libation to mark the importance of the event for the family and polis. This woman may be his mother since her hair is tied up, but it is generally hard to distinguish visually between wives, mothers, and daughters in these pictures. For ephebes who were orphaned and whose family could not provide armor, the state could step in. Indeed, this intervention was sometimes necessary as marriage and fatherhood came after a man reached full citizenship and legal rights at age thirty. Given this relatively late start to fatherhood, many ephebes and men in their twenties would not have living fathers and their inheritance and the future of the *oikos* would be under a guardian.

In addition to education and military training, youths also developed social networks through performances in religious festivals and especially through the symposion **(see Figure 5.20, page 119)**. Many of these scenes show a mixture of youths and adult men sharing couches, as in the mural from the Tomb of the Diver **(see Figure 10.20, page 255)**. Here one youth is holding a lyre and embraces an adult sharing the couch. The other symposiasts hold cups, and two of them raise their cups toward an approaching youth on the adjacent wall of the tomb. Singing, reciting, and talking created a close-knit group. The revelry could leave the andron with the symposiasts dancing and singing boisterously in an activity called the *komos*. These komast scenes appear early in black-figure pottery **(see Figure 5.23, page 122)** and continue in red-figure work such as the fifth-century kylix by the Euaion Painter **(Figure 13.12)**. One youth provides music with his lyre, while another offers an oinochoe of wine to an adult holding a skyphos. The men at the ends of the scene twist and kick to the music, and the procession carries on to the other side of the cup. This exuberant performance is less scripted and more informal than the type of dancing and singing associated with religious performances, and suggests that public display and near nudity were allowable for men in ways they were not for women.

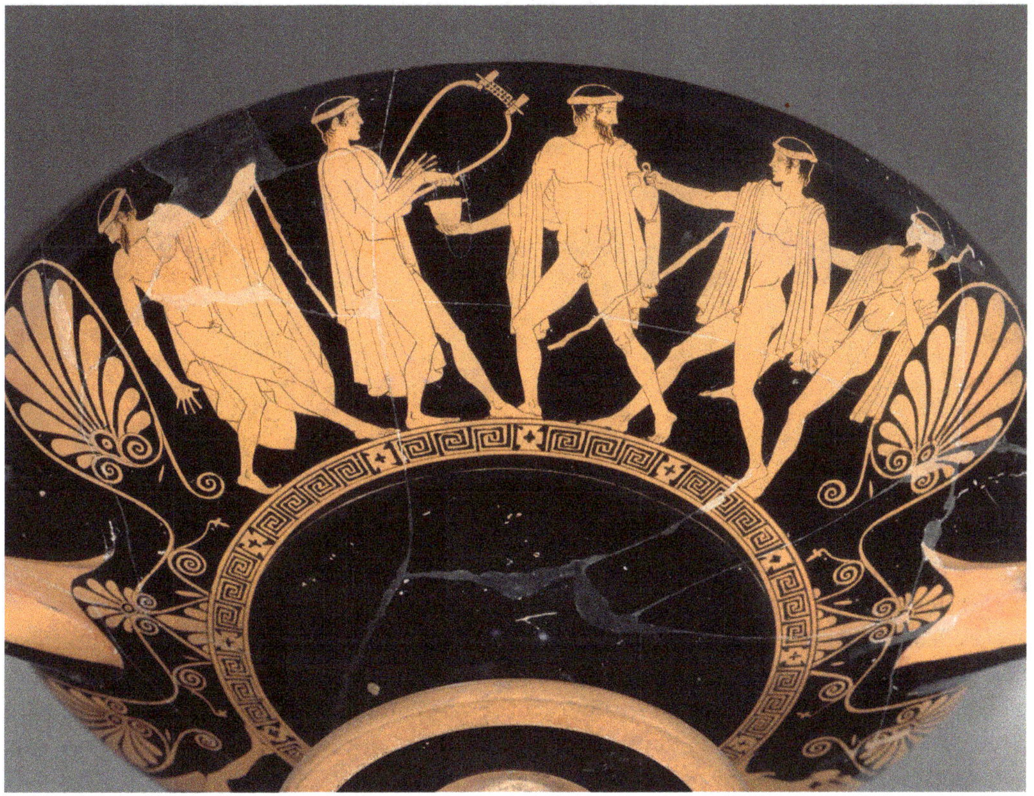

13.12 Attic red-figure kylix attributed to the Euaion Painter, 450–440 BCE. Diameter 12 in (30.5 cm). Boston, Museum of Fine Arts 01.8078. Komast scene. Photograph © 2014 Museum of Fine Arts, Boston.

The sympotic scenes not only point out differences in activities and behavior by gender in ancient Greece, they also raise the complex issue of sexuality. While a majority of people are heterosexual, the range of human sexuality is much broader and includes homosexuality and bisexuality. Having children is essential for both society and the *oikos*; the records of judicial speeches preserved from Athens show that inheritance and ownership problems arose if an heir were not available to the *oikos* or if the legitimacy of the heir presumptive were questioned. Gender roles helped to prepare men and women for performing these roles, but sexuality does not always align so neatly with gender identity and biological sex. To complicate this further, homosexuality was also linked to the gender roles assigned to men through the institution of **pederasty**. The exact nature of pederasty has been the subject of much debate, but Andrew Lear and Eva Cantarella (2008, 2) have described the custom as follows: "an adult man in ancient Greece could, with little or no risk of social disapproval, express sexual desire for another male, so long as the desired male was an adolescent (*pais*), whom the adult loved within the context of the socially codified and positively valued relationship which we call pederastic." In Athens and many Greek cities, adult men who interacted with youths in the symposion, ***palaistra***, school, and elsewhere not only mentored them in training and education, but developed homoerotic emotional relationships with them that could include sexual relationships as well. The social acceptance of homosexuality within pederasty, however, does not seem to have extended to all relationships between men. There were also regulations that were intended to prevent abuse of these functions and pederastic relationships. The asymmetry of this relationship between men and youths is also mirrored by the large age difference between husbands and wives, meaning that age, sexuality, and gender were aspects of one's identity and that adults could be expected to play multiple roles within Greek society. It also means that adult men might have to take on multiple sexualities in fulfilling all of their social and gender roles.

pederasty
the homosexual or homoerotic relationship between a male adult and youth

palaistra
a space for athletic activity in the gymnasion, usually for wrestling and boxing

While pederasty was practiced in many Greek cities, most of the literary and visual sources come from Athens, and in particular on painted pottery. While there are some explicitly sexual scenes,

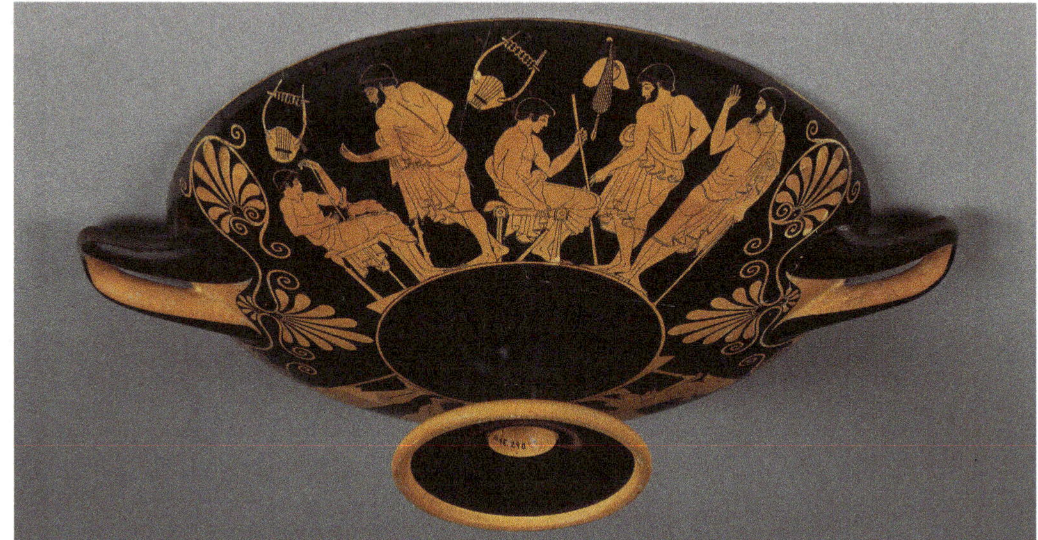

13.13 Attic red-figure kylix signed by Douris, 480 BCE. Diameter 12¼ in (31.2 cm). Malibu, Getty Museum 86.AE.290. Courtship scene. Photo: The J. Paul Getty Museum, Villa Collection, Malibu, California (photo inverted with permission).

both heterosexual and homosexual, these are small in proportion to the number of courtship scenes, like that seen on a kylix by Douris **(Figure 13.13)**. The exterior of this cup shows two youths seated on stools with adult men standing before them and another man off to the right. There are lyres hanging on a wall behind and above each youth, recalling music school scenes with adult teachers and their young students, whose *paidagogos* accompanies them. The net bag, sponge, and aryballos hanging on the wall refer to the physical part of education, but this is not an education scene. The hare in the lap of the youth on the left shows that this is a courtship scene, with the man in front of him offering the gift of a hare to gain his favorable attention. The pair in the center appear more contemplative or in conversation, but the direct gaze of the adults toward the youths signals their interest and effort. It is important to note, however, that these youths do not look back at the men, but lower their gaze. Even though they are the object of attention, they must behave with *aidos* and show proper decorum in responding to the courtship. As noted earlier, successful athletes were expected not to look at an audience while being crowned, but were to remain detached in their demeanor while receiving the adoring gaze of the spectators. It is interesting to note that youths, like women, were to lower their gaze and not respond directly when seen and desired by adult men.

eromenos
term for the "beloved," the youthful partner in a pederastic relationship

erastes
term for the "lover," the adult partner in a pederastic relationship

These images in art are idealized constructions and make an institutional custom appear uniform. In practice, however, pederasty covered a complex range of gender and sexual behaviors and orientations among individuals. Sexual and erotic activity was common, but, like marriage, was bounded and shaped by social conventions. The youth, the *eromenos* or beloved, needs to transform his identity from that of a child to that of a citizen, building a social network that will support him and his *oikos*. The adult, the *erastes*, is both teacher and lover; through shared activities at the symposion, the hunt, and the palaistra, he models the values, restrained behavior, and nobility expected of male citizens. In an era of fighting in hoplite formations that required rigorous discipline in maintaining an unbroken rank, trust in one's comrades was critical. Men who had shared social activities and developed emotional bonds with each other would develop the trust and mutual dependence required in battle or other actions. Perhaps the most monumental example of this ethos is the statue of the Tyrannicides that we have already discussed in Chapters 5 and 10 **(see Figure 5.9, page 108)**. Aristogeiton was the *erastes* of Harmodios, his *eromenos*. When Hipparchos, the brother of the tyrant Hippias, slandered Harmodios's sister after being rejected when he courted Harmodios, the pair acted together to avenge the insult and killed Hipparchos. Their deed became the symbol of the later democracy, but it began with their pederastic relationship and their willingness to die together in the action.

INTERACTION: CLASS, CIVIC, AND ETHNIC IDENTITY

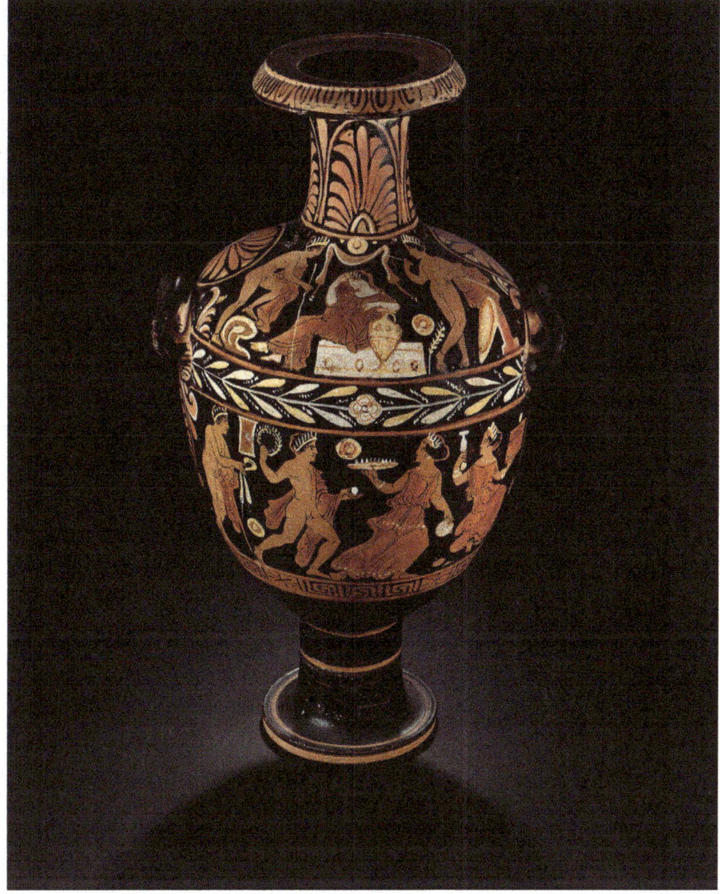

13.14 Campanian red-figure hydria attributed to the Manchester Painter, 350–330 BCE. 22¹¹⁄₁₆ in (57.6 cm). London, British Museum 1949,0926.1. Body: ritual procession of men and women; shoulder: woman (Elektra?) at tomb with youths (Orestes and Pylades?).

The picture from the literary sources in fifth- and fourth-century Athens suggests a strong degree of gender segregation, but the reality was more varied and complex. Beyond performing together in formal rituals, there are many scenes on vase paintings showing men and women interacting in other settings or with more animation. A Campanian red-figure hydria from the fourth century, for example, shows a mixture of women and youths gathered in an open setting (**Figure 13.14**). They wear wreaths and bear several different kinds of objects that might be used ritualistically, and the mood is one that is very festive and seemingly informal. On the shoulder is a woman, perhaps Elektra, sitting on a tomb with two youths standing nearby. Whereas we associate women with the maintenance of tombs and memorializing the dead, it is not always clear that the men and youths we see at tomb scenes are the deceased or living members of the family. Indeed, the Apulian loutrophoros with the grave naiskos that we saw in the last chapter (**see Figure 12.19, page 308**) shows a youth kneeling to offer a mirror to the deceased woman; he is the only figure who seems to be attending to the tomb at all. That these examples are from south Italian vase painting and not Athens reminds us that the Greek world was diverse and dispersed, and that civic and ethnic identity also played a role in shaping individuals and groups. To conclude this chapter, then, we will look at some other dimensions of identity that cut across the range of gender and sexuality.

We have already mentioned differences in class when talking about the symposion scene in **Figure 13.1** or the stele of Mnesistrate. Whereas pederasty helped to shape gender and sexuality for Athenian men, it also established their identity among the Athenian elite, as we saw in Harmodios and Aristogeiton (**see Figure 5.9, page 108**). Lavish funerary monuments were one way that the elite could distinguish themselves, and we have to consider that this desire to distinguish one's class was a key patronage element in the development of the Geometric style in Athens. The Dipylon amphora was truly monumental for its time, far larger than any other vase or sculpture and more intricately made and decorated (**see Figure 4.7, page 78**). Standing in the cemetery, it would have distinguished itself visually and drawn attention to the class status claimed by the family who had set it up over the tomb. While there are many more monumental kraters (**see Figure 4.9, page 80**) than amphorae from this period, the importance of class is signaled by the inclusion of a large number of women in the prothesis scenes as well as men in the commemorative procession. Later, marble funerary monuments serve to mark elite class identity, whether for Phrasikleia in the sixth century (**see Figure 8.13, page 195**) or the grave monuments of the Koroibos–Kleidemides family in the fourth (**see Figure 5.27, page 126**). Indeed, this effort to distinguish class over citizenship sometimes led to laws or policies banning elaborate funerary monuments, called sumptuary laws, since these displays were powerful visual statements against the equality of citizens in the polis. Even when individual monuments were common, as in the relief of Dexileos (**see Figure 12.12, page 301**), the polis still exerted its prerogatives by placing the remains of Dexileos with those of the other fallen soldiers in a group tomb, making the monument a cenotaph rather than tomb, but still effective at evoking the status of his family.

Civic identity distinguishes members of one polis or region from others and was a key factor in monumental architecture and sculpture. As we saw in Chapter 10, in the funeral oration of 431/0 BCE Perikles asked Athenians to look on their city as lovers while remembering the dead from the first year of the Peloponnesian War. While Athenians and Spartans might have been allies against the Persians in 480, Perikles extolled the greater virtue and superiority of the Athenians. Athens not only acted differently from Sparta, but also looked much greater as a city **(see Figure 1.9, page 13)**. The Parthenon was not just a religious building, it was a symbol of the city's triumphs and prestige.

Indeed, one could link the succession of temples built from the seventh century onward as a competition among cities for cultural and even political preeminence. At a Panhellenic sanctuary like Delphi, there was competition in the construction of monuments and treasuries by the various poleis to proclaim their wealth, power, or status. The Siphnian Treasury dominated the view from the entry to the temenos when it was built, but lost some of its visibility when the Sikyonian Treasury was built in front of it, but lower down the slope **(see Figure 7.2, page 157; Figure 7.15, page 171)**. When the Athenians came to build their treasury after defeating the Persians at Marathon in 490 BCE, they managed to secure a spot at the turning of the Sacred Way where their building would be seen fully on both its south and east sides **(see Figure 7.14, page 170)**.

Another way of expressing civic identity emerged with the development of silver coinage, which, according to Herodotos (1.94), was invented in Lydia in Asia Minor. This probably happened about the end of the seventh century BCE, but the idea quickly spread to the Greek poleis as it greatly facilitated trade. Each polis minted its own coins, and consistency in weight and purity of silver would help the economic life of the city. By the later sixth century, poleis began striking coins with designs, and each city chose specific symbols that would be identifiable across the Mediterranean. Athens, for example, had a head of Athena wearing a helmet on the obverse of its coins and an owl on the reverse, while Corinth had Pegasos and Athena on its coins.

Greek colonies also minted coins to establish their own civic identity. A silver **stater** from the Achaian colony of Metapontum/Metaponto in southern Italy, for example, shows an ear of barley **(Figure 13.15)**. This colony was established sometime in the seventh century, with an urban center (***asty***) near the coast and a *chora* that extended inland to the northwest. The land here is relatively flat and fed by rivers coming from the mountains, making it an ideal area for agriculture. Grain became the foundation of the wealth of the polis, so much so that the geographer and historian Strabo, active at the end of the first century BCE and beginning of the first century CE, tells us that the Metapontans

stater
a coin usually made of silver whose weight and value were about two to three times those of a drachma

asty
the urban center of a Greek colony (see also *chora*)

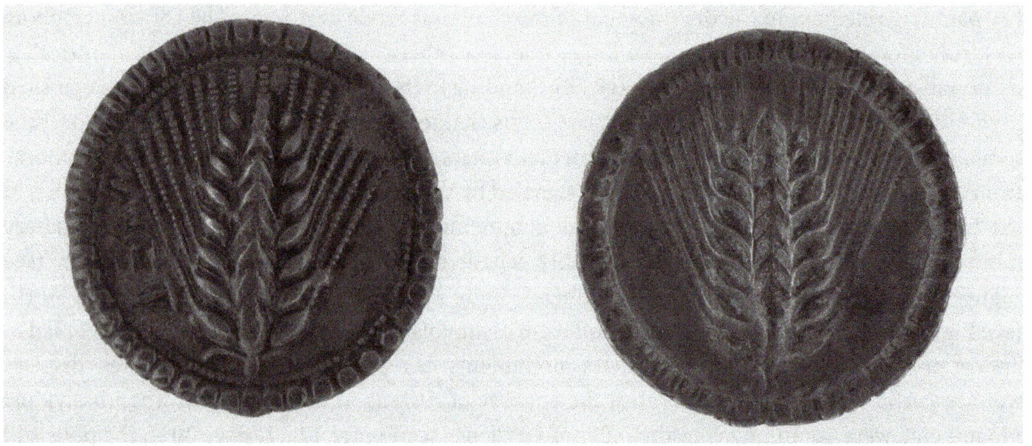

13.15 Silver stater from Metaponto, 540–510 BCE. Diameter: 1⅛ in (2.9 cm); weight: 8.19 g. Six-row barley head. New Haven, Yale University Art Gallery, Numismatic Collection Transfer, 2001; Purchased 1963, 2001.87.456. Photo: Yale University Art Gallery.

sent grain stalks made of gold as an offering to Delphi (Strabo 6.1.15). Thus the grain on the coin not only symbolizes the prosperity of the polis, but refers to its distinctive offering at one of the most important Panhellenic shrines.

Colonies like Metapontum/Metaponto included both Greek and non-Greek peoples as residents, and this raises another aspect of identity that might best be labeled ethnic. Cities such as Metapontum/Metaponto, Akragas/Agrigento, Syracuse/Siracusa, and Poseidonia/Paestum were founded in lands that were already settled by indigenous, non-Greek peoples. The relationship of native and immigrant varied widely across the Mediterranean, from hostility to coexistence and cooperation. At Metapontum/Metaponto, the earliest Greek settlers lived at Incoronata, a site already inhabited by the Oenotrians. At first the Greeks lived among the Oenotrians, but Incoronata was later transformed into a rural sanctuary with the development of the Greek *asty* and *chora* by the sixth century BCE. Imported Attic pottery bears witness to trade with mainland Greece, but the city had its own pottery industry that began to flourish in the second half of the fifth century, a fabric we now call Lucanian pottery **(see Figure 9.11, page 224)**. At first the style was very similar to contemporary Athenian pottery, but in the fourth century developed its own style and subject matter as it met local needs. The inhabitants of Metapontum/Metaponto included both Greeks and natives, and so we might look at items like grave goods to see how individuals expressed their ethnic identity in that city.

One particularly interesting tomb in the rural Pantanello cemetery, about 3 kilometers north of the *asty* of Metapontum, was an *a cappucina* burial lined with plaster containing the skeleton of a man, about twenty five to thirty years old. The grave goods of Tomb 106 **(Figure 13.16)** include three types of drinking cups in black glaze or banded ware, a Lucanian red-figure pelike, a stone alabastron, a bronze strigil, and a bronze belt. Based on the pottery style, the tomb is dated between 425 and 385 BCE. The pottery shapes are a common selection or kit for grave goods and provided wine for the deceased in the afterlife, to be poured figuratively from the pelike and drunk in the cups. The strigil, used to scrape oil and dirt from the body after athletic activity, is also found frequently in male graves and is an effective symbol of the deceased's participation in activities associated with Greek men and the palaistra. The bronze belt, however, is unusual and is a ceremonial type used by the Lucanians, the indigenous inhabitants of the interior of southern Italy (and who took control of Poseidonia/Paestum about 400 BCE) **(Figure 13.17)**. As Joseph Carter has noted, this is surely not a work that a Greek resident would have worn, meaning the deceased is probably Lucanian (Carter

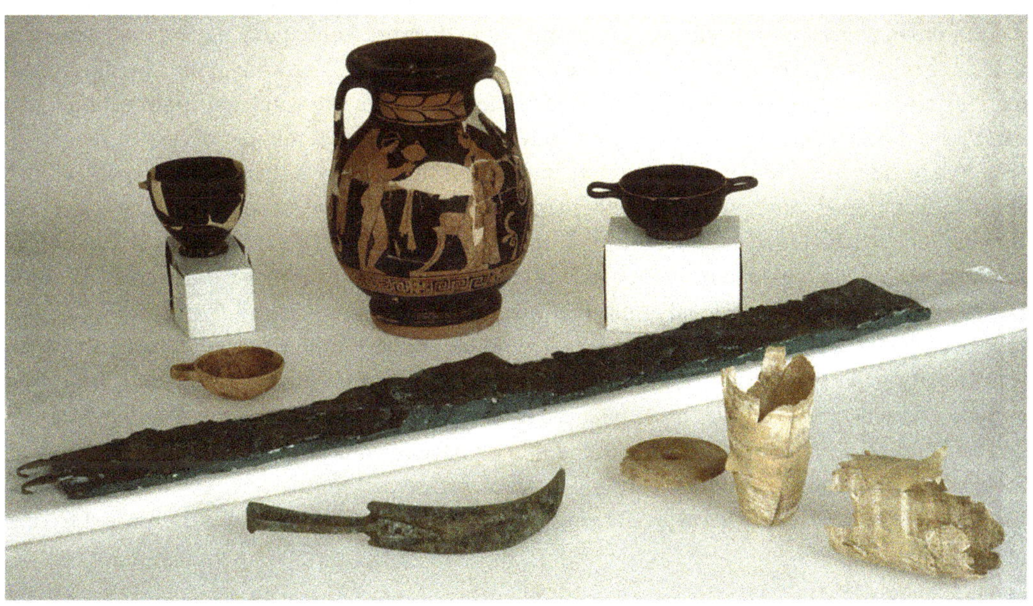

13.16 Grave goods from Tomb 106, Pantanello Cemetery at Metapontum/Metaponto, 425–385 BCE. Height of pelike 9¾ in (24.8 cm). Photo: Williams/Institute of Classical Archaeology.

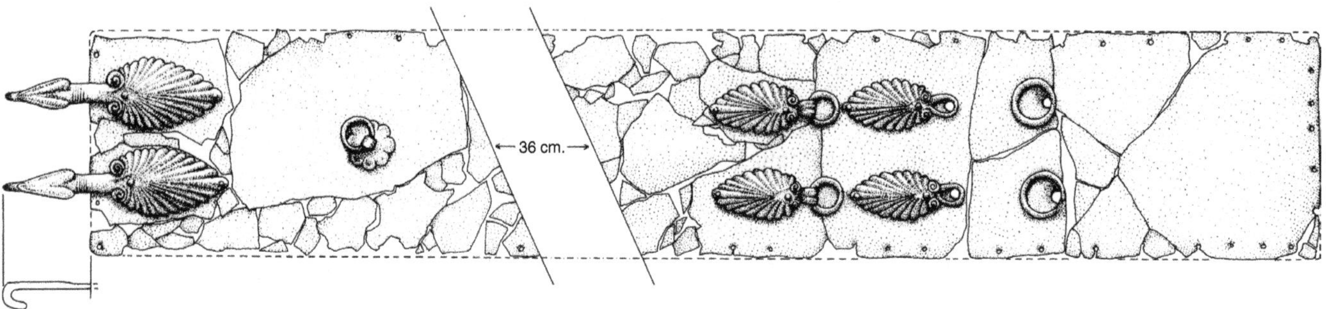

13.17 Reconstruction drawing of "Lucanian" bronze belt from Tomb 106, Pantanello Cemetery at Metapontum/Metaponto, 425–385 BCE. Width 3 in (7.5 cm). Drawing: S. Langston/Institute of Classical Archaeology.

2006, 220). There are several other graves in the Pantanello cemetery whose grave goods indicate their inhabitants were also Lucanians rather than Greeks. The grave goods, then, are a hybridization of customs and objects. The mixture of Greeks and non-Greeks in the same cemetery suggests to Carter that ethnicity could be fluid and that differing groups could share common beliefs and practices. For the Lucanian man in Tomb 106, his grave goods include artifacts of both cultures and his place in them.

One of those shared beliefs or customs may have been religious. The Pantanello cemetery has a number of graves whose goods indicate that many of the deceased were Orphic-Pythagorean-Dionysiac initiates. This religious movement is associated with the philosopher and mathematician Pythagoras, who moved to the Greek colony Croton in southern Italy about 530 BCE and died about 495 in Metapontum/Metaponto. He established a doctrine on the transmigration of the soul and practice of vegetarianism; his interest in the afterlife merged under his followers with ideas taken from Orphism and Dionysiac cults. We have already seen one aspect of this interest with the afterlife in the Derveni krater and tombs, and its practice spread throughout the Greek world **(see Figure 12.15, page 304)**. At Metapontum/Metaponto, this often shows up in grave goods through the inclusion of mirrors and lyres, and the lyre in the Tomb of the Diver in Poseidonia/Paestum may indicate that its inhabitant was an initiate **(see Figure 10.20, page 255)**. In Tomb 106, the pelike, attributed to the Amykos Painter who worked in Metapontum/Metaponto, shows Eros with a mirror standing before a woman, making an indirect reference to the religion, like the offerings shown on the Apulian loutrophoros with a grave naiskos **(see Figure 12.19, page 308)**. At first the subject – Eros, mirror, and a woman – may seem irrelevant to the man buried in the tomb, but since burials happened quickly, this may have been the best available means both for providing wine in the afterlife and for marking his status as an initiate. The back side of the vase shows two youths in conversation, so in some ways the pelike's subject matter is quite universal and usable in a number of circumstances.

If we consider the goods collectively, we can see that the identity of the man in Tomb 106 is a complex mixture. He identifies with activities associated with males in terms of his gender, but whether this included involvement with pederasty is not apparent, nor is his sexuality. The bronze belt suggests an elite class identity since such ceremonial objects are expensive and limited among Lucanian tombs. The goods signal a mixed ethnic identity of Lucanian and Greek and suggests a religious identity as an Orphic-Pythagorean-Dionsyiac initiate. This religion was one in which women were active participants, so that his religious beliefs may have made his gender identification and his interaction with women more nuanced in practice. It is entirely possible that the deceased had no hand at all in the selection of grave goods if he had died unexpectedly, but their choice by those who included them in the grave still shows how his identity was perceived by others. In either case, we can see how art marks, expresses, and models the range of identities for the ancient Greeks and their neighbors.

TEXTBOX: MONEY PURSES, SEX, AND IDENTITY

A number of scenes on Attic vases show a man or youth standing before a woman holding out a small sack in his hand, as can be seen on an epinetron from the mid-fifth century **(Figure 13.18)**. A seated woman is holding an alabastron up toward a youth, who holds out a small sack or purse toward her. We are not sure what is in the sack, but most scholars would see it as a money purse holding bronze and silver coins, although it is possible that it might contain other small objects such as knucklebones for a game. Coins were a new phenomenon in the sixth century and minted by many Greek cities, and the small purses become a frequent object in fifth-century images, suggesting their widespread adoption.

Many scholars have seen these scenes of a man with purse talking to a woman as negotiating the services of a ***hetaira***. Domestic signs in the picture, including items associated with weaving or an interior space, would place the scene in the house of the ***hetaira***, who would be carrying out domestic chores while not working professionally. Since discourse in public or in her own house with a man not in her family would be scandalous, the woman in such a picture must be a ***hetaira*** rather than a virtuous matron according to this view.

This interpretation shows the difficulty of decoding how images mark identity and relationships. A coin purse can indicate a transaction, but if the woman is holding an aryballos or wreath in her hand, the purchase may be for goods rather than services, as Sian Lewis has suggested (Lewis 2002, 93–94, 194–199). Certainly many women would have had to sell their production, such as textiles, if they were to make a living, either within or outside of an ***oikos***. So, too, some of the scenes might be courtships and the money would be an indicator of wealth or status, and hence of the eligibility of the suitor. Another factor to consider is that many of the pots having these scenes were made for export, and the painters may have thought the money purse would be an interesting image for consumers as coins were being minted throughout the Mediterranean by this time. In the case of the epinetron, it was found in Athens but was likely an object purchased by a woman, given its connection to textile production, making the association with a ***hetaira*** doubtful if we consider the role of agency in art. How an item like a coin purse would have served in real life as a marker of identity, and how we should interpret it within a picture such as this, is complex and varied, just like identity itself.

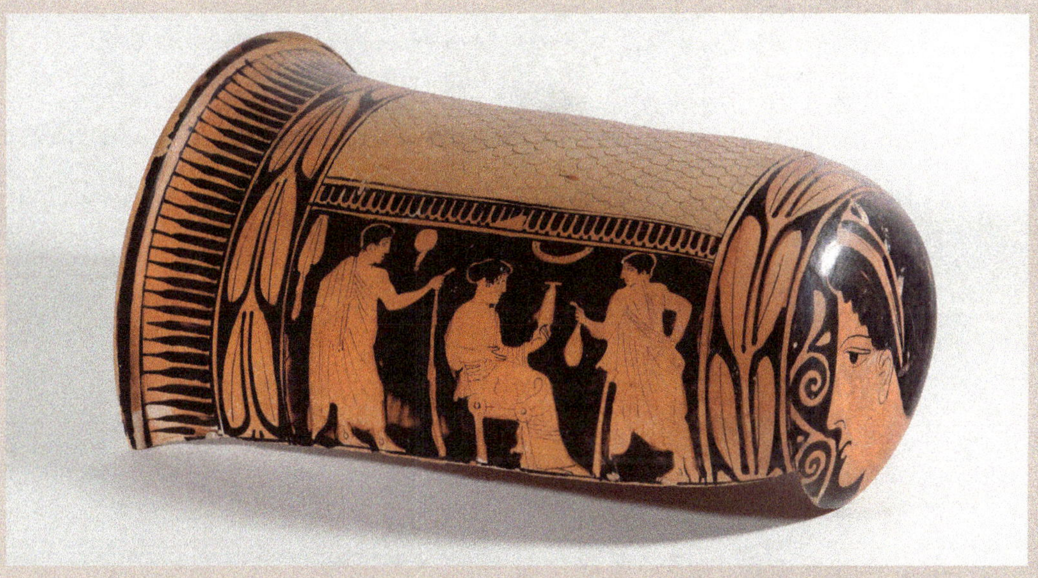

13.18 Attic red-figure epinetron attributed to the Painter of Berlin 2624, 450 BCE. Woman and youths. Berlin, Antikensammlung F2624. Photo: bpk/Antikensammlung, Staatliche Museen, Berlin/Ingrid Geske/Art Resource, NY.

REFERENCES

Carter, J. 2006. *Discovering the Greek Countryside at Metaponto*. Jerome Lectures, 23. Ann Arbor: University of Michigan Press.

Cole, S. E. 2013. "A Possible Egyptian Broad Collar on a Yale Kylix." *Yale University Art Gallery Bulletin* 2013, 126–129.

Fantham, E., H. P. Foley, N. B. Kampen, S. B. Pomeroy, and H. A. Shapiro. 1994. *Women in the Classical World: Image and Text*. Oxford: Oxford University Press.

Langdon, S. 2008. *Art and Identity in Dark Age Greece, 1100–700 B.C.E.* Cambridge/New York: Cambridge University Press.

Lear, A. and E. Cantarella. 2008. *Images of Ancient Greek Pederasty: Boys Were Their Gods*. London/New York: Routledge.

Lewis, S. 2002. *The Athenian Woman: An Iconographic Handbook*. London/New York: Routledge.

Nevett, L. C. 1999. *The House and Society in the Ancient Greek World*. Cambridge: Cambridge University Press.

FURTHER READING

Antonaccio, C. 2010. "(Re)Defining Ethnicity: Culture, Material Culture, and Identity." In S. Halles and T. Hodos, eds. *Material Culture and Social Identities in the Ancient World*, 32–53. Cambridge/New York: Cambridge University Press.

Blundell, S. 1995. *Women in Ancient Greece*. Cambridge, MA: Harvard University Press.

Connelly, J. B. 2007. *Portrait of a Priestess: Women and Ritual in Ancient Greece*. Princeton: Princeton University Press.

Dillon, S. 2010. *The Female Portrait Statue in the Greek World*. Cambridge/New York: Cambridge University Press.

Fantham, E., H. P. Foley, N. B. Kampen, S. B. Pomeroy, and H. A. Shapiro. 1994. *Women in the Classical World: Image and Text*. Oxford: Oxford University Press.

Ferrari, G. 2002. *Figures of Speech: Men and Maidens in Ancient Greece*. Chicago: University of Chicago Press.

Gruen, E S., ed. 2011. *Cultural Identity in the Ancient Mediterranean*. Los Angeles: Getty Research Institute.

Hall, J. M. 1997. *Ethnic Identity in Greek Antiquity*. Cambridge: Cambridge University Press.

Langdon, S. 2008. *Art and Identity in Dark Age Greece, 1100–700 B.C.E.* Cambridge/New York: Cambridge University Press.

Lear, A. and E. Cantarella. 2008. *Images of Ancient Greek Pederasty: Boys Were Their Gods*. London/New York: Routledge.

Lewis, S. 2002. *The Athenian Woman: An Iconographic Handbook*. London/New York: Routledge.

Llewellyn-Jones, L. 2003. *Aphrodite's Tortoise: The Veiled Woman of Ancient Greece*. Swansea: Classical Press of Wales.

Malkin, I. 2011. *A Small Greek World: Networks in the Ancient Mediterranean*. Oxford: Oxford University Press.

Neils, J. and J. H. Oakley. 2003. *Coming of Age in Ancient Greece: Images of Childhood from the Classical Past*. New Haven/London: Yale University Press.

Nevett, L. C. 1999. *The House and Society in the Ancient Greek World*. Cambridge: Cambridge University Press.

Oakley, J. H. and R. H. Sinos. 1993. *The Wedding in Ancient Athens*. Madison: University of Wisconsin Press.

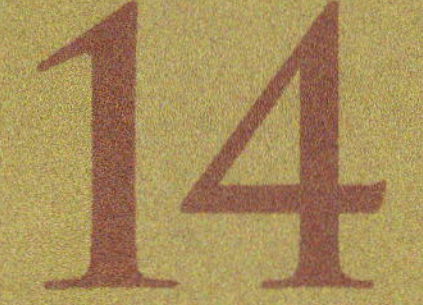

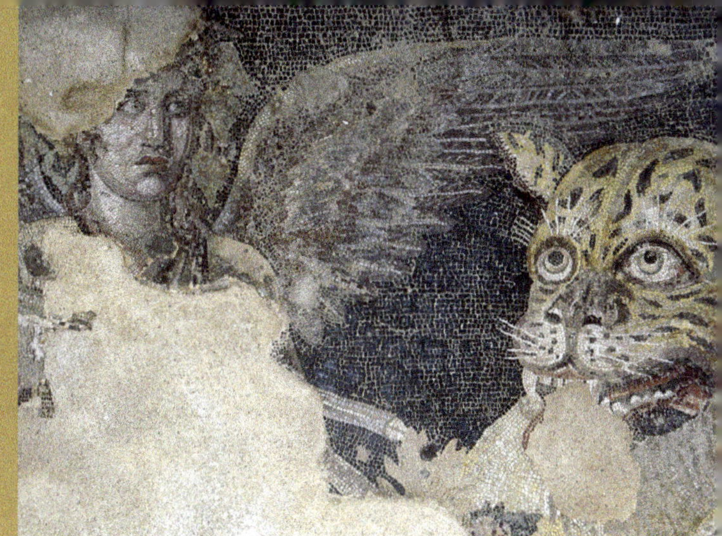

14

THE HELLENISTIC PERIOD

C. 330–30 BCE

Timeline
Characteristics of the Hellenistic Period
Cities and Architecture
Sculptural Styles and Dating
Theatricism and Narrative
Representations and Portrayal
Painting
The Private and Personal Realm
Textbox: The Riace Warriors as Hellenistic Sculpture
References
Further Reading

TIMELINE

	Architecture	Sculpture	Painting	Events
330–300	Alexandria becomes capital of Egypt, 320	Alexander Sarcophagus, 325–311	Stag Hunt mosaic, 330–300	330 Alexander defeats Persians 323 Death of Alexander
300–200	Temple of Apollo at Didyma, begun 300	Tyche of Antioch, original 296/293 Terracotta woman from Taras/Taranto, early 3rd cent. Coin of Arsinoë II, 261–246 Nike of Samothrace, late 2nd cent.	Centuripe vase, 3rd–2nd cent. Hadra hydria of Hieronides, 226–225 Panel of Hediste, 200	300 Foundation of Antioch 281 Foundation of Pergamon 270 Death of Arsinoë II 211 Roman sack of Syracuse/Siracusa
200–100	Great Altar of Zeus at Pergamon, 180–150 Asklepieion at Kos, 160	Sculpture from Lykosoura, 200–190 Aphrodite of Melos, 150–100	Mosaic in House of Dionysos at Delos, 166–100 Alexander Mosaic, late 2nd–early 1st cent.	168 Battle of Pydna 146 Battle of Corinth 133 End of Pergamene dynasty
100–1		Aphrodite from Delos, 100 Bronze head of man from Delos, early 1st cent. Head of Cleopatra VII, mid-1st cent. Sperlonga, mid-1st cent [11.14]		86 Sack of Athens by Sulla c. 80 Antikythera shipwreck 70–60 Mahdia shipwreck 31 Rome conquers Egypt

*Works for which an absolute chronological date can be suggested.

As we saw in Chapter 12, the fourth century witnessed the rise of Macedonia and its conquest of Greece under Philip II. Whether or not it is the tomb of Philip, the painted frieze from Tomb II at Vergina was an expression of royal prerogative, using hunting scenes to demonstrate the bravery and skill of the king and his retinue, particularly the two riders attacking the lion on the right side of the landscape (**see Figure 12.24, page 314**). The triumphant rider was a staple motif of Greek art, whether in the hunt or in battle, like the stele of Dexileos (**see Figure 12.12, page 301**), but the emphasis was now on the elite status of the king and royal family. The hunt had long been associated with royalty in Persia, Mesopotamia, and the Levant, and the use of the theme at Vergina proclaimed the Macedonian rulers as equals of the Persian kings. Indeed, Philip had been planning an invasion of the Persian empire before his assassination in 336 BCE, a task that his son Alexander the Great undertook after reasserting Macedonian control over Greece. Alexander crossed into Asia Minor in 334 and by 333 had control of the Levant and Egypt. He invaded Mesopotamia in 331 and had completely defeated the Persian king Darius by 330. Pushing eastward, he reached the Indus River and Indian Ocean by 325, when he turned back toward Mesopotamia. At his death in 323 the political geography of the Greek world had changed, and in the subsequent division of Alexander's empire among his generals, the cultural geography was similarly transformed.

The Alexander Sarcophagus is an example of this changed environment for Greek culture and art. The monumental marble coffin essentially forms a miniature treasury for its occupant and, like the Siphnian and Athenian treasuries at Delphi, has painted sculptural friezes on all four sides. On one end and the adjacent long side is a series of three hunts: riders attacking a lion from both sides, a group of hunters attacking a stag, and another group striking a panther on the short end. The other long side and end show battles between Persians (recognizable by their trousers, tunics, and soft caps) and Greeks (in armor or heroic nudity) (**Figure 14.1**). There are Greek riders at either end of the long side whose rearing pose and raised hands that once held bronze weapons recall the schema of Dexileos, except that their opponents are Persian riders who collapse under the assault. In the center are two more riders: a helmeted Greek rider on the left, who turns around to attack a kneeling Persian, and to the right a Persian rider who strikes at a nude Greek warrior on foot. Although one might expect someone like Alexander to be the central figure of the composition, he is actually the figure charging from the left side, wearing a lion-skin helmet. This motif, which is an attribute of Herakles, reflects not only the claim of the royal family to be descended from that hero, and hence descendants of Zeus, but also signifies the divinity of Alexander himself, who was declared a god by the oracle at Siwa in Egypt around 325 BCE. While the battle in the center of the sarcophagus shows continuing Persian resistance, the left side of the frieze shows the collapse of the Persians under Alexander's assault. There has been debate about whether the frieze represents an actual battle, such as the battles at Granikos (334) or Issos (333), during which Alexander personally led the flanking cavalry charges that defeated the Persians. Given the use of heroic nudity in the frieze, we should regard the composition as an epitome of Alexander's victories.

The style and proportions of the figures recall classical works like the stele of Dexileos or the riders on the Parthenon frieze (**see Figure 1.1, page 2**). Whereas the overlapping figures in the center create a dense composition, placing Alexander on the left isolates him visually and makes him a focal point, an effect that was heightened by the colored paint, traces of which are still visible. Given the style and subject matter, one might expect that the sarcophagus was made by a Greek sculptor for a Greek patron, and certainly the nickname for the work, the Alexander Sarcophagus, reinforces the expectation that it is a work for a Greek leader. In fact, the sarcophagus was found in the last of seven chambers in the royal tombs in Sidon in modern Lebanon. While there is no inscription, it is generally accepted that the sarcophagus was made for the last king of Sidon, Abdalonymos, whom Alexander had installed in 332 BCE as ruler following the defeat of the Persians in the Battle of Issos. Abdalonymos thus owed his power to Alexander's patronage. He managed to maintain his throne after Alexander's death in 323, until he was defeated in battle and died in 311, during the period when Alexander's generals fought over the division of the empire.

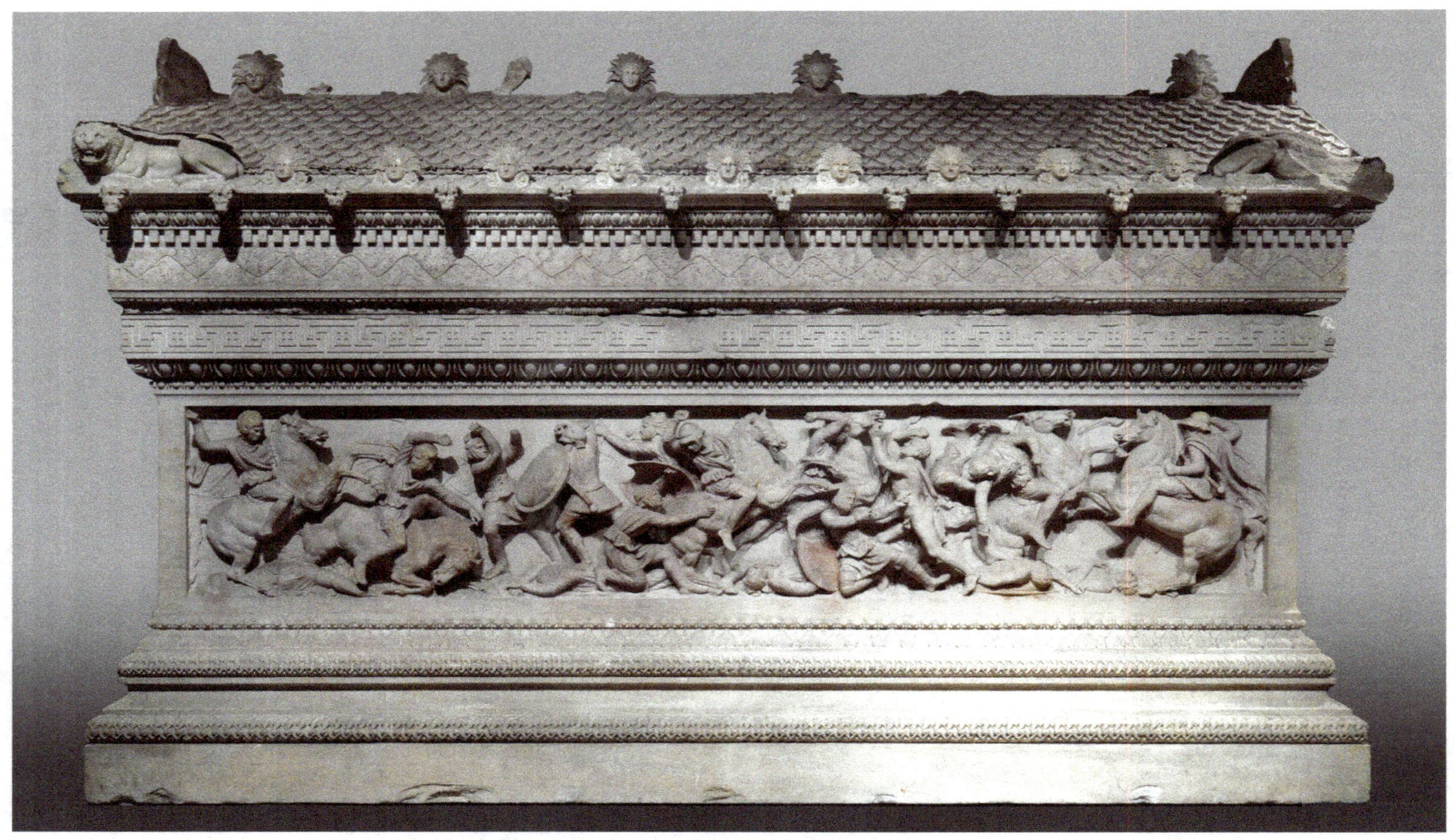

14.1 Alexander Sarcophagus from Sidon, *c.* 325–311 BCE. Istanbul, Archaeological Museum. 6 ft ¾ in (1.95 m); height of frieze 27 3/16 in (69 cm). Battle scene with Alexander the Great. Photo: © Vanni Archive/Art Resource, NY.

In contrast with the long side, the battle scene on the short end of the sarcophagus shows a Persian rider triumphing over a Greek warrior, and this is thought to be a portrait of Abdalonymos himself, perhaps during the period after his patron's death. Even though he had been installed on his throne by a Greek king, Abdalonymos had to fight the Greek successors of Alexander to maintain his kingdom. It is interesting, then, that Abdalonymos, if it is him, would choose to represent himself as a Persian, asserting his non-Greek identity. This is not to say that his identity is so simple as Greek or non-Greek, since in the long hunt scene on the other side of the coffin we see Abdalonymos attacking the lion personally, with Alexander riding in support behind him. The sarcophagus was likely made during the king's lifetime, and it therefore reflects both his identification with Alexander and his struggles with the new Greek rulers of the Levant and Egypt following Alexander's death.

Another representation of Alexander shows his nearly universal appeal during the Hellenistic period (**Figure 14.2**). A floor mosaic with an extraordinarily large central picture was found in an **exedra** in the House of the Faun in Pompeii, one of the most lavish houses in that city. Now mounted on a wall in the National Archaeological Museum in Naples, the mosaic is dated to the late second or early first century BCE and probably copies an early Hellenistic painting showing Alexander battling Darius. The ***opus vermiculatum*** mosaic uses small colored ***tesserae*** about 2–3 mm in size, meaning that it took over a million tesserae to compose the picture. While it is damaged in some areas, the durability of mosaic and the small sized "pixels" used here preserve much of the color and detail missing in paintings like the Tomb II fresco at Vergina.

The figures, about half-life-size, are set in a landscape space, with the Greeks charging from the left. Alexander is again on horseback, but is now wearing armor that shines with reflections of light off of its metal surface. His spear runs through a falling Persian rider wearing a gold tunic near the center of the panel. The use of such small tesserae allows for shading or ***chiaroscuro*** that makes the horses and figures solidly three-dimensional, an effect that is strengthened by the use of foreshortening and *skenographia*. The head of the Persian rider's horse is set pointing obliquely toward the front of the picture and the viewer, while to the right we see the highlighted rump of another horse running straight back into the picture. Behind that horse is Darius in his chariot car, elevated above the battle fray as his charioteer whips his horses to escape from Alexander's threat. Darius's outstretched right arm expresses dismay, not necessarily in fear for his own life, but perhaps in anguish over the loss of his soldiers, particularly the figure in the gold tunic. The battle is at a turning point, with Alexander sweeping in a new regime. Like the Alexander Sarcophagus, this is more likely an epitome of the battles Alexander fought against Darius, portraying him as an irresistible and charismatic warrior and leader.

The model for the mosaic was likely a painting done near the end of the fourth century BCE, but the mosaic itself was made for a wealthy patron in Pompeii, an area ruled by Rome but still inhabited mostly by the Samnites, a non-Roman Italic people. The Samnites occasionally fought against the Romans until they were finally defeated by the general Sulla in 80 BCE, after which a colony of Roman veterans was established in Pompeii. One might ask what the appeal of a Greek king would be in this environment, especially considering the huge cost of the mosaic. From a Roman perspective, as Cohen has discussed (1997), Alexander would have been a worthy model for the growth of the Roman empire during the Hellenistic period. If the mosaic were commissioned by a Roman after the defeat of the Samnites, one could see it as an assertion of the new power of Rome as equivalent to that of Alexander. If commissioned by a Samnite before that, Alexander could be a metaphor for the victory of a smaller kingdom over a huge empire, whether Persian or Roman, making it potentially an image of resistance. In either case, one can see that the narrative of Alexander could and did have appeal throughout the Mediterranean world for both Greek and non-Greek peoples.

The Alexander Mosaic in Pompeii serves to remind us of the changing political and military situation during the Hellenistic period. By the time of its creation, Rome's empire included most of the Mediterranean and by the end of the first century would control all of its shores. The Romans began to establish control over the Greek cities of southern Italy and Sicily during the third century,

exedra
a recess or alcove set off from the main body of a structure like a stoa or colonnade

opus vermiculatum
a mosaic technique that uses small square (<4 mm) tiles or stones called tesserae to create patterns and images

***tessera* (pl. *tesserae*)**
small squares used to make patterns and pictures in an *opus vermiculatum* mosaic

chiaroscuro
Italian term referring to the use of a range of tones in an image to create the appearance of three-dimensionality. It can also refer to the strong contrast between light and dark in a work that enhances dramatic effect

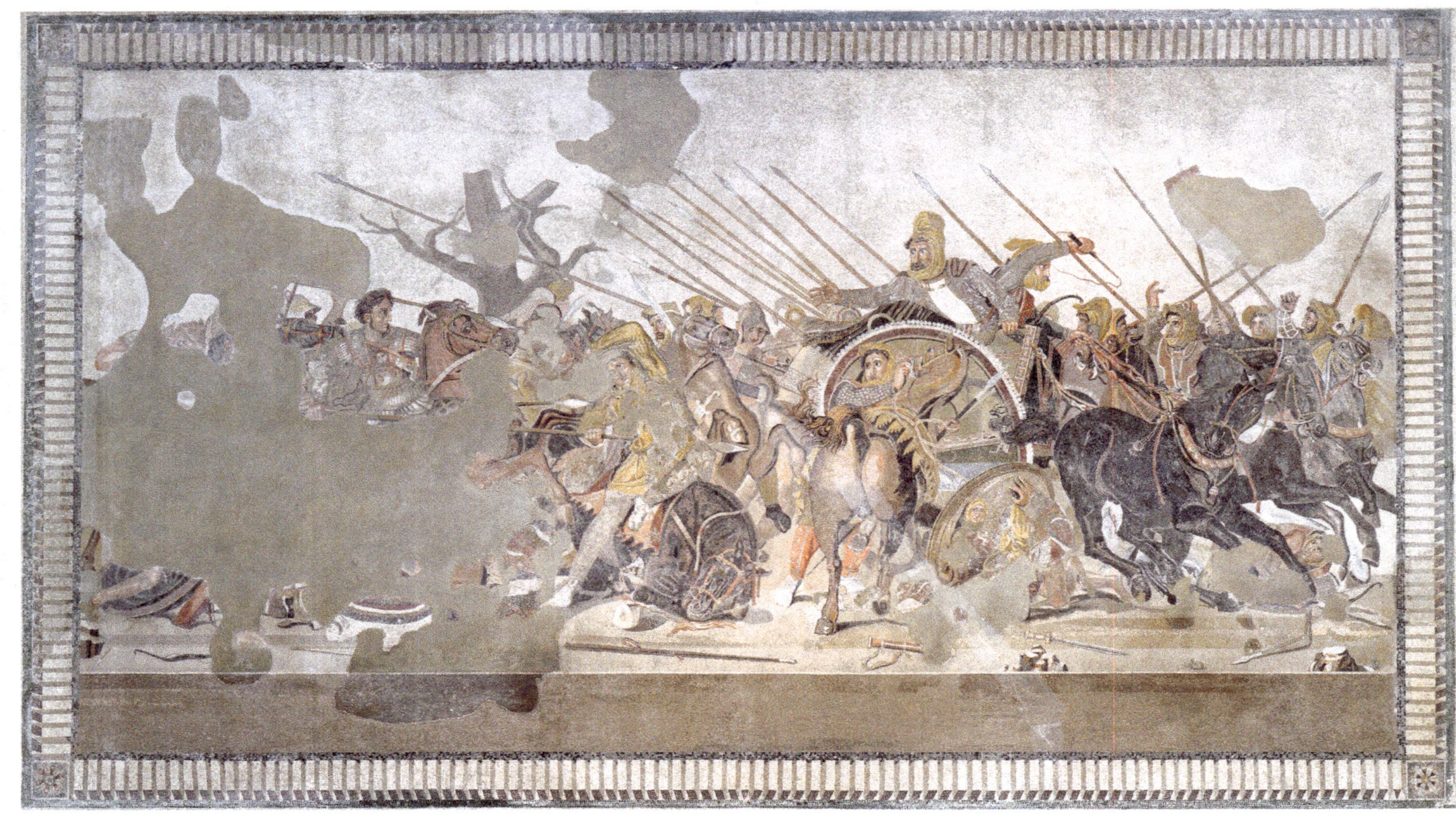

14.2 Alexander Mosaic from the House of the Faun, Pompeii, late 2nd–early 1st cent. BCE. Height of figure panel: 8 ft 10 11/16 in (2.71 m). Naples, Museo Nazionale Archeologico 10020. Battle between Alexander the Great and Darius. Photo: Scala/Ministero per i Beni e le Attività culturali/Art Resource, NY.

at the same time as they were fighting the Punic Wars with Carthage. During the late third century, the Romans conquered the Greek cities of Sicily, who were allied with the Carthaginians. Syracuse/Siracusa, the leading city of the Sicilian Greek poleis, was captured in 211 BCE, and in the subsequent sack of the city, the Romans brought many works of Greek art to Rome as trophies and booty. In 209, Rome sacked Taras/Taranto. After Rome destroyed Carthage itself in 202, it turned its attention to the Greek mainland. In Macedonia in northern Greece, Rome fought the successors of Alexander during the first half of the second century; this series of battles ended with the defeat of the Macedonian king Perseus at the Battle of Pydna in 168, bringing an end to the Macedonian kingdom. In southern Greece, many poleis had joined together in the Achaian League, a confederation that began in the early third century in the region of Achaia in the northern Peloponnesos, but expanded later to include most of the peninsula, including Corinth and Argos. The Romans defeated the Achaian League at the Battle of Corinth in 146, essentially completing their conquest of mainland Greece.

Alexander's conquest of Persia, the establishment of Greek kingdoms in the Near East and Egypt, and Rome's conquest first of the western Greek cities, then those of the mainland and Aegean, changed the geopolitical as well as cultural landscape in significant ways. Rather than a decentralized and shifting network of Greek cities and their neighbors, there were now kingdoms with more centralized control and patronage. Some of these trends are already apparent in the fourth century, but the scale and extent of the change are striking during the last three centuries of the millennium.

CHARACTERISTICS OF THE HELLENISTIC PERIOD

As we shall see in the discussion of Hellenistic sculpture below, it is difficult to divide the 300 years of the Hellenistic period into stylistic phases in order to illuminate its artistic developments. Multiple and diverse styles exist simultaneously, so that we cannot use style as reliably as a chronological marker and need to consider a work's expressive appeal. To approach the period, one needs to consider first what characteristics are common across styles, media, and geography that make Hellenistic art distinct from earlier periods of Greek art. As J. J. Pollitt has argued, there are five qualities that we should consider as fundamental to Hellenistic culture and its art (Pollitt 1986, 1–16).

Looking at the Alexander Sarcophagus and Alexander Mosaic as exemplars, one quality is the *cosmopolitan* character of Hellenistic culture. There were many new cities founded by the Greek rulers of the period, particularly in areas of Asia and Egypt where there had not been sizable Greek populations beforehand. While Greeks had founded many colonies starting in the eighth century BCE, the number of new sites was small during the classical period. In the Hellenistic period there was not only an increase in the number of new cities, there was also a substantial movement of people into the new cities. Some of these, like Alexandria in Egypt and Antioch in Asia Minor, were vastly larger than older major Greek cities like Athens or Syracuse/Siracusa. Just as Alexander had incorporated Persians and other nationalities into his court, the new cities had large and diverse populations of non-Greek residents, making them multicultural in their character.

As we saw in Chapter 12, fourth-century philosophy emphasized more universal characteristics of humanity, breaking down the identification with particular groups or the polis. The proclamation of Diogenes, the fourth-century Cynic philosopher, that he was a *kosmopolites*, or citizen of the world, becomes even more relevant in the time of Alexander and afterward. That Abdalonymos on his sarcophagus uses classicizing images of Alexander to proclaim his legitimacy as the ruler of Sidon is emblematic of this more multicultural outlook.

Along with cosmopolitanism, the Hellenistic age emphasized *individuality*. This, too, had its origins in fourth-century philosophers like Diogenes, but it was further developed by philosophical movements such as the Cynics, Stoics, and Epicureans, a new school founded by Epicurus (341–270 BCE). He argued that personal happiness was the object of life and that the individual should seek pleasure as a means for procuring happiness. Unlike modern notions of "Epicurean" indulgences in food and drink, his recommendations were actually for a more austere and ascetic lifestyle. In Hellenistic art one sees a greater range of emotions and behaviors being represented, and an interest in personalities like Alexander. The portrait becomes a more common subject for Hellenistic art as well.

Tyche
Greek goddess of fortune

Concurrent with individualism was a mental attitude that Pollitt has called an obsession with **Tyche**, the Greek personification of fortune (Fortuna in Latin). Writers and thinkers of the period emphasized how quickly the lives of humans could change, regardless of their virtue and accomplishments. Alexander is perhaps the ultimate individual favored by Tyche, as we see in the Alexander Mosaic, but more common were the examples of mighty figures, like Darius, who fell dramatically to defeat, disgrace, or death. Tyche spared none, and one can see that individuals would be concerned with trying to safeguard their own fate and would seek comfort in mystery cults that promoted the idea of a tranquil afterlife.

Hellenistic culture was also more *academic* than its predecessors, what Pollitt has termed a scholarly mentality. The libraries founded in Alexandria and Pergamon systematically collected the literature of the past and worked to restore literary masterpieces like the *Iliad* and *Odyssey* to their original state, free of corruptions in transmission, and to explain obscure language and characters. Philosophical schools collected the texts of their founders and sought to establish canonical views and interpretations. In art, we see the first real histories of art being compiled during this time (as we saw with Cicero's mini-history in Chapter 1), as well as an eclectic range of styles, some new and some old, that could exist side by side. As we shall see, Hellenistic artists produced works in a variety of older styles, including the archaic, Severe, classical, and Egyptian. The subject matter and purpose of a work of art served to determine the appropriate style to be used. It is during the Hellenistic period, too, that we find the production of systematic copies of works of art for elite patrons, like the Alexander Mosaic as a copy of an earlier painting.

Finally, we can also look at the increased importance of *theatricism* in Hellenistic art. We have already seen in classical art a theatrical element in the interaction of the viewer with an artwork, like the Tyrannicides, but the elements of staging and timing in subject matter and an emphasis upon dynamic movement and strong emotion greatly expand the dramatic as well as comic elements of Hellenistic art. Hellenistic art almost demands a viewer's direct response in a way that the Doryphoros never did. The world is now a stage in which art, architecture, and viewer interact more extensively and emotionally than they had in the past. Standing before the Alexander Mosaic, one can observe the thunderous charge of Alexander from the left side of the stage, sweeping everything before him, not just the speared figure, but Darius and the entire Persian army. In its original setting on the floor, one would have been standing on the plain where history was turning.

CITIES AND ARCHITECTURE

When Alexander died in Babylon in 323 BCE, there was no clear successor and his generals, called the Diadochi or "successors," fought with each other and divided the empire amongst themselves over the next quarter-century. Ptolemy appropriated the body of Alexander and took it to Egypt, there establishing the Ptolemaic dynasty that would last three centuries until the death of Cleopatra VII in 31. Seleukos took control of the Babylonian section of the Persian empire and by 301 had extended his control to Syria, where he founded the city of Antioch as a new capital in 300. Antipater had been viceroy in Europe and asserted control over Greece until his death in 319. Afterward his son Kassander defeated Alexander's mother Olympias for control of Macedon. Lysimachos was given Thrace, controlling the Black Sea area and, after 301, Asia Minor, until his death in battle in 281. One general, Antigonos, was the satrap of Phrygia in Asia Minor and after Antipater's death sought to reunify the entire Macedonian empire, a struggle that lasted until his death in battle in 301. Alexander's legacy was shifting Greek military and political control over a large, multicultural area from Greece to Afghanistan to Egypt.

Ptolemy initially took the body of Alexander to Memphis in Egypt, but later moved it and his capital to the new city of Alexandria, founded by the conqueror himself in 331 BCE. The city was laid out on a grid, with wide north–south and east–west avenues creating an X–Y axis dividing the city into quarters with a large agora at the center **(Figure 14.3)**. The island called Pharos protected the harbor and was connected to the city by a causeway, and on it was built the lighthouse of Alexandria, at least 300 feet (91.4 m) high and one of the seven wonders of the ancient world. The palace quarter ("Palast" on the plan) with its own harbor occupied the northeast section of the city, and there were numerous sanctuaries as well as a large park. The Temple of the Muses (Museion) housed the famous library of Alexandria where ancient literature was collected, studied, and edited. Estimates of the city's population range widely, but it probably had at least a half-million residents including slaves, making it double the size of Athens, which with Syracuse/Siracusa had been the largest Greek city of the classical period. The orthogonal plan of Alexandria follows some of the principles found in new Greek cities back in the archaic period, such as Poseidonia/Paestum **(see Figure 5.3, page 103)**, but its scale and that of Antioch were unprecedented.

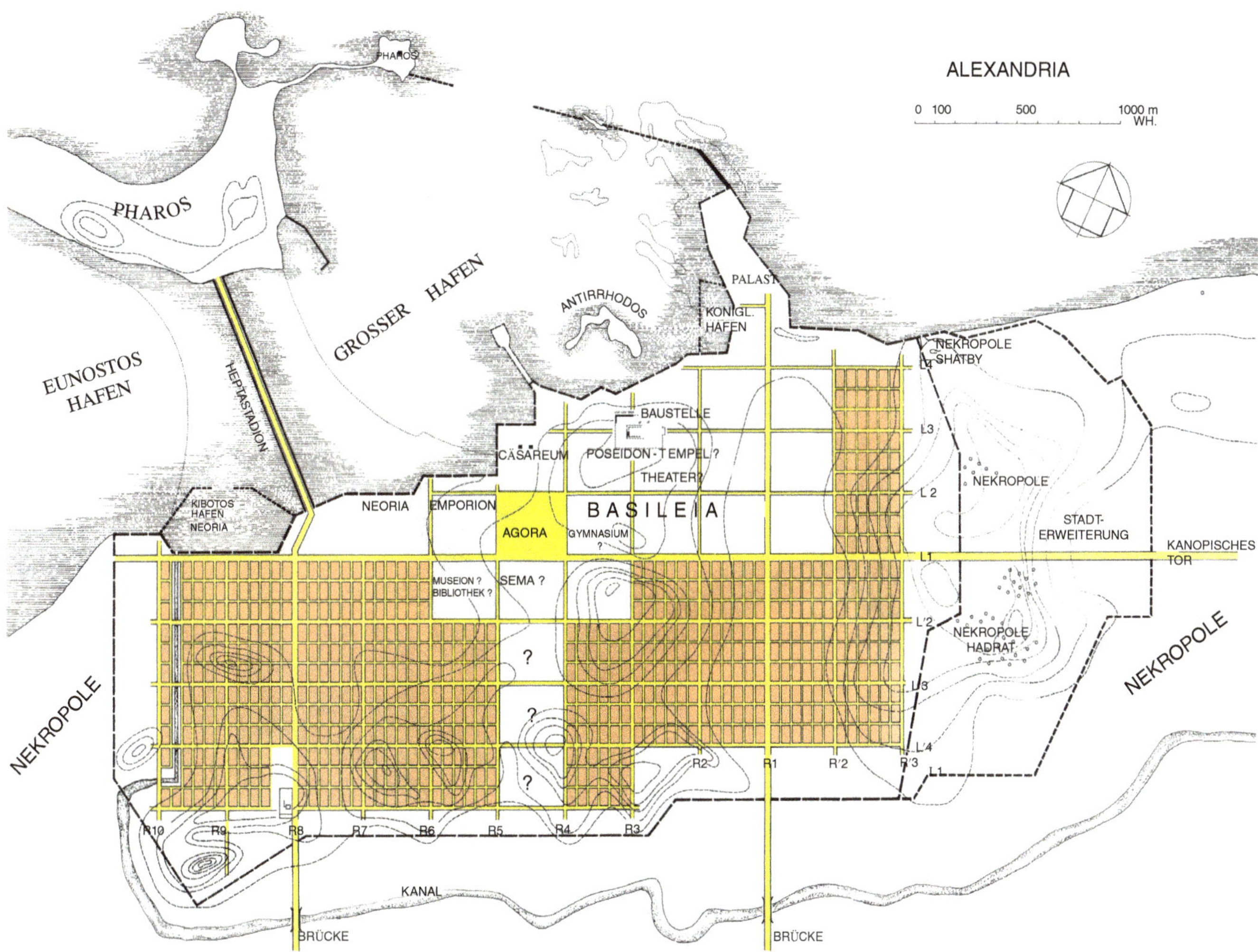

14.3 Plan of early Ptolemaic Alexandria, Egypt, 3rd cent. BCE. After W. Hoepfner and E.-L. Schwandner, *Haus und Stadt in klassischen Griechenland* (Berlin/Munich, 1994), Abb. 225 (drawing by authors). Used with permission of Hans Goette and the Deutsches Archäologisches Institut, Berlin.

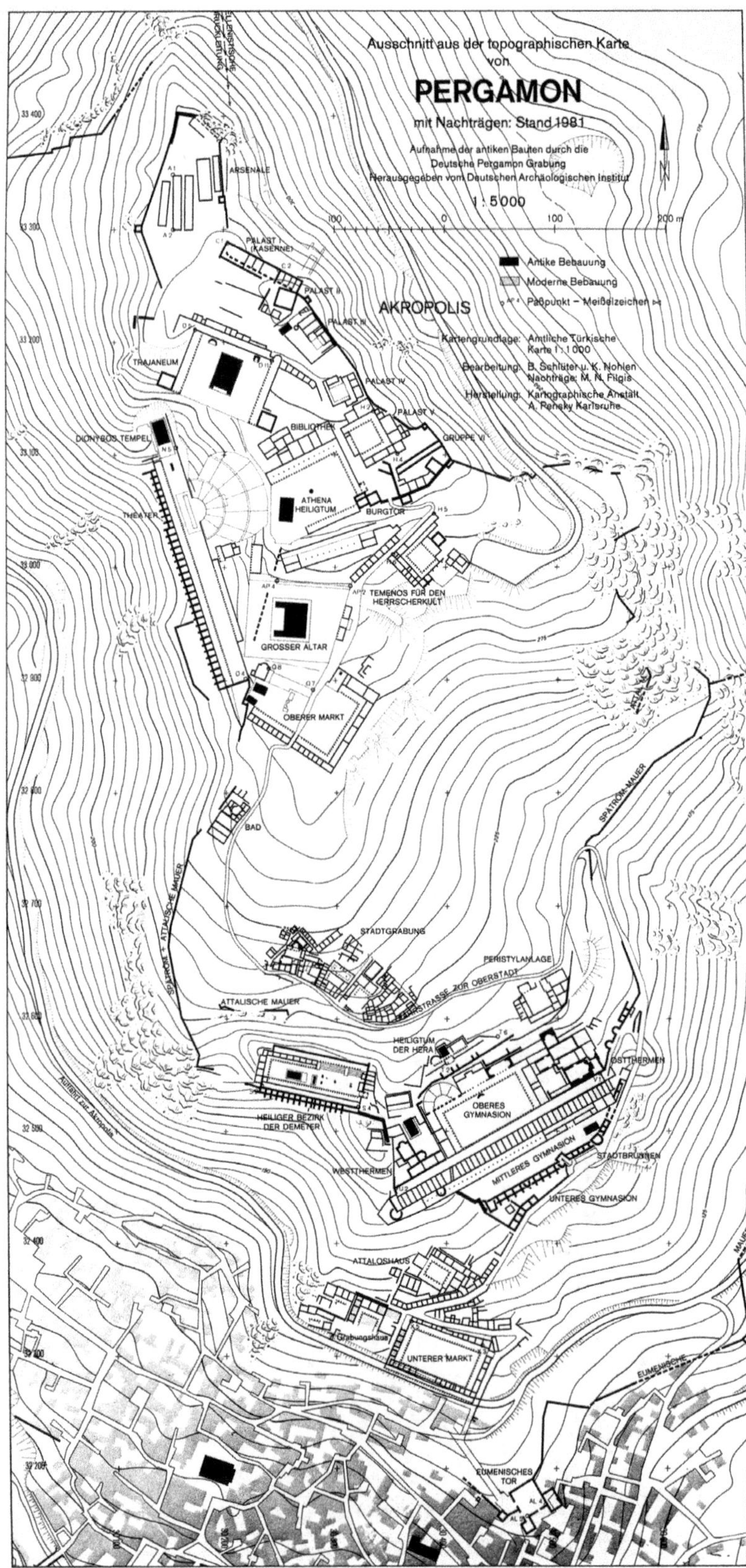

14.4 Plan of the acropolis at Pergamon, 3rd cent. BCE and later. After M. N. Filgis and W. Radt, *Die Stadtgrabung. Teil 1: Das Heroon, Altertümer von Pergamon* XV.1 (Berlin, 1986), Pl. 57, map by B. Schlüter, K. Nohlen, and M. H. Filgis. Used with permission of Hans Goette and the Deutsches Archäologisches Institut, Berlin.

Orthogonal grid planning was found at other sites, including Antioch and the much smaller town of Priene in Asia Minor **(see Figure 5.5, page 105)**. The grid here had to adapt to terrain that was more hilly than Alexandria or Antioch, but the east–west streets are able to maintain a usable grade while the north–south streets are much steeper and limited to pedestrian traffic.

Another city that rivaled Athens was Pergamon in Asia Minor. This was a small site that was built up by Philetairos, one of the generals of Lysimachos, who had entrusted Philetairos with the protection of his treasury of 9,000 talents. The steep terrain of the site was suitable for safeguarding this fortune, but following the death of Lysimachos in 281 BCE, Philetairos used the funds to turn Pergamon into an autonomous kingdom and to build up the city itself. He and his successors, particularly Attalos I (r. 241–197), Eumenes II (r. 197–158), and Attalos II (158–138), transformed the site into one of the most spectacular Hellenistic cities. The last Pergamene ruler, Attalos III (138–133), left the city to the Romans in his will. At the time, Pergamon was a royal city that rivaled Athens in both size and splendor, but Rome was less interested in further development of the city.

As can be seen in the plan of the city **(Figure 14.4)**, most of the monumental buildings were concentrated in the upper acropolis, which housed the palace and barracks along the highest ridge on the east and north sides. On the west side of the acropolis, facing the valley, large terraces lined with stoas were built that housed the library ("Bibliothek"), second only to Alexandria in importance **(Figure 14.5)**. Below these terraces, a large theater that could seat 10,000 spectators was cut into the steep bank and lined with a stoa more than 200 meters long that created a visual base for the vista. Access to the acropolis was at the southern foot of the mount ("Eumenisches Tor (Gate)"). The road led upward through a market to a middle city that featured a gymnasion and sanctuary of Demeter. From here, the road switched back and further up the mountain to reach the entrance to the upper city at a market just below the Great Altar. As can be seen in the plan and model, the main road through the acropolis twisted and turned along the summit until it reached the palace and barracks on the north.

The colonnaded terraces essentially served as stages for works like the Great Altar of Zeus **(Figure 14.6)**. That structure, now partially reconstructed in Berlin, had a monumental frieze almost 400 feet (121.9 m) long showing the Gigantomachy **(see Figure 9.4, page 215)**. While the altar is one of the major surviving works of Hellenistic architectural sculpture that we will discuss further below, Pergamon was filled with many sculptural groups commemorating its victories over the Gauls and others in the third century BCE. The lavish marble structures and terraces of the acropolis would have impressed visitors and viewers from below, long before they were able to progress though the gates at the bottom of the ridge into the city itself.

We have seen that Periklean Athens was conscious of the spectacle that its buildings created, and it is not surprising to find that the Pergamene kings also had connections to Athens as civic patrons. Several bronze groups commemorating mythological battles, called the Lesser Attalid dedication, were placed on the Acropolis, probably by Attalos I around 200 BCE, but possibly later by Attalos II. This second Attalos paid for the Stoa that bears his name in the Agora of Athens, which was reconstructed in the 1950s to house the Agora Museum and excavation facilities **(see Figure 5.6, page 105)**. Indeed, the effect of the Stoa of Attalos and the adjoining south stoas was to transform the somewhat irregular space of the classical agora into a more regular and monumental form with marble stoas in the Hellenistic period. By becoming significant patrons for buildings and art in Athens, the Pergamene kings asserted a claim not just to political control of their kingdom, but as cultural leaders in the broader Greek world with their city as a cultural capital.

The staging of architecture and landscape is found at other sites, such as the Asklepieion on the island of Kos (which had purchased the clothed statue of Aphrodite by Praxiteles, while neighboring Knidos bought the nude Aphrodite). Like the Asklepieion at Epidauros, that at Kos is outside of the city. Set on a hillside at the site of a spring, the sanctuary had a cypress grove as the sacred focal point. The earliest structures were located at what is now the second terrace, with a small temple and altar, and possibly an abaton for the healing process **(Figure 14.7)**. The cypress grove stood above this space,

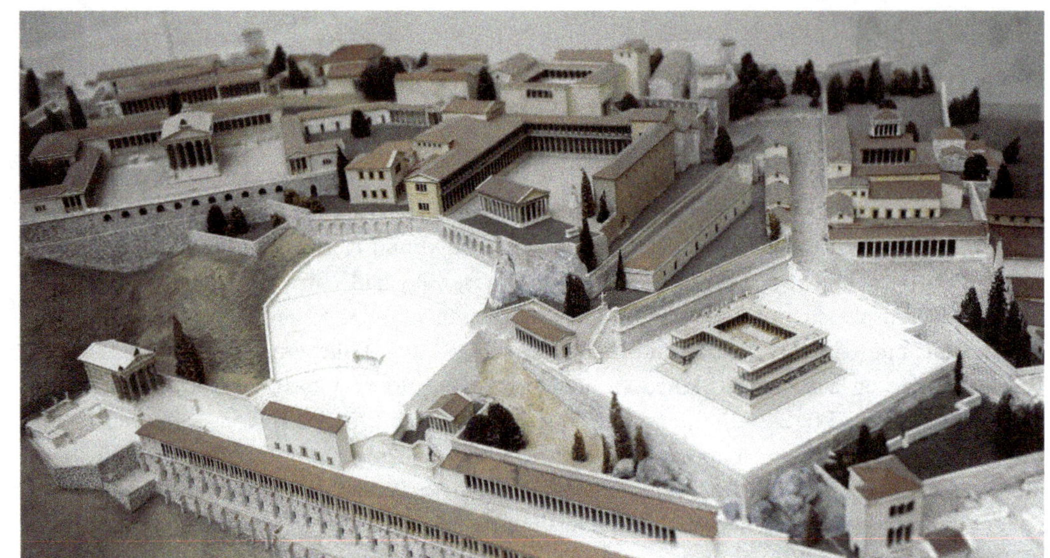

14.5 Model of Pergamon: view of western side of acropolis with Great Altar of Zeus to the right. Berlin, Pergamonmuseum. Photo: Album/Art Resource, NY.

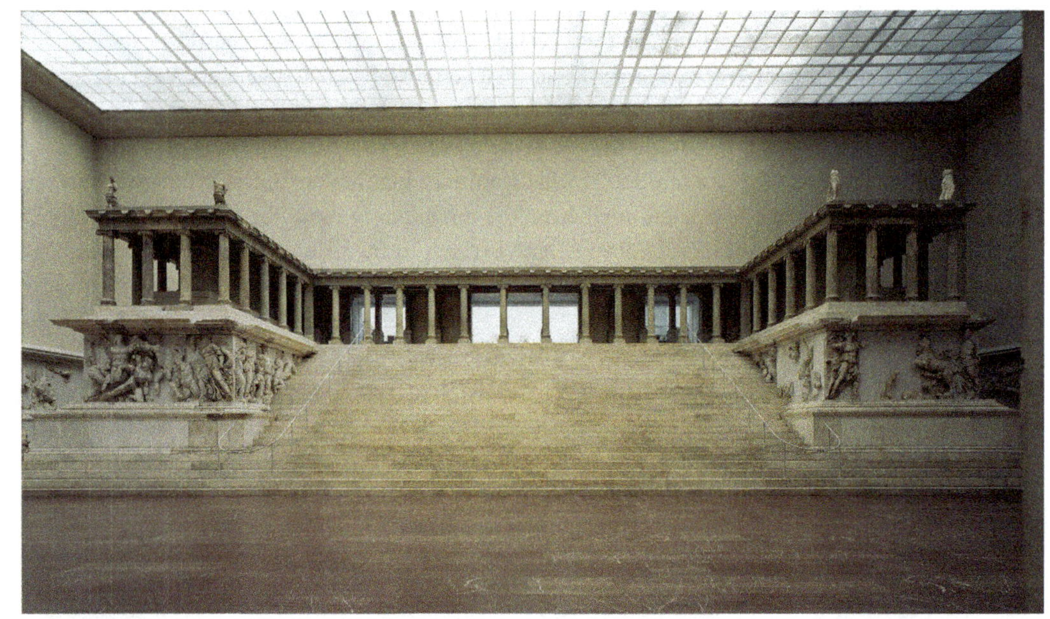

14.6 Great Altar of Zeus at Pergamon, *c.* 180–150 BCE, post-restoration 2004. Height of altar: 31 ft 8$^{5}/_{16}$ in (9.66 m). Berlin, Pergamonmuseum. Photo: bpk, Berlin/ Antikensammlung, Staatliche Museen/Johannes Jaurentius/Art Resource, NY.

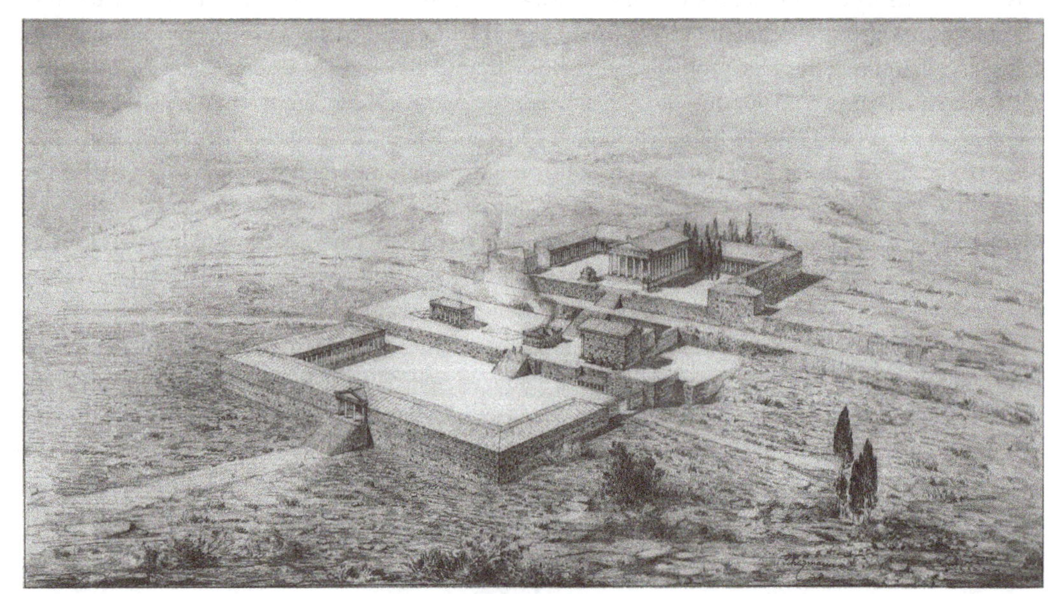

14.7 Asklepieion at Kos, *c.* 160 BCE. Reconstruction after P. Schazmann, *Akleopieion. Baubeschreibung und Baugeschichte, Kos* I (Berlin, 1932), pl. 40. Used with permission of Hans Goette and the Deutsches Archäologisches Institut, Berlin.

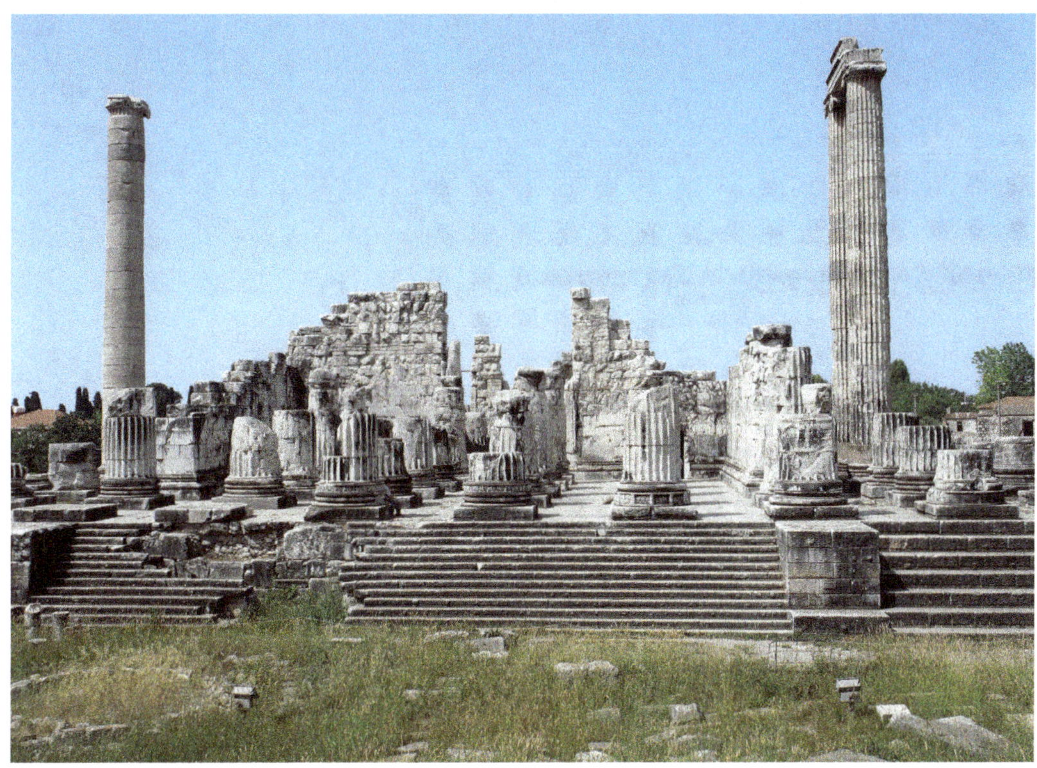

14.8 Temple of Apollo at Didyma, begun *c.* 300 BCE. Exterior with stairs leading to pronaos. Photo: Album/ Art Resource, NY.

framed by a wooden portico. Around 175–150 BCE, the upper terrace was rebuilt with new marble stoas framing a large temple in front of the cypress grove; a large marble staircase created a processional axis through the space. The result of this construction was to transform the sanctuary's organization of space to a longitudinal axis and make it more symmetric than it had been before. This offers a sharp contrast to the twisting and turning processional paths at sanctuaries like Delphi, Olympia, and the Acropolis at Athens. The new temple would have been visible over the roof of the lower terrace and propylon, making it a constant visual goal for the visitor to the sanctuary seeking the healing power of Asklepios.

Theatricism in religious architecture consists not just of framing vistas, but also of creating unexpected encounters for the visitor and enhancing the dramatic potential of the supplicant seeking healing or a prophecy. The cult of Apollo at Didyma had been famous in the archaic period for an important oracle; this had been destroyed by the Persians in 494 BCE and its priests sent into exile. The cult was revived by Alexander the Great and its cult image returned from Persia by Seleukos, who began construction of a new temple around 300 (**Figure 14.8**). At 51.1 meters wide and 109.3 meters long, it is one of the largest Ionic temples. The building has a double colonnade and its columns, 19.7 meters high, were the tallest that have ever been found in Greek architecture. Work on the building was protracted and continued through the Hellenistic period, but the building was never finished.

The temple's base consisted of seven huge steps, elevating the platform about 4 meters above the ground. A smaller set of more normally sized steps was set on the main axis and led to a pronaos (**Figure 14.9**). At the monumental door between the pronaos and naos, however, the floor rises about 1.5 meters, barring entrance. Beyond the threshold was not a naos but a small room with three openings to the exterior opposite the door that is best described as an elevated porch. A second set of steps led down from this porch into the interior of the temple, which was an open courtyard housing a small temple with four columns in antis (**Figure 14.10**). This small structure housed the spring where the priestess gave the oracle; the interior stairs provided access to the porch for the priests, who could use the porch as a stage to make pronouncements to visitors assembled in the pronaos. Actual access to the courtyard and small temple from the pronaos was via small doorways set near the corners of the pronaos; these doors led to a barrel-vaulted sloping tunnel that went down

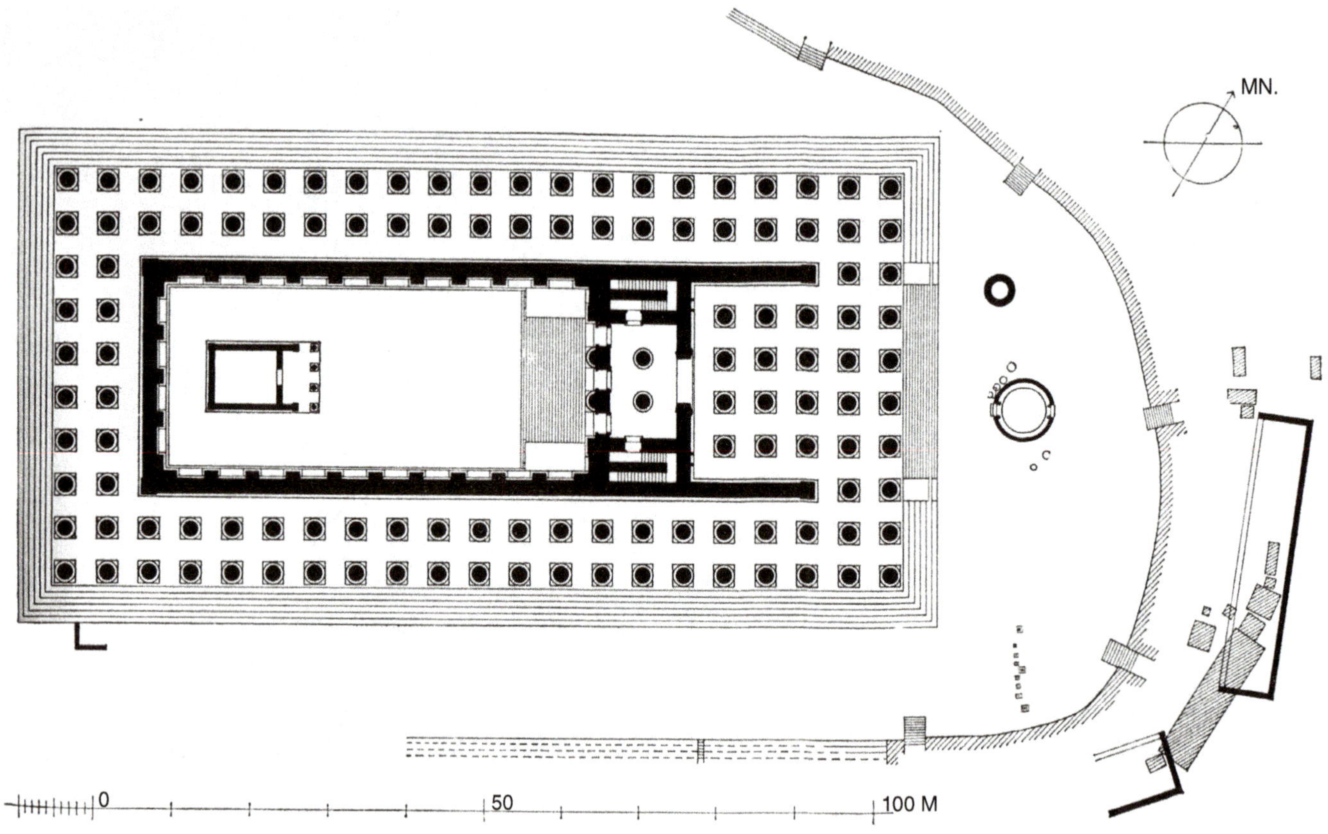

14.9 Temple of Apollo at Didyma, begun *c.* 300 BCE. Plan. After H. Berve and G. Gruben, *Greek Temples, Theaters, and Shrines* (New York: Harry N. Abrams, 1963), p. 463, fig. 129. Used with permission of Hirmer Verlag.

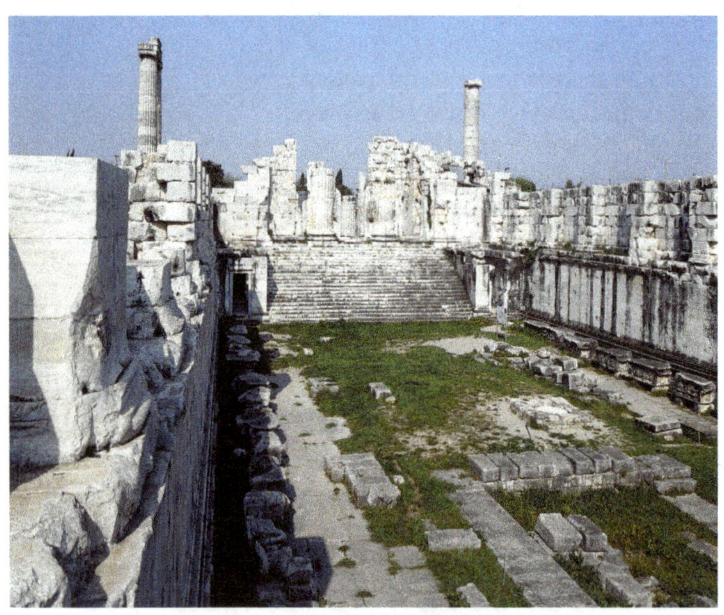

14.10 Temple of Apollo at Didyma, begun *c.* 300 BCE. Interior. Photo: Marie Mauzy/Art Resource, NY.

to the ground level of the interior courtyard. At the bottom, the doors emerged into corners of the courtyard at the foot of the interior stairs. The net effect for a visitor would be to go from the light area outside the temple into a shaded but well-lit porch, and from there into a dark, narrow, descending space that emerged once more into the sunlight, but now inside the building and looking at a building within a building.

Much of Hellenistic temple architecture was less theatrical and followed more closely the norms established in previous centuries. One architect, Hermogenes of Priene, who was active in the late third and early second centuries, was noted by Vitruvius for his refinements of the rules of proportions and symmetry, but only fragments of his temple at Magnesia survive. Indeed, there had always been elements of theatricism associated with religious performances and their sites, and grid planning was nothing new for city planning. What is different in Hellenistic architecture is a wider variation with the schema of Greek architecture and a greater manipulation of scale and viewing points to create effective and affective vistas and experiences. Like the architectural program of Periklean Athens, large financial resources were needed for lavish and monumental architecture. In the Hellenistic age resources were more readily available through royal and elite patrons, who were willing to expend significant funds to exercise individual or dynastic agency through the creation of impressive monuments.

SCULPTURAL STYLES AND DATING

The diversity of style that we saw in fourth-century sculpture becomes much more pronounced in the Hellenistic period. Given the relatively few works that can be precisely dated, this stylistic variety means that Hellenistic sculpture is difficult to discuss in terms of its chronological development. The choice of style for individual works seems more connected to its subject matter, type, function, and context, so we will explore Hellenistic sculpture more thematically than in previous chapters.

The sculpture recovered from two shipwrecks illustrates well the issues and variety of Hellenistic styles and dating. We have already seen one work, the fourth-century bronze youth recovered from the shipwreck at Antikythera, an island halfway between Crete and the southeast coast of the Peloponnesos (**see Figure 12.7, page 295**). Based on its cargo, the date of the shipwreck is generally set around 80 BCE, so it is probable that this statue had been taken from a site, whether by looting or other form of appropriation, and was being shipped westward, perhaps to Italy where so much fifth- and fourth-century Greek sculpture was sent following Roman conquests. There were other fourth-century bronze works in the Antikythera cargo, but there were also several marble copies of classical works, including one of the Aphrodite of Knidos (**compare Figure 12.11, page 300**), that were probably produced not long before being placed on the ship. By the early first century the number of classical originals to be had was undoubtedly shrinking, and workshops began producing neoclassical copies or adaptations to meet continuing demand for sculpture.

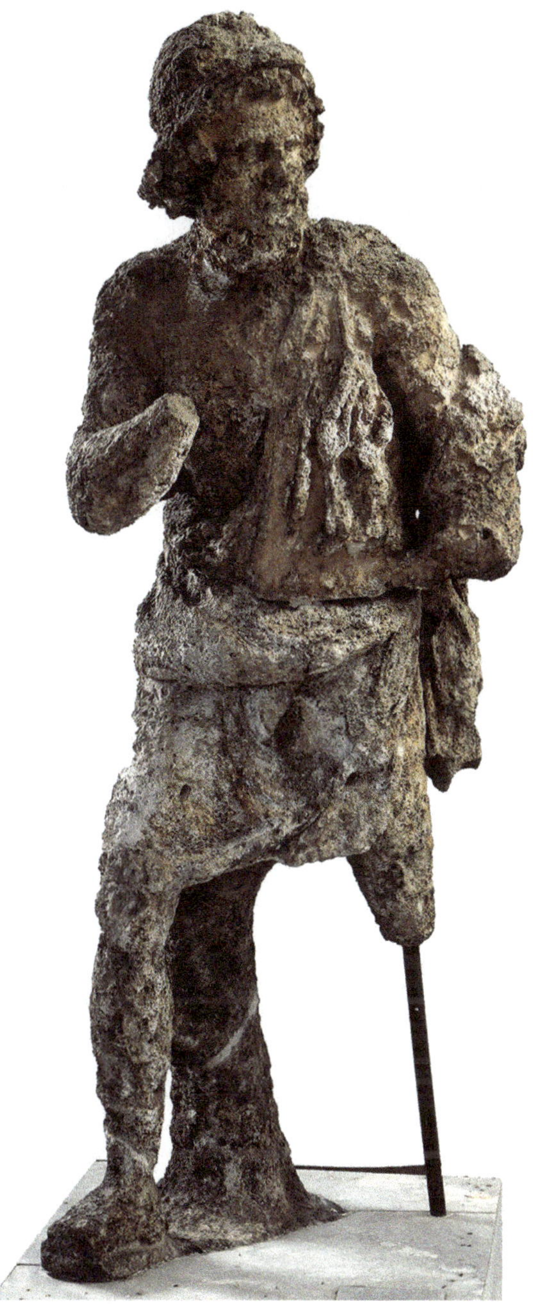

14.11 Odysseus from Antikythera shipwreck, first quarter of 1st cent. BCE. 6 ft $7^{15}/_{16}$ in (2.03 m). Athens, National Archaeological Museum 5745. Photo: National Archaeological Museum, Athens (Kostas Xenikakis) © Hellenic Ministry of Education and Religious Affairs, Culture and Sports/Archaeological Receipts Fund.

The Antikythera cargo included several marble statues that are identified as Trojan War heroes, such as the figure of Odysseus (**Figure 14.11**). Trojan themes became popular for large sculptural ensembles in the first century, especially among the Romans, who traced their origins back to the Trojan prince Aeneas, who had escaped from the destruction of Troy and came with his son to Italy via Carthage. While the Odysseus statue has endured much damage from exposure to the ocean environment, one can still see that the composition is more dynamic than much of classical sculpture. Odysseus has a wide striding pose and looks back over his shoulder. The statue was likely part of a group that enacted a dramatic moment in a Trojan episode, perhaps the stealing of the Palladion, the cult statue of Athena in her temple at Troy. The figure does not move in a single direction across a flat plane, but looks in one direction while moving in another on a fully three-dimensional stage. The composition uses more diagonals in the positioning of torso and limbs, creating an asymmetry and tension in the figure that add to its drama. Sculptural ensembles are not new, and it is possible that the Riace

Warriors belonged to such a grouping, but whereas there might be some psychological tension with those figures, they are not vigorously acting out a dramatic moment in the way that the Antikythera figures would as part of an ensemble.

While the stylistic details of the statue are hard to read because of the erosion and damage, it resembles works in the so-called **baroque style** of Hellenistic art. The term, deriving from the name used to describe seventeenth-century European art and artists like Caravaggio, Rubens, and Rembrandt, emphasizes the strong contrast of light and dark, the use of diagonals, and dramatic poses and expressions, and is applied to works like the Pergamon altar **(see Figure 9.4, page 215)**. The term, like Daedalic for seventh-century sculpture, is problematic but appears frequently in the literature and does have a descriptive value. Dating the Antikythera Odysseus on the basis of style, however, is difficult because it, like the contemporary classical-style copies on the same ship, was being produced by workshops for clients across the Mediterranean, and perhaps even by the same workshop. Essentially, a theatrical or baroque style was used for a dramatic narrative, while a neoclassical style was used for a replica of Aphrodite that was likely seen on its own, not as part of an ensemble.

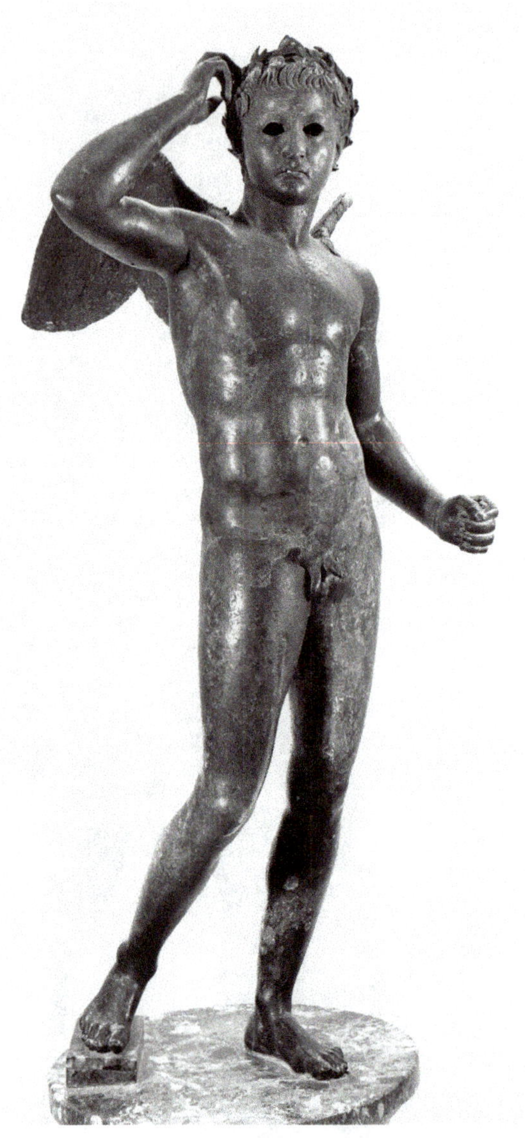

14.12 Eros (once called Agon) from Mahdia shipwreck, late 2nd–early 1st cent. BCE. Bronze, 4 ft 7⅛ in (1.40 m). Tunis, Bardo F106. Photograph: D-DAI-ROM-Neg. 61.436.

A second shipwreck at Mahdia, on the coast of Tunisia, probably dates to a decade or two after the Antikythera shipwreck, about 70–60 BCE. Its cargo was also quite varied, and included large marble kraters **(compare Figure 11.11, page 280)** and architectural elements, including capitals with chimera motifs and Ionic columns made in Athens. There were also classicizing marble statues, an archaistic bronze herm of Dionysos, and several bronze statues. One of these, an Eros (once identified as "Agon" or the personification of athletic competition), is a classicizing statue **(Figure 14.12)**. It bears some similarities to the work of Polykleitos or some of the youths on the Parthenon frieze **(compare Figure 1.1, page 2)**, but there is an exaggeration in the curve of the limbs and torso and a softer quality to the musculature that suggest a Hellenistic date.

In the same cargo was a series of small dancing dwarves that are in a more dramatic style, with extended limbs and strong diagonal composition that would have been completely unstable in stone **(Figure 14.13)**. The facial expression is more animated than the Eros and while the musculature does not bulge like that of the giants of the Pergamon altar or the Antikythera Odysseus, the multiple directions of movement and gaze have a similar three-dimensionality. The widespread interest in a non-ideal type of figure, a dwarf that by definition does not meet the idealized canon of proportions of the Doryphoros, is new in sculpture during the Hellenistic period, although not in other media like vase painting. The combination of subject matter and dance movement is often labeled **rococo** to distinguish a lighter type of theatrical style than the baroque. Rococo sculpture has many elements of the baroque, such as strong movement and diagonals, but the subject matter is lighter, more humorous, or erotic. Analysis of the bronze core of one of the dwarves, no. F215, shows that its materials are very similar to the Eros statue, suggesting that both the classicizing and rococo bronzes of the Mahdia cargo might have been made in the same workshop. Their differences in style, scale,

baroque style
style of Hellenistic sculpture defined by its dynamic compositions using diagonal lines, exaggerated musculature and poses, powerful emotional expression, and strong contrast of light and dark

and composition suggest that a workshop was not limited to a single style in its production at this time. Whether the bronzes were made at the same time as the architectural elements, which had likely been commissioned for a specific building project and must date to around the time of the shipwreck, or were somewhat older "antiques" dating around 100 BCE, is unclear, but certainly clients had eclectic interests in subject matter and styles that workshops and dealers supplied.

The Antikythera and Mahdia shipwrecks speak to a change in the production and consumption of sculpture in the Hellenistic period. Whereas raw materials and nearly finished sculpture had been transported long distances in the archaic and classical periods, the extent to which both materials and sculptors moved about in the Hellenistic period was larger. Athens remained an important center of production, particularly for works in a classicizing style, and much of its production was shipped to Roman clients in the Mediterranean. In light of this, the date of other works found at sea, like the Riace Bronzes **(see Figure 10.5, page 241)**, is open to question. As discussed in the textbox for this chapter, it is possible that the Riace Bronzes are not fifth-century originals but first-century works made for the Hellenistic market.

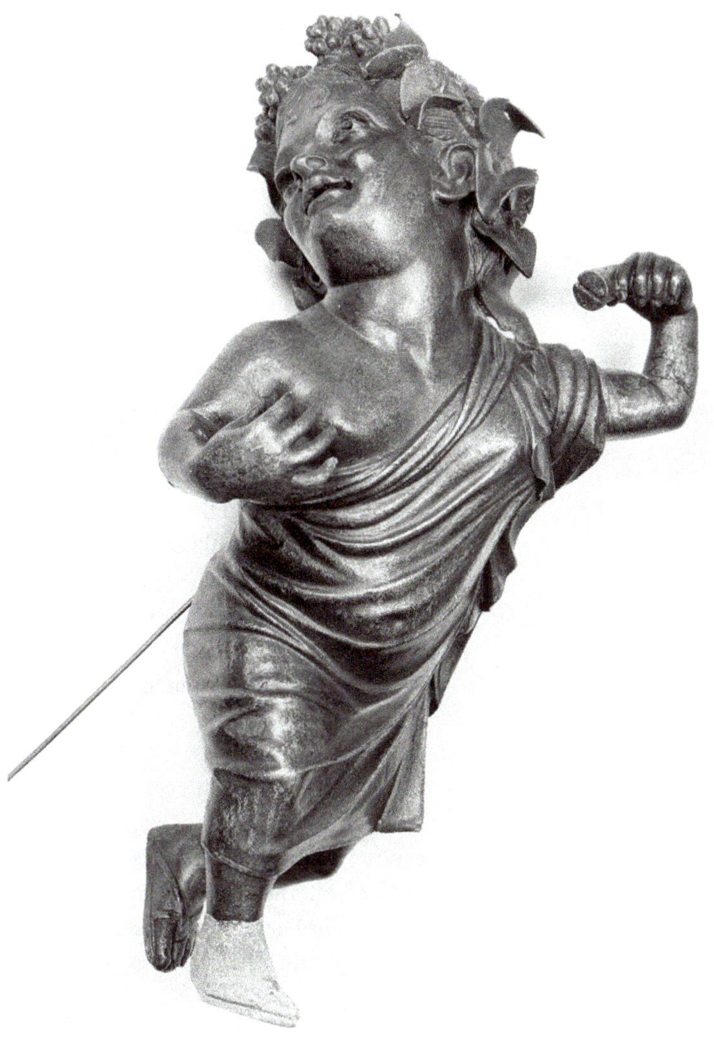

14.13 "Dancing Dwarf" from Mahdia shipwreck, late 2nd–early 1st cent. BCE. Bronze, 12⅜ in (31.5 cm). Tunis, Bardo F215. Photograph: D-DAI-ROM-Neg. 61.455.

Indeed, the Roman empire became a crucial factor in Hellenistic art, in part through political events and in part through patronage. During the late third century, the Roman sacking of Syracuse/Siracusa, one of the greatest classical Greek cities in size and artistic importance, and two years later of Taras/Taranto saw large quantities of Greek art taken to Rome and to the villas and houses of its leaders as trophies and booty. Indeed, Rome became flooded with Greek art, a trend that continued as Rome turned its attention to the Greek mainland in the second century. The sack of Corinth in 146 brought yet more works to Rome, and the Roman taste for Greek work provided a steady demand that was met by the production of new works in classicizing and other styles, as the Antikythera and Mahdia shipwrecks demonstrate.

In approaching Hellenistic sculpture, then, we shall consider format and subject matter more than chronology and stylistic development as we have done in other chapters. We will begin with the more dramatic styles typically used in narrative sculpture, to which the term baroque has often been applied. A more private and light-hearted version of the style, often called rococo, should also be viewed as part of a theatrical mode of sculpture like the baroque. Whereas commemorative sculpture in the form of grave monuments and votive statues is not unusual, there is a new effort to represent a more lifelike and realistic version of individuals that becomes, at least on a royal level, true portraiture in the Hellenistic period in a style that is often labeled realistic. The sacred continues to be an important subject for sculpture and cult statues continue to be made, but there are several different styles associated with this context, including a neoclassical (or classicizing), **neo-severe (severizing)** style, and **neo-archaic (archaizing)** style, as well as more theatrical compositions.

rococo
style of Hellenistic sculpture named after European rococo art and characterized by lighter or erotic themes and a more decorative or humorous than dramatic appeal

neo-severe style or severizing
term for sculpture that imitates qualities of the Severe Style of the early classical period but was produced in later periods

THEATRICISM AND NARRATIVE

We noted earlier the prominent placement of the Great Altar of Zeus at Pergamon, and the sculptural program from the building is one of the most significant of the Hellenistic period, both as an example of the baroque style and for providing grounds for dating **(see Figure 14.6)**. A fragmentary inscription, BASILISS(A) or queen, refers to Apollonis as queen mother and therefore links the structure to one of her sons, Eumenes II (r. 197–158 BCE) or Attalos II (158–138). Whether work began after the Battle of Apamea in 188, which confirmed Attalid rule over Pergamon, or after the wars with the Gauls in 168–166, is less certain, although the subject of the exterior frieze, a Gigantomachy, is likely meant to symbolize an important victory. An interior frieze lining the court at the top of the steps shows the life of Telephos, son of Herakles and the mythological ancestor of the dynasty. The central section of the monument was not finished, suggesting a *terminus ante quem* of 133, when the last Pergamene king, Attalos III, transferred the kingdom to Roman rule on his death. Work likely took a couple of decades for completion, and the signatures of at least fifteen sculptors survive from the Gigantomachy frieze, confirming that a large workshop was organized for the project. Taking all of this into account, a date of 180–150 BCE is usually assigned to the altar and it is considered to be a victory monument in a manner analogous to the Parthenon three centuries earlier.

As noted in Chapter 9 (see page 214), the Gigantomachy frieze is monumental in scale and wraps completely around the altar. It is first approached from its back and leads the viewer around the side and up the steps at the front **(see Figure 9.4, page 215; Figure 14.5)**. The nude giants have dramatically diagonal poses, with limbs and bodies frequently moving in different directions. The musculature is exaggerated in size and bulging; deep drilling and undercutting create a strong contrast between light and dark. The faces are rendered with worry lines, recessed eyes, and open mouths that capture the pathos of attacked figures. The faces of the gods are smoother and more serene yet still focused, but the undercutting of their drapery and their lunging poses give them decisive movement and action. These are figures that do not seem frozen in a pose, but stopped in an instant of motion, and this quality distinguishes the baroque style.

There is certainly an element of theatricism and viewer engagement with the Pergamon altar. Whereas architectural sculpture is often at some distance above a viewer and, outside of pediments, usually smaller than life-size in scale, the Gigantomachy frieze is 2.3 meters high, making its figures even larger than heroic-scale statues like the Doryphoros. Sitting only about 3 meters above the ground and carved in very deep, three-quarter relief, these figures, especially the giants, seem as if they are about to spill out into the viewer's immediate space, and indeed share the space as the steps mount toward the entrance above **(see Figure 9.4, page 215)**.

The baroque or theatrical style seems particularly well suited to narrative subjects, as we see in the poses of the Trojan War figures from the Antikythera shipwreck **(see Figure 14.11)** and also in the figures from the grotto at Sperlonga that we saw in Chapter 11 **(see page 281 and Figures 11.14 and 11.15, page 283)**. These five sculptural groups were made by three Hellenistic sculptors from the island of Rhodes, Hagesandros, Athenodoros, and Polydoros. The style of the sculptures is very similar to the Pergamon altar, and this has led to controversy over dating the Sperlonga ensemble, which was clearly made for the specific site. Were these three artists second-century artists in Rhodes whose work was copied in the first century for the grotto, or were they Greek artists working in the middle of the first century for Roman clients, probably the imperial family, using a style like that of the Pergamon altar? On the whole, the latter alternative seems more plausible, but the debate shows that the theatrical style had a lasting appeal throughout the Hellenistic period.

Another well-known example of this theatrical style is the Nike of Samothrace, dramatically placed today near the top of a long staircase in the Musée du Louvre **(Figure 14.14)**. Here its position recreates to some degree its original placement in an open-ended cella above the seats of the theater

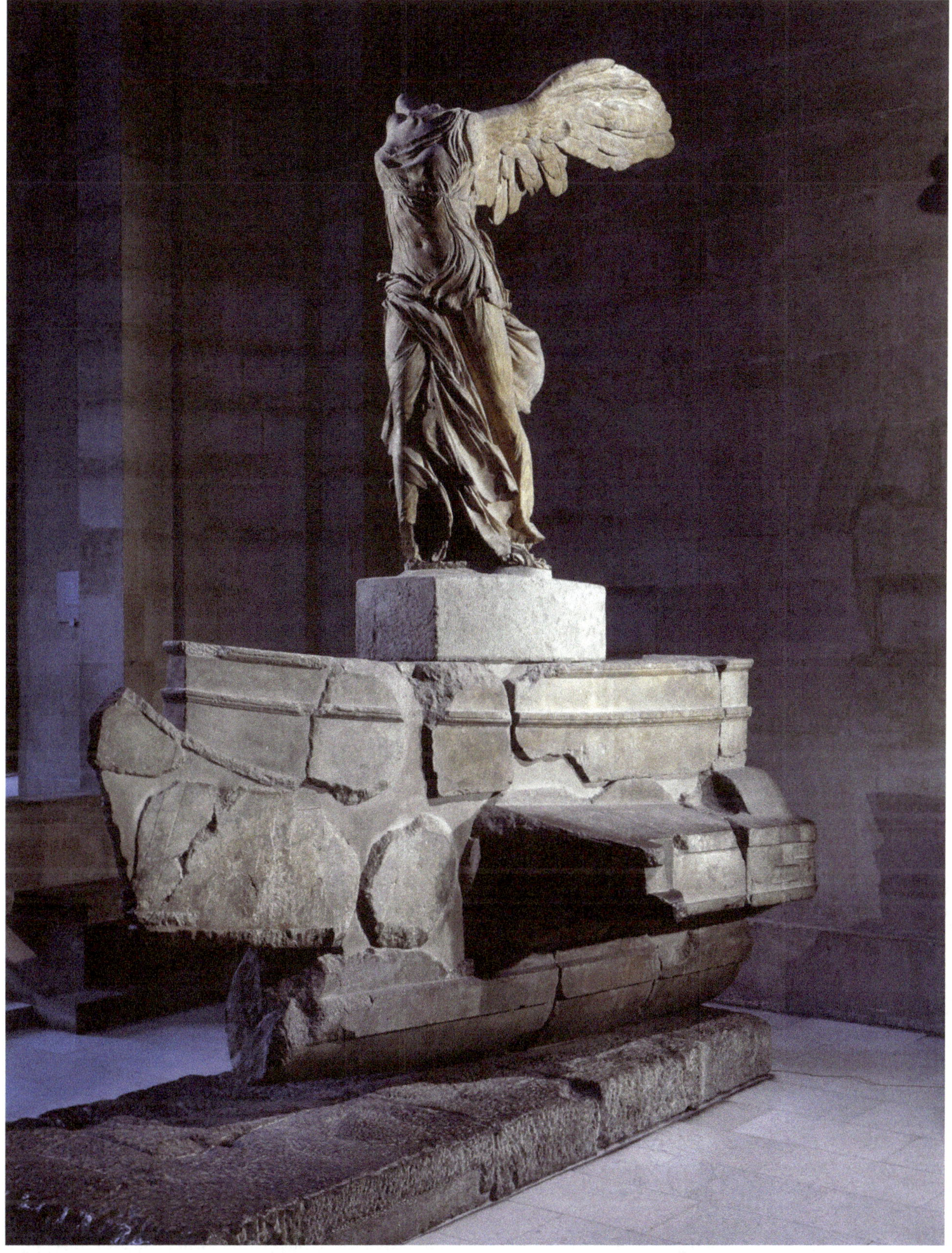

14.14 Nike of Samothrace, later 3rd–early 2nd cent. BCE. Height of figure: 8 ft ½ in (2.45 m). Paris, Musée du Louvre MA2369. Photo: Gianni Dagli Orti/The Art Archive at Art Resource, NY.

at the sanctuary of the Great Gods on the island of Samothrace. The original viewing points of the figure would have been limited by its enclosure walls, but a view of its left side would have been available to many of those below in the theater or walking toward it, or at the same level to those in the nearby stoa dedicated by the Ptolemies. The figure itself is 2.45 meters high and set on the prow of a ship, making the total height over 5.5 meters. The marble pavement of the floor of the enclosure was carved to represent rippling water, and the effect suggests that Nike has landed on the prow of the ship as it sails, with the result that her drapery is whipped around and behind her from the speed of both her flight and the ship moving forward on the sea.

The effect of wind-blown drapery is similar to the Nike by Paionios at Olympia from the late fifth century **(see Figure 10.8, page 245)**. Here, too, the drapery pulls tight against the body in front and billows behind, and the pose is one in which the feet point down to alight, conferring victory at that instant. Indeed, it has been argued that the roots of the Hellenistic baroque can be found in classical works like this, and in some ways the heavier drapery of the Nike of Samothrace and her more firmly planted feet make it seem less dramatic. Whereas the right hand of the Olympia Nike is thought to have held a branch to award victory, the 1950 discovery of the hand of the Samothrace Nike shows that it was not holding anything, but held her palm outward.

Indeed, there has been some doubt as to whether this is a victory monument as was originally thought, since there is no dedication to tie it to a specific patron or battle. Andrew Stewart has suggested that we should look at the monument metaphorically, as a Ship of State, with the goddess bringing the boat safely into harbor and greeting those in the harbor (Stewart 1993). Conversely, with the ship pointed north, it faces the sea as if sailing out and we could look at it metaphorically as an embarkation. Whether or not the monument commemorates a victory affects estimates for its date. The marble of the ship is from the island of Rhodes and an inscription found nearby preserves the last letter of the name of someone from Rhodes, so it has been seen as a Rhodian monument, perhaps for its victory in the battles of Myonnesos and Side in 190–189 BCE. The statue itself is made of marble from Paros, so the source of the marble is not sufficient alone to attribute the patronage of the statue. Disassociating it from a Rhodian victory, recent scholarship has tended to date the sculpture a generation earlier, to the late third century.

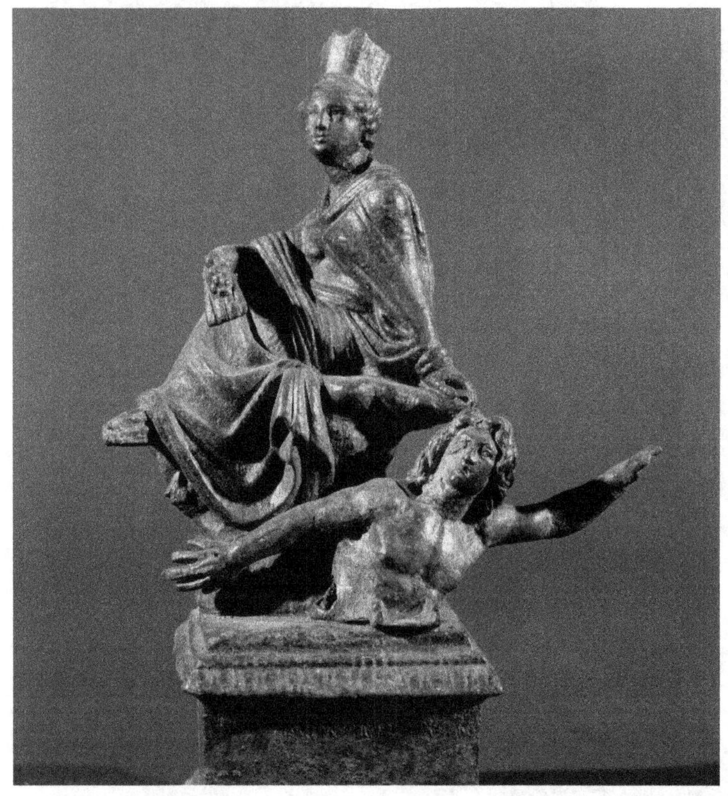

14.15 Bronze figure of Tyche of Antioch, 1st–2nd cent. CE Roman copy in bronze after the original by Eutychides, shortly after 300 BCE. Height of figures, 4½ in (11.5 cm). Paris, Musée du Louvre Br. 4453. Photo: Erich Lessing/Art Resource, NY.

Another example of a dynamic personification in sculpture belongs to the beginning of the third century, when the sculptor Eutychides was commissioned to make a Tyche for the new city of Antioch, founded in 300 BCE by Seleukos I as the capital of his Levantine empire. The original bronze sculpture must have been made shortly after 300 and no longer exists, but later copies in marble and at a smaller scale in bronze, coins, and glass attest to the main features of the work and its enduring appeal as a personification of both a city and fortune **(Figure 14.15)**. The original figure was set on a rock, at the base of which the river god Orontes sprung forth with open arms. Tyche herself forms a pyramid created by her bent and crossed legs and arms. She wears a wall crown, a symbol of the walls protecting a city and also an attribute of Cybele, a fertility/mother goddess from Anatolia, pointing to the syncretism of Hellenistic religion. Originally Tyche held a palm branch in her right hand, a symbol of victory for

Greeks but also of abundance and prosperity for a Near Eastern audience. Eutychides, a student of Lysippos, created a work that is an elaborate metaphor for the great fortune that the new capital city hoped to achieve, and Antioch did quickly become one of the great cities of the Hellenistic and later Roman worlds. While not set as a narrative, the theatrical presentation of metaphor, of a goddess resting on the heights of a city and protecting it, creates a dynamic and engaging work. Indeed, the elaborate symbolism and metaphor are part of the intellectual mentality of Hellenistic culture that could appeal meaningfully to its varied audiences.

A theatrical approach to sculpture does not have to be full of angst and can include lighter-hearted representations as well. The dwarves from the Mahdia shipwreck (**see Figure 14.13**) share the same use of diagonal and unbalanced arrangement of the body, extended limbs, and sharply turned head that we see in the Tyche of Antioch or Odysseus from the Antikythera shipwreck, but the subject matter is now dance and an unusual type of physique. Given their smaller scale, these works were intended for a more private and intimate type of setting like a garden or villa, as were the many Neoattic marble kraters made at this time and also included in the Mahdia cargo. Such figures might seem comic to our eye at first, and dwarves were often part of burlesque scenes in earlier Attic vase painting, but we should be wary of concluding that a Hellenistic or Roman viewer would also see them in that way, particularly dancing figures that might be part of a religious festival in which their otherness might also signify a sacred quality.

The label rococo could also be applied to a small marble statue group found on the island of Delos (**Figure 14.16**). Delos had become a free port in 166 BCE, a place where merchants from Rome, Greece, and the Near East gathered and conducted business; over the next eighty years there was energetic building activity that included sculptural, fresco, and mosaic decoration in both public and private buildings. The Poseidoniastes of Berytos, a club of Syrian merchants, built a complex that included both shrines and residential areas. In a long room of the residential section of their complex, constructed just before 100, was found the under-life-size sculpture known as the "slipper-slapper" group: Aphrodite raises a slipper toward the god Pan as an Eros hovers between them. An inscription tells us that a Syrian, "Dionysos son of Zenon, son of Theodoros, of Berytos on behalf of himself and his children [dedicated this] to his ancestral deities."

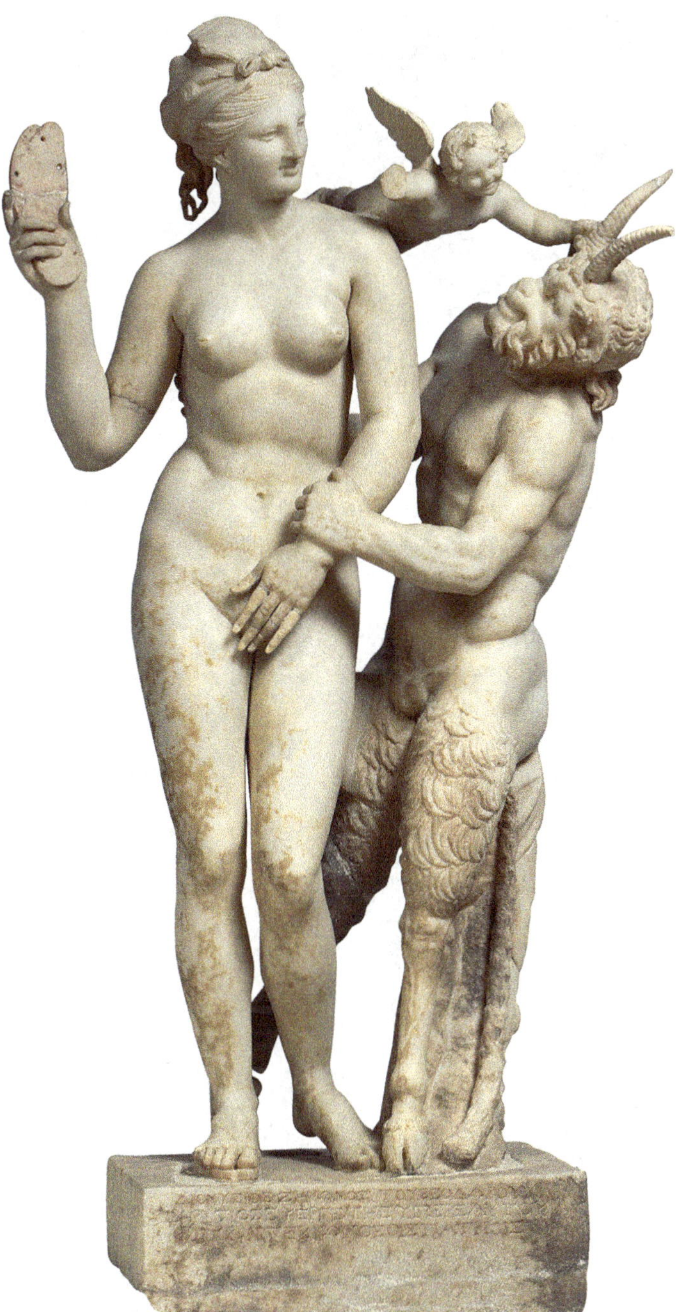

14.16 Aphrodite with slipper group from Delos, *c.* 100 BCE. 4 ft 2 13/16 in (1.29 m). Athens, National Archaeological Museum 3335. Photo: National Archaeological Museum, Athens (Giannis Patrikianos) © Hellenic Ministry of Education and Religious Affairs, Culture and Sports/Archaeological Receipts Fund.

The work is less open, extended, and three-dimensional than the other Hellenistic sculpture we have seen; considering the narrow proportions of the room for which it was commissioned, it was meant to be seen primarily from the front. The pose and body of Aphrodite recall the Praxitelean Aphrodite of Knidos (**see Figure 12.11, page 300**), but her hair and headdress are unusual and the hands have been adapted to the action of responding to the grasp of Pan. The muscular arms of the god certainly attempt to pull the arm and body of Aphrodite toward himself, and his face is turned

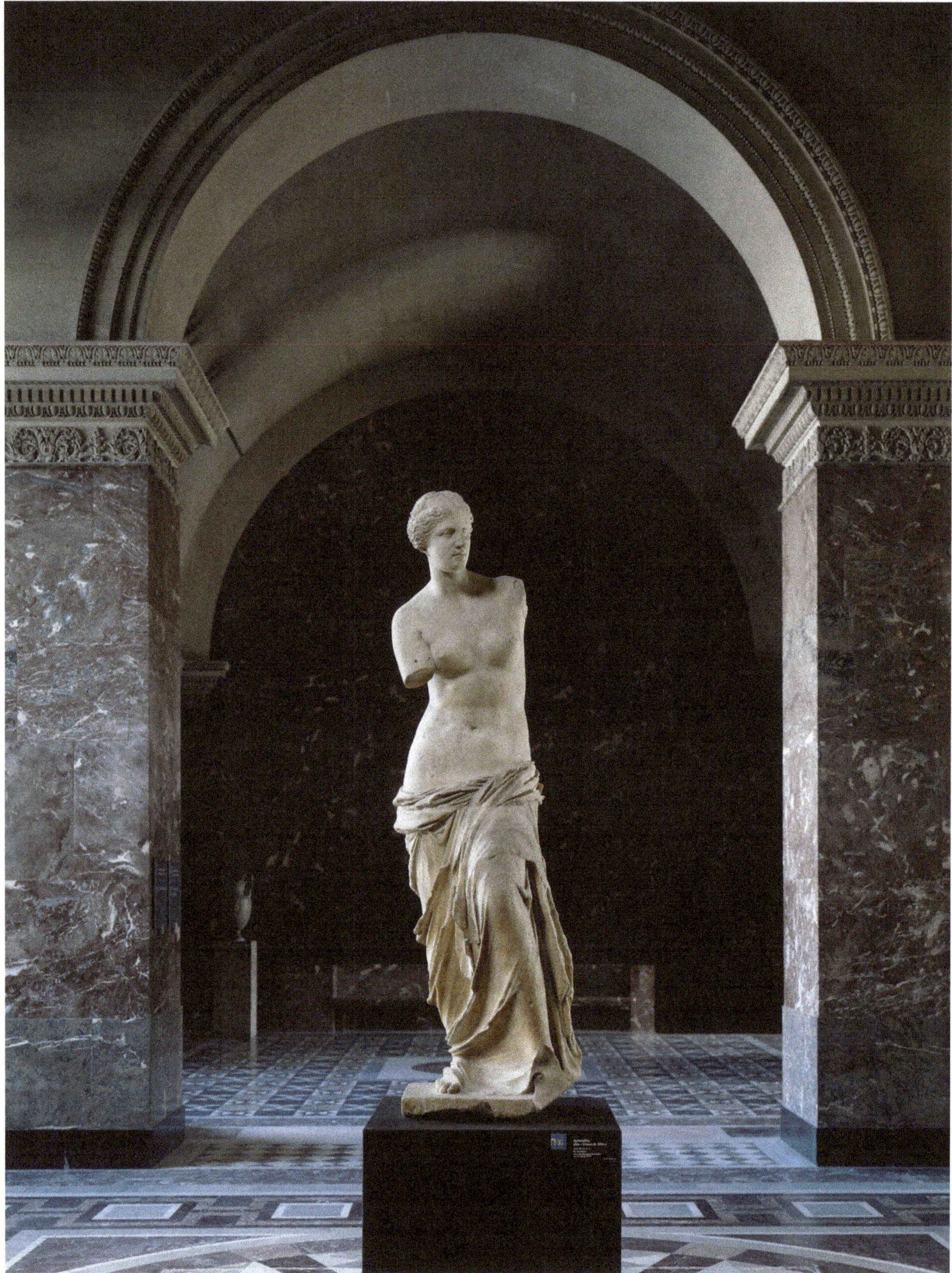

14.17 Aphrodite of Melos, *c.* 150–100 BCE. 6 ft 8⁵⁄₁₆ in (2.04 m). Paris, Musée du Louvre MA399/400. Image: © RMN-Grand Palais/Art Resource, NY.

upward with desire for her. His smaller size diminishes his menace, as does the smiling Eros who tugs at Pan's horn in a way that playfully mimics Pan's own grasp of Aphrodite's back. Here one senses a comic intent, but understanding the humor of another culture and time is notoriously difficult. Is Pan controlling or being controlled? Is Aphrodite defensive or manipulating? Is this about erotic attraction, or is it meant perhaps to evoke thoughts about fertility and primal forces? Is it serious or is it satire, or perhaps both simultaneously? What role did the patron, a Syrian, play in the development of the theme, and was the cosmopolitan population of Delos, its potential viewing audience, a factor in the composition? To be effective, satire and parody require a normative situation or expectation to create an effective contrast. Recasting a normative model like the Aphrodite of Knidos into the role of a slipper-slapper would seem to have a comic intent, but like much satire, there may be a serious point behind the playfulness that is less apparent to us today.

REPRESENTATIONS AND PORTRAYAL

The sculpture that we have seen thus far consists usually of multiple figures acting together in a narrative or tableau. There continued to be a need for single statues during the Hellenistic period, including figures of deities and representations of individuals, but these show more animation than earlier classical and archaic sculpture, even when they are imitating a classical or archaic style.

The nude or nearly nude Aphrodite is a popular subject for Hellenistic statues. The earliest close replicas of the Aphrodite of Knidos begin to appear at the end of the second century, but before then there are a number of other Aphrodite statues that share some of the stylistic features of the Praxiteles sculpture. Perhaps the most famous example is the Aphrodite from the Aegean island of Melos, the "Venus de Milo," which was excavated in 1820 (**Figure 14.17**). A base, now lost, records the name of the artist: "…andros son of [M]enides of [Ant]ioch-on-the Maeander made [it]," a sculptor who is otherwise unknown in the literary record. The statue stood in the middle of a niche of a gymnasion with herms on either side, and fragments of an upper arm and hand holding an apple were also recovered. The apple, *melos* in Greek, makes a pun on the name of the island, and one might regard the statue as an allegorical personification for the island, serving like the Tyche of Antioch. The placement of a classicizing statue of Aphrodite in a gymnasion fits with changes in the role of that institution in Hellenistic culture, as Rachel Kousser has argued (Kousser 2005). As centers of academic education and physical and military training, their curriculum emphasized literature of earlier periods by Homer and classical playwrights, and statues of Hermes and Aphrodite as well as benefactors were common elements of the gymnasion's artistic program. Based on style and context, the Melian statue is dated sometime after 150 BCE, in the last half of the second century.

The statue itself was made from two large pieces of marble doweled together, one for the lower section of drapery and the other for the nude torso. The upper body has the same soft treatment of skin, rounded abdomen and limbs, and richly textured hair that we see in the Aphrodite of Knidos. While not a copy of the Knidian Aphrodite, the similarities suggest the importance of the Praxitelean style for representing an idealized female beauty. The statue, however, has some Hellenistic elements that show it to be classicizing, rather than classical. The S-curve of the figure is more pronounced than the Praxitelean canon and the curve of her right hip more elongated. The legs are set in a more dynamic position with the left knee projecting, and there is more torsion in the figure. The drapery is certainly more baroque in its character, with heavy folds and deep channels that give the appearance of falling under its weight. In contrast to the Knidian Aphrodite, this statue seems poised in a moment of unveiling, with only the goddess's right hand holding back the cascade of drapery to the ground.

This retrospective, neoclassical stylistic quality is seen in other works, particularly in sculpture with a religious or social function, and is an aspect of the academic or scholarly mentality of the Hellenistic age. For example, a monumental group of figures was dedicated as cult statues at the sanctuary of Despoina at Lykosoura that show classicizing elements mixed with Hellenistic baroque

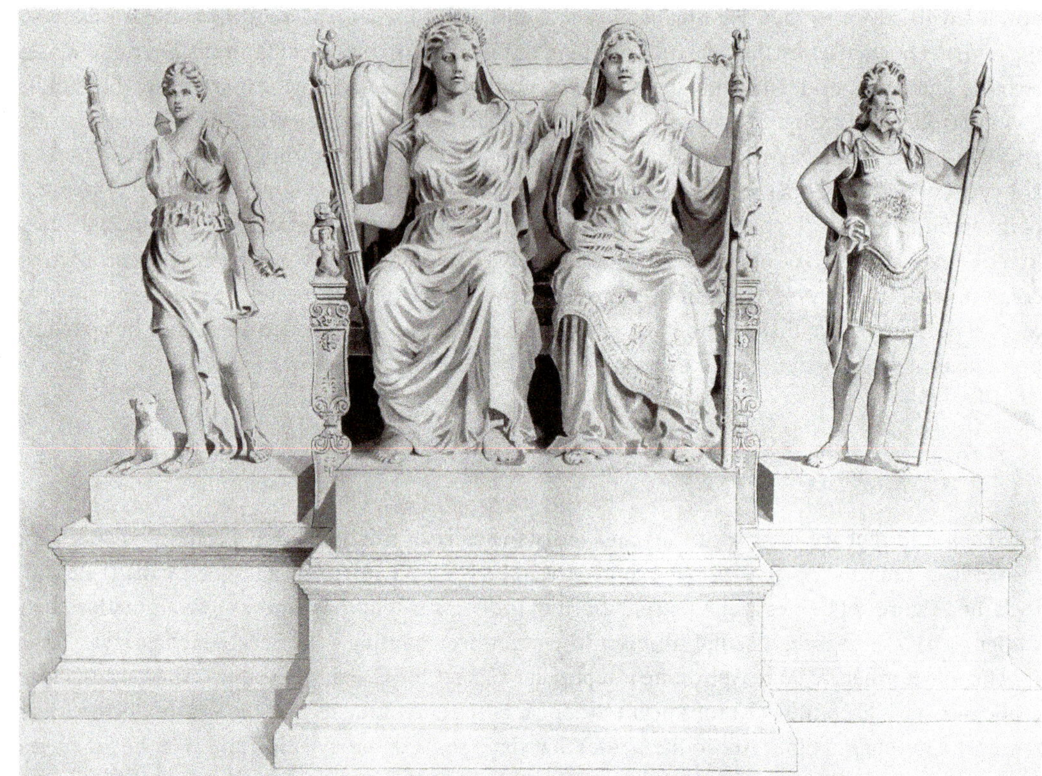

14.18 Reconstruction of cult statues by Damophon of Messene from the sanctuary of Despoina at Lykosoura, *c.* 200–190 BCE. Reconstruction after G. Dickens and K. Kourouniotis, "Damophon of Messene: II," *Annual of the British School at Athens* 13 (1906/1907), pl. 12. Reproduced with permission of the British School at Athens.

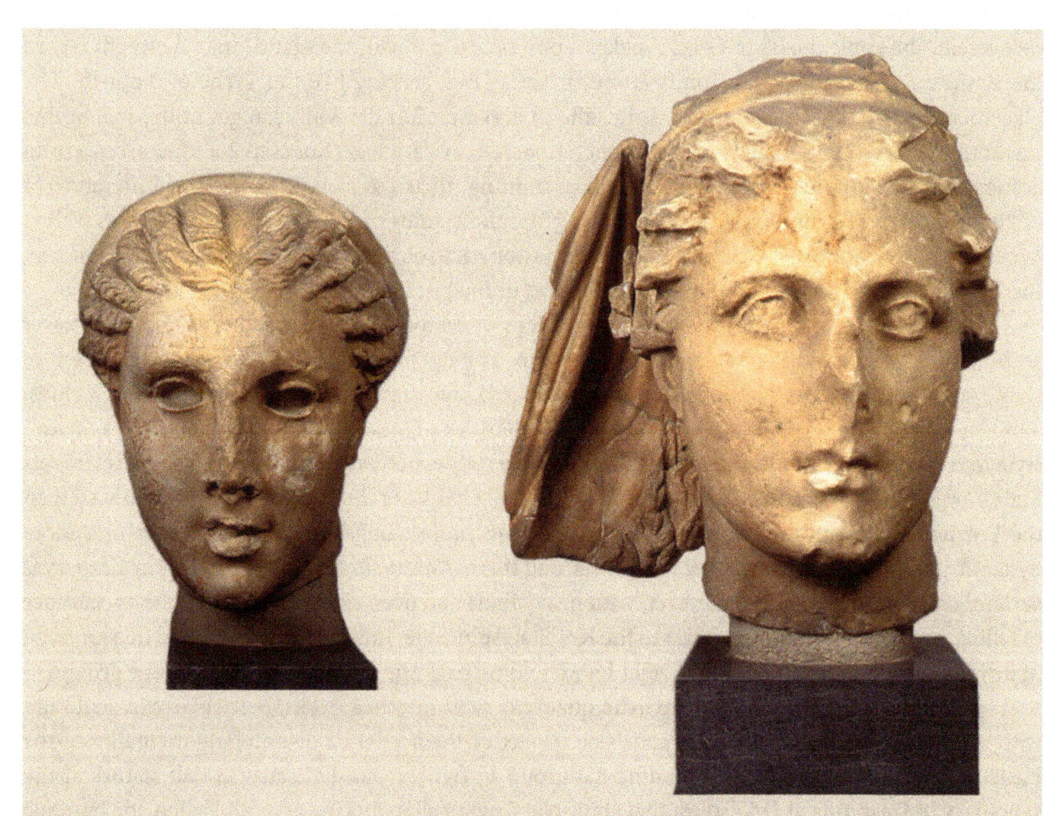

14.19 Artemis and Demeter from cult statues at Lykosoura, *c.* 200–190 BCE, by Damophon of Messene. 29½ in (0.75 m). Athens, National Archaeological Museum 1734–1736. Photo: National Archaeological Museum, Athens (Klaus-Valtin von Eickstedt) © Hellenic Ministry of Education and Religious Affairs, Culture and Sports/Archaeological Receipts Fund.

features (**Figure 14.18**). Demeter sits on the left on an elaborate throne, holding a torch and placing her hand over the shoulder of her daughter Despoina (meaning "mistress," a term used for Persephone, who was also called Kore by the Greeks). A much smaller Artemis and the Titan Anytos flank the pair. The sculptural group was seen by Pausanias (8.37.1–6), who tells us it was made by Damophon of Messene, who did several other cult statues in southern Greece in the late third and early second century BCE (Themelis 1994). A recently published inscription records that Damophon forgave the Lykosourans a debt of 3,546 tetradrachms (4-drachma coins, or 14,184 drachmas) due to him for the contract of the sculpture, suggesting that he, like Timotheos at Epidauros, was very well paid for his work and recognized as a public benefactor for his munificence.

Looking at the surviving heads of Artemis and Demeter (**Figure 14.19**), one can see that there is a smooth roundness of the features and heavily lidded eyes that recall the fifth-century Severe Style of Olympia or mid-fifth century classical works like the Doryphoros or Parthenon metopes. The hairstyle of both women, however, is more contemporary, including the melon coiffure of Artemis and the rich, wispy hair of Demeter. The effect is lively but serene, as would befit cult statues.

An archaizing style is also found in Hellenistic art, such as a tripod base from the Athenian Agora dated to *c.* 100 BCE (**Figure 14.20**). Three processing figures, Dionysos and two maenads, appear on the three sides. The maenad shown here holds a phiale in her hand and virtually floats on tiptoes. The folds of the drapery, especially the hems, are set as a series of nested smooth curves and swallowtails that fall in nearly perfect symmetry. The effect easily recalls archaic treatment of kore drapery (**see Figure 8.14, page 196**). The decorative effect of the pattern is enhanced by the outward curvature of the garments' edge, which is a Hellenistic stylization and clearly signals this work as retrospective rather than original. The archaizing style would appear to have had a religious as well as decorative value that made it appropriate for dedications like tripods or processional reliefs. Many of the most revered cult images were old and simple in form, *archaios*, making the imitation of the archaic style appropriate for dedications or votive offerings.

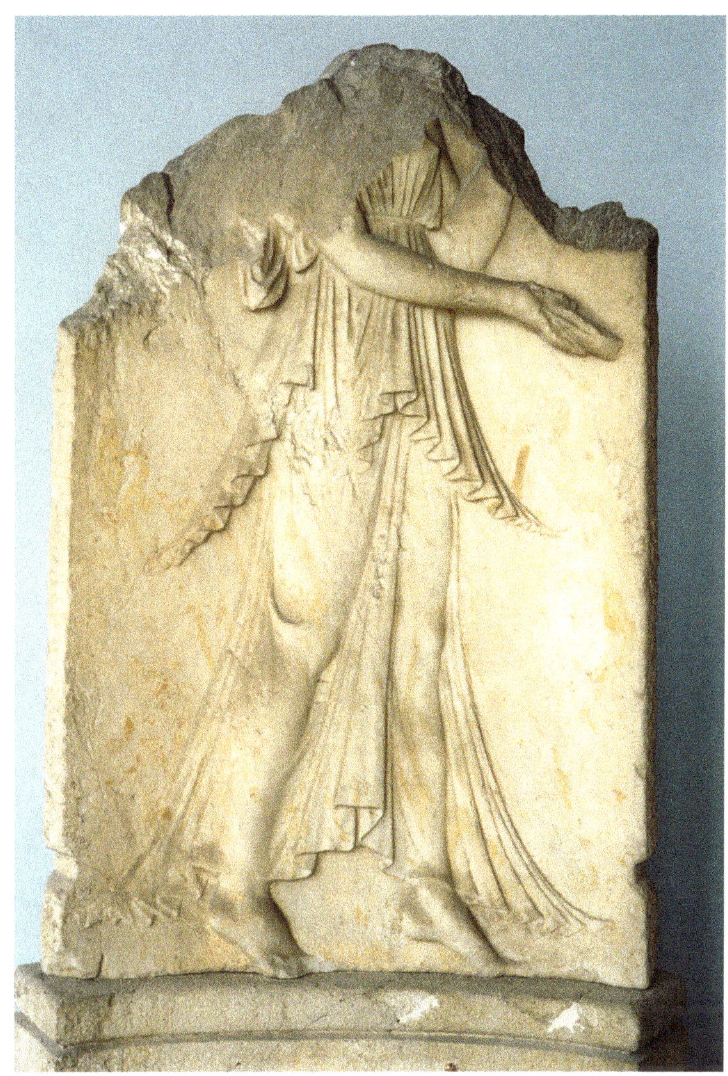

14.20 Tripod base fragment from Agora, Athens, *c.* 100 BCE. 3 ft 6¹⁵⁄₁₆ in (1.09 m). Athens, Agora Museum S370. Maenad. Photo: American School of Classical Studies at Athens: Agora Excavations.

A classicizing style was also appropriate for representations of people. Statues that represented individuals, at least symbolically, go back to the seventh and sixth centuries BCE, as can be seen in the Kore of Nikandre (**see Figure 6.3, page 134**) and the Kore of Phrasikleia (**see Figure 8.13, page 195**). These statues did not resemble the true look of their subjects, of course, but signified their idealized form and status. The use of honorific statues for individuals expanded significantly in the Hellenistic period, as we have already seen in the last chapter with the third-century statue of the priestess Aristonoë from the sanctuary at Rhamnous (**see Figure 13.8, page 329**). This statue is classicizing in its pose and features, with fewer of the baroque elements that we see at Lykosoura. One change from classical figures, however, is the heavier, thicker drapery of her undergarment, as seen at her feet, and the thinness of her mantle, through which we can see traces of the heavier undergarment, a drapery-through-drapery stylistic effect that belongs to the Hellenistic period.

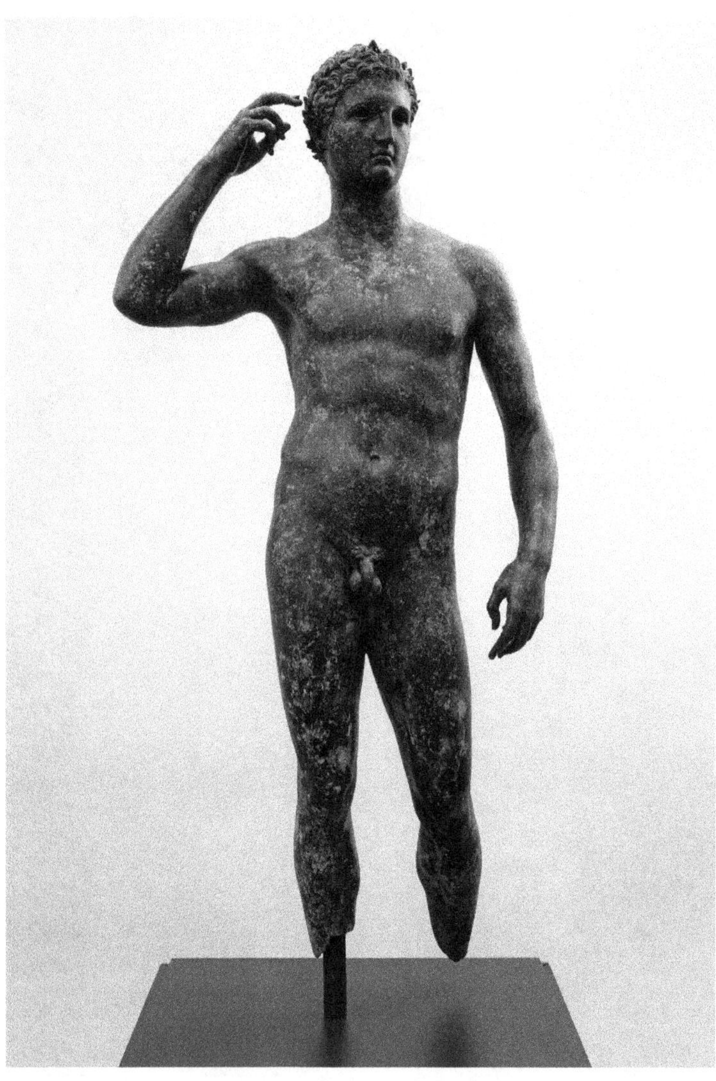

14.21 Getty athlete (neoclassical), 3rd cent. BCE. 4 ft 11 7/16 in (1.51 m). Malibu, Getty Villa 77. AB.30. Photo: The J. Paul Getty Museum, Villa Collection, Malibu, California.

A bronze statue recovered from the Mediterranean Sea and now known as the Getty athlete is representative of a victor statue, a nude athlete wearing a wreath dedicated at sanctuaries like Olympia and Delphi **(Figure 14.21)**. Originally associated with the Lysippan workshop, analysis of the statue's core now suggests that it dates to the third or possibly early second century BCE. The statue evokes the same ideal type of male figure as the Doryphoros, but the modeling of the abdomen is softer and there is a more pronounced S-curve to the figure that is late classical in origin. That a statue like this was first regarded as late classical when discovered attests to how close to their models classicizing sculptors could work to invoke the idealized ethos of the archetypes.

A different type of athletic statue is seen in the bronze statue of a boxer, housed today in the Terme Museum in Rome **(Figure 14.22)**. This statue was found in construction fill at the base of the Quirinal Hill in Rome, but its original context or how it got to Rome is not known. His hands wrapped for boxing, the figure sits at rest and looks up toward an unseen figure. The bulging muscles and twisted pose recall elements of the baroque style, but his pose is one of weariness and his face is not tortured with emotion, but instead marked with the cuts, broken nose, and cauliflower ears of the boxing arena, enhanced by using copper on the bronze surface to show blood from his wounds. Boxing was a crown sport at the Olympic and other games, but rather than an idealized and unblemished victor, we have here someone bearing the realistic signs of a sport marked by blood and death; possibly he is a professional athlete or slave rather than an elite athlete. The sharp turn of his head is a dramatic touch, and whether he was part of a statue group or not, he clearly indicates another person in the tableau and makes the viewer a third party in the scene. Whether he is looking at an unseen opponent, trainer, or owner, his posture puts the boxer into a subservient position, both to them and to the viewer, someone who seems not to control his destiny like the Getty athlete. The purpose of such realistic works is unclear, as is whether the figure is meant to evoke sympathy or some other emotion in the mind of the viewer.

The Terme boxer was found not far from another work now in the same museum, the so-called Hellenistic ruler or Terme ruler **(Figure 14.23)**. This figure has a well-muscled body like the boxer, and the placement of the right hand on the back of the hip recalls statues of the weary Herakles of Lysippos. The figure is not standing fully upright, but leans forward slightly, as if weary. He holds onto a spear set into the ground, and this type of standing, spear-planted pose was developed under Alexander the Great as an expression of his role as a conquering ruler, claiming rule over "spear-won" lands. The head seems small in proportion to the body, and its turning motion implies some unseen element. The eyes and face have an intense focus to them that seems vigilant rather than triumphant.

Like the boxer, the face of the ruler has a distinctiveness in his features suggesting that this is an individual's portrait rather than a mythological hero or triumphant athlete. How closely one should associate a realistic appearance with the actual person's appearance is an issue of some debate. Literary

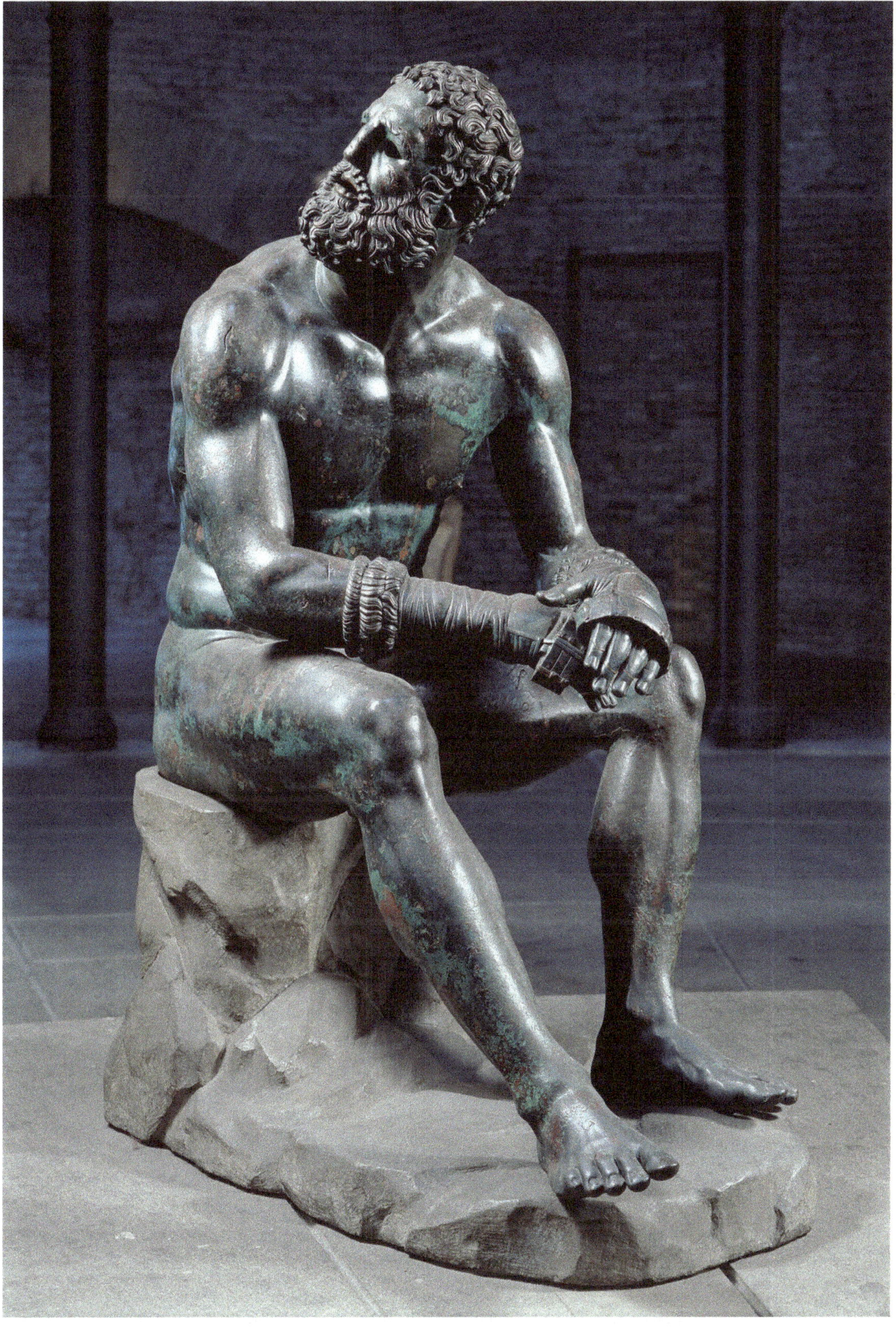

14.22 Terme boxer, 2nd–early 1st cent. BCE. 4 ft 2⅜ in (1.28 m). Rome, Museo Nazionale Romano (Palazzo Massimo alle Terme) 1055. Photo: Scala/Ministero per i Beni e le Attività culturali/Art Resource, NY.

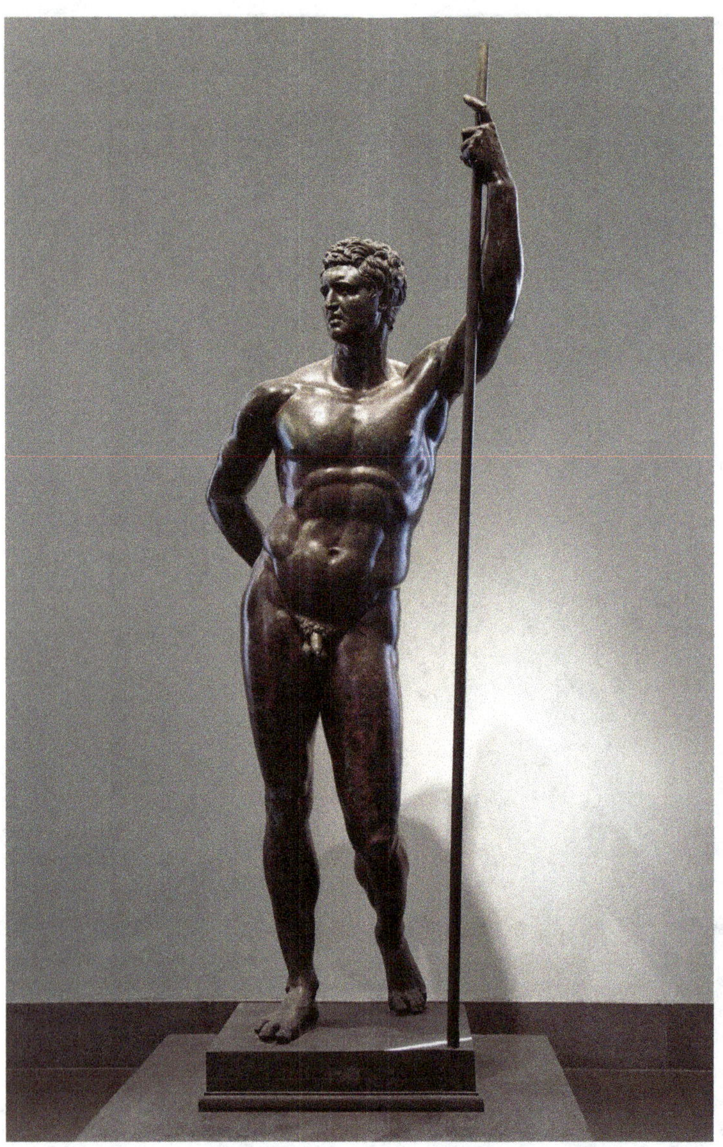

14.23 "Hellenistic Ruler," 2nd cent. BCE. 7 ft 3⅜ in (2.22 m). Rome, Museo Nazionale Romano (Palazzo Massimo alle Terme) 1049. Photo: Vanni/Art Resource, NY.

sources describe how Alexander worked with the leading artists of his day to create official portraits, and there is a consistency in representations of Alexander that suggests there might be some element of his actual appearance surviving in later images such as the Alexander Sarcophagus **(see Figure 14.1)** and the Alexander Mosaic **(see Figure 14.2)**. In particular, the leonine mane of hair and the anastole, or tuft of hair that stands up at the front, are said to have been prominent features of Alexander's portraits, as was an uplifted gaze. Whether or not these closely resemble Alexander's actual appearance, they created a distinctive typology that is both individualized and quickly recognizable for a viewer and was emulated by later Hellenistic kings and conquerors. For the Terme ruler, the realistic head seems strange when combined with the figure's nudity, but it would serve to emphasize the divine aspect of the Hellenistic ruler. There is no diadem on his head, making his identity as a king uncertain, and in the end the figure is enigmatic.

Ruler portraits serve a political purpose above all, and we should consider that some of the realistic and individualized detail of their portraits was meant to convey the vitality and authority of the ruler, rather than his or her unique appearance. The portraits of the Ptolemaic kings and queens in Egypt, for example, had to appeal to a variety of audiences and the royal images could be altered to address one segment of the population. A head of Cleopatra VII (69–30 BCE), the last ruler of Egypt before it was conquered by the Romans under Augustus, has an idealized set of features that make her appear like a goddess such as Aphrodite **(Figure 14.24)**. Her face is narrower than Aphrodite's, with no hint of a smile and a more focused gaze, but the soft, fine facial features, smooth skin, and richly textured hair share Aphrodite's idealized beauty. This head was made to sit on a separately carved body, probably a draped figure. This head and similarly styled profiles on coins were meant for a Greek audience, but we have other coins and other portraits of Cleopatra that show her with a hooked nose and less beautiful proportions. These may have been developed for a Roman audience, and certainly Roman writers did not describe her as beautiful, although they recognized her sharp intelligence, wit, and charm.

Egyptianizing style
a work made in imitation of a traditional Egyptian style, especially in the Hellenistic period

Ptolemaic rulers also had to address an indigenous Egyptian audience, and for their portraits in Egyptian temples and other public places workshops used an **Egyptianizing style** that invokes the forms and symbols of 2,500 years of Pharaoh portraits **(Figure 14.25, page 370)**. A small limestone statue of a third-century queen, Arsinoë II (d. 270 BCE), was made for her posthumous cult during the second half of the second century. The inscription, written in hieroglyphs, names her as a goddess; both king and queen in the Egyptian tradition were divine and often brother and sister, a tradition that the Ptolemies continued as Arsinoë II was married to her brother Ptolemy II. The tight sheath dress and straight stance with the left foot slightly advanced imitate traditional Egyptian sculpture **(see Figure 6.5, page 136; Figure 6.6, page 137)**, but the hairstyle is a hybridized mixture of Egyptian and Greek elements and the cornucopia in her left arm is a Greek symbol of abundance and fertility. The statue was made for the queen's cult, which was meant to invoke the aid of the once-mortal goddess for the continued prosperity of the land and dynasty. Arsinoë had both Hellenistic and Egyptianizing statues made of her during her lifetime and posthumously by her husband, who had instituted her cult. Coins that he issued, such as a gold octadrachm (eight drachmas) dating to 261–245, show a Hellenizing portrait on one side and, on the reverse, a double cornucopia, a symbol invented for her posthumous cult **(Figure 14.26, page 370)**. The coin circulated among the elite and addressed a different viewer than the cult statue, in a sense speaking a different language to make the same point about Arsinoë's divine status.

Not only did ruler portraits become prominent in the Hellenistic period, but portraits generally became common, particularly in the case of officials, priests and priestesses, and wealthy patrons who sponsored building projects. We have already seen the third-century portrait statue of the priestess Aristonoë, dedicated by her son in the sanctuary of Themis/Nemesis at Rhamnous **(see Figure 13.8, page 329)**. Like Cleopatra, her face is generalized and idealized, but her body is shown in an active position, with the right arm once extended, probably holding a phiale to perform an offering. Hellenistic portraits of women, like the grave stele of Phila **(see Figure 13.9, page 330)**, show more signs of action, authority, and agency than their classical predecessors, but the conventions of body pose are limited in range.

Portraits could be made of marble or bronze, but few of the later have survived apart from their marble bases inscribed with their names. A bronze head from Delos was part of a full-size figure and was found in the excavation of the Old Palaistra **(Figure 14.27, page 371)**. What is remarkable is the truly animated expression and detailing of the hair and features, which make the representation seem genuinely individual. The deep groove in the forehead, the turn of the head, the crow's feet by the eyes, and the open, slightly downturned mouth together work to create a vivid portrayal and have earned it the nickname of the "worried man." Who or what the man was, and whether the portrait was truly individualized or conforming to a type, remain unclear, although given the cost of a bronze statue, it was likely someone belonging to the elite of Delos. The head is usually dated to around or just after 100 BCE, in the middle of Delos's greatest period of prosperity before it was sacked in 88 and again in 69.

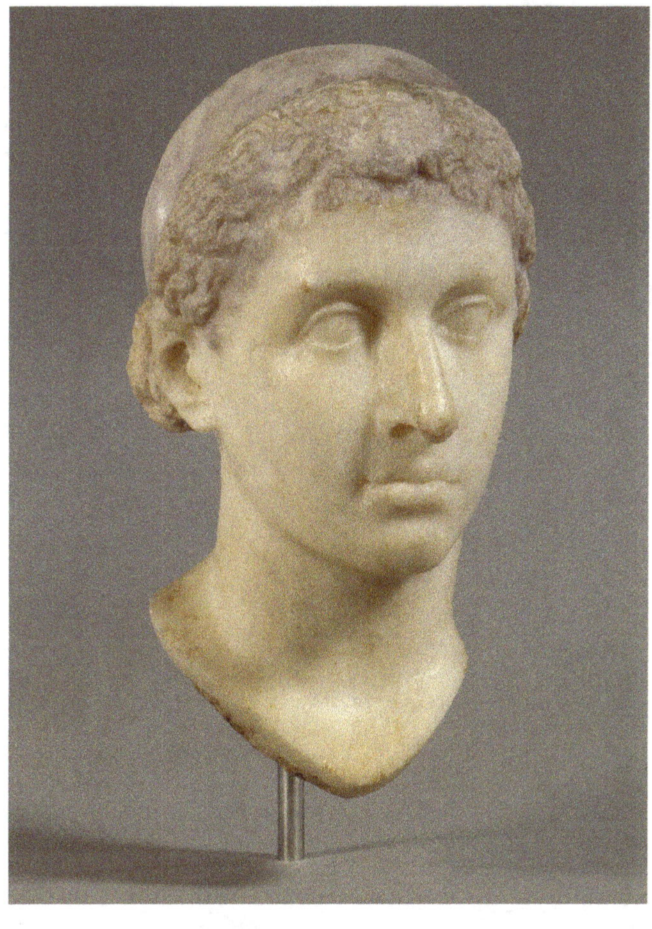

14.24 Head of Cleopatra VII, mid-1st cent. BCE. 11⅝ in (29.5 cm). Berlin, Antikensammlung, Staatliche Museen 1976.10. Image: bpk, Berlin/Antikensammlung/Johannes Laurentius/Art Resource, NY.

PAINTING

So far we have been looking mostly at sculpture that would have been found in public places. Some statues, like the figures from the Antikythera and Mahdia shipwrecks, were probably destined for individual patrons, Romans and elite Greeks who during the Hellenistic period built villas that could accommodate large-scale work as part of a decorative program. The large villas and houses were also decorated with extensive frescoes and mosaics. Several houses with large surviving mosaic floors have been excavated at Pella, the Macedonian capital where Alexander the Great was born in 356 BCE, and these show that the medium developed the ability to show representational scenes beyond the pebble mosaics seen at Olynthos and other fourth-century sites **(see Figure 12.22, page 311)**. Even the largest houses at Olynthos, however, were relatively modest compared to the size of some Hellenistic villas, like the Villa of the Helen Abduction at Pella, which, at 2,350 m^2, was more than four times the area of the typical house at Olynthos.

The Pella villa dates to the late fourth century BCE and had three dining rooms and two large pebble mosaic floors, one showing a stag hunt signed by its artist, Gnosis **(Figure 14.28, page 372)**.

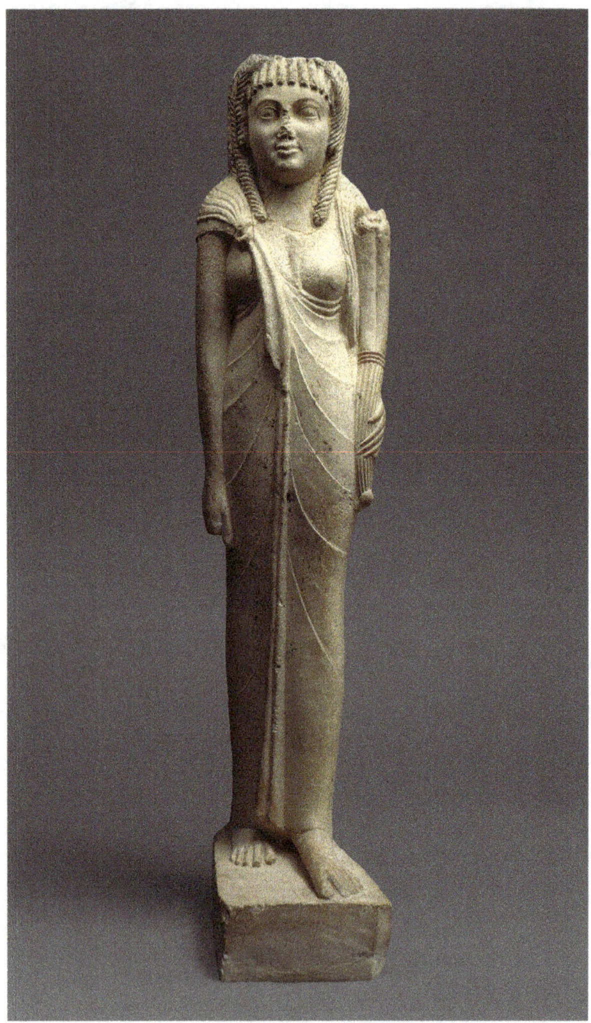

14.25 Statue of Arsinoë II (d. 270) for her posthumous cult, *c.* 150–100 BCE. Limestone, paint, gold leaf 15¼ in (38.7 cm). New York, Metropolitan Museum of Art 20.2.21. Image copyright © The Metropolitan Museum of Art. Image source: Art Resource, NY.

Around the border of the room is a winding vine pattern on which the klinai would have stood. In the center of the room and oriented toward the doorway is a panel whose figures are heroic in scale. Two nude youths with billowing capes and a dog attack a stag, a scene that was found on Tomb II at Vergina and is one of the favored hunt themes among the Macedonian elite. The ability to show a range of colors is limited in a pebble mosaic, since it can only use the natural color of small stones, but by careful sorting Gnosis has been able to show shading/*chiaroscuro* in the figures, giving them a three-dimensional mass missing in earlier mosaics. Further, the figures move on a ground plane that recedes into the background, giving them an actual stage on which to hunt. The hunter on the right stands behind a projecting rock, while his dog is in front, effectively surrounding the stag. There is one opening in the trap for the animal, and it looks toward the front plane where the viewer stands at the entrance to the room, making the viewer a party to the hunt. The shared experience of the hunt becomes the shared experience of the symposiasts, who themselves had likely participated in elite hunts like this.

Pergamon was also noted for its mosaics and was home to one of the more famous mosaicists of antiquity, Sosos, who was active in the second century BCE. By this time a new mosaic technique was common that used small squares or tesserae (*opus vermiculatum*), and the ability to work with a small size of tiles and a wider range of colors greatly expanded the potential for mosaics to be illusionistic (see the Alexander Mosaic in **Figure 14.2**). From the second half of the second century we can see the technique used in a mosaic from the House of Dionysos on Delos. This house has a peristyle central court with a mosaic in the center where it was part of an **impluvium** (**Figure 14.29, page 372**). In this position it would have been visually prominent to any visitor upon entering the house, rather than tucked away in a side room. Like many houses in Delos, there is no andron but several large rooms that would have been used for entertaining and leisure. Rather than places of domestic production like the houses at Olynthos,

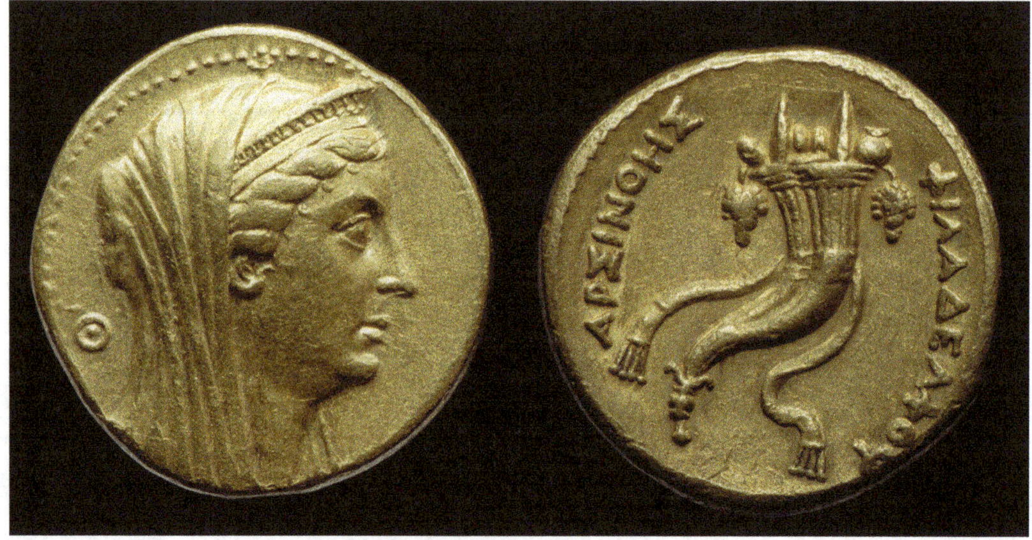

14.26 Coin of Arsinoë II, *c.* 261–246 BCE, minted by Ptolemy II. London, British Museum 1987,0649.135. Photo: © The Trustees of the British Museum.

Hellenistic houses became retreats for their owners and worth the investment of resources in their decoration.

As can be seen in the detail of the mosaic **(Figure 14.30, page 373)**, it is made of small tesserae, some just 1 mm square, with blacks, whites, yellows, browns, and reds; the face and neck of the rider are in three-quarter view and modeled to a three-dimensional effect. The sharp turn of the feline head actually brings its gaze toward the southwest corner of the peristyle, the main point of entry into the courtyard from the street. A youthful figure riding a leopard should be Dionysos, and the subject would be appropriate as the house was located in the theater district of Delos, where a number of mosaics have theater motifs, including masks, muses, and Dionysos. However, there are some unusual elements in this mosaic: the figure is smaller in scale than is typical and has a pair of wings; the cat is more tiger than leopard in its markings. The winged figure also carries a branch or **thyrsos**, an attribute usually found with maenads, followers of the god. Indeed, the gender of the figure is somewhat ambiguous, as is its identity, and perhaps this reflects the syncretism of Greek and Levantine ideas and visual signs.

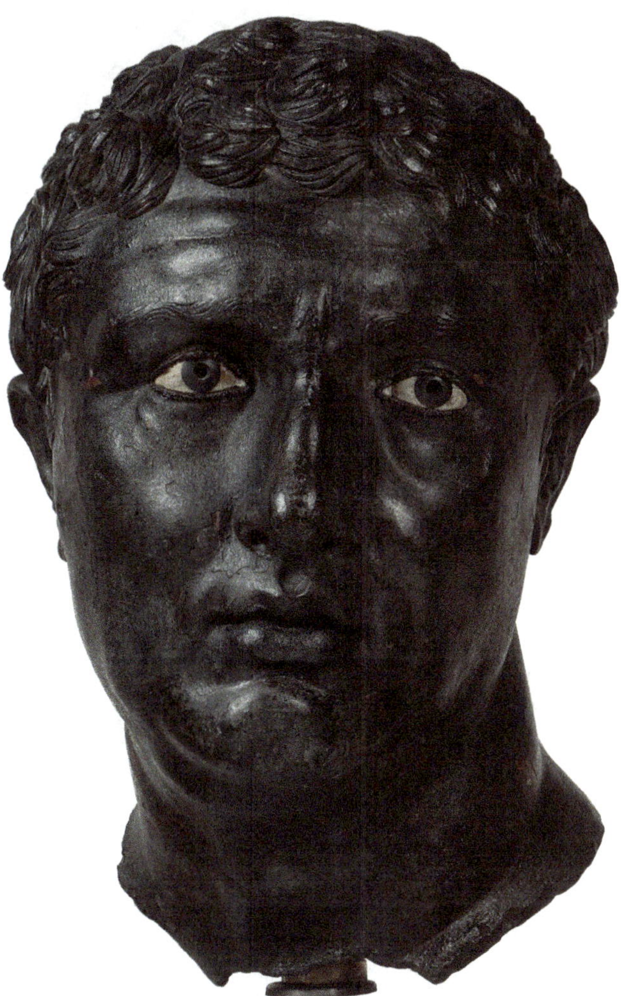

14.27 Bronze head of a man, from Delos, early 1st cent. BCE. 12 13/16 in (32.5 cm). Athens, NM Br 14612. Photo: National Archaeological Museum, Athens (Giannis Patrikianos) © Hellenic Ministry of Education and Religious Affairs, Culture and Sports/Archaeological Receipts Fund.

As floor decoration set in mortar, mosaics survive better than the painted walls of Hellenistic houses, but we can catch glimpses of small painted decoration in a few houses and larger paintings in some tombs like those from Vergina. Additionally, painted marble grave stelai were popular and a number have survived from sites like Alexandria in Egypt and Demetrias in northern Greece. Most of these stelai are conventional in their subject matter, showing the deceased either sitting on a couch or standing with an attendant or family member. One stele from Demetrias dating to around 200 BCE is remarkable for both its composition and subject matter, the Stele of Hediste, today in the Volos Archaeological Museum **(Figure 14.31, page 374)**. The better preserved upper section of the panel shows a woman, Hediste, lying on a couch with her breasts bare above the blanket. She is seen in an angled view from above and behind her in profile view is her husband. Further back in space, cut off by the room's door frame, is a nurse or midwife holding an infant. Even further back and perspectively smaller in scale is an attendant, whose open mouth indicates surprise, and some branches suggesting a courtyard or garden, creating three layers of a household interior. The tableau expresses quite vividly the grief of the household over the death of a young mother and her child.

The inscription at the bottom eloquently confirms this tragic situation and names both the Fates and Tyche as responsible for the deaths of mother and child:

> The Fates spun out a painful thread from their spindles for Hediste, when she, as a bride, encountered childbirth.
> Oh enduring is she, not intended to embrace her infant, nor even to water the lip of her own offspring with the breast.
> One light looked upon them both and Tyche led them both into a single tomb, coming upon them indistinguishably. (Tr. Salowey 2012, 254)

The sway of Tyche over individuals speaks to the Hellenistic spirit, and the dramatic portrayal of reactions to Hediste's death brings viewers into the experience, as we look on from the other side of the couch.

impluvium
a catch basin in the floor of an atrium-style house that would collect water from rain

thyrsos
a large fennel stalk with a pine-cone type of head carried by followers of Dionysos

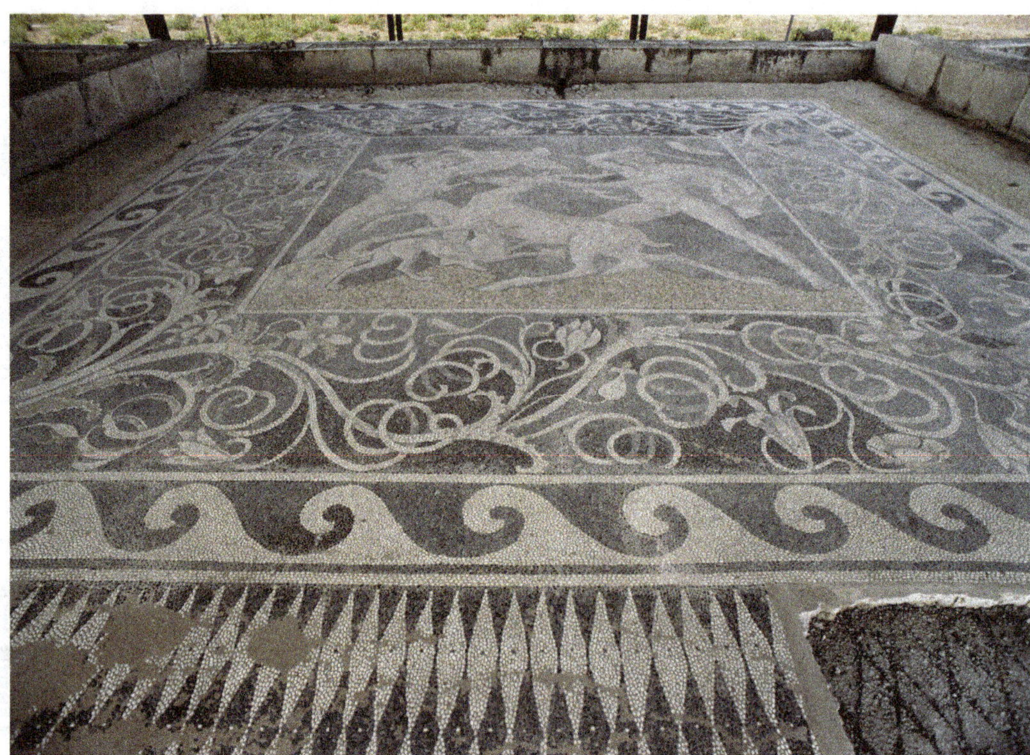

14.28 Stag Hunt mosaic by Gnosis from Pella, *in situ*, *c.* 330–300 BCE. Central panel, 10 ft 2 1/16 in (3.10 m). Photo: © Vanni Archive/Art Resource, NY.

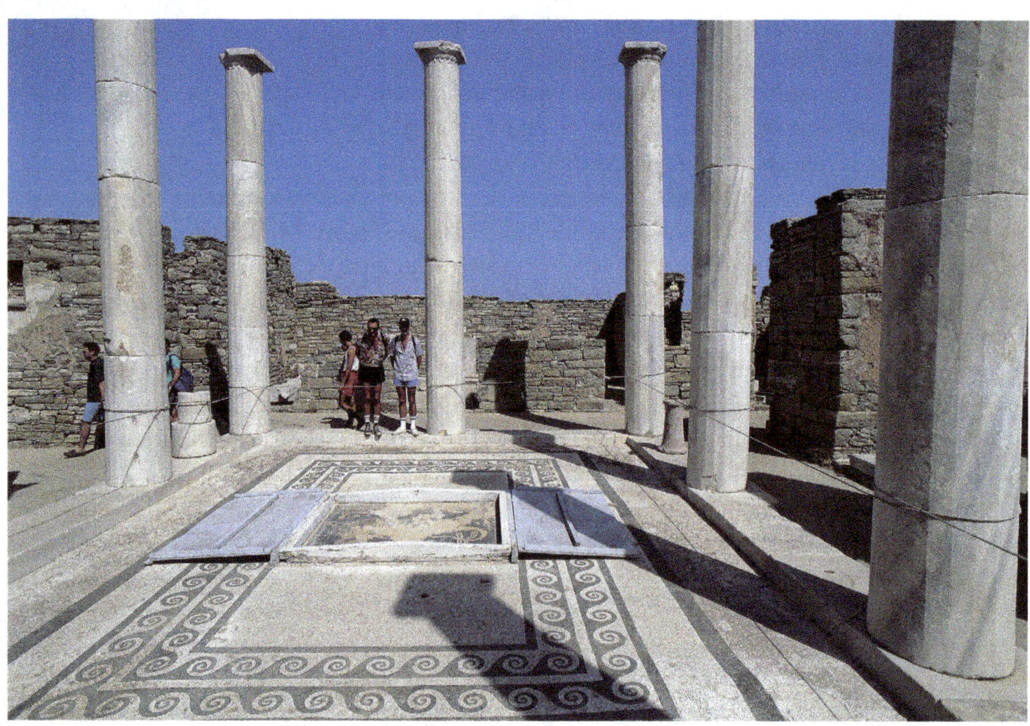

14.29 Courtyard of the House of Dionysos at Delos with mosaic, *c.* 166–100 BCE. Photo: © DeA Picture Library/Art Resource, NY.

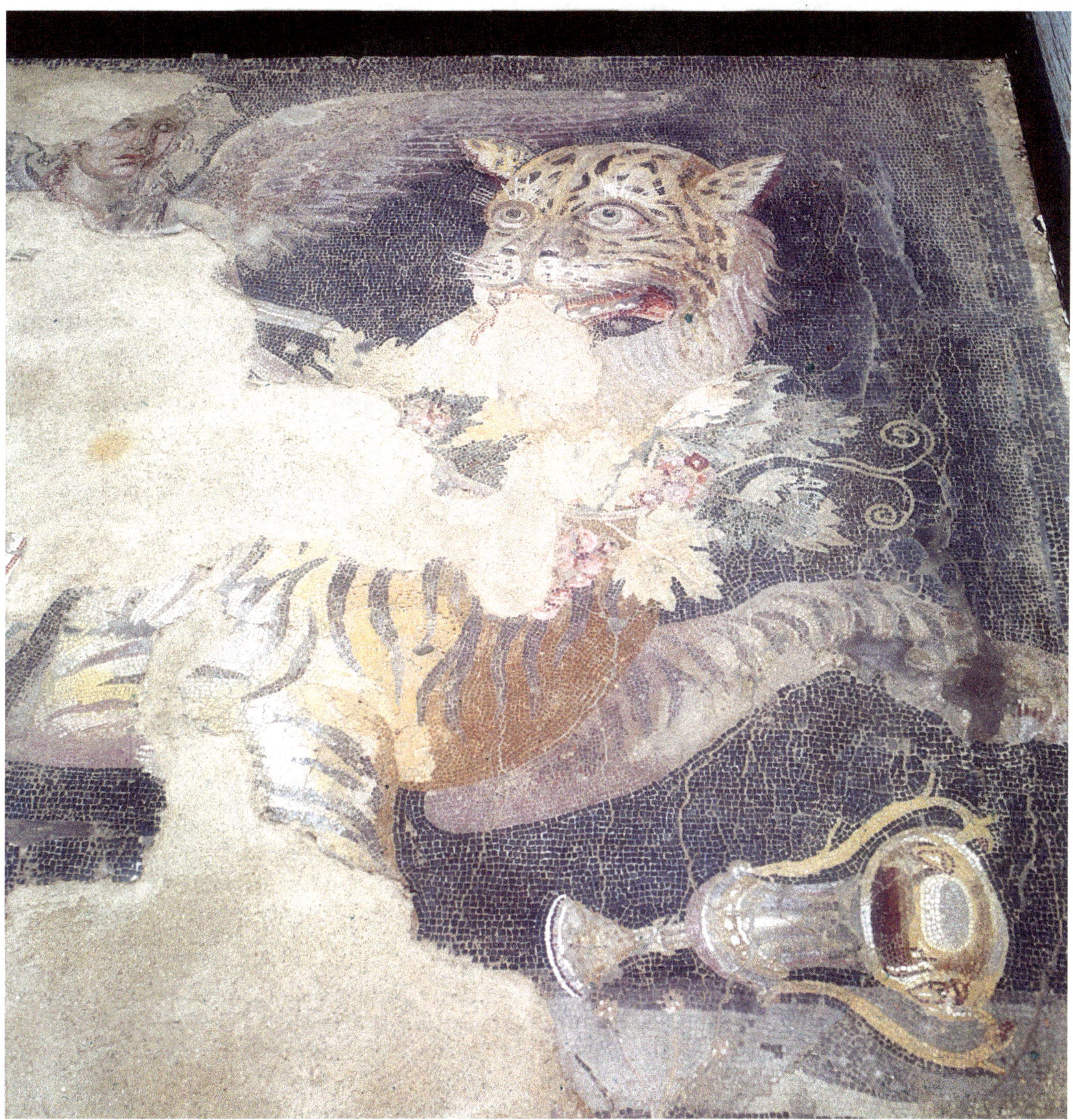

14.30 Detail of mosaic from House of Dionysos, Delos, *c.* 166–100 BCE. Height of panel, 4 2¹³⁄₁₆ in (1.29 m). Dionysos (?) riding tiger. Photo: HIP/Art Resource, NY.

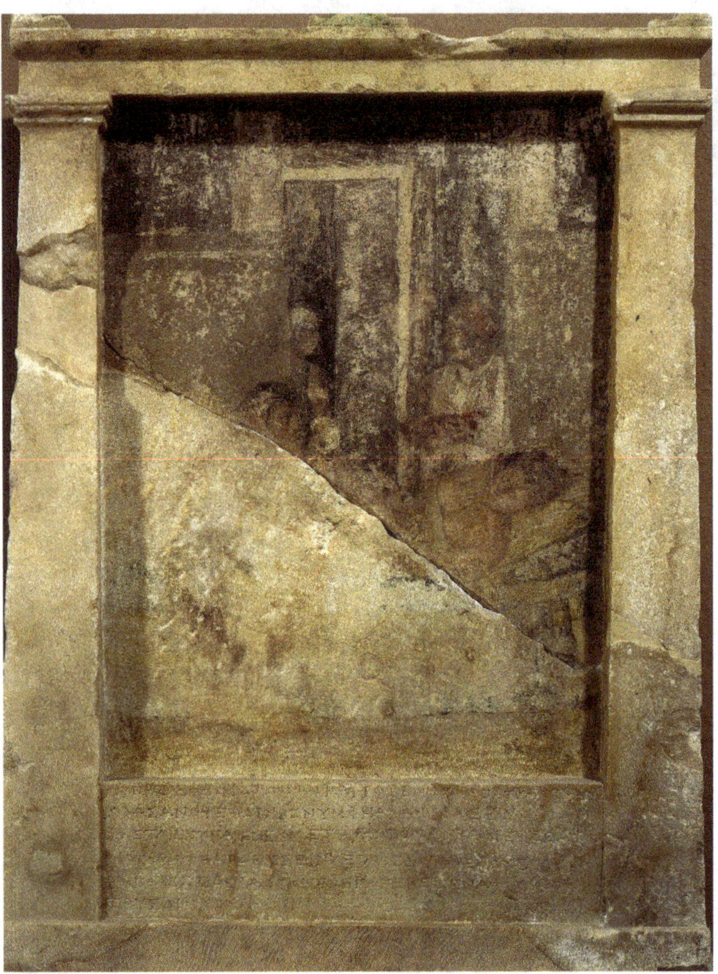

14.31 Painted Stele of Hediste from Necropolis of Demetrias, Greece, *c.* 200 BCE. 28¾ in (73 cm). Volos Archaeological Museum. Photo: Gianni Dagli Orti/ The Art Archive at Art Resource, NY.

THE PRIVATE AND PERSONAL REALM

Smaller-scale works in bronze, gems, pottery, and terracotta would have been found in the private and domestic settings that we have just seen, as well as in sanctuaries as votive offerings and in tombs as offerings for the dead to console them in the afterlife. Cremation burial is more common during this period and some special wares are created as burial urns. The most elaborate of these were produced in south Italy and Sicily, with **Centuripe vases**, named for the Sicilian site where many were found, the most well known **(Figure 14.32)**. Although these look like jars with lids, they are one-piece vessels and feature architectural moldings and acanthus leaves applied to the surface. They are brightly colored, often with a red background and figures painted in yellow, green, blue, and pink pastels. The scene here is a wedding with the bride surrounded by attendants bearing objects. The colors are applied to the vase after firing, creating an effect similar to fresco or painted stone. Highlights give a sense of volume to the figures, and the faces are in three-quarter view, giving further three-dimensionality to the bodies. Whether or not the urn was used for someone who was married or, like Phrasikleia, was a maiden who died before marriage is not certain from the object itself.

In Egypt, a special form of hydria were also used as a cremation urn. Called a **Hadra hydria**, this type of vessel is decorated with vegetal and pattern ornament drawn with black glaze on the cream surface **(Figure 14.33)**. Mostly found in Alexandria, many of these bear inscriptions that show they were used for the remains of foreigners who died in Egypt. The inscription on this example tells us that it contains the remains of Hieronides of Phocaea, who died in 226–225 BCE leading an embassy to king Ptolemy III Euergetes (r. 246–221), giving us a rare precise dating for the Hellenistic period. The writing on these cinerary vessels suggests that they were meant to be seen after they were placed in the tomb. Interestingly, it has now been determined that the Hadra hydriai were not made in Alexandria but in Crete, and were exported to Egypt for this funerary use, another indication of the cosmopolitan quality of the Hellenistic period.

We saw in Chapter 11 that pottery continued to be produced in Athens in the third century and later after the end of red-figure ware, following metalware models and relying on more purely decorative motifs than figural scenes **(see Figure 11.9, page 278)**. The so-called West Slope ware was exported and was one of several ornate, black-gloss wares like Gnathian ware that were produced in the Hellenistic period (**see Figure 12.20, page 309** for a fourth-century example of Gnathian ware). Mold-made bowls with incised or relief decoration were produced in several areas of the Hellenistic world and are commonly called Megarian bowls **(see Figure 11.10, page 279)**. These shapes imitate metal vessels, particularly Persian, and like metal work include both incised and relief decoration on their surface. Some, like the example from Athens, show one or more narrative scenes in a frieze, and sometimes include texts from poems to accompany the pictures. These wares, like plain pottery, could be found in both tombs and households.

Centuripe vases
cinerary pottery decorated with architectural relief and painted figures made in Sicily during the Hellenistic period

Hadra hydria
a type of hydria made in Crete but used widely in Egypt as a cinerary urn, with dark slip decoration painted on the light surface

Terracotta figures continued to be produced in large numbers, and many of these served either as votive offerings in sanctuaries or as grave goods in tombs. Brightly colored figures of women were particularly popular and were appropriate subjects for the tombs of young women or offerings upon significant events like a wedding. Some of these, like the figure of a heavily draped woman found in a tomb in Taras/Taranto, vividly preserve their colors (**Figure 14.34**). Like marble portraits of women, the standing figures fall into several large types. This young woman has her right arm bent sharply upward, creating a sling out of her heavy mantle. The projecting and now missing left arm pulled the rest of the drapery sharply in the other direction, creating a very energetic pattern of drapery folds that animate what is still a standing figure. Like many Hellenistic statues, her head is turned sharply and her gaze, even at this small scale, is clear and focused. The pose is more animated than similar archaic and classical terracotta figures.

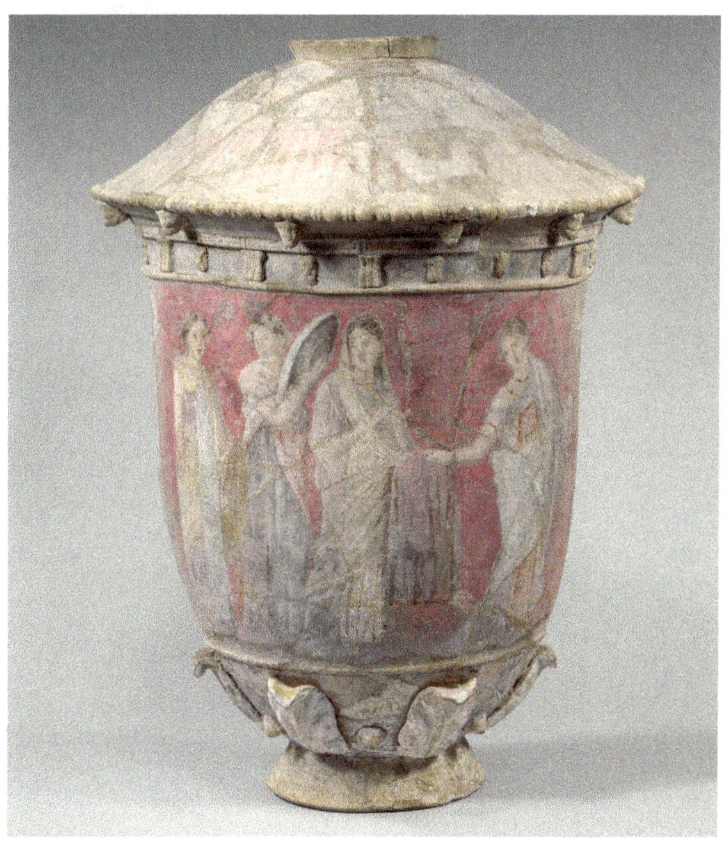

14.32 Centuripe vase with wedding scene, 3rd–2nd cent. BCE. 15½ in (39.4 cm). New York, Metropolitan Museum of Art 53.11.5. Photo: Image copyright © The Metropolitan Museum of Art. Image source: Art Resource, NY.

Terracottas like this are often called Tanagra figures generally, after the Boeotian site where many of them were first found in the nineteenth century, and became widely collected. These highly detailed and colorful figures were first produced in fourth-century BCE Athens, but their production spread to Boeotia; there were also significant production centers in Myrine (Anatolia), Alexandria, and southern Italy, including Taras/Taranto and Naples. In addition to standing women, Tanagras also included, among other subjects, actors and characters drawn from theater, dancers, children, and young girls playing. A terracotta showing a young child held in the lap by an old nurse is a charming and intimate scene that was a stock element of contemporary comedies (**Figure 14.35**). The faces, expressions, and proportions of the nurse and child are not idealized, and their large smiles suggest humor and delight. These and other terracottas show an interest in representing a wide range of character types, and can be associated with the rococo element of Hellenistic sculpture, like the dwarves from the Mahdia shipwreck (**see Figure 14.13**).

We saw in the introductory chapter an example of two seated women leaning together in an intimate conversation that is also characteristic of the genre (**see Figure 1.6, page 10**). The women do not have attributes, but could be a mother and daughter, perhaps Demeter and Persephone. Whether goddesses who protected young women or mothers, or simply women shown in an animated exchange, these were appropriate grave gifts or votive offerings for girls and young women and show them as vital and dynamic.

Dancers were also popular figures in terracotta and other media, including small bronzes like the Mahdia dwarves. One of the most unusual examples is a small bronze called the "Baker Dancer" in the Metropolitan Museum (**Figure 14.36**). The woman is wearing a heavy chiton with deep folds and has a thinner mantle wrapped over her body and head, making a veil. She pulls one corner of the mantle away from her body, which stretches the cloth to reveal the furrows of the chiton below in the drapery-through-drapery effect. We have already seen this feature in Tanagra-type figures; it also appears in marble sculpture and may have originated in the later third century BCE. The dancer's right arm is bent and enveloped in cloth to make a sling like the Taranto woman, but the pose here is much more complicated as the dancer is twisting her body toward her left while turning her head back toward the right, creating a pyramidal mass from some viewing points.

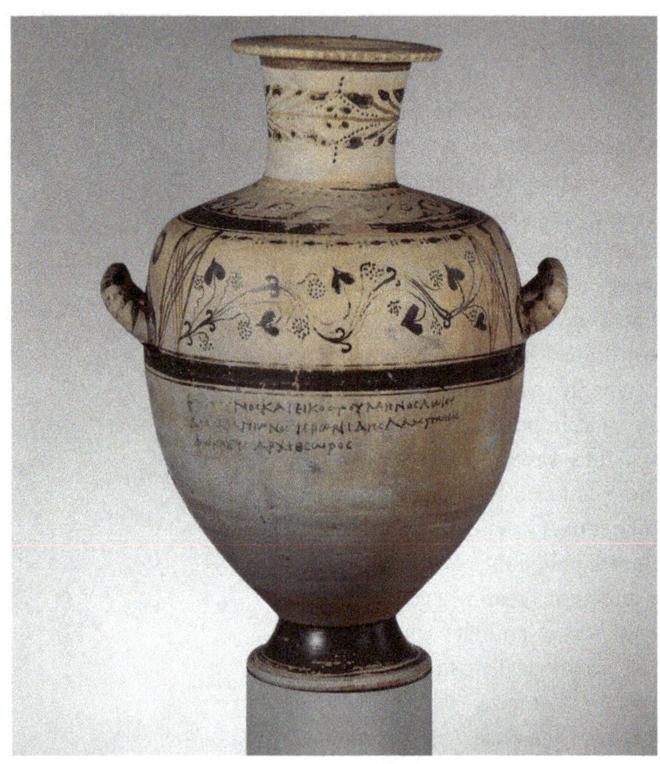

14.33 Hadra hydria, *c.* 226–225 BCE. 16⅝ in (42.2 cm). New York, Metropolitan Museum of Art 90.9.5. Urn of Hieronides of Phocaea. Photo: Image copyright © The Metropolitan Museum of Art. Image source: Art Resource, NY.

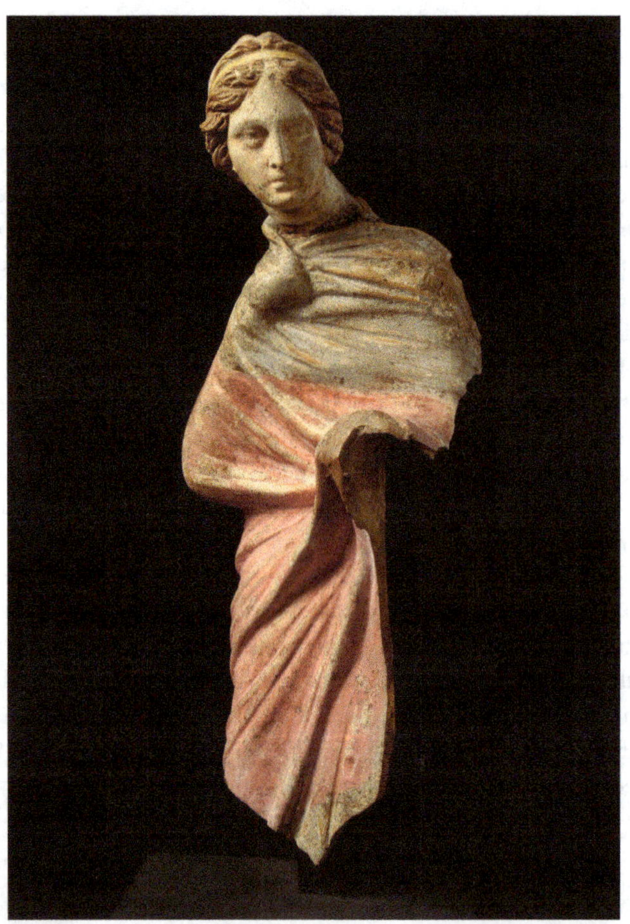

14.34 Terracotta woman from Corso Umberto, Taras/Taranto, early 3rd cent. BCE. Taranto, National Archaeological Museum 112640. Photo: Museum.

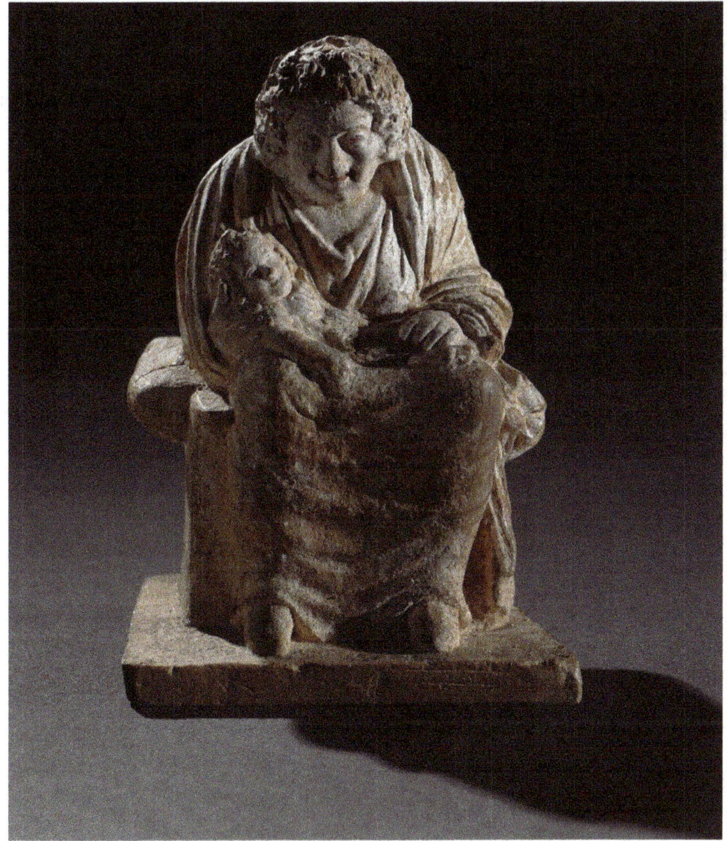

14.35 Terracotta seated nurse holding child, late 4th cent. BCE. 4¼ in (10.8 cm). London, British Museum 1874,1110.18. Photo: © The Trustees of the British Museum.

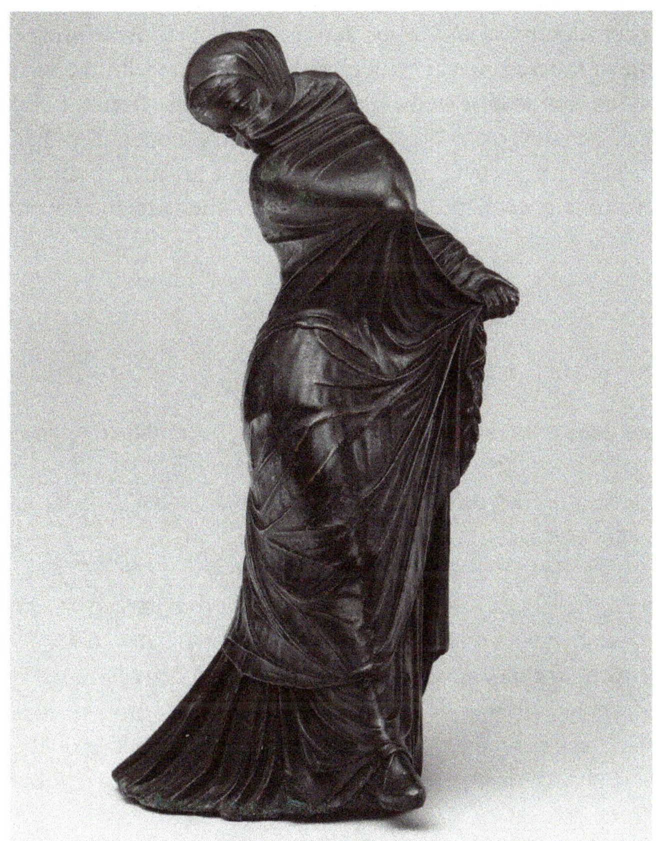

14.36 "Baker Dancer," 3rd–2nd cent. BCE. Bronze, 8 1/16 in (20.5 cm). New York. Metropolitan Museum of Art 1972.118.95. Photo: Image copyright © The Metropolitan Museum of Art. Image source: Art Resource, NY.

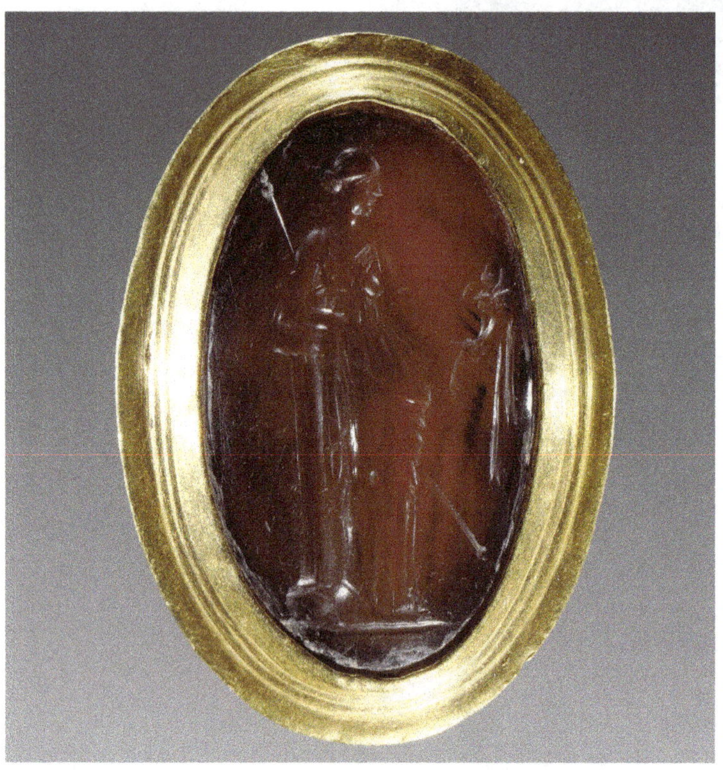

14.37 Ring with intaglio gem, c. 220–100 BCE. Gold and carnelian, 1½ in (3.8 cm). Malibu, Getty Villa 92.AM.8.9. Tyche. Photo: The J. Paul Getty Museum, Villa Collection, Malibu, California.

These types of veiled dancers were popular in Alexandria and the bronze is said to be from Alexandria, although it is without a findspot. This type of figure is often found in terracotta, but this example remains unique in bronze work, and the quality of the bronze is fine and detailed. Whether this figure was for domestic viewing or, like her terracotta counterparts, made as a tomb or sanctuary offering, is uncertain, but it does capture the drama of dance and mime and gives a glimpse of the entertainment of elite courts and households.

A very small work combines many of the characteristics that we have seen in Hellenistic art, a gem set in a gold ring that is part of an ensemble thought to be again from Alexandria **(Figure 14.37)**. The carnelian bezel is carved intaglio with a female figure leaning against a short column. She holds a cornucopia, an attribute of Tyche, but it is a double cornucopia and she holds a scepter as well. These link the figure to Arsinoë II, as we saw earlier, making this figure signify not only a goddess, but also the divine nature of the Ptolemaic dynasty. The pose recalls also the Aphrodite of Melos **(see Figure 14.17, page 362)** and shares with her the exaggerated line of the hips to give the standing figure a more open pose, holding her attribute out toward the viewer. In an age in which individuals worried about the vagaries of Tyche, such a ring could serve as a talisman to protect its owner. The owner, too, could also express reverence for the Greek rulers of Alexandria and Egypt, and the hope of receiving prosperity from both gods and kings. This type of syncretism and symbolism is in keeping with the intellectual character of Hellenistic culture. The cornucopias are held out at some distance from the body, but the shoulders and head are set back, and the pose could suggest, at least to a modern eye, that they are only tentatively offered to a beholder, and could be snatched back in a moment. Even standing, we might see the figure as maintaining a dramatic tension, raising doubt as to the benefits conferred to any individual.

TEXTBOX: THE RIACE WARRIORS AS HELLENISTIC SCULPTURE

The Riace Warriors **(see Figure 10.5, page 241)** were discovered by a diver in 1972 and then retrieved and restored by the Italian authorities. No traces of a shipwreck or other material were found that might provide a means for dating the statues, which relied upon stylistic and technical analysis after the works were cleaned and restored. Most scholars dated the works to the fifth century BCE on that basis.

There are not, however, very many comparanda in bronze from this or any other period of Greek art. One important scholar of Greek sculpture, Brunilde Ridgway, came to a different conclusion regarding the style and dating: "they were made simultaneously (not some thirty years apart, as several authors maintain), and no earlier than ca. 100 B.C., although possibly later. In my opinion, they are eclectic creations imitating primarily a basic heroic type of the fifth century that had great currency throughout antiquity" (Ridgway 2002, 200). Among other features, she points to the heavy eyelids, the open mouth, the use of silver for the teeth, and the dark patina of the surface, which is similar to the bronzes found in the Mahdia shipwreck and different from the shinier surface of works from the fifth century (see Ridgway 1984).

As we saw with the Odysseus statue from the Antikythera shipwreck, Greek workshops were producing marble statues for export to the Roman market, and the Sperlonga sculptures suggest that Greek artists also came to Italy to work for Roman patrons. Whereas the bronze youth from the Antikythera shipwreck would seem to have been a fourth-century statue that was being appropriated from somewhere for a Roman patron, the supply of bronzes through plunder and expropriation must have been dwindling by the first century BCE. Four monumental bronze statues that were found in the Piraeus harbor of Athens, probably buried in the sack of Sulla in 86 BCE, have also been attributed to the Hellenistic period as made for the Roman market (Ridgway 2002, 129 with bibliography).

The Riace Warriors were presented in this book as belonging to the fifth century, but it must be acknowledged that there is potential for a different dating, particularly if other comparanda with secure dating based on provenance are discovered in the future. It also suggests that classicizing can be just as evocative as classical art.

REFERENCES

Cohen, A. 1997. *The Alexander Mosaic: Stories of Victory and Defeat*. Cambridge/New York: Cambridge University Press.

Kousser, R. 2005. "Creating the Past: The Vénus de Milo and the Hellenistic Reception of Classical Greece." *American Journal of Archaeology* 109, 227–250.

Pollitt, J. J. 1986. *Art in the Hellenistic Age*. Cambridge/New York: Cambridge University Press.

Ridgway, B. S. 1984. "The Riace Bronzes: A Minority Viewpoint." In *Due Bronzi da Riace*, Bollettino d'Arte Serie Speciale 3, vol. 2, 313–326. Rome: Bollettino d'Arte.

Ridgway, B. S. 2002. *Hellenistic Sculpture III: The Styles of ca. 100–31 B.C.* Madison: University of Wisconsin Press.

Salowey, C. A. 2012. "Women on Hellenistic Grave Stelai: Reading Images and Texts." In S. L. James and S. Dillon, eds. *A Companion to Women in the Ancient World*, 249–262. Malden, MA/Oxford: Wiley Blackwell.

Stewart, A. 1993. "Narration and Allusion in the Hellenistic Baroque." In P. J. Holliday, ed. *Narrative and Event in Ancient Art*, 130–174. Cambridge/New York: Cambridge University Press.

Themelis, P. 1994. "Damophon of Messene: New Evidence." In K. A. Sheedy, ed. *Archaeology in the Peloponnese: New Excavations and Research*, 1–37. Oxford: Oxbow Books.

FURTHER READING

Cohen, A. 1997. *The Alexander Mosaic: Stories of Victory and Defeat*. Cambridge/New York: Cambridge University Press.

Cohen, A. 2010. *Art in the Era of Alexander the Great: Paradigms of Manhood and Their Cultural Transmission*. Cambridge/New York: Cambridge University Press.

Dillon, S. 2006. *Ancient Greek Portrait Sculpture: Contexts, Subjects, and Styles*. Cambridge/New York: Cambridge University Press.

Jeammet, V., ed. 2010. *Tanagras: Figurines for Life and Eternity. The Musée du Louvre's Collection of Greek Figurines*. Paris: Fundación Bancaja.

Kaltsas, N., E. Vlachogianni, and P. Bouyia, eds. 2012. *The Antikythera Shipwreck: The Ship, the Treasures, the Mechanism*. Athens: National Archaeological Museum.

Kousser, R. M. 2008. *Hellenistic and Roman Ideal Sculpture: The Allure of the Classical*. Cambridge/New York: Cambridge University Press.

Miles, M. M. 2008. *Art as Plunder: The Ancient Origins of Debate about Cultural Property*. Cambridge/New York: Cambridge University Press.

Miller, S. G. 2014. "Hellenistic Painting in the Eastern Mediterranean, Mid-Fourth to Mid-First Century B.C." In J. J. Pollitt, ed. *The Cambridge History of Painting in the Classical World*, 170–237. Cambridge/New York: Cambridge University Press.

Pollitt, J. J. 1986. *Art in the Hellenistic Age*. Cambridge/New York: Cambridge University Press.

Ridgway, B. S. 1990. *Hellenistic Sculpture I: The Styles of ca. 331–220 B.C.* Madison: University of Wisconsin Press.

Ridgway, B. S. 2000. *Hellenistic Sculpture II: The Styles of ca. 200–100 B.C.* Madison: University of Wisconsin Press.

Ridgway, B. S. 2002. *Hellenistic Sculpture III: The Styles of ca. 100–31 B.C.* Madison: University of Wisconsin Press.

15

EPILOGUE

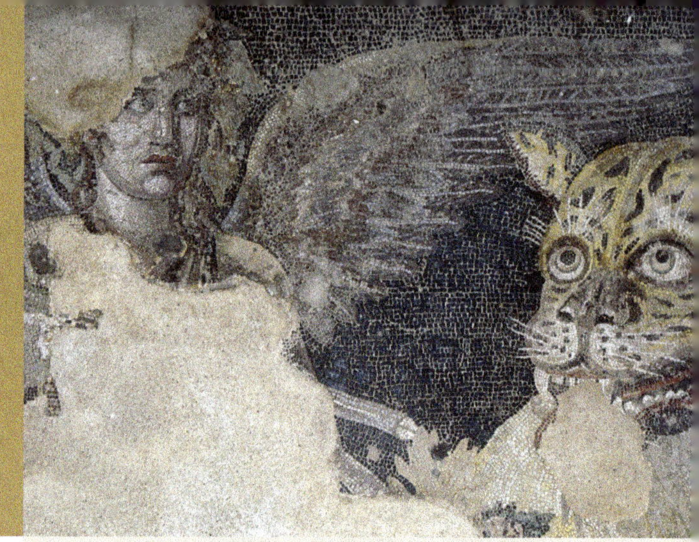

A History of Greek Art, First Edition. Mark D. Stansbury-O'Donnell.

We saw in the last chapter that the Greek world and the production of art and architecture greatly expanded in the Hellenistic period to new sites such as Antioch, Pergamon, and Alexandria, and that Greeks ruled a diverse population in many parts of the Mediterranean and Near East until the Roman and Persian empires asserted control by the end of the first century. The scale of this expansion as seen in the size of the cities and the production of art is remarkable, but the interaction of the Greek culture with the other peoples of the Mediterranean and beyond is a continuous aspect of their history going back to the Bronze Age. In the second millennium, art from Minoan and Mycenaean palatial cultures was exported throughout the Mediterranean and materials and works from Egypt and the Near East were imported. Even through the so-called Dark Ages contacts with Cyprus and other sites continued at some level, and in the later eighth century the new Greek poleis began sending colonists to start new cities throughout the Mediterranean. In the seventh and sixth centuries Greek art was exported thousands of miles from Spain to the Crimea and was produced outside the boundaries of mainland Greece in Magna Graecia.

In other words, Greek art did not exist in isolation and one should consider that the cultures of the ancient world were in continuous communication and exchange with one another, sometimes through war and conquest, sometimes through trade and migration, and often through both. Whereas some early histories of Greek art tended to see it as self-generated, springing as it were full-grown like Athena out of the head of Zeus, Greek art and culture were engaged in dialogue with other cultures, influencing and being influenced through the reciprocal contact. To conclude our exploration of Greek art history, we should consider briefly the interaction of Greek art and culture with those of its neighbors, and with our own culture today.

The three vessels in **Figure 15.1** were found in 1890 in a tomb in Athens, along with seven other vases, including the cup in **Figure 10.22 (page 258)**. Based on the style of the figural pottery, the works are dated around 460–450 BCE and came from one or possibly two closely related workshops associated with the potter Sotades, who signed the phiale on the right *Sotades epoie*, "Sotades made [me]." The sides of the pots have been carefully worked to create precise series of concentric flutes from the rim to the bottom. The flutes have been painted with three colors, black, white, and a matt red slip; the edges of the flutes are abraded and show the natural red of the clay. The mastoid cup shape, named after its resemblance to the breast, began to appear in Attic pottery in the late sixth century but its origins are thought to derive from metal cups of similar shape used in Near Eastern, especially Persian, dining. The drinkers would hold the vessel supported by the fingertips while reclining on a couch. The phiale is also a shape that derives from Near Eastern prototypes and was established in the Greek pottery repertory in the sixth century. The function of the vessel, however, was different from its model. In the Near East it served as a drinking cup like the kylix or mastoid cup, but in Greece the phiale became a ritual vessel for pouring offerings of wine onto an altar or the ground **(see Figure 9.18, page 232)**.

Most Greek examples of the shapes do not include the fluting seen here, which imitates the fluting found in Persian metalwork, like the rhyton in **Figure 15.2**. This object serves as a funnel, with wine poured into the top and then flowing out of a hole at the base for pouring into the cup of the drinker. It is a luxury service item in Near Eastern dining, and this example preserves the decorative fluting and use of gilding to create a high-status work to be used in a gathering of elite members of the Persian

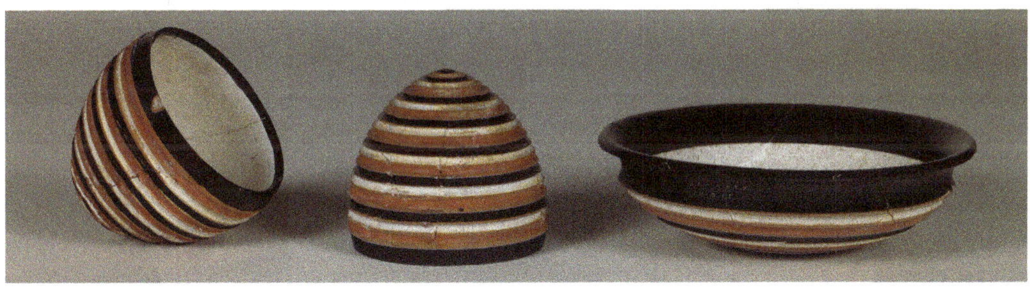

15.1 Two Attic mastoi; Attic phiale signed by Sotades, *c.* 460–450 BCE. Diameter of phiale: 6⅝ in (16.8 cm). London, British Museum 1894,0719.3; 1894,0719.4; 1894,0719.2. Photo: © The Trustees of the British Museum.

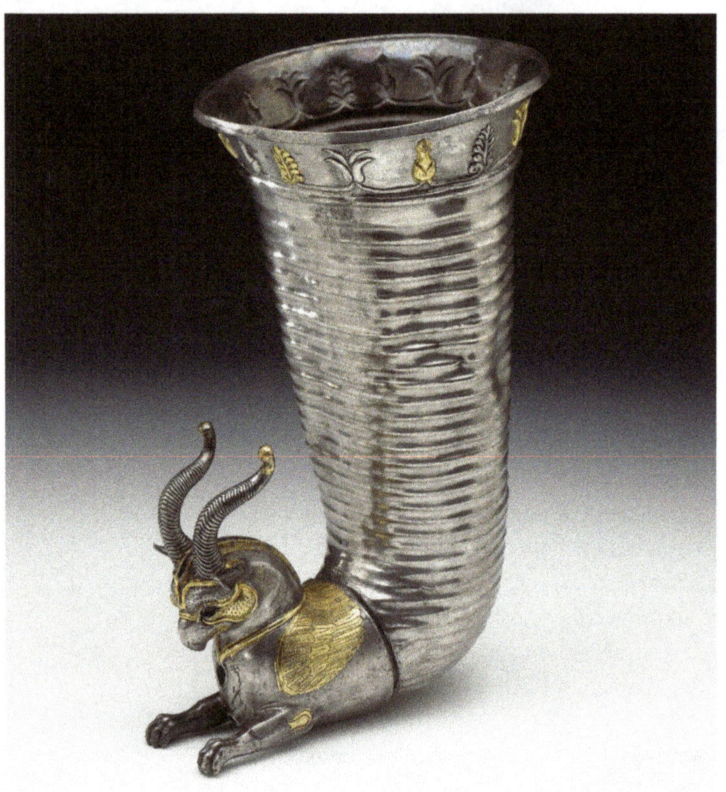

15.2 Achaemenid silver griffin rhyton from Erzincan, Turkey, 5th cent. BCE. 9¹⁄₁₆ in (23 cm). London, British Museum 1897,1231.178. Photo: © The Trustees of the British Museum.

empire. In comparing color and decoration to the mastoids and phiale of Sotades, one can see how art historians have thought that the Greek potter was imitating the shapes and effects of Persian metalwork in Attic clay.

In considering the relationship of the Sotades pots to Persian metalwork, one needs to examine not only the artistic details that suggest a connection, but also the motivation, as Margaret Miller has explained, both for the artist and for the family who purchased the works to serve as grave goods (Miller 1997). First, one can consider whether works like the Sotades cups are **imitations**, within the limitations of using a different medium, or adaptations. An imitation follows closely the shape and details of the model, whereas an **adaptation** would involve more significant changes to the shape and form of the model, perhaps using selected details out of context or using the model for a different purpose to create a **hybridized** work. With both imitation and adaptation, one has to ask whether the "copy" is meant to enhance the prestige or power of the owner/user or to denigrate or neutralize the status of the model and its culture, or some range or combination of motives.

In the case of the Sotades cups, we should probably consider these as imitations since the function and shape of the mastoid cup have not changed significantly, and creating the fluting is an added level of work and not a technique typical of ceramics, unlike metalwork. Even if the function of the Greek phiale is different from its Near Eastern prototype, in this case it is still imitation rather than adaptation, which would require greater change to the model. For example, Greek potters also produced animal-shaped rhyta similar to the Persian example, but transformed their pottery versions into closed vessels for drinking rather than a funnel for pouring. Sometimes stands were added, further adapting the original to the requirements of sympotic drinking. Whereas the symposion at its beginning imitated luxury Near Eastern dining, by the fifth century it was a more widespread custom and adapted to the ideology of the polis. The kylikes from the Agora well **(see Figures 1.10A and 1.10B, page 14)** that were introduced in the first chapter show that the practice remained formal, but was not elitist as it had been originally.

In both imitation and adaptation, the motivation can be quite varied. Metalware vessels were prestige objects, both for their intrinsic material value and for their associations with elite cultural groups such as Persian nobility. The Sotades cups, while not as valuable as metalware, were yet special and distinctive products that would have been recognized as such by family and participants in the funerary ritual. Their display and deposit at the tomb would proclaim the status of the deceased, just as imported work had done in the tomb of the Rich Lady **(see Figure 4.6, page 76)**.

Elsewhere we have other evidence of the adaptation of Persian art and style in Greek art, such as the *kanephoros* shown in the procession to Apollo on the fifth-century krater by the Kleophon Painter **(see Figure 7.17, page 174)**. She wears a sleeved garment, the **chitoniskos**, that is unlike the sleeveless peplos or chiton/himation garments seen in Greek painting and sculpture. There is also a fringe at the edge of the garment below the knee, another characteristic of Near Eastern textiles. The motifs on the garments, however, have been adapted, including the stylized birds above the fringe. Overall, her garment is modeled on the sleeved tunic but the decoration has been adapted for Greek use. The Persians were a powerful empire with many allies and contacts among the Greek poleis, and their art could be sources of emulation for enhancing the prestige of Greeks owning imitations or adaptations.

imitation
the reproduction of a model from one culture or period in a second period or culture, given differences in medium or technique

adaptation
the merger of elements from an artistic model or source with indigenous elements or types to create a hybridized work

hybridization
a blending of artistic elements from two cultures, with elements of both cultural styles and subject matter discernible in the work

chitoniskos
sleeved garment like a tunic

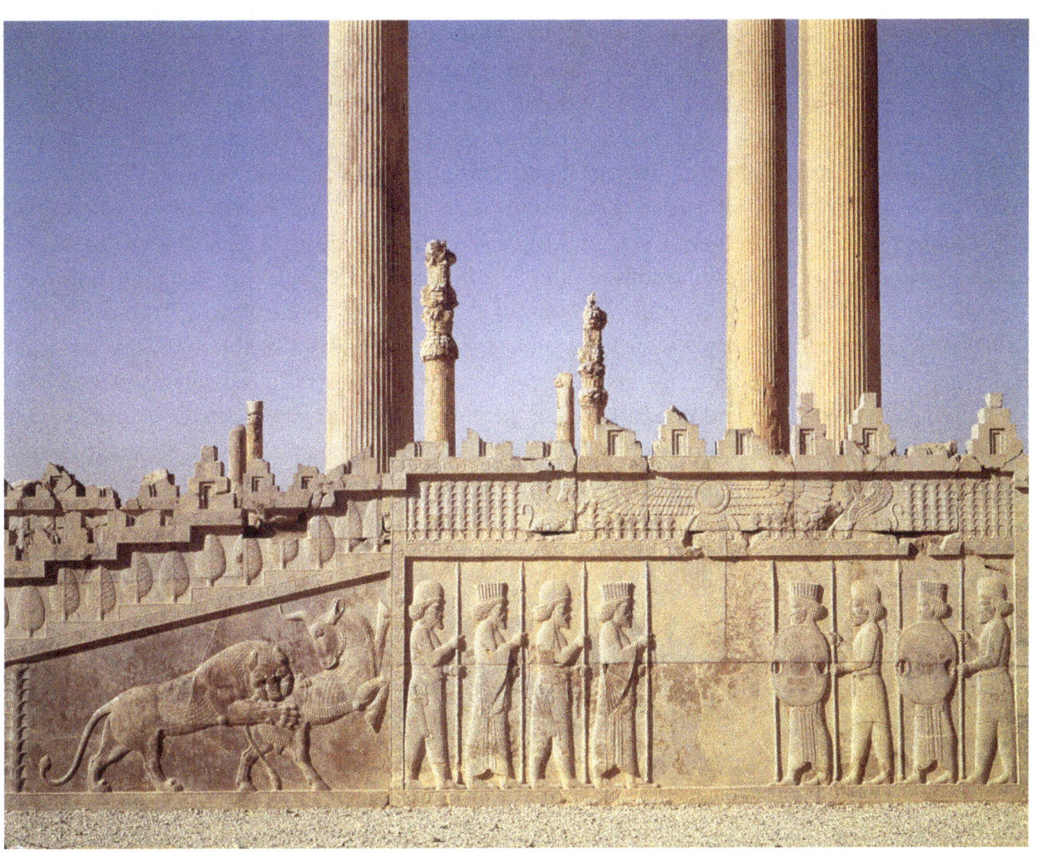

15.3 East stairway to the Apadana (audience hall) of Darius and Xerxes at the Persian palace at Persepolis, Iran, *c.* 520–460 BCE. Persian guards and lion attacking bull. Photo: Bridgeman-Giraudon/Art Resource, NY.

We can see another example of the complexity of the Persian and Greek artistic relationship by turning to the Persian palace at Persepolis. The Achaemenid empire had been founded in 557 BCE by Cyrus the Great (d. 530), who captured Babylon in 539 and from there extended his control to the Levant and Anatolia. His successor Cambyses (r. 530–522) extended the empire to Egypt by 522, followed by Darius (r. 522–486) into eastern Europe, including Thrace and Macedonia. Around 515 Darius founded the palace at Persepolis as one of the capitals of the Persian empire. The most prominent feature of the complex was the Apadana or audience hall **(Figure 15.3)**. This building had a nearly square base rising almost 4 meters above the flanking courtyards. Access to the Apadana was through a monumental gate leading into the courtyard, but the path followed a bent-axis organization involving a number of turns or switchbacks along the way, rather than a straight processional path. The Apadana served as a place where the subject territories of the empire would bring their tribute to the King of Kings. The stone staircases, parapets, and podium walls of the Apadana were carved with reliefs whose subjects included palace guards, processions of tribute bearers, and images of lions attacking bulls, as can be seen in the picture of the east stairway. The visitor to the palace would be reminded at every step, turn, and stop of the power of the Persian king.

The use of reliefs in palaces had ample precedent in the Assyrian empire, as the guardian figure in Chapter 6 demonstrated **(see Figure 6.2, page 133)**, but the use of limestone and other hard stone at Persepolis indicates a more ambitious and difficult decorative program, as was the design of the Apadana. The ceiling of the audience hall was a hypostyle structure, supported by thirty-six tall stone columns with capitals, creating an interior space that was almost 60 meters square. The height and volume of the Apadana were unprecedented in ancient architecture and signified powerfully the ambitions of the Achaemenid kings.

hypostyle
term signifying multiple columns aligned on a grid on the interior of a structure to support the roof and ceiling

As was true of Greek sculpture and architecture in the seventh century BCE, there was no established tradition of precision stone cutting and carving in Persian art and architecture in the sixth century when the building program began. To build their palaces, Darius and other Persian kings drew upon the expertise and materials of their subject nations, creating in the process a multicultural workforce. An inscription of Darius at the Achaemenid palace at Susa in Persia, which also included an Apadana, tells us that the workers who built that structure included several conquered peoples from Anatolia, and specifically that "The stone-cutters who wrought the stone, those were Ionians and Sardians" (Frankfurt 1970, 349). If we compare the carving style of the reliefs at Persepolis to late sixth-century relief sculpture from Greece, such as the Siphnian Treasury at Delphi **(see Figures 8.1 and 8.2, pages 183, 184)**, one can readily see similarities in the rendering of the features that support Darius's claim that Ionians were cutting and carving stone for the Persian palaces. The spacing and posing of the Persepolis figures are more formal than the narratives of the Siphnian Treasury, as would be suitable for their different purpose. One interesting point of comparison is the lion attack motif at Persepolis and in Greek art, and its adaptation in the lion attacking a giant on the Siphnian Treasury **(see Figure 9.1, page 212)**. In most of these, the lion and victim are shown in profile, but the twist of the lion's head as it bites into a bull or giant presents an artistic problem of foreshortening that was not fully resolved in the sixth century, as the Siphnian Treasury shows. In both cases we end up with a combination of a frontal and elevated view of the lion's face, a profile body, and the use of the mane to mask the turning of the neck.

This might seem to be a case of Greek art influencing Persian art. Certainly the fluted columns and some of the architectural ornament derive from Ionian architecture, but the relationship is more complicated than that. The lion attack had been a staple of Greek art since the eighth century, but it was also a common motif in Assyrian and Near Eastern art as an expression of royal power. The subject matter of the Persepolis reliefs, guards and tribute bearers, also draws upon Near Eastern traditions that the Persians have adapted for their purposes. Ultimately, we have to think about the purpose of the palace as an expression of Persian rule over a vast and diverse kingdom, and that the artists, materials, and subjects found in the art and architecture at Persepolis have been subsumed to serve Persian purposes. We might consider this a case of adaptation that expresses dominance over the source while serving to create a structure that was an easily recognizable symbol of Persian power.

The processional friezes at Persepolis have led to theories in turn about the influence of Achaemenid art on classical Athens, and in particular the Parthenon. The processional frieze of the Parthenon **(see Figure 1.1, page 2; Figure 10.12, page 249; Figure 10.15, page 250)** is without precedent in Greek architectural sculpture, as is the placement of an Ionian frieze on the cella of a Doric temple. The Periklean building program was on one level a memorial to the victory of Athens over Persia; an adaptation of the procession bearing tribute to the king to one bringing an offering to the goddess Athena would resonate with elements of Athenian propaganda, but the idea remains hypothetical (Root 1985).

Another building of Perikles also shows a formal connection to Persian architecture, the Odeion next to the Theater of Dionysos at the southeast foot of the Acropolis **(see Figure 7.4, page 160)**. This building was a hypostyle hall, just slightly rectangular rather than square (62.4 × 68.6 m), that was used, at least in later times, for music contests. Its archaeological details are very sketchy: the Periklean structure was destroyed in the sack of Athens by the Roman general Sulla in 86 BCE and then rebuilt. In Plutarch's second-century CE biography of Perikles (*Vita Perikles* 13.10), the writer tells us that "They say that it is the image (*eikona*) and the imitation (*mimema*) of the tent of the Persian King" (tr. Miller 1997, 221). Like the hypostyle halls of the palaces, the Persian king's campaign tent was a huge structure with many poles and rooms within it, but Margaret Miller has argued that we should look to the Apadana of the Persian kings as the model for the Odeion. Certainly the construction of a nearly square, stone hypostyle building in Athens was unprecedented in the fifth century BCE and its size is similar to the Apadana at Persepolis, making it the largest interior space in Greece at the time. To much later viewers, it continued to look foreign rather than Greek.

In building the Odeion, Perikles may have been asserting the power and prestige of Athens as the center of its own empire. Persia offered a model for imperial architecture and, by building it, Perikles distinguished Athens as distinct and different from the other cities of Greece, including powerful cities like Sparta, Corinth, and Thebes. This would appear to be a case of adaptation and emulation, and it seems likely based on the testimony that the building continued to look "Persian," and therefore distinctive, to its viewers in later centuries. It is interesting to consider that even though Greek artists worked on and contributed to the Persian Apadana, the influence of Greek art on Persian culture is modest at best, whereas the influence of Persia on Greece at various levels is varied and stronger. We need to recognize that Greek art did not exist in isolation or spring fully formed on its own, but that it existed within a network of ancient cultures whose current of ideas, materials, and style ebbed and flowed throughout the Mediterranean and Near East.

Some examples of Greece's cross-cultural relationships have appeared in many of the previous chapters. For example, it has been suggested that the kouros from Palaikastro emulates the Egyptian canon of proportions **(see Figure 2.14, page 37)**, and certainly its use of hippopotamus ivory is just one piece of evidence of the trade in materials and objects from the Bronze Age that we saw in Chapters 2 and 3. In the Geometric period we see Near Eastern artists and materials coming to Greece **(see Figure 4.6, page 76; Figure 4.14, page 85; Figure 11.12, page 281)** and Near Eastern motifs like the heraldic animals flanking a sacred tree being exported in a Greek Geometric style **(see Figure 4.11, page 82)**. The scale of exchange escalated in the seventh century with the imitation and adaptation of new motifs like the sphinx **(see Figure 6.13, page 143)**, griffin **(see Figure 6.9, page 139; Figure 6.14, page 143)**, sacred trees, and Mistress of Animals **(see Figure 6.17, page 145)**, and in some cases the imported ideas are exported, sometimes back to the east **(see Figure 6.10, page 140; Figure 6.11, page 141; Figure 6.14, page 143)**. Monumental stone sculpture was adapted by the Greeks, in terms of both form and stonework techniques **(see Figure 6.3, page 134; Figure 6.4, page 135)**, although the study of the proportional systems and carving techniques of statues suggests that there were multiple points of origin and not a single source or model. Painted figural pottery from Greece, especially with narrative scenes, became a widely dispersed commodity in the Mediterranean, and in Etruria there are limited adoptions of the Greek black-figure and red-figure technique. That exchange went in both directions is seen in the adoption of Etruscan shapes in Greek pottery workshops for sale in the Etruscan market **(see Figure 11.8, page 277)**.

With the fourth century we saw that red-figure pottery workshops became prolific in southern Italy and Sicily, but these painters were creating for a local market that was sometimes Greek, but frequently mixed (as in the case of Metapontum/Metaponto and Poseidonia/Paestum) or primarily non-Greek (in Apulia). New shapes and subjects were developed to meet this market. Elsewhere the classical style became more international, with Mausolos hiring Greek sculptors to decorate his Mausoleion **(see Figure 12.4, page 292)**, and new patrons and religious ideas became important in the northern Greek kingdoms. In the course of the Hellenistic period the Greek rulers shaped their images for both a Greek audience **(see Figure 14.26, page 370)** and local audience **(see Figure 14.25, page 370)**. Alexandria and Antioch were now two of the greatest Greek cities, though very diverse in their populations.

Finally, Romans became the occupiers of Greece and both "collectors" and patrons of Greek art. The Greek classicizing style becomes the idealizing style of Roman statues and the Doric, Ionic, and Corinthian orders were adopted wholesale for the facades of Roman buildings made of brick and concrete. Rome continues the classical tradition, assimilating the style and some models of Greek art **(see Figure 10.7, page 243; Figure 12.11, page 300)**, but created new categories and types of sculpture to make it truly Roman. The reuse of Roman building materials and constant discovery of statues from the Roman empire meant that the Greco-Roman classical past would continue to be discovered and rediscovered after antiquity, leading to Greece being viewed as the birthplace of western art.

Like many stories, the legacy of Greece is complex and changing. Neoclassical architecture and sculpture in the nineteenth century borrowed liberally from Greek styles and forms. The modernism

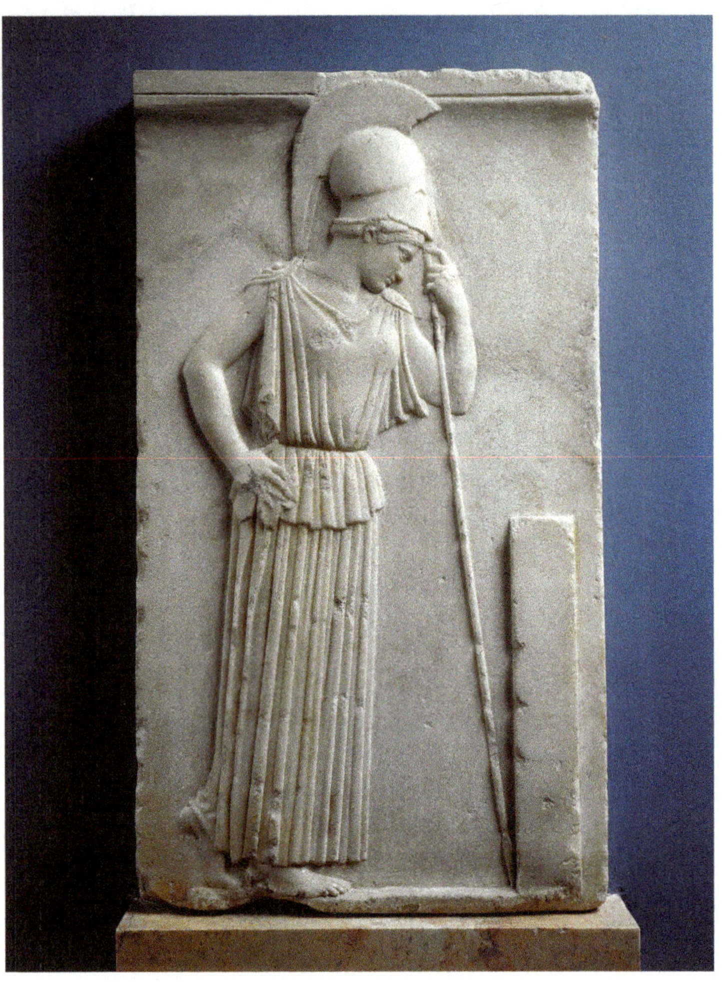

15.4 "Mourning Athena" relief, *c.* 470 BCE. 18⅞ in (48 cm). Athens, Acropolis Museum 695. Photo: Marie Mauzy/Art Resource, NY.

of the twentieth century put it out of favor, only for it to return in a transformed pastiche of postmodernism. Today, the aesthetic standard of Greek art is no longer reason alone for why we should study its history, but understanding its purpose and meaning to the culture that produced it is still important. Indeed, we might look at one final work of Greek art to offer a rationale for its relevance today. A votive relief from the Acropolis dating about 470 BCE shows Athena leaning on a spear with her helmet raised up on the crown of her head **(Figure 15.4)**. Her head is bowed and her eyes glance toward a slab seen in profile; it too is a stele like the object itself. We cannot see the front of the stele she looks at, but most scholars agree that it would have an inscribed text that she is reading. The most attractive theory is that the names of Athenian citizens who had recently died in battle were inscribed on it, like the casualty lists that we mentioned in the discussion of the monument of Dexileos **(see Figure 12.12, page 301)**. Athena's finger touches her hair, and while this is not the gesture of tearing one's hair in grief found in funerary images, which would not be appropriate for a goddess, it does suggest that she could be mourning the deceased, hence the nickname of the stele. As we have seen in many monuments of Greek art, it was important to remember the deceased, particularly their names and accomplishments. Athena, an immortal viewer, remembers these names for the generations to come.

One of the purposes of history is also to remember and understand why events happened, and for art history, to comprehend why and how works of art and architecture were made. Herodotos, the first Greek historian, sets out precisely his purpose in writing about the war between the Greeks and Persians in his first sentences:

> I, Herodotos of Halicarnassus, am here setting forth my history, that time may not draw the color from what man has brought into being, nor those great and wonderful deeds, manifested by both Greeks and barbarians, fail of their report, and, together with all this, the reason why they fought one another. (Herodotos 1.1; tr. Grene)

Herodotos's literary image of fading color over time resonates particularly well with the decay and destruction of art and buildings, but the fragments of Greek art and architecture still remain and ask us to remember what they are and the people who made, used, and saw them.

This power of names and memory continues to endure in our culture, as can be seen strikingly in a contemporary monument, Maya Lin's Vietnam Veterans Memorial in Washington, DC, dedicated in 1982. The design is deceptively simple, a granite wall set in a V-shape, with the names of the Americans who died in Vietnam inscribed chronologically on it **(Figure 15.5)**. The design was not without criticism after it was built as it lacked any figural sculpture, traditional in war monuments like the Iwo Jima memorial. The design, however, is extraordinarily effective in focusing our attention on the names of those who died in a controversial and divisive war. Three decades after its dedication, the monument still has the power to move, drawing thousands of visitors and creating an experience that might be said to contribute to a catharsis for those who view it. Names and people still have the

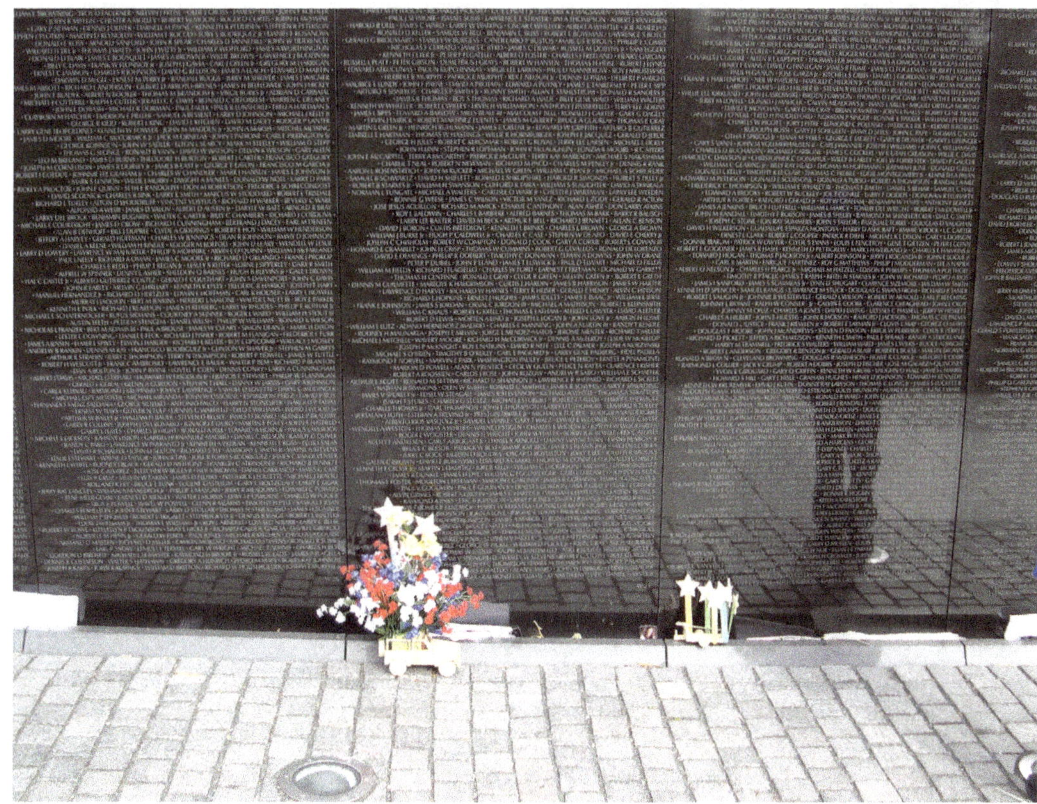

15.5 Maya Lin, Vietnam Veterans Memorial, Washington, DC, dedicated 1982. Photo: author.

ability to resonate in our culture, just as they did in Greece, and standing in front of the slabs of the Vietnam Veterans Memorial demonstrates that. When we look at the temples, ruins, and art of the Greeks, we need to think about those who looked and created before us and remember them, and perhaps continue to learn from them as well.

REFERENCES

Frankfurt, H. 1970. *The Art and Architecture of the Ancient Orient*. Harmondsworth: Penguin Books.

Herodotos. 1987. *The Histories*, tr. D. Grene. Chicago: University of Chicago Press.

Miller, M. C. 1997. *Athens and Persia in the Fifth Century BC: A Study in Cultural Receptivity*. Cambridge: Cambridge University Press.

Root, M. C. 1985. "The Parthenon Frieze and the Apadana Reliefs at Persepolis: Reassessing a Programmatic Relationship." *American Journal of Archaeology* 89, 103–120.

FURTHER READING

Gunter, A. G. 2009. *Greek Art and the Orient*. Cambridge/New York: Cambridge University Press.

Halles, S. and T. Hodos, eds. 2010. *Material Culture and Social Identities in the Ancient World*. Cambridge/New York: Cambridge University Press.

Miller, M. C. 1997. *Athens and Persia in the Fifth Century BC: A Study in Cultural Receptivity*. Cambridge: Cambridge University Press.

Villing, A. 2005. "Persia and Greece." In J. Curtis and N. Tallis, eds. *Forgotten Empire: The World of Ancient Persia*, 236–249. London: British Museum Press.

GLOSSARY

***a cappucina* tomb** Italian term designating a tomb made by lining a pit or trench with terracotta panels

abacus the square block that sits on top of the capital and supports the architrave

abaton the building in a sanctuary of Asklepios where the sick would be "incubated" as part of the healing ritual

abstract the representation of a subject in art in a simplified, reduced, or schematic form

acroterion (or akroterion) (pl. acroteria) ornament or sculpture placed at the corners or peak of a roof

adaptation the merger of elements from an artistic model or source with indigenous elements or types to create a hybridized work

agalma term meaning an object of delight such as a statue dedication. *Kalon agalma* means beautiful agalma

aglaos term signifying brilliance or radiance, especially of sculpture

agora the central open area of a Greek city where markets and administrative structures were found, as well as dedications and shrines

aidos term meaning modesty or sense of shame, usually signified by a downward gaze

alabastron a small perfume container, with a tall profile and rounded bottom

Amazonomachy term for a battle between Amazons and Greeks

amphictyony a group made up of members of neighboring states that oversaw a sanctuary such as Delphi

amphora (pl. amphorae) a multi-purpose storage vessel with two handles on the side and a narrower neck above a wide shoulder or belly

amphoriskos a small amphora or storage vessel

anakalypsis the gesture in the wedding in which the bride unveils herself to the groom. In art this is typically seen as a reference when a woman pulls her mantle away from her face or shoulder

anathema Greek word indicating the setting up or dedication of something for the gods

andron word meaning men's room, used to designate the dining room in the house where the symposion was held

anoikismos the founding or relocation of a city or cities by the movement inland of previously settled populations

anta (pl. antis) term for the projecting end of a wall

antefix vertical tile of terracotta or stone that covers the ends of the roof tiles. Antefixes can also serve as rain spouts

Anthesteria Dionysiac festival celebrating the new wine from the fall harvest

aparche an offering of "first fruits," that is, from the initial success or harvest

***apobates* (pl. *apobatai*)** a competition that involved a fully dressed warrior jumping out of and into a moving chariot

apotropaic a visual composition or motif that serves to protect a person or place from harm

archaic period Greek art produced between *c.* 720/700 and 480 BCE. From *archaios*, meaning "old"

archaios Greek word for old, used to denote something old in style, such as art of the seventh and sixth centuries, hence the archaic period

architrave the lower section of the entablature that rests on column capitals

aryballos a small perfume container with a single handle and narrow spout and with a pointed or globular body

ashlar masonry square-cut stone, usually in the form of long rectangular blocks

Asklepieion a temple dedicated to Asklepios

assemblage a group of objects found together in an archaeological context or deposit such as a grave

Astarte Phoenician goddess of fertility and sex often represented as a nude figure

asty the urban center of a Greek colony (see also *chora*)

Athena Promachos Athena "foremost fighter," featuring an armored Athena striding forward with a spear

Attic art coming from Athens, named for Attica, the name for the city of Athens and its surrounding rural areas

aulos a double flute played through a mouthpiece set on the ends and strapped around the neck, with each flute held in a different hand

baroque style style of Hellenistic sculpture defined by its dynamic compositions using diagonal lines, exaggerated musculature and poses, powerful emotional expression, and strong contrast of light and dark

bead-and-reel decorative pattern made of alternating round or ovular beads and narrow vertical disks (reel)

bilingual vase painting vases in which one side is painted in black-figure technique and the other in red-figure technique, often with the same subject matter

black-figure a style of painted pottery in which the silhouette of the figure is painted with black slip. Anatomical and other details are lines incised through the black surface; colors of red and white can be added on top of the black slip

black-glaze a style of painted pottery in which the surface is covered entirely with black slip

boule a council of citizens chosen to make decisions for the polis. This was a smaller group than the *ekklesia*

bouleuterion the meeting place of the *boule*

Bronze Age The era of Greek culture characterized by the use of bronze for tools and weapons, *c.* 3100–1075 BCE
burnishing rubbing an unfired, leather-hard vessel with a hard, smooth object to give it a smooth, polished surface
caryatid a statue of a woman that serves as a support in place of a column. It is a feature of the Ionic order of architecture and can also be a support handle for a mirror
cella the central room of a temple where the cult statue would be placed. Also called a naos
centauromachy literally, a centaur-battle, a term used to describe battles between centaurs and humans, and particularly the battle of the centaurs with the Lapiths at the wedding of their king, Peirithoös
Centuripe vases cinerary pottery decorated with architectural relief and painted figures made in Sicily during the Hellenistic period
chamber tomb a burial in which the remains are placed inside an open chamber, either vaulted or cut into rock or soil
chiaroscuro Italian term referring to the use of a range of tones in an image to create the appearance of three-dimensionality. It can also refer to the strong contrast between light and dark in a work that enhances dramatic effect
chiastic composition or chiasmus the placement of similar components on a diagonal axis in the composition, like the Greek letter chi (χ)
chiton a thin rectangular garment that is buttoned at the shoulders and hangs down, sometimes belted at the waist. Warriors can wear a short chiton under armor. Long chitons are worn by both women and men, although more rarely by the latter
chitoniskos sleeved garment like a tunic
chora the area of the Greek countryside and farmland outside of the polis
chous (pl. choes) small wine pitcher used in the Anthesteria
chronology, absolute the dating of a work to a specific calendar year(s) through external evidence, or a range of years on the basis of comparison to works with known dates
chronology, relative the dating of a work by its relationship to other works, either before, after, or at the same time
chryselephantine a work made of gold and ivory, often used for cult statues
chthonic related to or belonging to the underworld
cist grave a form of burial in which the grave is lined with stone slabs, leaving an open cavity for the body or ossuary and associated grave goods
classical period Greek art produced between *c.* 480 and 330 BCE
clerestory an upper story of a wall with openings or windows into the main space
comparanda known works of art that are used as benchmarks to identify or analyze the qualities of a work through comparison
continuous narrative narrative image in which multiple scenes are set in a continuous frieze or picture, repeating some of the participants from one scene to the next
contraction the practice in Doric architecture of adjusting the distance between columns at the corners to compensate for the placement of the triglyphs and metopes
contrapposto representation of the human figure showing the shifting and balancing of weight, usually with the weight borne on one leg and the other leg bent
corbel a form of vaulting in which each course of the vault projects progressively further inward until it meets the sloping ceiling from the other side
cornice the edge of the roof or pediment, called a raking cornice when sloped
Corridor House a type of Early Helladic structure with main rooms on the first floor that were flanked by corridors on either side that led to the upper story of the structure
cultural patrimony according to UNESCO, works of art and architecture, "which, on religious or secular grounds, is specifically designated by each State as being of importance for archaeology, prehistory, history, literature, art or science" (see textbox for Chapter 10)
Cycladic the designation for the Bronze Age on the Aegean islands
cyclical narrative narrative image in which multiple scenes are set in separate panels or pictures, repeating some of the participants from one scene to the next
Cyclopean walls made of massive, roughly worked stones, often with uneven courses
Daedalic a term derived from the mythological figure of Daidalos, used to signify early sculpture and relief of the seventh century, particularly the flat heads and triangle-shaped hair and faces
dekate a tithe offering
diachronic looking at things and events in chronological order
dinos a spherical mixing bowl without handles that sat on a stand
Dionysiac subject matter relating to the god Dionysos, his followers of satyrs and maenads, or activities associated with his festivals or the symposion
dithyramb a hymn that was sung and danced by a chorus
Doric order one of the orders of Greek architecture developed particularly for temples. It features columns with cushion capitals and no bases and a frieze made up of alternating triglyphs and metopes
Doryphoros "Spear-Bearer," a bronze sculpture of *c.* 450–440 BCE by Polykleitos now found only in copies
dromos a long and narrow passage leading to the vaulted chamber of a tholos
echinus the round cushion-shaped section of the Doric capital
egg-and-dart decorative molding made of alternating ovoid eggs framed by fanning spikes (darts)
Egyptianizing style a work made in imitation of a traditional Egyptian style, especially in the Hellenistic period
ekklesia the assembly of Athenian citizens voting on civic issues requiring a quorum of 6,000
ekphora the procession bearing the body of the deceased from the home to the tomb
emporion Greek term for a large market or trading center
engraving a metalwork technique in which lines are incised into the metal to create details or patterns
entablature the superstructure of a building above the colonnade, which includes the architrave, frieze, cornice, and pediment

entasis the vertical tapering and swelling of columns
epaulia term designating the reception held by a bride in her new home on the day after the wedding procession
ephebos term for a young man of eighteen to twenty years in age
epiblema a large and heavy mantle
epinetron a device worn over the knee to protect against abrasion and cuts from working with wool
erastes term for the "lover," the adult partner in a pederastic relationship
eromenos term for the "beloved," the youthful partner in a pederastic relationship
erotes term for the small winged youths who appear in art, sometimes in pairs, and recall Eros, son of Aphrodite
ethos Greek word meaning character
eu (to eu) term used by Polykleitos meaning ideal perfection or goodness
exedra a recess or alcove set off from the main body of a structure like a stoa or colonnade
faience glazed ceramic ware produced by a mixture of sand, fluxes, water, and calcium carbonate compounds
fascia a series of long, flat moldings, especially on the architrave of the Ionic and Corinthian orders
filigree metalworking technique in which wires are twisted into shapes and soldered to a surface
Final Palatial the period of Bronze Age Minoan culture following the second destruction of the palaces, during which only the palace at Knossos continued to be active, LM II–LM IIIA, *c.* 1490–1300 BCE
findspot the location where an object is found, including the site, locale, and the specific deposit or context such as a grave, well, debris pile, or construction fill
florid style term used for late classical art in which drapery is shown thin and tightly clinging to the body, often with many small folds that reveal the anatomy
Folded-Arm Figure (FAF) marble female figure produced in the Early Cycladic period, characterized by arms folded across the torso, a pubic triangle, a flat curved face with nose ridge, and slightly bent legs
***fossa* tomb** Italian term designating a tomb made by digging a hole or trench into the ground for the body or ashes, and then covered over, sometimes with a stone slab on the surface. Also called trench or pit burial
fresco wall painting in which the pigments are applied to the wet plaster (true or buon fresco) or applied with a binder on the surface of dry plaster (dry fresco)
frieze the second course of the entablature, between the architrave and cornice
frying pan a class of terracotta objects in Early Cycladic art consisting of a disk with short handle and covered with incised decoration. The actual purpose of this object is not known
genius (pl. genii) a winged human figure, often a guardian, having its origins in Near Eastern art
Geometric period Greek art produced between *c.* 900 and 700 BCE
Gigantomachy the battle between the giants, sons of Gaia and Uranus, and the Olympian Gods
Gnathian ware overpainted pottery ware produced in Apulia in the fourth and third centuries
gorgoneion the decapitated head of the Gorgon Medusa, shown frontally and used as a shield device or apotropaic figure
granulation metalworking technique in which small beads of gold are soldered to a surface as decoration
grave goods artwork and other objects placed in a grave with the remains of the deceased
grave offerings objects left by mourners at a tomb, either on it or in an offering trench, as part of a ritual sacrifice or visit to the tomb
gymnasion (pl. gymnasia) a building associated with physical and philosophical education, usually consisting of an open area flanked by porches or colonnades
gynaikonitis the women's quarters of the household
gyne term designating an adult married woman and mother
Hadra hydria a type of hydria made in Crete but used widely in Egypt as a cinerary urn, with dark slip decoration painted on the light surface
handmade pottery pottery made without the use of a wheel, such as through coils
hekatompedon a term designating a large, or 100-foot, temple
Helladic the designation for the Bronze Age on the mainland of Greece
Hellenistic period Greek art from the time of Alexander the Great (d. 323 BCE) to the reign of the Roman emperor Augustus (r. 31 BCE–14 CE), generally *c.* 330–30 BCE
heraldic composition symmetrical composition that shows figures like lions or sphinxes facing toward a central axis, which might include an object such as a column or sacred tree. Often used as an apotropaic device
heroön a shrine dedicated to a hero, frequently a Bronze Age tomb in later periods
hetaira Greek term for a woman who was hired to provide entertainment for the symposion, which could include sex as well
himation term used to designate a heavy cloth mantle worn over another garment, usually over one shoulder and hanging at an angle
hoplite term for Greek infantry soldier whose equipment included a helmet, breastplate or cuirass, and metal greaves on the shins. Hoplites carried one or two spears and wore a sword on a belt
hybridization a blending of artistic elements from two cultures, with elements of both cultural styles and subject matter discernible in the work
hydria a three-handled vessel used for carrying and pouring water
hypostyle term signifying multiple columns aligned on a grid on the interior of a structure to support the roof and ceiling
idealized, idealistic the representation of a subject as perfect in its proportions, beauty, or form
Iliad epic poem of Homer recounting the beginning of the tenth year of the Trojan War and the deaths of Sarpedon, Patroklos, and Hektor and the anger of Achilles. Generally dated to the later 8th cent. BCE
Iliupersis term for the fall of Troy or Ilium as it was known

imitation the reproduction of a model from one culture or period in a second period or culture, given differences in medium or technique

impluvium a catch basin in the floor of an atrium-style house that would collect water from rain

incision cutting lines into the surface to create patterns or figural decoration. See also **engraving**

intaglio the creation of a design by incision or engraving on a surface, producing raised lines when pressed into a soft surface like clay

isonomia Greek term designating the equality before the law of citizens

kalathos a basket to hold wool during its preparation for weaving. Small terracotta versions with openwork sides could serve as grave goods

Kamares Ware a Minoan pottery style produced in the Protopalatial period and featuring a dark slip background with painted motifs in white, yellow, and red

kanephoros basket-bearer, an important role in a ritual in which a woman bears a basket of sacrificial instruments in the ritual procession

kanous basket for ritual instruments carried in a procession by a *kanephoros*

kantharos a steep-sided, footed drinking cup with high projecting handles

Kastri Group a phase of Early Cycladic culture named after the site at Kastri on Syros and representing a new group of people in the area, *c.* 2200–2000 BCE

Kerch style Attic pottery produced in the fourth century featuring a rich use of color and exported in large numbers to the Black Sea

Keros-Syros Group a phase of Early Cycladic culture named after the cemetery on Syros, *c.* 2700–2200 BCE

kerykeion the wand held by Hermes or a herald, topped by a closed circle and open circle at its top. Also called the *caduceus* in Latin

kithara a large stringed instrument similar to a lyre, usually with a squared base and curved upright arms

***kline* (pl. *klinai*)** wooden couches with one arm and covered with cushions that were used for dining and drinking in the symposion. They might also serve as a bier for the prothesis

komos the movement of revelers at a symposion, which might take the form of a procession, boisterous dancing, and carousing

kore (pl. korai) a young woman or maiden, used to denote statues of clothed standing female figures in the seventh, sixth, and fifth centuries

kottabos a symposion game in which the sediment or dregs from the wine are tossed at targets in the andron

kouros (pl. kouroi) a male youth, used to denote statues of standing nude young men

krater large, open vessel for the mixing of wine and water

kylix (pl. kylikes) a drinking cup with a broad shallow bowl, usually on a stemmed foot, with two handles on the side

lawagetas Linear B/Mycenaean term meaning "leader of the people," perhaps a war leader

leaf-and-tongue decorative molding made of alternating leaf shapes framed by a running tongue

lebes gamikos a vase consisting of a deep bowl with handles on a stand, used for a wedding

lekanis a broad shallow bowl used for food. It can have a lid or cover

lekythos an oil container, usually with a cylindrical body, with a foot and single handle attached to a narrow neck and flanged opening. A more spherical body is called a squat lekythos

Levant the area of the eastern Mediterranean that includes present-day Israel, Jordan, Lebanon, and Syria

Linear A a writing script developed by the Minoans in Protopalatial Crete

Linear B writing script developed by the Mycenaeans in the Late Bronze Age that proved to be an old form of Greek

lotus and palmette ornamental pattern consisting of alternating lotus blossoms with spiked petals and palmettes with a fan of rounded fronds

louterion a basin made of metal or clay used to heat water for a bath or ritual purification

loutrophoros a tall closed container with a long and narrow neck. The *loutrophoros-hydria* with three handles was generally used for water in ritual washing of the bride; the *loutrophoros-amphora* with two handles served funerary purposes

mamoros term designating the shine of marble

mean (*to meson*) the middle or balance between opposites

meander a rectilinear design also known as a key pattern that creates a motif that winds or doubles back on itself before going forward

Megarian bowl term for a mold-made bowl with relief decoration on the exterior and produced during the Hellenistic period in Athens and other centers

megaron a rectangular structure featuring a square room with four columns, a small vestibule, and a porch with two columns set on a longitudinal axis

metic term for a foreign resident in a city. These were free individuals, but with limited legal rights

metope a square panel between triglyphs in a Doric frieze that is frequently used for painted or sculpted decoration

metroon building housing the civic archive

mimesis the imitation or representation of an object in a work of art so that it resembles the original model

Minoan the designation for the Bronze Age on Crete

Minyan ware a smooth, burnished, gray or yellow, wheel-thrown pottery produced on the Greek mainland in the Middle Helladic period

monoscenic narrative narrative picture in which the action occurs at a single time and place

mosaic a medium used for decorating floors in which small pebbles or tesserae are set in mortar to create decorative and figurative compositions

motif (pl. motifs) a form, design, or pattern, frequently repeated as a decorative device

mud brick building bricks made of mud, clay, and/or sand mixed with straw and dried hard in the sun. Walls of mud brick would be covered with plaster to make them more durable

mutule decorative element above the triglyph and below the cornice

naiskos a small, temple-like enclosure with a shallow space, frequently used for shrines or grave monuments and enclosing sculpted figures

naos the central room of a temple where the cult statue would be placed. Also called a cella

naturalistic the representation of a subject in art as being lifelike in its appearance

neo-archaic style or archaizing term for sculpture that imitates the abstract and schematic qualities of sixth-century sculpture in later periods

Neoattic term for classicizing sculpture produced in Athens for export, especially in the first century BCE

neoclassical or neoclassicizing a style that imitates the qualities of fifth- and fourth-century classical sculpture but is produced in later periods like the Hellenistic

Neolithic period literally the new stone age, characterized by the use of stone tools, farming, and domesticated animals. It is the last period before the Bronze Age, *c.* 7000–3100 BCE in Greece

Neopalatial the period of Bronze Age Minoan culture that saw the rebuilding of the palaces following their destruction at the end of the Protopalatial period, *c.* 1750–1490 BCE

neo-severe style or severizing term for sculpture that imitates qualities of the Severe Style of the early classical period but was produced in later periods

Nike the goddess of victory. Also an attribute of another god or goddess who brings victory, such as Athena Nike

nymphe term designating a wife or bride

oikos Greek term designating the household and its activities

oinochoe a pitcher used for pouring wine, with one handle, a defined shoulder, and often a trefoil mouth

olpe a pitcher used for pouring wine, usually with a round opening and continuously curved body

opisthodomos the back room of a Greek temple. It abuts the naos but does not usually open to it

opus vermiculatum a mosaic technique that uses small square (< 4 mm) tiles or stones called tesserae to create patterns and images

orchestra the circular area at the center of the theater where dramas were performed

Orientalizing period Greek art produced from about 720/700 to 625/600 BCE

overpainting pottery painting technique in which the colored pigments are painted on the glazed or slip surface, rather than put on the bare surface of the clay

paidagogos term for teacher of boys and youth

***pais* (pl. *paides*)** Greek term for child

Palace Style term for the LM II style of pottery produced at Knossos

palaistra a space for athletic activity in the gymnasion, usually for wrestling and boxing

Panathenaia the annual ritual in Athens honoring Athena as patron goddess of the city. It featured an elaborate procession from the Dipylon Gate to the Acropolis on the Panathenaic Way

Panathenaic amphora special Attic black-figure amphora with a pointed end that contained oil as prize for victory in the Panathenaic Games. The amphora had Athena and an owl on one side and a representation of the event on the back

Panathenaic Way the processional route of the Panathenaia in Athens, going from the Dipylon Gate to the Acropolis and going through the agora

panoramic narrative narrative image in which different actions take place at the same time but in different places

***pastas* house** house with a colonnaded porch across one side of the courtyard that continued as a hall across the house

pathos Greek term indicating the emotions of a figure, which can be read through facial expression and body movement

pederasty the homosexual or homoerotic relationship between a male adult and youth

pediment the triangular gable at the ends of a building, part of the entablature

pelike a vessel with a bulbous body and narrow neck used for containing and pouring liquids

peplos a heavier woman's garment made of wool, consisting of a single piece of cloth folded over to create a double layer over the chest and pinned together

peripteral a colonnade that goes all the way around a building, especially in the case of temples

peristyle a structure with columns that enclose it, such as a peristyle temple with columns on all four sides of the exterior or a peristyle courtyard with colonnaded porches on all four sides

peristyle house house whose courtyard is flanked by colonnaded porches on three or four sides

phiale a wide shallow bowl, usually with a knob in the center, used for pouring libations

phlyax a type of comic or burlesque play popular in fourth- and third-century southern Italy

phratry term designating a social or tribal group within the Greek polis

pilgrim's flask a small vessel with a round body and narrow neck and two loop or stirrup handles at the neck

pithos (pl. pithoi), pithoid a storage vessel with high shoulders and a pointed bottom, usually set into a circular opening in a bench or floor

polis (pl. poleis) the Greek city-state

polos a small cylindrical hat worn by women

polygonal masonry walls made of irregularly shaped stones that are finished with a smooth surface, giving the appearance of polygonal shapes

Polykleitos sculptor active in the second half of the fifth century BCE

porne Greek term for a prostitute

Postpalatial the period of Bronze Age Minoan following the Mycenaean control of Crete and their center at Knossos, *c.* 1300–1075 BCE

Potnia Theron term meaning "Mistress of the Animals," usually a frontal female figure holding two animals in either hand

Prepalatial the period of Bronze Age Minoan culture before the establishment of the palaces, *c.* 3100–1900 BCE

progressive narrative narrative image in which time progresses as one moves from one part of the image to another, but without repetition of any characters

pronaos an open porch on the end or side of a building leading to the *naos*, the interior room

propylon term signifying a gate marking the entry into the temenos of a sanctuary
***prostas* house** house with a small porch on the courtyard and usually no columns
prostyle temple or structure with columns projecting on the end or ends of the building
prothesis funerary rite in which the body of the deceased is laid on a bier and prepared for burial. The body is usually flanked by mourners
Protocorinthian the period of Corinthian art following the Geometric period, *c.* 725–625 BCE
Protopalatial the period of Bronze Age Minoan culture that saw the establishment of the first palaces, *c.* 1900–1750 BCE. The period ended in a cataclysmic destruction of the palaces, which were rebuilt
provenance the history of findspot and ownership for a work of art
psyche the spirit, soul, or shade of a person
punch or punching a metalwork technique in which a tool is pressed into the surface to create a design. The end of the tool can be carved with a design that is transferred to the surface
Pythia the priestess of Apollo at Delphi
pyxis (pl. pyxides) a small cylindrical container with a lid used to store small items such as jewelry
quadriga term for a chariot drawn by four horses
realistic the representation of a subject as it is, including individual traits or imperfections
red-figure a style of painted pottery in which the silhouette of the figure is left as the exposed surface of the clay and the background is painted with black slip. Anatomical and other details are drawn or painted on the red figure
regula peg-shaped elements below the triglyph
repoussé a metalwork technique in which the decoration is hammered from behind to create a raised relief
rhythmos a Greek term that signifies the compositional pattern of a work or figure, and, in connection with movement, an expression of how the parts of the body move to carry out an action
rhyton a conical shape drinking cup, sometimes with a base in the shape of an animal, head, or figure
rococo style of Hellenistic sculpture named after European rococo art and characterized by lighter or erotic themes and a more decorative or humorous than dramatic appeal
rosette a circular ornamental motif made of petals, with lines converging to the center
sakkos hair net or bag worn by mature women to cover their hair when worn up
sarcophagus a stone coffin for inhumation burial sometimes set into a chamber tomb and having relief decoration on the exterior
scotia a concave molding, especially on the base of an Ionic or Corinthian column and sandwiched by a torus molding above and below
seal a small object made of stone or metal used to make impressions on clay or wax used to seal containers, marking ownership and security of the contents. Seals were decorated with designs to distinguish individual owners
Severe Style a style of the early classical period that, while more lifelike than archaic art, was characterized by simplified body features and less ornamental surfaces
shaft grave a tomb with a chamber below ground that is accessed through a vertical shaft filled in after burial
silhouette painting technique in which the figure is shown as a silhouette with no or minimal anatomical detail other than limbs and head
sima gutter inside the edge of the roof
sistrum a rattle made in Egypt with beads set on wires stretched between U-shaped or squared arms
skene stage housing behind the orchestra in the Greek theater
skenographia Greek term meaning "scene painting," it refers to the use of a perspectival system to represent a three-dimensional space in a picture
skiagraphia Greek term meaning "shadow painting or drawing," it refers to the use of highlights and shading (chiaroscuro) to suggest the three-dimensionality of an object in a painting
skyphos a deep drinking cup with steep sides, a flat bottom or foot, and two handles on the side. Large versions could also be used as mixing bowls
slip a dilute solution of clay, sometimes with a pigment, that is applied to the surface of a clay vessel to create painted decoration. A slip differs from a glaze, in that the latter is glossy, hard, and relatively impervious. Some slips, like the black of Attic pottery, can vitrify during firing to give a glaze-like appearance
Special Palace Tradition Minoan pottery produced in the LM IB period at Knossos. It has several different stylistic divisions Marine, Floral, Abstract or Geometric, and Alternating
stadion a race course in a sanctuary, with banked sides for spectators
stamnos a large storage vessel with two side handles and a wide mouth that could be used for storing or serving wine
stamp and stamped designs making a decorative motif or design by pressing an incised, hard stamp into the surface of clay, metal, or other malleable material
stater a coin usually made of silver whose weight and value were about two to three times those of a drachma
stele (pl. stelai) a vertical stone slab used as a tomb stone or commemorative marker; it could be covered by relief, inscription, or painting
stereobate steps defining the platform of the temple
stirrup jar a small liquid container with a narrow opening and stirrup-shaped handles between the neck and body, sometimes with a third handle at right angles
stoa a rectangular colonnaded porch, sometimes with a second story, that served a variety of civic or religious needs in the agora or sanctuary
stomion entrance to a tholos tomb at the end of the dromos
stratigraphy the analysis of a site by the deposits found in defined layers of remains
style a system of renderings used to form the details of a subject or a set of forms and shapes used to fashion an object
stylobate platform of the temple on which the colonnade sits

symmetria regarding proportions in art, commensurability or the appropriate relationship among the parts

symposion (pl. symposia) a formal drinking party in which men would recline on *klinai* (couches) and drink wine, converse, dance, recite poetry, or otherwise revel. Symposia usually took place after important public festivals or occasions

synchronic things and events that exist at the same time, even if they were made at different times

synoptic narrative narrative picture that includes figures, actions, or objects that belong to different moments of a narrative

Tanagra figures terracotta figures produced from the fourth to first centuries BCE, named after the site in Boeotia where they were first found in large quantities

techne the Greek term for art, meaning skill, craft, or cunning of hand

temenos the boundary of a sanctuary

tempera painting technique in which the pigments are dissolved in egg white and applied to the surface. When applied to plastered walls it is called dry fresco, to distinguish it from true fresco (see **fresco**)

terminus a fixed calendar date determined by documentary evidence

terminus ad quem a calendar date at which an object was made

terminus ante quem a calendar date before which an object was made

terminus post quem a calendar date after which an object was made

terracotta objects made of fired clay, generally small figures, most of which are made with molds and can be painted

tessera (pl. tesserae) small squares used to make patterns and pictures in an *opus vermiculatum* mosaic

theoria viewing or being a spectator at a ritual performance

tholos (pl. tholoi) a circular-shaped building, including vaulted tombs or free-standing structures, sometimes with exterior colonnades as at Epidauros

threnody a song sung at the burial lamenting the deceased

thyrsos a large fennel stalk with a pine-cone type of head carried by followers of Dionysos

Titanomachy the battle of the gods and the Titans, the generation of gods before the Olympians. They included Kronos, Oceanus, Rhea, Themis, and Mnemosyne

torus a convex or rounded molding, especially on the base of an Ionic or Corinthian column

treasury a small building housing dedications at a sanctuary, usually rectangular in plan with a naos and pronaos with columns in antis

trench tomb see ***fossa* tomb**

triglyph vertical panel with three vertical bands that stands between metopes in the Doric frieze

tripod a bronze or ceramic vessel with a cauldron supported by three legs and having handles on the shoulder. Originally used as cooking vessels, monumental bronze tripods became prizes in competitions and dedications in sanctuaries

tumulus a large mound built over a grave or structure

Tyche Greek goddess of fortune

Tyrannicides "Tyrant-Killers," a term used for Harmodios and Aristogeiton who killed the tyrant Hipparchos in Athens in 514 BCE

Vasiliki Ware a pottery ware found in eastern and southern Crete in the period EM IIB, *c.* 2400–2200 BCE, and characterized by mottled slip surfaces and so-called teapots with long angular spouts

votive offering an offering to a god or shrine to fulfill a vow or recognize a benefit

wanax Linear B/Mycenaean word for king

West Slope ware overpainted pottery ware produced in Athens during the third century

wheel-thrown pottery pottery made by shaping a vessel as it rotates on a spinning wheel

white-ground vase painting form of vase painting, especially in Athens, in which a slip of white calcareous clay was placed on a vase. Figures were then drawn with outlines and washes of color

INDEX

abacus 161–162, 164
abaton 289, 291, 351
Abdalonymos 343, 345, 347
abduction 66, 94, 142, 182, 313, 325
abstract (style) 5–8, 25, 32, 37, 39, 51, 60–64, 73, 87, 94, 139, 190–192, 358
a cappucina tomb 123, 337
Achilles (subject) 66–67, 79, 85, 123, 182–184, 198, 204–207, 217, 218, 219–220, 222–224, 297, 307; Figs. 8.1, 8.23, 8.24, 9.10
Achilles Painter 257, 260; Fig. 10.23
Achilles, shield of 70, 263
acroterion 162–163, 181, 185, 244, 248, 268–271, 279, 290, 296; Fig. 11.2
adaptation, cultural 132, 135, 137, 163, 225, 382, 384–385
adult status 36, 74, 124, 231, 256, 324–325, 329, 331–334
Aeschylus 211, 224, 227, 234, 237, 242, 257, 281, 310
agalma 175, 194, 196
Agamemnon (subject) 41, 57–58, 67, 198, 222–225, 227, 238, 242, 281, 297, 310; Figs. 8.18, 9.11
agency 127–128, 177, 292, 339, 355, 369
agora (place) 15, 70, 103, 229, 349
see also Athens, Agora
aidos 127, 323, 334
Aigina (site) 142, 207, 238–240; Figs. 10.2, 10.3, 10.4
Ajax the Greater (subject) 67, 198, 205, 214, 217, 220, 226, 233, 257; Figs. 8.18, 8.24, 8.25, 9.5
Ajax the Lesser (subject) 67, 198, 218; Figs. 8.18, 9.7
Akragas/Agrigento (site) 161–162, 164, 166–167; Figs. 7.5, 7.13
Akrotiri (site) 21, 39–43, 46; Figs. 2.18, 2.19, 2.20
alabastron (object) 139, 337, 339; Figs. 5.22, 6.9
Alexander Mosaic 345–347; Fig. 14.2
Alexander Sarcophagus 343–345, 347; Fig. 14.1
Alexander the Great 103, 159, 288, 292, 294, 313, 317, 343–349, 353, 366, 368–369; Figs. 14.1, 14.2
Alexandria (Egypt) 278, 347–349, 351, 371, 374–375, 378, 381, 385; Fig. 14.3
al-Mina (site) 83, 137, 142
altar (object) 86, 99–100, 105–106, 145–147, 154–158, 214, 289, 291, 351–352, 356, 381; Fig. 9.4
altar (subject) 52, 57–59, 172–173, 199, 218, 302, 329; Figs. 3.2, 7.16, 8.21, 9.7
Amazonomachy (subject) 106, 188–189, 229, 248, 269, 292, 296–297; Figs. 11.1, 12.9
Amazons 66, 117, 323, 325
ambiguity, in narrative 173, 196, 230–231, 233, 301, 328
Ampharete, stele of 254, 272, 299, 301, 328; Fig. 10.20
amphictyony 170
amphora and amphoriskos 14–15, 51, 72–79, 85, 88, 89–90, 99, 119, 123, 142, 201, 205–206, 214, 218, 220, 222, 229–230, 276–277, 310, 335; Figs. 1.10a, 3.1, 4.2, 4.3, 4.4, 4.5, 4.7, 4.8, 5.22, 6.15, 8.24, 8.25, 9.5, 9.15, 11.8
amphora, Panathenaic 110–111, 274, 277; Fig. 5.11
amphoriskos 71–72; Fig. 4.1
anakalypsis 227
anathema 175
Anatolia (region) 24, 31, 67, 135, 360, 375, 383–384
Anavyssos (site) 122–123
andron 112–115, 118–120, 310–311, 321, 328, 332, 370
animal frieze (subject) 137, 140, 142, 150, 276
anoikismos 102
antefix 162
Antenor (artist) 109
Anthesteria 324
anthippasia (event) 110
Antikythera (shipwreck) 272, 294, 355–358, 361, 369, 379
Antikythera youth 294–296, 355; Fig. 12.7
Antioch 317, 347–349, 351, 360–361, 363, 381, 385
aparche 175
Apelles (artist) 2–3, 9, 311, 313
Aphrodite (deity) 142–143, 176
Aphrodite (subject) 8–9, 251–253, 296, 306–307, 313, 361–363, 368; Figs. 10.16B, 12.17, 14.16, 14.17
Aphrodite of Knidos 166, 281, 298–299, 301–302, 317, 321, 331, 351, 355–356, 368; Fig. 12.11
Aphrodite of Melos (Venus de Milo) 109, 363, 378; Fig. 14.17
apobates 248–250
Apollo (deity) 95, 107, 117, 133, 146, 155, 163, 166, 175, 191, 222, 227, 289, 296, 353–354
Apollo (subject) 36, 88, 135, 173, 182–183, 186, 190, 197, 212, 302, 382; Figs. 7.17, 8.1, 8.6, 8.16, 9.1
apotropaic device 53, 57, 144, 185–186
Apulian pottery 118, 277–278, 281, 305, 307–310, 338, 385; Figs. 12.18, 12.19, 12.20
arch 58, 161, 167, 256
archaic period 6, 8–9, 15, 237–239, 255, 363, 365
archaios 95, 110, 181, 238
archaizing style 357, 365
architrave 161–165, 254, 293
Ares 109, 122, 191, 213, 226, 252
Argive (regional style) 83–84, 242
Argives 83–84, 191
Argos (site) 72, 83–84, 109, 190, 243, 347
Aristion of Paros (artist) 194; Fig. 8.13
Aristogeiton 109, 177, 222, 334–335; Fig. 5.9
see also Tyrannicides
Aristonoë, priestess 329–330, 365, 369; Fig. 13.8
Aristophanes 325
Aristotle 5, 103, 282
arrephoros 325
Arsinoë II 368–370, 378; Figs. 14.25, 14.26
Artemis (deity) 133–134, 136, 144, 175, 184, 218, 272, 294, 324–325, 327, 329
Artemis (subject) 134, 182, 186, 212, 251, 365; Figs. 8.6, 9.1, 10.16A, 14.18, 14.19
Artemision, Cape, statue of god 11–12, 240, 242; Figs. 1.7, 1.8
aryballos (object) 139–140, 176, 224, 334, 339; Figs. 5.22, 6.9, 6.10
ashlar masonry 34–35, 50, 53, 55, 146, 150, 163, 167
Asklepios 85, 103, 166, 169, 171, 267–268, 288–291, 296, 351–353
assemblage 9–10, 15, 61, 124
Assyria and Assyrian art 86, 133, 136–137, 140, 383–384
Astarte 8, 85, 133
Asteas (artist) 225, 310; Fig. 12.21
Athena (deity) 100, 102, 103, 117, 159, 169, 185, 217, 218, 227, 249, 298, 355, 384
Athena (subject) 15, 110–111, 142, 172–173, 182, 186, 188, 198, 230, 246, 249, 251–253, 257, 278–279, 306–307, 336, 386; Figs. 5.11, 6.15, 7.16, 8.1, 8.6, 8.18, 10.2, 10.3, 10.9, 10.22, 11.11, 12.17, 15.4
Athena Nike, Temple, Acropolis 12–13, 253; Fig. 10.18
Athena Promachos (subject) 100, 110–111; Fig. 5.11
Athens 60–62, 71–84, 94–95, 99–103, 105–111, 124–127, 150, 158–160, 169, 170–173, 177, 181, 188–189, 219, 224, 247–250, 268–269, 276–284, 288, 335–336, 357, 384–386; Figs. 5.1, 5.2
Athens, Acropolis 7, 12–13, 15, 60, 99–102, 105–106, 159, 172–175, 194, 196, 207, 237–238, 246–254, 267–270, 279, 384, 386; Figs. 1.9, 5.1, 5.2, 7.4, 7.8, 10.10

A History of Greek Art, First Edition. Mark D. Stansbury-O'Donnell.

Athens, Acropolis, Erechtheion 12–13, 159, 164–165, 198, 254, 270–272, 279; Figs. 1.9, 7.8, 7.9, 11.3
Athens, Acropolis, Nike Temple 159, 253–254, 260
Athens, Acropolis, Parthenon 3, 12, 99–100, 159, 247–254, 267–269, 282, 290, 336, 343, 356; Figs. 1.1, 10.10, 10.11, 10.12, 10.13, 10.14, 10.15, 10.16, 10.17
  design 163, 169, 247–248; Fig. 10.13
  frieze 3–5, 7, 9, 12–13, 218, 221, 233, 244, 250, 254, 260, 323, 325, 332, 384; Figs. 1.1, 10.15
  metopes 248–249, 299, 365; Fig. 10.14
  pediment 251–253, 296, 299; Figs. 10.16, 10.17
  sculpture generally 66, 95, 248–253, 260–261, 284; Fig. 10.11
Athens, Acropolis, Propylaia 12–13, 99, 159, 253–254; Fig. 1.9
Athens, Agora 13–14, 60–62, 70–76, 99–102, 105–110, 115–116, 118–119, 123–124, 171, 176–177, 221–222, 267–268, 327, 351, 355; Figs. 5.1, 5.2, 5.6, 5.7, 5.8
  Hephaisteion 100, 105–106, 169, 269–270
  Stoa of Attalos 102, 106–107, 109, 351; Figs. 5.6, 5.8, 7.4
  Stoa Poikile 106, 255
Athens, Areopagos Hill 73, 102, 105
Athens, Dipylon Cemetery 78, 80, 85, 122, 133, 142, 299
Athens, Dipylon Gate 77, 100–102, 125, 299, 301
Athens, Kerameikos 9–10, 71–72, 77, 102, 125–126, 189, 299, 302, 305, 335; Fig. 5.27
Athens, Lysikrates Monument 165, 293, 303; Fig. 12.5
Athens, Odeion 384
Athens, Persian destruction 102, 109, 159, 173, 189, 238, 252, 288
Athens, Pynx 12–13, 100, 102, 159, 252
Athens, sack of 15, 109, 173, 196, 229, 238, 288, 384
athletes, athletic ideal 88, 109, 122, 243–244, 296, 331, 333–334, 337, 366
athletic contests 154–156, 159, 173, 177, 229, 248, 250, 330, 356
Attalos I of Pergamon 351
Attalos II of Pergamon 109, 351, 358
Attic (regional style) 22, 71–82, 84, 94–95, 231, 276–280, 305, 309–310, 331–332, 381–382
Attic black-figure 13–15, 18, 110–111, 201–202, 205–206, 277, 280; Figs. 1.10, 5.11, 8.23, 8.24, 9.5, 9.6, 9.16, 11.8
Attic Geometric 71–82, 94–95, 327; Figs. 4.1, 4.2, 4.3, 4.5, 4.7, 4.8, 4.9, 4.10, 4.23, 9.2, 13.5
Attic red-figure 13–15, 18, 256, 260, 277, 280, 305–307; Figs. 1.10, 5.19, 7.17, 9.3, 9.7, 9.8, 9.9, 9.10, 9.13, 9.18, 10.22, 10.24, 10.26, 11.5, 12.17, 13.1, 13.3, 13.6, 13.7, 13.11, 13.12, 13.13, 13.18
Attic white-ground 256, 260, 277, 305; Figs. 1.2, 5.26, 10.21, 10.23, 10.25
attribution 11, 17–18, 25, 297, 318

Auge 297, 302; Fig. 12.14
Augustus 2, 16, 368
aulos 172, 321

baroque style 214, 281, 356–360, 363–365
battle (subject) 40, 106, 140–141, 213, 218, 231, 233, 343–347; Figs. 2.20, 6.11, 8.1, 9.2, 9.16, 9.17, 14.1, 14.2
  see also Amazonomachy; Gigantomachy; Titanomachy
beard, as marker 109, 173, 227, 301, 322–323, 325, 331–332
Beazley, John D. 17–18
Berlin Painter 18
bilingual pottery 205–206; Fig. 8.25
black-figure pottery 13–15, 110–111, 138–140, 181, 199–206, 256, 276–277, 280, 332
  see also Attic black-figure; Corinthian pottery; Lakonian art
black-glaze pottery 13–15, 274, 305, 309; Fig. 11.6
Black Sea (region) 50, 61, 137, 150, 200, 211, 277, 303, 305, 348
Boeotia 191, 225, 288, 375
Boeotian pottery 172; Fig. 7.16
boule 107, 109, 171
bouleuterion 106–107, 109
bride 94, 125, 194, 227, 254, 260, 303, 325–328, 371, 374
bridegroom 94, 224, 227, 325
Briseis (subject) 222–223; Fig. 9.10
Bronze Age (general) 19–46, 50–67, 70, 95, 291, 385
bronze, material 6, 11–12, 44–45, 60, 86–90, 109, 114, 132, 136, 158, 173, 175, 196–199, 229–230, 237, 240–243, 272, 294, 317, 351, 355–356, 369, 375, 378; Figs. 1.7, 1.8, 2.22, 4.15, 4.16, 4.17, 4.18, 4.19, 6.6, 10.6, 12.7, 14.12, 14.13, 14.15, 14.21, 14.22, 14.23, 14.27, 14.36
bucchero ware 201, 276–277; Fig. 11.8
burnishing (pottery technique) 22–23, 26, 28, 31, 39

Cabiran Ware 225–226; Fig. 9.12
Cabiros (site) 225–226
Caeretan pottery 150, 200, 280, 284; Fig. 11.13
Calydonian boar hunt 199–200, 201, 219; Figs. 8.22, 8.23
Campanian pottery 305, 310, 335; Fig. 13.14
Canon (treatise and statue) 243, 282, 288, 294, 296, 356
caryatid 12–13, 164, 181, 254
caryatid, mirror 198, 242, 244, 302, 323, 327, 330–331; Figs. 8.19, 10.6, 13.10
cavalcade (subject) 110, 218, 250
cella *see* naos
cemetery 24–26, 256, 302, 324, 335, 337–338
centaur (subject) 84–85, 88–89; Figs. 4.13, 4.19
centauromachy 88–89, 142, 229, 244, 248, 292; Figs. 4.19, 6.12, 10.14
Centuripe vases 374; Fig. 14.32
Chadwick, John 50
chamber tomb 26, 41, 52, 57–58, 60–62, 135, 230, 256

chariots (subject) 63–64, 79, 87, 110, 140, 182, 205, 212, 226–227, 230, 278, 292, 313, 325, 345; Figs. 3.13, 4.9, 5.11, 6.11, 8.1, 8.2, 8.23, 9.1, 9.15, 10.16A, 11.10, 13.3, 13.25, 14.2
Charon (subject) 125; Fig. 5.26
Cheramyes, kore of 175, 176, 192–194, 196; Fig. 8.12
chiaroscuro (shading) 255, 345, 370
  see also skiagraphia
chiastic composition 243–244
Chigi Painter, olpe by 140–142, 146, 213, 218, 275–276, 313, 331; Fig. 6.11
children and childhood (*pais*) 74, 77, 144, 273, 324–325, 328, 330–331, 333, 375
Chios (site) 142
chiton 192, 194, 198, 242, 260, 297, 301, 323–324, 328, 375, 382
chitoniskos 382
chora 102, 154, 336–337
chorus and choral performance 37, 84, 171, 242, 291, 293, 325
chous 226, 324; Figs. 5.22, 9.13, 13.3
chronology 3, 7, 15–16, 23–24, 46, 181–182, 357
  absolute 3, 7, 23–24, 46, 86
  relative 3, 7, 21, 23, 46, 59–61
Chrysaor (subject) 184–185, 211; Fig. 8.3
chryselephantine statue 36, 197, 269, 282, 290; Fig. 8.18
chthonic 85, 176
Cicero 2–6, 255, 279
cist graves 25–26, 41, 72, 123, 255–256, 303
city planning 99–103, 105–109, 159, 292, 349–351, 354
classical period and style 6, 16, 95–96, 237–262, 281–282, 288–317, 384–385
classicizing style 279, 347, 356–357, 363–366, 379, 385
Cleopatra VII 298, 348, 368–369; Fig. 14.24
clerestory 53
clothing 88, 173, 192, 223, 301, 307, 322–323, 327, 331
coins 323, 336–337, 339, 369; Figs. 13.15, 14.26
colonies 99, 102, 137, 142, 150, 156, 184–186, 233, 274, 307, 310, 336–338, 345, 347
color
  in painting 2–3, 13–15, 39–40, 59, 118, 139–140, 146, 200, 256, 276–277, 370
  in sculpture 9, 185, 194–197, 199, 207; Figs. 8.15, 10.3
columns, Minoan 35, 41, 53, 57
comedy and comic representation 155, 171, 186, 200, 225, 280, 309–310, 325, 331, 348, 361, 363
comparanda 21, 85, 242, 296, 378–379
compass 72, 75
context, general 5–9, 11–13, 15–16, 24–25, 41, 46, 63, 99–127, 154–177, 190–191, 220–222, 233, 262–263, 294, 299, 324, 333, 355, 357, 366, 382
  see also domestic context
continuous narration 219
contraction 244, 247
contrapposto 237–238, 242, 243, 255, 260, 296, 298

cooking vessels 21, 71, 115; Fig. 5.16
copying and copy hypothesis 132, 135, 279–281, 317–318, 348, 363, 382
corbel 57–58
Corinth (site) 139–140, 150, 163, 184, 199–201, 268–269, 275–276, 278, 290, 310, 336, 347, 357, 385
Corinthian order 164–166, 169, 171, 291, 293, 303, 385; Figs. 7.6, 7.10, 12.2, 12.4
Corinthian pottery 119–120, 146, 199, 200, 201, 276–277; Figs. 5.21, 5.23
see also Protocorinthian pottery
cornice 161–164
Corridor House 28–29
courtship scenes 334
courtyard 32–36, 53, 91, 93, 111–114, 119, 353–354, 371–372, 383
cremation burial 72, 89–90, 123–124, 303, 374
Crete, Cretan (region) 21–27, 32–39, 45, 50–52, 60, 85–86, 88, 146, 150, 280, 355, 374
cult 36–37
Cult Center, Mycenae 55, 58–59, 64; Fig. 3.9
cult statue 36, 145–146, 155, 167, 173, 177, 185–186, 249, 271, 282, 290, 297–298, 353, 355, 357, 363–365; Fig. 14.18
cultural interaction 51, 61, 85, 132–133, 347, 382–385
cup (drinking) 31, 40–41, 60–62, 72–73, 119–121, 199–200, 217, 220–221, 225, 321–322, 381–382
see also kylix/kylikes; skyphos
Cybele 9, 360
Cyclades (region) 23–27, 39–43, 144
Cycladic art
Bronze Age 23–27, 39–43, 284
post-Bronze Age 144; Fig. 6.18
cyclical narration 219, 223
Cyclopean masonry 57–58
Cynics 288, 347–348
Cypro-Phoenician art 136, 137, 139–140; Fig. 6.8
Cyprus 50, 63–64, 82–84, 89, 132, 136, 142, 222, 381

Daedalic (style) 96, 133–135, 139, 144, 150, 190, 356
Daidalos 135, 150, 237
Damophon (artist) 282, 365; Figs. 14.18, 14.19
Daochos Monument, Delphi 296; Fig. 12.8
Darius I (r. 522–486) 383–384
Darius III (r. 336–330) 343, 345; Fig. 14.2
Dark Ages 55, 65, 70, 95, 102
see also Early Iron Age
deer (subject/motif) 45, 83, 140, 142, 313, 324; Figs. 2.23, 4.11, 6.10, 13.3
dekate 175
Delos (site) 133–136, 175, 192, 247, 329, 361, 363, 369–373
Delphi 70, 110, 117–118, 132–134, 137, 154–159, 166, 170–173, 190–191, 197, 269, 290, 296, 325, 336–337, 384; Figs. 7.1, 7.2
Athenian Treasury 156–157, 170–171, 188–189; Figs. 7.14, 8.7
omphalos 155, 166, 173, 325
Sacred Way 132, 156, 158, 170–171, 182, 184, 188, 197, 221, 336; Fig. 7.15
Siphnian Treasury 156–157, 170–171, 181–184, 186, 188, 194, 206, 212–213, 219, 239, 323, 336, 384; Figs. 7.15, 8.1, 8.2, 9.1
Temple of Apollo 170, 173
Demeter 74, 125, 251, 278, 313, 351, 365, 375; Figs. 10.16A, 11.10, 12.25B, 14.18, 14.19
Demetrias (site) 371
dendrochronology 46
Derveni krater 303, 313, 338; Fig. 12.15
Dexileos (monument, Athens) 126, 231, 272, 292, 299, 301–302, 332, 335–336, 343, 386; Figs. 12.12, 12.13
diachronic 15–16, 99, 165, 167
Diadochi 348
Didyma, Temple of Apollo 353–354; Figs. 14.8, 14.9, 14.10
dinos (object) 120, 199, 328
Diogenes 347–348
Dionysiac subject 15–16, 303, 310, 324, 328
Dionysos (deity) 3–4, 16, 156, 159, 171–173, 221, 226
Dionysos (subject) 212, 293, 298, 303, 317–318, 356, 365, 371; Figs. 12.15, 12.26
Dioskouroi 182, 191, 213; Fig. 9.3
Dipylon Master and Workshop 77–79, 88, 99, 335; Figs. 4.7, 4.8
Dipylon shield 79
dithyramb 156
Diver, Tomb of, Poseidonia/Paestum 120, 255–256, 332, 338; Fig. 10.20
dogs (subject) 140, 201, 370
domestic context 25, 61, 63, 79, 99, 111–122, 124–125, 327–329, 370, 374, 378
Doric Order (architecture) 79, 146, 161–165, 167, 173, 181, 244, 290–291, 311, 384–385
Doryphoros (spear-bearer) 3–5, 109, 243–244, 247, 249, 260, 294, 296, 317, 331, 348, 356, 358, 365–366; Fig. 10.7
double axe (subject) 52, 83, 142
dromos 58–60

Early Iron Age 13, 16, 70, 79, 86, 95
earthquake 32, 58, 66, 154, 156
echinus 161, 164
Egypt 23–24, 32, 36–37, 46, 61, 66, 176, 199, 288, 343, 345, 347–349, 368, 371, 374, 378, 381, 383
Egyptian art 6, 40–41, 85, 134–137, 142, 199, 321, 348, 368, 385; Figs. 6.5, 6.6
canon of proportions 134–135, 385
ekklesia 12–13, 100, 102
ekphora (subject) 123
Elektra (subject) 125, 224–225, 281, 310, 335; Figs. 9.11, 13.14 (?)
Eleusis (site) 76, 125, 127, 142, 212–213, 230, 233, 267
Elis (site) 227, 244, 302
elite (social status) 28–29, 31–32, 37, 41, 45, 52–53, 55, 57, 59–60, 70, 73, 76–77, 79, 84, 87, 91, 119, 122, 134, 192, 254, 272, 279, 281–282, 301, 303, 305, 324, 329–331, 335, 338, 343, 348, 355, 369–370, 378, 381–382
engraving 41, 76, 140, 206
entablature 161–164, 247–248, 293, 313
entasis 161, 164
epaulia 260, 327–328; Fig. 10.24
ephebe/*ephebos* (youth) 36, 40, 124, 190–191, 231, 332
Ephesos (site) 135, 272, 294, 296
Epicurus and Epicurean philosophy 348
Epidauros 165, 166, 169, 171–172, 225, 267–271, 279, 282, 288–293, 296–297, 299, 303, 323, 351, 365; Figs. 11.1, 11.2, 12.1, 12.2, 12.3
Abaton 289, 291
Theater 288, 291–292; Fig. 12.3
Thymele 289–291; Fig. 12.2
epinetron (object) 260, 327, 339; Figs. 10.24, 13.18
erastes 334
Eretria (site) 83, 310
eromenos 334
erotes 198, 242, 338, 356, 361, 363; Figs. 14.12, 14.16
ethnicity 338
ethos 88, 233, 242, 255–257, 262, 334, 366
Etruria (region) and Etruscans 124, 140, 181, 200, 201, 229–231, 233, 256, 263, 274, 277, 280, 322, 385
Etruscan art 201, 256, 276–277, 280
eu 243
Euboea (region) 79, 82–84, 90, 137
Eumenes II (of Pergamon) 351, 358
Euphronios (artist) 189, 206–207, 255, 262, 284, 321; Figs. 8.26, 10.26
Euripides 117, 211, 224, 233, 281
Eurystheus 200, 280; Fig. 11.13
Euthydikos, kore of 175–176, 196, 238; Fig. 7.18
Eutychides 360–361
Evans, Arthur 21, 50
Exekias (artist) 198, 204–206, 214, 216–217, 220, 226, 257, 280–281, 284; Figs. 8.24, 9.5

faience (material) 36, 76, 85
fascia 164
filigree (technique) 76, 85
Final Palatial Period (Minoan) 23–24, 50–52, 60
findspot 8, 11–12, 142, 378
florid style 244, 254, 260, 296, 306
Folded-Arm Figure (FAF) 24–25
foreshortening 189, 207, 240, 255, 260, 262, 294, 306, 313, 345, 384
forum (Roman) 279
fossa tomb 72, 123
Foundry Painter 18, 207, 331–332; Fig. 13.11
fresco (technique) 35, 40–45, 50, 52–53, 58–60, 64–65, 311, 313–317, 361, 374
frieze, architectural 161–165, 181–184, 214, 221, 247–250, 254, 270, 292–293, 297, 313, 351, 358
frontality 132, 144, 185–188, 198–199, 205–207
"frying pan," 23, 25–27
funerals, funeral games 79, 87, 205, 219
funerals and funerary rites 76–79, 90, 122–125, 159, 217, 223, 250, 253, 272, 301, 329, 336, 338

Galen 243
gaze 213, 262, 299–301, 310, 323, 330–331, 334, 356, 368, 371, 375
Gell, Alfred 127–128
gender 73–74, 77–79, 87–88, 198, 298, 321–325, 330–335, 338, 371
genius (subject) 137
Geometric period 6–8, 70–95, 122–124, 132, 134, 139, 142, 212–213, 233, 288, 325–327, 329, 335, 385
Gigantomachy (subject) 182, 206, 212–215, 229
gilding 136, 140, 307, 381
Gnathian Ware 278, 309, 374; Fig. 12.20
gold (material) 32, 35–37, 43–45, 70, 116–117, 144–145, 150, 166, 175, 196–197, 247, 274–275, 282, 303, 305–307, 311, 337, 345, 369, 378
goldsmith 76, 85, 280
gorgoneion (motif) 185; Fig. 8.5
Gorgons (subject) 142–144; Fig. 6.15
Gournia (site) 21, 33–35; Fig. 2.10
granulation (technique) 76, 85, 144
grave goods 6, 9, 11, 21, 25, 43–45, 60–61, 63, 72–76, 79, 87, 90, 94, 99, 117, 122–124, 198, 222, 303, 307, 310, 326–327, 337–338, 375, 382; Figs. 13.5, 13.16
grave marker/stele 77, 122–125, 142, 191, 194, 222, 254, 272, 301, 322, 324, 328, 330, 369
grave offerings 122–124, 327–328
graves, types 25, 43–45, 57, 60, 72–73, 90, 122–127
  see also a cappucina tomb; cist graves; *fossa* tomb; sarcophagus
grid in sculpture 134–135, 243
grid or orthogonal city planning 102, 103, 292, 349, 351, 354, 383
griffin (subject/motif) 53, 58, 118, 136, 139, 143–145; Figs. 6.9, 6.16, 15.2
gymnasion/gymnasia 5, 103, 109, 155, 333, 351, 363
gynaikonitis 328–329
gyne 328–329

Hadra hydria 374; Fig. 14.33
Hagesandros, Athenodoros, and Polydoros (sculptors) 281, 358; Figs. 11.14, 11.15
Halikarnassos (site) 103, 292, 323
Halikarnassos, Mausoleion 292, 296–297, 385; Figs. 12.4, 12.9
handles on vessels 22–23, 31, 73–75, 87, 115, 120, 126, 142–144, 198, 220, 276–277, 328
hare (subject/motif) 140–141, 198, 331, 334
Harmodios 108–109, 117, 177, 222, 334–335; Fig. 5.9
  see also Tyrannicides
Hawes, Harriet 21
Hegeso, stele of 127–128, 254, 299, 302, 330; Fig. 5.28
hekatompedon 144–147, 247
Hektor (subject) 67, 70, 72–73, 198, 218, 307; Fig. 8.16
Helen (subject) 66, 94, 144, 191, 218, 307
Helladic (period) 23, 27–31, 43–45, 50–67
Hellenistic period 2, 6, 10, 15–16, 95, 103, 107, 113, 115, 169, 214, 278–282, 343–379
Hephaistos 70, 156, 173
Hera (deity) 102, 145–148, 158, 163–164, 167, 173, 175, 186, 192, 244, 268, 318
Hera (subject) 3, 7–8, 86–87, 196, 306; Figs. 1.3, 12.17
Herakles 15, 66, 85–86, 88, 119, 182–183, 186, 188, 199, 200, 206–207, 212, 226–227, 229–231, 238, 244, 246, 252, 257, 280, 297, 302, 323, 358, 363; Figs. 5.21, 5.23, 8.1, 8.6, 8.16, 8.26, 9.15, 10.9, 11.13, 12.14
heraldic composition 53, 57, 83, 85, 136, 139, 185, 198, 385
Hermes 3, 105, 118, 146, 211, 217, 224–225, 278, 298, 306–307, 317–318, 363; Figs. 1.2, 9.11, 11.10, 12.6, 12.17, 12.18, 12.26
Hermogenes of Priene 354
herms 105, 363
Herodotos 16–17, 21, 66, 170, 182, 190–191, 208, 336, 386
heroön 90, 103, 167, 229–230
hetaira 323, 339
himation 192, 194, 223, 256, 301, 323, 382
Hipparchos 109, 222, 238, 334
Hippias 109, 334
Hippodamos of Miletos 103
Hittite Empire 67
Homer 8, 17, 21, 70, 205, 223, 263, 297, 363
hoplites (subject) 140, 182, 248, 331–332, 334
horse (subject) 63, 73, 83–84, 86–87, 89, 110, 139–140, 176, 182, 218, 226–229, 250, 301, 313; Figs. 4.15, 8.20, 12.12, 14.1, 14.2
houses 26, 28–30, 34, 40–43, 70, 90–93, 99–102, 103–105, 111–115, 118–119, 167, 311, 325–328, 339, 345, 369–372; Figs. 4.20, 4.22, 5.12, 5.13, 5.14, 5.15, 14.29
hunting (subject) 44–45, 140–141, 199–200, 201, 219, 292, 313, 331, 334, 343, 345, 369–370; Figs. 2.22, 6.11, 8.22, 12.23, 12.24, 14.28
husband (status) 135, 301, 323, 325, 328–330, 369, 371
hybrid and hybridization 45, 133, 338, 382
hybrid figure 89, 136, 144, 218
hydria 120, 200, 218, 224, 255, 273–274, 280, 298, 335, 374; Figs. 5.22, 9.7, 11.5, 11.13, 13.14, 14.33
hypostyle hall 383–384; Fig. 15.3

idealization and idealized figures 5, 8–9, 94–95, 122, 127, 134, 140, 196, 233, 238, 243, 249–250, 254, 296, 298–299, 323, 327, 330, 334, 356, 363, 365–366, 368, 369, 375
identity 8, 11–13, 29, 45, 71, 79, 94, 122, 169, 173, 175, 177, 321–329, 345
Iliad 8, 16–17, 53, 65–66, 70, 72–73, 79, 87, 90, 93, 95–96, 205, 211, 222–224, 348
Iliupersis (subject) 66, 146, 207, 218–219, 242, 248, 255, 269; Figs. 6.18, 9.7
imitation (artistic and cultural) 132, 140, 142, 280, 365, 368, 382, 384–385
incision (technique) 22, 29, 37, 125, 134, 140
influence, artistic 384–385
inhumation 52, 72, 79, 89, 123
inscriptions 35, 95, 109–110, 119, 123, 125–127, 133–136, 175–176, 182, 190–196, 200, 205, 214, 222, 230–231, 244, 254, 267, 271, 274, 278, 281–282, 293, 296, 299, 301, 303, 326–330, 343, 358, 360–361, 365, 368, 371, 374, 384
intaglio (technique) 29, 37, 378
Ionian art and architecture (style) 191–192, 198, 384
Ionic Order (architecture) 161–165, 171, 181, 254, 353, 356, 385
isonomia 93
Issos, Battle of 343
Isthmia (site) 156
ivory 21, 32, 35–36, 60, 70, 85, 89, 132–133, 136, 138–139, 166, 196–197, 247, 275, 292, 311, 385; Figs. 2.14, 4.14, 6.1, 6.7

Kalamis (artist) 2
kalathos 76, 327–328, 330
Kallimachos 165
Kalymnos (site) 61, 63
Kanachos (artist) 2–5, 8
kanephoros 109, 118, 172–173, 325, 329, 382
kanous (object) 172–173
kantharos (object) 120, 277–278; Fig. 11.9
Kassandra (subject) 66, 198, 218, 331; Figs. 8.16, 9.7
Kastri Group 23
Kephisodotos 281–282
Kerberos 200, 280; Fig. 11.13
Kerch style 277, 305–306; Fig. 12.17
Keros-Syros Group 23–26
Kirke (subject) 114, 205, 217–218, 220–221, 222, 225–226; Figs. 9.6, 9.12
kithara 9–10, 302
Kleisthenes 109
Kleobis and Biton (subject) 190–192; Fig. 8.9
Kleophrades Painter 18, 110–111, 207, 218–219, 242, 255; Figs. 5.11, 9.7
kline 119, 124, 310, 370
Knidos 166, 281, 298–299, 351
Knossos (site) 21, 23–24, 32–37, 46, 50–52, 55, 60, 62, 85; Figs. 2.11, 2.12
Kober, Alice 50
komos and *komasts* 120, 199, 332; Figs. 5.23, 13.12
kore 125, 133–136, 150, 173, 175, 192–197, 207–208, 231, 237–238, 325–326, 329, 365; Figs. 6.3, 7.18, 8.12, 8.13, 8.14, 8.15
Korfu/Korkyra (site) 137, 184–186; Fig. 8.3
Kos (site) 298, 351–353; Fig. 14.17
kottabos 120
Kourion, Cyprus (site) 83
kouros 36–37, 122–123, 134–135, 184, 190–192, 194, 196, 237–238, 278, 331, 385; Figs. 2.14, 5.24, 6.4, 8.9, 8.10, 8.11
krater 3–4, 52, 63–64, 77, 83–84, 90, 119–120, 124, 173, 199, 206–207, 220, 224–225, 230–231, 256–257, 262–263, 278–279, 284, 303, 307, 310, 321, 323, 325, 332, 338, 382; Figs. 3.13, 4.9, 4.11, 4.12, 5.22, 7.17, 8.23, 8.26, 9.16, 9.18, 10.22, 10.26, 11.11, 12.15, 12.18, 12.21
Kritios and Nesiotes 108–109, 237, 239; Fig. 5.9

Kritios Boy (statue) 196, 237–240, 243, 255; Fig. 10.1
Kroisos 122–123, 126, 191, 292; Fig. 5.24 (?)
kylix/kylikes 13–15, 120, 124, 201, 217, 220–221, 222, 223, 257, 284, 321–323, 332, 334, 381; Figs. 1.10, 3.11, 5.22, 8.22, 9.6, 9.8, 9.10, 10.21, 13.1, 13.11, 13.12, 13.13

Lakonian art 199–200, 201, 331; Figs. 8.22, 13.10
lamps 115, 166–167, 197
Laocoön 281
Lapiths (tribe) 142, 229
 see also centauromachy
lawagetas 55
lebes gamikos 328; Fig. 13.7
Lefkandi (site) 72, 83–85, 89–90, 145, 163, 167; Fig. 4.20
lekanis 172; Fig. 7.16
lekythos 72, 124–125, 224, 257, 260, 262, 278, 309, 327; Figs. 5.22, 5.26, 10.23, 10.25, 12.20, 13.6
leopard (subject/motif) 140, 212, 371
Lerna 23, 27–31; Figs. 2.5, 2.6, 2.7
Levant (region) 8, 31, 45, 60, 65, 84, 132–133, 136, 144, 150, 343, 345, 347, 361, 381, 383
libation 86, 119, 173, 177, 233, 329–330, 332
Libon of Elis (artist) 159, 244
linear (painting style) 309
Linear A (script) 35, 50
Linear B (script) 50, 52–55, 59, 65, 67, 95
lion and lion hunt (subject) 44–45, 140–141, 313, 331, 343, 345, 383–384; Figs. 2.22, 12.23, 12.24
Lion Gate, Mycenae 55–58, 70, 163, 185; Fig. 3.6
loom and loom weights 26, 114–115, 221, 225, 327; Figs. 5.19, 9.12
looting of art 21, 58, 111, 242, 262, 279, 284, 355
lotus 45, 136, 139–140, 142, 165, 195
louterion 94; Fig. 4.23
loutrophoros (object) 121, 126, 307, 309, 328, 335, 338; Figs. 5.22, 5.27, 12.19
Lucania and Lucanians 256, 337–338
Lucanian art 224, 256, 277, 280–281, 305, 309–310, 337–338; Figs. 9.11, 13.16, 13.17
luxury goods 35, 43, 60, 70, 111, 136–137, 276, 311, 381–382
Lydia (region) 133, 336
Lykosoura (site) 166, 282, 363–365; Figs. 14.18, 14.19
Lysimachos 348, 351
Lysippos 293–296, 361, 366

Macedonia 171, 288, 290, 311, 343, 347, 383
maenad 118, 173, 201, 365; Figs. 7.17, 11.8, 14.20
Magna Graecia (region) 142, 169
Mahdia shipwreck 356–357, 361, 369, 375, 378; Figs. 14.12, 14.13
maiden's kit 74
Mantiklos 6, 95, 133, 175–176; Fig. 7.19
Marathon, Battle of 158–159, 170, 188–189, 336
marble 23–25, 123, 133–135, 156, 170, 181, 190–191, 194–196, 207–208, 247–249, 254, 267–274, 278–279, 290, 294, 317, 335, 351, 353, 355–356, 360–361, 363, 369, 371, 375, 379
marble copies 109, 243, 279, 298, 317–318, 331, 345, 355, 360
Marcus Agrippa 109
Marinatos, Spyridon 21
Marine style pottery 37, 39, 51, 64; Fig. 2.17
marriage ritual 94, 194, 200, 223, 227–229, 325–328, 332
mastoid cup 381–382; Fig. 15.1
Mausolos 103, 292, 385
mean (*to meson*) 243–244, 251
meander 30, 73, 75–77, 85, 132, 142, 194
Medusa (subject) 146, 184–186, 211, 218, 294; Figs. 8.3, 8.4, 8.6
Megara Hyblaea (site) 142, 185, 191, 278
Megarian Bowl 278, 374; Fig. 11.10
megaron 43, 53–55, 57, 59, 70, 167
Melos (site) 109, 363
 see also Aphrodite of Melos (Venus de Milo)
Memnon (subject) 66, 182, 206, 219, 231; Fig. 8.1
memorial (*sema*, *mnema*) 100, 177, 194, 292, 384, 386–387
Menelaos (subject) 94, 144
Mesopotamia 83, 136, 144, 343
metalwork (medium) 23, 35, 43, 63, 76, 142–144, 303, 317, 381–382
Metapontum/Metaponto 336, 338, 385
metope 79, 146, 162–163, 186–189, 219, 231, 244, 246
metroon 107, 109
Mikon 255
mimesis 237–238, 262, 282, 288
Minoan (period) 23–26, 32–40, 43–45, 46, 51–52, 53–57, 381
Minos (king) 21, 23, 34–35
Minotaur 34, 94, 135, 188, 198, 219, 221; Fig. 9.8
Minyan Ware 28, 31, 61; Fig. 2.8
mirrors (bronze) 198, 201, 231, 242, 302, 309, 323, 327, 335, 338; Figs. 8.19, 10.6, 12.14, 13.10
Mistress of Animals 59, 133, 144–145, 185, 385; Fig. 6.17
Mnesikles 164
Mnesistrate, Stele of 301, 309, 322–324, 330, 335; Fig. 13.2
modesty *see aidos*
money *see* coins; purses
monoscenic narration 214
mosaic 111, 310–311, 313, 345–348, 361, 369–373; Figs. 12.22, 14.2, 14.28, 14.30
motifs, use of 22–23, 32, 40, 60, 63–64, 72–73, 118, 132–133, 136, 142, 194, 278, 280, 303, 309, 343, 371, 374, 382, 384–385
mourners (subject) 77, 85, 88, 122, 125, 223
mud brick 26–27, 34–35, 89, 111, 163
music and musicians 52, 81, 120, 122, 154, 156, 173, 181, 199, 243, 331–332, 334, 384
mutule 162–164
Mycenae (site) 21, 46, 50–51, 55–59, 64–65, 67, 70
Mycenae, Treasury of Atreus 57–58; Figs. 3.7, 3.8
Mycenaean art and architecture 44–45, 50–66, 72, 83, 90, 163, 167
Mycenaeans 36, 43, 45, 50–51, 70, 159
Mykonos (site) 144
Myrina (site) 9, 11, 375
Myron (artist) 279
Myrtos (site) 26–28, 33–34; Fig. 2.4

naiskos 231, 308–309, 335, 338
naos 161, 163, 166, 171, 244, 247–248, 252, 353; Fig. 7.11
narrative 37, 76, 144, 181, 184–186, 188, 197–198, 200–201, 211–233, 238, 242, 246, 250, 262, 313, 357–361, 363, 374, 385
 art vs. literature 222–225, 374
 context 221–222, 229–230
naturalism, naturalistic representation 5–6, 9, 11, 39–40, 173, 192, 213, 217, 237–238, 254–255, 293, 299, 309
Naukratis (site) 135, 137, 142–143, 199
Naxos (site) 133–134, 137, 175, 190, 329
Near East, art, influence 45, 76, 90, 385
Near East, region *see* Levant
Nemea (site) 156
neo-archaic style *see* archaizing style
Neoattic sculpture 279, 361; Fig. 11.11
neo-classical style *see* classicizing style
Neolithic Period 24
Neopalatial Period (Minoan) 23–24, 32–39, 52
Neoptolemos (subject) 207, 218, 255; Fig. 9.7
neo-severe style *see* severizing style
network theory and networks 150, 267, 334, 347, 385
Nikandre Kore 133–136, 140, 150, 175–176, 329, 365; Fig. 6.3
Nike (subject) 244, 253–254, 260, 296, 302–303, 358–360; Figs. 10.8, 10.18, 11.12, 14.14
Nikosthenes (potter) 201, 276; Fig. 11.8
Nilotic landscape 40; Fig. 2.20
Niobid Painter 257, 323, 332; Figs. 9.18, 10.22
nudity 3, 8, 85, 88, 133–134, 198, 298, 301–302, 321, 323, 330–332, 343, 351, 363, 366, 368
nymphe 194, 325

octopus (subject) 39–40, 51, 60, 64; Figs. 2.17, 3.1, 3.15
Odysseus (subject) 114, 117–118, 143, 158, 205, 217–218, 220–221, 225–226, 246, 260, 281, 307, 355–356, 361, 379; Figs. 6.15, 9.6, 9.9, 9.12, 11.15, 14.11
Odyssey 143, 211, 217–218, 222, 348
oikos 325, 327–328, 332–334, 339
oinochoe 14–16, 120, 142, 233, 332; Figs. 1.10b, 5.22, 6.13
Oinomaos 86, 226–229, 244; Fig. 9.14
olpe (object) 120, 140, 146, 213, 274–276, 313, 331; Fig. 6.11
Olympia 6–8, 70, 86–89, 110, 154, 158–159, 170–172, 175, 191, 242, 244–246, 275, 282, 290, 296, 360, 366; Fig. 7.3
 Philippeion 159, 171, 290, 292–293
 Statue of Zeus 36, 166, 197; Fig. 7.12
 Temple of Hera 318
 Temple of Zeus 166, 226–227, 244, 247, 268–269; Figs. 7.12, 9.14, 10.9
Olympian Gods 182, 184–185, 212, 248
Olympic Games 110, 156, 158, 191, 229, 296, 366
Olynthos (site) 103, 111–113, 118, 310–311, 369–370; Figs. 5.4, 5.12, 5.13, 12.22

opisthodomos 166–167, 244, 246
optical effects and refinement 240, 248, 288, 294, 296
see also contraction; entasis
opus vermiculatum 345, 370
orchestra 172, 225, 291–292
Orestes (subject) 224–225, 227, 281, 310, 335; Figs. 9.11, 13.14 (?)
Orientalizing period 16, 132–150
originality 132, 281, 296, 298, 317–318, 348, 365, 382
Orphic-Pythagorean-Dionysiac religion 303, 338
Orvieto (site) 230–231
ossuary 26, 124
outline painting (technique) 52, 139–140, 142, 146, 199, 206
overpainting 277–278, 305, 309

Paestan Ware 225, 305, 310; Fig. 12.21
paidagogos 331, 334
painted sculpture 24, 134, 182, 192, 194–196, 207–208, 238, 343, 374
painterly (style) 309, 313
painting (panel, mural) 2–3, 6, 12, 41–45, 52–53, 64–65, 199, 206, 311, 313, 317, 329, 345, 361, 374
Paionios of Mende (artist) 244, 253, 296, 360; Fig. 10.8
Palace Style pottery 51, 60, 62, 64
palaces 23–24, 32–35, 43, 45, 50–51, 52–58, 60, 63, 65–66, 70, 93, 111, 167, 349, 351, 383–384
Palaikastro (site) 36–37, 50, 385
palaistra 333–334, 337, 369
palmette (motif) 136, 139–140, 165
Pan (subject) 361, 363; Fig. 14.16
Panathenaia 100, 105, 109–111, 117, 159, 222, 233, 249, 252
Panathenaic games 105, 110, 274, 277
Panathenaic Way 100, 105–107, 109, 177
Panhellenic 70, 87, 132, 150, 154, 156, 170, 191, 329, 336–337
panoramic narrative 217–218, 313
Paris (subject) 66, 94, 140, 306–307; Fig. 12.17
Paros (site), Parian marble 181, 244, 246, 269, 278, 360
Parrhasios 305, 311
Parthenon *see* Athens, Acropolis, Parthenon
pastas (house type) 112–114
pathos 242–243, 255, 260, 262, 296–299, 358
patrimony, cultural 11, 262–263
Patroklos 70, 72–73, 79, 87, 90, 205, 219, 223
patron/patronage 6, 12, 32, 45, 51–52, 71, 73, 77, 87, 94–95, 128, 136, 282, 288, 293, 310, 317, 335, 343, 345, 347, 357, 360, 363, 379
Pausanias 17, 57, 86, 156, 170, 181–182, 188
pederasty 109, 333–335, 338, 340
pediment 156, 159, 162, 248
sculpture 163, 181–186, 207, 226–228, 238–239, 244, 251–253, 269–271, 297–299
Pegasos (subject) 184–186, 211, 311, 336; Figs. 8.3, 8.4, 8.6, 12.22
Peirithoös (subject) 142, 257
Peisistratos 109
Peleus 200, 205, 219, 327; Figs. 8.23, 9.18
pelike 13, 119, 213–214, 224, 260, 281, 306, 310, 337–338; Figs. 1.10b, 5.22, 9.3, 9.11, 12.17, 13.16
Pella (site) 369–370, 372
Peloponnesian War 102, 159, 244, 253, 277, 281, 288–289, 299, 336
Peloponnesos 27, 83, 163, 169, 227, 347, 355
Pelops 86, 226–229, 244; Fig. 9.14
Penelope (subject) 117–118, 221, 224–225, 260, 307; Fig. 5.19
Penelope Painter 260; Figs. 5.19, 9.9
peplos 218, 242–243, 248–250, 252, 323, 382
Pergamon 109, 348, 351–352, 358, 370, 381; Figs. 14.4, 14.5, 14.6
Great Altar of Zeus 214, 351, 356, 358; Figs. 9.4, 14.6
Perikles, Periklean program 159, 246–247, 250, 252–253, 264, 267–269, 336, 384
peripteral colonnade 161, 164–165
peristyle 107, 109, 145–146, 166–167, 267, 370–371
peristyle (house type) 112
Persephone (Kore) 74, 194, 251, 278, 313, 325, 365, 375; Figs. 10.16A, 11.10, 12.25
Persepolis 383–384, 387
Perseus (subject) 142, 146, 184, 185–186, 294; Figs. 6.15, 6.23, 8.6
Persia 15, 17, 21, 106, 246, 288, 313, 343, 347, 353, 384–385, 387
Achaemenid Dynasty 382–384
Persian War 21, 158, 181, 188, 229
perspective 200, 213, 255, 262, 294, 313
Phaistos (site) 32–33, 50
Pheidias 166, 247, 267, 271, 293
phiale 173, 177, 197, 224–225, 233, 274–275, 302, 329, 332, 365, 369, 381–382; Figs. 11.7, 15.1
Phiale Painter 18; Fig. 1.2
Philetairos 351
Philip II of Macedon 103, 111, 159, 171, 288, 290, 292, 311, 313, 343
phi-type terracotta figure 63; Fig. 3.14
Phoenicia and Phoenicians 70, 85, 137
Phoenician art 76, 83, 136, 139; Fig. 6.7
see also Cypro-Phoenician art
Phrasikleia, kore of 125, 127, 194–196, 207, 254, 326–327, 335, 365, 374; Fig. 8.13
pilgrim's flask (shape) 39, 60–61; Figs. 2.17, 3.11
Pioneers 206, 321
Pisa (site in Greece) 226–229
pithos, pithoi (object) 60, 113, 123, 144, 200, 280; Fig. 6.18
Plato 5, 103, 122, 282, 287
Pliny the Elder 17, 271, 281–282, 294, 296–298, 305–306
Plutarch 17, 267, 384
polis 70, 79, 88, 91–95, 109–110, 122, 170, 254, 263, 267–268, 288, 301, 313, 330–332, 335–337, 347, 382
polychrome painting 142
Polygnotos (mural painter) 158, 255–257, 262
Polygnotos, Group of (pottery painter) 273; Fig. 11.5
polygonal masonry 156
Polykleitos (sculptor) 2–5, 9, 109, 243–244, 271–272, 288, 290, 293, 317, 356; Fig. 10.7
Polykleitos the Younger (architect) 172, 290–292; Figs. 12.2, 12.3
Polyphemos (subject) 218, 221, 222, 281; Figs. 6.15, 11.15
Pompeii 21, 39, 311, 313, 345–346
Poseidonia/Paestum (site) 102, 163, 167, 186, 198, 225, 229–230, 244, 255–256, 268, 281, 288, 309–310, 337–338, 349, 385; Figs. 5.3, 7.7
Tomb of the Diver 120, 255–256, 332, 338; Fig. 10.20
Postpalatial Period (Minoan) 23–24, 50
Potnia Theron (subject) 144
pottery analysis 21–23, 46, 75, 276, 281, 284, 307, 309–310, 337, 381–382
pottery, handmade 22, 31
pottery, wheel-thrown 22, 28, 31–32
Praxiteles 281–282, 293, 298–299, 302, 317–318, 351, 363; Fig. 12.11
Prepalatial Period (Minoan) 23–24
Priam (subject) 66, 118, 198, 207, 218, 255, 307; Figs. 8.16, 9.7, 12.18
Priene (site) 103, 111–112, 115, 169, 351, 354; Figs. 5.5, 5.17
priest 158, 173, 222, 248, 323
priestess 9, 36, 52, 59, 63, 133, 155, 173, 175, 248, 302–303, 325, 329, 353, 365, 369
Prinias (site) 146, 150; Fig. 6.24
procession 37, 79, 94, 100, 105, 117–118, 120, 123, 146, 159, 172–173, 199, 218, 221, 222, 248–250, 260, 325–327, 332, 335, 382, 384
procession, chariot 63, 79, 325, 329
production 63–64, 102, 115, 133–134, 163, 238, 244, 267–282, 305, 317, 327–328, 339, 348, 357, 370, 375
progressive narrative 218, 250
prostas (house type) 112
prostyle temple 165
prothesis 77–80, 123–124, 329, 335; Figs. 5.26, 7.7, 7.8, 7.9
Protoattic pottery 142–143, 200; Fig. 6.15
Protocorinthian pottery 139–141, 176; Figs. 6.9, 6.10, 6.11
Protogeometric period 71–73, 79, 84, 86, 89–90
protome (object) 143–144; Fig. 6.16
Protopalatial period (Minoan) 23–24, 32–33, 35
provenance 10–11, 25, 262–263, 275, 379
psi-type terracotta figure 63; Fig. 3.14
psyche 8
Ptolemy I (r. 323–282) 348–349
Ptolemy II (r. 282–246) 368, 370
Ptolemy III Euergetes (r. 246–221) 374
punching (technique) 43
purses 323, 339
Pylos, Palace of Nestor 53–55, 70; Figs. 3.3, 3.4, 3.5
Pythagoras 243, 338
Pythia 155–156, 158, 166
Pythian Festival and Games (Delphi) 156
pyxis 73, 325; Figs. 5.22, 13.4

quadriga *see* chariots

radiocarbon dating 46
realism and realistic style 5, 9, 288, 296, 299, 357, 366, 368
red-figure pottery 13–15, 115, 181, 189, 205–207, 256, 260, 273–274, 277, 280, 305–309, 321, 374, 385
regula 162
repoussé (technique) 43, 136, 197
Rhamnous (site) 267, 329, 365, 369
Rhodes 8–10, 61, 139–140, 144–145, 198, 281, 358, 360
rhythmos 135, 189, 207, 240, 242, 255
rhyton 37, 381–382; Figs. 2.15, 15.2
Riace Warriors 240–243, 249, 272, 279, 355, 357, 378–379; Fig. 10.5
riders (subject) 110, 139–140, 182, 205, 231, 248, 250, 299, 313, 332, 343, 345, 371
ring (object) 37, 303, 378; Figs. 2.16, 12.16, 14.37
ritual 36–37, 43, 52–55, 83–86, 94, 122, 154–156, 166, 172–177, 192, 194, 196, 221, 229, 289, 291, 301, 325, 327–329, 331, 381–382
  see also funerals and funerary rites; procession; sacrifice, ritual; wedding and procession
rococo style 356–357, 361, 375
Rome and Roman Empire 2–3, 5, 11, 15–16, 242, 278–279, 281, 293–294, 317, 345, 347, 351, 355, 357–358, 361, 366, 368, 379, 381, 384–385
rosette (motif) 60, 132, 139, 142, 144, 146, 194

sacred tree 53, 82–83, 136, 139, 385
sacrifice, ritual 60–61, 86, 123, 145–146, 154–155, 158–159, 172–173, 177, 199, 233, 250, 289, 292, 325
Samos 135–137, 144, 175, 192–194, 198
  Heraion 144–148, 163; Figs. 6.19, 6.20, 6.21
sanctuaries 86–87, 94, 99–105, 132, 134–137, 142, 145–146, 154–162, 170–177, 190–192, 196–197, 246, 275, 288–289, 298–299, 336–337, 351, 353
Sappho 198
sarcophagus 52, 123, 292, 311, 313, 343–345, 347, 368; Figs. 3.2, 14.1
satyr 173, 201, 226, 227, 237, 276, 279, 293, 303; Fig. 9.13
sauceboat 23, 27–28, 31
Schliemann, Heinrich 21, 50, 66
scotia 164–165
seals and seal impressions 28–31, 35, 37, 76, 136; Figs. 2.7, 2.16
Seleukos I 348, 353, 360
Selinus/Selinunte (site) 142, 185–188, 198, 219; Figs. 8.5, 8.6
Severe Style 196, 237, 246, 264, 348, 365
severizing style 357
sex 119, 321–323, 333, 339
sexuality 298, 322, 331, 333, 335, 338
Shaft Graves 43–45, 50–51, 53, 55, 57, 89
shame 298, 302, 323, 331
  see also aidos
shield band (object) 197–199, 214; Figs. 8.16, 8.17
shine (of materials) 116–117, 197, 345
ship (subject) 25–26, 40, 43, 94, 325; Figs. 2.3, 2.20, 4.23
Sicily (region) 99, 102, 137, 142, 150, 161, 169, 185, 191, 277–279, 281, 288, 305, 307, 309–310, 327, 345, 347, 374, 385
  see also Akragas/Agrigento; Megara Hyblaea; Selinus/Selinunte; Syracuse/Siracusa
Sidon (site) 343–344, 347
signatures 194, 201, 205, 358
silhouette (technique) 77, 88, 94, 139–140, 143, 206
silver 44, 136, 138, 140, 170, 182, 267–269, 274, 282, 336, 339, 378, 382
Siphnos, site 170, 181–182
sistrum 37
skenographia 255, 262, 345
skiagraphia 255–256, 262
Skopas 293, 297–298
skyphos 14–15, 76, 79, 120, 221, 260, 332; Figs. 1.10b, 4.10, 5.19, 5.22, 9.2, 9.12
slip (ceramic) 13, 15, 22–23, 32, 39–40, 139–140, 199, 200, 206, 256, 260, 278, 374, 381
Smyrna (site) 330
social class 70, 87, 192, 281–282, 321–324
Sombrotidas, kouros of 191, 278
Sosos (artist) 370
Sotades (potter) and Sotades Painter 256, 381–382; Figs. 10.21, 15.1
Sounion (site) and kouros 134, 190, 198, 267; Fig. 6.4
southern Italy 99, 102, 150, 185, 200, 224, 240, 244, 277, 280, 282, 303, 305, 307, 309–310, 336–338, 345, 375, 385
  see also Metapontum/Metaponto; Poseidonia/Paestum; Taras/Taranto
Sparta and Spartans 106, 137, 158–159, 199, 229, 244, 246, 250, 253, 288, 299, 301, 323, 325, 330, 336, 385
Special Palace Tradition (ware) 37
sphinx 136, 139–140, 142, 198, 385; Figs. 6.7, 6.10, 8.16
stadion 155–156, 159, 172, 289
stamnos 119, 142, 274; Figs. 5.22, 6.12
stamped technique 25, 201
stele/stelai 43, 124–128, 254, 262, 272, 274, 299–301, 322, 324, 328, 330, 343, 369, 371; Figs. 5.28, 10.19, 12.12, 13.2, 13.9, 14.31
stereobate 161–162
stirrup jar 61, 64, 72; Fig. 3.15
stoa 100, 103, 106–109, 118–119, 146–148, 154–155, 158, 169, 255, 289, 351, 360
Stoics 106, 288, 348
stomion 58, 60
Strabo 336–337
stratigraphy 21
style 5, 6–9, 11, 13–15, 17–18, 22–23, 26, 45–46, 52, 60–64, 71–72, 76, 83–84, 110, 133, 135–137, 142–144, 181–182, 186, 192, 206, 211–214, 225, 237–240, 244, 246, 260, 267, 270, 276–281, 293–296, 298–299, 303, 307, 313, 317–318, 337, 347–348, 355–358, 363–366, 378, 381–382, 384–385
stylobate 161–162, 164, 166–167, 169, 248
Sulla 345, 379, 384
symmetria 243, 247
symposion 15–16, 112, 115, 118–122, 140, 199, 207, 221, 222, 225, 231, 233, 255–256, 274, 276, 298, 321–323, 331–335; Figs. 5.20, 5.21, 10.20, 13.1
synchronic 15–16, 154
synoptic narration 218, 225
Syracuse/Siracusa (site) 137, 142, 150, 185–186, 191, 337, 347, 349, 357
Syria (region) 43, 45, 76, 83, 85–86, 135–137, 142, 280, 348, 361, 363, 383–384
Syros 25–26

Tanagra figures 10–11, 302, 375; Figs. 1.6, 14.34
Taras/Taranto 137, 139–140, 210, 231, 278, 303, 305, 307, 309–310, 347, 357, 375–376
tau-type terracotta figure 63; Fig. 3.14
teapot 22–23, 26; Fig. 2.1
techne 6
Tegea, Temple of Athena Alea 297–299, 302; Fig. 12.10
Telemachos (subject) 117–118, 221, 260; Fig. 5.19
Telephos 297–298, 302, 358; Fig. 12.10A
temenos 146–147, 155–159, 171, 197, 229, 292, 336
temple 70, 86, 99–107, 145–149, 154–170, 173, 184–187, 226–229, 238–239, 244–248, 252–254, 267–269, 288–291, 294, 296–297, 336, 351–355
Tenian-Boeotian Group 144
Terme Boxer 5, 366; Fig. 14.22
terminus 7–8, 23, 181
terminus ad quem 8
terminus ante quem 8, 15, 182, 189, 244, 358
terminus post quem 8, 188
terracotta (medium) 25–28, 71, 74–76, 123–124, 128, 144, 146, 163, 185, 198, 242, 278, 305, 375–378
terracotta figures 6–11, 63–64, 84–88, 175–176, 305, 375; Figs. 3.14, 4.13, 7.20, 8.20, 14.34, 14.35
tesserae 310, 345, 370–371
textiles 36, 70, 76, 115–118, 196, 260, 311, 327–328, 339, 382; Figs. 5.18, 5.19
Thasos 113–115; Figs. 5.14, 5.15
thatch roof 28, 89, 146, 163
theater (building) 103, 155–157, 159–160, 171–173, 225, 288, 291–292, 351, 358, 360, 371, 375, 384; Fig. 12.3
Thebes (site) 94, 175, 278, 288, 325, 385
Themistokles 189
theoria 177
Thera 21, 39–43
  eruption 23–24, 32, 37, 46, 50
Thermon, Temple of Apollo 146, 163, 184; Fig. 6.22, 6.23
Theseus (subject) 94, 109, 142, 188–189, 198, 218, 219, 220, 221, 242, 252, 257; Figs. 8.7, 8.16, 9.8
Thetis 200, 205, 219, 232, 327; Figs. 8.23, 9.18
tholos 43, 52, 57–58, 60, 85, 107, 109, 165, 171, 256, 280, 288–293; Fig. 12.2
three-quarter view 37, 182, 188–189, 206–207, 213, 260, 306–307, 313, 358, 371, 374
threnody 77, 329
Thucydides 17, 253, 267

Timanthes (artist) 2
Timotheos (artist) 270–271, 296–297, 365; Fig. 11.2
Titanomachy (subject) 184–185
tombs 25–26, 43, 45, 52, 57–58, 60–63, 72–76, 85, 89–90, 122–126, 139–140, 194, 224–225, 230–233, 255–257, 261–264, 280–282, 291–292, 299, 301–303, 305, 309–315, 326–327, 335–338, 371, 374–375, 381–382
torus 164–165
tragedy and tragic performance 155, 171, 217, 242, 281, 309–310
transportation/shipping of art 21, 116, 134, 231, 246, 268–271, 273–274, 276, 278, 294, 355–356
treasury 155–157, 170–171, 186, 336, 343, 384
see also Delphi, Athenian Treasury; Delphi, Siphnian Treasury
triglyph 79, 162–163
tripod (object) 87–89, 95, 143–144, 156, 166, 175, 293, 365; Fig. 4.16
tripod (subject) 79, 139, 166, 174, 182, 325; Figs. 4.10, 7.17, 8.1
Troilos (subject) 66, 201, 219; Fig. 8.23
Trojan War 43, 144, 158, 205, 218–219, 227, 238, 248, 297, 307, 355, 358; Fig. 6.18
Troy 21, 46, 50, 57, 67, 106, 297
tumulus 28–29, 86, 90, 256, 311, 313
Tyche 348, 360–361, 363, 371, 378; Figs. 14.15, 14.37
Tyrannicides (object) 109–110, 117, 128, 177, 222, 237–240, 272, 317, 334, 348; Fig. 5.9
tyrants 109, 238, 275, 288, 301, 334

Ulu Burun (site) 50

Vapheio (site) 43–45
vase painting (general) 13, 18, 59–66, 71–84, 137–143, 199–207, 256–262, 306–310, 331–332, 335, 374
Vasiliki Ware 22–23, 26, 32; Fig. 2.1
Ventris, Michael 50
Vergina (site) 116–117, 282, 311–315, 325, 343, 345, 370–371; Figs. 5.18, 12.23, 12.24, 12.25
verus/veritas 3, 5
viewer 6, 11–13, 77, 94–95, 109, 120, 123, 128, 170, 175, 182–186, 188–189, 192, 194, 197, 208, 211, 214, 220–225, 229, 233, 237–242, 246–252, 293, 297–299, 323, 325, 330–331, 348, 358, 361, 366–370, 378, 386
Vitruvius 17
votive offerings 6, 8, 84, 86–87, 117, 128, 132–134, 136, 145, 158, 173–177, 194, 196, 198, 237, 244, 357, 365, 374–375, 386

walls (city) 66, 70, 100–103, 288
wanax 53, 57
weaving 26, 76, 114–116, 325, 327, 331, 339
see also textiles
wedding and procession 94–95, 177, 200, 205, 219, 220, 223–224, 227, 233, 260, 325–326, 328, 374–375; Fig.13.4
West Slope Ware 277–278, 305, 309, 374; Fig. 11.9
white-ground vase painting 124, 256–257, 277, 305; Figs. 1.2, 5.26, 10.21, 10.23, 10.25
wife (status) 127, 133, 135, 175, 194, 221, 233, 303, 325, 327–328
Wild Goat Style 142; Fig. 6.13
wine, consumption 3, 13–16, 119–120, 173, 220–221, 226, 251, 276, 324, 337–338, 381
see also symposion
women, patrons or owners/dedicants 133–134, 329–331, 339
see also kanephoros; priestess
women, tombs 60, 73–77, 89, 126–127, 165, 194, 254, 262, 302–303, 311, 313, 323–324, 371, 375
workshop 35, 52, 55, 58, 70–71, 85, 102, 112, 166, 199, 200, 205, 246, 254, 270, 273, 276, 280–281, 297, 318, 356–358, 366

Xenophon 122

Zagora, Andros (site) 90–93, 99, 113, 134, 167; Figs. 4.21, 4.22
Zeus (deity) 36, 158–159, 166, 214, 226, 244, 343, 381
Zeus (subject) 7–8, 11–12, 87–88, 117, 182, 227–229, 323; Figs. 1.7, 1.8, 7.12, 8.1
Zeuxis (artist) 2–3, 282, 305, 311

Printed in the USA
CPSIA information can be obtained
at www.ICGtesting.com
JSHW050753281223
54267JS00011B/351